S0-ERT-998

God is Great (October 3): Palestinian women in Beirut weep over the image of Mohammed al-Durrah, the 12-year-old boy shot dead in his father's arms by Israeli forces (Associated Press).

[Top] *Dimpled Chads* (November 23): Broward County Canvassing Board member Judge Robert Rosenberg studies a ballot card in the disputed Florida election (Popperfoto/Reuters).

[Bottom] *Celebrations in Sydney* (October I): Fireworks light up the city harbour during the closing ceremony of the XXVII Olympiad (Popperfoto/Reuters).

[Top] *Enduring Division* (June 14): North Korean leader Kim Jong Il (right) and South Korean President Kim Dae Jung conclude their summit in Pyongyang (Popperfoto/Reuters).

[Bottom] *Liberation in Yugoslavia* (October 5): Crowds storm the parliament building in Belgrade during the overthrow of the Milosevic regime (Associated Press).

Awaiting Rescue (March 1): Villagers In Mozambique seek safety on their rooftops after the Limpopo River burst its banks (Associated Press).

THE
ANNUAL REGISTER

A Record of World Events
2000

Edited by
D. S. LEWIS

assisted by
AILEEN HARVEY

FIRST EDITED IN 1758
BY EDMUND BURKE

Keesing's Worldwide
PRINT · CD-ROM · ONLINE

THE ANNUAL REGISTER 2000
Published by Keesing's Worldwide, LLC, 4905 Del Ray Avenue, Suite 402,
Bethesda, MD 20814, United States of America

ISBN 1-886994-39-0

(Keesing's Worldwide, LLC 2001
All rights reserved; no part of this publication may be reproduced,
stored in a retrieval system, or transmitted in any form or by any
means, electronic, mechanical, photocopying, recording or otherwise
without either the prior permission of the Publishers or a licence
permitting restricted copying issued by the Copyright Licensing Agency,
90 Tottenham Court Road, London, W1P 9HE, UK

British Library Cataloguing in Publication Data
The Annual Register—2000
1. History—Periodicals
909.82'8'05 D410

Library of Congress Catalog Card Number: 4-17979

Set in Times Roman by
NEW AGE GRAPHICS, BETHESDA, MARYLAND, USA

Printed in the UK by
MPG BOOK DIVISION, BODMIN

CONTENTS

	CONTRIBUTORS	viii
	IGO ABBREVIATIONS	xiv
	PREFACE TO 242nd VOLUME	xv
	EXTRACTS FROM PAST VOLUMES	xvii

I OVERVIEWS OF THE YEAR

1	Global Issues and Regional Realities	1
2	The International Economy	8

II WESTERN AND SOUTHERN EUROPE

1	i United Kingdom 16 ii Scotland 37 iii Wales 39 iv Northern Ireland 41	16
2	i Germany 47 ii France 52 iii Italy 56 iv Belgium 60 v The Netherlands 61 vi Luxembourg 63 vii Ireland 64	47
3	i Denmark 67 ii Iceland 68 iii Norway 69 iv Sweden 71 v Finland 72 vi Austria 73 vii Switzerland 77 viii European Mini-States 79	67
4	i Spain 81 ii Gibraltar 84 iii Portugal 86 iv Malta 89 v Greece 90 vi Cyprus 93 vii Turkey 96	81

III CENTRAL AND EASTERN EUROPE

1	i Poland 99 ii Baltic Republics 102 iii Czech Republic 105 iv Slovakia 107 v Hungary 109 vi Romania 111 vii Bulgaria 114	99
2	i Albania 117 ii Bosnia & Hercegovina 119 iii Croatia 121 iv Macedonia 122 v Slovenia 123 vi Yugoslavia 124	117
3	i Russia 128 ii Belarus, Ukraine, Moldova 133 iii Armenia, Georgia, Azerbaijan 136	128

IV AMERICAS AND THE CARIBBEAN

1	United States of America	138
2	Canada	157
3	Latin America: i Argentina 161 ii Bolivia 163 iii Brazil 164 iv Chile 165 v Colombia 167 vi Ecuador 169 vii Paraguay 170 viii Peru 171 ix Uruguay 173 x Venezuela 173 xi Cuba 175 xii Dominican Republic and Haiti 176 xiii Central America and Panama 177 xiv Mexico 181	161
4	Caribbean: i Jamaica 182 ii Guyana 183 iii Trinidad & Tobago 183 iv Barbados 184 v Belize 185 vi Grenada 185 vii The Bahamas 186 viii Windward and Leeward Islands 186 ix UK Dependencies 188 x Suriname 190 xi Netherlands Antilles and Aruba 191 xii US Dependencies 191	182

V MIDDLE EAST AND NORTH AFRICA

1	Israel	193
2	i Arab World and Palestinians 197 ii Egypt 200 iii Jordan 202 iv Syria 204 v Lebanon 206 vi Iraq 208	197
3	i Saudi Arabia 210 ii Yemen 213 iii Arab States of the Gulf 215	210
4	i Sudan 220 ii Libya 223 iii Tunisia 224 iv Algeria 226 v Morocco 228 vi Western Sahara 229	220

VI EQUATORIAL AFRICA

1	i Horn of Africa 231 ii Kenya 234 iii Tanzania 236 iv Uganda 237	231
2	i Ghana 239 ii Nigeria 241 iii Sierra Leone 243 iv The Gambia 245 v Liberia 246	239
3	i West African Francophone States 246 ii Central African Franc Zone States 254	246

VII CENTRAL AND SOUTHERN AFRICA

1	i Democratic Republic of Congo 259 ii Burundi and Rwanda 261 iii Guinea-Bissau, Cape Verde and São Tomé and Príncipe 263 iv Mozambique 265 v Angola 268	259
2	i Zambia 269 ii Malawi 270 iii Zimbabwe 271 iv Botswana, Lesotho, Namibia and Swaziland 274	269
3	South Africa	282

VIII SOUTH ASIA AND INDIAN OCEAN

1	i Iran 287 ii Afghanistan 289 iii Central Asian Republics 292	287
2	i India 298 ii Pakistan 302 iii Bangladesh 305 iv Nepal 306 v Bhutan 308 vi Sri Lanka 309	298
3	i Mauritius 311 ii Seychelles, Comoros and Maldives 313 iii Madagascar 315	311

IX SOUTH-EAST AND EAST ASIA

1	i Myanmar (Burma) 317 ii Thailand 319 iii Malaysia 320 iv Brunei 322 v Singapore 322 vi Indonesia 323 vii Philippines 326 viii Vietnam 328 ix Cambodia 329 x Laos 330	317
2	i China 331 ii Hong Kong SAR 337 iii Taiwan 338 iv Japan 341 v South Korea 345 vi North Korea 347 vii Mongolia 349	331

X AUSTRALASIA AND THE PACIFIC

1	i Australia 352 ii Papua New Guinea 356	352
2	i New Zealand 357 ii Pacific Island States 360	357

XI INTERNATIONAL ORGANISATIONS

1	United Nations	366
2	i Defence Organisations 376 ii Economic Organisations 383	376
3	i The Commonwealth 388 ii Francophonie and CPLP 390 iii Non-Aligned Movement and Developing Countries 393 iv Organisation of the Islamic Conference 395	388
4	European Union	396

CONTENTS

5	i Council of Europe 404 ii Organisation for Security and Co-operation in Europe 406 iii European Bank for Reconstruction and Development 409 iv Nordic, Baltic and Arctic Organisations 410 v Other European Organisations 412	404
6	i Arab Organisations 415 ii African Organisations and Conferences 418 iii Asia-Pacific Organisations 422 iv American and Caribbean Organisations 426	415

XII RELIGION — 431

XIII THE SCIENCES

1	Scientific, Medical and Industrial Research	437
2	Information Technology	443
3	The Environment	448

XIV THE LAW

1	i International Law 455 ii European Community Law 459	455
2	Law in the United Kingdom	462
3	Law in the USA	468

XV THE ARTS

1	i Opera 470 ii Music 472 iii Ballet & Dance 475 iv Theatre 478 v Cinema 482 vi Television & Radio 485	470
2	i Visual Arts 489 ii Architecture 492	489
3	Literature	494

XVI SPORT — 500

XVII DOCUMENTS AND REFERENCE

1	EU Charter of Fundamental Rights	509
2	US Supreme Court Ruling on result of Presidential Election in Florida	518
3	UK Labour Government	524
4	US Democratic Administration	525
5	International Comparisons: Population, GDP and Growth	526

XVIII OBITUARY — 527

XIX CHRONICLE OF PRINCIPAL EVENTS IN 2000 — 559

INDEX — 576

MAPS AND TABLES

US Presidential Election Results	148
US Gubernatorial Election Results	149
United Nations Peace-keeping Missions	374

CONTRIBUTORS

EXTRACTS FROM PAST VOLUMES   **M. R. D. Foot,** Former Professor of Modern History, University of Manchester

PART I
GLOBAL ISSUES AND REGIONAL REALITIES
THE INTERNATIONAL ECONOMY

John M. Roberts, Former Vice-Chancellor of the University of Southampton and Warden of Merton College, Oxford
Robert Ostergard Jr., PhD, Research Fellow at the Institute of Global Cultural Studies and the Center on Democratic Performance and Visiting Assistant Professor of Political Science, Binghampton University
Thomas C. Muller, Co-editor, *Political Handbook of the World.*

PART II

UNITED KINGDOM   **Institute of Contemporary British History** (Harriet Jones, BA, MSc, PhD, Director, ICBH; Michael Kandiah, BA, MA, PhD, Director, Witness Seminar Programme; Virginia Preston, BA, Deputy Director)

SCOTLAND   **Charlotte Lythe,** MA, Senior Lecturer in Economic Studies, University of Dundee

WALES   **Gwyn Jenkins,** MA, Keeper of Manuscripts and Records, National Library of Wales, Aberystwyth

NORTHERN IRELAND   **Sydney Elliott,** BA, PhD, Senior Lecturer in Politics, The Queen's University, Belfast

GERMANY   **Simon Green,** PhD, Lecturer in German Politics, Institute for German Studies, University of Birmingham
Charlie Jeffery, PhD, Deputy Director, Institute for German Studies, University of Birmingham

FRANCE   **Martin Harrison,** Professor of Politics, University of Keele

ITALY   **Stephen Gundle,** PhD, Head of Italian Department, Royal Holloway, University of London

BELGIUM, NETHERLANDS, LUXEMBOURG   **Marc Cole-Bailey,** Writer on European affairs

REPUBLIC OF IRELAND   **Louis McRedmond,** MA, BL, Journalist, historian and broadcaster

DENMARK, ICELAND, NORWAY, SWEDEN, FINLAND   **Alastair H. Thomas,** Professor of Nordic Politics, University of Central Lancashire

AUSTRIA   **Angela Gillon,** Researcher in West European Affairs

SWITZERLAND   **Hans Hirter,** PhD, Editor, *Année Politique Suisse*, University of Bern

EUROPEAN MINI-STATES   **Stefania Zerbinati,** MA, Researcher in European Affairs

SPAIN, GIBRALTAR   **Elisenda Fenés,** Freelance writer specialising in Spanish affairs

PORTUGAL   **Antonio de Figueiredo,** Knight Commander of Portugal's

CONTRIBUTORS

	Order of Freedom; Portuguese author, freelance journalist and broadcaster
MALTA	D. S. Lewis, PhD, Editor, *The Annual Register*
GREECE	Richard Clogg, MA, St Antony's College, Oxford
CYPRUS	Robert McDonald, Writer and broadcaster on Cyprus, Greece and Turkey
TURKEY	A. J. A. Mango, BA, PhD, Orientalist and writer on current affairs in Turkey and the Near East

PART III

POLAND	A. Kemp-Welch, BSc(Econ), PhD, Senior Lecturer, School of Economic and Social Studies, University of East Anglia
ESTONIA	Andres Kasekamp, BA, MA, PhD, Associate Professor, University of Tartu, Estonia
LATVIA, LITHUANIA	Mel Huang, Baltics Editor, the *Central European Review*
CZECH REPUBLIC, SLOVAKIA	Sharon Fisher, MA, Analyst specialising in East European political and economic affairs
HUNGARY	Marc Cole-Bailey, (see Pt. II, European Mini-States)
ROMANIA	Gabriel Partos, Eastern Europe Analyst, BBC World Service
BULGARIA, ALBANIA	Richard Crampton, PhD, Professor of East European History and Fellow of St Edmund Hall, University of Oxford
FORMER YUGOSLAV REPUBLICS	John B. Allcock, MA, PhD, Head of Research Unit in South-East European Studies, University of Bradford
RUSSIA, BELARUS, UKRAINE, MOLDOVA AND CAUCASUS	Stephen White, PhD, DPhil, Professor of Politics, University of Glasgow

PART IV

UNITED STATES OF AMERICA	Neil A. Wynn, MA, PhD, Reader in History and American Studies, University of Glamorgan
CANADA	David M. L. Farr, Emeritus Professor of History, Carleton University, Ottawa
LATIN AMERICA, CARIBBEAN	Peter Calvert, MA, PhD, Professor of Comparative and International Politics, University of Southampton

PART V

ISRAEL	Joel Peters, BSc, DPhil, Senior Lecturer in Politics and Government, Ben Gurion University of the Negev, Israel
ARAB WORLD, EGYPT, JORDAN, SYRIA, LEBANON, IRAQ	Christopher Gandy, Formerly UK Diplomatic Service, writer on Middle Eastern affairs
SAUDI ARABIA, YEMEN, ARAB STATES OF THE GULF	George Joffé, Senior Research Fellow, School of Oriental and African Studies, University of London
SUDAN	Ahmed Al-Shahi, MLitt, DPhil, Former lecturer in Social Anthropology, University of Newcastle Upon Tyne
LIBYA, TUNISIA, ALGERIA, MOROCCO, WESTERN SAHARA	Richard Lawless, PhD, Emeritus Reader in Modern Middle Eastern Studies, University of Durham

PART VI

HORN OF AFRICA	**Patrick Gilkes,** Writer and broadcaster on the Horn of Africa
KENYA, TANZANIA, UGANDA	**William Tordoff,** MA, PhD, Emeritus Professor of Government, University of Manchester
GHANA, SIERRA LEONE,	**Jeffrey Haynes,** BA, PhD, Professor of Politics, London Guildhall University
THE GAMBIA, LIBERIA, NIGERIA	**Guy Arnold,** Writer specialising in Africa and North-South affairs
FRANCOPHONE AFRICA	**Kaye Whiteman,** Former publisher, *West Africa*

PART VII

DEMOCRATIC REPUBLIC OF CONGO, BURUNDI & RWANDA, MOZAMBIQUE	**Patrick Harries,** PhD, Professor of African History, University of Basel, Switzerland
GUINEA BISSAU, CAPE VERDE, SÃO TOMÉ AND PRÍNCIPE	**Douglas Mason,** BA, M.Phil, MA., Editor, Africa Department, The Economist Intelligence Unit
ANGOLA, ZAMBIA	**Alex Vines,** Senior researcher, Africa division, Human Rights Watch
MALAWI	**Penny Dale,** BA, MA, freelance writer on Southern African affairs
ZIMBABWE	**R. W. Baldock,** BA, PhD, Editorial Director, Yale University Press, writer on African affairs
BOTSWANA, LESOTHO, NAMIBIA, SWAZILAND, SOUTH AFRICA	**Elizabeth Sidiropoulos,** BA Hons, MA, Director of Studies South African Institute of International Affairs, Johannesburg

PART VIII

IRAN	**Keith McLachlan,** BA, PhD, Emeritus Professor, School of Oriental and African Studies, University of London
AFGHANISTAN	**Matthew Sagar,** freelance writer on Central Asia
CENTRAL ASIAN REPUBLICS	**Shirin Akiner,** PhD, Lecturer in Central Asian Studies, School of Oriental and African Studies, University of London
INDIA, BANGLADESH, NEPAL, BHUTAN	**Peter Lyon,** BSc(Econ), PhD, Reader Emeritus in International Relations and Senior Research Fellow, Institute of Commonwealth Studies, University of London; editor, *The Round Table*, the Commonwealth journal of international affairs
PAKISTAN	**David Taylor,** Senior Lecturer in Politics with reference to South Asia, School of Oriental and African Studies, University of London
SRI LANKA	**Charles Gunawardena,** Former Director of Information, Commonwealth Secretariat, London
MAURITIUS, SEYCHELLES, COMOROS, MALDIVES, MADAGASCAR	**Kaye Whiteman,** (see Pt. VI, Francophone Africa)

PART IX

MYANMAR (BURMA), THAILAND, VIETNAM, CAMBODIA, LAOS	**Robert H. Taylor,** PhD, former Professor of Politics, School of Oriental and African Studies; consultant on South East Asian affairs

CONTRIBUTORS

MALAYSIA, BRUNEI, SINGAPORE	**Michael Leifer,** BA, PhD, Emeritus Professor of International Relations, London School of Economics and Political Science
INDONESIA, PHILIPPINES	**Norman MacQueen,** BA, MSc, DPhil, Head of Department of Politics, University of Dundee
CHINA, HONG KONG, TAIWAN	**Phil Deans,** BA, PhD, Lecturer in Chinese Politics, School of Oriental and African Studies
JAPAN	**Ian Nish,** Emeritus Professor of International History, London School of Economics and Political Science
NORTH AND SOUTH KOREA, MONGOLIA	**Alan Sanders,** FIL, Former Lecturer in Mongolian Studies, School of Oriental and African Studies, University of London

PART X

AUSTRALIA	**James Jupp,** MSc(Econ), PhD, FASSA, Director, Centre for Immigration and Multicultural Studies, Australian National University, Canberra
PAPUA NEW GUINEA	**Norman MacQueen,** (see Pt. IX. Indonesia, Philippines)
NEW ZEALAND, PACIFIC ISLAND STATES	**Stephen Levine,** PhD, Associate Professor and Head of School, School of Political Science and International Relations, Victoria University of Wellington

PART XI

UNITED NATIONS	**David Travers,** BA(Wales), Lecturer in Politics and International Relations, Lancaster University; Specialist Advisor on UN to House of Commons' Foreign Affairs Committee
DEFENCE ORGANISATIONS	**Paul Cornish,** PhD, Newton Sheehy Lecturer in International Relations, Centre of International Studies, University of Cambridge; Fellow, Wolfson College, Cambridge
ECONOMIC ORGANISATIONS	**Robert Ostergard Jr and Thomas C. Muller,** (see Pt. I, The International Economy)
COMMONWEALTH	**Derek Ingram,** Consultant Editor of *Gemini News Service*; author and writer on the Commonwealth
NON-ALIGNED MOVEMENT AND GROUP OF 77	**Peter Willets,** PhD, Professor of Global Politics, Department of Sociology, The City University, London
ORGANISATION OF THE ISLAMIC CONFERENCE	**Darren Sagar,** MA, Deputy Editor, *Keesing's Record of World Events*
EUROPEAN UNION	**Michael Berendt,** Expert on affairs of the European Union
COUNCIL OF EUROPE	**Christopher Shaw,** MA, Secretary to UK delegation to Parliamentary Assembly of the Council of Europe
ORGANISATION FOR SECURITY AND CO-OPERATION IN EUROPE	**Adrien G. V, Hyde-Price,** BSc(Econ), PhD, Institute of German Studies, University of Birmingham
EUROPEAN BANK FOR RECONSTRUCTION AND DEVELOPMENT	**Michael Kaser,** MA, DLitt, DSocSc, Emeritus Fellow of St Antony's College, Oxford, and Honorary Professor, University of Birmingham
NORDIC/BALTIC/ARCTIC ORGANISATIONS	**Alastair H. Thomas,** (see Pt. II, Denmark, etc.)
OTHER EUROPEAN ORGANISATIONS	**Marc Cole-Bailey,** (see Pt. II, Belgium, etc.)
ARAB ORGANISATIONS	**George Joffé,** (see Pt. V, Saudi Arabia, etc.)

AFRICAN ORGANISATIONS AND CONFERENCES	**Kaye Whiteman,** (see Pt. VI, Francophone Africa)
ASIA-PACIFIC ORGANISATIONS	**Darren Sagar,** (see above)
AMERICAN AND CARIBBEAN ORGANISATIONS	**Peter Calvert,** (see Pt. IV, Latin America, etc.)

PART XII
RELIGION	**Geoffrey Parrinder,** MA, PhD, DD, Emeritus Professor of the Comparative Study of Religions, University of London

PART XIII
MEDICAL, SCIENTIFIC AND INDUSTRIAL RESEARCH	**Tim Curtis,** Regional Editor, *Keesing's Record of World Events*, writer on international affairs
INFORMATION TECHNOLOGY	**Kristian Saxton,** Freelance writer on Information Technology; IT professional
ENVIRONMENT	**Julian Coleman,** Journalist, broadcaster and radio producer specialising in the environment, development and science

PART XIV
INTERNATIONAL LAW	**Christine Gray,** MA, PhD, Fellow in Law, St John's College, Cambridge
EUROPEAN COMMUNITY LAW	**N. March Hunnings,** LLM, PhD, Editor, *Encyclopedia of European Union Law: Constitutional Texts*
LAW IN THE UK	**David Ibbetson,** MA, PhD, Fellow and Tutor in Law, Magdalen College, Oxford
LAW IN THE USA	**Robert J. Spjut,** ID, LLD, Member of the State Bars of California and Florida

PART XV
OPERA	**Charles Osborne,** Author; opera critic, *The Jewish Chronicle*
MUSIC	**Francis Routh,** Composer and author; founder director of the Redcliffe Concerts
BALLET & DANCE	**Jane Pritchard,** Archivist, Rambert Dance Company and English National Ballet
THEATRE	**Jeremy Kingston,** Theatre critic, *The Times*
CINEMA	**Derek Malcolm,** Cinema critic, *The Guardian*
TV & RADIO	**Raymond Snoddy,** Media Editor, *The Times*
VISUAL ARTS	**Anna Somers-Cocks,** Editor, *The Art Newspaper*
ARCHITECTURE	**Paul Finch,** Editor, *The Architect's Journal*
LITERATURE	**Alastair Niven,** Principal, King George V and Queen Elizabeth Foundation of St Catharine's; formerly Director of Literature, British Council

PART XVI
SPORT

Paul Newman, Sports Editor, *The Independent*

PART XVII
OBITUARY

James Bishop, Editor-in-Chief, *The Illustrated London News*

PART XVIII
CHRONICLE OF 2000

Editorial Staff at Keesing's Worldwide

MAPS AND DIAGRAMS

Michael Lear, MJL Graphics, N. Yorks, YO14 9BE

ACKNOWLEDGMENTS

THE Editor gratefully acknowledges his debt to a number of individuals and institutions for their help with sources, references and documents. Acknowledgment is also due to the principal sources for the national and IGO data sections (showing the situation at end 2000 unless otherwise stated), namely *Keesing's Record of World Events* (Keesing's Worldwide), *Worldwide Government Directory* (Keesing's Worldwide), the *2000/20001 World Development Report* (Oxford University Press for the World Bank) and the *Financial Times* (London). The Board and the bodies which nominate its members disclaim responsibility for any opinions expressed or the accuracy of facts recorded in this volume.

THE Publisher, Editor and Advisory Board mourn the passing of Professor Michael Leifer, who died on March 23, 2001, having been for many years a much-valued contributor to the *Annual Register*.

ABBREVIATIONS OF NON-UN INTERNATIONAL ORGANISATIONS

AC	Arctic Council
ACP	African, Caribbean and Pacific states associated with EU
ACS	Association of Caribbean States
AL	Arab League
ALADI	Latin American Integration Association
AMU	Arab Maghreb Union
ANZUS	Australia-New Zealand-US Security Treaty
AP	Amazon Pact
APEC	Asia-Pacific Economic Co-operation
ASEAN	Association of South-East Asian Nations
Benelux	Belgium-Netherlands-Luxembourg Economic Union
BSEC	Black Sea Economic Co-operation
CA	Andean Community of Nations
Caricom	Caribbean Community and Common Market
CBSS	Council of the Baltic Sea States
CE	Council of Europe
CEEAC	Economic Community of Central African States
CEFTA	Central European Free Trade Agreement
CEI	Central European Initiative
CIS	Commonwealth of Independent States
COMESA	Common Market of Eastern and Southern Africa
CP	Colombo Plan
CPLP	Community of Portuguese-Speaking Countries
CWTH	The Commonwealth
EBRD	European Bank for Reconstruction and Development
ECO	Economic Co-operation Organisation
ECOWAS	Economic Community of West African States
EEA	European Economic Area
EFTA	European Free Trade Association
EU	European Union
G-8	Group of Eight
GCC	Gulf Co-operation Council
IOC	Indian Ocean Commission
Mercosur	Southern Cone Common Market
NAFTA	North American Free Trade Agreement
NAM	Non-Aligned Movement
NATO	North Atlantic Treaty Organisation
NC	Nordic Council
OAPEC	Organisation of Arab Petroleum Exporting Countries
OAS	Organisation of American States
OAU	Organisation of African Unity
OECD	Organisation for Economic Co-operation and Development
OECS	Organisation of Eastern Caribbean States
OIC	Organisation of the Islamic Conference
OPEC	Organisation of the Petroleum Exporting Countries
OSCE	Organisation for Security and Co-operation in Europe
PC	Pacific Community
PFP	Partnership for Peace
PIF	Pacific Islands Forum
SAARC	South Asian Association for Regional Co-operation
SADC	Southern African Development Community
SELA	Latin American Economic System
UEMOA	West African Economic and Monetary Union
WEU	Western European Union

PREFACE

The 242nd volume of the *Annual Register* has as its central theme the illusion of change. For many the year 2000 was regarded as the dawn of the new millennium. For purists it represented the last year of the twentieth century and the closing of the second millennium. In either case the celebrations which marked this artificial boundary in human evolution were at odds with the continuity which characterised the year's events. New century or not, the trends which had been so evident in the late twentieth century, particularly since the end of the Cold War, remained painfully apparent.

It is not possible here to summarise the year's events in full, but only to note some of its more salient images. The glimpse of a possible resolution to the open sore in the Middle East, even if based upon the triumph of pragmatism over justice, proved a mirage which disappeared under fusillades of Palestinian stones and Israeli bullets. For a nation still awaiting statehood it was a bitter blow. The picture of the 12-year old Palestinian boy, Mohammed al-Durrah, his face frozen with terror in the last moments of his life, before being riddled with bullets whilst huddling in his father's arms, provided one of the most haunting and poignant images of the year and achieved a macabre iconic status.

Elsewhere, too much of the world remained ravaged by a Malthusian mixture of war, famine, disease and disaster. The collapse of the conference on climate change in the Hague in November symbolised a year which saw considerable climatic instability. For those with ears to hear it sounded an unmistakable warning of the perils attendant upon ignoring the environmental consequences of humankind's rapacious exploitation of the planet. However, even from the misery of Mozambique's disastrous floods there emerged a tiny symbol of hope in the form of a child born in a tree being winched to safety in her mother's arms.

In the USA there was an illustration of the absurdities of temporal power as two uninspiring candidates struggled for the most powerful elected office in the world amid a plethora of legal suits relating to the degree to which ballot papers had been indented. As the world became familiar with the technicalities of "hanging" and "dimpled" chads the debacle illustrated both the strengths and weaknesses of liberal democracy.

Elsewhere, too many oppressive and unrepresentative regimes continued to trample upon the rights of their citizens. There was détente on the border between the two Koreas, but no prospect of change in the isolated and poverty-stricken North. There was a new President in Russia, but as in so many of the former Soviet states the country's bleak evolution continued to prove that the simple substitution of capitalism for communism did not constitute automatic progress. There were brave attempts to bring war criminals to justice, but the most culpable remained at large. The British government, to its enduring shame, refused to extradite for trial General Pinochet, the former Chilean dictator whose regime in the 1970s had elevated torture, murder and repression into routine tools of statecraft.

Amid this depressing catalogue of continuity, however, there was an undeniable triumph of the human spirit as the people of Yugoslavia rose up to tear down a regime based on violence and mendacity. It served to underline a simple but eternal truth in a rapidly fracturing and imperfect world: that the humanity of people, and the rights which pertain to that humanity, can be denied, abused and suppressed, but cannot be destroyed.

D.S. Lewis
Cambridge, May 2001.

EXTRACTS FROM PAST VOLUMES

230 years ago

1770. *Epidemic in Poland.* Poland still continues to groan under all the calamities of a war, in which her share is only to suffer. While labouring under the yoke of foreign cruelty and oppression, and convulsed in every part by the domestic rage of her citizens, these complicated evils have this year been increased, by the addition of that most dreadful scourge, the pestilence. This distemper broke out in some villages on the frontiers of Turkey, from whence it soon spread into the adjoining provinces of Poland, and made the most cruel ravages in Podolia, Volhinia, and the Ukraine.

229 years ago

1771. *Dispute between England and Spain over the Falkland Islands.* [debate in the House of Commons, London, January 22] It was said that. . . Spain having offered an affront to England in dispossessing her of a fort and island in time of peace, the national satisfaction to be demanded was restoration of what had been taken, and disavowal, on the part of the Spanish King, of the enterprise of his governor; and that both these points having been obtained, the honour and dignity of England have been fully supported and satisfied. . . The claim of title to Falkland's Islands has been a matter of dispute. . . from its being first set up. . . the claims on either side are so equivocal and uncertain, as to afford room for endless discussion, while the question of moral or legal right may be forever unsettled.

212 years ago

1782. *American War of Independence.* [22 February] It was resolved to make another attempt in the House of Commons, to bind the hands of the executive government by a strong and explicit declaration of the opinion of parliament. With this view, General Conway moved, that an address should be presented to his majesty, to implore his majesty to listen to the advice of his commons, that the war in America might no longer be pursued, for the impracticable purpose of reducing the inhabitants of that country to obedience by force.

200 years ago

1800. *Napoleon Bonaparte.* It is a question of not a little curiosity, what is the reason why Buonaparte affects to consider himself as under the peculiar protection of fortune? When he had to do with barbarians, to talk of fate, and fortune, might not be bad policy? But in fortune he has expressed his confidence to the *French army,* and even the *French nation and legislature,* who if they are not even deists are much less polytheists.

170 years ago

1830. *First fatal railway accident.* [15 September, Parkside, near Liverpool] The intervening space between the railways is exactly four feet, but as the Ducal Car overhung it about two feet and the Rocket engine about six inches, there was only a space of eighteen inches left - sufficient, however, to enable a person to stand without injury or damage. Mr. Holmes while affixing himself in this manner to the Ducal Car, had time to perceive the irresolution of the right hon. gentleman, and he called out to him "For God's sake, be firm, Mr. Huskisson". Mr. Huskisson grasped hold of the door of the Ducal car, the moment before the Rocket passed; this door, when open projected so far upon the neighbouring railway, that it was struck by the Rocket; the consequence was, that it swung rapidly round, overbalanced Mr. Huskisson, and caused him to fall on the railway of the Rocket, when his right leg instantly came in contact with the wheel of the engine, and was crushed.

150 years ago

1850. *Death of Sir Robert Peel.* [June] It is impossible to exaggerate the feelings of profound emotion with which the intelligence of Sir Robert [Peel]'s death was received throughout the country. All remembrance of the political offences of his earlier career were forgotten; nothing was remembered but his great practical reforms, and the power of mind and strength of purpose which made him the leading statesman of Europe and the master-mind of English polity.

143 years ago

1857. *Indian Mutiny.* [a young officer reports, Delhi] About 5 o'clock in the afternoon, all of a sudden, the Sepoys who were with us in the Mainguard, and on whom we had been depending to defend us in case of attack, began firing upon us in every direction: a most awful scene, as you may imagine, then ensued - people running in every possible way to try and escape.

124 years ago

1876. *Controversial US presidential election.* At last the two Conventions met, and the names of Hayes [Republican] and Tilden [Democratic] were proclaimed as the party representatives. The November elections took place, and resulted in a Democratic triumph far greater than had been expected. [Total votes Democrats 4,290,1187, Republicans, 4,042,726.]. . . Now, on the side of Mr. Tilden were 184 electors, whose return was not challenged, and but one vote more was needed to obtain for him the absolute majority ; while Mr. Hayes, in order to win, was bound to gain to his side all three of the disputed Southern States. Naturally the utmost intensity of feeling prevailed when the undecided nature of the result was known, and after the telegrams sent to Europe, announcing Mr. Tilden's election had been dispatched. But nothing could have been more exemplary than the conduct of governors and governed during the crisis, the citizens of the United States showing themselves orderly and law-abiding under the strongest temptations to factious excess.

100 years ago

1900. *Boer War.* Sir Henry Fowler, addressing his constituents at Wolverhampton, after a review of the history of South Africa in the past, spoke of the Jameson raid as one of the greatest outrages ever committed, an act of criminal folly only calculated to serve the purpose President Kruger had in view - to get rid of the supremacy of the British Crown in South Africa. People talked of a capitalist war, and said we had gone into the war with a view of making money, but the gold-mining industry in the Transvaal would have to pay a very heavy tax when the war was over to meet the heavy expenditure which this country had had to incur in the prosecution of that war.

99 years ago

1901. *Obituary of Verdi.* Giuseppe Verdi, the Italian composer, was born in 1813 at Roncole, a village in the Apennines. He received his first lessons in music from the village organist, and by his aid was enabled to go to Milan to pursue his studies. He was, however, rejected at the Conservatoire for want of sufficient musical ability.

94 years ago

1906. *Launch of first Dreadnought.* HMS Dreadnought. Her speed would be 21 knots. In two notable points she marked a new departure. She was the first large warship fitted with turbine engines, and the admiral and all officers were berthed forward of the engines instead of astern. Her construction had been expedited so that her trials might afford experience in time to apply it in the construction of her sister ships; but its rapidity proved that Great Britain could keep well ahead of other nations. She left Portsmouth for her steam trials on October 1, 1906, precisely 364 days after her first keel plate had been laid; and both her steam and [10 x 12"] gun trials were in every way satisfactory.

81 years ago

1919. *Development of air transport.* [16 January] A flight from London to Edinburgh was made during the night by a pilot and observer of the Royal Air Force.

[10 March] An air mail service started between London and Paris.

[14-15 June] Captain J. Alcock, D. S. C., and Lieutenant William Brown, R.A.F., flying a Vickers-Vimy machine succeeded in crossing the Atlantic from Newfoundland to Clifden [Co Galway] in 16 hours 12 minutes, thereby winning the prize of 10,000*l*. offered by the *Daily Mail.*

[10 December] Captain Ross Smith in a Vickers Vimy Rolls-Royce aeroplane completed the flight from London to Australia in just under twenty-eight days, thus winning a prize of 10,000*l*. offered by the Australian Government.

55 years ago

1945. *Death of F.D. Roosevelt.* Without warning, on April 12, news came from Warm Springs, Georgia, that Mr Roosevelt had died of a cerebral haemorrhage. The shock to America was immense. At the moment when American troops were racing into Germany and inching into Okinawa the death of the Commander-in-Chief came like a tragic Lincolnian paradox. . . . A Presidency longer in duration, more crowded with incident, buttressed with more power and affecting the lives of more American citizens than any other in history, had come to an end in a moment when everyone's assumption about the future still rested on the silent premise that Mr Roosevelt would continue to be the tenant of the White House.

51 years ago

1949. *Middle East conflict.* Thus Israel faced the year 1950 opposed to the will of the UN, surrounded by sullen enemies, and burdened by tens of thousands of immigrants who daily worsened the economic position, which appeared to be incurable. Yet there was no sign that the Government would limit immigration, or accept a compromise which could lead to a permanent settlement in the middle East. Certainly Israel would never give up Jerusalem of her own free will.

41 years ago

1959. *Brazilian protest.* President Juscelino Kubitschek shocked the orthodox economists: instead of curbing inflation, he persisted in using it as a means of accelerating the nation's economic expansion. The voters of Sao Paolo gave evidence of their disgust at their ruler's failure to stop the rise in the cost of living when, in October, they elected a rhinoceros from the zoo to the municipal council (the victorious animal was disqualified).

35 years ago

1961. *First man in space.* After several rehearsals with dogs and other living material Russia won the first, and propaganda-wise most important, lap of the space-race. Major Gagarin was successfully orbited on 12 April. The later and less spectacular American achievement, Commander Alan Shepard's flight up through the atmosphere and down again—he did not go into orbit—still stole some of the glory from Russia by being carried out in the full glare of world-wide publicity. Gagarin's successful flight was not announced until he had returned to earth.

10 years ago

1990. *Restoration of liberty in Czechoslovakia.* Freedom of speech, including cultural liberalization and uncensored media, became complete. Hundreds of new periodicals began publication. The educational system was democratized at all levels. Foreign travel both into and out of the country, as well as international cultural exchanges, grew exponentially. Visa requirements were abolished through agreements with most Western countries. Blank spots in modem history were being filled and communist clichés about the past were being revised. All religions were given a free hand. Repertoires of theatres and cinemas reflected the newly-won freedom. These developments gave the public an overwhelming sense of liberty.

THE ANNUAL REGISTER

FOR THE YEAR 2000

I OVERVIEWS OF THE YEAR

1. GLOBAL ISSUES AND REGIONAL REALITIES

No doubt it was always tempting to believe that the year ending the century and the second Christian millennium must have a unique importance, and, although already widely celebrated 12 months earlier, the moment was still felt to be special when it finally came. Yet, in looking back, it is not easy to see what the year 2000 can be said to signify in world history. Of dramatic moments and striking turns it seemed to have few. There were the Olympic Games, certainly a world event, but the most avid enthusiast for them could hardly claim more than that it was good that they should have taken place in a regular way and so splendidly. It was also an odd year that provided the unusual spectacle of the president of the United States, the prime minister of the United Kingdom and a dozen or so other Western leaders being condemned to 20 years imprisonment each. But, as the tribunal which sentenced them was a court in Belgrade trying them in absentia, it seemed merely bizarre, not important, and went largely unnoticed.

Most of the last year of the twentieth century, in fact, seemed no more remarkable in world history than many another year. Its continuity with the past was only too vividly apparent; there were many problems left disappointingly unresolved. Yet what some might think amongst its most portentous occurrences often did not strike the imagination of multitudes. The completion before the expected date, for instance, of the Human Genome project—or of perhaps 90 per cent of it, for there remained some uncertainty about what actually had been achieved—was clearly important, even if it was only the beginning of a very long road towards practical application in medical advances. But probably fewer noticed it than were disturbed by reports of growing frequency of the spread of the disease of BSE amongst the cattle herds of Europe. For very few was it a striking event, and that was true of much else in the year that was nevertheless important.

Something that certainly demands more attention than it received was the year's virtually complete failure to make ground in the management of climate change. The failure was crystallised in an abortive conference at the Hague which witnessed a sustained collision of European and American views (and Saudi Arabia playing a spoiling hand). When the conference finished, it left no agreement on a timetable for ratifying the 1997 Kyoto protocol on climate control, about which a US report on compliance in June had made gloomy reading.

The US administration had not even been able to get as far as putting legislation before Congress to give effect to what it had accepted two years before. In December a pessimistic report on carbon dioxide levels in the atmosphere said that they were higher than for 20 million years. There were warnings, too, that the rate of climatic deterioration was going to accelerate during the coming century if nothing were done. On another part of the environmental front, the UN was told that there was now a danger that illegal fishing would soon wipe out some coveted species. The Hague conference in fact epitomised a decade of failure in environmental protection. Even the uproar in the streets which accompanied it was hardly encouraging. It tended merely to parade, like the disturbances in Washington and Prague at the time of the IMF and World Bank meetings in those cities, a worldwide "rent-a-mob" distrust of governments and a demonisation of the complex phenomena lumped together as "globalisation". The protests did not move masses nor shake governments.

AIDS was another issue over which public opinion was everywhere slow to stir but, encouragingly, governments began to show just a little more interest in it than hitherto. The year 2000 brought the first meeting ever of the Security Council on any health issue, and AIDS was the subject. As the year drew to an end, a tiny gleam of good news came from sub-Saharan Africa, where two-thirds of the world's 36 million victims of the disease were to be found: it was reported that in Uganda (and, less certainly, elsewhere) rates of new infection were at last falling. Nonetheless, in South Africa alone, it was reckoned that there were over 4 million cases of the disease, and there was plenty of evidence of the durability and complexity of the obstacles standing in the way of tackling it. It was easier to whip up fear and excitement about BSE in developed countries.

Unsurprisingly, the year's headlines were usually filled instead by reminders of the world's violence. Africa still provided some of the most gross examples, notoriously in the Democratic Republic of the Congo, an area the size of western Europe disputed between rebels and a government of sorts whilst five other African states stirred the pot and the world passively waited to hear of another outbreak of genocidal strife. Less bloodily, but still violently and sadly, what had once been one of the more promising African countries, Zimbabwe, provided mounting evidence of decline and disorder. In February a new constitution, intended to strengthen further the hand of an already authoritarian president, Robert Mugabe, was rejected in a referendum, but soon afterwards there began a wave of illegal occupations of the farms of white Zimbabweans which the authorities did nothing to restrain, and which slid into murderous attacks on individuals known to be supporters of the opposition party. Mugabe meanwhile ploughed ahead towards one-party rule, exploiting racial polarisation for all it was worth by attacks on the white farming community, and undeterred by electoral setbacks. Given the huge dependence of what remained of his country's economy on agriculture, this not only led him into conflict with the country's Supreme Court, but speeded the descent of the country into economic privation as the year went on.

It was only a small offsetting item in the Africa account that peace was at last made between Ethiopia and Eritrea, and that civil strife was more or less contained in Sierra Leone at the end of a turbulent year. Meanwhile, in Asia, Kashmir continued a running sore, with almost daily skirmishes between Indian and Pakistani forces. In Indonesia the spectre of massacre threatened to spread from the Moluccas to the main islands. Even in Europe, Spain had a bad year with ETA terrorism and, though at a mercifully much less fierce and lower level of violence (if not of acrimony), the seeming elusiveness of a solution to Northern Ireland's problems tempted some back to the gun and bomb. All too evidently, few if any of the tidy solutions to the world's problems so eagerly awaited as 1999 ended had been realised. Even such progress as was made with some of them was qualified. The G-8 discussion of third world development and debt relief was disappointing; the new goals it announced for the achievement of universal primary education and reducing the ravages of malaria, tuberculosis and AIDS smacked of pious aspiration rather than of promise.

Given such facts, it is hardly surprising that world attention was still largely focused at the end of the year on the unchanging fact of the dominant influence of the USA. Some doubt about its long-enduring economic boom was beginning to influence opinion by the end of the year, it is true, but by then there had also been a major political change which raised further uncertainty. Amid obsessive attention from the US media (and to some extent from that of the world), the chronicle of a disputed presidential election was at last formally closed just before Christmas. Other countries shared the relief of Americans that an end to the process had at last been reached. But it could hardly be the end of speculation about a wider, implicit story. The legal resolution of the argument over the validity or inadequacy of Florida's ballot arrangements and vote-counting procedures had never eclipsed speculation about what the policy outcomes of prolonged irresolution would be. George Bush was clearly going to move into the White House in 2001, but that would now happen under circumstances much more embittered than they had been even as little as two months earlier. That meant greater uncertainty and, therefore, concern worldwide over the way that the new administration in Washington would behave. President Bill Clinton, for example, had postponed a decision about an anti-ballistic missile defence system—a new 'Star Wars' programme as some saw it, recalling the years of President Ronald Reagan—after test failures, but what the incoming president would do about it was now more unclear than ever. Bush had lost something like a month's time in selecting and installing his own officials and advisers, and would find facing him in January a more or less deadlocked Congress. The incoming administration was thus a more disconcertingly unknown quantity than usual. It was against this background of new uncertainties that the world would have to confront too many sores awaiting salve or solution.

Not all of these, fortunately, directly or closely involved other great powers. Russia was in any case likely to remain much preoccupied with domestic affairs. Two tragic disasters, the loss of a nuclear submarine and the burning of a television tower in Moscow, were widely read as symptoms of the rundown state of the country after years of inadequate investment and maintenance. As expected though, Vladimir Putin won the Russian presidential election in March with over

50 per cent of the popular vote. (He had engagingly announced soon after accepting the acting presidency that his predecessor had stepped down early in order to give him a "head start" in the electoral campaign.) Fighting continued in Chechnya, another running sore, but presidential rule was imposed there in June. Other signs also suggested an advance towards a greater degree of order and well-being. The new president set about curbing the powers of over-mighty provincial governors and created new Federal Districts. There was a successful renegotiation of some foreign-held Soviet debt, Putin made a good impression at the G-8 meeting, and the economy continued to pick up. Even relations with the West appeared marginally better, though still shadowed by uncertainty over US intentions regarding defence systems.

In the case of China, though the shadow of Belgrade in 1999 still hung over relations with the USA, something of a corner was turned in May when the US House of Representatives voted to treat the world's most populous country as a normal trading partner once it was admitted to the WTO, albeit with reservations about its human rights record. To these reservations the Chinese of course at once objected. With the exception of Taiwan there was no issue over which China's government continued to show more sensitivity than possible interference in its internal affairs. Yet, with US encouragement, China continued to move slowly towards entry to the WTO, though its attitude towards Taiwan appeared to harden early in the year. The change in Taiwanese politics registered by the replacement of a KMT president in May by one (the first) who was not a member of that party, did not seem to change this.

The European Union, whatever some had hoped, emphatically did not behave or look like a great power. It spent an agitated and somewhat self-absorbed year, after beginning hopefully with a sense of emergence from the embarrassments of recent scandals, the presentation of ambitious plans for reform of its institutions, and a plea from its new president for their complete overhaul during his five-year term. On the credit side, there ensued some changes in the EU's working and even some new degree of cohesion in certain areas. The year also brought a minor triumph in the first imposition of discipline on a member state. For disregarding EU (environmental) legislation Greece was fined by the European Court of Justice. As for the working of the common currency, even if that was not an entirely satisfactory experience, the loss of the euro's value against the US dollar had at least begun to show some recovery as the year drew to a close. Greece, one of the four member countries still outside the single currency system, announced that it would join it in the coming New Year, though another, Denmark, held a referendum which endorsed its earlier decision not to do so.

Two other matters meanwhile gave particular trouble. One was concern about the principles and possible shape of a European military capacity independent of NATO. In due course this seemed to be temporarily laid to rest, though only after alarming the USA and raising the spectre of a damaged and weakened NATO. The other concerned the future constitution of the EU. Like the first matter, this aroused intense dispute and provoked increasing uneasiness as time passed. Impatience was mounting in central and eastern Europe amongst potential new members of the Union (negotiations with six selected "fast-track" aspirants to membership had, after all, begun as long ago as November 1998—see AR 1998, pp.434-35). The six-monthly meeting of heads of governments in December at Nice, of which much had been hoped in furtherance of enlargement, was a disappointing anti-climax; the difficulties which it revealed in arriving at agreement and the entrenched positions which were taken up in debate made further delay in the enlargement process seem all too likely. It also brought to a head French alarm over possible constitutional changes which might leave Germany with greater voting power than France. Nor was any beginning made with the radical reconstruction—far less with the dismantling—of the Common Agricultural Policy, yet eastern European countries with heavy economic commitments to agriculture were waiting to be admitted. Nice also confirmed that when almost all the current member states had particular interests to defend they would find the old Gaullist device of the national veto the best way of doing so, whether to protect the French film industry or British social policy.

All this is perhaps to suggest that for major players on the world stage, nothing much changed in 2000. The Western politics of international moral intervention of the 1990s seemed to have become less attractive. A general election in Austria in the autumn of 1999 had pushed forward the right-wing Freedom Party, to the electoral discomfiture of the Social Democrats, and early in 2000 it took up half the seats in a new coalition Cabinet. Some leaders of the party were said to have expressed extremist and even pro-Nazi sentiments and the EU at once announced a downgrading of the ministerial relations of all of its members with Austria, suggesting that this state of affairs would continue whilst members of the Freedom Party continued in their ministerial posts. Nonetheless, the will to maintain this coercive stance towards a sovereign state soon crumbled. Such diplomatic sanctions as it had sustained were lifted in September.

Certainly, no temptation to base intervention on principle was shown by any of the former Kosovo partners where the Middle East was concerned. Here could be found the most obviously enduring and deeply rooted international problems left unsolved by the century. Iraq continued to be formally ostracised and subjected to sanctions, though with decreasing international support for the USA and Britain (which wanted to maintain them), and with no visible effect on its ruler. As for Iran, symptoms of what was hoped to be liberalising change were eagerly welcomed, but did not turn out to amount to much in practice. The graver instabilities of the region, though, lay further to the west. When the year began, there had been some grounds for cautious optimism. Israel had seemed ready to talk to Syria, and negotiations were going on with the Palestinians about the activation of matters agreed in principle in the previous autumn (AR 1999 pp. 560-63. There were signs of greater recognition of realities on both sides. The Israelis decided to withdraw from the south Lebanon "security zone" without waiting for a definitive peace agreement with Syria, and did so in May. Prime Minister Ehud Barak had showed a promising flexibility in abandoning the long-standing Israeli insistence on an unqualified sovereignty over the city of Jerusalem, and President Yassir Arafat seemed to relax a little also, no longer demanding, for instance, that all the land occupied by Israel in 1967 should be returned to the Palestinians. There was still a prudent silence too over the much-feared proclamation of a independent Palestinian state. It even appeared that, were a bilateral settlement with Israel not to be forthcoming, the Palestinians would be willing to consider, as a last resort, some internationalised future for Jerusalem.

Unhappily, the ground for hopefulness always tended to crumble away in acrimonious delays and misunderstandings over agreement previously thought to have been achieved in principle, notably on matters of specific territory. Twice, the set date for making a framework agreement slipped by, before violence on the West Bank and in the Gaza strip began again to raise the temperature. It had already done so when further summit talks took place under the personal supervision of President Clinton at Camp David in July. Like the collapse of his parliamentary majority, the disorder was not fatal to Barak's government, but it seriously distracted it from the business of domestic reform and secularisation and damaged his power to negotiate. A provocative visit by an intransigent Israeli politician of the opposition to the Temple Mount was the last straw for many Palestinians. In November Barak felt that he had to call for new elections in the New Year to try to shake off the persistent parliamentary weakness which had always encumbered him.

Hope had by then withered to vanishing point in a headlong decline of Israeli-Palestinian intercourse into armed conflict, between Israeli security forces and settlers on the one side and rioting crowds of enraged Palestinians—whose responsiveness or lack of it to the Palestinian authorities was impossible to assess—on the other. By the end of the year a new intifada was under way and there were hundreds of deaths, mainly Palestinian, bombings in Israel's streets, shootings and murders in border zones. The Oslo road seemed to have reached its end. Yet, as the year closed, plans were again going forward for still more meetings under US auspices between representatives of the two peoples. Clearly, efforts would go on being made in Washington right up to the moment when Clinton finally left office. But the omens did not look good.

At least in Europe and the Balkans some long-running troubles seemed to move towards settlement. Ethnic violence in 2000 still brought death to Kosovans and embarrassment and casualties to the NATO-led international peace-keeping force there, but war criminals continued to be brought into the dock in the court at the Hague. The murder in Belgrade of one notorious thug and atrocity-monger paradoxically gave grounds for hope: perhaps the thieves who ran the country were falling out with one another, for it was not established who had killed him or why. Sanctions continued to be imposed against Yugoslavia. Then came a change. In September Slobodan Milosevic lost a presidential election in which there had been plentiful evidence of improper pressure by his supporters. A general strike and a popular rising culminating in the storming and occupation of the parliament building and the state television headquarters seemed finally to persuade the soldiers that they need not step in to save him and he reluctantly left office. A message of support from Moscow to the successful opposition candidate, Vojislav Kostunica, no doubt also helped and with his inauguration the lifting of sanctions began almost at once. There was still plentiful cause for concern, for the realities of power in Belgrade were such that as the year closed much of the administration, and particularly the security apparatus, was still in the hands of criminals put there during the Milosevic regime and a huge task of purification faced the new parliamentary rulers of Serbia. But an era had ended.

There were grounds for optimism in Asian affairs too, in what looked like the beginnings of a normalisation of relations between the two Koreas. If it could be achieved, this would be a major break with recent history and the laying to rest of one of the last ghosts of the Cold War. A new relationship indeed appeared to be emerging slowly. Private economic initiatives and then official approaches from the South opened the way to the first meeting of the two presidents since the appearance of the two individual states 42 years earlier. Agreement on economic co-operation and on approaching together the problems of reunification came out of this, and, more meaningfully, an end to the violently antagonistic propaganda exchanges which had previously characterised relations between North and South. Soon, ministers began to talk to one another and families, hitherto divided by the Cold War, exchanged officially orchestrated visits. In September it was announced that the North Korean president would in fact visit South Korea in 2001. There were also signs, in the shape of discussion of matters of common interest, of decreasing tension between North Korea and the USA, which conceded some slight slackening of its economic sanctions. The North Koreans confirmed the moratorium which they had already announced on test-flying of ballistic missiles (though it was clear that they would continue to work on them). Nothing was achieved, though, by way of improving North Korea's relations with Japan.

The year 2000 thus closed on a world which had recently undergone radical change, and was still undergoing it, even if it had been less dramatic than some had hoped. Clearly, too, such change was not confined to the last year of the century. What the year's own confusions and disappointments reflected was the reality of historical change in a longer perspective. As 2001 began, it could be seen that more than a chronological millenium had closed. Over the years, international life had seemed slowly to slip away somewhat from the Hobbesian clarity provided by the long domination of the dogmas of state sovereignty and nationality. Limited and partial but strong commitments to different links and associations were connecting countries and populations in new ways. Perhaps world politics was on the move to more overlapping and confusing jurisdictions and obligations, and a broader acceptance of (or at least lip-service to) common principle than in the past. Old simplicities had become less unquestionable. Big changes can also sometimes be expressed by relatively minor facts. Amongst the candidates of the Polish presidential election of October 2000 was to be found Lech Walesa, hero of the heady struggles of the 1980s. Even in 1990, there had already been signs that he was losing ground in the popular affection, and that his day was passing. Ten years later he received less than 1 per cent of the votes cast in the presidential election. Evidently Poland—like most of the world—had changed a lot, but not in one year alone.

2. THE INTERNATIONAL ECONOMY

TAKEN as a whole, 2000 was another successful year as global output rose by more than 4 per cent on the strength of robust GDP growth in the USA (5 per cent) and solid performances in the European Union (3.4 per cent), Latin America (4 per cent) and Asia and the Pacific (3.7 per cent). However, the annual figures alone fail to capture the high drama of the year and the sharp decline in mood and performance in its later months. By the fourth quarter, the earlier unbridled confidence had given way to pervasive pessimism under the influence of two interrelated factors—a steep increase in oil prices (attributed for the most part to OPEC production cuts in 1999) and a sudden economic reversal in the USA. "Recession" was slipping into the vocabulary of analysts and policymakers in Washington in December, and most other capitals had joined in a fretful watch to see if the "new economy's" first slowdown would become a meltdown; if the "landing" would be soft or hard.

Nowhere was the split economic personality of 2000 more apparent than in the USA, the "engine" that had powered the impressive growth achieved in much of the world in 1999. Optimism ran high at the beginning of 2000, particularly after it quickly became clear that midnight on New Year's Eve had not triggered the Y2K calamity that some had feared would disrupt financial markets, businesses, and vital governmental operations to such an extent that the global economy would be sent into a tailspin. With computers still faithfully serving their masters, enthusiasm, some might say headiness, centred on the technology sector and the related seemingly boundless expectations for "e-commerce". The Nasdaq composite index of high technology stocks, which had risen by 80 per cent in 1999, surged to an all-time high of 5,048 in early March 2000. With GDP growing at an annualised rate of 6 per cent (the highest for 17 years), officials in Washington focused most of their energy on the ongoing campaign against potential overheating. Worried about inflationary pressures, the Federal Reserve Board, under the direction of Chairman Alan Greenspan, boosted the interest rate on federal funds in March and May, the fifth and sixth hikes since June 1999. Shortly after the second increase, however, warning signs began to surface that perhaps the brakes had been applied too hard, particularly in view of soaring energy prices and the resultant constraints on disposable household income. The manufacturing sector was the first to wilt, the strength of the dollar against other world currencies contributing to reduced export demand. At the same time, analysts started to urge investors to withdraw from certain "new economy" stocks and return to more traditional investments out of concern that the recent high tech frenzy had represented unacceptably speculative behaviour or even, as one analyst put it, "irrational exuberance".

Oil prices reached a 10-year high of US$37.80 per barrel in September, causing a political headache for the Clinton administration, and especially for Vice President Al Gore, the Democratic Party's candidate for the November presidential election. Heavy diplomatic pressure from Washington and other Western capitals secured modest production increases from OPEC, but prices moderated only slightly as a result. Meanwhile, the stock market continued its free-fall as reports poured in from the technology sector of low sales and weak profits and it became evident that many of the new dot.com firms had, embarrassingly, failed to adhere to sound business practices. By December the rout of the dot.coms was in full force, and late in the month the Nasdaq hit its low for the year of 2,340, down more than 50 per cent from its peak. Consumer spending and confidence also plummeted, resulting in an annualised GDP increase in the fourth quarter of only 1.4 per cent, the poorest quarterly performance in more than five years. Amongst other things, the slowdown provided the incoming Republican administration of President-elect George W. Bush with additional ammunition in its campaign for a large tax cut, once justified as a payback to taxpayers in view of recent spectacular budget surpluses but now also promoted as necessary to stimulate the economy. Meanwhile, Canada's economic strength (4.3 per cent GDP growth for the year) was credited with having contributed significantly to the easy re-election of Prime Minister Jean Chrétien in November (see IV.2).

For much of the rest of the world, the major question at the end of 2000 was how contagious the US cold would be. The EU had reason to believe that it was better protected than other regions. For one thing, Europe had not experienced the surge in high tech investment that had so occupied US investors, thus making the EU less susceptible to a backlash. Also, nearly 80 per cent of EU trade was conducted between member states. In any event, the OECD projected that the EU would register about 3.4 per cent growth in GDP for 2000, more than a percentage point higher than in 1999. (Many of the figures for 2000 used in this article were preliminary or projections.) Meanwhile, unemployment, a serious problem for the EU since its inception, declined to about 9 per cent, whilst inflation remained manageable at about 1.5 per cent. Analysts also suggested that tax cuts (notably in France, Germany and Italy) and other structural reforms (such as the deregulation of certain sectors) that were instituted in 2000 would help to sustain economic progress. In a related vein, the March 2000 EU summit set target dates for liberalising market mechanisms for a number of products as well as for revising labour regulations, although the latter remained a source of controversy in several key countries. The EU leaders in December also agreed to consider the creation of a so-called "European company statute", which proponents had sought for decades as a means of helping corporations to operate more efficiently across the EU. In addition, EU leaders in 2000 endorsed efforts to revamp the Union's "cumbersome machinery" for negotiating international trade agreements.

On a more worrisome front, the euro declined against the dollar for most of 2000, prompting the spectre of a loss of public support for the fledgling currency. (Upon Greece's accession to the EU's Economic and Monetary Union (EMU) on January 1, 2001, the euro was the common monetary unit for all EU members except Denmark, Sweden and the UK and was due to replace national currencies entirely from January 1, 2002.) After rejecting proposed intervention to prop up the euro as unnecessary several times earlier in the year, the European Central Bank finally agreed in September to buy up billions of euros in conjunction with the central banks of Canada, Japan, the UK and the USA in an effort to halt a slide that had seen the currency fall 30 per cent against the dollar since its introduction on January 1, 1999. "Euro-land" supporters received additional bad news in September when the Danes voted against proposed accession to the EMU (II.3.i), a decision that was considered likely to improve the prospects of the "euro-sceptics" in Sweden and the UK.

Despite the euro's valuation and accession problems, it received credit in 2000 for facilitating monetary stability and serving as a catalyst for structural reform, particularly regarding national budget deficits. In addition, the weakness of the euro produced at least one economic benefit by making European exports more attractive to the rest of the world. Germany in particular benefited from the boom, and its exports grew by 13 per cent for the year, underpinning annual GDP growth of 3.1 per cent (the best since unification and more than double the 1999 rate). As one means of promoting additional economic expansion, the German government in July 2000 passed an extensive reform package designed to reduce personal and corporate taxes. Meanwhile, France, the other dominant euro-zone economy, achieved GDP growth of 3.2 per cent in 2000, up from 2.4 per cent in 1999. The improvement was built in part on the creation of an estimated 500,000 new jobs, which, despite the fact that many were part-time or temporary, helped to bring the unemployment rate down to 9.2 per cent by the end of the year. With an eye towards the national elections scheduled for 2002, French politicians were jockeying to take credit for the new jobs, many of which were attributed to government incentives, youth employment programs and a shorter working week (II.2.ii).

Of the EU countries outside the euro-zone, the UK appeared the most likely to be influenced by fluctuations in the USA, the destination of 15 per cent of UK exports. Consequently, it was not surprising that the UK experience in 2000 mirrored that of the USA. A strong performance in the first half of the year contributed to yearly GDP growth of about 3.0 per cent, although the 0.3 per cent increase in the fourth quarter was the lowest since 1998. Manufacturing output increased 1.6 per cent, the best performance for that sector since 1994, whilst inflation was held to about 1.2 per cent, permitting the Monetary Policy Board of the Bank of England to leave interest rates unchanged for most of the year. In another positive development, unemployment declined to 5.3 per cent (well below the EU average) with some sectors even experiencing labour shortages. In view of the country's ongoing economic stability, UK Conservatives appeared to retain substantial popular support for their position that entry into the EMU would be imprudent.

In Russia, President Vladimir Putin was credited in 2000 with having brought life to the economy after only one year in office, his successes including the imposition of a degree of fiscal discipline and the restructuring of the tax code. According to the government's figures, GDP grew by 7.6 per cent in 2000, largely due to the positive effect on energy-rich Russia of rising oil prices and better export competitiveness resulting from past devaluation of the rouble. (Export value grew to US$100.4 billion for the year, whilst the trade surplus doubled to US$67 billion.) The government also reported that real incomes, which had plunged in 1999, rose by 9.1 per cent during 2000, whilst unemployment fell to 10.2 per cent. The privatisation of some state-run enterprises was viewed as influential in industrial growth of 9.2 per cent.

In the light of its stronger financial position, Russia adopted a much tougher stance late in the year in regard to the issue of the repayment of some US$48 billion in Soviet-era debt. Moscow hinted that it might not make the payments due to Paris Club creditors in early 2001 unless substantial rescheduling was negotiated. (About one-quarter of the Russian budget was currently committed to servicing the external debt.) However, lenders insisted on further cuts in government expenditure, reform of the banking sector and the curtailment of various monopolies. Complicating matters at the end of the year was a US report which argued that much of the aid which had been donated in the 1990s had been squandered due, in part, to pervasive corruption in Russia.

Former Soviet republics and satellite states in 2000 registered the second consecutive year of recovery from the Russian financial crisis of 1998. Growth for Central and Eastern Europe was estimated at 4.2 per cent, whereas for the Baltic countries it was 3.6 per cent, and for the Commonwealth of Independent States (CIS) it was 5.2 per cent. Central and Eastern Europe and the Baltic states were helped by increased investment from and exports to the EU, whilst producers in the CIS benefited from high oil prices. Meanwhile, political developments in south-eastern Europe, including the overthrow of Yugoslavian President Slobodan Milosevic and the installation of a reform-minded government in Croatia, were seen as laying the groundwork for future economic improvement. The European Bank for Reconstruction and Development reported that the transition countries in 2000 made their greatest progress in economic reform since 1997, although institutional reform still lagged behind market liberalisation and privatisation. The Bank declared recovery in the region to be "in full swing", supported by the return of private foreign investment.

The Asian and Pacific economies continued their surprisingly swift recovery in 2000 from the regional financial crisis of 1998, despite the fact that their stock markets reversed direction in consonance with the USA. (The Nikkei share price index in Japan dropped 27 per cent in 2000, after gaining 37 per cent in the previous year). China, Taiwan and South Korea were the regional powerhouses as north-east Asia's growth rate reached 8.3 per cent, compared with 5.8 per cent in south-east Asia. This disparity was attributed in part to the fact that foreign investment had poured into the north-east but had fallen by half in the south-east since the crisis. Foreign investment exceeded US$39 billion in China in 2000, helping to sustain a growth rate above 8 per cent. The government also continued to pump money into the economy through massive infrastructure construction. Despite maintaining many elements of its old protectionist policies, China achieved several breakthroughs in trade relations in 2000 with Europe and the USA. Perhaps the most important was the US government's decision to grant China permanent normal trading status, a move which was expected to facilitate China's eventual accession to the World Trade Organisation, although negotiations in that regard remained contentious at the year's end.

Other prominent Asian success stories in 2000 included South Korea where 8.7 per cent growth was fuelled by strong exports, and Singapore, which achieved 8.9 per cent growth. India suffered a disappointing harvest, its growth of slightly more than 6 per cent being offset by inflation that was running at 8 per cent annually by the end of the year. The administration of Prime Minister Atal Bihari Vajpayee, who had been viewed as reform-minded upon his installation in 1998, was described in 2000 as having lost momentum in that regard, in part due to difficulties in the coalition government. Political turbulence was also cited as a factor in the less than anticipated growth of 4.2 per cent in Indonesia, where separatists in Irian Jaya and Aceh battled for the opportunity to follow East Timor towards independence, and 3.6 per cent in the Philippines, where the beleaguered President Estrada's administration faced charges of poor governance on several fronts. In a more promising political development, many observers suggested that the historic summit of the leaders of North and South Korea in June would lead to extensive economic interaction, desperately needed in North Korea where the government had finally begun to retreat from its communist orthodoxy by permitting farmers to sell some of their products for personal profit and by expanding free-trade areas in the country for foreign investors.

The most glaring underachiever in Asia in 2000 was Japan, the world's second largest economy, which limped along at only 1.5-2 per cent annual growth despite the massive government stimulus program launched in late 1999. Industrial output and capital expenditure declined, in part due to a slowdown in consumer spending; unemployment reached 4.8 per cent in November, almost setting a record high. Exports to the USA began to slow in the second half of the year, threatening the country's fragile recovery from the startling 2.8 per cent contraction in 1998. Critics charged that the national government was "confused" as to how to address the economic distress.

Much as in Asia, economic performance in Latin America and the Caribbean in 2000 was a mixture of good and bad news. Final figures were expected to show overall growth in the region at a healthy 4 per cent for the year; however, many countries continued to struggle with deep-seated problems that had lingered since the early 1990s, such as widespread poverty, high unemployment and suffocating levels of debt.

Brazil, one of the region's economic giants, managed a significant turnaround from 1999, when it had been forced to devalue the real and had achieved less than 1 per cent growth. Taking advantage of increased competitiveness arising from the devaluation, the country was able to boost exports and attract more foreign investment. Under the additional influence of interest rate cuts, production for the first 11 months of 2000 was up 6.4 per cent from 1999; some 900,000 new jobs were reportedly created during the same period. Growth for the year was expected to reach 4 per cent. However, caution remained warranted at the end of the year regarding the debt burden as the government, facing IMF demands to maintain fiscal discipline, was forced to devote nearly half of its next budget to servicing external and domestic debts.

Mexico experienced an historic year in 2000. Amongst other things, the election of opposition party candidate Vicente Fox as President in July and the termination of 71 years of virtual one-party rule eased fears that political instability and domestic turmoil might hinder Mexico's further integration into the North American Free Trade Agreement. Growth shot up to 7 per cent for the year, supported by the influx of capital from US companies, the related surge of exports to the USA and higher oil prices. Meanwhile, inflation declined as the result of higher interest rates and the rising value of the peso. However, towards the end of the year it was apparent that Mexico was facing a policy dilemma on the oil front. Although rising prices were a boon to the domestic economy, they threatened the country's export markets, particularly the USA.

Argentina was less fortunate in 2000 than Brazil and Mexico. Although the administration of new President Fernando de la Rúa (sometimes governing by decree in the face of Congressional opposition) initiated labour reform, deregulated several economic sectors and otherwise attempted to promote development, overall growth for the year was less than 0.5 per cent. Some analysts blamed these economic difficulties in part on Argentina's currency policy, which not only pegged the peso to the US dollar, but also limited the supply of pesos to the amount of hard currency held on reserve. In effect, the dollar peg turned much of the nation's monetary policy over to the USA, the increases in interest rates in early 2000 by the USA Federal Reserve, for example, having a negative impact on the Argentinian economy. Experts also argued that the dollar kept the peso overvalued, thereby hindering Argentina's export competitiveness in world markets. Facing a myriad of such difficulties, the government was forced at the end of the year to negotiate a US$39.2 billion bailout with international financial institutions to avoid defaulting on its debt repayments.

In Africa, economic progress in 2000 remained constrained by a wide range of factors, including the AIDS crisis, which continued to represent not only an unspeakable humanitarian tragedy but also a potential long-term economic disaster, and an overwhelming debt burden. Regarding the latter, at the end of the year the World Bank and the IMF announced that 18 African countries had qualified for a new debt-relief initiative, although some observers wondered if many of the countries would be able to adhere to the spending discipline required to obtain the relief. Once again compounding difficulties for the continent during 2000 was the world commodities market. The energy sector aside, the price for most African commodities fell during the year, although the drop was not nearly as drastic as in 1999, when the price of coffee, cocoa and cotton had plummeted by up to 50 per cent. In view of the continued depression in the commodities market, African leaders warmly welcomed the US government's approval in May 2000 of the African Growth and Opportunity Act (AGOA), described as the largest trade bill passed by the US Congress since it had approved membership of the WTO in 1994. The Act provided for the unilateral reduction of US tariffs on a broad range of African goods as well as the elimination of import quotas for African textiles made with African or American materials. Amongst other things, supporters hoped that the measure would open up American markets for African manufacturing products, previously subject to tariffs of up to 17 per cent. President Bill Clinton lifted the first tariffs under the AGOA in December.

In South Africa, sub-Saharan Africa's most prosperous country, the administration of President Thabo Mbeki in 2000 continued to face the legacy of apartheid, which included an estimated 33 per cent unemployment rate and a severe maldistribution of wealth. The government attempted to combat the country's economic malaise by privatising government enterprises, reducing the national budget deficit, earmarking funds for road-building and other infrastructure development and adopting reforms designed to attract overseas investors by cutting the cost of doing business in South Africa. Nevertheless, it was estimated that growth reached only about 2.6 per cent for the year, compared with 3.6 per cent in 1999.

In late November 2000 Mbeki and other African leaders announced plans to launch a "Millennium Africa Recovery Plan" in conjunction with Europe, Japan and the USA. However, the scepticism elicited by this latest initiative to boost investment in the continent underscored the fact that "globalisation", still the word on everyone's lips, had far to go in bridging the North-South economic divide. The World Bank reported that capital flow to developing countries had recovered somewhat in 2000 but was concentrated on a select group of countries, including Brazil, China and Mexico. For their part, African leaders protested that the commitment of OECD countries to globalisation was less clear when it came to reducing the agricultural subsidies which gave their farmers a competitive edge.

The feeling amongst developing countries that they had been excluded from the New Economy remained a recurrent theme in 2000, having bubbled over at the ill-fated WTO meeting in Seattle in late 1999 (AR1999, pp. 412-13). Amongst others, the philanthropist financier George Soros supported anti-globalisation protesters, arguing that the developed countries had created an "uneven playing field". Within the World Bank severe discord was reported regarding the appropriate approach to global economic development (see XI.2.ii). In addition, criticism intensified in a number of quarters regarding the implications of globalisation for environmental and labour standards. On a related front, the UN World Employment report said that 160 million people were unemployed in 2000, some 20 million more than prior to the 1998 financial crisis in Russia and Asia. The technology revolution had yet to penetrate much of the world, UN bodies argued, and half of the world's population still lived on less than US$2 per day.

Such concerns were viewed as having contributed to stagnation in 2000 in the WTO regarding the proposed launching of new global trade negotiations, whilst the EU, Japan and the USA appeared farther apart than ever over their numerous disputes. Meanwhile, integrationist progress on the regional level in the developing world was held hostage to political and even military (as in central Africa) conflict. Further evidence that 2000 was "a bad year for world governance" appeared in the failure of climate control talks at The Hague to reach an agreement on curbing greenhouse gas emissions (see XIII.3). Those casting about for more positive developments perhaps could find a sliver of hope in the Global Compact launched in July at the UN by a group of some 50 transnational companies and a number of labour organisations after 18 months of discussions. In addition to outlining nine principles to guide transnationals in meeting their "corporate responsibilities" in the global economy, the Compact illustrated the UN's new commitment to co-operation with business, heretofore perceived as an adversary in many matters.

The 2000 Nobel Prize in the Economic Sciences was shared by Daniel McFadden of the University of California, Berkeley, and James Heckman of the University of Chicago. In recognising McFadden, the Nobel Committee cited his contributions to the development of the theory and methodology in an area of econometrics (economic modelling and statistics) known as discrete choice analysis. The committee lauded Heckman for his groundbreaking work in microeconometric theory and methodology involving different selection problems. Heckman's analysis had had a significant impact on applied economic research and other social sciences.

II WESTERN AND SOUTHERN EUROPE

1. UNITED KINGDOM—SCOTLAND—WALES—NORTHERN IRELAND

i. UNITED KINGDOM

CAPITAL: London   AREA: 245,000 sq km   POPULATION: 59,700,000
OFFICIAL LANGUAGES: English; Welsh in Wales   POLITICAL SYSTEM: parliamentary democracy
HEAD OF STATE: Queen Elizabeth II (since Feb '52)
RULING PARTY: Labour Party (since May '97)
HEAD OF GOVERNMENT: Tony Blair, Prime Minister (since May '97)
MAIN IGO MEMBERSHIPS (NON-UN): NATO, CWTH, EU, WEU, OSCE, CE, OECD, G-8
CURRENCY: pound sterling (end-'00 US$1=£0.67)
GNP PER CAPITA: US$22,640, US$20,883 at PPP ('99)

WHILST the Labour government elected in May 1997 remained politically dominant in 2000, it no longer seemed as invulnerable as it had in previous years. In spite of the fact that the economy was buoyant, with virtually full employment and low inflation, Prime Minister Tony Blair and his Cabinet colleagues faced a series of difficult and uncomfortable challenges during the course of the year.

The Millennium Dome was the most spectacular of these, a giant and very visible folly. In spite of the fact that the Dome had attracted some six million visitors, these constituted only half of the numbers needed to pay for the extraordinary costs of building and running it. If there were going to be a moment when Blair was vulnerable to political attack, this was the year. Try as he might, however, Conservative Party leader William Hague made little headway in the opinion polls, apart from brief distortions caused by specific events such as the petrol crisis in September. One of the problems was that under Hague's leadership, the Conservatives appeared to be more concerned with retaining the populist and right-of-centre approval of their own grass roots, than in engaging with the majority of opinion in the country. It seemed extremely unlikely that the Conservatives would return to power at the next general election, and more probable that voter apathy would do more to harm the government's majority than would the Opposition.

The UK's success in the Sydney Olympics, where it finished 10th in the league table of winners with a total of 28 medals (see XVI), was a great source of popular celebration, and an indication that the money invested in sporting facilities and education by the national lottery was paying dividends. But as the dull and chilly summer weather gave way to the rainiest autumn season since records began, the national mood at the end of the millennial year was subdued rather than optimistic.

ELECTIONS, GOVERNMENT CHANGES AND PARTY AFFAIRS. Labour remained ahead in the opinion polls throughout the year, but its showing in actual elections was less assured. In London, choosing mayoral candidates dominated the early months of the year. Steve Norris, former Transport Minister, was chosen as the Conservative candidate on January 17, but the real question was whether Ken Livingstone, or Tony Blair's favoured candidate, Frank Dobson, the former Health Secretary, would represent Labour. Dobson was eventually chosen on February 20 by 51.5 per cent of the vote in Labour's electoral college to Livingstone's 48.5 per cent, after Glenda Jackson was eliminated. Livingstone immediately denounced the result as "tainted", since he had achieved a majority amongst party members and union sections of the ballot. The result only increased the widespread perception that the Labour leadership had manipulated the entire electoral process in order to prevent Livingstone (who all the opinion polls showed to be the most popular candidate) from winning the party nomination (see AR 1999, pp. 19-20). Despite his earlier statement that he would not run as an independent, Livingstone, encouraged by his supporters, announced his candidacy on March 6.

The mayoral campaign then really became a family fight, between Dobson and Livingstone (who was formally expelled from the party on 3 April). Livingstone's popular lead remained huge throughout the campaign. In the event, only 223,884 people voted for Dobson, with Livingstone taking 776,427 votes; the latter won a majority of 212,290 over Norris (564,137 votes) on the second count. Susan Kramer, the Liberal Democrat candidate, came fourth with 203,452 votes. In the elections for the Assembly members, the Conservatives and Labour parties each won nine seats, the Liberal Democrats four and the Green Party three. Turnout was 33.6 per cent.

Countrywide, turnout in the local elections averaged around 30 per cent but fell as low as 15 per cent in some wards. The results for Labour were worse than predicted. The Conservatives emerged with overall control of 16 extra councils, Labour lost eight overall, whilst the Liberal Democrats lost one. A total of 560 Labour councillors lost their seats, on Labour's worst local election night since 1992, and the Conservatives gained nearly 600 seats. Nonetheless, Labour remained in control of 149 local authorities in Great Britain, with a total of 8,530 councillors, compared with 91 authorities and 6,740 councillors for the Conservatives and 27 authorities and 4,480 councillors for the Liberal Democrats. A total of 151 local authorities had no overall control.

On the same night that they improved their position in local government, however, the Conservatives suffered defeat by the Liberal Democrats in the by-election at Romsey, a south coast, semi-rural constituency, caused by the death of the sitting Conservative MP Michael Colvin. The Liberal Democrat candidate, Sandra Gidley, won with a majority of 3,311 on a 55 per cent turnout, with over 50 per cent of the vote. Hague's failure to hold Romsey suggested that an anti-Tory majority could still be mobilised even in the party's heartland constituencies. It was only the second time in 100 years that the Tories had lost a seat to the Liberals whilst in opposition.

Other by-elections during the year held fewer surprises. Three Westminster by-elections were held on 23 November, in Glasgow Anniesland, Donald Dewar's seat until his death on October 11 (see II.1.ii), Preston, vacant after the death of Audrey Wise, and West Bromwich, vacant after Betty Boothroyd's resignation as Speaker of the House of Commons. All three were held by Labour, despite Scottish Nationalist (SNP) hopes that they would win in Glasgow and a strong Tory challenge in West Bromwich. In December, a by-election in Falkirk West, whose MP, Dennis Canavan, had resigned from the Labour Party, was also won by Labour, though its majority was cut from 13,783 to 705 votes with a 16.15 per cent swing to the SNP.

Opinion polls through the year also suggested that voters continued to prefer Labour as the governing party. MORI polls for the *The Times* put Labour on 50 per cent in February, 47 per cent in June, 51 per cent in August and 48 per cent in November. There was a dramatic drop around September, though, at the time of the petrol crisis, to 37 per cent , with the Conservatives rising to 35 per cent from 29 per cent and the Liberal Democrats to 21 per cent from about 15 per cent during the rest of the year. By December, however, Labour's position had recovered.

In February Hague reshuffled his shadow Cabinet. Michael Portillo, the former Defence Secretary who had only recently returned to Parliament, was made shadow Chancellor. John Redwood, environment spokesman, and John Maples, shadow Foreign Secretary, were dropped, and replaced by Archie Norman, former Asda supermarket chief, and Francis Maude. Further changes were made in September, when Oliver Letwin, who became an MP in 1997, was promoted to shadow Chief Secretary, and Angela Browning moved from trade and industry, where her performance had been criticised, to become shadow leader of the Commons, whilst David Heathcoat-Amory took over from her. In August, a high-profile Conservative supporter, once tipped as Tory candidate for mayor of London, defected to the Labour Party. Ivan Massow, a gay millionaire insurance broker, claimed that the Tories had become "intolerant and just plain nasty" under William Hague.

The party conferences in the autumn took place as the government was being rocked by the petrol crisis, and its opinion poll lead was being sharply eroded. At the Liberal Democrat conference in September, Charles Kennedy said that his party would offer voters some hypothecated taxation—thereby allowing individuals to choose whether they want a specific sum spent on health, education or another public service. "We will", he said, "let people, not politicians, decide how some of their tax revenues are spent". Kennedy also used his speech to call on Tories to defect from William Hague if they believed in "tolerance, decency, fair play", and described Hague as "the world's first unpopular populist". He did not go into detail on Liberal Democrat plans to raise some taxes, but reaffirmed commitments to abolish prescription charges and student tuition fees and give pensioners up to £15 a week extra.

At the Labour conference the following week, there was dissent in the party over pensions policy. Chancellor Gordon Brown, in a strong speech, set out a partial about-turn on pensions but failed to avert a rare defeat later in the week, when party veteran Barbara Castle attacked government policy. Although in his pre-Budget report in November he did not restore the link to earnings, Brown raised pensions by over twice the rate of inflation. Tony Blair's speech at the conference included an impassioned appeal to the "basic decent instincts" of the British people to give Labour a second term to complete its modernisation programme.

He said that New Labour represented the marriage of "realism and idealism", compared with tax-cutting Tory cynicism, and claimed that he had an "irreducible core" of moral values which informed his politics. He admitted that the Dome had been a mistake, and that more must be done for pensioners, but was not very conciliatory to the fuel protestors, who were at that point dominating the political scene, arguing that "I have also had to listen over underfunding in the NHS, over extra investment in schools, over more police on the beat, over public transport". The world was full "of competing causes, most of them good. . . it's not an arrogant government that chooses priorities, it's an irresponsible government that fails to choose."

At the Conservative conference, William Hague's speech on October 6 attempted to reach out to disaffected Labour voters, saying that his party had learned from past mistakes and wanted to govern pragmatically "for all the people". He called for an immediate election, saying that he wanted to govern with "common sense" instincts—a reference to his three-year "common sense revolution" in the party—saying that being tough on crime, believing in lower taxes and defending national independence were an essential part of achieving better schools and hospitals, and thriving inner cities. He attacked Blair's government as "arrogant, out of touch and divided", run by a "metropolitan elite" and said that it was taking Britain down the road to a European superstate. Only by voting for the Tories, he said, could people keep the pound and ensure that "there still will be a Britain".

Donations to political parties remained an issue in 2000 as both parties looked to raise £15-20 million for the election campaign. The Tory Party treasurer, Michael Ashcroft, was made a life peer after his resignation as Belize's ambassador to the UN and his relocation to Britain. He gave his party another £1 million in the year to March, including the conversion of a £250,000 loan into a gift, plus £390,000 of gifts in kind, the party's biggest private benefactor. Nevertheless, the party remained £5 million in debt. Labour's largest donations came from Lord Sainsbury, publisher Paul Hamlyn and financier Christopher Ondaatje each of whom donated £2 million, but a smaller donation of £33,000 from prospective Millennium Dome buyer Robert Bourne provoked the most interest, though the party claimed it was merely the last instalment of a donation which had been pledged before the Dome was built. The Neill/Nolan anti-sleaze reforms on party funding were due to come into force in February 2001, and would oblige the parties to disclose donations of more than £5,000 and bar foreign donors.

On October 24, as the new session of Parliament got under way, a new Speaker was elected, amid calls for a reform of the archaic process in which candidates were eliminated one by one. The "Father of the House", Sir Edward Heath presided over the election. He rejected calls for reforming the electoral mechanism, even though 12 candidates were standing. These were eventually reduced, after almost seven hours, to Michael Martin, the first Roman Catholic to be elected Speaker since the Reformation.

The government's legislative programme, set out in the Queen's Speech on December 6, contained 15 main bills and four draft pieces of legislation. Amongst the matters included were child curfew schemes for those aged 9 to 15 years; new powers for seizing criminals' assets; a ban on the promotion and advertising of tobacco; new moves on literacy and numeracy for 11 to 14 year-olds and a major programme to improve adult literacy; £500 million for the best-run NHS trusts; increased public-private partnerships for primary health care, particularly inner-city GPs; a requirement for house-sellers to produce a buyers' pack, including a survey; a draft Safety Bill covering rail safety measures recommended by the Cullen inquiry into the Paddington rail crash; a bill to control arms exports; and a fraud bill to allow the withdrawal or reduction of benefit from anybody convicted twice of a benefit offence within three years. The long-awaited Hunting Bill was also included, offering MPs a free vote in choosing between an almost total ban on hunting with dogs, a compulsory regulatory system which would force hunts to obtain licences, or a voluntary system of self-regulation.

Late in the year, as expectations of a spring 2001 general election were high, the issue of US-style live TV debates resurfaced and seemed to have a greater chance of being realised than when John Major had turned them down at the last general election. The BBC and ITV made a joint approach to the leaders of the three main political parties. Hague, whose lively performances in the House of Commons made it seem likely that he would benefit from such an exercise, voiced his support. The government was much less enthusiastic.

MILLENNIUM PROJECTS. In 1994 the Conservative administration, led by John Major, had set up the Millennium Commission to make grants available to projects that would celebrate the ending of the twentieth century. The money was to come from the national lottery, which had identified Millennium projects as one of its five categories of "good works" that it would expect to finance. Following the 1997 general election, the incoming Labour government expressed its commitment to this vision. Millennium Commission grants, worth in total over £1.2 billion, funded a wide variety of projects which constituted a programme of year-long celebrations throughout the length and breadth of the United Kingdom. According to Chris Smith, the Millennium Commission Chairman and Culture Secretary, this would "create a lasting legacy which will be felt for generations to come." The scope and nature of these Millennium projects were wide-ranging but secular, a fact which caused some consternation to Christian leaders.

Millennium funding paid for celebrations at the beginning and end of the year. Across the country, but most dramatically in London, the skies were lit by spectacular fireworks at midnight to mark the coming of the year 2000. To mark the end of the year, further celebrations were scheduled in 32 towns and cities, funded by grants totalling £25 million. Although some events at the end of the year had to be cancelled, the festivities included a beach run in Blackpool, an aerial tightrope walk in Coventry and the UK's biggest tea dance in Plymouth. In between, the Commission awarded a total of £200 million to tens of thousands of individuals working on community projects. It also helped to fund 200 new buildings, and numerous environmental projects and visitor attractions. Money was also earmarked for ethnic minority groups. Four major grants were awarded to such groups: the Centre of Excellence for Black Women, the Windrush Heritage and Millennium Project, the Leadership Development Centre, and the Beta First Community Leadership Centre. International Women's Day in March was celebrated by a number of Millennium-funded projects, including drama and dance.

Whilst community-led projects lay at the heart of the Millennium celebrations, the fund was also used to pay for a number of spectacular and lasting public projects. The Tate Modern, for example, was opened by the Queen on May 11. A grant of £50 million was used to transform the former Bankside Power Station into one of the most significant museums of modern art in the world. Housing nearly 600 works by such artists as Dali, Picasso and Warhol, its works were displayed in themed groups rather than chronological order, an innovative curatorial approach. The Tate Modern was astonishingly successful, and attracted record numbers of visitors, to the envy of competing museums and galleries in the capital. Another major art centre, the Lowry, was opened in April in Salford, near Manchester, with the aid of a £15.65 million grant from the Millennium Commission. Dedicated to the legacy of the primitive Mancunian painter of working class life, it included an art gallery and a 1,750 seat theatre. Perhaps the most successful of the millennial attractions was the British Airways funded "London Eye" on the south bank of the River Thames. An enormous ferris wheel, the eye provided spectacular views along the river, and was visible for miles around.

Some projects were less successful, and for many people, the millennium celebrations would be remembered for their embarrassing misjudgments and controversies. The touted "river of flame" failed on New Year's Eve 1999 in London, to the consternation of the crowds gathered on the banks of the Thames. On 9 May, shortly after the Queen opened the Millennium Bridge—the first new bridge to cross the River Thames since the opening of Tower Bridge in 1894, and London's only solely pedestrian bridge—it had to be closed because it was found to sway alarmingly when people began walking across it. However, the most controversial Millennium project to be funded by the Commission, and certainly the most expensive, was the Millennium Dome in Greenwich. The Dome, an enormous tent-like construction held up by 12 spires, was internally divided into a series of themed "zones". Before it opened on New Year's Eve 1999, Prime Minister Tony Blair had claimed that it would be "the greatest show on earth", and the natural focus for the world's millennium celebrations. The Dome was going to be, in Blair's words, a metaphor to "show Britain as a country confident about the future". However, from the night it opened it appeared to be trouble. Thousands of invited guests—many from the media—were forced to queue for hours before gaining admission. The Minister for the Dome, Lord Falconer, was forced to issue a public apology, and the entire debacle was seen as a most unauspicious baptism.

The Dome was also widely criticised for its contents, which many saw as lacking focus. The zones were often uninspired and bland and, for the more popular areas, there were long queues. The result was public disenchantment and, as much of the media portrayed the Dome as a monument to the arrogance and emptiness of New Labour, the public voted with their feet and stayed away from the attraction. Costings for the project had been based on the estimate that the Dome would attract 12 million paying visitors (including 2 million from abroad) during the year. It was on this basis that the Dome was granted a further £50 million when its original £400 million grant had been spent by December 1999. In January the Commission found that it had to allocate the Dome another £60 million. Even by admitting large numbers of school children for free, the 12 million visitors estimate proved hopelessly unattainable and the Chief Executive of the Dome, Jennie Page, was sacked within weeks, to be replaced by Pierre-Yves Gerbeau, who had previously run Disneyland Paris. Visitor numbers remained low, however, and the management had to go back to the Commission in April for another £29 million. By this point, public and political sympathy for the project was at an end. In July 2000 a Select Committee of the House of Commons lambasted the ministers and managers of the Dome for their ineptitude. In September the Dome was granted another £45 million by the Millennium Commission to keep it open until the end of the year, but only because it was estimated that it would be more expensive to close it down immediately. In November the National Audit Office, in an official report, scathingly criticised the "weaknesses in financial management and control" of the Dome's management company. It had been hoped that some revenue could be recouped if a suitable buyer were found, but this proved increasingly difficult. In September Nomura International, the Japanese venture capital company, made a £106 million bid to create an urban entertainment resort, but quickly pulled out after seeing financial reports. In November the government agreed to give preference to the bid from Legacy, owned by controversial Irish developers, John Ronan and Richard Barrett, who had previously been substantial donors to the Labour Party. The future of the Dome was unresolved by the end of the year. However, during the final days in December 2000, an unexpected rush of visitors pushed up visitor totals to 6.5 millon. This made the Dome the most popular visitor attraction in Britain during 2000, and many of the visitors who were surveyed were enthusiastic about its attractions.

ASYLUM SEEKERS, IMMIGRATION AND RACE RELATIONS. Controversy over the numbers of asylum seekers gaining entry to Britain dominated public debate over immigration and race relations in 2000. In January, new figures confirmed that a record number of 71,160 asylum seekers had entered Britain in 1999, compared with 46,000 in 1998. This rising trend contributed to the wave of media attention and high political temperature that characterised the subject throughout the year. Home Office hopes that the new Asylum and Immigration Act, which came into effect in April, would help to reduce the numbers of applications were not realised by the end of the year. Applications during the last three months of 2000 averaged 6,680 per month, 1 per cent higher than for the same period of 1999. Overall however, numbers seemed to have stabilised. The government's promise to cut the backlog of asylum applications was put in doubt at the beginning of the year, when it was announced that these had risen above 100,000 for the first time. But by the end of 2000, it was clear that the new legislation was having a significant impact on the speed with which applications were dealt with. By the end of December, the number of outstanding applications had fallen to 66,195, 35 per cent lower than at the end of 1999. The majority of applicants came from Iraq, Sri Lanka, Iran, Afghanistan, Somalia and Eastern Europe, in particular the Federal Republic of Yugoslavia.

The Asylum and Immigration Act was intended to lift the unequal burden borne by local authorities, such as Tory-controlled Kent, which by the spring had an estimated 5,000 asylum seekers to support, including some 700 unaccompanied children under 18. Under the terms of the Act, applicants would become the responsibility of a National Asylum Support Service. A key aspect of the plan was forcibly to disperse asylum seekers around the country and to replace their eligibility for benefits with a voucher system to meet their essential needs. Maximum weekly voucher payments were £26.60 for a child under 16, £36.54 for an adult and £57.37 for a couple, representing 70 per cent of the equivalent income support levels for a British citizen, and including a £10 voucher redeemable for cash. Vouchers were issued in denominations of £10, £5, £1 and 50p and could be used to buy food, clothes and other items only in 15,000 designated stores. Shops in the scheme were not allowed to give change, an aspect which drew particular criticism. The harsher aspects of the new system were justified by the Home Office on the grounds that the application process would be much quicker under the terms of the Act, and that the measures would help to deter economic migrants whilst simultaneously providing safe refuge for genuine claimants.

Controversy over these plans, on practical as well as humanitarian grounds, was already apparent before they were put into effect. In March the Home Secretary, Jack Straw, was forced to announce the postponement of the full dispersal programme because of the difficulty of finding appropriate housing. Many councils held back from offering accommodation amid concern that the gap between central funding and the true cost of supporting asylum seekers would force them to cut services or increase council tax. By June the Audit Commission was warning that many of the people who the Home Secretary intended to move would simply return to London unless more were done to help councils receive them. Dispersing asylum seekers to areas of the country with no significant existing ethnic minority population was already proving to be unworkable within only weeks of the introduction of the new legislation. In August, for example, violent attacks on asylum seekers forcibly dispersed to Hull from Kent, meant that a number of people had to be removed for their own safety. This impression was confirmed in September, when Liverpool withdrew its support for the scheme, with a spokesman for the housing executive calling the Home Office arrangements "farcical"'. In the same month, the Government announced its intention to reconsider the working of the voucher scheme, in order to avert a revolt at the Party Conference led by transport union leader Bill Morris, a leading national critic of the new legislation.

Continuing public anxiety over the record numbers of applications made it difficult for the government to backtrack on its "get tough" policies, however. Moreover, the Conservatives did not hesitate to incorporate the immigration issue into its populist strategy in the year before a new general election. Nevertheless, mounting criticism from human rights organisations and religious leaders by the middle of the year led the government to shift its focus away from the individual asylum seeker and onto the role of organised criminal gangs smuggling people into Britain. It was announced at the beginning of the summer that the intelligence services were being mobilised to counter such activity. The scale of this problem was underscored by the discovery of 60 Chinese migrants trapped in a sealed lorry container in Dover at the end of June. A shocking counterpoint to the anti-refugee press coverage of the preceeding months, 58 of the migrants were already dead when the doors of the container were finally thrown open. In a Commons statement, Straw said that the discovery of the bodies on the truck, which travelled to Britain on a P&O Stena ferry from Zeebrugge, Belgium, was a "stark warning" to other would-be immigrants prepared to put their lives in the hands of organised crime. In July mounting public concern that failed applicants were absconding rather than leaving the country was met by the announcement of new Home Office targets for the removal of 30,000 illegal immigrants from the country annually. The Home Office was reported to have estimated that more than 100,000 asylum seekers had disappeared into the community since 1990 and that only 7,000 rejected applicants had left the country in 1999. Gordon Brown's announcement in the same month of an extra £400mn a year for three years to be used to cut the waiting list of applicants, meanwhile, drove the cost of the UK's asylum policy to more than £1.2 billion per year.

Public antipathy towards new immigration was ironic, given the labour shortages in key industries that continued to be a barrier to economic growth in the UK. At the beginning of September, the government announced its intention to relax immigration controls for the first time in 30 years in order to allow up to 100,000 workers to settle in Britain. The scheme, to be piloted in April 2001, would give priority to those with skills needed in Britain or to those with firm job offers. Visas would be awarded on the basis of a points system that considered factors such as education and family ties. It was also anticipated that many of those new migrants would come from countries such as India, where the combination of high numbers of IT workers and low wages would make economic migration an attractive option.

Controversy over asylum and immigration had a significant impact on race relations in the UK, with reports of violent attacks on asylum seekers or recent immigrants occurring with worrying regularity. This was most tragically brought to public attention at the end of the year with the fatal stabbing of 12-year old Damilola Taylor on a deprived housing estate in Peckham, South London. Damilola, who had come to Britain with his mother and epileptic sister from Nigeria six months earlier to receive medical assistance, was attacked on his way home from an after-school computer class and died in the stairwell of a apartment block near his home. The incident could not have provided more graphic evidence of the contrast between the bright hopes of well-educated immigrant families, and the deprivation and exclusion which they encountered in many districts throughout the country.

The 1999 Macpherson Report into the circumstances surrounding the death of black teenager Stephen Lawrence continued to have a significant impact on race relations issues in the UK in 2000 (see AR 1999, pp. 30-33). Royal Assent was given to the Race Relations (Amendment) Bill on November 30. This satisfied some of the key Macpherson recommendations by extending the 1976 Race Relations Act to cover the functions of public authorities in general, including the police. The Act placed a general duty on public authorities to promote racial harmony and was enforceable by the Commission for Racial Equality. The Act also made chief police officers vicariously liable for acts of racial discrimination by police officers under their direction and control.

Policing continued to be a source of controversy in race relations, fuelled by several high profile gaffes. At the beginning of the year Neville Lawrence, the father of Stephen, filed a complaint after being stopped and questioned by officers investigating a robbery on December 27th. The Home Secretary's commitment to employ more than 20 per cent of officers from non-white ethnic groups was far from being fulfilled, as police authorities continued to find it difficult to recruit and retain officers from ethnic minority backgrounds. Metropolitan police statistics were shown to have exaggerated the success of ethnic minority recruitment policies at the end of the year by including white recruits from Irish and Canadian backgrounds, for example, in its minority recruitment statistics. The parents of Stephen Lawrence, who in February refused an offer of £180,000 to settle the damages claim brought by them against the Metropolitan Police, were awarded £320,000 in October. In December, a Sikh police sergeant wrongly accused of sending hate mail to himself won record damages of £150,000 from the Metropolitan Police.

As the year ended, it seemed certain that asylum seekers, immigration and race relations would continue to feature highly on the political agenda in 2001, after public opinion research showed that voters remained worried about the numbers of people seeking residence in Britain. More than two thirds of voters remained convinced that Britain was perceived as a "soft touch" for immigrants, in spite of the harsh provisions of the Immigration and Asylum Act. According to a MORI survey, people thought asylum seekers had, on average, £113 a week to live on instead of a real figure of about £36, and public estimates of the number of immigrants were five times greater than the true number. In the week before Christmas, William Hague was warned by Gurbux Singh, the chairman of the Commission for Racial Equality, that he risked "throwing away" the good race relations which it had taken years to build up in Britain. His comments followed a speech in which the Conservative leader blamed the Macpherson Report for undermining morale in the Metropolitan Police. In an attempt to forestall the playing of the race card in the forthcoming general election, Singh wrote to all the party leaders asking for a new charter like the one signed by Tony Blair and John Major before the last general election, in which they had promised not to exploit race during the campaign.

TRANSPORTATION CONTROVERSIES. The UK's transportation problems appeared to go from bad to worse in 2000 as controversy ranged from air and rail safety to the price of petrol. As the year ended, the nation's railway system was grinding to a halt due to a combination of flooding and speed restrictions in the aftermath of a serious derailment near Hatfield, in Hertfordshire. There were signs, however, that the situation would improve in the future as important measures were introduced to overhaul the transport infrastructure of the country in the medium to long term after years of under-investment. Public controversy, meanwhile, focused on the role of private sector funding in this process.

In Parliament the year saw the passage of Deputy Prime Minister and Secretary of State for the Environment, Transport and the Regions John Prescott's long-awaited Transport Act. The measure, introduced on December 1, 1999, gave effect to the government's strategy for an integrated transport policy as set out in the White Paper "A New Deal for Transport: Better for Everyone" (Cm 3950), published in July 1998. It provided for improving local passenger transport services, reducing road congestion and pollution, and established the Strategic Rail Authority (SRA), which was given duties to promote rail use, secure the development of the network, and contribute to the development of an integrated transport system. Most controversially, however, the legislation included proposals for a public-private partnership for the National Air Traffic Services Ltd (NATS). This meant that ownership of NATS would transfer from the Civil Aviation Authority (CAA) to the Secretary of State, a strategic partner from the private sector, and NATS employees. Safety would remain the responsibility of the CAA, which would regulate the new regime. There was widespread fear that the part "privatisation" of NATS would prove as problematic as it had done for the railways, and that the drive for profits would compromise the excellent safety record of British air traffic control. The plan was condemned by a report of the all-party transport committee, and initially rejected by the House of Lords. But supporters of the scheme argued that realistically the only way for the government to raise the £1.4 billion needed to update the computer and technological infrastructure necessary to handle the increase in air traffic was through attracting private investors. The Lords finally passed the bill in November after the Minister of State for Transport, Lord Macdonald of Tradeston, agreed to further consultation before implementing a scheme. Royal Assent for the Transport Act was given on 30 November. The Act, together with a 10-year plan for investment unveiled by Prescott on July 20, represented the most significant new policy and spending initiatives in transport for a generation. Public and private sector capital investment were forecast to increase by 75 per cent in real terms compared with the previous decade.

This welcome news, however, was overshadowed by other events. Air France Concorde flight AF4590 crashed just north of Paris on July 25, killing all 109 people on board and four on the ground. Whilst investigations into the cause of the disaster proceeded, British Airways and Air France grounded their fleets of Concorde and the plane's airworthiness certificate was withdrawn. It was at first uncertain whether the supersonic aircraft, which was symbolic for being a successful Anglo-French technological collaboration, would ever fly again. Concern over its heavy fuel consumption and nitrogen oxide emissions made it seem more like an environmental dinosaur than the queen of the skies. By the end of the year it seemed likely that flights would resume, but the long-term future of Concorde remained in the balance.

The high cost of petrol was responsible for one of the most unexpected and dramatic events of the year. Relatively small numbers of protesters successfully blockaded oil refineries from the end of the first week of September and rapidly brought the country to a standstill. This state of affairs lasted for nearly a week, taking the government entirely by surprise. The crisis had its origins in two phenomena. The first was a rise in taxes on petrol which could be traced back to the 1993 budget, when Conservative Chancellor Norman Lamont had first introduced the principle of a "fuel duty escalator", involving an annual increase in road fuel duties above the rate of inflation. In his first budget of November 1997 Gordon Brown continued the principle of the escalator, and indeed increased it to at least 6 per cent. However, in November 1999 the Chancellor scrapped the escalator, which by that time had dramatically increased the proportion of tax in the cost of petrol and infuriated motoring lobby groups. The second factor was the decision by OPEC, the cartel of oil-producing countries, to cut the level of oil production in March 1999 in an attempt to boost the price of crude oil. By March 2000, the rising cost of crude was leading to substantial increases in petrol prices throughout Europe.

In the UK, groups particularly affected by the rise demanded that the government reduce petrol tax. The government, meanwhile, blamed the rise on rising oil prices. In August protests erupted throughout France, whilst the cost of petrol rose to more than 80p per litre in the UK, with tax making up around 72 per cent of the total price. An early attempt to organise a petrol boycott failed to make an impact in the UK, and commentators discounted the possibility that French-style protests could spread across the channel. This complacency proved ill-founded just weeks later, as the continuing rise in the cost of crude led British protesters—mostly road hauliers and farmers—to follow the lead of their French neighbours and establish blockades of their own. On September 7 approximately 100 people blocked access to the Stanlow oil refinery in Cheshire. Protests spread across the country in the following days until the closure of several refineries caused panic buying by motorists throughout the country. By September 11 Britain was facing widespread fuel shortages. This situation became increasingly frustrating for the Prime Minister over the following two days. Whilst the Privy Council granted the government emergency powers to regulate fuel supplies, tanker drivers refused to leave their depots, claiming intimidation by protesters. Blair, who on September 12 promised to get fuel supplies moving again within 24 hours, was initially ignored.

It was not until September 14 that protesters began to abandon the blockades, amid signs that public opinion was beginning to turn against them, and set a 60-day deadline for government action on petrol prices. The government, alarmed at the possibility of further protests, convened a "fuel task force" to deal with future emergencies, led by the Home Secretary Jack Straw, at the end of the month. By November, the credibility of the protesters had been badly damaged by the Government's campaign against them, as well as by reports of links with the far-right British National Party. Fatally divided, the plan for a slow-driving convoy of lorries from Jarrow to London failed to make a significant impact in the middle of the month. Meanwhile, in his pre-budget report, the Chancellor offered a £1.5 billion package to appease motorists, including a 3p cut in tax on low-sulphur fuel and a system for charging overseas trucks using British roads. On November 13 the protesters' 60-day deadline expired, but it seemed that the great fuel protests had fizzled out.

Only two weeks after the refinery blockades were lifted, a train derailment near Hatfield killed four people, bringing the total number of deaths in rail accidents to 94 since 1988. Concern over rail safety soon turned to panic, however, when it was discovered that the Hatfield crash was caused by a damaged rail that had shattered under the stress of the passing high speed train. Speed restrictions were immediately imposed on around 300 sections of similarly affected track thorughout the country, bringing rail travel to a crawl in the weeks before Christmas, and leading millions of travellers to take to the roads. Railway timetables were further disrupted in areas affected by flooding resulting from the record autumn rains.

The official inquiry into the Hatfield accident would subsequently confirm that both Railtrack and Balfour Beatty, its maintenance contractor, were aware of the cracked rail nearly a year before the crash. They were given a six month warning of the problem by site engineers, but failed to act. This made it seem likely that corporate manslaughter charges would be brought against senior executives of both companies. Already in August the rail regulator, Tom Winsor, was sufficiently concerned about the increasing number of broken rails on the network that he commissioned an independent audit on the way that the privatised train system was run. That report, which came out only days after the Hatfield derailment, was highly critical of Railtrack's relationship with its sub-contractors. Gerald Corbett, Railtrack's chief executive, resigned on November 17, with a reported £400,000 golden handshake. With public spending on the railways set to more than double by 2006, the promise that privatisation would lead to less public spending was proving unfounded. Furthermore, the fact that so much of that investment seemed to be spent on dividends and executive bonuses was leading to a profound popular shift away from support for the industry's privatisation.

The example of Railtrack, which contributed to resistance to private sector involvement in NATS, also made it difficult for the government to persuade Londoners to adopt a public-private partnership model for London's underground railway services. The new mayor, Ken Livingstone, had resisted PPP as part of his election platform, and his case was bolstered by the events of October. Livingstone's appointment of former New York City subway boss Robert Kiley, as his new transport commissioner, was widely seen as an astute decision. Already by the end of the year, and before Kiley was officially in the post, there were indications that the government was having problems attracting private sector funding for the tube. Kiley, who made no secret of his opinion that the government scheme was "fatally flawed", was holding talks with Prescott in December, and there were signs that a compromise arrangement would be found in the new year.

ENVIRONMENTAL CONCERNS The threat of global warming, which a decade ago had seemed remote and theoretical, became a focus for concern in the UK in 2000. Unrelenting autumn rains brought recurring flooding to low lying areas throughout the country. Around 6,500 homes were affected by flooding, and the rains were estimated to have cost UK farmers £500 million as crops rotted in sodden fields. Although scientists were reluctant to say categorically that the recent extremes of the normally benign British weather were the result of global warming, evidence was mounting that suggested that this was indeed the case. The Climatic Research Unit at the University of East Anglia reported that there had been a marked shift towards more intense periods of winter rainfall in recent decades and predicted that the UK would face an increase in the occurrence of extreme precipitation in the future. More flooding in the coming years would have an important impact on housing policy and the construction and design of better flood defences. Increasing concern about climate change had still not translated into political action, however, and there was no sign that either the Labour or the Conservative parties were willing to risk votes by adopting policies which would inevitably involve sacrifice in the short-term to safeguard the environment in the future.

In May British Nuclear Fuels announced the immediate closure of its Hinkly Point nuclear reactor in Somerset, and the phased shutdown of the remaining seven aging Magnox stations. This would include the closure of the older of the two reprocessing works at Sellafield in 2012, which was responsible for two-thirds of the radioactive discharges into the Irish Sea, and which had caused so much anger in Ireland and in the Nordic countries. The closure programme would involve 3,200 jobs, and 8 per cent of the country's electricity production. The closures put in jeopardy the government's targets for reducing by 20 per cent its carbon dioxide emissions by 2010. Emissions had decreased by 9 per cent already since 1990, because of the switch to gas from coal. But the closure of so much of the country's nuclear capacity would be likely to increase emissions once more. The decision left the privatised British Energy running the UK's remaining nuclear reactors.

In March the publication of a Countryside and Rights of Way Bill delighted ramblers and environmental groups, who had campaigned for 60 years for the right to roam over open land in England and Wales. The legislation also provided for protection for the 4,068 sites of special scientific interest (SSSIs) and wildlife. In spite of attempts to block the legislation by landed interests in the House of Lords, the new law was given the Royal Assent in the Autumn, although it fell short of the demands of some ramblers and questions remained concerning its enforceability.

Resistance to GM food trials in Britain continued in 2000. Whilst the government hoped to have trials underway in 25 fields for maize and oilseed rape and 30 more for either sugar or fodder beet by the end of this year, protests led by environmental groups such as Greenpeace threatened to disrupt the testing timetable altogether. In March, two weeks after the government announced the location of 31 farms in England and Scotland that had signed up for the trials, two of the farms pulled out as a result of pressure from local people. Greenpeace issued a hit list of 26 farms for targetting by protesters. The courts proved to be reluctant to impose harsh penalties on people charged with damaging such experimental crops, having regard to the sensitive nature of the public debate on genetic modification. In September, 28 Greenpeace protesters were acquitted of causing criminal damage to crops in Norfolk, including Lord Melchett, executive director of Greenpeace and former government minister in the Callaghan administration. The government, although increasingly sensitive to this popular hostility, remained committed to undertaking safe testing trials in order to determine the long-term viability of GM crops.

The long-awaited report of the Bovine Spongiform Encephalopathy (BSE) Inquiry was published at the end of October. Its findings included criticism of the previous government for playing down the links between BSE-infected beef and the variant Creutzfeldt-Jakob Disease (vCJD) and for misleading the public about the risks posed by so-called "mad cow disease". The 1989 ban on specified bovine offal entering the human food chain had been poorly enforced and there was poor communication between the government departments on the growing evidence of the links between BSE and vCJD. Although the beef on the bone ban was lifted in the UK in December 1999, the crisis was far from over as, one by one, the disease was discovered to have spread to other European countries in the final months of the year. The full impact of the disease on human health remained unknown and would do for some years. By the end of the year there had been around 80 deaths from vCJD in the UK since 1995, but there remained considerable uncertainty over its incubation period.

THE ECONOMY IN 2000. As the New Year approached, there were widespread fears that the UK's financial sector would prove to be particularly vulnerable to the so-called "Y2K" or millenium bug, as so much of the City's business was conducted electronically. Consequently a concerted effort was made, co-ordinated by the Bank of England, the UK's central bank, to ensure that Britain's central and European payments systems infrastructure did not collapse. There was also some concern that public anticipation of economic disruption would place undue demands upon automated cash machines over the new year period, and that debit and credit cards would not function properly. However, automated cash machines withdrawals turned out to be considerably less than estimated and, whilst some credit and debit card readers did fail to work, few other difficulties emerged.

The decline of the manufacturing industries continued, as the UK motor car industry sustained two sharp shocks. In April German car manufacturer BMW announced plans to shut down the Rover plant in Longbridge, West Midlands. This would have extinguished one of the oldest automobile brand names in Britain, resulting in thousands of job losses in the region. However, following government intervention, BMW announced its readiness to sell the company to the Phoenix consortium. The second shock came in May, when Ford announced that it would no longer produce cars at its plant at Dagenham, East London. Ford attempted to make this news more palatable by stating that the Dagenham plant would henceforward become the principal site for the production of diesel engines in Europe and that its design centre would be relocated from Italy to England. Further manufacturing sector problems included the news that RJB, the country's biggest coal producer, was facing losses of £130 million. and needed £70 million in aid to avert closure. The government eventually agreed to help on the understanding that these problems were short term. Additionally, the European Commission in December approved a £17.5 million funding package to secure the future of the Longannet coal mine in Fife, Scotland. The year ended with the prospect of a dramatic contraction of what remained of the British steel industry with Corus, the Anglo-Dutch successor company to British Steel, expected to announce the closure of several steel plants across the UK.

In the middle of the year there was a spectacular set back for the so-called "new" economy industries as share prices for dot.com companies plummeted. In Britain some companies, like boo.com, collapsed entirely, whilst the values of others, like lastminute.com, were halved. However, the importance of the internet as a market place remained strong, as virtually every UK business and institution continued to invest in online development and marketing, in spite of the fact that it remained unclear how the internet could be made to produce a profit. Meanwhile, the Office of National Statistics reported that the number of homes with internet access grew to 6.5 million, or one in four, during 2000, double the number in 1999. There remained, however, a clear "digital divide" in the UK, in terms of both location and family income. In Northern Ireland just 11 per cent of people had access to the internet, and only 14 per cent were online in Scotland and the north-east. London, the south-east and the east of England enjoyed the highest levels of access, with 25 per cent, 24 per cent and 22 per cent respectively. Only 3 per cent of the poorest households had access to the internet, whilst 48 per cent of the richest households were online.

There was some restructuring in various sectors of British industries as a result of mergers and acquisitions. The expenditure on acquisitions of UK companies by other UK companies was dramatically higher than in previous years: in both the first and fourth quarters of 2000 this peaked at around £35 billion. The merger of Glaxo Wellcolm and SmithKline Beecham resulted in GlaxoSmithKline, with an estimated 7 per cent of the world's pharmaceutical market. The other notable acquisition was that of the building society, Woolwich, by Barclays Bank for £1,931 million. This acquisition reflected the continuing tight competition in the British banking sector. Lending to households by smaller banks and by new entrants grew rapidly, as did lending to companies by smaller banks and those previously concentrating on mortgage lending.

Retail and service industries were also affected by changing market conditions. The UK's largest clothing retailer, Marks and Spencer, which had been experiencing falling sales over the past few years, began the year with a 5.3 per cent sales slump over the Christmas shopping period. The company attempted to fight back by employing top-name designers and sought to make its image more contemporary by dropping its St Michael label. However this had not attracted customers back into its stores by the end of 2000, and its continuing financial troubles had a knock-on effect upon many large clothing suppliers. Many, such as William Baird, Daks Simpson and Cooper & Roe, found their contracts with Marks and Spencer cancelled as it switched to non-UK clothing manufacturers to reduce costs. Whilst throughout the year the overall percentage growth of retail sales remained healthy, virtually all retailers found that their profit margins were under pressure as consumers became more sensitive to price.

Although the London Stock Exchange (LSE) remained Europe's most attractive share-trading location, it and the London International Financial Futures and Options Exchange (Liffe) found their once pre-eminent positions continuously challenged. In an attempt to re-establish its position the LSE had lately pursued a policy of alliances with European stock exchanges but in the end this proved largely abortive. Its 1998 alliance with eight other European stock markets failed to consolidate. In May 2000 it announced plans to merge with its biggest rival, Frankfurt's Deutsche Börse, to form iX. At the same time it also announced that Nasdaq had signed a memorandum of understanding with iX to create a pan-European high-growth market. Shareholders in the newly-demutualised London Stock Exchange and Deutsche Börse would hold 50 per cent each of iX's issued share capital, and trading costs were expected to be substantially reduced. However, the stock exchange's smaller brokers scuppered the deal, in the belief that iX would smother the trade in domestic equities. As a consequence the Chief Executive of the LSE, Gavin Casey, resigned. The strategy of the stock exchange was left in ruins, and its vulnerability was highlighted in the middle of the year when the Swedish OM group, which runs the Stockholm stock exchange, made an unsuccessful takeover bid.

During the first half of 2000 some business leaders complained, as they had done in previous years, that the government's determination to control inflation solely by manipulating the interest rate had led to an overvaluation of the pound which had undercut profitability on exports and had generally made UK exports uncompetitive. However, the government argued that businesses needed to make greater improvements in productivity. Indeed poor British productivity growth continued, with a trend rate of 1.5 per cent. To improve productivity growth the Chancellor in October 2000 announced his intention to improve access to the Internet across the country and thus boost information technology skills. However, in the second half of 2000 the value of the pound began to fall. Sterling's slide against the US dollar during August and September was dramatic, about 6 per cent, with an overall fall of around 12 per cent over the year. The pound's valuation against the euro remained stable. The political debate about whether Britain should join the euro continued, with the Conservatives maintaining a firm line against entry. The Labour government's position remained publicly equivocal, even though opinion polls revealed that most people were against giving up the pound.

The Bank of England's Monetary Policy Committee continued to identify the control of inflation as the benchmark guide for its actions. On January 13 the Bank increased the rate by 0.25 per cent to 5.7 per cent and the next month the interest rate crept up by another 0.25 per cent to 6.0 per cent. This rate was maintained for the rest of the year—the longest period the interest rate had remained stable in a decade—as inflationary pressure on the UK domestic economy eased. In fact, for much of the year inflation was at, or even below, the government's target of 2.5 per cent. In August it fell to a 25 year low at 1.9 per cent. Although unemployment continued to fall throughout the year, being around the 5 per cent mark, there was little sign of wage pressure in the economy. The headline rate of growth in average earnings fell and, at around 4 per cent, was well below the 4.5 per cent the Bank of England had previously identified as compatible for meeting the government's inflation target.

The Bank of England noted in its second Financial Stability Review (December 2000) that, in general, the economy had performed well during the year. The UK had remained vulnerable to external conditions, notably the slowing down of the US economy and changes in the world price of petroleum, but it had pulled through. The Bank was of the opinion that potential areas of concern were the debts incurred by the telecom sector, and the rising household and corporate sector debt. Even so the Bank felt that, in aggregate, the sectoral balance sheets through the year had remained considerably stronger than in the late 1980s and early 1990s.

In November 2000 the International Monetary Fund reported that in its opinion "the overall performance of the UK economy remains impressive". There was much justification for this view even though some sectors of the economy were in difficulty. The growth of the GDP had been roughly around the expected 3 per cent, and according to European Union statistics published in late-2000 the size of the British economy had overtaken France's and was now the fourth largest in the world. Whilst the manufacturing and traditional industries shrank, the service and financial sectors remained overwhelmingly strong and employment continued to grow at a healthy pace. The Labour government's management of the economy continued to remain comparatively business-friendly and fiscally prudent, reflecting Prime Minister Blair's vision of a "third way", and Chancellor of the Exchequer Brown's "balanced approach" to achieving long term economic prosperity.

EXTERNAL RELATIONS AND DEFENCE. After the war in Kosovo ended in June 1999, the NATO-led K-For (Kosovo Force) was established as a security presence in the province. About 3,900 British troops served with the 50,000-strong international force throughout the year, and there was no immediate prospect of K-For's disbandment. An international police force was also set up, to which the UK sent about 100 officers, and UK funding was given to projects for improving the security of returning Serbs. Municipal elections were held under the supervision of the UN in October. The largely peaceful overthrow of Slobodan Milosevic in October, and his replacement by President Kostunica, who had won the Serbian elections (see II.2.vi), encouraged Western hopes that relations with the Federal Republic of Yugoslavia could now be rebuilt and progress made on Kosovo in acordance with Kostunica's pledge to seek a diplomatic solution. The EU, with the UK's enthusiastic participation, dropped sanctions against Serbia and began to provide aid and look for trade development.

Elsewhere, British troops were called into action in Sierra Leone (see VI.2.iii). The former colony, originally founded as a settlement for freed slaves, had been a source of embarrassment to the government in 1998 when the UK was accused of encouraging the supply of arms, in defiance of UN regulations, to protect President Ahmed Tejan Kabbah, who was restored to power in February that year. In May 2000, some 1,000 British troops were sent to Freetown as foreign nationals were evacuated in the face of renewed civil war between Foday Sankoh's rebel Revolutionary United Front (RUF) and Kabbah's government. The peace agreement between the government and Sankoh's RUF broke down when UN forces moved into the diamond-mining areas which the rebels refused to give up. The UK deployment was reduced after the capture of Kabbah, although some 300 personnel remained, helping to train Sierra Leone's army. This number was increased again in October when a brigadier's headquarters were set up in Freetown (the capital), and in November when *HMS Ocean* was sent with 500 troops to support the UN peacekeepers as a fragile ceasefire was signed. There was no immediate likelihood of withdrawal. In January 2001 Brigadier Jonathan Riley said that the end of the war was in sight but that he expected UK troops to be stationed in the country for at least another year.

During the year efforts were made towards curbing the trade in "conflict diamonds" which provided illegal arms to organisations such as the RUF in Sierra Leone and UNITA in Angola. Such trade was an important factor in prolonging conflict in parts of Africa. A World Diamond Council was formed and its inaugural meeting was held in Tel Aviv in September, where it planned various measures to exclude conflict diamonds from sale. The UK actively backed a number of schemes including monitoring the diamonds leaving Sierra Leone and a certification scheme for rough diamonds. A conference was held in London in October, with 36 governments and the World Diamond Council present, and in October the issue was debated in the UN General Assembly.

Another former colony, Zimbabwe, was much in the UK news in the first half of the year, amid violence against opposition parties and the seizure of land from white farmers. The Secretary of State for Foreign and Commonwealth Affairs, Robin Cook, made regular statements deploring intimidation and offering help if there was a "return to the rule of law" and the Zimbabwe government was willing to work with the opposition parties. President Robert Mugabe, in turn, blamed Britain along with Zimbabwe's white minority for the economic problems being experienced in the country. He continued with his programme of forcible land seizures and his attempts to intimidate groups such as the Movement for Democratic Reform, which won 57 seats in the June elections (themselves accompanied by violence and from which Mugabe banned many foreign observers). In January, the government was accused of failing once again to have an "ethical foreign policy" when it authorised the export of Hawk jet parts to Zimbabwe for use in the civil war in the Congo.

In its election manifesto, the Labour Party had promised to ban the sale of arms to regimes that might use them for internal repression or international aggression, but this proved a rather flexible promise in practice. An Amnesty International report published in September criticised the government's failure to control the arms trade, undermining its own efforts to prevent or resolve conflicts abroad by exporting to countries such as Zimbabwe and Indonesia. A proposed bill to control the trade had been dropped, and Amnesty called for a personal commitment from Blair to take it forward. A bill to control the arms trade was promised in the Queen's Speech in December, but time was unlikely to be found for it before the next election. The report did, however, welcome the support provided for the UN in Sierra Leone, the human rights work done by many of Britain's overseas missions and efforts to abolish the death penalty.

The major developments in Europe during the year were the agreement to enlarge the European Union, with its consequences for voting rights over policy, and discussions of a European defence identity. An Anglo-French declaration on defence co-operation in December 1999 was followed in 2000 with discussions about what this might entail and how it would relate to NATO. A decision to form a European Rapid Reaction Force (ERRF) was taken at the Helsinki summit in December 1999, and in November 2000 EU defence ministers agreed that by 2003 the Union should be able to field up to 60,000 ground troops within 60 days and maintain them for up to a year. The total force would consist of 100,000 troops, 400 aircraft and 100 ships, with the UK's contribution including 12,500 ground troops, 72 combat aircraft and 18 ships. Germany would provide at least 13,500 troops and France around 12,000. There would be a small central headquarters, initially headed by Lieutenant General Rainer Schuwirth of Germany with a British deputy, Major-General Graham Messervy-Whiting.

Conservative critics immediately labelled it a "European army" which would undermine NATO and erode British sovereignty. Ministers argued instead that it made sense to pool expensive military assets in common operations, but that it was not a standing European force. Individual countries would decide whether their forces would take part in any particular operation, and the ERRF would only operate (to give assistance to civilians threatened by a crisis outside the EU, to respond to UN calls for peacekeeping forces or to intervene to separate warring factions) if NATO had decided not to get involved. Although there were fears that this would undermine the US commitment to NATO, the agreement was cautiously welcomed by the Clinton administration. There had been suggestions from the USA that Europe should do more towards its own defence, for example in Kosovo, where 7,000 US troops were currently serving.

The Nice summit, the longest in EU history (XI.4), was intended to produce a defining treaty, agreeing long-overdue institutional reforms which were required to allow eastern European countries to join from 2004, something which the UK had long been promoting. At the end of the five-day negotiations at Nice, however, there were still arguments about what exactly had been agreed. Some of the smaller EU countries were angry at the way the larger ones, Britain, France and Germany, had tried to maintain their power and influence in an enlarged community. Belgium was unlikely to be mollified by the news that most EU summits would be held in Brussels in future. The UK government was criticised at home for giving up Britain's veto over various aspects of policy, but Blair argued that most of these were about the efficiency of economic management and the single market, where majority voting was in Britain's interest. In general, the summit had moved towards a "more rational way of decision making", he argued, and this would allow enlargement to take place.

During the year, ministers continued to defend the 10-year-old sanctions regime in place against Iraq, in the face of increasing criticism and division amongst the international community. The reopening of Baghdad international airport in September saw humanitarian and political visits from countries including France (which favoured a suspension of non-military sanctions) and various Arab countries. Russia and China argued that the sanctions were counterproductive and served only to deny essential imports to the Iraqi population whilst blocking the development of Iraq's oil and gas reserves. The UK remained firmly on the side of the USA, however, continuing to provide combat aircraft to patrol the no-fly zones in northern Iraq, and regularly bombing Iraqi military targets. Ministers argued that the "oil for food" programme would prevent Iraqi suffering if Saddam Hussein allowed it to operate correctly, and that sanctions could not be dropped until UN weapons inspectors, charged with locating and destroying Iraq's nuclear, biological and chemical arms, had been allowed to return to Iraq to complete their work.

Queen Elizabeth II undertook two state visits in 2000. She travelled with Prince Philip, Duke of Edinburgh to Australia in late March, and to Italy in October. The Queen and Prince Consort of Denmark made a state visit to Britain in February, which included a trip to Edinburgh to meet Scotland's First Minister, Donald Dewar. King Abdullah and Queen Rania of Jordan were due to make a state visit in November, staying with the Queen at Windsor Castle, but pulled out in October as the peace process in the Middle East broke down (see V.2.i). Abdullah, who ascended to the throne in February after the death of his father, King Hussein, was taking an active part in trying to keep the peace process going and prevent violence spreading to Jordan.

After 17 months of legal and diplomatic arguments, on March 2 former dictator of Chile Augusto Pinochet was put on board a Chilean airforce jet and sent home rather than extradited to Spain at the request of a Spanish judge (see AR 1999, p. 40). The decision to do so was made by Home Secretary Jack Straw, on health grounds, after Pinochet's lawyers had unsuccessfully argued that he should be immune to prosecution as a former head of state. Diplomatic relations with Chile, which maintained that the former dictator should only be tried there, were badly strained by the case, as it and other South American governments interpreted his arrest as Spain, and by default Britain, imposing a form of moral colonialism on Chile. Negotiations between Britain, Spain and Chile finally led to the general being freed on humanitarian grounds. The Chilean embassy made representations that his health had significantly deteriorated. Tests were finally carried out in January, and Straw announced he was "minded" to halt extradition proceedings. The Spanish government responded by refusing to pass on a request for judicial review of this decision, but then the Belgian government stepped in to do so. Judges ruled that the reports had to be disclosed to the extraditing countries, in confidence, but they immediately appeared in Spanish newspapers. This, however, meant it was finally clear to the Spanish public that Pinochet should be allowed to go home, and in March he did so, facing instead possible trial in Chile.

In November the Ilios, British Indian Ocean Territory islanders, who had taken the British government to court over their removal from the Chagos Islands to allow a major US strategic air and naval base to be built on Diego Garcia, won their case that this exile was unlawful. Robin Cook announced that the government would not appeal against the judgement, would continue its work on the feasibility of resettling the Ilois and put in place a new immigration ordinance, which would allow the Ilois to return to the outer islands whilst observing the obligations under the treaty signed in 1966 with the USA, which gave them a lease until 2016. The US opposed the return of the islanders to the two other previously inhabited islands in the archipelago, Peros Banhos and Salomon. By the end of the year the situation remained unresolved, but the government was considering extending British citizenship to Ilois citizens of British Dependent Territories.

International negotiations to follow up the Kyoto protocol on climate change took place in The Hague in November, but failed to produce any deal. Negotiations foundered on the extent to which countries like the USA could trade their emissions with other countries, thereby avoiding having to make cuts at home. Instead of an agreement, there was a much-publicised row between John Prescott, the Deputy Prime Minister, and Dominique Voynet, the French Environment Minister, when Prescott thought a deal had been agreed with the USA but other European countries were dubious about the extent to which "carbon sinks"—forests planted in developing countries—would be allowed. Talks in Canada and Brussels in December attempted to restore the process, but failed. Prescott said that the EU had missed a unique opportunity, but carefully no longer blamed Voynet for this, claiming his relationship with her was now "wonderful".

ii. SCOTLAND

CAPITAL: Edinburgh   AREA: 78,313 sq km   POPULATION: 5,120,000
OFFICIAL LANGUAGES: English & Gaelic   POLITICAL SYSTEM: devolved administration within UK
HEAD OF STATE: Queen Elizabeth II (since Feb '52)
RULING PARTIES: Labour & Liberal Democrats (since May '99)
HEAD OF GOVERNMENT: Henry McLeish (Labour), First Minister (since Oct '00)

UNDOUBTEDLY the main political event in Scotland in 2000 was the death of Donald Dewar, the First Minister. Dewar had undergone heart surgery in May, but appeared to have fully recovered and had resumed his duties before his sudden collapse and death on October 11. Labour and opposition leaders alike were unreserved in their tribute to his political skills and personal integrity, and to his role as the principal architect, as UK Secretary of State for Scotland in 1997-99, of the Scottish devolution project. His funeral, on October 16, had many of the characteristics of a state occasion, and Scotland mourned the loss of a man who was widely described as the "father of his country" (see XVIII).

During Dewar's illness, and for a short period until a successor could be found, Deputy First Minister Jim Wallace, (of the Scottish Liberal Democrats) fulfilled his official functions. The full formal arrangements for electing a replacement leader of the Scottish Labour Party proved impossible to satisfy in the time period available for the First Minister to be elected. A compromise procedure, which critics saw as having calculatedly ensured a win for Prime Minister Blair's preferred candidate, accordingly resulted in the election of Henry

McLeish as interim party leader. He was duly elected as First Minister on October 26, and took office immediately.

Earlier in the year, the leadership of the opposition in the Scottish parliament also changed. Unexpectedly, Alex Salmond announced that he felt that 10 years of leadership of the Scottish National Party (SNP) was long enough, and on September 23 John Swinney was elected to succeed him.

The various by-elections conducted during the year brought little systematic comfort to any of the main parties, and were characterised by low turnouts. There were two by-elections for the Westminster parliament—in Glasgow Anniesland on November 23, to replace Dewar, and in Falkirk West on December 21, to replace Dennis Canavan who had decided to focus his activities solely on the Scottish Parliament. Labour held both seats, although in Falkirk West they only narrowly held off a challenge by the SNP. Two Scottish parliament by-elections were also held: one in Ayr on March 16, in which the Scottish Conservatives took the seat from Labour, and one in Glasgow Anniesland (Dewar had represented the constituency in both Westminster and Edinburgh) on November 23, which was held by Labour.

Controversy continued during the year over the apparently spiralling cost of the new Scottish Parliament building. Reports presented to the Scottish parliament documented the problems with the construction, but a debate in early April confirmed the decision to build on the proposed site in Holyrood whilst tightening up on the budget available. The architect whose design was being used, Enric Miralles, died on May 3, but the project team envisaged no problems in completing the work.

The summer and early autumn saw increasing concern about the operation of the new Scottish Qualifications Agency (SQA). A total of 2.7 per cent of the candidates for examinations conducted by the SQA did not get accurate results on time. This created uncertainty for the affected candidates, problems for their acceptance for further or higher education courses, and a general lack of confidence in all exam results. The SQA had been created as a result of the merger of two bodies, one responsible for academic and the other for vocational education at schools and colleges. The constituent parts of the new body involved different cultures and locations which it proved hard to reconcile. These problems were compounded by the introduction of the new qualification "Higher Still", marks for which came partly from schools assessment and partly from examination. However, the computer equipment necessary to handle the information proved unequal to the task, and this problem was exacerbated by management failures. Various reforms were introduced to try to ensure that the 2001 examination results would be free from similar problems.

Perceptions of Scottish justice were mixed in 2000. The trial of the two Libyans accused of the 1988 Lockerbie bombing (see AR 1988, p. 38) began in the Netherlands on May 3. Camp Zeist, a former US airbase near Utrecht, became Scottish territory for the purposes of the trial which, by the end of the year, was nearing its conclusion. Its conduct won widespread approval. By contrast, the trials associated with the murder in 1998 of Surjit Singh Chhokar created considerable disquiet; 3 men were accused of the crime, but they were not tried together. In the first trial, the defendant blamed the other two and was found not guilty. At a later trial the other two men blamed the first and they too were acquitted. After the conclusion of the second trial, on November 29 the Scottish Executive set up two separate inquiries, one into the arrangements for liasing with Chhokar's family and a second into the decision-making processes in the case. Also during the year the Scottish practice of selling warrants under court orders to extract payment from debtors came under attack. Tommy Sheridan's success in convincing the Scottish parliament that the system was inequitable led on December 6 to the approval of a bill to abolish the procedure.

The future of Scotland's national football stadium, Hampden Park, was assured in early April after a financial rescue package. The park was owned by Scotland's oldest football club, Queen's Park, which was finding it increasingly difficult to meet the cost of refurbishment. Under the recovery plan, the stadium would continue to be owned by the club, but would be managed by the Scottish Football Association. Another long-standing Scottish institution, shipbuilding on the River Clyde, was saved by a combination of a Ministry of Defence order in July and a commercial contract in December. As the year came to an end, however, the outlook for the Scottish fishing and fish processing industry was very uncertain. The European Union (EU)'s Common Fisheries Policy quotas were substantially tightened in 2000 in an attempt to conserve dwindling fish stocks. Whilst some attempts had been made to favour Scottish fisheries, grave doubts were expressed about whether the industry could survive under the new quotas.

iii. WALES

CAPITAL: Cardiff   AREA: 20,755 sq km   POPULATION: 2,940,000
OFFICIAL LANGUAGES: Welsh & English   POLITICAL SYSTEM: devolved administration within UK
HEAD OF STATE: Queen Elizabeth II (since Feb '52)
RULING PARTIES: Labour & Liberal Democrats (since Oct '00)
HEAD OF GOVERNMENT: Rhodri Morgan, First Minister (since Feb '00)

IN the course of the year, the dictum "power devolved is power retained" was challenged by the National Assembly for Wales. During 1999 the minority Labour administration had found it difficult to bring a degree of stability to the fledgling Assembly. Its leader, the Assembly's First Secretary, Alun Michael, was threatened by a motion of no-confidence on the grounds that he had failed to secure from the Treasury additional matched funding to take advantage of the European Objective One status granted to the most deprived parts of Wales.

The dissatisfaction with Michael, who was perceived as being the UK Prime Minister's messenger boy in Wales rather than an independent-minded leader, ran deeper than the specific issue of matched funding. In February he tried desperately to stave off impending defeat but received no support from the Chancellor of the Exchequer, Gordon Brown, who repeatedly stated that the issue of matched funding would be addressed in July during the Comprehensive Spending Review. The Prime Minister, Tony Blair, tried to broker a last-minute deal with the Liberal

Democrats to save the First Secretary, allegedly saying to the Liberal leader Charles Kennedy, that the alternative to Alun Michael, Rhodri Morgan, would be a "disaster". However, the Liberal Democrat members at the National Assembly were as dissatisfied with Michael as the other opposition parties and were at that juncture unwilling to contemplate a pact.

On February 9, in an embarrassing episode for the government, the Prime Minister defended Michael in the House of Commons at the very same time as Michael was tendering his resignation in the National Assembly. Michael had gambled that his Labour colleagues would remain loyal to him and that he would be re-elected leader but it soon became apparent that the majority were content to seek a new First Secretary. In this, Michael, Blair, as well as most of the London press, which in any case tended to treat the Assembly with disdain, had misjudged the genuine feelings of Assembly members, who wished to be led by someone not controlled by 10 Downing Street and Labour headquarters at Millbank. The man who moved smoothly into that role was Rhodri Morgan, "a well-educated dissident with trouble written all over him", as one commentator described him.

The new First Secretary, a few days after being referred to as a potential "disaster", was quickly embraced by Blair, who subsequently admitted that he had misjudged the situation in Wales. "Essentially you have to let go of it with devolution", he stated in a newspaper interview. It became clear too that not only the Labour Party in Wales but also the other parties had a leader with whom they could feel relatively comfortable. However, Morgan and his colleagues appreciated that there was much work to be done to establish the credibility of the Assembly and this would only be achieved by delivering more effective government in Wales.

Initially Morgan made few changes to his Cabinet, although the much-criticised Secretary for Agriculture, Christine Gwyther, was replaced during the summer by Carwyn Jones. In October Morgan reached an agreement with the Liberal Democrats, which secured a majority for a new coalition administration in the Assembly. The Liberals were given two Cabinet posts, with the party's leader Mike German becoming Deputy First Minister and his colleague, Jenny Randerson, becoming Minister for Culture and Sport. The use of the new title Minister, as opposed to Secretary, replicated the titles of Cabinet posts in Scotland. The coalition was underpinned by a Partnership Agreement, which committed the Cabinet to a series of Liberal Democrat policies, but the price paid by Labour did provide it with the stability to proceed with its programmes without the threat of further defeat at the hands of opposition parties in the Assembly.

The main opposition party, Plaid Cymru: the Party of Wales, also experienced a change of leadership. The charismatic Party President, Dafydd Wigley, stepped down on health grounds and was replaced by another North Walian, Ieuan Wyn Jones, who was elected by an overwhelming majority of party members.

In July, though much too late to save Alun Michael, the Chancellor announced a substantial increase in funding for Wales, including an additional £421 million which would be used to match Objective One structural funds. However, there was constant criticism of the complicated and time-consuming methods used to select projects for European funding and there were genuine fears that opportunities were being lost.

In September the contract to build a part of the new A380 superjumbo Airbus was secured by the British Aerospace Factory at Broughton, Flintshire, thanks to the assistance of a £19.5 million subsidy package from the National Assembly. It was expected that this would lead to the creation of 1,700 new jobs, 300 more than was originally envisaged. The news from the steel industry was less encouraging. A total of 1,400 jobs were shed in plants at Llanwern, Port Talbot, Shotton, Ebbw Vale, Llanelli and Gorseinon by the Anglo-Dutch steel giant Corus and, at the end of the year, there were real fears that several plants were in danger of imminent closure.

To a large extent the impetus and leadership of the petrol blockade which threatened to paralyse Britain in September originated in Wales. Brynle Williams, a Welsh-speaking livestock farmer from Flintshire, was prominent in a protest that effectively expressed the frustration of farmers, road hauliers and country people in general with the high price of fuel and its effect on their livelihood.

However, none of the serious issues which concerned the people of Wales attracted the attention of the world's press in a way comparable to that given to the marriage of the Swansea actress Catherine Zeta Jones to the Hollywood film star, Michael Douglas. Nevertheless the huge red dragon flag which flew over the entrance of New York's opulent Plaza Hotel, where the wedding took place in November, was a reminder that even the smallest of nations could produce talent and beauty on the world's stage.

iv. NORTHERN IRELAND

CAPITAL: Belfast   AREA: 18,843 sq km   POPULATION: 1,692,000
OFFICIAL LANGUAGES: English, Irish & Ulster Scots   POLITICAL SYSTEM: devolved administration within UK
HEAD OF STATE: Queen Elizabeth II (since Feb '52)
RULING PARTIES: Ulster Unionist Party (UUP), Social Democratic and Labour Party (SDLP), Democratic Unionist Party (DUP) & Sinn Féin (since Dec '99)
HEAD OF GOVERNMENT: David Trimble, First Minister (since July '98)

THE optimism of the New Year was quickly dispelled when UK Prime Minister Tony Blair refused to publish the report from General de Chastelain, the Canadian official responsible for co-ordinating the weapons decommissioning process, on February 2 because it contained no significant developments. A fresh response from the Irish Republican Army (IRA) interlocutor on February 11 was received after a 5.00 p.m. deadline set by Peter Mandelson, the UK Secretary of State for Northern Ireland, and the devolved institutions were suspended from midnight. The suspension prevented the Ulster Unionist Council (UUC) the next day from withdrawing the Ulster Unionist Party (UUP) from the Executive, but the IRA withdrew its interlocutor from contact with the Independent International Decommissioning Body and withdrew its offer of February 11. The decision to suspend the institutions produced considerable criticism from Sinn Féin, the Social Democratic and Labour Party (SDLP) and the Irish government.

The first hint of movement occurred on March 16 when First Minister David Trimble said that it was possible to have a return to power sharing ahead of the decommissioning of weapons. This statement caused him problems from those opposed to the Belfast ("Good Friday") Agreement of April 1998 (see AR 1998 pp. 45-6, 556-67), both within his party and outside it. At the UUC meeting in March, the Rev. Martin Smyth challenged for the party leadership and polled better than expected with 43 per cent of the vote. The meeting also made the return of power sharing with Sinn Féin conditional on the retention of the name of the Royal Ulster Constabulary (RUC) in the Northern Ireland police bill giving effect to the Patten Report (see AR 1999 p.51).

There were hints that the idea of putting weapons "beyond use", instead of straightforward decommissioning, was being explored. A visit by Blair to Belfast and Dublin on April 18 tried to assess the state of party opinion. Both the British and Irish premiers emphasised their commitment to the Good Friday Agreement and by April 27 agreement had been reached on having direct talks between the parties in London from May 2. A new IRA statement on May 6 said that it would put its weapons "completely and verifiably. . . beyond use" and that it would permit international inspectors to monitor some of its arsenals, naming Cyril Ramaphosa from the African National Congress in South Africa and Martti Ahtisaari, former President of Finland, as acceptable persons. The IRA statement was welcomed by Trimble as a fresh opportunity for peace, and he called a meeting of the UUC for May 20. The UK and Irish governments agreed to the restoration of devolution on May 22, subject to a positive response from the UUP and other political parties.

There followed an apparent series of choreographed steps. Firstly, on May 9 the Chief Constable announced the closure of two security bases at Cookstown and Londonderry (Strand Road) and the dismantling of three observation bases, including one at Crossmaglen. The number of troops at 14,000 would not be immediately reduced. (Some 500 went subsequently on June 3.) Then, on May 15 Ramaphosa and Ahtisaari visited Northern Ireland for talks with the parties, leaving with a promise to return in a few weeks to begin monitoring. The state of opinion within the UUP forced Trimble to postpone the UUC meeting for a week, until May 27, whilst assurances were sought from the UK government that the police bill would reflect the fact that the Police Service of Northern Ireland incorporated the RUC. At the UUC meeting on May 27 a carefully worded motion, which made it clear that Trimble would resign if defeated, was passed by 459 votes (53 per cent) to 403 (47 per cent). The decision enabled devolution to be restored at midnight on May 30 and ministers resumed their offices the next day. Finally, on June 26 an IRA statement said it had re-established contact with General de Chastelain and that a confidence building inspection of a number of arms dumps had been carried out. A statement from the arms inspectors, Ramaphosa and Ahtisaari, confirmed that they were satisfied that the weapons which they had inspected could not be used without detection, and gave a commitment to carry out regular re-inspections.

Upon resuming work after its suspension, the Executive had very little time to make an input into the Comprehensive Spending Plan of the Labour Government for the next three years. The public expenditure announcement on July 19 by Gordon Brown showed an increase of £1 billion for Northern Ireland in the three years 2001-04. The resources at the disposal of the NI Executive rose from £5,306 million in 2000-01 to £6,294 million in 2003-04 (excluding cash social benefits). The Executive launched a consultation process on the Northern Ireland Budget, which would be the first delivered by a local Minister for 26 years.

There was deep division within the Assembly over the police bill, and concessions to SDLP and Sinn Féin on the powers of the police board and recruitment quotas, announced on June 6, angered unionists. A Democratic Unionist Party (DUP) motion to exclude the two Sinn Féin ministers failed on July 6 as the Assembly rose for the summer. Two UUP members, as well as two others who had resigned the party whip, supported the DUP motion and enabled the Rev. Ian Paisley to claim the support of 55 per cent of unionists in the Assembly. On July 27 the two DUP Ministers, Peter Robinson and Nigel Dodds, resigned from Regional Development and Social Development respectively and were replaced with Gregory Campbell and Maurice Morrow.

Recent summers had been dominated by the tensions of the marching season, especially in Drumcree. Whilst there were disturbances in early July over the decision of the independent Parades Commission that the Drumcree march could not follow its preferred route, the climax of the marching season, the July 12th anniversary of the Battle of the Boyne, passed off with little disturbance.

However, an Ulster Freedom Fighters (UFF)/Ulster Defence Association (UDA) parade on the Shankill road on August 19 sparked off a bloody feud between the UDA and the Ulster Volunteer Force (UVF) which was to dominate loyalist politics for four months. There had been fears about the relationship between the two groups since the shooting dead of Andrew Cairns in Larne on July 11 by the UFF. When the August parade infringed locally agreed arrangements on the flying of "colours" there was a confrontation and a retreat by the marchers. Later the UFF shot and wounded six UVF supporters in bar, and when two men were shot dead on August 21 Mandelson ordered troops back onto the streets of north Belfast. Within the lower Shankill there were attacks on the homes of supporters of both rival organisations. The finger was pointed publicly at the UFF 2nd Battalion, C Company led by Johnny Adair. Consequently, on August 22 Adair became the first early release prisoner to have his license revoked and was returned to prison. However, this action did not end the killings, nor prevent the intimidation of families or the spread of the action to Newtownabbey, Carrickfergus and Coleraine. Attempts to arrange talks for September 6 were aborted. By 16 December, when loyalist leaders finally called for an end to the feud, some 8 persons had been killed and over 200 families forced to flee from their homes.

The Northern Ireland Assembly returned from its summer recess on September 9 against the background of the continuing loyalist feud which underlined its lack of power to regulate law and order. It lost arguably its most high profile member when John Hume, leader of the SDLP, announced his resignation on July 31 and was later replaced by Annie Courtney from the same party. It also suffered the humiliation of having Mandleson intervene to announce regulations on the flying of the union flag on designated days, after its failure to reach agreement over the issue. Furthermore, an academic study found that 55 per cent of Assembly committees were operating "behind closed doors", in marked contrast to their counterparts in Scotland and Wales.

A parliamentary by-election in South Antrim, the second safest UUP seat, caused by the death of Clifford Forsythe, highlighted the fragility of UUP support in the province. DUP candidate the Rev. William McCrea narrowly overturned a 1997 UUP majority of 16,611 votes to win in a constituency which the DUP had not bothered to contest since 1983. The result raised fears of an UUP electoral meltdown, and allowed Trimble's critics, who had been relatively quiet since May, to look forward to renewing their criticism at the annual conference on October 7.

In the interim some unilateral actions by Mandelson added to the unionist belief that the implementation of the Belfast Agreement was one-sided. On September 29 he announced the abandonment of extradition proceedings against fugitive IRA members and further demilitarisation measures, including the closure of six bases in Fermanagh and a reduction in troop levels by 5,500 to 8,000. The IRA's failure to offer any reciprocal gesture provided ammunition for Trimble's critics, as did Mandelson's warning on the eve of the UUP party conference that if devolution collapsed the result would be more involvement by the Republic of Ireland in the government of Northern Ireland.

At the UUP party conference on October 7 there were calls for another withdrawal from the Executive and a reversion to a policy of "no guns no government". Trimble successfully resisted this, however, saying that he would not "go down the road of ditching the Good Friday Agreement". Two days later, in the Assembly, he defeated a DUP no-confidence vote by 52 votes to 26, with no defections from his own party.

There was some positive news about the institutions of government in October. On October 9 the final institution, the Civic Forum, met for the first time in the Waterfront Hall under the chairmanship of Chris Gibson. On October 17 the Minister for Finance, Mark Durkan, set out a budget of £5,773 million and its allocation. A week later the Executive's *Programme for Government* was published. It covered 87 pages and set out 230 actions to be pursued. There were significant debates in the Assembly on issues such as the selection procedure at 11 plus and cross party concerns expressed at the degree of freedom to adopt or adapt UK legislation.

A BBC *Panorama* investigation by John Ware into the Omagh bombing by the Real IRA (see AR 1998 p. 49) was broadcast on October 9 and pointed the finger at four main suspects. The inquest into the bombing, which had closed six days earlier, had been told that 6,500 people had been questioned, 81 arrested but only one charged (in the Republic) since August 1998.

The IRA shot dead Joseph O'Connor, a commander in the Real IRA, outside his west Belfast home on October 13, giving rise to fears of fresh republican violence. However, on October 26, shortly before a scheduled UUC meeting, the

IRA's arms dumps were re-inspected and both Ramaphosa and Ahtisaari reported that they were satisfied. Attention then focused on whether this was enough for the UUC to allow Trimble to remain as First Minister.

Blair visited Northern Ireland on October 26 and chaired a Joint Ministerial Council meeting on Health. It was also attended by Trimble and Seamus Mallon but was boycotted by the Minister for Health in the NI Executive, Bairbre de Brun (Sinn Féin), who described it as a "support Trimble" visit. A poll published by Ulster Marketing Surveys for the Belfast Telegraph on the eve of the UUC meeting showed that 69 per cent (71 in 1998) still supported the Good Friday Agreement; Catholics were the more committed at 94 per cent (99) while Protestants were now negative at 47 per cent (51). The poll also clearly identified Jeffrey Donaldson as the alternative UUP leader with 29 per cent support against Trimble's 59 and Martin Smyth's 4 per cent.

At the UUC meeting on October 27 a Donaldson motion to withdraw from the Executive by December 1 was defeated by a motion seeking a more pro-active stance from the de Chastelain Commission and a bar on Sinn Féin ministers attending NSMC meetings. Thus, although Trimble triumphed with a clear majority of 445 votes (54.3%) to 374 votes (46.7%), the concession which he made over banning Sinn Féin ministers stoked up other immediate problems. Until November 1 the north-south implementation bodies and the areas for co-operation had been meeting (except for Transport where a DUP minister was involved) without controversy. In accordance with the banning order the First Minister refused to nominate Bairbre de Brun to a meeting on health to be held in Enniskillen on November 3. His right to do this was challenged by the minister, her party, the Deputy First Minister, the Irish government, the Irish Minister for Health, Michael Martin and, broadly speaking, nationalist Ireland. The meeting proceeded as a bilateral meeting instead. This tactic was repeated with Martin McGuinness and an education sector meeting with his Dublin counterpart, Dr Michael Woods, on November 24 but, given McGuinness's status in the republican movement, it was regarded even more seriously. A legal challenge opened on November 15 and resumed on December 15.

The tension between the Labour government and the Northern Irish parties over policing issues intensified towards the end of the year as the police bill completed its final stages in the Lords. On November 13 one of the members of the Patten Commission, Professor Clifford Shearing, broke silence and accused the government of "gutting" the report. His comments were welcomed by the SDLP and Sinn Féin spokesmen on policing. On November 19 Pat Doherty, vice chairman of Sinn Féin, linked progress on decommissioning with policing reform when he said that the handing of the policing issue had "ruined the context" for his party to ask the IRA to re-engage with the de Chastelain Commission. The Police (Northern Ireland) bill passed its third reading in the Lords on November 21 with both Sinn Féin and the SDLP saying they would not encourage young nationalists to join the new Police Service of Northern Ireland.

The final piece of legislation linked to the Belfast Agreement was the Disqualifications Act, which was passed on November 30. The bill enabled members of the Daíl to sit in the House of Commons or the Northern Ireland Assembly but prohibited office holding in Northern Ireland and the Republic. The legislation removed the disqualification incurred when the Republic had left the Commonwealth in 1949. The legislation had been opposed by Conservatives and Ulster Unionists and had been defeated in the Lords on November 20.

It was confirmed that President Clinton would make a friendly farewell visit to Ireland and the UK on December 12-14 before leaving office. Prior to the visit the murder of a protestant taxi driver on December 5, allegedly by republicans, resulted in the wounding of a catholic taxi driver and the shooting dead of a catholic building worker. Nevertheless, Clinton met the political parties at Stormont on December 13 and had detailed talks with the parties before addressing the public in the new Odyssey millennium entertainment centre. There were no immediate political developments from the visit. Indeed, the interception of a car bomb close to Belfast city centre on December 14 and the re-opening of Sinn Féin's legal challenge against the First Minister the next day seemed like a return to normal business. The only positive event was the call by loyalist leaders on December 16 for the ending of the feud which had cost 12 lives during the year.

Despite the underlying problems the Assembly rose for the Christmas recess on December 19 after voting its members another 2.9 per cent pay rise. On Boxing Day it was announced that four fugitive republican prisoners had been granted the royal prerogative of mercy to enable them to return to Northern Ireland without threat of arrest. On December 29, Ronald Hill, who had been in a coma since the Enniskillen bombing in November 1987, died and became the 12th fatal victim of that atrocity.

During the year the economy of Northern Ireland continued to improve. It attracted overseas investment and maintained the lowest unemployment rate for 25 years, and was described as the fastest growing regional economy in the UK. GDP continued to rise and within it the manufacturing sector remained significant, in contrast to the UK in general. However, the strength of sterling and its position outside the euro zone had an adverse impact on manufacturing exporters. Textiles, clothing, food processing and shipbuilding continued to decline. The construction industry was relatively buoyant, but agricultural income fell for the fifth successive year.

2. GERMANY—FRANCE—ITALY—BELGIUM—
THE NETHERLANDS—LUXEMBOURG—IRELAND

i. GERMANY

CAPITAL: Berlin   AREA: 357,000 sq km   POPULATION: 82,000,000
OFFICIAL LANGUAGE: German   POLITICAL SYSTEM: federal parliamentary democracy
HEAD OF STATE: President Johannes Rau (since July '99)
RULING PARTIES: Social Democratic Party (SPD) & Alliance 90/Greens
HEAD OF GOVERNMENT: Gerhard Schröder (SPD), Federal Chancellor (since Oct '98)
MAIN IGO MEMBERSHIPS (NON-UN): NATO, EU, WEU, OSCE, CE, CBSS, AC, OECD, G-8
CURRENCY: Deutsche Mark (end-'00 £1=DM3.11, US$1=DM2.08)
GNP PER CAPITA: US$25,350, US$22,404 at PPP ('99)

THE most prominent theme in German politics in 2000 was that of financial scandal. In late 1999, investigations against the former treasurer of the Christian Democratic Union (CDU), Walther Leisler Kiep, and the party's accountant, Horst Weyrauch, over tax evasion had unexpectedly revealed financial irregularities on a much larger scale and at the highest levels of the party. These investigations ensnared former Chancellor Helmut Kohl in December 1999, when he admitted to having received personally some DM2 million in illegal donations between 1993 and 1998 (see AR 1999, pp. 57-8). Kohl's stubborn and unrepentant refusal to name the donors concerned—as was required by laws which his own government had enacted—became one of the enduring images of the year. It led not only to the destruction of the personal reputation of the "Chancellor of German unity" but also to his resignation from the office of CDU honorary president and to an unprecedented (and ultimately fruitless) criminal investigation against a former head of government.

The scandal also opened the floodgates for other rumours and disclosures. Doubts were raised over the Kohl government's sale of the East German Leuna chemical works to Elf Aquitaine in 1994, with rumours that this was accompanied by substantial backhanders to the CDU. In January 2000 it was even alleged—though as yet without evidence—that France's former President Mitterrand had personally sanctioned payments to the CDU to help the party win the 1994 Bundestag election. In late January a similar pattern of illegal party donations, this time squirreled away into secret bank accounts in Switzerland and Liechtenstein, emerged in the CDU's regional branch in Hesse. These illegal funds—worth DM19.2 million—tarnished the reputation of Roland Koch, the CDU Minister-President (governor) of Hesse (one of the Länder, the autonomous states which comprised the German federation). Hitherto Koch had been one of the few rising stars of the CDU who had a nationwide profile.

The party finance scandal also claimed Kohl's long-time ally and successor as CDU leader, Wolfgang Schäuble as a victim. Whilst Schäuble had distanced himself from his former mentor in the wake of the revelations, he was forced to admit to having himself received a cash donation to the CDU of DM100,000, which the party failed to register in accordance with party finance law. Schäuble was then forced to resign on February 16 in a rebellion by the party's North

Rhine-Westphalian legislators, who were fearful of the detrimental effect of the controversy on the party's chances in their upcoming state election scheduled for May 14.

Schäuble's successor, Angela Merkel, faced a tall order. Not only did she have to rebuild the reputation of the party, but also absorb the consequences of the DM41.3 million fine imposed on the CDU for its financing irregularities (although the fine was later suspended by the courts). Merkel was in some sense well-placed to lead the process of renewal. Relatively young at 45 years of age, she was distanced from the discredited "Kohl system". As an easterner, she also offered the possibility of shoring up the party's fortunes with the fickle east German electorate. She was, though, on the liberal wing of the CDU and her election provoked some concern on the right of the party and, in particular, in its Bavarian sister organisation, the Christian Social Union (CSU). The CSU leader, Edmund Stoiber had used the CDU's difficulties to give himself and his party's harder-edged conservatism a higher profile, amidst periodic hints that he might challenge Merkel for the mantle of Christian Democratic candidate for the Chancellorship at the next Bundestag election in 2002.

The crisis in the CDU proved fortuitous for the Social Democratic Party (SPD) under Chancellor Gerhard Schröder. Schröder's performance, and that of his government, had been lacklustre since the unexpectedly clear-cut election victory of 1998. Internal programmatic disunity, an unpredictable coalition partner in the form of the Greens and a general whiff of opportunism surrounding Schröder had prevented a clear policy direction from emerging. The result had been a series of election defeats during 1999 which reflected above all an inability to mobilise the SPD core electorate amongst unionised workers.

The tribulations of Kohl, Schäuble and Merkel created a change of mood, which set the scene for the two Land elections held in 2000: in Schleswig-Holstein in the far north and in the industrial powerhouse of North Rhine-Westphalia. The Schleswig-Holstein election of February 27 took place just days after Schäuble's resignation. It offered voters their first opportunity to pass judgement on the sensational revelations of the previous three months. The state had been governed by the CDU continuously for 39 years until 1988, when the SPD had won it in the aftermath of another infamous scandal involving the then CDU Minister-President, Uwe Barschel. Until late 1999, the CDU's chances of victory had looked good. It had chosen the bullish former Defence Minister, Volker Rühe, to lead its campaign, and the incumbent SPD-Green government under Heide Simonis, the only female Minister-President in Germany, was trailing badly in the polls. But once the details of the CDU's finance scandal became public, the scales quickly tipped the other way, as the almost daily revelations of illegal dealings dominated the campaign.

The results were not, though, as bad as the CDU might have expected and were considerably better than the 30 per cent predicted by some analysts. The party did leak some support to the liberal Free Democratic Party (FDP), but was able to limit its losses. The previous SPD-Green coalition was easily re-confirmed in office, though with the Greens losing some support. A similar pattern of results

Schleswig-Holstein election (February 27, 2000)

Party	% of votes 2000	seats 2000	(% of votes 1996)	(seats 1996)
Social Democratic Party	43.1	41	(39.8)	(33)
Christian Democratic Union	35.2	33	(37.2)	(30)
Green Party	6.2	5	(8.1)	(6)
Free Democratic Party	7.6	7	(5.7)	(4)
SSW*	4.1	3	(2.5)	(2)
Others	3.8	-	(6.7)	(-)
Total	100.0	89	(100.00)	(75)

*The SSW represents the Danish minority in Schleswig-Holstein and was exempt from the 5 per cent threshold for representation.

emerged in the Land election on May 14 in North Rhine-Westphalia, traditionally considered a key "barometer" election in identifying future electoral trends. North Rhine-Westphalia was by far the most populous state in Germany, with over 16 million inhabitants. It also contained the electoral heartlands of both the CDU and SPD: not only had the SPD traditionally polled its best results in the industrial cities around the Ruhr valley, but the CDU's rhenish catholic heritage, as epitomised by Konrad Adenauer, the first West German Chancellor, also had its origins in the state. Since 1995 an SPD-Green coalition, first under Johannes Rau and since 1998 under Wolfgang Clement, had been in power. It had lately been beset by disputes over transport and energy policy, especially over the future of the Garzweiler open-cast mining project, and as the election approached the SPD also found itself embroiled in accusations of sleaze over the use of Westdeutsche Landesbank's private jets by Rau and the state Finance Minister, Heinz Schleuber.

North Rhine-Westphalia election (May 14, 2000)

Party	% of votes 2000	seats 2000	(% of votes 1995)	(seats 1995)
Social Democratic Party	42.8	102	(46.0)	(108)
Christian Democratic Union	37.0	88	(37.7)	(89)
Green Party	7.1	17	(10.0)	(24)
Free Democratic Party	9.8	24	(4.0)	(-)
Others	3.3	-	(6.7)	(-)
Total	100.0	231	(100.0)	(221)

The election was not a tremendous success for the SPD which had difficulties in mobilising its core voters, although, with a popular Minister-President in the figure of Clement, it was able to remain the largest party by a comfortable margin. The CDU's result was surprisingly good. With many in the party fearing a heavy defeat, more or less maintaining its share of the vote was seen as something of a triumph. The best result was that of the FDP, which more than doubled its vote, easily clearing the five per cent hurdle to re-enter the Land parliament. Under its leader, the brash former federal Economics Minister Jürgen Möllemann, the FDP ran an unashamedly populist campaign which capitalised on voter dissatisfaction with the other three parties. Given that the FDP's political profile and performance under leader Wolfgang Gerhardt had been considered lacklustre at best, Möllemann seemed set to use his success as a launchpad for a national role as the next Bundestag election approached.

The Greens were once again punished heavily by voters for what was perceived as their weak performance in government, and both the party and its candidate, state environment minister Bärbel Höhn, suffered from very low public approval ratings. The poor performance of the Greens was indicative of a wider problem they faced in preserving the purity of their anti-establishment origins amidst the exercise of governmental power. Persistent internal bickering over issues such as nuclear power and the internal structures of the party undermined their support and led to the partial estrangement of their foremost electoral asset—federal Foreign Minister Joschka Fischer—from the party grass roots. Möllemann's public flirtation with the SPD after the election in North Rhine-Westphalia signalled also that the SPD had another option as junior coalition partner. The Greens thus found themselves in a strategic bind with no obvious way out.

The other major party in Germany was the Party of Democratic Socialism (PDS), which had succeeded the former East German Communist Party and remodelled itself as a broad-based regional party of the east. It benefited from the scandals involving the mainstream CDU (and to a lesser extent the SPD), and retained high levels of support across the east. The PDS was generally considered to have suffered a setback, though, when its two most prominent leaders, Lothar Bisky and the charismatic Gregor Gysi, announced their intention to resign their party posts in April. Doubts exist about the quality of the next generation of leaders and in particular about their ability to boost the PDS presence in western Germany.

Thus, the domestic political outlook at the end of 2000, halfway through the current parliamentary term, was somewhat unclear. The SPD-Green government had scored some notable successes in securing far-reaching reforms in several areas. In particular, Schröder's Finance Minister Hans Eichel, who proved himself to be an astute political fixer, successfully piloted through a radical and long-awaited shake-up of the tax system during the summer. Breakthroughs on other key issues—the phasing out of nuclear power and the government-business compensation package for victims of slave labour in Germany in the Nazi era—confirmed a new potency in the government. On the other hand, however, the Greens were unable to reap the political benefit of these achievements, and their weakness casts doubts over the prospect of a renewed "red-green" coalition after the 2002 election. Moreover, the confirmation of the FDP as an alternative coalition partner strengthened the SPD's hand. With Schröder set to follow a strategy of competence and continuity, the onus appeared to be on the CDU/CSU to set the political agenda. One such possible area was immigration. This was a theme that the CDU highlighted in North Rhine Westphalia in response to the federal government's decision to introduce "green cards" to allow up to 10,000 non-EU, and in particular Indian, IT specialists German entry and work permits for up to five years in order to address a labour shortage in the high-tech sector. It resulted in the overtly populist election slogan "Kinder statt Inder" ("Children, not Indians"), advocating a focus on investment in education rather than immigration.

The baton was taken further in the debate about the German "Leitkultur" ("dominant culture") launched by the CDU in October. On October 18 Friedrich Merz, the CDU/CSU leader in the Bundestag, publicly supported the idea that immigrants should be expected to assimilate into the dominant value system of the German majority. This sparked an intense public debate between academics, intellectuals and politicians, which covered not only whether this was a reasonable expectation, but also the more important question of how this "Leitkultur" could be defined in practice. This new controversy came against the background of a long-standing debate between parties of the left and right over whether Germany should consider itself a multicultural society. Although this debate had also taken place elsewhere in Europe, it was particularly sensitive in Germany, because of its Nazi past. The result was an often contradictory policy under which immigrants were encouraged to maintain their own cultural identity, but were simultaneously expected to assimilate into the German cultural identity before being granted citizenship.

The immigration issue also took on a European Union dimension. The planned eastern enlargement of the EU offered the prospect of removing border controls and opening up free movement of labour between Germany and its eastern neighbours, but also threatened to facilitate illegal immigration and transnational criminality. Concerns about the effects of free movement and immigration on German labour markets, social cohesion and organised crime were issues of considerable public concern. High unemployment in the five new Länder excited anxieties both about the export of jobs and investment to lower-cost labour markets. There was also a strong association in the public mind between certain kinds of crime, like car theft and prostitution, and the openness of Germany's eastern borders. These anxieties were skilfully exploited by right-wing parties, in particular by the CSU in Bavaria.

The other key European policy issue in 2000 was the Intergovernmental Conference (IGC) scheduled for completion at the Nice Summit in December (see XI.4). The IGC was concerned with the "leftovers" of the previous Amsterdam IGC, in particular the streamlining of the EU's institutional structures prior to enlargement. The outcome at Nice was widely regarded as a major success for the German government. The institutional architecture of the EU was originally intended to diffuse issues of relative power and large countries were significantly under-represented. This question became more crucial as enlargement and the entry of a large number of small and poor states loomed. Agreement was reached at Nice on reweighting votes in the Council of Ministers, with each of the four large states being allotted 29 votes whilst the figures allotted to the smaller states went up much less steeply. Although France resisted German demands for increased voting-power in recognition of its larger population than any of the other big states, German weight in the European Parliament was decisively increased, with Germany keeping its entitlement of 99 MEPs, as opposed to the reduced quota of 74 for the other large states. More crucially, a dual majority system was introduced for qualified majority voting (QMV) in the Council whereby, on request, a majority would be checked to ensure that it represented 62 per cent of the EU's population. This ensured that Germany needed the support of only two other large states to put together a blocking minority. This option was not open to the remaining large states.

The outcome of Nice was a clear success for the Schröder government. It paved the way for enlargement and de facto established Germany as primus inter pares amongst European states. It also provided an avenue for the German Chancellor to be seen to play the key role in brokering agreement, thereby adding to Schröder's growing reputation as an effective political manager and giving him the foreign policy gravitas traditionally expected of German Chancellors. It thus bolstered his reputation at home and helped him to enter the second half of the parliamentary period looking in better political shape than at any point hitherto.

ii. FRANCE

CAPITAL: Paris   AREA: 552,000 sq km   POPULATION: 58,900,000
OFFICIAL LANGUAGE: French   POLITICAL SYSTEM: presidential parliamentary democracy
HEAD OF STATE AND GOVERNMENT: President Jacques Chirac (RPR), since May '95
RULING PARTIES: Rally for the Republic (RPR) holds presidency; Socialist Party (PS), French Communist Party (PCF), Greens and other groups form government
PRIME MINISTER: Lionel Jospin (PS), since June '97
MAIN IGO MEMBERSHIPS (NON-UN): NATO, EU, WEU, OSCE, COE, OECD, G-8, Francophonie
CURRENCY: franc (end-'00 £1=Fr10.44, US$1=Fr6.99)
GNP PER CAPITA: US$23,480, US$21,897 at PPP ('99)

As the new millennium broke, France presented two contrasting faces: dazzling celebratory pyrotechnics in Paris and widespread devastation from the worst storms of the century. Many thousands of homes were without heat or light, railways and roads were blocked and many of the best-known historical sites suffered damage. Eighty-eight people died and over 100 million trees were felled. France had been "wounded", declared President Jacques Chirac. The Prime Minister summoned ministers from holiday to "display solidarity" and to oversee the recovery. Power and communications were largely restored by mid-January, though the forest devastation remained. Another major disaster also marked the year: the crash of an Air France Concorde on takeoff in July with the loss of 113 lives.

This was an intensely political year. Political eyes—though not those of a disenchanted public—were fixed on elections due in 2002. Jacques Chirac for the right, Prime Minister Lionel Jospin for the left, locked in an uneasy "cohabitation", searched constantly to gain ground. An early casualty of this struggle was a constitutional amendment to reform the administration of justice. Despite the initial support of President and Prime Minister and a large majority in the Assembly, genuine misgivings about "a dictatorship of the magistrates" mingled with machinations within the President's own party, forcing him to halt the process. However, reforms not requiring a constitutional amendment were agreed, including measures to strengthen the presumption of innocence and to reduce opportunities for political interference in the administration of justice.

The early months were difficult for the government. Haulage company owners blockaded roads over fuel prices and the introduction of the 35-hour week, the latter being the major social reform of the Jospin administration. The government granted them partial exemption from the new law. Surgeons and anesthetists struck over their "chronically underfunded" system. Haulage drivers angry at concessions to their employers blockaded motorways and ports. Other workers demonstrated because their bosses were exploiting the legislation to impose more flexible working. Meanwhile, the employers' confederation attacked the legislation as too costly and complicated. A book by the chief doctor of the Santé prison condemning conditions there as an "inhumane nightmare" sparked a debate on prison reform. Her account was confirmed by recent VIP prisoners (mostly incarcerated for corruption). The Justice Minister, Elisabeth Guigou, announced the closure of three prisons and the renovation of the Santé, with its alarming suicide rate. However, critics contended that nothing less than a complete rethink of the system was needed. In January the Education Minister, Claude Allègre, announced new measures to tackle violence in schools, accepting that previous measures had failed. But proposals to impose reform on the teachers were abandoned in the face of union opposition, as were attempts to agree on the implementation of the 35-hour week in the civil service. Proposals by the Finance Minister, Christian Sautter, to unify tax assessment and tax collection collapsed after a strike by ministry staff.

Jospin's own reputation for competence was dented in February when he made a rare foray into foreign affairs, normally a presidential domain. Visiting the Middle East he was stoned by Palestinian students after branding attacks on Israeli troops in South Lebanon as "terrorist acts". He was publicly rebuked by Chirac. Despite increasing economic prosperity, his standing at the polls slipped. He was seen as indecisive, failing to back ministers when they ran into resistance from vested interests and temporising over the thorny issue of pensions reform. Several ministers paid the price. Former Premier Laurent Fabius became Finance Minister, providing the government with a balance lacking since Dominique Strauss-Khan's forced resignation in 1999 (see AR 1999 p. 61). Jack Lang, another big figure from the Mitterrand era, took the difficult education post. Jospin insisted that this was "not a change of policy but a deepening of policy".

Meanwhile, the enduring odour of scandal still hung over political life. In January, former President Mitterrand was revealed to have authorized the Elf-Aquitaine oil company to pay 100 million francs to Helmut Kohl for his 1994 election campaign. Some 21,000 million francs was allegedly milked from Elf between 1989 and 1994 for illegal political funding. In March the president of the Constitutional Council and former Foreign Minister, Roland Dumas, resigned when sent for trial on corruption charges. Later, Jean-Christophe Mitterrand, son of the late President, was embroiled with in a scandal over illegal arms deals with Angola. The Communist Party's general secretary also faced charges over illegal political funding. The discredited mayor of Paris, Jean Tiberi, was rejected as Gaullist candidate for re-election and expelled from the party. His wife came up for trial on corruption charges in November, her previous trial having collapsed for technical reasons. Accusations now crept ever closer to the President, himself a former mayor of Paris. In September, he was directly accused, by a onetime member of his party's central committee, with involvement in illegal political funding. Jean-Claude Méry, who died in 1999, left an accusatory videotape which curiously surfaced in *Le Monde* in murky circumstances via the ex-Finance Minister, Dominique Strauss-Khan, who was himself facing corruption charges. After a long silence Chirac declared himself "deeply hurt" by the allegations, denounced the investigation as "show justice", and declined to answer detailed questions.

It seemed that a change in the constitution might work in Chirac's favour. Which was why, though long a defender of seven-year presidential terms, he now backed a reduction to five years proposed by former President (and his sworn political enemy) Valéry Giscard d'Estaing. (Almost 70 in 2002 compared with Jospin's 62, it was widely believed that Chirac would be seen as too old to serve a full seven years.) Although it was denounced by some Gaullists as betraying a founding principle of the Fifth Republic by tilting the constitutional balance in a more parliamentary direction, the amendment was approved by 72.9 per cent of those voting in September, but the 30.7 per cent turnout was the lowest of any referendum under the Fifth Republic.

As so often in France, more came to light on unhappy episodes in the past. In January a former security service agent confirmed that the Moroccan opposition leader, Ben Barka, had indeed been kidnapped, tortured and murdered with the aid of French agents in Paris 35 years earlier, then buried at Orly on the site of a mosque. In March the government refused to compensate victims of the collaborationist wartime Vichy regime on the legalistic ground that a 1944 decree had declared that regime's acts null and void. In April an official commission reported that property and cash worth over 8,000 million francs had been seized from the Jewish community during the war; 2,000 million francs were still held by the government. A compensation scheme was promised. And former general Jacques Massu, 93, finally acknowledged and regretted the use of torture, so long officially denied, by the French army during the Algerian war of 1954-62.

Meanwhile, in July the government made a bold attempt to settle the interminable problem of Corsica. Jospin proposed a "sharing of competences", with Corsica gaining greater power over education, culture, the environment and economic development. Initially administration and regulatory power would transfer, then—subject to a probationary period and law and order being firmly established—a constitutional revision would confer limited law-making powers on a new political and administrative body. The Minister of the Interior, Jean-Paul Chevènement, hostile to giving more power to an area that was "a byword for corruption and criminality", felt that he had been put in "an impossible position" and resigned. Giscard d'Estaing declared the government had abdicated in the face of violence and the Gaullists said that the proposals undermined "national unity and the indivisibility of the Republic". The proposals were overwhelmingly approved by the Corsican Assembly. Whether the more extreme nationalists would give it a fair wind remained less certain. Predictably, a coalition of Basques, Bretons and movements from the Caribbean departments now sprang up to demand similar treatment to the Corsicans.

In August farmers, hauliers and fishermen took direct action over fuel prices, rapidly bringing the country almost to a standstill. Initially resolute, the government then capitulated, provoking the Green Environment Minister to threaten resignation. Jospin's approval rating dropped 20 points overnight. In October his Employment Minister, Martine Aubry—architect of the 35-hour week—resigned to prepare her mayoral campaign at Lille, precipitating a further reshuffle. She was replaced by Elisabeth Guigou, with Marylise Lebranchu moving into her place as Minister of Justice. Earlier, Daniel Vaillant had succeeded Chevènement as Interior Minister.

France had long prided itself on its handling of the BSE problem. In February it rejected criticism from the European Commission that it had failed to do enough to protect consumers. However, by October, 78 cases of BSE had been reported, with two deaths from nvCJD. Whilst this was far below British levels, a consumer panic ensued when it emerged that potentially infected meat had found its way into the shops. Beef sales plummeted. Random BSE testing was hastily introduced on cattle due to be slaughtered, along with a ban on animal fats in cattle food.

Such crises and conflicts were largely offset by the wellbeing arising from the buoyancy of the economy—the fastest growing in Europe. By mid-year, unemployment had at last fallen below 10 per cent, ending the year at 9.1 per cent (though this was still above the EU average). GDP increased by a comfortable 2.8 per cent (albeit also below the EU average), prices rose a mere 1.4 per cent (less than the average for the EU), and earnings rose by 5.3 per cent. The achievement was generally credited to a combination of government measures to bring young people into employment, low interest rates and low public debt. Inward investment was strong; e-commerce was thriving, and the 35-hour week now seemed more popular and successful. In September Fabius introduced a popular budget, offering a 112,000 million franc package of tax cuts aimed at stimulating growth, a reduction in income tax in all brackets by between 1.5 and 3.5 per cent over three years, but mainly benefitting middle and low taxpayers, and lower taxes on small and medium firms. Other reforms were aimed at making it more worthwhile for people on benefits to take jobs.

Comparable success could not be claimed for the French presidency of the European Union during the second half of the year. The political ambitions of President and Prime Minister, and their policy differences, led to both incoherence and to a tenacity in promoting French interests that was widely resented by other members, not least at the Nice summit. The Franco-German alliance came under severe strain. Jean-Paul Chevènement caused offence by suggesting that Germany had not entirely turned its back on the Nazi period. More generally, it seemed that France was finding it difficult to adjust to a situation in which Germany was now the dominant partner. In negotiations over the proposed European rapid reaction force, France was again at odds with her neighbours in pressing for it to have its own planning staff, independent of NATO, thereby potentially enlisting it in the longstanding aim of countering US power.

The year ended as it began, with internal politicking to the fore. In December Jospin pressed for a change in the electoral calendar so that parliamentary elections would follow rather than precede the presidential election. The right saw this as a blatant bid to improve his chances of the presidency; both his Green and Communist coalition partners were also unhappy. Most parties were now struggling with new "parity" legislation aimed at equalizing women's access to employment. Henceforth, any party fielding more men than women in local, regional, general or European elections would have its state funding cut. Whilst the principle had wide support, finding suitable women candidates proved difficult. Meanwhile, it seemed increasingly likely that Jospin and Chirac would be the two finalists in the presidential contest. The Socialists were the only credible contenders on the left, and Jospin had regained much popularity by the year's end. By contrast, the right had sundered into acrimonious fragmentation and, as yet, all pleas for a united front against the left went unheeded amid the clash of political egos and ambitions.

iii. ITALY

CAPITAL: Rome   AREA: 301,000 sq km   POPULATION: 58,000,000
OFFICIAL LANGUAGE: Italian   POLITICAL SYSTEM: parliamentary democracy
HEAD OF STATE: President Carlo Azeglio Ciampi (since May '99)
RULING PARTY: Left Democrats (DS) head centre-left coalition
HEAD OF GOVERNMENT: Giuliano Amato (independent), Prime Minister (since April '00)
MAIN IGO MEMBERSHIPS (NON-UN): NATO, EU, WEU, OSCE, CE, CEI, OECD, G-8
CURRENCY: lira (end-'00 £1=L3,080.79, US$1=L2062.39)
GNP PER CAPITA: US$19,710, US$20,751 at PPP ('99)

ITALY enjoyed another year of progress towards financial and economic stability. The cloud of crisis which had hung over the country's public accounts lifted sufficiently for the budget to contain the first provisions for paying back Italians for the sacrifices which they had made since 1992. Only a slight increase in inflation, to 2.4 per cent in March, and the slow growth in employment in the south caused some concern.

The year in politics, however, was marked by considerable upheaval and disputes. Massimo D'Alema's leadership of the government was overturned, and there was significant realignment within the party system. The later months of the year were marked by election campaigning in preparation for the contest which was due in early 2001. Amidst these activities, little progress was made towards reforming the electoral system or resolving "conflicts of interest" issues involving those in public life, two concerns which had been pressing for at least four years.

Local elections held on April 16, to choose regional presidents and assemblies, proved disastrous for D'Alema's administration. The opposition, headed by Silvio Berlusconi, campaigned vigorously and sought to turn the contest into a judgement on the performance in government of the ruling centre-left coalition and the abilities of D'Alema, leader of the former-Communist Left Democrats (DS), as Prime Minister. Although the centre-left was at first wary of accepting this challenge, it remained confident of victory. The opinion polls were positive and it fielded some prominent candidates in key regions. (The mayor of Naples, Antonio Bassolino, resigned to run in Campania; and the mayor of Venice, Massimo Cacciari, did the same to stand in the Veneto.) Incautiously, therefore, D'Alema accepted his opponent's challenge and stated on television that he would resign if defeated. The results of the vote came as a shock to the government as the centre-left lost control of Liguria and Lazio and saw a decline in its support in Puglia, Calabria and the Abruzzo. Berlusconi's Forza Italia emerged as the largest party, and the north was won by the centre-right alliance between the Liberty Pole (Forza Italia and the National Alliance) and the Northern League. Overall, the centre-right took eight regions to the centre-left's seven. The only left-wing candidate to score an impressive victory was Bassolino, whose record as mayor of Naples formed the cornerstone of the left's success in the surrounding region. Faced with no alternative but to acknowledge defeat, the Prime Minister tendered his resignation on April 17.

President Carlo Azeglio Ciampi wasted little time in appointing the Treasury Minister, Giuliano Amato, as D'Alema's successor. A former close ally of the disgraced Socialist leader Bettino Craxi (whose death in January in Tunisia gave rise to much debate), Amato had initiated the process of economic renewal through sacrifice when he first became Prime Minister in 1992. Now he was charged with continuing this work as well as with managing the referenda which were scheduled to take place in the spring and with implementing electoral reform. The Amato government differed little in composition from its predecessor. The former Finance Minister, Vincenzo Visco, took over at the Treasury, whilst the Finance portfolio went to the Socialist Ottaviano Del Turco.

Buoyed by success in the regional elections, Berlusconi regarded victory in the forthcoming national elections as being within his grasp. In consequence, his coalition pursued a policy of non-cooperation with the government on many issues. Already in the first two months of the year, a government proposal to adopt new rules on equal treatment of the parties in the media during elections had been rejected by the Liberty Pole as unnecessarily restrictive. When these rules were approved by parliament, Berlusconi threatened to block all reform plans. He also made repeated attacks on the judiciary. Although the opposition leader was acquitted in May of charges that he had bribed government financial inspectors looking into the affairs of his companies, and in June of bribing a judge for a favourable ruling on a takeover battle, he maintained his attitude of hostility towards judges, whom he accused of being politicised and, in his most startling attack, of being little better than delinquents.

The referenda which took place in May 21 provided an opportunity for the opposition to score a further victory over the government. The issues were various, several having been devised by the Radical Party to exploit growing public disaffection with politics and to capitalise on its European election success of 1999. The most significant issue to be put to the vote was undoubtedly the bid to alter the electoral system by abolishing the 25 per cent of parliamentary seats which were distributed between the parties on a proportional basis. This would have made the electoral system function on a simple-majority basis and, in the view of its promoters, would have strengthened the bi-polar nature of the party system. Support for the measure came from both left and right (in particular from the National Alliance), whilst smaller parties of all persuasions opposed it as a threat to their legislative representation. Although he had initially backed the reform, when it came to the vote Berlusconi announced his opposition and urged voters to abstain. When a mere 33 per cent of Italians voted (the quorum for the result of the referendum to be valid was 50 percent), he claimed victory. The issue of the reform of the country's imperfect electoral system was thus returned to the politicians and once more became the subject of horse-trading between them. By the end of the year no significant action had been taken.

The same was true of the conflict of interest question. Ever since Berlusconi had entered politics in 1994—the year in which he had achieved his first electoral success at the head of a right-wing coalition—there had been concern that a powerful media magnate could hold public office whilst retaining his business interests. Although this was felt to be bad for democracy and the centre-left coalition had vowed to address the issue when it won power in 1996, no decisive steps had yet been taken in this regard. With a new election looming, the matter became pressing but more difficult to address in a manner that was not open to accusations of partisanship.

The only area in which some steps towards reform were accomplished was devolution. In September the Liberty Pole and Northern League-dominated regional assembly in Lombardy decided, controversially, to hold a consultative referendum to seek approval for its claim to greater powers. In November, however, the Senate pre-empted the assembly's move by approving a design for a new constitutional law that would devolve powers to the regions, provinces and communes. This was seen as a first step towards the adoption of a federal system.

Faced with these various setbacks, which were compounded by poor leadership, internal divisions and the lack of a clear agenda, the centre-left was obliged to consider how it could re-establish its popularity with the electorate. Broadly speaking, the year saw two movements develop amongst the parties within the coalition. On the one hand, the DS leader, Walter Veltroni, continued to promote his idea of a single force embracing all of the left-wing parties. Although neither the Green Party nor the Party of Italian Communists (both part of the governing alliance) were happy with this proposal, it remained an aspiration. Prime Minister Amato was seen as the ideal broker to seek a new departure of this type. On the other hand, the centre parties in the coalition, including the Democrats for the Olive Tree (Democrats), Italian Renewal and the Italian People's Party, succeeded in creating a common platform and symbol (the daisy). Their alliance was significantly bolstered by the emergence of the

Democrat mayor of Rome, Francesco Rutelli, as the centre-left's candidate for Prime Minister. An able administrator who had successfully managed the challenge of the Jubilee, but above all a politician of youthful good looks who was untainted by any association with the old party system, Rutelli was seen as preferable to Amato. Although the latter was highly-regarded, his links to the Craxi era and lack of popular appeal rendered him an inappropriate choice for what promised to be an uphill struggle. Amato nonetheless remained as Prime Minister and promised his backing to the chosen candidate.

The centre-right remained stable for most of the year; only the nascent alliance with the Radicals foundered. Berlusconi launched a highly personal poster campaign towards the end of the year that was designed to anticipate the official start of the election campaign. However, the European Union's strong reaction to the accession of the far-right Austrian Freedom Party to government raised questions about the role of the Northern League in the opposition. Although few questions had been raised (and no sanctions imposed) when the Liberty Pole, including Forza Italia and the ex-fascist National Alliance, came to power with the Northern League in 1994, the climate had since changed. Both within Italy and outside, there was concern about the policies of the League on immigration and cultural diversity. A sign of change came in March when the League called for force to be used to stop immigrants from entering Italy. Walter Veltroni denounced the League as unfit to govern after it supported a protest against the building of a mosque in Lodi, and the DS regularly compared its leader, Umberto Bossi, to Jorg Haider of the Austrian Freedom Party (see II.3.vi).

A further development in Italy's party system occurred when Sergio D'Antoni, the leader of CISL, the Catholic trade union confederation, began to attract together significant numbers of former Christian Democrats. In November he resigned his trade union post to devote himself to the construction of a new party named European Democracy. Backed by seven times Prime Minster Giulio Andreotti and other prominent politicians, he aspired to create a force that could occupy the middle-ground in the 2001 elections. He pledged that no electoral agreements would be struck with either side.

A confused political situation was briefly worsened towards the end of the year by two bombs. The first, allegedly the work of a fragment of the Red Brigades, was discovered on December 18 on the roof of the Milan Duomo, and was defused by police only three hours before it was timed to explode. Four days later, a second bomb exploded in the hands of a far-right activist as he was placing it in the offices of communist newspaper, *Il Manifesto*. These events brought back memories of the political violence which had marred Italian political life in the 1970s and 80s.

The worst floods that the country had experienced since 1994 devastated northern Italy in October and November. Torrential rain resulted in widespread flooding and landslides, which killed at least 33 people and forced tens of thousands to leave their homes. On October 16 the government declared a state of emergency in the regions of Valle d'Aosta, Piedmont and Liguria; soon extending this to include the River Po valley.

iv BELGIUM

CAPITAL: Brussels   AREA: 33,000 sq km   POPULATION: 10,300,000
OFFICIAL LANGUAGES: French, Flemish & German   POLITICAL SYSTEM: federal parliamentary democracy based on language communities
HEAD OF STATE: King Albert II (since Aug. '93)
RULING PARTIES: Flemish Liberals and Democrats (VLD/Flemish), Liberal Reform Party (PRL/Walloon), Socialist Party (SP/Flemish), Socialist Party (PS/Walloon), Flemish Greens (Agalev) & Walloon Greens (Ecolo)
HEAD OF GOVERNMENT: Guy Verhofstadt (VLD), Prime Minister (since July '99)
MAIN IGO MEMBERSHIPS (NON-UN): NATO, EU, WEU, Benelux, OSCE, CE, OECD, Francophonie
CURRENCY: Belgian franc (end-'00 £1=BFr64.18, US$1=BFr42.97)
GNP PER CAPITA: US$24,510, US$24,200 at PPP ('99)

DURING 2000 the underlying tensions between the Francophone and Flemish regions of Belgium came to the fore. The Flemish Bloc (VB), a far right-wing nationalist party which advocated separatism for Flanders (the Dutch speaking region of Belgium) and an end to immigration into the country, achieved major gains in local elections held on October 8. The party, led by Filip Dewinter, secured 33 per cent of the vote in Antwerp (and two extra seats) although, despite its status as the largest party, it failed to capture control of the city council which remained dominated by a coalition of smaller political parties. The VB also secured impressive gains in other towns in Flanders and even in Brussels, a city with an overwhelming Francophone majority. In a further development, the federal Council of Ministers on October 17 approved an agreement giving Flanders and Wallonia (the French speaking region) greater autonomy over taxation. The agreement was brokered by the Prime Minister, Guy Verhofstadt in response to pressure from Flanders for more economic independence from Wallonia, and represented a significant change to Belgium's federal constitution.

In economic affairs, the federal Council of Ministers on October 17 approved the 2001 budget providing for tax reform and the first fiscal surplus for more than 50 years. The budget proposed tax cuts which would reduce annual taxation by BFr135 billion by 2005. Cuts in social expenditure, together with economic growth, were projected to produce a fiscal surplus in 2001 following a balanced budget in 2000. The government's fiscal plans had suffered a setback in September, when widespread protests by farmers and lorry drivers forced it to offer a package of social and fiscal measures to compensate protesters for the rising costs of fuel, although it did not accede to demands for a 15 per cent cut in fuel taxes. The year was also notable for the creation on September 22 of Euronext, a pan-European stock exchange, through the merger of the stock exchanges of France, Belgium and the Netherlands. The merger was designed to facilitate cross-border transactions in the wake of the introduction of the euro. The new exchange was Europe's second largest after London in terms of market capitalisation and the number of companies listed.

During the year the food and agricultural sector, which had been adversely affected by health scares in 1999 (see AR 1999, p. 68) was further troubled by evidence that Bovine Spongiform Encephalopathy (BSE or mad cow disease) might have infected some sheep in Belgium. Three flocks of East Friesian sheep exported from Belgium to the USA were destroyed in July by the US Department of Agriculture after preliminary tests on several sheep showed signs of the disease.

In the international sphere, the centre-left ruling coalition led by the Flemish Liberals (VLD) sought to raise the priority given to human rights in foreign policy. Accordingly, Belgium was one of four countries which unsuccessfully sought the extradition of Gen. (retd) Augusto Pinochet Ugarte, the former dictator of Chile, from the UK in January 2000. The government also clashed with the government of Iran when it emphasised, in March 2000, that it would not intervene in a Belgian examining magistrate's consideration of criminal charges against Ali Akbar Hashemi Rafsanjani, the former President of Iran, following a complaint from an Iranian-born Belgian citizen that Rafsanjani had been party to torture and illegal imprisonment. In addition, the Belgian legislature on May 2 launched an investigation into the murder of the former Congolese Prime Minister Patrice Lumumba in 1961, following allegations from a historian that the murder had been arranged by the then Belgian government.

The government's regard for human rights was visible at home also. A three week amnesty was declared in January for the regularisation of illegal immigrants resident in Belgium who came forward, provided that they met certain criteria, including having children at school in Belgium or originating from "high risk" countries. In an embarrassing development however, the UN issued a report on March 13 which blamed Belgium, along with Bulgaria and seven African countries, for lax controls which allowed the repeated violation of UN sanctions imposed on the rebel National Union for the Total Independence of Angola (UNITA) with particular regard to the illegal export of diamonds from that country.

v. THE NETHERLANDS

CAPITAL: Amsterdam   AREA: 41,000 sq km   POPULATION: 16,070,000
OFFICIAL LANGUAGE: Dutch   POLITICAL SYSTEM: parliamentary democracy
HEAD OF STATE: Queen Beatrix (since April '80)
RULING PARTIES: Labour Party (PvdA), People's Party for Freedom and Democracy (VVD) & Democrats 66 (D66)
HEAD OF GOVERNMENT: Willem Kok (PvdA), Prime Minister (since Aug. '94)
MAIN IGO MEMBERSHIPS (NON-UN): NATO, EU, WEU, Benelux, OSCE, CE, OECD
CURRENCY: guilder (end-'00 £1=G3.51 US$1=G2.35)
GNP PER CAPITA: US$24,320, US$23,052 at PPP ('99)

DOMESTIC politics during 2000 were dominated by social issues, a number of which pertained to issues of equality and individual rights. On December 12 the Senate enacted legislation which granted homosexual couples in legal partnerships (recognised by Dutch law since 1998) the same rights as heterosexual couples with respect to marriage, adoption or divorce. The legislation had been passed by the lower house of the bicameral legislature in September 2000. The development was strongly opposed by churches and religious political parties, which argued that it threatened the sanctity of Christian marriage.

The second major piece of legislation to be enacted during the year was a bill, approved by a majority of 104 votes to 40 in the lower house of the legislature on November 28, to legalise physician-assisted suicide, a practice which had previously been unofficially tolerated, but which left physicians open to potential prosecution. The bill, which required the approval of the upper house before becoming law, enabled persons aged 16 years and over to commit suicide with the assistance of a physician if the person was in continuous and incurable pain and had sought a second medical opinion. The legislation, which did not allow a physician personally to administer a fatal drug, received the backing of most parties, including the three in the coalition government, but was not supported by the opposition Christian Democrats and three small Calvinist parties.

On June 27 the lower house of the legislature narrowly approved a non-binding motion which called for the decriminalisation of the wholesale trade in cannabis. The motion, which did not have Cabinet approval, was passed by a narrow margin of 73 votes to 72. It was aimed at removing the anomaly whereby licensed "coffee shops" were allowed to hold and sell small quantities of cannabis whilst their suppliers remained open to prosecution. However, after the vote the Justice Minister Benk Korthals indicated that he would not draw up legislation to comply with the motion.

In economic policy, the government on September 17 announced a 455 million guilder package of measures to ease the cost of high fuel prices, a response to a blockade of The Hague, the seat of government, by hauliers and farmers. The package gave temporary rebates on diesel duty to operators of large commercial vehicles, to be followed in 2001 by reductions in duty on low-sulphur diesel to encourage the use of more environmentally friendly fuel. The protests drew some sympathy from ministers of the centre-left government, who blamed oil companies for rising fuel prices.

The country was shocked by the deaths of 20 people, including four firemen, in a huge explosion at a fireworks factory on May 13 in the eastern city of Enschede. The explosion, which destroyed hundreds of houses in the city and injured almost 600 people, led to calls for changes in the law regarding the storage of dangerous materials in residential areas. Another tragedy, the discovery in the UK port of Dover of the bodies of 58 Chinese illegal immigrants who had died of asphyxiation whilst being smuggled into the UK inside a Dutch registered lorry in June (see II.1.i), focused attention on the activities of criminal gangs in Holland which profited from smuggling migrants into various destinations in northern Europe.

The question of the alleged culpability of Dutch UN peacekeeping troops for the massacre of Muslim civilians in the UN designated "safe area" of Srebrenica in 1995 (see AR 1995, pp. 125-6) continued to be a cause of controversy in foreign and domestic affairs during the year. The Dutch Public Prosecutor's Office announced on December 21, 1999, that it had not found evidence to support the contention that Dutch peacekeeping troops had actually assisted Serb forces to carry out the massacre. However, this was not the end of the issue. In July 2000 a group of 40 prominent Dutch authors sent an open letter to the government which called for a public apology to those who had survived the massacre and the establishment of a full parliamentary inquiry into the circumstances of the killings. The authors argued that the question of whether Dutch soldiers could have done more to save lives had not been adequately addressed.

vi. LUXEMBOURG

CAPITAL: Luxembourg AREA: 3,000 sq km POPULATION: 440,000
OFFICIAL LANGUAGE: Letzeburgish POLITICAL SYSTEM: parliamentary democracy
HEAD OF STATE: Grand Duke Henri (since Oct '00)
RULING PARTIES: Christian Social People's (PCS) & Democratic (DP) parties
HEAD OF GOVERNMENT: Jean-Claude Juncker (PCS), Prime Minister (since Jan '95)
MAIN IGO MEMBERSHIPS (NON-UN): NATO, EU, WEU, Benelux, OSCE, CE, OECD, Francophonie
CURRENCY: Luxembourg franc (end-'00 £1=LFr64.18, US$1=LFr42.97)
GNP PER CAPITA: US$43,570, US$37,420 at PPP ('98)

PUBLIC life in Luxembourg during the year was dominated by the abdication, after a 35 year reign, of Head of State Grand Duke Jean, 79, on October 7 and the succession of Crown Prince Henri, 45, who had exercised considerable constitutional powers, delegated by his father, since April 1998 (see AR 1998, pp. 69-70). The coronation of Henri and his wife, Maria Teresa, was postponed until the middle of 2001, however, because Henri's younger brother had been seriously injured in a car accident near Paris in September. The political role of the Head of State was limited to appointment of the Prime Minister, although he could also refuse to accept the resignation of a Cabinet or the dissolution of parliament.

Authorities in Luxembourg announced in May that they had frozen eight bank accounts, which contained more than US$600 million belonging to the late Nigerian dictator Sani Abacha. The offshore accounts were believed to contain the proceeds of bribes and Nigerian public money embezzled by the Abacha family and its associates. In a related development, the Chamber of Deputies voted on October 25 to approve a relaxation of Luxembourg's bank secrecy rules in order to improve co-operation with the US Internal Revenue Service (IRS) over US nationals with bank accounts in the Duchy. Under the changes, Luxembourg banks would become "qualified intermediaries" of the IRS and would be obliged to withhold from US depositors tax which was owed in the USA, and to reveal depositor identities to the IRS.

The highlight of diplomatic activity during the year was the visit in July of the Chinese Prime Minister, Zhu Rongji, who visited the Duchy as part of a six-nation European tour to boost China's ties with the European Union, and European support for China's application for membership of the World Trade Organisation (WTO).

In an unusual incident for Luxembourg, a country with a reputation for very low rates of violent crime, a mentally disturbed gunman held two dozen children and three teachers hostage for 30 hours at a day care centre in Wasserbillig, near the German border. It was a controversial aspect of the case that police, who ended the siege on June 2 by shooting and wounding the perpetrator, were disguised as television cameramen.

vii. REPUBLIC OF IRELAND

CAPITAL: Dublin   AREA: 70,000 sq km   POPULATION: 4,000,000
OFFICIAL LANGUAGE: Irish & English   POLITICAL SYSTEM: parliamentary democracy
HEAD OF STATE: President Mary McAleese (since Nov '97)
RULING PARTY: coalition of Fianna Fáil (FF) & Progressive Democrats (PD)
HEAD OF GOVERNMENT: Bertie Ahern (FF), Prime Minister/Taoiseach (since June '97)
MAIN IGO MEMBERSHIPS (NON-UN): EU, OSCE, CE, OECD
CURRENCY: punt (end-'00 £1=IR1.25, US$1=IR0.84)
GNP PER CAPITA: US$19,160, US$19,180 at PPP ('99)

THE remarkable acceleration of recent years in the Republic's economy continued unabated during 2000. With economic growth of 8.75 per cent, unemployment down to 4 per cent, a budget surplus double that of the previous year (itself a record), the national debt so reduced that the debt-to-GDP ratio was the second lowest in the EU, and indicators ranging from new car sales to earnings from tourism showing the highest-ever returns, the many prophets of woe who had forecast recession in the first year of the millennium seemed to have been confounded. Yet, by December the cautionary voices still predominated. What worried economists particularly was the rate at which the long-anticipated inflation took hold and burgeoned throughout the year from 3.4 per cent at the outset to 7 per cent at the close. Whilst some of this could be attributed to circumstances outside Irish control, such as oil prices, the cost of imports consequent on the strength of sterling, and measures undertaken by the European Central Bank to assist sluggish continental economies, the government attracted criticism for adding to the problem by lowering taxes in the December budget and thereby stimulating domestic spending.

The government had to a degree pre-empted the argument by stressing the advantage of using tax concessions rather than wage increases to meet trade union complaints that inflation was eroding the benefits of a new national agreement on pay, the Programme for Prosperity and Fairness (PPF), concluded between the government, most trade unions, and employers in January. In fact, however, as early as March and through the summer and autumn, industrial disputes and demands for pay rises to off-set inflation grew more intense. Unions which were parties to the PPF by and large got their increases through a pay review under the terms of the agreement, and received the promised tax reductions in the budget as well. Unions outside the PPF met more resistance from employers and government. Secondary teachers were embroiled in an acrimonious conflict with the education ministry by the year's end which threatened disruption of the school-leaving examinations in 2001 if unresolved.

The government at the same time came under fire from the major churches for neglecting the opportunity to promote social inclusion in Irish society through giving priority to the elimination of poverty and the provision of adequate health services. The Conference of Religious in Ireland (the heads of Roman Catholic religious orders) alleged, with convincing statistical analysis, that resources had had been given "in superabundance to those who were already better off", thereby ensuring that the gap between rich and poor was "substantially widened". The churches were also active, together with *ad hoc* voluntary bodies, in urging the government to adopt a coherent policy for coping with the influx of asylum-seekers from Eastern Europe and Africa, arriving in the Republic at a rate of nearly a thousand a month. Whilst the Minister for Justice, John O'Donoghue, could claim that considerable advances were made during the year in providing accommodation, financial resources and administrative structures to deal with the problem, he still drew criticism for dispersing immigrants throughout the country without sufficient consultation with local communities, for delaying decisions on individuals who were denied the right to work until their legal status was determined and for an insensitive approach to deportation when adverse judgements were reached.

Other events also buffeted the governing coalition of Fianna Fáil and the Progressive Democrats. In May a former Supreme Court judge, once associated with Fianna Fáil, who had had to retire the previous year when faced with allegations of interference in the process of a lower court, was nominated by the government for appointment as a vice-president of the European Investment Bank, a vacancy in Ireland's gift that year. Although the judge later declined the nomination, the widespread indignation over what was seen as political favouritism was seen by many as the direct cause of the election of an independent socialist in a June by-election in South Tipperary, with the Fianna Fáil candidate relegated to third place in what had been a stronghold of the party. Public outrage at abuses of political privilege was also stoked by evidence of payments by businessmen to a number of politicians at national and municipal level, as well as the salting away of funds in secret overseas accounts, revealed at the on-going judicial tribunals (see AR 1999, pp. 72-73). The facts unearthed in these proceedings during 2000 included also decisions by banks in the 1980s and early 1990s to forego the full repayment of loans made to prominent public figures, and a similar leniency towards them by the Revenue Commissioners in enforcing tax regulations.

Although Fianna Fáil politicians, including the former Taoiseach Charles Haughey, featured prominently in the tribunal investigations, the government survived. The general prosperity mitigated public dissatisfaction, whilst the parliamentary opposition failed to dent the stability of a minority administration supported by four independent members of parliament. The Progressive Democrats refused to break with their Fianna Fáil coalition partners despite repeated media rumours that they would do so in order to reiterate their commitment to rectitude in public life, the principle upon which they had been founded. The Taoiseach, Bertie Ahern, proved adroit in accommodating the requirements of the independents at constituency level and of the Progressive Democrats in national policy. He avoided decisions which were likely to be divisive between his government partners and supporters, delaying action on demands for a referendum on abortion and putting a brake on the further decentralisation of the civil service. In foreign affairs, his manifestly amicable rapport with US President Bill Clinton and UK Prime Minister Tony Blair seemed to serve both himself and the country well.

Foreign affairs were in fact an area of solid achievement. Sustained diplomatic lobbying came to fruition in October when Ireland won a two-year term on the United Nations Security Council, being elected ahead of Norway and blocking a bid by Italy for one of the two available seats. The Irish claim rested mainly on its long involvement in UN peacekeeping, a role which also was invoked by Ahern and the Minister for Foreign Affairs, Brian Cowan, to justify a government undertaking that the Republic would participate in the European Union's proposed Rapid Reaction Force. Rumblings of discontent from proponents of an absolutist interpretation of Irish neutrality failed to spark any noticeable public disapproval. Within the EU, the exclusion of company tax from matters to be decided in future by qualified majority voting was of vital importance to Ireland, where a low corporate tax regime had attracted much of the foreign investment underlying the current prosperity. Whilst this decision at the Nice summit in November (see XI. 4) had to be credited primarily to the British stance, it enabled Ahern to bring home very good news, overshadowing the envisaged loss at a future date of Ireland's right to a permanent seat on the EU Commission.

In Irish-British relations, Northern Ireland remained the subject of overwhelming mutual concern (see II.1.iv). David Trimble's survival in the face of several attempts to undermine his leadership of the Ulster Unionist Party was welcomed by virtually all shades of opinion in the Republic, and the restoration of the Northern Assembly at the end of May, after months of suspension, evoked as much relief in Dublin as in London. The activities of the so-called "Real IRA" caused particular anxiety because of the supposed location of the movement's bases of operation south of the border with Northern Ireland, but the diligence of the Garda Siochana, the Republic's police force, in uncovering a number of arms and explosive dumps bore witness to the state's determination to stamp out subversive violence. The uncertain fragility of the peace process, threatened on the one hand by IRA intransigence over the decommissioning of weapons and on the other by Unionist intransigence over police reform, found reflection in the different emphases of Dublin and London, with Ahern urging full implementation of the Patten report on Northern policing and Blair stressing the importance of decommissioning.

One hopeful development was that issues of common economic and social concern were processed through the North-South bodies, involving politicians and officials from both jurisdictions on the island of Ireland. However, even this was frustrated to a degree by Trimble's decision to bar Sinn Féin ministers from these discussions, pending progress on decommissioning. It was a decision which the Irish government saw as highly unhelpful even if, privately, Trimble's difficulties were understood. In December President Clinton visited Dublin and the southern border town of Dundalk before going on to Belfast and Chequers. How far his exhortations in favour of peace, co-operation and common-sense would achieve results remained to be seen but he was received in the Republic with genuine affection as the US President who, above all former holders of that office, had shown practical concern to assist in resolving the Irish troubles.

3. DENMARK—ICELAND—NORWAY—SWEDEN—FINLAND—AUSTRIA—SWITZER-
LAND—EUROPEAN MINI-STATES

i. DENMARK

CAPITAL: Copenhagen   AREA: 43,000 sq km   POPULATION: 5,400,000
OFFICIAL LANGUAGE: Danish   POLITICAL SYSTEM: parliamentary democracy
HEAD OF STATE: Queen Margrethe II (since Jan '72)
RULING PARTIES: coalition of Social Democrats (SD) & Radical Liberals (RV)
HEAD OF GOVERNMENT: Poul Nyrup Rasmussen (SD), Prime Minister (since Jan '93)
MAIN IGO MEMBERSHIPS (NON-UN): NATO, EU, NC, CBSS, AC, OSCE, CE, OECD
CURRENCY: Danish krone (end-'00 £1=DKr11.88, US$1=DKr7.95)
GNP PER CAPITA: US$32,030, US$24,280 at PPP ('99)

FOLLOWING the endorsement of Economic and Monetary Union (EMU) by the Swedish Social Democrats, and the revaluation of the Greek drachma, on January 19 the governor of the Danish central bank, Bodil Nyboe Andersen, announced her emphatic support for the single European currency, the euro. On March 9, as the Greek government applied to join the euro, the Danish government announced (a year sooner than expected) that a referendum on joining would be held on September 28. Opinion polls showed the electorate to be about 60 per cent in favour. The pro-euro campaign, supported by all the mainstream parties, emphasised the advantages of a single-currency bloc with Denmark's main trading partners, and pointed out that the krone had been tied to the euro and its predecessor, the ecu, since 1982. The anti-euro side argued that this showed that no change was needed. The far right Danish People's Party stressed sovereignty issues, claiming that the single currency would lead to a loss of Danish identity, more immigration and German domination. The "No" argument from the left was that EMU threatened Denmark's generous social security system. The "No" lobby also gained from the Danish Economic Council's statement in May that the benefits of the euro were "minimal and uncertain", and from the euro's continuing weakness throughout the year.

In the event, the result was a narrow rejection of the euro, and a major defeat for the pro-euro majority in the Folketing (legislature) and for Prime Minister Poul Nyrup Rasmussen (Social Democrat) and his Radical Liberal Cabinet partners. In an 87.5 per cent turnout of the country's 4 million voters, 53.1 per cent opted to retain the krone as the national currency and 46.9 per cent voted for the euro. Thus Denmark, with Sweden and the UK, remained outside the single currency, with Denmark being the only EU country to have put the issue to a referendum. Rasmussen accepted the verdict with disappointment and stated that his government would not seek its speedy reversal. Following the vote the central bank raised its base interest rate to protect the krone's position against the euro.

In regard to immigration, a package of 78 regulations intended to accelerate the integration of immigrants was introduced by the government in February. Human rights groups objected particularly to a regulation which raised the minimum age for bringing in a foreign spouse from 18 to 25 years, a move widely interpreted as an attempt to lower the foreign birth rate. The package also allowed cities to set quotas on the ethnic composition of housing projects, and provided for immigrants who refused to attend Danish language classes to lose their benefits.

On a less controversial note, the Øresund Bridge was officially opened on July 1 by Queen Margrethe II of Denmark and King Carl XVI Gustaf of Sweden. The 17 km long fixed link carried a four-lane motorway and double-track railway via causeway, tunnel and bridge from central Copenhagen to Malmö, Sweden's third city. Financed jointly by the Danish and Swedish governments, it took four years to build and was expected to carry upwards of 3 million vehicles annually.

Queen Ingrid, mother of Queen Margrethe II, died at Fredensborg Castle on November 7, aged 90 (see XVIII). Another casualty of the year was Poul Hartling, Minister of Foreign Affairs 1968-71, Prime Minister 1973-75 and UN High Commissioner for Refugees (UNHCR) 1978-85, who died on April 30, aged 85. Hartling's tenure as High Commissioner saw a massive expansion of the UNHCR's workload, especially in south-east Asia (following the wars in Indochina), Afghanistan, central America and Africa, and his efforts and moral leadership were recognised in the award to UNHCR of the 1981 Nobel Peace Prize.

The year ended with the Prime Minister announcing an extensive Cabinet reshuffle on December 21. Five ministers moved to new posts and a further five joined the Cabinet as replacements. Mogens Lykketoft, 53, (Social Democrat-SD) moved after seven years as Finance Minister to become Foreign Minister, and Pia Gjellerup, 41, (SD) moved from Trade to become Finance Minister, the first woman to hold this office in Denmark. Although the party balance was unchanged, the Radical Liberals lost the senior post of Foreign Minister, held by Niels Helveg Petersen. The new Cabinet of 12 men and eight women was seen as a generational shift in preparation for the election due by March 2002.

Extensive personnel changes were also announced in the diplomatic service on December 19, aimed at strengthening it in preparation for Denmark's chairmanship of the European Union during the second half of 2002.

ii. ICELAND

CAPITAL: Reykjavík AREA: 103,000 sq km POPULATION: 280,000
OFFICIAL LANGUAGE: Icelandic POLITICAL SYSTEM: parliamentary democracy
HEAD OF STATE: President Ólafur Ragnar Grímsson (since Aug '96)
RULING PARTIES: Independence (IP) & Progressive (PP) parties
HEAD OF GOVERNMENT: Davíd Oddson (IP), Prime Minister (since April '91)
MAIN IGO MEMBERSHIPS (NON-UN): NATO, EFTA/EEA, NC, OSCE, CE, OECD
CURRENCY: króna (end-'00 £1=IKr126.59, US$1=IKr84.74)
GNP PER CAPITA: US$28,010, US$22,830 at PPP ('98)

THE year saw a number of cultural celebrations, including the Millennium of Christianity Festival, inaugurated in Akureyri, northern Iceland, in April 1999, which was scheduled to last until Easter 2001. Its numerous events included the opening of a cultural centre dedicated to the medieval saga writer Snorri Sturluson, and the première in October of an opera by Atli Heimir Sveinsson portraying the adoption of Christianity in Iceland in 1000 AD. The year also saw numerous commemorations of the discovery of America by the Icelander Leifur Eiríksson in 1000 AD, including some 250 events in the USA and 200 in

Canada. This amounted to the largest promotion of Icelandic culture ever undertaken in America.

On a less happy note, following the revelation that British nuclear fuels company BNFL had falsified data on plutonium-uranium mixed oxide (MOX) shipped from Japan for reprocessing at Sellafield in the UK, Foreign Minister Halldór Asgrimsson on February 26 asked for Sellafield to be closed because of the threat posed by radioactive discharges to Iceland's main industry, fishing. Similar concerns were expressed in Denmark and Sweden.

At the EU Capabilities Commitment Conference on November 21 Ásgrímsson stated Iceland's willingness to co-operate with the EU over humanitarian assistance, search and rescue, as well as peacekeeping missions. Although Iceland had no armed forces, it was agreed that civilian assets and capabilities could be made available. Some 50 professionals from Iceland had been deployed in Bosnia and Kosovo, and it was agreed that the Icelandic Crisis Response Unit—a roster of up to 100 police officers, engineers, doctors and nurses, lawyers, management experts and other technical personnel—would offer a 25-strong team which would be able to join in peacekeeping missions at short notice.

Iceland chaired the European Free Trade Association/European Economic Area (EFTA/EEA) during 2000. Implementation of the Schengen Agreement progressed well, and Iceland and Norway agreed to co-operate with EU states over political asylum on the basis of the Dublin Agreement.

iii. NORWAY

CAPITAL: Oslo   AREA: 324,000 sq km   POPULATION: 4,500,000
OFFICIAL LANGUAGE: Norwegian   POLITICAL SYSTEM: parliamentary democracy
HEAD OF STATE: King Harald V (since Jan '91)
RULING PARTY: Labour Party
HEAD OF GOVERNMENT: Jens Stoltenberg (Labour), Prime Minister (since March '00)
MAIN IGO MEMBERSHIPS (NON-UN): NATO, EFTA/EEA, NC, CBSS, AC, OSCE, CE, OECD
CURRENCY: Norwegian krone (end-'00 £1=K13.17, US$1=K8.82)
GNP PER CAPITA: US$32,880, US$26,522 at PPP ('99)

PRIME Minister Kjell Magne Bondevik announced the resignation of his three-party minority government on March 9 after being defeated in a confidence vote in the Storting (legislature). The challenge arose from the opposition's proposal to build two gas-fired power stations, which the government wanted to postpone until the technology had been developed to make the plants pollution-free. The Labour Party, with 65 of the 165 seats in the Storting, formed a new government on March 17. It was led by Jens Stoltenberg who, at the age of 41, became Norway's youngest Prime Minister.

A dynamic former Foreign Affairs Minister (1996-97), Stoltenberg had become leader of the Labour Party in February when he replaced Thorbjørn Jagland, who had served as Prime Minister in 1996-97. The latter became Foreign Affairs Minister in the new administration, and Bjørn Tore Godal, himself a former Foreign Minister, was appointed as Defence Minister. The 19-member

Cabinet included 8 women. Upon taking office Stoltenberg expressed his intention to privatise partially Statoil, Norway's largest industrial company, and the telecoms group Telenor.

Away from politics, the year began with tragedy as a high-speed inter-regional train crashed head-on into a local train on a stretch of single track about 100 km north of Oslo on January 1. There were 19 deaths from the impact and the subsequent fire which blazed through both trains. The cause of the accident was believed to have been the failure of the driver of the local train to stop at a red signal.

A more widely publicised accident allowed Norwegian divers to observe the deterioration of the Russian navy when one of the latter's nuclear-powered submarines, the *Kursk*, sank on August 12 during manoeuvres in the Barents Sea (see III.3.i.). Having initially rejected all offers of help, Russian officials finally requested foreign assistance on August 16, whereupon a British rescue mini-submarine and its crew, together with a team of 12 Norwegian and British deep-sea divers from the Stolt Offshore company, set out from Trondheim on board the Norwegian ship *Seaway Eagle*. Reaching the *Kursk* on August 20, the divers succeeded on August 21 in opening one of the rear hatches, but found that the submarine was flooded and all of its 118 crew and officers had drowned. The disaster happened in 108 meters of water about 180 km north-east of Murmansk, close to Norwegian waters, and aroused considerable Norwegian concern over the environmental implications.

Other foreign developments saw a Norwegian diplomatic delegation visit Sri Lanka in January in an effort to mediate in the conflict between the government the Liberation Tigers of Tamil Eelam (LTTE). This was followed on February 16 by a visit to Colombo from Norway's Foreign Minister, Knud Vollebæk, which appeared to have made some progress in encouraging the government to conduct peace negotiations with the rebels. In February the UN donated emergency aid, the bulk of it from Norway and the UK, to Mongolia, for herders suffering the consequences of severe winter conditions (see IX.2.vii), whilst on October 10 the UN elected Norway, together with Colombia, Ireland, Mauritius and Singapore to serve two-year terms as non-permanent members of the Security Council, commencing January 1, 2001.

Although the economy remained buoyant during the year, a six-day strike by over 84,000 members of the confederation of trade unions ended on May 9 with a settlement which was seen as costly and likely to cause overheating. The strike followed the rejection by union members of a fifth week of holiday and a 4 per cent wage increase in 2000 and 2001. Finance Minister Karl-Eirik Schjøtt-Pedersen announced large spending cuts on May 12—including reduced spending on defence and foreign aid—in an effort to keep down price and wage inflation, and unemployment, as economic growth increased. The defence cuts included the cancellation of orders for 20 new Eurofighter aircraft.

The year ended with the announcement by Crown Prince Haakon on December 1 that he intended to marry 27 year-old Mette-Marit Tjessem Højby on 25 August 2001. Although the couple had been together for over a year the match was not without some controversy. Højby, an engineering student, had a three-year old son, Marius, from a previous relationship.

iv. SWEDEN

CAPITAL: Stockholm   AREA: 450,000 sq km   POPULATION: 8,867,000
OFFICIAL LANGUAGE: Swedish   POLITICAL SYSTEM: parliamentary democracy
HEAD OF STATE: King Carl XVI Gustav (since Sept '73)
RULING PARTY: Social Democratic Labour Party (SAP)
HEAD OF GOVERNMENT: Göran Persson, Prime Minister (since March '96)
MAIN IGO MEMBERSHIPS (NON-UN): EU, NC, CBSS, AC, PFP, OSCE, CE, OECD
CURRENCY: Swedish krona (end-'00 £1=K14.09, US$1=K9.44)
GNP PER CAPITA: US$25,040, US$20,824 at PPP ('99)

DURING the course of 2000 Sweden took hesitant steps towards a closer involvement with the European Union. The Swedish Social Democratic Labour Party (SAP) for the first time formally endorsed membership of European economic and monetary union (EMU) on January 14. The SAP Congress on March 10 voted by 234 to 133 to adopt participation in EMU as an official policy, with the backing of Prime Minister Göran Persson but in the face of opposition from several Cabinet ministers. The motion stipulated that a referendum should be held before any legislation was proposed, and this was not expected before the 2002 parliamentary election. In March the government negotiated an extension of three-and-a-half years for its tough alcohol import restrictions. The European Commission had insisted that the law be brought in line with more liberal EU single market regulations by July 1, but lobbying by Finance Minister Bosse Ringholm helped to secure the delay.

The Swedish economy remained strong during the year. The government's draft budget for 2001, published on September 20, continued the policy of tax cuts initiated by the 2000 budget. With a booming economy and buoyant tax revenues, the government proposed income tax reductions totalling SKr12.5 billion in 2001 (US$1=9.5803 SKr on Sept. 22, 2000), with increased social expenditure, notably on higher child benefit payments. A budget surplus of SKr 76 billion (3.5 per cent of GDP) was forecast for 2001, compared with a projected surplus of SKr 71 billion (3.4 per cent of GDP) in 2000. On the other hand, a controversial increase in diesel fuel tax was confirmed. The additional SKr0.10 per litre made the Swedish price the second-highest in Europe, but ministers justified the move on environmental grounds. Following protests by road hauliers and farmers, on September 20 the government promised to examine the current tax burden on both of these sectors.

Persson's Cabinet saw only one significant change during the year. Justice Minister Laila Frievalds resigned from the government on September 21 after being criticised within the SAP for opting to buy her council-owned apartment in central Stockholm, this being contrary to SAP policy in the capital, where the party was in opposition. She had held the post since 1988. Her portfolio was entrusted to Deputy Prime Minister Lena Hjelm-Wallén, until the appointment on October 11 of Thomas Bodström.

A two-year old tragedy was resolved on June 9 when four Iranian youths were convicted of starting the October 1998 fire in the Macedonian Cultural Centre in the Göteborg (Gothenburg) suburb of Hisingen, where over 400 young people were attending a Halloween disco (see AR 1998 p. 80). Due to overcrowding and poor safety measures, 63 people had died and over 200 had been injured in the fire. The crime appeared to have been motivated by an earlier altercation, rather than by racism. A 19-year-old was sentenced to eight years' imprisonment, and two people aged 21 and 19 years each received prison terms of six years. A fourth person, who had been a minor at the time of the fire, was sentenced to three years' juvenile detention. Three of the defendants were found to have had previous criminal convictions.

In foreign affairs a slight thaw in Sweden's relationship with Turkey was signalled when Anna Lindh, the Swedish Foreign Minister, visited the country in mid-February. Sweden had been the EU member most reluctant to allow Turkey to become a candidate for EU-membership because of concerns over its record on human rights.

In January Hans Blix, former Director-General of the International Atomic Energy Agency, was appointed head of the UN Monitoring, Verification and Inspection Commission (UNMOVIC), created in December 1999. The new panel, appointed on March 10, was more broadly representative of UN membership than that of the organisation's predecessor, the UN Special Commission (UNSCOM), which had been dominated by experts from the USA, the UK and other industrialised countries. Blix insisted on March 2 that he would resume UNSCOM's inspection of suspected Iraqi weapons' sites as soon as the Iraqi authorities allowed UN inspectors to return to the country.

v. FINLAND

CAPITAL: Helsinki   AREA: 338,000 sq km   POPULATION: 5,200,000
OFFICIAL LANGUAGE: Finnish   POLITICAL SYSTEM: presidential democracy
HEAD OF STATE: President Tarja Halonen (SSDP), since February '00
RULING PARTY: Social Democratic Party (SSDP), National Coalition (KOK), Left-Wing Alliance (VAS), Swedish People's Party (SFP) & Green Union (VL)
HEAD OF GOVERNMENT: Paavo Lipponen (SSDP), Prime Minister (since April '95)
MAIN IGO MEMBERSHIPS (NON-UN): EU, NC, CBSS, AC, PFP, OSCE, CE, OECD
CURRENCY: markka (end-'00 £1=Fmk9.46, US$1=Fmk6.33)
GNP PER CAPITA: US$23,780, US$21,209 at PPP ('99)

THE year began with a presidential election. The results of the first round on January 16 were not decisive: Tarja Halonen of the Finnish Social Democratic Party obtained 40.0 per cent of the vote, former Prime Minister Esko Aho of the Centre Party obtained 34.4 per cent, and the remainder was shared between five other candidates. As no candidate polled over 50 per cent, a second round run-off contest was held between the two leading contenders on February 6. It was won by Halonen, who polled 51.6 per cent of the votes cast and thereby became Finland's first female President. As Foreign Minister Halonen had been widely admired for her effective leadership and her emphasis on human rights and welfare issues. The new President's six-year term was expected to continue Finland's pro-EU but anti-NATO stance.

Halonen succeeded Martti Ahtisaari, who had played a prominent role in the negotiations to end the Kosovo conflict in 1999, but who had not been renominated by his party. Nevertheless he continued to participate in international affairs.

In May he began to act as one of the two independent inspectors nominated by the Irish Republican Army (IRA), to monitor its hidden arsenals, as part of the process of decommissioning weapons (see II.1.iv.).

Finland was indirectly caught up in a remote conflict in the Philippines when two Finns were amongst the hostages seized by Islamic separatist rebels in April. A letter on August 22 from the presidents of Finland, France, Germany and South Africa urged President Estrada to refrain from any action which could jeopardise the lives of the captives. The Finnish hostages were amongst a few who were released on September 9 under negotiations mediated by Libya (see IX.1.vii).

vi. AUSTRIA

CAPITAL: Vienna   AREA: 84,000 sq km   POPULATION: 8,100,000
OFFICIAL LANGUAGE: German   POLITICAL SYSTEM: federal parliamentary democracy
HEAD OF STATE: Federal President Thomas Klestil (since Aug '92)
RULING PARTIES: People's (ÖVP) and Freedom (FPÖ) parties
HEAD OF GOVERNMENT: Wolfgang Schlüssel (ÖVP), Federal Chancellor (since Feb '00)
MAIN IGO MEMBERSHIPS (NON-UN): EU, OECD, CE, PFP, CEI, OECD
CURRENCY: schilling (end-'00 £1=Sch21.89, US$1=Sch14.66)
GNP PER CAPITA: US$25,970, US$23,808 at PPP ('99)

THE year 2000 saw the "grand coalition" finally laid to rest after some 50 years of almost uninterrupted power. When months of negotiations in the wake of the October 1999 general election failed to produce agreement between the Social Democrats (SPÖ) and the People's Party (ÖVP), the latter's leader, Wolfgang Schüssel, abruptly turned to Jörg Haider's radical right-wing Freedom Party (FPÖ) as a potential coalition partner. After brief negotiations, and in spite of a chorus of international disapproval, an ÖVP-FPÖ coalition government was formed on February 4, with Schüssel as Chancellor.

The new government emphasised its commitment to democratic values, minority rights and the objectives of the European Union, including enlargement. Haider himself—who had made himself notorius with statements indicating personal sympathy with the Nazi past—was not included in the new administration. Nevertheless, in a statement issued on January 31, the 14 other EU member states warned that high-level bilateral contacts with Austria would be frozen if the FPÖ were given a role in government, that no EU support would be given to Austrian candidates seeking positions in international organisations, and that Austrian ambassadors in EU capitals would have no access to ministers. These measures were duly implemented, and Israel also withdrew its ambassador from Austria.

Austrian shock and indignation were intense. The authorities protested that over 70 per cent of Austrians had *not* voted for Haider in the election, and that the ÖVP-FPÖ coalition was a democratically-constituted government. They complained that the EU was following a policy which was being driven by the domestic agenda of certain member states which were seeking to contain the threat from their own far-right parties. They challenged the EU's legal right to take such action against a member, and claimed that such a course would not have been followed if the same situation had arisen in a larger member state. Although the government reluctantly accepted that it would have to live with the sanctions for the time being, it continued to insist on Austria's good record in the EU and on human rights, and to argue that the FPÖ should not be demonised but judged instead by its performance in government.

By mid-year, it was becoming evident that the other EU members were having second thoughts about their action, and on June 28 it was announced that three "Wise Men" would be appointed to examine Austria's human rights record. They would also seek to determine whether the new administration was respecting "European values" and would scrutinise the democratic credentials of the FPÖ. This committee, led by Martti Ahtisaari, the former Finnish President, was appointed on July 12 and completed its report on September 8. It concluded that the EU's sanctions had proved effective, that the Austrian government had not failed in its commitment to uphold European democratic values, and that the sanctions, if maintained, would become counterproductive. The report criticised some aspects of FPÖ activity, describing it as "a right-wing populist party with extremist characteristics". Nevertheless, the EU measures were quickly lifted on September 12, forestalling Austria's decision that a national referendum should be held in the autumn on EU membership and on removal of the sanctions.

These events naturally had significant domestic repercussions. The former Chancellor, Viktor Klima, resigned as party chairman of the SPÖ and retired from politics on February 17; he was replaced by Alfred Güsenbauer. Less predictably, Jörg Haider decided on February 28 to resign as FPÖ party chairman in favour of his deputy, Susanne Riess-Passer, the Austrian Vice-Chancellor, in order, ostensibly, to concentrate on his duties as governor of Carinthia. In fact, he continued to control the party and to court the attention of the international press, making no secret of the fact that his ultimate objective remained the chancellorship. By the end of the year, however, his prospects and those of the FPÖ were looking rather less bright. Amongst the reasons for this were Chancellor Schüssel's marked gain in stature and popularity during the year; and a scandal involving the Justice Minister, Dieter Böhmdorfer, who had already been criticised in the Wise Men's report. It was now alleged that, in his former capacity as a lawyer for the FPÖ and Haider, he and his associates had paid police officers for confidential information on political opponents.

Participation in the government also caused the FPÖ some problems, with old and new supporters alike complaining about unfulfilled election pledges, tax increases and sharp cuts in government spending. The party's support dipped accordingly in two provincial elections towards the end of the year. In Styria on October 10, the ÖVP increased its vote by 10 per cent, whereas FPÖ support dropped from 29 per cent at the 1999 federal election to 12 per cent. In Bürgenland on December 3, in spite of FPÖ attempts to capitalise on the economic effects of eastward EU enlargement, the SPÖ and Green Parties increased their vote at the expense of both ÖVP and FPÖ, with the latter losing its only seat in the provincial parliament.

In spite of a controversial start to its term in office, and some turnover amongst inexperienced FPÖ ministers (three of the six had to be replaced along the way, and Böhmdorfer's position was looking weak by the end of the year), the coalition proved relatively cohesive, and had some success in changing Austria's political and economic culture. It was helped by a strong economic performance, with annual growth of 3.3 per cent, and inflation and unemployment rates both estimated at approximately 3.1 per cent (a full percentage point rise in the case of the former, as a result of higher oil prices; a half percentage point decline in the latter). The young and very able FPÖ Finance Minister, Karl-Heinz Grasser, pursued with dedication, but only mixed success, budgetary policies aimed at reducing the traditional deficit to zero by 2002. Pension reform proposals were presented to Parliament on May 30, and the government made some progress on privatisation—most notably by selling the country's biggest state-owned bank, Bank Austria, to a German owner—without provoking public uproar.

There was public support for the government's declared intention of reining back vested interests, which had come to dominate the traditional system of consensual social partnership, and of reducing the power of the Proporz system, by which jobs were allocated on party political lines—although the former policy seemed to be pursued with more energy than the latter. However, liberals expressed concern over new legislation on immigration, introduced in May; the withdrawal of state art funding in certain areas; and laws aimed at controlling the media, all of which critics saw as bearing Haider's imprint. In December the FPÖ's appetite for litigation against its critics drew an unprecedented protest from the legal profession, when 1,300 Austrian judges and public prosecutors signed a letter of protest against the party's "unconcealed political pressure" on legal enquiries.

Undoubtedly one of the coalition's major achievements was to make swift and effective progress on agreeing payments to Nazi slave labourers, and on negotiating a settlement on restitution for businesses and properties seized from Austrian Jews before and during World War II. On October 24 bilateral agreements were signed with the USA and five east European countries for the disbursement of a voluntary compensation fund of US$399 million amongst the 150,000 Austrian survivors of Nazi labour camps. Austrian industry agreed to contribute about half of this total, on the condition that it was given guarantees against future court action, and the Holocaust Fund was formally constituted on December 20.

On the following day the Austrian special representative on the return of Aryanised property visited Washington DC to present proposals for a $150 million compensation plan for those who had lost rented flats, plus another $150 million for the loss of other property confiscated by the Nazis. This was rejected as too low an offer, and negotiations were still in progress at the end of the year. Other noteworthy events were the opening in Vienna on April 7 of the European monitoring centre on racism and xenophobia; the unveiling on October 25, also in Vienna, of the Holocaust memorial, designed by the British artist, Rachel Whiteread; and the opening on November 5 of Vienna's new synagogue.

In external relations Austrian attention focussed mainly on the EU, although the

Foreign Minister, Benita Ferrero-Waldner, acquired a new role when Austria took over the chair of the Organisation for Security and Co-operation in Europe (OSCE) on February 10. The security debate over Austria's relationship with NATO rumbled on, but the public was more preoccupied with EU enlargement and its possible effects on future prosperity and employment. The government continued to maintain that it remained fully committed to the enlargement project, and on March 17 appointed a former Vice-Chancellor, Erhard Busek, as its special representative on this issue. Nonetheless, Haider continued to argue that accession should be delayed until candidates had achieved parity with Austrian wage levels.

Enlargement also contributed to friction with the Czech Republic over the commissioning of its nuclear power station at Temelin, which began operating in October. The Austrian government had threatened to block progress on the Czech EU entry application pending a resolution of the dispute, and Austrian antinuclear activists repeatedly blocked border crossing points with the Czech Republic. An agreement on safety and environmental impact was finally signed by the two governments on December 12, whilst Presidents Klestil and Havel tried to dispel remaining bitterness and suspicion in joint articles published in Austrian and Czech newspapers on December 29.

Another problem which prompted blockades by environmental campaigners was the remorseless rise in EU freight traffic across the Brenner Pass and through Tirol, the volume of which had increased up by 50 per cent since Austria had joined the EU. Austrians were infuriated when the European Court thwarted the government's attempts to reduce this traffic by ruling on September 26 that Austrian tolls were too high and discriminated in favour of native hauliers. However, another long-running dispute with the European Court was resolved on November 1, when Austria finally bowed to EU pressure and abolished its anonymous bank accounts.

On March 30 a distinguished and respected figure disappeared from national life when the former President, Rudolf Kirchschläger, died at the age of 85 (see XVIII).

Sadly, Austrians will always remember the year 2000 for the terrible fire in the Kitzsteinhorn tunnel on November 11, which killed 155 mainly young people at the ski resort of Kaprun, already hard hit by the loss of 11 skiers killed by an avalanche in March. The fire was the country's worst peace-time disaster and Chancellor Schüssel called for two days of national mourning as a mark of respect to its victims.

vii. SWITZERLAND

CAPITAL: Berne   AREA: 41,300 sq km   POPULATION: 7,200,000
OFFICIAL LANGUAGES: German, French, Italian & Rhaeto-Romanic
POLITICAL SYSTEM: federal canton-based democracy
RULING PARTY: Christian Democratic People's (CVP), Radical Democratic (FDP), Social Democratic (SPS) and Swiss People's (SVP) parties
HEAD OF GOVERNMENT: Adolf Ogi (SVP), 2000 President of Federal Council and Minister of Defence
MAIN IGO MEMBERSHIPS (NON-UN): OECD, OSCE, CE, EFTA, PFP
CURRENCY: Swiss franc (end-'00 £1=SFr2.42, US$1=SFr1.62)
GNP PER CAPITA: US$38,350, US$27,486 at PPP ('99)

FEDERAL Councillor Adolf Ogi announced in the autumn his retirement from the government, where he had sat as the sole representative of the Swiss People's Party (SVP) for the last 13 years. The announcement triggered a wave of political manoeuvring as the main parties grappled for advantage.

At the end of 1999, when the whole Federal Council had been re-elected, the SVP had tried without success to form an all-conservative coalition by ejecting the Social Democrats (SPS) from government (see AR 1999, p. 86). Following Ogi's decision to step down, however, it was the SPS which sought to throw out the SVP and form a centre-left government with the Radical Democratic (FDP) and the Christian Democratic People's (CVP) parties. However, these two parties were no more interested in breaking the traditional formula for the distribution of the seven seats in the government than they had been the previous year. Therefore they agreed to elect a representative of the SVP as Ogi's replacement, although they indicated that they would not necessarily support the official SVP candidate if that party nominated only right-wingers. In the event the SVP presented two candidates: Rita Fuhrer and Roland Eberle, both of whom represented the party's conservative mainstream, whereas Ogi had been more liberal in his stance. The SPS, having failed to convince the FDP and the CVP to oust the SVP from government, did not propose its own candidate, but backed Cécile Bühlmann from the Green Party.

The majority of the FDP and the CVP voted for Samuel Schmid, an experienced legislator proposed by the Bernese section of the SVP and an outspoken critic of the national SVP's shift towards a more right-wing position. He was eventually elected, and was to replace Ogi as Defence Minister on January 1, 2001. The SVP leadership, although displeased with this outcome, accepted Schmid as the party's new representative in the Federal Council, but announced a more critical stance toward the government than in the past.

Further adjustments to the Federal Council occurred in December, when the Federal Vice-President and Minister of Transport and Environment, Moritz Leuenberger (SPS), was elected to the annually rotating post of President for 2001. As the open discontent of other party-leaders with her performance continued, the leader of the SPS, Ursula Koch, finally resigned from her post. Christiane Brunner, MP and former trade union leader from Geneva, replaced her.

The most important political issue in 2000 was the referendum on ratifying the bilateral treaties (see AR 1999, p. 87) with the European Union (EU) which was held on May 21. Swiss citizens accepted the seven treaties in a single vote, with 67 per cent voting in favour. The forgoing campaign had been much less heated than that of 1992, when the citizens voted against the integration of Switzerland into the European Economic Area (EEA) (see AR 1992, p. 81). Voter turnout was 48 per cent, far lower than it had been in 1992, when it had been 79 per cent. Only the smaller right-wing parties and some rather obscure isolationist groups had campaigned against the treaty. The SVP, the only major party opposed to integration into the EU and EEA, was split: the national party was in favour of a "Yes" vote, but half of its cantonal parties proposed voting "No". Unlike the 1992 poll, this time there was no difference on the issue between the linguistic regions. With two exceptions (Schwyz and Italian-speaking Ticino) all cantons were in favour, although the majorities were larger in the French-speaking part of Switzerland. This positive result did not signify a shift in the public attitude towards EU-membership, however, as opinion polls taken immediately after the referendum showed those advocating full integration were still in the minority.

Switzerland's newly-ratified bilateral treaties with the EU included the right of free access to labour markets. Adherence to this agreement would have been put seriously at risk by the approval of an initiative put to popular vote on September 24. It proposed that the quota of foreigners living in Switzerland (currently almost 20 per cent of the population) should not exceed 18 per cent. The proposal was backed by the smaller right-wing parties and, without much enthusiasm, by the SVP. It was clearly rejected, with 64 per cent voting against.

Also put to a referendum during the year were proposed reforms of the old-age pension scheme. In 1995 growing problems with the economy had led to a government decision to raise the retirement age for women gradually from 62 years to 64 (see AR 1995, p. 81). The trade unions and the Green Party, traditional opponents of this policy, now each proposed instead a general option to retire at the age of 62 and still be entitled to a full state pension. On November 26 the citizens rejected both almost identical initiatives. The referendum result demonstrated once again the gulf in political preferences between the main linguistic regions of Switzerland. Both proposals had been accepted by the French-speaking population, but clearly rejected by the German-speaking cantons.

Amongst the year's most debated issues was the Swiss army and its role in the world. In a referendum held on November 26 the citizens voted against an initiative from the SPS which was intended to halve military expenditure. Parliament accepted the government's proposal that Swiss troops deployed in international peace forces be armed for self-protection. This was designed to prevent a repetition of the embarrassing spectacle during the crisis in the former Yugoslavia, where Swiss troops engaged in construction work and transport services had had to be protected by the Austrian army. Isolationist forces associated with the SVP and left-wing pacifists criticised the decision as being another step towards NATO membership. Each collected separately the required number of signatures for a referendum on the issue, to be held in June 2001.

The economy grew even faster than it had in 1999. According to first estimates, GNP growth exceeded 3 per cent. Unemployment dropped to 70,000 in December (1.9 per cent of the workforce) and enterprises from all sectors complained of a shortage in the workforce.

viii. EUROPEAN MINI-STATES

Andorra
CAPITAL: Andorra la Vella   AREA: 445 sq km   POPULATION: 70,000
OFFICIAL LANGUAGE: Catalan   POLITICAL SYSTEM: parliamentary democracy
HEAD OF STATE: President Jacques Chirac of France & Bishop Joan Martí Alanis of Urgel (co-princes)
HEAD OF GOVERNMENT: Marc Forné Molné, President of Executive Council (since Dec '94)
MAIN IGO MEMBERSHIPS (NON-UN): CE, OSCE
CURRENCY: French franc & Spanish peseta

Holy See (Vatican City State)
CAPITAL: Vatican City   AREA: 0.44 sq km   POPULATION: 875
OFFICIAL LANGUAGES: Italian & Latin   POLITICAL SYSTEM: theocracy
HEAD OF STATE: Pope John Paul II (since '78)
HEAD OF GOVERNMENT: Cardinal Angelo Sodano, Secretary of State (since Dec '90)
MAIN IGO MEMBERSHIPS (NON-UN): OSCE
CURRENCY: Vatican lira (at par to Italian lira)

Liechtenstein
CAPITAL: Vaduz   AREA: 160 sq km   POPULATION: 34,000
OFFICIAL LANGUAGE: German   POLITICAL SYSTEM: parliamentary democracy
HEAD OF STATE: Prince Hans Adam II (since Nov '89)
RULING PARTY: Patriotic Union (VU)
HEAD OF GOVERNMENT: Mario Frick, Prime Minister (since Dec '93)
MAIN IGO MEMBERSHIPS (NON-UN): EFTA/EEA, OSCE, CE
CURRENCY: Swiss franc (end-'00 £1=SFr2.42, US$1=SFr1.62)
GNP PER CAPITA: US$45,000 ('98 est.)

Monaco
CAPITAL: Monaco-Ville   AREA: 1.95 sq km   POPULATION: 33,000
OFFICIAL LANGUAGE: French   POLITICAL SYSTEM: constitutional monarchy
HEAD OF STATE: Prince Rainier III (since '49)
HEAD OF GOVERNMENT: Patrick Leclercq, Minister of State (since Jan '00)
MAIN IGO MEMBERSHIPS (NON-UN): OSCE
CURRENCY: French franc

San Marino
CAPITAL: San Marino   AREA: 60.5 sq km   POPULATION: 27,500
OFFICIAL LANGUAGE: Italian   POLITICAL SYSTEM: parliamentary democracy
HEAD OF STATE AND GOVERNMENT: Captains-Regent Giuseppe Arzilli and Marino Bollini (Oct '00-Mar '01)
RULING PARTIES: Christian Democratic and Socialist parties
MAIN IGO MEMBERSHIPS (NON-UN): OSCE, CE
CURRENCY: Italian lira

In ANDORRA, the centre-right Liberal Union government led by Marc Forné Molné remained securely in power during 2000. Although Andorra was one of the smallest states in Europe, in September the government signed a treaty which transferred sovereignty over 15 sq km of territory to France. The land provided the French with access to a road tunnel which was under construction and which was intended to provide the primary road link between Andorra and France, and offer an alternative to the existing Puerto d'Envalira route.

In the HOLY SEE (Vatican) a huge car park was inaugurated by the Pope in January. It was a five-storey building constructed underneath the Gianicolo Hill, next to Vatican City. The car park, dubbed "God's Garage", was the centre of a controversy after archaeologists and environmentalists discovered nearby the ruins of an ancient frescoed villa, which had belonged to the Emperor Nero's mother Agrippina. The frescoes were protected, but other mosaics and ceramics were ignored (and destroyed) during construction.

A visit by the Austrian far-right leader Jörg Haider, the governor of Carinthia, to the Vatican for the lighting of a Christmas tree brought hundreds of protesters to St. Peter's Square. The Vatican, embarrassed by the controversy, stated that in 1997, when the province of Carinthia had offered the Christmas tree, Haider had not been governor. Nevertheless, in what was seen as a bid to soothe the critics, the Pope did not participate in the lighting ceremony.

In LIECHTENSTEIN money laundering was a common element in several developments. In June a bank owned by the principality's ruling family was implicated in a police investigation. The investigation followed the arrest of several financial managers who were believed to have used the bank to launder money for Columbian drug cartels and the Russian mafia. A leading Liechtenstein politician was also alleged to be linked to the scandal. Banks within the principality came under heavy European and international pressure to co-operate in the global fight against money laundering. Liechtenstein was expected to participate in measures ensuring an open exchange of information, which involved all European banks. The aim of this project was to crack down on tax evasion.

During the year Liechtenstein helped Nigeria to recover part of the more than US$4 billion stolen by former dictator Sani Abacha and hidden in the principality under the names of various associates. Several bank accounts were frozen. In the light of recent events, the government prepared new legislation and reforms to stop the fraudulent misuse of its banks. A new law abolished the practise of allowing annonymous bank accounts.

In MONACO the issue of bank secrecy was also important during 2000, with the French authorities accusing the territory of concealing vital information about secret bank accounts and refusing to co-operate in the fight against illicit money transfers. This provoked an angry response from Prince Rainier, who accused France of a lack of respect for the principality and its people, and who asked for more independence from Paris. The Prince declared his wish to appoint the head of Monaco's government independently, rather than being limited to a choice of three names selected by the French Foreign Ministry.

A seaweed known as Caulerpa taxifolia, which had escaped about 16 years ago from the Oceanographic Institute of Monaco, was found to have destroyed large swathes of the Mediterranean seabed and to have spread, via the anchors of ships, as far as California. The methods used by the principality to destroy the escaped seaweed had been costly, and not very efficient, and the growth rate of the weed was very high (up 3.5 inches per day).

SAN MARINO was one of the first countries to declare its commitment to eliminating harmful tax practices after the Organisation for Economic Co-operation and Development (OECD) issued a statement in June. Andorra, Liechtenstein, Monaco and San Marino were amongst the territories identified in the statement as tax havens. According to the OECD, criminals and tax evaders used the secrecy laws and loose regulatory regimes of the territories to conceal financial dealings forbidden in their home countries. The blacklisted countries were given until the end of the year to co-operate with the OECD and until 2005 for the completion of their reform.

SPAIN—GIBRALTAR—PORTUGAL—MALTA—GREECE—CYPRUS—TURKEY

i. SPAIN

CAPITAL: Madrid   AREA: 506,000 sq km   POPULATION: 40,100,000
OFFICIAL LANGUAGE: Spanish   POLITICAL SYSTEM: parliamentary democracy
HEAD OF STATE: King Juan Carlos (since Nov '75)
RULING PARTY: Popular Party (PP)
HEAD OF GOVERNMENT: José María Aznar López, Prime Minister (since May '96)
MAIN IGO MEMBERSHIPS (NON-UN): NATO, EU, WEU, OSCE, CE, OECD
CURRENCY: peseta (end-'00 £1=ptas264.74, US$1=ptas177.22)
GNP PER CAPITA: US$14,000, US$16,730 at PPP ('99)

SPAIN suffered a year marked by the return of ETA violence. With the end of its self-proclaimed ceasefire the Basque separatist group launched one of its most sustained offensives in the last 10 years. It soon became clear that the group had used the 14-month break in hostilities to reorganise itself. The human cost of the campaign was high: 27 fatalities, including four ETA members killed when the bomb they were handling exploded. There were also three deaths which resulted from the activities of the extreme left-wing First of October Armed Revolutionary Group (GRAPO). Spain had not seen so many terrorist deaths since 1992, when ETA had launched an intensive campaign to coincide with the holding of the Olympic Games in Barcelona. The geographical spread of the some 40 attacks, extending far beyond the Basque Country to Catalonia, Madrid and Andalusia, also indicated an organisation with a formidable infrastructure. The arrest of dozens of ETA activists and the dismantling of six commando units failed to halt, or even stall, this wave of violence.

ETA's actions seemed almost intended to court mass revulsion. Some speculated that it sought to provoke a more extreme retaliation from Madrid which would radicalise Basque nationalists. The government did indeed stiffen anti-terrorist legislation and tried to isolate democratic Basque nationalist parties. Spain's ruling Popular Party (PP) also forced the expulsion of the Basque Nationalist Party (PNV) from the International Christian Democrats. The most sinister aspect of the new campaign was the steady expansion of ETA's list of "legitimate" targets, traditionally confined to members of the military and police. It now included both Socialist and PP politicians, academics, judges, businessmen and journalists. Concern over the issue of terrorism continued to grow to the point where 81.5 per cent of the population considered it the country's main problem. Despite the fear, however, more and more citizens turned out for street protests which called on ETA to stop the killing.

The renewed campaign claimed its first victim in January and loomed large on Spain's political agenda throughout the year. Amongst the victims were the former civil governor of Guipúzcoa, Juan María Jáuregui; the president of the Guipúzcoa employers' organisation, José María Korta; journalist José Luis López de Lacalle; the chief prosecutor of the High Court of Andalusia, Luis Portero; Supreme Court judge José Francisco Querol; and the former Socialist Minister Ernest Lluch, whose killing on November 21 had an unexpected effect—in Barcelona nearly a million people marched in protest against his murder, calling on the political establishment to unite and achieve peace through dialogue. This call pushed the ruling PP and the main opposition Socialist Workers' Party (PSOE) into signing a controversial anti-terrorist pact on December 12, to which they hoped other democratic forces would subscribe. However, nationalist parties rejected the pact, alleging that it was designed to isolate moderate Basque nationalists, and that ultimately it was a pact against democratic nationalism. Other parties also resented their exclusion from the negotiating table.

The government's anti-terrorist pact should also be understood within the context of a local pre-electoral battle. Since the PNV in February had suspended the legislative agreement under which the party derived support from ETA's political wing, Euskal Herritarrok (EH), because of its refusal to condemn ETA violence, opposition parties had tried to force early elections in the Basque Country. Buoyed by his unexpected absolute majority in March's general elections, Prime Minister José María Aznar intended the PP to overtake the PNV as the leading party in the region and see his tough-minded Interior Minister, Jaime Mayor Oreja, installed as the first non-nationalist premier. His critics saw this strategy as playing straight into ETA's hands, as it risked polarising Basque society. The gulf between Madrid-based parties and Basque nationalists had become glaringly apparent, placing Basques on the verge of a social fracture.

Meanwhile, collaboration with France and Mexico on the issue of terrorism resulted in the capture and extradition of a number of leading figures, including Ignacio Gracia Arregui, widely believed to be ETA's overall leader, and the dismantling of ETA's logistical structure. In November French police also captured the leading members of GRAPO.

The year 2000 was also an electoral year, in which the PP obtained for the first time an absolute majority in the legislature. The party, which during its first term in office had had to rely on the support of the nationalists, was now able to realise old projects such as a tough immigration bill and a Humanities decree, aimed at standardising the teaching of language, literature and history throughout Spain's multicultural territory. In the elections held on March 12 the ruling PP secured 183 seats—up from 156 in the last legislature—in the 350-member Chamber of Deputies, whilst the PSOE dropped to 125 seats from 141. The PSOE's allies in the communist-dominated United Left (IU) coalition slumped to eight seats from 21. It was the left's worst electoral defeat since the return of democracy. As soon as the results became known, PSOE's leader Joaquín Almunia announced his resignation. After weeks of exploratory discussions, the PP formed an alliance in the legislature (but not a formal coalition) with Convergence and Union (CiU)—which depended upon the PP in the Catalan autonomous parliament—and the Canary Islands Coalition (CC), but not with the PNV (as it had done after the 1996 election).

The election results were as follows (1996 results in parentheses):

Party	seats in Chamber	% of vote in Chamber	seats in in Senate
Popular Party (PP)	183 (156)	44.6 (38.8)	126
Socialist Workers' Party (PSOE)	125 (141)	34.1 (37.5)	62
United Left (IU)	8 (21)	5.5 (10.6)	0
Convergence and Union (CiU)	15 (16)	4.2 (4.6)	8
Basque Nationalist Party (PNV)	7 (5)	1.5 (1.3)	6
National Galician Bloc (BNG)	3 (2)	1.3 (0.9)	0
Canary Islands Coalition (CC)	4 (4)	1.1 (0.9)	5
Andalusian Party (PA)	1 (0)	0.9 (-)	0
Catalan Republican Left (ERC)	1 (1)	0.8 (0.7)	0
Initiative for Catalonia (IC) - Greens (V)	1 (0)	0.5 (-)	0
Basque Solidarity (EA)	1 (1)	0.4 (0.5)	0
Aragonese Junta (CHA)	1 (0)	0.3 (0.0)	0
Others	0 (3)	4.8 (4.2)	1

Total, 350 (350), 100.0 (100.0), 208*

*40 of the Senate's members were designated by the regional legislatures.

Several factors explained the PP's overwhelming victory. One was the economic success of Aznar's four years in office, which should be seen in the context of the fiscal austerity required for the adoption of the euro. Another was the PSOE's leadership crisis and the disenchantment of the left and centre-left electorate, who did not comprehend the electoral pact signed by the PSOE and the IU. The abstention rate was more than seven percentage points higher than in the previous election. In simultaneous elections to the 109-seat Regional Assembly in Andalusia the PSOE obtained the most votes.

On April 27 Aznar announced a new, expanded Cabinet, promoting three ministers. Mariano Rajoy Brey became First Deputy Prime Minister and Minister of the Presidency, Rodrigo Rato y Figaredo became Second Deputy Prime Minister and kept the Economy portfolio, whilst Josep Piqué i Camps received the Foreign Affairs portfolio.

The leadership of the opposition PSOE was resolved on July 23 when José Luis Rodríguez Zapatero, a 39-year-old lawyer and legislator from northern Castille, was elected as the new leader by a very narrow margin. José Bono Martínez, a political heavyweight who for 17 years had been president of the autonomous government of Castille-La Mancha, had been expected to win the leadership. Rodríguez Zapatero promptly installed a new generation in the national executive committee, excluding veterans and left-wingers. His priority, he said, was to modernise the party so that it could carry out effective opposition. A generational change also took place within the IU. Julio Anguita, its historic leader, retired as the party's secretary general. Gaspar Llamazares was elected as his successor.

It was also a year in which Spain started to face the issue of immigration. It became evident that the state was not prepared to react in the face of the unstoppable influx of illegal immigrants, mainly from Latin America and northern Africa, who crossed the Strait of Gibraltar in record numbers in search of better living conditions. According to the Asociación Pro Derechos Humanos, some 200 people drowned in their attempt to reach the Spanish coast, whilst around 20,000 were intercepted during the attempt. The avalanche of immigrants provoked some scenes of racism, the worst of which was an explosion of xenophobic violence in El Ejido, in February, where immigrants saw their houses and cars burnt amid the passivity of the police and the town mayor. The government exacerbated the problem, introducing changes to the Aliens bill, which had been agreed with the rest of the legislative parties the previous year. The new measures curtailed the social rights (such as the right of association, the right to unionise and the right to strike) of immigrants who lacked residency permits. This decision provoked the resignation of the Minister of Labour and Social Security Manuel Pimentel Siles.

The tragic note of the year was the death of 28 people, mostly teenagers, who were killed when a bus collided head-on with a lorry in the village of Golmayo near the northern city of Soria on July 6. The cause of the accident was thought to be a call on a mobile telephone. Some 20,000 people attended the funerals, in a rare display of mass bereavement.

On the economic front, inflation returned as a concern. Official figures for 2000 showed an inflation rate of 4 per cent, well above the euro-zone average. In late 2000 Spain also suffered its first confirmed cases of "mad cow disease" (BSE). The two infected cows came from the north-western region of Galicia.

ii. GIBRALTAR

CAPITAL: Gibraltar   AREA: 6.5 sq km   POPULATION: 33,000
OFFICIAL LANGUAGE: English   POLITICAL SYSTEM: Crown Colony, parliamentary democracy
HEAD OF STATE: Queen Elizabeth II
GOVERNOR-GENERAL: David Durie
RULING PARTIES: Gibraltar Social Democrats (GSD)
HEAD OF GOVERNMENT: Peter Caruana, Chief Minister (since May '96)
CURRENCY: Gibraltar pound (at a par with UK pound)

THE most important political event of the year was the general election to the national legislature, the House of Assembly, held on February 10. Peter Caruana, the Gibraltar Chief Minister, had surprised political rivals on January 10 by calling the snap election, thereby giving the minimum notice required by law. The centre-right Gibraltar Social Democrats (GSD), led by Caruana, retained their overall majority in the unicameral legislature. Final results showed that the GSD obtained over 58 per cent of the vote, compared with the 53 per cent that the party had won in the 1996 election. The opposition alliance—consisting of the Gibraltar Socialist Labour Party (GSLP) and the Liberal Party (LIB)—led by former Chief Minister Joe Bossano, won just over 40 per cent. The electoral system's limit on the number of candidates which any party could field (eight), however, meant that the composition of the new House remained unchanged.

For the first time in recent years the election campaign focused more on local issues than on relations with neighbouring Spain and the UK. Peter Cumming, an independent candidate campaigning for a negotiated settlement with Spain over its sovereignty claim, polled just over 0.5 per cent of the vote.

The election results were as follows:

Party	% of vote	seats
Gibraltar Social Democrats (GSD)	58.3	8
Gibraltar Socialist Labour Party (GSLP)/Liberal Party (LIB)	40.6	7
Others	1.1	0
Total	100	15*

*The House of Assembly comprised a Speaker (appointed by the Governor), two ex-officio members and 15 elected members serving a four-year term.

In April David Durie, a senior UK Department of Trade and Industry official, became Governor of Gibraltar in succession to Sir Richard Luce. Luce had been appointed in 1997. In the same month another significant development took place when the UK and Spain reached an agreement over Gibraltar's administrative status. The agreement ended a long-running dispute between the two countries and unblocked a raft of stalled European Union (EU) legislation, including a directive on cross-border takeovers, which had been held up because of Spain's refusal to recognise the devolved Gibraltar government as a "competent authority" in EU affairs. Spain had always insisted on dealing directly with the UK rather than with Gibraltar's elected government. The UK, Spain and Gibraltar all made concessions, and each praised the breakthrough as a deal "without winners or losers". Under the agreement, which did not affect the sovereignty of Gibraltar, passports, identity cards and driving licences issued by the territory would henceforth be recognised by Spain; banks and other financial institutions based in Gibraltar would be able to spread their services throughout the EU; communications between Spain and Gibraltar would be conducted through a special "post-box" at the UK Foreign Office in London; there would be increased police co-operation between Gibraltar and Spain; and all Gibraltarian documents, diplomatic contacts and financial and judicial decisions which extended outside the territory would have to be endorsed by the UK.

At the end of the year the conflict over the threat posed to Gibraltar and surrounding areas by *HMS Tireless*, a nuclear submarine, remained unresolved. The submarine, which on May 12 suffered a reactor leak during operations in the Mediterranean, arrived on May 19 in Gibraltar amidst much local and Spanish concern that the disabled vessel posed a threat to health and safety. Despite Gibraltarian and Spanish demands that the UK tow the ship home, the Royal Navy maintained its intention, announced on June 26, to repair the reactor in Gibraltar.

iii. PORTUGAL

CAPITAL: Lisbon   AREA: 92,000 sq km   POPULATION: 10,000,000
OFFICIAL LANGUAGE: Portuguese   POLITICAL SYSTEM: presidential/parliamentary democracy
HEAD OF STATE: President Jorge Sampaio (since March '96)
RULING PARTY: Socialist Party (PS)
HEAD OF GOVERNMENT: António Guterres, Prime Minister (since Oct '95)
MAIN IGO MEMBERSHIPS (NON-UN): NATO, OECD, EU, WEU, OSCE, CE, CPLP
CURRENCY: Portugese escudo (end-'00 £1=Esc318.99, US$1=Esc213.54)
GNP PER CAPITA: US$10,600, US$15,147 at PPP ('99)

To a larger extent than in previous years, EU-related issues were the dominant feature in Portuguese politics throughout 2000. For only the second time since its admission in 1986, Portugal occupied the presidency of the EU Commission from January 1 to June 30. The special European Council on "Employment, Economic Reform and Social Cohesion", held in Lisbon on March 23, was widely hailed as a success, not only for the resolutions on common social policies, but for marking the empowering of the Council, over the Council of Ministers and the Commission itself. Praise for the Portuguese presidency was renewed after the concluding summit at Vila da Feira, in northern Portugal, on June 19.

In the succeeding French presidency, however, Portugal had more reasons for concern than satisfaction. The discussions concerning the prospective phased EU enlargement towards Eastern Europe included proposals for the redistribution and weighing of votes and the extension of qualified majority voting, thereby further reducing the influence in the Commission of smaller countries, like Portugal, with the loss of its single permanent Commissioner. The proposed reforms announced at the Nice summit in mid-December also clearly implied this diminution in the power of smaller countries. The Portuguese, whose diplomacy towards the EU had been led by one of the ablest of a new generation of diplomats, Dr Seixas da Costa, were not caught unprepared, and indeed had a leading role in the protests against what amounted to a further assertion of the dominance of the Commission by the three largest powers

The Portuguese availed themselves of the opportunity provided by their six-month presidency to bring to the fore some of the interests inherited from their historical overseas expansion. With five Portuguese speaking African countries now grouped in the CPLP (Community of Portuguese Language Countries) together with Brazil, Portugal succeeded in promoting an EU-Africa ministerial meeting preparatory to a long-planned EU-Africa summit of heads of state, which subseqently took place in Cairo on April 3-4. Although almost unnoticed in the international press, its usefulness was duly recognised by the EU Commission which at the Vila da Feira summit gave its approval to a Portuguese offer to host a further EU-Africa summit in Lisbon in 2003. Another significant bilateral meeting at ministerial level, this time between the EU and India, in which both Prime Minister Guterres, as EU acting President, and Chris Patten, as EU foreign relations Commissioner, took part, was held on June 28 just as the presidency was to pass to the French.

This more intense than usual government involvement in EU issues took place against a background of slower economic growth in 2000, a rise in oil prices, labour unrest and predictions of forthcoming recession. Moreover, the coincidental passing of the 25th anniversary of Portugal's radical withdrawal from its far-flung empire provided a good point of reference against which to measure the country's post-colonial achievement. Since the collapse of the Salazar regime and the former colonial empire in 1974-75 little international attention had been paid to Portugal's quiet but impressive transition to a more integrated role in Europe. In colonial times Portugal had been ranked as one of the poorest western European countries, and even at the time of admission to the EU, its GDP was only 56 per cent of the community's average. By the beginning of 2000, however, this figure had risen to 74 per cent, and the country's infrastrutural modernisation, urban expansion, housing and consumer booms were comparable with those in Ireland, or Greece. However, with the rate of economic growth falling to 3 per cent in 1999 and 2000, and the central Banco de Portugal warning that this trend would continue in 2001, many independent reports estimated that it would take Portugal at least 20 years to close the gap with average EU states.

There were significant strides during 2000 in the areas of education, from nursery schools to universities and teaching hospitals. But too much of Portugal's economic growth was dependent on public works: spectacular bridges over the wide Tagus estuary in Lisbon, metropolitan railways at Oporto, new stadiums for the 2004 Euro football championship, a second airport in Lisbon and a much needed extension of the airport at Madeira. The rise in oil prices in March and the prospect of public protests such as those seen in other EU countries also forced the government to freeze increases in petrol prices up to the end of 2000. The lost revenue from fuel taxes and the increased cost of imports led to cuts in public spending on social services and to additional privatisation, thus discrediting even further the socialist credentials of the PS government led by Guterres. Moreover, despite the visibility of the boom in public works and almost full employment, there remained an undercurrent of frustration and economic uncertainty. With inflation expected to reach 2.7 per cent, up from the target of 2 per cent, the government issued frequent calls for wage restraint and increased productivity.

Notwithstanding the economic uncertainty, the year saw continued political stability, with the centre-right PSD-led opposition divided and ineffectual, and the extreme left unable to make much impact amongst the younger consumer generation. The notions that national governance was subject to EU authority, and that the privatised media was devoted to entertainment rather than enlightenment, were seen by some commentators as explaining the widespread indifference to ideology and party-political activity within Portugal.

The passing of the 500th anniversary of the arrival of Alvares Cabral to Brazil was more noted by protests than the sort of celebrations which had taken place during the Columbus commemorations in 1992. The word "discovery" was replaced by "finding" but even this and other concessions did not prevent the commemorative ceremonies at Porto Seguro, the historical point of arrival, attended by both the Presidents of Brazil and Portugal, from being marred by protests by anti-imperialist, enviromentalist and Amerindian groups.

History and religion provided the other highlights of the year. With the handing over of Macau to China at the end of 1999, the situation in East Timor remained like a dramatic post-script to the withdrawal from empire. Having been one of the most remote and forgotten outposts of the empire, even Indonesia's brutal invasion in 1975 had passed largely unnoticed amongst the traumatic events of the withdrawal from Angola, Mozambique and the other African colonies. But with the worldwide reports of the devastation that ensued after the Timorese opted for independence from Indonesia in the UN-sponsored referendum in 1999 (see AR 199, pp. 347-8), the initial shock turned into a national obsession. Discharging its obligations as the administrative power recognised by the UN, the President, Prime Minister and other leading Portuguese figures made a point of visiting East Timor, and under the co-ordination of a specially appointed Commissioner, Antonio Melancias, Portugal contributed significantly to the UN programme to rebuild East Timor.

On May 12-13 a visit by Pope John Paul II was surrounded by an even greater significance than usual for a country of 10 million, 90 per cent of whom were baptised Catholics. The theological importance of the visit to the shrine of Our Lady of Fatima was the beatification of an octagenarian nun, Sister Lucia, the only survivor of three illiterate shepherd children who claimed to have seen and heard Our Lady of Fatima in a field near the village of Fatima. The first two vision-messages were interpreted as forecasting the end of World War I and the outbreak of World War II, but a "Third Secret" remained undisclosed, thereby encouraging the belief that it was of even greater import. Upon disclosure at the time of the papal visit, it turned out that the secret was a message which was interpreted as forecasting an attempt on the life of a "Bishop dressed in white. . . which gave the impression of being the Holy Father". This was seen as a prediction of the unsuccessful assassination attempt against Pope John Paul ll in 1981. These developments, however, did not deter, and might even have reinforced, dissidence amongst Catholics who in the past few years had denounced the cult of Fatima as a relic of the past which continued to survive only because of the million or so pilgrims and visitors which it attracted each year.

The year ended with the campaign for the presidential elections in which the amiable and urbane President Jorge Sampaio, 61, fought for re-election for a further 5-year term against four other candidates: the centre right candidate Ferreira do Amaral, the Communist Party's Antonio Abreu, the Leftwing Bloc's Fernando Rosas, and the extreme-left wing Garcia Pereira of the revolutionary

PCP-MRPP. The poll was scheduled for January 14, 2001, which made the constitutionally prescribed period of the electoral campaign begin in December, with a brief lull for the Christmas and New Year. Most commentators predicted a comfortable win for Sampaio.

iv. MALTA

CAPITAL: Valletta   AREA: 316 sq km   POPULATION: 384,000
OFFICIAL LANGUAGES: Maltese & English   POLITICAL SYSTEM: parliamentary democracy
HEAD OF STATE: President Guido de Marco (since April '99)
RULING PARTY: Nationalist Party (NP)
HEAD OF GOVERNMENT: Edward Fenech Adami, Prime Minister (since Sep '99)
MAIN IGO MEMBERSHIPS (NON-UN): NAM, CWTH, OSCE, CE
CURRENCY: Maltese lira (end-'00 £1=ML0.65, US$1=ML0.44)
GNP PER CAPITA: US$9,440, US$13,610 at PPP ('98)

SIGNIFICANT progress was made during 2000 in the key area of Malta's relationship with the European Union (EU). On February 16 the EU formally opened accession negotiations with six further countries, including Malta, in an official ceremony held at the headquarters of the EU's Council of Ministers in Brussels. Minister of Foreign Affairs Joe Borg described it as "a historic day for Malta, comparable in significance with the day when the decision was taken to seek independence and later when the decision was taken for Malta to become a republic". At a ceremony to mark the occasion EU Commissioner Gunther Verheugen, who was responsible for enlargement, confirmed that Malta could now begin detailed negotiations with the EU and expressed the view that the island would soon catch up with those countries with which accession negotiations had already begun. Verheugen also noted that Malta had completed the screening process (see AR 1999, p. 98) very swiftly and he complimented the Maltese government on the manner in which work had been conducted so far. Borg welcomed the news as the beginning of the final phase that would lead to Malta's full EU membership and reiterated his government's stated aim that Malta should be amongst those countries which joined the EU in the next phase of enlargement.

Progress in this area continued during the year and on November 8 the EU Commission published a detailed report, documenting the progress made by the 13 applicant countries towards meeting accession requirements, and setting out a "road map" for the completion of negotiations. The report judged that Malta (together with Cyprus) was the best equipped of the 13 aspirant countries to join as both had "functioning market economies". However, the Commission's report into Malta's state of readiness also contained a number of areas of concern, including environmental issues (particularly sewerage, landfill and transport questions), and the size of the public sector (particularly the annual M£15 million state subsidy received by the island's dry docks). Furthermore, although the report set a target date of mid-2002 for the completion of negotiations, so that new members could be admitted from January 1, 2003, it was widely believed that, given the time required for each existing state to ratify new admissions and the complexities of EU institutional reform prior to enlargement, the earliest feasible accession date for new EU entrants would be 2004.

This represented a serious problem for the government of Prime Minister Eddie Fenech Adami which was committed to holding a referendum on the issue of EU membership once the negotiations with Brussels had been concluded. With a general election due by February 1, 2004, the government was keen to have concluded negotiations and to have held the referendum prior to going to the polls in search of a fresh mandate.

As part of its EU accession preparations the government continued its fiscal squeeze during 2000 in a bid to reduce the budget deficit. By the end of the year Finance Minister John Dalli estimated that the deficit would amount to no more than 6.5 per cent of GDP, compared with the 11.7 per cent which the government had inherited in 1998. However, the national debt, including parastatal companies, remained at around 60 per cent of GDP, the maximum allowed under the Maastricht Treaty for countries wishing to enter the EU's single currency. Overall growth for the year was a modest 4.5 per cent, although unemployment was estimated to have fallen to 4.5 per cent of the workforce following the creation of 4,000 jobs in the past two years. The government also remained committed to the privatisation programme outlined in the November 1999 White Paper, although the precise mechanics of the sale remained undetermined.

The comparatively modest rate of economic growth, together with the tight controls on public spending and the imposition of measures to combat tax evasion, helped to increase political infighting during the year. The opposition Labour Party remained fiercely opposed to EU membership, preferring to champion Malta as an off-shore tax haven. Its leader, Alfred Sant, still smarting over the manner in which he was ousted from government in 1998 (a backbench rebellion had forced a general election which he had unexpectedly lost—see AR 1998, p. 100), suggested that, if his party were to win the next election, he might disregard the result of any referendum which had been held on EU membership.

v. GREECE

CAPITAL: Athens   AREA: 132,000 sq km   POPULATION: 11,000,000
OFFICIAL LANGUAGE: Greek   POLITICAL SYSTEM: parliamentary democracy
HEAD OF STATE: President Kostas Stephanopoulos (since March '95)
RULING PARTY: Pan-Hellenic Socialist Movement (PASOK)
HEAD OF GOVERNMENT: Kostas Simitis, Prime Minister (since Jan '96)
MAIN IGO MEMBERSHIPS (NON-UN): NATO, EU, WEU, OSCE, CE, BSEC, OECD
CURRENCY: drachma (end-'00 £1=Dr542.17, US$1=Dr362.94)
GNP PER CAPITA: US$11,770, US$14,595 at PPP ('99)

THE year began with early elections. On February 4 Prime Minister Kostas Simitis announced that elections would be held on April 9. The justification for holding the poll five months earlier than stipulated by the constitution was the need for the government to secure a fresh mandate for its key policy objective, entry into the EU's Economic and Monetary Union (EMU), which was scheduled to take place at the beginning of 2001. In this connection Greece on March 9 made a formal application to become the 12th member of the EMU, a move which, according to opinion polls, enjoyed the support of some 70 per cent of the electorate. The economic and fiscal policies of the Simitis government had brought the rate of inflation down to 2.1 per cent, within the range stipulated by the Maastricht treaty.

Simitis's strategy of holding early elections very nearly backfired. His Panhellenic Socialist Party (PASOK) secured the narrowest of wins (43.8 per cent to 42.7 per cent of the popular vote) over Kostas Karamanlis's conservative New Democracy (ND) party. Indeed, early results had appeared to indicate a ND victory and jubilant supporters took to the streets in premature celebration. Despite the closeness of the result the electoral system gave PASOK a comfortable majority in parliament: 158 seats to the ND's 125 in the 300-member chamber. The Communist Party of Greece (KKE) with a 5.5 per cent share of the vote secured 11 seats, whilst the 3.2 per cent secured by the left-wing Alliance of Leftist and Progressive Forces gave it 6 seats. The Democratic Social Movement (DIKKI), a dissident offshoot of PASOK, with 2.7 per cent of the vote narrowly failed to reach the 3 per cent threshold for representation in parliament. PASOK's winning of a third successive term of office was without precedent in the country's electoral history.

New members of the government included Nikos Christodoulakis as Minister of Development; Michalis Stathopoulos as Minister of Justice; and Anastasios Giannitsis as Minister of Labour and Social Affairs. Theodoros Pangalos, who had been obliged to resign as Foreign Minister in the wake of the Ocalan affair (see AR 1999, p. 101), returned to office as Minister of Culture, and announced that his first priority would be securing the return of the Elgin Marbles from the British Museum. In November, however, he was dismissed for criticising the government, and replaced by Evangelos Venizelos.

Shortly after the election, Greece reacted angrily to a US State Department report that ranked the country as second only to Colombia in the risk of anti-American terrorist attacks. It described Greece as the "weakest link" in counter-terrorist efforts in Europe and revealed that the US spent more on security for its diplomats in Athens than in any other capital city in the world. A month later, the "17 November" group, one of the last surviving Marxist-Leninist guerrilla organisations in Europe, claimed its 22nd victim, Brigadier Stephen Saunders, the British defence attaché. On June 8 he was shot at close range whilst his car was stuck in a traffic jam. "17 November" subsequently declared that the killing was in retaliation for the British government's prominent role in launching bombing attacks on Yugoslavia during the Kosovo war. The Greek government issued a 1 billion drachma reward for information leading to the apprehension of the killers, who had operated with impunity over the previous 25 years. Scotland Yard detectives were seconded to assist the Greek police in the manhunt and the UK Foreign Secretary, Robin Cook, made an appeal for information on Greek television.

The ease with which such attacks were carried out raised questions over the ability of the authorities to ensure security at the Olympic Games due to be held in Athens in 2004. On a number of occasions during the year the International Olympic Committee expressed concern at the slow rate of preparation for the 2004 Games. Gianna Angelopoulou-Daskalaki, who had led the campaign for the award of the Games to Greece, was placed in charge of the organising committee, which was plagued by a number of high-level resignations.

In the spirit of the much improved climate of relations between Greece and Turkey as a consequence of what had come to be known as "earthquake diplomacy" (see AR 1999, p. 101-2), Georgios Papandreou in January paid the first official visit to Turkey undertaken by a Greek Foreign Minister for 38 years. The following month, his Turkish counterpart, Ismail Cem, declared that more had been done to promote good relations between the two countries during the previous six months than in the last 40 years. Initiatives continued to be taken to improve co-operation over non-contentious issues such as tourism, technological and economic co-operation, and combatting drugs and terrorism; but no substantive progress was made towards a resolution of the persistent problem of Cyprus. In early June, Turkish troops participated for the first time in NATO exercises held on Greek soil, whilst in October six Greek F-16 warplanes landed at a Turkish air force base for the first time since 1972. But they were withdrawn, amidst acrimony and following mock dogfights, from NATO's "Destined Glory 2000" exercise after Turkey insisted that the warplanes could not fly over the Greek islands of Ikaria and Lemnos. These had been demilitarised by provisions in the Lausanne Treaty of 1923, which in the Greek view had been overridden by the Montreux Convention of 1936.

Archbishop Christodoulos, Archbishop of Athens and all Greece, and the Holy Synod of the Church of Greece in June organised massive rallies in Athens and Thessaloniki in protest against the government's decision to remove religious affiliation from the identity cards which were compulsory for all citizens. The move brought Greek practice into line with that of its European partners. At the rally in Thessaloniki on June 14 the Archbishop told a huge crowd waving Greek flags, the Double-Headed Eagle of the Byzantine Empire and crucifixes that the proposal constituted an attack on the very fundamentals of Greek identity and insisted that "our inspiration comes largely from the East and not from the West which is undermining our traditional values". In December Christodoulos denounced EU proposals to strengthen the provisions for the freedom of worship in the European Convention on Human Rights as part of a plan to "de-Christianise Europe".

On September 27 the island ferry *Express Samarina* was wrecked on a well-charted and lighted rocky outcrop near the island of Paros. The ship sank within 30 minutes and 81 of the 530 passengers and crew on board were drowned. Amidst allegations that members of the crew had left the bridge to watch a football match on television, the captain and four crew members were charged with manslaughter. The disaster prompted many allegations of the use of unseaworthy ships on the profitable lines to the islands, and 65 ferries were held in port pending safety checks. Questions were also asked about the near monopoly position established by Minoan Flying Dolphin Lines, which owned 86 ships, and the company's managing director, Pantelis Sfinias, subsequently committed suicide. Amongst other measures the government promised to accelerate the opening up of island ferry services to competition from other European ferry operators. This was now to be permitted from 2002 instead of 2004 as had been agreed previously. The maximum age of ships permitted to operate in the Aegean was to be reduced from 35 to 30 years. After claims of collusion between Minoan Lines and the Ministry of Merchant Marine, the Minister, Christos Papoutsis, declared that no more cartels would be permitted in coastal shipping and that the Aegean would not be allowed to become anyone's private lake.

In November the European Court of Human Rights, by a majority of 15-2, upheld the claim of ex-King Constantine that the Greek state had in 1994 illegally confiscated properties in Greece belonging to the former royal family. One of the two dissenting judges was Greek. Constantine had asked for US$1.4 billion if his properties (summer palaces at Tatoi near Athens and on the island of Corfu and a forested estate at Polydendri in central Greece), were not returned. The Greek government countered that this sum was exceeded by unpaid taxes in respect of the properties. The Court gave the parties six months to reach agreement, failing which it would itself impose a settlement.

Spyros Markezinis, a prominent politician, died on January 4. Markezinis won early renown in 1953, when, as Minister of Co-ordination, he instituted the devaluation of the drachma which contributed significantly to Greece's post-civil war reconstruction. His reputation was subsequently tarnished when, in 1973, he briefly became Prime Minister at the instigation of Colonel Georgios Papadopoulos, the leader of the military junta then ruling Greece, as part of a move towards a "guided democracy". He was one of the very few politicians prepared to work with the military.

vi. CYPRUS

CAPITAL: Nicosia   AREA: 9,251 sq km   POPULATION: 866,300 ('99): 666,800 Greek Cypriots in the south & 199,500 Turkish Cypriots and Turks in the north (acc. to respective Planning Bureaus)
POLITICAL SYSTEM: separate presidential/parliamentary democracies in Republic of Cyprus and in Turkish Republic of Northern Cyprus (recognised only by Turkey)
HEAD OF STATE AND GOVERNMENT: President Glafkos Clerides (since Feb '93); in the north, Rauf Denktash has been President since Feb '75, Dervis Ergolu, Prime Minister (since Dec '98)
RULING PARTIES: Democratic Rally (DISY) heads coalition with United Democrats (EDI) and independents in Greek Cyprus; National Unity Party (UPB) and Communal Liberation Party (TKP) form coalition in TRNC
MAIN IGO MEMBERSHIPS (NON-UN): (Greek Cyprus) NAM, OSCE, CE, CWTH
CURRENCY: Cyprus pound (end-'00 £1=C£0.91, US$1=C£0.61); in TRNC Turkish lira
GNP PER CAPITA: Greek Cyprus US$12,765 ('00); TRNC US$4,553 ('99)

UN-SPONSORED negotiations for a constitutional settlement, which had commenced in New York in December 1999 (see AR 1999, pp.103-106), continued throughout 2000 with no success. The negotiations took the form of "proximity talks", with the leaders of both communities coming together in a common venue—but not face-to-face—for discussions with the UN Secretary General Kofi Annan and his Special Advisor on Cyprus, Alvaro de Soto. The Greek Cypriots insisted that any settlement should be based upon the principles set out in Security Council Resolution 1251 of June 29, 1999, which referred to the Republic of Cyprus as a bi-communal, bi-zonal federation within a single state, with a single sovereignty and a single international identity and a single citizenship. The Turkish Cypriots insisted on prior recognition of the sovereignty of the Turkish Republic of Northern Cyprus (the northern third of the island, secured by the presence of more than 30,000 Turkish troops) and the formation of a confederation with the Greek Cypriot controlled territory in the south.

Talks were held in Geneva (January 31-February 8, July 5-12 and July 24-August 4, and November 1-10), and also in New York (September 12-26). The New York session almost collapsed after the Secretary General in his opening remarks said that the "equal status" of the parties should be reflected in any settlement. The Greek Cypriot leader, Glafkos Clerides, said this could be interpreted as the first step towards a recognition of the TRNC. After the November talks the Turkish Cypriot leader, Rauf Denktash, said he would attend no more sessions until the sovereignty of the TRNC was recognised.

The talks were supposed to be held under a news blackout, but during the September round a 30-page Turkish Cypriot document containing an outline of a proposed settlement was leaked to the press. It called for a confederation of two "partner states", each with its own constitution. The confederation would exercise only those powers explicitly assigned to it by the states. The population would be "citizens" of the confederation but "nationals" of the partner state, which would exercise powers over immigration and the issuing of passports. The external representation of the confederation would reflect its "bi-national" character and would be subject to a subsidiary agreement to be negotiated later. The states would decide on their own government arrangements and exercise their own laws, regulations and executive powers. There would be a "border" between the states which would be adjusted to allow the return of some refugees. There would be restricted border crossings. Persons affected by the territorial adjustment would have the right to remain in the area concerned, whilst those wishing to relocate would receive compensation from an "international" fund. In October, however, the Greek Cypriot House of Representatives adopted a resolution rejecting any settlement "containing the seeds of confederation or the establishment of two states".

During the November round of talks, the UN produced a series of "non-papers" which also were also leaked. According to press reports, these referred to two "component states" and said that, though largely self-governing, these could not enact "provisions or rules" that would "contradict the basic law of the state". Political equality would be defined as "effective participation" in the government of the common state. There would be a president and vice president from different component states elected for a five-year, non-renewable term by an electoral college with representation from both states (numbers not specified). One state could not provide more than two successive presidents. There would be a nine member Council of Ministers with executive powers in which each state would provide at least three members. The legislature would consist of two 60-member chambers—one reflecting the population ratios, but with at least 20 members for each state, and the other in which each component state would have 30 members. The settlement would provide for the return of an "appreciable amount" of territory to the southern sector with the repatriation of "the largest possible number" of Greek

Cypriot refugees and the dislocation of "as few as possible" Turkish Cypriots. There could be "some restrictions" on Greek Cypriots residing in the north and the number of Turkish Cypriots in the south. The settlement would "commit Cyprus to the European Union".

On December 16 the assembly of the TRNC passed a resolution condemning the talks as "meaningless at this stage".

Notwithstanding this lack of progress on the construction of a new constitutional framework, the Republic of Cyprus (together with Malta) continued to be the most advanced of the candidates for EU enlargement, with provisional closure at the end of the year of negotiations on 16 of the 31 chapters of the *acquis communitare* and "progress" on a further nine. The Greek Cypriots sought to join the EU by January 1, 2003. The Nice summit communiqué said that it was hoped that membership could be proffered to some applicants in time for them to participate in the elections to the European Parliament in June 2004. Under the enlargement arrangements agreed at the Nice summit in December (see XI.4), Cyprus was assigned four of the 345 votes in the Council, one Commissioner (until there were 27, when their number would be capped and the posts filled by rotation), six places on the Economic and Social Committee and six seats in the Council of the Regions. The Turkish Cypriot leadership continued to refuse to participate in the negotiating process. The Helsinki summit in December 1999 had established that a constitutional settlement was not a precondition for accession.

The year 2000 was one of political and economic turmoil in the TRNC. In the April 15 presidential elections, Denktash did not get a clear majority in the first round, for the first time in his 27 years in that office. He polled 43.7 per cent compared with 30.1 per cent for his closest rival, the National Unity Party Prime Minister, Dervis Ergolu. This should have led to a run off on April 22 but Eroglu withdrew, claiming "interference" after the Turkish government endorsed Denktash. The latter demanded that Eroglu resign as leader of the coalition government with the Communal Liberation Party (TKP), but he refused.

Deputy Prime Minister Mustafa Akinci, head of the TKP, clashed with the head of the Turkish garrison, Brig. Gen. Ali Nihat Ozeyranli, who accused Akinci of "treason" after he called for the police and fire brigade to be transferred to civilian control. The publisher of *Avrupa*, a newspaper opposed to Denktash and the Eroglu-led government, was arrested with five others on charges of "espionage" after he supported Akinci. The charge was thrown out in court but the incident led to the formation by 44-opposition groups of a Platform Against Oppression, which organised three demonstrations in north Nicosia late in July.

During the first half of the year six banks were declared insolvent in the TRNC and put under public administration, with the loss of some US$200 million by 40,000 depositors. Activists from amongst their number joined the political protests, and on July 24 some 3,000 demonstrators occupied the parliament building and demanded compensation. Police used water cannon and truncheons to break up the demonstration, injuring 18 and arresting 60. The activism abated after the administration hinted that a state of emergency might be declared.

vii. TURKEY

CAPITAL: Ankara AREA: 775,000 sq km POPULATION: 68,600,000
OFFICIAL LANGUAGE: Turkish POLITICAL SYSTEM: parliamentary democracy
HEAD OF STATE: President Ahmet Necdet Sezer (since May '00)
RULING PARTY: Democratic Left (DSP), Nationalist Action (MHP) & Motherland (ANAP) parties
HEAD OF GOVERNMENT: Bülent Ecevit (DSP), Prime Minister (since Jan '99)
MAIN IGO MEMBERSHIPS (NON-UN): NATO, OSCE, OECD, CE, OIC, ECO, BSEC
CURRENCY: Turkish lira (end-'00 £1=TL1,001,294.3, US$1=TL670,300.0)
GNP PER CAPITA: US$2,900, US$6,126 at PPP ('99)

THE year 2000, which marked the 50th anniversary of Turkey's first free parliamentary elections on 14 May 1950, was dominated by the need to establish an effective democratic administration in order to qualify for membership of the European Union (EU). The ruling coalition government headed by Bülent Ecevit, leader of the centre-left Democratic Left Party (DSP), and comprising also the right-wing Nationalist Action Party (MHP) and the centre-right Motherland Party (ANAP), faced considerable difficulties in the implementation of its reform programme, but succeeded in maintaining its cohesion and retained considerable external support, even though its domestic popularity waned.

In January Ecevit successfully avoided EU condemnation by persuading his coalition partner, the deputy Prime Minister and leader of the MHP, Devlet Bahçeli, to agree to a stay of execution of the death sentence passed against the Kurdish rebel leader Abdullah Öcalan, pending a review of the case by the European Court of Human Rights in Strasbourg. The Court had decreed a stay of execution but Bahçeli had opposed this on the grounds that it effectively deprived the Turkish legislature of the right to confirm the death sentence (see AR 1999, p. 108).

Ecevit's handling of the election of the President of the republic, however, was less sure. His proposal to amend the constitution in order to allow a second term of office to the incumbent, the veteran centre-right politician Süleyman Demirel, was endorsed by his coalition partners, but rejected by parliament on April 5. Ecevit then put forward a compromise candidate, the chief justice of the constitutional court, Ahmet Necdet Sezer, who was accepted by the leaders of all the political parties, although not by all their followers in parliament. Nevertheless, Sezer was elected on a third ballot on May 5 and took office on May 16.

The new President's insistence on the strict letter of the law brought him into conflict with Ecevit during the parliamentary summer recess when he rejected as unconstitutional a number of government decrees. The most controversial of these provided for a fast-track dismissal of civil servants who were deemed to have engaged in subversive activities. The measure had been recommended by the National Security Council, the body which acted as a conduit through which the military presented its views to the government. After withdrawing the decree the government promised to present it as a bill to parliament, but no action had been taken on it by the end of the year.

The coalition partners then had great difficulty in agreeing the text of an amnesty law, which Ecevit had promised to enact when he assumed office, but which had been vetoed by President Demirel at the first attempt. A compromise text, which benefited common law criminals at the expense of prisoners sentenced for crimes against the state, was similarly returned to parliament by President Sezer, but entered into force at the end of December, after parliament had backed it for a second time. With half of the country's prisoners being released, political prisoners, most of whom were members of the militant Revolutionary People's Liberation Party/Front (DHKP/C), began hunger strikes in protest at the decision to move them from communal dormitories to cells in modern prisons. After failing to end the hunger strikes by persuasion, the government sent security forces to occupy the prisons. At least 30 protesters died in the resulting violence, many by setting themselves on fire.

Both before and after the prison riots, the DHKP/C mounted hit-and-run attacks on the police. The government had greater success in combatting two other militant organisations: the radical Kurdish nationalist Kurdistan Workers Party (PKK) and the Islamic Hezbollah. The PKK largely obeyed the decision of its imprisoned leader Öcalan to end its armed campaign, and the number of violent incidents in the Kurdish-inhabited areas subject to emergency rule fell by 80 per cent. Turkish security forces continued meanwhile to hunt down PKK insurgents both inside the country and across the border in northern Iraq. The organisation of Hezbollah, the roots of which were also in the Kurdish area, where it had acted as a counterweight to the PKK, was broken up after its leader Hüseyin Velioglu was shot dead by security forces in Istanbul on January 17. The bodies of more than 60 Hezbollah victims were subsequently discovered in raids on the organisation's safe houses throughout the country.

As the Turkish press published allegations that some Hezbollah militants had been trained in Iran, President Sezer decided not to attend the summit in Tehran on June 10 of the Organisation of Economic Co-operation (ECO), comprising Islamic countries in the Middle East and Central Asia. Instead he made his first official visit abroad to the Turkish Republic of Northern Cyprus (TRNC, recognised only by Turkey) on June 23, and followed it up in October with a trip to the Turkic republics of Central Asia. Throughout the year, Turkish diplomacy tried to promote the projects, backed by the Clinton administration, to build pipelines for the transport of oil and natural gas to Turkey from Azerbaijan and, if possible, from across the Caspian sea. But financial arrangements for the projects remained in doubt. In the meantime, work started on the on-shore portions of the Blue Stream pipeline which was to bring Russian natural gas to Turkey across the Black Sea.

Following the Helsinki summit in December 1999, when the EU had accepted Turkey as a candidate for full membership, the Commission published its accession partnership document and its annual report on Turkey in November (see XI.4). There was friction over references to a settlement in Cyprus and in the Aegean dispute with Greece. Under a compromise formula both problems were named as subjects of the political dialogue, and were thus kept apart from the Copenhagen criteria which Turkey had to meet before membership negotiations could begin. The Turkish national programme in response to the EU accession partnership document had still not been finalised as the year ended. In December a new obstacle emerged as, disregarding pleas by President Clinton, Turkey vetoed the proposal that there should be a structured arrangement whereby a European common defence initiative could have access to NATO facilities. Turkey insisted that it should participate in EU defence planning instead of being consulted only when its interests were affected.

However, economic rather than political problems occupied centre stage. Hopes rose at the beginning of the year as the government began implementing the programme agreed with the IMF to bring down consumer price inflation from 69 to 25 per cent. The Istanbul stock exchange index rose to a record level, whilst interest rates briefly became negative. However, as inflation fell more slowly than anticipated, the Turkish lira appreciated in real terms, with the result that imports rose rapidly whilst exports stagnated, and fears developed that the external deficit was becoming unsustainable. As the economy grew more quickly than forecast, the government was slow in clamping down on consumer credit, whilst delays in privatisation prevented a rise in foreign direct investment.

The difficulties experienced by banks, which had earlier relied heavily on high-yield treasury paper, were exacerbated when a vigorous campaign against banking fraud led to the state take-over of failing banks. In November a general loss of confidence in the management of the economy caused a flight of capital estimated at US$6 billion, and overnight money rates climbed to 2,000 per cent. The situation was saved in December when the IMF accepted a new letter of intent from the Turkish government and granted credit facilities in excess of US$10 billion. As estimates put growth for the current year at 6 per cent or more, the government secured parliamentary approval of a more restrictive budget for 2001.

Whilst the November crisis highlighted deficiencies in the implementation of the anti-inflationary programme and presaged more difficult conditions for the coming year, 2000 did witness real improvements in the economy. Consumer price inflation fell by 30 points to 39 per cent, and the primary budget surplus was expected to exceed 6 per cent of GNP. But investors had a bad year with share prices falling by nearly half, when adjusted for consumer price inflation. Although public investment was severely curtailed, Istanbul airport acquired a gleaming new international terminal, and the first section of the city's underground passenger transport system was opened to the public.

For most Turks, however, the most notable achievement of the year was the success of Istanbul's Galatasaray football club, which won both the UEFA Champions Cup and Super Cup. The former victory, the first ever by a Turkish team, was marred, however, by the fatal stabbing of two supporters of the visiting British team Leeds United in Istanbul in April, prior to the first leg of the semi-final.

III CENTRAL AND EASTERN EUROPE

1. POLAND—BALTIC REPUBLICS—CZECH REPUBLIC— SLOVAKIA—HUNGARY—ROMANIA—BULGARIA

i. POLAND

CAPITAL: Warsaw AREA: 323,000 sq km POPULATION: 39,000,000
OFFICIAL LANGUAGE: Polish POLITICAL SYSTEM: presidential democracy
HEAD OF STATE: President Aleksander Kwasniewski (since Dec '95)
RULING PARTIES: Solidarity Election Alliance Movement (AWS) & Freedom Union (UW)
HEAD OF GOVERNMENT: Jerzy Buzek (AWS), Prime Minister (since Oct '97)
MAIN IGO MEMBERSHIPS (NON-UN): NATO, OSCE, CE, PFP, CEI, CEFTA, CBSS
CURRENCY: new zloty (end-'00 £1=Zl6.17, US$1=Zl4.13)
GNP PER CAPITA: US$3,960, US$7,894 at PPP ('99)

THE coalition which had ruled Poland since September 1997 (see AR 1997, p.105) collapsed after 30 months in office, leaving a minority government with an uncertain economic and social programme. Its privatisation bill was vetoed by President Aleksander Kwasniewski, who convincingly won a second term in the autumn elections. Whilst parliamentary legislation for European Union membership was speeded up, sections of the public became more sceptical about the benefits of early entry.

Strains within the ruling coalition emerged in the lower house of Parliament (the Sejm) on January 22 when 22 members of the senior coalition partner, the centre-right confederation the Solidarity Electoral Alliance (AWS), voted with the opposition to remove Treasury Minister Emil Wasacz. He survived in office, against accusations of reneging on pledges to favour local businesses and the public in the sale of state assets, by two votes. Following the censure motion, the junior coalition partner, the Freedom Union (UW) called for stricter voting discipline amongst the AWS to ensure the safe passage of an agreed programme for economic reform and spending cuts. The party also called for the replacement of Prime Minister Jerzy Buzek.

After weeks of fruitless negotiation, the ruling council of the Freedom Union voted to withdraw from the Cabinet. Its four ministers included the Minister of Finance (and Deputy Prime Minister) Leszek Balcerowicz, the main architect after 1989 of economic reform. Buzek refused to accept their resignations, however, or to offer his own. Instead he called for further talks, but these also foundered over the selection of a mutually acceptable alternative to Buzek as Prime Minister. Rather than accept the AWS leader, Marian Krzaklewski, as Premier, the Freedom Union withdrew from government on June 6.

Buzek announced that he would continue in a minority administration, still committed to EU membership, and pledged to work for economic and political stability. These general goals were given more substance by the appointment of Jaroslaw Bauc (previously Deputy-Finance Minister) to replace Balcerowicz. His reassertion of previous policies, including tight budgetary constraints, helped to calm the financial markets. Amongst other replacements, Bronislaw Komorowski became Minister of National Defence and Wladyslaw Barcikowski replaced Bronislaw Geremek as Foreign Minister.

Despite the changes, political controversy soon returned. On July 14 the lower house of parliament narrowly adopted a law on the sale of state assets. It approved a massive enfranchisement programme, under which the public would receive share vouchers in companies to be privatised, and state-owned apartments would become the property of those occupying them. The ruling AWS declared that this would compensate every adult Polish citizen for the losses which they had endured during the communist period. But opposition deputies, supported by independent experts, warned that such massive transfers would cause chaos in the housing market and chronic imbalances in the state's finances. The Freedom Union argued that public money would be better used to fund welfare programmes.

The proposed sell-off was passed by the upper house (the Senate) on August 8. When it was sent to him for approval, President Kwasniewski used his veto, stating that the bill was "politically unwise, economically miscalculated and socially unjust". The loss of the legislation led to vociferous protests from the governing AWS, but satisfied the main opposition parties, including Kwasniewski's own Democratic Left-Alliance (SLD). Tensions continued with the announcement that the next presidential election would be held in October. This prompted political action from the potential contenders.

One newcomer, the National Peasant Bloc, a radical coalition which had appeared early in the year, declared its opposition to current economic and social policies. Whilst it was to contest the presidency, and declared a long-term goal of achieving parliamentary representation, its immediate tactics included extra-parliamentary protest. On August 21 a 30-day arrest warrant was issued in eastern Poland for its leader Andrzej Lepper, head of the Peasants' Self-Defence trade union. After five days in detention for consistent failure to attend court summonses in relation to a frontier customs blockade in January 1999, he was released after promising to remain within the law. He abandoned his idea of asking neighbouring Belarus for political asylum.

There was also a renewed attempt to arraign prominent presidential candidates for alleged collaboration with the ancien regime. On August 11 President Kwasniewski was acquitted when five secret police (SB) agents told a Warsaw court that he had not been an informer for the former communist security service. Similar charges against ex-President Walesa, the founder of the Solidarity movement in 1980, were shown to have been fabrications by the secret police, designed to discredit his international reputation.

The presidential election, held on October 8, resulted in a clear victory for the incumbent. President Kwasniewski surpassed the 50 per cent needed to win outright, receiving 53.92 per cent on the first ballot. His first post-communist predecessor, Lech Walesa, finished seventh with 1.01 per cent of the vote. Walesa declared his withdrawal from politics, though he continued as honorary chairman of his party, the Christian Democracy of the Third Republic. Second place went to an independent and Western-oriented economist, Andrzej Olechowski (17.30 per cent). His pro-European outlook and advocacy of the free market found rapport amongst businesses and with young voters. His support from intellectual circles was assisted by the absence of any candidate from the Freedom Union. The candidate of the ruling AWS, Marian Krzaklewski, came third with 15.57 per cent. Despite the withdrawal in his favour of former Prime Minister Jan Olszewski, Krzaklewski blamed his defeat on the disunity of the right, stating that the AWS could not compete effectively as a "coalition of dispersed parties". Followers insisted that he would continue as leader despite the electoral defeat. But political opponents called for the ruling AWS to resign from government and submit itself to early elections, not due to be held until 2002.

Rejecting that challenge, the government announced an acceleration of its timetable for adopting standard EU legislation. In early November Jacek Saryusz-Wolski, who had been appointed Minister for European Integration on April 18, stated that the legislation planned for 2002 would be completed in 2001. It was hoped that Poland would thereby remain on track for admission to the EU in its next round of enlargement. Anxiety had been aroused by a European Commission report of November 8 on candidate countries (see XI.4). Whilst praising Poland's overall economic performance of steady growth and progress towards a restructured and market-based economy, it singled out for criticism the country's slowness in enacting enabling legislation, and noted that agricultural reform had not been tackled at all.

Although Integration Minister Saryusz insisted that the government would devote more attention to persuading the public of the benefits of EU membership, scepticism grew in rural areas. The Polish Peasants' Party estimated that only 600,000 of the country's 2 million private farms would survive the joining process, leaving the rest bankrupt or dependent on the possibilities of Polish social security payments or subsidies from Brussels. Meanwhile, they argued that Polish supermarkets were swamped by cheap EU food imports, whilst Polish access to Western markets was being blocked.

Other problems of transition were successfully addressed. From late April Polish currency was removed from its link to a basket of currencies consisting of the US dollar and the Euro and had floated freely. The country's markets were thereby made more accessible to Western capital. But mobility of labour remained a problem. Whilst struggling Polish enterprises encouraged employees to seek gainful employment in western Europe, the government feared a backlash, above all in Germany, against such skilled immigrant labour. The concern also grew that, given the dimensions of Poland's economy and its unresolved problems, smaller countries requiring less adjustment might be admitted first.

ii. ESTONIA—LATVIA—LITHUANIA

Estonia

CAPITAL: Tallinn   AREA: 45,000 sq km   POPULATION: 1,400,000
OFFICIAL LANGUAGE: Estonian   POLITICAL SYSTEM: democratic republic
HEAD OF STATE: President Lennart Meri (since Oct '92)
RULING PARTIES: Pro Patria Union, Moderate & Reform parties
HEAD OF GOVERNMENT: Mart Laar (Pro Patria), Prime Minister (since March '99)
MAIN IGO MEMBERSHIPS (NON-UN): OSCE, CE, PFP, CBSS
CURRENCY: kroon (end-'00 £1=K24.91, US$1=K16.67)
GNP PER CAPITA: US$3,480, US$7,826 at PPP ('99)

Latvia

CAPITAL: Riga   AREA: 64,000 sq km   POPULATION: 2,400,000
OFFICIAL LANGUAGE: Latvian   POLITICAL SYSTEM: democratic republic
HEAD OF STATE: President Vaira Vike-Freiberga (since July '99)
RULING PARTIES: coalition of Latvia's Way (LC), People's Party (TP),
    For Fatherland and Freedom-LNNK (TB/LNNK) & New Party (JP)
HEAD OF GOVERNMENT: Andris Berzins (LW), Prime Minister (since May '00)
MAIN IGO MEMBERSHIPS (NON-UN): OSCE, CE, PFP, CBSS, WTO
CURRENCY: lats (end-'00 £1=L0.92, US$1=L0.62)
GNP PER CAPITA: US$2,470, US$5,938 at PPP ('99)

Lithuania

CAPITAL: Vilnius   AREA: 65,200 sq km   POPULATION: 3,715,000
OFFICIAL LANGUAGE: Lithuanian   POLITICAL SYSTEM: democratic republic
HEAD OF STATE: President Valdas Adamkus (since Feb '98)
RULING PARTIES: coalition of New Alliance (NS) and the Liberal Union (LLS)
HEAD OF GOVERNMENT: Rolandas Paksas (LLS), Prime Minister (since Oct '00)
MAIN IGO MEMBERSHIPS (NON-UN): OSCE, CE, PFP, CBSS
CURRENCY: litas (end-'00 £1=L5.97, US$1=L4-pegged)
GNP PER CAPITA: US$2,620, US$6,093 at PPP ('99)

THE year in domestic politics in ESTONIA was relatively calm. The three-party governing coalition consisting of the Pro Patria Union, Moderates, and Reform Party remained remarkably stable. Three opposition parties, representing mainly the rural population and pensioners, merged to form the largest party, the People's Union. The most heated political battle took place in the city council of the capital, Tallinn, where incumbent mayor Juri Mois (Pro Patria) managed to outbid the formidable leader of the opposition Centre Party, Edgar Savisaar, for the support of ethnically Russian city council members. Towards the end of the year, attention began to turn to the selection of a new president to succeed the erudite Lennart Meri in elections scheduled for the following year.

President Meri appeared to lose his political touch with a series of unfortunate personnel choices. In the spring, the council of the Bank of Estonia surprisingly chose Vello Ventsel over incumbent president Vahur Kraft. Ventsel, however, mysteriously withdrew before taking up the post, arousing suspicions of past KGB connections. Meri refused to confirm the council's second new choice and Kraft was eventually re-appointed. During the summer months, the President's replacement of the Commander of the Armed Forces, General Johannes Kert, evoked strong opposition. During the autumn, three candidates put forward by

Meri for the post of Legal Chancellor and Ombudsman were all rejected by parliament and the post remained vacant.

Several important steps were taken to encourage the integration of the large Russian-speaking minority into Estonian society. The state integration programme was adopted by the government, temporary residence permits were replaced by permanent ones for non-citizens and stateless persons, and changes were made in language legislation, relaxing the requirements for the use of Estonian in the private sector.

After the downturn resulting from the Asian and Russian financial crises of 1998, the economy registered a return to rapid growth. Following years of heated debate, and bitter polemics during the summer, the government finally privatised Estonia's power plants, selling them to the US company, NRG Energy. A second major issue of contention was the Privatisation Agency's selection of a preferred bidder for the nation's railways at the end of the year.

In foreign affairs, the top priority for the government was preparation for NATO membership which optimists hoped would be decided in 2002. This meant an increase in defence spending and the implementation of the Membership Action Plan. Negotiations for accession to the European Union (EU) continued at a good pace, with Estonia receiving one of the most favourable reports of the candidate countries from the European Commission in November, placing the country amongst the frontrunners from eastern Europe for EU membership.

The year 2000, like most others in the past decade in LATVIA, was riddled with scandal and controversy. Yet also, as in past years, the country continued to develop and progress despite the infighting amongst the politicians. The economy recovered strongly from the Russian economic crisis of 1998-99 with quarterly growth over five per cent, although its success was tempered by a budgetary policy which was heavily criticised by the conservative central bank.

The political world in the first part of the year was rocked by the so-called "paedophilia scandal". An ad hoc committee, chaired by Social Democratic legislator Janis Adamsons, which had been investigating alleged government links to a widening paedophilia scandal in the beauty pageant industry, named three prominent politicians—including the then Prime Minister, Andris Skele (TP) and ex-Justice Minister Valdis Birkavs (LC)—as being involved. Pressure from the scandal, combined with allegations of questionable activities in gathering his multi-million-dollar wealth, caused Skele's downfall to the extent that he began the year as Prime Minister but ended it as the country's least popular politician.

The fall of Skele's governing coalition in April caused a political vacuum, with many predicting an early election. Even after a new coalition was formed (comprising the LC, TP, TB/LNNK, and JP, and not dissimilar from that which had supported Skele), President Vaira Vike-Freiberga refrained from endorsing it until she was convinced of its stability. Having been endorsed by the President, Andris Berzins (Latvia's Way), the popular mayor of Riga, became Prime Minister. Though at first widely viewed as a "caretaker" or the "puppet" of his party, Berzins asserted his position strongly, and by the year's end had established control of the party.

Privatisation failed to proceed in 2000 and contributed heavily to the downfall of the Skele government. The fate of the Latvian Shipping Company (LASCO) had played a key role in the fall of several governments in recent years, and continued to apply strong negative pressure on the Berzins administration throughout the second half of 2000. Public pressure via a petition campaign all but ended plans to restructure and privatise the power utility Latvenergo, the biggest company in the Baltics. Smaller privatisation projects also contributed to a general sense of distrust and distance amongst the four coalition parties, leading many analysts to suspect that the government collapse of 2000 was likely to repeat itself in 2001.

Despite the problems faced by the government throughout the year, President Vike-Freiberga maintained her strong individual style of leadership. Unlike most political figures in Latvia, Vike-Freiberga was free from the entanglement of special interests groups (especially the oil transhipment lobby) and was not adverse to criticising erring politicians and officials alike. Central Bank chief Einars Repse also played a key role in maintaining stability, pursuing tight monetary policy and advocating a strict fiscal regime for the government.

Political relations with Russia were severely shaken in 2000 by the trial of former Soviet partisan Vasili Kononov for war crimes. Kononov, convicted of killing villagers during World War II, became the symbol of tension between the two countries, as protests mounted in Russia and amongst Russian speakers in Latvia for his release. Provocative protests by Russian nationalists in Latvia and Russia, as well as a series of attacks against Latvian diplomatic property in Russia, increased the tension. However, economic ties remained stable, as the oil transhipment route via Latvia continued to be one of Russia's lifelines—especially with the high price of oil in world markets.

LITHUANIA experienced a significant political shift throughout 2000, apparent in both the March local council elections and the October parliamentary elections. The formerly dominant parties, such as the Homeland Union (TS) and the Christian Democrats (LKDP), saw their popular support drop drastically. The TS, the ruling party in 1999, lost over 60 seats in the parliamentary elections and became a very minor right-wing opposition party.

The winners of this political shift were parties of the centre, mostly the centre-left New Alliance (NS) and the free-market Liberal Union (LLS). These two parties, following the October elections, formed the new ruling coalition along with some minor groups. At the same time another centrist group, the Centre Union (LCS), fared dramatically badly in the elections despite having originally reaped the most reward from the political shift of 1999-2000; ironically, much of its support was lost to the NS and LLS, which had originally been its pre-election partners.

The year also revitalised the left, leading to a planned merger between the Labour Democrats (LDDP) and the Social Democrats (LSDP), under the latter's banner. A return from political retirement by ex-President Algirdas Brazauskas led the joint left to a modest victory in the parliamentary elections, but it failed to gain enough seats to form the government. The agrarian-based Peasants Party

(LVP) fared well in the local elections, but had lost momentum by October.

The new government, formed by the "New Policy" coalition of NS and LLS, trod a tightrope in the months following the election. The parliament chose NS leader Arturas Paulauskas as chairman by only a handful of votes. However, the confirmation of the government programme of Prime Minister Rolandas Paksas (leader of the LLS) fared worse, receiving only 70 votes out of a possible 141 but being approved because of the number of abstentions. Some ambitious legislative proposals made before the elections were dropped, whilst other key items barely survived the hostile parliament. The consolidated left played the role of an active opposition and, during the early days of the Paulauskas parliament, veteran legislators on the left managed to control the parliamentary agenda over the head of the inexperienced Paulauskas (who had never before served in parliament). However, the governing coalition, even before the elections, enjoyed the support of President Valdas Adamkus, and his office began to seek an expanded role for the presidency through its influence with the "New Policy" coalition.

Both the old and new governments continued to pursue Lithuania's goal of joining NATO and the European Union. The Paksas government remained committed to military integration, including in the 2001 budget an ambitious increase in defence spending to over 1.9 per cent of GDP. EU integration gained a boost with the promise partially to shutdown the controversial Ignalina Nuclear Power Plant. Lithuania, after protracted negotiations over its rural subsidies, finally gained WTO membership at the end of 2000.

Lithuania did not recover from the 1998-99 economic crisis as well as its Baltic neighbours, with disappointingly slow growth in the early half of the year. The supply of crude oil from Russia remained problematic for the giant Mazeikiu Nafta processing complex, putting pressure on the economy as a whole. Plans to privatise the last state-owned banks hit a snag at the year's end, as one process collapsed and the other faced further domestic opposition.

iii. CZECH REPUBLIC

CAPITAL: Prague   AREA: 79,000 sq km   POPULATION: 10,300,000
OFFICIAL LANGUAGE: Czech   POLITICAL SYSTEM: parliamentary democracy
HEAD OF STATE: President Václav Havel (since Jan '93)
RULING PARTY: Czech Social Democratic Party (CSSD)
HEAD OF GOVERNMENT: Milos Zeman (CSSD), Prime Minister (since July '98)
MAIN IGO MEMBERSHIPS (NON-UN): NATO, OSCE, CE, PFP, CEI, CEFTA, OECD
CURRENCY: koruna (end-'00 £1=Kor56.21, US$1=Kor37.63)
GNP PER CAPITA: US$5,060, US$12,289 at PPP ('99)

THE Czech political and economic scene continued to be somewhat shaky in the year 2000, despite increased stability over the previous year. On January 26 the ruling Social Democrats (CSSD) and opposition Civic Democratic Party (ODS) decided to strengthen their "opposition agreement" that had been introduced after the June 1998 parliamentary elections. The changes provided for greater co-operation on the state budget, electoral reform, and preparations for European Union (EU) accession. The international community welcomed the enhancement of the agreement since it decreased the likelihood that the CSSD minority government would fall before its term was over; however, the pact continued to cause anxiety to other opposition parties, President Václav Havel, and within the CSSD itself. Critics feared that the changes to the opposition agreement gave the ODS-CSSD team a monopoly on political power and threatened to erode the checks and balances that exist within a healthy democratic system, particularly since the changes were combined with attacks on the small parliamentary parties, on presidential powers, on the work of police units fighting financial crime, and on the independence of the Czech National Bank (CNB).

The 2000 state budget was finally approved in early March after two failed attempts, but the ODS made its support conditional on a Cabinet reshuffle. In February Bohumil Fiser was named Health Minister, taking over from Deputy Prime Minister Vladimir Spidla, who had been serving as temporary caretaker in the post. Four ministers lost their portfolios after the budget's approval: Transport Minister Antonin Peltram was replaced by Jaroslav Schling; Regional Development Minister Jaromir Cisar by Petr Lachnit; Interior Minister Vaclav Grulich by Stanislav Gross; and Minister Without Portfolio Jaroslav Basta by Karel Brezina.

The "opposition agreement" also led parliament to amend the electoral law and to approve constitutional changes aimed at decreasing presidential powers. The new electoral legislation introduced elements of the first-past-the-post system and was, therefore, advantageous to larger parties such as the CSSD and ODS. After the parliament overrode a presidential veto of the electoral law in July, Havel filed a complaint with the Constitutional Court.

The ODS and CSSD also changed the law on the Czech National Bank (CNB), restricting the president's right to appoint the bank's governor. Havel vetoed the bill in late October, and CNB governor Josef Tosovsky resigned the following day. In late November a crisis arose between Havel and the government when the President appointed Zdenek Tuma as the CNB's new governor, without obtaining Prime Minister Milos Zeman's counter-signature. The lower house overrode Havel's veto of the CNB legislation in December, and the President took the case to the Constitutional Court later that month, claiming that the amendments infringed on the bank's independence.

Despite CSSD-ODS efforts to control the political scene, the CSSD experienced a bitter defeat on November 12 in elections to the Senate and to the 13 new regional assemblies that corresponded to the country's new administrative setup. In fact, the future of the "opposition agreement" was called into question since the CSSD and ODS lost their Senate majority. Former Senate chairman Petr Pithart, a representative of a coalition of four smaller centre-right opposition parties, regained his previous position in December after a two-year break. Moreover, some public opinion polls indicated that the four smaller parties, which in late September agreed to run as a coalition in the 2002 lower house elections, would win even under the new electoral legislation.

In other political developments, in late February Karel Kuhnl was elected chairman of the Freedom Union, one of the key partners in the four-party opposition coalition. In March the leadership of the secret services was taken over by Zeman and two Cabinet ministers. In late May the parliament approved a law to restitute Jewish property confiscated after the Nazi occupation. A serious political controversy arose in late December when the supervisory board of the public service station Czech Television (CTV) named Jiri Hodac as CTV director. Employee trade unions and members of the news department opposed Hodac's appointment, claiming that he had political ties to the ODS, and they announced a series of protests. CTV was temporarily taken off the air as rival news teams produced competing broadcasts.

On the economic front, the Czech Republic emerged from two years of recession, and GDP growth was forecast at 2-2.7 per cent despite a summer drought that damaged the country's agricultural production. Unemployment reached 8.8 per cent by year's end, whilst annual inflation grew by 3.9 per cent. The Czech banking sector was the most troubled area of the economy in 2000. In February the government announced plans to bail out Komercni banka, the country's biggest bank, and a majority share of Ceska Sporitelna was sold to Austria's Erste Bank. In mid-June the ailing IPB bank was placed under forced administration as masked police officers occupied its Prague headquarters, triggering criticism from the Japanese firm Nomura, which had purchased the bank in 1997. Because of its reliance on ODS support, the CSSD government was criticised for its failure to make any meaningful progress in bringing criminal charges against perpetrators of financial crime during previous ODS governments.

Regarding foreign affairs, the Cabinet strove to speed up the adoption of legislation needed for the country's EU accession. Relations with neighboring countries were mostly good, although tensions with Austria intensified when the Czech Republic's Temelin nuclear power plant approached completion and was ready to become operational (see also II.3.vi.). In September, an annual meeting of the International Monetary Fund/World Bank was held in Prague, and the city became the site of major environmentalist and anti-globalisation protests (see XI.2.ii).

iv. SLOVAKIA

CAPITAL: Bratislava   AREA: 49,000 sq km   POPULATION: 5,400,000
OFFICIAL LANGUAGE: Slovak   POLITICAL SYSTEM: parliamentary democracy
HEAD OF STATE: President Rudolf Schuster (since June '99)
RULING PARTIES: coalition of Slovak Democratic Coalition (SDK), Party of the Democratic Left (SDL), Party of the Hungarian Coalition (SMK) & Party of Civic Understanding (SOP)
HEAD OF GOVERNMENT: Mikulas Dzurinda (SDK), Prime Minister (since Oct '98)
MAIN IGO MEMBERSHIPS (NON-UN): OSCE, CE, PFP, CEI, CEFTA, OECD
CURRENCY: Slovak koruna (end-'00 £1=K70.02, US$1=K46.88)
GNP PER CAPITA: US$3,590, US$9,811 at PPP ('99)

SLOVAKIA remained on its reform path in the year 2000, although it continued to struggle with economic and political difficulties. Membership talks with the European Union (EU) moved ahead relatively quickly, and Slovakia's accession to the Organisation for Economic Co-operation and Development (OECD) in the autumn was deemed to be the government's greatest success since taking power in October 1998.

Relations amongst the four government parties were strained in mid-April, when parliamentary chairman Jozef Migas and several other members of the ruling Party of the Democratic Left (SDL) backed an unsuccessful no-confidence vote by the opposition. Although some SDL representatives criticised Migas's actions, he was re-elected party chairman in July after dropping demands for a Cabinet reshuffle. In November tension mounted within the Slovak Democratic Coalition (SDK), the largest of the ruling parties, after Prime Minister Mikulas Dzurinda established a new party, the centre-right Slovak Democratic-Christian Union. Some SDK representatives joined Dzurinda, but several groups of deputies resigned from the SDK parliamentary caucus in protest. Despite such developments, remarkable unity was demonstrated by the ruling parties in mid-December, when the 2001 state budget was approved by a three-fifths parliamentary majority.

Opposition activity increased after former Prime Minister Vladimir Meciar was arrested on April 20 by masked police and briefly detained in an effort to force him to testify in several cases. Nonetheless, attendance at a series of anti-government rallies was low. The opposition also instigated instability by initiating a referendum on early parliamentary elections. However, the referendum, which was held on November 11, was declared invalid since just 20 per cent of registered voters participated.

The opposition called a number of no-confidence votes in government members, but none was successful. However, two ministers were replaced as a result of decisions taken within the ruling parties themselves. Roman Kovac took over in July from Healthcare Minister Tibor Sagat after President Rudolf Schuster had nearly died the previous month during a colon operation at a Slovak hospital. The incident had prompted severe public criticism of the Slovakian healthcare system, particularly after Schuster was transferred to neighbouring Austria, where his life was saved by Austrian doctors. In December, Defence Minister Pavol Kanis announced his resignation following complaints over personnel policies at his ministry and his construction of a luxurious villa, and the SDL nominated Jozef Stank to replace him.

Political tension also arose from the issue of national minorities, and the chairman of the Party of the Hungarian Coalition, Bela Bugar, several times threatened to remove his party from the government if the position of ethnic Hungarians was not strengthened. At the same time, a solution to the Romani question became increasingly urgent as Slovak Roma continued to seek asylum abroad.

The government's economic reforms began to show results in 2000, and annual GDP growth was predicted at 2.1 per cent, mainly because of strong exports. Nonetheless, annual inflation rose to 12.0 per cent, whilst unemployment remained a difficult problem, and was forecast to reach 18.6 per cent in December. The year brought a large influx of foreign investment, most notably through the sale of the east Slovak steel giant VSZ to US Steel, Deutsche Telekom's purchase of 51 per cent of its Slovak counterpart, and the sale of a majority share of Slovenska Sporitelna to Austria's Erste Bank. In an attempt to restore confidence in the state administration, the government introduced a program to fight corruption.

Regarding foreign relations, Slovakia launched membership negotiations with the European Union in February, and during the year the country opened 16 of the 31 chapters of the *acquis communautaire* with the aim of catching up with its neighbours in the accession process. Slovakia's relations with neighbouring countries remained good, and co-operation was especially strong with the Czech Republic, Hungary, and Poland.

v. HUNGARY

CAPITAL: Budapest   AREA: 93,000 sq km   POPULATION: 10,050,000
OFFICIAL LANGUAGE: Hungarian   POLITICAL SYSTEM: parliamentary democracy
HEAD OF STATE: President Ferenc Madl (since Aug '00)
RULING PARTIES: Young Democrats (Fidesz) head coalition with Independent Smallholders' Party (FKGP) & Hungarian Democratic Forum (MDF)
HEAD OF GOVERNMENT: Viktor Orban (Fidesz-MPP), Prime Minister (since July '98)
MAIN IGO MEMBERSHIPS (NON-UN): NATO, OSCE, CE, PFP, CEI, CEFTA
CURRENCY: forint (end-'00 £1=Ft421.76, US$1=Ft282.34)
GNP PER CAPITA: US$4,650, US$10,479 at PPP ('99)

FERENC Madl, 69, was elected President of Hungary, in succession to Arpád Göncz, by the unicameral National Assembly in a third round of balloting on June 6. Although Madl was the sole candidate, he had failed to achieve the necessary two-thirds majority in the first two ballots and had only been elected because the third ballot had required a simple majority of the votes cast. At his inauguration on August 4, Madl, who had been defeated by Göncz in the presidential election of 1995 and who had served as Minister of Education and Culture in the 1990-94 coalition government, pledged to promote reconciliation within Hungarian society and to support Hungary's entry into the European Union (EU).

The most significant of several ministerial changes made during the year was the appointment, announced on December 13, of Mihaly Varga as Minister of Finance (with effect from 1 March 2001) in succession to Zsigmond Jarai, who was to assume the post of Governor of the National Bank of Hungary (the central bank). Following the announcement of his appointment, Varga said that he would continue his predecessor's financial policies, concentrating on the reform of state finances in general and of the healthcare system in particular. Varga's statement acknowledged mounting public dissatisfaction with the state healthcare system, in which medical staff were paid very low wages, and which had proved unable to improve Hungary's ranking as the country with the lowest life expectancy in Europe after Russia. Allegations of corruption within the bureaucracy claimed two ministers during the year. Ferenc Ligetvari was dismissed as Minister of the Environment in November, having held the post since June 16 in succession to Pal Pepo. Both ministers were reported to have been dismissed for failing to control financial irregularities within an environment management institute.

The year saw the beginning of two initiatives designed to reshape the right wing of Hungarian politics. In the first, Ibolya David, the Justice Minister and chairwoman of the Hungarian Democratic Forum (MDF), announced the creation of a new union of moderate right-wing forces, the "Right Hand of Peace 2000", on February 2. The aim of the new grouping, which included the MDF, the Democratic People's Party and the Entrepreneurs' Party, was to create a new centre-right power base which could balance the power of the Young Democrats (Fidesz), the dominant party in the ruling centre-right coalition. In the second initiative, two former agriculture ministers, Jozsef Ferenc Nagy and Jeno Gerbovits, both members of Hungary's first government of the post-communist era, announced the foundation on October 12 of a new smallholders' party. According to the two former ministers, the new party had been established in order to create a party for smallholders "without Jozsef Torgyan", the Agriculture Minister and leader of the Independent Smallholders' Party (FKGP), a junior partner in the ruling coalition. Torgyan had been criticised for his authoritarian style of leadership and blamed for the fact that the FKGP was trailing badly in the opinion polls.

GDP growth was an impressive 5.7 per cent in 2000, following a healthy 4.2 per cent in 1999. Inflation fell during the year to 9.8 per cent from 10.3 per cent in 1999, and unemployment fell to 8 per cent at the end of the year from 9.6 per cent in 1999 (see AR 1999, p. 122). Furthermore, Hungary's reputation was enhanced by a report by the European Bank for Reconstruction and Development (EBRD), released in May 2000, which identified it as one of five countries in the region—along with Poland, Estonia, Latvia and Lithuania—whose recoveries after the emerging markets crises of 1998-99 were based on "sound" fiscal policies. Robust GDP growth was recorded despite widespread flooding in eastern Hungary in early April 2000. The flooding, caused by heavy rains which burst the banks of several rivers in the region, including the River Tisza, resulted in damage estimated at some 6 billion forints. In order to cope with the crisis, the government on April 14 reduced all government budgets by 2.1 per cent and redirected the resources (some 37.3 billion forints) to assist the flooded areas.

The economy of the Somes-Tisza-Danube region suffered an earlier setback in January when the Baia Mare gold mine in northern Romania discharged 100,000 tonnes of sludge water, polluted with cyanide and heavy metals, into the river system. At least 100 tonnes of dead fish were recovered from the rivers and the Hungarian and Yugoslav governments organised a massive clean-up operation. Although the cyanide decomposed quickly, environmentalists were concerned that the long-term effects of the heavy metals on the river system (and thus the local fishing industry) could be far more serious. Government efforts to secure compensation from the owners of the mine, the Australian company Esmeralda Exploration and a state owned Romanian company, were hampered by the fact that the Australian company had gone into voluntary receivership in March. A further spill of water contaminated by heavy metals occurred on March 10 at the Baia Borsa coal mine in Romania, polluting the Tisza River in Hungary and Yugoslavia.

Relations between the European Union (EU) and Hungary, one of the "priority candidate" countries for accession to the EU, were dominated by the vexed question of the establishment of a timetable for the accession of candidate countries. In particular, Viktor Orban, the Prime Minister of Hungary, was reported to be concerned that difficulties with Poland over agricultural reform would hold back all six countries scheduled to join in the first round of EU enlargement. EU institutional reforms and the endorsement of a European Commission "road map" for enlargement in November went some way to placating the concerns of the Hungarian government, although it was still the case that accession could not occur before 2003.

Relations with France and the EU were strained during the year by France's consideration of asylum applications from more than 40 Roma Gypsies who had arrived in France in July 1999 from the village of Zamoly in western Hungary. The refugees claimed to have been persecuted by the Hungarian authorities, and they filed a complaint with the European Court of Human Rights (ECHR) accusing the government of tolerating discrimination against the nation's estimated 700,000 Roma people. In an effort to diffuse the issue, officials from the Czech Republic, Hungary, Poland, Slovakia, and Romania met in Prague on October 27, under the auspices of the Visegrad group (see XI.5.v.), to discuss measures to ensure the better treatment of Roma minorities.

Hungary's relationship with Russia was damaged during 2000 by remarks made by Orban on October 30 1999 during a visit to Canada, in which he expressed the opinion that his government would be prepared in an "emergency situation" to allow the deployment of nuclear weapons on Hungarian territory by the North Atlantic Treaty Organisation (NATO). The remarks were heavily criticised by the Russian government and by leftist opposition parties in Hungary, which claimed that the country's recent accession to NATO (see AR 1999, p. 120-1) had not committed it to allowing the deployment of nuclear weapons on Hungarian soil.

vi. ROMANIA

CAPITAL: Bucharest   AREA: 238,000 sq km   POPULATION: 22,300,000
OFFICIAL LANGUAGE: Romanian   POLITICAL SYSTEM: presidential democracy
HEAD OF STATE: President Ion Iliescu (since Dec '00)
RULING PARTY: Party of Social Democracy of Romania (PDSR)
HEAD OF GOVERNMENT: Adrian Nastase (PDSR), Prime Minister (since Dec '00)
MAIN IGO MEMBERSHIPS (NON-UN): OSCE, CE, CEI, PFP, BSEC
CURRENCY: leu (end-'00 £1=L38,726.8, US$1=L25,925.00)
GNP PER CAPITA: US$1,520, US$5,647 at PPP ('99)

THE year, which was dominated by elections and political campaigning, produced a big electoral swing back to the post-communist left, the defeat and decimation of the governing centre-right coalition, and the emergence of the ultra-nationalists as the main party of opposition. If the victory of the Party of Social Democracy of Romania (PDSR), was widely expected before the November elections, the failure of the Christian Democratic National Peasants

Party (PNTCD), the leading force within the outgoing government, even to get back into parliament came as a surprise. However, the real shock was the success of the Greater Romania Party (PRM) in becoming the strongest challenger to the PSDR.

Initial concern in Romania and abroad over the PRM's strong electoral performance and its likely post-election influence was somewhat allayed when Ion Iliescu, the PDSR's candidate, scored a convincing victory over Corneliu Vadim Tudor of the PRM in the second round of the presidential contest in early December. Further relief came when the new minority administration concluded a protocol with two moderate parties which agreed to support it in parliament without joining the government.

Although the elections were held at the end of the year, electioneering began early with President Emil Constantinescu and other centre-right politicians denouncing the PDSR in February for being a crypto-communist party. They also claimed that the PDSR had maintained a "hot line" with Moscow during Iliescu's two terms as president from 1990 to 1996. The PDSR denied the allegations and hit back against the governing coalition, which it blamed for widespread corruption, incompetence and inefficiency. These accusations gained greater credibility with the collapse in May of FNI, Romania's largest investment trust. Since the State Savings Bank was one of the major investors in FNI, much of the public anger at the collapse—including violent protests—was directed against the government.

With the financial turmoil uppermost in most investors' minds, the PDSR came first in the elections for mayors as well as for local and county councils in June, polling 26.45 per cent in the mayoral vote. Meanwhile, the Democratic Convention—which was dominated by the PNTCD and was the main grouping within the governing coalition—was pushed into fifth place with 7.29 per cent. The disastrous performance by the PNTCD and its closest allies, as well as continuing infighting between and within the governing parties, persuaded Constantinescu to announce in July that he would not be contesting the forthcoming presidential elections which were widely seen as likely to end in his embarrassingly decisive defeat.

President Constantinescu's decision turned out to be a prudent move in the light of the subsequent election results. Iliescu led in the first round, held on November 26, ahead of Tudor, whilst each of the two mainstream centre-right candidates gained only around 10 per cent of the vote. In the second round Iliescu was able to profit from the widespread fear of his ultra-nationalist rival to score a landslide victory with 68.8 per cent of the vote against Tudor's 33.2 per cent.

The same pattern was seen in the parliamentary elections, also held on November 26, from which the PDSR emerged as the largest party, followed by the PRM. Three other groups secured a foothold in the Senate and the Chamber of Deputies: the National Liberal Party (PNL), which had earlier broken with the outgoing governing coalition; as well as the Democratic Party (PD) and the Democratic Union of Hungarians in Romania (UDMR) both of which had remained within it.

Party	% of votes	seats in Senate	% of votes	Seats in Chamber of Deputies
Party of Social Democracy of Romania	37.09	65	36.61	155
Greater Romania Party	21.01	37	19.48	84
Democratic Party	7.58	13	7.03	31
National Liberal Party	7.48	13	6.89	30
Democratic Union of Hungarians in Romania	6.90	12	6.80	27

The brunt of the electorate's dissatisfaction was directed against the revamped Democratic Convention 2000 (and, above all, against its main component, the PNTCD), which failed by a wide margin to clear the 10 per cent threshold required for electoral alliances to achieve parliamentary representation. As such, it paid the price for three years of economic decline, continuing high inflation and unemployment, as well as for the intra-government squabbling, lack of clear leadership and a tolerance of corruption during its term of office.

Although the PDSR recovered its position as the strongest party, its own record of economic mismanagement and hesitancy in introducing reforms during the period 1990-96 was still too fresh in many voters' minds to give it a convincing victory. Instead, a large section of the disillusioned electorate, including many who were undecided right up to polling day, cast their ballots for the third option—Tudor's mixture of nationalist and populist policies.

The newly-inaugurated President Iliescu appointed his long-standing deputy, Adrian Nastase, as Prime Minister in December. A former Foreign Minister and President of the Senate, Nastase was an experienced politician who had been groomed as a successor to Iliescu. The new administration was the first since the restoration of democracy following the anti-Ceausescu revolution of 1989 to be a minority government. However, the PDSR concluded separate agreements with the PNL and UDMR under which the two opposition parties undertook—in exchange for various concessions—to refrain from supporting no-confidence votes in the government for a period of 12 months.

The new government was facing a tough economic legacy. Economic growth returned in 2000 after three years of decline, but the 2 per cent rise in GDP was barely one-third of what Romania required on a sustained basis to catch up with the more advanced ex-communist countries in central Europe. Unemployment, though slowly falling, remained stubbornly high at 10 per cent of the labour force. However, both official GDP and unemployment figures needed to be treated with caution because they did not take into account the expanding informal economy which, according to different estimates, amounted to 30-50 per cent of the formal economy. Meanwhile, inflation—at 40 per cent—was well above the 27 per cent projected by the government, even if much of that was due to factors beyond its control, such as the rise in world oil prices and a disastrous drought at home.

The continuing poor state of the economy was highlighted once again by the European Commission's latest annual report in November on the countries preparing for membership of the European Union (EU) (see XI.4). The report noted that Romania had still not met two of the key criteria for membership—having a functioning market economy and being able to withstand competition within the single European market. But whilst the Commission remained sceptical about the government's economic record, in a historic move formal accession talks on Romania's EU membership had already got underway in February. The opening of negotiations was part of the EU's reward for the Romanian government's strong support for NATO during the conflict in Kosovo. Talks on the first five, relatively uncontroversial, chapters of the EU's body of law, the *acquis communautaire*, were concluded in May, thereby opening the way for negotiations over another eight chapters. EU officials warned, however, that accession remained a distant objective for Romania.

Romania's relations with its neighbours were generally free of the controversy of earlier years. However, relations with Hungary, Ukraine and Yugoslavia came under some strain in February and March following two environmental incidents. Both the Danube and Tisza rivers suffered severe pollution from cyanide and heavy metals after waste material was accidentally released into their tributaries in Romania. Hungary claimed that on each occasion the Romanian administration had failed to give adequate warning about the spillage. On a more positive note, after years of argument, Romania and Bulgaria finally reached agreement on the location of a second bridge over the Danube. The bridge, to be built with EU assistance, would connect Calafat in Romania with Vidin in Bulgaria.

vii. BULGARIA

CAPITAL: Sofia AREA: 111,000 sq km POPULATION: 8,200,000
OFFICIAL LANGUAGE: Bulgarian POLITICAL SYSTEM: parliamentary democracy
HEAD OF STATE: President Petar Stoyanov (since Jan '97)
RULING PARTIES: Union of Democratic Forces (UDF) & People's Union (PU),
 allied as United Democratic Parties
HEAD OF GOVERNMENT: Ivan Kostov (UDF), Prime Minister (since May '97)
MAIN IGO MEMBERSHIPS (NON-UN): OSCE, CE, PFP, CEI, CEFTA, BSEC, Francophonie
CURRENCY: lev (end-'00 £1=L3.11, US$1=L2.08)
GNP PER CAPITA: US$1,380, US$4,914 at PPP ('99)

THE main task facing Bulgaria's government in 2000 remained to move further towards fulfilment of the conditions for entry into the European Union (EU). In February Foreign Minister Nadezhda Mihailova expressed confidence that Bulgaria would become a member by 2007, and in March a Foreign Ministry spokesman said that the country was ready to start accession talks on eight out of the 31 chapters of the *aquis communautaire*. The following month, however, Prime Minister Ivan Kostov warned against undue euphoria, saying that the road to EU membership would still be long and difficult.

Bulgaria's determination to reform its economy was not in doubt and earned plaudits in influential quarters. In February the World Bank's chief representative for Bulgaria said that all 10 World Bank projects in the country were being implemented properly, whereas three years previously this had been the case with only 40 percent of such projects. In May a senior official of the IMF described Bulgaria's economic behaviour as "exemplary". Good conduct brought its rewards, especially in the form of grants and loans. The EU gave a grant of US$125.5 million in January; in April it gave just over US$200 million to improve safety at the nuclear power facility at Kozlodui and in May it gave a further US$46.8 million per annum for the next six years to improve agriculture. The World Bank gave a general loan of US$200 million in February and in June a further loan of US$63 million to finance improvements in healthcare.

Nevertheless, economic indicators continued to be mixed. The trade deficit remained high, over half a billion dollars in the first half of the year, and foreign direct investment, after a noticeable improvement in the first part of the year, slowed towards its end. On the other hand, in the first quarter of the year the foreign debt fell by just over nine per cent, from US$9.984 billion to $9.07 billion, and at the end of December it was announced that in 2000, for the first time since 1989, the trade balance had been positive.

The World Bank and other international organisations stated clearly that overcoming corruption was one of the chief problems facing the Bulgarian government. In February a parliamentary deputy of the Euro-left party was jailed for six years for extortion, and in April scandal approached the Prime Minister when his son-in-law was accused of profiteering from privatisation deals. On April 18 a government spokesman, Mihail Mihailov, was forced to resign after being accused of accepting bribes. Kostov reacted swiftly, admitting that he had made mistakes in not pursuing corruption with sufficient energy, and putting before parliament a bill which required senior state officials and civil servants to declare their wealth at the start and end of their period in office. However, scandals continued to emerge: at the end of the month the executive director of Bulgaria's second largest oil refinery was arrested on charges of embezzlement, and a much more embarrassing blow befell the government on June 9 when its own chief negotiator with the EU, Aleksandar Bozhkov, resigned following a report from the prosecutor-general's office. Bozhkov had been Industry Minister, with responsibility for privatisation, when the media had dubbed him "Mr 10 percent".

Corruption and criminality were also revealed in the business world. On August 21 Bulgaria expelled five foreign businessmen, four of whom were Russian. More were deported in September. They were said to have brought into Bulgaria vast amounts of money of unclear origin. This crack-down on money laundering occasioned some tension with Russia. When the authorities in Moscow requested information from the Bulgarian National Security Service on the decision to expel the Russians, the Bulgarian government responded sharply, reminding Russia that the Warsaw Pact no longer existed and that Bulgaria had "put an end to the practice of sharing its national security considerations with other states." The expulsions and the clamp down on suspected money-laundering were indications that Bulgaria would not tolerate its territory being used for nefarious financial transactions. These tough measures helped to secure the lifting of the EU visa requirement for visiting Bulgarians in December.

The most difficult problem facing Bulgaria in foreign affairs was the case of the six Bulgarians detained in Libya since February 1999. In February 2000 it was announced in Tripoli that the six—five nurses and a doctor—were to be tried on charges of conspiring against Libyan national security by deliberately infecting 393 children in a Benghazi hospital with the HIV virus. The situation was not helped by injudicious remarks by the Bulgarian Minister of Justice, Teodosii Simeonov, who told journalists in Sofia that he could predict the outcome of the trial in "a white country" but not in Libya. He later apologised for the remark, but at the end of the year the six were still in detention, awaiting a trial which had already been postponed seven times, and which carried the possibility of the death penalty if the accused were convicted.

Bulgaria was also involved in a dispute with the UN Security Council over a UN report which alleged that the country had supplied arms to the UNITA rebels in Angola. A commission of enquiry set up by the Ministry of Justice in Sofia rejected the allegations in May.

An important development for Bulgaria was the agreement in March with Romania, after nine years of intermittent and sometimes acrimonious negotiation, to build a second bridge across the Danube. It was agreed that the location of the bridge should be Vidin-Calafat, at the western end of the common frontier, and that the majority of the funding was to come from Bulgarian sources. The bridge would help to relieve congested routes through the Balkans.

There was tension with another Balkan neighbour, Macedonia, early in the year. On February 29 the Bulgarian Constitutional Court banned the Ilinden United Macedonian Organisation-Party for Economic Development and Integration of the Region. The second part of the name had been chosen because in Bulgarian it formed the acronym, PIRIN, the name of a region where some inhabitants claimed to be of Macedonian nationality—a claim rejected by the Bulgarian authorities. The Macedonian government registered its disapproval but the dispute was contained.

On the domestic front, the ruling Union of Democratic Forces (UDF) lost popularity. At the time of the corruption scandals of April, a Gallup International Poll showed that 52 percent of the population did not trust the government. Social deprivation had much to do with the declining popularity of the administration. Despite some economic advances, unemployment remained high, at around 18 per cent, and by the end of the year the average stipend was only US$110 per month. The UDF's hold on power, however, was not seriously threatened and it easily survived a vote of censure in May.

There were a few problems with ethnic minorities, but these did not pose a serious threat to stability. In January the leader of the mainly Turkish Movement for Rights and Freedom called for a change in the statement in the constitution that Bulgaria was a "mono-ethnic" state. There were also complaints from the Roma community of police brutality. On the other hand, Bulgarian television began relaying some programmes in Turkish in February and in the following month Islamic classes were introduced in elementary schools in 22 towns and cities.

2. ALBANIA—BOSNIA & HERCEGOVINA—CROATIA—
MACEDONIA—SLOVENIA—YUGOSLAVIA

i. ALBANIA

CAPITAL: Tirana   AREA: 29,000 sq km   POPULATION: 3,600,000
OFFICIAL LANGUAGE: Albanian   POLITICAL SYSTEM: parliamentary democracy
HEAD OF STATE: President Rexhep Mejdani (since July '97)
RULING PARTY: Socialist Party of Albania (PS) holds presidency and heads government coalition
HEAD OF GOVERNMENT: Ilir Meta (PS), Prime Minister (since Oct '99)
MAIN IGO MEMBERSHIPS (NON-UN): OSCE, PFP, CE, CEI, BSEC, OIC
CURRENCY: lek (end-'00 £1=AL213.24, US$1=142.75)
GNP PER CAPITA: US$870, US$2,892 at PPP ('99)

LOCAL elections in October provided the first chance for a national political poll in Albania since the ruling Socialist Party of Albania (PS) came to power after the anarchy of 1997. For many the PS had not brought the changes which they expected, and it had failed in its efforts to prove that Sali Berisha, the leader of the main opposition party, the Democratic Party of Albania (PD), bore personal responsibility for the collapse of the pyramid investment schemes which had triggered the 1997 crisis (see AR 1997 pp. 122-4).

Nevertheless, in the first round of voting, on October 1, the PS took control of 258 of the 398 local authorities, whereas the PD won 118. For the first time the PS captured control of the capital, Tirana, previously a PD stronghold. Berisha claimed that up to 800,000 people had been illegally excluded from the registers but OSCE spokesman Giovanni Porta stated that "everything reported by our observers is positive." Prime Minister Ilir Meta of the PS said: "These were not only the fairest, most democratic, and most transparent elections the country has ever had, but also the calmest." The PD boycotted the second round of the contest on October 15. The OSCE noted that there was less transparency in this vote than there had been in the first round, and it complained specifically of nationalist rhetoric in the southern town of Himara where all Albanian parties had supported the local PS candidate in order to defeat the largely Greek Human Rights Union Party.

The main problem facing the PS both before and after the October vote was organised crime. This at times took a violent form. On August 2 the police chief of Shkoder was killed in a gunfight with a suspected murderer, and in November a sniper fired shots into the apartment of the newly-elected mayor of Tirana, who was not hurt. In the same month, OSCE spokesman Porta left the country after receiving threats. In September there had been a failed grenade attack on Berisha in the southern town of Fier; the PD blamed the local police, who in turn maintained that the attacker was the chairman of the PD branch organisation in a nearby village. In December there was a bomb explosion in Frushe Kruje shortly before the Prime Minister was due to visit the town.

Organised crime continued to flourish, particularly in the smuggling through Albania of prostitutes, drugs, stolen cars, weapons and illegal immigrants wishing to enter western Europe. In March the Albanian government requested Italy's help in combating crime, and common efforts to control illegal activities also featured in agreements concluded with Montenegro in April and with Bulgaria in May. Towards the end of the year, however, things had not improved and Benita Ferrero-Waldner, the Austrian Foreign Minister and current head of the OSCE, called on the government to step up its fight against human trafficking. Albania, Ferrero-Waldner said, needed "to develop a national strategy on enforcement and interdiction as well as on prevention and protection of the victims."

The economy performed reasonably well in 2000. In June a senior IMF official praised Albania for its pursuit of "sound" macroeconomic policies. By the middle of the year GDP was growing at around seven per cent, inflation was close to zero and there were ample foreign currency reserves. The social cost of economic progress did not diminish and unemployment hovered around the 17 per cent level throughout the year. The government used the good economic indicators to continue its campaign for closer integration into Euro-Atlantic structures. On February 2 the Minister for Foreign Affairs, Paskal Milo, announced that the government was launching an intensive campaign for entry to the European Union (EU). In March he insisted that Albania and Macedonia should receive "special support from the Stability Pact" because those two states had been most affected by the Kosovo crisis and unless they were given such preferential treatment there could be no stability in southeastern Europe.

Kosovo remained a crucial factor in Albania's Balkan policy. On a number of occasions the Albanian authorities made it clear that they would offer no support to efforts by Albanians to destabilise the Preshevo valley in south-west Serbia. Milo also denied that there was any aspiration to incorporate Kosovo into a "Greater Albania", although Prime Minister Meta did say in November that at the EU Balkan summit in Zagreb he would represent all ethnic Albanians. In May President Rexhep Meidani became the first Albanian head of state ever to visit Kosovo; the following month Berisha was denied permission to do likewise on security grounds. The good relations with the US government, established during the Kosovo emergency of 1998-9, were maintained. In April President Meidani gave General Clark, NATO's supreme commander in Europe, the Order of Skanderbeg, the highest Albanian award that a foreigner could receive, and in August the visa section of the US embassy in Tirana was reopened. The entire embassy had been closed in 1998 because of the danger of terrorist attack from the Middle East.

Albania enjoyed generally good relations with other Balkan states. Greece's Foreign Minister, Georgios Papandreou, visited Greek villages in southern Albania in March, and President Petar Stoyanov of Bulgaria paid an official visit in May. In February Turkey agreed to provide US$39 million in military aid to the end of 2004. On February 28 the border between Albania and Montenegro was reopened; it had been closed in 1998. This, however, was an agreement between Albania and the Yugoslav republic of Montenegro, not endorsed by Yugoslavia. In protest the Yugoslav government ordered the army to close the frontier, which it did the following day. Further talks between the Albanian and Montenegrin governments reopened the crossing but it was subject to interruption until President Slobodan Milosevic of Yugoslavia had been removed from office in October (see III.2.vi.).

ii. BOSNIA & HERCEGOVINA

CONSTITUENT REPUBLICS: Federation of Bosnia & Hercegovina and Republika Srpska (Serb Rebublic)
CAPITAL: Sarajevo   AREA: 51,129 sq km   POPULATION: 4,500,000
OFFICIAL LANGUAGE: Serbo-Croat   POLITICAL SYSTEM: federal republic
HEADS OF STATE & GOVERNMENT: Zivko Radisic (Chairman of the presidency, Serb); Halid Genjac (Muslim); Ante Jelavic (Croat)
PRESIDENTS OF REPUBLICS: Ejup Ganic (Muslim-Croat Federation); Mirko Sarovic (Republika Srpska)
PRIME MINISTERS: Martin Raguz (Republic of Bosnia & Hercegovina); Edham Bicakćić (Muslim-Croat Federation); Milorad Dodik (Republika Srpska)
MAIN IGO MEMBERSHIPS (NON-UN): OSCE, CEI
CURRENCY: marka (end-'00 £1=M3.11, US$1=M2.08)
GNP PER CAPITA: n/a

ELECTIONS within Bosnia-Hercegovina yielded contrasting results during the year. Local elections held on April 8 confirmed the dominant position of the Serbian Democratic Party (SDS) within Republika Srpska (RS), and that of the Croatian Democratic Union (HDZ) within areas with ethnic Croat majorities. Elsewhere, the Muslim Party of Democratic Action (SDA) lost ground to multi-ethnic parties, especially the Social Democrats.

However, legislative elections in the Republika Srpska and the Muslim-Croat Federation on November 11 saw a weakening of the hold of the major ethnic parties in all areas. The HDZ retained a secure hold on power only in the canton of Western Hercegovina (less securely in Livanjski). In no single canton did the SDA win a majority of seats. In Republika Srpska the SDS candidate Mirko Sarovic secured the post of President, defeating Milorad Dodik. Sponsorship of the latter by the office of the UN High Representative in a succession of controversial situations had undermined the his popularity even within his own party (Party of Independent Social Democrats—SNSD). The SDS gained only 31 of the 83 seats in the Republika Srpska legislature, however, and gains by moderate nationalists and multi-ethnic groups compelled Sarovic to form a coalition government. Coalition governments around a core of Social Democrats also emerged from the elections in the Muslim-Croat Federation, and from the all-Bosnia union elections, where the legislature was composed of members drawn from the Federation and from the Republika Srpska.

Encouragement was given to those working for an integrated multi-ethnic Bosnia by the signature on May 10 of an agreement between the Ministers for Education of both parts of the republic, making provision for the publication of common history text-books. The first Islamic building to be constructed in the RS since the war of 1992-95 (a mosque in Kozarac) was opened on August 26.

The difficulties arising from the republic's ethnic diversity continued to be reflected in the protracted negotiations over the formation of the joint presidency. Following a legal challenge to the constitutionality of the law on the Council of Ministers in February, a Council of Ministers was only endorsed by the union House of Representatives on June 22. On October 14 Alija Izetbegovic retired from the collective presidency. He had founded the SDA, led the government of independent Bosnia-Hercegovina throughout the war of 1992-

95, and served as a member of the joint presidency since the Dayton settlement of 1995 (see AR 1995, pp. 126-8; 559-62).

The continuing involvement of the international community in the future of Bosnia was confirmed on June 21, when the UN Security Council voted to extend the mandate of S-FOR for a further 12 months. The slowness of the flow of returning refugees to their homes continued to create anxiety for the international agencies involved with the region, and reflected the persistence of inter-ethnic suspicions. Five years after the end of the war, Bosnia-Hercegovina still hosted 543,000 refugees and internally displaced persons, with 197,000 refugees of Bosnian origin in the Federal Republic of Yugoslavia, and 21,000 in Croatia. Other European states still provided temporary homes for 101,000 refugees and asylum seekers from the union.

International impatience with the slowness of the process of economic reform was expressed on March 8 by the IMF's resident representative in Sarajevo, who indicated that the availability of stand-by loans might be delayed if changes in the legal framework required by the Fund were not made. These concerns, repeated at the Board of the Peace Implementation Council in April, provoked sharp political controversy within the union, in which the World Bank was accused of blocking the privatisation process. The privatisation of 34 large enterprises was delayed following complaints from international officials about the lack of transparency in the process, and in April the Austrian company Rogner withdrew from a hotel construction project because of dissatisfaction with the legal framework for investment. On May 12 the UN High Representative Wolfgang Petritsch imposed legislation designed to give investors a secure framework. The fourth tranche of the IMF's stand-by loan was deferred in November because of the failure to meet the Fund's conditions, only partly attributable to the constitutional complexity of the union.

The process of calling indicted war criminals to account was advanced significantly on April 3 by the arrest in Pale of Momcilo Krajisnik, former Speaker of the Serb National Assembly and an associate of Radovan Karadzic and Gen. Ratko Mladic. He appeared on trial in The Hague on April 7, charged with genocide, crimes against humanity, violations of the laws and customs of war, and other offences. The trial in The Hague of five Bosnian Croats, accused of involvement in the Ahmici massacre in April 1993, concluded on January 14, with sentences ranging from six to 25 years' imprisonment.

iii. CROATIA

CAPITAL: Zagreb   AREA: 57,000 sq km   POPULATION: 4,600,000
OFFICIAL LANGUAGE: Croatian   POLITICAL SYSTEM: presidential republic
HEAD OF STATE AND GOVERNMENT: President Stipe Mesic (since Feb '00)
RULING PARTIES: Social Democratic Party of Croatia (SPH) & Croatian Social Liberal Party (HSLS) lead coalition
PRIME MINISTER: Ivica Racan (SPH), since Jan '00
MAIN IGO MEMBERSHIPS (NON-UN): OSCE, CE, CEI
CURRENCY: kuna (end-'00 £1=K12.08, US$1=K8.09)
GNP PER CAPITA: US$4,580, US$6,915 at PPP ('99)

ELECTIONS on January 4 to the lower house (Zastupnicki dom) of the Assembly (the Sabor), rescheduled after the death of former President Franjo Tudjman (see AR 1999, pp. 134, 592-3), revealed important changes in the political climate. The Croatian Democratic Union (HDZ), which had ruled since 1989 under Tudjman's leadership, was ousted by Ivica Racan's Social Democrats (SPH). Other nationalist parties also lost ground. A new government was formed from a five-party coalition, including Drazen Budisa's Croatian Social Liberal Party (HSLS). In the second round of elections for the presidency, on February 7, Stipe Mesic, representing a four-party centrist coalition, received 56 per cent of the vote, after a very effective personal campaign.

Prime Minister Racan signalled a clear difference of direction by announcing a programme for economic reform, and his determination to eliminate corruption. In February Ivan Herak, the former Minister for Tourism, and Miroslav Kutle, a prominent businessman, were arrested on charges of corruption. On October 16 the trial began in Zagreb of 18 alleged members of the "Zagreb Mafia". In November corruption charges were also laid against Nevenka Tudjman, the daughter of the former President.

International acknowledgement of the new direction in Croatian politics soon came with a visit to Zagreb by the President of the European Commission, Romano Prodi, on January 14. On March 29 an IMF team arrived in Zagreb to negotiate new arrangements, and Croatia acceded on May 25 to the "Partnership for Peace" programme. Zagreb hosted the second Balkan summit on November 24.

The new government also took a radically different position with respect to the International Criminal Tribunal for the Former Yugoslavia (ICTY), accepting the request of the Chief Prosecutor, Carla del Ponte, to examine a suspected mass grave of Serbs killed by Croatian forces in 1991. President Mesic also made available a large amount of Croatian government documentation relevant to the work of the Tribunal both in Croatia and Bosnia-Hercegovina. The law on minority rights was amended on May 11, and a reform of the intelligence services was launched, with the appointment of a new head. The murder in August of Milan Levar (an important prosecution witness at The Hague) was linked to several Croats suspected of war crimes, and the government responded during September with a wave of arrests, the most significant of which was Ignac Kostroman.

The clearest signal of the ending of the Tudjman era came on November 9, when a package of constitutional reforms was passed in the Sabor, reducing dramatically the hitherto considerable powers of the state president.

The new policies were not universally popular, however, and veterans of the 1991-95 wars mounted demonstrations of protest in several cities. The policy of co-operation with the ICTY occasioned particular controversy, placing serious strain on the ruling coalition. On September 28 a group of senior military officers published an open letter to President Mesic, criticising the policy of collaboration with the ICTY. Nevertheless, in October a series of trials began in which the Croatian government prosecuted a number of individuals on charges relating to the conduct of the war in Bosnia (especially the Ahmici massacre of 1993) and incidents during the retaking of the former Serb-controlled Krajina (see AR 1995, p.121).

On January 13 the United Nations Security Council voted to extend the UN observer mission in the Prevlaka Peninsula (disputed with Montenegro) until July 15 (see AR 1995, p. 124). Croatia's other outstanding border dispute following the disintegration of the former Yugoslavia, the border with Slovenia in the Bay of Piran) also remained unresolved at the year's end (see AR 1994, p. 135).

Dissatisfaction with the strains of economic reconstruction was reflected in a strike of more than 100,000 public sector workers on December 8. The ongoing presence of around 21,000 refugees from Bosnia, and 34,000 internally displaced persons, continued to be exploited by nationalist parties.

iv. MACEDONIA

CAPITAL: Skopje   AREA: 26,000 sq km   POPULATION: 2,100,000
OFFICIAL LANGUAGE: Macedonian   POLITICAL SYSTEM: presidential republic
HEAD OF STATE AND GOVERNMENT: President Boris Trajkovski (since Dec '99)
RULING PARTIES: coalition of Internal Macedonian Revolutionary Organisation-Democratic Party for Macedonian National Unity (VMRO-DPMNE), Democratic Alternative (DA) & National Democratic Party (NDP)
PRIME MINISTER: Ljubco Georgievski (VMRO-DPMNE), since Nov '98
MAIN IGO MEMBERSHIPS (NON-UN): OSCE, PFP, CE, CEI
CURRENCY: Macedonian denar (end-'00 £1=D98.98, US$1=D66.26)
GNP PER CAPITA: US$1,690, US$4,339 at PPP ('99)

RELATIONS between the Slav Macedonian majority and the large Albanian-speaking minority continued to be a major factor in Macedonian politics, coloured by anxiety about the danger of the spread into Macedonia from Kosovo of Albanian secessionism. The escape to Kosovo in April of Xhavit Hasani, a leading figure in the Kosovo Liberation Army (UÇK), was widely interpreted as the result of a deal struck between the Macedonian government and the UÇK, in return for the repatriation of four Macedonian soldiers captured in Kosovo. On July 24 the Sobranie approved a law officially establishing the Albanian-language university (see AR 1995, p. 122).

A new left-of-centre opposition coalition was formed in mid-May, involving the Social-Democratic Alliance of Macedonia (SDSM), led by Branko Crvenkovski, the Liberal Democratic Party (LDP), led by Risto Penov, and, subsequently, the ethnic Albanian League for Democracy (LD). The stability of Macedonia's democracy was brought into question in September, however, when local elections were marred by several security incidents and evidence of widespread intimidation, resulting in one death.

The republic's ongoing abandonment of the economic heritage of communism was given a further impetus in April with the passage through the Assembly (the Sobranie) of a programme to restore property expropriated by the former regime to its original owners. Amongst the largest and earliest beneficiaries of the scheme, estimated to cost around US$740 million, would be religious foundations, both Orthodox and Muslim.

The renovated pipeline in January resumed deliveries of oil to the Skopje refinery, from Thessaloniki in Greece. The Macedonian government also sold a majority holding in the republic's largest bank, Stopanska banka, to the National Bank of Greece. These developments, reflecting the steady growth of Greek interest in the Macedonian economy, contrasted starkly with the earlier conflict between the two states over the use of the name "Macedonia" (see AR 1992, pp. 126-7; AR 1993, pp. 127-8; AR 1994, p. 134; AR 1995, p. 122; and AR 1998, p. 141).

The World Bank on July 11 announced a strategy of investment in Macedonia including loans of US$136.3 million, covering structural reform in public enterprises and public administration. The announcement occasioned fierce controversy, however, as it was estimated that implementation of the reforms could result in up to 5,000 redundancies, particularly from over-staffed government departments.

Skopje was the venue for the Balkan summit which took place on October 25, when the heads of the Balkan states (excluding Slovenia) met with the EU External Relations Commissioner Chris Patten and the Co-ordinator of the Stability Pact, Bodo Hombach. Welcoming Yugoslav President Vojislav Kostunica to his first international gathering, the summit appraised the recent changes in the Federal Republic of Yugoslavia (see III.2.vi).

v. SLOVENIA

CAPITAL: Ljubljana   AREA: 20,000 sq km   POPULATION: 1,800,000
OFFICIAL LANGUAGE: Slovene   POLITICAL SYSTEM: presidential republic
HEAD OF STATE AND GOVERNMENT: President Milan Kucan (since April '90)
RULING PARTIES: Liberal Democracy of Slovenia (LDS), United List of Social Democrats (ZLSD) & Democratic Party of Pensioners (DeSUS)
PRIME MINISTER: Janez Drnovsek (LDS), since Nov '00
MAIN IGO MEMBERSHIPS (NON-UN): OSCE, CE, PFP, CEI
CURRENCY: tolar (end-'00 £1=T339.80, US$1=T227.48)
GNP PER CAPITA: US$9,890, US$15,062 at PPP ('99)

FAILURE to reach agreement with Croatia over Slovenia's long-standing border dispute in the Bay of Piran (see AR 1994, p. 135) was one of the reasons behind the resignation on January 21 of the Foreign Minister, Boris Frlec. He was replaced by Dimitrij Rupel. This thorny issue remained unresolved at the end of the year.

After protracted attempts to re-form a government, and following defeat in a vote of confidence, Prime Minister Janez Drnovsek resigned on April 8. Attempts to form a new government dragged on through May, and it was not until June 7 that a new Cabinet was endorsed by the State Chamber, under the Premiership of

Andrej Bujak, supported by a coalition of the Slovenian People's Party, the Social Democratic Party, and independents.

The continuing instability of Slovenia's centre-right was reflected in the formation on August 4 of a new party, led by Bujak and his Foreign Minister Lojze Peterle. The New Slovenia-Christian People's Party was formed from elements of the Slovenian People's Party and of the Christian Democrats. The general election of October 15, however, showed that the electorate had little confidence in the new party, which secured only eight of the 90 seats in the State Chamber. Drnovsek's Liberal Democrats secured 34 seats, and were returned to power in coalition with the United List of Social Democrats and the Pensioners' Party. The election turned largely upon economic issues, and in particular the prospects for the early entry of Slovenia into the European Union (EU). After further protracted negotiations, to which personalities as much as programmes constituted the chief obstacles, Drnovsek's new Cabinet was finally sworn in on November 30.

Despite Slovenia's determination at the diplomatic level to turn its back on its "Balkan" heritage, there was noteworthy growth during the year in its economic links with Macedonia (where Nova ljubljanska banka acquired an interest in Tutunska banka), Montenegro (where Triglav purchased a major share in Lovcen osiguranje), and Bosnia-Hercegovina (where Mercator opened a large commercial centre in Sarajevo).

vi. FEDERAL REPUBLIC OF YUGOSLAVIA

CONSTITUENT REPUBLICS: Montenegro (13,812 sq km), Serbia (88,316 sq km)
CAPITAL: Belgrade   AREA: 102,128 sq km   POPULATION: 10,200,000
OFFICIAL LANGUAGE: Serbo-Croat   POLITICAL SYSTEM: federal republic
HEAD OF STATE & GOVERNMENT: President Vojislav Kostunica (since Oct '00)
RULING PARTIES: Democratic Opposition of Serbia (DOS) & Socialist People's Party of Montenegro
PRESIDENTS OF REPUBLICS: Milan Milutinovic (Serbia); Milo Djukanovic (Montenegro)
PRIME MINISTER: Zoran Zizic since Nov '00   Mirko Marjanovic (Serbia); Filip Vujanovic (Montenegro)
MAIN IGO MEMBERSHIPS (NON-UN): OSCE, CEI, EBRD
CURRENCY: new Yugoslav dinar (end-'00 £1=YD20.39, US$1=YD13.65)
GNP PER CAPITA: n/a

THE year 2000 saw a transformation in Yugoslavian politics with the popular overthrow of President Slobodan Milosevic, whose regime in recent years had spawned economic ruin, military defeat and international odium for the people of Yugoslavia.

The year began with the assassination on January 15 of Zeljko Raxnjatovic in the lobby of the Belgrade Intercontinental hotel. Better known by the nom de guerre "Arkan", he was wanted by Interpol for several offences before his return to Yugoslavia in 1986. He organised the infamous paramilitary unit, the "Tigers", the activities of which in Croatia and Bosnia-Hercegovina between 1991 and 1995 resulted in his indictment for war crimes by the International Criminal Tribunal for the former Yugoslavia. After the war his energies were divided between politics (as founder of the extreme nationalist Party of Serbian Unity) and organised crime. His death (like many such) remained unsolved by the year's end, but was variously attributed to the growing political distance between himself and the family of Milosevic, or to criminal rivalries.

Following the earlier, unsolved disappearance of the former leader of the Serbian League of Communists, Ivan Stambolic, Yugoslav political life was marked by a succession of assassinations of other prominent figures. On February 7 the Federal Minister of Defence, Pavle Bulatovic, was shot in a Belgrade restaurant. A close associate of Milosevic, he had held his post for seven years. The head of the state airline, JAT, Zika Perovic, was killed on April 25, and the following day a prominent businessman, Zoran Uskokovic, was also murdered, as was Bosko Perosevic on May 13. An attempt on the life of the opposition politician Vuk Draskovic, on holiday in Montenegro, on June 16, failed. (See also AR 1999, p. 140)

Slobodan Milosevic was re-elected as head of the Socialist Party of Serbia, at its congress on February 17—the sole candidate for the post—defying both the NATO bombing campaign of 1999 and his indictment for war crimes by the International Criminal Tribunal for the Former Yugoslavia (ICTY). However, signs of the increasing effectiveness of the democratic opposition were seen when 16 parties reached agreement on January 10 on a unified strategy against the regime. On April 14 this Democratic Opposition of Serbia (DOS) coalition was able to mount a demonstration estimated to number 100,000 in Belgrade. In May the leadership of the movement against Milosevic began to pass, however, from the orthodox political parties to the student movement Otpor (Resistance). Thereafter, increasingly hostile demonstrations took place in several provincial cities, including Nis, Novi Sad and Milosevic's home town of Pozarevac.

In an attempt to suppress this movement the regime took repressive action against the independent media, especially the TV channel Studio B, and radio stations B92 and Index (see also AR 1997, p. 134 and AR 1998, p.146). Raids, arrests and the beating of Otpor activists were regular occurrences, particularly after campaigning for the presidential election began in earnest in September. The regime attempted to reinforce the sense of threat to Serbia with a well-publicised trial of 143 ethnic Albanians, alleged to be members of the Kosovo Liberation Army (UÇK), charged with various offences related to terrorism. The defendants were sentenced on May 22 to prison terms ranging from seven to 13 years. Surprisingly, however, a proposed stringent new anti-terrorist law was withdrawn on June 29 after Vojislav Seselj (Milosevic's coalition partner and head of the Serbian Radical Party—the SRS) refused to support it. Further intensification of the atmosphere of external threat took place with the arrest on August 3 of two British police officers working with the OSCE in Kosovo, and two Canadians based in Pristina, on charges of attempted terrorism. A similar purpose was served in mid-September by the mounting of a show trial in absentia in Belgrade of 14 leading Western political figures and diplomats on charges of "crimes against humanity and international law" in relation to the 1999 NATO bombing campaign (see AR 1999, pp. 139-141). All were found guilty, and "sentenced" to long prison terms.

After a protracted period of dissention between the opposition parties, the leader of the Democratic Party of Serbia (DPS), Vojislav Kostunica emerged as the agreed presidential candidate on behalf of the DOS, recognising his clear leadership in opinion polls over Vuk Draskovic. The combined efforts of a united parliamentary opposition and Otpor rapidly made ground against Milosevic.

Following the ballot of September 24 for the presidency of Yugoslavia, markedly differing results were claimed by the government and opposition, amid widespread accusations of intimidation and ballot-rigging. Despite estimates by independent observers that Kostunica had won the presidential contest in the first round, the Federal Election Commission announced on September 26 that the margin of victory was sufficiently small to require a second round. International pressure on Milosevic to accept defeat mounted during the following week, and DOS found itself supported from some surprising quarters—particularly the Serbian Orthodox Church, and Vojislav Seselj leader of the SRS and a former ally of Milosevic. Senior military figures declared that they would not intervene in the electoral process. On September 29 a massive campaign of demonstrations and strikes was launched. A key contribution was made by the miners of the Kolubara and Kostolac mines, together responsible for around 40 per cent of Serbia's energy requirements, who defeated the efforts of the security forces to take over their mines and threatened to bring the country to a standstill.

On October 5 a huge demonstration in Belgrade broke through police cordons and occupied the Assembly building, and later the same day set alight the headquarters of Radio-Television Serbia. Units of the security forces began to join the demonstrators. Recognising the inevitable, Milosevic surrendered power on the following day, his decision being prompted in part by a pointed withdrawal of support by the Russian government. Vojislav Kostunica was inaugurated as President of Yugoslavia on October 7.

A difficult period followed for the newly-elected government. Kostunica had been elected as head of state, but it was necessary to negotiate a compromise with a parliament in which the largest party was still the SPS, until new elections could be held. These were scheduled for December 23. A power-sharing deal was agreed, in which DOS held the majority of portfolios, but the republican and federal premierships were retained by the SPS. Despite fears that a coup might be attempted by dissident military and police units loyal to Milosevic, these arrangements were respected. Elections to the Serbian Assembly (the Skupstina) were held, as scheduled, on December 23, and saw the DOS coalition secure an overwhelming majority, thereby completing its peaceful transition from opposition to government.

Prior to Milosevic's overthrow, the effectiveness of the international campaign of economic sanctions was repeatedly subjected to question in the early part of the year. In an attempt to encourage opposition forces, the European Union (EU) revised its sanctions policy on February 14, lifting the ban on international air links with Serbia, but issuing an extended list of the names of party and government officials who would be prohibited from travelling to the EU. The UN Economic Commission for Europe published a report on May 3 which was openly critical of the sanctions regime as "counter-productive". The fall of Milosevic in October saw the immediate lifting of the greater part of the array of economic sanctions against Yugoslavia, especially the international oil embargo, but not including prohibitions against travel abroad by the Milosevic family and others closely associated with the former President. On October 26 the US government approved aid arrangements to Yugoslavia amounting to $100 million. Russia extended further credits, and the EU granted membership of the Stability Pact. The four Western police officers and OSCE staff arrested in August were released on October 6. International acceptance of the new regime remained less than complete until the end of the year, however, because of the new government's refusal to co-operate fully with the International War Crimes Tribunal, and because of the continuing tension in Kosovo.

Yugoslavia applied for admission to the UN on October 27, tacitly abandoning the position upon which Milosevic had insisted, of the fundamental continuation of Yugoslavia as a legal entity, despite the secession of four of its constituent republics. This quietly opened the way for a negotiated settlement of several significant outstanding disputes between the legatees of the former Yugoslav federation. On November 27 Yugoslavia was admitted to the OSCE. In December Yugoslavia was readmitted to the European Bank for Reconstruction and Development, and to the International Monetary Fund.

The NATO-led peace-keeping force in Kosovo (K-FOR) was repeatedly put to the test during 2000 (see AR 1999, pp. 141-142). The northern city of Mitrovica was the scene of repeated clashes between Serbs and Albanians. The most serious rioting occurred in mid-February, after which a meeting of the NATO Council on February 25 voted to increase the 30,000-strong force. The Serbian authorities were widely regarded as responsible for the outbreaks of violence. There were further serious clashes in the city in August, when troops from the peace-keeping force took over control of the "Zvecan" smelting plant, which UN officials had declared unsafe.

On April 18 the European defence force "Eurocorps", created in 1995 in response to the Bosnian crisis (see AR 1995, p. 125), took over responsibility for peace-keeping operations in Kosovo, although continuing to operate within the NATO structure.

During the year the pattern of violence in Kosovo shifted, from Serb aggression in early months to Albanian aggression later in the year. Dissatisfied with the degree of protection which ethnic Serbs in the province were receiving from the peace-keeping force, Serb representatives withdrew from the UN Interim Mission in Kosovo (UNMIK) on June 4. On June 15 a large cache of Albanian arms and ammunition was discovered by UK troops. Although sporadic inter-communal violence continued in Kosovo throughout the year, in November the focus of attention shifted to three municipalities in southern Serbia lying outside of the province, but with substantial ethnic Albanian populations—Presevo, Medvedja and Bujanovac. Here UNMIK units found themselves collaborating with the Serbian security forces in the attempt to control action by the UÇK to bring these areas into a future, secessionist Albanian state. On December 15 the head of UNMIK, Bernard Kouchner, resigned the post which he had held since July 1999.

The US-based Human Rights Watch issued a report in January criticising NATO for breaches of international law during its bombing campaign. On August 18 forensic experts working for the ICTY reported that they had exhumed 3,000 bodies during their investigations in Kosovo, and anticipated the recovery of around 2,000 more. Their estimate of the death-toll amongst ethnic Albanians in Kosovo, during the 1999 conflict, was between 4,000 and 5,000—significantly smaller than the numbers claimed by NATO governments during the bombing campaign.

The succession of wars in the region had generated an enormous refugee burden for Yugoslavia. By the year's end the federation was hosting around 712,000 ethnic Serbs displaced from Bosnia-Herzegovina, the former Croatian Krajina and Kosovo. The absence of around 111,000 refugees and asylum seekers from the FRY in other European states represented a considerable loss of the educated labour-force.

Montenegro continued its hesitant movement towards independence during the year, and created a central bank, having adopting the Deutsche Mark as its official currency in November 1999 (see AR 1999, p. 143). This was declared illegal by the federal constitutional court on January 26, but the ruling was effectively ignored. On April 25 a trade and cultural agreement was signed between Montenegro and Albania, by-passing federal institutions. Montengrin aspirations for greater independence were abetted openly by the EU, which on May 8 announced an "emergency aid" package for the republic of US$460 million.

Local elections in two Montenegrin cities on June 11 resulted in some gains for the pro-Milosevic Yugoslav Coalition. In the elections of September 24, however, fewer than a quarter of the electorate voted. The government of Milo Djukanovic urged Montenegrins to boycott the contest, thereby reinforcing the impression that secession from the federation would be only a matter of time. One of President Kostunica's first actions, on October 17, was to visit Podgorica for discussions with President Djukanovic, although no progress was reported in resolving the problematical relationship between Montenegro and the federation. At the EU-sponsored Balkan summit, held in Zagreb on November 24, Djukanovic insisted on participating as a head of state, and not as a member of the "Yugoslav" delegation.

3. RUSSIA, EASTERN EUROPE AND THE CAUCASUS

i. RUSSIA

CAPITAL: Moscow   AREA: 17,075,000 sq km   POPULATION: 146,000,000
OFFICIAL LANGUAGE: Russian   POLITICAL SYSTEM: federal republic
HEAD OF STATE AND GOVERNMENT: President Vladimir Putin (since May '00)
RULING PARTIES: fluid coalition
PRIME MINISTER: Mikhail Kasyanov (since May '00)
MAIN IGO MEMBERSHIPS (NON-UN): CIS, OSCE, G-8, CE, PFP, CBSS, BSEC, AC
CURRENCY: rouble (end-'00 £1=R42.80, US$1=R28.65)
GNP PER CAPITA: US$2,270, US$6,339 at PPP ('99)

THE year 2000 began positively for Russia as the enfeebled and latterly discredited President Boris Yeltsin was succeeded by Vladimir Putin, who was committed to the vigorous promotion of Russian state interests at home and abroad. There were also real signs of economic recovery after a decade of almost unbroken contraction. Putin promised a "dictatorship of the law", including a recentralisation of state authority at what appeared to be the expense of the mass media, the financial-industrial oligarchs—who had been disproportionately powerful during the later Yeltsin years—and regional leaders throughout the federation.

Bolstered by the result of the December 1999 Duma election, in which the pro-Kremlin Unity party had secured a strong second place (see AR 1999, pp. 147-8), Boris Yeltsin had unexpectedly resigned on December 31, six months before his second term was due to come to an end. Under the terms of the constitution his responsibilities passed to Prime Minister Putin, already Yeltsin's designated successor, and the election date was brought forward from June 4 to March 26. Putin enjoyed enormous advantages as the incumbent, and the succession appeared to be a carefully crafted deal under which the new acting President would be all but guaranteed an electoral victory. This would in turn secure the position of the Yeltsin "family" and the powerful interests which were associated with it. Putin's first decree was certainly consistent with this interpretation: it gave the former President lifelong immunity from prosecution, together with three-quarters of a presidential salary, a personal staff, medical care, a government dacha, and benefits for his immediate family—all of which was difficult to reconcile with the constitution or the rule of law.

The early election meant that other candidates were seriously disadvantaged. It also meant that there was less chance that the campaign in Chechnya, with which Putin's political fortunes were closely associated, would begin to go wrong—or at least, that the heavy losses that were being incurred in subduing the rebel province would become impossible to conceal. In the end, 10 other candidates managed to fulfil the criteria for registration: the Communist and Yabloko leaders, Gennadii Zyuganov and Grigorii Yavlinsky; the governors of the Samara and Kemerovo regions, Konstantin Titov and Aman Tuleev; former chief prosecutor Yuri Skuratov; a wealthy businessman, Umar Dzhabrailov; the head of "For Civic Dignity", Ella Pamfilova (also the first women to compete for the presidency); film director Stanislav Govorukhin; the leader of Spiritual Heritage, Alexei Podberezkin; and a former Kremlin official, Evgenii Savostyanov. The Liberal Democrat leader, Vladimir Zhirinovsky, was originally disqualified because of an irregularity in his property declaration, but was reinstated after an appeal to the Supreme Court. Savostyanov, however, withdrew his candidacy in favour of Yavlinsky at the last possible moment. This left voters with a choice between 11 candidates, the same number as had contested the 1996 presidential election.

The leading contenders, according to opinion polls and in the view of the candidates themselves, were Putin, Zyuganov and Yavlinsky. Of these, Putin was clearly the strongest; indeed almost from the outset the only question that was asked about his victory was whether it would take place in the first round or whether a run-off against the second-placed candidate (presumably Zyuganov) would be necessary. The former Foreign Minister, Evgenii Primakov, who had previously announced his intention to stand, withdrew his challenge, and Moscow mayor Yuri Luzhkov called openly for a Putin victory. So too did the leaders of Fatherland-All Russia, which had been seen as the principal challenge to the Kremlin in the Duma elections. The Union of Rightist Forces refused to endorse Titov, and several of the party's leaders called openly for a Putin victory. Kemerovo governor Tuleev, who had stood on the Communist ticket in 1996, called for his supporters to vote for Putin if there was a second round, rather than for Zyuganov. For most of the candidates it was a question not of winning but of avoiding the need to repay the public funds that they had been allocated for their campaign, an obligation which would arise for anyone who won less than 3 per cent of the vote.

Putin refused to campaign directly, and did not issue an election manifesto. However, some impression of his priorities could be gained from an article which he published on the government website on the eve of the new millennium, as well as from an "Open letter to Russian voters" that appeared in the national press on February 25. He also gave a series of interviews to three journalists, which were published in the form of a book, entitled *First Person*, in the middle of March. Two themes in particular were reiterated in these writings, and they featured strongly in other statements which he made about Russia's political and economic predicament: the need for a strong state, and the importance of a properly functioning market economy. There was no danger to democracy from a strong state, Putin insisted, as "the stronger the state, the stronger the individual". Nor was there any conflict between a strong state and a market economy as the state was necessary to regulate the market, to ensure the rights of property, to protect the entrepreneur, and to make a better job of collecting taxes. The acting President also emphasised the dangers of a "second Yugoslavia" in Russia were fundamentalist Islam to be allowed to spread from Chechnya to the middle Volga, and more generally he promised to restore Russia's place as a great and respected power amongst the world's leading nations.

The Central Electoral Commission announced the final results on April 5, but it had been clear from about midnight on the day of the election itself that Putin would secure a narrow majority on the first ballot. In the end, he took 52.9 per cent of the vote on a turnout of 68.7 per cent of the electorate. Zyuganov, as expected, came second with 29.2 per cent, which was a somewhat more substantial share of the vote than had been predicted and one that he insisted would have been higher if the election had been conducted honestly. Grigorii Yavlinsky came third, as had also been expected, but with no more than 5.8 per cent, which was less than the 7.3 per cent which he had secured in 1996 and slightly less than his party had obtained in the Duma elections. None of the other candidates gained the 3 per cent that would have allowed them to retain the state funds which had been made available for their campaigns. Putin was formally inaugurated on May 7, relinquishing at the same time the position of Prime Minister that he had held jointly with the acting presidency. His successor as Prime Minister was former first deputy premier and Finance Minister Mikhail Kasyanov, whose nomination was confirmed by the Duma on May 17.

Vladimir Putin, at 47, was clearly a much younger and healthier man than his predecessor. He had a law degree from Leningrad University, where one of his mentors had been the reforming mayor, Anatolii Sobchak, and he spoke excellent German. At the same time he had been a career officer in the foreign intelligence service of the KGB, and had been the head of its successor, the Federal Security Bureau, from the summer of 1998. He had little experience of democratic practices, nor apparently much appetite for them. He had risen to power, moreover, at the head of a military campaign against "terrorism" in Chechnya and throughout the federation. Putin appeared to have two main priorities as President: to strengthen executive authority throughout the federation, and to introduce a "dictatorship of the law" that made life increasingly difficult for independent journalists and their organisations.

There were no indications, during the election campaign, nor as the year progressed, that the province of Chechnya was close to the restoration of federal authority, and actions undertaken by the armed forces were a source of considerable embarrassment in Russia's relations with Western states, which drew attention to what appeared to be massive violations of human rights, including the routine torture and rape of detainees. The Council of Europe, after undertaking its own investigation, withdrew Russia's voting rights.

The new President's earliest legislative initiatives concentrated on curtailing the powers of the elected governors of Russia's 89 republics and regions. On May 13 he issued a decree forming seven federal districts or "super-regions", which largely corresponded to the country's military districts. These districts would be headed by presidential envoys who would supervise local regions' compliance with federal legislation, and would be funded from Moscow, making it more difficult for regional governors to impede their work. The new presidential envoys included only two civilians; the rest were senior officers from the military or security services. In a televised address on May 17 Putin proposed further changes that would extend the president's powers to remove incompetent governors and would deprive governors of their automatic right to seats in the Federation Council, the upper house of the parliament. Under legislation adopted in July, regional governors and presidents would be replaced in the Federation Council by two representatives: one nominated by the governor and approved by the regional legislature, the other elected from amongst candidates nominated either by the Speaker of the regional legislature or by a third of its deputies. A new consultative body, the State Council, was formed in September with a membership that included the heads of all republics and regions, and was designed to advise the president mainly on issues relating to the relationship between the central administration and the regions..

There was considerable concern at home and abroad about Putin's policy towards the media, which appeared to have the objective of reducing or even eliminating the freedom to criticise government policy. In a statement in February, the Union of Journalists drew attention to restrictions on coverage of the Chechen campaign and warned that government policy, from being a threat to freedom of speech, had grown into its "open and regular suppression". A leaked official document, published in the press in May, suggested that the new administration wished to use the security police to "control the political process" and to silence opposition media by "driving them to financial crisis". Then, in May, armed police raided the offices of the Media Most conglomerate in Moscow, whose various publications had taken an independent line on the Chechen war and on Putin's election as president. In a still more dramatic development, the head of Media Most, Vladimir Gusinsky, was himself arrested on June 13 and placed in Moscow's forbidding Butyrki prison on fraud charges. He was released after three days. In July the charges against him were dropped because of lack of evidence, and he left the country. It later emerged that Gusinsky had been pressured to agree to the sale of Media Most to the gas monopoly Gazprom, to which Media Most was heavily in debt, in order to secure his release, in a deal that had been brokered by the Minister for the Media. Further fraud charges against Gusinsky were made in November, and he was arrested in Spain in mid-December to face extradition proceedings. A new national doctrine on information security, published in September, aimed to strengthen "moral values" in a manner that was reminiscent of Soviet times, and it strengthened concerns that further attempts would be made to subordinate the printed and broadcast media to government requirements.

Putin suffered his only serious public relations setback during the year in mid-August, when he responded in what appeared to be a belated and callous manner to the sinking of the *Kursk*, a nuclear submarine, during manoeuvres in the Barents Sea. The first official reports were that all 118 hands had lost their lives immediately, although this later turned out not to have been the case and that some of the doomed crew members had survived the initial explosion only to die of suffocation as the stricken vessel lay helplessly on the ocean floor. Repeated rescue efforts failed and offers of foreign assistance were initially declined. Putin remained on holiday at a Black Sea resort for the first six days of the disaster, thereby exciting severe domestic criticism. There were two more calamities during August: a bomb explosion in a Moscow underpass, which killed 12 people, and a fire at the Ostankino television tower, which interrupted transmissions throughout the country for some days. This sequence of disasters pointed to the wider and more intractable problem of an ageing and sometimes collapsing infrastructure and seemed to symbolise the country's post-Soviet decline.

A new and somewhat more abrasive position on foreign policy began to emerge during the year, following a worsening of relations with Western countries after the 1999 NATO bombing campaign in Yugoslavia. In January a new national security doctrine was published, which declared that "the West, led by the United States" aimed to dominate world affairs and that Russia had, therefore, lowered the threshold for the use of Russian nuclear weapons, which could now be used "to repel armed aggression if all other means of rendering a crisis situation have been exhausted or turn out to be ineffective". Similarly, a new military doctrine, approved by President Putin in April, allowed Russia to use nuclear weapons if "the very existence of the country" was threatened. A new foreign policy doctrine, published in July, emphasised the connection between external objectives and domestic foreign policy requirements.

Putin was an active participant in international gatherings, making an assured debut at the G8 summit in Okinawa in July. He also attended a summit meeting with the European Union (EU) at the end of October, and an APEC meeting in Brunei in mid-November. Relations with traditional Soviet allies, such as Cuba, India and North Korea, were given more attention than before, and Russia was one of the five members of the CIS customs union (with Belarus, Kazakhstan, Kyrgyzstan and Tajikistan) that concluded a new Eurasian Economic Union in October, modelled on the EU.

ii. BELARUS—UKRAINE—MOLDOVA

Belarus
CAPITAL: Minsk   AREA: 208,000 sq km   POPULATION: 10,100,000
OFFICIAL LANGUAGES: Belarusan & Russian   POLITICAL SYSTEM: presidential
HEAD OF STATE AND GOVERNMENT: President Alyaksandr Lukashenka (since July '94)
RULING PARTY: Belarussian Patriotic Movement (BPR)
PRIME MINISTER: Uladzimir Yarmoshyn (since Feb '00)
MAIN IGO MEMBERSHIPS (NON-UN): CIS, OSCE, PFP, CEI
CURRENCY: Belarusian rouble (end-'00 £1=BR1,818.70, US$1=BR1,217.50)
GNP PER CAPITA: US$2,630, US$6,518 at PPP ('99)

Ukraine
CAPITAL: Kyiv   AREA: 604,000 sq km   POPULATION: 50,222,000
OFFICIAL LANGUAGE: Ukrainian   POLITICAL SYSTEM: democratic republic
HEAD OF STATE AND GOVERNMENT: President Leonid Kuchma (since July '94)
RULING PARTIES: Inter-Regional Reform Bloc (MBR) links ruling circle
PRIME MINISTER: Victor Yushchenko (since Dec '99)
MAIN IGO MEMBERSHIPS (NON-UN): CIS, OSCE, CE, PFP, BSEC, CEI
CURRENCY: hryvna (end-'00 £1=H8.12, US$1=H5.43)
GNP PER CAPITA: US$750, US$3,142 at PPP ('99)

Moldova
CAPITAL: Chisinau (Kishinev)   AREA: 34,000 sq km   POPULATION: 4,500,000
OFFICIAL LANGUAGE: Moldovan   POLITICAL SYSTEM: democratic republic
HEAD OF STATE AND GOVERNMENT: President Petru Lucinschi (since Jan '97)
PRIME MINISTER: Dumitru Braghis (since Dec '99)
MAIN IGO MEMBERSHIPS (NON-UN): CIS, OSCE, CE, PFP, BSEC, CEI
CURRENCY: leu (end-'00 £1=ML18.52, US$1=ML12.40)
GNP PER CAPITA: US$370, US$2,358 at PPP ('99)

THERE were conflicting tendencies in the former Soviet republics during 2000. Whilst Russia, the most influential power in the region, showed signs of economic improvement, there was less evidence of renewal elsewhere in the region. National incomes had already dropped by as much as two-thirds over the decade of post-communist rule; and there was increasing concern that high levels of crime and corruption, together with a loss of research capacity, would make such trends difficult to reverse. There were indications, particularly in Ukraine and Moldova, that ruling elites in the post-Soviet republics were giving increased attention to their relationship with Russia in these difficult circumstances.

IN BELARUS, Russia's closest ally, supporters of the opposition came under continued pressure. A large-scale demonstration took place peacefully in March, although some journalists and foreign observers as well as opposition activists were arrested. President Alyaksandr Lukashenka, who had been out of the country at the time, subsequently dismissed the Interior Minister and described the arrests as "a misunderstanding and a mistake". Former Prime Minister Mikhas Chygir received a three-month prison sentence in May for what he insisted were politically motivated charges. In June two opposition leaders received suspended prison sentences for their part in organising a demonstration the previous October. The Prime Minister was himself dismissed in February and replaced by the mayor of Minsk, Uladzimir Yarmoshyn.

Attempts were made during the year to develop a "public dialogue" with a wide range of political opinion, but with limited success. A particular focus of political activity was the parliamentary election that was due to be held in October, under a revised electoral law. According to the official returns, some 60.6 per cent of the electorate took part (opposition sources reported a figure of 45 per cent), but more than 200 would-be candidates were denied registration on procedural grounds, and media coverage was conspicuously one-sided. Russia's President Putin congratulated his Belarusian counterpart on the "successful holding of free and democratic parliamentary elections", and President Lukashenka himself claimed that the exercise had been "absolutely democratic", even "beautiful and elegant". Western governments were less impressed, and most of them continued to regard the Supreme Council, elected before the controversial referendum of November 1996 (see AR 1996, pp. 132-3), as the country's legitimate parliament.

The government of UKRAINE had changed hands in late December 1999 with the appointment of Viktor Yushchenko as Prime Minister (AR 1999 p. 151). Further appointments followed in December 1999 and January 2000. A continuing impasse in relations with the Ukrainian parliament, the Supreme Council, which in January found itself split over the election of a new Speaker, led President Kuchma to announce a constitutional referendum to take place on April 16. The referendum, he claimed in a television address, would ensure the "systematic and efficient work of the legislature" and the "co-ordinated action and joint accountability of the Supreme Council and the Cabinet of Ministers". Two of the questions that had originally been proposed for the referendum were ruled unconstitutional. The four remaining questions secured the support of over 80 per cent of those who voted; they included increased powers for the President to dissolve parliament, and the establishment of an upper parliamentary chamber that would represent the regions.

There was a further government change at the end of September when Foreign Minister Borys Tarasyuk was dismissed and replaced by Anatolii Zlenko, ambassador to France and himself a former Foreign Minister. President Kuchma explained the move as having been caused by a changing global situation, but it was understood as an implicit rejection of the strongly pro-Western line that had been pursued by Tarasyuk in favour of an approach that placed rather more emphasis on relations with Russia and other post-Soviet republics.

The Ukrainian parliament approved the new government's "Reforms for Prosperity" programme in early April, endorsing its emphasis on privatisation and a balanced budget. One of the new government's more controversial decisions was to announce the closure in December of the Chernobyl nuclear power station, the site of world's worst-ever disaster in 1986. The decision was unpopular with locals, who had found the power station a steady source of employment, but it was welcomed by Western governments, which had provided much of the finance that made it possible.

Kuchma and senior ministers were mired in controversy at the end of the year, after the decapitated and mutilated body of an independent journalist was found in a village south of Kiev in early November. Tape recordings obtained and made public by Kuchma's opponents appeared to leave little doubt that the Ukrainian President, his head of staff and the Internal Affairs Minister had been discussing how to remove the journalist, Heorhiy Gongadze, from public life, if not necessarily to murder him. Kuchma himself continued to insist that the tapes were "a forgery, possibly with the participation of foreign special services" (a remark widely understood as a reference to Russia). But for outside observers the episode was part of a worrying slide towards a pattern of government that was increasingly unscrupulous in the face of economic difficulties that it had shown little ability to resolve.

In MOLDOVA the government had changed hands in December 1999 with the appointment of Dumitru Braghis as Prime Minister (AR 1999, p. 151). There were far-reaching changes in the constitution in July when President Petru Lucinschi was obliged to approve a law that transformed Moldova into a parliamentary republic, with a president who would in future be elected by parliament rather than a popular vote. Lucinschi himself, in a non-binding referendum in May 1999, had been able to claim popular support for his alternative proposal to transform the republic into a presidential republic. By the end of the year, however, the Moldovan parliament had not been able to generate a two-thirds majority in favour of a single nomination to the presidential post that would fall vacant in January 2001, and the Constitutional Court ruled that Lucinschi had the "right and duty" to dissolve the parliament in such circumstances.

Identified as "Europe's poorest country" by *The Economist* in July, the Moldovan economy fell further behind after extreme frosts in late November. Moves were meanwhile being made to privatise the country's wine and tobacco industries in order to secure international financial assistance.

iii. ARMENIA—GEORGIA—AZERBAIJAN

Armenia
CAPITAL: Yerevan AREA: 30,000 sq km POPULATION: 3,900,000
OFFICIAL LANGUAGE: Armenian POLITICAL SYSTEM: democratic republic
HEAD OF STATE AND GOVERNMENT: President Robert Kocharian (since Feb '98)
RULING PARTIES: Pan-Armenian National Movement heads ruling coalition
PRIME MINISTER: Andranik Markarian (since May '00)
MAIN IGO MEMBERSHIPS (NON-UN): CIS, OSCE, PFP, BSEC, CE
CURRENCY: dram (end-'00 £1=D823.73, US$1=D551.43)
GNP PER CAPITA: US$490, US$2,210 at PPP ('99)

Georgia
CAPITAL: Tbilisi AREA: 70,000 sq km POPULATION: 5,400,000
OFFICIAL LANGUAGE: Georgian POLITICAL SYSTEM: democratic republic
HEAD OF STATE AND GOVERNMENT: President Eduard Shevardnadze (since Oct '92)
RULING PARTIES: Citizens' Union coordinates fluid coalition
MAIN IGO MEMBERSHIPS (NON-UN): CIS, CE, OSCE, PFP, BSEC
CURRENCY: lari (end-'00 £1=L2.93, US$1=L1.96)
GNP PER CAPITA: US$620, US$3,606 at PPP ('99)

Azerbaijan
CAPITAL: Baku AREA: 87,000 sq km POPULATION: 8,200,000
OFFICIAL LANGUAGE: Azeri POLITICAL SYSTEM: democratic republic
HEAD OF STATE AND GOVERNMENT: President Geidar Aliyev (since June '93)
RULING PARTY: New Azerbaijan Party (YAP)
PRIME MINISTER: Artur Rasizade (since July '96)
MAIN IGO MEMBERSHIPS (NON-UN): CIS, OSCE, PFP, BSEC, OIC, ECO, CE
CURRENCY: manat (end-'00 £1=M6,656.37, US$1=M4,456.00)
GNP PER CAPITA: US$550, US$2,322 at PPP ('99)

IN ARMENIA there were two changes in government during the year. In February Aram Sarkisian was appointed Prime Minister, with the key ministers of Defence, National Security, Interior, Justice and Foreign Affairs all retaining their positions. But on May 2 President Robert Kocharian dismissed Sarkisian and the entire Cabinet, and on May 12 the leader of the Republican Party of Armenia, Andranik Markarian, was appointed in his place. Both President and Prime Minister promised to end the infighting that had destabilised Sarkisian's administration. Markarian also promised to continue the economic policies of previous administrations, whilst seeking to carry out constructive reforms and combat corruption.

The new Cabinet was appointed on May 20, and most members of the outgoing administration once again retained their posts. Markarian's programme, announced to parliament in June, called for the doubling of pensions, allowances and salaries of state workers by 2003 and for export growth of 25 per cent. He also announced his intention of doubling GDP over the following 7-8 years whilst preserving macroeconomic stability.

In neighbouring GEORGIA Eduard Shevardnadze was overwhelmingly re-elected President for a further five-year term on April 9, with 79 per cent of the vote, against 17 per cent for his nearest challenger, the Communist leader

Dzhumber Patiashvili. In his campaign Shevardnadze had stressed the need to eradicate corruption, which was widely seen as one of the main factors holding back the republic's economic recovery. In accordance with the constitution, the government of Vazha Lortkipanidze resigned on May 1 following the inauguration of the new President. In his inaugural speech Shevardnadze promised to press forward a campaign against incompetent and corrupt officials, and to pay outstanding wage and pension arrears. Gia Arsenishvili, previously the presidential representative in Kakheti province, was nominated to the premiership on May 5. The new Premier announced that his priorities would be economic reform, combating the shadow economy and creating jobs. His nomination was approved by parliament on May 11.

Parliament also approved Shevardnadze's plans to restructure the government by reducing the number of ministries from 21 to 18. All but four of the outgoing ministers were renominated to their positions; two, however, were rejected by parliament. Arsenishvili signed a protocol on stabilisation measures with the Prime Minister of the separatist region of Abkhazia in July, under the aegis of the United Nations.

In the third Caucasian republic, AZERBAIJAN, there was a parliamentary election on November 5 at which the ruling New Azerbaijan Party (YAP), headed by President Heidar Aliev, was overwhelmingly successful. According to the official returns, the YAP won 62.5 per cent of the party-list vote. The other parties that exceeded the 6 per cent threshold were the Azerbaijani Popular Front with 10.8 per cent, the Communist Party of Azerbaijan with 6.7 per cent, and the Civic Solidarity Party with 6.3 per cent. International observers declared that the election had fallen below acceptable standards, although it represented an improvement on the polls which had taken place in 1995 and 1998. The problems they identified included the rejection of about half of all would-be candidates in single-seat constituencies, and other "serious irregularities". Opposition parties called for the election to be annulled in these circumstances, and began a campaign of public demonstrations; but by the end of the year there was no indication that their campaign would be successful.

IV THE AMERICAS AND THE CARIBBEAN

1. UNITED STATES OF AMERICA

CAPITAL: Washington, DC   AREA: 9,364,000 sq km   POPULATION: 277,600,000
OFFICIAL LANGUAGE: English   POLITICAL SYSTEM: democratic federal republic
HEAD OF STATE AND GOVERNMENT: President Bill Clinton, Democrat, (since Jan '93)
PRESIDENT ELECT: George W. Bush, Republican, (from Jan '01)
RULING PARTIES: Congress is controlled by the Republicans
MAIN IGO MEMBERSHIPS (NON-UN): NATO, OSCE, OECD, G-8, OAS, NAFTA, APEC, AC, CP, PC, ANZUS
CURRENCY: dollar (end-'00 £1=US$1.49)
GNP PER CAPITA: US$30,600, US$30,600 at PPP ('99)

IN a presidential election year the news is always dominated by the race for the White House but this year turned out to be exceptional. Both leading candidates, Vice President Al Gore (52) for the Democrats and Texas Governor George W. Bush (54) for the Republicans, had to fight closely contested primaries to ensure their selection. From the outset it was clear that the public found it difficult to choose between Gore, perceived as a rather wooden, policy "wonk", tainted by association with the Clinton administration, and Bush who was seen as inarticulate, intellectually lightweight and lacking in experience. As a consequence, the election campaign seesawed between the two, with neither able to establish a decisive lead.. The election itself produced probably the most controversial result since 1876. Although Gore polled a majority of the popular vote (50.2 million compared with Bush's 49.8 million), contested votes in Florida delayed a final decision. Only after a series of legal challenges was it finally determined that Bush had carried the state and, in so doing, had won sufficient votes in the electoral college to become president. This was the first time such a result had occurred since 1886, and it raised questions about the electoral process itself, both in the way that votes were recorded and the manner in which they were then translated into electoral college votes.

Away from politics, the United States experienced its fair share of bad weather during the year. On February 14 the most destructive tornadoes to hit Georgia in 50 years killed at least 22 people in and around the town of Camilla. Storms also damaged property and caused injuries in Arkansas, Mississippi, Tennessee, and Florida. In May a controlled fire set by the National Park Service blew out of control near Los Alamos, New Mexico, forcing the evacuation of 25,000 people. Several buildings at the Los Alamos National Laboratory, the nuclear research establishment famous for its association with the Manhattan project, were destroyed. A heatwave affected various southern states in July and at least 12 deaths were attributed to heat in Texas. Several western states faced their worst summer fires since the 1950s, and the government mobilised three army battalions to assist the massive firefighting effort in August.

On December 17 storms with gusts of wind up to 200 mph tore through several southern states. At least 12 people were killed and hundreds were left homeless after tornadoes hit parts of Alabama in and around the city of Tuscaloosa. Nine people died in earlier storms in Arkansas and many areas were disrupted by breakdowns in power supplies. Bad weather later in December brought heavy snowfalls and ice storms to parts of Texas, Arkansas, Oklahoma, and Louisiana. One man, Thomas Truett, had a miraculous escape after being found alive despite having been buried in his snow-covered car for 16 days in a remote forest in Oregon. Once he had recovered Truett faced charges of having deserted from the US air force.

In April a Marine Corps Osprey aircraft crashed in Arizona as a result of pilot error, killing all 19 passengers. Nineteen people were also killed on May 21 when a Jetstream aircraft crashed near Scranton International airport, Pennsylvania, following engine failure. In July the National Transportation Safety Board reported that the crash of the aircraft flown by John F. Kennedy Jr. in which he, his wife, and sister-in-law had died (see AR 1999, p. 155) was due to pilot error. In a report published in August the Board concluded that the crash of TWA flight 800 in July 1996 was due to an explosion in the fuel tank caused by an electrical short-circuit (see AR 1996, p. 138-39).

Attention was briefly diverted from the weather and politics in February when 22.8 million viewers watched "Who Wants to Marry a Multi-Millionaire" on Fox television. Fifty women competed to be chosen by Rick Rockwell, a Californian property developer, to be his bride. The winner was Darva Conger. In addition to a husband, she won a two-week honeymoon in the Caribbean, a car and a $35,000 ring. When it transpired that Rockwell was not as wealthy as he claimed and had a history of violence the marriage was quickly annulled.

ELECTIONS. The election process began with the various contests to determine the respective party candidates, starting with the Iowa caucus on January 24. The outcome confirmed that George W. Bush and Al Gore were the leading candidates for the the Republican and Democratic parties respectively. Governor Bush had a clear victory over Steve Forbes and Alan Keyes, but his principal rival, Senator John McCain had not campaigned in the state. Vice President Gore established a clear lead over his challenger, Senator Bill Bradley, even though the latter had spent more on advertising and had campaigned vigorously in the state.

The race for the Republican nomination became more competitive on February 1 when McCain beat Bush by 49 per cent of the vote to 31 per cent in the New Hampshire primary, a much wider margin than anticipated. However, Bush was the clear winner in Delaware, by 51 to 25 per cent, and by 53 to 42 per cent in the crucial vote in South Carolina on February 19. Forbes withdrew from the race after the Delaware result in which he secured only 20 per cent of the vote.

The contestants within each party resorted more and more to negative personal attacks rather than debating policy. After victories in Michigan and Arizona on February 22, and gaining support from Democratic or independent voters in "open" primaries, McCain claimed that he was building a "new Republican majority". On February 28 he referred to members of the anti-Catholic religious right, such as Pat Robertson and Jerry Falwell, as "agents of intolerance" and "corrupting influences on religion and politics". He also described Bush, who had earlier visited Bob Jones University, the fundamentalist college in South Carolina, as a "Robertson Republican". Nonetheless, Bush won in the contests in North Dakota, Virginia and Washington on February 29.

There was some bitterness too in the Democratic contest as Gore was compared to Richard Nixon and criticised over the campaign finance scandal of 1996 (see AR 1997, p. 151-2) by his challenger Bill Bradley. The Vice President defeated Bradley in New Hampshire but only by a margin of 4 per cent. In Delaware he won by 57 per cent to 40 per cent, but neither man had campaigned in the state.

On February 11 Jesse Ventura, the former wrestler who became the Reform Party's leading elected official as governor of Minnesota in 1998, announced he was leaving the party, which he described as "hopelessly dysfunctional". Ventura indicated that he would lead an Independent Party. It appeared likely that the conservative former Republican, Pat Buchanan, would become the Reform Party's presidential nominee. Meanwhile, on February 21 the veteran consumer rights campaigner, Ralph Nader, announced that he intended to seek the presidential nomination of the Green Party.

On February 6 Hillary Clinton finally declared her long-anticipated candidacy for a Senate seat representing New York and so became the first First Lady ever to run for political office. On February 11 Rudolph Giuliani, the combative Republican mayor of New York City, confirmed that he would run against her. However in April Giuliani announced that he would have to reassess his position following a diagnosis that he was suffering from prostate cancer. On May 3 he admitted to having an affair with Judith Nathan, and on May 19 he withdrew from the Senate campaign on personal and health grounds. The Republican Long Island Representative Rick Lazio indicated that he would stand against Clinton. The main plank of his campaign was that he was not Hillary Clinton.

The primary elections continued with 16 Democratic and 13 Republican primaries in the "Super Tuesday" contests on March 7. Al Gore won every contest, including Bill Bradley's home state of Missouri, and on March 9 Bradley announced his withdrawal from the campaign. In his speech Bradley suggested that the issues upon which he had campaigned—gun control, healthcare reform, and campaign finance reform—had not been defeated. Whilst he promised Gore his "full support", his statement fell short of a total endorsement for the Vice President. Victories in the remaining 13 primaries in March ensured that Gore had secured some 300 more delegates than the 2,170 required to be sure of his party's nomination.

Despite victories in Connecticut, Massachusetts, Rhode Island, and Vermont, McCain announced on March 9 that he was suspending his campaign. He had failed to attract the support of Roman Catholics in states such as New York, and in open contests, such as Georgia, Bush had secured more support from independent voters. Bush's nine victories gave him a substantial overall lead in the number of delegates to the Republican Party convention. However, McCain did not formally endorse his opponent until May 9, and for a while it was believed that he might attempt to use his bloc of delegates at the convention to extract concessions from the Bush camp. He ruled out any possibility of running as Bush's vice-presidential candidate. Victories in the further eight primaries in March, however, ensured that Bush already had more delegates than the 1,034 needed to secure the nomination. With the nominations a foregone conclusion, the remaining primaries in April and May only served to confirm the victories of Bush and Gore.

Throughout May Bush sought to clarify his policies for the electorate. In a speech to the National Press Club on May 23 he suggested that he would take "a new approach" to the issue of nuclear weapons and would consider unilateral cuts in the number of the US warheads. He called for the development of a more comprehensive missile defence system than that proposed by the Clinton administration. In other speeches he proposed reforms of the social security system to enable individuals to invest a proportion of their payroll taxes in personal savings accounts based on the stock market. He also suggested tax allowances to offset the cost of long-term medical care.

Opinion polls during May showed that Bush had recovered from the set-backs of the primary campaign and had re-established a clear lead over Gore. Gore's campaign appeared to be damaged by his support of the administration's attempts to normalise trade relations with China and by his difficulty in distancing himself from attempts to return Elian Gonzalez to his father (see below).

In June Gore attempted to boost his campaign's performance with a number of policy statements and by replacing his campaign chairman. Campaigning in Cincinnati on June 15, Gore outlined a programme which doubled his original proposal of $250 billion in tax relief over 10 years to help middle-income families send their children to college. He later unveiled a voluntary retirement savings plan related to the stock market not unlike that suggested by Bush, but said the difference was that his would be separate from social security. On June 21 he said that he would raise tax thresholds to exempt more small farms and businesses from estate taxes. Gore's team attempted to deflect criticism of the Clinton-Gore administration in the light of petrol price rises by highlighting Bush's past links with the oil industry and the backing that he and the Republicans received from oil companies.

The Gore team continued to struggle in the face of fresh controversy surrounding the campaign finance scandal of 1996. Following the revelation by Republican Senator Arlen Specter that Justice Department officials were pushing for the appointment of an Independent Counsel to investigate Gore's role, Attorney General Janet Reno announced on June 23 that she would not be rushed into such a decision.

A further set-back to the Gore campaign came with the nomination of Ralph Nader as the Green Party's candidate during the party convention on June 24-25. It was believed that Nader could attract some liberal Democratic votes away from Gore. On the other hand, Gore's campaign was strengthened on July 13 when his former rival Bill Bradley formally endorsed his bid for the nomination.

On July 25 Bush named 59-year-old Dick Cheney as his vice-presidential running mate. Cheney had previously served as Secretary of Defence under Bush's father, President George Bush between 1989 and 1993. He had also been the chief executive of the Halliburton company, the largest oilfield services company in the world. His appointment added experience to the Bush team, particularly in foreign affairs and defence policy, areas in which the Republican contender was seen as weak.

The Bush-Cheney team was officially endorsed without dispute at the Republican national convention in Philadelphia on July 31-August 3. The convention was carefully stage-managed to reinforce Bush's image as a compassionate conservative appealing to all races. This message was expressed most forcibly by the African American former chair of the Joint Chiefs of Staff, Colin Powell, in his speech on July 31 urging delegates to "reach out to minority communities". In his acceptance speech on August 3, estimated to have been watched by a television audience of over 25 million, Bush repeated his opposition to abortion and his campaign promises to cut taxes, reform social security and Medicare, oppose new gun control measures, and build an anti-missile defence system. He promised to extend prosperity to "every forgotten corner of the country", and to "change the tone of Washington". The result of the convention was a surge in Bush's lead over Gore in the opinion polls to margins of between 11 and 19 per cent.

However, Gore recovered some of this lost ground with his nomination on August 7 of the Connecticut Senator Joseph Lieberman (58) as his vice-presidential running mate. The selection was significant not only because Lieberman was the first Jewish vice-presidential candidate, but also because he had been openly critical of President Clinton during the Lewinsky affair. Speaking before an audience of religious ministers in a televised programme on August 10, Clinton himself said that Gore "didn't fail in his ministry because I did", and that "no fair minded person should blame him for any mistake that I made". The President apologised yet again for the scandal but said that he believed that the majority of Americans had forgiven him.

The Gore-Lieberman ticket was formally endorsed at the Democratic national convention in Los Angeles, on August 14-17. The convention, again watched by huge television audiences, heard Clinton's valedictory address, in which he stressed the strength of the US economy and urged people to protect it by electing Gore.

In his acceptance speech on August 17 Gore distinguished between his and Bush's proposals to cut taxes and reform social security by arguing that his favoured working people whilst Bush's would benefit the wealthy and privileged. Distancing himself from the Clinton administration, he declared "I stand here tonight as my own man and I want you to know me for who I truly am". He caught many people by surprise when he gave his wife a long and passionate kiss rather than the perfunctory public embrace which was customary on such occasions. His performance overall gave his campaign a significant new "bounce" as he took a narrow lead in the opinion polls.

On August 12 the Reform Party convention, meeting in Los Angeles, nominated Pat Buchanan as its presidential candidate. He promised to "defend America's history, heritage, and heroes against the visigoths and vandals of multiculturalism". Some disaffected members of the party, alienated by Buchanan's conservatism, nominated alternative candidates.

Following his success at the Democratic convention and buoyed by his lead in the opinion polls, Gore revealed further policy details in September, including proposals to use government funding to cut the cost of prescription drugs, and attacked drug manufacturers for "price gouging". On September 6 he announced a detailed economic plan in which he promised to reduce poverty levels, eliminate the publicly-held federal debt, provide tax cuts for middle-income families, eliminate gender-based pay differentials, and increase home ownership and college attendance. Whilst such proposals seemed to strengthen the Vice President's lead, doubts about his tendency to embellish facts (or, as his opponents claimed, to tell outright lies) resurfaced when he was criticised for exaggeration in the claims he made in August that the anti-arthritis drugs used by his mother-in-law cost more than drugs prescribed for his dog.

Bush also suffered some set-backs in the form of criticism of Dick Cheney's relationship with oil interests, and for stock options negotiated in a retirement package which raised a possible conflict of interest if he were elected. Even more damaging was the remark Bush made to Cheney at a rally in Illinois on September 4 when, believing the microphones were switched off, he described a *New York Times* reporter as a "major league asshole". There was also criticism of a televised advert attacking the Gore prescription plan in which the word RATS appeared for a fraction of a second, suggesting the use of subliminal methods. Bush's subsequent inability to pronounce the word "subliminal" did not help his campaign.

There was also considerable national interest in the contest between Hillary Clinton and Rick Lazio in New York. Clinton suffered some setbacks during her campaign but remained ahead in the polls. Her relationship with the Jewish community was threatened once more (see AR 1999, p. 161) when a book published in July claimed she had once referred to an aide as a "Jew bastard". Mrs Clinton denied the accusation and consolidated her lead in a series of televised debates. In the first of these, on September 13, Lazio appeared too aggressive when he brandished papers pledging not to accept unregulated financial contributions from single issue groups in her face, demanding her signature. In the second debate, the following month, Hillary Clinton responded to a question about why she had remained with her husband despite his infidelities by saying that she had made choices which were right for her, based on "my religious faith" and "my strong sense of family".

The first of three televised presidential debates between Gore and Governor Bush took place on October 3 at the University of Massachusetts, Boston. In the course of the debate the differences on issues such as the role of government, taxation, and abortion rights were clearly defined. Although Gore was believed by 56 per cent of viewers in one opinion poll to have out-performed Bush, he alienated many viewers with his exaggerated off-camera sighs and exclamations in response to some of Bush's remarks. Bush apparently won support by not making any gaffes and by being more articulate than his public image often suggested.

Gore's political opponents accused him of making several "misstatements" during the debate, and pointed to his habit of embellishing facts. In the course of the debate, amongst other things, he denied having questioned Bush's qualifications to be President, though he had done so; claimed to have travelled to Texas with the head of the Federal Emergency Management Agency in 1996, which he had not; and claimed a special role for himself in initiating the special mission in Kosovo that had been instigated by other officials in Europe, Russia and the USA. The Democratic camp replied that such minor errors of fact did not alter the substantive points which the Vice President had made in the debates.

The only debate between the vice-presidential candidates took place in Danville, Kentucky and was televised nationally on October 5. Cheney and Lieberman discussed their parties' differences, particularly over taxation, in a civil and good-humoured manner.

The second presidential debate on October 11 focused primarily on foreign policy. Whilst Gore defended an interventionist policy in which US troops could be used overseas in peacekeeping or "nation building" roles, Bush advocated a more limited role in which American forces would only intervene to protect clear US interests. Bush said that he "would like to" withdraw US troops from the Balkans and that "Europeans should be taking over the peacekeeping role". Although neither candidate emerged ahead, it was widely felt that Gore, accused of being too aggressive in the first meeting, was too passive in the second.

The final debate, in the form of a "town hall meeting" in which uncommitted voters could question the candidates, was held in St. Louis on October 17. In a generally more lively performance, Gore reiterated his campaign promises to fight vested interests, which he claimed Bush represented. Bush in return described Gore as "a big spender". However, neither candidate emerged from the debates with a clear lead. Opinion polls throughout the year suggested that the candidates were running neck and neck much of the time, despite some seesawing which saw the lead change eight times between January and November. Following the Democratic primary in August, Gore pulled ahead and at the start of October was leading Bush by 51 per cent to 40 per cent. Many believed that his campaign had finally taken off. However, by the start of November it appeared that Bush was again well ahead with a lead of 51 per cent to 39 per cent. A Gallup poll on the eve of the election, however, put Bush only narrowly ahead by 47 per cent to 45 per cent.

Revelations at the start of November that Bush had been convicted for drunk driving in 1976 and had omitted to declare this when called to serve on a jury in a similar case in 1996 only momentarily slowed the Republican campaign. The candidate repeated his earlier admission of a wild youth but reiterated that such behaviour was in the past and that he had given up alcohol. Meanwhile President Clinton, who had been kept deliberately in the background, finally appeared on the campaign trail in support of the Vice President, albeit to mainly black audiences in a few states. Despite these developments, observers still felt the outcome of the election was too close to call.

Predictions of a close result proved fully justified. After a campaign that had lasted more than 18 months and cost in the region of $3 billion, the presidential election ended in chaos and confusion following the vote on November 7. In one of the closest races in recent times, with a turnout of 53 per cent (some 100 million voters), Al Gore had a majority of about 250,000, with 49 per cent of the vote compared to Bush's 48 per cent. However, the outcome was determined by the electoral college vote on a state-by-state basis and large states where the contest was known to be close, such as Pennsylvania, Michigan and Florida, would be crucial. Early in the evening various television stations announced that, on the basis of their exit polls, Gore had won these crucial states and it was predicted that he would be the clear victor. As the evening progressed, however, the media retracted these predictions and declared the race as too close to call. It became clear that the Green Party candidate, Ralph Nader, had obtained about 3 per cent of the vote, crucially depriving Gore of majorities in some key states with large electoral college votes. With Gore having obtained 267 electoral college votes and Bush 246, Florida's 25 votes became crucial to determining the outcome within the 538-member electoral college. In the early hours of the morning the presidency appeared to be Bush's when it emerged he had a tiny majority of the vote in Florida. It would be the first time since 1888, and only the third time in history, that a candidate had won an overall majority in the electoral college despite his opponent having achieved an overall majority of the popular vote.

During the early hours of November 8 Gore telephoned his opponent to concede, only to retract this shortly afterwards when a recount was automatically called in Florida because of the close margin of Bush's victory—1,200 votes. It was estimated that the recount of the six million votes would be completed by 5pm on November 9.

In the course of the recount it emerged that there were possible irregularities in the Florida election. The most serious charges concerned a precinct in Palm Beach where unusual ballots had been designed, apparently to help the elderly to read them. The larger ballot, known as the butterfly ballot, was spread over two pages with a central column to record votes. As a consequence of this design it was alleged that some voters had mistakenly punched a hole against the name of Pat Buchanan when they had intended to vote for Gore. Some of these had then tried to correct the error by punching out a second hole against Gore's name, thereby invalidating their ballot. A total of 19,000 ballots were declared spoiled, and the number of votes for Buchanan in that precinct (3,400) was three times higher than in neighbouring wards. There were claims too that some voters, mainly African American or Hispanic, had been turned away from polling stations. The black civil rights leader, Rev. Jesse Jackson said that there was "a bad smell" about the election.

With various legal challenges being launched against accepting the original count, Florida's several thousand postal votes, most of which had still to arrive, also became an issue. They would not be counted before Friday November 17. The result of the initial mechanical recount gave Bush a majority of just 327 but because it was believed that the computers had wrongly read 17,000 votes as no votes, the Gore camp insisted on a further hand recount of those disputed ballots. The Bush camp indicated that they would seek an injunction to halt the hand recount. They also suggested that they might call for recounts in Wisconsin, Iowa, and New Mexico, where Gore had won by narrow majorities.

The Bush campaign was heartened on November 13 when the Florida secretary of state, Katherine Harris, herself a renowned Republican, ordered all recounts to be completed by 8pm the next day. Following Democratic protests that such a task was impossible, the Florida Supreme Court ruled on November 16 that there was "no legal impediment to recounts continuing". With 65 of the 67 counties and the overseas postal ballots counted by November 18, Bush was still ahead by 960 votes. The Florida Supreme Court upheld the Gore camp's insistence that manual recounts be used to check disputed computer punch cards on November 21. However, the court ruled that such counts must be completed by November 26. During this process a whole new vocabulary entered popular parlance with references to "chads" (the punched out portion of a computer card), "dimpled chads" (not punched out but marked), and "hanging chads" (only partially punched out).

On November 22 officials in Miami-Dade County declared that they would suspend the recount as they could not meet the Court's deadline. The Gore camp believed votes in that county could make a significant difference to the outcome of the contest and signalled that they would go to court to force the recount to continue. The Bush camp received a setback of a different nature when it was announced that Dick Cheney had been admitted to hospital with chest pains. Cheney, who had suffered from numerous heart problems since his first heart attack at the age of 37, underwent minor surgery and was soon released from hospital.

Katherine Harris on November 26 refused requests to extend the 5pm deadline and declared the official outcome of the Florida election to be a victory for Bush by a margin of 537 votes. Gore launched a series of further legal challenges in the Florida courts in order to have the recount completed and to have a number of disallowed votes counted. The Bush team meanwhile launched an action through the federal Supreme Court to have all hand recounts disallowed.

The federal Supreme Court on December 4 ruled that the decision to extend the recount of ballots had been wrong, but asked the Florida Supreme court to re-examine the reasoning behind its decision in order to determine whether the decision was based on Florida state or federal law. In the meantime it restored Bush's 930 vote majority. Local Florida courts subsequently rejected calls for recounts and demands by Democratic Party activists to have incorrectly completed absentee ballots invalidated.

On December 9 the federal Supreme Court ruled by a margin of five votes to four to stop manual recounts across the sate of Florida (as had been ordered by the state's Supreme Court on December 8). The final legal intervention came at 10pm on December 12 when the Supreme Court ruled (once again by five votes to four) to refer the matter back to the state Supreme Court, a decision which effectively ended the legal process by removing any hope that a recount could be concluded before the December 12 deadline for certification of the state's electoral college representatives. The Court divided on political lines: the majority consisting of Chief Justice William Rehnquist, Justices Sandra Day O'Connor, Antonin Scalia, Anthony Kennedy and Clarence Thomas. The dissenting justices were Stephen Breyer, David Souter, Ruth Bader Ginsberg, and John Stevens. Justice Stevens said the only loser in the election was "the nation's confidence in the judge as an impartial guardian of the rule of law".

Following the Supreme Court's decision Al Gore appeared in a televised address early the next morning to announce his concession to Bush, with whom he had spoken earlier. Gore made it clear that he "strongly" disagreed with the court's decision but accepted the finality of the outcome. He declared that "what remains of partisan rancour must now be put aside", and offered to meet Bush as soon as possible to "start to heal the divisions of the campaign". Bush spoke later and indicated that he was "thankful for America and thankful that we are able to resolve our electoral differences in a peaceful way". He promised to work to "unite and inspire the American citizens" and said that he had not been elected "to serve one party, but to serve one nation". He promised to work to serve all interests and to win the respect of all, regardless of their political affiliations. On December 18 the electoral college met and confirmed Bush's victory by 271 to 267 votes despite calls from some people for Republican electors to reflect the popular vote and switch their votes to Gore.

The Democrats secured a number of victories in the congressional and gubernatorial elections. In New York Hillary Clinton emerged a comfortable winner with 55 per cent of the vote to Lazio's 43 per cent, becoming the first wife of a President elected to the Senate. In her victory speech she thanked her family for their support, and promised to "reach across party lines to bring progress for all of New York's families". In the light of Gore's poor campaign performance many people saw Hillary Clinton as a potential candidate for the presidency in 2004.

Amongst the other Senate victories was that in New Jersey where the multi-millionaire Democratic businessman Jon Corzine won a Senate seat after spending $60 million of his own money; in Delaware the Democratic governor, Tom Carper, defeated the incumbent Republican Senator and chair of the Senate finance committee, William Roth; in Florida Bill Nelson defeated Bill McCollum, one of President Clinton's prosecutors; and in Minnesota Mark Dayton defeated the incumbent, Rod Grams. Republicans won in Virginia where Governor George Allen defeated the sitting candidate, Chuck Robb, and John Ensign won in the contest for the vacant seat for Nevada. In Missouri Democratic Governor Mel Carnahan was elected to the Senate three weeks after he had died in a plane crash. His death had occurred too late for the ballot to be changed, and it seemed likely that his wife would take his place. The final contest in Washington state—which after a recount gave Democrat Maria Cantwell victory over the Republican incumbent Slade Gorton—divided the Senate evenly 50-50 between the two parties. The Republicans held on to their majority in the House of Representatives, winning 221 seats to 212, with two independents.

Gubernatorial elections were also held in 11 states on November 7, seven of which were held by Democratic incumbents. The Democrats successfully defended all seven and gained one governorship from the Republicans in West Virginia. The Democratic victory meant that the new distribution of governor-

IV THE AMERICAS AND THE CARIBBEAN

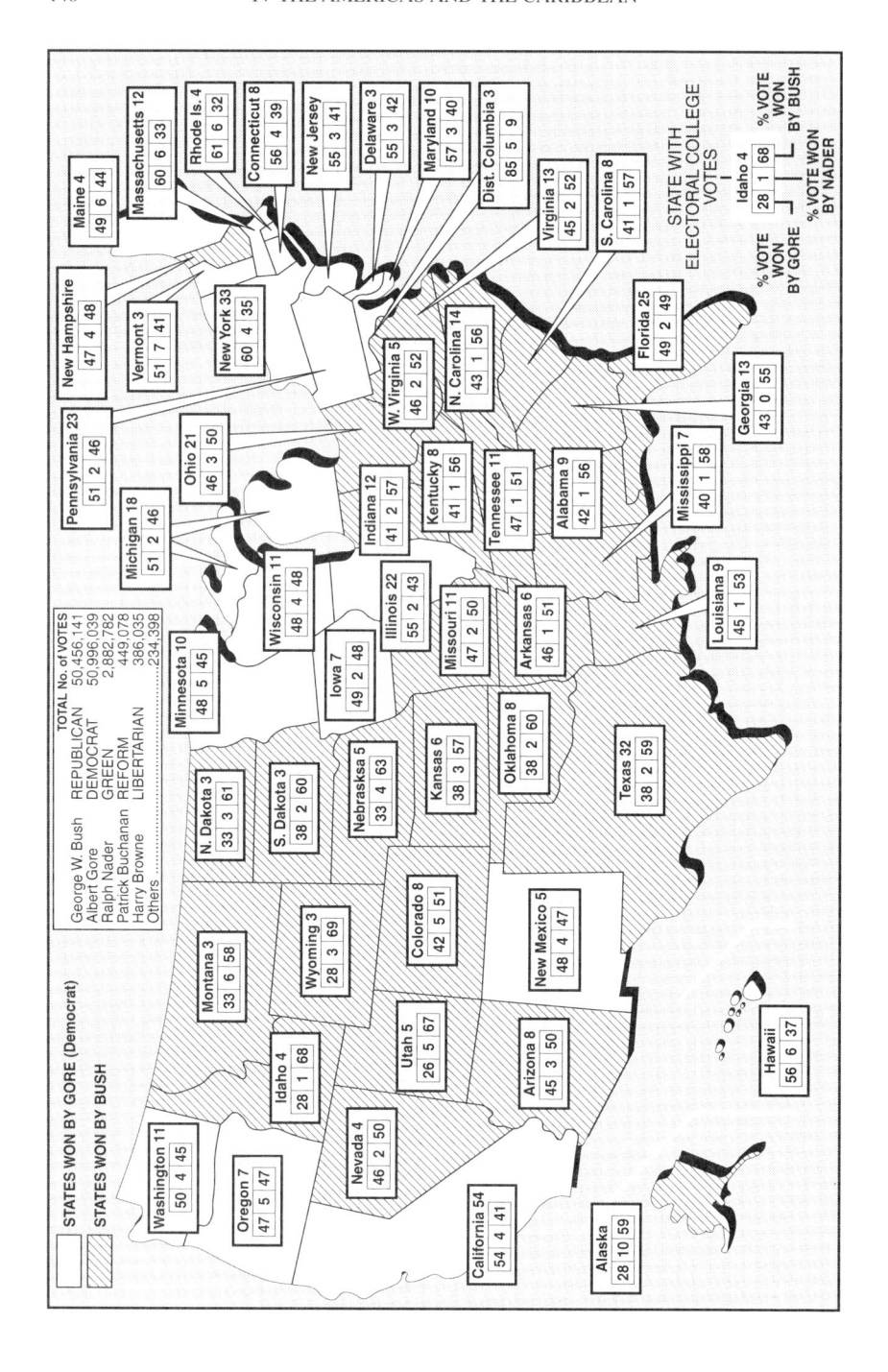

STATES WON BY GORE (Democrat)
STATES WON BY BUSH

STATE WITH ELECTORAL COLLEGE VOTES

Idaho 4 | 28 | 1 | 68

% VOTE WON BY GORE | % VOTE WON BY NADER | % VOTE WON BY BUSH

	TOTAL No. of VOTES
George W. Bush REPUBLICAN	50,456,141
Albert Gore DEMOCRAT	50,996,039
Ralph Nader GREEN	2,882,782
Patrick Buchanan REFORM	449,078
Harry Browne LIBERTARIAN	386,035
Others	234,398

Maine 4 — 49 | 6 | 44
Massachusetts 12 — 61 | 6 | 32
Rhode Is. 4 — 60 | 6 | 33
Connecticut 8 — 56 | 4 | 39
New Jersey 15 — 55 | 3 | 41
Delaware 3 — 55 | 3 | 42
Maryland 10 — 57 | 3 | 40
Dist. Columbia 3 — 85 | 5 | 9
Virginia 13 — 45 | 2 | 52
S. Carolina 8 — 41 | 1 | 57
New Hampshire 4 — 47 | 4 | 48
Vermont 3 — 51 | 7 | 41
New York 33 — 60 | 4 | 35
Florida 25 — 49 | 2 | 49
W. Virginia 5 — 46 | 2 | 52
N. Carolina 14 — 43 | 1 | 56
Georgia 13 — 43 | 0 | 55
Pennsylvania 23 — 51 | 2 | 46
Ohio 21 — 46 | 3 | 50
Michigan 18 — 51 | 2 | 46
Indiana 12 — 41 | 2 | 57
Kentucky 8 — 41 | 1 | 56
Tennessee 11 — 47 | 1 | 51
Alabama 9 — 42 | 1 | 56
Mississippi 7 — 40 | 1 | 58
Wisconsin 11 — 48 | 4 | 48
Illinois 22 — 55 | 2 | 43
Missouri 11 — 47 | 2 | 50
Arkansas 6 — 46 | 1 | 51
Louisiana 9 — 45 | 1 | 53
Minnesota 10 — 48 | 5 | 45
Iowa 7 — 49 | 2 | 48
N. Dakota 3 — 33 | 3 | 61
S. Dakota 3 — 38 | 2 | 60
Nebraska 5 — 33 | 4 | 63
Kansas 6 — 38 | 3 | 57
Oklahoma 8 — 38 | 2 | 60
Texas 32 — 38 | 2 | 59
Montana 3 — 33 | 6 | 58
Wyoming 3 — 28 | 3 | 69
Colorado 8 — 42 | 5 | 51
New Mexico 5 — 48 | 4 | 47
Idaho 4 — 28 | 1 | 68
Utah 5 — 26 | 5 | 67
Arizona 8 — 45 | 3 | 50
Hawaii 4 — 56 | 6 | 37
Washington 11 — 50 | 4 | 45
Oregon 7 — 47 | 5 | 47
Nevada 4 — 46 | 2 | 50
California 54 — 54 | 4 | 41
Alaska 3 — 28 | 10 | 59

IV.1. UNITED STATES OF AMERICA 149

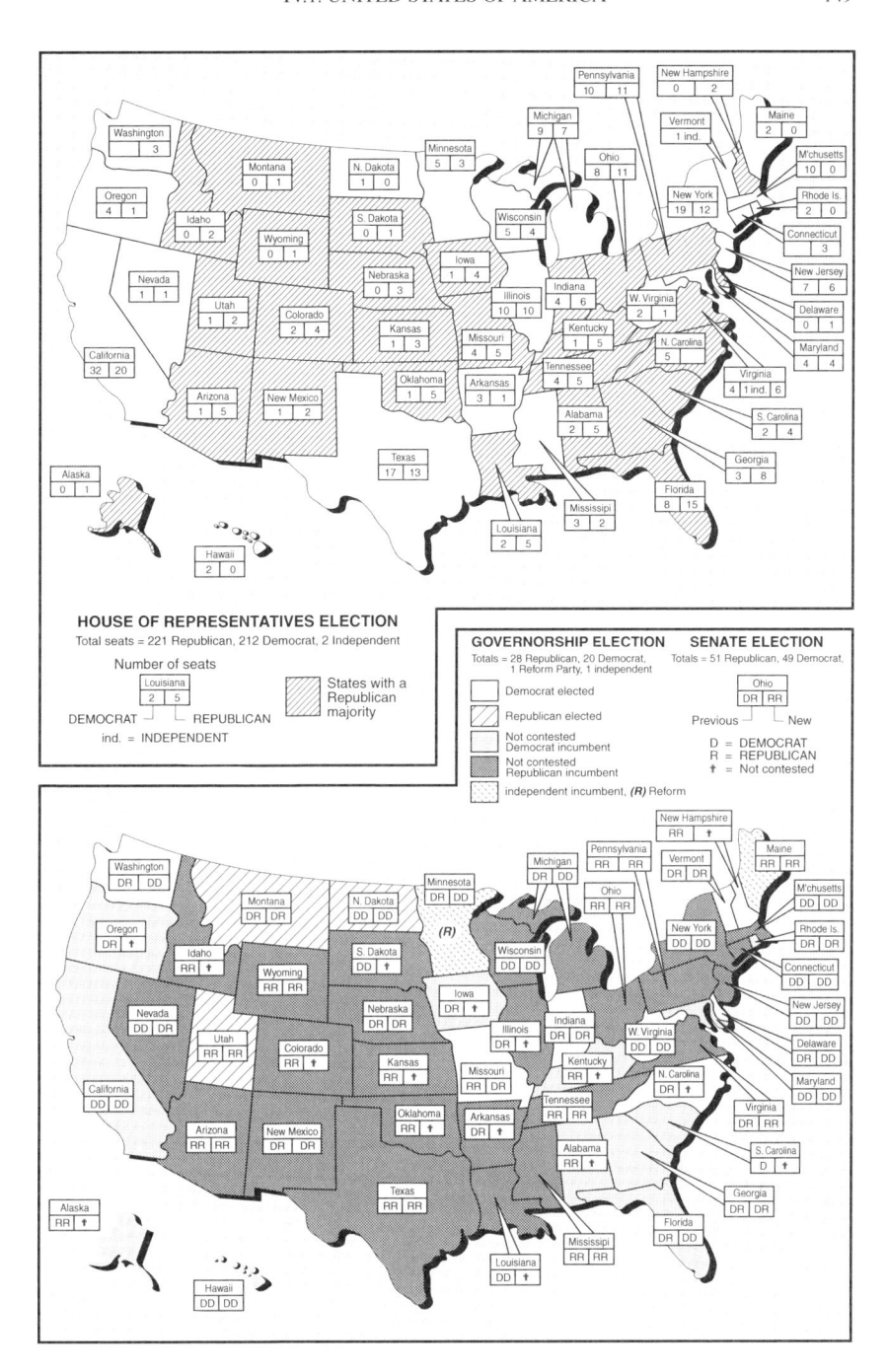

HOUSE OF REPRESENTATIVES ELECTION
Total seats = 221 Republican, 212 Democrat, 2 Independent

Number of seats

Louisiana
2	5

DEMOCRAT — REPUBLICAN
ind. = INDEPENDENT

States with a Republican majority (hatched)

State results (Democrat | Republican):
- Washington: 3 | —
- Oregon: 4 | 1
- California: 32 | 20
- Nevada: 1 | 1
- Idaho: 0 | 2
- Montana: 0 | 1
- Wyoming: 0 | 1
- Utah: 1 | 2
- Arizona: 1 | 5
- Alaska: 0 | 1
- Hawaii: 2 | 0
- N. Dakota: 1 | 0
- S. Dakota: 0 | 1
- Nebraska: 0 | 3
- Colorado: 2 | 4
- New Mexico: 1 | 2
- Minnesota: 5 | 3
- Iowa: 1 | 4
- Kansas: 1 | 3
- Oklahoma: 1 | 5
- Texas: 17 | 13
- Wisconsin: 5 | 4
- Illinois: 10 | 10
- Missouri: 4 | 5
- Arkansas: 3 | 1
- Louisiana: 2 | 5
- Michigan: 9 | 7
- Indiana: 4 | 6
- Kentucky: 1 | 5
- Tennessee: 4 | 5
- Alabama: 2 | 5
- Mississippi: 3 | 2
- Ohio: 8 | 11
- W. Virginia: 2 | 1
- N. Carolina: 5 | —
- S. Carolina: 2 | 4
- Georgia: 3 | 8
- Florida: 8 | 15
- Pennsylvania: 10 | 11
- New York: 19 | 12
- Vermont: 1 ind.
- New Hampshire: 0 | 2
- Maine: 2 | 0
- M'chusetts: 10 | 0
- Rhode Is.: 2 | 0
- Connecticut: 3 | —
- New Jersey: 7 | 6
- Delaware: 0 | 1
- Maryland: 4 | 4
- Virginia: 4 | 1 ind. | 6

GOVERNORSHIP ELECTION
Totals = 28 Republican, 20 Democrat, 1 Reform Party, 1 independent

- Democrat elected
- Republican elected
- Not contested Democrat incumbent
- Not contested Republican incumbent
- independent incumbent, (R) Reform

SENATE ELECTION
Totals = 51 Republican, 49 Democrat

Ohio
DR	RR

Previous — New

D = DEMOCRAT
R = REPUBLICAN
† = Not contested

State Governorship | Senate (Previous | New):
- Washington: DR | DD
- Oregon: DR | †
- California: DD | DD
- Nevada: DD | DR
- Idaho: RR | †
- Montana: DR | DR
- Wyoming: RR | RR
- Utah: RR | RR
- Colorado: RR | †
- Arizona: RR | RR
- New Mexico: DR | DR
- Alaska: RR | †
- Hawaii: DD | DD
- N. Dakota: DD | DD
- S. Dakota: DD | †
- Nebraska: DR | DR
- Kansas: RR | †
- Oklahoma: RR | †
- Texas: RR | RR
- Minnesota: DR | DD (R)
- Iowa: DR | †
- Missouri: RR | DR
- Arkansas: DR | †
- Louisiana: DD | †
- Wisconsin: DD | DD
- Illinois: DR | †
- Indiana: DR | DR
- Kentucky: RR | †
- Tennessee: RR | RR
- Alabama: RR | †
- Mississippi: RR | RR
- Michigan: RR | RR
- Ohio: RR | RR
- W. Virginia: DD | DD
- N. Carolina: DR | †
- S. Carolina: D | †
- Georgia: DR | DR
- Florida: DR | DD
- Pennsylvania: RR | RR
- New York: DD | DD
- Vermont: DR | DR
- New Hampshire: RR | †
- Maine: RR | RR
- M'chusetts: DD | DD
- Rhode Is.: DR | DR
- Connecticut: DD | DD
- New Jersey: DD | DD
- Delaware: DR | DD
- Maryland: DD | DD
- Virginia: DR | DR

ships was 19 for the Democrats and 29 for the Republicans. The number of independent governors remained unchanged at two.

Once his victory was secure Bush began filling the nearly 7,000 federal government appointments, beginning with members of his Cabinet. His first appointment on December 16 was that of Colin Powell as Secretary of State, the first African American to hold the post. Bush described General Powell, as "an American hero, an American example and a great American story". On December 17 Bush named Condoleezza Rice as the first black national security adviser and judge Alberto Gonzales as White House counsel. These were widely regarded as symbolic appointments to win over black and Hispanic support in the face of continued challenges to the legitimacy of the election result from groups led by Jesse Jackson.

Bush appeased the Republican right when he nominated the right-wing former Missouri Senator, John Ashcroft, for the post of Attorney General on December 22. He also named the moderate governor of New Jersey, Christine Todd Whitman, to head the Environmental Protection agency. At the end of the month Bush selected the welfare-reforming governor of Wisconsin, Tommy Thompson, as Secretary of Health and Human Services, and the former attorney general of Colorado, Gale Norton, as Secretary of the Interior. Another black man, Rod Paige, was named Education Secretary.

OTHER DOMESTIC ISSUES. In his seventh and final State of the Union address delivered before Congress on January 27, President Clinton emphasised the economic achievements of his administration in presiding over the longest period of uninterrupted economic growth in the nation's history. Politically he claimed that he had "restored the vital centre" and had "replaced outdated ideologies with a new vision". He went on to propose measures to repay the national debt by 2013, tax cuts of $250 billion over 10 years for middle- and low-income groups, spending of $110 billion over 10 years to increase access to healthcare insurance, and a system of licensing for handgun purchases.

Capital punishment became an issue during the year. On January 31 Republican Governor George Ryan of Illinois declared a moratorium on capital punishment because of national evidence of widespread miscarriages of justice involving defendants unable to pay for adequate legal representation. Twelve people had been executed in Illinois since the death penalty was restored in 1977. The conservative Pat Buchanan called for a nationwide moratorium on capital punishment on the same grounds during a conference on religion and the death penalty on April 7. In May the New Hampshire state legislature became the first since 1976 to vote to abolish capital punishment, but the Democratic governor, Jeanne Shaheen, vetoed the move.

A study, released on June 12, of state death penalty sentences between 1973 and 1995 found that more than two-thirds had been overturned on appeal. The report, by a Columbia University law professor, concluded that the use of the death penalty was "fraught with error". On June 14 Gore said that he would be willing to consider a review of the administration of the death penalty, but he re-affirmed his support for the principle of capital punishment and ruled out a moratorium on the use of the federal death penalty. On July 7 it was announced that President Clinton had postponed the first federal execution since 1963 because of procedural, racial, and geographical concerns over the fairness of capital punishment. Capital punishment also came to the fore during the election campaign as several executions were carried out in Texas including that of a woman, a man of low IQ, and another who had only been 17 when he had committed murder. In all, more than 150 executions occurred in Texas whilst Bush was governor.

There was considerable public protest in New York city on February 26 following the acquittal of four white New York Police Department officers by a jury in Albany, New York. The four policemen had been charged with second-degree murder following the shooting of Amadou Diallo, an unarmed black man, in February 1999 (see AR 1999, p. 163). Criticism of the NYPD continued following the fatal shooting of two unarmed black men in separate incidents on March 2 and March 16. Criticism of the police, and of Mayor Giuliani's support for aggressive policing, increased after three white officers were convicted by a federal jury on March 6 for offences relating to an assault on Abner Louima, a Haitian immigrant, in August 1997 (see AR 1997, p. 159). On June 27 former police officer Charles Schwarz was sentenced to 15 years in prison for his part in the assault and cover-up. Two other officers were sentenced to five years each for conspiring to obstruct justice.

Matters related to the Whitewater and other linked investigations continued to surface during the year. On March 16 Robert Ray, the Whitewater Special Prosecutor, reported that there was no "credible" evidence that Hillary Clinton or senior officials had been involved in the circumstances under which the White House had secured FBI files on leading public figures in 1996. The report concluded that the files had been mistakenly acquired by junior White House workers. However, on March 19 Ray confirmed, in a statement which many people considered politically motivated, that his office was considering whether to indict President Clinton on charges relating to the Lewinsky and Jones cases once he had left office. Democrats were particularly angry when it was reported on August 17 that Ray had convened a grand jury to consider the case, although it transpired that a judge had inadvertently given this information to a journalist.

On May 22 the Arkansas Supreme Court's Committee on Professional Conduct recommended that President Clinton be disbarred from practising law in the state because of his "serious misconduct" in giving false testimony concerning his relationship with Monica Lewinsky during the Paula Jones case in 1998 (see AR 1998, pp. 159-62,164-5). On May 24 it was announced that charges against Linda Tripp for wiretapping were to be dropped by the state of Maryland. It was Tripp who had revealed details of telephone conversations with Lewinsky, including her affair with Clinton. In a third development, on May 26 a panel of the US Court of Appeals in the District of Columbia declined to overrule an earlier finding that Clinton had committed an infringement of the Privacy Act in making public letters sent to him by Kathleen Willey (see AR 1998, pp. 161-2).

On September 12 Ray announced that there was "insufficient evidence to prove to a jury beyond reasonable doubt" that President Clinton or Hillary Clinton had committed any criminal acts in the various land deals which became known as the Whitewater affair (see AR 1996, p. 144). The timing of this announcement, and its failure to exonerate the Clintons totally, led to criticism that it was intended to influence the election campaigns.

There was considerable public and media interest over the affair of Elian Gonzalez, the six-year-old Cuban boy who became the centre of a legal struggle for his custody. Elian had been rescued with two other survivors off the coast of Florida in November when the ship in which he and his mother were fleeing Cuba sank (see AR 1999, p. 189). As Elian's mother had drowned, the boy's relatives in Miami argued that he should remain in the USA. However, on January 5 the US Immigration and Naturalisation Service (INS) ruled that the boy's father, Juan Miguel Gonzalez, had exclusive legal authority over his son, and the child should be returned to him in Cuba. Elian's relatives, supported by anti-Castro groups amongst the Cuban exile community, opposed the decision and began legal action in the local and federal courts to prevent Elian's return to his homeland.

Juan Miguel Gonzalez arrived in the USA on April 6 to claim custody of Elian, but the boy's Florida-based relatives, a number of whom had criminal convictions, refused to give him up. Their attempted manipulation of pubic opinion over the issue reached new heights on April 13 when they released a videotape, which was shown on major television networks, in which Elian said that he did not want to return to Cuba. Amid fears that the boy was being psychologically damaged by the dispute and was being used as a pawn by anti-Castro interests, the US authorities moved to end the impasse. Acting on the authority of Attorney General Janet Reno, armed agents of the INS seized Elian in the early hours of the morning of April 22 and reunited him with his father. The action was followed by angry demonstrations in Miami and further legal action. However, on June 28 the US Supreme Court dismissed requests for an asylum hearing, thus leaving Elian free to return to Cuba with his father.

The USA once again experienced a number of shooting incidents throughout the year. A seven-year old shot and killed six-year old Kayla Rowland at Buell Elementary School in Mount Morris township, Michigan, on February 29. On March 9 five-year-old Sacorya Johnson was shot dead by a seven-year-old using an air rifle in Monroeville, Alabama. On March 17 the largest manufacturer of handguns in the US, Smith & Wesson, announced that it would fit child resistant safety locks to its products.

On March 1 a black man who had indicated that he wanted "to kill all white people" shot one person dead and wounded four others in a Pittsburgh suburb. On March 22 another gunman wounded four people in an attack on a church in Pasadena, Texas, before killing himself. The day before the ceremonies to mark the anniversary of the Columbine school shootings (see AR 1999, pp.164-65) Richard Glassel shot and killed two people in a retirement home near Peoria, Arizona, following a dispute about his hedge. On April 24 Antoine Jones, a 16-year-old, shot and wounded seven children aged between 11 and 16 in Washington National Zoo during a gang dispute. On April 28 a white unemployed lawyer, Richard Baumhammers, killed five people during an apparently racially-motivated attack in the suburbs of Pittsburgh. Five people were also killed in a robbery in a burger bar in Queen's, New York city, on May 24.

On December 26 Michael McDermott, a 42-year-old employee at Edgewater Technology in Wakefield near Boston, shot and killed seven of his colleagues at work. McDermott was disarmed and arrested by police, and charged with seven counts of murder the following day. He pleaded not guilty. It appeared that he was angered by his employer's threat to withhold unpaid taxes from his wages. Seven people were also killed in another shooting incident involving four masked men in Philadelphia on December 29 in what appeared to be a drug-related crime. The killers were not apprehended.

The issue of guns was raised during the presidential campaign as Gore criticised Bush for failing to support gun controls in Texas. Bush did say that, if elected, he would approve legislation requiring trigger locks on all new guns and would renew the ban on certain types of assault weapons. Demonstrations were held in 60 cities on May 19 as part of the "Million Mom March" to protest against the failure to enact more stringent federal arms control legislation. Meanwhile the National Rifle Association reported a sudden growth in membership which reached a record 3.6 million that month.

Following his earlier ruling on April 3 in the US District Court in Washington DC that the software giant Microsoft corporation had repeatedly acted in violation of the Sherman Anti-trust Act (see AR 1999, p. 168), Judge Thomas Penfield Jackson on June 7 ordered the company to submit plans for its breakup. Accepting the Justice Department's claims against the company, Jackson said that "Microsoft has proved untrustworthy in the past". However, he gave the corporation until October to submit proposals and to allow time for an appeal, and on June 20 he referred the appeal by Microsoft directly to the US Supreme Court.

Cases against the tobacco industry continued through out the year. On March 27 a San Francisco grand jury awarded a terminally ill smoker US$20 million in punitive damages against the Philip Morris and R.J.Reynolds cigarette manufacturers. The same jury had earlier awarded $1.7 million in compensatory damages on the grounds that the companies had "acted with malice" in misleading the public about the dangers of smoking. On April 7 another jury in Miami awarded $6.9 million in damages against the same companies for two plaintiffs who had developed cancer as a result of smoking. A second Miami jury in July awarded $145 billion in punitive damages to an estimated 500,000 ill Florida smokers. Observers doubted whether the full amount, the largest ever punitive award, would ever be paid given the time likely to be spent in appeals and further hearings.

A report by Senator John Danforth revealed on July 21 that the fatal fire which ended the Waco siege in Texas in April 1993 (see AR, 1993 p. 159) was due to the actions of the Branch Davidian sect inhabitants and not the attacking federal agents. The report also indicated that sect members probably shot 20 of their own number, including five children, prior to the compound's destruction.

On September 11 it was reported that Wen Ho Lee, the physicist at the Los Alamos nuclear laboratory implicated in charges of possible espionage with

China had agreed to plead guilty to a charge of improperly handling classified information in return for a sentence of 275 days, a period which he had already spent in detention. Both the judge who heard the case in Albuquerque, New Mexico, and President Clinton expressed misgiving about the handling of the case and the charges themselves. Some commentators suggested that Lee had been singled out because he was an Asian American and that he had been mistreated in prison. He was released on September 13.

In December Timothy McVeigh, the man convicted of the Oklahoma City bombing which killed 168 people in 1995 (see AR 1995, p. 154), asked the Denver court (where he had been convicted) to halt all further appeals against his conviction and to set a date for his execution. The Court granted his request and an execution date was due to be set early in the new year.

THE ECONOMY. On January 4 President Clinton nominated Alan Greenspan for his fourth term as chairman of the Federal Reserve. Greenspan, who had first been appointed by Ronald Reagan in 1987, was widely believed to have contributed to the strong state of the US economy by his handling of monetary policy. Both Vice President Gore and Governor Bush supported his re-nomination.

According to Labor Department figures released in January, core inflation had fallen to 1.9 per cent in 1999, the lowest rate since 1965. Unemployment had remained constant in December 1999 at 4.1 per cent. In January unemployment was recorded as 4 per cent, the lowest figure since 1970, and a 5 per cent increase in labour productivity was reported for the last quarter of 1999. Overall annual productivity rose by more than 2 per cent for the fourth consecutive year.

On January 10 the largest ever take-over occurred when Time Warner, the huge publishing, news, and entertainment corporation, merged with the world's biggest internet provider, America Online. Ted Turner, the major stockholder of Time Warner who was to become vice chairman of AOL Time Warner, approved the $350 billion deal. Steve Case, chairman on AOL, became head of the new company.

On February 7 President Clinton submitted his budget proposal for the fiscal year 2001 (beginning on October 1) to Congress. The $1,840 billion budget projected surpluses over the next 10 years of $2,900 billion, with a surplus of $179 billion for 2000, and $171 billion for 2001. The President proposed tax cuts for those on middle and low incomes, and tax increases on tobacco and corporate interests. Federal health insurance was to be extended to cover five million low-income workers, an additional $300 billion was to be spent on Medicare over 10 years, and spending on education was to be increased to recruit an additional 100,000 teachers. Military spending was to increase and pay for the armed forces was to rise by 3.7 per cent.

Further positive statistics concerning the economy were released in May. Stock market prices as reported on the Nasdaq index were also 40 per cent higher than in June 1999. Fears of possible inflationary pressures led the US Federal Reserve to raise interest rates from 5.5 to 5.75 per cent in February, to 6 per cent in March, and to 6.5 per cent on May 16, the sixth rise since June 1999.

On September 21 a record US trade deficit of $31.89 billion was reported for July. This was attributed to high oil prices and the strength of the Euro. In order to bring prices down President Clinton on September 22 ordered the release of 30 million barrels of crude oil from the country's strategic reserve.

Figures released on September 26 suggested that the percentage of US citizens defined as living in poverty—surviving on less than US$17,000 p.a. for a family of four—had fallen from 12.8 to 11.8 per cent between 1998 and 1999, whilst median real income had grown by 15 per cent between 1984 and 1999.

Some fears that the US economy might be on the brink of a down-turn surfaced towards the year's end with two banks cutting 5,000 jobs in the light of poor trade figures and a fall in spending. Other companies including Eastman Kodak, General Motors, and News Corp announced recruitment freezes. Surveys of consumer confidence indicated the fourth largest monthly decline since such investigations began in 1978.

FOREIGN AFFAIRS. President Clinton was particularly active in the field of foreign affairs during 2000, in what many observers believed was an attempt to leave a lasting positive record of his presidency. He visited several countries, including India on March 19, the first President to visit the country since Jimmy Carter in 1978. The visit marked the improving relations between the two countries and brought trade agreements and a relaxation of the sanctions imposed by the US government after India's nuclear tests in 1998. During the course of his visit Clinton urged India and Pakistan to resume negotiations over the disputed territory of Kashmir. Clinton also visited Bangladesh on March 20, and Pakistan, briefly, on March 25.

President Clinton met President Vladimir Putin of Russia for a summit meeting on June 3-5. An agreement on arms control, setting up a joint early warning centre, and arranging for the disposal of stocks of plutonium was signed, but no agreement was reached on the controversial National Missile Defence system proposed by the USA. In the first ever address by a US President before the Duma, Clinton warned "We are not destined to be adversaries but it is not guaranteed we will be allies".

In a show of support for President Olusegun Obasanjo, President Clinton visited Nigeria on August 26-28, the first such visit since Carter in 1978. He declared that Nigeria was "pivotal to Africa's future", and expressed backing for Nigeria's peacekeeping role in Sierra Leone.

The President also made a brief visit to Colombia on August 30 to support the war against drugs. On August 22 the he had approved a $1.3 billion aid package to Colombia to assist in the anti-drug campaign.

Accompanied by his wife and daughter, Clinton visited Vietnam from November 16-19 in a culmination of the restoration of relations between the two countries. In a speech of reconciliation the President said the American people were now coming to see Vietnam "as a country, not a war". He received the remains of several US servicemen killed during the war. Some 950 US personnel were still recorded as missing in action in the conflict.

Clinton and his family arrived for a two-day visit to the Republic of Ireland and the United Kingdom on December 12. On the first day he received a rapturous, often emotional, welcome in Dublin and in the border town of Dundalk before going on to Belfast. Clinton used the visit to try to revitalise the peace process with which he was so closely associated (see II.1.iv). Speaking in Dundalk on December 12 he urged the audience to "stand up for peace today, tomorrow, and for the rest of your lives". In Belfast on December 13, he said that "those who reject peace should know there is no place for them to hide".

There were a number of other developments in foreign relations: on June 27 the House of Representatives voted to relax sanctions against Cuba by lifting the embargo on food and certain medicines. However, the ban on US tourists going to Cuba remained. Clinton supported the measure but was reluctant to approve it on the grounds that it limited presidential authority to impose future embargoes.

Clinton achieved a considerable foreign policy objective in September when the Senate approved a bill granting permanent normal trading relations to China. The bill, previously passed by the House of Representatives in May despite widespread criticism by human rights groups, ended the annual review process of China's status and put the country on an equal footing with other US trading partners.

Much of President Clinton's foreign policy energy focused on the Middle East peace process. The US government hosted peace negotiations in which Clinton acted as mediator between Israel's Prime Minister Ehud Barak and the Syrian Foreign Minister Faruq al Shara' in West Virginia from January 3-10. The President met Barak in Washington, DC, on April 11 and met Palestinian President Yassir Arafat later in the month to encourage the resumption of the Middle East peace process. He also met President Hafez al-Assad of Syria in Geneva on March 26.

From July 11 to July 19 Clinton hosted what he called a "make or break" summit meeting between Barak and Arafat and even fruitlessly delayed his departure to the G-8 annual summit in Japan until July 20 in the hope that an agreement could be reached. He held further separate meetings with the two leaders whilst at the UN millennium summit in New York on September 6. In his address to the summit he urged both sides to reopen negotiations and take the "hard risks for peace". Secretary of State Madeleine Albright held further meetings with Barak and Arafat in Paris on October 4 prior to the summit meeting attended by Clinton at Sharm el-Shaikh. Both meetings produced commitments to a ceasefire but only after prolonged and heated negotiation. Israeli and Palestinian negotiators met in Washington DC in late December and Clinton met them personally on December 23 as he intensified efforts to reach a settlement. No agreement was forthcoming, however, and on December 28 Clinton ruled out further talks with Israeli and Palestinian leaders "unless both sides accepted the parameters" which he had laid out.

2. CANADA

CAPITAL: Ottawa   AREA: 9,971,000 sq km   POPULATION: 31,200,000
OFFICIAL LANGUAGES: English & French   POLITICAL SYSTEM: federal parliamentary democracy
HEAD OF STATE: Queen Elizabeth II (since Feb '52)
GOVERNOR-GENERAL: Adrienne Clarkson (since Oct '99)
RULING PARTIES: Liberal Party (since Oct '93)
HEAD OF GOVERNMENT: Jean Chrétien, Prime Minister (since Oct '93)
MAIN IGO MEMBERSHIPS (NON-UN): NATO, OECD, OSCE, G-7, OAS, NAFTA, APEC, CP, CWTH, Francophonie
CURRENCY: Canadian dollar (end-'00 £1=C$2.24 US$1=C$1.50)
GNP PER CAPITA: US$19,320, US$23,725 at PPP ('99)

IN a third general election in seven years, held on November 27, Canadians gave a comfortable majority to the Liberal government headed by Prime Minister Jean Chrétien. The party captured 172 of the 301 seats in the federal House of Commons and gained 41 per cent of the country's popular vote. The showing represented a distinct improvement over the party's performance in the 1997 election. Opposition parties continued to be badly fractured, as they had been since the Chrétien Liberals had first won office in 1993. An attempt to unify the right under a new party, the Canadian Alliance, was only marginally successful.

The victory was a personal triumph for the veteran Jean Chrétien, 67, who had been in Parliament almost continuously since 1963. Coming from the industrial town of Shawinigan, Chrétien had based his political career on a strong attachment to a united Canada. He was a cautious politician, preferring pragmatic solutions to bold initiatives. Long years in office had given him an authoritarian style and he had called this election against the wishes of many in his party. The results justified his political acumen. The election was well-timed. The Canadian economy was strong and over the past seven years his government had eliminated a burdensome deficit and produced healthy surpluses. Discontent in Quebec appeared to be waning. Furthermore, an autumn election had the advantage of catching the newly-created political party of the right off-guard.

The year had seen a sustained effort on the part of the Leader of the Opposition, Preston Manning of the Western-based Reform Party, to consolidate the forces of the right. Manning had created the Reform Party a decade earlier to express the sense of alienation felt by the four western provinces at the domination of Canadian affairs by the two largest provinces, Ontario and Quebec. In January 2000 Manning persuaded members of the Reform Party to merge their organisation into a new party, to be called the Canadian Alliance. The leadership of the new party was determined by a direct election amongst its members which saw Manning displaced by Stockwell Day, 49, who had been Treasurer of the Progressive Conservative Party (PCP) government of Alberta. Day had balanced the books of his native province and produced impressive surpluses, which had made Alberta a fiscal leader amongst Canada's 10 provinces. Coming from an evangelical Christian background, Day held conservative views on social questions such as abortion and homosexual rights. He gained a seat in Parliament for British Columbia in a by-election in September, only two months before Chrétien called the general election.

Day was placed on the defensive from the very beginning of the campaign. Chrétien accused the new party of having a hidden agenda which would introduce private medicine into the state medical system. He painted the Canadian Alliance as a party of extremists and Day as a leader without experience in federal politics. Although the Alliance swept the west and held on to its standing as the leading opposition party, increasing its share of seats from 60 to 66, it won only two seats in Ontario and none in Quebec and the Maritime provinces. Nationally, it won 24 per cent of the popular vote and it was clear that it still faced the task of selling conservative policies, somewhat similar to those put forward by the Republican Party in the USA, to the Canadian voter. For the time being Canadians clearly felt more comfortable with the centrist position of the Liberals.

One of Reform Party leader Manning's hopes had been to forge a partnership with the PCP, which had been in power for nine years before Chrétien assumed office. Although a diminished force in national politics, the Conservatives still possessed supporters across the country. The party had been led since 1998 by Joe Clark, a former Prime Minister who had held important Cabinet positions in the PCP administration of Brian Mulroney. When Manning, and later Day, suggested that the two parties of the right merge in an effort to defeat the Liberals Clark rebuffed the approaches. In the November election the PCP lost ground to the Alliance in the West and to the Liberals in Quebec. In 1997 it had won 20 seats, but now it fell to 12, just sufficient to retain its official party status. Clark could take some comfort from winning a seat in Calgary, Alberta, in the heart of Alliance territory, but the future of the party looked insecure.

The most surprising outcome of the voting occurred in Quebec, which had been dominated politically by the Bloc Québecois, a federal party advocating secession for the province. Its support in Quebec fell and its number of seats dropped from 44 to 38, all from French-speaking areas. The Liberal Party made strong gains, winning traditional seats in English-speaking ridings and picking up new seats in French-speaking districts. Its share of the popular vote equalled that gained by the Bloc in the province. Although the provincial administration was still controlled by the separatist Parti Québecois, the federal results showed that a third referendum on secession was unlikely.

Canada's social democratic party, the New Democratic Party (NDP), fared poorly in the national contest. It had won 21 seats in 1997, but its share now it dropped to 13, mostly from the Maritime provinces and the West. It had mounted a strong defence of the national public health system but this sentiment had also been put forward by the other parties. Its advocacy of other measures intended to promote an agenda of social justice had failed to appeal to Canadians at a time of national prosperity.

The Chrétien government, which had dealt cautiously with the Quebec separatist movement since taking office, took a firmer stance in 2000. Drawing on a 1998 Supreme Court of Canada opinion, which affirmed certain principles governing a legitimate procedure for secession, it embodied these conditions in the Clarity Act. This measure provided that the House of Commons should approve any question on independence which might be submitted to the voters of Quebec in a referendum. It also stated that a vote for secession should be supported by a decisive (although unspecified) majority. Only then would the government of Canada be required to enter into negotiations with the province on secession. In two previous referenda on secession, in 1980 and in 1995, the issue had been clouded for voters by the use of the term "sovereignty", combined with the prospect of Quebec's continued association with the rest of Canada. The purpose of the Clarity Act was to remove any such ambiguities from any future question which might be posed to Quebec's voters. The measure was passed in the House of Commons in March, although bitterly opposed by the Bloc Québecois. The act received hearty endorsement across Canada, however, and even in Quebec, especially amongst younger residents, it found favour.

Canadians gave much attention in 2000 to strains in their prized public health system. Established a generation ago and costing C$80 billion a year, the plan was supported by grants from the federal government but administered by the provincial governments. The Canada Health Act laid down principles, such as accessibility and portability, underpinning the plan and the federal government assumed the prime responsibility for upholding the statute.

In 2000 Canadian medicare faced two major challenges. One was the decision of certain provinces, such as Alberta and Quebec, to allow the introduction of private clinics to provide particular services. These services would be paid for partly by the public plan and partly through fees charged to recipients. The central government criticised these moves but did not to act against them. The other challenge was more important in the short run: there was inadequate funding for a system serving an expanding and ageing population. In 1993, when the Liberals came to office, they reduced health grants to the provinces, claiming that the need to bring a budget deficit under control had a higher priority. This retrenchment had gone on steadily to the dismay of the provinces. They argued that if the central government was unwilling to fund healthcare adequately then it should not have the authority to lay down conditions for the operation of the system. With a federal election looming and three years of growing budget surpluses, the Chrétien government took action. A conference was held on September 11 in Ottawa, attended by the Prime Minister and the First Ministers of all the provinces and territories. Chrétien announced that grants for healthcare, education and social programmes would be increased by C$23.4 billion over the next five years.

An unprecedented wave of sympathy spread across Canada with the death of Pierre Elliot Trudeau on September 28 at the age of 80 (see also XVIII). Trudeau had been Prime Minister for 15 years between 1968 and 1984. Intelligent, articulate and sophisticated, he had championed a bilingual federal Canada against the appeal of nationalism in his native province. In 1982 he had repatriated the Canadian constitution from its birthplace in the British Parliament and included in it a Charter of Rights and Freedoms. The thousands of Canadians who mourned his passing had been touched by that vision.

The Canadian economy grew strongly in 2000, recording an increase in GNP of almost 5 per cent, a figure only slightly below the rate achieved in the USA.

Exports to that booming market made up 80 per cent of Canada's sales abroad and featured a range of new products such as telecommunications equipment and computer-related items. High energy costs drove up the consumer price index to 3.2 per cent in November but for the most part inflation remained under control. Employment figures were rosier than in past years, with a jobless rate of 6.8 per cent in December.

Finance Minister Paul Martin delivered two budgets during the year: the annual one on February 28 and a pre-election statement on October 18. Both concentrated on lowering taxes for individuals and corporations. The changes were intended to meet the tax-cutting policies of the opposition Canadian Alliance and to combat the loss of skilled Canadians to the USA, attracted by lower US tax rates. Tax cuts were given to all Canadians, with particular attention to those of low and middle incomes. Tax reductions in the second budget roughly doubled those announced in February, amounting to $100 billion over the next five years. A change that benefited all was the elimination of "bracket creep", the phenomenon under which inflation continually pushed tax-payers into higher categories. For the third year in a row, Martin was able to forecast a budget surplus. For the fiscal year 1999-2000 (ending March 31) the surplus was revised upwards several times, levelling off at $12 billion. For the following year it was estimated that it would reach the same amount.

Canada's Foreign Minister, Lloyd Axworthy, did not stand for re-election in November. Chrétien replaced him with John Manley, who was moved from the post of Minister of Industry. Axworthy had emphasised "human security", or the protection of the individual in the relations between states. His sponsorship of a convention in 1997 banning the use of anti-personnel land mines was a notable example of this emphasis. Canada's two-year occupancy of a non-permanent seat on the United Nations Security Council, 1999-2000, gave it the opportunity to bring the plight of civilians caught in violent conflicts to the Council's attention, although achievements in these areas were limited.

A related topic was also brought before the Security Council by Canada in 2000. This was the trade in "conflict diamonds" which financed rebel movements in such African states as Angola, Sierra Leone and the Democratic Republic of the Congo. Canada's representative to the UN carried out a fact-finding mission to these countries early in the year and brought back a report specifically naming individuals who were engaged in the trade in "blood diamonds". The Security Council imposed sanctions in July against the buying or selling of diamonds unless they were legally certified by their country of origin.

3. LATIN AMERICA

ARGENTINA—BOLIVIA—BRAZIL—CHILE—COLOMBIA—ECUADOR—
PARAGUAY—PERU—URUGUAY—VENEZUELA—CUBA—DOMINICAN REPUBLIC AND
HAITI—CENTRAL AMERICA AND PANAMA—MEXICO

i. ARGENTINA

CAPITAL: Buenos Aires   AREA: 2,780,000 sq km   POPULATION: 37,900,000
OFFICIAL LANGUAGE: Spanish   POLITICAL SYSTEM: federal presidential democracy
HEAD OF STATE AND GOVERNMENT: President Fernando de la Rúa Bruno (since Dec '99)
RULING PARTY: Radical Civic Union-National Solidarity Front (since Dec '99)
MAIN IGO MEMBERSHIPS (NON-UN): OAS, SELA, ALADI, Mercosur
CURRENCY: peso (end-'00 £1=AP1.49, US$1=AP0.998)
GNP PER CAPITA: US$7,600, US$11,324 at PPP ('99)

DURING the course of the year there were grim reminders of Argentina's recent history of military dictatorship. President Fernando de la Rúa announced in January that decisions on the extradition of 48 personnel connected with the 1976-83 military dictatorship, requested by the Spanish judge Baltasar Garzón, would be left to the courts. The latter then rejected all of the requests. However, on March 9 Navy Capt (retd) Alfredo Ignacio Astiz, who had boasted in the magazine *Tres Puntos* of his crimes during the "dirty war", received a three-month suspended sentence for "violating public peace", and in April the President dismissed all of the members of the highest military court, the Consejo Supremo de las Fuerzas Armadas, after they had claimed jurisdiction in all military cases involving theft and the clandestine adoption of children, a crime not covered by the 1978 amnesty. The bodies of 90 victims of the "dirty war", all shot at close range, were found in a mass grave in Lomas de Zamora Cemetery. In May Gen. (retd) Antonio Domingo Bussi, former Governor of Tucumán, was voted morally unfit to sit in the Chamber of Deputies.

The year began in economic crisis and by August unemployment had reached 15.4 per cent of the workforce. With the agreement of the outgoing secretary general of the General Confederation of Labour (CGT), Rodolfo Daer, in February, the Chamber of Deputies passed legislation to introduce greater flexibility in labour relations. The bill was strongly contested by his nominated successor Hugo Moyano, however, and in March a split developed as a faction led by Daer challenged Moyano's appointment. On May 5 the CGT staged a general strike to protest against the law, and although it was finally approved on May 11, the unrest continued.

Plans to attract investment by deregulating both the health sector and telecommunications went ahead in June. Nonetheless, the rapidly growing fiscal deficit inherited from former President Carlos Saúl Menem precluded the government from spending to ease social discontent, and on May 19 new cuts were ordered in public expenditure. The resulting nationwide general strike on June 9 brought much of the country to a standstill. In the new budget published in September the government proposed to reduce the fiscal deficit in 2001 from US$5,300 million to US$4,100 million, with an overall cut in government expenditure of US$700 million. The Alliance in Congress then declared an economic emergency and passed an anti-evasion law and a law to reduce corporate taxes. On November 14, in a televised address, the President announced that the country faced "a veritable catastrophe". Although the IMF agreed to give emergency help estimated at US$12,000 million, it was on the severest conditions, including the abolition of the existing state pension scheme and the freezing of federal transfers to the provinces. On November 23 a 36-hour strike brought the capital and other major cities to a halt.

In March the government launched an investigation into charges of corruption against some 30 members of Menem's Justicialist (PJ) government. Then in August charges were brought against former Defence Minister Antonio Erman González and former Foreign Minister Guido di Tella of having withheld evidence about illegal arms sales to Croatia and Ecuador.

The government scored a political victory in early May, when Aníbal Ibarra of the Alliance decisively defeated Domingo Cavallo of Encounter for the City for the mayoralty of the federal capital. However, the government itself was shaken by scandal when in September it was alleged that ministers had tried to bribe opposition senators to pass the labour legislation which had been approved in May. The President reacted with a significant Cabinet reshuffle on October 5, appointing Christian Colombo to replace Rodolfo Terragno, who had been openly critical of the government's behaviour, as Chief of the Cabinet (Prime Minister). The President's brother, Jorge de la Rúa, was appointed Justice Minister. Nonetheless the bribery scandal led on October 6 to a split in the Alliance, with Vice President Carlos "Chacho" Alvarez resigning in protest at the decision to retain two ministers implicated in the scandal. Under pressure from Alliance members, the departure of the two individuals followed: Alberto Flamarique, Secretary to the Presidency, left immediately, and on October 20 Fernando de Santibañes, resigned as head of the Secretariat for State Intelligence (SIDE).

Abroad, on September 1 the Chilean Senate finally ratified the 1997 mining treaty providing for the joint exploitation of Andean deposits. In October the President paid a state visit to Spain.

ii. BOLIVIA

CAPITAL: La Paz and Sucre   AREA: 1,099,000 sq km   POPULATION: 9,000,000
OFFICIAL LANGUAGES: Spanish, Quechua, Aymará   POLITICAL SYSTEM: presidential democracy
HEAD OF STATE AND GOVERNMENT: President Hugo Banzer Suárez (since Aug. '97)
RULING PARTIES: Democratic Nationalist Action (AND) heads coalition with Civic Solidarity Union (UCS), New Republican Force (NFR) & Movement of the Revolutionary Left (MIR)
MAIN IGO MEMBERSHIPS (NON-UN): OAS, ALADI, SELA, AG, CA, NAM
CURRENCY: boliviano (end-'00 £1=B9.50, US$1=B6.36)
GNP PER CAPITA: US$1,010, US$2,193 at PPP ('99)

AT the start of the year, a one-third increase in water charges in the Department of Cochabamba sparked off a series of violent demonstrations, culminating in two days of rioting in which more than 30 police 100 rioters were injured. The government of President Hugo Bánzer Suárez therefore agreed on February 6 to rescind the decision. However, the New Republican Force (NFR), headed by the mayor of Cochabamba, Manfred Reyes Villa, which had opposed the government's policy on water, was expelled from the ruling coalition.

Early in February the IMF and the World Bank agreed to afford Bolivia relief under the enhanced Heavily Indebted Poor Countries (HIPC) scheme, amounting to some 30 per cent of the debt disbursed at the end of 1998, or some US$1,300 million. After a week of general unrest, on April 8 the government proclaimed a state of emergency, and five people were killed in clashes between police and security forces. A police strike on April 9 was called off within 48 hours when the government conceded a 50 per cent pay rise for lower paid ranks. On April 20 the state of emergency was lifted.

On March 10 the Information Minister, Jorge Landívar, was forced to resign after the US Ambassador, Donna Hrinak, undiplomatically accused him of securing the acquittal of a drugs suspect, Marino Diodato. Diodato was also the husband of President Bánzer's niece and the faux pas aroused anti-American sentiment in leading circles. Landívar was replaced by Ronald McLean Abaroa, a former Foreign Minister. Less than two months later, in a Cabinet reshuffle on April 25, McLean was moved to Finance and Guillermo Fortún of the ADN became Interior Minister; a further reshuffle on October 20 created a new post of Minister of Peasants, Indigenous Peoples and Ethnic Affairs.

In a dramatic accident, Antonio Arguedas Mendieta, who as Interior Minister in 1966-69 had arranged for copies of Maj. Ernesto "Che" Guevara de la Serna's diary to be smuggled to Cuba, and who was stated to be behind a recent bombing campaign by the anti-Communist Commandos against Corruption, Cocaine and Castroism (C-4), was killed in March after a home-made bomb he was carrying exploded.

In September a total of 10 people were killed as the government faced a further wave of protests from peasants and public sector workers. The protests were ended on October 6, following talks which made it plain that the coca eradication programme, costing the country some 6 per cent of GDP, was not negotiable.

During an official visit to Brazil in March, the President signed a new gas supply agreement. Though Bolivia was currently only supplying 88,000 cubic metres of gas a day (cu m/d), the contract for 2000 was 210,000 cu m/d and the target for 2004 was 850,000 cu m/d.

iii. BRAZIL

CAPITAL: Brasília   AREA: 8,547,000 sq km   POPULATION: 173,000,000
OFFICIAL LANGUAGE: Portuguese   POLITICAL SYSTEM: federal presidential democracy
HEAD OF STATE AND GOVERNMENT: President Fernando Henrique Cardoso (since Jan '95)
RULING PARTIES: Brazilian Social Democratic Party (PSDP) heads coalition with Liberal Front Party (PFL), Brazilian Progressive Party (PPB), Popular Socialist Party (PPS) & Brazilian Democratic Movement Party (PMDB)
MAIN IGO MEMBERSHIPS (NON-UN): OAS, ALADI, SELA, Mercosur, AP, CPLP
CURRENCY: real (end-'00 £1=R2.91, US$1=R1.95)
GNP PER CAPITA: US$4,420, US$6,317 at PPP ('99)

THE 500th anniversary of the first official Portuguese landing in Brazil on April 22 1500 was preceded by several days of protests by indigenous and landless groups, in which three people were killed. Disruptions by these groups continued to trouble the government throughout the year. Earlier in April, the courts had overturned the 1997 conviction of Landless Peasant Movement (MST) activist José Rainha Júnior (see AR 1997, p. 170). On May 2 more than 30,000 MST demonstrators occupied land and federal buildings in eight states, but withdrew after failing to reach agreement with the government. In September the movement resumed its campaign of mass occupations of public buildings and private land. When federal troops were sent to defend the President's own estate, Córrego da Ponte, Buritis, the governor of Minas Gerais, former President Itamar Franco, demanded their withdrawal. The demonstrators withdrew on September 26 and soon afterwards the government agreed to make loans at low interest rates to fund crop planting.

There were a few changes to the Cabinet. Elcio Alvares, who had been appointed head of the new unified Defence Ministry in 1999, was dismissed by President Fernando Henrique Cardoso in January. His successor, former Justice Minister Geraldo Magela Quintão, confirmed the sale to a French consortium of a 20 per cent stake in the aircraft manufacturer Embraer, privatised in 1995. The deal was a major source of contention between the government and the airforce. In April José Carlos Dias resigned following a dispute with the anti-narcotics secretariat (Senad) and was replaced as Justice Minister by José Gregori.

On March 15 the Supreme Court dismissed the contention that the government's social security reforms were unconstitutional and the President's proposal to increase the federal minimum wage from R$136 to R$151 a month was ratified by Congress in May. Support in Congress for the President's legislative programme had been consolidated in February by an alliance between his Brazilian Social Democratic Party (PSDB) and the Brazilian Labour Party (PTB), bringing the PTB into the ruling coalition, though only until August.

After one of six people held hostage on a bus in Rio de Janeiro had been killed in a shootout with police, the President announced a national plan to combat rising crime on June 20, including a temporary ban on all sales of firearms, later struck down by the Supreme Court (November 19). A congressional report on organised crime and drug trafficking released on November 30 implicated nearly 200 officials, and more police officers than drug dealers.

July saw presidential embarrassment when it was alleged that funding for construction contracts in São Paulo had been corruptly obtained with the complicity of Eduardo Jorge Caldas Pereira, secretary-general of the presidency (1995-98). In the first round of municipal elections, held on October 16, significant gains were made across the country by the Liberal Front Party (PFL) and the Workers Party (PT), which won 13 municipalities including São Paulo.

The state oil company Petrobrás was fined US$28.4 million following the escape in January of some 1.3 million litres of crude oil into Guanabara Bay, damaging an area of some 50 sq. km. Despite this, on July 16 a further 4 million litres of oil escaped from a burst pipe in a Petrobrás refinery into the River Barigui, threatening the celebrated Iguaçu Falls. In June the government's second round auction of oil licences raised US$262 million, the majority of the licenses going to Petrobrás. In early August a state of emergency was declared after the worst floods for 25 years killed at least 48 people and made more than 100,000 homeless in Alagoas and Pernambuco.

iv. CHILE

CAPITAL: Santiago   AREA: 757,000 sq km   POPULATION: 15,500,000
OFFICIAL LANGUAGE: Spanish   POLITICAL SYSTEM: presidential democracy
HEAD OF STATE AND GOVERNMENT: President Ricardo Lagos Escobar (since March '00)
RULING PARTIES: Concertación coalition composed of Party for Democracy (PPD), Socialist (PS),
   Christian Democratic (PDC), & Social Democratic Radical (PRSD) parties
MAIN IGO MEMBERSHIPS (NON-UN): OAS, ALADI, SELA, APEC, NAM
CURRENCY: Chilean peso (end-'00 £1=Ch857.07, US$1=Ch573.75)
GNP PER CAPITA: US$4,740, US$8,370 at PPP ('99)

IN the second round of voting on January 16 (see AR 1999, p. 180), Ricardo Lagos Escobar of the Socialist Party (PS), running as candidate of the centre-left Concertación alliance, defeated Joaquín Lavín Infante, of the Independent Democratic Union (UDI), part of the right-wing Alliance for Chile. Lagos, who became Chile's first socialist President since the overthrow of Salvador Allende Gossens in 1973 (see AR 1973, p. 96), took 51.31 per cent of the vote to 48.69 per cent for Lavín, and was sworn in as President on March 11. He appointed a Cabinet which reflected his governing coalition with José Miguel Insulza (PS) as Interior Minister; María Soledad Alvear (Christian Democrat—PDC) as Foreign Affairs Minister; and Nicolás Eyzaguirre of the Party for Democracy (PPD) as Finance Minister.

In October it emerged that some 74 senior employees of state enterprises had been given substantial "severance" payments by the outgoing government before being re-employed. Seven resigned and 14 others refunded the payments. In municipal elections on October 29 the ruling Concertación gained over half the votes cast, but the share of the right-wing Alliance for Chile rose from 32.5 per cent in 1996 to 40.1 per cent, and Joaquín Lavín was elected Mayor of Santiago.

Gen. (retd) Augusto Pinochet Ugarte, held under house arrest in the UK pending extradition to Spain, underwent medical tests on January 5. In February the medical report was given, on orders of the UK High Court, to the centre-right Spanish government and was promptly leaked to the press. The report, which asserted that Pinochet was suffering from brain damage and memory loss, apparently as a result of a series of minor strokes in late 1999, formed the basis of the later decision by UK Home Secretary Jack Straw to order the Pinochet's release and immediate return to Santiago (see II.1.i.). On his arrival on March 3, the General was welcomed by the commander-in-chief of the Army, Maj-Gen Ricardo Izurieta, in a formal ceremony organised by the armed forces, and also received an ovation from supporters. Although the outgoing government of Eduardo Frei Rúiz-Tagle (who himself on retirement became, like Pinochet, a senator-for-life with immunity from prosecution) had campaigned for Pinochet's release on health grounds, his Foreign Minister, Juan Gabriel Valdés, called the welcome ceremony a "disgrace" and invited those countries which had opposed his release to bring their cases in the Chilean courts.

Television coverage showed that Pinochet's health had apparently improved markedly during his journey home. Under Chilean law, however, neither physical disability nor mental incapacity would debar the former dictator from standing trial, although he could escape punishment if he proved to be senile, something that his family hotly denied. On March 6 Judge Juan Guzmán Tapia asked the Appeals Court to lift Pinochet's immunity from prosecution and on March 8 the State Defence Council (the public prosecutor) registered for the first time as a party to the cases involving the so-called "caravan of death"—an elite army unit which was alleged to have "disappeared" 72 political prisoners in the weeks following the 1973 military coup. When hearings began on April 16, President elect Lagos called on the armed forces to respect the decision of the courts, which he said he was committed to support. However it still came as a surprise when in August the Supreme Court, by 14 votes to 6, upheld the May decision of the Court of Appeals to lift Pinochet's parliamentary immunity, thereby clearing the way for his prosecution. Following a further appeal from Pinochet's family which was later denied, on September 29 Judge Guzmán announced that the medical tests of Pinochet's fitness to stand trial would be delayed until early 2001. Earlier in April he had also ordered the arrest and prosecution of Gen. (retd) Carlos Forrestier, who had been governor of Tarapacá when 10 political prisoners were arrested in the city of Iquique in 1973. They were never seen again.

Fresh revelations continued to sap Pinochet's credibility. In March the US Justice Department re-opened its investigation into the General's complicity in the murder in 1976 of Orlando Letelier in Washington DC. In April, imprisoned military officers who had previously remained silent, published secret military documents which directly linked the former dictator to an army hit squad which operated in the 1980s. Gen. (retd) Manuel Contreras, former head of Dina (Pinochet's secret police), confirmed that he had received orders directly from the General, thus implicating him in the murder in Buenos Aires in 1974 of Gen. Carlos Prats and his wife. On October 17 former Air Force General Fernando Matthei disclosed that Pinochet did not deserve the credit for returning Chile to civilian rule, as other senior officers had restrained him from ordering a military coup following his defeat in the 1988 plebiscite (see AR 1988, p. 77). Although the armed forces had acceded to a draft agreement, published on June 13, that was designed to protect their anonymity whilst they co-operated in helping to trace a thousand "disappeared", they later retreated from the agreement.

Raúl Rettig, chair of the Truth and Reconciliation Commission (CVR) which in 1991 established that at least 3,146 people were murdered or disappeared during Pinochet's dictatorship, died on April 30, aged 90 (see XVIII).

v. COLOMBIA

CAPITAL: Santa Fe de Bogotá   AREA: 1,139,000 sq km   POPULATION: 42,000,000
OFFICIAL LANGUAGE: Spanish   POLITICAL SYSTEM: presidential democracy
HEAD OF STATE AND GOVERNMENT: President Andrés Pastrana Arango (since Aug '98)
RULING PARTIES: Social Conservative Party (PSC) heads Great Alliance for Change
MAIN IGO MEMBERSHIPS (NON-UN): OAS, ALADI, SELA, AG, CA, ACS, NAM
CURRENCY: Colombian peso (end-'00 £1=Col3,340.14, US$1=Col2,236.00)
GNP PER CAPITA: US$2,250, US$5,709 at PPP ('99)

COLOMBIA passed the year suffering from an acute combination of civil unrest, lawlessness and poverty. Negotiations continued between the government of President Andrés Pastrana Arango and the Revolutionary Armed Forces of Colombia (FARC) on the structure of future peace talks and, following the proposal on January 11 by US President Bill Clinton of a two-year aid programme, and US Secretary of State Madeleine Albright's brief visit four days later to Cartagena de Indias, agreement was reached at the end of January.

Meanwhile on January 17 National Liberation Army (ELN) guerrillas inflicted severe damage in attacks on the national grid in Antioquía. Millions of people later switched off their lights in a protest for peace, but in retaliation for the ELN disturbances right-wing paramilitaries killed some 50 people near Ovejas on the night of February 19-20, the night before talks with the FARC resumed in the demilitarised zone. Links between military intelligence, paramilitaries and assassins hired to threaten and even kill human rights workers were censured in a report by Human Rights Watch on February 24. However, four leaders of non-government organisations were convicted in March of channelling Amnesty International and EU aid to the ELN.

The peace talks themselves proceeded fitfully. Bombings in small towns near Bogotá in March were seen as evidence of a new strategy by the FARC command of putting pressure on urban areas rather than the countryside, the guerillas' traditional stronghold. Following death threats from the FARC, Francisco Santos Castillo, the new editor of *El Tiempo*, left the country. On April 13 the FARC agreed to discuss a ceasefire, but when it proposed to levy a so-called "peace tax", the chief government negotiator resigned and was replaced by Camilo Gómez, one of the President's inner circle. On April 30 the FARC made a second attempt to relaunch itself as a political party, the Bolivarian Movement for a New Colombia.

Meanwhile on April 20 the government agreed to create a second demilitarised zone in parts of Bolívar and Antioquia for talks with the ELN. Unlike the FARC zone this would be subject to restrictions including international verification. The proposal was held up by local protests but finally endorsed by the paramilitary United Self Defence Forces of Colombia (AUC) on May 28, by which time peace talks with the FARC had again been suspended. Talks with the ELN took place in Geneva on July 24-25, shortly after a group of European countries had agreed to support the US-sponsored "Plan Colombia" to combat drugs and violence. On September 14 President Pastrana announced plans to increase the size of the armed forces to 42,000 by the end of 2000 and to 52,000 by the end of 2001.

Talks resumed with the FARC on September 22 but they stalled in October when 58 soldiers died in fighting in northern Antioquia, and were suspended by the FARC on November 18 in protest at the US-backed "Plan Colombia". In a tragic conclusion to the year, on December 29 Diego Turbay, president of the Congressional Peace Commission, and six of his colleagues died in an ambush in the FARC demilitarised zone.

Armando Pomárico, president of the Chamber of Representatives and a key supporter of the President, was forced to resign on March 25. He was accused of having failed to exercise sufficient control over the allocation in December 1999 of contracts for building and maintenance work, but denied corruption, and on March 31 the President reintroduced anti-corruption proposals previously voted down by Congress. In May further allegations of corruption led to the resignation and replacement of four ministers, including the Interior Minister, Néstor Humberto Martínez, who was succeeded by former Vice President Humberto de la Calle Lombana, serving as Ambassador in London. On July 11 another reshuffle brought seven new Liberal (PL) ministers into the Social Conservative Party (PSC) Cabinet. These included Juan Manuel Santos Calderón at Finance and Augusto Ramírez Ocampo at Economic Development. Tax reform proposals submitted in September, however, were criticised as inadequate and the government's investment plan was ruled unconstitutional by the Constitutional Court. In elections held on October 29 amid considerable violence, the ruling PSC lost heavily. The opposition PL won 15 governorships and smaller parties 10, but the PSC won none. The PL also won control of 13 departmental capitals compared with the PSC's two.

Reports that Venezuelan forces had crossed the frontier on October 13 and burnt houses and coca plantations near Tres Bocas, Norte de Santander, were denied by the Venezuelan government. However, when on November 25 Colombia recalled its Ambassador to Venezuela, it was because FARC representatives had been invited to a conference in Caracas.

vi. ECUADOR

CAPITAL: Quito   AREA: 284,000 sq km   POPULATION: 13,000,000
OFFICIAL LANGUAGE: Spanish   POLITICAL SYSTEM: presidential democracy
HEAD OF STATE AND GOVERNMENT: President Gustavo Noboa Bejarano (since Jan '00)
RULING PARTIES: Popular Democracy (DP) heads coalition
MAIN IGO MEMBERSHIPS (NON-UN): OAS, ALADI, SELA, AG, CA, NAM
CURRENCY: US dollar (adopted Sept '00, at approx 25,000 sucre to the dollar)
GNP PER CAPITA: US$1,310, US$2,605 at PPP ('99)

AT the very start of the year Ecuador's government was overthrown in a populist coup. On January 18 the Confederation of Indian Movements (Conaie) mobilised the largest demonstration to date against the government of President Jamil Mahuad Witt. His neo-liberal economic policies included a highly controversial project to adopt the US dollar as the country's currency, which, when announced on January 9, had instantly led to price rises of between 50 and 300 per cent. With the connivance of elements in the armed forces, led by Cols. Lucio Gutiérrez, Jorge Brito and Fausto Cobos, on January 21 the demonstrators seized the Congress and Supreme Court buildings. Mahuad abandoned the Palacio Carondelet and took refuge in a nearby air force base and a "junta of national salvation" was proclaimed, consisting of Conaie leader Antonio Vargas, former president of the Supreme Court Carlos Solórzano, and Col Gutiérrez, who soon ceded his role as chair to the commander of the armed forces and acting Defence Minister Gen. Carlos Mendoza.

This new order was, however, short-lived. Following strong representations from the USA and other American states, on January 26 Congress declared that Mahuad had abandoned his post and Vice President Gustavo Noboa Bejarano was duly sworn in as President, thus preserving constitutional conventions. Warrants were issued against the military officers involved in the coup, whose motive seemed to have been anger at the ending in 1999 of the futile 30-year border dispute with Peru and the consequent reduction in military spending. On January 24 Gen Telmo Sandoval was appointed as new armed forces commander in place of Mendoza. Pedro Pinto Rubianes was appointed Vice President, Jorge Guzmán Ortega Minister of Finance and Public Credit, and Heinz Moeller Minister of Foreign Affairs.

The Interior Minister, Franciso Huerta Montalvo, resigned on April 25 after his colleagues failed to ratify his agreement with Conaie on measures to help indigenous peoples. Congress on May 31 approved an amnesty for both military officers and civilians who had taken part in the January coup. But Gen Sandoval and other senior colleagues had by then also been forced to resign, having tried to conceal the fact that the intended beneficiary of the coup was to have been Gen. (retd) Francisco Moncayo Gallegos, who in regional and local elections held on May 21 ran as candidate of the Democratic Left (ID) and emerged as the new mayor of Quito.

The new government, to general surprise, went ahead with "dollarisation", which was approved by Congress on February 29, as well as adopting measures to liberalise the labour market and open the country's oil, electricity and telecommunications industries to foreign investment. The IMF objected that the proposed legislation could concentrate all banking in government hands. Widespread and escalating protests were not quelled by the decision on March 29 to raise the national minimum wage from US$53 to US$73 per month. On April 19 the Fund approved a 12-month standby credit for SDR336.73 million (worth US$303 million) to finance dollarisation, but the Finance Minister resigned on May 23 because of disagreements with the President over the size and scope of the structural adjustment package he had subsequently proposed, and in June Luis Yturralde was appointed in his place. The privatisation bill became law by default in August after the majority Popular Democracy (DP) lost its hold on Congress as a result of defections. The President's Social Christian Party (PSC), however, failed to elect the new Speaker, a post which went to Hugo Quevedo who had just been expelled from the PSC, and on September 4 Conaie announced an indefinite general strike against privatisation and dollarisation. Though plans for the privatisation of Petroecuador were suspended, the dollar finally replaced the sucre as the national currency on September 8.

Fears that insurgency might spread from Colombia were confirmed when on October 12 the Colombian FARC kidnapped 10 foreign nationals (connected to oil companies) near Pompeya, two of whom later escaped. At the same time fighting in Putumayo, in Colombia, sent a wave of refugees into Ecuador and prompted serious international concern.

vii. PARAGUAY

CAPITAL: Asunción   AREA: 407,000 sq km   POPULATION: 5,800,000
OFFICIAL LANGUAGE: Spanish   POLITICAL SYSTEM: presidential democracy
HEAD OF STATE AND GOVERNMENT: President Luís González Macchi (since March '99)
RULING PARTIES: Colorado Party (ANR-PC) heads coalition with National Encounter (EN)
MAIN IGO MEMBERSHIPS (NON-UN): OAS, ALADI, SELA, Mercosur
CURRENCY: guarani (end-'00 £1=G5,295.52, US$1=G3,545.00)
GNP PER CAPITA: US$1,580, US$4,193 at PPP ('99)

THE start of the year was characterised by political conflict and unrest. On February 6 the Authentic Radical Liberal Party (PRLA) voted to pull out of the national unity government of President Luis González Macchi. In consequence Foreign Minister José Félix Fernández Estigarribia resigned and was replaced on February 15 by Juan Estaban Aguirre Martínez of the Colorado Party (ANR-PC). Moves to impeach the comptroller-general, Daniel Fretes Ventre, on corruption charges were voted down by the Chamber of Deputies, but on March 24, the anniversary of the fall of President Raúl Cubas Grau (AR 1999, p. 184), there were mass demonstrations in favour of "better government".

Three people were wounded on May 18 in an attempted coup by supporters within the First Cavalry Division of Gen (retd) Lino César Oviedo Silva, who had fled from Argentina (where he had been given political asylum in March 1999—see AR 1999, p. 184) on December 9, 1999. The coup failed, as, under pressure from Brazil and the USA, the armed forces command resumed control. Oviedo himself was arrested in Brazil on June 11.

The government announced a package of measures, initially valued at $US20 million, for aid, land colonisation and infrastructural improvements in support of the country's 250,000 peasant farmers. Protests continued against the planned privatisation of telephones, drinking water and the railway, but a 48-hour general strike on June 22-23, backed by three of the four national labour federations, crumbled without achieving any results. On November 14 Congress approved the privatisation programme.

Elections for Vice President had been scheduled for August 13, and the President had promised that the post would go to a member of the opposition, but the Colorados clearly intended to contest this. On April 9 the ANR-PC chose as its candidate Félix Argaña, son of the former controversial Vice President Luis María Argaña Ferrero, for whose assassination in March 1999 (AR 1999, p. 183) Luis Alberto Rojas was later arrested. In the election on August 13 Argaña was narrowly defeated by Julio César Franco (PRLA), who obtained 47.78 per cent of the votes cast compared with 46.98 per cent for Argaña. His brother, Nelson Argaña, resigned as Defence Minister on the following day and was replaced by Rear Adml. José Ocampos Alfaro, hitherto commander-in-chief of the armed forces. In a further Cabinet reshuffle on October 10 Francisco Oviedo became Finance Minister and Julio César Fanego was appointed Interior Minister.

viii. PERU

CAPITAL: Lima   AREA: 1,285,000 sq km   POPULATION: 26,000,000
OFFICIAL LANGUAGES: Spanish, Quechua, Aymará   POLITICAL SYSTEM: presidential democracy
HEAD OF STATE AND GOVERNMENT: President Valentín Paniagua (since Nov '00)
RULING PARTY: Popular Action (AP) party
MAIN IGO MEMBERSHIPS (NON-UN): OAS, ALADI, SELA, CA, AP, NAM
CURRENCY: new sol (end-'00 £1=S5.27, US$1=S3.53)
GNP PER CAPITA: US$2,390, US$4,387 at PPP ('99)

IN May President Alberto Fujimori was officially re-elected as President for a third term. Although the 1993 constitution clearly prohibited this (see AR 1998, p. 192), the National Election Board (which was dominated by Fujimori's supporters) ruled on January 1 that Fujimori was eligible to stand. In March the Board refused appeals to disallow his candidature even when it had become clear that over a million signatures on his nomination papers had been forged. Although those most closely involved in the forgery scandal were forced to resign from the Peru 2000 list of candidates, the first round of elections went ahead on April 9. These were widely seen as being deeply fraudulent and the count dragged on for days before it was officially declared that Fujimori had failed to gain an overall majority in the first round. The official count gave him 49.87 per cent compared to 40.24 per cent for his main rival, the 54-year old economist, businessman and former World Bank official, Alejandro Toledo, of Perú Possible (Perú Posible). Candidates of the former dominant parties, the Peruvian Aprista Party (APRA) and Popular Action (AP), got 1.38 per cent and 0.43 per cent respectively.

Fujimori won the run-off on May 28 comfortably with 51.2 per cent of the votes cast, since on May 18 Toledo had withdrawn from the contest in disgust over its conduct. As voting was compulsory, 17.7 per cent voted for Toledo and 31.1 per cent lodged spoilt ballots. Fujimori was sworn in on July 28 amidst violent protests in which six people died and 43 more disappeared. In his new Cabinet, one of his opponents, Federico Salas Guevara, became President of the Council of Ministers (prime minister), and Carlos Boloña Bohr became Economy and Finance Minister, a post which he had held until 1993.

In simultaneous legislative elections on April 9 Fujimori's Peru 2000 party polled 42 per cent of the vote but lost its overall majority in the 120-seat Congress. Toledo's Peru Possible party polled 23 per cent and finished strongly in second place.

With the economy in crisis and unemployment at around 30 per cent, public discontent continued to run high. In a surprise announcement on September 16 Fujimori stated his intention to hold fresh elections in April 2001 in which he would not be a candidate. Fujimori's right-hand man, Vladimiro Montesinos, who as head of the National Intelligence Service (SIN) was deeply implicated in the blackmail, harassment and torture which had helped maintain Fujimori in power for the previous five years, had been caught on camera in the act of trying to bribe an opposition congressman. Montesinos fled the country, but his application for political asylum in Panama was refused and on October 23 he returned to Peru. Thereafter he went into hiding, whilst the President, clad in a smart leather jacket, personally led a group of soldiers through the streets, ostentatiously failing to find him.

Talk of a possible coup waned after October 28 when the President dismissed Montesinos' associates, the head of the armed forces, Gen José Villanueva Ruesta, and the navy and air force commanders. But two days later a brief rebellion, led by Lt Col. Olanta Humala, took place at Toquepala, a mining town in the South, as a protest against a military and political establishment tainted by corruption and drug trafficking. The resignation of First Vice President Francisco Tudela came too late to dissociate him from the discredited regime, since a further videotape of Montesinos boasting how he had successfully rigged Fujimori's election victory led to a revolt in Congress and key Fujimori supporter Martha Hildebrandt, President of the Chamber of Deputies, was ousted. The President flew to Brunei to attend the Asia-Pacific Economic Co-operation (APEC) summit, and then flew on to Tokyo. Having been safely assured that he was still regarded as Japanese by his hosts (something that he had angrily denied on many occasions), he resigned the presidency on November 17.

Congress contemptuously refused to accept Fujimori's resignation, instead declaring him to be "morally unfit" to be President. Second Vice President Ricardo Márquez resigned on November 20 and 64-year old Valentín Paniagua of the Popular Action Party (AP)—former Minister of Justice in Fernando Belaúnde Terry's second government, who had been elected President of Congress on November 16—became interim President. He was sworn in on November 22 and appointed a Cabinet headed by former UN Secretary General

Javier Pérez de Cuéllar. The new government dismissed a whole cohort of senior military figures and some police officers associated with Montesinos, whose empty beach hideout was discovered in December. It also began an extensive investigation into allegations against the previous regime, and in late December enacted three anti-corruption bills.

ix. URUGUAY

CAPITAL: Montevideo   AREA: 177,000 sq km   POPULATION: 3,370,000
OFFICIAL LANGUAGE: Spanish   POLITICAL SYSTEM: presidential democracy
HEAD OF STATE AND GOVERNMENT: President Jorge Batlle Ibáñez (since March '00)
RULING PARTIES: Colorado Party holds presidency and heads a government which includes the Blanco (National) Party
MAIN IGO MEMBERSHIPS (NON-UN): OAS, ALADI, SELA, Mercosur, NAM
CURRENCY: peso Uruguayo (end-'00 £1=UP18.68, US$1=UP12.51)
GNP PER CAPITA: US$5,900, US$8,280 at PPP ('99)

JORGE Batlle Ibáñez of the Colorado Party (PC) was sworn in as President on March 1. Continuity with the government of his Colorado predecessor, Julio María Sanguinetti, was emphasised by his decision to retain four Cabenet ministers, including Didier Operti (PC) at Foreign Affairs and Guillermo Stirling (PC) at Interior. Five of the 13 posts went to the Blanco (National) Party (PN), the junior partner in the ruling coalition.

In April the President dismissed the army chief of staff, Gen. Manuel Fernández, after the latter had stated in a press interview that he expected once again to have to fight against the old Marxist-Leninist enemy. He had already been passed over as commander-in-chief in favour of Gen. Juan Geymonat.

In local elections held on May 14 the two traditional parties, the PC and the PN, carried all 19 Departments except for the capital, Montevideo, where the Progressive Encounter/Broad Front (EP-FA) retained control. In October the House of Representatives, against strong FA opposition, approved a five-year budget including provisions to privatise 40 per cent of the state telecommunications company Ancel.

x. VENEZUELA

CAPITAL: Caracas   AREA: 912,000 sq km   POPULATION: 23,400,000
OFFICIAL LANGUAGE: Spanish   POLITICAL SYSTEM: presidential democracy
HEAD OF STATE AND GOVERNMENT: President Hugo Chávez Frias (since Feb '99)
RULING PARTY: Patriotic Front coalition
MAIN IGO MEMBERSHIPS (NON-UN): OAS, ALADI, SELA, CA, ACS, OPEC, NAM
CURRENCY: bolívar (end-'00 £1=Bs1,045.29, US$1=Bs699.75)
GNP PER CAPITA: US$3,670, US$5,268 at PPP ('99)

AT the start of the year political tensions were running high as the new constitution was implemented. President Hugo Chávez Frías ruled by decree pending presidential elections. Internal dissension in Venezuela's two traditional parties, precipitated by their defeat in the December 1999 constitutional referendum (see AR 1999, p. 187), led to the resignation of the entire executive committee of Acción

Democratica (AD) on January 10 and a split in the Social Christian Party (COPEI). At its last session the National Constituent Assembly (ANC), the reforming body convened in 1999, approved a controversial resolution to allow the reinstatement of military officers who had taken part in the attempted coup of 1992, one of whom, Eliecer Otayza, an ANC member, had been appointed head of the Intelligence and Prevention Services Directorate (DISIP) the previous day. The following day, January 31, the ANC president, Luís Miquilena, was installed as chair of a 21-member interim legislative body. The ANC was then dissolved. The bicameral legislature, the National Congress, had already been dissolved, as had the Supreme Court which was replaced by a Supreme Tribunal of Justice appointed by the ANC. This new body decided on May 25 to postpone the elections until July.

Meanwhile the ruling Patriotic Front faced strong censure from within. Some of President Chavez's old military colleagues criticised corruption and especially the influence of Miquilena. Civilian politicians in turn disliked what they perceived as undue military influence, a view which was strengthened by the appointment on February 1 of Col. (retd) Luis Alfonso Dávila to the Interior in place of the civilian Ignacio Arcaya. In April charges of corruption were filed against Miquilena by the public prosecutor, though, in a separate case, his accuser, Lt. Col. (retd) Jesús Urdaneta Hernández, was also charged with illicit enrichment. On October 4 the Chief Superintendent of Customs was arrested together with 11 other tax officials. Relations between the military and civilians had also not been helped when in January the government announced an investigation into reports that during the December 1999 floods in the Department of Vargas, soldiers had summarily shot looters.

In the elections on July 30 the President, running as candidate of the Fifth Republic Movement (MVR) in alliance with the Movement Towards Socialism (MAS), was elected to a new six-year term with 59.7 per cent of the votes cast, compared with 37.7 per cent for his former colleague Lt.Col. (retd) Francisco Arias Cárdenas. Claudio Fermín, a former mayor of Caracas, representing the newly-founded National Encounter (EN), polled only 2.7 per cent. However, whilst the MVR took 93 and the MAS six of the 165 seats in the new National Assembly, Democratic Action (AD) emerged as the second-largest party in the legislature with 32 seats. The remainder were divided between Project Venezuela (PRVZL) with eight seats, the Social Christian Party (COPEI) five, First Justice five, Radical Cause three, indigenous groups three, and others 10. (Later in the year a split opened up in the AD as the secretary-general, Timoteo Zambrano, tried to oust the party leader, Henry Ramos Allup.) The MVR won 12 and the MAS three of the 23 state governorships. There were several accusations of fraud and troops were dispatched to quell disturbances in Mérida where the incumbent governor had been defeated.

President Chávez was sworn in on August 16, shortly before the successful conclusion of "Operation Journey" which resulted in the seizure of more than 25 tonnes of cocaine and 43 arrests. On November 7 the new National Assembly voted by 114 to 48 to grant the President power to legislate by decree for a year in industrial and economic policy. Only a day earlier he had appointed the tenth head of the Seniat tax agency to hold the office in less than two years.

xi. CUBA

CAPITAL: Havana   AREA: 115,000 sq km   POPULATION: 11,600,000
OFFICIAL LANGUAGE: Spanish   POLITICAL SYSTEM: communist republic
HEAD OF STATE AND GOVERNMENT: President Fidel Castro Ruz (since Jan '59)
RULING PARTIE: Cuban Communist Party (PCC)
MAIN IGO MEMBERSHIPS (NON-UN): ACS, SELA, NAM
CURRENCY: Cuban peso (end-'00 £1=Cub31.37, US$1=Cub21.00)
GNP PER CAPITA: n/a

RELATIONS between Cuba and the USA did not improve much during 2000. On January 1 military aircraft were scrambled when a Cessna light aircraft piloted by a US citizen flew over Havana. Meanwhile tension remained high over the future of Elian González, the boy rescued from the sea off the Florida coast in November 1999 after his mother had drowned (AR 1999, p. 188). The decision of the US Immigration and Naturalization Service (INS) that his Cuban father, Juan Miguel González, had sole legal authority over the child was hotly contested by the boy's relatives in Florida, backed by powerful anti-Castro exile groups (see IV.1). Finally on April 22, on the orders of US Attorney General Janet Reno, armed INS agents seized the boy and reunited him with his father. Whilst congratulating Reno on her action, President Fidel Castro Ruz dismissed any suggestion that it could lead to better relations with the USA, and indeed both eventual US presidential candidates (who at the time were contesting primary elections) had publicly sided with the boy's Miami relatives. The US Supreme Court, however, dismissed without comment both a request from the relatives for a hearing and an emergency request to block the boy's departure. He and his father returned to Cuba on June 28.

Meanwhile, on February 17 Mariano Faget, a Cuban-born US immigration officer, was arrested and accused of passing confidential information about defectors to Cuba. Two days later the US government declared José Imperatori, the Cuban Vice-Consul at the Cuban Interest Section of the Swiss embassy in Washington DC, persona non grata. When he refused to leave they expelled him to Canada and he returned to a hero's welcome in Havana.

Elections were held on April 23 and 30 for more than 14,000 members of local councils. In early May the government put a temporary freeze on new foreign investment in residential property. On May 5 the Havana City People's Provincial Court ordered the US government to pay the Cuban people compensation amounting to US$121,000 million for the damage done by the economic blockade. Subsequently, though the US Congress voted to allow sales of food and medicines to Cuba (as well as to other embargoed states) provided that no US credit was used to finance the transactions, Cuban officials maintained that the entire embargo was unjust and should be raised. Demonstrations against the embargo on July 26, the 47th anniversary of the Moncada uprising, were the largest for some years, and on November 9 the United Nations General Assembly called for an end to the embargo by the record majority of 167 votes to 3, with 4 abstentions.

On October 8 six UK citizens were detained in Havana on suspicion of espionage. They claimed to be employees of a London detective agency engaged by a private client to investigate the marital affairs of Michael Nahmad, a prominent Panamanian businessman. However Nahmad was believed to have served the Cuban government in helping evade the US embargo, and the detainees were denied consular access for some three weeks before President Castro personally arranged their release.

In November Castro paid a five-day state visit to Venezuela and concluded a five-year agreement with President Hugo Chávez Frías to supply a third of Cuba's oil needs on preferential terms, which included credit and, if necessary, part payment in goods and services.

xii. DOMINICAN REPUBLIC AND HAITI

Dominican Republic
CAPITAL: Santo Domingo   AREA: 49,000 sq km   POPULATION: 8,800,000
OFFICIAL LANGUAGE: Spanish   POLITICAL SYSTEM: presidential democracy
HEAD OF STATE AND GOVERNMENT: President Hipólito Mejía (since Aug '00)
RULING PARTY: Dominican Revolutionary Party (PRD)
MAIN IGO MEMBERSHIPS (NON-UN): OAS, SELA, ACS, ACP
CURRENCY: Dominican Republic peso (end-'00 £1=DP24.08, US$1=16.12)
GNP PER CAPITA: US$1,910, US$4,653 at PPP ('99)

Haiti
CAPITAL: Port-au-Prince   AREA: 28,000 sq km   POPULATION: 8,100,000
OFFICIAL LANGUAGE: French   POLITICAL SYSTEM: presidential democracy
HEAD OF STATE AND GOVERNMENT: President Jean-Bertrand Aristide (since Nov '00)
RULING PARTY: Lavalas Family (FL) movement
PRIME MINISTER: Jacques Édouard Alexis (since Jan '99)
MAIN IGO MEMBERSHIPS (NON-UN): OAS, SELA, ACS, ACP, Francophonie
CURRENCY: gourde (end-'00 £1=G31.37, US$1=G21.00)
GNP PER CAPITA: US$460, US$1,407 at PPP ('99)

PRESIDENT Leonel Fernández Reyna of the DOMINICAN REPUBLIC made a number of senior military appointments on March 3, in which Maj. Gen. José Elías Valdez Bautista became commander of the army. Five people were killed in the run-up to the presidential elections on May 16, when the candidate of the centre-left Dominican Revolutionary Party (PRD), Hipólito Mejía Domínguez, obtained 49.86 per cent of the votes cast. The two other candidates, Danilo Medina of the ruling Dominican Liberation Party (PLD), with 24.95 per cent, and Joaquín Balaguer Ricardo, of the right-wing Christian Social Reform Party (PRSC), with 24.64 per cent, then withdrew and Mejía was sworn in as President on August 16. In the new Cabinet Hugo Tolentino Dipp became Foreign Minister and Fernando Alvarez Bogaert was appointed as Finance Minister.

On January 21 the US government proclaimed its intention to withdraw all units from HAITI, where it had maintained a substantial military presence in support of the civilian government since 1994 (see AR 1994, p. 195). Under UN Security Council Resolution 1277 (1999) the UN Civilian Police Mission in Haiti (MIPONUH) would remain in place until March 15, when it was to be replaced by an International Civilian Support Mission (MICAH) with wider responsibilities for police training and the promotion of democracy. Political assassinations led to many key figures going into hiding; April alone saw 12 deaths, including those of the outspoken radio journalist, Jean Léopold Dominique, shot dead outside Radio Haiti-Inter in Port-au-Prince on April 3, and the opposition politician, Ducertain Armand, hacked to death on April 25 by intruders. On October 16 six senior police officers sought and were later given asylum in the Dominican Republic after allegedly conspiring to overthrow the government.

Under international pressure the legislative elections originally scheduled for November 1999 were finally set for May 2. Sadly, numerous irregularities cast doubt on the apparent success of the ruling Lavalas Family (FL) candidates and after violent demonstrations the head of the Provisional Electoral Council (CEP) fled to the USA and the second round of voting was postponed. President Rene Préval thereupon confirmed the first-round results and set the second round for July 9. The poll was boycotted by the opposition and the international community. The official results gave 18 of the 19 seats contested in the Senate and 72 of the 83 in the Chamber to the ruling FL, but it was not until November 24 that the National Assembly formally ratified the nomination of Jacques Edouard Alexis as Prime Minister. Opposition parties also boycotted and international observers refused to monitor the presidential elections on November 26, when former President Jean-Bertrand Aristide, 47-year old leader of the FL, was officially stated to have polled 92 per cent of the votes cast.

In December the first outbreak of polio was reported in both Haiti and the Dominican Republic since 1991.

xiii. CENTRAL AMERICA AND PANAMA

Guatemala
CAPITAL: Guatemala City   AREA: 109,000 sq km   POPULATION: 13,000,000
OFFICIAL LANGUAGE: Spanish   POLITICAL SYSTEM: presidential democracy
HEAD OF STATE AND GOVERNMENT: President Alfonso Antonio Portillo Cabrera (since Jan '00)
RULING PARTY: Guatemalan Republican Front
MAIN IGO MEMBERSHIPS (NON-UN): OAS, SELA, CACM, ACM, NAM
CURRENCY: quetzal (end-'00 £1=Q11.62. US$1=Q7.78)
GNP PER CAPITA: US$1,660, US$3,517 at PPP ('99)

El Salvador
CAPITAL: San Salvador   AREA: 21,000 sq km   POPULATION: 6,030,000
OFFICIAL LANGUAGE: Spanish   POLITICAL SYSTEM: presidential democracy
HEAD OF STATE AND GOVERNMENT: President Francisco Flores Pérez (since June '99)
RULING PARTY: National Republican Alliance (Arena)
MAIN IGO MEMBERSHIPS (NON-UN): OAS, SELA, CACM, ACS
CURRENCY: Salvadorian colón (end-'00 £1=C13.06, US$1=C8.74)
GNP PER CAPITA: US$1,900, US$4,048 at PPP ('99)

Honduras

CAPITAL: Tegucigalpa   AREA: 112,000 sq km   POPULATION: 6,300,000
OFFICIAL LANGUAGE: Spanish   POLITICAL SYSTEM: presidential democracy
HEAD OF STATE AND GOVERNMENT: President Carlos Roberto Flores Facussé (since Jan '98)
RULING PARTY: Liberal Party of Honduras (PLH)
MAIN IGO MEMBERSHIPS (NON-UN): OAS, SELA, CACM, ACS, NAM
CURRENCY: lempira (end-'00 £1=L22.56, US$1=L15.10)
GNP PER CAPITA: US$760, US$2,254 at PPP ('99)

Nicaragua

CAPITAL: Managua   AREA: 130,000 sq km   POPULATION: 5,400,000
OFFICIAL LANGUAGES: Spanish   POLITICAL SYSTEM: presidential democracy
HEAD OF STATE AND GOVERNMENT: President Arnoldo Alemán Lacayo (since April '97)
RULING PARTY: Liberal Alliance (AL)
MAIN IGO MEMBERSHIPS (NON-UN): OAS, SELA, CACM, ACS, NAM
CURRENCY: gold córdoba (end-'00 £1=C19.27, US$1=C12.90)
GNP PER CAPITA: US$430, US$2,154 at PPP ('99)

Costa Rica

CAPITAL: San José   AREA: 51,000 sq km   POPULATION: 3,700,000
OFFICIAL LANGUAGE: Spanish   POLITICAL SYSTEM: presidential democracy
HEAD OF STATE AND GOVERNMENT: President Miguel Angel Rodríguez Echeverría (since May '98)
RULING PARTY: Social Christian Unity Party (PUSC)
MAIN IGO MEMBERSHIPS (NON-UN): OAS, SELA, CACM, ACS
CURRENCY: Costa Rican colón (end-'00 £1=C474.21, US$1=C317.45)
GNP PER CAPITA: US$2,740, US$5,770 at PPP ('99)

Panama

CAPITAL: Panama City   AREA: 76,000 sq km   POPULATION: 2,900,000
OFFICIAL LANGUAGE: Spanish   POLITICAL SYSTEM: presidential democracy
HEAD OF STATE AND GOVERNMENT: President Mireya Elisa Moscoso de Gruber (since Sept '99)
RULING PARTIES: Anulfist Party (PA) heads Union for Panama coalition
MAIN IGO MEMBERSHIPS (NON-UN): OAS, SELA, NAM
CURRENCY: balboa (end-'00 £1=B1.49, US$1=B1)
GNP PER CAPITA: US$3,070, US$5,016 at PPP ('99)

ON January 14 Alfonso Portillo of the Guatemalan Republican Front (FRG) was sworn in as President of GUATEMALA, appointing Gabriel Orellana as Minister of Foreign Affairs and Manuel Maza Castellanos as Minister of Finance. Former dictator, Gen. (retd) José Efraín Ríos Montt (FRG) was elected President of the National Congress (on May 13 he was also re-elected secretary-general of his party).

In the first of a spate of high profile arrests, in mid-January three army officers were detained on suspicion of complicity in the assassination in 1998 of Bishop Juan José Gerardi Conadera, although a priest, Fr Mario Arantes Nájera, was charged with the murder on January 21. In February Gerardi's former cook, Margarita López, was charged with being an accessory to the crime. Former President Fernando Romeo Lucas García (1978-82), his brother and army chief of staff and the then Defence Minister were formally charged on May 3 with the massacre of more than 800 farm workers. On May 6 the chief of staff of the armed forces, Col. César Augusto Ruiz, was dismissed for allegedly plotting to overthrow the government. He was replaced by Col Eduardo Arévalo Lacs. The following day the government revealed the existence of a secret database holding some 650,000 names, set up jointly by the government and the armed forces around 1985 and computerised in 1996.

On August 9 the President formally admitted government responsibility for the atrocities committed during the civil war by signing an agreement with the IACHR which opened the way to compensation in 17 specific cases. Yet earlier in July he had brought into his Cabinet as Interior Minister Gen. (retd) Byron Barrientes, who had been accused of human rights abuses under Gen. Ríos Montt. Proceedings against the General and 19 of his colleagues for allegedly retrospectively altering an alcohol tax law ("Guategate") were suspended because of a conflict of interest by the Supreme Court on September 12.

Eduardo Peñate Polanco, the human rights prosecutor of EL SALVADOR, resigned on February 8, before a report on his conduct could be considered by the National Assembly. He faced accusations of corruption and perversion of justice in a previous post. The opposition Farabundo Martí Liberation Front (FMLN) hotly contested the decision of the Legislative Assembly on July 7 to allow the US Government to establish an anti-narcotics base at Comalapa International airport. The Assembly had previously ratified a constitutional amendment to permit an extradition treaty with the USA. On November 22 the government announced the decision to adopt the US dollar as the national currency.

The Defence Minister of HONDURAS, Edgardo Dumas Rodríguez, on February 3 confirmed the army commander, Col. José Isaías Barahona, in his post, but appointed new commanders of the navy and air force and a new Inspector General, Col. Marco Antonio Bonilla Reyes, amongst some 60 senior appointments. On July 10 the International Development Association (IDA) confirmed its support for some US$556 million in debt relief for Honduras under the Highly Indebted Poor Countries (HIPC) debt relief scheme. Elizabeth Chiuz Sierra was replaced as Security Minister in August by Gautama Fonseca.

The National Assembly of NICARAGUA on January 20 approved constitutional reforms, under which elections due in 2001 would choose a constitutional assembly instead of a new president to succeed Arnoldo Alemán Lacayo. However the provision that reduced the threshold to avoid a runoff in the presidential election from 45 per cent to 35 per cent was widely believed to favour the opposition Sandinista National Liberation Front (FSLN), and was seen as a concession made in return for a permanent seat in the legislature for Alemán upon his retirement and consequent immunity from prosecution. Between January and March tension with Honduras remained high, leading to armed clashes, but the dispute was resolved on March 7 by an agreement brokered by the Organisation of American States (see IX.6.iv.).

Gen. Javier Carrión, formerly chief of staff, was appointed commander-in-chief of the army on February 21, replacing Gen. Joaquín Cuadra. In June Ramón Kontorosky was appointed Defence Minister in place of José Antonio Alvarado, who had resigned after he had accused the government of suppressing demands for democracy and his citizenship had been annulled. Alvarado subsequently resigned from the Constitutional Liberal Party (PLC—a constituent part of the Liberal Alliance—AL) and formed a new party, the Liberal Democratic Party (PLD), in July. On May 31 Gen. Manuel Salvatierra, a veteran of the campaign against the US-backed "contras", became the first Nicaraguan defence attaché for 21 years to be accredited to Washington DC. In October Interior Minister René Herrera resigned to contest the legislative elections of 2001; he was replaced by Agriculture Minister José Marenco. The president of Congress, Ivan Escobar, and the Vice President, Enrique Bolaños, also resigned to run for the presidency; they were replaced by Oscar Moncada and Leopoldo Navarro, respectively. In municipal elections held on November 5 the PLC won control of 97 of the 151 municipalities with some 42 per cent of the votes cast. The opposition FSLN won 49, including the capital, Managua, and other key cities.

A non-binding referendum held in COSTA RICA in March showed substantial support for a proposal by former President and Nobel laureate Oscar Arias Sánchez to permit presidents to serve a second term, but the Supreme Court confirmed on September 5 that he was barred from running for office again under a 1969 constitutional amendment and a proposal to amend the constitution was later withdrawn. The Legislative Assembly approved legislation for the deregulation of electricity and telecommunications. In an exchange of letters in June President Miguel Angel Rodríguez Echeverría reached agreement with President Alemán of Nicaragua which resolved their dispute over rights of navigation on the San Juan River. Under the terms of the agreement the position was restored to that which had existed prior to July 1998, when armed Costa Rican police officers could patrol the river if they gave Nicaragua prior notice.

On January 1 the government of PANAMA assumed responsibility for the Panama Canal. Later in the month an agreement was negotiated with the USA for finance and training for anti-drugs forces. The IMF in June approved a 21-month standby arrangement for SDR64 million (US$83.8 million) to support the government's economic programme for the year. On August 22 President Mireya Elisa Moscoso de Gruber reshuffled her Cabinet, but made only minor changes.

xiv. MEXICO

CAPITAL: Mexico City   AREA: 1,958,000 sq km   POPULATION: 99,000,000
OFFICIAL LANGUAGE: Spanish   POLITICAL SYSTEM: federal presidential democracy
HEAD OF STATE AND GOVERNMENT: President Vincente Fox Quesada (since Dec '00)
RULING PARTY: National Action Party (PAN)
MAIN IGO MEMBERSHIPS (NON-UN): OAS, SELA, ALADI, ACS, APEC, NAFTA, OECD
CURRENCY: Mexican peso (end-'00 £1=MP14.35, US$1=MP9.61)
GNP PER CAPITA: US$4,400, US$7,719 at PPP ('99)

THE hold on Mexican politics of the former "official" party, established by Plutarco Elías Calles and his supporters in 1929, was finally broken in 2000. In presidential elections held on July 2, Vicente Fox Quesada of the Alliance for Change—comprising his own centre-right National Action Party (PAN) and the small Mexican Green Ecology Party (PVEM)—won with 43.4 per cent of the votes cast. He defeated Francisco Labastida Ochoa of the Institutional Revolutionary Party (PRI) with 36.9 per cent, following the decision on June 14 of Porfirio Muñoz Ledo of the Authentic Party of the Mexican Revolution (PARM) to withdraw from the contest and endorse Fox. Cuauhtémoc Cárdenas Solórzano of Alliance for Mexico, led by his centre-left Party of the Democratic Revolution (PRD), trailed in third place with 17 per cent.

However, the Alliance for Change fell short of an overall majority in either house of Congress. In the Chamber of Deputies the results were: Alliance for Change 223 (PAN 208, PVEM 15), PRI 209, PRD 52, and others 16. In the Senate the results were: PRI 60 seats, Alliance for Change 51 (PAN 46, PVEM 5), PRD 15, and others two. The chairs of the congressional committees were subsequently allocated between the parties proportionately, although it was noted that the PRI retained control of finance and foreign affairs in the Chamber and of defence in both houses.

Fox, a former Coca Cola executive, had been elected a Deputy in 1988, gaining notoriety by publicly accusing President Carlos Salinas de Gortari of having won the presidency through fraud. Fraud was also blamed for his own defeat in the 1991 gubernatorial contest in Guanajuato. However in 1995 he had won the governorship by a large margin and on July 2 his party's candidate, Juan Carlos Romero Hicks, retained the office, and the PAN's Sergio Estrada Cagijal won the governorship of Morelos, whose previous governor, Jorge Carrillo Olea, had been deposed by the State Supreme Court in April for misappropriation of state property. By contrast the victory of the PRI's candidate in gubernatorial elections in Tabasco on October 15 gave rise to widespread accusations of ballot-rigging.

At his inauguration on December 1 the new President pledged to consolidate Mexico's progress towards democracy, to combat poverty, reform education, decentralise federal powers, ensure accountability and fight crime. Amongst key Cabinet appointments were those of Jorge Castañeda at External Relations, Santiago Creel at *Gobernación* and Francisco Gil at Finance and Public Credit. In November the PAN candidate, Francisco Ramírez Acuña, won the governorship of Jalisco. Meanwhile during a brief visit to Mexico from exile in Ireland, Salinas published memoirs blaming his successor, President Ernesto Zedillo Ponce de Leon, both for mishandling the 1994 financial crisis which he had bequeathed him and for the PRI's election defeat.

In January Bishop Samuel Rúiz of San Cristóbal de las Casas, Chiapas, retired at the age of 75. However, his role as mediator between the government and the Zapatista National Liberation Army guerrillas was not, as he had hoped, inherited by his coadjutor, Raúl Vera, who was transferred by the Vatican to another post. Moves were announced to petition the federal government to allow the coastal region of Soconuzco to secede from Chiapas and form a new state with its capital at Tapachula. In May Gen. Julio César Santiago Díaz and two senior police officers were sentenced to eight years' imprisonment for their role in the "Acteal massacre" of December 1997, when 45 Tzotzil Indians were killed (AR 1997, p. 185). Following his inauguration President Fox sent to Congress the 1996 peace deal concluded by the outgoing administration but never ratified, and on December 30 he personally oversaw the release of 17 Zapatistas held at Tuxtla Gutierrez, with 86 more prisoners expected to be freed in the new year.

On December 18 some 50,000 people in the Valley of Mexico had to be evacuated when Popocatépetl erupted, lighting up the night sky and hurling rocks and ash over a wide area.

4. THE CARIBBEAN

JAMAICA—GUYANA—TRINIDAD & TOBAGO—BARBADOS—BELIZE—GRENADA—
THE BAHAMAS—WINDWARD & LEEWARD ISLANDS—UK DEPENDENCIES—
SURINAM—NETHERLANDS ANTILLES AND ARUBA—US DEPENDENCIES

i. JAMAICA

CAPITAL: Kingston   AREA: 11,000 sq km   POPULATION: 2,700,000
OFFICIAL LANGUAGE: English   POLITICAL SYSTEM: parliamentary democracy
HEAD OF STATE: Queen Elizabeth II
GOVERNOR-GENERAL: Sir Howard Cooke
RULING PARTY: People's National Party (PNP)
HEAD OF GOVERNMENT: Percival J Patterson, Prime Minister (since March' 92)
MAIN IGO MEMBERSHIPS (NON-UN): OAS, SELA, ACS, Caricom, ACP, CWTH, NAM
CURRENCY: Jamaican dollar (end-'00 £1=J$67.37, US$1=J$45.10)
GNP PER CAPITA: US$2,330, US$3,276 at PPP ('99)

WITH the economy in crisis, on February 16 Parliament approved ending the communications monopoly hitherto held by the UK firm Cable and Wireless. On February 21 the Prime Minister, Percival Patterson, of the People's National Party (PNP), reshuffled his Cabinet. By moving Portia Simpson Miller from Labour to Tourism he signalled his intention to revive the country's biggest earner of foreign exchange, while Anthony Hylton was appointed to Foreign Trade.

On September 12 the Judicial Committee of the Privy Council in London ruled that the sentences of six prisoners held pending execution in Jamaica should be commuted to life imprisonment. The decision renewed calls for the creation of a separate Caribbean court of appeal to replace the UK Privy Council as the country's highest judicial authority.

ii. GUYANA

CAPITAL: Georgetown   AREA: 215,000 sq km   POPULATION: 860,000
OFFICIAL LANGUAGE: English   POLITICAL SYSTEM: cooperative presidential democracy
HEAD OF STATE AND GOVERNMENT: President Bharrat Jagdeo (since Aug '99)
RULING PARTY: People's Progressive Party-Civic (PPP-C)
PRIME MINISTER: Sam Hinds (since Dec '97)
MAIN IGO MEMBERSHIPS (NON-UN): OAS, SELA, AP, ACS, Caricom, ACP, CWTH, NAM
CURRENCY: Guyana dollar (end-'00 £1=G$269.63, US$1=G$180.50)
GNP PER CAPITA: US$770, US$2,680 at PPP ('98)

IN advance of talks on Venezuela's claim to the Essequibo, due to start in May, President Hugo Chávez of Venezuela stepped up pressure on Guyana by stating that he "could not accept" the installation of a satellite launching facility in the disputed area. The application by Beal Aerospace Technologies of Texas had been given preliminary approval by the government in March and on May 19 the contract was signed.

A territorial dispute with Surinam was inflamed after the Surinamese navy on June 3 forced a Canadian oil exporation company to remove an oil rig from a sea area which Surinam regarded as within its territorial waters. The company, CGX Energy, had been granted a concession to drill by the Guyanese government in 1998. The government of President Bharrat Jagdeo reacted with angry statements and deployed troops along its frontier with Surinam on the Corentyne (Corentijn) river. On September 26 a Surinamese gunboat was reported to have crossed the Corentyne into Guyanese territory and fired on a Guyanese vessel, spurring opposition demands for increased defence spending.

In other developments, new legislation to combat money-laundering was passed by the National Assembly in February. Breaches carried penalties of a fine of up to $5,500 or up to seven years in prison. In September the Information Minister, Moses Nagamootoo, who had held the equivalent post since 1996, resigned to pursue studies abroad.

iii. TRINIDAD & TOBAGO

CAPITAL: Port of Spain   AREA: 5,128 sq km POPULATION: 1,337,000
OFFICIAL LANGUAGE: English   POLITICAL SYSTEM: parliamentary republic
HEAD OF STATE: President Arthur N.R. Robinson (incapacitated); Ganace Ramdial, acting president (since Feb '98)
RULING PARTIES: United National Congress (UNC) & National Alliance for Reconstruction (NAR)
HEAD OF GOVERNMENT: Basdeo Panday (UNC), Prime Minister (since Nov ,95)
MAIN IGO MEMBERSHIPS (NON-UN): OAS, SELA, ACS, Caricom, ACP, CWTH, NAM
CURRENCY: Trinidad & Tobago dollar (end-'00 £1=TT$9.32, US$1=TT$6.24)
GNP PER CAPITA: US$4,430, US$6,720 at PPP ('98)

THE murder of a leading member of the ruling United National Congress (UNC), Hansraj Sumairsingh, on December 31 1999 was linked to his concern about corruption in the government's relief programme. Suspicion fell on the Local Government Minister, Dhanraj Singh, who had made threats against Sumairsingh, but it was not until October 12 that, at the request of Prime Minister Baseo Panday, that he was dismissed by acting President Ganace Ramdial.

The government signed an agreement in March for the expansion of Atlantic LNG's natural gas installation at Point Fortin. Although the Minister for Energy, Finbar K. Gangar, hailed it as the largest inward investment ever in the country (or indeed in the Caribbean area), there were protests from opposition parties and the trade unions.

On November 2 the Prime Minister called a general election for December 11. A complicating factor was that he himself might be declared bankrupt, as the result of a judgment in the High Court on October 11. The Court had ordered him to pay US$135,000 in libel damages to his former colleague in the National Alliance for Reconstruction (NAR) government, Ken Gordon, chairman of the Caribbean Communications Network (CCN), for comments made in a speech in May 1997, but he gave notice of his intention to appeal to the UK Privy Council. In the elections, Panday's ruling United National Congress (UNC) won 19 seats, the conservative People's National Movement (PMN) 16 and the National Alliance for Reconstruction (NAR) one.

However, a constitutional crisis ensued when President Arthur Robinson declined to act on the advice of Prime Minister Panday that he appoint some seven of the defeated government candidates either to the Cabinet or to the 31-member Senate—16 of the members of which were constitutionally appointed by the Prime Minister. The issue was still unresolved at the year's end.

Abroad, Foreign Minister Ralph Maraj and other Caribbean government ministers called on US Secretary of State Madeleine Albright to respect their support for ACP/EU partnership and opposition to WTO trade measures at the second meeting between US and Caribbean Foreign Affairs Ministers in New Orleans on March 29. An agreement was reached in talks at Port of Spain on September 26 to promote trade and investment relations with Guyana. On September 27 BP Amoco confirmed the discovery, previously reported in May, of a large offshore natural gas field with proven resources of 56,600 million cubic metres (three trillion cubic feet).

iv. BARBADOS

CAPITAL: Bridgetown   AREA: 430 sq km   POPULATION: 264,000
OFFICIAL LANGUAGE: English   POLITICAL SYSTEM: parliamentary democracy
HEAD OF STATE: Queen Elizabeth II
GOVERNOR-GENERAL: Sir Clifford Husbands
RULING PARTY: Barbados Labour Party (BLP)
HEAD OF GOVERNMENT: Owen Arthur, Prime Minister (since Sept '94)
MAIN IGO MEMBERSHIPS (NON-UN): OAS, SELA, ACS, Caricom, ACP, CWTH, NAM
CURRENCY: Barbados dollar (end-'00 £1=Bd$2.97, US$1=Bd$1.99)
GNP PER CAPITA: US$7,890, US$12,260 at PPP ('98)

IN an unexpected Cabinet reshuffle on April 1, Prime Minister Owen Arthur, of the Barbados Labour Party (BLP), dismissed George Payne, the Minister for Tourism. No explanation was given for the decision and Noel Anderson Lynch was appointed in his place. Opposition Democratic Labour Party (DLP) members continued to criticise the government for the island's high level of crime, especially violent crime, which was widely attributed to the increasing aggressiveness of the drug cartels. The opposition was also persistently critical of the performance of Health Minister Senator Philip Goddard. Work continued on the Port Charles Marina project in Speightstown.

v. BELIZE

CAPITAL: Belmopan   AREA: 23,000 sq km   POPULATION: 246,000
OFFICIAL LANGUAGE: English   POLITICAL SYSTEM: parliamentary democracy
HEAD OF STATE: Queen Elizabeth II
GOVERNOR-GENERAL: Sir Colville Young
RULING PARTY: People's United Party (PUP)
HEAD OF GOVERNMENT: Said Musa, Prime Minister (since Aug '98)
MAIN IGO MEMBERSHIPS (NON-UN): OAS, SELA, ACS, Caricom, ACP, CWTH, NAM
CURRENCY: Belize dollar (end-'00 £1=Bz$2.94, US$1=Bz$1.97)
GNP PER CAPITA: US$2,610, US$3,940 at PPP ('98)

TENSION along the border with Guatemala escalated after an army patrol killed a Guatemalan peasant who had strayed across the undemarcated frontier. The new Guatemalan Foreign Minister, Gabriel Orellana, then formally revived Guatemala's long-standing claim to half of Belize's national territory, which had been suspended in 1986. On the eve of talks between the two countries to resolve the dispute, on February 24 a four-member patrol was captured by Guatemalan troops in the frontier area and accused of entering Guatemala illegally. The talks were called off, despite the efforts of Prime Minister Said Musa to negotiate the release of the men.

vi. GRENADA

CAPITAL: St George's   AREA: 344 sq km   POPULATION: 93,000
OFFICIAL LANGUAGE: English   POLITICAL SYSTEM: parliamentary democracy
HEAD OF STATE: Queen Elizabeth II
GOVERNOR-GENERAL: Sir Daniel Williams
RULING PARTY: New National Party (NNP)
HEAD OF GOVERNMENT: Keith Mitchell, Prime Minister (since June '95)
MAIN IGO MEMBERSHIPS (NON-UN): OAS, SELA, ACS, Caricom, OECS, ACP, CWTH, NAM
CURRENCY: East Caribbean dollar (end-'00 £1=EC$4.03, US$1=EC$2.70)
GNP PER CAPITA: US$3,170, US$4,720 at PPP ('98)

IN response to the storm surges generated by Hurricane Lenny in November 1999, the Caribbean Development Bank agreed in April to lend Grenada US$9 million to rehabilitate sea defences in the Grand Mal and Palmistra/White Gate regions. A further loan of US$10 million was agreed by the World Bank in August. Meanwhile at the South Summit in Havana, Cuba, on April 13, Prime Minister Keith Mitchell called for the reform of the World Trade Organisation (WTO). In a Cabinet reshuffle in August he created a new Ministry of Implementation.

Phyllis Coard, who had been held a prisoner in Richmond Hill prison for 17 years for her involvement in the coup which overthrew and killed Maurice Bishop in 1983, was released on licence to undergo surgery for cancer of the colon and receive chemotherapy in Jamaica.

vii. THE BAHAMAS

CAPITAL: Nassau   AREA: 14,000 sq km   POPULATION: 265,000
OFFICIAL LANGUAGES: English   POLITICAL SYSTEM: parliamentary democracy
HEAD OF STATE: Queen Elizabeth II
GOVERNOR-GENERAL: Sir Orville Turnquest
RULING PARTY: Free National Movement (FNM)
HEAD OF GOVERNMENT: Hubert Ingraham, Prime Minister (since Aug '92)
MAIN IGO MEMBERSHIPS (NON-UN): OAS, ACS, Caricom, ACP, CWTH
CURRENCY: Bahamian dollar (end-'00 £1=B$1.49 US$1=B$1)
GNP PER CAPITA: US$10,460 at PPP ('98)

SIR Lynden Pindling, first Prime Minister of the independent Bahamas, died on August 26 in Nassau (see XVIII). He led his country to independence from Britain in 1973, and served five terms of office, from 1967 to 1992.

viii. WINDWARD AND LEEWARD ISLANDS

Antigua & Barbuda

CAPITAL: St John's   AREA: 440 sq km   POPULATION: 69,000
OFFICIAL LANGUAGE: English   POLITICAL SYSTEM: parliamentary democracy
HEAD OF STATE: Queen Elizabeth II
GOVERNOR-GENERAL: Sir James B. Carlisle
RULING PARTY: Antigua Labour Party (ALP)
HEAD OF GOVERNMENT: Lester Bird, Prime Minister (since March '94)
MAIN IGO MEMBERSHIPS (NON-UN): OAS, ACS, OECS, Caricom, ACP, CWTH
CURRENCY: East Caribbean dollar (end-'00 £1=EC$4.03, US$1=EC$2.70)
GNP PER CAPITA: US$8,300, US$9,440 at PPP ('98)

Dominica

CAPITAL: Roseau   AREA: 48,400 sq km   POPULATION: 70,500
OFFICIAL LANGUAGE: English   POLITICAL SYSTEM: parliamentary republic
HEAD OF STATE: President Vernon Shaw (since Oct '98)
RULING PARTIES: Dominica Labour (DLP) & Dominica Freedom (DFP) parties
HEAD OF GOVERNMENT: Pierre Charles, Prime Minister (since Oct '00)
MAIN IGO MEMBERSHIPS (NON-UN): OAS, ACS, OECS, Caricom, ACP, CWTH, Francophonie
CURRENCY: East Caribbean dollar (see above)
GNP PER CAPITA: US$3,010, US$3,940 at PPP ('98)

St Christopher (Kitts) & Nevis

CAPITAL: Basseterre   AREA: 260 sq km   POPULATION: 39,100
OFFICIAL LANGUAGE: English   POLITICAL SYSTEM: parliamentary democracy
HEAD OF STATE: Queen Elizabeth II
GOVERNOR-GENERAL: Sir Cuthbert Sebastian
RULING PARTY: St Kitts-Nevis Labour Party (SKNLP)
HEAD OF GOVERNMENT: Denzil Douglas, Prime Minister (since July '95)
MAIN IGO MEMBERSHIPS (NON-UN): OAS, ACS, Caricom, OECS, ACP, CWTH
CURRENCY: East Caribbean dollar (see above)
GNP PER CAPITA: US$6,130, US$7,940 at PPP ('98)

St Lucia

CAPITAL: Castries   AREA: 616 sq km   POPULATION: 153,000
OFFICIAL LANGUAGE: English   POLITICAL SYSTEM: parliamentary democracy
HEAD OF STATE: Queen Elizabeth II
GOVERNOR-GENERAL: Perlette Louisy

RULING PARTY: St Lucia Labour Party (SLP)
HEAD OF GOVERNMENT: Kenny D. Anthony, Prime Minister (since May '97)
MAIN IGO MEMBERSHIPS (NON-UN): OAS, ACS, OECS, Caricom, ACP, CWTH, NAM
CURRENCY: East Caribbean dollar (see above)
GNP PER CAPITA: US$3,410, US$4,610 at PPP ('98)

St Vincent & the Grenadines
CAPITAL: Kingstown   AREA: 390 sq km   POPULATION: 119,000
OFFICIAL LANGUAGE: English   POLITICAL SYSTEM: parliamentary democracy
HEAD OF STATE: Queen Elizabeth II
GOVERNOR-GENERAL: Charles James Antrobus
RULING PARTY: New Democratic Party (NDP)
HEAD OF GOVERNMENT: Arnhim Eustace, Prime Minister (since Oct '00)
MAIN IGO MEMBERSHIPS (NON-UN): OAS, ACS, OECS, Caricom, ACP, CWTH
CURRENCY: East Caribbean dollar (see above)
GNP PER CAPITA: US$2,420, US$4,090 at PPP ('98)

IN ANTIGUA & BARBUDA, the government of Prime Minister Lester Bird continued efforts to comply with international requirements for the prevention of money laundering, in an attempt to get sanctions lifted.

In DOMINICA the general election on January 31 gave the opposition Dominica Labour Party (DLP) 10 of the 21 seats in the House of Assembly. The ruling centre-left United Workers Party (UWP) of Prime Minister Edison James, who had held power since 1995, won only nine seats and the Dominica Freedom Party (DFP) two. Roosevelt "Rosie" Douglas, the 58-year old DLP leader, was sworn in by President Vernon Shaw on February 3 as Prime Minister and Minister of Foreign Affairs, having formed a coalition government in which the DLP president, businessman Ambrose George, became Finance Minister, and the junior coalition partner, the DFP, received three portfolios.

In the following months, the new government pursued pragmatic policies designed to attract badly-needed inward investment. In late April Douglas's government announced that it would resume the controversial practice, introduced by the previous government, of selling passports to non-nationals. Though much disliked by the USA and Canada, this practice of "economic citizenship" was defended as raising much-needed revenue. When Dominica's representative voted with Japan at the International Whaling Commission to prevent the establishment of a South Pacific whaling sanctuary, Atherton Martin, the Agriculture, Planning and Environment Minister, resigned. He was replaced on July 11 by Lloyd Pascal, while the Prime Minister assumed personal responsibility for the banana industry.

Rosie Douglas's death on October 1, of a heart attack, was so unexpected that it gave rise to rumours of foul play. He was succeeded on October 3 by the deputy leader of the DLP and acting Prime Minister, Pierre Charles.

On February 13 Denzil Douglas, Prime Minister of ST CHRISTOPHER (KITTS) & NEVIS called an early general election. At the election on March 6, the ruling St Kitts-Nevis Labour Party (SKLP) carried all eight seats in St Kitts. On Nevis the Concerned Citizens Movement (CCM) retained two seats and the Nevis Reformation Party (NRP) one. The conservative People's Action Movement (PAM) lost its only seat, its leader, former Prime Minister Kennedy Simmonds, having suffered from accusations of corruption supported by a report of an inquiry conducted by the UK lawyer Sir Louis Blom-Cooper. In the new Cabinet appointed on March 9 the Prime Minister retained the Finance portfolio and his deputy, Sam Condor, that of Foreign Affairs. Sir Lee Moore, former Prime Minister of the Associated States of St Kitts-Nevis and Anguilla, who had relinquished the leadership of the SKLP in 1989, died on May 6 aged 61.

The Prime Minister of ST LUCIA, Kenny Anthony, announced a Cabinet reshuffle on March 2, the first in almost three years. Whilst a number of duties were reallocated, the only new appointment was that of Melissa Rambally to the portfolios of Tourism and Civil Aviation. Two men who attacked worshippers in the Basilica of the Immaculate Conception in Castries on December 31 claimed to be Rastafarians fighting corruption in the Catholic Church but were denounced by Rastafarian leaders. They sprayed several of the more than 400 worshippers with petrol and set them ablaze with a blowtorch before advancing to the altar where they attacked several people with machetes, killing an Irish nun.

On September 26 the 69-year old Prime Minister of ST VINCENT & THE GRENADINES, Sir James Mitchell, who had led his party to four successive election victories, agreed to step down as Prime Minister. He had already agreed on May 4, under an arrangement brokered by the Caribbean Community (CARICOM), to hold early elections to quell political unrest, which had been fanned by government decisions to award higher pay and pensions to MPs. He then relinquished the leadership of the New Democratic Party (NDP) to Finance Minister Arnhim Eustace at a party convention held on August 20. On October 27 Eustace was sworn in as Prime Minister.

ix. UK DEPENDENCIES

Anguilla
CAPITAL: The Valley   AREA: 96 sq km   POPULATION: 12,800
OFFICIAL LANGUAGE: English   POLITICAL SYSTEM: representative democracy
GOVERNOR-GENERAL: Peter Johnstone
RULING PARTIES: Anguilla National Alliance (ANA) & Anguilla Democratic Party (ADP) form United Front coalition
HEAD OF GOVERNMENT: Osbourne Fleming (ANA), Chief Minister (since March '00)
MAIN IGO MEMBERSHIPS (NON-UN): OECS, Caricom (obs.)
CURRENCY: East Caribbean dollar (end-'00 £1=EC$4.03, US$1=EC$2.70)

Bermuda
CAPITAL: Hamilton   AREA: 53 sq km   POPULATION: 64,000
OFFICIAL LANGUAGE: English   POLITICAL SYSTEM: representative democracy
GOVERNOR-GENERAL: Thorold Masefield
RULING PARTY: Progressive Labour Party (PLP)
HEAD OF GOVERNMENT: Jennifer Smith, Prime Minister (since Nov '98)
MAIN IGO MEMBERSHIPS (NON-UN): Caricom (obs.)
CURRENCY: Bermudian dollar (end-'00 £1=Bm$1.49, US$1- Bm$1)

British Virgin Islands
CAPITAL: Road Town   AREA: 153 sq km   POPULATION: 19,000
OFFICIAL LANGUAGE: English   POLITICAL SYSTEM: representative democracy
GOVERNOR-GENERAL: Francis J. Savage
RULING PARTY: Virgin Islands Party (VIP)
HEAD OF GOVERNMENT: Ralph O'Neal, Chief Minister (since May '95)
MAIN IGO MEMBERSHIPS (NON-UN): OECS (assoc.), Caricom (assoc.)
CURRENCY: East Caribbean dollar (see above)

Cayman Islands
CAPITAL: George Town, Grand Cayman   AREA: 259 sq km   POPULATION: 43,000
OFFICIAL LANGUAGE: English   POLITICAL SYSTEM: representative democracy
GOVERNOR-GENERAL: Peter John Smith
MAIN IGO MEMBERSHIPS (NON-UN): Caricom (obs.)
CURRENCY: East Caribbean dollar (see above)

Montserrat
CAPITAL: Plymouth   AREA: 102 sq km   POPULATION: 3,600
OFFICIAL LANGUAGE: English   POLITICAL SYSTEM: representative democracy
GOVERNOR-GENERAL: Anthony John Abbott
HEAD OF GOVERNMENT: David Brandt, Chief Minister (since Aug '97)
MAIN IGO MEMBERSHIPS (NON-UN): OECS, Caricom, ACS
CURRENCY: East Caribbean dollar (see above)

Turks & Caicos Islands
CAPITAL: Cockburn Town   AREA: 430 sq km   POPULATION: 17,500
OFFICIAL LANGUAGE: English   POLITICAL SYSTEM: representative democracy
GOVERNOR-GENERAL: Mervyn Jones
RULING PARTY: People's Democratic Movement (PDM)
HEAD OF GOVERNMENT: Derek H. Taylor, Chief Minister (since Jan '95)
MAIN IGO MEMBERSHIPS (NON-UN): Caricom (assoc.)
CURRENCY: East Caribbean dollar (see above)

IN January the Prime Minister of ANGUILLA, Herbert Hughes, called a new general election to resolve the constitutional deadlock which had arisen when the Finance Minister, Victor Banks, of the Anguilla Democratic Party (ADP), resigned. His departure had led to a paralysis of the government as the opposition boycotted the House of Assembly, thereby denying the government a legislative quorum. Less a year after the previous election (see AR 1999, p. 203), the March poll resulted in a victory for the United Front, a new opposition coalition between the Anguilla National Alliance (ANA) of Osbourne Fleming and Banks's ADP, with two seats each. Hughes's Anguilla United Party (AUP) retained two seats and the seventh went to an independent, Edison Baird, who had been an ADP minister in the previous government. Osbourne Fleming was appointed Chief Minister on March 6 when the new Executive Council was sworn in by Governor Peter Johnstone, who had been appointed on January 29 to succeed Robert Harris.

Amnesty International welcomed legislation passed by the government of BERMUDA to abolish the death penalty and judicial corporal punishment. The government of Prime Minister Jennifer Smith, of the Progressive Labour Party (PLP), had had a clear majority for the Act in the House of Assembly but the vote was tied in the Senate and was eventually carried by 6 votes to 5 only on the casting vote of the Chair. It was signed by Governor Thorold Masefield on December 23 1999. The concerns of opposition United Bermuda Party (UBP) senators about sentencing procedures remained to be addressed, but there had in any case been no execution on the island since 1977.

On September 26 Ralph O'Neal, Chief Minister of the BRITISH VIRGIN ISLANDS, appointed as his deputy J. Alvin Christopher, previously Minister of Communications and Works. He replaced Eileen Parsons, who had been dismissed for allegedly plotting with the opposition National Democratic Party (NDP) to replace O'Neal.

The CAYMAN ISLANDS was amongst the 15 countries named on June 22 as potential havens for money-crime by the Financial Action Task Force on Money Laundering, an international body created in 1989 by the G-7 countries. In addition, a report published in June by the Organisation for Economic Co-operation and Development (OECD) contained a formal complaint against all six UK dependencies. Accordingly, the UK government was reported on October 29 to have given the six Caribbean Overseas Territories an ultimatum to devise improved procedures to combat money laundering and to increase co-operation with international regulators.

In January persistent seismic activity in the Soufriere Hills on the island of MONTSERRAT showed that a new lava dome which had formed on the south-east side of the crater in December 1999 was continuing to grow. By May a large mass had formed at the head of the Tar river valley and rockfall activity continued at a high level. On September 14 there was a small eruption, sending pyroclastic flows down the eastern flanks of the volcano and a cloud of ash some 10,000 feet into the air. A second, smaller explosion occurred the following day. However, life continued to return to normal in the habitable part of the island in the wake of 1997's massive eruption (see AR 1997, p.198), and the traditional Christmas Festival was a great success.

In January Mervyn Jones was appointed Governor of TURKS & CAICOS, replacing John Kelly.

x. SURINAME

CAPITAL: Paramaribo   AREA: 163,000 sq km   POPULATION: 451,800
OFFICIAL LANGUAGE: Dutch   POLITICAL SYSTEM: republic
HEAD OF STATE: President Ronald Venetiaan (since Aug '00)
RULING PARTY: New Front for Democracy (NF) heads coalition
HEAD OF GOVERNMENT: Vice-President Jules Ajodhia (since Sept '00)
MAIN IGO MEMBERSHIPS (NON-UN): OAS, SELA, AP, ACS, Caricom, ACP, NAM
CURRENCY: Suriname guilder (end-'00 £1=SG1,465.42, US$1=SG981.00)
GNP PER CAPITA: US$1,660 ('98)

THE year began with the government in serious difficulties. Economic crisis had led to the resignation of the entire Cabinet in December 1999 and President Jules Wijdenbosch continued to rule at the head of a minority government. Charges of torture were filed in January in the Netherlands against former military ruler

Desiré "Desi" Bouterse. At elections on May 25 the opposition New Front for Democracy (NF), led by former President Ronald Venetiaan, won 32 seats in the 51-member National Assembly. The Millennium Combination (MC), an alliance of Bouterse's ruling National Democratic Party (NDP) with two smaller parties, secured only 10 seats and the Democratic National Platform 2000 (DNP 2000), a splinter group of the NDP led by the outgoing President, only three.

Venetiaan, who had served previously from 1991 to 1996, was again elected President on August 4 and sworn in on August 12. At the same time Jules Ajodhia was sworn in as Chairman of the Council of Ministers, in succession to Pratanpnarain Radhakishun. Humphrey Hildenberg, Siegfried Gilds, Marie Levens and Ronald Assen were also appointed to the portfolios of Finance, Justice and Police, Foreign Affairs, and Defence respectively.

xi. NETHERLANDS ANTILLES AND ARUBA

Netherlands Antilles
CAPITAL: Willemstad (Curaçao)   AREA: 800 sq km   POPULATION: 250,000
OFFICIAL LANGUAGES: Dutch, Papiamento & English   POLITICAL SYSTEM: parliamentary, under Dutch Crown
GOVERNOR-GENERAL: Jaime M. Saleh
RULING PARTIES: National People's Party (PNP) heads coalition
HEAD OF GOVERNMENT: Susanne Camelia-Römer (PNP), Prime Minister (since May '98)
CURRENCY: Neth. Antilles guilder (end-'00 £1=AG2.66, US$1=AG1.78)
GNP PER CAPITA: n/a

Aruba
CAPITAL: Oranjestad   AREA: 193 sq km   POPULATION: 69,000
OFFICIAL LANGUAGE: Dutch   POLITICAL SYSTEM: parliamentary, under Dutch Crown
GOVERNOR-GENERAL: Olindo Koolman
RULING PARTIES: Aruban People's Party (AVP) & Aruban Liberal Organisation (OLA)
HEAD OF GOVERNMENT: Jan Hendrick (Henny) Eman (AVP), Prime Minister (since July '94)
CURRENCY: Aruba florin (end-'00 £1=AFl2.67, US$1=AFl1.79)
GNP PER CAPITA: US$16,640 ('98)

THE island of Sint Maarten voted in a referendum on June 23 to follow the example set by ARUBA in 1996 and leave the NETHERLANDS ANTILLES federation to become a separate country within the kingdom of the Netherlands. The proposition was supported by all three of the island's political parties and, on a 55 per cent turnout, almost 70 per cent of voters were in favour.

xii. US DEPENDENCIES

Puerto Rico
CAPITAL: San Juan   AREA: 9,103 sq km   POPULATION: 3,880,000
OFFICIAL LANGUAGES: Spanish & English   POLITICAL SYSTEM: democratic commonwealth
GOVERNOR-GENERAL: Sila María Calderón
RULING PARTY: New Progressive Party (PNP) have majority in the senate
CURRENCY: US dollar (end-'00 £1=US$1.49)

US Virgin Islands
CAPITAL: Charlotte Amalie   AREA: 342 sq km   POPULATION: 146,000
OFFICIAL LANGUAGE: English   POLITICAL SYSTEM: democratic dependency
GOVERNOR-GENERAL: Charles Turnbull (independent)
CURRENCY: US dollar (end-'00 £1=US$1.49)

DESPITE US President Clinton's decision, announced on December 3 1999, to phase out naval operations on Vieques Island off PUERTO RICO over the next five years, protests at the possibility of the navy's continued use of the island for live firing carried on into January and the occupation of the naval firing range by more than 200 demonstrators led by Rubén Berríos Martínez of the Independence Party continued. However, the USA's offer of US$40 million in aid persuaded Governor Pedro Juan Rosselló González to agree to let the navy resume training with blank ammunition in March. A referendum on the use of live ammunition would be held later. If the voters agreed, the territory would receive a further US$50 million; if they refused, the navy would leave the island by May 1 2003 rather than by 2005 as originally agreed. On May 4 US federal agents evicted the demonstrators from the firing range in a well-organised operation.

In the elections on November 7 the 58-year old mayor of San Juan, Sila María Calderón, of the liberal Popular Democratic Party (PDP), was elected governor, the first woman to hold the post of chief executive. She obtained 48.5 per cent of the votes cast compared with 45.7 per cent for Carlos Pesquera of the conservative and pro-statehood New Progressive Party (PNP). In addition the PDP gained control of both houses of the legislature, the results for the Cámara de Representantes (the lower house) being: PPD 27 seats (49.2 per cent), PNP 23 seats (46.4 per cent) and the Puertorican Independence Party (PIP) one seat (4.4 per cent). Unlike her predecessor, Governor Rosselló, Calderón, a business executive and former vice president of Citibank in Puerto Rico, supported Puerto Rico's special status as a US Commonwealth and strongly opposed the campaign for the territory to become the 51st US state. Her election was also seen as a popular rejection of the agreement between Rosselló, the White House and the Navy Department to allow the navy to stay on Vieques until 2003. Navy Secretary Richard Danzig therefore refused to implement the promise to transfer 8,000 acres of navy land on Vieques to the government of the territory on December 31.

The government of the US VIRGIN ISLANDS was able to report that in the two years (1999-2000) public employment had been cut from 12,000 to 10,200, saving US$33 million. Rum taxes were up by US$75 million and the Bureau of Internal Revenue had collected US$40 million more in the fiscal year 2000 than in the previous year. There had been a 20 per cent increase in the number of tourists visiting the territory and crime was down by 15 per cent.

V MIDDLE EAST AND NORTH AFRICA

1. ISRAEL

CAPITAL: Jerusalem   AREA: 21,000 sq km   POPULATION: 6,300,000
OFFICIAL LANGUAGE: Hebrew   POLITICAL SYSTEM: parliamentary democracy
HEAD OF STATE: President Moshe Katzav (since July '00)
RULING PARTY: minority government led by Israel Labour Party & Centre Party
HEAD OF GOVERNMENT: Ehud Barak (Labour), acting Prime Minister (since July '99)
MAIN IGO MEMBERSHIPS (NON-UN):
CURRENCY: new shekel (end-'00 £1=Sh6.04, US$1=Sh4.04)
GNP PER CAPITA: US$15,940, US$17,310 at PPP ('98)

FOR Israel it was a year of turbulence and turmoil. Few would have predicted at the turn of the year that Ehud Barak, who had enjoyed an overwhelming victory at the polls in May 1999, would be forced to resign and would be facing the prospect of electoral defeat at the hands of Ariel Sharon. Likewise few could have imagined that Israel and the Palestinians, having set a target of September 13 for signing a peace agreement and bringing about an end to the conflict, would by the end of the year find themselves in a state of virtual war.

The year began with high hopes of a breakthrough between Israel and Syria. This optimism had been fuelled by the historic meeting between Ehud Barak and Syrian Foreign Minister Faruq al Shara' in Washington DC, in the middle of December 1999. Although that meeting had proven to be largely symbolic, the two sides had agreed to reconvene in Shepherdstown, Virginia at the start of January for further high-level negotiations aimed at drawing up a peace treaty. But the Shepherdstown meeting broke up after eight days, having achieved little. The parties were scheduled to return to the USA for a further round of talks on January 20, but they left Shepherdstown further apart than at the start of the meeting. The Syrians were angered by the leak to the media of a draft peace treaty which had been drawn up by the Americans suggesting Syria's willingness to engage in normalisation with Israel and to comply with a number of Israeli security concerns. They were also angered by what they saw as Israeli stalling concerning the demarcation of the border between the two sides and declared that they would not return to the negotiating table before receiving written guarantees that the border would be based on the June 4, 1967 line. Diplomatic efforts to bring the Syrians back to the negotiating table appeared to have been successful when President Clinton announced at the end of March that he would be meeting with Syrian President Hafez al-Assad in Geneva. The three-hour meeting ended in failure, however, effectively bringing negotiations between Israel and Syria to a halt. Any prospects for further progress on this track in 2000 disappeared when President Assad died at the beginning of June (see V.2.iv).

Developments on the Syrian track at the beginning of the year were intimately linked with a general shift in Israeli policy in southern Lebanon. Ehud Barak had promised during his election campaign to withdraw Israeli troops from Lebanon within a year of taking office. He had spoken, however, of a withdrawal in the context of an agreement rather than a unilateral withdrawal. Such was the desire of the Israeli public to end their country's 18 year-long imbroglio in Lebanon that the Israeli Cabinet announced, at the beginning of March, that it would be withdrawing Israeli troops from the self-declared "security zone" in southern Lebanon by the beginning of July, regardless of whether an agreement had been reached with Syria or the Lebanese government.

In mid-April Israel informed the United Nations that it had set July 7 as the intended date for its departure from Lebanon. However, events on the ground developed their own momentum. In mid-May Israel began to move its troops southwards towards the Israeli border, handing over its fortified positions in the "security zone" to members of its own client militia, the Southern Lebanon Army (SLA). The SLA forces suddenly disintegrated, leaving Israel's planned withdrawal in disarray and its forces hurriedly retreating to the international border. On May 24, six weeks ahead of schedule, Israel's occupation of southern Lebanon came to an undignified end as the last of its troops, accompanied by around 6,500 fleeing SLA members, crossed the border. On June 18 the UN Security Council endorsed a report by UN Secretary-General Kofi Annan that Israel had fulfilled the provisions of UN Security Council Resolution 425 and had withdrawn its troops from Lebanon. The Lebanese border remained quiet until the beginning of October when Hezbollah kidnapped three patrolling Israeli soldiers and fired rockets into Israel. Tensions mounted when, on October 15, Hezbollah announced that it was holding an additional Israeli who had apparently been abducted whilst travelling in Europe. Efforts by Kofi Annan to secure the release of the four captured Israelis proved unsuccessful.

With the completion of the Israeli withdrawal from Lebanon and the collapse of the Syrian track, diplomatic efforts reverted to the peace process between Israel and the Palestinians. The year began with Israel and the Palestinians in deadlock over the implementation of the September 1999 Sharm el-Sheikh agreement. By February 2000 negotiations had ground to a halt, and the February 13 deadline for the drawing up of a "Framework Agreement" on final settlement issues passed with the two sides refusing to meet. It took a month of intensive mediation by the USA, with the help of Egypt, to bring the two sides back together. Again they travelled to Sharm el-Sheikh to establish a new timetable for ending the conflict. They now aimed to complete the Framework Agreement by May and to complete all negotiations by September 13. It came as no surprise to anyone that the new May deadline passed without the signing of a Framework Agreement.

In an effort to break the deadlock and push forward the peace process, President Clinton announced at the beginning of July that he would be convening a "make or break" summit at Camp David. For the first time since the signing of the Oslo Declaration in 1993, Israel and the Palestinians began to address the critical final status issues at the heart of the conflict: the future of Jerusalem, the future status of Palestinian refugees, the future of Israeli settlements in the West Bank and Gaza, and the territorial dimensions of a future Palestinian state. Originally intended to last eight days, the Camp David summit between Israeli Prime Minister Barak and Palestinian President Yassir Arafat continued for 15 days. Whilst the summit ended without a signed agreement, the prevailing view was that the two sides had made considerable progress towards reaching a peace treaty. The principal stumbling block in the negotiations was the question of the future status of Jerusalem and in particular the question of sovereignty over the Temple Mount/Haram al Sharif in Jerusalem's Old City.

August and September witnessed intensive efforts by Israel and the Palestinians to garner international support for their negotiating positions and diplomatic efforts to bring the two sides together to complete the process embarked upon at Camp David. On September 26 Ehud Barak and Yassir Arafat met at Barak's home in an effort to kick-start the peace process. It was their first meeting since Camp David and reports described it as the "best ever" between the two leaders. Two days later, however, following a visit to the Temple Mount/Haram Al-Sharif by the hard-line leader of the Likud opposition party, Ariel Sharon, serious rioting broke out in Jerusalem leaving four Palestinians dead and over 200 wounded. Sharon's visit to the Temple Mount was seen by Palestinians as deliberate provocation aimed at asserting Israeli sovereignty over the holy sites in Jerusalem at a sensitive moment in the negotiations. Violent clashes between Israeli troops and Palestinian police and civilians quickly spread to other towns in the West Bank and Gaza, effectively shattering the peace process. The violence soon spread to Israel itself, when protests by Israeli Arabs, in solidarity with the Palestinians, led to Israeli police shooting and killing 13 demonstrators. Efforts to bring about a cease-fire between the two sides proved ineffective. Some 2,500 people were wounded and over 150, the vast majority of them Palestinian, were killed in October as the clashes intensified.

Intensive diplomatic efforts, including the direct intervention of US President Bill Clinton, brought Israel and the Palestinians to Sharm-el-Sheikh in the middle of October. The Sharm summit ended with both sides agreeing to bring about an end to the violence and to resolve their differences through negotiation. But such was the new level of distrust between Yassir Arafat and Ehud Barak that President Clinton could only secure a verbal understanding, and not a signed agreement. At the end of the summit the two leaders left refusing to shake hands. The two sides did, however, agree to the setting up of a fact-finding committee, to be headed by former US Senator George Mitchell, which would investigate the causes of the outbreak of violence and report its findings to the US President. The verbal understandings at Sharm-el-Sheikh did not translate into facts on the ground, however, and the Palestinian uprising (the intifada) and violence continued unabated for the remainder of the year.

The uprising broke out with Barak already facing mounting domestic pressures and presiding over a minority government. Whilst he had won an overwhelming majority in the elections in May of the previous year, his ruling coalition consisted of an uneasy balance of six parties, each with its own concerns and agenda. In June, an ongoing dispute over the funding of their educational network led the Sephardi religious party, Shas, with 17 seats, to threaten to leave the government and support opposition efforts to bring about new elections. In order to prevent Shas abandoning the coalition, Yossi Sarid, leader of the left-wing civil rights party Meretz, resigned as Education Minister and left the government, though the party continued to support Barak's coalition inside parliament.

Barak's coalition effectively collapsed prior to his departure in July for Camp David and the summit meeting with Yassir Arafat when three parties—Shas, the nationalist National Religious Party and the Russian party, Yisrael B'Aliyah—left the government in protest at Barak's conduct of the peace negotiations. As a result, Barak flew to the USA heading a minority adminstration of only 30 members, just one quarter of the total membership of the Israeli parliament. He returned from Camp David to be greeted with the news that his Foreign Minister, David Levy, who had refused to participate in the summit, had announced that he too was leaving the government. Barak's embattled administration received a further blow at the end of July when Moshe Katsav, a member of the Likud, defeated Shimon Peres, against all expectations, to become the new Israeli President. Katsav replaced Ezer Weizmann, who had been forced to resign after a police investigation failed to clear him of receiving undeclared gifts and monies worth US$300,000 in the 1980s when he was a government minister.

When the Palestinian uprising broke out, Barak's first move was to call for the formation of a government of national unity to attend to the crisis facing the country. Whilst the creation of such a government held great appeal for the Israeli public, Barak and Sharon were unable to agree upon the terms and the division of responsibility in such an administration. Consequently, the calls for national unity went unheeded. Instead the opposition parties worked towards bringing down Barak's fragile government and securing enough votes in parliament to force new elections. By the end of November Barak could no longer stave off the inevitable. Rather than face defeat in a vote to dissolve parliament, he announced that he was in favour of a general election. Agreeing to dissolve the Knesset was not Barak's only option, however, and on December 9 he instead offered his resignation, thus creating the opportunity for new elections to be held solely for the post of Prime Minister. It was left to the Israeli parliament to decide between the two options. It chose not to disband itself and to opt for a special election for the premiership, to be held on February 6, 2001.

The fall of Barak's government prompted the return from self-imposed political exile of former Prime Minister and head of Likud, Binyamin Netanyahu, who declared his candidacy for the Prime Ministerial contest. Netanyahu, however, was in favour of a general election; once that option was rejected he withdrew his candidacy, leaving Ariel Sharon to contest the race with Ehud Barak.

2. ARAB WORLD AND PALESTINIANS—
EGYPT—JORDAN—SYRIA—LEBANON—IRAQ

i. THE ARAB WORLD AND THE PALESTINIANS

THE hopes raised in 1999 for a settlement between the Palestinians and the new Israeli Prime Minister were unfulfilled in 2000. Ehud Barak's policy seemed in the end dictated crucially by his resolve to stay in office. The ageing Palestinian leader, Yassir Arafat, capricious, opportunist and unmethodical, increasingly lost support amongst younger Palestinians. But in Syria, Jordan and Morocco, death brought to power younger men with new ideas. The USA retained its decisive influence in Israel but did not always dare to use it; continental Europe had often little sympathy with the US line but could not easily pursue one of its own; Russian power and resolve to intervene in the region continued to decrease.

The strength of the Palestinians' case for replacing Israel in the Occupied Territories was weakened by their inefficiency, disunity and sometimes corruption. Already in February young Palestinians were again throwing stones, this time at their own leaders—and also at France's Prime Minister for having described the Lebanese Hezbollah as terrorists. There were student disorders in Jerusalem and elsewhere. Arafat and his authorities reacted with arrests and beatings and often refused those arrested access to lawyers. "The Palestinian Authority (PA)," said a Palestinian academic, "is becoming like any other Arab regime maintaining its own interests". Its security services closed a radio station which had criticized Arafat and Palestinian human rights activists accused the PA of collaborating with Israeli and other intelligence services at the expense of democracy.

Palestinian discontent followed unsuccessful Arafat-Barak negotiations and was increased by the severity—often including torture—of the conduct of Israeli security forces towards Palestinians. At first the two sides agreed on a further transfer to the PA of land in the Occupied Territories, but Barak delayed the handover after accusing the Palestinians of foot-dragging. After acrimony between Arafat and Barak, the Palestinian side announced in February that the talks had been frozen.

In February the Vatican opposed any unilateral Israeli decision on Jerusalem's future as being legally and morally unacceptable. At Arafat's meeting in Rome with the Pope, the Vatican recognised the PLO's authority, and the Arab side reaffirmed Jerusalem's international status, with free access to the Holy Places for Christians, Jews and Muslims. Barak, on the other hand, wanted the Holy Places issue postponed. Visiting the Occupied Territories in March, the Pope told Arafat that the Palestinians deserved a homeland of their own. The local Christians, uncomfortably situated, were increasingly emigrating, both for economic reasons and for fear of Muslim fundamentalism. Meanwhile younger Arabs were increasingly opposed to Arafat and his regime. Journalists condemned rigged elections in Arab trade unions, and teachers thought themselves unfairly treated.

By March 21, however, Palestinians and Israelis had agreed on a land transfer which would bring 43 per cent of the West Bank under partial or total Palestinian control. In mid-April Barak for the first time publicly envisaged a demilitarised Palestinian state of more than half the West Bank but not extending to pre-1967 borders. Growing Jewish settlement in the Occupied Territories and falling popular support, whether Jewish or Arab, remained crucial obstacles to agreement. Furthermore, Arafat's influence with Palestinians was diminishing and Barak's loss of his Knesset majority restricted his scope for compromise.

US attempts to bring the two sides together culminated in an unsuccessful Washington meeting in late July. Palestinian and Israeli leaders faced difficulties from their own sides, as when an Israeli official stated that the fundamental UN resolution 242 was irrelevant, or the PLO empowered the executive to declare, immediately, a sovereign state, a move which was endorsed by Arafat. Also contentious was a proposed massive return of Arabs who had been driven from their lands into exile: Arafat's security chief had admitted that the exiles would in any case largely not want to return. In mid-September the Israelis confiscated more Arab land for road-building.

Russia and China urged caution on Arafat whilst the USA strove to reduce tension. On September 27, after a US-organised Israeli-Arab meeting, Barak admitted the possibility of sharing authority in east Jerusalem. At this point, however, everything broke down. On September 28 the arch Israeli intransigent, Ariel Sharon, was allowed into Jerusalem's Haram al Sharif or Temple Mount, a site particularly sacred to Muslims. The visit provoked a new intifada. In response Israeli forces fired on stone-throwing Palestinians, helicopters attacked Palestinian targets in the Occupied Territories, and Arab olive groves were bulldozed. In early October Israel, by cutting off the Occupied Territories from Israel proper, deprived 100,000 Palestinians of their livelihoods.

By October 31 over 130 Palestinians had been killed in the violence. A few Israelis had also died, generally victims of firing by anti-Arafat extremists. By early December, estimated Arab deaths had risen to 258 and Israeli to 35. This strengthened extremists on both sides and discouraged peace-making, though responsible Arabs appealed repeatedly for an end to violence, and Arafat claimed to be working to prevent firing from residential areas in the Palestinian controlled zone.

Finally, the USA's attempt to re-launch Israeli-Palestinian negotiations succeeded—two months after Sharon's entry to the Haram. Whilst Arafat was visiting Moscow on November 25, Barak spoke with him on the telephone. Later, reversing his previous refusal to co-operate until Arab violence had ceased, Barak met a US-led international committee aimed at promoting a settlement and accepted its intervention. The committee met in New York on December 3.

But 10 days later, in the worst fighting since September's intifada began, Israeli forces killed four Palestinian policemen. The next day, December 15, was even worse, as six Palestinians, including three Fatah men, were killed. This was an inauspicious background for talks in Gaza and Washington involving Clinton, Arafat, Barak and others. By the year's end these talks had reached no conclusion, although they had examined a reported US plan whereby the Palestinians would drop their demand for a mass return to their lost homes and Israel would meet at least some Palestinian desiderata in east Jerusalem.

By now, however, there was popular opposition on both sides to the negotiations. Ordinary Palestinians rejected the compromises necessary for peace and Barak faced similar difficulties from the intransigent Israeli right. He called elections and then resigned his office. Neither Arafat nor Barak could now control his erstwhile supporters. Two months of violence and death had encouraged extremists on both sides and US influence was insufficient to relaunch the interrupted negotiations. Israel had damaged the Palestinian economy by refusing to admit Arab labour and by severing communications between Israel and the Occupied Territories, moves which were widely seen as an unjust form of collective punishment. An Israeli academic spoke against both sides, Arafat for using violence to extort concessions and ignoring the role of economic advancement in promoting peace, his security forces for practising extortion, kidnapping and torture of their own people, and the Israelis for lowering living standards in the Occupied Territories and thus reducing the Palestinian will to compromise.

Arafat's belated resistance to Israeli demands had increased his influence, whilst Barak's contemplated concessions had weakened his. The violence following Sharon's intervention had also weakened those Arab governments, like Egypt and Jordan, which had favoured negotiation. Now, bowing to popular pressure at home, they began to break or reduce their relations with Israel. Egypt withdrew its ambassador from Jerusalem and Qatar and Morocco closed the Israeli missions in Doha and Rabat.

In economic developments, the over-use of water by Jewish settlements in the Occupied Territories steadily drained the aquifers there, although deposits of natural gas were discovered off-shore which could meet Palestinian needs for 25 years. The European Union (EU) discovered and condemned Israel's export to Europe, under concessions available only to Israel itself, of products from Jewish settlements in the Occupied Territories. Paradoxically, the Palestinian stock market, being dominated by shares of companies holding monopolies, proved to be the Arab world's best performing exchange.

ii. EGYPT

CAPITAL: Cairo   AREA: 1,001,000 sq km   POPULATION: 66,000,000
OFFICIAL LANGUAGE: Arabic   POLITICAL SYSTEM: presidential democracy
HEAD OF STATE AND GOVERNMENT: President Mohammed Hosni Mubarak (since '81)
RULING PARTY: National Democratic Party (NDP)
PRIME MINISTER: Atif Mohammed al Ubayd (since Oct '99)
MAIN IGO MEMBERSHIPS (NON-UN): AL, OAPEC, OAU, OIC, NAM
CURRENCY: Egyptian pound (end-'00 £1=E£5.81, US$1=E£3.89)
GNP PER CAPITA: US$1,400, US$3,303 at PPP ('99)

PRESIDENT Husni Mubarak, now over 70 and in power since 1981, remained much concerned with Arab-Israeli relations and the stalemated peace process during 2000. But he could not influence events decisively nor carry his people wholeheartedly with him. Egypt was compromised by its dependence on US finance. The Arab-Israeli crisis of the autumn 2000 nonetheless forced Mubarak to curtail relations with the USA's friends in Israel and reduced Egypt's foreign exchange income. The government faced Muslim-Christian feuding in Upper Egypt and was weakened when some senior figures were found guilty of corruption. More positively, there was a perceptible relaxation of governmental control on press and public opinion generally.

Mubarak's involvement in the Arab-Israeli peace process brought frequent consultation, and some disagreement, with the US administration. Spring saw him visit the USA twice and President Clinton visited Cairo in August. In July the Egyptian government's arrest of a liberal Egyptian-American intellectual, Sa'aduddin Ibrahim —on implausible charges of spying for the US—evoked damaging protests from the USA and from Middle Eastern commentators abroad. Egypt, like most Arab states, rejected the USA's uncompromising hostility towards Iraq, and Saddam Hussein himself was permitted to attend an Arab League meeting in Cairo. Disagreement persisted even over Palestine, an issue upon which Egypt had been closer to the USA than most Arab states. The US government disliked Egypt's support for alleged Palestinian intransigence over the status of Jerusalem, particularly when Foreign Minister Amr Musa said that Israeli sovereignty over west Jerusalem should be matched by Arab sovereignty over the east. Egypt also criticised the continued allied air attacks on Iraq and opposed the continued imposition of sanctions.

President Mubarak's entente with Israel was increasingly unpopular in Egypt. Protesting at Ariel Sharon's incursion into the Haram al Sharif in Jerusalem (see V.1. and V.2.i.) and Israel's anti-Palestinian severities, Egyptian crowds demanded a rupture with Israel and action against US-owned firms. In November, Egypt, one of the few Arab governments with relations with Israel, recalled its ambassador, despite a US plea not to do so. An Egyptian and an absent Russian were at the same time charged with spying for Israel.

In February John Paul II became the first Pope to visit Egypt. He retraced the steps of Moses on Mount Sinai and met the President, the Coptic Patriarch and the Shaikh of Al Azhar. However, the year opened with anti-Coptic violence in Upper Egypt. Christians allegedly fired on Muslims from a church steeple and in retaliation Muslim mobs attacked Coptic shops and about 20 people were killed, nearly all of them Copts. The local Coptic majority was more prosperous than—and so resented by—its Muslim neighbours.

Throughout the year, Islamic fundamentalist agitation persisted. In February some professional men were arrested as Muslim Brothers. In early May a book was denounced by a newspaper as blasphemous; this was followed by an Islamist student demonstration which the police violently suppressed. The students were later released, the book withdrawn and the newspaper suspended. By September many Muslim Brothers had been arrested and over 200 were retained in custody.

The judiciary began to assert its independence and intervened to correct excesses by the security forces during the year. The Supreme Court ruled the current parliament technically unconstitutional because elections to it had not been properly supervised. In July the courts quashed the government's suspension of a political party and its newspaper. A protracted corruption trial brought heavy sentences for government MPs, including one ex-minister.

The routine prolongation in February of the state of emergency was not unanimously approved by parliament. Egyptian media were no longer so easily controllable and the public could always watch foreign television. In March the director of the official information service lifted restrictions on foreign press and broadcasting: there was, he said, no way to stop people abroad criticising Egypt.

In anticipation of parliamentary elections, the National Accord Party was founded, with government approval, as the fifteenth party. In July the Constitutional Court ruled that elections must be supervised by judicial, not governmental, officials. At the autumn elections, the government won more seats than before but over half the members had stood as independents and rejoined the government party only after their election. The new assembly was more pluralistic than usual: a Nasserist and a Wafdist won important parliamentary posts from government candidates.

Egypt's foreign exchange imbalance again caused concern during the year as the crisis in Palestine reduced tourism within the whole of the Middle East region, and thus diminished Egypt's foreign exchange earnings. It faced the usual pressure to devalue its currency but as this would raise prices and hurt consumers Mubarak ruled it out. Although the government had begun, falteringly, selling off the industries nationalised under Nasser, much remained in government hands and thus remained over-manned and inefficient. Other economic developments included a fight by Egyptian cement companies to resist a take-over drive by foreign capital, indignation in Cairo over a UK bank's unfavourable report on the economy, and the flight of an investment banker whose shares fell suddenly by 75 per cent—upon which a newspaper remarked "little thieves hang but great ones escape".

Prince Hasan Aziz Hasan, a cousin of King Faruq who had stayed in Egypt after the revolution of 1952, died in Cairo on April 17 aged 76. The son of a Spanish Catholic mother and educated in Turkey, Lebanon and England, he had a notably British accent and was a talented painter and musician.

iii. JORDAN

CAPITAL: Amman   AREA: 89,000 sq km   POPULATION: 5,300,000
OFFICIAL LANGUAGE: Arabic   POLITICAL SYSTEM: monarchy
HEAD OF STATE: King Abdullah ibn al-Husain (since Feb '99)
PRIME MINISTER: Ali Abu al-Rageb (since June '00)
MAIN IGO MEMBERSHIPS (NON-UN): AL, OIC, NAM
CURRENCY: Jordanian dinar (end-'00 £1=JD1.06, US$1=JD0.71)
GNP PER CAPITA: US$1,500, US$3,542 at PPP ('99)

AT the beginning of the year 2000 Abdullah ibn al-Husain had been King for less than a year, since ascending to the throne in February 1999. Internally, his focus was on the country's economic development. Externally, Jordan's biggest challenge was its co-existence with Israel and its attitude to Israeli treatment of the Palestinians in the Occupied Territories. Many Jordanians of Palestinian origin had never reconciled themselves to Jordan's recognition of Israel or to Israel's continued occupation of the West Bank, which had been seized from Jordan during the 1967 war. The autumn crisis in the Occupied Territories sharpened this opposition.

The new King sustained the relations with Iraq which were vital to Jordan's economy and were emotionally important to many Jordanians. In June he replaced Prime Minister Abdul-Raouf Rawabdeh with Ali Abu al-Rageb, a former Minister of Industry and Trade and a US-educated liberal. Nevertheless, the growing conflict in the Occupied Territories towards the end of the year increased Jordan's financial problems by reducing the lucrative influx of Western tourists to the Middle East.

However strong were people's anti-Israel feelings, Jordan's finances were awkwardly dependant on the USA, wherein the powerful Jewish lobby exerted strong pro-Israeli pressure. Even so, King Abdullah's 1999 visits to Damascus and the Gulf had already suggested that he would now bring Jordan closer to other Arab states. On August 22, after the King met Palestinian President Yassir Arafat, Jordan insisted that East Jerusalem must be placed under Arab sovereignty. Soon afterwards, Jordanian-Israeli tension rose when the new Intifada brought clashes between Palestinian demonstrators and Israeli security forces, with high rates of casualties amongst the former group (see V.1. and V.2.i.). Trade unions attacked those Jordanians whom they accused of supporting normalisation with Israel. There were demands to close the Israeli Embassy and attacks in Amman on Israeli diplomats. On December 17 the Prime Minister said that Jordan would only accept a solution that gave Palestinians the right to recover their former homes and receive compensation for their losses. In late December Jordan worked with Egypt and the Palestinian authorities in an effort to end the killing of Palestinians in the Occupied Territories.

Jordan-Iraq relations remained at first difficult, as the latter complained of sundry unfriendlinesses, and they further deteriorated in June when Iraq executed a Jordanian subject. But Iraq was of prime economic importance for Jordan, and the King and his government began a reconciliation, unwelcome to the USA but popular with the public. Iraq's deputy Prime Minister, Taher Yasin Ramadan, visited Amman in July. The reconciliation was supported by businessmen who stood to benefit from it. As the first Jordanian Prime Minister to visit Iraq in 10 years, Ali Abu al-Rageb, a successful businessman and former minister with good contacts in Baghdad, took a large delegation there in November. He was welcomed like a head of state and promised to work to end sanctions. Iraq undertook to meet Jordan's oil needs for 2002 at a concessionary price. The Jordanian media praised the government's efforts to end the sufferings of the Iraqi people caused by the sanctions.

Turning to internal affairs, eight new ministers were appointed in January, including a new Minister of Court reputedly less liberal than his predecessor. The Prime Minister, Abdul Rauf Rawabdeh, stayed in office—despite insinuations of corruption—until June when he was dismissed and replaced by his critic Ali Abu al-Rageb. The King wanted the government to promote equality between people from the East and West Banks and to give the latter—and educated people in general—more influence within government. Traditional instincts on the East Bank were illustrated in May when a tribal leader and MP demanded the enforcement of Muslim law. Similarly, in February, the East Bank-dominated parliament refused to stiffen the law against killing unfaithful wives. More surprising was a December eruption of anti-Israeli feeling among the Bedouin of East Jordan.

In September two ex-Prime Ministers founded a new political group, the Arab Democratic Front, which aimed to stimulate political life. King Abdullah's sometimes unorthodox methods were illustrated in January when he personally investigated a widow's complaints of ill-treatment and disguised himself to see how a hospital was handling patients—a cartoonist showed him in 10 different costumes, including one as a bearded fundamentalist and another as a US tourist.

Jordan's economy remained in a precarious state during the year. Tourism, a main source of foreign exchange, fell heavily after the outbreak of the Intifada. In January the government earned US$508 million by selling 40 per cent of its telecommunications to a French firm which spent heavily on improving them. The government, supported by the International Monetary Fund, accelerated privatisation, although this risked increasing unemployment, which already affected 30 per cent of the labour force.

iv. SYRIA

CAPITAL: Damascus   AREA: 185,000 sq km   POPULATION: 17,300,000
OFFICIAL LANGUAGE: Arabic   POLITICAL SYSTEM: presidential
HEAD OF STATE AND GOVERNMENT: President Bashar al-Assad (since July '00)
RULING PARTY: Baath Arab Socialist Party
PRIME MINISTER: Mohammed Mustafa Mero, since March '00
MAIN IGO MEMBERSHIPS (NON-UN): AL, OAPEC, OIC, NAM
CURRENCY: Syrian pound (end-'00 £1=S£79.92, US$1=S£53.50)
GNP PER CAPITA: US$970, US$2,761 at PPP ('99)

HAFEZ al-Assad, President of Syria for nearly 30 years, died on June 10 (see XVIII). Under his rule, Syria had retained a significant military presence in Lebanon and the determination to use it. Though ready to make concessions for peace with Israel, he had been committed to regaining the territory lost by Syrian the 1967 war. His funeral was widely attended by, amongst others, the Presidents of France and Turkey and by the US Secretary of State.

Assad's successor, his son Bashar al-Assad, differed from his father in background and character. A Western-educated doctor, he had not been expected, until his brother Basil died in 1994, to enter government. Amongst the national problems which he inherited were the Israeli-Palestinian stalemate (see V.1 and V.2.i.) and relations with Lebanon. Bashar's accession was smooth and-foreseeably-his position was confirmed massively in a referendum. His first pronouncements followed his father's line on foreign affairs but less so in internal matters where he was discernibly less autocratic and showed greater indulgence towards the regime's political opponents.

President Mubarak of Egypt paid a surprise visit to Damascus in January, reportedly to improve relations after he had suspected Syria of rushing, without consulting him, into a rapprochement with Israel. Syrian forces still occupied Lebanon, though less numerous in Beirut than in the past. In January, rioting Islamic extremists (see V.2.v.) were suppressed by Syrian troops acting "on Lebanon's behalf". But, under the new President, Syrian behaviour in Lebanon seemed to grow more conciliatory as autumn advanced. Lebanese banks were allowed to operate in Syria, and the Syrian government admitted that it was holding 50 Lebanese prisoners. In December the Lebanese President revealed that he had long been negotiating with Syria for their release. On December 11 a total of 54 Lebanese and eight Palestinian prisoners were freed and returned to Beirut. Human rights activists maintained that this represented less than the total of those who had been imprisoned.

The new President's first visit abroad was to Egypt in early October. There were negotiations with Iraq on trade, pipelines and rail links, and August saw the first train from Baghdad reaching Aleppo. Syria began piping water to Jordan and liberalising its trade there.

The situation in Israel loomed throughout the year. Late in 1999 the Syrian government had arrested Islamists and left-wingers in preparation for expected (but ultimately unsuccessful) negotiations with Israel, and had allowed Arabs in occupied Golan to meet their Syrian relatives. Talks with Israel began in the USA in January, when Faruq al Shara', the Foreign Minister, met Israeli Prime Minister Ehud Barak. The latter's government would not defy its domestic opposition by negotiating the evacuation of the Golan, although Israel had previously contemplated doing so in return for financial compensation. On March 26 Hafez al-Assad met US President Clinton in Geneva (a concession by a man normally reluctant to travel) but again found little on offer but a list of minimum Israeli requirements. There was still no question of restoring the 1967 frontier nor returning the Golan, (or surrendering control of the northern shore of Lake Tiberias) and instead, Israel approved the construction of yet more Jewish settlements in the area.

In November the Syrians boycotted the European-Mediterranean conference in Marseilles because Israel was expected to attend. The following month the USA warned Syria and Lebanon that Israel might attack Syrian forces in Lebanon if Hezbollah continued operations against Israel. The year thus ended without progress, although there was promise in the new President's desire to avoid fresh conflict with Israel and to improve Syria's relations with the West, including the USA.

President Hafez al-Assad's lifetime saw important personnel changes. Mahmud Zu'bi, long a central figure in government, was replaced as Prime Minister in March, after being accused of corruption, and deprived of all his property. He later committed suicide. A new Cabinet was sworn in on March 14 under Prime Minister Muhammad Mustafa Mero, formerly governor of Aleppo. Some of his ministers had been recommended by the President's son, Bashar al-Assad, seen as an advocate of economic and administrative reform.

After Hafez al-Assad's death his rebellious brother Rifa'at al-Assad (see AR 1999, p. 219) claimed to succeed him but he was kept away from the funeral and a warrant for his arrest was issued. In mid-June the Ba'ath held its first full congress for 15 years and its nomination of Bashar as President was endorsed by referendum on July 10. His inaugural speech on July 17 followed the paternal line on Israel but he spoke dismissively of Arab unity, an enthusiasm of his father's. Syria's proliferating bureaucracy, he admitted, had been a source of economic failure and must be pruned.

He also appeared to be discouraging an emerging personality cult when he banned the display of his portrait, and began a campaign against abuses of power for personal gain. He also relaxed the previous clamp-down on opposition when in July he released communists and Muslim Brothers from prison. From August onwards, freedom seemed to be increasing as, for instance, the activities of civil rights groups were permitted. Meanwhile the Lebanese press demanded a lifting of the Syrian state of emergency and the release of over a thousand political prisoners. In November Bashar al-Assad, to mark the 30th anniversary of his father's presidency, amnestied several hundred political prisoners and authorised an increase in press freedoms.

In November there were clashes, seemingly unconnected with national politics, between Druze and Bedouin, in the south around Suwaida. The fighting left over 20 dead-mostly Druze, the Bedouin being the better armed.

The Ba'ath under Hafez al-Assad had been obsessed with Arab nationalism and doctrinaire socialism and had neglected the economy, which suffered from poor management, undue state control and corruption. The 1999 budget, only published in January 2000, showed a deficit of over 10 per cent. Exports and agricultural production were falling. By contrast Bashar cultivated Western-trained economists and businessmen, and was a keen advocate of the symbols of Western economic advancement such as the internet and mobile telephones.

v. LEBANON

CAPITAL: Beirut   AREA: 10,000 sq km   POPULATION: 3,400,000
OFFICIAL LANGUAGE: Arabic   POLITICAL SYSTEM: presidential, power-sharing
HEAD OF STATE AND GOVERNMENT: President Émile Lahoud (since Nov '98)
PRIME MINISTER: Rafiq al-Hariri (since Oct '00)
MAIN IGO MEMBERSHIPS (NON-UN): AL, OIC, NAM, Francophonie
CURRENCY: Lebanese pound (end-'00 £1=L£2,251.16, US$1=L£1,507.00)
GNP PER CAPITA: US$3,700, US$4,129 at PPP ('99)

THE year saw few real changes in Lebanon's political situation. Syria's forces remained within the country and the Syrian government retained its paramount position of influence. Israel withdrew its troops (together with their Lebanese collaborators) but its aircraft continued to attack Hezbollah partisans who fired into Israel. Elections produced a new government (under a Syrian-connected billionaire) which faced the same difficulties, including thousands of Palestinian refugees who had nowhere else to go. The economy too remained problematic, with the cost of servicing the national debt exceeding total state revenue.

There was heavy fighting in January around the self-declared Israeli Security Zone in south Lebanon. In early February Israel bombed power stations in Beirut, Tripoli and Baalbek, with President Mubarak of Egypt joining President Lahoud in condemning the air-raids. The Israelis appeared to expect Hezbollah to stop fighting after incurring severe casualties, but the bombardments appeared only to make them more determined.

In the face of such resolute (and increasingly skilful) resistance, Israel found that its occupation was incurring unacceptable casualty rates and was increasingly unpopular at home. Therefore, the government of Prime Minister Ehud Barak decided to honour its election pledge and withdraw its troops from the self-declared Security Zone in south Lebanon. The Lebanese offered to accept a United Nations force in the south, but said that any peace must include Israeli withdrawal from the Golan and give Palestinian refugees the right to return to their homes. In May, two months ahead of the planned date, Israeli troops began to withdraw, handing over positions to their client militia, the South Lebanese Army (SLA). It soon became apparent that the SLA could not defend the zone, however, and both Israeli units and SLA forces ended up making an unconditional and rapid retreat from Lebanon (see V.1). The SLA commander accused Israel of betraying him, but Lebanon's Prime Minister Salim al-Hoss rejected his plea for an amnesty and confirmed that SLA members who remained would be dealt with in accordance with the judicial process.

Thousands of Lebanese made the Israelis' departure a national holiday. Near the border some were then killed by land mines, whilst others were fired on by

Israeli units. Prisoners who had been kept by the SLA in Khiam gaol were freed, and evidence was uncovered of the appalling conditions in which they had been imprisoned and the torture which had been routinely applied to them.

The UN Secretary-General, Kofi Annan, had previously urged Israel to leave Lebanon, disband the SLA, release Lebanese prisoners and stop reconnaissance flights over Lebanon. In late May the Security Council endorsed Annan's verification that Israeli forces had been withdrawn, although Prime Minister Hoss disputed this. When Israel's forces left Lebanese territory (except for a few farms which remained occupied near the frontier), Lebanese troops began to replace them, joining a UN detachment. There were still 350,000 unassimilated Palestinian refugees in Lebanon, mostly herded in camps—an unacceptable addition to the Muslim community in a delicate confessional balance. Hoss said they must be given the right to return to their homes in Palestine.

Peace did not return when the Israeli troops withdrew. Lebanon would not use its forces to protect Israel, which in October was again attacked by Hezbollah fighters. Israeli aircraft responded by overflying Lebanon at will. The US government warned both sides against escalating the situation. The year closed without any solution to the problem of four Israelis held by Hezbollah, whom the latter were prepared to exchange for 19 Lebanese and many other Arabs held in Israeli jails.

The Syrian occupation continued, countering Islamic extremists, but was gradually relaxed. Finally, in December, some 50 Lebanese prisoners in Syrian jails were freed and allowed home (see V.2.iv.). The occupation naturally aroused protest and in April Maronites loyal to the exiled Michel Aoun (see AR 1997, p. 216) clashed with police whilst demonstrating against it. Walid Jumblatt, leader of the Druze, joined in further anti-Syrian protests and Maronite bishops said that Syria was dictating Lebanon's decisions for her and should leave.

The government quarrelled with the Libyan ambassador and a display of Libyan *amour propre* ended in his withdrawal. Four of the Japanese Red Army who had arrived in Lebanon in 1997 with forged passports (see AR 1997, p. 216) were expelled; a fifth was given political asylum.

Autumn saw an unexpected electoral win for the billionaire former Prime Minister Rafiq al Hariri. In south Lebanon the two Shia parties, Amal and Hezbollah, long-term allies, won all of the region's seats. The previous Prime Minister, Salim al-Hoss, lost his seat. The public dissatisfaction with his term of office stemmed from economic recession; increased debt, and an unwillingness to undertake radical change. Parliament reassembled on October 16. Hariri was accused, by Jumblatt and prominent Maronites, of subservience to Syria in forming his government. His deputy was another billionaire from the Gulf and eight key ministers were closely associated with him. Proteges of Nabih Berri (himself still Speaker of Parliament) held five portfolios, including Foreign Affairs.

Economically, the country remained in considerable difficulties. Hoss's government could not control its spending and in May the budget deficit was 52 per cent of expenditure (the target being 37 per cent). Accumulated debt was 135 per cent of GDP, with the burden of debt servicing exceeding government revenue.

Half of the government expenditure went on salaries, with many jobs being distributed according to religion and patronage. The national airline for instance, with only nine aircraft, had some 4,500 employees. By August an estimated 15,000 people were emigrating monthly, and there were now worldwide an estimated 12 million expatriates whose remittances were sustaining the economy.

Saeb Salam, six times Prime Minister of Lebanon, died in Beirut on January 20 aged 95 (see XVIII). A Sunni Moslem, and after Suez a strong pro-Nasser nationalist, he supported Muslim-Christian co-existence throughout the 1975-90 civil war. He retired to Switzerland, returning only in 1994. Raymond Edde died in Paris on May 10 aged 87. A moderate Maronite and twice a minister, he had stood unsuccessfully for President in 1976. That same year he left for exile in Paris after surviving a Phalangist assassination attempt.

vi. IRAQ

CAPITAL: Bagdad AREA: 438,000 sq km POPULATION: 23,000,000
OFFICIAL LANGUAGE: Arabic POLITICAL SYSTEM: presidential
HEAD OF STATE AND GOVERNMENT: President Saddam Hussein (since July '79),
    also Prime Minister & Chairman of Revolutionary Command Council
RULING PARTY: Baath Arab Socialist Party
MAIN IGO MEMBERSHIPS (NON-UN): AL, OPEC, OAPEC, OIC, NAM
CURRENCY: Iraqi dinar (end-'00 £1=ID0.47 US$1=ID0.31)
GNP PER CAPITA: n/a

CHANGES in Iraq's fortunes benefited the regime of President Saddam Hussein during 2000. The declared US intention to overthrow him with sanctions and propaganda was supported only by the UK, and that half-heartedly. Other governments, including Iraq's neighbours, increasingly disregarded US wishes and severely undermined the sanctions. The victims of the crumbling blockade, the poor and the weak, blamed the allies more than Saddam and the misery of the sanctions (particularly their impact on children) had the effect of rallying support to his cause.

Domestic news was scarce and unreliable. In January 40 members of the armed forces were reportedly executed for disloyalty, but in general Saddam's grip on the state's security apparatus appeared undiminished. After elections, won easily by the Ba'ath, a new parliament opened in April, with 30 appointees to represent Kurdish areas outside the Iraqi administration's control (or, as the government said, areas "occupied by the Americans"). Kurdistan was being regularly used for the export of Iraqi oil (as were Iranian territorial waters in the Gulf), otherwise, Kurdistan was more tranquil: Allied policy appeared to have relieved Iraq of a burden.

Allied policy towards Iraq was ostensibly based on UN sanctions. The UN inspectors were initially satisfied with Iraq's co-operation, although they insisted that their inspections must be unscheduled. But soon the long-standing disagreement in the Security Council (UNSC) between the Anglo-Americans and the other permanent members embarrassed the UN Secretary General: sanctions, he said, were hurting civilians (see XI.1.). The UNSC unanimously doubled the funds for upgrading the oil industry and the UN Reparations Committee postponed settling the Kuwaiti claim against Iraq.

The first candidate to head the UN Special Committee on Iraq (UNSCOM)—Richard Butler having resigned—was rejected by three of the five permanent members of the Security Council. The monitoring committee's new Swedish head faced disagreements between the great powers, and several international officials concerned with Iraq resigned in protest.

The USA demanded a change of government in Iraq, on the basis that Saddam should be tried for war crimes, and it promised another US$4 million to overthrow him. At the same time, US companies were buying and selling Iraqi oil. The Anglo-American attitude was generally attacked, and not only in Iraq (a US national who had formerly run the sanctions committee, now called the measures misguided), and the sanctions policy was opposed by the other permanent Security Council governments. The Russians, stressing the damage to their economy, denounced the interception of their tankers and negotiated with Iraq over missile components. France called sanctions "cruel, ineffective and dangerous". Both, defying the USA and UK, sent missions to Iraq. As the year went on, the Anglo-American ostracism of Iraq was increasingly disregarded. In October the Iraqis were admitted to an Arab League summit for the first time in 10 years.

Iraq's neighbours resented the USA's support for Israel. The Syrian government attacked sanctions and US efforts to isolate Saddam. It re-opened the Syria-Iraq railway link, imported Iraqi oil for its refineries (at a discounted price), and allowed the oil to transit Syrian territory to the Mediterranean. Iraq was also visited by Iran's Foreign Minister—for the first time in 10 years—and Jordan's Premier.

Saudi-Iraqi rapprochement was more difficult. US forces remained in Saudi bases and Iraqi leaders accused the Saudis—and the Kuwaitis—of helping the Ango-Americans. But when Saudi dissidents highjacked a Saudi aircraft carrying a Saudi prince (and 40 Britons) and landed it in Baghdad, Saddam liberated the hostages, entertained them lavishly, and sent them on their way. Relations with Kuwait also remained strained. The Kuwaiti government denied holding Iraqi prisoners, and demanded US$21 billion in reparations and the return of Kuwaiti property seized during the war.

There was widespread sanctions-busting through Jordan (which received Iraqi oil at reduced prices), Dubai, Iran and even Turkey. It was hard to prevent Iraqi oil being transported through the Gulf, since movements by small ships were virtually uncontrollable. Sanctions often produced international disagreements. Ships with Iraqi oil were seized by Iran and the US navy, but smuggling continued and benefited privileged individuals. There was also a surge in travel to and from Iraq. Many foreign delegates attended the Baghdad trade fair, and in November Iraqi Airways resumed regular flights.

Having gone some way towards making the decade-old air embargo redundant, the Iraqi government turned its attention to the oil component of the sanctions regime—the procedure by which Iraqi revenues under the UN's "oil-for-food" arrangement were held in a UN escrow account, and then spent subject to item-by-item approval by the UN sanctions committee. This arrangement meant in effect that the USA and the UK controlled Iraq's budget through their veto powers, ostensibly to prevent expenditure on rearmament. In an attempt to undermine these veto powers, in late November companies lifting Iraqi crude were asked to pay a 40 cent per barrel surcharge directly into a government account, rather than through the UN escrow account. The UN rejected the move and Iraq suspended all oil exports. However, the effect of the suspension on market prices was negligible, partly due to Saudi and Kuwaiti pledges to cover any shortfall, and in mid-December exports were resumed and the "oil-for-food" programme was renewed for a further six-months. Nonetheless, Iraq claimed that it had won a "political" victory in the form of commitments from France and Russia to work harder to end the sanctions regime as it stood.

Although UN sanctions and Anglo-American anti-Iraqi policy hardly weakened the Saddam regime, it greatly increased the sufferings of ordinary Iraqis. Since sanctions had begun in 1991, child mortality had reportedly doubled because of power and water shortages in hospitals, malnutrition and increasing communicable disease.

3. SAUDI ARABIA—YEMEN—ARAB STATES OF THE GULF

i. SAUDI ARABIA

CAPITAL: Riyadh   AREA: 2,150,000 sq km   POPULATION: 21,600,000
OFFICIAL LANGUAGE: Arabic   POLITICAL SYSTEM: monarchy
HEAD OF STATE: King Fahd ibn Abdul Aziz (since June '82), also Prime Minister
HEAD OF GOVERNMENT/HEIR APPARENT: Crown Prince Abdullah ibn Abdul Aziz (since June '82).
   Also First Deputy Prime Minister
MAIN IGO MEMBERSHIPS (NON-UN): AL, OPEC, OAPEC, GCC, OIC, NAM
CURRENCY: Saudi riyal (end-'00 £1=SR5.60, US$1=SR3.75)

THROUGHOUT 2000 Saudi Arabia had to deal with the problem of controlling world oil prices as they rose from the depths reached in 1998 to levels which caused increasing alarm within the developed world. Initially, other OPEC members showed considerable reluctance to increase production in order to modify prices, but the Saudi authorities in March were able to persuade them to increase output by 7 per cent or 500,000 barrels a day (b/d). This led to an overall rise of 1.45 million b/d over the production quota levels of a year earlier, which was in reality only a rise of 774,000 b/d because of quota-breaking in 1999. Iran, in protest at US heavy-handedness, refused to sign the agreement but agreed to abide by it. Still prices did not fall, despite a further 708,000 b/d increase in OPEC production agreed in late June, so Saudi Arabia allowed 162,000 b/d more oil than its quota limit onto the market. OPEC agreed a further 800,000 b/d production increase in early September. US pressure for increased production had become intense and Saudi Arabia, as virtually the only OPEC member apart from Kuwait with excess capacity, had in effect recovered its role as swing producer. It promised to increase production from the August level of 8.5 million b/d towards its capacity limit of 11 million b/d if prices continued to rise beyond the OPEC upper price limit of US$28 per barrel.

Saudi Arabia also sought to improve its own hydrocarbon sector performance by creating a new Supreme Petroleum and Mineral Affairs Council in January. The new council, which was, in theory, chaired by King Fahd, was to define and approve national policy and set prices and production levels. To the disappointment of international oil companies, which two years ago had hoped that they might get access to Saudi concession acreage, it was made clear that the council would block attempts to allow them into upstream petroleum production. Instead, in April, after the council had decided to allow foreign entry into upstream gas production, 15 international oil companies were invited by Crown Prince Abdullah to submit bids. Up to US$30 billion was expected to be invested as a result. Their plans, designed to provide feedstock to the power, desalination, petrochemical and general industrial sectors by raising gas production and treatment by 1.6 billion cubic feet per day, were outlined by Saudi officials in July, and were submitted to the council at the end of August.

At the end of February the Saudi authorities exhibited their displeasure with the behaviour of the Japanese-run Arab Oil Company, which operated offshore in the Neutral Zone, by cancelling its 280,000 b/d 40 year-old concession. The result was that Japan lost 30 per cent of the crude which it obtained from fields under its direct control. The company continued to retain the Kuwait part of the concession but its former Saudi concession area was taken over by Aramco. The cancellation arose after the collapse of last minute negotiations over a US$2 billion financing package for a 1,400 km railway project in the Saudi Arabia. Japan had offered a low interest loan for the project, together with a US$5.75 billion 10-year investment programme, a proposal which did not satisfy Saudi aspirations in view of the Arab Oil Company's past record of low investment in its concession. As a result of the withdrawal of the concession, Japanese petrochemical producers cancelled investment plans in the country.

A new Royal Family Council, under Crown Prince Abdullah, was instituted in June, apparently to pave the way for King Fahd's retirement from active public life. The new council was openly supported by pro-Abdullah members of the royal family, but Prince Sultan, the second deputy premier and Defence Minister, and Prince Naif, the Interior Minister, were not members, suggesting that the "Sudairi Seven" did not support the initiative. Otherwise the domestic scene remained calm throughout the year, except for two car bombings in Riyadh in November involving UK expatriates in Saudi Arabia. Despite fears that the attacks had targeted foreigners—a concern strengthened by a lone gunman's attack on an expatriate housing compound at the same time—the Saudi authorities insisted that the bombings involved an illegal alcohol production ring within the expatriate community and had no political implications.

There were major economic reforms throughout the year. Legislative preparations were made in January for Saudi Arabia's attempt to join the World Trade Organisation, expected in 2001, involving reforms to tariff structures, trade in services, subsidies, incentive and labour regulations. Further legislative and regulatory reforms were proposed, also in January, to encourage portfolio equity investment and to regulate a future stock market. At the same time, Saudi Arabia acquiesced in Gulf Cooperation Council decisions over a future common external tariff which, at 5.5 per cent for basic goods and 7.5 per cent for luxury goods, was below the Saudi proposals of first 8 and 12 per cent and then 6 and 8 per cent respectively. A new investment law, designed to encourage foreign direct investment, was issued in April which would allow 100 per cent foreign ownership of Saudi companies, rather than 49 per cent, as in the past. The law also provided for a new permissive regulatory body, the General Investment Authority, under the chairmanship of the head of the Royal Commission for Yanbu and Jubail, Prince Abdullah bin Faisal bin Turki, to replace the former Foreign Capital Investment Committee. There were problems with the new law, however, because it lacked adequate mechanisms to encourage investors. Eventually, in December, the Supreme Economic Council overrode the new authority to approve 29 investment licences worth SR3.85 billion, whilst 87 applications, worth SR5.17 billion, remained under consideration.

A new five-year plan was published in late August for the period from 2000 to 2005. It proposed overall GDP growth of 3.16 per cent per year, with the private sector growing at 5.04 per cent. It sought to eliminate budget deficits and to encourage economic growth and the Saudisation of the workforce. It aimed to create 817,000 new jobs by the end of the plan period in order to counter unemployment, which was running at between 15 and 20 per cent of the workforce. The private sector was expected to drive the plan and the non-oil sector was to grow from 3 per cent of the economy to 76 per cent by 2004. In fact, improved oil revenues—an estimated US$64.8 billion, compared with the budget estimate of US$29 billion—led to hopes that a fiscal surplus would be achieved during the financial year for the first time in 17 years, thus allowing the country to begin to pay off long term debt, estimated to be equivalent to 115 per cent of GDP. This expected outcome ran counter to the earlier budget forecast made in February which, on the basis of a low oil price of US$16 per barrel, had anticipated a budget deficit of SR28 billion, with revenues of US$157 billion and expenditure rising by 12 per cent over 1999 to SR185 billion—of which only SR9.1 billion was expected to go to capital expenditure. In fact, the budget significantly underestimated oil prices and the trade surplus in 2000 was expected to be substantially larger than the 1999 figure of US$22.77 billion, itself double the previous year's figure, leading to a current account surplus in the current year, compared with a deficit of US$1.7 billion in 1999.

Saudi Arabia's privatisation programme ran into trouble after electricity tariffs were cut in October, thereby discouraging potential private investors from the new Saudi Electricity Company which had been formed in January by merging regional state companies, preparatory to privatisation. Preparations for the privatisation of the national airline, Saudia, went ahead in December, however, with the appointment of consultants.

The year also saw major improvements in Saudi Arabia's regional relations. In June a border agreement was signed with Yemen, bringing to an end the 67 year-long conflict over the frontiers between the two countries and Saudi Arabia's push for a corridor to the Indian Ocean. The matter of the maritime delimitation with Iran in the Gulf was raised after a dispute over the location of an Iranian drilling rig which Saudi Arabia claimed was in its territorial waters. The maritime delimitation dispute with Kuwait was also settled in June. In one area, however, the outlook was not so encouraging; Saudi Arabia increasingly found itself at loggerheads with the USA over the latter's policies towards the ongoing dispute between the Palestinians and Israel, particularly after a new spate of violence began in the Israeli Occupied Territories at the end of September (see V.1 and V.2.i.). By the end of the year, Saudi Arabia had taken several steps to align itself with the Palestinian cause. At the Arab League summit in October, Saudi Arabia proposed and contributed to two funds, totalling US$1 billion, to support the Palestinian Authority. Furthermore, Crown Prince Abdullah expressed his support for Yassir Arafat's stance over Jerusalem, warning the USA that any move of the US embassy to Jerusalem would result in Arab retaliatory measures against US policy towards Iraq and US businesses operating in Saudi Arabia. In December, the Defence Minister, Prince Sultan, formerly a strong pro-USA advocate, blamed the US administration for the crisis in the Occupied Territories, and US Secretary-of-Defence, William Cohen, on his last visit to the region before the end of the Clinton administration in November, was warned of the damage being done to the USA's position in the region by its uncritical support of Israel.

ii. YEMEN

CAPITAL: Sana'a   AREA: 528,000 sq km   POPULATION: 18,500,000
OFFICIAL LANGUAGE: Arabic   POLITICAL SYSTEM: presidential
HEAD OF STATE AND GOVERNMENT: President (Field Marshall) Ali Abdullah Saleh (since May '90)
RULING PARTIES: General People's Congress (GPC) & Yemeni Alliance for Reform (Islah)
PRIME MINISTER: Abdulkarim al-Iryani (since April '98)
MAIN IGO MEMBERSHIPS (NON-UN): AL, OIC, NAM
CURRENCY: Yemeni rial (end-'00 £1=YR245.57, US$1=YR164.39)
GNP PER CAPITA: US$350, US$688 at PPP ('99)

DURING 2000 the Yemeni government was finally able to end its long-standing border dispute with Saudi Arabia which had existed since the Treaty of Taif in 1934, and which had allowed Saudi Arabia to influence domestic Yemeni politics and contribute significantly to the traditional weakness of central government. Indeed, even in February 2000 there had been a clash between Yemeni and Saudi forces in the border region which left 10 Yemeni soldiers dead and Saudi forces in control of Jabal Jahfan, seven kilometres inside Yemeni territory. Yemeni ministers visited Riyadh to encourage their Saudi counterparts to establish a timetable for a resolution of the border agreement which had been under negotiation since 1994. The USA, through the assistant Secretary-of-State, Edward Walker, offered to mediate as it had done in February 1995, when it had persuaded both sides to sign a memorandum of understanding in order to settle the dispute—although nothing substantial had occurred for the next five years.

On June 12 final agreement over the border was reached, culminating in the ratification of the agreement by both governments, thus bringing to an end a process of negotiation which had begun when Crown Prince Abdullah of Saudi Arabia had visited Yemen on the 10th anniversary of unification in May 1990. The agreement that delimited the border was, surprisingly, in Yemen's favour. A private company would be responsible for demarcating the frontier and both sides were to withdraw their military forces 20 kilometres from the border. Yemen anticipated that the agreement would lead to a significant cut in military expenditure, which had been running at 15 per cent of GDP and represented 32 per cent of the state budget. The Yemeni government also hoped for increased tourism and foreign investment, as well as enhanced co-operation with Saudi Arabia in oil and gas joint ventures, a shared refinery and oil export terminal, and joint petrochemical ventures. These expectations were probably over-optimistic, but it seemed that Saudi Arabia might well provide increased aid, in addition to allowing more Yemeni migrants into the Kingdom and possibly agreeing to a free trade area arrangement with Yemen. It would not, however, promote Yemeni membership of the Gulf Cooperation Council—something which the Yemeni government would have dearly liked.

The new border agreement did not imply an immediate improvement in Yemeni domestic security. On June 10, two days before the treaty was signed, a Norwegian diplomat was killed in crossfire as police battled with his four kidnappers at a road block, whilst attempting to free him. He had been kidnapped with his son when trying to collect his car from a repair shop in Sana'a, the Yemeni capital. Some months earlier, in March, the Polish ambassador to Yemen, Krzyztof Suprowicz, was kidnapped by the Qiyari tribe just outside the capital and held for three days until a detained tribesman was freed. In October Hatim Muhsin bin Farid, the latest leader of the banned Aden-Abayan Army, notorious for its attacks on tourists in December 1998, was sent to prison for seven years. The prosecution appealed against the decision because the court found that charges of possessing heavy weaponry and of leadership of the banned movement had not been proved.

On October 12 a US warship moored in Aden harbour, the *USS Cole*, was attacked by two suicide bombers in a small craft packed with explosives, resulting in the death of 17 sailors, the wounding of 37 and the infliction of severe damage to the hull of the ship. US missions in the region claimed to have been expecting an attack and had closed, fearing an assault by Osama bin Laden, who was duly blamed for the attack on the *Cole*. Two days later the UK embassy in Sana'a was attacked when a bomb was thrown over the perimeter fence at 6 am. Although a diesel generator was destroyed, there were no casualties and observers suggested that there was no direct link with the *Cole* attack.

Five weeks after the attack on the *Cole*, six Yemenis were arrested; two were accused of having organised the bombing and the other four of having assisted with it through the provision of forged documents. The dead bombers, of whom one at least was Yemeni, were said to have fought in Afghanistan, and it was suspected that one might have been involved in the bombing of US embassies in Kenya and Tanzania in August 1998 (see AR 1998 pp. 262-3). In the wake of the arrests, Yemen and the USA signed an anti-terrorism convention which allowed FBI agents in Yemen to attend the interrogations of the accused, although they could only question them in writing.

Four new oil concessions were offered along the coast, bringing to 36 the total number of blocks on offer, alongside the 27 operating concessions involving 29 foreign companies. Oil output by the end of the year was expected to have reached around 470,000 barrels a day (b/d), an increment of 30,000 b/d. Oil reserves stood at 5.7 billion barrels, with 15,000 billion cubic feet of natural gas. Oil revenues were essential for ensuring that the current account was in surplus, and generated two thirds of the country's budget revenues. Foreign exchange revenues, on the back of buoyant oil prices, rose to US$910 million in the first six months of the year, compared with only US$495 million in the same period of 1999. Inflation was kept under control at 16.7 per cent, despite cuts in drought subsidies. However, the benefits of good economic management were wiped out by Yemen's very high birth-rate, which grew by 3.5 per cent during the year.

iii. ARAB STATES OF THE GULF

United Arab Emirates (UAE)
CONSTITUENT REPUBLICS: Abu Dhabi, Dubai, Sharjah, Ras al-Khaimah, Fujairah, Umm al-Qaiwin, Ajman
CAPITAL: Abu Dhabi   AREA: 77,000 sq km   POPULATION: 2,990,000
OFFICIAL LANGUAGE: Arabic   POLITICAL SYSTEM: federation of monarchies
HEADS OF STATE & GOVERNMENT: Sheikh Zayad bin Sultan al-Nahayyan (Ruler of Abu Dhabi), President of UAE (since Dec '71)
PRIME MINISTER: Sheikh Maktoum bin Rashid al-Maktoum (Ruler of Dubai), Vice-President and Prime Minister of UAE (since Nov '90)
MAIN IGO MEMBERSHIPS (NON-UN): AL, OPEC, OAPEC, GCC, OIC, NAM
CURRENCY: UAE dirham (end-'00 £1=Dh5.49, US$1=Dh3.67)
GNP PER CAPITA: US$18,220, US$19,720 at PPP ('98)

Kuwait
CAPITAL: Kuwait   AREA: 18,000 sq km   POPULATION: 2,000,000
OFFICIAL LANGUAGE: Arabic   POLITICAL SYSTEM: monarchy
HEAD OF STATE: Sheikh Jabir al-Ahmad al-Jabir al-Sabah (since Dec '77)
HEIR APPARENT: Crown Prince Sheikh Saad al-Abdullah al-Salim al-Sabah, Prime Minister (since Feb '78)
MAIN IGO MEMBERSHIPS (NON-UN): AL, OPEC, OAPEC, GCC, OIC, NAM
CURRENCY: Kuwaiti dinar (end-'00 £1=KwD0.46, US$1=KwD0.31)
GNP PER CAPITA: US$22,110, US$24,270 at PPP ('98)

Oman
CAPITAL: Muscat   AREA: 300,000 sq km   POPULATION: 2,800,000
OFFICIAL LANGUAGE: Arabic   POLITICAL SYSTEM: monarchy
HEAD OF STATE: Sheikh Qaboos bin Said (since July '70)
MAIN IGO MEMBERSHIPS (NON-UN): AL, GCC, OIC, NAM
CURRENCY: rial Omani (end-'00 £1=RO0.58, US$1=RO0.39)
GNP PER CAPITA: US$4,950, US$8,690 at PPP ('97)

Qatar
CAPITAL: Doha   AREA: 11,400 sq km   POPULATION: 671,000
OFFICIAL LANGUAGE: Arabic   POLITICAL SYSTEM: monarchy
HEAD OF STATE: Sheikh Hamad bin Khalifa al-Thani (since June '95)
MAIN IGO MEMBERSHIPS (NON-UN): AL, OPEC, OAPEC, GCC, OIC, NAM
CURRENCY: Qatar riyal (end-'00 £1=QR5.44, US$1=QR3.64)
GNP PER CAPITA: US$11,570 ('97)

Bahrain

CAPITAL: Manama AREA: 685 sq km POPULATION: 740,000
OFFICIAL LANGUAGE: Arabic POLITICAL SYSTEM: monarchy
HEAD OF STATE: Sheikh Hamad bin Isa al-Khalifa (since March '99)
HEAD OF GOVERNMENT/HEIR APPARENT: Sheikh Khalifa bin Sulman al-Khalifa, Prime Minister (since Jan '70)
MAIN IGO MEMBERSHIPS (NON-UN): AL, OAPEC, GCC, OIC, NAM
CURRENCY: dinar (end-'00 £1=BD0.56, US$1=BD0.38)
GNP PER CAPITA: US$7,660, US$13,700 at PPP ('98)

ALL the Arab Gulf states enjoyed significantly improved economic results during the year because of the consistent buoyancy in oil prices. The improvement in oil revenues affected both their external accounts and their budgetary outcomes. Thus, in Oman the budget deficit in 2000 was only 2 per cent of GDP and was 60 per cent lower than forecast at OR140 million, compared with its level of 8 per cent of GDP in 1999, even though expenditure during the year had risen by 13 per cent over the 1999 level to OR2.44 billion. Revenue, forecast at OR2.09 billion on the basis of an oil price of US$14.5 per barrel, was bolstered by an oil income of US$2.93 billion in the first nine months of the year, 52 per cent more than in 1999. The windfall profits were set to go to the State General Reserve Fund, which could be used to finance budget deficits and which, like the Fund for Future Generations in Kuwait, was used for foreign investment.

In the United Arab Emirates GDP growth throughout the year was anticipated to reach 7.1 per cent because of the increase in oil revenue towards US$7 billion, with inflation at 2.5 per cent. The federal budget was expected to be buoyant, with adequate funding for projects such as the Thurayyah satellite telecoms project, the Dolphin project, the Dubai Internet City and the Adnoc Offshore Summit project.

In Kuwait, where the financial year ran from July to June, the budget for 2000 began with very robust expectations as oil revenues were estimated to reach a record US$16 billion. The budget surplus was predicted to be over US$4 billion, compared with a US$6.6 billion deficit in 1998 and, after 10 per cent of oil revenue—worth US$2.25 billion—had been transferred to the Fund for Future Generations, the net surplus was still expected to be around US$3 billion. Expenditure was expected to be US$13.5 billion, compared with revenue of at least US$17.5 billion. Real GDP growth was set at 3.5 per cent, although the National Assembly was expected to slow down the reconstruction campaign.

In Qatar the budget, published in April, built upon the surplus achieved in the 1999 financial year and the US$13 million deficit in the 1998 financial year by forecasting a very cautious oil price level throughout the year of $15 per barrel. This cautious approach was largely because of the privatisation of 45 per cent of Q-Tel which, if excluded from the budget, would have produced a deficit of 7 per cent of GDP. As a result oil revenue was set at US$2.5 billion, a level that did not allow for any increase in expenditure, not least because of past accusations of over-investment. Expenditure was set at QR15.4 billion (US$4.23 billion), revenue at QR12.6 billion (US$3.46 billion) and the budget deficit was expected to reduce by 23 per cent to QR2.8 billion (US$769 million)—although with elevated oil prices, the outcome seemed likely to be much better, with a surplus of up to

US$500 million. The country's main financial problem was foreign debt. Direct government debt was more than US$4 billion, and government-guaranteed debt raised the total to US$11 billion—120 per cent of GDP. Repayment between 2000 and 2002 was set at US$1 billion per year, a factor which threatened to push the budget back into deficit.

In Bahrain, where GDP growth was 4.8 per cent in 1998 and 4 per cent in 1999 in real terms, the budget deficit for the 2000-2001 financial year was expected to be BD314 million, partly because Bahrain's oil production had fallen to 36,800 barrels a day (b/d) although 263,000 b/d—62 per cent free of charge—were imported from Saudi Arabia, largely to be processed by the Sitra refinery, where capacity was to be upgraded to 250,000 b/d.

Whilst the Gulf members of OPEC supported the organisation's attempts throughout the year to maintain oil prices within the US$22-to-US$28 per barrel price range agreed upon at the OPEC summit in September, both Bahrain and Oman—who were not members—sought to expand production. Omani production reached 900,000 b/d at the end of the year with the prospect of capacity reaching 1 million b/d by 2004, and plans were laid in March for a new 75,000 b/d refinery at Sohar, which would start operating in 2004. New emphasis was also placed on natural gas, with plans to expand liquified natural gas (LNG) production by 50 per cent to serve the Indian, Japanese and South Korean markets, as the first shipments of LNG for Korea left the processing plant at Qalhat in April. Domestic use of gas was to be enhanced by a new pipeline between Sohar and Salalah, for which contracts were awarded in August. The pipeline would serve two new industrial centres and would power projects including a US$2.5 billion aluminium smelter, the US$970 million India-UAE joint venture fertiliser plant and two new build-operate-transfer power plants. Development, in short, was to be pushed ahead. In this context Oman joined the World Trade Organisation in October and, despite a subdued stock market throughout the year, sought to attract increased foreign direct investment with the promise of 70 per cent foreign ownership of companies, rising to 100 per cent in the financial sector, as from February 2001.

In Bahrain, the outlook was more clouded as its diverse economy sought to adjust to declining crude production by expanding the refineries and placing increasing emphasis on the financial sector, which currently generated as much income as the hydrocarbon sector. Results in the financial sector were mixed, with Arig (the Arab Insurance Group) reporting a loss for 1999 and ABC (the Arab Banking Corporation, which had been hit by the Asian crisis at the end of the 1990s) reporting a profit both from the parent company and from its Islamic banking and Algerian subsidiaries.

Qatar, on the other hand, was far more bullish, after GDP growth of 8.9 per cent in 1999 and a balance of payments surplus of US$0.9 billion. It allowed its ambitious investment plans to continue on the back of its 640,000 b/d oil quota—with plans for an expansion of its oil production capacity to 900,000 b/d by the end of 2000 and 1.03 million b/d by the end of the following year being revived—and the start of significant gas exports.

In Kuwait the economic year was dominated by "Project Kuwait" and safety problems in the country's refineries. Project Kuwait was an ambitious plan to attract international oil companies into the country's northern oil fields along the Iraqi border. Although the oil ministry claimed that this was because of the need to bring in the latest technology—the scheme would generate an additional 500,000 b/d, raising Kuwait's production capacity to 3 million b/d by 2005—in reality the objectives were more strategic in nature in that the country could be certain of Western military support in the case of future Iraqi aggression if Western oil companies were operating there. Nine companies were short-listed at the end of the year for the US$14 billion project, even though constitutional issues had not been resolved. Kuwait's constitution did not permit foreign ownership of its oil resources, so 20-year operating and servicing agreements, renewable for a further 10-year period, had been proposed instead. Kuwait's National Assembly also disliked the project, insisting in February 2000 that it had sole prerogative over the award of such agreements.

Safety at the country's major refineries was called into question in mid year when two workers died in a gas leak in Mina al-Shuaiba refinery. Five persons died and 50 were injured in an explosion at Mina al-Ahmada refinery which was subsequently closed for repairs costing US$330 million.

In the United Arab Emirates particular attention was paid during the year to expanding electricity production, with a US$1 billion syndicated loan for the Taweelah-1 site at the end of the year, just after a similar loan for the Taweelah-2 project. A further project—Taweelah-3—was under discussion which would supply 25 per cent of Abu Dhabi's electricity needs within four years. Dubai, given its restricted access to crude oil, had turned instead to tax-free zone operations and was carving out a lead in information technology, with 607 IT companies already operating there, earning US$624 million a year. In late October, the Crown Prince opened the latest venture, Dubai Internet City, of which the first phase had cost US$200 million. Two more projects were planned—Dubai Media City for publishing and broadcasting and Dubai Ideas Oasis for new IT products. Dubai clearly intended to establish a lead, both inside and outside the region in this new but risky field. A new federal stock market law permitted the opening of a new trading floor in Dubai in March. This was intended to end over-the-counter trading there, in an effort to attract foreign investment, although, outside the free trade zones where 100 per cent foreign ownership was permitted, foreigners could only hold 49 per cent of company equity.

In foreign affairs, apart from the ongoing problem of Iraq—Saudi Arabia and Kuwait resolutely refused to deal with Saddam Hussein, whilst the United Arab Emirates, Qatar and Oman took a more relaxed view—the scene was dominated by the two long-standing disputes with Iran: the crisis over the Greater and Lesser Thunbs islands, of which Abu Dhabi continued to dispute the annexation by Iran in 1971; and over Abu Musa where Sharjah repudiated Iran's unilateral rejection in 1992 of the 1971 Memorandum of Understanding. Although the other Gulf states had been generally supportive, their growing links with Iran caused the United Arab Emirates to threaten to suspend its membership of the Gulf Cooperation Council in November.

The other major issue was the continuing maritime boundary dispute between Bahrain and Qatar, which had been placed before the International Court of Justice at The Hague. In an unexpected gesture of reconciliation at the end of 1999, the Emir of Qatar, Sheikh Hamad bin Khalifa al-Thani, had visited Bahrain. His visit was returned by the Bahraini emir on January 6 and the two rulers agreed to establish a joint committee to resolve the dispute, so that they could withdraw the case from the International Court of Justice. The Qatari ruler's sudden visit had been stimulated by the Bahraini ruler's decision to boycott the Gulf Cooperation Council summit in Doha in December 1999 because of the dispute. The initiative broke down, however, in late May, despite another surprise visit by the Emir of Qatar to Bahrain, when Qatar filed documents with the Court—an act that was seen as a breach of faith by Bahrain. The Court's judgement was expected in early 2001.

In domestic terms, the situation in Bahrain was dominated by the policies introduced by the new ruler. In a move to end the Sunni-Shi'a divide, political prisoners were released and exiles were allowed to return. In late September a new 40-member *shura* (consultative) council was established, thus fulfilling a promise the new emir had made in May. The first batch of 19 members included four women, a representative of the Asian community and a Jew. The council was only to have advisory powers but, after 2004, it was to be elected. The council started work in October, three months after the former intelligence head, Peter Henderson, had retired. At the end of the year, on Bahrain's national day, the emir announced that further constitutional reform would create a bicameral parliament in which the *shura* council would become the upper chamber. The lower chamber, which would have legislative powers, would be elected by universal suffrage. At the same time, Bahrain would become a monarchy. After the changes were approved in December by referendum, a committee was set up under the Crown Prince to implement them within three years. The Bahraini scene was clouded in late August by the crash of a Gulf Airways Airbus A320 with 143 persons on board as it was attempting to land. All on board died in the crash.

In August Qatar took over the chair of the Islamic Conference Organisation from Iran and, at the organisation's ninth summit in Doha in November, calls were made for Islamic countries to break diplomatic ties with Israel. Saudi Arabia and Iran sought to make this mandatory for member states, particularly if the USA moved its embassy to Jerusalem. Despite Iraqi and Sudanese pressure, Egypt and Turkey resisted a call for a jihad against Israel. The gathering agreed to create an Islamic common market. In February the Qatari courts announced sentences against those who had participated in the failed coup against the emir in 1996. Thirty persons were convicted and given life sentences, rather than the death sentences which the prosecution had sought, and 85 people were acquitted.

In Kuwait an alleged sabotage network was uncovered in November. Its members, who included Kuwaitis and Moroccans, had planned to attack US targets in protest at the USA's policy towards Israel. The Kuwaiti members of the conspiracy, who included a major in the armed forces, responsible for organising an arms dump for the group, were members of Islamic Jihad, whilst the Moroccans were said to have been in contact with Osama bin Laden's organisation, al-Qa'ida. Earlier in the year, in May, the Kuwaiti Supreme Court had upheld the verdict of high treason passed against Ala al-Khalaji, the Kuwaiti who had been made the head of the Iraqi puppet regime during the occupation of Kuwait in 1990. Al-Khalaji had voluntarily returned to Kuwait from Norway to argue the case. His death sentence was later commuted to life imprisonment. The Kuwaiti National Assembly, which had become very active in recent years, in December 1999 rejected a series of decrees issued by the emir in the summer of 1999. It also rejected a proposal that women should be allowed to vote and to stand for election, a decision which was later upheld by the Supreme Court.

In Oman new elections to the consultative council took place in September—the previous elections had occurred in 1997. In the United Arab Emirates, a major arms contract was signed in March when the federation decided to buy 80 F-16 C/D Desert Falcons for US$6.4 billion from the Lockheed Martin Corporation. The deal had been under negotiation since the mid-1990s and delivery was set for between 2004 and 2007.

4. SUDAN—LIBYA—TUNISIA—ALGERIA—
MOROCCO—WESTERN SAHARA

i. SUDAN

CAPITAL: Khartoum   AREA: 2,500,000 sq km   POPULATION: 31,400,000
OFFICIAL LANGUAGE: Arabic   POLITICAL SYSTEM: Islamist/military regime
HEAD OF STATE AND GOVERNMENT: President (Gen.) Omar Hasan Ahmed al-Bashir (since Oct '93), previously Chairman of Revolutionary Command Council (since June '89)
RULING PARTY: National Congress Party (NCP)
MAIN IGO MEMBERSHIPS (NON-UN): AL, OAU, COMESA, OIC, ACP, NAM
CURRENCY: Sudan dinar (end '00 £1=SD386.45, US$1=SD258.70)
GNP PER CAPITA: US$290, US$1,360 at PPP ('98)

THROUGHOUT the year the conflict intensified between President Omar Hasan Ahmed al-Bashir and Hasan al-Turabi, the leader of the Islamic National Front (INF). To consolidate his position and to weaken the influence of the INF on the government, the President in January appointed a new Cabinet, which he subsequently reshuffled in July. The government also extended the state of emergency, imposed in 1999, until the end of the year.

In May President al-Bashir called a meeting of the ruling National Congress Party (NCP) to launch his campaign for the forthcoming presidential election, a move objected to by al-Turabi, the secretary general of the party. The President then suspended the membership of the entire NCP and all party chiefs throughout the country. In an ineffectual gesture of retaliation, al-Turabi dismissed the President and a number of his aides from the NCP. Although al-Turabi did not himself stand as a candidate in the presidential elections, he announced in September that his newly formed political party, the Popular National Congress Party (PNCP), would contest both the presidency and the parliamentary elections.

The elections were held in December and were boycotted by northern opposition parties and the Sudan People's Liberation Army (SPLA). The turnout was very low and President al-Bashir was re-elected for a further four-year term.

In the light of the need for a rapprochement and reconciliation with northern opposition groups and the SPLA, the President argued in favour of a move towards democracy and a secular state, whilst Hasan al-Turabi objected strongly to the latter. In a gesture of reconciliation the President issued a decree in July pardoning those who had raised arms against the state. However, he also emphasised the need to face the military situation in the south and the government continued to send volunteer students and others to fight there. In a show of discontent with al-Bashir's policies, al-Turabi called in September for an end to the war in the south, accusing the President of having abandoned the cause of Islam.

Egypt, Libya and Eritrea made extensive efforts to reconcile the Sudanese government with all of its opposition groups. In response; the first major political party to reach an agreement with the government was the Umma Party, which at a meeting in Asmara, the capital of Eritrea, decided to leave the National Democratic Alliance (NDA) and agreed to a ceasefire with the government. The leader of the Umma Party, Sayyid Sadiq al-Mahdi, returned to Sudan in November after four years of self-exile. He affirmed the need to restore multi-party democracy, the right of southern Sudanese to self-determination and the need to adapt Islamic sharia law to the country's changing circumstances. The reconciliation with Mahdi was seen as a considerable coup for the government.

Despite pressure from Egypt, Eritrea and Libya, and a meeting with President al-Bashir, Sayyid Muhammed Othman al-Mirghani, the leader of the NDA and the Democratic Unionist Party (DUP), remained in exile. He accused the government in December of not being serious about national reconciliation, a view echoed by the SPLA.

Meanwhile, the armed conflict continued. Forces of the NDA, known as the New Sudan Brigade and comprising SPLA military units and NDA fighters, raided the eastern town of Kassala and temporarily occupied the religious centre of Hamish Koreib. A member of the fundamentalist group al-Takfir wa-al-Hijra (Atonement and Exile) opened fire in December in a mosque on the outskirts of Omdurman, killing 23 people and wounding 55 others. This was the second attack on the mosque by the group despite the government's claim that it had successfully suppressed the group.

The SPLA, under the leadership of Col John Garang, continued its military operations against government forces in the south. A number of military garrisons and towns changed hands with casualties being sustained by both sides. During fighting between the SPLA and government forces around the Bentiu oil field the latter forced members of the Nuer tribe to vacate their villages, ostensibly for security reasons, although it was suspected that the move was prompted by a government desire to exploit the oil.

Riak Machar, hitherto an ally of the central government, resigned from his government-supported positions as Chairman of the Southern Sudan States' Coordination Council (SSCC), assistant to President al-Bashir and Chairman of the United Democratic Salvation Front. He left for Kenya, but remained undecided as to whether to join the SPLA or establish his own anti-government forces.

The Inter-Government Authority for Development (IGAD) meetings in February, May and December, resulted in indecision, and the organisation looked weak and ineffectual. The difficulty faced by IGAD was that of reconciling two divergent views—the government's desire to maintain sharia law, and the SPLA's insistence on the separation of the state and religion.

With a view to improving relations with Uganda, Sudan repatriated 51 Ugandans who had been kidnapped by Uganda's Lord's Resistance Army (LRA). In a reciprocal gesture of appeasement, the Ugandan Parliament asked President Yoweri Museveni to sever links with the SPLA. In January Eritrea restored diplomatic relations with Sudan, and President al-Bashir visited Eritrea in February to normalise relations. President Isayas Afewerki of Eritrea responded with a visit to Sudan in October, in pursuance of his efforts to reconcile Sudan's government with its opposition groups. The military confrontation between Ethiopia and Eritrea in May forced thousands of Eritrean civilians to seek refuge in Sudan and the latter appealed for international help to deal with the influx.

The provision of international aid to people in the south who had been displaced by the civil war was hampered when Western humanitarian agencies pulled their operations out rather than sign separate memoranda with the government and the SPLA. Eight Norwegian church aid workers were killed in January when their vehicle was attacked on the border with Uganda. It was thought that Uganda's LRA was responsible.

Sudan succeeded in persuading Canada not to propose the intervention of the United Nations in the conflict in southern Sudan. The USA sent two officials in March and a delegation in September to assess the peace process in the south, the internal political difficulties and Sudan's links with terrorism. However, Sudan protested against a visit, made without the official permission of Susan Rice, the US Assistant Secretary of State for African Affairs, to assess humanitarian aid and reports of human rights violations in SPLA-controlled areas. In October the USA blocked Sudan's election to the African seat on the UN Security Council because of its alleged links with terrorism.

In March the government signed a loan agreement with the Kuwait-based Arab Fund for Economic and Social Development for US$114 million for road and irrigation projects. The decision of the International Monetary Fund (IMF) in August to lift the suspension of Sudan's voting and related rights as a result of the country's improved economic performance was welcomed. But the IMF insisted that Sudan must increase its repayments to the organisation and other creditors in order to regain access to the financial resources of the IMF.

ii. LIBYA

CAPITAL: Tripoli   AREA: 1,760,000 sq km   POPULATION: 6,700,000
OFFICIAL LANGUAGE: Arabic   POLITICAL SYSTEM: socialist 'state of the masses'
HEAD OF STATE: Col. Moamer Kadhafi, 'Leader of the Revolution' (since '69)
HEAD OF GOVERNMENT: Mubarak Abdullah al-Shamikh, Secretary-General of
   General People's Committee (since Dec '97)
MAIN IGO MEMBERSHIPS (NON-UN): AL, OPEC, OAPEC, AMU, OAU, OIC, NAM
CURRENCY: Libyan dinar (end-'00 £1=LD0.81, US$1=LD0.54)
GNP PER CAPITA: n/a

EARLY in the year, Libya's government underwent a structural transformation. In March Col Moamer Kadhafi announced that most of the government secretariats (in effect ministries) were being abolished and their functions devolved to the municipal and provincial levels. The move continued a decentralisation policy which had been introduced in the late1980s but which was interpreted in part as a means of deflecting blame for the country's mounting social and economic problems away from the leadership to local officials. The Libyan leader declared that the secretariats of Foreign Liaison and International Co-operation, Finance, and Justice and Public Security would be retained and two new secretariats created, one for African Unity and another bringing together Information, Culture and Tourism. Policy on the vital area of hydrocarbons was transferred to the National Oil Company. A new and much smaller General People's Committee (in effect the Cabinet) was formed with Mubarak Abdullah al-Shamikh as Secretary (a post broadly equivalent to that of Prime Minister).

Whatever the changes to the formal political structure, however, real power remained with Kadhafi and a close circle of confidants. At this time Kadhafi also spoke of the need to establish a "constitutional reference", which was interpreted by many as a call for the appointment of a "head of state", a title that had not been used since 1977, and one consistently rejected by Kadhafi himself. In a reshuffle in October, the secretaries for Justice and Public Security, and Finance were dismissed and the Information secretariat abolished. By the second half of the year the devolution process had made little progress.

The trial of the two Libyans accused of the 1988 Lockerbie bombing finally began in May (see II.1.ii.). It was alleged that they were members of the Libyan intelligence service and had spent four years planning the attack. Both defendants pleaded not guilty. The defence alleged that members of a small Palestinian guerrilla group, the Popular Front for the Liberation of Palestine-General Command, acting as agents of the Iranian government, had planted the bomb in revenge for the shooting down of an Iranian civilian airliner over the Gulf by a US warship in July 1988. In August Britain and the USA released the text of a letter from the UN Secretary-General to Col Kadhafi, written before the handover of the two suspects, promising that they would not be used to "undermine the Libyan regime". Scottish legal officers insisted that these assurances would in no way inhibit the prosecution's case. After 73 days of evidence and more than 230 witnesses the prosecution completed its submission in late November. Much of the evidence presented was highly circumstantial and a number of key witnesses proved unreliable or offered testimony which appeared to undermine the prosecution's case.

Nevertheless, an attempt by the defence to have the case against one of the defendants, Lamen Khalifa Fhimah, dropped because of insufficient evidence was rejected by the judges.

Relations with the European Union (EU) remained uneasy. In January the President of the European Commission, Romano Prodi, withdrew an invitation to Kadhafi to visit Brussels, and in April the Libyan leader used his main speech to the EU-Africa summit in Cairo to castigate Africa's former colonisers. Yet Libya continued to be courted by individual European states, and in August won praise from the French and German governments for its role in securing the release of Western hostages held by Muslim separatists in the Philippines. Libya was allowed to participate in the Euro-Mediterranean meeting in Marseilles in November. In June Russia announced that it was resuming arms sales to Libya.

Kadhafi's African ambitions, notably his project to establish a "United States of Africa", received a setback in early October when Libyan mobs attacked black African migrant workers, killing over 50 and causing thousands of others to flee the country. Undeterred, the Libyan leader embarked on a tour of the Arab world, presenting a "strategic proposal" for Arab unity with Africa. He then caused embarrassment by revealing on television the proposed Egyptian draft of the final declaration of the forthcoming Arab League summit in Cairo, denouncing it as a sell-out and challenging Arab leaders to "take steps that would satisfy the angry Arab masses".

During the year the authorities announced plans to attract US$10 billion in investment over the next five years, mostly from foreign companies, in order to expand the vital oil and gas sector and to modernise the country's crumbling infrastructure.

iii. TUNISIA

CAPITAL: Tunis   AREA: 164,000 sq km   POPULATION: 10,100,000
OFFICIAL LANGUAGE: Arabic   POLITICAL SYSTEM: presidential
HEAD OF STATE AND GOVERNMENT: President Gen. Zine el-Abidine Ben Ali (since Nov '87)
RULING PARTY: Constitutional Democratic Rally (RCD)
PRIME MINISTER: Mohammed Ghannouchi (since Nov '99)
MAIN IGO MEMBERSHIPS (NON-UN): AL, AMU, ICO, OAU, OIC, NAM
CURRENCY: Tunisian dinar (end-'00 £1=TD2.07, US$1=TD1.38)
GNP PER CAPITA: US$2,100, US$5,478 at PPP ('99)

IN February unrest broke out in the south-east of the country as anti-government demonstrations by high-school students and young unemployed Tunisians turned violent. Whilst the authorities insisted that the unrest had only lasted for a few hours and was limited to a small area, other sources claimed that the rioting lasted for several days and spread beyond the south-east.

On April 6 Habib Bourguiba, Tunisia's first President, under house arrest since being deposed by Zine el-Abidine Ben Ali in 1987, died at the age of 97. His funeral was a deliberately low-key affair, and the authorities ordered state television not to broadcast live coverage of the ceremony. Nevertheless, tens of thousands of Tunisians lined the route of the funeral procession, and in Sfax, Tunisia's second city, hundreds of students demonstrated against the Ben Ali regime.

Tunisia's human rights record was once again in the spotlight in April when journalist Taoufiq Ben Brik began a hunger strike in protest at police harassment. Ben Brik had earlier been charged with diffusion of false information and defamation of the country's institutions after he wrote several articles for the European press which were critical of the Ben Ali regime. The affair attracted unprecedented attention in the international press with French newspapers in particular devoting considerable coverage to human rights abuses in Tunisia, and several senior European political figures, including President Jacques Chirac of France, raising the issue with the Tunisian authorities. Within Tunisia dissidents became more outspoken in their criticism of the regime and argued that civil society was finally reawakening to resist the regime's "strategy of fear". In early May, apparently under strong European pressure, the authorities backed down, returned Ben Brik's passport and lifted the ban on his travelling abroad. In response Ben Brik ended his hunger strike and left for France.

The affair led to a number of other hunger strikes by human rights activists and political prisoners. In June two members of the banned Parti Communiste Ouvrier Tunisien (Tunisian Communist Workers' Party) and in August a member of the outlawed al-Nahda party, Taoufiq Chaib, were released from prison after staging hunger strikes. But these events did not signal greater tolerance by the regime. In July officials from Amnesty International and the International Federation of Human Rights were refused permission to visit Tunisia, and Moncef Marzouki, spokesman for the Conseil National des Libertés en Tunisie (National Council for Liberties in Tunisia), was dismissed from his university post after publicly criticising the Tunisian authorities during a visit to Europe.

In municipal elections held at the end of May the ruling Rassemblement Constitutionnel Democratique (Democratic Constitutional Assembly—RCD) retained control of all the municipal councils, winning 93 per cent of the 4,128 seats contested. Official figures put turnout at 84 per cent, down from 92.5 per cent in 1995. The ruling party, which put up candidates in every constituency, stood unopposed in 175 of the 257 constituencies, with the opposition parties fielding candidates in only 60 constituencies and independent candidates standing in 22. Although independent and opposition candidates won 243 seats compared with only six (out of 4,090) in 1995, they had been expected to win over 800 seats following the introduction of new electoral rules in 1997.

Relations with France became strained over the Ben Brik affair, which provoked the strongest French criticism of Tunisia since Ben Ali came to power. The European Parliament continued to press for greater political reform but resisted calls from MEPs demanding that the EU association agreement with Tunisia should be suspended. New agreements were signed with Italy on defence co-operation and the employment of Tunisian workers. Tunisia's efforts to revive the moribund Arab Maghreb Union, notably by trying to reconcile Morocco and Algeria, made little progress, but bilateral relations with Libya were strengthened, and in June the two countries agreed to establish a free trade zone. Early in the year the first senior Tunisian official visited Tel Aviv for talks with the Israeli Foreign Minister, but in late October, in the wake of violent clashes between Israel and the Palestinians (see V.1 and V.2.i.), Tunisia again closed its interest section in Israel and imposed a freeze on the normalisation of relations with the Jewish state. At the beginning of the year, Tunisia began a two-year term on the United Nations Security Council.

In January tariffs were removed on the first group of European industrial goods also produced in Tunisia. The Tunisian Employers Association voiced concern that despite the ongoing modernisation programme, Tunisian enterprises were not yet prepared for direct competition.

iv. ALGERIA

CAPITAL: Algiers   AREA: 2,382,000 sq km   POPULATION: 31,800,000
OFFICIAL LANGUAGE: Arabic   POLITICAL SYSTEM: quasi-military regime
HEAD OF STATE AND GOVERNMENT: President Abdelaziz Bouteflika (since April '99)
RULING PARTIES: National Democratic Rally (RND), National Liberation Front (FLN),
   Movement for a Peaceful Society (MPS) & En-Nahda Movement (MN) form coalition
PRIME MINISTER: Ali Benflis, since Aug '00
MAIN IGO MEMBERSHIPS (NON-UN): AL, OPEC, OAPEC, AMU, OAU, OIC, NAM
CURRENCY: dinar (end-'00 £1=AD106.68, US$1=AD73.42)
GNP PER CAPITA: US$1,550, US$4,753 at PPP ('99)

IN early January, after urgent high level negotiations between the authorities and the leadership of the Islamic Salvation Army (AIS), a new agreement was reached which provided a full amnesty for the group's fighters, estimated to number some 3,000. For its part, the AIS agreed to disband permanently, although in the short term several hundred fighters were to be enrolled in an "auxillary unit" under army command and deployed against those Islamist militants who had rejected President Abdelaziz Bouteflika's 1999 peace initiative, notably the Armed Islamic Group (GIA). Shortly after the mid-January deadline for the amnesty the Interior Minister announced that 80 per cent of members of armed groups had surrendered to the authorities. Amnesty International, which was allowed to send a delegation to Algeria in May, later criticised the President's peace initiative, arguing that it meant that in practice neither side in the conflict was going to be punished for acts of brutality. Amnesty called on the authorities to investigate all past and present atrocities and to bring those responsible to justice. The President's peace plan was not accompanied by any new political initiatives, and a lifting of the ban on the Islamic Salvation Front (FIS) was ruled out. In May the Interior Minister refused to legalise Wafa (Fidelity and Justice), headed by former presidential candidate Ahmed Taleb Ibrahimi, on the grounds that the new party was merely a reconstitution of the banned FIS under another name, and in November the authorities closed the party's offices throughout the country.

Although relative calm prevailed in the capital, Algiers, and most major cities, large swathes of the countryside remained insecure, with around 200 civilians, soldiers and rebels being killed every month. At the end of the year there was a marked upsurge in the level of violence; some 300 civilians were killed during the first two weeks of December, including the massacre of 16 students at a lycée in Médéa, all attributed to the GIA. The authorities released no information about the latest atrocities but they were widely reported in the private press, which voiced strong criticism of the President, insisting that his peace initiative had failed. Sections of the press claimed that certain Islamist militants had taken advantage of the amnesty to re-establish their underground networks. Some analysts argued rather that the resurgence of violence reflected the latest power struggle between Bouteflika and the military hierarchy, suggesting that the GIA was acting on the orders of the security services to discredit Bouteflika's policy of reconciliation. Rumours circulated in Algiers that the leading generals were planning to replace him.

The Prime Minister, Ahmed Benbitour, resigned in August after only eight months in office and was replaced by Ali Benflis, Bouteflika's Chief of Staff and one of the President's closest allies. The new government remained a coalition of seven political parties, and there were only a few ministerial changes, notably the appointment of Abdelaziz Belkadem, a senior member of the National Liberation Front (FLN), as Foreign Minister. The new Prime Minister immediately set up six ministerial co-ordination groups to draw up the details of his government's programme and was expected to press ahead with reforms.

Despite growing problems at home, Bouteflika succeeded in improving Algeria's image abroad and ending the diplomatic isolation imposed on it by the West after the 1992 military takeover. He made a full state visit to France in June, the first of its kind by an Algerian President, during which he was given every honour, and in July the Spanish premier, José María Aznar, became the first European leader to visit Algiers since 1992. There were also visits by several senior US officials during the year to discuss political, economic and military issues, and President Bill Clinton praised Bouteflika's leadership at home and Algeria's role in securing an end to the conflict between Ethiopia and Eritrea. Diplomatic relations with Iran were restored after a meeting between Bouteflika and President Khatami at the United Nations Millenium Summit in New York in September. But the Western Sahara dispute continued to prevent any significant improvement in relations with neighbouring Morocco. Algeria strongly denied an Israeli statement in March that Israel had agreed to provide assistance in counter-terrorism to Algeria following a secret meeting in Italy between emissaries from the two countries.

Government technocrats proceeded with the modernisation of the economy, often ignoring the social consequences. Social tensions mounted as a small minority flaunted its wealth ostentatiously whilst the majority suffered impoverishment and daily hardships, with high levels of unemployment, acute housing shortages and deteriorating public services, especially in the spheres of education and health.

v. MOROCCO

CAPITAL: Rabat   AREA: 447,000 sq km   POPULATION: 29,900,000
OFFICIAL LANGUAGE: Arabic   POLITICAL SYSTEM: monarchy
HEAD OF STATE AND GOVERNMENT: King Mohammed VI (since July '99)
RULING PARTY: Socialist Union of Popular Forces (USFP) heads broad coalition
PRIME MINISTER: Abderrahmane Youssoufi (USFP), Prime Minister (since Feb '98)
MAIN IGO MEMBERSHIPS (NON-UN): AL, AMU, OIC, NAM
CURRENCY: dirham (end-'00 £1=D15.78, US$1=D10.56)
GNP PER CAPITA: US$1,200, US$3,190 at PPP ('99)

WHILST modernising and changing the style of the monarchy, King Mohammed VI left no doubt that, like his father, he intended to reign and rule. The King continued to dominate the political sphere, making appointments to all key posts and formulating political strategy. The King's energy and high-profile activities contrasted sharply with the opposition-led government, which appeared lethargic and silent and was subject to increasing public criticism. Premier Abderrahmane Youssoufi's administration could point to some solid achievements, but it had failed to push through important legislation, notably on labour relations and women's rights, and, amidst sharply deteriorating socio-economic conditions, it was seen as weak on economic management. After a long-awaited reshuffle in early September, the Cabinet was reduced in size from 42 to 33 ministers and junior ministers but its political composition remained unchanged and all but four of its members had served in the previous administration. Prime Minister Youssoufi retained his post, as did the four ministers appointed by the Palace. Doubts were expressed that the creation of three economic "super-ministries" would improve the efficiency of the new administration.

Meanwhile an active civil society began to play a more prominent role in the political sphere, and was pressing for further changes and reforms, provoking tensions with the authorities. Despite the government's payment of some US$14 million in compensation to past victims of repression, human rights associations insisted that there could be no reconciliation without justice and demanded that those responsible for human rights abuses should face trial. There was mounting discontent amongst trade unions and workers over pay, and a general strike was only averted in April after the government agreed to costly concessions. Unemployed graduates continued to demonstrate, and in June violent clashes broke out in Rabat between protestors and police. Abdelsalam Yassine, the leader of the country's largest Islamist group, was released in May after spending some 10 years under house arrest, although his movement, Adl Wal Ihsan (Justice and Charity), remained illegal. In early December scores of Islamists were arrested when police broke up demonstrations across the country organised to protest at the restrictions placed on the group's activities.

Sections of the independent press acted as the driving force for change and set out to test the limits of press freedom. It quickly became apparent that comments on the monarchy, the army, and the Western Sahara remained out of bounds. Reporters sans Frontières claimed that during the first six months of the year seven newspapers were banned by the authorities. In early December the three most outspoken and popular weekly magazines, *Le Journal*, its Arabic counterpart

Assahifah, and *Demain*, were banned indefinitely after they published a letter written in 1974 to Abderrahmane Youssoufi which implied that leading personalities in the Socialist Union of Popular Forces (USFP) had been involved in the 1972 failed military coup against King Hassan. The affair unleashed a political storm. Premier Youssoufi insisted that the ban had been imposed not because of the letter but because the three weeklies had attacked the monarchy and the army, endangering the transition to democracy. Some of his critics claimed that the ban exposed the growing influence of senior figures in the security apparatus who were opposed to greater democracy, and their close alliance with the leadership of the USFP.

King Mohammed's first official overseas visit was to Paris in March, where he asked France to support Morocco's request for a partnership with the European Union (EU). The King was well received in Washington in June, re-emphasising the strong ties between Morocco and the USA. Spanish premier José María Aznar visited Morocco in May, and King Mohammed made a state visit to Madrid in September, when the two countries agreed to work to settle their differences, notably Morocco's refusal to renew the EU fisheries accord, racist attacks on Moroccan workers in Spain and the future of the Spanish enclaves of Ceuta and Melilla. King Mohammed held talks with President Abdelaziz Bouteflika of Algeria at the EU-OAU summit in Cairo in April but the Western Sahara dispute continued to prevent any significant improvement in relations (see V.4.iv. and V.4.vi.). In late October, following renewed violence between Israel and the Palestinians, Morocco closed its interest section in Tel Aviv. Earlier, some half a million Moroccans had demonstrated in Rabat in support of the Palestinians, the largest protest march in the country since the 1991 Gulf War.

Severe drought led to another poor harvest with real GDP growth forecast to fall below 1 per cent. Official predictions that Morocco could become self-sufficient in energy after the discovery of oil and gas at Talsint in the Sahara in August were regarded by analysts as premature.

vi. WESTERN SAHARA

CAPITAL: Al Aaiún   AREA: 284,000 sq km   POPULATION: 164,000 ('98)
STATUS: regarded by Morocco as under its sovereignty, whereas independent
Sahrawi Arab Democratic Republic (SADR) was declared by Polisario Front in 1976

DURING the course of the year, the United Nations Secretary-General, Kofi Annan, appeared to have concluded that proceeding with the long-delayed referendum on the future of the disputed territory was no longer a viable option. He secured approval from the Security Council to explore other ways and means to find a solution. The Secretary-General's frustration and pessimism was understandable. After almost a decade and costs close to US$500 million, the UN Mission for the Referendum in Western Sahara (MINURSO) had succeeded in establishing a list of 86,381 eligible voters but faced more than 133,000 appeals from applicants— mostly presented by Morocco—whose eligibility to vote had been rejected. The

Moroccan government was insisting that the vast majority of these cases should be reviewed individually, a process that could take up to two years. Annan also pointed out that the UN had made no provisions for enforcing the result of a referendum should one side refuse to accept it.

It was against this background that the Secretary-General asked former US Secretary of State James Baker to resume his role as special envoy, with a mandate to explore with the parties concerned "all ways and means to achieve an early, durable and agreed solution to the dispute". Autonomy for the Western Sahara under Moroccan sovereignty appeared to be the UN's favoured option and one encouraged by the USA and France. But a number of meetings mid-year between Baker and representatives of Polisario and the Moroccan government failed to make any progress. Although Baker had tried to persuade them to discuss a political solution other than the referendum plan, neither side expressed any interest in doing so. Indeed Moroccan officials now insisted that all Sahrawis in the "southern provinces" and not just those found eligible under the criteria set by the UN must be allowed to vote in a referendum or Morocco would withdraw from the process. Polisario, for its part, insisted that the problems confronting the referendum were not insurmountable and that it would support any proposals put forward by the UN to allow the appeals process to begin. Polisario's refusal to consider any solution outside the referendum framework was firmly supported by its principal backer, Algeria. At a further meeting in late September chaired by Baker, Morocco indicated its willingness to begin talks on autonomy for the Western Sahara, but Polisario continued to reject any alternative to the referendum which it was confident of winning. However, Polisario faced declining diplomatic support in Africa and Latin America and there were reports of unrest among Sahrawi civilians under Polisario control.

VI EQUATORIAL AFRICA

1. HORN OF AFRICA—KENYA—TANZANIA—UGANDA

i. ETHIOPIA—ERITREA—SOMALIA—DJIBOUTI

Ethiopia
CAPITAL: Addis Ababa   AREA: 1,104,000 sq km   POPULATION: 66,000,000
OFFICIAL LANGUAGE: Amharic   POLITICAL SYSTEM: presidential
HEAD OF STATE: President Negaso Gidada (since Aug '95)
RULING PARTY: Ethiopian People's Revolutionary Democratic Front (ERPDF) coalition
HEAD OF GOVERNMENT: Meles Zenawi, Prime Minister (since Aug '95)
MAIN IGO MEMBERSHIPS (NON-UN): OAU, COMESA, ACP, NAM
CURRENCY: birr (end-'00 £1=Br12.29, US$1=Br8.23)
GNP PER CAPITA: US$100, US$599 at PPP ('99)

Eritrea
CAPITAL: Asmara   AREA: 118,000 sq km   POPULATION: 3,900,000
OFFICIAL LANGUAGES: Arabic & Tigrinyam   POLITICAL SYSTEM: presidential
HEAD OF STATE AND GOVERNMENT: President Isayas Afewerki (since May '93)
RULING PARTY: People's Front for Democracy and Justice (PFDJ)
MAIN IGO MEMBERSHIPS (NON-UN): OAU, COMESA, ACP, NAM
CURRENCY: nakfa, at par with Ethiopian birr (see above)
GNP PER CAPITA: US$200, US$1,012 at PPP ('99)

Somalia
CAPITAL: Mogadishu   AREA: 638,000 sq km   POPULATION: 11,700,000
OFFICIAL LANGUAGES: Somali & Arabic   POLITICAL SYSTEM: presidential - interim government
HEAD OF STATE AND GOVERNMENT: President Abdiqasim Salad Hasan (since Aug '00)
PRIME MINISTER: Ali Khalif Galayr (since Oct '00)
MAIN IGO MEMBERSHIPS (NON-UN): AL, OAU, ACP, OIC, NAM
CURRENCY: Somalia shilling (end-'00 £1=Ssh3,913.75, US$1=Ssh2,620.00)
GNP PER CAPITA: n/a

Djibouti
CAPITAL: Djibouti   AREA: 23,000 sq km   POPULATION: 750,000
OFFICIAL LANGUAGES: Arabic & French   POLITICAL SYSTEM: presidential
HEAD OF STATE AND GOVERNMENT: President Ismail Omar Guellah (since April '99)
RULING PARTY: Popular Rally for Progress (RPP)
PRIME MINISTER: Barkat Gourad Hamadou (since Sept '78)
MAIN IGO MEMBERSHIPS (NON-UN): AL, OAU, ACP, OIC, Francophonie, NAM
CURRENCY: Djibouti franc (end-'00 £1=DFr261.12, US$1=DFr174.80)
GNP PER CAPITA: n/a

FOR the first four months of the year, there was little fighting along ETHIOPIA's disputed border with Eritrea. Both sides affirmed their acceptance of the peace framework negotiated by the Organisation of African Unity (OAU), but disagreed over technical arrangements for its implementation. In May, following a breakdown in proximity talks sponsored by Algeria and the USA, and despite a United Nations

Security Council arms embargo, Ethiopia launched an offensive and made substantial gains. These included retaking Zalembessa and Bada, whilst Badme, the other area in dispute, had been recaptured by Ethiopia in February 1999. Ethiopian troops also penetrated deep into Eritrea to seize Senafe and Barentu. Faced with defeat, on May 25 Eritrea announced its withdrawal from the areas taken in 1998.

Under strong international pressure, on June 18 both sides agreed to a cease-fire. A formal peace agreement was signed on December 12, allowing for the deployment of a 4,200-strong UN peacekeeping force in a 25-kilometre security buffer zone, inside Eritrea, until the border should be demarcated. The first UN military observers arrived in September, and by the end of December half of the peacekeeping force had been deployed but technical disagreements over the security zone remained. Ethiopia continued the deportation of Eritreans and Eritrea rounded up over 7,000 Ethiopians in May. Both sides complained about the treatment of detainees, and compensation remained an unresolved issue. Repatriation of prisoners started before the end of the year, and Ethiopia began the demobilisation of 50,000 men.

Both sides continued their propaganda war, however, and their support for each other's dissidents. Ethiopia continued to back the Eritrean opposition, the Alliance of Eritrean National Forces (AENF). In September, Eritrea hosted a conference in Asmara at which six Ethiopia opposition groups, all Oromo, united in the United Liberation Forces of Oromia. An earlier Oromo Liberation Front (OLF) offer of a cease-fire to facilitate food deliveries had been ignored by the government. OLF activity led to joint Kenyan-Ethiopian security operations along the border. An upsurge of anti-government activity in eastern Ethiopia was blamed on al-Itahaad and the Ogaden National Liberation Front. Furthermore, in August, the externally based opposition Tigray Democratic Union announced that it was launching an armed struggle.

Neither side detailed its costs in the war, but it was estimated that the total killed exceeded 70,000. Both countries spent several hundred million US dollars buying aircraft from Russia, and other arms from China, Bulgaria, Libya and Israel. An International Monetary Fund (IMF) report on Ethiopia in June indicated that the war had caused a sharp decline in expenditure on health and education, and in capital funding for the regions, which fell by 40 per cent. Donors were reluctant to provide aid during the conflict. The budget was postponed until October when the World Bank and the IMF indicated a resumption of aid. In December, the World Bank announced details of a US$400 million credit, and began studies to see if Ethiopia qualified for the "Highly Indebted Poor Countries" initiative. During the year there were serious food problems. By mid-year, 10 million people needed food aid, though famine was contained. Drought was the main cause, but the war displaced hundreds of thousands of people on each side and led to major logistical problems. A series of major forest fires in southern areas lasted from March to May, destroying 70,000 hectares of forest.

Ethiopia hosted the eighth Nile Basin conference in June, building on the Nile Basin Initiative, the commitment for co-operation agreed by the Nile riparian states in 1999. A ministerial meeting in Khartoum in August agreed a framework for joint usage of water.

Federal and state elections were held in May. The ruling Ethiopian Peoples' Revolutionary Democratic Front (EPRDF) won its expected easy victory, taking 479 seats in the 548 seat House of Representatives. Despite the numerous substantiated allegations of fraud, intimidation and violence, Prime Minister Meles Zenawi was formally re-elected in October.

Human rights continued to come in for substantial unfavourable comment from the US State Department in its report of February 2000. At the end of the year Ethiopia still had more journalists in jail (eight) than any other country in Africa. Former Prime Minister Tamrat Layne, dismissed in 1997, was given an 18-year prison sentence in March for corruption. The trials of those accused of human rights abuses under the previous military regime were also accelerated. The establishment of an official Human Rights Commission and an Ombudsman was approved in July. In October, a US$64 million national campaign was launched against HIV/AIDS—Ethiopia officially had 350,000 AIDS patients and over three million carriers of the HIV virus.

In February the Tigrai People's Liberation Front (TPLF), the major element in the EPRDF, celebrated the 25th anniversary of its foundation with a festival in Tigrai region.

In November, the remains of former emperor, Haile Selassie, murdered in August 1975, were finally laid to rest in Holy Trinity Cathedral in Addis Ababa.

Ethiopia's advances in May caused hundreds of thousands to flee, disrupting planting in western ERITREA, the country's main grain producing area. Numbers needing food aid reached a million, with another 500,000 affected by drought. Once the fighting ended Eritrea was again able to access aid, and in December the government announced that it had secured funding for its US$287 million emergency recovery programme.

Substantial criticism of government policies appeared after June. A group of Eritrean intellectuals wrote a letter to President Isayas in September, criticising the accumulation of power in the presidency and calling for transparency and accountability in government as well as the immediate implementation of the constitution, allowing for more political parties. Following similar criticism in the National Assembly, the government announced that multi-party elections would be held in December 2001.

President al-Bashir of Sudan visited Asmara in January, and President Isayas Aferwerki went to Khartoum in October, but relations remained uneasy. Sudanese opposition offices in Eritrea remained open, and Sudan blamed Eritrea for an opposition attack on Kassala in November. Relations with Djibouti, broken after President Isayas insulted President Hassan Gouled Aptidon in 1998, were restored in March. In December a major reorganisation of the Foreign Ministry was carried out and several new embassies were opened.

In SOMALIA there were hopeful signs of recovering stability during 2000. A Somali reconciliation and government conference opened at Arta in Djibouti in May. A 245 member Transitional National Assembly was finally chosen in August by a complex clan-based system and, on August 27, Abdiqasim Salad Hasan, a former Deputy

Prime Minister and Minister of the Interior under Siad Barre, was sworn in as President. The regional Inter-Governmental Authority for Development (IGAD), the Arab League, the UN and the EU endorsed the results. Faction leaders and "warlords", stayed aloof, as did the self-declared Republic of Somaliland and the separate administration of Puntland. They condemned the conference and its government as unrepresentative of political reality.

In October Assembly members and the government began a move to Mogadishu, but by the end of the year they had yet to establish full control over the city. In November one of the Assembly members was assassinated, and attempts to set up a police force made little immediate progress. President Abdiqasim visited Ethiopia in November, but failed to satisfy concerns over links with Islamic groups and Ethiopia continued to support several factions opposed to his government.

A poor harvest in mid-year, with flooding on the Juba and Shebelli rivers in May, put an estimated 1.2 million people at risk from food shortages and an estimated 600,000 required urgent food aid in October.

In DJIBOUTI in February the last faction of the Afar opposition Front for the Restoration of Unity and Democracy (FRUD-Armee), headed by former Prime Minister Ahmed Dini, signed a cease-fire. Ahmed Dini returned to Djibouti at the end of March but little progress was made towards implementing FRUD demands, which included an accurate census, increased decentralisation and an unlimited multi-party system (the current limit was four parties).

The ruling People's Rally for Progress held its eighth congress in February, appointing President Ismail Omar Guellah as chairman. In October Prime Minister Barkat Goured returned to Djibouti after six months treatment for a heart condition.

Drought meant that the World Food Programme provided food aid for 100,000 people for the first six months of the year.

Police units launched an unsuccessful coup in December, after the dismissal of police commander Gen. Yacin Yabeh. Yacin tried to take refuge in the French naval base but was promptly handed over to the government. Two weeks later, in an apparent search for illegal aliens, over 5,000 people were arrested; the majority of whom were deported to Ethiopia.

ii. KENYA

CAPITAL: Nairobi   AREA: 580,000 sq km   POPULATION: 32,000,000
OFFICIAL LANGUAGES: Kiswahili & English   POLITICAL SYSTEM: presidential
HEAD OF STATE AND GOVERNMENT: President Daniel arap Moi (since Aug '78)
RULING PARTY: Kenya African National Union (KANU)
MAIN IGO MEMBERSHIPS (NON-UN): OAU, COMESA, ACP, CWTH, NAM
CURRENCY: Kenya shilling (end '00 £1=Ks116.59, US$1=Ks78.05)
GNP PER CAPITA: US$360, US$975 at PPP ('99)

PRESIDENT Daniel arap Moi reverted to his earlier decision to hand over the constitutional reform process to a parliament dominated by the Kenya African National Union (KANU). He thus effectively derailed the broad-based review initiated in 1998, which many KANU MPs were still thought to favour, particularly in relation to the President's sweeping powers over the legislature and judiciary. By skilfully exploiting Luo-Kikuyu rivalry, he risked turning the constitutional reform debate into an ethnic contest. He obtained the support of Raila Odinga, leader of the Luo-based National Democratic Party (NDP), who led a parliamentary commission of NDP and KANU members on reform of the basic law. This parliamentary initiative was challenged by a church-led, interfaith constitutional reform movement which pressed for a people-oriented approach; it avoided association with the opposition parties, but was nevertheless accused by KANU loyalists of being a front for power-hungry Kikuyu politicians. The reformers, backed by the independent press, wanted to reduce the executive's very considerable powers and feared that a parliament-fronted constitution would extend Moi's term in office, which was due to expire in 2002. Meanwhile, the country's leaders struggled for political power. KANU was split into competing factions and more than 12 parties were angling for the presidency. Simon Nyachae, a former Minister of Finance who had resigned from the Cabinet in 1999 (see AR, 1999, p. 249), announced his candidacy, but did not state the party on whose ticket he proposed to stand.

Chris Okemo, the Finance Minister, presented the budget in June. Commentators accepted that the tariffs which he imposed on raw materials and his other relief measures would give a boost to industry, that removing more than 200,000 Kenyans from the tax band would help the poor, and that the retrenchment of 25,000 civil servants over the next two years would provide long-term savings. But the increase in VAT from 15 to 18 per cent (13 to 16 per cent for hotels) was criticised on the ground that it would put up prices across the board and would damage tourism. The Minister argued that the rise in VAT was necessary to meet revenue targets and to further tariff and trade harmonisation policies in the East African Commission (EAC). Whilst Kenya had probably done more than Tanzania and Uganda, its EAC partners, to implement these policies, this particular budget achieved little in that direction. One concession that he did make was a reduction of the excise duty on beer by 5 per cent (to 85 per cent), which slightly narrowed the gap across the three countries (the duty was between 60 and 70 per cent in Tanzania and Uganda). The budget, along with the reform initiatives taken by Richard Leakey, the head of the civil service, and other civil service technocrats did enough to convince the International Monetary Fund (IMF) and other major donors to resume aid. In August the IMF approved a three-year Poverty Reduction and Growth Facility arrangement.

Rising social tensions included escalating crime and violence, the unrelenting spread of the AIDS virus, and severe drought in some areas. An equal rights bill in favour of women and minority groups was opposed by Muslim women as contravening Islamic law, and was dropped. Mungiki, a religious sect which had originated 15 years previously in the Kikuyu-dominated Central Province, grew in size and influence, maintained its reputation for violence and was seen to be taking an increasingly political stance.

iii. TANZANIA

CAPITAL: Dar es Salaam/Dodoma   AREA: 945,000 sq km   POPULATION: 36,180,000
OFFICIAL LANGUAGES: Kiswahili & English   POLITICAL SYSTEM: presidential
HEADS OF STATE & GOVERNMENT: President Benjamin Mkapa (since Nov '95)
RULING PARTY: Chama cha Mapinduzi (CCM)
PRESIDENT OF ZANZIBAR: Amani Abeid Karume (since Oct '00)
PRIME MINISTER: Frederick Sumaye (since Nov '95)
MAIN IGO MEMBERSHIPS (NON-UN): OAU, SADC, ACP, CWTH, NAM
CURRENCY: Tanzanian shilling (end-'00 £1=Tsh1,202.51, US$1=Tsh805.00)
GNP PER CAPITA: US$240, US$478 at PPP ('99)

FOLLOWING a lacklustre campaign, the elections for the Union presidency and parliament were conducted in an orderly and peaceful manner on October 29. President Benjamin Mkapa benefited from Tanzania's fast growing economy and the failure of the opposition parties to unite behind a single candidate. He gained an easy victory in the presidential election over his three challengers, receiving 71.7 per cent of the votes cast, as against the 61.8 per cent which he had achieved in 1995. The ruling party, Chama cha Mapinduzi (CCM), also triumphed, winning 90 per cent of the 222 directly elected seats in the National Assembly. (There were also 40 special seats for women and 10 additional seats under a recent constitutional change.) The Civic United Front (CUF), the CCM's main challenger and allegedly a Muslim-oriented party, captured two elected seats on the mainland and 16 on the Zanzibar island of Pemba, but only the two mainland MPs were willing to serve in the Union parliament. The other opposition parties fared badly. Frederick Sumaye was reappointed Prime Minister. The 27-strong Cabinet contained many new faces and was dominated by members of the professional classes.

Whilst the mainland elections were accepted by international observers as free and fair, those to Zanzibar's House of Representatives, also on October 29, were seriously flawed, being characterised by violence and blatant ballot rigging. The CUF, which had made greater autonomy within Tanzania its main election platform, demanded that the elections should be re-run in all of the islands' 50 constituencies. The Zanzibar Electoral Commission agreed to this request in respect of 16 constituencies in the Urban West region (in western Zanzibar) and arranged for fresh elections on November 5. A number of violent incidents (some of the later ones were shown on television) occurred at various stages of the electoral process. The CCM was declared to have won every seat in Unguja, the main island, and four in Pemba, where the CUF had swept the board in 1995; the CUF captured 17 constituencies on this occasion. The second round of elections was boycotted by the opposition parties, thereby allowing the CCM to win all 16 seats and giving it a two-thirds majority in the House of Representatives. In the Zanzibar presidential contest, Amani Abeid Karume, the CCM's candidate, obtained 67 per cent of the vote against 33 per cent for the CUF's Seif Shariff Hamad. The new President, in conciliatory mood, included three ministers from Pemba (and one woman) in his 12-member Cabinet and dropped all the ministers and deputy ministers who had served in the Salmin Amour administration. He also freed the 18 CUF leaders who had been charged with treason and imprisoned for three years without trial. Nevertheless, tension remained high in Zanzibar and there was no early prospect of a rapport between the rival camps.

This political setback came at a time when President Mkapa's administration was being praised by the international community for its economic achievements—low inflation, a 5 per cent GDP growth rate, a steady rise in average incomes, the privatisation of two-thirds of public companies, and good investment opportunities. Although corruption remained a problem, the government was making a serious effort to combat it. The 2000-01 budget presented to the Union parliament by Daniel Yona, the Finance Minister, in mid-June, proposed to continue with the programme of fiscal reforms which had recently earned the country macro-economic stability. The social services sector was to receive 25 per cent of estimated expenditure, the amount spent to be recovered from debt relief funds under the World Bank's Highly Indebted Poor Countries (HIPC) initiative. A total of 20 per cent of expenditure was to go to the defence and legal sector, 18 per cent to the economic sector and 37 per cent to the other sectors. The Minister announced that the number of taxes on oil products would be reduced; he waived customs duties on 26 commodities; and upheld duties on petrol, beer, cigarettes, soft drinks, liquor and small vehicles. There were no specific measures for regional integration and the three East African Community member-states seemed to be pulling in different directions on the crucial issue of harmonising trade policies.

After 38 years of research, Tanzania finally succeeded in controlling river blindness or onchocerciasis by using an effective drug called mectizan. Its own programme was supported by the Africa Programme for Onchocerciasis Control (APOC).

iv. UGANDA

CAPITAL: Kampala   AREA: 241,000 sq km   POPULATION: 22,600,000
OFFICIAL LANGUAGE: English   POLITICAL SYSTEM: presidential
HEAD OF STATE AND GOVERNMENT: President Yoweri Museveni (since Jan '86)
RULING PARTIES: National Resistance Movement (NRM) heads broad-based coalition
PRIME MINISTER: Apolo Nsibambi (since April '99)
MAIN IGO MEMBERSHIPS (NON-UN): OAU, COMESA, ACP, CWTH, OIC, NAM
CURRENCY: new Uganda shilling (end-'00 £1=Ush2,640.30, US$1=Ush1,767.50)
GNP PER CAPITA: US$320, US$1,136 at PPP ('99)

IN a referendum in June, just over 90 per cent of voters cast their ballots in favour of retaining the country's no-party "Movement" system advocated by President Yoweri Museveni, but condemned by pluralists as creating a de facto one-party state. Those in the Democratic and other parties who campaigned for the re-introduction of multi-partyism were denied access to state funds and called for a boycott of the referendum; this helped to account for the low turnout (47.2 per cent of registered voters). The prevailing system therefore continued: political parties could exist but could not function, and the fiction was that there was a single programme upon which they were all agreed. It was, claimed the President, a democratic system because anybody could compete for political office on the basis of individual merit.

In August the unexpected happened: the Constitutional Court declared the Referendum and Other Provisions Act of 1999 null and void on the grounds that it had been passed into law on July 1, 1999, by an inquorate legislature. In spite of this ruling, against which the government was to appeal, the Attorney General announced that the Constitutional Court's decision did not invalidate the referendum results. The legislature was embarrassed and the President accused the judiciary of being insensitive "to the aspirations of the ordinary people". He subsequently announced his intention to stand for re-election in 2001 in order to professionalise the army, prepare the country for an orderly succession, and contribute towards the building of the regional market.

Like Tanzania, Uganda followed Kenya's lead and ratified the East African Community treaty. The only serious step that the three governments took towards harmonising tariff structures was to reduce excise duty on malt beer from 90 to 85 per cent, thereby narrowing the gap across the three countries. There was no sign of the emergence of a regional infrastructure policy and each government tended to channel resources into defence and security rather than into regional integration. These matters were of major concern to Uganda, whose forces were committed to defending the country's northern and western borders against rebel attacks and to supporting the rebel Congolese Rally for Democracy (RCD) in the Democratic Republic of the Congo (DRC) (see VII.1.i.). Tension in the latter was high because the Ugandan and Rwandan forces backed different RCD factions, leading in April to further confrontation between them over territory in Kisangani. More promisingly, Uganda and Sudan agreed to restore the diplomatic relations that had been broken off in 1994 and to make arrangements to prevent the northern border areas being violated by rebels on either side. Western donors were unhappy about Uganda's continuing involvement in the DRC and worried that defence expenditure might spiral out of control. They were given assurances, however, that it would not exceed 2 per cent of GDP.

The budget was introduced in parliament by Gerald Ssendaula, Minister of Finance and Economic Planning, in June. It aimed to achieve a GDP growth rate of at least 7 per cent, keep inflation at 5 per cent, maintain macro-economic stability, privatise public enterprises, undertake public utility reforms, and eradicate poverty. Of the total budget of Ush1,516 billion, 27 per cent was allocated to education, 7.6 to health, 9.3 per cent to roads, and 1.4 to agriculture. Money was also set aside to provide coffee seedlings and cotton seeds for the poor. The Minister said that expenditure had been slashed because of the poor performance of the Uganda Revenue Authority, severe drought (which afflicted much of East Africa), the sharp rise in fuel prices and the drop in world coffee prices. The International Monetary Fund (IMF) expressed satisfaction that the government had adhered to its monetary policy, had sought to reduce poverty, and had dramatically increased enrolment in primary education. An improved debt relief package announced by the IMF and the International Development Association promised to reduce Uganda's annual debt servicing by between two-thirds and three-quarters.

A thousand or more people, including women and children, were massacred in south-west Uganda on the orders of the leaders of a cult called the Movement for the Restoration of the Ten Commandments of God. The probable cause of the atrocity was the demand of cult members for the return of their money and possessions when the leadership's prophesy that the world would end on December 31, 1999, had not materialised. Elsewhere, a total of 68 people had died by the end of October following the reappearance in northern Uganda of the highly contagious Ebola virus.

2. GHANA—NIGERIA—SIERRA LEONE—THE GAMBIA—LIBERIA

i. GHANA

CAPITAL: Accra   AREA: 239,000 sq km   POPULATION: 19,200,000
OFFICIAL LANGUAGE: English   POLITICAL SYSTEM: presidential
HEAD OF STATE AND GOVERNMENT: President Jerry Rawlings (since Nov '92),
    previously Chairman of Provisional National Defence Council (since '81)
PRESIDENT ELECT: John Kufuor (New Patriotic Party)
RULING PARTIES: National Democratic Congress (NDC) heads coalition
MAIN IGO MEMBERSHIPS (NON-UN): OAU, ECOWAS, ACP, CWTH, NAM
CURRENCY: cedi (end-'00 £1=C10,867.40, US$1=C7,275.00)
GNP PER CAPITA: US$390, US$1,793 at PPP ('99)

DURING 2000, Ghana was focused on the end of year presidential elections. After taking power two decades earlier by coup d'etat, President Jerry John Rawlings was due to stand down as President. Constitutionally, he was unable to serve more than two terms as national leader. Rawlings was first elected in 1992 in a ballot which the opposition alleged was rigged. It made the same accusation over his re-election in 1996, but he seemed to retain much of his popularity until the economy faltered.

By 2000 the country seemed largely tired of its President, particularly as economic problems became increasingly serious. Whilst most Ghanaians believed the country was better off in 2000 than it had been when Rawlings first took power, there was also considerable disillusionment that 17 years of structural adjustment programmes had failed to stave off an economic crisis partly caused by a collapse in world prices for the country's main exports: cocoa and gold. Despite years of reform, Ghana's economy remained weak and dependent upon Western aid and other financial inputs, with limited benefits to most ordinary people. Many Ghanaians suspected that the economic reforms—portrayed as transforming Ghana into one of the best and freest economies in Africa—had really amounted to selling out the country to foreign financiers.

Whilst the election campaign was fought by seven political parties, only two—Rawlings' National Democratic Congress (NDC) and John Agyekum

Kufuor's National Patriotic Party (NPP)—had a realistic chance of winning power. The first round of presidential voting took place on December 7. Kufuor managed a small lead over Rawlings' preferred successor, Vice-President, John Atta Mills, winning 48 per cent of the vote to Mills's 45 per cent. Because of the closeness of the result, the head of the Electoral Commission, Kwadwo Afari-Gyan, decreed a run-off between the two leading candidates. Candidates from the other five parties managed to acquire between them less than 7 per cent of the votes and were eliminated from the second round of voting.

The run-off election was held on December 28. Kufuor achieved an emphatic victory over Mills, winning 56 per cent compared with 44 per cent. The election's result was not only significant for Ghana but also for Africa. In more than 40 years of independence, this was Ghana's first ever handover of power from one elected regime to another. Praising the elections, which were generally perceived as free and fair despite having been marred by sporadic violence, United Nations Secretary General Kofi Annan, a Ghanaian, said: "With these elections, Ghana has demonstrated that democracy and its institutions are taking root in Africa". When Kufuor's victory became clear on December 30, thousands of jubilant Ghanaians flooded the streets of Accra, Kumasi and other towns and cities to celebrate.

Whilst many of Ghana's west African neighbours such as Sierra Leone, Liberia and Guinea faced a debilitating combination of armed rebellions and economic stagnation, there were widespread expectations of a political and economic upturn in Ghana under the new President. Having previously stood against Rawlings in 1996, the 62 year old Kufuor now inherited a tough political legacy, after two months of bruising and divisive election campaigning. A lawyer who had studied at Oxford University, Kufuor had served as Ghana's deputy Foreign Minister at the age of 30. He dropped out of politics after a military coup, but served briefly as secretary for local government after Rawlings seized power at the end of 1981. He was seen as having run a vigorous campaign despite a lack of resources, particularly by venturing into the ruling NDC's rural strongholds to overturn his party's urbanite image.

Following his election, President-elect Kufuor and his fellow NPP leaders called for restraint—no doubt fearful of retaliation from hard-liners and their military associates in the outgoing Rawlings regime. In an address on Ghana's national radio station, GBC, on December 30, he noted the difficulties facing his administration, particularly the "deteriorating economy" and "depreciating currency". Nevertheless, he was conciliatory towards the former leader, saying, "We must move forward into the new century as one nation and one people with one manifest destiny. . . There will be no room for witch-hunting. . . I reiterate my intention to accord President Rawlings all the respect and support that is due to him. . . when he retires, and I will ensure that he is treated as I would like to be treated at the end of my term of office".

ii. NIGERIA

CAPITAL: Abuja   AREA: 924,000 sq km   POPULATION: 132,000,000
OFFICIAL LANGUAGE: English   POLITICAL SYSTEM: presidential
HEAD OF STATE AND GOVERNMENT: President (Gen. Retd) Olusegun Obasanjo (since May '99)
MAIN IGO MEMBERSHIPS (NON-UN): OAU, ECOWAS, OPEC, ACP, OIC, NAM, CWTH
CURRENCY: naira (end-'00 £1=N164.32, US$1=N110.00)
GNP PER CAPITA: US$310, US$744 at PPP ('99)

DURING 2000, his first full year in office, President Olusegun Obasanjo faced major problems on three fronts: growing sectarian violence between Muslims and Christians; the task of turning around an economy which had become hopelessly overdependent on oil; and a level of corruption that had become an international byword.

The religious divide between Muslims and Christians widened sharply during a year in which eight northern states introduced sharia law: these were Zamfara, Kano, Kaduna, Niger, Sokoto, Kebbi, Yolo and Borno. Christian-Muslim riots occurred as a result of these moves to establish sharia law in the north and in February some 400 deaths followed clashes in and around Kaduna. Further violence in the east of the country took place when Ibo Christians and Hausa Muslims fought each other in the towns of Aba and Umahia, and about 50 people were killed. After the Kaduna killings President Obasanjo appealed for calm and said that sectarian violence threatened international goodwill for Nigeria and undermined the country's transition to democracy. At the end of February, in an effort to halt the escalating violence, the governors of 18 northern states met and promised not to pursue the implementation of sharia law. However, shortly after the meeting, the governors of Zamfara, Sokoto and Kebbi states went back on the agreement (of the 18 governors), announcing that they would continue to implement sharia law.

On March 29 President Obasanjo said he would not forbid Nigerian states to implement sharia law, despite the violence that it had unleashed and despite the fact that amputations under sharia breached an agreement between the federal government and the states and violated the constitution. He said, referring to an amputation for theft in Zamfara, that it was up to individuals and not the federal government to challenge the legitimacy of the state of Zamfara's actions in the courts. A further meeting of 19 state governors at the beginning of April discussed the implications of imposing sharia. The meeting decided to establish a panel of Muslim and Christian leaders in order to harmonise sharia with the federal legal code. At the beginning of May the state governments which had adopted sharia agreed at a meeting of the National Council of State to revert to the penal code that had been in force since independence. But despite such meetings and agreements the implementation of sharia continued, and the issue as a whole—the steady process of the northern states adopting sharia law in defiance of the Nigerian constitution, the accompanying violence and growing Christian fears, as well as the weak response of the President and federal government—raised a number of doubts about the integrity of the federal state.

On May 7 President Obasanjo approved the delayed budget for 2000. This came only after an agreement had been reached with the National Assembly to deal with various disputed matters in a supplementary bill. The main point of dispute was the decision of parliamentarians to award themselves US$220 million, equivalent to the national education budget. In August the International Monetary Fund (IMF) approved a 12-month standby credit for Nigeria for SDR788.94 million (US$1.07 billion) to support the 2000-01 economic programme. The government said that it would treat the credit as a precautionary measure and had no plans to draw on it. The IMF claimed that the loan had been granted because of the "progress made toward restoring macroeconomic stability [by the government] during their first year of office".

The draft budget for 2001 was given a hostile reception by the National Assembly. Government spending was set at N892 billion (apart from debt servicing) against projected revenue of N1,444 billion. The government's main objective was economic restructuring, although the budget in fact did little to address the problem of the country's crumbling infrastructure. The privatisation programme (non-oil) under the Bureau of Public Enterprises (BPE) was scheduled to sell 39 enterprises during the existing Phase 6 of privatisation: these included hotels, paper and sugar mills, service companies, utilities and vehicle assembly plants. The privatisation of the National Electric Power Authority (NEPA) was scheduled for early 2001. The government was also prepared to offer stakes in Nigeria Airways and the state telecom company NITEL.

In March President Obasanjo dismissed the head of NEPA and his management team for their failure to deal with national power blackouts; in their place he appointed a nine-man board to ensure that NEPA eliminated power cuts and operated at full capacity by the end of 2001. He also promised that NEPA would be privatised.

Oil remained inextricably intertwined with Nigerian politics, and there was ongoing resentment amongst local populations affected by the activities of the oil companies. In March armed youths seized control of a Shell gas plant in the Delta region, taking 30 oil workers and four soldiers hostage. The students demanded that Shell tar the local roads. Troops later stormed the plant although there were no casualties. In April new violence erupted in the Delta region against Shell, the principal oil operator; this time the violence was orchestrated by members of the Movement for the Survival of the Ogoni People (MOSOP). The demonstrators tried to prevent Shell from building a road as part of its reconciliation programme with the local communities. MOSOP claimed that there had been insufficient consultation and that the road was not a development priority. The police later arrested the MOSOP leader, Ledum Mitee, on charges of gun-running and corruption. At the end of July 165 Shell workers were taken hostage on two oil rigs in the Niger delta region. The hostage takers were 50 Ijaw youths demanding work.

In response to huge fuel price rises at the beginning of June riots occurred in Lagos, Abeokuta and Ibadan. The government was forced to climb down and reduce the rises to a few naira instead of the original 50 per cent. About 250 people, many of them women and children, were killed in the explosion of a vandalised petrol pipeline at Adage, near Warri, on July 11. They were engaged in collecting fuel from the leaking pipe. During 1999 there had been about 500 cases of vandalism of pipelines. On July 16 a second explosion of a pipeline in similar circumstances some eight kilometres away resulted in another 100 deaths.

In a move that would affect later privatisation, the government called upon the Nigerian National Petroleum Company (NNPC) to adopt a policy of greater openness and release its accounts. The government said that it aimed to increase oil output from the 2000 level of 2 million barrels per day (b/d) to 5 million b/d by 2010. Bidding was opened for 22 ultra deep and continental shelf blocks that, once in production, should increase the country's reserves from the existing 20 billion barrels to around 50 billion barrels.

The Bonny Liquefied Natural Gas (LNG) field came on stream in September 1999 after the investment of US$3.8 billion. The field's initial capacity was 7.15 billion cubic metres a year; this was expected to increase to 10 billion by 2002. Reserves stood at 3,400 billion cubic metres. The government hoped to harness flared gas in order to diversify exports away from an over-reliance upon oil. The NNPC, Shell, Elf and Agip formed the gas consortium. The Finima plant on Bonny Island, designed to produce LNG from associated gases, was expected to reach an output by 2002 derived entirely from associated gases, thereby making Nigeria a major world supplier of LNG.

US President Bill Clinton visited Nigeria in August. In an effort to show support for President Obasanjo's reform programme Clinton told the National Assembly that Nigeria was "pivotal to Africa's future" and that the world "needs Nigeria to succeed".

iii. SIERRA LEONE

CAPITAL: Freetown   AREA: 72,000 sq km   POPULATION: 4,700,000
OFFICIAL LANGUAGE: English   POLITICAL SYSTEM: presidential
HEAD OF STATE AND GOVERNMENT: President Alhaji Ahmed Tejan Kabbah (since March '96)
MAIN IGO MEMBERSHIPS (NON-UN): OAU, ECOWAS, OIC, ACP, CWTH, NAM
CURRENCY: leone (end-'00 £1=Le2,836.72, US$1=Le1,899.00)
GNP PER CAPITA: US$130, US$414 at PPP ('99)

As the civil war dragged on, a return to political normality continued to elude Sierra Leone. On February 7, faced with deteriorating conditions, the United Nations Security Council voted to increase the number of UN peacekeeping troops in Sierra Leone from 6,000 to 11,000. By the end of the year there were 13,000 UN troops in the country, the largest peacekeeping operation in the world. Such a presence was seen as necessary to fill the security vacuum left by the phasing out of the Nigerian-led Economic Community of West African States (ECOWAS) force.

Under the terms of the July 1999 Lomé peace agreement, the rebel group, the Revolutionary United Front (RUF), acquired seats in government and a general amnesty for the many atrocities which it had committed during the civil war, in return for the dismantling of its army. However, the accord collapsed in early May 2000 when the RUF abducted 500 peacekeepers belonging to the UN Mission to Sierra Leone (UNAMSIL). This was followed by a full-scale resumption of fighting between the RUF and the Sierra Leone Army (SLA) and its militia allies. In Freetown, on May 8, an unarmed crowd of 10,000 demonstrators marched on the house of the leader of the RUF, Foday Sankoh, to demand the release of the UN hostages. Sankoh's bodyguards fired on the demonstrators after some had thrown stones and at least 19 people were killed. During the ensuing gun battle with the Special Security Division of the Sierra Leone police, Sankoh, who was still nominally a Vice President in the transitional government as a result of the Lomé agreement, managed to escape in the chaos.

The shooting of the demonstrators and a UN claim, later proved false, that the RUF had taken the town of Waterloo, 30 kilometres from Freetown, prompted the deployment to Sierra Leone of 1,000 UK troops on May 8. The presence of the British troops put the rebels on the defensive and led to a series of military defeats for the RUF. The RUF released 139 of the UN hostages in mid-May, and the men arrived in neighbouring Liberia on May 15. Two days later, on May 17, Sankoh was captured by pro-government militias in Freetown whilst trying to leave the city in disguise. Slightly wounded during his arrest, he was handed over to British troops and placed in custody at an undisclosed location. President Ahmed Tejan Kabbah announced that Sankoh's immunity from prosecution would be lifted and that he would stand trial. The remaining UN hostages were released by the RUF on May 28. Combat continued, however, with the RUF engaging with both SLA and UNAMSIL troops.

On August 22 the RUF announced that Sankoh had been replaced as leader by its field commander, Issay Sessay, a move to which the incarcerated Sankoh had allegedly given his approval. The RUF said that it was now willing to recommit itself to the peace agreement and disarm its forces. However, prospects for peace were dealt a serious blow when the West Side Boys (WSB), a militia nominally allied to the government, kidnapped 11 British soldiers on August 25. The abductions occurred when the soldiers were travelling through the Occra Hills, the main WSB stronghold, near Freetown. Following negotiations, five of the soldiers were released on August 30. The remainder were freed on September 9 when British troops stormed the WSB headquarters, killing at least 25 WSB fighters and capturing a number of others.

The UK government sent 500 further troops to Sierra Leone in November. This new deployment augmented the British military presence and was seen as a reaction to deepening doubts over the commitment of the rebels to honour a cease-fire signed on November 10. The key test of the RUF's commitment to the cease-fire was straightforward enough: if it gave up control of the diamond fields that had fuelled its brutal nine-year war, the end of the conflict could well be within grasp. The November accord kept open the possibility that the Lomé agreement could be revived and the RUF returned to a power-sharing government. Whilst the Kabbah government welcomed the November cease-fire and the rebels' pledge to demobilise, it was sceptical about whether either would last. A government spokesman said that the regime had "no intention of relaxing its stance".

At the end of the year many issues remained to be resolved. Amongst them were the fate of Foday Sankoh, who faced the prospect of trial before an international court for crimes against humanity. There were also concerns about whether the RUF's representative at the November peace talks, Col Jonathan Kposowa, actually spoke for the fractured RUF leadership. Finally, there were serious doubts about whether the RUF would give up control of its lucrative diamond mines in order to make the putative accord work.

vi. THE GAMBIA

CAPITAL: Banjul   AREA: 11,300 sq km   POPULATION: 1,370,000
OFFICIAL LANGUAGE: English   POLITICAL SYSTEM: presidential
HEAD OF STATE AND GOVERNMENT: President (Col) Yahya Jammeh (since Sept '96),
    previously Chairman of Armed Forces Provisional Revolutionary Council (from July '94)
RULING PARTY: Alliance for Patriotic Reorientation and Construction (APRC)
MAIN IGO MEMBERSHIPS (NON-UN): OAU, ECOWAS, ACP, CWTH, OIC, NAM
CURRENCY: dalasi (end-'00 £1=D22.82, US$1=D15.28)
GNP PER CAPITA: US$340, US$1,430 at PPP ('98)

WHILST President Yahya Jammeh claimed to have reinstated democratic rule and honest government in The Gambia, his assertions were strongly disputed by opposition parties and the independent press. They claimed that both civil liberties and political rights were in decline.

Such claims were given credence when student-led, anti-government riots broke out in the capital, Banjul, on April 10-11. The government allegedly instructed the security forces to use live ammunition, and 13 young demonstrators were killed, amongst them Omar Barrow, a popular local journalist. Interior Minister Ousman Badgie insisted that officers had used rubber bullets during the disturbances and announced that the government was investigating reports that some demonstrators had been armed. The heavy-handed response was condemned by the main opposition party, the United Democratic Party (UDP). President Jammeh ordered a week of national mourning following the deaths.

The trigger for the riot was a public outcry following the release of an autopsy report on the death in March of a student, Ebrahima Barry. Whilst the report attributed his death to natural causes, many Gambians believed that he had been tortured and murdered by security personnel. Schools remained closed for the remainder of April as student demonstrations spread throughout the country.

In June the UDP's leader, Oussainou Darboe, and 21 of his followers were arrested on murder charges after the death of a party colleague. As political tension rose, Jammeh's government ended the year widely perceived by many ordinary people, the independent media, and opposition parties as an intolerant regime which would not countenance public expressions of discontent. The forthcoming presidential elections, due early in 2001, were expected to be a significant test of Jammeh's popularity.

v. LIBERIA

CAPITAL: Monrovia   AREA: 97,750 sq km   POPULATION: 2,900,000
OFFICIAL LANGUAGE: English   POLITICAL SYSTEM: republic
HEAD OF STATE AND GOVERNMENT: President Charles Taylor (since July '97)
RULING PARTY: National Patriotic Party of Liberia (NPPL)
MAIN IGO MEMBERSHIPS (NON-UN): OAU, ECOWAS, ACP, NAM
CURRENCY: Liberian dollar (end-'00 £1=L$1.49, US$1=L$1)
GNP PER CAPITA: n/a

PRESIDENT Charles Taylor maintained his tight grip on power via his control of a loyal armed guard and a small circle of notoriously corrupt associates. One of his principle assets was control of the booming diamond export trade, greatly boosted by the civil war in neighbouring Sierra Leone (see VI.2.iii.), a war fomented and fuelled by Taylor through his protegé, Foday Sankoh, who was until May 2000 leader of the Revolutionary United Front (RUF), the rebel group in Sierra Leone. Because of Taylor's support for the RUF, the UK government managed in June to persuade fellow European Union (EU) governments to block the first tranche of a US$55 million EU aid package to Liberia.

During the year Taylor's government had problems with the local independent and foreign media. In mid-March the government ordered the closure of two leading independent radio stations, Star Radio and Radio Veritas. The Press Union of Liberia condemned such moves, but Taylor responded by saying that he would not tolerate attempts by media organisations to "propagate hate messages". The ban on Star Radio continued, although that on Radio Veritas was lifted on March 24.

In August four journalists working for the UK television station, Channel 4, were arrested by security forces and charged with espionage. The four were alleged to have collected sensitive information to support claims that the Liberian government was involved in diamond trading and gun-running in neighbouring Sierra Leone. Pressure from the UK government, following allegations of torture, resulted in the release of the four at the end of August after they had agreed to apologise to the Liberian nation.

3. WEST AFRICAN FRANCOPHONE STATES—CENTRAL AFRICAN FRANC ZONE

i. SENEGAL—MAURITANIA—MALI—GUINEA—CÔTE D'IVOIRE—
BURKINA FASO—TOGO—BENIN—NIGER

Senegal
CAPITAL: Dakar   AREA: 197,000 sq km   POPULATION: 9,800,000
OFFICIAL LANGUAGE: French   POLITICAL SYSTEM: presidential democracy
HEAD OF STATE AND GOVERNMENT: President Abdoulayé Wade (since April '00)
RULING PARTIES: Front for Changeover (FAL) coalition
PRIME MINISTER: Moustapha Niasse (since April '00)
MAIN IGO MEMBERSHIPS (NON-UN): OAU, ECOWAS, UEMOA, ACP, OIC, NAM, Francophonie
CURRENCY: CFA franc (end-'00 £1=CFAFr1,043.69, US$1=CFAFr698.69)
GNP PER CAPITA: US$510, US$1,341 at PPP ('99)

VI.3.i. WEST AFRICAN FRANCOPHONE STATES

Mauritania
CAPITAL: Nouakchott   AREA: 1,026,000 sq km   POPULATION: 2,500,000
OFFICIAL LANGUAGES: French & Arabic   POLITICAL SYSTEM: presidential
HEAD OF STATE AND GOVERNMENT: President (Col) Moaouia Ould Sidi Mohammed Taya (since Jan '92), previously Chairman of Military Council of National Salvation (from Dec '84)
RULING PARTY: Democratic and Social Republican Party (PRDS)
PRIME MINISTER: Cheikh El-Avia Ould Mohammed Khouna (since Nov '98)
MAIN IGO MEMBERSHIPS (NON-UN): OAU, UEMOA, AMU, AL, ACP, OIC, NAM, Francophonie
CURRENCY: ouguiya (end-'00 £1=O374.90, US$1=O250.97)
GNP PER CAPITA: US$380, US$1,522 at PPP ('99)

Mali
CAPITAL: Bamako   AREA: 1,240,000 sq km   POPULATION: 11,200,000
OFFICIAL LANGUAGE: French   POLITICAL SYSTEM: presidential
HEAD OF STATE AND GOVERNMENT: President Alpha Oumar Konaré (since April '92)
RULING PARTY: Alliance for Democracy in Mali (ADEMA)
PRIME MINISTER: Mande Sidibe (since Feb '00)
MAIN IGO MEMBERSHIPS (NON-UN): OAU, ECOWAS, UEMOA, AL, ACP, OIC, NAM, Francophonie
CURRENCY: CFA franc (see above)
GNP PER CAPITA: US$240, US$693 at PPP ('99)

Guinea
CAPITAL: Conakry   AREA: 246,000 sq km   POPULATION: 8,090,000
OFFICIAL LANGUAGE: French   POLITICAL SYSTEM: presidential
HEAD OF STATE AND GOVERNMENT: President (Gen.) Lansana Conté (since Dec '93); previously Chairman of Military Committee for National Recovery (from April '84)
RULING PARTY: Party of Unity and Progress (PUP)
PRIME MINISTER: Lamine Sidimé, since March '99
MAIN IGO MEMBERSHIPS (NON-UN): OAU, ECOWAS, ACP, OIC, NAM, Francophonie
CURRENCY: Guinean franc (end-'00 £1=GFr2,808.34, US$1=GFr1,880.00)
GNP PER CAPITA: US$510, US$1,761 at PPP ('99)

Côte d'Ivoire
CAPITAL: Abidjan   AREA: 322,000 sq km   POPULATION: 16,000,000
OFFICIAL LANGUAGE: French   POLITICAL SYSTEM: presidential
HEAD OF STATE AND GOVERNMENT: President Laurent Gbagbo (since Oct '00)
RULING PARTY: Ivorian Popular Front (FPI)
PRIME MINISTER: Affi N'Guessan, since Oct '00
MAIN IGO MEMBERSHIPS (NON-UN): OAU, ECOWAS, UEMOA, ACP, NAM, Francophonie
CURRENCY: CFA franc (see above)
GNP PER CAPITA: US$710, US$1,546 at PPP ('99)

Burkina Faso
CAPITAL: Ouagadougou   AREA: 274,000 sq km   POPULATION: 12,000,000
OFFICIAL LANGUAGE: French   POLITICAL SYSTEM: presidential
HEAD OF STATE AND GOVERNMENT: President (Capt.) Blaise Compaoré (since Dec '91); previously Chairman of Popular Front (from Oct '87)
RULING PARTY: Congress for Democracy and Progress (CDP)
PRIME MINISTER: Kadre Desiré Ouedraogo (since Feb '96)
MAIN IGO MEMBERSHIPS (NON-UN): OAU, ECOWAS, UEMOA, ACP, OIC, NAM, Francophonie
CURRENCY: CFA franc (see above)
GNP PER CAPITA: US$240, US$898 at PPP ('99)

Togo

CAPITAL: Lomé AREA: 57,000 sq km POPULATION: 4,800,000
OFFICIAL LANGUAGES: French, Kabiye & Ewem POLITICAL SYSTEM: presidential
HEAD OF STATE AND GOVERNMENT: President (Gen.) Gnassingbé Eyadéma (since '67)
RULING PARTY: Rally of the Togolese People (RPT)
PRIME MINISTER: Messan Agbeyome Kodjo (since Aug '00)
MAIN IGO MEMBERSHIPS (NON-UN): OAU, ECOWAS, UEMOA, ACP, NAM, Francophonie
CURRENCY: CFA franc (end-'00 £1=CFAFr1,043.69, US$1=CFAFr698.69)
GNP PER CAPITA: US$320, US$1,346 at PPP ('99)

Benin

CAPITAL: Porto Novo AREA: 113,000 sq km POPULATION: 6,400,000
OFFICIAL LANGUAGE: French POLITICAL SYSTEM: presidential
HEAD OF STATE AND GOVERNMENT: President Mathieu Kérékou (since March '96)
MAIN IGO MEMBERSHIPS (NON-UN): OAU, ECOWAS, UEMOA, ACP, NAM, Francophonie
CURRENCY: CFA franc (end-'00 £1=CFAFr1,043.69, US$1=CFAFr698.69)
GNP PER CAPITA: US$380, US$886 at PPP ('99)

Niger

CAPITAL: Niamey AREA: 1,267,000 sq km POPULATION: 11,000,000
OFFICIAL LANGUAGE: French POLITICAL SYSTEM: republic
HEAD OF STATE AND GOVERNMENT: President Mamadou Tanja (since Dec '99)
RULING PARTY: National Movement for a Development Society (MNSD)
PRIME MINISTER: Hama Amadou (since Jan '00)
MAIN IGO MEMBERSHIPS (NON-UN): OAU, ECOWAS, UEMOA, ACP, OIC, NAM, Francophonie
CURRENCY: CFA franc (see above)
GNP PER CAPITA: US$190, US$727 at PPP ('99)

THE year 2000 was an annus mirabilis for SENEGAL and its people, probably the most significant year in its 40 years of independence. After many multi-party elections over the years had failed to yield a change of government, to the point where people had almost ceased to believe that it might happen, this year, finally, saw a new administration.

The presidential elections of February 29 were thus critical for Senegal. The opposition leader, Abdoulayé Wade, 74, had said for some time that this would be his last attempt at the presidency, after four previous campaigns. His main opponent was President Abdou Diouf, who had been in power for 19 years. Diouf entered the election with a number of problems, in spite of the advantage of incumbency. Following the 1999 defection of Djibo Ka, one of the major barons of the ruling Socialist Party (PS), who had declared his candidacy in the elections, an even more considerable figure, former Foreign Minister Moustapha Niasse also announced that he would run. Furthermore, under opposition pressures, Diouf had been obliged to reform the electoral system, creating a fully operational national election observatory (the ONEL) under Louis Pereira de Carvalho.

The campaign was stormy, not least because the December 1999 coup in neighbouring Côte d'Ivoire (see AR 1999, pp. 266-8) had caused alarm when it was observed that France had not been willing to intervene to reverse the overthrow of the government. Wade made a number of wild assertions about the risks of military intervention, followed by a call on the army to prevent election violence. The key development was, however, the grouping together of opposition candidates into an alliance for the second round of voting. This came after Diouf had failed to obtain the 50 per cent necessary to win the contest outright in the first round. He obtained 42 per cent of the vote, with Wade securing 31 per cent, Niasse 17 per cent and Ka 7 per cent. In the three weeks before the second round there were rumours that Diouf's hardline supporters, notably his chief of staff and party boss Ousmane Tanor Dieng, were planning to rig the vote, but in the event it passed off peacefully and transparently. The key factor was that Niasse maintained his opposition to Diouf (the platform was TSD— Tout Sauf Diouf), thus permitting Wade to win 58.49 per cent (969,332 votes) against Diouf's consistent 41.51 per cent. The return by Djibo Ka to the PS camp in the interim period made no difference as his supporters maintained their opposition to Diou.

Whilst the government newspaper *Le Soleil* would not admit that the result was the product of anything more than the "irreversible aspiration for change", the impact of the election was far-reaching. It was a major tonic for Senegalese politics, which had languished in the apparent inevitability of one-party rule for over 50 years, despite the multi-party framework. Furthermore, throughout west Africa and beyond, it was seen as a boost for democracy in the continent at a time when one was particularly needed. The contrast with the instability in Côte d'Ivoire was particularly pronounced.

Wade was sworn in as President at the beginning of April, and immediately appointed Niasse as Prime Minister, with a galaxy of new ministers. Some of these were from smaller opposition parties, but there were others who were brought in from outside politics, including a notably large number of fluent English-speakers—amongst these were the Foreign Minister, the Finance Minister and the Secretary General to the government, Idrissa Seck. The latter was perceived as a new strongman in the style of Ousmane Tanor Dieng, and there was soon friction between him and Niasse.

Wade found that even the élan of a new administration was not enough to solve the problem of the secessionist rebellion in the southern province of Casamance. Initial peace moves were rebuffed by a further wave of violence. Through a series of unproductive peace meetings, some of which involved The Gambia, (a major if sometimes untrustworthy player), it was soon apparent that part of the solution still depended upon the difficult situation in neighbouring Guinea-Bissau. It was only the demise in November of the Gambian-born head of Guinea-Bissau's army, Gen Ansumane Mane, (seeVII.1.iii.), who had openly been supporting an extremist faction of the secessionist forces, that appeared to open the way for a further attempt at a settlement.

MAURITANIA's only elections during the year were for one third of the seats in the Senate in June, in which the ruling Democratic and Social Republican Party (PRDS) won 13 of the 17 seats. Overall it was a year of political fractiousness, in which an authoritarian government all too frequently resorted to the mailed fist when confronted with opposition. The leader of one of the main opposition parties, Ahmed Ould Daddah (the son of Mauritania's first President and founding father Mokhtar Ould Daddah) was arrested and released twice during the year—the second time after returning from a visit to Paris at the invitation of the French government. In October he was accused of advocating violence, and his party, the Union of Democratic Forces-New Era (UFD-EN), was banned.. It was alleged that in France he had been in contact with a "terrorist organisation", the clandestine group, Conscience and Resistance.

The international prestige of President Alpha Konaré of MALI continued to grow, especially when at the end of the year he finally took on the chairmanship of the Economic Community of West African States (ECOWAS), a position which he had coveted for some time. At the same time, his domestic position was reinforced by his continued public determination to give up his post after two terms in 2002, when Mali's next presidential and parliamentary elections were due.

To ensure the smooth running of the coming elections, the National Assembly adopted a revision of the constitution proposed by the President and by an all-party political forum, making anyone of Malian nationality eligible to stand for the presidency. This measure authorised those with dual nationality to stand, and was in stark contrast to the more restrictive position of Côte d'Ivoire.

In GUINEA it proved to be an increasingly tough year for the regime of President Lansana Conté. Although a superficial appearance of democracy was maintained with local government elections in June, which the ruling Peoples Unity Party (PUP) won predictably (but not very fairly), the five-month trial of Alpha Condé, the leader of the main opposition party cast a long shadow over much of the year. He had been arrested during the violence which had followed the presidential election of December 1998, which he alleged that Conté had won unfairly (see AR 1998 p. 279). In September, Condé was jailed for five years on a charge of having fomented a rebellion in the period following the election. He had been arrested in 1998 near the Ivoirian border, prior even to the declaration of the results, and the government accused him of leaving the country to prepare an "external destabilisation" of the regime. When the much delayed trial finally began in April, Condé refused to defend himself, saying that the charges were "fantasist". He was an intellectual, he said, and his fight was that of ideas, and that his arms were "the pen and the word".

Parliamentary elections, scheduled for the end of November, were postponed indefinitely and domestic politics were increasingly overshadowed by problems on the borders with Liberia and Sierra Leone. Large numbers of refugees had gathered there, some over several years during the conflict in Liberia in the early 1990s, and more following the recent civil war in Sierra Leone(see VI.2.iii.). In September the government claimed there had been an invasion and detained more than a thousand Sierra Leoneans and Liberians from the refugee camps. Prime Minister Lamine Sidimé, appealed to the international community to intervene in the face of aggression. By the end of the year, relations with the Taylor regime in Liberia had sunk to a low ebb. There were reported to be some 350,000 refugees in camps along the south and eastern borders, in a region where shadowy "rebel" groups carried out a series of cross border attacks, the most serious being on the eastern Guinean town of Kissidougou in December. The Conté regime blamed Charles Taylor and the rebels of the Revolutionary United Front (RUF) in Sierra Leone for the attacks, and the year ended in an atmosphere of crisis and uncertainty.

COTE D'IVOIRE's disastrous end to 1999, when the government of President Konan Bédié was overthrown in an almost accidental military coup, meant that the country entered the year 2000 in a mood of uncertainty and foreboding. Although the new President, Gen. Robert Gueï, began with considerable goodwill, based on his apparent stance as a reluctant ruler and a commitment to an early return to civilian rule, there remained widespread anxiety about the volatility of the armed forces—which had shown that they were subject to considerable indiscipline and political division.

Initially it was felt that the dominant influence in the new government was Alassane Ouattara, the former Premier who had been banned from standing in the 1995 election (on the dubious grounds that he was more Burkinabe than Ivoirian) and had been a thorn in the side of Bédié ever since. It soon became clear, however, that Ouattara's influence was limited and that Gueï had other ideas about how the transition to civilian rule was to take place. In view of the bitter opposition to Ouattara manifest throughout southern Cote d'Ivoire, Gueï persuaded himself that he had a historic mission to stand in the elections.

A constitutional referendum which entrenched the nationalist notion of *Ivoirité* which had first been propounded by Bédié was postponed from April to August, whereupon it achieved a substantial majority. Meanwhile, pro-Ouattara elements had been dropped from the government, and there had been two outbursts of discontent from other ranks in the army which took all of Gueï's own authority to control. An unexplained assassination attempt on Gueï in September was blamed on the two senior pro-Ouattara generals, Abdoulaye Coulibaly and Lassana Palenfo, both of whom were dismissed and took refuge in the Nigerian embassy. Then, on October 6, the courts once again ruled that Ouattara would not be allowed to stand for election. This led to a boycott of the October election by Ouattara's party, the Rassemblement Democratique Republicain (RDR), which meant that there was a low turn-out on the day, especially in the north, the RDR's stronghold, and 62 per cent of registered voters abstained from the poll.

The unfair distortion of the results which this produced was submerged, however, in the dramatic events which followed. The main contestants in the election were Gueï himself, standing as an independent candidate, and the main opposition leader Laurent Gbagbo, who had come to a "pact with the devil" with Gueï in supporting the continued campaign for *Ivoirité*, and the ban on Ouattara. In the event the two fell out seriously, as Gueï, in a flagrant attempt to hijack the election, sacked the electoral commission and proclaimed himself the winner. His own Prime Minister, Souleymane Diarra, resigned in protest and thousands of supporters of Gbagbo took to the streets in such a show of popular disapproval that after several hours of street battles, some key army units defected, and Gueï was obliged ignominiously to leave the country by helicopter, having been on the brink of swearing himself in as President.

After Gueï's flight, Diarra re-emerged to reinstate the electoral commission and pronounce Gbagbo the winner, with 59 per cent of the vote compared with 31 per cent for Gueï. But even as Gbagbo was being sworn in, a new drama was unfolding. Ouattara's supporters had taken the opportunity of Gueï's departure to stage demonstrations of their own, calling for new elections, but these had been bloodily repressed and some 50 young RDR supporters were found to have been massacred by security forces. Although an inquiry was set up, and Ouattara and Gbagbo met to appeal for calm, the tension and bitterness in the country was considerable, and the situation was not helped by Gbagbo's maintenance of the ban on Ouattara from standing in the parliamentary elections on December 14 (postponed for a week because of the tense situation). Once again the RDR announced a boycott, and this time it was so complete that in most of the northern constituencies voting did not take place. Once again the Ivorian Popular Front (FPI) of Gbagbo won a convincing majority, with the discredited Democratic Party of Cote d'Ivoire (the former ruling party) finishing in second place.

For as long as Ouattara and the RDR remained excluded from political life, however, the FPI's victory appeared hollow, and the country remained seriously split along both religious and ethnic lines. The economic and financial results for the year were disastrous, with mounting debt, huge deficits, and growing dislocation and commercial recession. Violence and xenophobia continued to rise, and increasing alarm was expressed by poorer neighbouring countries, many of which had come to depend on the famous 40 year post-independence Ivorian success story.

In BURKINA FASO the legacy of the journalist Norbert Zongo, murdered in December 1998 (see AR 1998, p. 281), continued to plague Burkinabe political life. The trial in September of five members of the security services, and their imprisonment for terms of 10-20 years, scarcely mollified the many critics of the way in which the government had handled the affair, especially as accusations of complicity in the murder had been made against the family of President Blaise Compaoré, whose brother's alleged murder of his chauffeur had come under Zongo's scrutiny. There were new demonstrations on the second anniversary of Zongo's death in December, despite government attempts to ban them.

In September the ruling party won a comprehensive victory in local elections, which was not surprising since they were boycotted by the opposition parties. Compaoré seemed to be sweeping domestic discontentment aside, just as he chose to ignore increasing allegations that he was involved in international diamond smuggling both from Angola and from Sierra Leone, the latter via his close ally President Charles Taylor of Liberia.

President Gnassingbé Eyadéma of TOGO, one of Africa's last surviving old fashioned military dictators, grimly clung on to power in spite of domestic bankruptcy and continuing international pressures to democratise his regime. Whilst the ban on aid to Togo from most of the major donors, spearheaded by the European Union, was maintained, Eyadéma continued his rearguard action in the apparent hope that office would somehow help him recover prestige. Just as in 1998-9 he had used the chair of the Economic Community of West African States (ECOWAS) to give him more credibility, so in 2000 he milked to the maximum the fact that he hosted the Organisation of African Unity (OAU) in Lomé in July, and then became chair of that organisation. Any prestige that he may have hoped to accrue from this position, however, was severely dented by two United Nations reports accusing him of receiving diamonds from the Angolan rebel leader Jonas Savimbi in return for diplomatic support.

The crucial political issue of the year was Eyadéma's pledge to French President Jacques Chirac in July 1999, at the time of the signing of an "Accord-Cadre" with the five main opposition parties, that new parliamentary elections would be held (previous elections in March 1999 had been boycotted by the opposition). Throughout 2000, however, there was no sign of the elections taking place. Opposition parties charged Eyadéma with shelving the promised poll to preserve his total majority in the National Assembly. In all probability new elections, especially if held under intense international scrutiny, would lose him that majority. As it was, he could use his majority to change puppet Prime Ministers with impunity, as he did in September when he replaced Joseph Kokou Koffigoh with his son-in-law, Messan Kodjo Abgeyome. By the end of the year, however, the pressures had become so considerable that he was obliged to ask the Independent Electoral Commission (CENI) to set out an electoral calendar, although it was not expected that the fresh elections would be held before October 2001.

It was a quiet year in BENIN. The major politicians were largely manoeuvring for position in the run-up to the presidential elections scheduled for March 2001. It seemed certain that President Mathieu Kérékou, now in his mid-sixties and in failing health, would run again, but not so certain that he would win. Victory was especially doubtful given the unstable economic situation, and because his previous win, over incumbent President Nicéphore Soglo, had depended on an alliance with one of the southern parties. Soglo was apparently also intent on running again, as was the President of the National Assembly, but it was thought that much would depend on the shifting combinations of Benin's febrile multi-party politics.

At the end of the year 2000 NIGER was taking stock of the first year in power of President Oumarou Tandja, whose election in the Presidential poll at the end of 1999 (see AR 1999, pp. 269-270) put an end to the short period of military rule experienced in the mid-1990s. A new government under Amadou Hama, who had also been Prime Minister in the regime overthrown in 1996, set about re-establishing international credibility, especially with France, which resumed co-operation in January 2000, and with the International Monetary Fund and the World Bank. There were signs of growing friction towards the end of the year, including demonstrations by militant Muslims, and there was also concern at restrictions on the media.

ii. CHAD—CAMEROON—GABON—CONGO—CENTRAL AFRICAN REPUBLIC—EQUATORIAL GUINEA

Chad

CAPITAL: Ndjaména   AREA: 1,284,000 sq km   POPULATION: 7,020,000
OFFICIAL LANGUAGES: French & Arabic   POLITICAL SYSTEM: presidential
HEAD OF STATE AND GOVERNMENT: President (Col.) Idriss Déby (since Dec '90)
RULING PARTIES: Patriotic Salvation Movement (MPS), Union for Renewal and Democracy (URD) & National Union for Development and Renewal (UNDR)
PRIME MINISTER: Nagoum Yamassoum (since Dec '99)
MAIN IGO MEMBERSHIPS (NON-UN): OAU, CEEAC, ACP, OIC, NAM, Francophonie
CURRENCY: CFA franc (end-'00 £1=CFAFr1043.69, US$1=CFAFr698.69)
GNP PER CAPITA: US$200, US$816 at PPP ('99)

Cameroon

CAPITAL: Yaoundé   AREA: 475,000 sq km   POPULATION: 15,500,000
OFFICIAL LANGUAGES: French & English   POLITICAL SYSTEM: presidential
HEAD OF STATE AND GOVERNMENT: President Paul Biya (since Nov '82)
RULING PARTY: Democratic Rally of the Cameroon People (RDPC)
PRIME MINISTER: Peter Mafany Musonge (since Sept '96)
MAIN IGO MEMBERSHIPS (NON-UN): OAU, CEEAC, ACP, OIC, NAM, Francophonie
CURRENCY: CFA franc (see above)
GNP PER CAPITA: US$580, US$1,444 at PPP ('99)

Gabon

CAPITAL: Libreville   AREA: 268,000 sq km   POPULATION: 1,273,000
OFFICIAL LANGUAGE: French   POLITICAL SYSTEM: presidential
HEAD OF STATE AND GOVERNMENT: President Omar Bongo (since March '67)
RULING PARTY: Gabonese Democratic Party (PDG)
PRIME MINISTER: Jean-François Ntoutoume-Emane (since Feb '99)
MAIN IGO MEMBERSHIPS (NON-UN): OAU, CEEAC, OPEC, ACP, OIC, NAM, Francophonie
CURRENCY: CFA franc (see above)
GNP PER CAPITA: US$3,950, US$6,660 at PPP ('98)

Congo

CAPITAL: Brazzaville   AREA: 342,000 sq km   POPULATION: 3,160,000
OFFICIAL LANGUAGE: French   POLITICAL SYSTEM: presidential
HEAD OF STATE AND GOVERNMENT: President Denis Sassou-Nguesso (since Oct '97)
RULING PARTIES: Congolese Movement for Democracy and Integral Development (MCDDI) is now included in ruling coalition
MAIN IGO MEMBERSHIPS (NON-UN): OAU, CEEAC, ACP, NAM, Francophonie
CURRENCY: CFA franc (see above)
GNP PER CAPITA: US$670, US$897 at PPP ('99)

Central African Republic

CAPITAL: Bangui   AREA: 623,000 sq km   POPULATION: 3,800,000
OFFICIAL LANGUAGE: French   POLITICAL SYSTEM: presidential
HEAD OF STATE AND GOVERNMENT: President Ange-Félix Patassé (since Sept '92)
RULING PARTIES: Central African People's Liberation Party (MPLC) heads broad coalition
PRIME MINISTER: Anicet Georges Dologuélé (since Jan '99)
MAIN IGO MEMBERSHIPS (NON-UN): OAU, CEEAC, OPEC, ACP, OIC, NAM, Francophonie
CURRENCY: CFA franc (see above)
GNP PER CAPITA: US$290, US$1,131 at PPP ('99)

Equatorial Guinea
CAPITAL: Malabo   AREA: 28,000 sq km   POPULATION: 455,000
OFFICIAL LANGUAGES: Spanish & French   POLITICAL SYSTEM: presidential
HEAD OF STATE AND GOVERNMENT: President (Brig.-Gen.) Teodoro Obiang Nguema Mbasogo (since Aug '79)
RULING PARTY: Democratic Party of Equatorial Guinea (PDGE)
PRIME MINISTER: Angel Serafin Seriche Dugan (since March '96)
MAIN IGO MEMBERSHIPS (NON-UN): OAU, CEEAC, ACP, NAM, Francophonie
CURRENCY: CFA franc (see above)
GNP PER CAPITA: US$1,500, US$4,400 at PPP ('98)

FOR CHAD, one of Africa's poorest and most disadvantaged countries, this was the year when the possibility of a better future appeared on the horizon. It came in the shape of the final approval in June of the World Bank's contribution to financing a 1,050 km pipeline, to run from planned oilfields at Doba, in southern Chad, to Kribi on the Cameroon coast. The total cost of the oil project was estimated at US$3,700 million, to be financed mainly by international banks on behalf of a consortium, 65 per cent of which was owned by the US multi-nationals Exxon and Chevron. It was the largest investment project currently being planned in Africa. The World Bank seal of approval was necessary for the consortium (which also included the Malaysian state oil firm Petronas). The project was officially inaugurated in October, with work beginning almost immediately, and a target date for operation of the end of 2003.

The euphoria surrounding the project was lessened, however, when a furore arose at the end of November after President Déby admitted that US$3.5 million of a US$25 million bonus paid out by two new consortium members had been used to purchase arms because of the difficult security situation. This led to the World Bank and the International Monetary Fund (IMF) delaying the approval of Chad's qualification as a Highly Indebted Poor Country, which would have brought US$7.45 million of debt relief, in the context of a poverty-relief programme. The matter was the more agonising for the World Bank in that the Chad deal was supposed to have been a model of project revenue management that was meant to avoid this sort of situation. One problem was that the management agreement only applied to revenue from when the oil began to flow. The World Bank's need to safeguard its standing meant that in future these controls would be applied immediately, although there was no question of delaying the project.

International commercial backing was the more surprising in that since October 1998 the regime of President Idriss Déby had been struggling against an intractable rebellion led by one of his former colleagues, Youssouf Togoïmi, in the difficult terrain of the Tibesti plateau, in the Saharan north of the country. There were three periods of serious combat, in February, July and December, all ending indecisively, with each side making absurd claims concerning the losses suffered by the other. In July the government briefly lost the fort of Bardai, and in December senior officers on both sides were reportedly killed in what was probably the bloodiest clash of the year when fighting took place on the Libyan border.

Mediation in September by the Libyan leader Col Kadhafi, in which both protagonists went to the resort of Syrte for long discussions, collapsed after the attacks on west Africans in Libya (see V.4.ii.), which meant that many Chadians were deported. Officially the two governments tried to maintain good relations, but in the Chadian capital there was increasing concern that the Libyan leader might be hedging his bets and providing financial support for the Togoïmi rebels. Furthermore, although the return to rebellion of the southerner Moïse Ketté ended after six months with his death in an ambush, there remained fears that in the vulnerable oil regions of the south, already disaffected with Déby's rule, another hero figure might emerge and the discontents of the area surface again.

There was little indication in a generally tense political atmosphere that Chad was ready or prepared for the presidential and parliamentary elections due in the course of the year 2001, or that Déby, increasingly under strain, really wanted them to go ahead.

Even in a year without elections, political tensions rumbled on in CAMEROON, especially in the troubled Anglophone provinces of the south-west and the north-west. At the beginning of the year there were alarming signs of secessionist effervescence, with a wave of arrests of militants who had staged attacks on or before New Year's eve, and the political fractiousness continued through the year. The main focus of opposition protests was the call for an independent electoral commission, a condition for Cameroon's joining the Commonwealth in 1995 which had never been implemented. A Commonwealth Secretariat mission in September produced only vague responses, and in November there were threats of demonstrations in support of the idea. In December the government met the opposition half-way, securing passage through the National Assembly of a bill setting up a National Election Observatory (ONEL) modelled on that which had been successful in Senegal.

Meanwhile the economy continued to improve after the difficulties of recent years. Cameroon had plenty of resources, including oil and gas, but the consensus was that these had been badly managed. The inclusion of Cameroon in the list of Highly Indebted Poor Countries (HIPC) for which the World Bank and the IMF approved conditional debt relief at the end of the year was a testimony to the new favour that the country had found in the international donor community, despite continuing concerns over poor governance and corruption.

It was a quiet year politically for GABON, although there were various preparations for local and legislative elections due before the end of 2001. In power since 1967, but apparently still not losing his touch, President Omar Bongo remained master of the political scene, skilled at setting opposition parties against each other and at foiling the over-ambitious in his own camp. Bongo was also still manoeuvring to play a leading regional role. He involved himself, unsuccessfully, in mediation in the intractable conflict in the Democratic Republic of Congo, and played a more successful hand in the central African regional grouping, CEMAC, where he managed to foil Cameroon by securing the projected regional stock exchange for Libreville. He also played a continuing role in mediating the dialogue between parties in neighbouring Congo.

Miraculously, the truce and cease-fire between the army and rebels in CONGO, which had been worked out in November 1999, held firm throughout the year, although it sometimes looked rough around the edges. One material factor in preserving the truce was the military defeat of the "Ninjas" of former Premier Bernard Kolélas, who had been operating in the south-west of the country, by Angolan troops, also responsible for helping President Denis Sassou Nguesso back to power in 1997. This meant that the conflict-battered country could little by little began to think about reconstruction and rebuilding national unity. The agreement involved setting up a "national dialogue", demilitarising rebel militias, and a reorganisation of the army. The "cocoyes" militia, supporting former President Pascal Lissouba and operating in the far west of the country, was also involved in the settlement. Slowly the population of Brazzaville, some 250,000 of whom had fled the fighting early in the year, returned, and the key road connecting the capital with the river port of Kinkole was reopened. The United Nations Development Programme immediately provided some US$1.3 million for a programme to demobilise the militias. A meeting of single-state and international donors in October provided for longer term commitments on condition that the peace process held.

The national dialogue, presided over by President Bongo of Gabon, eventually succeeded in producing a draft constitution for submission to a referendum in 2001, which would signal the return of the country to democracy after a three year transition under Nguesso. The opposition parties continued to contest strongly the government's decision to exclude two former leaders, Kolélas and Lissouba from the dialogue process.

Although the final withdrawal from the CENTRAL AFRICAN REPUBLIC at the beginning of the year of Minurca—the UN intervention force which had replaced the francophone peace-keepers—was held to presage a new era of stability, the basic causes of political problems were still present. The most important of these was the disastrous state of the economy, which meant that government finances were in chaos and salaries were usually several months in arrears. Added to this, a mounting fuel shortage caused a state of near permanent breakdown, especially in the capital Bangui. Attempts by President Ange-Félix Patassé to forge a new consensus with the opposition did not materialise, and by the end of the year there was a simmering state of revolt, symbolised by a one-day general strike called "CAR ghost country". There were new rumours of possible plots and coups, and the government found hidden arms caches, a portent that there might be worse trouble to come in 2001.

EQUATORIAL GUINEA's uneasy mix of brutal autocracy and ever greater wealth arising from oil revenues continued to display the country's contradictions. Protests over the mistreatment and harassment the government's opponents remained vociferous. Meanwhile, local government elections, boycotted by the three main opposition parties because of the prospect of massive vote-rigging, produced the expected 95 per cent victory for the ruling Equatorial Guinea Democratic Party (PDGE).

There were still expectations that a continuing rise in the standard of living might eventually bring spin-off benefits in terms of liberalising the political situation, which in the past few years had, under donor pressure, moved to a nominally multi-party system. It was not known how far Mobil, the US oil multinational which held the lion's share of oil contracts both offshore and on land, had been exercising clandestine influence to erase political tensions, but there was little sign of overt persuasion.

The economic statistics, however, were impressive. The country was producing possibly as much as 150 barrels a day of crude oil, and the national per capita income had increased from about US$360 to US$1,310 within five years. When oil first started flowing in 1997, GDP rose by 102 per cent. There had also been large growth in secondary business to support the oil sector, and at least 800 foreign businesses were reported to be operating in the country.

VII CENTRAL AND SOUTHERN AFRICA

1. DEMOCRATIC REPUBLIC OF CONGO—BURUNDI AND RWANDA—
GUINEA-BISSAU, CAPE VERDE AND SÃO TOMÉ & PRÍNCIPE—
MOZAMBIQUE—ANGOLA

i. DEMOCRATIC REPUBLIC OF CONGO

CAPITAL: Kinshasa   AREA: 2,345,000 sq km   POPULATION: 53,000,000
OFFICIAL LANGUAGE: French   POLITICAL SYSTEM: presidential
HEAD OF STATE AND GOVERNMENT: President Laurent Kabila (since May '97)
RULING PARTY: fluid
MAIN IGO MEMBERSHIPS (NON-UN): OAU, CEEAC, ACP, Francophonie, NAM
CURRENCY: Congo franc (end-'00 £1=CFr6.72 US$1=CFr4.50)
GNP PER CAPITA: US$110, US$750 at PPP ('98)

AT the start of the year, six months after the signing of the Lusaka peace accords in July 1999 (see AR 1999, pp. 276-7), there was no sign of an end to the war in the Democratic Republic of Congo (DRC). The active engagement of neighbouring Rwanda in the war continued to be provoked by the presence in the DRC of armed Interahamwe militiamen and former members of the Rwandan armed forces, who had been responsible for the Rwandan genocide of 1994. Uganda similarly sought to protect its frontiers from rebel encroachment by occupying eastern areas of the DRC and by aiding the opponents of President Laurent Kabila's regime in Kinshasa. The nature of the war as a regional conflict, rather than simply a civil war confined to one country, was further confirmed by the growing military support supplied to the DRC government by Zimbabwe and Angola and, to a lesser extent, Namibia.

The disregard shown for the Lusaka accords was underlined in January when Kabila called for the unconditional withdrawal of foreign forces and, a month later, offered an amnesty to all rebels who accepted his authority. This was rejected by the Congolese Liberation Movement (MLC) and the Congolese Rally for Democracy (RCD), which in March threatened to seize Ilebo, a major communication centre on the Kasai river about 350 miles east of Kinshasa. The Lusaka ceasefire was also broken on an almost daily basis in the provinces of Katanga in the south, Kivu in the east, and Equateur in the north-east. More than half of the country continued to be occupied by the rebels and their Rwandan and Ugandan backers.

On April 8 the combatants agreed to another ceasefire and, the following month, the US representative to the United Nations (UN), Richard Holbrooke, visited Kinshasa to prepare the way for UN observers and support troops. But the introduction of peacekeepers was held up as opposing forces refused to withdraw from established positions in a way that would allow the UN forces to be deployed. In mid-August the Southern African Development Community held an emergency summit in Lusaka aimed at breaking the deadlock. This brought together representatives of all the major participants in the conflict. But the meeting collapsed when Kabila stormed out after refusing to accept Ketumile Masire, the former President of Botswana, as a mediator. Kabila was also piqued by the refusal of his allies at the conference to call for the withdrawal of Rwandan and Ugandan troops from the DRC. Following the collapse of the talks, the President officially suspended the Lusaka accords, called for direct negotiations with Rwanda, Uganda and Burundi, and rejected the deployment of UN peacekeepers.

Part of the reason for Kabila's new intransigence stemmed from what he saw as a favourable turn in the course of the war. In the north-east, renewed fighting between Rwandan and Ugandan units in May and June had led to the demilitarisation of Kisangani and the deployment of UN peacekeepers in the third-largest city in the DRC. By the end of June, only Rwandan-backed RCD-Goma troops remained in Kisangani. Encouraged by his opponents' divisions, Kabila seemed to close the door to a negotiated settlement when in July he launched an offensive in Equateur against Uganda's allies in the MLC. Kabila initially succeeded in dislodging the MLC under Jean-Pierre Bemba from some of its positions along the frontier with the Central African Republic. At the same time, the President established a Transitional Parliament in Kinshasa which effectively excluded any form of political opposition since he nominated its 300 members. However, Kabila's inflexibility was dependent on his maintaining the upper hand in the military conflict. When in mid-August and September government troops suffered a series of reverses at the hands of the MLC on the Oubangu river, and the new parliament ruled out any political solution to the conflict, Kabila's intractable position became a major problem for both allies and opponents.

Kabila finally agreed in principle to the deployment of UN troops in government-held territory. But in the final months of the year, various new peace initiatives failed to bring tangible results. As 2001 began, the deadlock on the diplomatic front was accompanied by another military reverse for the government when the RCD, backed by Rwandan troops, seized Pweto on Lake Mweru in the south-east. Some 3000 Zimbabwean and Congolese troops fled across the Zambian border, leaving Kasenga as the only large town between the RCD and Lubumbashi, the capital of Katanga and Kabila's major stronghold.

ii. BURUNDI AND RWANDA

Burundi
CAPITAL: Bujumbura   AREA: 28,000 sq km   POPULATION: 7,200,000
OFFICIAL LANGUAGES: French & Kirundi   POLITICAL SYSTEM: presidential
HEAD OF STATE AND GOVERNMENT: President (Maj.) Pierre Buyoya (since July '96)
MAIN IGO MEMBERSHIPS (NON-UN): OAU, CEEAC, ACP, NAM, Francophonie
CURRENCY: Burundi franc (end-'00 £1=BrF1,165.81, US$1=BrF780.42)
GNP PER CAPITA: US$120, US$553 at PPP ('99)

Rwanda
CAPITAL: Kigali   AREA: 26,000 sq km   POPULATION: 8,100,000
OFFICIAL LANGUAGES: French, Kinyarwanda & English   POLITICAL SYSTEM: transitional
HEAD OF STATE AND GOVERNMENT: President Paul Kagame (since April '00)
RULING PARTIES: Rwandan Patriotic Front (FPR) & Republican Democratic Movement (MDR) head coalition
PRIME MINISTER: Bernard Mazuka (since April '00)
MAIN IGO MEMBERSHIPS (NON-UN): OAU, CEEAC, ACP, NAM, Francophonie
CURRENCY: Rwanda franc (end-'00 £1=RFr536.32, US$1=RFr359.03)
GNP PER CAPITA: US$250 ('99)

THE regime of President Pierre Buyoya in BURUNDI, established through a coup d'état in 1996 (see AR 1996, p. 267), continued to face armed opposition from abroad and dissent at home. The sixth round of peace negotiations at Arusha, aimed at ending the six-year old civil war, had collapsed when Julius Nyerere fell ill and died in October 1999 (see AR 1999, p. 279). Nyerere was replaced as mediator by the former South African President, Nelson Mandela. Progress was achieved at a meeting held in Arusha in February 2000 when Buyoya responded to Mandela's criticisms of his rule by promising to curtail Tutsi domination of military and political life in Burundi. In April Buyoya promised to dismantle the "regroupment villages" that had been established in 1996 in an attempt to withhold popular support for Hutu rebels operating across the border from the neighbouring Democratic Republic of Congo (DRC) and Tanzania. About 800,000 small farmers, mainly Hutu opponents of the regime, had been assembled in these "fortified villages" where living conditions had sparked Mandela's criticism. During this time, armed units of the Forces for the Defence of Democracy (FDD) and the National Council for the Defence of Democracy (CNDD), two Hutu rebel groups, attacked regroupment villages in the south and Hutu militias succeeded at one stage in entering the outer suburbs of Bujumbura.

Mandela visited Burundi in April and June to meet a wide range of local authorities and visit regroupment camps and political prisoners. In July the CNDD-FDD announced its willingness, for the first time, to enter into the peace negotiations brokered by Mandela. On August 28 a power-sharing agreement was reached in Arusha between the government, the military and a number of political parties representing Hutu and Tutsi interests. This agreement was signed in the presence of Mandela, US President Bill Clinton, and more than a dozen other heads of state. But the compromises made by Buyoya had to be balanced against the interests of the Tutsi-led army. And the tentative nature of the agreement was underlined by the absence of the three Hutu guerrilla forces and several Tutsi political parties. No firm steps were taken towards establishing a transitional parliament, choosing a new President, or opening the army to Hutu recruits. Nor was the future of the regroupment camps tackled or a decision taken about the freeing of political prisoners.

Support for Pierre Buyoya began to fray at the start of 2001 as Col Epitace Bayaganakandi, a former Interior Minister, emerged as a new champion of Tutsi interests. The war was also showing signs of turning against Buyoya. For, as the first timid signs of peace appeared in the (DRC) (see VII.1.i.), attacks by Burundian Hutu forces on the Tutsi suburbs of Bujumbura were escalating, and military reprisals against the civilian population were heightening the ethnic tension around the capital. Many feared an escalation of the war as Rwandan Hutu extremists, responsible for the 1994 genocide in that country, entered the conflict in Burundi. Members of the Interahamwe and the former Rwandan army were thought to be adding strength to the attacks launched from the DRC by the FDD. Although the peace talks in Arusha continued, they were accompanied by increasingly ominous signs of war.

The long shadow of the 1994 genocide in RWANDA, when some 800,000 Tutsis and moderate Hutus were killed (see AR 1994, pp. 292-4), continued to dominate life in the country. In December 1999 an independent report commissioned by the United Nations blamed the organisation for having failed to act on the eve of the genocide, and for having failed to halt the killings once they had begun. In April reburial ceremonies were held for up to 200,000 victims of the genocide, and steps were taken towards erecting a monument in honour of those who lost their lives during the slaughter.

Warrants issued throughout the year by the International Criminal Tribunal for Rwanda (ICTR) led to the arrest, in several countries, of those accused of perpetrating the genocide. At the same time, Georges Ruggiu, a Belgian who had worked as an announcer on the extremist Hutu "Mille collines" radio station, was sentenced to 12 years' imprisonment by the ICTR in Arusha. Ruggiu's inflammatory broadcasts, the court decided, had made a important contribution to the genocidal atmosphere in Rwanda in 1994. A life sentence imposed by the ICTR upon former Prime Minister Jean Kambanda was upheld in October by the UN Appeals' Court in the Hague. Despite these and other convictions, some 125,000 individuals remained in prisons and detention centres awaiting trial for their part in the genocide. The conditions of their detention were criticised in April in an Amnesty International report. In a few instances, such as that of the Catholic bishop, Augustine Misago, detainees accused of genocide were acquitted by the courts.

Paul Kagame, the leader of the Rwandan Patriotic Front which had seized power in 1994, increased his hold on power during 2000. In January the speaker in the National Assembly, Kabuye Sebarenzi, was obliged to resign after the assembly raised unconfirmed charges of corruption against him. A month later the same institution brought about the resignation of the Prime Minister, Pierre-Celestin Rwigyema, and in March that of Pasteur Bizimungu, the moderate Hutu who had held the office of President since the seizure of power in 1994. Paul Kagame immediately succeeded him as President, a move which was ratified by the pro-Tutsi National Assembly in April.

The war in the DRC continued to engage the energies and finances of Rwanda's government. Some 10-15,000 soldiers of the Hutu-dominated former Rwandan army, together with large numbers of Interahamwe militiamen, had become an important element in the pro-government forces within the DRC. With this major threat on his border, Kagame remained highly dependent on the support of the Rwandan military. His position was equally dependent on the large-scale aid received from Western countries, and if the Rwandan government was seen to be too unrepresentative of the broader population, or too intransigent in its dealings with the DRC, this aid could be decreased. So, as the year came to an end, Kagame walked a tightrope between maintaining a strong, autocratic government capable of suppressing the external threat, and maintaining at least the image of a government concerned with reconciliation and national integration.

iii. GUINEA-BISSAU—CAPE VERDE—SÃO TOMÉ & PRÍNCIPE

Guinea-Bissau
CAPITAL: Bissau   AREA: 36,000 sq km   POPULATION: 1,258,000
OFFICIAL LANGUAGE: Portuguese   POLITICAL SYSTEM: presidential
HEAD OF STATE AND GOVERNMENT: President Kumba Yalla (since Feb '00)
RULING PARTIES: Social Renewal Party (PRS) heads coalition
PRIME MINISTER: Caetano N'Tchama, since Feb '00
MAIN IGO MEMBERSHIPS (NON-UN): OAU, ECOWAS, ACP, OIC, NAM, CPLP
CURRENCY: CFA franc (end-'00 £1=CFAFr1,043.69, US$1=CFAFr698.69)
GNP PER CAPITA: US$160, US$750 at PPP ('98)

Cape Verde
CAPITAL: Praia   AREA: 4,000 sq km   POPULATION: 434,000
OFFICIAL LANGUAGE: Portuguese   POLITICAL SYSTEM: presidential
HEAD OF STATE: President Antonio Mascarenhas Monteiro (since March '91)
RULING PARTY: Movement for Democracy (MPD)
HEAD OF GOVERNMENT: Antonio Gualberto do Rosario (since Oct '00)
MAIN IGO MEMBERSHIPS (NON-UN): OAU, ECOWAS, ACP, NAM, CPLP
CURRENCY: Cape Verde escudo (end-'00 £1=CVEsc176.64, US$1=CvEsc118.25)
GNP PER CAPITA: US$1,165 ('99), US$2,950 at PPP ('98)

São Tomé & Príncipe
CAPITAL: São Tomé   AREA: 965 sq km   POPULATION: 151,000
OFFICIAL LANGUAGE: Portuguese   POLITICAL SYSTEM: presidential
HEAD OF STATE AND GOVERNMENT: President Miguel Trovoada (since March '91)
RULING PARTIES: Movement for the Liberation of São Tomé and Príncipe-Social Democratic Party (MLSTP-PSD)
PRIME MINISTER: Guilherme Pósser da Costa (since Dec '98)
MAIN IGO MEMBERSHIPS (NON-UN): OAU, CEEAC, ACP, NAM, CPLP
CURRENCY: dobra (end-'00 £1=Db3,570.18, US$1=Db2,390.00)
GNP PER CAPITA: US$342 ('99), US$1,350 at PPP ('98)

PRESIDENT Kumba Yalla took power in GUINEA BISSAU on February 17 following a second round of voting in January in which he defeated Malam Bacai Sanha, the interim President and candidate of the former ruling party, the African Party for the Independence of Guinea-Bissau and Cape Verde (PAIGC). A coalition government was formed between the Social Renewal Party (PRS) and the other main opposition party, the Guinea-Bissau Resistance-Ba-Fata Movement (RGB-MB) on January 24. Caetano N'tchama, a close associate of the President, was named Prime Minister, and Helder Vaz, the President of RGB-MB, became Minister of Economy.

The new administration struggled to assert its authority over the former military government, headed by the army chief of staff, Gen. Ansumane Mané, which refused to disband formally, claiming that it was an autonomous centre of power. In May the commander of the navy, Mohammed Lamine Sanha, defied government authority by refusing to obey orders for his own dismissal. A compromise was finally reached with the intervention of Gen. Mané.

The coalition was also dogged by internal instability. On September 5 President Yalla dismissed five Cabinet members belonging to the RGB-MB, but was forced to reinstate them a week later following threats by the party to withdraw from the government.

Efforts were made to improve relations with Senegal, strained over close relations between the Guinea Bissau army and secessionist rebels from the Casamance region. President Yalla held talks with Senegal's new President Abdoulaye Wade in Dakar on August 17 and agreed to improve co-ordination on border security.

Relations with the army were plunged into crisis on November 16 when President Yalla made 30 senior appointments in the military, most of them Balantas, the ethnic group which dominated the new government. Gen. Mané declared the promotions void, naming himself commander in chief of the armed forces, a position which constitutionally belonged to the President. The situation reached a violent resolution late in the month as fighting broke out in central Bissau on November 23, in which the rebel forces were routed. A week later Mané and a small group of supporters were shot dead by an army patrol some 30 km north of Bissau.

In CAPE VERDE the governing Movement for Democracy (MPD) was riven by internal division for much of the year because of a leadership struggle to succeed Prime Minister Carlos Veiga. In municipal elections on February 20 the party lost ground to the opposition African Party for the Independence of Cape Verde (PAICV) and a number of independents.

Veiga supported the Vice Prime Minister, Antonio Gualberto do Rosário, as his successor, and he was officially nominated at the party's congress in June. Another leadership contender, Jacinto Santos, the former mayor of Praia, the capital, resigned in July to form a new movement, the Party of Democratic Renovation, taking with him his supporters. On July 29 Prime Minister Veiga stood down temporarily and appointed do Rosário as his replacement. This move precipitated a constitutional crisis, as it was claimed that the right to appoint the

Prime Minister belonged only to the president. In October constitutional legalities were observed when Veiga formally resigned and the President appointed do Rosário as Prime Minister. The ruling party ended the year still divided on this issue, and was looking vulnerable in the approach to the elections scheduled for January 2001.

Cape Verde improved its position in the UN Human Development Index for 2000, ranking the third highest in Africa after Mauritius and South Africa. The result reflected extensive investment in human capital over the past 10 years, particularly in health and education.

In São Tomé And Príncipe, the government of Prime Minister Guilherme Pósser da Costa continued to cohabit uneasily with President Trovoada. The former reshuffled his Cabinet on May 9, reducing it from 11 to nine following the resignation of two ministers.

Manoeuvring intensified over the contest to succeed President Trovoada who was due to complete his final term in office in 2001. The leader of the Movement for the Liberation of São Tomé and Príncipe (MLSTP), Manuel Pinto da Costa, indicated that he would seek the nomination of his party. The opposition coalition, the Democratic Platform, composed of four parties, stated that it would attempt to find a single candidate.

Progress was made toward macro-economic stability after years of economic stagnation. Targets agreed with the International Monetary Fund (IMF) and World Bank were met, and a new loan agreement with the IMF and debt relief under the Heavily Indebted Poor Countries (HIPC) initiative were both approved. On August 28 São Tomé agreed to settle its border dispute with Nigeria concerning off-shore areas where the US company Exxon/Mobil was undertaking oil exploration. The two countries agreed to exploit jointly the disputed area. Positive exploration results released by the US company indicated that production of petroleum resources might begin in 2005.

iv. MOZAMBIQUE

CAPITAL: Maputo   AREA: 802,000 sq km   POPULATION: 17,300,000
OFFICIAL LANGUAGE: Portuguese   POLITICAL SYSTEM: presidential
HEAD OF STATE AND GOVERNMENT: President Joachim Alberto Chissano (since Nov '86)
RULING PARTY: Front for the Liberation of Mozambique (Frelimo)
PRIME MINISTER: Pascoal Mocumbi (since Dec '94)
MAIN IGO MEMBERSHIPS (NON-UN): OAU, COMESA, SADC, ACP, CWTH, OIC, NAM, CPLP
CURRENCY: metical (end-'00 £1=M25,656.1, US$1=M17,175.0)
GNP PER CAPITA: US$230, US$797 at PPP ('99)

Mozambique's economic growth rate of close to 10 per cent remained unchecked as the country entered the new millennium. A favourable tax regime, cheap labour, fertile soil and the strategic position of the port of Maputo drew considerable foreign investment to the south of the country. Most notably, with investments of almost UK£2.5 billion, the Maputo Corridor, linking the capital with South Africa, stood out as the largest infrastructure project in southern Africa.

This impressive economic growth was derailed, however, as the country was struck by the biggest environmental catastrophe of the year. Heavy rains began towards the end of January and a month later, as the floodgates of the dams on the Nkomati and Limpopo rivers were raised, huge quantities of water poured down the Limpopo valley and effectively cut the country in two. Further up the coast, cyclone Eline hit the port of Beira with winds of up to 160 mph. Damage to the infrastructure was extensive. The towns of Xai Xai and Chokwe on the Limpopo were flooded, and contact with the stricken areas was reduced as railways, roads and bridges were swept away, and telecommunications destroyed. Some 400,000 head of cattle drowned, 141 schools were destroyed, and a third of the maize crop was lost. Up to one million people were displaced by the floodwaters, and about 700 lost their lives. The incidence of malaria rose as the waters extended the breeding grounds of the anopheles mosquito, and cholera came to some areas following the destruction of clean sources of drinking water.

International aid to combat the disaster came initially from the neighbouring Southern African Development Community (SADC) countries, and television viewers were presented with dramatic pictures of the rescue missions mounted by South African helicopters. At a Donors' conference in Rome, in May, Mozambique received pledges of support totalling US$453 million. But the effectiveness of this aid would depend both on the payment of pledges and on the ability of a weak administration to undertake the reconstruction of damaged rural infrastructure.

Despite the destruction wrought by the floodwaters, the government still estimated a GDP growth rate of 3.8 per cent for the year and an inflation rate of 12 per cent. This was partly due to the growing strength of the mining sector, particularly in the central provinces where bauxite, graphite and coal were extracted. But it was largely a product of continued investor confidence in the country. In April the IMF supplied Mozambique with US$600 million in debt relief. This would reduce the country's once crippling debt repayments from US$73 million to US$24 million (0.4 per cent of GDP in 2000). In September, several SADC Presidents attended the official opening of the US$1.3 billion Mozal aluminium plant in Maputo. The plant, which had in fact opened ahead of schedule some three months earlier, would produce 250,000 tonnes of aluminium and would double the size of Mozambique's export earnings. Although the proposed iron and steel smelter to be built in Maputo, using Mozambican gas and South African ore, had been scaled down, JCI and Mitsubishi had entered into a similar project in Beira. In the north of the country, the Nacala corridor was officially opened by President Joachim Alberto Chissano and President Muluzi of Malawi in September. This project aimed to rehabilitate the port at Nacala and refurbish the railway feeding Malawi and eastern Zambia. The establishment of a full Ministry of Tourism in the new Cabinet confirmed the importance of this fastest growing sector of the economy.

Whilst the economy showed healthy signs of growth despite the flood damage, the political situation was more troubled. The main opposition party, the National Resistance Movement (Renamo) refused to accept the narrow victory won by the ruling Front for the Liberation of Mozambique (Frelimo) in the elections of December 1999. When the Supreme Court refused its demand for a hand recount of the ballots, Renamo threatened to establish its own government in the northern and central provinces, where most of its support was located. Tension mounted when Frelimo refused to offer posts in the Cabinet to Renamo and, in July, appointed its own governors in the six provinces won by the opposition. The investment of foreign aid in the south of the country, in an attempt to mend the flood damage, further enraged Renamo's supporters in the north and central regions. They also claimed that the government discriminated against Renamo supporters in the army and state-owned companies. Throughout the country, the political situation was further unsettled by the poor social services, low wages and high prices which accompanied the structural adjustment programme.

In May the leader of Renamo, Afonso Dhlakama, threatened to remobilise the party's guerrilla army and later that month five people were killed during an attack on a police station in Nampula. Negotiations between the government and the opposition began in secret in June. They collapsed in September when Renamo dismissed its principle negotiator, Raul Domingos, the man who had negotiated the peace accords which had ended the civil war in 1992. Domingos was reported to have based his negotiations for a settlement with government on the payment of a sum of US$1 million to Renamo and a monthly payment of US$10,000 to Dhlakama. But it was his reported request for a personal loan of US$500,000 that caused Renamo to sack Domingos and expel him from the party. Following the breakdown in negotiations, Renamo called on its followers to demonstrate in favour of a power-sharing agreement with the government. These demonstrations resulted in the death of about 40 people, including six policemen, and a large numbers of arrests. In November, some of these arrested Renamo supporters were placed in severely overcrowded cells in Montepuez, in the north of the country, and 83 of them died in detention, apparently from suffocation. Dhlakama continued to demand that Chissano consult him over the appointment of government ministers and that Renamo should be allowed to name the governors of those provinces which it had won in the election.

As the year ended, new flooding along the Zambezi and Limpopo rivers threatened to destroy the gains made during the dry season. Other problems remained, particularly the unresolved political tensions dividing government and opposition, and a growing economic disparity between the provinces in the south and those in the centre and north of the country. Corruption also emerged as a major issue during the year, highlighted by the murder in November of Carlos Cardoso, the country's foremost investigative journalist.

v. ANGOLA

CAPITAL: Luanda   AREA: 1,247,000 sq km   POPULATION: 12,200,000
OFFICIAL LANGUAGE: Portuguese   POLITICAL SYSTEM: presidential
HEAD OF STATE AND GOVERNMENT: President José Eduardo dos Santos (since Sept '79)
RULING PARTIES: Popular Movement for the Liberation of Angola-Workers' Party (MPLA-PT) heads nominal coalition
MAIN IGO MEMBERSHIPS (NON-UN): OAU, COMESA, SADC, ACP, NAM, CPLP
CURRENCY: new kwanza (end-'00 £1=Kw24.95, US$1=Kw16.70)
GNP PER CAPITA: US$220, US$632 at PPP ('99)

ANGOLA'S civil war continued throughout the year and the number of displaced persons grew to an estimated 3.8 million. Road access remained restricted throughout the country; only coastal roads, some southern provinces and routes within the security perimeters of major provincial cities were usable by humanitarian agencies.

An Angolan army counter-offensive pushed the National Union for the Total Independence of Angola (UNITA) out of its strongholds in the central highlands in late 1999. At the end of the year and for the first four months of 2000, the government continued to enjoy a string of military successes, whilst UNITA seemed disorientated, its actions limited to sporadic and largely ineffective attacks. As the year progressed, however, UNITA's guerrilla assaults became more effective. The level of UNITA violence against civilians, which increased significantly during the year, appeared to be an attempt to prevent the flight of refugees from areas under its control. Economic assets were also targeted. In August UNITA attacked a diamond mine near Camafuca, and in September it destroyed an oil well near Soyo, in the northwest of the country.

There were numerous allegations of continued violence by government forces, although less systematic than that perpetrated by UNITA. The government's late 1999 and early 2000 offensives included a scorched earth policy of burning villages and killing civilians, particularly in Cuando Cubango and Lunda Sul provinces. The renewed conflict was fuelled by new flows of arms into the country, although arms purchases by the government significantly declined. Ukraine, Russia and Israel remained the government's suppliers of choice, and Slovakia delivered a number of military aircraft in early 2000 that were purchased through an oil-backed loan.

A series of United Nations (UN) embargoes on UNITA remained in force and the UN Security Council's Sanctions Committee produced a 54-page report in May. It stated that President Gnassingbé Eyadéma of Togo and President Blaise Compaoré of Burkina Faso were playing an important role in supporting UNITA. The report also documented claims that Rwanda was an important location for gun-running and diamond trading. Libreville in Gabon was found to have been an important refuelling location for sanctions-busting planes after they had visited UNITA-controlled areas. It was found that most of the weapons imported by UNITA were from Bulgaria. UNITA's arms were believed to be funded largely by the illicit trade in diamonds.

In Luanda and along the coast, and in the southern province of Lubango, areas under government control, there was greater political tolerance and normality.

The privately owned media expanded its efforts throughout the year to inform Angolans about public affairs, criticise maladministration and corruption, and voice a variety of opinions. The government responded to these efforts by using its powers under the law, and sometimes going beyond the law, to stifle dissent, especially when it was critical of the President José Eduardo dos Santos.

In March the Episcopal Conference of Catholic Bishops of Angola and São Tomé and Príncipe issued a pastoral letter appealing to the government not to dismiss dialogue and to grant an amnesty in order to assist national reconciliation. The churches' advocacy on this issue resulted in a slight shift in the government position on negotiations. On June 19 President dos Santos reaffirmed the validity of the Lusaka Protocol and indicated that the UNITA leader Jonas Savimbi and his supporters could be "forgiven" if they renounced violence. In December the President announced that multi-party elections would be held in late 2002, 10 years after Angola's last and only multi-party legislative elections.

In April, as part of a larger agreement between the International Monetary Fund (IMF) and the government of Angola to reform the economy, the IMF and the government reached an agreement to monitor oil revenues, under World Bank supervision. Overall, oil revenues comprised 92 per cent of Angola's exports, had constituted 70-90 per cent of government revenue during the period 1994-99, and amounted to over 50 per cent of the country's GDP. This agreement was seen as a positive first step that might help to establish greater transparency and accountability within the government of Angola.

2. ZAMBIA—MALAWI—ZIMBABWE—BLNS STATES

i. ZAMBIA

CAPITAL: Lusaka   AREA: 753,000 sq km   POPULATION: 10,550,000
OFFICIAL LANGUAGE: English   POLITICAL SYSTEM: presidential
HEAD OF STATE AND GOVERNMENT: President Frederick Chiluba (since Nov '91)
RULING PARTY: Movement for Multi-Party Democracy (MMD)
MAIN IGO MEMBERSHIPS (NON-UN): OAU, COMESA, SADC, ACP, CWTH, NAM
CURRENCY: Zambian kwacha (end-'00 £1=Kw6,722.12, US$1=Kw4,500.00)
GNP PER CAPITA: US$320, US$686 at PPP ('99)

WITH neighbours such as Angola, the Democratic Republic of Congo and Zimbabwe in turmoil, Zambia enjoyed relative stability during the year. The government-owned Zambia Consolidated Copper Mines (ZCCM) and the South African Anglo American Corporation signed an agreement transferring ownership of 70 per cent of ZCCM to the South African mining giant in April. This sale brought to a conclusion years of negotiation over the privatisation of the mines, a process which had been characterised by frequent suspension of negotiations and disagreements over the terms of sale. Zambia had privatised more than 90 per cent of its state-owned companies over the last few years.

In October Zambia's Supreme Court declared founding President Kenneth Kaunda a Zambian citizen, thereby ending a protracted battle which had prevented him from contesting the 1996 election. In 1999 the High Court had upheld a private citizen's petition that he was a foreigner who had governed illegally. At the end of the year, senior officials in the ruling Movement for Multiparty Democracy (MMD) indicated that the party should remove constitutional obstacles before calling on President Chiluba to seek a third term. Presidential and parliamentary elections were scheduled for late 2001. In July the MMD expelled Environment Minister Ben Mwila and seven MPs for launching "premature" campaigns. Chiluba had banned campaigning for the MMD leadership until he had announced an election date.

The political opposition remained weak. In April the main opposition party, the United National Independence Party (UNIP), appointed Francis Nkhoma as its successor for former President Kenneth Kaunda, but by the end of December Nkhoma himself seemed likely to be replaced. The new opposition United Party for National Development (UPND) fared slightly better, winning a number of by-elections during the year. However, all opposition parties, as well as NGOs and other civic groups were regularly denied permission to assemble or had their meetings cancelled on public security grounds. The ruling MMD, by contrast, continued to hold meetings, rallies, and pro-government demonstrations without permits.

ii. MALAWI

CAPITAL: Lilongwe   AREA: 118,000 sq km   POPULATION: 11,000,000
OFFICIAL LANGUAGE: English   POLITICAL SYSTEM: presidential
HEAD OF STATE AND GOVERNMENT: President Bakili Muluzi (since May '94)
RULING PARTIES: United Democratic Front (UDF) heads coalition with Malawi National Democratic Party (MNDP) & United Front for Multi-Party Democracy (UFMD)
MAIN IGO MEMBERSHIPS (NON-UN): OAU, COMESA, SADC, ACP, CWTH, NAM
CURRENCY: Malawi kwacha (end-'00 £1=Kw120.10, US$1=Kw80.40)
GNP PER CAPITA: US$190, US$581 at PPP ('99)

A series of corruption scandals and political in-fighting during the year did little to combat further economic decline in one of the world's poorest countries. The deeply divided ruling party, the United Democratic Front (UDF), lurched from one crisis to the next. Revelations that the aid-dependent government had spent US$2.47 million on 39 top-of-the-range Mercedes Benz limousines for ministers and that further millions of government money had been embezzled by ministers and legislators soured relations with the aid donors and angered the public. President Bakili Muluzi delayed action, but finally was forced to promise to auction off the cars and two days later, on November 1, he dismissed his entire Cabinet. His new Cabinet had few fresh faces; notable exclusions, however, were two political heavyweights and presidential hopefuls, Cassim Chilumpha and Brown Mpinganjira. Both had been implicated in the Education Ministry's loss of US$2.5 million on dubious contracts; Chilumpha was Finance Minister at the time and Mpinganjira Education Minister. The latter was also expelled from the UDF. Since he was seen as the biggest rival to Muluzi, Mpinganjira's expulsion added to widespread speculation that Muluzi might well change the constitution in order to run for a third term in 2004. The corruption scandals underpinned student resolve to fight an increase of 3,000 per cent in university fees, which resulted in riots and marches.

The fortunes of the opposition Malawi Congress Party (MCP) fared little better. The party failed to persuade the courts to overturn Muluzi's narrow victory in the 1999 presidential elections, and its leader, Gwanda Chakuamba, was controversially suspended from parliament for a year. Simmering tensions between Chakuamba and his bitter rival and deputy, John Tembo, who had been the right-hand man of the former dictator Hastings Kamuzu Banda, eventually exploded. At rival party conventions held on August 6, each man was elected party leader by his supporters. Although the courts ruled effectively in Chakuamba's favour, the party remained evenly divided and thus incapable of mounting an effective opposition.

Some economic respite came at the end of the year in the form of interim debt relief of US$30 million from the International Monetary Fund, under the Heavily Indebted Poor Countries scheme (HIPC). But other good news proved elusive: in an import-led economy, the price of basic goods rose by about 30 per cent because of government overspending, rising oil prices and the loss of half of the currency's value, whilst the price of tobacco, the main export, tumbled.

iii. ZIMBABWE

CAPITAL: Harare   AREA: 391,000 sq km   POPULATION: 13,300,000
OFFICIAL LANGUAGE: English   POLITICAL SYSTEM: presidential
HEAD OF STATE AND GOVERNMENT: President Robert Mugabe (since Dec '87);
   previously Prime Minister (from April '80)
RULING PARTY: Zimbabwe African National Union-Patriotic Front (ZANU-PF)
MAIN IGO MEMBERSHIPS (NON-UN): OAU, COMESA, SADC, ACP, CWTH, NAM
CURRENCY: Zimbabwe dollar (end-'00 £1=Z$82.31, US$1=Z$55.10)
GNP PER CAPITA: US$520, US$2,470 at PPP ('99)

THE year began with a popular setback for President Robert Mugabe and his ZANU-PF government. A referendum was held on February 12 to ratify proposed amendments to Zimbabwe's 20-year-old constitution, which dated from the country's independence (see AR 1979, p. 257). The amendments would have increased the President's powers, but the vote was decisively lost by the government. Although the result—a 55 per cent vote against the ruling party—was publicly accepted by Mugabe, it unleashed a campaign of retribution, intimidation and government-sponsored lawlessness which by the end of the year had reduced Zimbabwe to the status of a pariah nation.

The principal targets of the government's hostility were the country's 4,500 white farmers, who together owned 11 million hectares of the best agricultural land, whilst the remaining 16 million hectares were shared by over one million black farmers. Although the need for a radical redistribution of land had long been acknowledged, the government had done little to address it. With a view to recovering its popularity in time for the general election which was due in April (but eventually postponed until June), the ruling party condoned the mass invasion of white farms by landless squatters, many of whom claimed to be veterans of Zimbabwe's war of liberation in the 1970s. By March 3, 142 white-owned farms had been occupied, often violently, and early in April a white farmer, David Stevens, was killed, the first of five who were murdered during the year while defending their land.

Mugabe attributed the land crisis to the inequities of the country's colonial past, and called on the UK government to compensate white farmers for the loss of their property. Relations between the two countries deteriorated swiftly after unexplained interference by Zimbabwean officials in British diplomatic bags at Harare airport, an action described by the British Foreign Office as "uncivilized and paranoid". At a meeting with Mugabe at the beginning of April, during the Europe-Africa Conference in Cairo, the UK Foreign Secretary, Robin Cook, raised the possibility of funding a land compensation scheme in return for a commitment by ZANU-PF to the rule of law. In the same month the Zimbabwe Farmers' Union secured a court ruling that the farm invasions were illegal, a judgment which the Attorney General, Patrick Chinamasa, dismissed as unenforceable. Before the dissolution of Parliament on April 11 the government rushed through legislation legitimising the seizure of designated farms without compensation.

The election campaign was conducted in an atmosphere of high tension and resulted in 31 deaths, most of whom were government opponents. Its tone was set at the beginning of April when, in the presence of the police, an opposition demonstration in Harare was viciously set upon by ZANU-PF supporters. Eleven protestors were injured in an incident described by British Foreign Office Minister Peter Hain as "thuggery licensed from on high". Rallies organised by the Movement for Democratic Change (MDC), established as a political party less than a year earlier (see AR 1999, p. 288), attracted enthusiastic crowds, despite reports of government surveillance and the intermittent harassment of its candidates, including the brief arrest of its leader, Morgan Tsvangirai, on May 5.

On the eve of the election, held on June 24-25, the chairman of ZANU-PF, John Nkomo, claimed that his party would form the next government, irrespective of the ballot. "President Mugabe", he declared, "is an institution". In the event a high turnout of over 65 per cent of registered voters brought a very close result. The MDC, with 47.06 per cent of the votes cast, won 57 seats. ZANU-PF, with 48.45 per cent, won 62 seats, thereby giving Mugabe the statutory right to nominate 30 additional discretionary legislators in the 150-member parliament, but denying him the two-thirds majority required to amend the constitution. Significantly, the opposition won a clean sweep in the urban centres, whilst the government's support came entirely from rural areas where, according to reports from independent observers, intimidation was high and election monitoring had proved very difficult. On the basis of exit polls, the South African-based Helen Suzman Foundation declared that a significant proportion of the rural electorate had voted in terror and against its wishes. Tsvangirai, himself contesting a rural constituency, failed to win the seat. The MDC tabled a legal challenge to the result in that and 38 other constituencies.

The government's response to its unexpectedly narrow victory was swift. Revenge campaigns were reported in opposition-held constituencies, and in September police twice raided the Harare headquarters of the MDC, and the premises were subsequently bombed. In October the opposition was denied the statutory Z$30 million due to it under the Political Parties (Finance) Act in respect of its share of the electoral vote. The same month the President declared a Clemency Order extending an amnesty to thousands of politically motivated crimes which had been perpetrated, predominantly by his own party's supporters, in the six months before the election. Tsvangirai, however, was threatened with arrest on the grounds of "inciting violence" at a celebration to mark his party's first year of existence. The MDC in turn instituted impeachment proceedings against Mugabe on a charge of "wilful violation of the constitution and gross misconduct".

On July 14 100 white-owned farms were designated for immediate sequestration, with a further 2,197 listed for appropriation by the end of the year. Pressure from Thabo Mbeki, the South African President, brought only a brief halt in the activities of the vigilante armies, led by Chenjerai "Hitler" Hunzvi, and on September 29 Mbeki's predecessor, the former President Nelson Mandela, publicly criticised Mugabe's "use of violence and the corroding of the rule of law". On November 13, following a ruling by the Zimbabwe Supreme Court that the land resettlement programme was unconstitutional and illegal, Mugabe openly attacked the judiciary and declared the government to be at war with the commercial farmers.

The political crisis inevitably damaged the country's already fragile economy. The decline in foreign investment and continued withholding of International Monetary Fund (IMF) loans (see AR 1999, p. 287) depleted foreign currency reserves and resulted in petrol and electricity shortages throughout the year, with consequent steep rises in the cost of food, transport and other basic items. Production in the severely disrupted agricultural sector fell by 30 per cent. Inflation persisted above 60 per cent and two-thirds of the working-age population was unemployed. On August 1 the Minister of Finance and Economic Development, Simba Makoni, announced a 24 per cent devaluation of the Zimbabwe dollar to prevent it from going into freefall. Makoni, one of a group of younger, able technocrats appointed to the Cabinet after the election, said in October that Zimbabwe's involvement in the war in the Democratic Republic of the Congo (see VII.1.i.) had cost the country Z$10,000 million since 1998 and that this level of expenditure was unsustainable (see AR 1999, p. 289). His budget in November duly reduced defence spending by 13.4 per cent.

At the ZANU-PF party congress the same month, the issue which preoccupied much of the country—how to get rid of the 76-year-old Mugabe before the presidential election which was due in early 2002—was not even mentioned. But in September, whilst in New York on a visit to the United Nations, Mugabe was served with a US$400 million legal suit for human rights violations.

Tourism, Zimbabwe's third largest foreign currency earner after agriculture and mining, was critically hit by the political turmoil and by the country's negative depiction in the world's press. The Central Statistical Office reported 200,000 fewer visitors to the country than in 1999, and the occupancy rates of most hotels dropped to between 20 and 40 per cent of capacity. In early December, at the height of the summer season, the world famous Victoria Falls Hotel had guests in only seven of its 182 luxurious rooms.

iv. BOTSWANA—LESOTHO—NAMIBIA—SWAZILAND

Botswana

CAPITAL: Gaborone   AREA: 582,000 sq km   POPULATION: 1,700,000
OFFICIAL LANGUAGE: English and Setswana   POLITICAL SYSTEM: presidential democracy
HEAD OF STATE AND GOVERNMENT: President Festus Mogae (since March '98)
RULING PARTY: Botswana Democratic Party (BDP)
MAIN IGO MEMBERSHIPS (NON-UN): OAU, SADC, SACU, ACP, CWTH, NAM
CURRENCY: pula (end-'00 £1=P8.01, US$1=P5.36)
GNP PER CAPITA: US$3,240, US$6,032 at PPP ('99)

Lesotho

CAPITAL: Maseru   AREA: 30,000 sq km   POPULATION: 2,400,000
OFFICIAL LANGUAGES: English & Sesotho   POLITICAL SYSTEM: monarchy
HEAD OF STATE: King Letsie III (since Jan '96)
RULING PARTY: Lesotho Congress for Democracy (LCD)
HEAD OF GOVERNMENT: Bethuel Pakalitha Mosisili, Prime Minister (since June '98)
MAIN IGO MEMBERSHIPS (NON-UN): OAU, COMESA, SADC, SACU, ACP, CWTH, NAM
CURRENCY: maloti (end-'00 £1=M11.31, US$1=M7.57)
GNP PER CAPITA: US$550, US$2,058 at PPP ('99)

Namibia

CAPITAL: Windhoek   AREA: 824,000 sq km   POPULATION: 1,800,000
OFFICIAL LANGUAGES: Afrikaans & English   POLITICAL SYSTEM: presidential democracy
HEAD OF STATE: President Sam Nujoma (since March '90)
RULING PARTY: South West Africa People's Organisation (SWAPO)
HEAD OF GOVERNMENT: Hage Geingob, Prime Minister (since March '90)
MAIN IGO MEMBERSHIPS (NON-UN): OAU, SADC, SACU, ACP, CWTH, NAM
CURRENCY: Namibian dollar (end-'00 £1=N$11.31, US$1=N$7.57)
GNP PER CAPITA: US$1,890, US$5,369 at PPP ('99)

Swaziland

CAPITAL: Mbabane   AREA: 17,350 sq km   POPULATION: 998,600
OFFICIAL LANGUAGES: English & Siswati   POLITICAL SYSTEM: monarchy
HEAD OF STATE: King Mswati III (since '86)
HEAD OF GOVERNMENT: Sibusiso Barnabas Dlamini, Prime Minister (since July '96)
MAIN IGO MEMBERSHIPS (NON-UN): OAU, COMESA, SADC, SACU, ACP, CWTH, NAM
CURRENCY: lilangeni/pl. emalangeni (end-'00 £1=E11.31, US$1=E7.57)
GNP PER CAPITA: US$1,400, US$3,580 at PPP ('98)

CONFLICT continued to plague parts of southern Africa in 2000, and often embroiled neighbouring states. The spillover effects of the civil war in Angola were felt in Botswana and Namibia. The same was true of the conflict in the Democratic Republic of Congo, where Namibia had troops fighting on the side of President Laurent Kabila, together with Angola and Zimbabwe.

However, the region also experienced positive economic growth. Botswana ranked third and Namibia fourth in the World Economic Forum's Africa Competitiveness Report. A new revenue-sharing deal was finally worked out in the Southern African Customs Union and would be implemented in April 2001. The successor agreement to Lomé IV-bis was signed in Cotonou, Benin, in June. Of the BLNS states, only Lesotho was classified as a least developed country. The Southern African Development Community (SADC) Free Trade Agreement

(FTA) came into effect on September 1 (see XI.6.ii.). Initial members were South Africa, Botswana, Lesotho, Malawi, Mauritius, Mozambique, Namibia, Swaziland, Tanzania and Zimbabwe. However, Mozambique, Tanzania, Malawi and Zambia (although it had not yet joined the FTA) would be partially exempt for the first five years from tariffs covering clothing and textiles.

At the start of 2000, the Vice-President of BOTSWANA, Ian Khama, took a year's sabbatical amid speculation that there was discontent within the ruling Botswana Democratic Party concerning his initial appointment to the position. The original inclusion of Khama in the Cabinet had been seen as a way to strengthen President Mogae's support in the rural areas and to rid the party of the factionalism that had wracked it since the departure of Ketumile Masire. Khama was recalled to government in August. Although he lost his portfolio as Minister of Presidential Affairs, he was placed in charge of improving the efficiency of the government, and, more importantly, he became responsible for overseeing the implementation of the eighth National Development Plan (NDP).

Shortly before Khama's return, Mogae announced that he would stay on as President for the full two terms, thus quashing rumours that his resignation was imminent and helping to consolidate his position within the party. With the next legislative elections due by October 2004, there was no serious challenge to the BDP from the opposition parties, which were riven by infighting.

In response to growing criticism of discrimination against the San community of the central Kalahari region, Mogae established a commission to examine whether the constitution discriminated against minority tribes. The government had for many years tried to force the San from their land in order to make way for a diamond mine and tourist facilities. Unlike Namibia and South Africa, Botswana had not signed any agreements with its San community which recognised them as co-owners of the land, which was rich in game and mineral deposits, especially diamonds.

Regional instability continued to make its presence felt in Botswana in the form of refugees from the Angolan civil war and from secessionist activity in the Caprivi Strip in Namibia. Since 1999, when the Namibian government gave permission to Angola to conduct operations against UNITA forces from within its territory, several hundred Namibians and Angolans had sought refuge in Botswana, some as a result of reprisals by UNITA forces. The security crackdown in Caprivi as a result of separatist tensions there exacerbated the flow.

Botswana and South Africa established a joint commission on defence and security. A sign of the close links between the two security establishments as well as the similarity in the countries' approaches to regional problems, the commission was to focus on co-operation in defence matters as well as customs and immigration. The joint commission expressed concern over internal developments in Mozambique and Swaziland, and called on the SADC to assist in finding lasting solutions to their problems. Botswana also condemned the worsening political and economic situation in Zimbabwe, and installed an electric fence along the border. Although its purpose was ostensibly to control livestock movements between the two countries, it would also have the effect of reducing the influx of refugees from Zimbabwe.

Botswana's economic growth rate for 2000 was projected at 5.5 per cent. Its foreign reserves at the end of 1999 were US$6.2 billion, equivalent to about 29 months of import cover. Although the economy had been well managed, it was in need of diversification into industrial and service activities to reduce its reliance on the primary sector: diamonds and beef. However, the attraction of foreign direct investment had been slow, partly because of the small market size, conflicts in the region and high HIV/Aids infection rates. In 1999 foreign direct investment amounted to US$112 million.

The two greatest challenges facing President Mogae's government were AIDS and unemployment. The United Nations organisation UNAids estimated that more than one in three people in Botswana now had HIV/Aids—an HIV infection rate of 36 per cent. In August Mogae announced that the government would provide free HIV/Aids drugs at public health facilities for people with the illness. The government also announced an ambitious weekly counselling programme, which was expected to cost US$4.5 million in the first three years.

Botswana's unemployment rate of about 20 per cent included a high proportion of people who were unskilled and "unemployable". This, together with high HIV/AIDS rates, limited the country's potential for developing high value sectors. The closure of the Motor Company of Botswana (MCB), owned by Hyundai, which had become the second largest export earner after diamonds, was a blow both for employment and for plans to diversify the economy. The failure of the Motor Company also raised concerns about government assistance to foreign companies, since MCB had received subsidies and tax breaks. Another company, Haltek, a polyester-weaving plant which received an overseas development grant and equity investment from the Botswana Development Corporation, was facing problems even before it began full operations.

In March the government presented an updated white paper on privatisation. Air Botswana was expected to be privatised in 2001 and the government established a Public Enterprise Evaluation and Privatisation Authority to identify parastatals to be privatised.

As with much of the southern African region, Botswana experienced some of the worst floods in 30 years in early 2000. Some 160,000 people were affected, most of them living below the poverty line. However, the government said that it would not be able to compensate the victims because of a lack of funds, as it would have to concentrate on repairing damage to infrastructure such as roads, bridges, schools and clinics.

An agreement was reached between the LESOTHO government and the Interim Political Authority (IPA) in December 1999, which seemed to pave the way for elections by June 2000. The IPA had been established in the aftermath of the political upheavals in Lesotho and the military intervention by South Africa and Botswana in 1998 (see AR 1998, p. 306). The agreement establishing the IPA was sponsored and guaranteed by the Southern African Development Community, the

Commonwealth, the United Nations and the Organisation of African Unity (OAU). Its mandate was to review the electoral code, which currently enshrined the "first-past-the-post" system, in order to allow the support of opposition parties to be reflected more fully in the legislature. As such the December 1999 agreement provided for a system where the current 80 constituency seats would be retained and an additional 50 seats would be allocated on a proportional basis. However, when the amending legislation was brought before parliament—dominated by the Lesotho Congress of Democracy (LCD)—it was altered and made to stipulate that these measures would have to be accepted by a national referendum.

Throughout 2000, as the LCD government was perceived to be delaying elections, opposition parties warned of wide-scale unrest unless they were held. However, attempts by the Basotho National Party in August to organise a national stay-away in an attempt to pressurise the government into agreeing to early elections failed, partly because the government threatened tough action against those who participated.

The international community was involved in mediation efforts as a result of political wrangling amongst the parties in the IPA. A visit by a Commonwealth team in May found that the voters roll was outdated and that, therefore, a new voter registration process would have to be undertaken, which would take some 10 months to complete. The UN Development Programme (UNDP) launched a governance and democratisation programme in June at a cost of some US$250,000. In addition, a Canadian technical adviser, Barbara Reinhardus, was sponsored by the UNDP to join the Independent Electoral Commission (IEC). The other international expert on the IEC was a Swede, Jorg Elklit. The IEC set May 26 2001 as the date for elections, although the form of the electoral system had yet to be resolved.

A commission of inquiry headed by Judge Ramon Leon was set up in April to investigate the causes of the unrest in 1998. Although the LCD hoped to gain political mileage out of revelations concerning the activities of opposition politicians, the commission also heard testimony which implicated amongst others, the former LCD Prime Minister and founder of the party, Ntsu Mokhehle, who was accused of being an apartheid agent and of ordering the killing of political rivals.

In a step which indicated a return to some normality in the Lesotho Defence Force, in May the last of the SADC troops withdrew with the completion of Operation Maluti. Botswana and South Africa had provided training to five companies in the Lesotho Defence Force to improve its professional standards. Furthermore, the trials of policemen and the courts martial of soldiers following the 1998 unrest were finally completed.

Once elections were held the greatest challenge to the government would be creating conditions that would stimulate economic growth and thus reduce unemployment, estimated at 40-45 per cent of the workforce. In 1989 South African mines had employed 129,000 Lesotho workers. By the beginning of 2000 this figure had fallen to 64,000, as some mines were forced to close down or reduce their workforce. The proportion of GDP constituted by remittances from miners fell accordingly.

Some progress was made with privatisation. Seventy per cent of the Lesotho Telecommunications Corporation was sold to Mountain Kingdom Communications, and the Lesotho Electricity Corporation was restructured to prepare it for privatisation.

Although only the first phase of the Lesotho Highlands Water project was completed, Lesotho had already become self-sufficient in electricity. To date the project had created some 3,500-4,000 jobs and rural infrastructure had improved. Negotiations on subsequent phases were underway between South Africa and Lesotho. In May the trial began of members of the Highlands Water Authority accused of misusing funds. Investigations revealed that international construction companies had made payments to influence the award of tenders.

In NAMIBIA the Democratic Turnhalle Alliance (DTA) and the United Democratic Front (UDF) formed a coalition in April, thus becoming the official opposition in parliament, although the Congress of Democrats had come second in the December 1999 elections. The DTA and the UDF indicated that this coalition would be a first step towards forming a single party.

Land seizures and expropriations in neighbouring Zimbabwe during 1999 and 2000 did not spread to Namibia. The government reiterated to farmers that it would continue to reform land ownership through a "willing-buyer, willing-seller" principle. However, subsistence farmers and members of the ruling party, the South West African People's Organisation (SWAPO) called for the existing land reform programme to be accelerated. The secretary general of SWAPO, Hifikepunye Pohamba, warned farmers that if they continued to be unwilling to sell land, then the government would be forced to expropriate it, although he added that this would be done in line with the constitution and subject to the payment of "just compensation". Commercial farmers in Namibia (numbering some 4,000, most of whom were white) owned some 36.5 million hectares, 44 per cent of Namibian land.

Having granted permission to Angola in 1999 to use Namibia's northern territory to launch attacks against UNITA, the government saw an increase in instability on its border during 2000. In June a dusk-to-dawn curfew was imposed along the Okavango River and the Caprivi strip. By mid-2000 UNITA's retaliatory attacks in Namibian territory had caused the death of some 50 Namibians. The presence of Angolan government forces in northern Namibia created problems for the local population. Local councillors claimed that the troops were increasingly ill-disciplined. Their presence had also proved ineffective in protecting the border. In August most of the Angolan troops withdrew and troops of the Namibian Defence Force were sent into southern Angola to remove UNITA bases. The activities of the Angolans as well as the Caprivi secessionists weakened the local economy in the Kavango region, especially tourism. Some 2,000 shops were forced to close down after looting by UNITA and Angolan forces. Furthermore, there were allegations of Namibian security force brutality against the local inhabitants. Some 2,000 members of the Kxoe community fled from western Caprivi into Botswana, complaining of persecution by security forces searching for members of the Caprivi Liberation Army.

In December President Sam Nujoma appointed Maj. Gen. Solomon Hawala as the new chief of the Namibian Defence Force. In the 1980s Hawala had been in charge of the interrogation of SWAPO members who were alleged to be South African spies, many of whom were executed or tortured. Concerns were expressed that the defence force could become more politicised with his appointment, especially given the security situation along the border with Angola. Namibia's security forces also continued to be involved in the civil conflict in the Democratic Republic of Congo, and had some 2,000 troops within the country.

In June the government adopted a set of guidelines for Namibia's privatisation programme. One of the key elements of the programme was to provide low-income Namibians with the opportunity to hold shares in partially privatised state firms. Although the government had not yet published a list of potential privatisation candidates, Namibia Power Corporation, Telecom Namibia, Namwater (which was planning a major coastal de-salination plant), and Air Namibia were expected to be amongst the first to be partially privatised.

Namibia attracted about US$114 million in foreign direct investment in 1999, compared with US$77 million in 1998, and was ranked fourth in competitiveness in Africa by the Africa Competitiveness Report. The South African Anglo American Corporation agreed to proceed with the development of the Skorpion zinc mine and smelter, which was expected to be one of the lowest-cost zinc producers in the world. Total capital investment was estimated at about US$454 million and the project would be the largest such mining investment since the 1970s. In order to convince Anglo American to locate the refinery in Namibia, the government granted the plant export processing zone status.

As a major diamond producer Namibia was instrumental, together with other diamond-producing countries, in seeking practical measures to enforce the international certification of diamonds. Diamond certification would make it difficult for diamond dealers from conflict-ridden areas (such as UNITA in Angola and the RUF in Sierra Leone) to sell their diamonds to fuel their war machines, whilst not endangering the legitimate mining operations of countries such as Namibia and Botswana. The US Congress had threatened to enact a bill which would have required certificates of origin for all rough stones sold on the global market.

With the implementation of the EU-SA Free Trade Agreement in January and the need to phase out the Southern African Customs Union external tariffs within the next five years to comply with World Trade Organisation requirements, it was clear that Namibia would have to seek other ways of boosting its revenue. However, the government had not yet produced a proposal on diversifying sources of revenue. Namibia was already experiencing difficulties in meeting budget deficit targets as a result of increased defence expenditure—due to its involvement in the DRC and instability in northern Namibia—and an increase in the proportion allocated to health, education and infrastructure as part of its poverty alleviation programme.

The suppression of freedom of expression and clamping down on the media and the labour movement continued in SWAZILAND during 2000. Nonetheless, the year was characterised by protests against King Mswati's absolute monarchy. The Constitutional Review Commission, appointed by the King in 1996 to recommend whether Swaziland should adopt a multiparty democracy, submitted a report to him in November. The content of the report was not made public, although pro-democracy organisations were not in its recommendations as most of the 33 members of the CRC were from the royal family or were traditional chiefs. Furthermore, the Commission had not allowed group submissions, preferring instead submissions from individuals. Media coverage of the hearings was also banned.

In February *The Swaziland Observer*, a state-owned daily newspaper, was shut down because it had been critical of the government. Its most recent act had been the publication of a letter written by Swaziland's commissioner of police to former South African commissioner George Fivaz, who was to help Swaziland combat drug trafficking. The journalist who had written the story refused to disclose his source and was threatened with criminal charges. The general suppression of press freedom was criticised by four media freedom organisations in a letter to the Swazi Prime Minister, Sibusiso Dlamini. They also called on the government to drop the charges against the former editor of a weekly newspaper, the *Times on Sunday*, for his article on King Mswati's new bride in 1999.

Although the Swaziland Investment Promotion Authority had been established in 1998 to attract investment, its efforts had been undermined by the political climate in the country. In 1998 Swaziland attracted foreign direct investment of US$51 million. In 1999 there was a net outflow of US$4 million. In an attempt to attract investors, the Finance Ministry announced in October a 10 year cut in corporate tax from 37.5 per cent to 10 per cent for eligible companies. Such companies would also be exempt from withholding tax on dividends for 10 years.

The role of the un-elected Swazi National Council, which represented traditional authorities, in over-ruling government decisions throughout the year adversely affected the relationship between the private sector and the Swazi authorities. In June parliament passed amendments to the Industrial Relations Bill, as had been requested by the International Labour Organisation (ILO), which had threatened Swaziland with sanctions. The National Council, however, amended the legislation after it had been passed by parliament. The ILO and the US trade representative insisted that the anti-trade union amendments be removed. The USA threatened to withdraw Swaziland's eligibility for the Generalised System of Preferences (GSP), under which the country imported and exported goods from and to the USA duty free. Under the GSP Swaziland exported 20,000 tonnes of sugar to the USA, a commodity which was the country's largest export and its second largest employer after the public sector.

The Federation of Swaziland Employers, the Swaziland Chamber of Commerce and Industry, the SFTU and the Swaziland Federation of Labour, called on the government to comply with the ILO and US demands. The Labour Advisory Committee, comprising workers, employers and government representatives, also recommended the removal of the clauses. The SFTU called for a national stay-away to pressurise the government, and although many interest groups initially supported the action, a court order making it illegal discouraged forced them to withdraw their support. The matter was eventually resolved in December when, after a further amendment to the Industrial Relations Act, and the USA announced that Swaziland would remain inside the GSP. In addition, the government conditionally lifted a ban on trade union meetings. However, only members could be in attendance and only labour-related matters could be discussed.

Although the opposition remained far from united, the debate over the Industrial Relations Act had pitted the Swazi National Council against the more modernist and reform-minded business and labour community as well as elements within the government. The government's initial response to growing cries for political reform was to clamp down on such activity, including the banning of trade union meetings. The opposition movement received support from the Congress of South African Trade Unions (Cosatu) in South Africa, the African National Congress and the South African Communist Party. In October they led a demonstration of some 15,000 people against rights abuses in Swaziland.

Meeting in the South African town of Nelspruit in November, because they were banned from doing so in Swaziland, pro-democracy activists adopted a declaration calling on King Mswati to end the ban on political parties and the state of emergency that had been in force since 1973. The "Nelspruit Declaration" also called for the establishment of an interim government, which would be representative of all sections of society.

The curtailment of political activity saw Swaziland excluded from the first list of eligible countries under the USA's Africa Growth and Opportunity Act, which came into effect in October. Aspiring countries, which would benefit from access to the US clothing and textiles market, had to meet stringent criteria relating to political pluralism. Therefore, whilst the continuation of GSP preferences had required an amendment to the labour law, inclusion in AGOA required not only that, but also tangible progress towards democratisation.

A government poverty assessment report estimated that 43 per cent of the rural population and 30 per cent of the urban population lived below the poverty line. About 16 per cent of those employed (109,000) worked in the informal sector in 1998. Although the economy grew by 3.1 per cent in 1999, it was barely keeping up with population growth, which was 2.9 per cent in 1997. Furthermore, AIDS was already affecting productivity, with some 30 per cent of the population testing HIV positive and a health service which was unable to apply even basic preventative measures to curb the spread of the disease.

3. SOUTH AFRICA

CAPITAL: Pretoria   AREA: 1,221,000 sq km   POPULATION: 44,000,000
OFFICIAL LANGUAGES: Afrikaans, English & nine African languages
POLITICAL SYSTEM: presidential democracy
HEAD OF STATE AND GOVERNMENT: President Thabo Mbeki (since June '99)
RULING PARTIES: African National Congress (ANC) & Inkatha Freedom Party (IFP)
MAIN IGO MEMBERSHIPS (NON-UN): OAU, SADC, SACU, CWTH, NAM
CURRENCY: rand (end-'00 £1=R11.31, US$1=R7.57)
GNP PER CAPITA: US$3,160, US$8,318 at PPP ('99)

THE year saw some minor changes to the political scene in South Africa. Party politics underwent realignment, with a consolidation of the two parties which had majority white support. In June the Democratic Party (DP) and the New National Party (NNP) formed an alliance, the Democratic Alliance (DA), to contest the local government elections. The NNP's decision to join forces with the Democratic Party had been spurred by a spate of defections to the DP over previous months. The ruling African National Congress (ANC) characterised the merger as a coming together of "right-wingers for a final onslaught", whilst liberal commentators and some members of the DP feared that the party's alliance with the NNP, which had been the party of apartheid, might sully the DP's liberal values. It was anticipated that the merger of the two parties, which were also joined by the small white Federal Alliance of Louis Luyt, would maximise the white vote, retain the coloured vote and attract more Indian voters.

Under the terms of the constitution, the DP would continue to be the official opposition in parliament until the next general election in 2004. The constitution prohibited members of parliament from crossing the floor or parties from merging, therefore the parties would continue to sit separately in the federal and the provincial legislatures. Tony Leon, leader of the DP, became leader of the new Democratic Alliance, whilst the leader of the NNP, Marthinus van Schalkwyk, became deputy leader. Joe Seremane, national chairman of the DP, retained that position within the Alliance.

South Africa's second democratic local government elections were held in December. The elections were held under new municipal demarcations, which reduced the number of municipalities from 843 to 237 and created six large metropolitan councils to be run by executive mayors. The elections were preceded by much acrimony between traditional leaders and the government. The former complained that they had not been consulted during the demarcation process and feared that the changes would undermine their authority. Although their representation on local councils was increased from 10 to 20 per cent, grievances persisted and President Thabo Mbeki said that the powers and role of traditional leaders would be examined after the local government elections.

The elections proceeded without any serious problems and were declared free and fair by the Independent Electoral Commission. A relatively low voter turnout was registered (about 48 per cent), compared with the national election in June 1999 (see AR 1999 p. 297), although participation was on a par with the previous local election in 1995. Some surveys ascribed the low rate of participation to a conscious "protest stay-away" amongst supporters of the ANC. Just under 60 per cent voted for the ANC, compared with 66 per cent in the 1999 general election. The DA received more than 22 per cent, an increase of some five percentage points over the combined total of the DP and the NNP in the general election. Although the voting pattern did not break the racial mould—most blacks voted for the ANC, whilst most whites and other minorities (including coloured and Indian) voted for the DA—the Alliance was able to make some inroads into traditionally ANC support bases, as some black voters switched allegiance.

Nevertheless, the ANC won 170 municipalities (including five of the six metropolitan areas). Eighteen went to the Democratic Alliance (including Cape Town), 36 to the Inkatha Freedom Party and one to the United Democratic Movement, whilst in 12 municipalities no overall majority was achieved. Thus, although the ANC continued to command overwhelming support, the strong showing of the opposition demonstrated that the government needed to accelerate its delivery of jobs and improved living conditions. The disillusionment of some, especially the urban poor and the young, was reflected in the large number of people who chose not to vote.

Since the advent of the Mbeki government in 1999 (see AR 1999, pp. 297-8) there had been a renewed focus on race in public debate. This was heightened by the broadcast on national television of footage of white policemen setting dogs on three black men, illegal immigrants from Mozambique. The six policemen were arrested on November 2 and charged with attempted murder. The public discovery of the incident, which had occurred in 1998, caused a vast outcry amongst South Africans, both white and black, and it revived concern about continued racism within the police force. Race issues generally were prominent on the government's agenda. In the first full year of the Mbeki administration there was an acceleration in the transformation of government departments to reflect more accurately the country's demographics. The Human Rights Commission, a statutory body, organised a conference on racism in August, and South Africa was due to host the third world conference against racism, racial discrimination, xenophobia and related intolerance in 2001.

In addition, the Promotion of Equality and Prevention of Unfair Discrimination Act was passed during the year. The act prohibited discrimination on 17 grounds including race, gender, sexual orientation, disability or religion. It outlawed "hate speech" and established "equality courts". The Act also shifted the onus to the respondent defending an action to prove that discrimination did not take place. The Equality Act was to prevail over all law other than the constitution.

Differences between the ANC and its alliance partners, the Congress of South African Trade Unions (Cosatu) and the South African Communist Party, increased in intensity in 2000, but were not expected to threaten the alliance. The concerns expressed by the trade union movement related mainly to three issues: firstly, the restructuring of state assets and their privatisation; secondly, proposed amendments to certain labour regulations that would make some dismissals easier and provide flexibility in working hours, overtime and overtime pay; and thirdly, the effectiveness of the Gear policy, which had imposed fiscal austerity without creating the projected number of jobs. Cosatu threatened to embark on a series of strikes in 2001 unless the government withdrew proposed amendments to labour legislation.

The generation of jobs, together with the issues of education and HIV/AIDS continued to be the largest challenges facing the government. According to the expanded definition of unemployment, the rate had dropped slightly in 1999 to 36.2 per cent (under the strict definition, it dropped to 23.3 per cent), compared with 37.5 per cent in 1998 (25.2 per cent). There had been a steady erosion of the income gap between whites and blacks. Whereas in 1975 only 2 per cent of the richest 10 per cent of the population were black, this figure had grown to 22 per cent by 1996. The percentage of whites in the top 10 per cent had declined from 95 to 65. However, the gap between wealthy blacks and poor, unemployed blacks was growing.

Despite South Africa's high unemployment rate, it experienced a shortage of highly skilled people, primarily the result of the Bantu education system. A new Immigration Bill aimed to redress the shortage but imposed a levy on companies for every foreign worker they employed. The Bill, however, went some way towards addressing the skills needs of a globalising economy.

In 2000 South Africa had one of the fastest growing HIV/AIDS rates in the world. By the end of the year, some six million people were HIV positive, according to estimates by ING Barings. The United Nations organisation UNAID projected a fall in the life expectancy of South Africans from 65 years in 1998 to 48 in 2010. The percentage of the South African workforce with HIV/AIDS was expected to rise from 11 per cent in 1999 to 18 per cent in 2005.

When Thabo Mbeki came to power in June 1999, he made the attainment of an African Renaissance the cornerstone of his foreign policy. This was linked to the advocacy of a reformed international rules-based system, which would discriminate less against Africa and the other countries of the southern hemisphere, both politically and economically. Thus Mbeki championed the Highly Indebted Poor Countries (HIPC) initiative, the reform of the UN, and a stronger voice for the developing world in the World Trade Organisation.

However, two issues dwarfed most other foreign policy initiatives in 2000. The first was the growing crisis in Zimbabwe where "war veterans" overran many white farms, usually violently, encouraged by President Mugabe's government on the basis of a need to effect land reform (see VII.2.iii.). The South African government attempted to use "quiet diplomacy" to encourage Mugabe to restore law and order. This was not successful. Although it seemed doubtful whether more would have been achieved by condemning Mugabe openly, there were calls for Mbeki to make a clear statement of the South African government's stance on developments in Zimbabwe. Amongst the South African white farming community, Mbeki's delay in condemning the farm invasions—he finally broadcast a message to the nation in mid-May reiterating South Africa's commitment to the rule of law—raised fears about similar occurrences. This anxiety was compounded by a statement made by Land and Agriculture Minister Thoko Didiza, who said that that the state was considering expropriating privately owned farms, since market-based land reform had not delivered "quality land at the right price". Unlike Zimbabwe, South Africa had in place a land restitution and redistribution policy, which had begun to deliver. By June 1999 some 13,400 households had recovered about 264,615 hectares of land at a cost of R53 million. By February some 47 million hectares of land, benefiting over 40,000 households, had been redistributed. The land invasions in Zimbabwe and the support they received from the rural poor did, however, introduce a sense of urgency to the process of land restitution and redistribution in South Africa.

The crisis in Zimbabwe caused the value of the rand to drop, and it was feared that South Africa's quiet diplomacy would affect investor confidence in the economy. Zimbabwe was also South Africa's most important trading partner in Africa, with two-way trade of R6,385 million in 1999. This too was adversely affected by the rapid decline in the Zimbabwean economy as a result of the crisis.

The second foreign policy issue that dominated the headlines was the HIV/AIDS controversy. Mbeki, having followed some of the "dissident" debates amongst academics that HIV did not necessarily cause AIDS, announced that state hospitals would not provide AZT treatment to people with HIV. The perception internationally that the President was attempting to micro-manage, and his insistence on following "dissident" opinion on a matter which most people believed had been sufficiently proven, created a negative image of the country abroad.

South Africa, with an economy three-quarters that of the Southern African Development Community (SADC) as a whole, was critical as an "anchor" for the region, especially since it was an important investor in its neighbours. Total trade with SADC grew by 13.6 per cent between 1998 and 1999, from R17,857 million to R20,301 million. It was expected that with the signing of the SADC free trade agreement in September, trade within the region would grow further.

However, South Africa's success in the region would increasingly depend on its ability to address its domestic problems of inadequate socio-economic delivery. Real GDP grew by 1.2 per cent in 1999, compared with 0.5 per cent in 1998. The National Treasury forecast growth of 2.4 per cent in 2000. But this was still insufficient to reduce unemployment, a problem which also reflected the structural difficulties of the economy. For example, although the economy was set to experience a shortage of 41,000 people in the information technology sector by 2003, most unemployed people were in fact unskilled. The challenge was how to retrain them so that they could benefit from the opportunities offered by new industries.

Foreign direct investment (FDI) into South Africa in 1999 amounted to US$1.4 billion, compared with US$ 561 million in 1998. However, in 2000 FDI dropped to US$492 million. This was partly the result of instability in Zimbabwe, combined with the HIV/AIDS controversy and low foreign direct investment in emerging markets around the world. Many investors who had no investments in Africa tended not to differentiate between stable and war-torn countries. In a survey by the United Nations Conference on Trade and Development (UNCTAD) and the International Chamber of Commerce, South Africa topped the list of the most attractive countries for FDI in Africa. Its stable macro-economic environment, coupled with fiscal rectitude, and its sophisticated infrastructure, were positive selling points. However, most of the foreign investment into South Africa since 1994 had been primarily through mergers and acquisitions. Greenfield investments had been largely absent, whilst local companies had also not invested. Furthermore, privatisation, which foreign investors regarded as a signal of a government's commitment to economic restructuring, had been slow. The strength of the trade unions in this regard had also influenced perceptions.

Privatisation was expected to gather momentum in 2001. The Minister for Public Enterprises, Jeff Radebe, estimated that privatisation should generate about R40 billion in revenue and should be completed by 2004. Private economists expected the revenue to amount to between R50 billion and R90 billion. One important privatisation in the medium term would be that of 30 per cent of the 24 power stations belonging to Eskom, which would introduce competition into the electricity sector.

On a positive note for trade, the EU-SA Trade, Development and Co-operation Agreement came into effect in January. Also, South Africa was on the first list of countries that would benefit from the enactment in the USA of the Africa Growth and Opportunity Act (AGOA) in May. According to some estimates, AGOA could create up to 66,000 jobs in the South African clothing industry.

VIII SOUTH ASIA AND INDIAN OCEAN

1. IRAN—AFGANISTAN—CENTRAL ASIAN REPUBLICS

i. IRAN

CAPITAL: Tehran   AREA: 1,633,000 sq km   POPULATION: 64,600,000
OFFICIAL LANGUAGE: Farsi (Persian)   POLITICAL SYSTEM: Islamic Republic
SPIRITUAL GUIDE: Ayatollah Seyed Ali Khamenei (since June '89)
HEAD OF STATE: President Mohammed Khatami (since Aug '97)
MAIN IGO MEMBERSHIPS (NON-UN): OPEC, ECO, CP, OIC, NAM
CURRENCY: Iranian rial (end-'00 £1=IR2,610.41, US$1=IR1,747.50)
GNP PER CAPITA: US$1,790, US$5,163 at PPP ('99)

PRESIDENT Mohammed Khatami endured mixed fortunes in 2000. The annual budget was much augmented in response to an improved inflow of oil revenues, but little progress was made in domestic political reform. The majlis elections of February 18 failed to produce a clear victory for the reformist factions within the regime. There was a 69 per cent turn-out of eligible voters, slightly down on the figure for the 1996 elections. In the first round of voting, 224 out of a total of 290 seats were filled, leaving 66 seats to be re-run on May 5. Verification of the elections was clouded by legal disputes over the ballot in Tehran. Although the outcome of the election gave the appearance of a majority to the reformists, the loose alliance of pro-Khatami groups did not represent a coherent political party with which to oppose the conservatives in the majlis, let alone confront the bastions of hardline power, such as the Council of Guardians, in the arenas beyond the jurisdiction of the majlis. In the aftermath of the elections, Ali Akbar Hashemi Rafsanjani resigned his disputed seat in the majlis and gave up his ambition of becoming the new Speaker of the Assembly. In his place Mehdi Karrubi, seen as a compromise figure between reformists and conservatives, was appointed as Speaker, indicating that, however much President Khatami's supporters might appear to dominate the majlis, the hardliners were as deeply entrenched there and as able to influence affairs as ever.

Those opposed to change used heavy-handed violence to underline their continuing strength within the fabric of the Islamic Republic. In March there was an assassination attempt on Saeed Hajjaran, a close political ally of the President. The reformist elements of the press were systematically intimidated by the Islamist judiciary, which closed down most newspapers that dared to attack hardline individuals or revolutionary institutions. By the end of the year, nine senior editors and journalists were in detention on a variety of insubstantial charges designed to ensure a muting of reformist opinion. Similarly, Iranians voicing independent views at conferences overseas were brought before the courts and some were summarily imprisoned, including Akbar Ganji, a journalist, and Hassan Yussefi Eshkevan, a reformist cleric, amongst others. An important political gain by the hardliners was the successful destabilisation of the Minister of Culture and Islamic Guidance, Ataollah Mohajerani, whose liberal approach to the press and academic freedoms was deeply resented. He resigned on December 14.

The Khatami government made some progress in motivating economic reforms such as the privatisation of parts of the large state agencies. In the political arena there was little change to encourage the President other than the removal of the head of the national Law Enforcement Authority, who was aligned against the reformists, and some consolidation of Cabinet portfolios into more liberal hands. The Ministry of Agriculture and the Construction Crusade Ministry were amalgamated in December, ending a damaging division of authority over farm affairs that had endured since the revolution in the late 1970s.

The clerical regime as a whole was diminished in popular esteem by the stalemate between the reformists and the conservatives and the resulting lack of real development in social welfare and living standards. The manipulation of the majlis election results by non-democratic organs of state was also an affront to an already frustrated but sophisticated electorate. The young people and educated classes increasingly voted by leaving Iran for the West. At home there were outbreaks of random unrest in several towns, including Haftgel in Khuzestan in January, Khorramabad in Lorestan in September and a major riot in Tehran in December—all indicating that severe social and political tensions lay simmering below the surface. The government itself admitted in October that the crime rate was rising rapidly throughout the country, with drug addiction and trafficking becoming a major social problem.

Iran's foreign relations maintained a good momentum. There was a thaw in Iran's relationship with the USA thanks to an enhanced level of exchanges in the field of sport and a softening in US trade restrictions in March that allowed a resumption of imports to the USA of Persian rugs, carpets, pistachio nuts and caviar. US sanctions as a whole were, however, kept in place. President Khatami and a high level delegation visited New York in September to take part in the UN Millennium Summit and to advance Iranian interests in the USA. Iranian contacts with Russia remained ambiguous. Despite the two countries' continuing convergence in policy on Afghanistan, Azerbaijan and Tajikistan, and the re-establishment of Russia as an important supplier of arms and nuclear technology, Iran was critical of the Russian role in Chechnya and suspicious of Russia's bias towards the economic and military renaissance of Iraq. In June Khatami was officially invited to visit Moscow by President Vladimir Putin. The Russian Minister of Defence, Igor Sergeyev, visited Iran in December, when new arms transfers to Iran were discussed.

A significant diplomatic development in 2000 was a 170-delegate mission led by the President to China, beginning on June 22. Agreements on co-operation in petroleum, petrochemicals and mining were the principal declared achievements of the visit, although defence was also a major item of discussion. President Khatami's wish for closer relations with the European Union states was advanced as a result of an increasing tempo of visits to Tehran by high ranking European officials and politicians, including the Spanish Prime Minister, José Aznar, in October. In July Khatami was an official visitor to Berlin, when the German government increased trade credits for suppliers to Iran to US$400 million. The trial and sentencing of 13 Jews by an Iranian court in July brought criticism in Europe but did not seriously interrupt the progress of Iranian-EU relations.

In the Middle East and Asia the Iranian charm offensive had mixed results. Some improvement affected links with the Arab states of the Persian Gulf area, with the Foreign Minister, Kamal Kharra-zi, visiting Iraq in October. Relations with Turkey were adversely affected by the arrest in Turkey of some 200 Iranian nationals in July and the interception of an Iranian cargo aircraft in Turkish airspace in October.

Advances in the economic domain came from an easing of foreign exchange shortages as oil revenues rose by more than 25 per cent over 1999 to US$20 billion, with an average oil production of 3.7 million barrels a day. The country's foreign debt was reduced to US$8 billion, whilst foreign exchange reserves grew to some US$10 billion. It was likely that expenditure on defence was also increased substantially. Iranian policy within OPEC was directed at stabilising oil prices at approximately US$25 per barrel. The strengthening of oil sector income helped to lift overall economic growth to 5 per cent in real terms, supported by a 7 per cent rise in the value of investment.

Agriculture was a poor performer, badly affected by drought across much of the country, but industry, principally state petrochemical plants and a broad spectrum of private manufacturing, fared particularly well. Hydrocarbon developments were encouraging, with new oil fields discovered and a growing number of major foreign oil companies such as Shell, BP and Statoil seeking to participate in new ventures in Iran.

Imports expanded to some US$14 billion during 2000, whilst exports were estimated at US$24 billion. Inflation fell to a reported 16 per cent. The only negative aspect of the economy was the government's failure to press on with structural reform, especially the privatisation of monolithic state enterprises. The government was also unable to reduce its inherited problem of heavy subsidies on energy, medicines and foodstuffs, which cost US$5.8 billion in the year.

ii. AFGHANISTAN

CAPITAL: Kabul   AREA: 650,000 sq km   POPULATION: 23,700,000
OFFICIAL LANGUAGES: Pushtu, Dari (Persian)   POLITICAL SYSTEM: Islamic state
LEADERSHIP: Mola Mohammed Omar, Leader of the Talibaan (in power since Sept '96), Mohammed Rabbani, Chairman of Ruling Council (since Sept '96)
MAIN IGO MEMBERSHIPS (NON-UN): ECO, CP, OIC, NAM
CURRENCY: afgani (end-'00 £1=Af7,095.55, US$1=Af4750.00)
GNP PER CAPITA: n/a

THE armed struggle between the government Talibaan militia and the anti-Talibaan coalition forces—the United Front for Salvation of Afghanistan (UIFSA), commanded by former Defence Minister Ahmed Shah Masud—continued throughout the year. The Talibaan maintained the upper hand in the conflict, controlling Kabul and up to 90 per cent of the country. Despite military efforts to secure a decisive victory during the summer months and the resumption of peace negotiations, both sides remained locked in an apparent stalemate.

The improved weather in early March saw a resumption of fighting and Talibaan forces launched a limited offensive to regain territory lost to the UIFSA in skirmishes throughout the winter months. Talibaan officials claimed to have made significant territorial and military gains in the fighting, which was concentrated north of Kabul. However, the UIFSA denied that the Talibaan had secured any advantage in the offensive and in the following months military operations by both sides remained limited as they mustered supplies in preparation for their summer offensives. Hopes for a peaceful settlement to the conflict had been raised in March when the Organisation of the Islamic Conference (OIC) hosted a meeting between representatives of both sides in Jeddah, Saudi Arabia. Agreement was reached to hold further direct talks in May, but these ended with little progress reported.

In early August the Talibaan launched a large-scale offensive in the north of the country. Heavy artillery bombardment and air attacks on UIFSA positions around Taloqan, the capital of Takhar province, failed to dislodge Masud's forces, who were able to launch their own counter-offensive later in the month. The UIFSA had captured this strategically-important town on Afghanistan's north-eastern border with Tajikistan in October 1998 (see AR 1998, p. 318) and it had enabled Masud to keep open key supply routes to the north. However, in early September large numbers of Talibaan troops attacked Taloqan on three fronts and quickly overran UIFSA positions. As many as 150,000 people fled the area during the fighting. The fall of Taloqan was a major blow for Masud as it severed supply routes into his stronghold in the Panjsher Valley. The ability of UIFSA forces to maintain a fighting force through the winter without adequate supplies was subject to question, although Masud managed to keep control of strategically important heights to the east of Taloqan, from where he had mounted the offensive to capture the town in 1998.

An Ariana (Afghan national airline) Boeing 727 airliner with 187 people on board was hijacked on a domestic flight from Kabul to the northern city of Mazar-i-Sharif in early February. The plane was then forced to fly to Tashkent, the capital of Uzbekistan, where some passengers were released. In Tashkent the hijackers demanded the immediate release of Ismail Kahn, the former governor of Herat known as the "Lion of Herat", who had been imprisoned by the Talibaan after their capture of Herat in 1995. The airliner then flew to Aktyubinsk in Kazakhstan where some passengers were freed, then on to Moscow, Russia, where further passengers were released, before it arrived at Stansted airport in the UK. Following the plane's arrival in the UK the hijackers did not repeat their earlier demand for the release of Kahn and, after the peaceful resolution of the hijacking after a few days, 69 of the aircraft's passengers made applications for political asylum in the UK.

The Talibaan faced further embarrassment in late March when Ismail Kahn, who was a close ally of Masud, escaped from a high security prison in Kandahar and fled to Iran. The Talibaan announced a substantial reward for the recapture of Kahn and also offered immunity from prosecution for anyone providing information on his whereabouts.

In September the Talibaan sent a delegation of officials to the USA to mobilise support for the regime's claim to Afghanistan's seat at the United Nations, which was currently held by the ousted government of former President Burhanuddin Rabbani. However, the efforts failed and the Talibaan remained diplomatically isolated throughout the year. The isolation increased in November when Pakistan, one of the Talibaan's closest allies, suddenly closed its border with Afghanistan. The decision followed an influx of 30,000 new refugees who had crossed the border in September to join the estimated 2,100,000 who had already fled the conflict. The regime also faced considerable international pressure over the presence in the country of Osama bin Laden, the Saudi-born Islamic militant who was wanted in the USA on terrorism charges which included the August 1998 bombing of US embassies in east Africa (see AR 1998 p. 261-2).

In February Talibaan officials announced that bin Laden had been critically ill with kidney failure and had ceded control of his Islamist organisation to his personal doctor and former head of the Egyptian Islamic Jihad, Ayman al-Zawahiri. No details of his condition emerged and the USA maintained efforts to force the Talibaan to surrender bin Laden to their control. The US and Afghan ambassadors to Pakistan held talks over bin Laden in Islamabad, the capital of Pakistan, in November, following reports of his alleged involvement in the October bombing of the *USS Cole* in Yemen (see V.3.ii.). Following reports in the media that the USA was prepared to carry out missile strikes against Afghanistan for harbouring him, bin Laden fled his base close to Kandahar and moved to a remote outpost in the Hindu Kush mountains. The pressure on the Talibaan regime to surrender bin Laden was intensified in December, when the UN Security Council voted to adopt Resolution 1333 imposing limited sanctions on the country. Drafted by US officials, the resolution gave Afghanistan 30 days to force bin Laden to surrender or an arms embargo would be imposed on the Talibaan and all Talibaan offices and Ariana Airlines offices abroad would be closed. Talibaan officials reacted angrily to the decision, claiming that the threatened embargo was in effect an undeclared war against Afghanistan. In retaliation the Talibaan closed the offices of a UN special mission to Afghanistan. Aid agencies described the situation as serious because many refugees had depended on the mission for food and shelter.

The year ended with a new round of peace talks between the UIFSA and the Talibaan, held in mid-December in Ashkabad, the capital of Turkmenistan. The negotiations, chaired by Fancesc Vendrell, UN Secretary General Kofi Annan's special envoy to Afghanistan, were the first direct talks to be held since 1999. However, no tangible progress was made and the Talibaan withdrew from the talks in protest over the imposition of UN sanctions.

iii. KAZAKHSTAN—TURKMENISTAN—UZBEKISTAN— KYRGYZSTAN—TAJIKISTAN

Kazakhstan

CAPITAL: Astana   AREA: 2,717,000 sq km   POPULATION: 15,000,000
OFFICIAL LANGUAGES: Kazakh & Russian   POLITICAL SYSTEM: presidential
HEAD OF STATE AND GOVERNMENT: President Nursultan Nazarbayev (since Feb '90)
RULING PARTIES: Fatherland Party (Otan) leads ruling alliance
PRIME MINISTER: Kasymzhomart Tokayev (since Oct '99)
MAIN IGO MEMBERSHIPS (NON-UN): CIS, PFP, OSCE, OIC, ECO
CURRENCY: tenge (end-'00 £1=T217.43, US$1=T145.55)
GNP PER CAPITA: US$1,230, US$4,408 at PPP ('99)

Turkmenistan

CAPITAL: Ashgabat   AREA: 488,000 sq km   POPULATION: 5,050,000
OFFICIAL LANGUAGE: Turkmen   POLITICAL SYSTEM: presidential
HEAD OF STATE AND GOVERNMENT: President (Gen.) Saparmurad Niyazov (since Jan '90)
RULING PARTIES: Democratic Party of Turkmentistan (DPT)
MAIN IGO MEMBERSHIPS (NON-UN): CIS, PFP, OSCE, OIC, ECO, NAM
CURRENCY: Turkmen manat
GNP PER CAPITA: US$660, US$3,099 at PPP ('99)

Uzbekistan

CAPITAL: Tashkent   AREA: 447,000 sq km   POPULATION: 25,660,000
OFFICIAL LANGUAGE: Uzbek   POLITICAL SYSTEM: presidential
HEAD OF STATE AND GOVERNMENT: President Islam Karimov (since March '90)
RULING PARTIES: People's Democratic Party (PDP)
PRIME MINISTER: Otir Sultonov (since Dec '95)
MAIN IGO MEMBERSHIPS (NON-UN): CIS, PFP, OSCE, OIC, ECO, NAM
CURRENCY: sum (end-'00 £1=S482.2, US$1=S322.80)
GNP PER CAPITA: US$720, US$2,092 at PPP ('99)

Kyrgyzstan

CAPITAL: Bishkek   AREA: 199,000 sq km   POPULATION: 5,100,000
OFFICIAL LANGUAGES: Kyrgyz & Russian   POLITICAL SYSTEM: presidential
HEAD OF STATE AND GOVERNMENT: President Askar Akayev (since Oct '90)
RULING PARTIES: Democratic Movement of Kyrgyzstan heads loose ruling coalition
PRIME MINISTER: Amangeldy Muraliyev (since April '99)
MAIN IGO MEMBERSHIPS (NON-UN): CIS, PFP, OSCE, OIC, ECO
CURRENCY: som (end-'00 £1=S72.06, US$1=S48.24)
GNP PER CAPITA: US$300, US$2,223 at PPP ('99)

Tajikistan

CAPITAL: Dushanbe   AREA: 143,000 sq km   POPULATION: 6,600,000
OFFICIAL LANGUAGE: Tajik   POLITICAL SYSTEM: presidential
HEAD OF STATE AND GOVERNMENT: President Imamoli Rakhmanov (since Nov '92)
RULING PARTIES: People's Democratic Party of Tajikistan & United Tajik Opposition head precarious coalition
PRIME MINISTER: Akil Akilov (since Dec '99)
MAIN IGO MEMBERSHIPS (NON-UN): CIS, OSCE, OIC, ECO
CURRENCY: Tajik rouble
GNP PER CAPITA: US$290, US$981 at PPP ('99)

PARLIAMENTARY elections were held in Kyrgyzstan and Tajikistan in early 2000. The Kyrgyz elections of February 20 produced only a handful of clear results. Several political parties were prevented from fielding candidates by last-minute changes in the election law, and the eligibility of others was challenged on the grounds that the nomination procedures might not have been legal. Monitors from the Organisation for Security and Cooperation in Europe (OSCE) expressed concern about the exclusion of opposition candidates from the run-offs, and allegations of pressure on voters. They stated that the elections had "failed to comply with OSCE commitments". In Tajikistan, the first-ever multi-party elections were held in February and March, for, respectively, the lower and upper houses of the legislature. The elections were monitored by teams from the United Nations (UN) and the OSCE. Both teams drew attention to a number of shortcomings, including the failure of the media to provide balanced coverage. The pro-presidential People's Democratic Party won the largest share of seats in the lower house.

On October 29 the incumbent President of Kyrgyzstan, Askar Akayev, was re-elected for a third term. His opponents deemed this to be unconstitutional, and there were numerous allegations of fraud. In Uzbekistan, President Islam Karimov was also returned to office for a further term. The elections, held on January 9, had a turnout of 95.9 per cent, of which 91.9 per cent of the votes (including— by his own account—that of the only challenger) were cast for Karimov.

Elsewhere in Central Asia the trend was towards extending presidential terms of office indefinitely. In January Turkmen President Saparmurad Niyazov—more generally known as the Turkmenbashy (Father of the Turkmens)— was confirmed in office for life by the Turkmen National Forum. In Kazakhstan, a law giving President Nursultan Nazarbayev extraordinary powers and privileges after the expiry of his present term of office in 2006 was passed by both houses of the Kazak Parliament in June. The measure evoked criticism from the opposition, some of whom blamed the country's rampant corruption and economic mismanagement on a system of government focused on one person—the President. Nazarbayev stressed that he did not intend to be "a Khan or a President for life". Yet he did not exclude the possibility of standing for a further term of office, as his current term was arguably only the first under Kazakhstan's new constitution, an interpretation which would make him eligible to stand again in 2006.

In Tajikistan the peace was continued to hold. The National Reconciliation Commission held its final session on March 26. The Commission, in which both government and opposition factions were represented, had been set up in summer 1997 to oversee the implementation of the peace accords which had ended the Tajik civil war. After the parliamentary elections the peace process was deemed to have been satisfactorily concluded. However, the chairman noted that problems still remained, including the repatriation of an estimated 108,000 Tajik refugees and the integration of Tajik opposition fighters into the Tajik armed forces.

During 2000 some progress was made towards the reconstruction and development of Tajikistan. Unexpectedly, Tajik President Imamoli Rakhmonov announced the introduction of a new currency, the somoni (subdivided into 100 diram), effective from October 30. The existing currency, the Tajik rouble, would remain legal tender until April 1 2001, with an exchange rate between the two currencies of 1 somoni to 1,000 TR (with 2.05 somoni equal to US$1). The introduction of the new Tajik currency caused "visible price rises and shortages", according to the Speaker of the Tajik National Assembly. This was an issue of grave concern as, according to international agencies, some 80 per cent of the Tajik population were living below the poverty line.

Economic forecasts for the region were somewhat more optimistic than in past years. Uzbekistan's GDP for the period January-September was 1,955 billion sum, 4.2 per cent up on the corresponding period in 1999, according to figures from the Uzbek Macroeconomics and Statistics Ministry. The non-state sector accounted for 70.3 per cent of total GDP. Foreign trade turnover during this period was US$4.458 million, with a foreign trade surplus of US$51.4 million. Foreign investments accounted for 22.7 per cent of the total volume of capital investment. Progress towards the convertibility of the Uzbek sum, however, was slow; according to President Karimov this would take another 3-5 years. Privatisation moved ahead at a steady pace. As of October 1, Uzbekistan had 178,000 small and medium-sized businesses (90 per cent of all registered enterprises), an increase of 11.4 per cent on the figure for October 1 1999.

Kazakhstan expected a positive trade balance of upwards of US$2 billion for 2000. Economic growth for the year was forecast to be 6-7 per cent. A growth rate of 15 per cent was expected in construction and 6 per cent in services. Inflation was expected to be somewhat above 9 per cent at the end of the year.

In Kyrgyzstan the economic crisis of 1998 appeared at last to have been overcome. During the first 10 months of the year, Kyrgyz GDP grew by 4.3 per cent, while the national currency, the som, lost only 6.7 per cent of its value (as opposed to a loss of 46 per cent in the comparable period in 1999). Inflation was brought down from 39 per cent in 1999 to an estimated 13 per cent. The budget deficit, which in August 1999 had amounted to 864.6 million som (2.5 per cent of GDP) would, it was hoped, be eliminated by 2003. However, according to members of the Kyrgyz Legislative Assembly, the Kyrgyz "black" economy had more than doubled in the past five years and now accounted for an estimated 40 per cent of GDP. Legislators attributed the rise principally to the heavy burden of taxation, particularly on the small and medium-sized business sectors. As a result of the heavy taxes, repeated efforts by the government to foster the development of these enterprises had had little effect.

The Tajik GDP during the first six months of the year, according to official data, was up 6.5 per cent in comparison with the corresponding period in 1999, and industrial output grew by 9 per cent. Arrears in salaries in sectors funded from the state budget were reduced, but pension arrears increased. Inflation over the period was 16.6 per cent. The Tajik Finance Ministry announced that in the first half of 2000 the budget deficit had been reduced to 257.7 million Tajik roubles (US$102,000), the equivalent of 0.1 per cent of GDP.

The agricultural sector in all the Central Asian states suffered numerous problems. There was a recurrence of the locust infestation of 1999 in Kazakhstan, though on a smaller scale. The Kazak grain yield in 2000 was 13 million tonnes, down from 14.2 million tonnes in 1999. However, the state sector was able to secure contracts for grain exports that included delivery of 100,000 tonnes each to Uzbekistan and Iran, whilst the private sector supplied over 100,000 tonnes to Afghanistan. In the southern tier (southern Kazakhstan, Tajikistan, Uzbekistan and Turkmenistan) agriculture was severely affected by drought, the worst since 1951. In Turkmenistan the grain harvest was disappointing and there was a drop of 20 per cent in the cotton harvest (1.03 million tonnes, as against 1.3 million tonnes 1999). In Uzbekistan, the cotton crop was down by 18 per cent; the rice harvest, too, was badly hit by the drought.

The Caspian Sea continued to be a subject of dispute. In June, Russian President Vladimir Putin and Kazak President Nursultan Nazarbayev issued a joint statement urging all the Caspian states to take a more active part in defining the new legal status of the Sea. Subsequently, Viktor Kaluzhny, Putin's special envoy on Caspian Sea issues, toured the littoral states, hoping to win support for the Russian proposal for a "phased approach". This proposal envisaged signing a convention on ecological issues and the protection of the biological resources of the Sea before addressing the possible division of the Sea into national zones. Kaluzhny emphasised the importance of the Caspian for Russia's security, but claimed that Russia had no "imperial ambitions" there. He rejected the Iranian proposal that the Sea be divided equally between the five littoral states. He did, however, gain Iranian support for the establishment of a centre for the strategic development of the Caspian Sea.

Progress was made in the development of the Karachaganak oil and gas field in western Kazakhstan. The field was being developed by an international consortium whose participants included UK company British Gas and Italy's Agip (each with a 32.5 per cent stake), US Texaco (20 per cent) and Russia's LUKoil (15 per cent). During the first eight months of the year, 4.5 tonnes of gas condensate were sold from the Karachaganak field, as against 2.1 million tonnes in the corresponding period in 1999. A contract, worth US$900 million, to build a 635 km gas pipeline from Karachaganak to the Caspian Sea port of Atyrau was awarded to an Italian-Greek consortium. The pipeline, due for completion in late 2003 or early 2004, would have an initial capacity of 10 million tonnes of condensate a year, eventually to rise to 12 million tonnes. The Italian-Greek consortium would also develop infrastructure systems and build a gas condensate refining plant with a capacity of 7 million tonnes of condensate a year.

The Presidents of the five member states of the Commonwealth of Independent States (CIS) Customs Union—Belarus, Kazakhstan, Kyrgyzstan,

Russia and Tajikistan—signed a treaty on October 10 to transform this body into the Eurasian Economic Community (EEC), to take effect from April 2001. The EEC would be empowered to represent the interests of member states in discussions with other countries and international organisations on matters relating to international trade and customs policy. Some commentators saw this as the first step towards the creation of a "Eurasian Union", as advocated in 1994 by Kazak President Nursultan Nazarbayev. Significantly, the Premiers of the five states agreed to draft a treaty on visa-free travel between member states.

The leaders of the so-called "Shanghai Five" states—China, Kazakhstan, Kyrgyzstan, Russia and Tajikistan—met in the Tajik capital, Dushanbe, on July 5. In a joint declaration, they registered their "resolve to fight jointly against international terrorism, religious extremism and national separatism", and also against arms and drug trafficking and illegal migration. The declaration confirmed "each state's true right of choice of their own course of political, economic and social development in line with their realities" and renounced "interference in each other's internal affairs" even on the pretext of "humanitarian intervention" and "human rights". They backed the Chinese government's "One China" policy, as well as Russia's actions in Chechnya, UN efforts for a political settlement of the Afghan conflict, and the "absolute necessity" of adhering to the 1972 Anti-Ballistic Missile Treaty. Uzbek President Islam Karimov, who was present as an observer, stressed that the security interests of his country coincided with those of the "Five", and welcomed the contribution of Russia and China to guaranteeing security in Central Asia.

China also participated in bilateral discussions with the Central Asian states. These included the first round of talks between working groups of experts on the use of rivers crossing the Kazak-China frontier. The results of the six-day session, held in November in Almaty, were fairly modest: a list was drawn up of all the rivers crossing the frontier, together with an outline of future work. The discussions failed to resolve Kazak fears about the effect of the Cherny Irtysh-Karamay canal being constructed by the Chinese as part of a major plan to develop western China. A co-operation accord on the improvement of cross-border passenger transport was concluded between the Kyrgyz and Xinjiang authorities. Agreement was also reached on the construction of a road to link eastern Tajikistan and China. Chinese military aid (worth about US$600,000) was made available to Uzbekistan.

The conflict in Afghanistan between the forces of the Talibaan and the Northern Alliance remained one of the main security concerns for the Central Asian states. There were a number of initiatives for peace. On December 7, Stephen Sestanovich, adviser on the CIS to the US Secretary of State, called for further discussions amongst the "six-plus-two" group—Iran, China, Pakistan, Tajikistan, Turkmenistan, Uzbekistan plus Russia and the USA—on how to end the conflict. He said that the USA would propose to the UN Security Council that new sanctions be introduced against the Talibaan. However, the Turkmen President argued against such a course of action. Instead, he invited representatives of both the Talibaan and the government of ousted President Burhanuddin Rabbani (which now controlled only a small part of northern Afghanistan) to visit Turkmenistan for talks during the celebrations for the fifth anniversary of Turkmen neutrality (December 10). A meeting between representatives of the two sides duly took place, the first face-to-face meeting since 1999.

Other Central Asian countries also made efforts to find a *modus vivendi* with the Talibaan. President Nursultan Nazarbayev pointed out that the existence of the Talibaan was an "undeniable reality". Thus, on November 21 the Kazak and Afghan Talibaan ambassadors to Pakistan held a long meeting in Islamabad, the first such official encounter. Their discussions covered issues of terrorism, drug trafficking, and the settlement of the Afghan conflict. The following week, the Uzbek Foreign Minister stated that Uzbekistan might open its borders with Afghanistan in the near future.

Another serious concern for the Central Asian states was the renewed activity of Islamist militants. They made an incursion into Uzbekistan and southern Kyrgyzstan in August, almost exactly a year after a similar incident in 1999. The militants, reportedly members of the banned Uzbek Islamist organisation known as the Islamic Movement of Uzbekistan (IMU), attacked from Afghanistan via Tajikistan. Yet unlike in 1999, when the militants made their aim explicit (namely, the establishment of an "Islamic empire" in Central Asia), the motives of the new invasion were unclear. Some reports linked the militants with the international drug trade. The Russian government offered its help, urging the need for united efforts to maintain the security of the region. Other CIS members, including Belarus and the Ukraine, also offered assistance.

The insurgents were driven out of Uzbekistan by mid-September, but they were not dislodged from Kyrgyzstan until early October. A victory parade was held in the Kyrgyz capital, Bishkek, on October 26. President Akayev announced that he would donate some US$20,000 to the families of the 35 Kyrgyz troops killed in action against the militants. The militants' losses were estimated at 120 dead and 200 injured. In September the US State Department placed the IMU on its list of international terrorist organisations. It was alleged that there were links between the IMU and the global terrorism network of Osama bin Laden. Kyrgyzstan and Uzbekistan concluded a bilateral defence agreement—the first to be signed between two Central Asian states—with the aim of strengthening regional security.

2. INDIA—PAKISTAN—BANGLADESH—NEPAL—BHUTAN—SRI LANKA

i. INDIA

CAPITAL: New Delhi   AREA: 3,288,000 sq km   POPULATION: 1,040,000,000
OFFICIAL LANGUAGES: Hindi & English   POLITICAL SYSTEM: parliamentary democracy
HEAD OF STATE: President Kocheril Raman Narayanan (since July '98)
RULING PARTY: Bharatiya Janata Party (BJP) heads multi-party coalition
HEAD OF GOVERNMENT: Atal Bihari Vajpayee (BJP), Prime Minister (since March '98)
MAIN IGO MEMBERSHIPS (NON-UN): SAARC, CP, CWTH, NAM
CURRENCY: rupee (end-'00 £1=Rs69.73, US$1=Rs46.68)
GNP PER CAPITA: US$450, US$2,149 at PPP ('99)

INDIA experienced a year of relative political stability (with the reorganisation of some states) combined with active diplomacy, but economic performance was overall somewhat sluggish. Kashmir continued to attract news attention as it was a year punctuated by localised violence in that much troubled northern mountainous state.

The year began shortly after the re-election of the coalition government led by the Bharatiya Janata Party (BJP—see AR 1999, p. 314). A day before the newly re-elected Prime Minister Atal Bihari Vajpayee swore in his Cabinet on October 13, 1999, news came of a military coup in Pakistan headed by Gen. Pervaiz Musharraf, who was widely regarded in Delhi circles as resolutely anti-Indian and as the main planner of Pakistan's attempt to capture a part of Kashmir around Kargil in the summer of 1999.

Early in the year the Subrahmanyam committee published a 227-page report on the 1999 conflict with Pakistan. The report said that failures of India's intelligence agencies had enabled the insurgent Islamic separatist guerrillas, supported by regular Pakistani troops, to entrench themselves in formidably defensible positions. It also criticised deficiencies in equipment and clothing which had compounded the problems which the Indian forces had faced in repelling the intruders. The committee recommended the acquisition of surveillance aircraft, communications-intercept and satellite-imaging capabilities for the national security system.

At least 35 Sikhs were murdered on March 20 at a village about 80 km southeast of Srinagar, the summer capital of the state of Kashmir and Jammu. A group of armed men dressed in Indian army uniforms had ordered the men out of their houses, ostensibly for an identity parade, and then shot them.

At the end of a five-day debate, the state assembly of Kashmir and Jammu on June 26 accepted a resolution of the National Conference (JKNC) government to improve state autonomy, thus endorsing a report by a state committee. The resolution was opposed by legislators from both the BJP and the opposition Congress (I) party, but the JKNC held two-thirds of the assembly's seats. The plan proposed that Kashmir revert to the special status which it had held between 1947 and 1953, when the state enjoyed complete autonomy except in matters of defence, foreign relations and communications.

The volatility of the Kashmir issue, evident throughout the year, intensified in the last quarter. Although there continued to be sporadic violence and killings on all sides, the Indian government in late December extended for another month the ceasefire which it had called unilaterally at the beginning of the Muslim holy month of Ramadan. Pakistan responded by saying that it was withdrawing "substantial numbers" of troops from the line of control in Kashmir. Kashmiris remained deeply divided between pro-Pakistan and pro-independence groups, with few takers for the autonomy status which was the most the government in New Delhi was likely to offer.

The enhanced majority that the BJP coalition government commanded heightened hopes, mostly unrealised, of more political stability as well as decisiveness in policy making. By the end of the year, however, worries about the health of the Prime Minister raised concerns about the chances of his government being able to serve out its full five year term.

The start of 2000 saw the government in the midst of a crisis after an Indian Airlines aircraft was hijacked from Kathmandu in Nepal to Kandahar in Talibaancontrolled Afghanistan. The government secured the safety of the passengers on board by agreeing to release jailed Muslim cleric Maulana Masood Azhar and two others held for fighting Indian rule in Kashmir. Azhar returned home to Pakistan, which India accused of masterminding the hijack.

In elections held in February for four state assemblies the opposition Congress party showed that it had still not recovered from its unprecedentedly poor performance in the 1999 general election. It still could not mount a serious challenge to the ruling National Democratic Alliance (NDA). There were mixed results, however, for Prime Minister Vajpayee's Bharatiya Janata Party (BJP), the core element in the NDA. In the agriculturally rich northern state of Haryana and in the poor eastern state of Orissa the BJP's allies won conclusive victories but BJP candidates performed badly—with the consequence that these allies were emboldened to demand a bigger role in the national government and a larger share of patronage for their states. The biggest shock for the BJP came, however, in the country's second most populous state, Bihar, in the northern plains. There, every pollster and Hindu party leader had predicted the downfall of Laloo Prasad Yadav, the shrewd and resilient politician whose state party had ruled Bihar for a decade but who faced a range of corruption charges. In the event, Yadav's party won 123 seats in the 324-seat state legislative assembly, one more than the BJP and its allies combined. A close result in the northern-eastern state of Manipur, after voting on February 22, was not resolved until March 2 when a United Front-Manipur State Congress Party (MSCP)-FPM coalition government was sworn in.

The year saw the launch of three new states, carved out of existing large states in fulfilment of projects which had been tabled for some years. The Union parliament agreed to the creation of the new states of Jharkhand (from southern Bihar), Chattisgarh (from Madhya Pradesh), and Uttaranchal (from Uttar Pradesh). This trend toward creating smaller states reflected the growing realisation that they were easier to administer and tended to develop faster, whilst perhaps also reducing the power of regional satrapies vis á vis the central government. The new states also reflected increasing regional and caste assertiveness. Jarkhand and Chattisgarh were dominated by tribal peoples. Uttaranchal was an upper-caste domain, many of whose citizens had felt threatened by the increasing confidence and political muscle of lower-caste politicians in Uttar Pradesh.

The heightened assertiveness of states was paralleled by that of the judicial system. A court convicted Jayalitha Jayaram, a former Chief Minister of Tamil Nadu, of corruption. This made her the highest-ranking politician in India to be convicted of such a crime—but not for long. In October the former Prime Minister (1991-96), P V Narasimha Rao, and one of his former Cabinet colleagues were convicted of bribing MPs.

The Congress party continued to be torn by infighting. Jitendra Prasad, a party leader from Uttar Pradesh, stood against the incumbent Congress president Sonia Gandhi (widow of Rajiv and daughter-in-law of Indira Gandhi) in party elections held in mid-November, but was defeated overwhelmingly.

India's diplomacy was markedly active and met with some successes during the year. Relations with the USA not only seemed to recover but were apparently put on a more cordial level than had seemed possible for several decades. Thus, the diplomatic highlight of the year came in March when Bill Clinton became the first US President to visit India whilst in office since Jimmy Carter in 1978. Clinton came with a large entourage of businessmen, especially those of Indian extraction. Both governments were at pains to improve relations which had been badly damaged by India's nuclear tests in 1998 (see AR 1998 p. 327-8). Throughout his five-day visit Clinton devoted much time and skill to charming his hosts, and both sides reiterated their countries' mutual commitment to democracy and pluralism. They agreed to institutionalise annual contacts and, by affirming that the line of control dividing Kashmir should be respected and terrorism deplored and opposed, the US President appeared to endorse India's position its dispute with Pakistan.

In September Vajpayee made a reciprocal visit to New York and Washington. The large number of successful Indian-born computer-analysts and Silicon Valley entrepreneurs present at the vast state banquet that Clinton gave for Vajpayee reflected the growing importance of the Indian diaspora in Indo-US relations. In an article published in the *International Herald Tribune* on September 21, Vajpayee wrote that India and the USA, the world's two biggest open societies, "can be natural allies in the 21st century". In the same article he added that "A unilateral moratorium on explosive tests, a policy of 'no first use', a tight export control regime and a willingness to engage with other countries on all aspects of international security are the principles of India's nuclear policy."

Russia's President Vladimir Putin paid a state visit in October and concluded a number of arms deals. On India's shopping list were advanced Sukhoi fighters for the air force, a refitted aircraft carrier and 300 new tanks. The Indian government signed arms deals with Russia worth US$3 billion for the joint production and marketing of Russian-designed weapons systems.

Though relations with Pakistan remained tense throughout the year, Sino-Indian relations showed some signs of easing. India's President Kocheril Raman

Narayanan visited Beijing and China's Foreign Minister, Tang Jiaxuan, visited New Delhi. The visits indicated a disposition to maintain a constructive bilateral dialogue even though no substantial progress was made on their border dispute. However, the escape of the third highest Tibetan Buddhist leader, the Karmapa Lama, from Tibet to India in January served as a reminder of how swiftly Sino-Indian relations could plummet when touchy issues were involved.

The year also saw visits to India by Geoffrey Hoon, the UK Defence Minister, France's Foreign Minister Hubert Vedrine and his German counterpart, Jozchka Fischer. In August Yoshiro Mori became the first Japanese Premier to visit India for a decade. In June Prime Minister Vajpayee led his country's delegation to Lisbon for the first summit between India and the European Union (see XI.4.).

India's relations with its neighbours in the South Asian Association for Regional Co-operation (SAARC) remained guarded at best and acrimonious at worst, partly—but not only—because India refused to accept the reconvening of SAARC's annual summit, which would have entailed India's Prime Minister meeting with Gen. Pervaiz Musharraf of Pakistan. In May India refused to send troops into Sri Lanka to help rescue 40,000 government troops trapped by advancing Tamil Tigers in the northern city of Jaffna.

Financial markets and economic experts alike had greeted the re-election of the BJP-led coalition in October 1999 with optimism. Its increased majority in parliament raised speculative hopes of a new era of decisiveness in economic policy making. By the close of the year 2000 it seemed, however, that the government had lost its momentum in this regard. In his annual budget speech in February Finance Minister Yashwant Sinha promised a stiff dose of reforms, but failed to live up to expectations. The budget proposed lower interest rates in the future, lowered peak tariffs, reduced a costly fertiliser subsidy and raised the ceiling on permissible foreign institutional investment in Indian companies from 30 to 40 per cent. However, many commentators pointed out that Sinha failed to tackle at all adequately the most serious problem facing the economy: the deficit. The government target was revised upward to 5.1 per cent, but even that appeared unattainable. An increase in defence spending by 28 per cent, the largest ever annual increase on defence, spurred by heightened tensions with Pakistan, also put pressure on the government's finances.

Furthermore, Sinha did not produce a clear timetable or programme for the privatisation of state-owned companies. In February the government made a start on privatisation by selling a loss-making bakery, Modern Foods, to the Anglo-Dutch Multinational, Hindustan Lever. Further progress was stalled by a wall of special interests: government ministries unwilling to cede control, powerful regional politicians vetoing privatisation and supporters of protectionism within the ruling coalition opposed to more foreign ownership.

Infrastructure continued to lag. As the world market for power-generation picked up, especially in developed markets such as the USA, India began to look less attractive to foreign companies. In Uttar Pradesh, thousands of state electricity workers went on strike to protest against a move by the state government to break up its loss-making State Electricity Board into separate units for the generation, transmission and distribution of power. The state government held firm, but was no closer to attracting serious investor interest in its power sector. Andhra Pradesh in southern India offered an exemplary glimmer of hope for reformers. Chief Minister Chandrababu Naidu refused to back down in the face of hunger strikes and mob violence protesting against his power sector reforms. The infrastructure area where the government moved fastest was telecoms, freeing long-distance telephony from government control earlier than expected.

The software industry emerged as the strongest example of the benefits to India of globalisation. In 2000 software firms Silverline Technologies, Wipro, and state-owned telecoms giant Videsh Sanchar Nigam all listed on US stock exchanges, as did ICICI Bank. Nevertheless, software was an island of modernity in a largely backward economy. As world oil prices began rising, India started to feel the pinch. Rising inflation and a lack of new investment seemed to auger an economic slowdown in 2001. The government maintained that GDP would grow by about 7 per cent in the fiscal year ending on March 31 2001. But with a poor monsoon likely to depress agricultural incomes, and with high world prices fuelling inflation and discouraging investment, most analysts estimated that growth would be less than 6 per cent.

The growth in imports by 22.5 per cent to nearly US$26 billion in the first six months of the fiscal year was misleading. Rather than reflecting an upturn in investment, most of the growth—about US$8 billion—was due to higher world oil prices. Exports, however, were up 22 per cent in the first half of the fiscal year to US$21.3 billion, stimulated by strong global demand for Indian textiles, leader gems and steel. Software, counted separately, was another aspect of dynamism in the economy. Software exports were expected to rise to about US$6 billion in the year ending March 31 2001, up from nearly US$4 billion the previous year.

Foreign investment remained relatively lukewarm. Foreign Direct Investment (FDI) inflows in the first four months of the fiscal year stood at US$799 million compared with US$448 million a year earlier. But this was not even close to the boom years of the mid-1990s, let alone the government's ambitious target of US$10 billion.

ii. PAKISTAN

CAPITAL: Islamabad   AREA: 796,000 sq km   POPULATION: 145,000,000
OFFICIAL LANGUAGE: Urdu   POLITICAL SYSTEM: military regime
HEAD OF STATE: President Mohammed Rafiq Tarar (since Dec '97)
HEAD OF GOVERNMENT: Gen. Pervaiz Musharraf, Chief Executive Officer of National Security Council (since Oct '99)
MAIN IGO MEMBERSHIPS (NON-UN): OIC, SAARC, ECO, CP, NAM
CURRENCY: Pakistan rupee (end-'00 £1=PRs86.04, US$1=PRs57.60)
GNP PER CAPITA: US$470, US$1,757 at PPP ('99)

THIS was a year in which, despite some ostensible movement, little real progress was made on any of the major issues confronting Pakistan. On the political front, Chief Executive Gen. Pervez Musharraf, who came to power via a military coup in October 1999 (see AR 1999, pp. 321-2), succeeded in containing the challenge to his position from the ousted politicians.

His immediate predecessor, Nawaz Sharif, was under arrest for most of the year on charges of hijacking and terrorism, which arose from his efforts to resist the coup, as well as facing corruption charges. On the latter he was found guilty in July and sentenced to 14 years' imprisonment, whilst on the former he was convicted in a special anti-terrorism court on April 6 and sentenced to 25 years' imprisonment. On appeal the Sindh High Court upheld the sentence, although it quashed the conviction for terrorism. It was made clear to Musharraf that a death sentence would be wholly unacceptable to the West, and on December 10 Sharif was allowed to go into exile in Saudi Arabia. His principal rival, Benazir Bhutto, was already in self-imposed exile whilst corruption charges continued to be levelled against her. The two leaders' parties, the Pakistan People's Party and the Pakistan Muslim League (PML-headed at this point by Nawaz Sharif's wife, Kulsoom Nawaz), together with some smaller parties, formed a Grand Democratic Alliance in November to conduct a programme of popular agitation, although some members of the PML were reluctant to take part and the government faced no major challenge on the streets. Musharraf's own strategy appeared to be to encourage the parties to regroup under alternative leaders who would be more willing to work with him.

The Chief Executive also took steps to extend his control over the other institutions of state. In January, following a precedent set by Gen. Zia-ul-Huq in 1981, he required the judges of the Supreme Court to swear new oaths of allegiance. The Chief Justice and five other judges refused to do so and as a result were forced to stand down. In May the Supreme Court issued a judgment which conferred legitimacy on Musharraf's regime by invoking the doctrine of necessity, but required a return to civilian rule by 2002. A major reshuffle of the top leadership of the army was carried out at the beginning of September. In particular, Lt Gen. Aziz Khan, who was reported to have played a key role in the October 1999 coup, was moved from his staff position to command an army corps. This was generally interpreted as a rebuff to the more strongly Islamicist elements in the army, although other key figures with equally strong Islamic connections remained in their existing positions. On a number of occasions Gen. Musharraf appeared to be under pressure from Islamicist elements within the army and outside. In July, for example, it was announced that the Islamic provisions in the otherwise suspended constitution would be revived, whilst the Supreme Court ruled that the government had to take steps to eliminate interest (riba) from the economy.

In line with the Supreme Court ruling, and in response to international pressure, Musharraf announced in March, on the eve of President Clinton's visit to Pakistan, that the return to democracy would begin with elections to local councils. The first round of these was held in 18 districts on a non-party basis on December 31. Turnout figures were relatively modest, and in the absence of political parties the contests appeared to have revolved around local rivalries. A feature of the elections was the reservation of one third of the seats for women candidates.

Throughout the year there were bomb blasts in various parts of the country, which killed more than 70 people, although no group claimed responsibility. There were also several cases of sectarian conflict between Sunni and Shia groups. In March a senior member of Nawaz Sharif's legal team was shot dead in his office.

Relations with India remained at a low ebb following the 1999 clashes in the Kargil region of Kashmir and the hijacking of an Indian plane to Afghanistan in December of the same year, but there was some movement in the later part of 2000. In late July the Hizbul Mujahideen, one of the main militant groups in Kashmir with strong Pakistani connections, declared a ceasefire, and an informal round of talks took place with the Indian authorities. However, these broke down over the group's demand that Pakistan be brought into the discussions and the ceasefire was abrogated. The Lashkar-e-Toiba, another leading group of militants, was generally believed to have been responsible for a wave of killings intended to abort the negotiations. In late November, India declared a ceasefire to coincide with the holy month of Ramadan and extended it once the initial period was over. Pakistan responded by announcing a partial pull-back from the line of control, and at the end of the year preparations were underway for a group of Kashmiri politicians from the All Parties Hurriyat Conference to visit Pakistan, following a private visit by one of its leaders, Abdul Ghani Lone. However, much of the activity during the year appeared to be about establishing positions for future negotiation.

In late March President Clinton made a long-awaited visit to South Asia, but unlike previous presidential visits no attempt was made to appear even-handed between India and Pakistan. It was only after some hard bargaining that a visit to Pakistan was negotiated. In the event, Clinton used his brief visit on March 25, which included a televised address to the Pakistani public, to make clear his support for the restoration of democracy and to urge Pakistan to abandon its support for terrorist action in Kashmir and for the Talibaan regime in Afghanistan.

Pakistan's long-term relationship with China cooled somewhat, as changes in the global situation took effect. In December China announced that it would cease to export missile technology, a blow to Pakistan's missile programme. In contrast, the UK announced a partial resumption of arms sales during the year, although many restrictions remained and there was continued political pressure from the European Union as a whole for Pakistan to return to civilian rule.

The economy stagnated during the year. The agricultural sector revived, especially cotton production, but otherwise growth rates were weak. There was a decline in inflows of foreign investment and a rapidly growing trade deficit. Continued pressure on foreign exchange reserves meant that there were regular contacts with the International Monetary Fund (IMF), aimed at restoring the programme of balance of payments support which had stalled in May 1999. The IMF in turn insisted on the implementation of an effective sales tax and an agricultural income tax as ways of broadening the tax base and reducing the fiscal deficit. The budget announced on June 17 duly introduced a general sales tax, but this provoked organised opposition from the retail sector. At the end of November the IMF eventually approved a stand-by loan of US$596 million which was intended to facilitate debt-rescheduling and other international aid.

iii. BANGLADESH

CAPITAL: Dhaka   AREA: 144,000 sq km   POPULATION: 134,000,000
OFFICIAL LANGUAGE: Bengali   POLITICAL SYSTEM: parliamentary democracy
HEAD OF STATE: President Shahabuddin Ahmed (since July '96)
RULING PARTY: Awami League heads coalition
HEAD OF GOVERNMENT: Sheikh Hasina Wajed, Prime Minister (since June '96)
MAIN IGO MEMBERSHIPS (NON-UN): SAARC, CP, OIC, CWTH, NAM
CURRENCY: taka (end-'00 £1=Tk80.81, US$1=Tk54.10)
GNP PER CAPITA: US$370, US$1,475 at PPP ('99)

Two developments, both principally domestic, stood out as leitmotifs of Bangladesh's politics for the year 2000. The first was continuing verbal skirmishes between the judiciary and Prime Minister Sheikh Hasina Wajed. In a radio interview with the BBC in August the Prime Minister said that the granting of bail in some cases was responsible for escalating violence and that she thought that lawyers and judges should be held accountable for this. The Supreme Court's bar association responded by filing another defamation suit against her. The court had reprimanded the Prime Minister in an earlier suit involving similar comments, and asked her to be more careful in her future use of language. But in November she asked publicly why the High Court had found it necessary to sit at midnight to grant bail to a newspaper editor accused of sedition.

The second development, which also peaked in August, concerned the High Court's sentencing of former President Hossain Mohammad Ershad, head of the opposition Jatiya Party, to five years in jail for corruption and requiring him to pay a fine of 55 million taka (almost US$1 million). Soon after the High Court's sentence on Ershad was announced, leaders of the former mainstream opposition alliance met at his residence and issued a statement pledging to contest together the next parliamentary elections, due by July 2001 and, if elected, to form a united-front government. Former Prime Minister, Khaleda Zia of the Bangladesh National Party, which led the alliance, Ershad, Golam Azam of the right-wing Jamaat-e-Islami and Maulana Azizul Huq of the Islami Oikya Jote all signed the statement. Hasina immediately described the agreement as "political hypocrisy" since it was Khaleda's former government, led by the BNP, that had filed charges against Ershad.

In foreign relations the year 2000 was one of modest successes for Hasina's government on the world scene but of setback, or at least continuing stalemate, in regional matters. In October 1999 Bangladesh had been elected to the United Nations Security Council for the second time as a non-permanent member for a two year term, beginning in January 2000. But Hasina's efforts to reactivate the seven-member South Asian Association for Regional Co-operation (SAARC) and to help improve Indo-Pakistan relations were fruitless. Indeed, relations with Pakistan cooled perceptibly in September immediately following some remarks made by Hasina at the UN's Millennium summit on September 7. She called for UN action against military regimes which seized power by overthrowing elected governments. She also said that Pakistan's army should be punished for "war crimes" committed in 1971, in what was then east Pakistan but later became Bangladesh. Pakistan's reaction was swift and unmistakable. Gen. Pervaiz Musharraf, the country's Chief Executive, did not turn up for a meeting with Hasina at the UN the next day which had been arranged at his request.

Annual GDP growth for Bangladesh averaged around five per cent in recent years, thanks largely to agriculture-led growth, whilst the manufacturing sector mostly stagnated. Favourable weather helped to produce good harvests for the two seasons following the country's worst-ever floods in 1998 (see AR 1998, p. 334-5). However, industry remained narrowly based, with ready-made garments and knitwear producing more than 70 per cent of total export earnings. There was no evidence that the government was serious about undertaking structural reform, or tackling the problem of endemic corruption. The taka was devalued by six per cent against the US dollar on August 13, the seventeenth devaluation since June 1996.

iv. NEPAL

CAPITAL: Kathmandu AREA: 147,000 sq km POPULATION: 25,000,000
OFFICIAL LANGUAGE: Nepali POLITICAL SYSTEM: parliamentary democracy
HEAD OF STATE: King Birendra Bir Bikram Shar Deva (since '72)
RULING PARTY: Nepali Congress Party (NCP)
HEAD OF GOVERNMENT: Girija Prasad Koirala (NCP), Prime Minister (since March '00)
MAIN IGO MEMBERSHIPS (NON-UN): SAARC, CP, NAM
CURRENCY: Nepalese rupee (end-'00 £1=NRs111.40, US$1=NRs74.58)
GNP PER CAPITA: US$220, US$1,219 at PPP ('99)

NEPAL'S politics in 2000 were characterised by governmental instability, the opportunist manoeuvering for office of a virtually self-supporting political elite, and persistent ideological and ethnic insurgencies, which fomented uneasy relations with neighbouring countries.

On March 20 King Birendra appointed Girija Prasad Koirala to the post of Prime Minister to form the country's ninth government in 10 years. Koirala, leader of the Nepali Congress Party, had held the job twice previously. Upon taking office he promised that his government would be clean, effective and "people-oriented", and the he would sack corrupt and inept ministers. His government soon proved to be no more effective than its predecessor, however, and whilst failing to tackle corruption and inefficiency, seemed also unable to curb incursions by Maoist rebels intent on overthrowing the monarchy and setting up a communist republic.

The guerrillas, who already controlled at least a dozen districts in the north-western parts of the kingdom, began intruding into the Kathmandu Valley, allegedly with the support of the Indian separatist group, the United Liberation Front of Assam. On August 9, in a major setback to Nepal's vital tourist industry, the rebels took hostage six Spanish tourists who were trekking to Mount Manasulu. They were released five hours later, after their captors had robbed them of 70,000 rupees (approximately US$1,000), but the incident caused the government to worry about its plan to attract 1 million foreign tourists in 2002, especially when, in their most severe attacks in the four year insurgency, the rebels had killed 14 policeman and wounded 40 more. Failure to quell the Maoist insurgency led the Home Minister to resign on September 29.

Meanwhile divisions within the ranks of the main parliamentary opposition, the Nepal Communist Party (United Marxist-Leninist), became patent. Party politburo members Bamdef Gautam and Sahana Pradahan split from the party; then prominent leaders Madhav Kumar Nepal and K.P Oli disputed publicly for the general secretary's post. Eventually Bharat Mohan Adhikari was appointed to the post as a temporary compromise.

Nepal's wary relations with its southern neighbour India remained uneasy, particularly over the question of the repatriation of more than 100,000 Bhutanese refugees of Nepalese ethnicity. The refugees first entered Baghdora in West Bengal, from where local police tracked them to Nepal's lowland south-eastern region of Jhapa. Nepal's Foreign Minister, Chakra Prasad Banstola, paid a three-day official visit to India and also visited the Bhutanese capital, Thimphu, for three days in May in vain efforts to organise the repatriation of the Bhutanese refugees. He said that the Bhutanese government had not been helpful over the issue.

A general strike was called at the end of the year, the latest in a succession of political and social crises, including riots and bomb attacks, to disrupt the mountain kingdom. The capital, Kathmandu, was shaken by three bombs on New Year's eve, all directed at the homes of leading political figures. The residence of Sushil Koirala, the National Congress's general secretary, was damaged by a pipe bomb thrown from a motorcycle in a suspected Maoist attack. Other bombs exploded at the homes of the Education Minister and the former Home Minister, but no one was injured in either attack.

In the last week of December there were three days of riots in Kathmandu and other cities over remarks allegedly made by the Indian film star Hrithik Rosham. It was rumoured that he had expressed his dislike of Nepal in a television interview, but a video showed that Nepal was not mentioned. Nonetheless, the rumour took hold on the streets and clashes with Nepal's riot police left four people dead. The riots were followed by a call for the resignation of Prime Minister Koirala, for failing to deliver on promises to end the Maoist rebellion. A resolution for his removal was signed by 56 Congress party deputies and a decision was expected early in the New Year.

Experiencing slow and patchy economic growth in 2000, as had been the pattern over recent years, Nepal's population nevertheless grew once again by about 2.4 per cent, the highest rate in South Asia. Heavy monsoon rains brought havoc to life and property in 72 of Nepal's 75 districts. More than 200 people died and about US$8 million in damage was caused to crops and infrastructure. An epidemic of encephalitis in rural areas killed 350 men, women and children. Timely intervention with Chinese vaccines helped to prevent the spread of the disease.

On November 15 representatives of most of the world's major faiths gathered in Kathmandu to pledge action to tackle forest and marine destruction, climate change and other environmental problems. The faiths celebrating "sacred gifts for a living planet" included Baha'is, Buddhists, Christians, Hindus, Jains, Jews, Muslims, Sikhs, Shinto's, Taoists and Zoroastrians. The meeting was organised by the Worldwide Fund for Nature to coincide with its annual conference.

On October 7 Davo Kalmicar, from Slovenia, became the first man to ski down Mount Everest.

v. BHUTAN

CAPITAL: Thimphu   AREA: 46,500 sq km   POPULATION: 760,000
OFFICIAL LANGUAGES: Dzongkha, Lhotsan & English   POLITICAL SYSTEM: monarchy
HEAD OF STATE: Dragon King Jigme Singye Wangchuk (sice '72)
MAIN IGO MEMBERSHIPS (NON-UN): SAARC, CP, NAM
CURRENCY: ngultrum (end '00 £1=Nu69.73, US$1=Nu46.68)
GNP PER CAPITA: US$400 ('97)

THE fourth, and present King, Jigme Singye Wangchuk, cotinued the modernisation policies begun by his father, Jigme Dorji Wangchuk (1952-72), which had seen Bhutan change from a centuries old theocracy resting on a dual authority of secular rulers and a lineage of reincarnating lamas, to a hereditary monarchy (since 1907), and thence to a country which had begun since the 1950s to modernise its economy and political system and reduce its isolation from the rest of the world. However, although Bhutan became more active internationally and received help from the United Nations (UN) and aid from Japan and a number of Western countries, India remained by far its most important single relationship, overseeing its foreign and defence policies.

Bhutan suffered one of its worst ever natural disasters in August when heavy rains washed away houses, roads and bridges on the southern foothills of the Himalayas. Massive landslides blocked the main highway from Phuntsholding on the Indian border in the south to the highlands and the capital, Thimphu. Hundreds, perhaps thousands, were made homeless by unprecedented flash floods. The official death toll was given as 49, although that was regarded by many as a gross understatement. Furthermore, the slowness with which the government reacted to the crisis, combined with suspicions that the official media did not frankly report the full extent of the disaster, severely compromised the credibility of the government and aroused concern amongst Bhutan's international donors.

The roads were eventually re-opened with Indian assistance, which once more emphasised the importance of links with its giant neighbour. Relations with the Indian government were marred, however, as in previous years, by the presence in southern Bhutan of various separatist insurgent groups from India's volatile north-eastern region. The Bhutanese authorities identified about 21 rebel bases, and in July deployed some 4,000 soldiers along the border with India's Assam state to prevent insurgents crossing into Bhutan. It was questionable, however, whether the Royal Bhutanese Army—only 6,000 strong—would be able to evict the rebels without support from India.

Bhutan's relations with the only other independent kingdom in the Himalayas, Nepal, remained strained and verged on hostility throughout the year. India stayed studiously neutral over the central issue of inter-ethnic violence between the two countries, violence which had caused the exodus from Bhutan of tens of thousands of ethnic Nepalese to camps in Nepal. Polemics and mutual accusation continued on this issue throughout the year.

Bhutan's literacy rate, 54 per cent, remained low but was improving. The government, with the approval of its international donors, had allocated substantial funds for education and health in recent years. In late March the country's first internet café was opened in the capital, Thimphu. It offered internet access, e-mail, printing and scanning facilities to the tiny Buddhist nation, which had launched its first television station less than a year earlier (see AR 1999, p 330).

vi. SRI LANKA

CAPITAL: Colombo AREA: 66,000 sq km POPULATION: 19,200,000
OFFICIAL LANGUAGES: Sinhala, Tamil, English POLITICAL SYSTEM: presidential democracy
HEAD OF STATE AND GOVERNMENT: President Chandrika Bandaranaike Kumaratunga (since Nov '94)
RULING PARTIES: Sri Lanka Freedom Party (SLFP) heads People's Alliance coalition
PRIME MINISTER: Ratnasiri Wickremanayake (since Aug '00)
MAIN IGO MEMBERSHIPS (NON-UN): SAARC, CP, CWTH, NAM
CURRENCY: Sri Lankan rupee (end-'00 £1=SRs123.54, US$1=SRs82.70)
GNP PER CAPITA: US$820, US$3,056 at PPP ('99)

THE year moved to a close offering some hope for ending Sri Lanka's ethnic problem, which had pitted the Liberation Tigers of Tamil Eelam (LTTE) against the government for nearly two decades in a violent bid by the former to carve out a separate state for minority Tamils. A Norwegian diplomat, Eric Solheim, acting as a facilitator with the consent of both parties, announced after meeting LTTE leader Velupillai Prabhakaran on November 1, that the Tigers were prepared for unconditional talks with the government. An LTTE statement from London immediately afterwards, however, cast doubt on the offer's unconditionality.

During the last government-LTTE talks, which took place in 1994 soon after Chandrika Bandaranaike Kumaratunga became President (see AR 1994, pp. 343-5), several months were spent on peripheral matters—ranging from the supply of food and medicines to the location of army camps—without any discussion of the basic issues of autonomy for predominantly Tamil areas. When the LTTE broke off the talks and resumed armed activity the government accused it of having cynically used the talks to restock its armoury and rebuild its cadre. It therefore responded to the latest LTTE offer warily, suggesting that it would want a time-bound schedule for completing political negotiations. The Tigers' declaration of a month's ceasefire from Christmas Eve brought no reciprocal action from Colombo, which called it a propaganda gambit, not even hinted at in LTTE discussions with Solheim. Significantly, however, the government did not reject the offer. The international community, or at least its Western members, who directly and through international financial institutions provided development funds to Sri Lanka, appeared to press both sides to seek a political settlement. In the West, organisations raising money for the separatist group faced increasing curbs and the LTTE itself faced the prospect of proscription in more countries besides the USA. Western spokesmen, whilst urging negotiations, declared themselves against Eelam, the separate Tamil state demanded by Prabhakaran.

Amongst the Sinhalese—who constituted 74 per cent of the population compared with the Tamils' 12.6 per cent—extreme nationalist groups mounted protests against the President's readiness to devolve power to the regions as a way of meeting Tamil aspirations. However, a new party, Sihala Urumaya (Sinhalese heritage), which was a combination of several groups that wanted a military solution to what they saw as a purely terrorist problem, secured just one seat in legislative elections on October 10. This suggested that the Sinhalese electorate was not averse to a political settlement. Chandrika Bandaranaike Kumaratunga, re-elected as President in December 1999, was able to ensure that her People's Alliance (PA) continued in power. It secured 107 seats compared with 89 for the United National Party (UNP), led by Ranil Wickremasinghe. The tally fell short of an overall majority but the PA was bolstered by the support of an anti-LTTE Tamil party and a Moslem party. The Janatha Vimukthi Peramuna (JVP), which had twice attempted to seize power through extremely violent insurrections (in 1971 and 1988-89), emerged with 10 seats as the third party in parliament—but hardly the "Third Force" which some had predicted.

Earlier in the year, PA-UNP discussions had held out the hope of a consensus on constitutional changes that would both devolve power to the regions and abolish the executive presidency. A bipartisan approach towards devolution was widely seen as likely to help negotiations with the Tigers, but after a promising start the talks failed. Kumaratunga's wish to serve out her second term as President whilst scrapping the presidency for the future was a major sticking point. The government brought to parliament its proposals for constitutional reforms but, with no prospect of achieving the required two-thirds majority, withdrew the bill.

Fighting between LTTE and government forces in the north ebbed and flowed during the year. A Tiger offensive in March and April forced the army to vacate several camps, including the important Elephant Pass base, leading to fears for Jaffna, the north's main city, and the 40,000 troops which could be trapped there. Helped by new weapons purchases, however, the army regained the initiative and recaptured some of the lost territory. There were further reports of the LTTE deploying young children on the frontline, contrary to undertakings given to the United Nations. Besides attacks on security forces in the east, the Tigers continued to target government members. In March a firefight in Colombo, involving LTTE cadres waiting to ambush a ministerial convoy resulted in 29 deaths (six police, eight Tigers and 15 civilians). There was also a suicide-bomb attack in a Colombo suburb in June that killed the Minister for Industrial Development, his wife and more than 20 others.

The government tightened censorship of the press after its military setbacks, although the Supreme Court quashed a ban placed on the independent *Sunday Leader* for alleged infringements of the code. The government also came under pressure from human rights groups after 24 suspected Tigers in a detention centre were killed in October.

Sirimavo Bandaranaike, the grand old lady of Sri Lankan politics, died on her way home after voting in the October 10 election. The world's first woman Prime Minister, she was thrice Prime Minister of Sri Lanka (see XVIII). Lawyer Kumar Ponnambalam, leader of the small Tamil Congress party, human rights activist and champion of the LTTE, was killed by a gunman on January 5; and Mohammed Ashraff, a government minister and a leader of the Muslim community, died in a helicopter crash on September 16.

The war claimed 5-6 per cent of Sri Lanka's GDP during the year. The rupee depreciated sharply, by 16 per cent against the US dollar; and inflation rose into double figures. Exports grew 17 per cent in the period to November, with buoyant tea and garment sales, but imports rose even faster, thereby widening the trade gap. Foreign reserves declined, and heavy government borrowing pushed up interest rates. Higher world oil prices caused rises in cooking gas prices, bus fares, freight and other costs, leading to consumer unrest and political protests.

3. INDIAN OCEAN STATES:

i. MAURITIUS

CAPITAL: Port Louis   AREA: 2,040 sq km   POPULATION: 1,200,000
OFFICIAL LANGUAGE: English   POLITICAL SYSTEM: parliamentary democracy
HEAD OF STATE: President Cassam Uteem (since June '92)
RULING PARTY: Mauritian Socialist Movement (MSM) & Mauritian Militant Movement (MMM)
HEAD OF GOVERNMENT: Sir Aneerood Jugnauth, Prime Minister (since Sept '00)
MAIN IGO MEMBERSHIPS (NON-UN): OAU, COMESA, SADC, OIC, ACP, CWTH, Francophonie, NAM
CURRENCY: Mauritian rupee (end-'00 £1=MRs41.56, US$1=MRs27.82)
GNP PER CAPITA: US$3,700, US$9,400 at PPP ('98)

THE dominant political event of the year was the general election of September 11, in which the opposition alliance between the Mauritian Socialist Movement (MSM) and the Mauritian Militant Movement (MMM) won a surprisingly comfortable victory. The alliance captured 54 seats out of 62 on both Mauritius and Rodrigues. The alliance of the Labour Party, of the outgoing Prime Minister Navin Ramgoolam, and the Xavier Duval Mauritian Party (PMXD) won only six seats. The MSM-MMM alliance took 51 per cent of the votes cast against 36 per cent for the Labour coalition. Eight parliamentary seats were allocated by the Election Supervisory committee to candidates who failed to secure election, on the basis of the "best losers". This gave the ruling coalition three extra seats, the main opposition party one more, whilst two seats went to the Mouvement Rodriguais, which contested the elections on Rodrigues. The two remaining seats went to arbitration. Thus, on September 26, at the request of President Cassam Uteem, Anerood Jugnauth, leader of the MSM-MMM coalition, was appointed as Prime Minister, an office which he had previously held in 1995. He appointed Paul Bérenger, the leader of the MMM as Deputy Prime Minister and Minister of Finance.

The background to Ramgoolam's defeat was a series of corruption scandals uncovered by a new body, the Economic Crimes Office (ECO), which implicated two popular ministers, Health Minister Kishore Deerpalsingh and Social Security Minister Vishnu Bundum, both of whom were forced to resign in August. Deerpalsingh claimed to possess evidence involving a "very senior politician" in a property deal, but the assembly was dissolved before he came to trial.

At the end of the year, an old story was revived with the judgment at the High Court in London, UK, on November 3 that the eviction of some 2,000 inhabitants of the Chagos islands, now an uninhabited dependency called the British Indian Ocean Territory (BIOT), was unlawful. Diego Garcia, one of the Chagos archipelago, was leased as a base to the USA. The islanders were sent to Mauritius, which claimed to have sovereignty over the Chagos archipelago, and intended to secure compensation from the US and UK governments for the "discrimination and human rights violations" suffered by the islanders, who were planning to return to their deserted homeland. Thus, following the ruling, further litigation looked inevitable.

The new Jugnauth government immediately entered into a conflict with the Federation of Civil Service Unions of Mauritius over the revocation of a 300 rupee monthly salary increase awarded by the previous government. The union sought an injunction to declare the revocation null and void, and a series of legal actions followed, with Finance Minister Bérenger sticking to his guns. Although the Mauritian economy was generally reported to be healthy, the remarkable growth rate of 25 per cent recorded in 1999 was down to 8.5 per cent in 2000. This was in part because of the poor sugar harvest in 1999-2000 due to drought. However, the government's success in diversification meant that poor sugar harvests were no longer so disastrous for the economy, not least because of the developing role of Mauritius as a financial and business centre.

ii. SEYCHELLES, COMOROS AND MALDIVES

Seychelles
CAPITAL: Victoria   AREA: 454 sq km   POPULATION: 79,000
OFFICIAL LANGUAGES: Seychellois, English & French   POLITICAL SYSTEM: presidential
HEAD OF STATE AND GOVERNMENT: President France-Albert René (since June '77)
RULING PARTIES: Seychelles People's Progressive Front (SPPF)
MAIN IGO MEMBERSHIPS (NON-UN): OAU, COMESA, OIC, ACP, CWTH, Francophonie, NAM
CURRENCY: Seychelles rupee (end-'00 £1=SRs9.35, US$1=SRs6.26)
GNP PER CAPITA: US$6,450, US$10,530 at PPP ('98)

Comoros
CAPITAL: Moroni   AREA: 1,860 sq km   POPULATION: 590,000
OFFICIAL LANGUAGES: Arabic & French   POLITICAL SYSTEM: military regime
HEAD OF STATE AND GOVERNMENT: Col. Azili Assoumani (since April '99)
PRIME MINISTER: Ahmed Amadi (since Nov '00)
MAIN IGO MEMBERSHIPS (NON-UN): OAU, COMESA, ACP, CWTH, AL, OIC, Francophonie, NAM
CURRENCY: Comoros franc (end-'00 £1=CFr788.73, US$1=CFr528.00)
GNP PER CAPITA: US$370, US$1,480 at PPP ('98)

Maldives
CAPITAL: Malé   AREA: 300 sq km   POPULATION: 282,000
OFFICIAL LANGUAGE: Divehi   POLITICAL SYSTEM: presidential
HEAD OF STATE AND GOVERNMENT: President Maumoon Abdul Gayoom (since Nov '78)
MAIN IGO MEMBERSHIPS (NON-UN): SAARC, CP, OIC, CWTH, NAM, SADC
CURRENCY: rufiya (end-'00 £1=R17.58, US$1=R11.77)
GNP PER CAPITA: US$1,230 ('98)

IN the SEYCHELLES there was increasing speculation during the year over the future of President France-Albert René, who had ruled since seizing power in a coup in June 1977. Although his regime had been legitimised through the introduction of multi-party politics in the early 1990s, the control of the country by his party, the Seychelles People's Progressive Front (SPPF), had remained fairly comprehensive. After his victory in the 1998 elections with a sweeping majority both in the presidential and legislative vote, political activity became fairly quiescent, but at the beginning of 2000 observers detected a certain loss of authority, almost for the first time. This was attributed in part to René's failing health, which caused him to withdraw from many public activities, and there was clear evidence that his party bosses were trying to prepare for the post-René era.

In this context an important constitutional amendment was approved by the National Assembly in May. It permitted the president to call elections when appropriate at any time from a year after the previous election, rather than observe the former fixed five-year term. Many saw it as a mechanism through which a presidential successor could be promoted from within the SPPF. René was said to favour as successor his Vice President, James Michel, who was given pride of place at the party congress in June, and was generally more visible than Rene himself. But Michel was said to have a number of important opponents within the party.

Meanwhile, the opposition Seychelles National Party (SNP), despite holding only three seats in the National Assembly, was seen as performing well under its new leader Waved Rankalawan.

The economy remained fragile, especially as the currency, the Seychelles rupee, continued to depreciate against the US dollar, and concerns continued over the existence of a parallel financial market. In spite of improved foreign exchange earnings from fishing and tourism, there was still a foreign exchange shortage, and international institutions continued to press both for further financial reform and for the privatisation of parastatals.

The military regime in COMOROS of Gen. Azali Assoumani, who had seized power in April 1999 (see AR 1999, pp. 336-7), continued to fumble its way through a series of crises whilst doing nothing to improve its international relations. It was most notably unable throughout the year to handle the unresolved question of the three-year-old secession of the island of Anjouan. In the wake of a reported abortive coup in March, a mid-April deadline for a return to civilian rule for the first anniversary of the coup was not met, in spite of an urgent reminder from the Organisation of African Unity (OAU) that Comoros should instantly conform to the decision of the 1999 Algiers summit, which required that it should return to civilian rule before the next summit—as had been promised by the junta soon after the coup took place. Likewise, Anjouan repeatedly failed to sign the 1999 Antananarivo Agreement providing for an end to the secession, with greater autonomy for all three islands, Grand Comore, Anjouan, and Moheli. Accordingly, a Comoro delegation was refused admission to the OAU Summit in Lomé, Togo, in July.

A referendum in June on the fourth island in the group, Mayotte, which was still administered by France at the request of its inhabitants, produced a 72.9 per cent vote in favour of a new status of "departmental community", replacing its current status as a simple department, reportedly to open up new possibilities of development. This move was condemned by the Comoro government, which said that "Mayotte can only belong to the Comoro islands".

On August 26 in Famboni, on the island of Moheli, the military government signed an agreement with the separatists, creating a new Comorian entity of unclear constitutional status. This was opposed by the OAU, which felt that it compromised the unity of the islands, and that it was at variance with the Antananarivo agreement. The accord said that the new "entity" would have a common religion (Islam) and nationality, a common currency, and a shared foreign and defence policy. The emphasis would be on "the development of island entities". Comoran and international experts would find a name for the new entity, and its constitution would be submitted for popular approval within 12 months. This was followed by a lifting of travel, communications and economic sanctions against Anjouan, which had been applied by the OAU over the secession, and had reportedly had a crippling effect on the economic life of the island, causing fuel and electricity shortages.

A new constitutional charter giving more power to Col. Assoumani had previously been adopted on August 6, amid rumours of a fresh attempt to destabilise his government. It stipulated that the head of state was "chosen by the army" and invested by the legislative council, and that "the present head of state continues in office". He was given the power to choose the Prime Minister and other ministers. In December a new government was established with Ahamadi "Bolero" Madi, 35, as Prime Minister, and composed only of supporters of the military junta, in spite of two weeks of negotiations between the Assoumani regime and a number of small opposition parties. This was a setback to the moderate wing of the regime.

On Anjouan in November, Lt. Col. Said Abeid Abderemane, the leader of the secessionist island, which continued to style itself independent, appointed a new legislature and government to replace those which he had dismissed.

In a quiet year President Maumoon Abdul Gayoom of the MALDIVES was able to concentrate on international relations, especially his continued appeals to consider the problems the Maldives faced with global warming. Gayoom took this plea to the United Nations (UN) Millennium Summit in New York in September.

Earlier in the year, in March, an important political exercise took place in the shape of the national census. Provisional results indicated an increase in population of 34,000 people since the census of 1995, with a current population of 270,000. This would mean a growth rate of 1.9 per cent, compared with 2.7 per cent five years earlier, and 3.4 per cent 10 years before. Final results were not expected until 2001.

There were concerns towards the end of the year over a financial downturn, leading to a foreign exchange shortage. This was due to declining international fish prices, and the rising cost of petroleum products during the year.

iii. MADAGASCAR

CAPITAL: Antananarivo   AREA: 587,000 sq km   POPULATION: 15,000,000
OFFICIAL LANGUAGES: Malagasy & French   POLITICAL SYSTEM: presidential
HEAD OF STATE AND GOVERNMENT: President (Adm.) Didier Ratsiraka (since Jan '97)
RULING PARTIES: Vanguard for Economic and Social Recovery (ARES) heads coalition
PRIME MINISTER: Tantely Andrianarivo (since July '98)
MAIN IGO MEMBERSHIPS (NON-UN): OAU, COMESA, OIC, ACP, Francophonie, NAM
CURRENCY: Malagasy franc (end-'00 £1=MFr9,291.43, US$1=MFr6,220.00)
GNP PER CAPITA: US$250, US$766 at PPP ('99)

MADAGASCAR'S multi-party democracy continued to function after its own fashion under the rule of President Didier Ratsiraka, who had formerly been its military ruler and had then presided over a single-party state. The "great red island" was seriously disrupted, however, by three heavy cyclones in February and March—Eline, Gloria and Hudah—all of which caused considerable damage. As they affected the northern part of the island, which produced most export products such as vanilla, coffee and pepper, there were fears of economic catastrophe, but the harvest figures for all three commodities stood up remarkably well, and Madagascar was able to retain its position as the world's leading vanilla producer, albeit with 850 tonnes instead of the estimated 1,200 tonnes.

There was criticism both domestically and internationally over the size of the country's security forces, estimated to exceed 28,000, and concern at the slow rate of privatisation of the large number of uneconomic state enterprises. Although the World Bank and IMF indicated that they were encouraged by growth rates since 1997 (which had averaged 4 per cent a year), and the improvement of fiscal discipline, there remained strong resistance to foreign investment in key sectors of the economy.

There was welcome news at the end of the year when Madagascar was included in the list of 22 poor countries included in the enhanced Heavily Indebted Poor Countries (HIPC) Initiative sponsored by the World Bank and the IMF. The move meant that debt servicing savings on the country's debt should average some US$62 million a year.

IX SOUTH-EAST AND EAST ASIA

1. MYANMAR (BURMA)—THAILAND—MALAYSIA—BRUNEI—SINGAPORE—
INDONESIA—PHILIPPINES—VIETNAM—CAMBODIA—LAOS

i. MYANMAR (BURMA)

CAPITAL: Yangon (Rangoon)   AREA: 677,000 sq km   POPULATION: 50,000,000
OFFICIAL LANGUAGE: Burmese   POLITICAL SYSTEM: military regime
HEAD OF STATE AND GOVERNMENT: Gen. Than Shwe, Chairman of State Peace and
   Development Council and Prime Minister (since April '92)
MAIN IGO MEMBERSHIPS (NON-UN): ASEAN, CP, NAM
CURRENCY: kyat (end-'00 £1=K9.75, US$1=K6.53)
GNP PER CAPITA: n/a

SECRET talks commenced in October between the ruling junta, the State Peace and Development Council (SPDC), and Daw Aung San Suu Kyi, the general secretary of the opposition National League for Democracy (NLD). This followed five years of unsuccessful efforts by UN Assistant Secretary-General Alvaro de Soto to improve the human rights situation and encourage dialogue between the government and the pro-democracy opposition which had won national elections in 1990 that were never recognised. De Soto was replaced during the year by former Malaysian diplomat Razali Ismail. Razali visited the country three times without fanfare, and approached his task in a more low key manner which seemed to be acceptable to all sides. Rajsmooer Lallah, the UN special rapporteur on human rights in Myanmar, resigned in frustration in November over the lack of support he had received from the international body's bureaucracy.

Aung San Su Kyi twice attempted to leave Yangon (the capital) in September to visit NLD workers in other parts of the country, but was blocked by the authorities on both occasions, leading to her isolation in the capital and the continued atrophy of her party. Senior NLD figures remained under house arrest in the capital following a year of great pressure on the party by the military, which sought to increase its own political support through the 10-million-strong Union Solidarity Development Association (USDA).

The recently created international concern about forced labour in Myanmar led the International Labour Organisation (ILO) to resolve in November that member states should review their policies toward the country. This followed an official ILO mission in May and a last minute and grudging reply to its recommendations by the government. The result had been a stand-off, with the government refusing to have any further dealings with the ILO, and the situation raised the spectre of international action against Myanmar's trade and financial links with countries with politically powerful trade union movements.

Thanks to the intervention of the UK oil company, Premier Oil, James Mawdsley, a British pro-democracy advocate who was arrested a third time for illegal entry into Myanmar, was released in October. Mawdsley's case had generated significant protests from Western governments. In an effort to improve the human rights situation in Myanmar, the Australian government began work with the newly-created Human Rights Commission to train government officials in international human rights law. Premier Oil also secured the right for an independent international NGO to monitor labour conditions in its area of operation, whilst the US oil giant UNOCAL won a case in the California courts accusing it of complicity in the use of forced labour.

The government's disputed efforts to reduce and eventually eliminate opium production in the northern part of the country continued during the year with the beginning of the relocation of 50,000 people in the Wa areas of Shan state to new agricultural land further south. By the end of the year, whilst many people had been relocated, a modest increase in guerrilla activity in the area suggested that some of the Wa leadership who had earlier entered into ceasefire arrangements with the government were unhappy with the programme, and that resistance was developing from other groups. Meanwhile, the Shan State Army-South, led by Col Yawdserk, continued its campaign against the government, accusing other Shan leaders of betraying the Shan people. Expatriate opposition groups accused the government of relocating the population in order to create ethnic tensions between the Wa and local Shan.

The Karen National Union (KNU), which remained the only established insurgent group not to have entered into a ceasefire with the government since 1988, changed leadership at the end of January as the organisation faced increasing military and political pressure from both Thailand and Myanmar. Bo Mya, the septuagenarian leader of the organisation for the past 25 years, was ousted. His joint posts as military and political head of the rebel group were split between Ba Thin, who became chairman, and Gen. Tambalaw, who assumed the role of chief of staff of the Karen National Liberation Army (KNLA). Whilst indicating their willingness to negotiate (without preconditions) with the government over a political settlement, the new leadership refused to surrender.

Whilst substantial international aid to the Myanmar economy had been stopped since 1988, Japan continued to develop its ties with the country and in May provided a substantial aid package in support of rural electrification, the development of small- and medium-sized businesses, and IT training. The economy of Myanmar continued to stagnate during the year, however, although thanks to a large rice crop and declining international prices, inflation was reduced to more manageable levels.

ii. THAILAND

CAPITAL: Bangkok   AREA: 513,000 sq km   POPULATION: 63,400,000
OFFICIAL LANGUAGE: Thai   POLITICAL SYSTEM: constitutional monarchy
HEAD OF STATE: King Bhumibol Adulydadej (Rama IX), since June '46
RULING PARTY: Democrat Party (DP) heads six-party coalition
HEAD OF GOVERNMENT: Chuan Leekpai, Prime Minister (since Nov '97)
MAIN IGO MEMBERSHIPS (NON-UN): ASEAN, CP, APEC, NAM
CURRENCY: baht (end-'00 £1=Bt64.80, US$1=Bt43.38)
GNP PER CAPITA: US$1,960, US$5,599 at PPP ('99)

WITH a general election looming in early 2001, a major step in the programme of democratisation set out in the 1997 constitution was taken in March when elections were held for the (previously appointed) 200-member Senate (the upper chamber of the bicameral legislature). The new body had a middle class, reformist cast to it. Seventy-eight winners were, however, immediately disqualified for electoral fraud by the Election Commission, although all but two of these were allowed to stand in subsequent by-elections. One of those who was banned from standing again was the wife of Deputy Prime Minister and Interior Minister, Maj.-Gen. Sanan Kajomprasart, who himself was forced to resign from the Cabinet and was convicted of corruption by the National Counter-Corruption Commission. As secretary general of the Democratic Party (a key element within the coalition government of Prime Minister Chuan Leekpai), Sanan's conviction, which was upheld by the Constitutional Court in August, undermined the stability of the embattled regime.

Forty-eight previously barred candidates in the Senate vote were subsequently elected in April but even after repeated re-runs four seats remained vacant in June, nearly causing the cancellation of the coterminous session of the House of Representatives (the lower chamber). In the latter part of the year, corruption allegations against the leader of the Thai Rak Thai Party, telecoms tycoon Thaksin Shinawatra, cast doubts over his ability to serve as Prime Minister, despite the popularity of his party in the polls. In the event, Thai Rak Thai won a clear majority in elections in January, 2001, a unique event in modern Thai politics. Former Deputy Prime Minister Samak Sundaravej, leader of the Pracharkorn Thai Party, won an overwhelming victory in the election for Bangkok governor in July.

Strains in relations between Thailand and Myanmar dominated foreign relations in 2000. In January, a group of Karen rebels seized a hospital at Ratchaburi and held the 700 patients hostage for a day before police stormed the building, killing 10 rebels. A flood of refugees and economic migrants into Thailand posed other problems during the year. In November a group of eight Burmese and two Thai prisoners held a number of prison officers hostage in a bold attempt at a break-out from a jail in Samut Sakhon province; all 10 prisoners were killed on the orders of the Cabinet. Relations improved at the end of the year following the visit of a high ranking Thai military delegation to Myanmar.

Three years after the financial crisis which had rocked the Thai and neighbouring economies in 1997 (see AR 1997, pp. 327-9), the government heralded the easing of restrictions on overseas investment by Thais by permitting Merrill Lynch Phatra Securities of Thailand to purchase US$50 million of Thai government bonds issued overseas. The case of the bankrupt Thai Petrochemical Industry (TPI) proceeded through the courts during the year. TPI, the country's largest debtor following the 1997 meltdown, was declared insolvent in March and was effectively restructured by the end of the year under a court-supervised scheme. This was the first major test of the effectiveness of the newly formed central bankruptcy court. Widespread flooding disrupted life and the economy in large parts of the south of the country in November.

iii. MALAYSIA

CAPITAL: Kuala Lumpur   AREA: 330,000 sq km   POPULATION: 23,100,000
OFFICIAL LANGUAGE: Bahasa Malaysia   POLITICAL SYSTEM: federal democracy
HEAD OF STATE: Salahuddin Abdul Aziz Shah, Sultan of Selangor (since April '99)
RULING PARTY: National Front coalition
HEAD OF GOVERNMENT: Dr Mahathir Mohamad, Prime Minister (since July '81)
MAIN IGO MEMBERSHIPS (NON-UN): ASEAN, APEC, CP, OIC, CWTH, NAM
CURRENCY: ringitt Malaysia (end-'00 £1=RM5.68, US$1=3.80)
GNP PER CAPITA: US$3,400, US$7,963 at PPP ('99)

IN May Prime Minister Mahathir Mohamad was re-elected unopposed for a further three years as president of the United Malays National Organisation (UMNO), the dominant party within the ruling Barisan Nasional (BN, National Front) coalition. Deputy Prime Minister Abdullah Ahmad Badawi was elected unopposed as UMNO deputy president. In the contest for the three offices of vice president, the successful candidates were Najib Razak, the Defence Minister, Muhammad Taib, the former Chief Minister of Selangor, and Muhyiddin Yassin, the Minister for Domestic Trade. Coincidentally or not, the latter three had been elected as vice presidents in 1993 as members of a so-called vision team which had been nominated by former deputy president of UMNO and former Deputy Prime Minister Anwar Ibrahim.

A special UMNO general assembly was convened in November at which Mahathir sought to amend the party's constitution in order to extend the interval between elections for senior offices from three to five years. In the event, the amendment was withdrawn in response to strong opposition from amongst the delegates. The election earlier in the month of Mohamed Dzaiddin Abdullah as chief justice by the nine Malay sultans was also interpreted as a political set-back for the Prime Minister.

Anwar Ibrahim's trial on a charge of sodomy resumed in January. Although the defence claimed that the charge had been fabricated as part of a political conspiracy, in April the judge rejected a request that Mahathir be required to testify. That month another court rejected Anwar's appeal against his conviction in April 1999 on charges of corruption (see AR 1999, pp. 342-43). Anwar was eventually found guilty of sodomy in August and was sentenced to nine years' imprisonment to run consecutively with the six years which he had received for corruption.

In June the ruling National Front (BN) coalition won a federal parliamentary by-election in Negri Sembilan with a substantially reduced majority after a spirited performance by the opposition Parti Keadilan Nasional (National Justice Party), led by Anwar's wife, Wan Azizah Wan Ismail. In November, however, in a corresponding contest, the Keadilan candidate won a state assembly by-election in Kedah in a constituency that had been held by the BN's precursor since independence. The BN's electoral reverse was not only attributed to Malay alienation at the alleged cruel treatment of Anwar but also to grievances on the part of the Chinese community.

On the eve of the November 1999 general election (see AR 1999, pp. 342-43), 11 leading Chinese organisations had put forward a set of civil rights demands defined with reference to the controversial "bumiputra policy" privileges enjoyed by the indigenous Malay community. These demands were rejected out of hand by Mahathir who went so far as to compare the 11 Chinese organisations to communists in his annual National Day speech delivered in August. The Prime Minister was unrelenting in his condemnation even after the Kedah by-election result, repeating his charge in the federal legislature in late December. At the same time, agitation against the Chinese demands was mounted by the Federation of Peninsula Malay Students. As a consequence, Deputy Prime Minister Abdullah was moved to call publicly for "an end to this reckless escalation of ethnic tension".

In July, members of Al-Ma'unah (Brotherhood of Inner Power), a previously unknown Islamic sect, entered two military arms depots in the state of Perak and seized a large quantity of heavy weapons through some of their number posing as officers. The episode came to a bloody end when anti-terrorist commandos overran the sect's jungle camp, but not before two hostages had been murdered. Twenty-seven adherents were arrested and charged with treason; their trial opened in September.

In April a group of 15 masked gunmen from the Philippine Islamic separatist Abu Sayyaf (Father of the Sword) movement landed on the Sabah resort island of Sipidan and kidnapped 21 people, including 10 foreign tourists, who were taken by speedboat to Jolo in the Philippines (see XI.1.vii.). Reports in mid-June that the Malaysian government was conducting secret negotiations over a ransom with the kidnappers caused tension between the Philippines and Malaysian governments. All of the Malaysian hostages were released by August. In September, however, an additional three Malaysians were kidnapped from Pandanan island, off the coast of Sabah. They were rescued in October after a Philippine military offensive against the Abu Sayyaf.

iv. BRUNEI

CAPITAL: Bandar Seri Bagawan   AREA: 5,765 sq km   POPULATION: 346,000
OFFICIAL LANGUAGES: Malay & English   POLITICAL SYSTEM: monarchy
HEAD OF STATE: Sultan Sir Hassanal Bolkiah (since '67)
MAIN IGO MEMBERSHIPS (NON-UN): ASEAN, APEC, OIC, CWTH, NAM
CURRENCY: Brunei dollar (end-'00 £1=Br$2.59, US$1=Br$1.73)
GNP PER CAPITA: US$25,090 ('98)

IN an out of court settlement in May, Prince Jefri Bolkiah, the younger brother of the Sultan, agreed to transfer to the state all assets which he had acquired whilst serving as Finance Minister and head of the Brunei Investment Agency. Legal proceedings against Jefri by the government had begun in February, and in March he had been sued for US$15 million.

v. SINGAPORE

CAPITAL: Singapore   AREA: 1,000 sq km   POPULATION: 3,700,000
OFFICIAL LANGUAGES: Malay, Chinese, Tamil & English   POLITICAL SYSTEM: parliamentary
HEAD OF STATE: President S.R. Nathan (since Sept '99)
RULING PARTY: People's Action Party (PAP)
HEAD OF GOVERNMENT: Goh Chok Tong, Prime Minister (since Nov '90)
MAIN IGO MEMBERSHIPS (NON-UN): ASEAN, APEC, CP, CWTH, NAM
CURRENCY: Singapore dollar (end-'00 £1=S$2.59, US$1=S$1.73)
GNP PER CAPITA: US$29,610, US$27,024 at PPP ('99)

IN April Prime Minister Goh Chok Tong confirmed his intention to step down from office after the next election to make way for a younger generation of politicians. In the previous month Goh had announced that his government would open a Speakers' Corner modelled on that in Hyde Park in London. The initiative was explained as an attempt to encourage political participation, but speakers would be required to obtain police permits in advance and would be bound by rigorous slander laws. The Speakers' Corner was opened on September 1 but failed to attract sustained public interest.

In August Senior Minister and former Prime Minister Lee Kuan Yew paid his first visit to Malaysia. Lee was received with conspicuous hospitality by a number of senior Cabinet ministers and held a private meeting with Prime Minister Mahathir Mohamad. At the end of his visit Lee gave a press conference in which he revealed that he had discussed outstanding bilateral issues with Mahathir, including water supply and the development of railway land in Singapore which was owned by Malaysia. In response to a question from a foreign journalist, Lee ventured the view that the Anwar Ibrahim affair (see IX.1.iii) had been "an unmitigated disaster" over which Mahathir had made several errors of judgement. Despite the long-standing testy relationship between Malaysia and Singapore, there was a striking absence of any negative response to Lee's remarks from the Malaysian government. Lee also said that if there was sufficient bilateral co-operation it would be possible to settle outstanding issues within two or three months. In November, however, whilst in Singapore for the informal summit of the Association of South-East Asian Nations (ASEAN), Mahathir dashed expectations of an early settlement and stated that details of a new agreement on water supply were still being discussed with the state government of Johor, which enjoyed jurisdiction over water piped to Singapore.

In April the stock exchanges of Singapore and Malaysia reached an agreement on the reversion to the market of Malaysian shares to the value of around US$5 billion. The shares had been traded in Singapore until frozen by the Malaysian government in September 1998.

During a visit to Singapore in November to attend the informal ASEAN summit, President Abdurrahman Wahid of Indonesia made a number of vehement criticisms of the island-state's leaders during a private meeting with fellow countrymen at his government's embassy. According to a transcript of his remarks which appeared in *The Straits Times*, his criticisms included the suggestion that the water supply from Malaysia should be withheld because Singapore allegedly profited from selling back treated water. Whilst Wahid's critical remarks about Singapore attracted press criticism in Indonesia, they found support amongst the media in Malaysia. In January Singapore had announced the development of its first "home-grown" desalination plant.

In May Deputy Prime Minister and Defence Minister Tony Tan entered into an agreement to allow Japan's Self-Defence Forces to use Singapore's military bases when engaged in evacuating Japanese civilians or in peacekeeping operations in south-east Asia.

vi. INDONESIA

CAPITAL: Jakarta   AREA: 1,905,000 sq km   POPULATION: 203,500,000
OFFICIAL LANGUAGE: Bahasa Indonesia   POLITICAL SYSTEM: presidential
HEAD OF STATE AND GOVERNMENT: President Abdurrahman Wahid (since Oct '99)
RULING PARTY: National Awakening Party (PKB) heads coalition
MAIN IGO MEMBERSHIPS (NON-UN): ASEAN, APEC, CP, OIC, OPEC, NAM
CURRENCY: rupiah (end-'00 £1=Rp14,452.50, US$1=Rp9,675.00)
GNP PER CAPITA: US$580, US$2,439 at PPP ('99)

THE year 2000 saw little progress in the realisation of the hopes which had accompanied the collapse of the Suharto regime in 1998 (see AR 1998, 355-57). Whilst significant institutional reform was undertaken, there was a generalised failure of leadership which did nothing to resolve the major challenges confronting the country—in particular the role of the military, the territorial integrity of the state and the management of inter-ethnic relations. The sense of continuing crisis was deepened by the apparently intractable character of the economic troubles that had afflicted the country—and the broader region—since the mid-1990s.

Central to Indonesia's problems was the politically inexperienced, physically infirm and at times deeply perplexing figure of President Abdurrahman Wahid, who had come to office in October 1999 (see AR 1999, p. 346). Wahid's unpredictable and shifting positions on a range of issues, from local autonomy to the proper way of dealing with the wrong-doers of the previous regime, encouraged continuing speculation about the durability of the new order and, in particular, the intentions of the military. In February Wahid moved to dismiss the powerful former armed forces commander Gen. Wiranto from his post as Security Minister following a damning report on the military's handling of the East Timor crisis of the previous year (see AR 1999, pp. 247-48). Sensing Wahid's weakness, Wiranto simply refused to go, thus triggering real fears of a coup. A compromise was eventually reached by which the General was "suspended" rather than removed, but it remained unclear which side, if either, had blinked first. At the end of February the victory appeared to be Wahid's when he successfully removed a large number of "old guard" officers from sensitive posts and appointed a civilian, Juwono Sudarsono, to the Defence Ministry. But over the following months conservatives within the military moved to neutralise the influence of the new breed of liberal officers who Wahid had sought to advance.

This continuing capacity and willingness of the military to act outside political control (already vividly illustrated in East Timor) was evident in the various parts of the archipelago where either separatism or ethnic conflict required a military response. In Aceh, in Sumatra, longstanding separatist pressures were met with an apparent new emollience by President Wahid and this gave rise to hopes of a viable political solution. In parallel with this, however, military abuses continued in the first months of 2000, fuelling the guerrilla campaign and undermining Wahid's political authority. Some political ground was made by the government in July when it brought 24 soldiers to court accused of carrying out massacres in the region in 1999. However, there was disappointment at the relatively lenient sentences passed and at the absence of senior officers from the indictment. A delicately negotiated ceasefire in Aceh was eventually implemented in the middle of the year, although it remained on a knife-edge at the end of 2000.

Suspicions of the military's intentions were also raised by its brutal response to the reinvigorated separatist movement in Irian Jaya (West New Guinea) and by its role in the violence between Christians and Muslims which continued throughout the year in the Moluccas. Here the complicity of elements of the military with extremist Muslim factions was suspected. Nor were suspicions of military misbehaviour restricted to unsettled provinces. A series of apparently motiveless bombings in Jakarta in the second half of the year which resulted in several deaths (and which included a particularly destructive attack on the stock exchange in September) appeared to be carried out with technical equipment and skill which many felt did not point to civilian culprits.

Amidst this instability much speculation about President Wahid's future surrounded the first meeting of Indonesia's highest legislative assembly, the People's Consultative Assembly (MPR), at the beginning of August. Although some sharp criticisms of the President's performance were made, no significant challenge to his position was forthcoming. In some part this was due to Wahid's unwonted and unexpected tone of humility before the assembly. Apologising for lack of progress on political reform and economic reconstruction, he reasonably pointed to the weight of the previous three decades of the Suharto regime and the impossibility of reversing its baleful consequences overnight. Perhaps more importantly for those contemplating change at the top was the lack of any able successor. His deputy and former rival Megawati Sukarnoputri offered even less of a prospect of stable and mature leadership. Although she was supposedly to take a greater amount of the day-to-day burden of presidential responsibility from the middle of the year, this did not appear to amount to any significant change in the distribution of power. Wahid thus emerged from this "trial by legislature" in a somewhat strengthened, though hardly impregnable position.

The popular standing of Wahid's administration had already had something of a boost earlier in the year from its evident determination to ensure that some form of justice be applied to ex-President Suharto and his corrupt circle. At the end of May the former President had been placed under house arrest pending his trial on corruption charges. As earlier attempts to indict Suharto had failed, this brought Wahid considerable plaudits, qualified only partly by his public undertaking to pardon the 79-year old former leader if he was found guilty. Formal charges were laid in August, although they were limited in scope, dealing only with several hundred millions of the billions of dollars which Suharto and his family were widely believed to have misappropriated over the years. At the opening of his trial, however, Suharto's lawyers sought an abandonment of the process on the basis of their client's age and ill-health. At the end of September, following an assessment by a panel of doctors, all charges against him were dropped, to the fury of many but the surprise of few. Some ground was recovered for the government the following month by the jailing of Suharto's son, Hutomo "Tommy" Mandala Putra, and President Wahid's subsequent refusal of clemency towards him.

Despite some promising signs in the earlier part of the year, the Indonesian economy continued to languish during 2000. Although the country's relationship with the IMF, which had deteriorated disastrously during the last phase of the Suharto regime, was fully repaired, the rupiah slid to a new low of 8,500 against the US dollar. The installation of a new economic team in the government in August had done little to retrieve the situation by the end of the year. Investor confidence, the single most important factor in recovery, was not encouraged by the accretion of problems facing the country and the inadequacy of the government's response to them during 2000.

The former Indonesian province of EAST TIMOR entered 2000 in a state of great uncertainty, but some optimism. Unequivocally freed from its quarter century of enforced integration with Indonesia, the territory was in essence now a United Nations protectorate pending the construction of the institutions of independent statehood. Throughout the year the United Nations Transitional Administration in East Timor (UNTAET) was responsible for these nation-building tasks whilst grappling with the huge problems of physical reconstruction after the destruction of 1999. UNTEAT also provided policing and security in the still tense post-conflict climate, particularly on the border with Indonesian West Timor.

Whilst considerable progress was made in 2000—in part as a consequence of the relatively unified indigenous political forces—serious difficulties remained even in the short-term. Prominent amongst these was the position of some 120,000 refugees in camps in West Timor, whose return was being obstructed by elements of the pro-Jakarta militias responsible for the 1999 violence, who had subsequently established an intimidating presence in the camps.

vii. PHILIPPINES

CAPITAL: Manila   AREA: 300,000 sq km   POPULATION: 77,000,000
OFFICIAL LANGUAGE: Filipino   POLITICAL SYSTEM: presidential democracy
HEAD OF STATE AND GOVERNMENT: President Joseph Ejercito Estrada (since June '98)
RULING PARTY: Struggle of the Nationalist Philippines Masses (LMMP)
MAIN IGO MEMBERSHIPS (NON-UN): ASEAN, APEC, CP, NAM
CURRENCY: Philippine peso (end-'00 £1=PP74.69, US$1=PP50.00)
GNP PER CAPITA: US$1,020, US$3,815 at PPP ('99)

IN 2000 the Philippines' disenchantment with the style and performance of President Joseph Estrada's administration, which had been mounting virtually since he took office in 1998 (see AR 1998, pp. 357-58), culminated in his impeachment by Congress, the bicameral legislature. A specific and detailed accusation of (long-suspected) corruption provided the immediate grounds for the move against him, but underlying this were more fundamental discontents about his political abilities.

During the term of the previous President, Fidel Ramos, a number of chronic security threats posed by Islamic separatists in the southern province of Mindanao and by various leftist guerrilla groups had receded after delicate and skilful negotiations (see AR 1997, p. 336). This carefully constructed accommodation began to unravel when Estrada came to power. In March heavy fighting broke out between government forces and the Moro Islamic Liberation Front (MILF) which, although resisting a final settlement with the government in the past, had maintained an effective ceasefire during the late 1990s. More significantly, the larger Mindanao National Liberation Front (MNLF) showed signs of rethinking the formal peace agreement that it had signed with the Ramos government in 1996 (see AR 1996, p.326).

Then, in April, a series of kidnappings took place in Mindanao, the most dramatic of which was that of a party of foreign tourists who were taken across the Sulu Sea to the island of Jolo from a resort in the Malaysian province of Sabah. Later the tally of foreign hostages increased when a group of French journalists covering the story were themselves abducted. The government proved incapable of resolving the hostage crisis, substituting bluster and inconclusive military operations for meaningful negotiation, whilst relying on external mediation, notably by Libya. Although the identity of the kidnappers—and their intentions—remained unclear, and simple criminality might have played a part, they were assumed to be associated with the small, fragmented but determined Abu Sayyaf group of militant Islamic separatists. Whilst most of the hostages had been released by the end of the year (after the payment of large ransoms) the situation in Mindanao remained extremely unstable. A triumphalist celebration of the "capture" of the MILF headquarters by the army in July was widely seen not merely as premature but deeply provocative.

This concern seemed to be justified when a bombing campaign began in Manila in the second half of the year, culminating in December in considerable loss of life when the public transport network was targeted. Beyond the Philippines, President Estrada's lack of political sensitivity and penchant for military solutions caused considerable concern for the home governments of the hostages, and most particularly for Malaysia whose important tourist industry was threatened by the separatist campaign in Mindanao.

Estrada's troubles deepened considerably in October when he was accused by a provincial governor, Luis Singson, of accepting some US$8 million in kickbacks from illegal gambling ventures and from a tobacco tax scam. For many who had followed Estrada's career the accusation was only too credible. On November 13 Congress, despite the strong presence of the President's onetime allies, voted for his impeachment. The matter was sent for trial in the Senate (the upper house of Congress) which began hearings in somewhat confused conditions—much delighted speculation centred on whether and how many of Estrada's several mistresses would be called to testify—in the second week of December. The completion of the process—and the determination of Estrada's future, if any—was expected in January 2001. A guilty finding would require a two-thirds majority of the 22-member Senate, and the likely outcome was far from clear. However, the questions surrounding Estrada went further than the specific accusations levelled by Singson. The deepening crisis of political violence along with the continuing decline of the economy (with both share prices and the value of the peso falling markedly in 2000) came together with issues of venality to highlight the general ineptness of his administration.

President Estrada's chances of survival were not improved by the presence of a willing, able and popular alternative in the person of the Vice President, Gloria Macapagal-Arroyo (see AR, 1998, p. 358). Although elected independently of Estrada and unassociated with his party, Macapagal-Arroyo (a US-educated economist) had accepted the post of Social Security Minister in his administration. Resigning as a minister (though not as Vice President) days after the accusations against the President were first made, she became the de facto leader of a coalition of anti-Estrada forces. This also included veterans of earlier "people's power" struggles such as Cardinal Jaime Sin, the Archbishop of Manila, and former President Corazon Aquino. Whatever the specific outcome of the Senate hearings, as the year ended, it seemed likely that if President Estrada were to remain in office until the end of his term in 2004, he would do so with greatly diminished authority.

viii. VIETNAM

CAPITAL: Hanoi   AREA: 332,000 sq km   POPULATION: 83,000,000
OFFICIAL LANGUAGE: Vietnamese   POLITICAL SYSTEM: socialist republic
HEAD OF STATE: President Tran Duc Luong (since Sept '97)
RULING PARTY: Communist Party of Vietnam (CPV)
PARTY LEADER: Lt Gen. Le Kha Phieu, CPV general secretary (since Dec '97)
PRIME MINISTER: Phan Van Kai, Prime Minister (since Sept '97)
MAIN IGO MEMBERSHIPS (NON-UN): ASEAN, NAM, Francophonie
CURRENCY: dong (end-'00 £1=Vnd21,681.0, US$1=Vnd14,514.0)
GNP PER CAPITA: US$370, US$1,755 at PPP ('99)

TWENTY-FIVE years after the defeat of the USA in Vietnam, relations with the US government improved significantly during the year and culminated in November with an official visit by President Bill Clinton. Clinton became the first US President to visit the country since Richard Nixon in 1969 and the first ever to set foot in a unified Vietnam. The question of US military personnel missing in action (MIA), an emotional political issue in the USA, continued to dog the relationship, but trade, investment and even eventual military co-operation were also on the agenda. US Defence Secretary William Cohen, in a visit in March, urged Vietnam to work with fellow members of the Association of South-East Asian Nations (ASEAN) to reach a settlement over their territorial disputes over the Spratly Islands in the South China Sea. US efforts to bolster ties with Vietnam were part of an effort to strengthen the region against Chinese pressures.

The signing of a bilateral trade agreement with the USA in July pointed to increasing economic reform and deregulation of the economy, whilst Vietnam and China improved relations by agreeing a land border treaty and holding a joint seminar on communist political control and market liberalisation. Vietnam's international debt structure improved during the year, largely as a result of an agreement with Russia over the US dollar value of the country's US$1.7 billion debt to its former wartime ally. The favourable terms meant that 90 per cent of the debt would be repaid via business concessions to Russia.

The opening of a stockmarket, also in July, with an initial listing of three companies—four by the end of the year—was met with a degree of euphoria not borne out by initial developments. However, the modern sectors of the economy did not have a bad year. Industrial production for the first 10 months was up nearly 16 per cent on the previous year, with the state sector still providing 42 per cent of output despite the more rapid growth of the domestic private and foreign sectors. Agricultural production was also good, as a result of increased investment in infrastructure and favourable weather conditions. The decline in world rice prices led Vietnam to agree with Thailand to create a rice pool in an attempt to stabilise prices.

In an effort to try to speed up the reform of Vietnam's creaking bureaucracy, Prime Minister Phan Van Kai appointed Deputy Prime Minister Nguyen Tan Dung, a former governor of the State Bank of Vietnam (the central bank), as deputy head of the government's Steering Committee for Administrative Reform (SCAR). The government's attention to the issue of corruption in public life was underscored in April when it allowed a small public demonstration against illegal activities to take place outside the provincial headquarters of the ruling Communist Party of Vietnam in the southern province of Dong Thrap. In January the appeal court in Ho Chi Minh City had upheld the convictions of 77 people who had been sentenced in mid-1999 on charges of fraud and appropriating state funds (see AR 1999, pp. 350-51). Two of the defendants, however, had their death sentences commuted to life imprisonment.

ix. CAMBODIA

CAPITAL: Phnom Penh   AREA: 181,000 sq km   POPULATION: 11,600,000
OFFICIAL LANGUAGE: Khmer   POLITICAL SYSTEM: monarchy
HEAD OF STATE: King Norodom Sihanouk (elected Sept '93)
RULING PARTIES: Cambodian People's Party (CPP) & United National Front for an Independent, Neutral, Peaceful and Co-operative Cambodia (FUNCINPEC)
HEAD OF GOVERNMENT: Hun Sen, Prime Minister (since July '97)
MAIN IGO MEMBERSHIPS (NON-UN): ASEAN, CP, Francophonie, NAM
CURRENCY: riel (end-'00 £1=R5,728.72, US$1=R3,835.00)
GNP PER CAPITA: US$260, US$1,286 at PPP ('99)

PLANS to introduce legislation to create special courts to try senior Khmer Rouge leaders for genocide, with foreigners providing a majority of the judges and working under UN supervision, were thwarted in January. The government instead suggested courts staffed by Cambodian nationals which would operate independently of, but funded by, the UN. Kofi Annan, the Secretary-General of the UN, had insisted on the internationalisation of the procedures and hence ruled the proposals unacceptable. A compromise was reached in May under which the majority of judges would be Cambodian, but joint foreign-Cambodian prosecution teams would be established.

Prime Minister Hun Sen suspended 20 government officials in February for their complicity in the illegal logging of forests for the lucrative foreign market. Such government action seemed to satisfy the international donor community which met in May and pledged an additional US$548 million in aid in exchange for the government's addressing the need for improved financial management, reductions in the military, and judicial reform.

Opposition leader Sam Rangsi staged a hunger strike for three days in October to draw attention to allegations of corruption in the provision of international aid to villagers who had suffered flooding from the Mekong river and Tonle Sap lake. Corruption also undermined the work of the Cambodian Mine Clearance Agency (CMCA) which was forced to lay off 70 per cent of its staff because of underfunding from foreign governments who were concerned about the misuse of their support. Years after the end of the civil war in Cambodia, and despite the best efforts of the CMCA, mines continued to cause around 1,000 casualties per year, many of them children.

x. LAOS

CAPITAL: Vientiane AREA: 237,000 sq km POPULATION: 5,800,000
OFFICIAL LANGUAGE: Laotian POLITICAL SYSTEM: people's republic
HEAD OF STATE: President (Gen.) Khamtay Siphandon (since Feb '98)
RULING PARTY: Lao People's Revolutionary Party (LPRP)
HEAD OF GOVERNMENT: Gen. Sisavath Keobounphanh, Prime Minister (since Feb '98)
MAIN IGO MEMBERSHIPS (NON-UN): ASEAN, CP, Francophonie, NAM
CURRENCY: new kip (end-'00 £1=K11,352.90, US$1=7,600.00)
GNP PER CAPITA: US$280, US$1,726 at PPP ('99)

RELATIONS with Thailand deteriorated in mid-year as disputes over their mutual border resurfaced. In August Lao troops seized two islands in the Mekong river (which constituted the border for some 800 km), alleging that they were the territory of Laos. In July dissidents crossed the river from Thailand and attempted to raise a protest in the name of the old Laotian royal family, whilst unexplained bombs went off in the capital, Vientiane. The growing unrest, which included a series of bomb blasts that hit hotels, restaurants and markets over a number of months in various towns, led to the reported imposition of an informal curfew in August. Bombs continued to explode in the capital later in the year, however, leading to speculation that government agents were planting them.

Seventy-six year-old President Khamtay Siphandon, a long time ally of Vietnam, faced increasing pressure within and without the ruling Lao People's Revolutionary Party to introduce reforms. The bomb blasts, which were linked to rumours about a resurgence of Hmong tribal insurgency, underscored the unrest which had been simmering in the country for the past year. Pockets of resistance, largely ineffectual, had emerged in both the north and south of the country. Meanwhile, heavy rains led to flooding along the Mekong in September.

Laos hosted a meeting of Association of South East Asian Nations (ASEAN) foreign ministers with their counterparts from the European Union (EU) in November. The meeting, the first in three years, had previously been blocked by the unwillingness of EU governments to participate in ASEAN meetings following the admission of Myanmar as a full member of the regional association in 1997. The meeting was remarkable for how little was accomplished, as indicated by the sparse attendance of major European figures.

The Laos economy continued to suffer from chronic under-investment and over regulation as the regime failed to introduce policies to generate either foreign or overseas investments in the country. The infrastructure remained rickety, with another airliner crash by the national carrier in October, underscoring the recommendation of some Western governments to avoid flying Lao Aviation.

2. CHINA—HONG KONG—TAIWAN—JAPAN—SOUTH KOREA— NORTH KOREA—MONGOLIA

i. PEOPLE'S REPUBLIC OF CHINA

CAPITAL: Beijing   AREA: 9,597,000 sq km   POPULATION: 1,330,000,000
OFFICIAL LANGUAGE: Chinese   POLITICAL SYSTEM: people's republic
HEAD OF STATE: President Jiang Zemin (since March '93)
RULING PARTY: Chinese Communist Party (CCP)
PARTY LEADER: Jiang Zemin, CCP general secretary (since June '89)
CCP POLITBURO STANDING COMMITTEE: Jiang Zemin, Li Peng, Zhu Rongji, Li Riuhuan, Hu Jintao, Li Lanqing, Wei Jianxing
CCP CENTRAL COMMITTEE SECRETARIAT: Hu Jintao, Ding Guangen, Wei Jianxing, Wen Jiabao, Zhang Wannian, Luo Gan, Zeng Qinghong
CENTRAL MILITARY COMMISSION: Jiang Zemin, chairman (since Nov '89)
PRIME MINISTER: Zhu Rongji (since March '98)
MAIN IGO MEMBERSHIPS (NON-UN): APEC
CURRENCY: renminbi (RMB) denominated in yuan (end-'00 £1=Y12.36, US$1=Y8.28)
GNP PER CAPITA: US$780, US$3,291 at PPP ('99)

THE year 2000 saw few dramatic changes within the People's Republic of China (PRC) but the underlying pressures caused by the government's economic reform programme continued to generate problems for the leadership of the ruling Chinese Communist Party (CCP). The worst of the deflationary pressures and economic slowdowns that had marked 1999 eased but were far from being conquered, and the social consequences of change remained a major issue for the CCP. The economy continued to grow, with estimates for the first three quarters of 2000 putting underlying growth at 8.1 per cent, but regional disparities and local hardships continued to increase. In order to meet these challenges the Chinese leadership began to reappraise the ideological basis of the CCP's position in society as well as initiating debates on more practical reforms with regard to social welfare and increased investment into western China. The major issue of the year outside the domestic arena was the victory of the opposition candidate, Chen Shui-bian, in the presidential election in Taiwan (see IX.2.iii) and the implications of this for China. Elsewhere, the international arena saw a gradual improvement of ties with China's main partners, Japan and the USA, and considerable progress with regard to entry into the World Trade Organisation (WTO).

SOCIETY AND GOVERNMENT. One area of particular concern for the CCP leadership was the number of incidents of significant social unrest. Hong Kong media reports suggested that there had been 1,680 major disturbances since the first half of 1998, 905 of which involved laid-off employees. The reports suggested that there had been a 70 per cent rise in demonstrations in 1999 compared with 1998. The Falun Gong issue was of a lower profile in 2000 than in 1999 (see AR, 1999 p. 355) although reports of arrests of Falun Gong demonstrators persisted throughout the year, in particular in April, at the anniversary of the 1999 Falun Gong rally when large-scale arrests were reported in and around Tiananmen Square in the capital, Beijing. Elsewhere, there were reports of small-scale demonstrations and riots, with two major incidents. The first was in Jiangxi province where up to 20,000 peasants were reported as being involved in riots over government fees and taxes. The second major social disturbance occurred in Nanjing in December and centred upon the removal of a memorial to victims of the 1937 Nanjing Massacre during the construction of a new hotel. The memorial was not reinstated and led to a number of clashes between demonstrators criticising the hotel management, local government and Japan. Demonstrations and protests also followed the banning of public funerals after the appalling fire on 25 December in Luoyang, in which 309 people were reported killed.

Anger in Luoyang was in part the product of a widespread perception that government corruption might have contributed to the shoddy workmanship that was believed to be the cause of the blaze. The high-profile anti-corruption drive of the CCP continued apace in 2000 with a number of senior officials being sentenced or charged: it was revealed that between January and August 104 high-ranking cadres of mayoral or department level or above (including four of ministerial rank) had been investigated. In February the former deputy governor of Jiangxi province, Hu Changqing was sentenced to death for accepting over 5 million yuan in bribes between 1995 and 1999. Ma Xiangdong, the executive vice mayor of Shenyang, was reported to be under investigation over money laundering charges, and Cong Fukui, the former executive deputy governor of Hebei, and Zhang Erchen, the former mayor of Shijiazhuang, were stripped of their positions as delegates to the National People's Congress (NPC, the unicameral legislature) over bribery and corruption charges. The most prominent case of all came in July when Cheng Kejie, former vice chairman of the NPC Standing Committee, was found guilty and sentenced to death for having received 41 million yuan in bribes when he was deputy secretary of the CCP central committee of Guangxi. Even greater corruption difficulties might lie ahead following the retirement of Gao Changli as Minster of Justice. The official reason given was ill health, but Gao had been linked to housing distribution fraud.

THE ECONOMY. During 2000 the CCP began to outline its main goals for the next five-year plan (2001-05). The objectives included: promoting the large scale development of the western regions; facilitating the development of the eastern regions to a level comparable with that of industrialised countries during the mid-1990s; transforming and modernising agricultural and livestock production; training as many as 2.8 million undergraduate students for appropriate employment; promoting high-tech industrial development and establishing a high-tech defence system; eliminating livelihood problems in impoverished areas; making six years of primary education the norm throughout the country; enabling between 80 and 100 large and medium cities to reach international environmental standards; attaining a GNP per capita target of US$1,800 by 2005; and establishing the free conversion of the currency in international markets. Furthermore, in August Zhang Zuoji, the Minister of Labour and Social Security, outlined five goals: (i) to establish stable channels to fund emerging social security arrangements; (ii) a nationwide unemployment scheme to guarantee basic living standards; (iii) the standardisation of minimum living standards for the urban population; (iv) to accelerate medical insurance reform; and (v) to introduce social security legislation. At the ninth NPC standing committee's 14th session, held in July, Premier Zhu Rongji called for the large-scale development of western China, focusing on accelerated infrastructure development, measures to preserve and conserve the natural environment, and the development of strong local industries.

China's drawn out negotiations to enter the WTO continued throughout 2000, but many of the outstanding issues were resolved and the key hurdles for the country's entry were cleared. In September the US Senate (the upper house of Congress) voted in favour of the landmark trade bill which granted permanent normal trading relations (PNTR) to China. The bill, passed by the House of Representatives (the lower house) in May, had caused considerable controversy in the USA because human rights groups had seen the procedure of an annual review of China's trade status as a useful political tool to apply pressure to China over the country's human rights record. The EU and China also resolved their outstanding issues over China's entry to the WTO in October.

A key economic problem throughout the year was the persistence of bad debts in the banking sector. The government implemented a policy of debt-equity swaps, which eased the problem to some extent, but this was criticised as being a superficial remedy. The issue was highly politicised and did not lend itself to easy solutions. The key regulatory banking body, the People's Bank of China, reported directly to the State Council and, therefore, represented political interests rather than those of the banks.

POLITICS. Ideology and ideological debate grew in significance during the year. The "three stresses" campaign continued (see AR 1999, p. 355) but was overtaken by the debate over the "Three Representations". The "Three Representations"—designed to define the role of the CCP in China's changing political and economic environment—stated that the party represented the interests of advanced social productive forces, advanced culture, and the majority of the Chinese people. This marked a clear shift away from the CCP's traditional claim to represent workers, peasants and soldiers. Widespread discussion of the issue followed a symbolic tour of Guangdong by President Jiang Zemin in April. This was followed by articles in the authoritative theoretical journal *Qiushi*. The "Three Representations" campaign was closely associated with Jiang, but the key proponent of the policy during 2000 was Hu Jintao, tipped by many observers as a potential successor to Jiang Zemin. Hu claimed in November that, "Comrade Jiang Zemin's ideology of the 'three representations' is a development of Deng Xiaoping's theory on building a socialist road with Chinese characteristics." Deng's theory had been enshrined as the CCP's core ideology and linking the two theories therefore increased the legitimacy of the "Three Representations". In December Hu Jintao called for the "Three Representations" campaign to be taken to the countryside amongst all county (city) departments, township, town and village leadership groups. Foreign observers commented on the likelihood of the "Three Representations" being incorporated into the CCP constitution at the 16th party congress, scheduled for 2002. Such a move would mean the elevation of the ideas of Jiang to a similar status as the thoughts of Mao Zedong and Deng Xiaoping within the formal ideological framework of the party. However, Hong Kong press reports suggested that there was considerable opposition to the "Three Representations" from party elders such as Wan Li, Bo Yibo, Yang Baibing, Wang Enmao and Wang Hanbin because of the excessive praise it supposedly gave to Jiang Zemin as an incumbent politician and because of the confusion that theoretical shifts could cause.

The most important issue on the political agenda in 2000 was the March 2000 presidential election in Taiwan, claimed as a province of China by the PRC. In February the State Council released a new White Paper on the Taiwan question, entitled *The One-China Principle and the Taiwan Issue*. The paper constituted the first official document to deal with the Taiwan issue since 1993. It stated that the PRC would use force to reunify Taiwan with China if (i) there was a separation of Taiwan from China in any name; (ii) Taiwan was invaded and occupied by a foreign power; or (iii) the Taiwan authorities refused peaceful settlement of the issue through negotiation. Compared with the events of the previous presidential election in Taiwan in March 1996, the PRC took a measured approach in 2000, restricting itself to verbal admonishment of the Taiwanese and warnings of the consequences for Taiwan if it were to turn to independence. The defeat of the ruling Nationalist Party (KMT) candidate Lien Chan and the victory of Chen Shui-bian of the opposition Democratic Progressive Party (see IX.2.iii) came as a surprise to the Chinese leadership, which adopted a "wait-and-see" posture towards the new administration. Comments on Chen's victory in the Chinese media were sparse, although typically accompanied by warnings of the consequences of "rash actions" by the new Taiwanese leadership. Most of Beijing's ire was directed at the new Vice President, Lu Hsiu-lien (Annette Lu) who was described as "the scum of the nation" and a "Japan-flattering traitor". An interim assessment of Chen emerged from Beidaihe in August; it called for a proactive and reactive stance, with the overall aim of bringing Taiwan to the negotiating table within three years. The end of the year saw a major breakthrough with the opening of the "three mini links" of direct contacts between the Chinese mainland and the Taiwanese-controlled offshore island of Kinmen, marking the first official direct contact across the Straits since the founding of the PRC in 1949.

However, tensions within the Chinese leadership were apparent following reports in the Hong Kong press that Zhang Wannian, vice chairman of the Central Military Commission and deputy head of the Central Leading Group for Taiwan Affairs, had claimed that war was likely over Taiwan in the period of the 10th five year plan (2001-2005). Within the PRC there were notable changes in the personnel designated to handle Taiwanese affairs which saw a marked increase in the formal influence of the People's Liberation Army (PLA) over Taiwan policy. Zeng Qinghong was replaced as secretary general of the CCP Central Leading Group on Taiwan Affairs by Lt-Gen. Xiong Guangkai, the deputy chief of the

PLA general staff. This followed the announcement that Maj.-Gen. Wang Zaixi was to be the new vice director of the State Council's Taiwan Affairs Office.

With regard to the PLA, October saw the publication of a White Paper on national defence. The paper cited the significance of living in an era of multipolarity, and stated that the core of China's defence policy was to achieve mutual equality, trust and co-operation with other nations. The paper was critical of the way that the pretexts of humanitarianism and human rights were being used to violate the United Nations charter and legitimise the use of force. The main points of the White Paper stated that the objectives of the PRC were: to consolidate national defence; to be independent and self-reliant; to maintain a strategy of active defence; to have a lean and strong military, built in the Chinese way; to combine the armed forces with the people; to subordinate national defence and place it at the service of the nation's overall economic development; and to safeguard world peace by resolutely opposing hegemonism. The White Paper was strongly critical of discussions in the USA regarding the construction of a system of National Missile Defence (NMD) and of proposals regarding Theatre Missile Defence (TMD). Foreign commentators remarked that the PLA was seen to have benefited from increased professionalism and also a new sense of purpose following NATO's intervention in Yugoslavia in 1999. Major advances had also been made by the PLA in divesting itself of its considerable business concerns. This followed a call from Jiang Zemin in July 1998 for the PLA to withdraw from commercial activities.

The issue of political succession gained prominence in 2000 as potential leaders jockeyed for position to succeed Jiang Zemin and the other senior leaders after the 16th CCP congress scheduled for 2002. One notable figure whose position appeared to take a knock was Jiang Zemin's preferred candidate, Zeng Qinghong. Zeng was passed over for permanent membership of the politburo following criticism of his role and work-style by other party members. Zeng was accused of being over-ambitious and of involving himself in areas outside his designated remit. His rival, Hu Jintao, reputed to be Deng Xiaoping's preferred successor to Jiang, was amongst those who criticised Zeng. Zeng, however, was able to consolidate his position within the party structures.

EXTERNAL AFFAIRS. The year 2000 was a success for the PRC's foreign relations, with visible improvements in key bilateral relations, and improvements in other ties. With regard to the USA, difficulties continued over NATO's bombing of the Chinese embassy in Belgrade in 1999 (see AR 1999, p. 360), although tensions were eased greatly after the USA agreed to pay compensation for the loss of life suffered. The approval of permanent normal trading relations (PNTR) for the PRC by the US Congress lifted a key barrier to China's entry to the WTO and also removed the difficult annual ritual of the renewal of most-favoured nation status from the agenda of bilateral ties. Several senior US figures visited the PRC in 2000, including Secretary of State Madeleine Albright who discussed the Taiwan question and PNTR in June, and the Secretary of Defence William Cohen who visited in July for talks with

China's Defence Minister, Chi Haotian. Chi stressed to Cohen the importance of the three China-US joint communiqués, especially with regard to the Taiwan question, and also re-stated the PRC's opposition to the USA's Theatre Missile Defence (TMD) proposals.

Relations with Japan saw an improvement after a difficult year in 1999. Japanese Foreign Minister Kono Yohei visited in August amid complaints from Japanese right-wing figures concerning Chinese violation of Japanese territorial waters and opposition to Japan's large Overseas Development Assistance budget dedicated to the PRC. The Chinese side again restated its concerns over Japan's role in the Taiwan issue. This meeting was followed by a visit of Chinese Premier Zhu Rongji to Japan in October. Zhu's visit was particularly noteworthy because of his insistence on avoiding focusing on the question of Japan's wartime aggression and on instead discussing the cordial relations that had developed since the 1970s. This was despite criticism at home of Zhus' stance.

China's relations with the European Union (EU) saw mixed results, in part the product of conflicts within the EU itself. In the summer, the European Parliament passed resolutions which were strongly critical of the PRC's stance over both Tibet and Taiwan, a move which brought angry criticism of European interference in China's domestic affairs. However, an EU-China summit in October passed without any serious disagreements between the two sides and saw the EU and the PRC resolve their final differences over China's WTO entry. Other regional relationships also saw improvements. A number of high-level meetings with Russian officials took place, including a meeting between Russian President Vladimir Putin and Defence Minister Chi Haotian. This was accompanied by a number of announcements demonstrating the deepening interaction between Russia and the PRC, especially with regard to the Chinese purchase of Russian military equipment and technology. Reports circulated throughout the year of the imminent arrival of advanced Russian SU-30 combat aircraft and of the possible purchase of Russian airborne early warning systems. Ties with India continued to recover from the hiatus caused by the Indian nuclear tests of 1998. A range of provincial level exchanges took place, such as the visit to India of the Guangdong governor Lu Ruihua in May, and further progress was made on the demarcation of the disputed Indo-Chinese border in October.

ii. HONG KONG SPECIAL ADMINISTRATIVE REGION

CAPITAL: Victoria   AREA: 1,092 sq km   POPULATION: 7,000,000
STATUS: Special Administrative Region of People's Republic of China (since 1 July 1997)
CHIEF EXECUTIVE: Tung Chee-hwa (since July '97)
ADMINISTRATIVE SECRETARY: Anson Chan (since July '97), previously Chief Secretary (since Sept '93)
MAIN IGO MEMBERSHIPS (NON-UN): APEC
CURRENCY: Hong Kong dollar (end-'00 £1=HK$11.65, US$1=HK$7.80)
GNP PER CAPITA: US$23,520 US$20,939 at PPP ('99)

THE year 2000 was a difficult one for Hong Kong, with the economy showing some signs of improvement but still struggling and with continuing uncertainty regarding the role of the central Chinese government in Hong Kong's local political affairs. Elections to the Legislative Council (Legco) did not result in major changes, although there were gains for the Democratic Alliance for the Betterment of Hong Kong (DAB), a party regarded as being pro-Beijing.

The economy grew in 2000, after three years of recession, but it was not without problems. There was a small decline in unemployment to around 5 per cent, but property values remained below the levels which they had reached in 1993. The strength of the US dollar in 2000 meant that the Hong Kong authorities needed to maintain high interest rates to defend the value of the Hong Kong dollar. This had the consequence of lowering domestic demand and prices, with the result that growth in GDP was accompanied by falling revenues.

Uncertainty over high-technology shares and doubts over the strength of growth in south-east Asia and the future of the US economy continued to damage confidence in Hong Kong. Elections for the Legco were held in September and resulted in some important shifts in the elected component of the council. The Democratic Party remained the largest single party with 12 seats, but saw its number of votes fall by 170,000 compared with 1998. By contrast, the DAB, widely regarded as being the closest of all the parties to the Chinese administration, saw a significant increase in its number of seats to 11. Media comment interpreted this as being the product of a growing sense of disillusionment with the negativity of the Democratic Party platform.

One of the highest profile issues of the year was the role of Hong Kong's media in the political life of the territory. Li Ka-shing, one of Hong Kong's leading industrialists who had close ties with the Chinese leadership in Beijing, was accused of obtaining secret information about legislative proceedings. Li accused politicians of orchestrating attacks against him, which led to bitter criticism of Li in the Hong Kong media from politicians and academics. China's concern over the Hong Kong media manifested itself in a number of ways. During and after the March presidential election in Taiwan (see IX.2.iii), Wang Fengchiao, deputy director of the Liaison Office, stated that the Hong Kong media should not advocate or disseminate information about Taiwanese independence. Later in the year Willy Wo Lap Lam, the China editor of the influential English language *South China Morning Post*, resigned amid speculation that the Chinese government had intervened to have him removed. In December Chinese President Jiang Zemin stated that the media in Hong Kong must pay attention to its social responsibilities, an announcement that was immediately criticised by Martin Lee, the leader of the Democratic Party, as an attempt to stifle open debate and criticism.

iii. TAIWAN

CAPITAL: Taipei   AREA: 35,981 sq km   POPULATION: 20,350,000
OFFICIAL LANGUAGE: Chinese   POLITICAL SYSTEM: presidential
HEAD OF STATE AND GOVERNMENT: President Chen Shui-bian (since May '00)
RULING PARTY: Democratic Progressive Party (DPP)
PRIME MINISTER: Chang Chun-hsiung (since Oct '00)
MAIN IGO MEMBERSHIPS (NON-UN): APEC
CURRENCY: new Taiwan dollar (end-'00 £1=NT$49.42, US$1=NT$33.08)
GNP PER CAPITA: US$13,235 ('99), US$16,100 at PPP ('99)

EVENTS in Taiwan in 2000 were dominated by the March presidential election and its consequences. The victory of Chen Shui-bian, the leader of the opposition Democratic Progressive Party (DPP), came as a surprise to many and had major implications for domestic politics within Taiwan, for relations across the Taiwan Straits with the People's Republic of China (PRC) and for Taiwan's international position. Following his inauguration, Chen was a faced with a multitude of difficulties at home derived from problems within his own party, the activities of his political opponents, and growing problems with the economy. With regard to external affairs, Chen took a cautious line to reassure nervous observers in the PRC and Taiwan's supporters in Japan and the USA. The economy was sluggish as uncertainly about the new administration influenced consumers, and particular problems emerged with regard to the banking sector.

The year began with attention firmly focused on the forthcoming presidential election. Opinion polls indicated a very close race between three main contenders: the incumbent Vice President, Lien Chan, standing for the ruling Kuomintang (KMT); Chen Shui-bian, head of the main opposition party, the DPP; and James Soong (Soong Chu-yu), a former senior KMT member who had split from the party in October 1999. The key issue in the run-up to the election was that of "black gold"—corrupt practices by KMT politicians and party members dating back over many years. Chen Shui-bian was able to exploit this issue as well as playing on the DPP policies of promoting greater social welfare, more equality and environmental protection. Cross-straits relations were also a factor, with the KMT promising to retain President Lee's controversial "special state-to-state" formula with regard to relations with China, whilst Soong promised to improve ties across the Straits. Chen, whose party was associated with the cause of Taiwan's independence, promised to take a constructive approach to cross-straits ties and down-played the DPP's pro-independence heritage. The KMT campaign was lacklustre and much energy was devoted to attacking the charismatic Soong. It was this split in the KMT vote between Soong and Lien that was to prove vital in allowing Chen to win a surprising, but very narrow victory. The final votes for the three main candidates were Chen Shui-bian (DPP) 4,977,737 (39.3 per cent); James Soong (independent) 4,664,932 (36.8 per cent); and Lien Chan (KMT) 2,925,513 (23.1 per cent).

Chen's victory resulted from a range of causes, including the split in the KMT, the effectiveness of the DPP's criticism of KMT practices, Chen's personal popularity and probity, and a general desire for change. Although they received the most attention in foreign media, issues of cross-straits relations were not the determining factor in the outcome of the election. Following the KMT's defeat, outgoing President Lee Teng-hui was forced to stand down as KMT party chairman ahead of schedule, and senior KMT figures were abused and attacked by angry party members. The bitterness and recrimination within the party over the KMT's defeat remained a constant in 2000.

Chen's inaugural address, given in May, sent mixed messages to observers. His claims that "Taiwan has stood up" appealed to DPP activists who had hoped for a clearer signal of Taiwan's growing distance from China, whilst his rejection of President Lee's "special state-to-state" formulation for cross-straits ties signalled a desire to initiate fresh dialogue with the Chinese government. However, the euphoria amongst DPP members and supporters at the election victory was to prove short-lived, as the difficulties associated with power, and especially the problem of developing a relationship with an opposition-dominated Legislative Yuan (legislature), became apparent. It initially appeared that President Chen had found a mechanism for easing many of his problems with the appointment of KMT stalwart and former Defence Minister Gen. Tang Fei as Premier. This move was designed to win a cross-party consensus and send a gesture of conciliation to the KMT and so ease pressure in the legislature. Tang's long established pro-reunification position also sent a signal to China that it need not fear any radical attempts to change Taiwan's status. Tang's period in office was short-lived, however, as he was dogged by poor health and caught in the cross-fire as the DPP and the opposition argued bitterly over the construction of Taiwan's fourth nuclear power plant. He stood down in October to be replaced by Chang Chun-hsiung, hitherto Deputy Premier and a DPP member.

The nuclear power plant controversy proved to be the biggest issue for the new government. For the DPP, with its long history of political activism, abandoning the nuclear power plant construction was a symbol of its new brand of politics. However, Premier Tang, backed by the KMT, refused to agree to abandonment. Tang's successor, Chang Chun-hsiung, immediately called a halt to work on the plant, a move which caused an uproar in the Legislative Yuan. The KMT and People First Party (PFP) claimed that by suspending work on the plant Chang had acted unconstitutionally and perhaps illegally and threatened to impeach the Premier and recall President Chen. The issue was then sent to the Supreme Court and a ruling on Chang's action was expected in early 2001. The DPP's domestic problems were exacerbated in November when the influential new weekly *The Journalist* carried a story claiming that Vice President Annette Lu (Lu Hsiu-lien) had informed the magazine that Chen was having an affair with one of his advisors. Lu strenuously denied the claims and initiated libel proceedings against the magazine.

President Chen's problems were not helped by a sluggish domestic economy. The jobless rate hit a record high of 3.27 per cent in December, and the currency, the New Taiwan dollar, fell in value by five per cent against the US dollar over the year. Stocks were damaged by the political uncertainty over the resignation of Premier Tang and the on-going conflict over the fourth nuclear power plant. The banking sector in particular suffered from a lack of confidence as local and international media reported serious structural difficulties and the danger of significant non-performing loans of the type that had damaged Japanese and other east Asian banking sectors.

There was some respite for the new regime, however, in international affairs. The relationship across the Taiwan Straits with the PRC showed a number of technical improvements despite an atmosphere of deep uncertainty. The Chinese leadership made clear its apprehension about the March elections through a series of warnings to the Taiwanese people in the run-up to polling (see IX.2.i). China's suspicion with regard to the new administration manifested itself more in attacks on Vice President Lu, but much of the concern prior to the election over the mainland's reaction proved groundless. By the end of the year a major symbolic breakthrough had been achieved with initiation of the "three mini-links" enabling direct contact between the Taiwanese-controlled island of Kinmen and the Chinese mainland, the first official direct contact in over 50 years.

Relations with the USA at the start of the year were dominated by the discussion in the US Congress (the bicameral legislature) over the Taiwan Security Enhancement Act, a law proposed by Taiwan's supporters in Washington and designed to codify the nature of the US security relationship with Taiwan. The controversial legislation was not passed, although it might return under the incoming Bush administration. The Clinton administration paid guarded compliments to Chen following his victory in the presidential poll, but continued to reassure the PRC that there would be no significant change in USA's China policy as a result of the victory. The US policy of supplying sufficient arms to Taiwan to maintain its defence continued. The Taiwanese broadly welcomed the election of President George W. Bush (see IV.1), although domestic opinion was divided over how this would influence cross-straits ties.

Relations with Japan were bolstered with the accession of Yoshiro Mori to Prime Minister (see IX.2.iv). Mori had longstanding ties with Taiwan and his Cabinet contained a range of pro-Taiwan members.

iv. JAPAN

CAPITAL: Tokyo AREA: 378,000 sq km POPULATION: 129,000,000
OFFICIAL LANGUAGE: Japanese POLITICAL SYSTEM: parliamentary democracy
HEAD OF STATE: Emperor Tsugu no Miya Akihito (since Jan '89)
RULING PARTIES: Liberal Democratic Party (LDP) leads coalition with New Komeito &
  New Conservative Party (Hoshuto)
HEAD OF GOVERNMENT: Yoshiro Mori, Prime Minister (since April '00)
MAIN IGO MEMBERSHIPS (NON-UN): APEC, CP, OECD, G-8
CURRENCY: yen (end-'00 £1=Y170.59, US$1=Y114.20)
GNP PER CAPITA: US$32,230, US$24,041 at PPP ('99)

THE year was marked by a few major events played out against the background of economic uncertainty and popular demoralisation. After initial high hopes of economic recovery, the economy remained stuck in a rut throughout the year. In the case of banks there was much restructuring and planned mergers in order to overcome the negative consequences of the bubble economy. Most conspicuously, the sales took place of the nationalised Long-term Credit Bank (see AR 1999, p. 370) to an international investment group led by Ripplewood Holdings of the USA, and of the Nippon Credit Bank to a consortium headed by Softbank. Moreover, a large number of companies, ranging from life and fire insurance companies to supermarkets and department stores, and pharmaceutical and construction companies, continued to be heavily burdened with debt and had to file for court protection from creditors.

In the early months of the year the Diet (the bicameral legislature) made heavy weather of the annual budget, which was only passed in March. Meanwhile, local government showed signs of significant change. For the prominent post of the governor of Osaka, the incumbent (Isamu Yamada, widely known by his former stage name "Knock") was forced to resign because of sexual irregularities which were prominently publicised by the court proceedings. His place was taken in February by Fusae Ota, the first woman governor in Japan. This was followed shortly afterwards by the success of a woman candidate in the contest for the governorship of Kumamoto prefecture. Shintaro Ishihara, the controversial governor of Tokyo, who had a reputation for expressing racist sentiments, introduced a plan to impose a temporary 3 per cent tax on gross profits of major banks as a device to solve the serious financial problems of the Tokyo Metropolitan area. Ishihara's plan constituted Japan's first proposal for local corporate taxation. It was opposed both by the banks, which instituted court proceedings, and by the central government whose tax-levying rights were challenged by it.

Prime Minister Keizo Obuchi of the Liberal-Democratic Party (LDP) expressed dissatisfaction with the unstable three-party coalition over which he presided and gave notice on April 1 that it would be broken up. At the time of his announcement Obuchi was heavily overworked because of the eruption on March 31 of Mount Usu, a volcano in south-west Hokkaido, and the consequential evacuation of over 13,000 people from the area. This crisis was soon overtaken by a political one when Obuchi suffered a stroke late on April 1 and lay in hospital in a coma on a life-support machine until his death on May 14. The press was displeased with the lack of transparency over Obuchi's condition and with passing of the interim premiership to the Cabinet Secretary, Mikio Aoki, Obuchi's nominee.

Obuchi, an experienced parliamentarian and LDP faction leader, had been Prime Minister since July 1998, having previously served as Foreign Minister. Although he was not charismatic, he was assiduous in performing his duties and travelled widely in the national interest. Modest and self-effacing, he enjoyed much goodwill amongst the electorate. He enabled his party to retain a majority in the two houses of the Diet by forging a coalition with the Liberal Party and the New Komeito and tried to grapple with the intractable problems of the Japanese economy, with some success.

Eventually the governing party appointed as Prime Minister Yoshiro Mori, the leader of one of the LDP factions, who worked initially with the outgoing Cabinet. Mori did not enjoy a traditional honeymoon period with the press because of certain incautious remarks, notably his description of Japan as "a divine country with the emperor at its centre". This seemed to be a flashback to pre-war attitudes and was widely criticised. Whilst Mori disowned the remark, this and a number of other statements continued to dog him. Nonetheless, he started his ministry with a series of overseas visits, to South Korea, the USA and Russia. The purpose of his hectic schedule was to conduct parleys in advance of the G-8 summit due to take place in Japan in July. In order to establish his own credentials and to capitalise on the popular goodwill towards Obuchi, who had probably died because of overwork for his country, he called a snap election for the House of Representatives (the lower house of the Diet) on 25 June. In a house of 480, the number of seats gained by the LDP dropped to 233 seats from 271 in the previous House, whilst the opposition Democratic Party of Japan (DPJ) gained 127 compared with 95. However, by reviving the coalition with New Komeito and the New Conservatives the LDP managed to maintain its working majority. The lower house was recalled and re-elected Mori as Prime Minister. On this basis he appointed his second Cabinet on July 4.

In late July the annual summit of the G-8 industrialised countries was held in Japan. Whilst subsidiary meetings were held in Kyushu, it was the government's deliberate intention to hold the main sessions on the island of Okinawa, which had since its return to Japan in 1972 regarded itself as a disadvantaged prefecture. The summit was efficiently organised; and the delegates were expensively entertained. Japan justified the expense on the grounds that the G-8 meetings meant more to Japan—which was not a member of NATO or a permanent member of the UN Security Council—than other G-8 members. The final communiqué made special reference to the elimination of poverty in developing countries, relief of third world debt and international assistance to developing countries facing the IT revolution. Much of the limelight was on President Vladimir Putin of Russia who was present at the summit for the first time.

In July the lengthy legal proceedings over the attack staged by members of the Aum Shinrikyo cult on the Tokyo Metro in 1995 (see AR 1995, p. 348) came to fruition. The judgments passed down by the Tokyo District Court included five death sentences for those responsible for releasing sarin nerve-gas. Meanwhile, the cult continued to exist under the new name of Aleph, although it had renounced violence.

President Putin, accompanied by a large delegation, paid a return visit to Japan on September 3-5. During his earlier visit in July, the Japanese had asked for a bilateral summit on the subject of the Northern Territories, the islands which Soviet forces had occupied in 1945 and had never returned. However, Putin had declined this on the grounds that his schedule was too busy. Whereas Putin's two predecessors (Gorbachev and Yeltsin) had expressed the wish that the issue of the Northern Territories could be resolved during 2000, Putin could not hold out any hope of an early date for ending the dispute. Nonetheless, some progress was made in co-operation on regional economic affairs, fisheries and joint consultation over search and rescue operations. The positive results of Putin's visit were marred by the arrest of a Japanese naval officer on charges of providing sensitive information to a Russian naval attaché, who had to return home. Overall, however, Russo-Japanese relations continued to improve during the year.

In a supplementary budget presented in September the government announced another in a long line of economic stimulus packages. It claimed that economic recovery was on track and pledged substantial capital for public works projects. The package, a 4,780 billion yen supplement to the budget providing for the construction of roads, bridges and tunnels, was approved in November despite being widely criticised in the Diet by those who felt that such measures would not lead to any increase in consumer spending and were merely increasing Japan's public indebtedness.

The second-half of the year was dominated by allegations of Mori's unpopularity as shown by his poor rating in public opinion polls and the critical coverage of his gaffes by the media. The good international reputation that he had won from the G-8 summit did not feed back into domestic politics. The opposition decided to capitalise on this by calling for a vote of no-confidence when the Diet re-opened in November. More serious for the governing party was the likelihood that one of the reformist factions within the LDP, led by Koichi Kato, might join with the opposition in ousting Mori. Eventually, after 10 days of horse trading, Kato and a number of others who had called for Mori's resignation abstained from voting under the threat of being deprived of LDP funds. The no-confidence motion was voted down in the House on November 21.

In early December Mori formed his third Cabinet in order to reward the loyalty of his supporters and managed to strengthen his personal position by including several heavyweight members. He persuaded former Prime Minister Kiichi Miyazawa to continue as Finance Minister, a post which he had held for over two years, and succeeded in enlisting another former Prime Minister and leader of the LDP's largest faction, Ryutaro Hashimoto, who took over the special portfolio of Administrative Reform. It was envisaged that Hashimoto's office would oversee the reorganisation of central government, and a regrouping of government ministries and agencies scheduled for early in 2001. Mori proclaimed a Rebirth Plan for the country; but it remained uncertain whether the reforms envisaged would overcome the Prime Minister's personal unpopularity and carry the party through to success in the House of Councillors (the upper chamber) elections which were due to be held in July 2001.

Japanese conduct prior to and during the Pacific War once again cast a shadow over foreign affairs during 2000. In January a highly controversial conference between historians and former soldiers was held in Osaka to discuss whether the 1937 "Rape of Nanjing" in China by Japanese Imperial troops was a fabrication. This was bitterly opposed by the Chinese government, which condemned the meeting, and it led to Chinese popular protests. During the official visit to Japan in October of the Chinese Premier, Zhu Rongji, he drew attention to the fact that China had not received an unequivocal written apology for Japan's aggression. The Japanese claimed that repeated apologies had already been made. In December an "international tribunal on Japan's wartime sexual slavery" was held in Tokyo, at which the Japanese government was urged to apologise and pay compensation for the many "comfort women" who had been forced to serve as unpaid prostitutes for the Imperial armed forces.

At the end of the year government reports confirmed that economic growth was slowing down in line with the slowdown of the US economy. Whilst there had been signs of economic recovery during 2000, they had been tentative and could not be sustained. Private consumption—which normally rose steeply in the Christmas and New Year periods—failed to rally. It was thought that the decline in lifetime employment and the general turmoil in the financial sector had made consumers more cautious. Although there was much talk of eventual reform, it was likely to be slow and circumspect under any LDP-led coalition. Nonetheless, Japan continued to attract foreign investment, which in the long-term might act as a catalyst for reform in the economic sector. It was also likely that the growing influence of foreign executives in Japanese corporations would result in the adoption of foreign methods. In some cases, notably the revival of Nissan Motors by Renault, the infusion of foreign management seemed already to have been beneficial.

Three serious natural disasters took place during the year. Apart from the eruption of Mount Usu in March, there was a serious eruption of the volcano in Miyakejima in the Izu island chain off Tokyo in July, and an earthquake in October in Tottori prefecture on the Japan Sea coast which measured 7.3 on the Richter scale.

The deaths took place during the year of two personalities who had been on the political stage for many years. The Dowager Empress Nagako, the widow of the Emperor Hirohito (in death known as Showa), died in June at the age of 97. Engaged in 1918, she married Hirohito, then the crown prince, in 1924, two years before he succeeded to the throne. They visited Europe in 1971 and the USA in 1975. After Hirohito's death in 1989, the Empress made almost no public appearances.

Noboru Takeshita, long an eminence grise of the LDP, died in June at the age of 76. He served as Finance Minister at a critical time, playing an important role in adjusting the yen-dollar ratio, and as Prime Minister in 1987-89. Thereafter he was, by virtue of heading the largest faction in the LDP, influential behind the scenes as "king-maker" and mediator between the various factions of his party (see XVIII).

v. SOUTH KOREA

CAPITAL: Seoul   AREA: 99,000 sq km   POPULATION: 48,000,000
OFFICIAL LANGUAGE: Korean   POLITICAL SYSTEM: presidential democracy
HEAD OF STATE AND GOVERNMENT: President Kim Dae Jung (since Feb '98)
RULING PARTY: Millennium Democratic Party (MDP), formerly the National Congress for New Politics, and United Liberal Democrats (ULD)
PRIME MINISTER: Lee Han Dong, since May '00
MAIN IGO MEMBERSHIPS (NON-UN): APEC, CP, OECD
CURRENCY: won (end-'00 £1=SKW1,889.66, US$1=SKW1,265.00)
GNP PER CAPITA: US$8,490, US$14,637 at PPP ('99)

IN preparation for the April 2000 general election, President Kim Dae Jung relaunched his National Congress for New Politics as the Millennium Democratic Party (MDP) in January. However, the MDP failed to win an outright majority in the elections and the opposition Grand National Party (GNP) remained the single largest party in the National Assembly (the unicameral legislature) winning 133 of the total 273 seats. Voter turnout was a mere 57.2 per cent, falling below 60 per cent for the first time in the country's history. Kim Jong Pil had resigned as Prime Minister at the start of the year in order to take charge of the election campaign for his United Liberal Democrats (ULD). The ULD had held 48 seats in the previous assembly but garnered only 17 in the election.

The election was widely characterised as a mid-term referendum on President Kim's economic reform programme. Despite an overall gain of 11 seats for the MDP, the result was seen as a considerable setback for Kim's presidency. By contrast, it boosted the profile and power base of GNP leader Lee Hoi Chang and left the GNP only four seats short of a simple majority. The President's position was not helped by the enforced resignation of Park Tae Joon, who had been appointed Prime Minister in January in place of Kim Jong Pil. Park resigned in mid-May, after being found guilty of tax evasion, and was replaced by ULD president Lee Han Dong.

The early April announcement of a forthcoming summit meeting between President Kim and North Korean leader Kim Jong Il was criticised by opposition politicians as having been timed in order to boost the MDP's election performance. Nevertheless, preparations for the summit began at the first North-South meeting of officials for six years in the truce village of Panmunjom. In a speech in Berlin in March, President Kim had offered, in exchange for dialogue, government aid to help rebuild the North Korean economy before reunification. The two Kims met in mid-June in the North Korean capital of Pyongyang where they concluded two days of festivities and talks with a joint declaration. They agreed in principle to promote economic co-operation and eventually to reunify the two countries without outside "interference". Families divided by the Korean war would meet in Seoul and Pyongyang. There were plans for a highway and the re-opening of the railway line across the demilitarised zone (DMZ), which would link Seoul via Pyongyang with China and Russia. Kim Jong Il was also invited to visit the South "at an appropriate time".

After the summit President Kim proclaimed "a new day for Korea", but warned that results would take time and patience to achieve. The opposition GNP criticised the declaration's failure to mention North Korean missiles and nuclear weapons and the return of South Korean prisoners of war. However, government officials insisted that there was "firm agreement on the prevention of war and establishment of peace on the Korean peninsula". The loudspeakers in the DMZ ceased broadcasting virulent propaganda, and the liaison office in Panmunjom was reopened after a closure of five years. In September, in a symbolic gesture of unity, athletes from North and South marched at the opening of the Sydney Olympics under one flag, depicting an outline of the Korean peninsula.

The vagueness of the joint declaration released in Pyongyang in June gave rise to doubt that anything much would change. Meetings of divided families were delayed by the North and limited to small numbers. At their Cheju island meeting in September, South Korean Defence Minister Cho Seong Tae sought confidence-building measures such as a military hotline, a reduction of tension in the DMZ, advance notification of military manoeuvres and the exchanges of observers, whilst North Korean Defence Minister Kim Il Chol would only discuss mine clearance for the North-South rail link. Later it emerged that Kim Il Chol had also called for the withdrawal of US troops from the South, despite President Kim Dae Jung's earlier claim that Kim Jong Il had agreed with him that US troops should remain even after North-South reconciliation, in order to avoid creating a "dangerous vacuum".

It was announced in October that President Kim Dae Jung had been awarded the Nobel Peace Prize for his struggle for democracy and the "sunshine policy" of reconciliation with North Korea. However, it was suggested by some that the champion of human rights was using repression at home to avoid annoying the North. Another Nobel Peace Prize winner-the Dalai Lama-was refused entry to South Korea shortly before Chinese Premier Zhu Rongji's visit to Seoul in November for an Asia-Europe summit. Religious leaders accused President Kim of caring more about Chinese pressure than his fellow-countrymen's wishes.

A North-South economic co-operation agreement in November outlined steps towards cross-border investment and remittances. At further talks in December the rebuilding of the North Korean economy was discussed. The government expressed its willingness to give the North another 700,000 tonnes of grain on credit. However, Kim Young Sam, Kim Dae Jung's predecessor as President accused Kim Dae Jung of being too compliant and warned that Kim Jong Il would exploit the South's generosity. The government was accused of trying to stifle the press and prevent critics of Pyongyang from being heard.

An IMF report in August said that the country had largely recovered from the 1997 financial crisis, but that a thorough clean-up of financial institutions was still needed. At mid-year the 17 big commercial banks had combined bad loans of around US$48,000 million, 11 per cent of the total loans, but had made provision against only a third of them.

Hyundai, the country's biggest *chaebol* or family-controlled conglomerate, with debts of US$46,000 million, was forced to restructure in May. Chung Yu Jung, the company's 84-year-old founder, retired after two of Hyundai's companies were refused renewal of loans. However, when 12 commercial banks met to discuss a credit crisis at one of the companies, Hyundai Engineering and Construction, 11 decided to keep their credit lines in place, and only one refused-Korea First Bank, the country's first foreign-owned bank. Hyundai Engineering and Construction, controlled by Chung's son, Chung Mong Hun, also survived, whilst a rescue package was put together from other Hyundai companies, including Hyundai Motor, chaired by Mong Hun's brother, Chung Mong Koo.

Daewoo Motor, the country's second biggest car-manufacturer, appeared about to collapse in November, after a bid by Ford was withdrawn and the Korea Development Bank refused more loans. However, other creditors continued to fund business and the plants remained in production whilst the receivers sought buyers.

During the year the Fair Trade Commission examined allegations that all four top *chaebol*—Hyundai, Samsung, LG and SK—had subsidised weak affiliates from the earnings of healthy ones without consulting minority shareholders. It was also investigating unregulated investment in businesses controlled by the sons of *chaebol* owners, in an effort to enforce the separation of management from ownership.

In December the Kookmin and Housing and Commercial banks announced a merger which would make them the country's largest bank, with assets worth SKW167,000 billion (US$147 billion). In protest at the merger and fearing job losses, 12,000 bank workers went on strike.

Between January and November the stock market fell by 50 per cent, and the won fell to a two-year low, yet annual GDP growth was still expected to reach 8.9 per cent.

vi. NORTH KOREA

CAPITAL: Pyongyang   AREA: 123,370 sq km   POPULATION: 24,400,000
OFFICIAL LANGUAGE: Korean   POLITICAL SYSTEM: people's republic
RULING PARTY: Korean Workers' Party (KWP)
PARTY LEADER: Kim Jong Il, KWP general secretary (since Oct '97)
PRIME MINISTER: Hong Song Nam (since Sept '98)
MAIN IGO MEMBERSHIPS (NON-UN): NAM
CURRENCY: won (end-'00 £1=NKW3.29, US$1=NKW2.20)
GNP PER CAPITA: US$573 ('98, J.P. Morgan)

THE summit meeting between Kim Jong Il and South Korean President Kim Dae Jung in June in Pyongyang was the first ever meeting between the leaders of North and South Korea (for details see IX.2.v). Although diplomatic manoeuvring between North Korea and the USA grew more intense, Kim's invitation to US President Bill Clinton to visit Pyongyang was not taken up, the US condition of progress in arms control talks not having been met.

At talks between the two sides in Berlin in January, North Korean officials were told that the USA wanted not a moratorium on long-range missile tests, but a complete end to missile building, testing, deployment and sales. The USA also wanted more stringent inspection of missile sites without having to submit to what it described as the North's extortionate demands for concessions and its "inflammatory language". Pyongyang agreed in February to send a high-level delegation to Washington DC to discuss the improvement of relations, but demanded that the US State Department first remove North Korea from its list of nations sponsoring terrorism. The USA eased trade sanctions against North Korea in June.

Kim Yong Nam, president of the presidium of the Supreme People's Assembly (SPA, the unicameral legislature), who was on his way to New York for the UN Millennium Summit of world leaders in September, abandoned his journey after his delegation was subjected to body searches by US airline staff at Frankfurt airport.

Cho Myong Nok, first vice chairman of the National Defence Commission, was received by US President Bill Clinton in October. Cho was the highest-level North Korean visitor to the USA to date. He presented to President Clinton North Korea's detailed response to US proposals for the improvement of relations. Their joint statement pledged the resolution of outstanding issues and opposition to terrorism. Madeleine Albright paid a visit to Pyongyang in October, the first by a US Secretary of State. Her arrival coincided with celebrations marking the 55th anniversary of communist rule. During talks, Kim Jong Il linked his moratorium on Taepodong-2 missile tests with North Korea's need for another country to launch its satellites, an idea which received little sympathy within either the USA or South Korea.

Some progress on the missile issue was made at a meeting between US and North Korean officials in New York in October. July talks with the North had ended in stalemate, the USA again refusing to pay US$1,000 million a year for an end to missile exports. At talks in Kuala Lumpur in November, the US negotiators were still seeking to persuade North Korea to abandon its missile programme, but "significant issues" remained unresolved, they said.

An upturn in relations with China was indicated when Kim Jong Il arrived unexpectedly at a farewell banquet given in March by Chinese ambassador Wan Yongxiang, the first sighting of the "Dear Leader" at a foreign embassy since he inherited power from his father Kim Il Sung in 1994. Just before his June summit with South Korean President Kim Dae Jung, Kim Jong Il visited Beijing for three days for talks with President Jiang Zemin and other senior Chinese leaders. On his first trip abroad since his father's death, Kim praised China's "successful experiment in socialism with Chinese characteristics" and went home with Chinese pledges of food and oil aid worth US$1,000 million.

Foreign Minister Igor Ivanov-the highest ranking Russian visitor in a decade-visited Pyongyang in February for talks with Foreign Minister Paek Nam Sun. When Russian President Vladimir Putin dropped in on his way to a G-8 meeting in Japan in July, Kim Jong Il once again suggested that North Korea would abandon missile development and sales if other countries would help it to launch satellites. Kim said later that his remarks had been a "joke".

Talks on the normalisation of North Korean relations with Japan opened in Pyongyang in April, but at a further session held in Tokyo in August North Korea demanded an apology and compensation for the Japanese occupation of Korea, whilst Japan demanded information about the abduction of Japanese citizens, which North Korea denied. A third session held in China in late October also ended in failure, although in the run-up to the talks Japan had announced a change of strategy by promising to send North Korea some 500,000 tonnes of rice over the next 18 months. In January Italy became the first G-7 nation to establish diplomatic relations with North Korea; the UK followed suit in December.

According to reports that emerged in February, real GDP growth went into the black in 1999 for the first time in 10 years, after declining by 1 per cent in 1998 and 7 per cent in 1997. Nonetheless, a report published by UN agencies in November estimated that in 2001 North Korea would be faced with a food shortage of 1,165,000 tonnes as a result of unexpected droughts and floods during the past year. The estimated shortage took into account a predicted harvest of 2,920,00 tonnes of grain and 700,000 tonnes of planned food aid and loans from South Korea. Widespread power shortages were blamed on the USA for delaying construction of the Korean Peninsula Energy Development Organisation (KEDO) reactors under the terms of the Geneva framework agreement of 1994.

vii. MONGOLIA

CAPITAL: Ulan Bator   AREA: 1,564, 116 sq km   POPULATION: 2,382,500 (2000 census)
OFFICIAL LANGUAGE: Halh (Khalkha) Mongolian   POLITICAL SYSTEM: republic
HEAD OF STATE AND GOVERNMENT: President Natsagiyn Bagabandi (since June '97)
RULING PARTY: Mongolian People's Revolutionary Party (MPRP)
PRIME MINISTER: Nambaryn Enhbayar (since July '00)
MAIN IGO MEMBERSHIPS (NON-UN): NAM, EBRD
CURRENCY: tögrög (end-'00 £1=T1,638.70, US$1=T1,097.00)
GNP PER CAPITA: US$350, US$1,496 at PPP ('99)

THE early months of the year witnessed the disintegration of political parties and alliances and the formation of new ones in preparation for the forthcoming general election. The majority party in the outgoing Great Hural (the legislature), the Mongolian National Democratic Party (MNDP), lost several leading members to the reborn Mongolian Democratic Party (MDP) and the Civil Courage Party (CCP) founded by Sanjaasürengiyn Oyuun in memory of her murdered brother Sanjaasürengiyn Zorig (see AR 1998, p. 386). The Mongolian Social Democratic Party (MSDP) abandoned the Democratic Alliance with the MNDP to stand alone, and the MNDP set up a new Democratic Alliance with the much smaller Mongolian Believers' Democratic Party (MBDP). The Mongolian People's Party (MPP), which under the chairmanship of Dembereliyn Ölziybaatar had merged with the opposition Mongolian People's Revolutionary Party (MPRP) (see AR 1999, p. 377), asserted its independence under Lama Dorligjavyn Baasan, who was re-elected chairman in April. On polling day, July 2, 603 candidates representing 17 parties stood for election.

In view of the disorder in the ruling parties, it was no surprise that the MPRP was swept back to power, winning 72 of the 76 seats in the Great Hural. The remaining seats went to Janlavyn Narantsatsralt (MNDP ex-Prime Minister), Sanjaasürengiyn Oyuun (CCP president), Badarchiyn Erdenebat (chairman of the Mongolian Democratic New Socialist Party), and an independent, Lamjavyn Gündalay. Prime Minister Rinchinnyamyn Amarjargal and all MSDP candidates, including party chairman Radnaasümbereliyn Gonchigdorj, the Speaker of the Great Hural, were defeated.

The new session of the Great Hural opened on July 19 with the election of the new Speaker, Lhamsürengiyn Enebish, secretary general of the MPRP. When proceedings moved on to the appointment of the new Prime Minister, however, the MPRP's nomination of the party chairman, Nambaryn Enhbayar, was held up by President Natsagiyn Bagabandi, who refused to approve it before the contentious issue of constitutional amendments was settled. The amendments had been adopted by the Great Hural the previous December (see AR 1999, p. 377), then vetoed by the President and rejected by the Constitutional Court. One of the amendments permitted Hural members to serve concurrently in the Cabinet, and Enhbayar was now a Hural member. After four days of wrangling, a new debate on the amendments was agreed in exchange for Enhbayar's nomination, which was approved by the Hural on July 26. Despite a "final" ruling by the full Constitutional Court rejecting the amendments in November, the Great Hural debated them again and adopted them once more, unchanged, in December, whereupon the President vetoed them again. The Hural concluded that his veto was unconstitutional, and dismissed it.

At a "great hural for uniting the parties for democracy" on December 6, the leaders of the MNDP, MSDP, MBDP, MDP and the Mongolian Democratic Renewal Party resolved to abolish their parties and found a new Democratic Party. Dambyn Dorligjav from the MNDP was elected chairman. Registered on December 26, the Democratic Party claimed an amalgamated membership of 160,000, twice the size of the MPRP.

Russian President Vladimir Putin visited Ulan Bator on November 13-14, on his way to an Asia-Pacific Economic Cooperation (APEC) conference in Brunei. The last top-level visit from Moscow had been that of Leonid Brezhnev in 1974. Presidents Bagabandi and Putin confirmed their countries' adherence to the Treaty of Friendly Relations and Co-operation concluded by Presidents Punsalmaagiyn Ochirbat and Boris Yeltsin in Moscow in 1993 (see AR 1993, p. 373), and signed an "Ulan Bator Declaration". This pledged that Mongolia and Russia "will not join any military-political alliances against one another, nor conclude any treaty or agreement with third countries harmful to the interests of the other's sovereignty or independence. Neither side will allow its territory to be used by a third state for purposes of aggression or other acts of violence harmful to the sovereignty, security and public order of the other." Russia confirmed its adherence to the five nuclear powers' declaration of guarantees for Mongolia's security in connection with its nuclear-weapons-free status. Mongolia supported Russia's efforts to prevent any revision of the 1972 Anti-Ballistic Missiles treaty.

Mongolia and Russia agreed to boost the productivity of joint ventures like the Erdenet copper combine and the Ulan Bator Railway. The terms for rescheduling Mongolia's recent debts to Russia were settled, but the long-disputed US$11,000 million debt which Moscow claimed to be owed for aid during the Soviet period was not written off as the Mongolian government had hoped. An agreement on co-operation in the peaceful use of nuclear energy prepared the way for Russian assistance with planning and building a nuclear power station in Mongolia. Russia supported Mongolia's involvement in the construction of international gas and oil pipelines and power lines in north-east Asia, but their final route remained uncertain and subject to Chinese agreement.

The drought in the autumn 1999 and severe winter in early 2000 over much of the country led to *zud* conditions in which animals starved to death for lack of grazing or fodder. Some 2.8 million perished, leaving over 2,300 herdsmen's families without a livelihood and thousands more greatly impoverished, despite emergency measures and widely publicised but mostly meagre international aid pledges.

X AUSTRALASIA AND THE PACIFIC

1. AUSTRALIA—PAPUA NEW GUINEA

i. AUSTRALIA

CAPITAL: Canberra   AREA: 7,741,000 sq km   POPULATION: 19,500,000
OFFICIAL LANGUAGE: English   POLITICAL SYSTEM: federal parliamentary democracy
HEAD OF STATE: Queen Elizabeth II
GOVERNOR-GENERAL: Sir William Deane
RULING PARTIES: Liberal-National Party coalition
HEAD OF GOVERNMENT: John Howard, Prime Minister (since March '96)
MAIN IGO MEMBERSHIPS (NON-UN): APEC, PC, PIF, CP, ANZUS, OECD, CWTH
CURRENCY: Australian dollar (end-'00 £1=A$2.69, US$1=A$1.8)
GNP PER CAPITA: US$20,050, US$22,448 at PPP ('99)

THERE were no elections at national or state level in Australia and, therefore, an unusual condition of party stability prevailed. However, Australian foreign policy was faced with the collapse of its long-standing strategy of maintaining an "arc of security" stretching from New Zealand through Papua New Guinea and Indonesia and on to Malaysia and Singapore. The continuing political unrest in Indonesia, and especially the secession of East Timor, damaged relations with Australia's nearest and largest neighbour (see AR1999, p. 380). Coups in the Solomon Islands and Fiji and social tensions in Papua New Guinea threatened the stability of states which Australia had cultivated and attempted to consolidate for many years. The difficult relationship with Malaysia was not visibly improved and there were even verbal tensions and disagreements between Australia and New Zealand over defence and immigration policy. In July the Australian high commissioner in Fiji was recalled and sanctions were imposed on sporting, aid and defence ties, in protest against the inclusion of coup supporters in the interim Fiji government (see X.2.ii.).

None of this had any measurable impact on domestic politics and the Liberal-National Party government held mostly even with the opposition Australian Labor Party (ALP) in the opinion polls, although tending to be behind more often than in front. The economy continued to be relatively sound. Unemployment reached an 11-year low at 6.3 per cent in August but started to rise slowly towards the end of the year, whilst manufacturing production dropped to its lowest level since 1992. The exchange value of the Australian dollar reached new lows but this helped to increase exports. The new goods and services tax (GST) came into operation on July 1 (see AR 1999, p. 380). This had little significant impact on the government's popularity, perhaps because it was preceded by an expensive public relations campaign to explain and justify it and to publicise associated reductions in direct taxation. The budget of May 9 recorded the fourth year in surplus and allowed for very substantial cuts in personal income tax. A report on social welfare by Patrick McClure in August suggested major changes, including an extension of the "work for the dole" principle, and its basic approach was immediately endorsed by the Cabinet. Community consultations on defence expenditure were launched in August as a preliminary to an official announcement that the changed international situation required greater defence spending. In May Maj.-Gen. Peter Cosgrove, who had commanded the International Force in East Timor, was appointed as commander in chief of the army after his role in East Timor ended in February.

The year was characterised by an unusual number of public celebrations and occasions, including the visit of Queen Elizabeth II in March, the Olympic Games in September (see XVI) and the officially orchestrated excitement leading up to the marking of the centenary of the Australian Federation on January 1, 2001. In July Prime Minister John Howard visited London with four former Prime Ministers and current political leaders to celebrate with the UK government the centenary of the signing of the United Kingdom Act which had created the Commonwealth of Australia. Sydney was the scene of massive and elaborate celebrations at the start of the year 2000, at the opening and closing of the Olympics, and at the beginning of 2001. The Sydney Olympics, despite initial problems and disputes, went off without a hitch, causing much self-congratulation, although unsurprisingly requiring additional public funding support. These rejoicings were of some political significance as Liberal Prime Minister Howard had his strongest base in Sydney. There were also massive and peaceful demonstrations for reconciliation with the Aboriginal minority, including marches across Sydney harbour bridge on May 28, and later in the other cities. These were essentially non-partisan, but the Prime Minister did not participate personally in any of them, unlike some of his Liberal Party colleagues and the leaders of the ALP and the Australian Democrats. Front bench Liberals were particularly prominent in the Melbourne march of December 4. There were more violent demonstrations in Melbourne on September 11 against the World Economic Forum.

Aboriginal affairs had considerable prominence, particularly after the launching of a reconciliation document which had been in preparation for nine years, in the Corroboree 2000 ceremony on May 27. The document's most contentious item called for a treaty between indigenous Australians and the Commonwealth government, which the latter immediately rejected. This treaty had been an objective of the new chairman of the Aboriginal and Torres Strait Islander Commission, Geoff Clarke, for some years. It was not urged by all members of the Council for Aboriginal Reconciliation, the body which had prepared the report. The government also found itself at variance with Aboriginal activists when it submitted to an official enquiry that there had never been a "stolen generation", a term applied to children removed from their parents during the preceding century. Another contentious issue was the imposition by the Northern Territory of mandatory prison sentencing for repeated offences. The Territory, which had the highest proportion of Aboriginal inhabitants, had an even higher proportion of Aboriginal prisoners and junior offenders, one of whom committed suicide whilst imprisoned for a minor offence under the new law.

Australia was criticised by the United Nations Human Rights Committee for its treatment of Aborigines and by the UN High Commission for Refugees for its mandatory detention of asylum seekers. This caused the government in April to conduct an audit of Australian participation in the UN international treaty system. Several times between June and September ministers advocated an overhaul of the UN committee system and expressed resentment at UN intervention in what they saw as domestic issues. In September Australia refused to endorse the UN optional protocol on the elimination of discrimination against women.

Increasing concern was raised by churches and other non-government organisations about conditions in the two isolated detention centres at Port Hedland and Woomera in which asylum seekers coming through Indonesia by boat were housed under the control of a private security company (see AR 1999, p. 379). Most of the inmates were from Afghanistan, Iraq or Iran and the majority were eventually given refugee status on temporary protection visas. However, the issues of long delays in processing, claims of harassment by centre staff, and the continued detention of women and children were increasingly raised towards the end of the year, especially through the national newspaper *The Australian*. In April remaining Kosovar refugees under temporary protection orders were returned to Kosovo despite many objections.

A new departure in immigration policy was advocated at the end of the year when the status of New Zealanders and their social security eligibility were raised by the Minister for Immigration, Philip Ruddock. He expressed concern that many New Zealand immigrants, now comprising the largest intake and not subject to visa control, had not been born there and might be "back door entrants", whilst the social security burden of supporting New Zealanders was inequitable between the two countries.

Party politics were marked by the continuing disintegration of the far-right One Nation party (see AR 1998, p. 389; 1999, p. 382) and by public exposure of the internal affairs of the ALP (and, to a lesser extent, of the Liberals) in Queensland. Signing up new party members to influence the selection of candidates was common practice, but fraudulently enrolling them as electors to qualify them was not, and was illegal. Revelations that this had happened in north Queensland led to an official enquiry and the resignation of several ALP state politicians, putting at risk the majority of the state ALP government. A different crisis led to the resignation of the chief minister of the Australian Capital Territory, Kate Carnell, who had authorised a large payment to renovate a sports stadium for Olympic soccer without getting legislative approval.

The ALP biennial national conference in Hobart in the first week of August endorsed greater state support for health and education, and a reversal of the current government's commitment to privatisation and deregulation. The party was less united on the issue of free trade in regard to Australian industry, with unions supporting the idea of "fair trade" to protect manufacturing and prevent it from moving offshore. Greg Sword, a trade union official, was elected as the party's new president. Trade unions had few successes during the year, the most important being the withdrawal of proposed industrial relations legislation after the Australian Democrats refused to allow it to pass through the Senate. This legislation would have greatly reduced the role of unions and increased that of individual contracts.

One Nation was deregistered in Queensland and in New South Wales, obliging its leader, Pauline Hanson, to repay A$500,000 of funds which had been granted to the party as a result of the Queensland election of 1998 (see AR 1998, p. 388). The party disintegrated into three distinct and mutually hostile groups: the City Country Alliance in Queensland, the One Nation party led by David Oldfield in New South Wales, and Pauline Hanson's remaining loyal supporters. Elsewhere, the leader of the National Party, Tim Fischer, resigned in January and was replaced by John Anderson.

Transport developments included an agreement between the federal central, South Australian and Northern Territory governments to proceed with the Alice Springs to Darwin railway, which would link the northern port with the rest of Australia and expedite trade with Asia. The proposed high speed train link between Sydney and Canberra was, however, rejected by the federal government. All these proposed railway developments were now in private hands, as was the new rail link between Sydney airport and the city, opened for the Olympics but reporting very light usage. Transport to the Olympic site at Homebush Bay also involved a new rail link and was without problems. Two new airlines, Impulse and Virgin Blue, entered the market on main routes. The government allocated A$1.2 billion in November for local council road works and promised a further A$400 million for outer metropolitan links. Concerns with air safety regulation were expressed towards the end of the year when several Ansett planes were grounded during the Christmas period for lack of inspection. Plans for a second Sydney airport were indefinitely suspended after a long campaign against aircraft noise.

There were serious floods in northern New South Wales during late November, whilst other areas were still experiencing drought conditions. Fifteen young people died in a fire at a backpacker hostel in Childers (Queensland) on June 23, most of them fruit pickers on working holiday visas. A temporary resident of the hostel was later arrested and charged with murder and arson. On May 7 the trial of those accused of murdering New South Wales state MP John Newman was aborted when the jury was discharged for failing to agree (see AR 1994, p. 395).

Amongst those who died during the year were Aboriginal activist Charles Perkins (64); Dame Roma Mitchell (86), the first woman to become a state governor; David Tonkin (71), the former Liberal premier of South Australia; Sir William Keys (77) ex-service leader; the novelist Nancy Cato (83); Bruce Gyngell (71), pioneer of Australian television; Sir Mark Oliphant (98), the nuclear physicist; the distinguished poets Alec Hope (92) and Judith Wright (85); and the founder of Australian demography, Mick Borrie (86).

In September Australia was visited by Nelson Mandela and he was awarded two honorary degrees. The Anglican archbishop of Perth, Peter Carnley, was installed as primate in a ceremony on April 30 which several conservative Sydney bishops did not attend.

ii. PAPUA NEW GUINEA

CAPITAL: Port Moresby   AREA: 463,000 sq km   POPULATION: 4,800,000
OFFICIAL LANGUAGES: Pidgin, Motu & English   POLITICAL SYSTEM: parliamentary democracy
HEAD OF STATE: Queen Elizabeth II
GOVERNOR-GENERAL: Sir Sailas Atopare
RULING PARTY: People's Democratic Movement (PDM) heads coalition
HEAD OF GOVERNMENT: Sir Mekere Morauta (PDM), Prime Minister (since July '99)
MAIN IGO MEMBERSHIPS (NON-UN): APEC, CP, PC, PIF, ACP, CWTH, NAM
CURRENCY: kina (end-'00 £1=K4.53, US$1=K3.04)
GNP PER CAPITA: US$800, US$2,263 at PPP ('99)

THE year 2000 was one of continuing economic difficulty, political instability and regional disorder for Papua New Guinea (PNG). As in the past, however, the country showed every sign of muddling on as a functioning (though deeply flawed) parliamentary democracy.

Successive Cabinet shuffles and shifting coalitions punctuated the year as Prime Minister Mekere Morauta struggled to remain in office at the head of a viable administration. The problem of government stability in an environment of insufficiently embedded party loyalties and rapidly changing alliances had dogged PNG politics since independence in 1975. Successive plans to address the problem through legislation and constitutional amendment had either foundered or been circumvented when implemented. In early March the discovery of a plot from within the government itself to precipitate a vote of no-confidence and effect a change of leadership led to a series of ministerial sackings and demotions. Another reshuffle followed in mid-April when the governing coalition was widened to pre-empt further assaults. In August Morauta attempted to tackle one of the roots of this instability by proposing legal restrictions on the ability of a member of parliament elected under one party banner to defect to another during the course of a parliament. Typically, this threat itself triggered another revolt within the ruling coalition which sabotaged the new legislation and led, at the beginning of November, to another major Cabinet overhaul. Finally, in December, more ministers were dismissed, including PNG's first Prime Minister, Sir Michael Somare, who lost his posts as Foreign Minister and Minister with responsibility for Bougainville.

Prior to his departure Somare had overseen some positive developments in the Bougainville saga. March saw the so-called "Loloata Understanding" between the central government and the president of the Bougainville People's Congress, Joseph Kabui, by which a new provincial administration would assume an ever-greater degree of autonomy from the government in Port Moresby prior to holding a referendum on the future of Bougainville. This was to include an option for independence. Apparent second thoughts on this last issue by the central government threw the entire peace process into doubt, and real fears grew of a return to violence on the part of the separatist Bougainville Revolutionary Army. At the end of November, however, it appeared that there was now a firm commitment to the referendum and, despite the new uncertainty injected into the situation by Somare's dismissal, the year ended with the prospects for a long-term settlement to the 12-year-old Bougainville crisis perhaps better than ever before.

Despite its periodic descent into political pantomime, Morauta's government continued to implement the structural adjustments to the economy which had been established as conditions for IMF support. The process of privatisation of state enterprises continued, and public spending—historically high by Third World standards—was reduced, with real social consequences. In November the 2001 budget was announced. In line with long-term adjustment plans this allowed for balanced income-expenditure of 4 billion kina (US$12 billion) and a modest growth rate of 3.1 per cent. Prospects for the successful realisation of these targets were, however, compromised by the announcement that the huge Ok Tedi gold and copper mine in Western Province—which had hitherto provided about 10 per cent of the country's GNP—was to be closed on environmental grounds.

2. NEW ZEALAND—PACIFIC ISLAND STATES

i. NEW ZEALAND

CAPITAL: Wellington   AREA: 271,000 sq km   POPULATION: 4,000,000
OFFICIAL LANGUAGE: English   POLITICAL SYSTEM: parliamentary democracy
HEAD OF STATE: Queen Elizabeth II
GOVERNOR-GENERAL: Dame Silvia Cartwright
RULING PARTIES: New Zealand Labour Party (NZLP) & Alliance
HEAD OF GOVERNMENT: Helen Clark, Prime Minister (since Dec '99)
MAIN IGO MEMBERSHIPS (NON-UN): ANZUS (suspended), APEC, PC, PIF, CP, OECD, CWTH
CURRENCY: New Zealand dollar (end-'00 £1=NZ$3.38, US$1=NZ2.26)
GNP PER CAPITA: US$13,780, US$16,566 at PPP ('99)

NEW Zealand's Labour-Alliance coalition government experienced an extended period of popularity following its November 1999 election victory. The government moved quickly to implement its core election promises. The country's elderly received a substantial increase in their pensions and university students were spared interest on their loans whilst still studying. New Zealand's accident insurance program was renationalised, the minimum wage was raised, and tax rates on higher incomes were increased. The government also enacted a new labour law giving trade unions more power in wage negotiations.

Labour's moves in these areas drew criticism from business groups. A fall in the value of the currency—below US$0.40 at one point—also contributed to a decline in business confidence. Other problems also emerged. The Minister of Maori Affairs, Dover Samuels, was dismissed in June following allegations about his private life that were ultimately unproven. Recriminations between Samuels and Prime Minister Helen Clark kept him out of the Cabinet, however, with Clark staking her job on her personal choice of his replacement. Another minister, Ruth Dyson, resigned her position in November after she failed a drink-driving test whilst returning home one evening from her Cabinet office.

Race relations proved another sensitive area. Protest threats at Waitangi led Clark to boycott the annual Treaty of Waitangi commemorations held in February, and she later announced that she would not be attending the following year either. Her criticism of alleged racism in the New Zealand police force in the wake of a shooting incident in May proved controversial, and the officer involved in the affair was cleared by investigators in August. The government's "closing the gaps" policies, intended to reduce economic and social disparities amongst New Zealand's indigenous Maori inhabitants, was modified to benefit all low-income groups after claims that it was racially divisive. Plans to write commitments to the Treaty of Waitangi into economic and social legislation were also criticised. A new law restructuring the public health system, passed in December, was clarified to make it plain that those of Maori origin were not entitled to preferential access to health services. A free trade agreement with Singapore was approved in December, despite concerns over a clause that allowed the government to give more favourable treatment to Maori.

Problems with both Cabinet management and race relations were evident in October when a Filipino family was wrongfully deported in the wake of a government decision to act against visitors who had overstayed their visas. The family had to be flown back to Auckland when it was discovered that an appeal had been lodged over the deportation order. The Minister for Immigration, Lianne Dalziel, at first defended the early morning raid and then attacked her own department for allegedly misleading her about the circumstances. The amnesty itself was questioned by Australia, which expressed concerns about the ability of such migrants to move there subsequently from New Zealand (see X.1.i.).

Foreign and security policy initiatives were also a prominent feature of the government's first year in office. A reassessment of defence spending needs and priorities led to the scrapping of arrangements made by the previous government to lease 28 F-16 fighter planes from the USA. Plans to upgrade surveillance aircraft were also discontinued. Deployments of New Zealand forces on peace monitoring operations in East Timor and the Solomon Islands contributed to government decisions to purchase new equipment for the army. New Zealand also adopted a high-profile stance in the Pacific, strongly condemning the Fiji coup attempt and the dismissal of the country's elected government. Prime Minister Clark played a leading role in the Pacific Islands Forum's decision to develop procedures to deal with future regional crises, and her unwillingness to take part in meetings in Fiji until the restoration of constitutional government prevented the Forum from agreeing on the site for its next meeting in 2001.

Future relations with Australia became a renewed subject for debate, with support growing in New Zealand for the introduction of a single currency. There were also plans for merging New Zealand's sharemarket with Australia's. Each of these moves was seen as a way of giving New Zealand's economy greater protection from external shocks. The government was also seeking to harmonise business and tax rules between the two countries.

Dame Silvia Cartwright, a High Court judge, was chosen as the country's next Governor-General, only the second woman to be appointed to the position. Her selection gave New Zealand's women a monopoly of the country's most powerful positions, including Prime Minister, Leader of the Opposition (Jenny Shipley) and Chief Justice (Dame Sian Elias).

Ties with the UK were further loosened with New Zealand abolishing the award of royal honours carrying titles of "Sir" and "Dame" and the Prime Minister describing the country's links to the British monarchy as "absurd". Evidence of further social change in New Zealand was to be found in a scheduled review of the legal status of cannabis, and in the introduction in September of a bill aimed at decriminalising prostitution. Parliament approved legislation in November putting property rights in same-sex relationships on the same basis as those which existed for married people. It also gave the same rights to "de facto" couples, defined as people who have lived together for three years or more.

By the end of the year the government had achieved most of its key campaign pledges, and polls showed the Labour Party holding a lead over its strongest adversary, the National Party. The coalition was also managing to demonstrate that New Zealand's proportional representation electoral system, used only for the second time in 1999, could produce stable government. This eased demands for further change at a time when a special parliamentary committee had been conducting a review of the system. Cabinet rules had been modified to relax the requirements for collective responsibility, making the rules consistent with coalition arrangements that gave the government's smaller partner, the Alliance, freedom to dissent from government policy. As a result, a more complex multi-party policy-making process had begun to emerge in Parliament. For instance, the new health legislation was passed only after Clark agreed to accept changes sought by the Green Party, the National Party, and, subsequently, the Alliance, which had earlier given the bill its approval.

The coalition held office through support from the Greens despite failure to negotiate a formal written agreement. However, both the Alliance and the Greens opposed the free trade agreement with Singapore and the measure could only be passed after the National Party gave it its support. Two Green MPs took part in protests in Melbourne, Australia, in September outside the World Economic Forum. The Green Party had compared Labour free-trade policies, which were opening up the private sector to globalisation, to the free-market policies of the previous 1984-90 Labour government, which had allowed New Zealand-owned assets to be sold to foreign owners. However, the coalition displayed its environmental credentials by acting to protect native forests on the South Island's west coast, five years earlier than planned. As for the Alliance, it was satisfied with government moves to introduce a new state-owned "People's Bank", a move to offset overseas control over the New Zealand banking and financial sectors. It was also pleased by the establishment of an Economic Development Ministry, headed by the Alliance's leader, Deputy Prime Minister Jim Anderton.

ii. PACIFIC ISLAND STATES

Fiji
CAPITAL: Suva   AREA: 18,375 sq km   POPULATION: 802,000
OFFICIAL LANGUAGES: Fijian, Hindi & English   POLITICAL SYSTEM: republic
HEAD OF STATE: President Ratu Josefa Iloilo (since July '00)
RULING PARTY: interim government
HEAD OF GOVERNMENT: Laisenia Qarase (since July '00)
MAIN IGO MEMBERSHIPS (NON-UN): CWTH, PC, PIF, CP, ACP
CURRENCY: Fiji dollar (end-'00 £1=F$3.25, US$1=F$2.18)
GNP PER CAPITA: US$2,110, US$3,580 at PPP ('98)

Kiribati
CAPITAL: Tarawa   AREA: 1,000 sq km   POPULATION: 90,000
OFFICIAL LANGUAGES: English & Kiribati   POLITICAL SYSTEM: republic
HEAD OF STATE AND GOVERNMENT: President Teburoro Tito (since Sept '94)
MAIN IGO MEMBERSHIPS (NON-UN): CWTH, PC, PIF, ACP
CURRENCY: Australian dollar (end-'00 £1=A$2.69, US$1=A$1.8)
GNP PER CAPITA: US$1,180, US$3,480 at PPP ('98)

Marshall Islands
CAPITAL: Dalap-Uliga-Darrit   AREA: 200 sq km   POPULATION: 69,000
OFFICIAL LANGUAGES: English & Marshallese   POLITICAL SYSTEM: republic
HEAD OF STATE AND GOVERNMENT: President Kessai Note (since Jan '00)
RULING PARTY: United Democratic Party (UDP)
MAIN IGO MEMBERSHIPS (NON-UN): PC, PIF
CURRENCY: US dollar
GNP PER CAPITA: US$1,540 ('98)

Federated States of Micronesia
CAPITAL: Palikir (Pohnpei)   AREA: 701 sq km   POPULATION: 126,000
OFFICIAL LANGUAGE: English   POLITICAL SYSTEM: independent republic in free association with USA
HEAD OF STATE AND GOVERNMENT: President Leo Falcam (since May '99)
MAIN IGO MEMBERSHIPS (NON-UN): PC, PIF
CURRENCY: US dollar (end-'00 £1=US$1.49)
GNP PER CAPITA: US$1,800 ('98)

Nauru
CAPITAL: Domaneab   AREA: 21.4 sq km   POPULATION: 11,000
OFFICIAL LANGUAGES: Nauruan & English   POLITICAL SYSTEM: republic
HEAD OF STATE AND GOVERNMENT: President Bernard Dowiyogo (since April '00)
MAIN IGO MEMBERSHIPS (NON-UN): CWTH, PC, PIF
CURRENCY: Australian dollar (see above)
GNP PER CAPITA: n/a

Palau (Belau)
CAPITAL: Koror   AREA: 460 sq km   POPULATION: 19,000
OFFICIAL LANGUAGE: English   POLITICAL SYSTEM: independent republic in free association with USA
HEAD OF STATE AND GOVERNMENT: President Tommy Remengesau (since Nov '00)
MAIN IGO MEMBERSHIPS (NON-UN): PC, PIF
CURRENCY: US dollar (end-'00 £1=US$1.49)
GNP PER CAPITA: n/a

Samoa

CAPITAL: Apia   AREA: 2,842 sq km   POPULATION: 170,000
OFFICIAL LANGUAGES: English & Samoan   POLITICAL SYSTEM: constitutional monarchy
HEAD OF STATE: Susuga Malietoa Tanumafili II (since Jan '62)
RULING PARTY: Human Rights Protection Party
HEAD OF GOVERNMENT: Tuila'epa Sa'ilele Malielegaoi, Prime Minister (since Nov '98)
MAIN IGO MEMBERSHIPS (NON-UN): CWTH, PC, PIF, ACP
CURRENCY: tala (end-'00 £1=T4.99 US$1=T3.34)
GNP PER CAPITA: US$1,020, US$3,440 at PPP ('98)

Solomon Islands

CAPITAL: Honiara   AREA: 28,000 sq km   POPULATION: 460,000
OFFICIAL LANGUAGE: English   POLITICAL SYSTEM: parliamentary democracy
HEAD OF STATE: Queen Elizabeth II
GOVERNOR-GENERAL: Sir John Ini Lapli
RULING PARTIES: Liberal Party (LP) heads Alliance for Change coalition;
    People's Progressive Party holds premiership
HEAD OF GOVERNMENT: Manasseh Sogavare, Prime Minister (since June '00)
MAIN IGO MEMBERSHIPS (NON-UN): CWTH, PC, PIF, ACP
CURRENCY: Solomon Island dollar (end-'00 £1=SI$7.71, US$1=SI$5.16)
GNP PER CAPITA: US$750, US$2,080 at PPP ('98)

Tonga

CAPITAL: Nuku'alofa   AREA: 750 sq km   POPULATION: 99,000
OFFICIAL LANGUAGES: Tongan & English   POLITICAL SYSTEM: monarchy
HEAD OF STATE: King Taufa'ahua Tupou IV (since Dec '65)
HEAD OF GOVERNMENT: 'Ulakalala Lavaka Ata, Prime Minister
MAIN IGO MEMBERSHIPS (NON-UN): CWTH, PC, PIF, ACP
CURRENCY: pa'anga (end-'00 £1=P2.69, US$1=P1.8)
GNP PER CAPITA: US$1,690, US$3,860 at PPP ('98)

Tuvalu

CAPITAL: Fongafle   AREA: 26 sq km   POPULATION: 11,000
OFFICIAL LANGUAGE: English   POLITICAL SYSTEM: constitutional monarchy
HEAD OF STATE: Queen Elizabeth II
GOVERNOR-GENERAL: Tomasi Puapua
HEAD OF GOVERNMENT: vacant
MAIN IGO MEMBERSHIPS (NON-UN): PC, PIF, ACP
CURRENCY: Australian dollar (end-'00 £1=A$2.69, US$1=A$1.8)
GNP PER CAPITA: n/a

Vanuatu

CAPITAL: Port Vila   AREA: 12,000 sq km   POPULATION: 181,600
OFFICIAL LANGUAGES: English, French & Bislama   POLITICAL SYSTEM: republic
HEAD OF STATE: President John Bani (since March '99)
RULING PARTY: Melanesian Progressive Party (MPP) heads coalition
HEAD OF GOVERNMENT: Barak Sope (MPP), Prime Minister (since Nov '99)
MAIN IGO MEMBERSHIPS (NON-UN): CWTH, PC, PIF, ACP, Francophonie
CURRENCY: vatu (end-'00 £1=V213.63, US$1=V143.01)
GNP PER CAPITA: US$1,270, US$3,160 at PPP ('98)

VIOLENCE and ethnic tensions affected several Pacific Island countries during the year. In FIJI, an attempted coup was begun on May 19, one year after the election of Mahendra Chaudhry as the country's first Prime Minister of Indian ancestry.

The armed take-over of Parliament by a Suva businessman, George Speight, lasted for nearly two months. The action brought about the removal from office of both Prime Minister Chaudhry and the President, Ratu Sir Kamisese Mara. Speight, who claimed that he was acting to protect indigenous Fijian rights, was eventually taken prisoner by the Fiji military, which held him with other coup participants on an island not far from the capital. The military's declaration of martial law paved the way for the discarding of Fiji's constitution and the appointment of an interim government with Josefa Iloilo as President and Laisenia Qarase as Prime Minister. Subsequently Chaudhry travelled to other countries seeking support for the reinstatement of his government.

The take-over of Parliament had led military forces to surround the parliamentary complex in an effort to isolate the rebel group. The group's hostages, the members of the Chaudhry government, were released in July as part of a deal giving amnesty to Speight and his men. Later that month the military stormed the rebel headquarters at a school on the outskirts of Suva, capturing the leaders of the insurrection. One rebel was killed in the assault and 32 were wounded. The action was taken following allegations of threats against the new President's life just prior to his scheduled appointment of a new government. Speight, two of his advisers, and his bodyguard were arrested by troops at a checkpoint near the rebel headquarters. They were charged with carrying arms in violation of the amnesty agreement.

Other incidents of hostage-taking occurred around Fiji and there were acts of intimidation directed against Indo-Fijians, some of whom fled their homes. In November 39 members of an elite army unit were charged with mutiny over a failed uprising at an army barracks in Suva. The rebels stormed an armoury and took over the barracks compound, but lost control of it six hours later after a gun battle with troops loyal to Fiji's military commander. Eight people were killed in the fighting.

The interim government in November announced the appointment of a commission to draft a new constitution. The new document was scheduled to be completed in 2000 following public hearings that were, at least initially, boycotted by Fiji's Indian communities. The government announced that it was planning to hold fresh elections in March 2002. In November Fiji's High Court ruled (with little immediate effect) that the new government was illegal and unconstitutional, and that the Chaudhry administration and the constitution should both be reinstated. In the aftermath of the ruling, Ratu Mara announced his resignation, backdating it to May 29, the day that martial law had been declared. The military-appointed government announced its intention to appeal against the decision to the Court of Appeal and also defended its abrogation of the 1997 constitution, saying that it had done so to save the lives of those held hostage and to restore law and order. A board of inquiry was also set up to investigate the causes of the Fiji rebellion and why, in particular, the security forces had allowed the coup to take place.

Less than three weeks after the beginning of the events in Fiji, with Chaudhry and his Cabinet still being held hostage, a second Pacific coup took place, this time in the SOLOMON ISLANDS. The coup was part of a struggle between the Isatabu Freedom Movement, which represented the indigenous residents of Guadalcanal, site of the capital, Honiara, and the Malaita Eagle Force, which represented migrants from Malaita, who had come to Guadalcanal for work. The Prime Minister, Bartholomew Ulufa'alu, was captured and placed under house arrest after members of the Malaita Eagle Force and paramilitary police invaded his home, forcing security officers to flee. He was later released following his agreement to resign, which permitted the election of a new Prime Minister and the formation of a new government. He was succeeded by Manasseh Sogavare, a former leader of the opposition, who was elected by a parliamentary vote of 23-21 at a meeting that some legislators were unable to attend.

A ceasefire agreement was signed in Honiara in August. Subsequently an accord was signed in October in Townsville, Australia, calling for a surrender of arms and ammunition by mid-December. About 70 people were killed in the fighting, whilst some 20,000 people were believed to have lost their homes. A New Zealand and Australian international peace monitoring team was deployed to supervise the hand-over of weapons and an amnesty was to be given to members of the two militias. The agreement also provided for the appointment by the government of a commission of inquiry to investigate the acquisition of land on Guadalcanal by non-Guadalcanal residents.

In the aftermath, the Solomon Islands government announced a plan to amend the country's constitution to permit the establishment of state governments. The move was an attempt to prevent some of the provinces from seceding altogether, leading to the break-up of the country. Both Malaita and Guadalcanal provinces were expected to be given considerably more autonomy, whether by devolution or by constitutional amendment.

Ethnic conflict was also critical in WEST PAPUA, on the western half of New Guinea island, where Melanesians had become more assertive in challenging continuing Indonesian rule. Two men were shot by Indonesian police in July while attempting to hoist the Papuans' Morning Star flag. The flag had been outlawed, but an agreement with Indonesia provided that it could be raised if it were not placed higher than the Indonesian national flag. In December, however, several more people were killed by Indonesian solders in separate flag-raising incidents. The Indonesian President, Abdurrahman Wahid, had been seeking to follow a more lenient approach, moving to change the province's name from Irian Jaya and permitting display of the separatist banner. However, other members of his government, including the military, took a more hard-line approach, arresting independence leaders with whom Wahid had opened a dialogue. More than 50 people, including Indonesian soldiers, were killed or wounded during the year in flag-related clashes. The intensification of the independence struggle in West Papua followed Indonesia's withdrawal from East Timor as well as violence involving separatist groups in other parts of the country (see IX.1.vi.).

Political changes in accord with established constitutional processes occurred in several Pacific Island states. In PALAU, Tommy Remengesau, the country's youngest Vice President when he was elected at age 36 in 1992, became its new

President as a result of November elections. Sandra Pierantozzi, in 1996 Palau's first woman Senator, became the country's first female Vice President.

In the MARSHALL ISLANDS, Kessai H. Note was elected President in January, the first time that a commoner rather than a high chief had been elected to the position. Note, a former Speaker of the Nitijela (the legislature) and a legislator since independence in 1979, was a member of the United Democratic Party, which had taken control of the Nitijela following the November 1999 elections.

Meanwhile, talks continued between the USA and both the Marshall Islands and the FEDERATED STATES OF MICRONESIA on the renewal of their separate Compact of Free Association agreements. Some members of the US Congress had said that further large-scale assistance required government reforms and changes in the use to which US aid was put. There were also moves in Congress to extend federal immigration laws to the NORTHERN MARIANAS, restricting some of the powers of the Commonwealth government.

In TONGA, the King appointed his youngest son, Prince 'Ulukalala Lavaka Ata, who had been serving as Minister of Foreign Affairs and Defence, as Prime Minister in January. He became only the country's 13th Prime Minister since the enactment of the Tongan constitution in 1876.

In other Pacific Islands there was electoral continuity rather than change. In the US overseas territory of AMERICAN SAMOA, voters gave Governor Tauese Sunia a second term in November. Although defeated, Rosalia Tisa Faamuli became the territory's first-ever female candidate for governor. In GUAM Governor Carl Gutierrez survived a recall resolution by an 8-7 vote—two votes short of the total needed to place the question on the November general election ballot—when he reached an agreement with five Republican legislators two hours prior to a vote on the steps which needed to be taken to improve relations between the executive and legislative branches of the island's government.

NAURU'S April general election was followed by the re-election in Parliament of incumbent Rene Harris as President. Nauru and VANUATU were the first countries to express support for the West Papua independence movement, raising the issue at the UN Millennium Summit in September and at the Pacific Islands Forum (PIF) meeting in October in Tarawa, Kiribati.

Moves by Pacific Island states to participate more widely in international affairs were continued as TUVALU became the 189th member of the United Nations. Its application was made possible in part by a business arrangement involving the internet, with the country earning US$50 million from an agreement to sell rights for 10 years to its ".tv" domain name. A portion of the receipts was to go towards payment of Tuvalu's annual UN subscriptions. Tuvalu also upgraded its membership of the Commonwealth, becoming a full member of the 54-nation group in September.

However, Tuvalu suffered its worst tragedy since gaining its independence in 1978 in March when 18 girls and a supervisor died in a fire at a girls' dormitory at a secondary school. In December Prime Minister Ionatana Ionatana died suddenly, being succeeded by Lagitupa Tuilimu, who took office as acting Prime Minister.

In SAMOA, two Cabinet ministers, Leafa Vitale and Toi Aukoso, were tried for their role in the killing of the Minister of Public Works and for plotting the assassination of the Prime Minister. Found guilty of planning the minister's murder, they were sentenced in April to death by hanging, although no executions had been carried out by Samoa since it became independent in 1961. In January Vitale's son, Eletise Vitale, had his death sentence for the killing of Public Works Minister Luagalau Levaula Kamu commuted to life imprisonment (with eligibility for parole in 10 years).

Although parts of KIRIBATI were already being affected by rising sea levels, the country continued its development as a site for satellite launchings. In January Japan signed an agreement with the Kiribati government to build a landing strip on Christmas Island for unmanned space shuttle flights. Two months later an unsuccessful attempt was made to launch a British communications satellite from a floating platform.

A summit in Japan in April between its Prime Minister, Yoshiro Mori, and leaders from 14 Pacific Island countries, the second of its kind (the first was in 1997), focused on issues of sustainable development and on environmental dangers facing Pacific Island countries. The participants committed themselves to a "common vision on Tomorrow's Pacific", stressing economic reform, private sector development, and global environmental issues such as climate change. Japan also offered to increase its aid programme, establishing a "good will" trust fund to be used to finance development projects in the fields of environment, energy and tourism.

There were moves by the USA to protect at least some Pacific environments. In December President Clinton announced a new reserve to safeguard over 80 million acres of fragile coral reefs and endangered wildlife. The reserve, extending 1,200 miles north-west of Hawaii, was the largest protected area ever created in the USA and included 70 percent of the country's reefs. A month earlier an organisation known as the Nature Conservancy had completed its purchase of Palmyra, an uninhabited island located about 1,000 miles south of Honolulu, Hawaii. The Conservancy planned to develop an eco-system management plan on the island, a US territory that was the home of various species of fish and a site for migratory birds.

XI INTERNATIONAL ORGANISATIONS

1. UNITED NATIONS AND ITS AGENCIES

DATE OF FOUNDATION: 1945 HEADQUARTERS: New York, USA
OBJECTIVES: To promote international peace, security and co-operation on the basis of the equality of member-states, the right of self-determination of peoples and respect for human rights
MEMBERSHIP (END-'00): 189 sovereign states; those not in membership of the UN itself at end-2000 were the Holy See (Vatican), Switzerland and Taiwan (Republic of China), although all except Taiwan were members of one or more UN specialised agency
SECRETARY GENERAL: Kofi Annan (Ghana)

THE highlight of the United Nations' year was the Millennium Summit, but there were also important institutional developments. The Security Council devoted the month of January to African issues. It declared that the HIV/AIDS crisis and trafficking in diamonds were threats to peace in Africa.. There was a determined drive to improve the targeting and enforcement of sanctions and to enhance peacekeeping. The Council established a new arms embargo, created a new peacekeeping force, despatched visiting missions and created working groups on sanctions, peacekeeping and the statutes of the international tribunals. Members of the Council also engaged in debate with leading members of the US Senate committee on foreign relations in an attempt to improve the UN's relations with the USA. The General Assembly adopted new assessment scales for the regular budget and for peacekeeping, and an important Convention against Trans-national Organised Crime.

MILLENNIUM SUMMIT. The Millennium Summit held in New York on September 6-8 attracted the largest ever gathering of statesmen: 100 heads of state (99 member states and the President of Switzerland), 47 heads of government, 3 Crown Princes, and numerous other dignitaries. It was co-chaired by President Sam Nujoma of Namibia, and President Tarja Halonen of Finland. There was a general debate in which the speakers were restricted to five-minute speeches. A declaration was adopted which set goals and commitments for the international community in the early part of the 21st century. It covered the following themes: peace, security and disarmament; poverty-eradication and development; protecting the common environment; human rights, democracy and good governance; protecting the vulnerable; Africa; and strengthening the UN. (The 55th General Assembly later discussed how this declaration might be implemented.)

The Security Council held a summit meeting on the same occasion, and the Bureau of the Economic and Social Council met for the first time at the level of heads of state. Four interactive roundtables took place. States were encouraged to sign or deposit instruments of ratification for multilateral treaties that they might have not yet joined, especially 25 core treaties that represented key UN objectives.

ELECTIONS. Harri Holkeri, the former Prime Minister of Finland, was elected President of the 55th Session of the General Assembly. Ruud Lubbers of the Netherlands was appointed the new High Commissioner for Refugees for three years beginning on January 1, 2001. He replaced Sadako Ogata of Japan, who retired at the end of 2000.

Colombia, Ireland, Mauritius, Norway and Singapore were selected by the General Assembly as non-permanent members of the Security Council for two-year terms beginning on January 1, 2001. Colombia and Singapore were supported by their regional groupings—the Latin American and Caribbean States and the African and Asian States—and were unopposed. But four rounds of voting were needed for Mauritius to defeat the Sudan for the third African and Asian seat. Although Sudan was the official candidate of the OAU, the USA lobbied hard against it because of its alleged support for terrorism. Ireland won on the first ballot but three rounds were required for Norway to defeat Italy to take the second Western Europe and Others group seat. The elected states replaced Argentina, Canada, Malaysia, Namibia and the Netherlands. They were to join Bangladesh, Jamaica, Mali, Tunisia and the Ukraine, elected in October 1999 (see AR 1999, p. 393) as non-permanent members of the Council.

On February 28 the Security Council adopted an initiative that it had first used informally in December 1999. It decided that it would in future invite the newly elected non-permanent members to familiarise themselves with the working practices of the Council by attending informal consultations of Council members for the month preceding their appointment.

NEW MEMBERSHIP. The General Assembly, on September 5 and November 1 respectively, endorsed the recommendations of the Security Council that Tuvalu (on which China abstained because Tuvalu had established diplomatic relations with Taiwan) and the Federal Republic of Yugoslavia be admitted as members of the UN. The General Assembly had stated in September 1992 that the Federal Republic of Yugoslavia (comprising Serbia and Montenegro) could not continue automatically to use the membership of the former Socialist Federal Republic of Yugoslavia in the General Assembly.

SPECIAL SESSIONS. The General Assembly held a special session in New York on June 5-9 on "Women 2000: Gender Equality, Development and Peace for the 21st Century". The Assembly reviewed the extent to which the 12 critical areas of the Beijing Platform had been realised. It adopted two resolutions and two texts—one a political declaration, the other on further actions and initiatives to implement the Beijing Declaration and Platform for Action. A second special session was held in Geneva on June 26-30 on Social Development.

The General Assembly on October 18 resumed for the sixth time its adjourned 10th emergency special session on illegal Israeli actions in occupied East Jerusalem and the rest of occupied Palestinian territory. (Three such meetings had been held in 1997, one in 1998 and another in 1999.) It adopted a resolution on October 20 by a recorded vote of 92 in favour, six against and

46 abstentions that demanded an end to the violence, especially the excessive use of force by Israeli forces against Palestinian citizens; urged all parties to implement the Sharm El-Sheikh Accord; insisted that Israel abide scrupulously by its legal obligations and its responsibilities under the Fourth Geneva Convention of 1949 on the Protection of Civilian Persons in Time of War in all the territories that it had occupied since 1967; and, finally, that supported the immediate creation of a mechanism of inquiry to establish all the relevant facts of the recent tragic events and to prevent a repetition. The USA had earlier abstained from voting in the Security Council on October 7 on resolution 1322, which had condemned acts of violence, and especially the excessive use of force, without specifically citing Israel.

The Commission on Human Rights convened a Special Session from October 17-19 on the situation of human rights in the occupied Palestinian territories. It decided, by a vote of 19 in favour, 16 opposed and 17 abstaining, to establish a commission to gather and compile information on violations of human rights and acts which constituted grave breaches of international humanitarian law by the Israeli occupying power. It also requested that the High Commissioner visit the occupied territories. She made such a visit, which also included stops in Israel, Egypt and Jordan, on November 8-16.

BUDGET AND FINANCE. Joseph E. Connor, the Under Secretary General for Management, told the Fifth Committee of the General Assembly that in 2000 the UN had lost ground financially. The financial health of all three components of the UN was not as good as it had been a year earlier. Cash had been reduced, unpaid assessments had risen and debt owed to member states had increased.

At the end of 2000 total cash in the regular budget and peacekeeping funds was US$1 billion—some US$100 million lower than at the end of 1999. The UN had been able to avoid a deficit in the regular budget because the USA had made a late payment that was equal to its current full year assessment. Therefore there was no need on this occasion to cross-borrow at the end the year from the cash in the peacekeeping fund to compensate for the regular budget deficit.

The total assessment for member states in 2000 had increased to US$3.4 billion. This was not the highest ever assessment figure but was close to the peak years of 1994 and 1995 and was a large increase on the 1999 total of US$2.064 billion.

Regular budget assessments were US$1.089 billion in 2000 and had remained constant. Indeed there had been no growth since 1994 and regular budget assessments levels were lower by US$100 million than they had been eight years earlier. Assessments for the international tribunals were US$166 million, which was higher than the previous year. Peacekeeping assessments in 2000 were US$2.1 billion, which was a very rapid rise from 1999. The size of these assessments had been erratic: they had been very large amounts in 1994 and 1995, then diminishing amounts each year from 1996 to 1999. The steep increase was mainly due to assessments for four large peacekeeping missions in Sierra Leone, East Timor, Kosovo and the Democratic Republic of Congo. All of these operations except for the DRC had assessments of over US$500 million.

In 2000, 141 members states had paid the regular budget assessments in full for that year and all preceding years. A further 27 states owed approximately one year or less in assessments. Only 19 states owed unpaid assessment of more than one year. The USA owed US$165 million or 74 per cent of the total unpaid assessments. Brazil owed US$22 million or 10 per cent of the total, and Argentina owed US$12 million or 5 per cent of the total. A further 43 states between them owed US$23 million or 11 per cent of the total. Arrears for the regular budget had been reduced by almost one half, from US$417 million in 1998 to US$222 million in 2000, a reduction of US$195 million.

For the first time ever, money had to be cross-borrowed to finance the UN's tribunals. Connor was concerned that this might be a developing problem. A total of 106 states had unpaid tribunal assessments at the end of 2000 but three member states—the USA, the Russian Federation and France— accounted for the largest amounts, each owing about US$12 million, which was approximately 25 per cent each of the uncollected total. Peacekeeping arrears were US$1.989 billion. There was real concern that the amount due and unpaid was rising rapidly. The USA and Japan had markedly increased their debt by the end of 2000. Fortunately several other states, and principally the Russian Federation, had made significant efforts to reduce their long outstanding debt.

At the end of 2000 the total amount of unpaid contributions was increasing. Three member states owed 89 per cent of outstanding regular budget arrears. Five member states owed 89 per cent of outstanding assessments for the international tribunals. Six member states owed 91 per cent of the outstanding peacekeeping assessments.

At the beginning of 2000 the UN had owed US$800 million to states that had contributed to peacekeeping operations. Most of that amount was for contingent-owned equipment and a smaller amount was owed for troop costs. But at the end of 2000 the debt had risen to US$917 million. During the year payments were completed to member states for 1999 costs and arrears—US$91 million and US$71 million respectively.

In 2000, however, member states peacekeeping costs were US$491 million, which greatly exceeded the estimate of US$365 million. Payments of US$165 million were made to member states. But no arrears collections were received during 2000 and, therefore, no reduction in the debt owed to members could be made. For the first time in several years the Secretary-General had been unable to pay fully the peacekeeping costs that states had incurred during 2000.

NEW ASSESSMENT SCALES. On December 23 the US delegation achieved a central feature of the Helms-Biden reform package. The General Assembly adopted new scales of assessment for 2001-03 by which the US assessment—which was the largest—was reduced from 25 per cent to 22 per cent. The USA had claimed that the 2000 scale was based on economic data that was as much as 10 years old; that the use of such data distorted the capacity of member states to pay, with the result that some states paid too much and others too little; that as a result of increasing discounts over many years many states were not being assessed according to their true capacity to pay; and that the present scale placed too much responsibility for United Nations finances in too few hands.

Negotiations, however, proved very difficult. The USA had to secure agreement amongst the member states that some would accept increases to compensate for the USA's reduction whilst ensuring that the ceiling decrease did not affect the poorer states which did not have the means to pay more. Moreover, many members found it an anathema that the USA, a very prosperous state, was seeking a reduction; others resisted what they saw as a US diktat and sought to defeat it. Agreement was only secured when the USA offered to compensate, for one year only, those states that now had higher assessments than had been anticipated when their annual budgets had been drawn up. The US$34 million required would come not from the US tax-payer but from US billionaire Ted Turner. After receiving a briefing from Richard Holbrooke—the US Permanent Representative—he said that if US$34 million would secure an agreement then he would contribute this money to ease states through the transition. It was also agreed to keep the new methodology for calculating assessments in place for six years to avoid a wasteful and protracted debate over the issue in 2003.

The USA also secured reform of the peacekeeping scales of assessment, which were another element in the Helms-Biden legislation, although it did not obtain the ceiling of 25 per cent that it sought. These scales would become effective in July 2001. The current peacekeeping scales had been adopted in October 1973, as an ad hoc compromise, when the Security Council had created the second United Nations Emergency Force. It consisted of four bands of payment: in Group A the Permanent Members peacekeeping costs were apportioned in accordance with the scale of assessment established for the regular budget, plus a premium to offset the discounts given to other members which took into account their special responsibilities for maintaining peace and security; in Group B, in which there were 25 states, payments for peacekeeping were at the rate of the regular budget contributions; in Group C, states' peacekeeping costs were reduced by 80 per cent compared to the regular budget assessment; and in Group D, states received a discount of 90 per cent.

The USA argued that 98 per cent of peacekeeping costs were borne by 30 members, with the other 159 collectively paying just 2 per cent; that the top five contributors paid more than 75 per cent of the expenses; that the global economic environment had changed drastically since 1973 and around 20 states with above average per capita incomes were receiving 80 per cent discounts; and that in the absence of any established criteria the assignment of peacekeeping discounts to UN members was totally arbitrary and frequently based upon anecdotal evidence.

The new scales had potentially 10 levels of assessment based upon a state's per capita income. The permanent members would continue to pay a premium; certain states would continue to pay at the rate of their regular budget assessments; and the least developed states would continue to receive 90 per cent. In between there were seven new levels, which offered discounts ranging from 7.5 per cent to 80 per cent. The scales would be updated every three years, with states moving between them depending upon their economic circumstances. In July 2001, when the new scales were to become effective, the US assessment would be reduced to 27.58 per cent of the total, saving over 100 million dollars. The US rate would continue to decline progressively and was expected to reach the desired 25 per cent in either 2006 or 2007.

SECURITY COUNCIL PROCEEDINGS. The Security Council met on September 7 for only the second time at the level of heads of state and government. Nine Presidents, five Prime Ministers and one Foreign Minister discussed how to strengthen the ability of the Council to address challenges to peace and security. The Council declared that it would enhance the UN's effectiveness in conflict prevention; that it would give equal priority to the maintenance of peace in all regions whilst giving special attention to Africa; that it would strengthen the UN's peacekeeping capacity; that illegal flows of small arms into conflict areas had to be prevented; that resolute action was required to address illegal exploitation and trafficking of high value commodities which contributed to the heightening or continuation of conflict; and that it would strengthen co-operation and communication between the UN and regional and sub-regional organisations.

In 2000 the Security Council revived the practice of special visiting missions—a practice that, apart from one mission to Indonesia and East Timor in 1999, had been largely dormant since 1995. Members of the Council visited Kosovo (April 27-29), the Democratic Republic of Congo (May 4-8), Eritrea and Ethiopia (May 9-10), Sierra Leone (October 7-14), and East Timor and Indonesia (November 9-17). The Security Council debated the report of each mission and then approved either a resolution or a presidential statement.

The Council held open meetings on Angola, Rwanda, Burundi, Somalia, Central African Republic, Guinea-Bissau, Israel/Lebanon, Israel/Syria, Bosnia and Hercegovina, Iraq, Afghanistan, Western Sahara, Georgia, Tajikistan, Cyprus, Solomon Islands and Papua New Guinea. Meetings were also held on the important issues of the International Criminal Tribunals, conflict prevention, disarmament, demobilisation and reintegration of ex-combatants, exit strategies for peacekeeping operations, humanitarian aspects of issues before the Council, violence against humanitarian personnel, protection of civilians in conflict, terrorism, and United Nation sanctions. There were special debates on: children and armed conflicts, women and peace and security, and HIV/AIDS and international peacekeeping.

PEACEKEEPING MISSIONS. The Security Council withdrew the United Nations Mission in the Central African Republic (MINURCA) on February 15 and the United Nations Mission of Observers in Tajikistan (UNMOT) on May 15, when their mandates expired. The Council approved the Secretary-General's intention to replace both missions with United Nations Peace-building Support Offices.

The Council authorised the United Nations Mission in Ethiopia and Eritrea (UNMEE) in two stages. On July 31 the Council adopted resolution 1312(2000), which approved the deployment of 100 military observers to Ethiopia and Eritrea—to prepare for the subsequent peacekeeping force. On September 15 the

Council in resolution 1320 authorised the deployment of up to 4,200 troops, including 220 military observers. The mandate was to monitor the cessation of hostilities between the two states, to assist in ensuring the observance of the security commitments made by the parties, to monitor and verify the redeployment of Ethiopian and Eritrean troops and to monitor their position once deployed, and to oversee the 25 km temporary security zone.

The UN adopted six important developments in peacekeeping. First in February it appointed child protection advisers to the peacekeeping operations in Sierra Leone and the Democratic Republic of Congo. In the same month the Council extended the mandate of the peacekeeping force in Sierra Leone to allow it to use force to ensure the freedom of movement of its personnel and to provide protection to civilians in its areas of deployment under imminent threat of physical violence. In April the Security Council discussed its role in the UN's failure to prevent the 1994 genocide in Rwanda. In May the Council endorsed the Secretary General's intention to confirm that Israel had withdrawn completely from Lebanon (see V.1. and V.2.v.) and to take steps to deal with all eventualities. In July the Council, in its first ever resolution on a health issue, urged member states to consider voluntary HIV/AIDS testing and counselling for troops to be deployed in peacekeeping and requested the Secretary General to take steps to provide training for peacekeeping personnel on the prevention of HIV/AIDS. In November the Council discussed and welcomed the Brahimi Report and adopted a wide-ranging resolution on peacekeeping. The panel on United Nations Peacekeeping Operations had been established by the Secretary General in March 2000 and issued its report on August 21. The Council had established a working group to review the report's recommendations, which included: the extensive restructuring of the Department of Peacekeeping Operations; a new information and strategic analysis unit to service all UN departments concerned with peace and security; an integrated task force at the UN headquarters to plan and support each peacekeeping mission from its inception; and more systematic use of information technology.

SANCTIONS. On May 17 the Security Council imposed, for a period of 12 months, an arms, technical assistance and training embargo on Ethiopia and Eritrea. The ban would be terminated if the Secretary General reported that a peaceful and definite settlement of the conflict had been concluded.

Sanctions against Iraq continued to be controversial. The permanent members remained divided about their efficacy, and some states indicated their displeasure by not informing the sanctions committee of their intention to send allegedly humanitarian flights to Iraq, which helped to end Iraqi aviation isolation. In March Hans von Sponeck, the humanitarian co-ordinator for Iraq, resigned citing the inadequacies of the oil for food programme. During the year, however, the Council took several steps to soften the impact of sanctions against Iraq. It decided that Iraq could spend up to US$600 million to purchase oil spare parts and equipment under the oil for food programme, twice extended the programme for 180 day periods, requested the Secretary General to provide a comprehensive report on the programme—including observations on whether Iraq had ensured the equitable distribution of medicine, health supplies, foodstuffs and materials and supplies for essential civilian needs—and, finally, the Council directed that its Iraq sanctions committee should approve lists for electrical and housing supplies to vulnerable groups in Iraq and that supplies of these items would not require committee approval.

There were also important developments in other sanctions regimes. Sanctions against Angola, Sierra Leone and Afghanistan were tightened. In the case of Angola the Expert Panel appointed in 1999 had detailed how the existing sanctions were being violated and by whom. The panel cited individuals, firms and the governments of Bulgaria, Burkina Faso, Gabon and Togo. The Security Council in April supported the great majority of the panel's suggestions for improving the sanctions. It also requested the Secretary-General to establish for six months a monitoring mechanism of five experts to conduct further investigations into sanctions violations. In July the Council imposed an embargo on Sierra Leone rough diamonds for 18 months and called upon the diamond industry to co-operate with the ban. It requested the Secretary-General to appoint a panel of experts to monitor the implementation of the ban and asked the sanctions committee to hold public hearings to assess the role of diamonds in the Sierra Leone conflict and the link between the trade in diamonds and that in arms.

In December by 13 votes in favour, and two abstentions (China and Malaysia) the Council imposed new sanctions against the Talibaan for continuing to support international terrorism. These included an arms embargo; the closing of all Talibaan offices abroad; the freezing of Osama bin Laden's assets; the closure of all offices of Ariana Afghan Airlines; a ban on flights to and from territory under Talibaan control; the halting of all illegal drug activities and a ban on the import of all precursor chemicals for narcotics production. Finally, the Secretary General was requested to appoint a committee of experts to make recommendations to the Council on how the arms embargo and the closure of terrorist training camps could be monitored, making use of any intelligence information supplied by member states to the Secretariat.

ARMS INSPECTIONS. The United Nations Monitoring, Verification and Inspection Committee (UNMOVIC) was established by Security Council resolution 1284 of December 17 1999. It had a similar mandate to its predecessor, the Special Commission (UNSCOM): to disarm Iraq of, and to prevent it from reacquiring, weapons of mass destruction and missiles with a range of more than 150 km. KofiAnnan appointed Hans Blix of Sweden to be the Commission's Executive Chairman after the Security Council was unable to agree upon the candidacy of Ambassador Rolf Ekeus. The Secretary-General after consultation with the Council also appointed 16 members to serve on the College of Commissioners, which provided advice and guidance to the Chairman. Unlike UNSCOM, the staff would be employed by the UN rather than seconded. Although UNMOVIC was unable to return to Iraq, the Chairman nonetheless prepared, and received the approval of the Security Council for, a plan for its operation.

UNITED NATIONS PEACEKEEPING MISSIONS

	Established	Present Strength	Renewal Date
UNTSO: United Nations Truce Supervision Organisation	June 1948	153 military; 110 international civilian; 115 local civilian.	
UNMOGIP: United Nations Military Observer Group in India and Pakistan	January 1949	45 military; 28 international civilian; 51 local civilian.	
UNFICYP: United Nations Peacekeeping Force in Cyprus	March 1964	1,215 military; 34 civilian police; 43 international civilian; 145 local civilian.	June 15, 2001
UNDOF: United Nations Disengagement Observer Force	June 1974	1,040 military; 35 international civilian; 96 local civilian.	May 31, 2001
UNFIL: United Nations Interim force in Lebanon	March 1978	5,744 military; 140 international civilian; 344 local civilian.	January 31, 2001
UNIKOM: United Nations Iraq - Kuwait Observation Mission	April 1991	1,104 military; 55 international civilian; 159 local civilian.	Mandate is reviewed by Security Council every six months Next review April 6, 2001
MINURSO: United Nations Mission for the Referendum in Western Sahara	April 1991	231 military; 112 local civilian; 34 civilian police; 287 international civilian.	February 28, 2001
UNOMIG: United Nations Observer Mission in Georgia	August 1993	102 military; 90 international civilian; 157 local civilian.	January 31, 2001
UNMIBH: United Nations Mission in Bosnia and Hercegovina	December 1995	1,816 civilian police; 4 military; 356 international civilian; 1,633 local civilian.	June 21, 2001

UNITED NATIONS PEACEKEEPING MISSIONS *continued*

	Established	Present Strength	Renewal Date
UNMOP: United Nations Mission of Observers Prevlaka	January 1996	27 military; 3 international civilian; 4 local civilian.	January 15, 2001
UNMIK: United Nations Interim Administration in Kosovo	June 1999	4,145 civilian police; 38 military; 1,132 international civilian; 3,588 local civilian.	Established for an initial period of 12 months; to continue unless the Security Council decided otherwise.
UNAMSIL: United Nations Mission in Sierra Leone	October 1999	12,522 military; 34 civilian police; 225 international civilian; 195 local civilian.	March 31, 2001
UNTAET: United Nations Transitional Administration in East Timor	October 1999	7,877 military; 1,420 civilian police; 945 international civilian; 1,853 local civilian.	January 31, 2001
MONUC: United Nations Organisation Mission in the Democratic Republic of the Congo	December 1999	245 military observers; 207 international civilian; 117 local civilian.	June 15, 2001
UNMEE: United Nations Mission in Ethiopia and Eritrea	July 2000	Authorised strength: 4,500 military including 200 military observers. Current strength: 188 military observers; 3,302 troops; 145 international civilian; 81 local civilian.	March 15, 2001

2. DEFENCE AND ECONOMIC ORGANISATIONS

i. DEFENCE ORGANISATIONS

North Atlantic Treaty Organisation (NATO)
DATE OF FOUNDATION: 1949   HEADQUARTERS: Brussels, Belgium
OBJECTIVES: To ensure the collective security of member states
MEMBERSHIP (END-'00): Belgium, Canada, Czech Republic, Denmark, France, Germany, Greece, Hungary, Iceland, Italy, Luxembourg, Netherlands, Norway, Poland, Portugal, Spain, Turkey, United Kingdom, United States (*total* 19)
SECRETARY GENERAL: Lord (George) Robertson of Port Ellen (UK)

Partnership for Peace (PFP)
DATE OF FOUNDATION: 1994   HEADQUARTERS: Brussels, Belgium
OBJECTIVES: To provide a framework for cooperation between NATO and the former communist and neutral states of Europe and ex-Soviet Central Asia
MEMBERSHIP (END-'00): Albania, Armenia, Austria, Azerbaijan, Belarus, Bulgaria, Estonia, Finland, Georgia, Irish Republic, Kazakhstan, Kyrgyzstan, Latvia, Lithuania, Mecedonia, Malta, Moldova, Romania, Russia, Slovakia, Slovenia, Sweden, Switzerland, Turkmenistan, Ukraine, Uzbekistan (*total* 25)

Western European Union (WEU)
DATE OF FOUNDATION: 1955   HEADQUARTERS: Brussels, Belgium
OBJECTIVES: To provide a framework for defence and security cooperation between European states
MEMBERSHIP (END-'00): Belgium, France, Germany, Greece, Italy, Luxembourg, Netherlands, Portugal, Spain, United Kingdom (*total* 10)
OBSERVER MEMBERS: Austria, Denmark, Finland, Ireland, Sweden
ASSOCIATE MEMBERS: Czech Republic, Hungary, Iceland, Norway, Poland, Turkey
SECRETARY GENERAL: Javier Solana Madariaga (Spain)

DEFENCE and security organisations have commonly been defined either as "soft" security collectives committed to dialogue, transparency and confidence building, or "hard" alliances providing collective defence by combined military forces. This division has become increasingly difficult to sustain since the end of the Cold War, with both types of organisation identifying similar problems and challenges: narcotics, organised crime, degradation of the environment, human trafficking, terrorism, the proliferation of weapons of mass destruction, the spread of HIV/AIDS, and the abuse of human rights. The Asia-Pacific region and Europe contain the majority of the world's active defence and security organisations. An assessment of the most significant of these organisations demonstrates how, in 2000, the boundary between "defence" and "security" became still more blurred.

SECURITY IN ASIA AND THE PACIFIC. In the Asia-Pacific region, the seventh meeting of the Association of South-East Asian Nations (ASEAN) Regional Forum (ARF) took place in Bangkok in July, attended for the first time by a delegation from the Democratic People's Republic of Korea (North Korea). In 1994 the ARF had set itself various "soft security" and transparency objectives, which would be approached in three stages: confidence-building measures; preventive diplomacy; and dealing with conflicts. The forum produced its first Annual Security Outlook in 2000, an unedited collection of voluntary contributions from the governments and organisations participating in the forum, and attempts were made to encourage more involvement by defence and military officials. Amongst issues of concern for the ARF were the implementation of a treaty on the South-East Asia Nuclear Weapon Free Zone, the territorial integrity of Indonesia, the future of East Timor, transnational crime and piracy, and the situation in the Solomon Islands and Fiji. Relations between North Korea and the South Korea (the Republic of Korea) improved markedly during 2000, much to the satisfaction of the ARF, although the stability of the South China Sea remained of special concern. The ARF urged states involved to settle any disputes by peaceful means and observe the UN Convention on the Law of the Sea, and welcomed the attempts by ASEAN and the People's Republic of China to implement a Regional Code of Conduct in the South China Sea.

Elsewhere in the Asia-Pacific region, the Australia, New Zealand and United States (ANZUS) Pact of 1951 limped along in 2000. New Zealand's loss of interest in an alliance with the USA deprived ANZUS of some of its diplomatic strength and authority, although co-operation between Australian and New Zealand armed forces continued. The US-Australia relationship also remained strong, and was described by US Secretary of Defence William Cohen as "the anchor to our policy in the Pacific region".

In some respects the ARF modelled itself on the Organisation for Security and Co-operation in Europe (OSCE). Europe's largest security organisation involving 55 "participating states" (including Yugoslavia, readmitted in November after an eight year suspension), the OSCE continued to deploy a wide range of field missions in 2000, in south-east Europe, the Baltic Republics and Eastern Europe, the Caucasus and Central Asia. In the autumn the organisation was closely involved in organising and monitoring elections in Kosovo, Bosnia and Hercegovina and Serbia. In Kosovo, the OSCE also helped in establishing and training the Kosovo Police Service. The OSCE took steps to strengthen its relationship with the North Atlantic Treaty Organisation (NATO), the two organisations having co-operated closely in the Balkans. In November the OSCE's main decision-making body—the Permanent Council—was addressed for the first time by NATO's Secretary-General, GeorgeRobertson.

NORTH ATLANTIC TREATY ORGANISATION. Talking was something of a preoccupation for NATO in 2000, in the form of various outreach and dialogue initiatives. The Mediterranean Dialogue (involving Algeria, Egypt, Israel, Jordan, Mauritania, Morocco and Tunisia) continued, as did the South-East Europe Initiative. On a larger, and more formal scale, the Euro-Atlantic Partnership Council (EAPC) with its 46 members continued to address a wide variety of issues from arms control to the lessons learned from the Kosovo campaign. Under the political aegis of the EAPC, the Partnership for Peace (PfP) pursued a more practical agenda, including defence budgeting, military exercises and planning for civil emergencies. At NATO's Washington Summit in 1999, it had been decided to enhance PfP to enable NATO and its partners to co-operate in peacekeeping operations. The political and military requirements for such operations continued to be discussed in the Planning and Review Process. The Washington Summit had also made it clear that the "open door" enlargement policy remained, and that new candidacies would be considered at the next summit, which would be held no later than 2002. Prospective applicants for NATO membership would be invited to participate in a Membership Action Plan. Whilst the NATO-Ukraine Commission made progress in 2000, NATO's relations with Russia were somewhat cooler. Following deep disagreement over NATO's handling of the Kosovo crisis in 1999, Russia had suspended diplomatic contact with NATO. But by February, the relationship had thawed sufficiently to allow the NATO-Russia Permanent Joint Council to meet again in Florence in May. Steps were also taken to establish a NATO Information Office in Moscow. Nevertheless, at Florence, the Alliance made it known that it was "deeply concerned" over events in Chechnya (see III.3.i). NATO also continued to work on adapting the Conventional Armed Forces in Europe Treaty, and voiced concern over the high levels of treaty-limited equipment deployed by Russia in the North Caucasus.

Operationally, NATO continued to lead the Stabilisation Force (SFOR) in Bosnia-Hercegovina and the Kosovo Force (KFOR). In 2000 the situation in Bosnia-Hercegovina was generally calmer, thanks in part to the efforts of the 20,000-strong SFOR. The number of murders was reduced, whilst the number of displaced persons returning to their homes was greater than in 1999. SFOR was also closely involved in apprehending indicted war criminals. NATO remained committed to the political reconstruction of Bosnia-Hercegovina, campaigning for the full implementation of the Dayton Peace Agreement and participating in the meetings of the Peace Implementation Council. In Kosovo, NATO had set itself the goal of "a peaceful, multi-ethnic, multi-cultural and democratic Kosovo". In early spring, this goal—and indeed the whole purpose of the intervention in 1999—looked in grave doubt. Whilst there were some successes—fewer killings, over one million refugees were returned to their homes, and the Kosovo Liberation Army handed in some weapons—a multi-ethnic civil society in Kosovo seemed to have come no closer. Kosovo's 100,000 Serbs shrank back into enclaves under NATO protection, leading to starkly divided communities such as Mitrovica. Organised crime proliferated, with trafficking in drugs and people, and Kosovar Albanian extremists stepped up their operations against Serb targets. With interest dwindling in European capitals, it appeared that "Balkan fatigue" had set in, with a reluctance to continue supporting the 37,000-strong KFOR.

EUROPEAN DEFENCE AND SECURITY Together with outreach and operations, NATO was busy during the year with its relations with the European Union (EU) and its plans for a security and defence capability. At NATO's Washington summit in April 1999, a compromise had been offered, based on proposals made three years earlier in Berlin. The so-called "Berlin-plus" offer came in four parts: "assured EU access to NATO planning capabilities"; "the presumption of availability to the EU of pre-identified NATO capabilities and common assets"; "identification of a range of European command options"; and "the further adaptation of NATO's defence planning system to incorporate more comprehensively the availability of forces for EU-led operations".

XI.2.i. DEFENCE ORGANISATIONS

The EU's response to NATO's overtures—the nascent Common European Security and Defence Policy (CESDP)—began to take shape at the December 1999 Helsinki meeting of the European Council (see XI.4.). A "headline goal" was agreed, whereby the EU would develop by 2003 the capacity to co-ordinate and deploy a force of 60,000 troops, at 60 days notice to move, and sustainable for up to one year. The force would be capable of carrying out a range of tasks from non-combat peacekeeping, to humanitarian and rescue missions, to combat-capable crisis-management operations or peacemaking. Since 1992 these scenarios had been known as the "Petersberg tasks", and had been incorporated into the 1997 Amsterdam Treaty on European Union (Article 17). Whilst the planners accepted the possibility of combat, it was nevertheless not envisaged that the force would be suitable for anything more demanding militarily, least of all full-scale collective defence.

At the organisational level, following agreement at the Köln European Council in June 1999 to absorb the Western European Union by the end of 2000, the EU agreed at Helsinki to establish various new committees and staff organisations (military and civil) in Brussels. A standing Political and Security Committee (PSC), at the ambassadorial level, would have competence in all aspects of the EU's foreign, security and defence policies. A Military Committee (MC), made up of the military representatives of the national chiefs of defence, would provide advice to the PSC and direction to the European Union Military Staff (EUMS). The EUMS would carry out "early warning, situation assessment and strategic planning for Petersberg tasks, including identification of European national and multinational forces". Importantly, these new arrangements would be voluntary for EU members and would be very firmly within the orbit of the intergovernmental European Council, making little or no concessions to closer styles of EU integration. Equally importantly, the EU offered reassurance to the USA and NATO that the EU "would only launch and lead a military operation if NATO decided that it did not want to spearhead a campaign". The main proponents of the revived European defence and security project, Prime Minister Blair of the UK and President Chirac of France, appeared to share the position recorded in the Helsinki declaration, to the effect that the aim was to create "an autonomous capacity to take decisions", to launch EU operations "where NATO as a whole is not engaged", and that the plan did not "imply the creation of a European army".

In the early months of 2000, the prospects for improving and deepening the relationship between NATO and the EU, in accordance with all the initiatives launched in 1999, seemed fair. In February NATO conducted a joint crisis management exercise with the WEU. The exercise explicitly addressed a Petersberg task scenario on the imaginary island of "Kiloland" and was open to the EU as an observer. The exercise was designed to test procedures by which the WEU would get some access to NATO equipment and assets. NATO also continued to pursue its Defence Capabilities Initiative (DCI), launched in April 1999. At NATO's Florence meeting in May 2000 the DCI was described as "essential to strengthening European defence capabilities and the European pillar of NATO, so that European Allies will be able to make a stronger and more coherent contribution to NATO. It will also improve their capability to undertake EU-led operations where the Alliance as a whole is not engaged". Operationally, NATO gave temporary command of KFOR to the Eurocorps headquarters (albeit with a great deal of infrastructure support from NATO).

On March 1 the EU established various "interim" political and military bodies to serve until the PSC, MC and EUMS were fully established within the EU's Council of Ministers. At the European Council meeting in Feira in June, the plans laid down in 1999 at Köln and Helsinki were confirmed. As far as military capabilities were concerned, the EU looked forward to a "Capabilities Commitment Conference" in November, where EU members would pledge their contributions both to the main, "headline goal" and to a set of "capability goals". If the EU's military capability were to be anything like effective by 2003, and if the EU were ever to be "in a position to intervene with or without recourse to NATO assets", it would be necessary to address deficiencies in key capabilities listed in a "force catalogue" which had been drawn up with the help of NATO.

The "Capabilities Commitment Conference" took place on November 20 in Brussels. EU governments made offers amounting to 100,000 troops, 400 aircraft and 100 ships. This notional pool of manpower and equipment suggested that the "headline goal" could indeed be achieved in time. It was noted, however, that the force would need to be improved before "the most demanding Petersberg tasks are to be fully satisfied", that certain operational capabilities (such as medical and other combat services) were still lacking, and that strategic capabilities needed improvement, including strategic air and sea transport, command and control and, particularly, strategic intelligence. Agreement was also reached on an "evaluation mechanism", designed to seek increases in commitments and to ensure that they materialised when needed. The conference declaration reassured anxious Atlanticists that there would be no "unnecessary duplication" (of functions and assets already provided by NATO), that the NATO/EU Working Group on Capabilities would ensure that the organisations would develop their capabilities in a coherent and complementary fashion, and reiterated that the initiative did not "involve the establishment of a European army".

If the capabilities conference made progress, it also exposed lingering tensions and uncertainties. At the Feira European Council, the EU had invited EU candidates and non-EU European members of NATO to offer contributions to the headline goal. Turkey—a member of NATO and so far thwarted in its bid to join the EU—responded with an increased offer of 6,000 troops, thus reopening the issue of participation by non-EU NATO members. It also became apparent that other difficulties—such as the "sequencing" of authority and initiative between NATO and the EU, the question of force and operational planning, arrangements for the transition of command and control, and the availability to the EU of NATO assets—were not yet resolved.

The next European Council meeting took place in Nice on December 7-9 (see XI.4). As the meeting drew near, it seemed there were still disagreements amongst EU members—most spectacularly between the UK and France—over the character and function of the CESDP and its relation to NATO. Tension between France and Britain had, reportedly, been simmering before the meeting and flared up after a press conference on December 8, in which Chirac declared that the European initiative would have to be "independent" of NATO. For Blair and the UK government, this announcement departed from the Anglo-French position set out at Helsinki, whereby the EU would enable itself to make decisions, but would not seek autonomy in military capability, and would not seek strategic independence from NATO. Chirac's lack of finesse played into the hands of Blair's Eurosceptic critics, as did a French damage-limitation exercise which announced that "European defence cannot be subordinated to NATO". British negotiators at Nice were also dismayed by France's attempts to make the defence initiative an area for "enhanced co-operation", whereby a group of EU states could decide to move towards deeper, more integrated forms of co-operation. For the UK, one of the instigators of the revived EU defence initiative, "enhanced co-operation" in defence meant the abandonment of many of the NATO/EU compromises developed so painstakingly since Helsinki, the estrangement of the UK from the project, and yet more ammunition for Eurosceptic critics in London.

In the end, diplomatic calm was restored. The European Council endorsed the process launched at Köln and continued through Helsinki and Feira to the Capabilities Commitment Conference. The Treaty of Nice made the standard commitment to "respect the obligations of certain Member States, which see their common defence realised in [NATO]", made clear that the European security and defence initiative concerned only the Petersberg tasks, and insisted that "the objective for the European Union is to become operational quickly". Reviewing its performance in the presidency (June-December 2000), the French government noted that one of its goals had been to "affirm" the "security and defence dimension" of the new, "political Europe". The French government clearly felt that it had achieved its goal. Claiming that "the basis of a Defence Europe has been built", the French review referred to "a genuine strategic partnership between the EU and NATO in crisis management", and made clear once again that "these commitments do not signify the creation of a European army".

However, the core issue—the nature of the relationship between the EU and NATO—had not yet been resolved. Recognising that "a definitive arrangement" between the two organisations was not yet available, EU governments had effectively decided to avoid the controversy for the time being, and move ahead where they could. And if there was muddling through in Europe, there was uncertainty in Washington. The outgoing Clinton administration had spent much of the year arguing against the notorious "three Ds"—*decoupling* Europe from the USA, *discrimination* against NATO allies which were not EU members, and *duplication* of efforts and capabilities. In March Clinton himself had addressed the NATO/EU relationship, calling for NATO to be guaranteed the "right of first refusal" when missions were being considered. But by the autumn, Washington seemed unclear as to the nature of the European effort and whether it would be beneficial to NATO. During a speech to NATO defence ministers in October, US Secretary of Defence WilliamCohen declared that the US agreed with the initiative "not grudgingly, not with resignation, but with wholehearted conviction", and even acknowledged it as "a natural, even inevitable part of the process of European integration". Two months later, however, Cohen took a far more cautious line, insisting that the European initiative would have to complement and be of benefit to NATO, which would otherwise "become a relic". It was this equivocation which had led GeorgeRobertson, NATO's Secretary General, to suggest earlier in the year that the USA suffered "from a sort of schizophrenia" where European defence was concerned. The confusion also threatened to consume NATO. France took its argument for "independence" for the European force to a meeting of NATO foreign ministers in mid-December, reportedly causing the relationship between the EU and NATO to come "close to collapse", and prompting Robertson to insist that the European initiative should be "NATO-friendly".

By the end of the year, NATO appeared to have ridden the storm, for the time being. The Nice summit was widely thought in NATO to be a "useful starting point on how the EU and the alliance would work together". What was also encouraging to NATO, and particularly to the USA, was the suggestion that European NATO allies planned to increase their defence spending in 2001. If one result of the Helsinki plan was that Europeans finally began to build up their combined defence capacity, then much of the Euro-Atlantic tension over defence burden-sharing—built up over decades—would at last have begun to relax. Without a serious effort at a more equitable sharing of the Alliance's defence burden, NATO might have begun to take on the appearance and practices of other security organisations around the world; a loose organisation, and a preoccupation more with dialogue and diplomacy than with defence and the application of military force.

But burden-sharing in NATO was always more than a discussion (often a dispute) about levels of defence spending and military capabilities, with accusations of "free-riding" and "hegemony" flying back and forth across the Atlantic. Fruitful discussion would require broad agreement on the political, strategic and even moral nature of the burden, and a willingness to shoulder it. It was difficult in 2000, as it had been since 1989, to imagine NATO—the embodiment of the strategic partnership between the USA and Europe—remaining at the heart of the European security and defence debate without such a sense of shared purpose.

By way of encouraging a sense of shared purpose, what was also needed was more responsibility in the conduct of the strategic debate, with a pledge by politicians and commentators no longer to indulge in that curious EU-rococo form of discussion which wilfully substituted rhetoric for reality, deconstructing each statement and word ("independence", "autonomy", "sequencing", "army", "strategic", "capability" etc.) in the quest for hidden meaning and malevolent political intent. By the end of 2000, where European security and defence organisations were concerned, there were two strategic aspirations in evidence, with many questions being asked about them, but just one reality. One aspiration was that of the USA, seeking a fairer division of the mutual security burden with its European allies by encouraging them to spend wisely and efficiently on a low-level collective military capability. The other was that of members of the EU, having decided to give themselves limited means to project military force. The reality was that without first acquiring such means—common, after all, to both strategic aspirations—the debate about the initiative, and all attempts to answer questions on the future of Europe and the future of the Atlantic partnership, would be, quite literally, lacking in any subtance.

ii. ECONOMIC ORGANISATIONS

International Monetary Fund (IMF)
DATE OF FOUNDATION: 1945   HEADQUARTERS: Washington DC, USA
OBJECTIVES: To promote international monetary co-operation and to assist member states in establishing sound budgetary and trading policies
MEMBERSHIP (END-'00): 182 UN members plus Switzerland (*total* 183)
MANAGING DIRECTOR: Horst Köhler (Germany)

International Bank for Reconstruction and Development (IBRD/World Bank)
DATE OF FOUNDATION: 1945   HEADQUARTERS: Washington DC, USA
OBJECTIVES: To make loans on reasonable terms to developing countries with the aim of increasing their productive capacity
MEMBERSHIP (END-'00): 182 UN members plus Switzerland (*total* 183)
PRESIDENT: James D. Wolfensohn (USA)

World Trade Organisation (WTO)
DATE OF FOUNDATION: 1995 (successor to General Agreement on Tariffs and Trade, GATT)   HEADQUARTERS: Geneva, Switzerland
OBJECTIVES: To eliminate tariffs and other barriers to international trade and to facilitate international financial settlements
MEMBERSHIP (END-'00): 140 acceding parties
DIRECTOR GENERAL: Mike Moore (New Zealand)

Organisation for Economic Cooperation and Development (OECD)
DATE OF FOUNDATION: 1965   HEADQUARTERS: Paris, France
OBJECTIVES: To promote economic growth in member states and the sound development of the world economy
MEMBERSHIP (END-'00): Australia, Austria, Belgium, Canada, Czech Republic, Denmark, Finland, France, Germany, Greece, Hungary, Iceland, Ireland, Italy, Japan, South Korea, Luxembourg, Mexico, The Netherlands, New Zealand, Norway, Poland, Portugal, Slovakia, Spain, Sweden, Switzerland, Turkey, United Kingdom, United States (*total* 30)
SECRETARY GENERAL: Donald Johnston (Canada)

Organisation of the Petroleum Exporting Countries (OPEC)
DATE OF FOUNDATION: 1960   HEADQUARTERS: Vienna, Austria
OBJECTIVES: To unify and co-ordinate member states' oil policies and to safeguard their interests
MEMBERSHIP (END-'00): Algeria, Indonesia, Iran, Iraq, Kuwait, Libya, Nigeria, Qatar, Saudi Arabia, United Arab Emirates, Venezuela (*total* 11)
SECRETARY GENERAL: Ali Rodriguez Araque (Venezuela)

INTERNATIONAL MONETARY FUND. After a lengthy and surprisingly public political battle, Germany's Horst Köhler, President of the European Bank for Reconstruction and Development, was selected as the IMF's new managing director in March. (Michel Camdessus of France, who had held the post for 13 years, had announced his retirement in November 1999, effective from February 2000.) German Chancellor Gerhard Schröder had initially touted Caio Koch-Weser, State Secretary in the German Finance Ministry, for the post, which had always been held by a European under an informal reciprocal arrangement whereby the USA had been permitted to appoint the head of the World Bank. Although the EU had rallied around Koch-Weser, the USA bluntly rejected his candidacy. Subsequently, Japan announced its own candidate in what was perceived as part of an ongoing attempt to increase Asian influence in the Fund, whilst a group of developing countries proposed Stanley Fischer, a naturalised US citizen who had served in the number two post at the Fund for many years and had been named acting managing director in February. Those essentially symbolic nominations were withdrawn, however, when the US administration accepted the compromise candidacy of Köhler, who had been praised for his role as Helmut Kohl's economic "point man" during the reunification of West and East Germany and had been influential in the successful launch of the EU's Economic and Monetary Union. Despite Köhler's eventual unanimous endorsement by the 24 members of the IMF's Board of Executive Directors, many countries reportedly remained disgruntled over the process, and in July the Board established a working group to suggest a formal structure for subsequent selections. Amongst other things, critics, including Camdessus, argued that the current system failed to give developing countries an appropriate voice in selecting the Fund's leadership.

The wrangling over the managing director's post came at a particularly inopportune time for the Fund, since it was already facing an unusual amount of criticism on several fronts. For one thing, the US Congress was pushing for extensive internal reform of the IMF, charging that Fund operations were inefficient and had deviated from the original stated mission. At the same time, developing countries attacked the much-publicised debt-relief program of recent years, noting that only one country had met the stringent requirements to qualify for the assistance. Additionally, the April joint meeting of the IMF and World Bank was the focus of extensive street demonstrations and other protests by a wide array of organisations opposed to the impact of globalisation on the environment and labour standards as well as the failure of the "new economy" to assist the world's poor. Regarding the latter, the IMF's new International Monetary and Financial Committee agreed that the benefits of globalisation had not been sufficiently extended. However, Köhler argued that the solution was not to "turn back the clock" on globalisation but rather to refine the operations of international financial institutions to help to secure sustained economic growth.

The IMF and World Bank issued a joint statement in September delineating their separate purposes, Köhler agreeing that "mission creep" within the Fund had created a sometimes confusing overlap with the Bank's activities. For its part, the IMF announced that it would refocus its energies toward fulfilling its original mission of promoting global economic stability by assisting countries with fiscal, monetary, and exchange rate policies, whilst the Bank would concentrate on facilitating the "institutional, structural, and social dimensions of development". The IMF said it would retain more money for dealing with emergencies and give greater attention to the role played by financial markets in generating crises such as those experienced in the late 1990s in Asia and Russia. Collaterally, the Fund announced it would cut back on the "conditionality" attached to its lending, acknowledging it had been "heavy-handed" in recent years in insisting that governments overhaul many aspects of their national economies before becoming eligible for IMF assistance. The Fund indicated it would adopt a more "consultative" approach with recipient governments in order to accommodate domestic "political realities".

However, the Fund also announced that it would charge higher interest rates and reduce the length of certain loans in an effort to wean middle-income countries away from long-term reliance on IMF lending, keeping in mind that the role of the IMF was to "support, not supplant" private sector lending. In addition, the Fund promised greater transparency in its operations and other reforms geared toward improving efficiency, as requested by the US Congress. Consequently, late in the year the USA announced its support for an IMF/World Bank decision to "streamline" procedures for poor countries to qualify for the debt relief programme announced in 1999. In December the IMF/World Bank declared 22 countries (18 in Africa, and four in Latin America) eligible for some US$34 billion in debt relief.

WORLD BANK. "Fierce debate" was reported within the World Bank in 2000 regarding its annual World Development Report. One camp of economists reportedly argued that overall economic growth within a country should be the exclusive goal of Bank lending and that emphasis should be retained on economic liberalisation in support of the free market. A second camp demanded that greater attention be given to distribution of wealth within a country and to the sometimes negative short-term effects of liberalisation on the poor. Ravi Kanbur, the leader of the team preparing the Report, abruptly resigned in June, reportedly out of concern that pro-market orthodoxy was being reinjected into the Report and that his team's endorsement of "empowerment" of the poor was being watered down. Some observers suggested that, in retrospect, Kanbur's resignation may have been an over-reaction, since the final Report retained much of the original language. Amongst other things, the Report urged "protection" for "vulnerable" groups when a country's economic policies were addressed. It also called for additional Bank focus on combating AIDS and other diseases as well as fighting government corruption.

Of the three major targets of anti-globalisation protesters (the Bank, the IMF, and the WTO), the Bank appeared to be the most responsive to those critics in 2000. Bank President James Wolfensohn and other officials acknowledged that previous loans, many of which had supported massive infrastructure projects, had often failed to help the poor. In addition, the Bank encouraged "dialogue" with the activists and expressed the hope that its lending levels would increase substantially in upcoming years, in contrast to the IMF, where a retrenchment was underway. The Bank's approach won the approval of many charitable non-governmental organisations but, at the same time, it continued to face pressure from the US Congress and others to slim down operations, particularly in regard to lending to middle-income countries. Some critics argued that those countries had become "dependent" on routinely extended Bank lending, which could be more appropriately supplied by the private sector. It was reported that the policy differences among Bank members was contributing to a morale crisis among employees, some of whom complained of a "fuzzy" mandate. The staff issues notwithstanding, Wolfensohn was reappointed in 2000 to a second five-year term.

WORLD TRADE ORGANIZATION. Following what one reporter called its "fall from grace" at the ministerial meeting at Seattle in late 1999, the WTO spent 2000 in a period of "convalescence" or, in a less charitable characterisation, "paralysis". Little was achieved in resolving the complicated issues that had surfaced so dramatically at the 1999 session. Friction continued between developed and developing nations over the latter's demand for greater WTO influence. The economic powerhouses, most notably the EU, Japan, and the USA, still could not agree on a timetable and agenda for a proposed new round of global trade negotiations. And protests by anti-globalisation activists persisted, attacking, amongst other things, the perceived negative effect of WTO activity on labour standards and environmental protection and arguing that the poverty in many countries was being exacerbated, not ameliorated, by WTO decisions. Further complicating the image problems for the organisation, a report prepared in mid-2000 for consideration by a UN subcommission described the WTO as a "nightmare" for developing countries and urged that it be brought under UN jurisdiction.

Despite the barrage of negative publicity, some WTO proponents suggested that a degree of positive momentum had developed by the end of the year, arguing that the recent global economic slowdown might spur interest in launching the new round of trade talks in 2001. Moreover, the long-awaited accession of China to the WTO appeared imminent in view of the agreement between the EU and China on the issue in May and the USA's decision in September to normalise its bilateral trade relations with China. Russia's President Vladimir Putin also announced that WTO accession for his country within two years was a top priority for his administration. Meanwhile, WTO negotiations continued, albeit without reports of any major breakthroughs, on the controversial subjects of agriculture and trade in services such as banking, insurance, and communications.

ORGANISATION FOR ECONOMIC CO-OPERATION AND DEVELOPMENT. In June the OECD published a list of 35 countries and territories whose offshore financial operations were considered "harmful" to global economic and political affairs because they provided a haven for tax evaders and other criminals. In a related vein, the OECD also charged 15 countries and territories with having been unco-operative in efforts to curb money laundering. The OECD told the "tax havens" that they would face sanctions within a year unless they reformed their systems by, amongst other things, creating greater transparency, establishing effective communication channels between the offshore banks and financial institutions in other countries, and eliminating regulations which provided preferential treatment to foreigners. However, the highly publicised "name and shame" campaign proved controversial as the targeted countries and territories complained of being "bullied" by "rich" OECD nations, some of whose banking sectors were also highly secretive and candidates for abuse. Under the influence of organisations to which many of the havens belonged (such as the Commonwealth and the Caribbean Community and Common Market), the tone of the argument had softened by the end of the year, the OECD possibly having accepted a more "consultative" approach that might lead to a multilateral treaty on the issue.

The OECD continued to face scrutiny in 2000 of its own financial affairs, an independent audit in August confirming the need for reform of the OECD's "outdated" budget and pension systems. In other activity during the year, the organisation adopted new voluntary standards for the conduct of international corporations and warned that the recent wave of mergers in the banking and insurance sectors was presenting a problem for international regulators by creating companies "too big to fail". Slovakia was accepted as the 30th OECD member in December.

ORGANISATION OF THE PETROLEUM EXPORTING COUNTRIES. The per barrel price of oil soared past US$30 in early 2000, and in March OPEC agreed to increase production by 1.7 million barrels per day in an effort to reverse that climb. However, prices remained high, and further OPEC increases of 708,000 and 500,000 barrels per day were approved in June and September respectively in the face of heavy international concern over the negative impact of energy prices on the global economy. Amongst other things, high fuel costs prompted extensive protests across Europe on the part of truckers and other consumers in early September and convinced US President Bill Clinton to release 30 million barrels of crude oil from US reserves on September 22. A fourth OPEC production increase of 500,000 barrels a day in October (approved after the per barrel price hit a 10-year high of US$37.80 in September) finally appeared to have stemmed the tide, the per barrel price falling to US$26 in December. By that time some OPEC members had begun to express the fear that prices might soon fall out of the OPEC target range of US$25-US$28 per barrel in view of the slowdown in the US economy and concurrent decline in energy demand. Consequently, observers speculated that the next OPEC initiative would involve a quota decrease, the members of the organisation apparently having developed renewed confidence in their ability to shape the oil economy based on their revived cohesion of recent years.

The heads of state of OPEC members gathered in Caracas, Venezuela, in September for only the second OPEC summit in history. (The first was held in 1975.) On the one hand, the OPEC leaders were careful to adopt a conciliatory tone with the West in order to avoid a repeat of the tension that had developed in the 1970s. At the same time, however, the summit exhibited an inclination to expand OPEC's political influence, insisting, for example, that European countries were responsible, at least in part, for increased prices because of the high taxes they levied on energy products. Venezuelan President Hugo Chávez, considered one of the major architects of OPECs recently restored unity, also blamed inappropriate "market speculation" with having contributed to the fact that prices had remained high throughout the year despite the series of OPEC quota increases. On yet another quasi-political front, OPEC expressed concern over the implications of international negotiations to curb global warming, arguing that oil-producing countries should be compensated in some form if treaties lead to a sharp decline in the use of oil.

In November the OPEC ministers elected Alí Rodríguez Araque, the Venezuelan Energy and Mines Minister, to succeed Rilwanu Lukman of Nigeria as OPEC Secretary General, effective January 1, 2001.

3. OTHER WORLD ORGANISATIONS

i. THE COMMONWEALTH

DATE OF FOUNDATION: 1931   HEADQUARTERS: London, UK
OBJECTIVES: To maintain political, cultural and social links between (mainly English-speaking) countries of the former British Empire and others subscribing to Commonwealth democratic principles and aims
MEMBERSHIP (END-'00): Antigua & Barbuda, Australia, The Bahamas, Bangladesh, Barbados, Belize, Botswana, Brunei, Cameroon, Canada, Cyprus, Dominica, Fiji (*suspended*), The Gambia, Ghana, Grenada, Guyana, India, Jamaica, Kenya, Kiribati, Lesotho, Malawi, Malaysia, Maldives, Malta, Mauritius, Mozambique, Namibia, Nauru, New Zealand, Nigeria, Pakistan (*suspended*), Papua New Guinea, St Kitts & Nevis, St Lucia, St Vincent & the Grenadines, Samoa, Seychelles, Sierra Leone, Singapore, Solomon Islands, South Africa, Sri Lanka, Swaziland, Tanzania, Tonga, Trinidad & Tobago, Tuvalu, Uganda, United Kingdom, Vanuatu, Zambia, Zimbabwe (*total* 54)
SECRETARY GENERAL: Don McKinnon (New Zealand)

ATTEMPTS to improve the quality of democracy and human rights in Commonwealth countries suffered a number of setbacks in mid-2000. The most serious was the overthrow of the Fiji government of Mahendra Chaudhry on May 19, involving his seizure by rebel leader George Speight (see X.2.ii.). Commonwealth response was swift. The Commonwealth Ministerial Action Group (CMAG) of eight Foreign Ministers met in London on June 6 and suspended Fiji "from the Councils of the Commonwealth"—similar action to that taken against Pakistan in 1999. A CMAG mission visited Suva several days later. In New York on September 15 CMAG met the now-released Chaudhry and the new Prime Minister, Laisenia Qarase. Later, Justice Pius N. Langa of South Africa was made Commonwealth Special Envoy to Fiji to facilitate the restoration of democracy.

In the Solomon Islands, on June 5, rebels seized Prime Minister Bartholemew Ulufa'alu and he resigned. However, the legislature chose his successor and the Solomons thus avoided Commonwealth suspension. These events took place almost as soon as Don McKinnon, former New Zealand Foreign Minister, had succeeded Chief Emeka Anyaoku, as Commonwealth Secretary General on April 1, and whilst a further crisis was brewing— the conflict over land reform in Zimbabwe, which seriously damaged relations with the UK (see VII.2.iii.). McKinnon's first weeks were crowded. He flew to Fiji and met Chaudhry, then still held hostage, and later to Harare to talk to President Robert Mugabe, who agreed to a Commonwealth Group observing the upcoming parliamentary elections. Later McKinnon saw Gen. Musharraf in Islamabad, warning him that Pakistan faced further measures if the Commonwealth's 2001 deadline for a return to democratic civilian rule was not observed.

The 33-strong Observer Group to Zimbabwe was led by Gen. Abdusalami-Abubakar, the former head of state of Nigeria, who had restored civilian rule there in 1999. The group's report deplored "the level and nature of politically-motivated violence" which preceded polling and the "impediments placed in the way of enabling the electorate to freely choose their representatives". It praised, however, the meticulous vote-counting process. CMAG guidelines precluded any Commonwealth action against Zimbabwe, pending consideration of stronger rules by the High Level Review of the Commonwealth being undertaken by 10 heads of government with President Thabo Mbeki of South Africa as Chairman. The Review's findings would not be discussed until the 2001 Brisbane summit.

In 2000 the Commonwealth also sent observer groups to Sri Lanka, Zanzibar and Trinidad and Tobago. On October 29 the Zanzibar mission, led by Gaositwe Chiepe, former Foreign Minister of Botswana, condemned the conduct of polling as "in many places... a shambles". In Sierra Leone, its other major trouble spot, the Commonwealth, a Moral Guarantor of the 1999 Lomé Peace Accord, confined its activities to training public service staff and police and strengthening parliamentary and democratic infrastructures. The retraining of diplomats was also begun. Militarily, the UN and UK remained the major players in the Sierra Leone. When McKinnon addressed the Millennium Summit in New York on September 13 he urged the UN to encourage good governance by following the Commonwealth practice of suspending leaders who overthrew democratically elected governments. In New York, at the same time, a seven-member Ministerial Group formed to monitor the dispute between Guyana and Venezuela held its first meeting, and the long-standing committee of eight ministers on Belize reviewed the dispute with Guatemala, promising technical help in dealing with the problem. A CMAG success came when President Yahya Jammeh of The Gambia promised to repeal Decree 89, which prevented political parties and senior politicians from previous governments from contesting elections. The decision followed a CMAG mission to The Gambia on November 19-22. A Commonwealth review team examined the difficult relationship between the islands of Antigua and Barbuda and made recommendations in November to Prime Minister Lester B. Bird. The same month a Commonwealth Eminent Persons Group went to Papua New Guinea to review its defence and security needs.

On the economic front, persistent attempts to persuade the World Bank to give higher priority to issues affecting small states led to the first annual Small States Forum sponsored by the Commonwealth and the World Bank and chaired by Prime Minister Owen Arthur of Barbados. The venue was Prague, where the World Bank/IMF annual meetings were taking place. World Bank President James Wolfensohn said that he wanted to reverse the international impression that small states received too little attention. On the issue of international debt, pressure from Commonwealth forums over many years, led by the UK—notably at Finance Ministers Meetings (held this year in Malta on September 19-21)—began to pay off. At the end of the year a World Bank-IMF deal promised a US$23 billion cut in the debt burden of 22 countries. Eight were Commonwealth members—Cameroon, The Gambia, Guyana, Malawi, Mozambique, Tanzania, Uganda and Zambia. Commonwealth anger erupted in Malta over the Organisation for Economic Co-operation and Development (OECD) threat to "name and shame" 35 countries—more than 20 of them in the Commonwealth—if they did not streamline their tax systems to comply with OECD standards by July 2001. They said that they had a right to determine their own tax policies.

Education Ministers met in Halifax, Nova Scotia, on November 27-30, Ministers Responsible for Women's Affairs in New Delhi on April 16-19, and Youth

Ministers in Honiara, Solomon Islands on May 24-26. Amongst many NGO meetings in 2000 was the first to bring together local government leaders, ministers and mayors. The talks in London, held from September 13-14, centred on strategies for strengthening and modernising local government.

From September 1 Tuvalu became a full member of the Commonwealth, enabling it to attend future summit meetings. Hitherto, it had been designated a Special Member—the last remaining member in this category. Winston Cox, former Barbados Central Bank Governor, became Commonwealth Deputy Secretary General (Development Co-operation) on September 1, succeeding Nick Hare of Canada. Cox would be in charge of the work of the Commonwealth Fund for Technical Co-operation (CFTC). Gracia Machel of Mozambique, wife of Nelson Mandela, became Chair of the Commonwealth Foundation in succession to Donald Mills of Jamaica.

ii. FRANCOPHONE AND PORTUGUESE-SPEAKING COMMUNITIES

International Organisation of Francophonie (OIF)
DATE OF FOUNDATION: 1997   HEADQUARTERS: Paris, France
OBJECTIVES: To promote co-operation and exchange between countries wholly or partly French-speaking and to defend usage of the French language
MEMBERSHIP (END-'00): Albania, Belgium (French-speaking community), Benin, Bulgaria, Burkina Faso, Burundi, Cambodia, Cameroon, Canada, Cape Verde, Central African Republic, Chad, Comoros, Democratic Republic of Congo, Republic of Congo (Congo-Brazzaville), Cote d'Ivoire, Czech Republic, Djibouti, Dominica, Egypt, Equatorial Guinea, France, Gabon, Guinea Guinea-Bissau, Haiti, Laos, Lebanon, Lithuania, Luxembourg, Macedonia, Madagascar, Mali, Mauritania, Mauritius, Moldova, Monaco, Morocco, New Brunswick (Canada), Niger, Poland, Quebec (Canada), Romania, Rwanda, St Lucia, São Tomé & Príncipe, Senegal, Seychelles, Slovenia, Switzerland, Togo, Tunisia, Vanuatu, Vietnam (*total* 54)
SECRETARY GENERAL: Boutros Boutros-Ghali (Egypt)

Community of Portuguese-Speaking Countries (CPLP)
DATE OF FOUNDATION: 1996   HEADQUARTERS: Lisbon, Portugal
OBJECTIVES: To promote political, diplomatic, economic, social and cultural cooperation between member-states and to enhance the status of the Portuguese language
MEMBERSHIP (END-'00): Angola, Brazil, Cape Verde, Guinea-Bissau, Mozambique, Portugal, São Tomé & Príncipe (*total* 7)
OBSERVER MEMBER: East Timor
EXECUTIVE SECRETARY: Dulce Pereira (Brazil)

FRANCOPHONIE. Although the year between biennial summits usually tended to be a quiet one for the International Organisation of Francophonie (OIF), 2000 in fact saw a considerable amount of activity, if not of a headline-grabbing kind. Of greatest significance was a series of workshops and conferences on the subject of democracy, an important innovation for an organisation that until its Hanoi summit in 1997 had been almost exclusively concerned with different aspects of the French language, including matters such as communications and the new technology.

In January a joint colloquium with the Commonwealth was organised in the Cameroonian capital, Yaoundé, on the subject of the problems of democracy and cultural pluralism. This was the first of several meetings arranged by the two organisations—both post-colonial structures with the particular vocation of meeting the needs of developing countries. The colloquium was jointly chaired by the two Secretaries General—Boutros Boutros-Ghali for the OIF, and Chief Anyaoku for the Commonwealth, shortly before he completed his term of office. Given the broad range of membership, it was possible to consider the experiences of countries like Canada, India, Northern Ireland, as well as Lebanon, Switzerland and Cameroon itself, whose President Paul Biya, addressed the gathering, recalling that the summit at Moncton, New Brunswick, the previous year had called for an engagement of the OIF on the subject of democracy.

The second meeting was a seminar in Chad on democratic institutions, and it was followed by two seminars in Paris on electoral issues. The series of meetings culminated in a large symposium in Bamako, capital of Mali, on "Democratic Practices, Rights and Freedoms". President Alpha Oumar Konaré of Mali called the meeting a "moment of truth and sharing", which called on the francophone community to correct the deficits seen in the last few years, which had translated themselves into "ethnic and religious conflicts, civil wars and situations of anarchy". The meeting also called on the OIF to follow the practice, already in force in both the Commonwealth and the OAU, of condemning military coups, and excluding those administrations established by their perpetrators. This measure, however, still fell short of the Commonwealth's committee to monitor democracy in its member states.

The "economic francophonie", a new aspect to the OIF which had also been resolved upon in Hanoi, did not manifest itself significantly, although there was work on planning the second meeting of Economy Ministers due in April 2001. There were also consultations between Trade Ministers, including talks at the African Trade Ministers meeting in Libreville in November, to try and work out positions for the World Trade Organisation. More activity was seen on the front of civil society, with meetings of francophone women (their first full conference), youth, and non-governmental organisations, as well as a number of cultural projects in the field of film, TV, media and the internet. The OIF also signed a convention of co-operation with the High Council of Francophonie, and the two organisations met for two days of reflection on the issue of the "dialogue of cultures", which was to be the theme of the next summit in Beirut in October 2001.

COMMUNITY OF PORTUGUESE-SPEAKING COUNTRIES. The main event of the year was the third summit meeting of the seven CPLP heads of state held in Maputo, Mozambique, in July. Preceded by preparatory inter-ministerial meetings, in which the development of the CPLP was compared with that of both the Commonwealth and the International Organisation of Francophonie (OIF), the summit included the election of the Brazilian Dulce Pereira as Executive Secretary. She succeeded (by alphabetical order of the country members) the former Angolan Prime Minister, Marcelino Moco, who was the organisation's first executive secretary in 1996. The main theme of the summit was "Co-operation, Development and Democracy in the Globalisation Age".

The year had started with the first meeting of CPLP women, from January 30 to February 1, in Salvador, in northern Brazil, on the theme of "Genre, Culture, Access to Power, Political Participation and Development". A wide-ranging series of subsequent meetings on education, inter-cultural communication, social sciences and journalism took place during the year in various towns in the CPLP countries. Co-operation amongst African member countries was productive on civil issues; in particular a new "Lusophone Citizenship" was proposed, which, whilst restricting immigration, would make it easier for professionals and students to move between member countries.

The CPLP showed its support of the democratic process in Lusophone countries. The newly independent state of East Timor was granted observer status and FRETLIN leader Xanana Gusmao attended the Maputo summit meeting, emphasising Lusophone solidarity. A joint observation committee, comprising members from each of the CPLP countries and a representative of the Executive Secretary, was sent to cover the presidential elections in Guinea-Bissau in January, whilst a public meeting at Oporto in February discussed the theme of "The importance of education in the building of peace in Angola".

Since its foundation in 1996—21 years after the independence of its five African member states—the CPLP had been a comparatively low profile organisation, and had not attracted much popular support. It was hoped that the new Executive Secretary, Dulce Pereira, who was a leading campaigner for feminist and negro causes in Brazil, might bring a more progressive outlook to the organisation, which had so far looked somewhat unrepresentative of its demographic black majority.

Despite adjustment during the year, the financial burden of the CPLP remained unevenly distributed, and continued to weigh heavily on Portugal. Although Brazil was by far the largest, and potentially the richest member state, Portugal's annual financial quota was still 20 per cent greater, despite a substantial increase in Brazil's contribution from US$200,000 to US$1.3 million, effective from 2000. Portugal was also to finance the building of the headquarters of the new Portuguese Language International Institute—designed by Sisa Vieira, one of Portugal's foremost architects—in Cape Verde, at an estimated cost of over US$1.5 million. President Chissano of Mozambique, the host of the Maputo summit meeting, commented that "the CPLP will have no future if it does not enter into economic co-operation". Portuguese Foreign Minister Jaime Gama was in agreement, stating that the summit was "devoted to renovation".

iii. NON-ALIGNED MOVEMENT AND DEVELOPING COUNTRIES

Non-Aligned Movement (NAM)
DATE OF FOUNDATION: 1961   HEADQUARTERS: rotating with chair
OBJECTIVES: Originally to promote decolonisation and to avoid domination by either the Western industrialized world or the Communist bloc; since the early 1970s to provide a authoritative forum to set the political and economic priorities of developing countries; in addition, since the end of the Cold War to resist domination of the UN system by the USA
MEMBERSHIP (END-'00): 115 countries (*those listed in AR 1995, p. 386, plus Belarus and the Dominican Republic*)
CHAIRMAN: President Thabo Mbeki, South Africa (since June '99; succeeded Nelson Mandela, who had held the post since Sept '98)

Group of 77 (G-77)
DATE OF FOUNDATION: 1964   HEADQUARTERS: UN centres
OBJECTIVES: To act as an international lobbying group for the concerns of developing countries
MEMBERSHIP (END-'00): 133 developing countries (*those listed in AR 1996, p. 385, minus South Korea, plus China, Eritrea & Turkmenistan*)
CHAIRMAN: President Olusegun Obasanjo (Nigeria)

THE regular triennial Conference of Foreign Ministers of the Non-Aligned Movement (NAM) was held in Cartagena, on April 8-9, and was followed immediately by the first-ever South Summit of the Group of 77 (G-77) in Havana, on April 10-14. Only 98 of the 115 member countries of the NAM were represented in Cartagena, making it the smallest meeting for some years. Those missing were Uzbekistan, nine micro-states, six other small countries and Yugoslavia, whose membership was suspended. There was also relatively low attendance at the South Summit. Less than half the 133 members were represented by their heads of state or government. It was notable that the Chinese were treated as a full member of the G-77 and Vice-Premier Li Lanqing led their delegation.

The NAM ministers agreed that the international situation could be regarded as a mixture of political threats and economic opportunities, provided that globalisation could be harnessed for all rather than leaving the developing countries marginalised. The organisation's traditional emphasis on nuclear disarmament and strengthening the United Nations was joined by a more immediate concern about the destabilising effects of the proliferation in small arms. Another priority was to maintain the independence of the International Criminal Court and extend its mandate, as soon as possible, to cover the crime of aggression.

In most current conflicts, notably the civil wars in Sierra Leone and in the Democratic Republic of Congo and the border war between Ethiopia and Eritrea, there was support for mediation and UN peace-keeping. The majority also took a neutral approach to the continuing tension between Iraq and Kuwait. However, in some conflicts the NAM was more partisan. Despite the Talibaan's control over most of Afghanistan, the previous government was still represented at Cartagena and the NAM insisted that "there is no military solution to the Afghan conflict". The conference endorsed UN action to support the Angolan government and to "send a clear sign to Savimbi that he is isolated". Similarly, the status quo in Cyprus was considered unacceptable, "primarily due to Turkish intransigence".

The NAM attributed the breakdown of the Seattle WTO Conference (see AR 1999, pp. 1-2 and 412) to resistance amongst developing countries to secretive negotiations that ignored their interests. It affirmed that "non-trade issues, such as social and environmental issues, should not be introduced in the agenda of the WTO". The priority for the next round of negotiations was to enhance developing country integration into the trading system. At the same time, international financial instability was seen as adversely affecting development and there was a call to regulate speculative activities, particularly through hedge funds.

Reports to the Foreign Ministers showed the NAM to be a strong and effective caucus in the United Nations, through the Co-ordinating Bureau on questions such as the Middle East, Kosovo and the Lockerbie trial, and through Working Groups on disarmament, peace-keeping, human rights, legal questions and Palestine. A relatively new forum, the NAM Troika of Colombia, South Africa and Bangladesh (the past, current and future countries to hold the chair) became more important, particularly for relating to other regional groups.

The G-77 South Summit produced a "Havana Programme of Action" with five sections. The first section did little more than establish very general principles for responding to globalisation. The second asserted the importance of "Knowledge and Technology", with a vague set of utopian aspirations that was of little relevance to more than a few of the largest countries. The section on South-South co-operation did propose some limited practical measures: to review the possibility of negotiations for a third round of the Global System of Trade Preferences; to formulate a programme of work for the G-77 Chamber of Commerce; to convene a Ministerial Meeting on Transit Transport Co-operation in 2003; and to organise a business forum and a South-South trade and investment fair in 2002. The fourth section on North-South relations outlined a comprehensive set of negotiating goals, but only took one minor step to consider how the South might negotiate more successfully.

The final section of the programme was on institutional follow-up. After more than three decades of debate since the idea of a secretariat for developing countries was first proposed at the third Non-Aligned summit in 1970, the Havana South Summit finally decided to upgrade the office of the Chairman of the G-77 in New York to "a compact executive secretariat". Each member country was asked to contribute an annual sum of US$5,000. There was also an appeal for a voluntary fund of at least US$10 million to assist implementation and follow-up. In contrast to the trivial level of resources requested from members, heavy demands were made upon the Chairman of the G-77 to give life to the Programme of Action.

Relations between the developing countries and the industrialised countries underwent substantial improvement during the year. The NAM had held various ad hoc meetings with the G-8 in the past. Immediately prior to the Okinawa G-8 summit in July this was extended for the first time, by holding a full series of parallel meetings: a preparatory meeting of senior officials, a ministerial meeting of the NAM Troika, the G-77 Chair and G-8 ministers, and then the first summit-level dialogue. In Tokyo on July 20, President Obasanjo of Nigeria, Chair of the G-77, President Mbeki of South Africa, Chair of the NAM, President Bouteflika of Algeria, Chair of the OAU, and Prime Minister Chuan of Thailand, Chair of

ASEAN, held a general discussion on debt and development with the G-8 leaders, followed by specialist exchanges on information technology, infectious diseases and human resources. In reporting back to the NAM in New York, the South Africans were pleased to declare that "for the first time the G-8 Summit focused on the agenda of the South".

The Dominican Republic was welcomed as a member of the NAM by the Cartagena Conference, following the endorsement of its application the previous September in New York. This brought the total to 115 members. The G-77 remained unchanged with 132 members plus China. The government of Iran took over the Chair of the G-77 from the Nigerians at the end of the year.

iv. ORGANISATION OF THE ISLAMIC CONFERENCE (OIC)

DATE OF FOUNDATION: 1970   HEADQUARTERS: Jeddah, Saudi Arabia
OBJECTIVES: To further co-operation among Islamic countries in the political, economic, social, cultural and scientific spheres
MEMBERSHIP (END-'00): Afghanistan, Albania, Algeria, Azerbaijan, Bahrain, Bangladesh, Benin, Brunei, Burkina Faso, Cameroon, Chad, Comoros, Djibouti, Egypt, Gabon, The Gambia, Guinea, Guinea-Bissau, Indonesia, Iran, Iraq, Jordan, Kazakhstan, Kuwait, Kyrgyzstan, Lebanon, Libya, Malaysia, Maldives, Mali, Mauritania, Morocco, Mozambique, Niger, Nigeria, Oman, Pakistan, Palestine, Qatar, Saudi Arabia, Senegal, Sierra Leone, Somalia, Sudan, Suriname, Syria, Tajikistan, Togo, Tunisia, Turkey, Turkmenistan, Uganda, Uzbekistan, United Arab Emirates, Yemen, Zanzibar (*total* 56)
SECRETARY GENERAL: Azeddine Laraki (Morocco)

LEADING officials of the 56 member countries of the Organisation of the Islamic Conference (OIC) attended its ninth summit meeting in Doha, the capital of Qatar, in mid-November. The organisation's eighth summit meeting had been held in Iran in December 1997 (see AR 1997, pp. 399-402). The main preoccupation of the summit, and that of its closing Doha declaration, was concern over the heavy fighting between Israel and the Palestinians which had erupted in September following a visit to Jerusalem's Haram al-Sharif (Temple Mount) by Ariel Sharon, the hard-line, nationalist leader of the Israeli opposition Likud (see V.1. and V.2.i.). The weeks leading up to the Doha summit saw violent clashes between Israeli troops and Palestinian police and civilians as the new Palestinian intifada gathered momentum.

The Doha summit resulted in the issuing of a declaration under the title of "The Aqsa Intifada, the Intifada for the independence of Palestine". Egypt and Turkey led a rejection of an attempt by Iraq and Sudan to include in the declaration an invocation of a jihad (holy war) against Israel. Nonetheless, the leaders agreed that the ninth summit was held in "extremely serious circumstances. . . due to the prevailing tragic conditions and brutal crimes perpetrated in the Palestinian territories. . . as a result of the war launched by Israel against the Palestinian people". Such "wanton premeditated and deliberate Israeli aggression" came within the framework of Israeli policy aimed at imposing a fait accompli and judaising Al-Quds Al-Sharif (Jerusalem), it was asserted, and would "have serious consequences for the Middle East and world security and peace".

The summit invited the OIC member states which had already established, or had started to take steps to establish, relations with Israel within the framework of the peace process to sever those connections—including closing missions and offices, cutting economic ties and stopping all forms of normalisation—until Israel fully and genuinely implemented UN resolutions relating to Palestine and Jerusalem, and the Arab-Israeli conflict, and until a just and comprehensive peace was established in the region. The leaders requested the states of the world to abide by UN Security Council Resolution 478 (1980) calling for the non-transfer of their diplomatic missions to Jerusalem. The leaders also requested the UN and the UN Security Council to provide the necessary international protection to the Palestinian people in the Palestinian territories to forestall "the grave violations they are subjected to until they are able to exercise their inalienable national rights in Palestine in accordance with the resolutions of international legality".

Furthermore, the OIC leaders requested the UN Security Council to set up an International Criminal Court to prosecute Israeli "war criminals" responsible for the massacre of Palestinians and other Arabs and to decide to sue them in accordance with the provisions of the Statutes on the International Criminal Court. They stressed, once again, that the condition for the establishment of a just and comprehensive peace in the region was, first and foremost, full Israeli withdrawal from all occupied Palestinian and Arab territories including Jerusalem and the Syrian Golan to the line of June 4, 1967, and from the Lebanese territories still under occupation, including the Shabaa farms, to the internationally recognised borders, in implementation of the resolutions of international legitimacy, particularly UN Security Council Resolutions 242, 338 and 425 and the principle of peace for land.

In his closing statement to the summit, the Amir of Qatar, Sheikh Hamad Bin Khalifa al-Thani, emphasised the importance of taking steps towards the OIC goal of creating an Islamic Common Market. Malaysia was chosen as the host for the next summit meeting.

4. EUROPEAN UNION

DATE OF FOUNDATION: 1952   HEADQUARTERS: Brussels, Belgium
OBJECTIVES: To seek ever-closer union of member states
MEMBERSHIP (END-'00): Austria, Belgium, Denmark, Finland, France, Germany, Greece, Ireland, Italy, Luxembourg, Netherlands, Portugal, Spain, Sweden, United Kingdom (*total* 15)
PRESIDENT OF EUROPEAN COMMISSION: Romano Prodi (Italy)
CURRENCY: euro, introduced on 1 Jan '99 by 11 members, with Denmark, Greece, Sweden & UK not participating (end-'00 £1=E1.59, US$1=E1.07)

THE prospect of further enlargement of the European Union from the current 15 member countries to as many as 27 cast its shadow over the EU's activities in the year 2000. No timetable for accession of the new members could be negotiated until some key institutional questions had been resolved, especially relating to the size of the European Commission, the voting rules in the Council of Ministers and the weighting to be given to each member state in an enlarged EU—all sensitive issues which were the unfinished business from the 1997 Amsterdam Council and all with significant political implications.

The balance of forces in the European Union continued to shift, with the Council of Ministers taking an increasingly dominant role at the expense of the Commission. The appointment of Javier Solana as Council Secretary General and standard-bearer for foreign policy and security issues reinforced the process. Evolution of policy areas such as defence strengthened the position of the big countries. There was less appetite for supra-national decision-making.

Relationships between member countries became more flexible and less predictable. The French and German governments, which had co-operated so closely since the earliest years of European integration, were no longer working together to drive policy. They seemed to share neither close personal relationships nor common policy goals. The UK's approach of seeking multiple alliances was rather successful, for instance working closely with France on aspects of defence identity, and with Spain and Portugal on economic policy.

PREPARING FOR ENLARGEMENT. The Inter-Governmental Conference (IGC) for adapting the European Treaties to the needs of an enlarged Union was launched under the Portuguese presidency in February and met periodically throughout the year. The avowed aim was to make the EU institutions capable of effective decision-making despite the accession of several new member states. For Commission President Romano Prodi this meant a strengthening of the traditional European Community method—wider use of qualified voting in the Council and a stronger role for the Commission—a view shared by many of the smaller member countries.

Other member states had their own special concerns. The British were determined to retain unanimity for decisions on all taxation policy issues; Germany wanted a stronger say than the other large countries to reflect its larger population; Spain was intent on protecting the benefits it had obtained from the EU budget; and France wanted a Charter of Rights enshrined in European law.

Attempts to widen the scope of the IGC to provide the Union with a formal constitution were not successful and by the time of the Nice summit (under the new French presidency) on December 7-11 there were four main points to settle: the number of votes each member state should have in the Council of Ministers (including the applicant countries), the level of national representation in the European Commission, the extension of qualified majority voting to new policy areas and the procedure which would allow a limited number of member states to advance more quickly than the others on a particular policy.

Nobody predicted quite how acrimonious the Nice discussions would be, and the meeting had to be extended for an extra two days to achieve a result. Changes were eventually agreed which would shift more power to the big countries, especially Germany, and increase the importance of the Council in relation to the Commission and the European Parliament. The internal dynamics of the meeting were complicated by the relationship between President Jacques Chirac and Prime Minister Lionel Jospin, who each wished to be seen as defending French interests, a lack of realistic preparation by the EU presidency, and a clumsy negotiating style by the French President.

The impact on policy-making from the anticipated accession of several small countries had long caused concern for the big member states, which could envisage situations where they might be outvoted in the Council because of the voting structure established in the Treaty of Rome. A minority of the enlarged EU's population could thus impose its will on the majority. The German government took this one stage further, demanding additional votes in the Council to reflect the size of its population—82 million against 59 million in both France and the UK.

Once the box was opened, other demands were made, such as the Netherlands' claim for more votes than Belgium (one of the considerations which had scuppered any decision at the 1997 Amsterdam summit). Agreeing the number of votes to be allocated to the applicant countries once they joined was also highly contentious. Although President Chirac was determined to fortify the position of the large countries, he was adamant that France and Germany—as the key founding members of the Union—should have an equal voting strength. The final outcome left the four largest countries, including Germany, with 29 votes each, and Spain (and Poland) with 27. The Netherlands received 13 and Belgium 12. As an additional safeguard for the large countries, it was agreed that if they should be out-voted in the Council, they could require that the decision be approved by governments representing 62 per cent of Europe's population before it could go ahead—thereby providing a blocking minority which could consist of Germany plus one other large member country. The smaller countries were granted a counter-safeguard—a simple majority of member states could block a decision regardless of their voting weight.

Representation on the European Commission was also to be changed. As from 2005 the College would consist of one nominee per member country up to a maximum of 26, so the big countries would lose their dual representation. Some additional powers were agreed for the Commission President in managing the College.

Extension of qualified majority voting was seen by most smaller countries and by the Commission as the key to more efficient decision-making in an enlarged EU, but several countries had their special interests and only a modest extension of qualified voting was agreed. The British succeeded in preserving unanimity for tax and social security, for passport changes and for asylum issues, but conceded in other areas where they claimed it was in their interests anyway. These included international trade in services, previously subject to unanimity, and judicial reform such as the rules of procedure of the European Court. Spain insisted on maintaining the veto on regional development spending beyond 2006—crucial in protecting its share of EU structural funds in an enlarged Union. France successfully defended unanimity for culture, audio-visual policy, education, health and social services; Greece and Denmark for maritime and air transport issues.

A major advance for the Commission was a new right to negotiate on behalf of the EU on services such as telecoms and financial services, where its competence had been limited by the Treaty.

Procedures were agreed to allow "enhanced co-operation", permitting groups of member states to push ahead in certain policy areas, but subject to limitations—there must be no threat to the internal market, other members must be entitled to join in later, and it would not apply to defence, where the UK argued that such flexibility might prejudice the decision-making procedure already agreed for the European defence identity and could threaten the NATO relationship. The British also feared that it could be used to give respectability to Eurocorps, the French-German-Spanish operating unit which did not include the UK.

Germany insisted that a date be set for a new IGC in four years' time, reflecting the desire of top German politicians, including Foreign Minister Joschka Fischer, to see a constitution for the European Union. There was an air of disillusionment in some quarters after the Nice IGC. The most important achievement of the conference was the removal of a significant barrier holding back the EU enlargement process, but it was also clear to both the European Commission and the European Parliament that the Nice agreement would make decision-making more complex in an enlarged EU and was a turning-away from the greater integration which they sought. It could certainly be seen as a pivotal moment in the evolution of the European Union, introducing a bigger say for the large member states, less scope for pushing through contentious legislation, and more inter-governmental co-operation.

The UK was pleased with the outcome—as demonstrated by an elated Prime Minister in the House of Commons. The Belgians accepted differentiation from the Dutch in return for qualified majority voting in appointments to the Commission. Germany benefited from the population threshold and a reallocation of European Parliamentary seats. The candidate countries were assured equality with the existing member states should they join the EU.

EUROPEAN DEFENCE IDENTITY. Significant progress was made during the year in establishing the structure for a European Security and Defence Policy (ESDP) within the European Union, although there were inevitable tensions concerning the relationship between the EU and NATO, both within the Union and between the EU and the USA. This was not surprising, considering that the long-term objective was to rebalance the defence and security needs of Europe in a way which would make Europe less dependent on the USA (see XI.2.i.).

The immediate challenge was to carry forward the Headline Goals agreed at Helsinki in December 1999 for development of the ESDP (see AR 1999, p. 432). An informal meeting of EU Defence Ministers at Sintra, in Portugal, in February, agreed that work should start on setting up a Military Committee consisting of defence chiefs from member states and the recruitment of a military staff within the Council of Ministers. These bodies would have the task of establishing the European Rapid Reaction Force, capable of mobilising up to 60,000 troops within 60 days and sustaining them for a year for peace-keeping, peace-making and crisis response tasks.

Towards the end of the Portuguese presidency, European leaders met in Feira. They reaffirmed their commitment to the ESDP and announced that a Capabilities Commitments Conference would be held in the autumn to establish what resources in men and materials each member state would be able to contribute to the Rapid Reaction Force. The French pushed this ahead during the succeeding presidency and on November 20 were able to register a commitment by the EU countries to contribute a pool of 100,000 troops, 400 aircraft and 100 ships. On the following day 15 non-EU countries, including Turkey, Norway and Iceland, agreed that they would also contribute to the Force. The UK, which was a prime mover with France in making a reality of these policies, offered 12,500 troops, 72 aircraft and 18 ships. Although the Force was not expected to be fully operational until 2003, it should have some capacity to act by mid-2001.

The more concrete the EU's plans became, the more the political and practical difficulties emerged. The UK government was faced with a domestic political campaign against the creation of a supposed "European army". France expressed its long-standing ambition for an autonomous European defence capability by seeking a larger military staff in the Council. Some US politicians and commentators condemned the plans for a Rapid Reaction Force as undermining NATO. In order to calm these tensions a distinction was drawn between the functions of NATO (collective defence) and the European Defence Identity (crisis management). A declaration in November said that there would be no duplication of NATO's work and that the move did "not involve the establishment of a European army". NATO Secretary General Lord Robertson expressed his support for the initiative, saying that: "The EU's desire to be more effective is sparking real improvements in capability that can only enhance NATO's overall effectiveness".

The relationship between the EU and NATO dominated the debate on the ESDP up to the Nice summit and the year ended with many questions unanswered. The UK government was able to secure a public relations success by claiming to have blocked French ideas for an independent planning and command capability, but the tensions remained. US Defence Secretary William Cohen supported the EU's efforts, but stressed the interdependence with NATO. Common planning was needed "as the only logical, cost-effective way to ensure the best possible co-ordination of limited forces and resources". He warned against seeing the two institutions as autonomous and competing.

Four NATO-EU working groups had been set up to handle the practical issues of co-operation, and following the Nice Summit the Foreign Ministers of the Atlantic Alliance met in the North Atlantic Council to discuss relationships, but they failed to agree a final communiqué because Turkey refused to agree that the EU should have permanent access to NATO assets in times of crisis. The Turks resented being excluded from the EU's discussions on defence despite their geopolitical position and military strength. The draft formal declaration on co-operation intended to conclude the meeting was therefore blocked.

EURO DECLINE. Europe's new currency, the euro, began the year at parity with the US dollar, after slipping during 1999. It declined further during 2000, reaching a low of US$0.89 by the end of the summer, and then recovering to US$0.92.

Exporters from the 11 countries of the euro-zone, which consisted of all member states except Denmark, Greece, Sweden and the UK, enjoyed the competitive position which the falling currency gave them on international markets, but the fall had a damaging political spin-off. Many UK commentators saw it as proof that the new currency was bound to fail, thereby fuelling opposition to Britain's membership of the euro club. The German government was initially comfortable with the boost that the low currency provided for sluggish growth, but became increasingly concerned as the slippage continued and public opinion in Germany grew more hostile. People compared the weakness of the euro with the Deutschmark's traditional strength. Ministers looked ahead to January 1, 2002, when euro notes and coins would replace national money and the public would be asked to prepare for the changeover.

The French were concerned with the currency's decline. In the view of French Finance Minister Laurent Fabius and others, the euro's weakness was partly a reflection of poor policy co-ordination, so he made common cause with his Belgian counterpart Didier Reynders to strengthen the euro-11, the grouping whereby the Finance Ministers of the euro-zone met together to discuss policy, now given the name of Euro Group. With France taking the EU presidency from July, and the Belgian minister due to preside over the Euro Group for the whole of 2001, they had a full 18 months to advance their aims. Greece was to join the group on July 1 in anticipation of full euro membership from the beginning of 2001, leaving Denmark, Sweden and the UK outside.

The two ministers wanted to extend the regular two-hour meeting of the Euro Group to a full day's discussions in advance of each Ecofin Council, which all 15 Finance Ministers attended. They also wanted a bigger say in the deliberations of the independent European Central Bank. Fabius said that the scope of the Euro Group's deliberations would be broadened to take account of everything connected with the smooth running of its members' economies and the euro exchange rate—including not only fiscal policies, but also tax matters, wage issues, pensions, financial market integration, and structural reform of particular interest to the Euro zone countries. The UK became increasingly concerned that the Euro Group would become an alternative power base to the full meeting of Finance Ministers, but could do little but refer to the 1997 Luxembourg agreement where Ecofin was affirmed as the centre for co-ordination of economic policies.

In order to raise public and market understanding of the single currency and euro zone economic policies, the Euro Group announced that the European Commission would from the autumn produce regular monthly indicators of the euro zone economy. The Euro Group itself began to discuss how to speed up preparations for the changeover to the euro—especially during the transitional period up to January 2002.

On September 28, when the euro was at its weakest, the Danes gave their verdict on Denmark's membership. They voted to reject the government's proposal to adopt the single currency, with 53.1 per cent voting against and 46.9 per cent in favour—a surprisingly high margin for the "nej" voters. The Danish Prime Minister, Poul Nyrup Rasmussen, was stung by the result, but said that "Denmark does not turn its back on Europe" and undertook to maintain Denmark's membership of the exchange rate mechanism. The Danes' decision reflected more than perceptions of monetary union. It focused voters' complex worries about European integration and its impact, stirring fears for the country's welfare system and a belief that it would encourage immigration and undermine Danish culture and identity. For the Swedish and British governments, with referendums in prospect, it was a disturbing result which threatened to delay their own tests of the electorate, whilst for the French and Germans it demonstrated the need for a two-tier Europe.

The Greek government was keen to adopt the euro and was working hard to make it possible. In May the European Commission published an analysis which noted that Greece had made striking economic progress and had achieved a high degree of sustainable economic convergence, so the country's economy met the four convergence criteria required. At the European Council at Feira, in June, it was formally decided that Greece should become part of the euro-zone on January 1, 2001 and would adopt euro notes and coins in 2002, at the same time as the other Euro Group members.

ENLARGEMENT. A more flexible approach to the timetable for enlargement was put into effect. Negotiations continued with the original six candidate countries—Hungary, Poland, Czech Republic, Estonia, Slovenia and Cyprus—and talks began in February with Bulgaria, Latvia, Lithuania, Malta, Romania and Slovakia, but the process was blighted until the present 15 member states had determined the future of the decision-making process in the IGC.

This issue was resolved at the December Nice summit, which also endorsed a Commission strategy paper setting out a detailed timetable for concluding EU accession negotiations. This so-called "road map" suggested that the remaining issues should be tackled with the most advanced countries stage by stage, in 2001 and 2002, with indicative schedules agreed, and negotiations with the most advanced candidate countries concluded during 2002. There was talk of an accelerated ratification process once negotiations were completed with a candidate country, but the realistic expectation was for up to 28 months for member states to ratify, which would mean no new accession before 2004 at the earliest.

Although more flexibility was built into the calendar, there remained concern as to Poland's position, with many issues to be resolved and an appreciation that it would be difficult to accept other candidates before the Polish negotiations had been completed. The Nice Summit called for a new impetus in the talks and registered its "hope" that new member states would be able to participate in the 2004 European elections.

AUSTRIAN ISOLATION. In February 14 member states of the European Union decided to isolate Austria following the formation of a coalition between the People's Party of Wolfgang Schüssel and Jörg Haider's Freedom Party (see II.3.vi.). The move was unprecedented. Such action had never before been taken against a fellow member state. It demonstrated a new-found willingness amongst EU states to act against members, signalling to the candidate countries of central and eastern Europe that those judged to be political extremists could not be brought into government without provoking fierce reaction from EU partners. It was "a symbol and a lesson for the world" said Portuguese Prime Minister Antonio Guterres, who was encouraged by Italy, Germany and President Chirac of France.

Others were concerned that the action would have precisely the opposite effect to that which had been intended, and that it would boost Haider's popularity in Austria. The move went down especially badly in Denmark where it underlined the impression of an overbearing European Union brow-beating a small member country and the affair might have boosted the vote against adopting the euro.

The action against Austria was decided on an inter-governmental basis. The European Commission and the Council's High Representative Javier Solana were only informed at the last moment. It was not a formal EU decision and it left the Commission in confusion. After noting the announcement, the Commission said that at this stage the working of the institutions was not affected and that it would maintain its working relationship with the Austrian government. President Prodi was all in favour of vigorous action, but the Austrian Commissioner, Frans Fischler, was extremely unhappy and issued a personal statement effectively opposing the moves in the Council. He welcomed the statement setting out the new Austrian coalition's principles and maintained that "Austria is not a stronghold of fascism, of intolerance, but a functioning democracy".

The affair soured the atmosphere within the European Parliament and in the Council of Ministers. When Austrian President Thomas Klestil visited the Parliament's plenary session, left-wing MEPs responded by walking out. The Austrian President (who had always sought alternatives to the coalition) said that he was determined to reject any unjustified criticism of his country and people. "I appeal to you to find a way out of this situation in the interests of all parties and the EU" he said. EP President Nicole Fontaine was uncompromising in reply. "Out of respect for memory we cannot accept the cheap values of the far right" she said, and went on to say that "Austria could be a full partner of the EU again, which it has never ceased to be legally speaking". The political parties, especially the centre-right European Peoples' Party, were seriously split.

Having placed themselves in a difficult position, ministers had to find a way to extricate themselves and so they appointed three "Wise Men" to examine Austria's human rights record. This group gave the country a clean bill of health, and the sanctions were lifted on September 12. The sanctions, said the French presidency, had been effective.

EXTERNAL RELATIONS. The European Union remained active in the Balkans. A European Agency for the Reconstruction of Kosovo, with headquarters in Thessaloniki and an operational centre in Pristina, began work to see that reconstruction schemes in the country were implemented rapidly and effectively. Some 36,000 troops from Europe were allocated to the NATO-led Kosovo Force (K-For), amounting to about four fifths of the total manpower; some E530 million was contributed as aid to the Balkans.

Following the electoral defeat of President Slovodan Milosevic, the EU lifted its oil embargo and flight ban on Serbia and called for political and economic links to be re-established. On October 13-14 European leaders welcomed newly-elected Yugoslav President Vojislav Kostunica to their informal summit in Biarritz. They supported his efforts to consolidate democracy and backed plans for urgent EU assistance to Serbia of about E200 million, particularly to meet food and energy requirements over the winter.

A joint declaration promised increasing dialogue and co-operation between the EU and Russia, including discussions on political and security matters, Russian membership of the World Trade Organisation, and energy. WTO membership was the main theme of relations with China.

ENTERPRISE EUROPE. The Lisbon summit on March 23-24 marked a significant new direction in European economic policy thinking, triggered by the wave of change brought about by new technologies and comparisons with the USA. There was a conviction that Europe must change its attitudes if the economies of its member states were to prosper and new jobs were to be created.

Stimulated by the British, Portuguese and Spanish, and enthusiastically espoused by the Scandinavians, a strategic goal was set for the EU to become by 2010 "the most competitive and dynamic knowledge-based economy in the world, capable of sustainable economic growth with more and better jobs and greater social cohesion". Full employment was the long-term aim. A range of targets was agreed to extend access to new technologies, especially the internet, to boost research and innovation, to lower the costs of running small and medium businesses, to improve the flexibility of financial markets and to improve education and training.

5. EUROPEAN ORGANISATIONS

i. THE COUNCIL OF EUROPE

DATE OF FOUNDATION: 1949 HEADQUARTERS: Strasbourg, France
OBJECTIVES: To strengthen pluralist democracy, the rule of law and the maintenance of human
   rights in Europe and to further political, social and cultural co-operation between member states
MEMBERSHIP (END-'00): Albania, Andorra, Austria, Belgium, Bulgaria, Croatia, Cyprus,
   Czech Republic, Denmark, Estonia, Finland, France, Georgia, Germany, Greece, Hungary,
   Iceland, Ireland, Italy, Latvia, Liechtenstein, Lithuania, Luxembourg, Macedonia, Malta,
   Moldova, Netherlands, Norway, Poland, Portugal, Romania, Russia, San Marino, Slovakia,
   Slovenia, Spain, Sweden, Switzerland, Turkey, Ukraine, United Kingdom (*total* 41)
SECRETARY GENERAL: Walter Schwimmer (Austria)

THE Council of Europe continued to reform itself and to prioritise its work in accordance with the recommendations of the Committee of Wise Persons and the financial constraints imposed by member states' policy of zero real growth. It redefined its political priorities as crisis management and rehabilitation, co-operation with other institutions, promotion of civil society and the compliance by member states with their commitments. This last activity was particularly evident in Ukraine, where the organisation worked hard to assist in resolving the confrontation between the executive and parliament.

The dominant issue throughout the year was the continuing Russian military action in Chechnya. The Council of Europe played a leading role in pressing for a cease-fire and then persuading the Russian authorities to investigate reports of human rights abuses through a specially established office, to which it contributed financial support and legal expertise. The Assembly consistently took a stronger line than the Committee of Ministers in condemning the use of excessive force by the Russian military and in April it took its protest a stage further by suspending the voting rights of the Russian delegation. It also called, unsuccessfully, for governments to take legal action against Russia for breaching the European Convention on Human Rights (ECHR). The Committee of Ministers focused on the progress being made through its preferred policy of maintaining a constructive dialogue.

Following the elections in the Federal Republic of Yugoslavia (FRY) in September, President Kostunica made a formal request for membership of the Council of Europe. The Committee of Ministers, which had previously ruled out early entry by the FRY, passed on the request to the Assembly for an opinion. In November the Committee of Ministers accepted the recommendations made by the Assembly in June and invited both Armenia and Azerbaijan to join the organisation. The two countries made undertakings to bring their legislation into line with Council of Europe standards and Azerbaijan was also required to respond to the criticisms of the international monitoring mission on the parliamentary elections there. Membership applications from Monaco and Bosnia and Hercegovina continued to be considered, whilst that of Belarus remained frozen. The monitoring procedure in respect of Latvia was brought to an end following the implementation of reforms there whilst procedures continued in respect of Albania, Bulgaria, Croatia, the former Yugoslav Republic of Macedonia, Georgia and Ukraine.

The Council of Europe participated in election monitoring during the year, in conjunction with the OSCE and its Office for Democratic Institutions and Human Rights (ODIHR). The presidential elections in Georgia in April were judged to have followed too soon after the parliamentary elections to enable all the lessons learnt to be implemented. The parliamentary elections in Serbia in December were judged to be largely in line with international standards, as were the municipal elections in Kosovo and Bosnia and Hercegovina in the autumn.

The Council of Europe marked the 50th anniversary of the signing of the European Convention on Human Rights in April and opened for signature a new protocol on the prohibition of all forms of discrimination. Separately, a European Landscape Convention was adopted, designed to promote the better protection and management of landscapes throughout Europe. The organisation also adopted a Convention to provide legal protection for broadcasters against illicit accessing of their services.

The Council of Europe continued to support the stability pact for south-eastern Europe. Work focused on promoting the training of judges and the independence of the judiciary as well as the reform of administrative law. However, the organisation was frustrated that it could not obtain the necessary financial backing from member states to support all of its proposals.

Close attention was paid throughout the year to the framing of the EU Charter of Fundamental Rights, which was signed at the Nice summit in December after a year of negotiations in which the Council of Europe was represented. Some Council of Europe member states feared that the Convention would rival and possibly undermine the existing European Convention of Human Rights. The document eventually agreed was a political declaration rather than a legally binding document but its status was earmarked for further review at the next Inter-Governmental Conference. The Assembly recommended that the EU accede to the European Court of Human Rights (ECHR) in order to guarantee consistent standards of human rights protection throughout the continent.

Finally, the Council of Europe continued to develop its relations with other international organisations such as the UN, EU and the OSCE. In this context, the agreement by the United Nations General Assembly to discuss its relations with the Council of Europe for the first time represented welcome recognition of the Council of Europe's role in the international institutional architecture.

ii. ORGANISATION FOR SECURITY AND CO-OPERATION IN EUROPE (OSCE)

DATE OF FOUNDATION: 1975   HEADQUARTERS: Vienna, Austria
OBJECTIVES: To promote security and co-operation among member states, particularly in respect of the resolution of internal and external conflicts
MEMBERSHIP (END-'00): Albania, Andorra, Armenia, Austria, Azerbaijan, Belarus, Belgium, Bosnia & Hercegovina, Bulgaria, Canada, Croatia, Cyprus, Czech Republic, Denmark, Estonia, Finland, France, Georgia, Germany, Greece, Holy See (Vatican), Hungary, Iceland, Ireland, Italy, Kazakhstan, Kyrgyzstan, Latvia, Liechtenstein, Lithuania, Luxembourg, Macedonia, Malta, Moldova, Monaco, Netherlands, Norway, Poland, Portugal, Romania, Russian Federation, San Marino, Slovakia, Slovenia, Spain, Sweden, Switzerland, Tajikistan, Turkey, Turkmenistan, Ukraine, United Kingdom, United States, Uzbekistan, Yugoslavia (*total* 55)
SECRETARY GENERAL: Giancarlo Aragona (Italy)

OVER recent years, the Organisation for Security and Co-operation in Europe (OSCE) had consolidated its position within the European security system. The OSCE was the only pan-European security organisation with a comprehensive mandate, and had a particular responsibility for preventive diplomacy, conflict management and post-conflict rehabilitation. Its growing importance in European affairs was evident from the record budget of 192 million euros allocated to it for 2000 by participating states. This represented an increase of more than 30 per cent over the 1999 budget of E153 million.

The bulk of this E192 million (roughly 86 per cent) was allocated to OSCE Missions and field operations, with approximately 79 per cent going to the three largest missions—in Kosovo, Croatia and Bosnia. At the same time, the OSCE sought to address a number of organisational and financial deficiencies that had plagued its operations in previous years. These included improvements in the budgetary and accounting processes, strengthening internal financial oversight controls and aligning OSCE working conditions with those of the United Nations system. Thanks to the impetus given to these reforms by the Norwegian OSCE chairmanship, the organisation was now better placed to secure high quality staff and had strengthened its operational capability.

The priorities of the OSCE for the year were spelt out by its new chairman, Austrian Foreign Minister Wolfgang Schüssel, to Permanent Representatives on January 13. The unique strengths of the OSCE, he argued, were its ability to present a "common platform" of all 54 participating states, its ability to "detect conflicts at an early stage and prevent them", its "defence of human and minority rights", and its support for "democracy, independent media and free and fair elections". The specific goals of the Austrian Chair were: to facilitate the return of 7.5 million refugees and internally-displaced persons in the OSCE area; to ensure the effective functioning of the Stability Pact for South-Eastern Europe; to find political, rather than military solutions to conflicts in the Caucasus; and to organise free and fair elections in Kosovo and Bosnia-Hercegovina.

The change of government in Austria on February 5 led to the appointment of a new Austrian Foreign Minister, Benita Ferrero-Waldner, who subsequently became the organisation's first woman Chairperson-in-Office. In her first address to the Permanent Council, on February 10, she stressed the continuity of Austrian priorities for the OSCE announced by her predecessor, and reiterated the challenges facing the OSCE in South-Eastern Europe, the Caucasus and Central Asia. In the light of the international controversy surrounding the participation of Jörg Haider's far-right Freedom Party in a coalition government with her own party, the Conservative People's Party (see II.3.vi.), Ferrero-Waldner called for participating states to give their full support to the Austrian Chairmanship and "work together for the achievement of a common security space based on the values of democracy, human rights and the rule of law".

The "acid test" for the OSCE's aspirations to achieve such a common security space was south-eastern Europe. The largest of the OSCE's field missions was that to Kosovo, which had been accorded a key role in post-conflict rehabilitation following the air war of 1999 (see AR 1999, p.436). The tasks of the mission were to help create democratic institutions, promote human rights, and support a free and fair media. Central to this was the organisation of local elections in October, a responsibility carried out, in the main, successfully. In addition, the OSCE ran the Kosovo Police Service School, the task of which was to train a multi-ethnic police force (with 10-15 per cent of the recruits being ethnic Serbs). The OSCE also helped in the establishment of a human rights Ombudsperson. At the same time, the OSCE had the harrowing responsibilities of helping to recover and identify the bodies of victims of mass killings, and of notifying the families concerned.

In Bosnia-Hercegovina, the OSCE deployed 750 election monitors to observe the municipal elections in April. It also launched an anti-corruption campaign in September which was linked to the general election held in November. Given that approximately 50 per cent of GDP in Bosnia-Hercegovina was currently generated by the "black" economy, it was no surprise that smuggling, bribery, fraud and embezzlement were rife, posing a significant threat to the consolidation of democratic institutions and the rule of law. In neighbouring Croatia, the OSCE's Office of Democratic Institutions and Human Rights (ODIHR) provided observers for the parliamentary and presidential elections held in January/February, polls which were held under new electoral legislation after criticisms of previous laws by both the OSCE and the Council of Europe.

OSCE observers monitored municipal elections in Macedonia in September and Albania in October, but it was in the Federal Republic of Yugoslavia (FRY) that the most dramatic developments occurred. After massive protests following rigged elections held on September 24, President Slobodan Milosevic was forced to resign, opening the way for a transition to democracy and international respectability for the Yugoslav government (see III.2.vi). Having been suspended from participation in the OSCE since 1992, Yugoslavia was formally reintegrated into the organisation at a meeting of the Permanent Council on November 10. The new Yugoslav Foreign Minister, Goran Svilanovic, took his seat in the Council and the flag of the FRY was raised, bringing the number of OSCE participating states back to 55.

Another area of special concern to the Austrian Chair of the OSCE was the Caucasus. The OSCE Minsk Group continued to work for peace between Armenia and Azerbaijan over Nagorno-Karabakh, and Chairperson-in-Office Ferrero-Waldner visited the two countries in July. She secured the release of the last remaining Azeri POWs, but no political settlement of the conflict was reached. In April she visited Moscow and—amidst tight security—Chechnya, where she called for a political solution to the conflict. She also sought to negotiate the return of the OSCE Assistance Group to Chechnya, which had been withdrawn after renewed fighting in December 1998. However, no agreement was reached with Moscow on this sensitive issue. In neighbouring Georgia, the mandate of the existing mission was expanded in December 1999 to include observation of the 81 km long border with Chechnya. Patrols by OSCE monitors began in February.

Divisions within Europe were much in evidence at the eighth OSCE Ministerial Council, which met in Vienna from November 27-28. Two declarations were agreed, one on the role of the OSCE in South-Eastern Europe, the other on limiting the flow of small arms and light weapons. However, no consensus was reached on a full Ministerial Declaration, and when Chairperson-in-Office Ferrero-Waldner provided a summary of the two-day meeting, Russia responded by declaring that it did not consider itself bound by any of its conclusions or recommendations. Russia objected to OSCE statements on Chechnya, Moldova and Georgia.

At the start of 2000 Wolfgang Schüssel had suggested that "If we can say at the end of 2000 that there are fewer trouble spots than at the beginning of the year, we shall have made progress". Sadly, the OSCE was not able to solve any outstanding conflicts. Nonetheless, it continued to provide an important instrument for pan-European diplomacy, preventive diplomacy, crisis management and post-conflict rehabilitation. In July it celebrated its 25th anniversary, and in his keynote address the guest of honour, Han-Dietrich Genscher, spoke of the vision and courage that had brought 35 heads of state and government together in the Cold War to sign the Helsinki accords. He called for the same courage and far-sightedness to tackle current global challenges. "If the participating states of the OSCE wish to face their responsibility for stability in a new world order, they must resolutely seize the unique chance offered them by their organisation... History does not usually repeat its offers and the opportunities that it holds out to us today will not always be there for the taking".

iii. EUROPEAN BANK FOR RECONSTRUCTION AND DEVELOPMENT (EBRD)

DATE OF FOUNDATION: 1991   HEADQUARTERS: London, UK
OBJECTIVES: To promote the economic reconstruction of former Communist-ruled countries on the basis of the free-market system and pluralism
MEMBERSHIP (END-'00): Albania, Armenia, Australia, Austria, Azerbaijan, Belarus, Belgium, Bosnia & Hercegovina, Bulgaria, Canada, Croatia, Cyprus, Czech Republic, Denmark, Egypt, Estonia, European Investment Bank, European Union, Finland, France, Georgia, Germany, Greece, Hungary, Iceland, Ireland, Israel, Italy, Japan, Kazakhstan, Kyrgyzstan, South Korea, Latvia, Liechtenstein, Lithuania, Luxembourg, Macedonia, Malta, Mexico, Moldova, Mongolia, Slovenia, Spain, Sweden, Switzerland, Tajikistan, Turkey, Turkmenistan, Ukraine, United Kingdom, United States, Uzbekistan, Yugoslavia (*total* 62)
PRESIDENT: Jean Lemierre (France)

THE IMF's choice in April of Horst Köhler as its Managing Director (see XI.2.ii.), required the European Bank of Reconstruction and Development (EBRD) to seek a new President less than half-way through his four-year term. It chose Jean Lemierre, the 49-year-old director of the French Treasury, supported by both France and Germany (at the IMF a German had succeeded a Frenchman), and went on to select a Pole to succeed Miklos Nemeth (Hungary) as one of the Vice Presidents. Hanna Gronkiewicz-Waltz had been Central Bank governor for eight years and became the first woman Vice President. The Bank already had a female Deputy Vice President in Noreen Doyle and the Team Director for Russia—the Bank's biggest borrower—was Dragicia Pilipovic-Chaffey.

Membership was enlarged by the admission of two more states with transitional economies. Mongolia entered in October, not as a recipient member, but as open to the EBRD's advice and to the likelihood of more bilateral credits from member-states. Following the ousting of President Milosevic in September (see III.2.vi.), Yugoslavia became a recipient member from January 2001. As a consequence of the adoption by the new Croatian government of policies of economic and political reform, the EBRD in November adopted a strategy to support privatisation, foreign direct investment and the commercialisation of state-owned infrastructure. Faced with Turkmenistan's regression from the "democracy, pluralism and market economy" to which the EBRD—uniquely amongst international financial institutions—was constitutionally committed, First Vice President Charles Frank (USA) led a mission to Ashgabat in April to express concern at Turkmenistan's lack of progress towards those objectives. President Niyazov (in Frank's words, "most disturbingly, made President for life in December 1999") refused to meet them and the Bank suspended making investments in the public sector there. This was the first time that the EBRD had taken such strong action against a recipient member, the closest previous action had been a brief suspension of public-sector loans to Russia to protest against the August 1991 coup, and the current practice of not lending to the public sector in Belarus. Visiting Moscow in October, Lemierre observed that in Russia "severe weaknesses in the rule of law continue to undermine investment, both domestic and foreign", and launched a new strategy for the country (which during the

EBRD's life had gained 3.1 billion euros, or 20 per cent, of aggregate Board approvals) to enlarge "the access of the private sector to international sources of funding".

The EBRD's annual meeting in Riga on May 20-22 focused on regional integration through investment, trade and cross-border co-operation and approved plans to augment its investment flow from E2.2 billion in 1999 to E2.5 billion in 2000. Results for the 12 months to June 2000 showed E2.2 billion, against E1.6 billion in the corresponding period to June 1999, with general administrative expenses kept for the half year to US$89 million and operating profits rising to US$134 million. Lemierre stated that in the CIS and the Balkans the EBRD would increase its level of business, but in the EU accession countries its investments would primarily be to sectors and regions not currently well served by private capital.

iv. NORDIC, BALTIC AND ARCTIC ORGANISATIONS

Nordic Council
DATE OF FOUNDATION: 1952   HEADQUARTERS: Stockholm, Sweden
OBJECTIVES: To facilitate legislative and governmental co-operation between member states, with particular reference to proposals of the Nordic Council of Ministers
MEMBERSHIP (END-'00): Denmark, Finland, Iceland, Norway, Sweden (*total* 5)

Baltic Council
DATE OF FOUNDATION: 1992   HEADQUARTERS: rotating
OBJECTIVES: To promote political, economic and social co-operation between the three Baltic republics
MEMBERSHIP (END-'00): Estonia, Latvia, Lithuania (*total* 3)

Council of the Baltic Sea States (CBSS)
DATE OF FOUNDATION: 1992   HEADQUARTERS: Stockholm, Sweden
OBJECTIVES: To promote political, economic and other co-operation between Baltic littoral and adjacent states
MEMBERSHIP (END-'00): Denmark, Estonia, Finland, Germany, Latvia, Lithuania, Norway, Poland, Russia, Sweden (*total* 10)

Arctic Council (AC)
DATE OF FOUNDATION: 1996   HEADQUARTERS: Ottawa, Canada
OBJECTIVES: To promote co-operation between Arctic states (involving indigenous communities) on environmental issues and on the social and economic development of the region
MEMBERSHIP (END-'00): Canada, Denmark, Finland, Iceland, Norway, Russia, Sweden, USA (*total* 8)

THE loss of ozone over the Arctic exceeded 60 per cent during the winter of 1999-2000, the worst loss ever recorded. This was reported on April 5 to the European Ozone Research Co-ordinating Unit. Although industrialised countries had phased-out the manufacture of ozone-destroying chemicals, the thinning and shrinking of the Arctic icecap caused by global warming resulted in colder conditions in the upper atmosphere which accelerated ozone destruction. US scientists reported that the temperature of the Arctic environment had risen by 6°C over the past 30 years, and in August scientists aboard a Russian icebreaker found open water at the North Pole.

In April the heads of government of the Council of Baltic Sea States (CBSS) countries endorsed a new structure for the Council, consolidating within its overall framework all regional intergovernmental, multilateral co-operation taking place amongst CBSS members. The CBSS Forum on the Northern Dimension was held in Schwerin in Mecklenburg-Western Pomerania, Germany, in August, and the Forum for NGOs was organised by the *land* of Schleswig-Holstein in Lübeck. A further step towards closer economic and academic links throughout the area was the opening on September 20 of the EuroFaculty at Kaliningrad State University, Russia, following similar centres at Tartu in Estonia, Riga in Latvia and Vilnius in Lithuania.

Finland served as Chair of the Arctic Council for 2000-02 and presided over a series of meetings and workshops covering: environmental concerns; biodiversity monitoring; the Arctic Council Action Plan; a special Telemedicine session at the 11th International Congress for Circumpolar Health; the Arctic Migratory Birds Workshop; and Bycatch of Seabirds by Commercial Fisheries in the Arctic Region. An International Oil and Ice Workshop 2000 was held and the Sustainable Development Working Group met at Fairbanks, Alaska, USA. The Saami Council met in Karesuvanto, Finland.

The Baltic Assembly held its 16th session in Tartu, Estonia, on May 25-27. A main focus of discussion, as in 1999, was the strengthening of Baltic co-operation in preparation for the entry of the three states to the European Union (see AR 1999, p. 440). The Assembly met again on December 7-9 in Vilnius, Lithuania, for its 17th session, when ministers discussed the integration of the Baltic States into NATO and the development of rail transport and tourism, and approved a US$307,602 budget for 2001.

At its 52nd session—held in Reykjavik, Iceland on November 6-8—the Nordic Council elected Svend Erik Hovmand of Denmark as its new rotating president for 2001. The Council heard the report of the specially appointed Advisory Panel on the Future of Nordic Co-operation, which advised an extension of co-operation to include security and foreign policy, and advocated closer involvement with Baltic countries. The panel further proposed that Nordic countries should "speak with a single voice in the EU". Initiatives on bio-ethics and food safety, social and healthcare policy, and the competitiveness of the region in the IT sector were also debated at the session.

v. OTHER EUROPEAN ORGANISATIONS

European Free Trade Association (EFTA)
DATE OF FOUNDATION: 1960   HEADQUARTERS: Geneva, Switzerland
OBJECTIVES: To eliminate barriers to non-agricultural trade between members
MEMBERSHIP (END-'00): Iceland, Liechtenstein, Norway, Switzerland (*total* 4)
SECRETARY GENERAL: William Rossier (Switzerland)

Central European Free Trade Association (CEFTA)
DATE OF FOUNDATION: 1992   HEADQUARTERS: rotating
OBJECTIVES: Reducing trade barriers between members with a view to their eventual membership of the European Union
MEMBERSHIP (END-'00): Bulgaria, Czech Republic, Hungary, Poland, Romania, Slovakia, Slovenia (*total* 7)

Visegrad Group
DATE OF FOUNDATION: 1991   HEADQUARTERS: rotating
OBJECTIVES: Reducing trade barriers between members with a view to their eventual membership of the European Union
MEMBERSHIP (END-'00): Czech Republic, Hungary, Poland, Slovakia (*total* 4)

Central European Initiative (CEI)
DATE OF FOUNDATION: 1992   HEADQUARTERS: rotating
OBJECTIVES: To promote the harmonisation of economic and other policies of member states
MEMBERSHIP (END-'00): Albania, Armenia, Azerbaijan, Bulgaria, Georgia, Greece, Moldova, Poland, Romania, Slovakia, Slovenia, Ukraine, Yugoslavia (*total* 17)

Black Sea Economic Co-operation Organisation (BSECO)
DATE OF FOUNDATION: 1992   HEADQUARTERS: Istanbul, Turkey
OBJECTIVES: To promote economic cooperation between member states
MEMBERSHIP (END-'00): Albania, Armenia, Azerbaijan, Bulgaria, Georgia, Greece, Moldova, Romania, Russia, Turkey, Ukraine (total 11)
DIRECTOR: ValeriChechelashvili

EUROPEAN FREE TRADE ASSOCIATION. Events relating to the European Free Trade Association (EFTA) during 2000 were dominated by the question of closer economic relations between Switzerland and the European Union (EU). In a referendum, held on May 21, an unexpectedly high number (67.2 per cent) of Swiss voters approved a series of free trade agreements, the most contentious of which allowed workers from EU countries to work in Switzerland. The Swiss Federal Assembly had ratified the free trade agreements in 1999, but opponents (a loose coalition of trade union and environmental groups) had been able to force the holding of a referendum on the agreement (see AR 1999, pp. 85-8; 442). Despite the endorsement of the bilateral agreements by the electorate, Switzerland remained outside the European Economic Area (EEA) and an application for full membership of the EU in the near future was thought to be unlikely.

In a further notable development, EFTA negotiators signed a free trade agreement with Mexico on November 27 in Mexico City. The agreement, scheduled to enter into force in July 2001, was EFTA's first trans-Atlantic agreement and included areas such as financial services, agricultural products and public procurement. The agreement provided for the phased reduction of tariffs on manufactured goods exported by EFTA nations to Mexico and their complete elimination by 2007—making EFTA manufactured exports to Mexico subject to the same regime as those from the European Union and the member nations of the North American Free Trade Agreement (NAFTA). In exchange, the agreement allowed tariff-free access to EFTA markets for Mexican manufactured exports with effect from July 2001.

The new Secretary General of EFTA, William Rossier, took over from his predecessor, Kjartan Jóhannsson on August 29. Rossier, a Swiss diplomat, had previously served as the Swiss Permanent Representative to the World Trade Organisation (WTO).

CENTRAL EUROPEAN FREE TRADE ASSOCIATION. The annual summit of the Central European Free Trade Association (CEFTA), held in Warsaw on November 15, was dominated by the question of the timetable for the accession to the EU of the priority candidate countries, three of which (Poland, the Czech Republic and Hungary), were members of CEFTA. The summit, chaired by the Polish Prime Minister Jerzy Buzek, issued a statement which urged the EU to expedite internal reform in order to facilitate the accession of new members and to set accession dates for the priority candidate countries at its December summit in Nice.

In a separate development, Romanian Foreign Minister Petre Roman stated during a visit to Belgrade on October 10 that Romania was prepared to sponsor Yugoslavian membership of CEFTA.

VISEGRAD GROUP The four nation Visegrad Group, the forerunner to CEFTA, had been established in 1991 and revived in 1998 due to tensions within CEFTA. For the members of the group, the year 2000 was a frustrating one during which it seemed as if they could do little more to further their prospective membership of the EU than press for a timetable for enlargement. Accordingly, at a meeting at Stirin Castle near Prague on June 9, the Prime Ministers of the four countries called on the EU to set a date for the completion of accession talks with the three Visegrad priority candidate states (Slovakia, the fourth Visegrad nation, was not one of the priority candidate countries).

Tensions emerged within the Visegrad group between Slovakia and Hungary over the strategy to be pursued towards the EU. At a meeting of the Visegrad Four on October 13, in Karlovy Vary, the Hungarian Prime Minister, Viktor Orban, stated that whilst the Visegrad members supported each others' negotiating positions: "no country can expect the others to wait for it to catch up". The comment was a rejection of the Slovakian position that the four countries should wait to accede to the EU at the same time and not in different waves.

At a meeting on January 19 in Pszczyna, Poland, the Presidents of the member nations expressed their support for Slovakia's bid to become a member of the North Atlantic Treaty Organisation (NATO), and urged NATO to announce a decision on Slovakian membership at its 2002 summit to be held in

Prague. Slovakia was the only Visegrad state which had not been admitted to NATO in March 1999 (see AR 1999, p. 405).

Officials from the Czech Republic, Hungary, Poland, Slovakia, and Romania (which was not a member of the Visegrad group) met in Prague on October 27 to consider measures which would ensure the better treatment of Roma (Gypsy) people in the region. The issue was an important one since discrimination against Roma people had been a source of tension between the Visegrad four and the European Union (see AR 1999, p. 442).

CENTRAL EUROPEAN INITIATIVE. The most significant development during the year relating to the Central European Initiative (CEI), the largest grouping of states in central and eastern Europe, was the formal accession of the Yugoslavia to the organisation, at the CEI annual summit in Budapest on November 23-25.

At the summit, held under the auspices of the Hungarian presidency, the heads of government of the member states reiterated the importance of the European integration process and enlargement of the European Union (EU) for the CEI member states and welcomed the Stability Pact for South Eastern Europe. With regard to policy co-ordination within the CEI, the heads of government recommended that environmental protection should become a priority for governments following a series of environmental accidents in member countries during the year.

BLACK SEA ECONOMIC CO-OPERATION ORGANISATION Following a relatively eventful 1999, the 11 nations of the Black Sea Economic Co-operation Organisation (BSECO) experienced a quieter year in 2000. Relations between Turkey and Armenia, strained by continued recriminations over the massacre of Armenian Christians in the Ottoman Empire in 1915, improved to the extent that it was announced in August that Armenia was to establish permanent representation to the BSECO headquarters in Istanbul in accordance with an agreement signed in April 1999. Both governments emphasised, however, that direct diplomatic representation between the two countries would not be established. Successive Turkish governments had made the normalisation of relations with Armenia conditional on Armenian acceptance of Azerbaijani sovereignty over the disputed territory of Nagorno-Karabakh.

6. ARAB, AFRICAN, ASIA-PACIFIC AND AMERICAN ORGANISATIONS

i. ARAB ORGANISATIONS

League of Arab States
DATE OF FOUNDATION: 1945   HEADQUARTERS: Cairo, Egypt
OBJECTIVES: To co-ordinate political, economic, social and cultural co-operation between member states and to mediate in disputes between them
MEMBERSHIP (END-'00): Algeria, Bahrain, Comoros, Djibouti, Egypt, Iraq, Jordan, Kuwait, Lebanon, Libya, Mauritania, Morocco, Oman, Palestine, Qatar, Saudi Arabia, Somalia, Sudan, Syria, Tunisia, United Arab Emirates, Yemen (*total* 22)
SECRETARY GENERAL: Ismat Abdel Meguid (Egypt)

Gulf Co-operation Council (GCC)
DATE OF FOUNDATION: 1981   HEADQUARTERS: Riyadh, Saudi Arabia
OBJECTIVES: To promote co-operation between member states in all fields with a view to achieving unity
MEMBERSHIP (END-'00): Bahrain, Kuwait, Oman, Qatar, Saudi Arabia, United Arab Emirates (*total* 6)
SECRETARY GENERAL: Jameel al-Hujilan (Saudi Arabia)

Arab Maghreb Union (AMU)
DATE OF FOUNDATION: 1989   HEADQUARTERS: Casablanca, Morocco
OBJECTIVES: To strengthen "the bonds of brotherhood" between member states, particularly in the area of economic development
MEMBERSHIP (END-'00): Algeria, Libya, Mauritania, Morocco, Tunisia (*total* 5)
SECRETARY GENERAL: Mohammed Amamou (Tunisia)

THROUGHOUT 2000 the ARAB LEAGUE was primarily concerned with the crisis in the Middle East peace process and Israel's proposed withdrawal from Lebanon. At the start of March, in response to renewed Israeli attacks on villages in southern Lebanon because of the activities of Hezbollah, Arab League foreign ministers met in Beirut for the first time in 30 years to demonstrate their solidarity with Lebanon. They called on all Arab states to freeze relations with Israel until there was movement on the issue of peace between Israel and the Palestinians and demanded that Israel should make its planned withdrawal from Lebanon—which went ahead in May—part of an overall Middle East peace settlement. The issue arose again at the start of May when the Arab League headquarters in Cairo condemned Israeli attacks on Lebanon that had left two civilians dead, and called for Arab states to withdraw from multilateral negotiations until there was genuine progress towards peace.

In mid-July, the League expressed its concerns over possible co-operation between India and Israel on nuclear issues after the Indian Foreign and Interior Ministers visited Israel and agreed to co-operate on anti-terrorism strategies, mainly directed towards countering the growing threat to Indian control in Kashmir. Soon, however, the focus switched back to the peace process when, in early September, Arab League Foreign Ministers warned that Arab states would break off diplomatic relations with any state recognising Jerusalem as the Israeli capital. By the end of the month the League was struggling to deal with a far greater crisis as serious hostilities broke out in the Occupied Territories (see V.2.i) and, at an Arab League ministerial meeting hastily called in Cairo to prepare for an emergency Arab summit, the gathering called for Israelis responsible for killing Palestinians to be put on trial.

At the emergency summit meeting in Cairo in late October, Israel was roundly condemned for the violence in the Occupied Territories, but moderate Arab states prevented demands for a total break with Israel being adopted by the meeting. Instead, the meeting called for the creation of a UN force for the Occupied Territories, a UN tribunal to try Israelis accused of killing Palestinians, and a fact-finding mission to visit the area. At the same time, two funds were created, one, with US$200 million, to help the families of the victims of the crisis and the other, with US$800 million, to support a Palestinian state and preserve Jerusalem. Towards the end of the year, after the outgoing Secretary General of the League, Ismat Abdel Meguid, had met the UN High Commissioner for Human Rights, Mary Robinson, in November to protest about Israeli brutality in the Occupied Territories, the League began preparations for another summit meeting over the Israel-Palestinian crisis, to be held in early 2001.

In an on-going separate initiative, the League continued to work for the construction of an Arab common market during the year, as part of its response to the EU's Barcelona Process initiative. In June, in the wake of the Israeli withdrawal from Lebanon, Foreign Ministers of the Damascus Declaration states—a virtually defunct organisation consisting of Gulf Co-operation Council countries, together with Egypt and Syria, and created in the wake of the war against Iraq in 1991 to guarantee Gulf security—met in Cairo to celebrate the "Lebanese victory".

During the year, the GULF CO-OPERATION COUNCIL (GCC), which was originally conceived as a regional security organisation based on economic integration, saw its economic dimension come to the fore. At the annual summit meeting in December, Council heads of state approved the decisions of a ministerial meeting the previous month to establish a common external customs tariff for the organisation at 5.5 per cent for ordinary goods and 7.5 per cent for luxury goods which, they proposed, should come into force in March 2005, after a five-year transitional period. The summit meeting, however, delayed the start of the transitional period by one year until January 2002 and failed to set a timetable for the introduction of a common currency, a measure that had originally been intended to accompany the introduction of the common external tariff. In view of the organisation's awareness of the pressure of economic globalisation—all of its members being members of the World Trade Organisation—this was a serious setback to measures for closer economic integration. Similar problems of delay persisted in on-going negotiations over a proposed free trade area with the EU and over new quota and tariff arrangements for Gulf petrochemical and aluminium exports to Europe.

In part, such delays reflected internal tensions within the Council. The United Arab Emirates, for example, had sought a lower external customs tariff of 4 and

6 per cent respectively on basic and luxury goods. Most of the tensions, however, related to political issues, particularly the on-going quarrel between the Emirates and Iran over sovereignty over the Greater and Lesser Tunb Islands (claimed by Abu Dhabi), and Abu Musa (claimed by Sharjah), which were strategically situated at the entrance to the Persian (or Arabian) Gulf. Iran had annexed the islands in 1971 and had, in a memorandum of understanding in that year, agreed to share sovereignty with Sharjah. In 1992 the Iranian authorities revoked this agreement, claiming all of Abu Musa. In response, the GCC states revived claims to all three islands and had consistently thereafter demanded an Iranian withdrawal and reference of the dispute to the International Court of Justice at The Hague or to another international tribunal.

Since 1998, however, the Arab states of the Gulf, led by Saudi Arabia, had worked to improve their relations with Iran. Iran, too, had suggested a meeting at foreign ministerial level to the United Arab Emirates, but the Emirates government had made it clear that it would accept the proposal only if Iran accepted international arbitration, an agreed agenda for such a meeting, and a timetable for resolving the dispute. The situation had led to fears in the Emirates that support within the GCC for its demands had begun to wane and, in November, it threatened to leave the organisation. After renewed promises of support, the Emirates agreed to remain and to accept the higher level of external customs tariff. As a result, the December summit meeting renewed calls on Iran to yield on the islands issue.

The United Arab Emirates made a further concession by acquiescing to Saudi Arabian demands that it support a call upon Iraq at the summit to comply with UN resolutions over sanctions and human rights—the Emirates was an advocate of renewed links with Iraq to return it to the Arab fold, despite Saudi and Kuwaiti opposition. The summit meeting's call echoed one made earlier in the year at a meeting of GCC foreign ministers in Jeddah, which demanded "practical steps" from Iraq over compliance with UN demands. That meeting also condemned an Amnesty International report on Saudi Arabia as lacking in objectivity and neutrality in what the meeting considered to be an "unjustified campaign". The condemnation underlined the degree to which the GCC was becoming a Saudi-dominated organisation as well as losing its significance as an instrument for collective defence. The latter point was highlighted by the fact that the December summit meeting, although it approved a common defence pact, did not provide for new institutions to operate the new agreement. In fact, defence was now provided on a national basis with Western support, precisely the outcome the GCC was originally designed to avoid.

ii. AFRICAN ORGANISATIONS AND CONFERENCES

Organisation of African Unity (OAU)
DATE OF FOUNDATION: 1963   HEADQUARTERS: Addis Ababa, Ethiopia
OBJECTIVES: To promote the unity, solidarity and co-operation of African states, to defend their sovereignty and to eradicate remaining traces of colonialism
MEMBERSHIP (END-'00): Algeria, Angola, Benin, Botswana, Burkina Faso, Burundi, Cameroon, Cape Verde, Central African Republic, Chad, Comoros, Democratic Republic of Congo, Congo, Côte d'Ivoire, Djibouti, Egypt, Equatorial Guinea, Eritrea, Ethiopia, Gabon, Gambia, Ghana, Guinea, Guinea-Bissau, Kenya, Lesotho, Liberia, Libya, Madagascar, Malawi, Mali, Mauritania, Mauritius, Morocco, Mozambique, Namibia, Niger, Nigeria, Rwanda, Sahrawi Arab Democratic Republic (Western Sahara), São Tomé & Príncipe, Senegal, Seychelles, Sierra Leone, Somalia, South Africa, Sudan, Swaziland, Tanzania, Togo, Tunisia, Uganda, Zambia, Zimbabwe (*total* 54)
SECRETARY GENERAL: Salim Ahmed Salim (Tanzania)

Economic Community of West African States (ECOWAS)
DATE OF FOUNDATION: 1975   HEADQUARTERS: Abuja, Nigeria
OBJECTIVES: To seek the creation of an economic union of member states
MEMBERSHIP (END-'00): Benin, Burkina Faso, Cape Verde, Côte d'Ivoire, Gambia, Ghana, Guinea, Guinea-Bissau, Liberia, Mali, Niger, Nigeria, Senegal, Sierra Leone, Togo (*total* 15)
EXECUTIVE SECRETARY: Lamine Kouyaté (Guinea)

West African Economic and Monetary Union (UEMOA)
DATE OF FOUNDATION: 1994   HEADQUARTERS: Ouagadougou, Burkina Faso
OBJECTIVES: To promote the economic and monetary union of member states
MEMBERSHIP (END-'00): Benin, Burkina Faso, Côte d'Ivoire, Guinea-Bissau, Mali, Mauritania, Niger, Senegal (*total* 8)

Southern African Development Community (SADC)
DATE OF FOUNDATION: 1992   HEADQUARTERS: Gaboro, Botswana
OBJECTIVES: To work towards the creation of a regional common market
MEMBERSHIP (END-'00): Angola, Botswana, Democratic Republic of Congo, Lesotho, Malawi, Mauritius, Mozambique, Namibia, Seychelles, South Africa, Swaziland, Tanzania, Zambia, Zimbabwe (*total* 14)
EXECUTIVE SECRETARY: Pakereesamy (Prega) Ramsamy (Mauritius), acting

Common Market for Eastern and Southern Africa (COMESA)
DATE OF FOUNDATION: 1993   HEADQUARTERS: Lusaka, Zambia
OBJECTIVES: To establish a full free-trade area
MEMBERSHIP (END-'00): Angola, Burundi, Comoros, Democratic Republic of the Congo, Egypt, Eritrea, Ethiopia, Kenya, Lesotho, Madagascar, Malawi, Mauritius, Mozambique, Namibia, Rwanda, Sudan, Swaziland, Uganda, Zambia, Zimbabwe (*total* 20)
SECRETARY GENERAL: Erastus Mwencha (Kenya)

Economic Community of Central African States (CEEAC)
DATE OF FOUNDATION: 1983   HEADQUARTERS: Libreville, Gabon
OBJECTIVES: To establish a full free-trade area
MEMBERSHIP (END-'00): Angola, Burundi, Cameroon, Central African Republic, Chad, Democratic Republic of the Congo, Congo, Equatorial Guinea, Gabon, Rwanda, São Tomé & Príncipe (*total* 11)
SECRETARY GENERAL: Louis-Sylvain Goma (Congo)

East African Commission (EAC)
DATE OF FOUNDATION: 1996 (reviving former East African Community)   HEADQUARTERS: Nairobi, Kenya
OBJECTIVES: To promote economic integration between member states
MEMBERSHIP (END-'00): Kenya, Tanzania, Uganda (*total* 3)

ORGANISATION OF AFRICAN UNITY. With a certain lack of enthusiasm, the heads of state and government of the Organisation for African Unity (OAU), at their 36th summit, in Lomé, in July, adopted a resolution supporting the Libyan-sponsored African Union (AU) Treaty. This move towards greater African unity had been initially proposed by Col. Moamer Kadhafi at a summit in September 1999. A draft of the treaty—the charter for the AU—was drawn up and finalised at a meeting attended by African Foreign Ministers in Tripoli from May 27 to June 3.

The new AU Charter would replace the 1963 OAU Charter and the 1991 Abuja Treaty setting up the African Economic Community. The bodies of the proposed African Union would be the Conference of the Union, the Executive Council, the Parliament, the Court of Justice, and Cultural Economic and Social committees, as well as financial institutions such as an African Central Bank. The stated purpose of the change was to face the threat of globalisation and the emergence of restrictive regional trading blocs and alliances.

Reports of the discussions at the summit indicated that some of the most important African countries, notably South Africa, Nigeria, Egypt, Algeria and Kenya did not favour moving immediately ahead with the Union. Of the 53 member countries, only 27 were ready to put their signatures to the draft document, and there was a feeling amongst even those who signed it that the treaty still needed a lot of further revision. Kadhafi attached great importance to the summit, and was said to have contributed some US$13 million towards the US$20 million costs. Many of the supporters of the treaty were west African states, notably Togo itself, whose autocratic President Gnassingbé Eyadéma took on the OAU chair for 2000-1. Several countries, such as Angola, the DRC, Namibia, and Zimbabwe protested against Eyadéma's continuing involvement with Angolan rebel Jonas Savimbi.

Amongst those who expressed reservations about the African Union project there was a feeling that Africa still had too many problems for it to start talking about continental unity. Leaders at the 1999 OAU summit had committed themselves "to intensify action for peace and to support efforts aimed at the peaceful settlement of conflicts, particularly through the strengthening of the OAU mechanism for conflict resolution". In 2000, however, there was only limited discussion of major conflicts such as those in Somalia and the DRC, but the summit participants welcomed progress made in the mediation between Ethiopia and Eritrea by the outgoing President Bouteflika of Algeria. The summit also decided to send a delegation to Côte D'Ivoire to mediate in the growing confrontation between the military leader Gen. Gueï and the political leader Alassane Ouattara (see VI.3.i.). The delegation was met by hostile demonstrators warning the OAU to stay out of Ivoirian affairs and it had only limited success. Gueï himself had been excluded from the summit by the new OAU ruling that those who had come to power by coups could not attend OAU summits (a prohibition which was also applied to the military ruler of the Comoros).

At the conclusion of the summit, OAU Secretary General Salim Ahmed Salim said that the Union was the logical extension of the OAU, moving towards a higher form of unity for the continent. But, he said, many of the institutions would have to wait for further consultations. It was also decided at the summit to send a troika of three leaders, the Presidents of Algeria, Nigeria and South Africa, on missions to developed country capitals to propound a Millennium African Partnership Initiative, which would revive the often touted idea of a Marshall plan for Africa that would further development based on Africa helping itself.

The problem of Africa's development was also high on the agenda of the first Europe-Africa summit (jointly organised by the EU and the OAU) held in Cairo at the beginning of April. It was reported that the Europeans had hoped that the summit would focus on political questions (democracy, human rights and good government) but the Africans, forming a united front, decided that the debt issue needed to be at the forefront. In this they were backed by the Jubilee 2000 campaign for a millennial cancellation of the debts of the world's poorest countries. The final Cairo Declaration included mention of ways to adapt African economies to the world economy and increase private investment, and commissioned an official report on African debt.

Several weeks prior to the Europe-Africa summit, the EU and the 70 African, Caribbean and Pacific (ACP) countries had completed a new 20-year trade and aid partnership agreement to replace the Lomé Convention, which expired on February 29. It was most notable for the phased ending of the principle of non-reciprocity—which had been at the heart of the Lomé agreement—signalling a possible end to some of the other privileges and protections enshrined in the former convention. This framework accord, individual parts of which would be subject to more frequent renegotiation, was subsequently signed on June 28 in Cotonou, Benin.

International concern at the state of the African continent, especially the issue of the HIV/AIDS pandemic—which ran as an unpleasant theme through all the major meetings of the year as more and more facts emerged on the extent of the problem—was also prominent at the UN Millennium Summit in September.

Organisations such as the African Development Bank and the Economic Commission for Africa both held assemblies at which plans for furthering African development were addressed. The Bank renewed the mandate of its President, Morocco's Omar Kabbaj for a further five years.

REGIONAL ORGANISATIONS. Of Africa's regional organisations, the 12-country Southern African Development community (SADC) was once again centre-stage for the wrong reasons, as it grappled unsuccessfully with the continuing civil war in the Democratic Republic of Congo (DRC). The SADC ceasefire, worked out in July 1999 in Lusaka, had still not been put into application by the end of 2000, and tensions between SADC member states, notably between those who passionately backed the DRC government—such as Zimbabwe, Angola and Namibia—and those which were less enthusiastic, started to affect other aspects of the grouping. However, the leaders put on a show of solidarity at the annual summit in Windhoek in August over Zimbabwean President Robert Mugabe's land reform policies. It also proved possible for the member governments to approve an agreement for a free trade area, which came into force at the beginning of September (although Angola, the DRC and the Seychelles had not yet signed). The objective was to eliminate tariffs for 85 per cent of intra-SADC trade by 2008 and to have a full free trade area by 2012. This agreement was counter-balanced by a similar Free Trade Area for the Common Market for Eastern and Southern Africa (COMESA)—which grouped many of the SADC members with eastern African countries—that came into force for the "first wave" of nine of COMESA's 20 members, at the end of October. This confused jigsaw was rendered more complex by Tanzania's withdrawal from COMESA, whilst remaining a member of SADC.

The Economic Community of West African States (ECOWAS) was able to feel that for the first time in some years it could focus on its economic aspects, since in March it had formally withdrawn its troops in the ECOMOG (ECOWAS Monitoring group) from Sierra Leone. In May, seven of its members (Nigeria, Ghana, Sierra Leone, the Gambia, Liberia, Guinea and Cape Verde) agreed to set up a "fast track" for currency union involving all the member countries not in the franc zone. Although the two-year deadline for implementation appeared short in view of the wide disparity of the currencies concerned, the move was endorsed at the organisation's summit in Bamako. This meeting also responded to pressures from the mounting crisis on the Guinea border by agreeing to send a small ECOMOG force of some 1,600 troops to patrol the border in view of the increasing number of cross-border attacks from unidentified rebel groups in both Sierra Leone and Liberia.

The prospect of progress on the regional currency front appeared to be endorsed by the franc zone members, who already belonged to the West African Economic and Monetary Union (UEMOA). This organisation continued to make strides towards further integration, although there was increasing concern that its progress might be hampered by the continuing crisis in Côte d'Ivoire in view of the economic disruption in that country, the economic power-house of UEMOA, and the damaging friction with its northern neighbours. The UEMOA also began to involve itself in the crisis-wracked francophone African airline Air Afrique, whose worrying finances threatened its survival.

The Economic and Monetary Community of Central African States (CEMAC)—the franc zone's central African grouping—continued to make modest progress, whilst still lagging behind its west African counterpart. The progress of the wider Economic Community of Central African States (CEEAC)—made up of the membership of CEMAC plus notably the DRC and Angola—proved blocked by the DRC's political crisis. Plans also still moved slowly towards the loose reconstitution of the former East African Community as an "association". On the whole, the dream that unity might come through regional groupings was still proving frustratingly slow and remained beset with difficulties.

iii. ASIA-PACIFIC ORGANISATIONS

Association of South-East Asian Nations (ASEAN)

DATE OF FOUNDATION: 1967   HEADQUARTERS: Jakarta, Indonesia
OBJECTIVES: To accelerate economic growth, social progress and cultural development in the region
MEMBERSHIP (END-'00): Brunei, Cambodia, Indonesia, Laos, Malaysia, Myanmar, Philippines, Singapore, Thailand, Vietnam (*total* 10)
SECRETARY GENERAL: Rodolfo C. Severino (Philippines)

Asia-Pacific Economic Co-operation (APEC)

DATE OF FOUNDATION: 1989   HEADQUARTERS: Singapore
OBJECTIVES: To promote market-oriented economic development and co-operation in the Pacific Rim countries
MEMBERSHIP (END-'00): Australia, Brunei, Canada, Chile, China, Hong Kong, Indonesia, Japan, South Korea, Malaysia, Mexico, New Zealand, Papua New Guinea, Peru, Philippines, Russia, Singapore, Taiwan, Thailand, United States, Vietnam (*total* 21)
EXECUTIVE: Timothy Hannah (New Zealand)

South Asian Association for Regional Co-operation (SAARC)

DATE OF FOUNDATION: 1985   HEADQUARTERS: Kathmandu, Nepal
OBJECTIVES: To promote collaboration and mutual assistance in the economic, social, cultural and technical fields
MEMBERSHIP (END-'00): Bangladesh, Bhutan, India, Maldives, Nepal, Pakistan, Sri Lanka (*total* 7)
SECRETARY GENERAL: Nacem ul-Hasan (Pakistan)

Indian Ocean Rim Association for Regional Co-operation (IORARC)

DATE OF FOUNDATION: 1997
OBJECTIVES: To promote co-operation in trade, investment, infrastructure, tourism, science, technology and human-resource development in the Indian Ocean region
MEMBERSHIP (END-'00): Australia, India, Indonesia, Kenya, Madagascar, Malaysia, Mauritius, Mozambique, Oman, Singapore, South Africa, Sri Lanka, Tanzania, Yemen (*total* 14)

Pacific Community (PC)

DATE OF FOUNDATION: 1947 (as South Pacific Commission)   HEADQUARTERS: Noumea, New Caledonia
OBJECTIVES: To facilitate political and other cooperation between member states and territories
MEMBERSHIP (END-'00): American Samoa, Australia, Cook Islands, Fiji, France, French Polynesia, Guam, Kiribati, Marshall Islands, Federated States of Micronesia, Nauru, New Caledonia, New Zealand, Niue, Northern Mariana Islands, Palau, Papua New Guinea, Pitcairn Islands, Samoa, Solomon Islands, Tokelau, Tonga, Tuvalu, United Kingdom, United States, Vanuatu, Wallis & Futuna Islands (*total* 27)
DIRECTOR GENERAL: Lourdes Pangelinan (Guam)

Pacific Islands Forum (PIF)

DATE OF FOUNDATION: 1971 (as South Pacific Forum)   HEADQUARTERS: Suva, Fiji
OBJECTIVES: To enhance the economic and social well-being of the people of the Pacific, in support of the efforts of the members' governments
MEMBERSHIP (END-'00): Australia, Palau, Cook Islands, Fiji, Kiribati, Marshall Islands, Federated States of Micronesia, Nauru, New Zealand, Niue, Papua New Guinea, Samoa, Solomon Islands, Tonga, Tuvalu, Vanuatu (*total* 16)
SECRETARY GENERAL: Noel Levi (Papua New Guinea)

ASSOCIATION OF SOUTH-EAST ASIAN NATIONS. In November the heads of government of the member states of the Association of South-East Asian Nations (ASEAN) held an informal summit in Singapore. ASEAN leaders had previously held an informal summit in the Philippines in November 1999 (see AR 1999, pp. 452-53). In Singapore the leaders agreed to phase out tariffs between member states on information technology goods by 2010 and ambitious plans were also made to construct regional high-speed internet connections. Of symbolic importance was the commissioning of a feasibility study of a proposed free trade area linking ASEAN with China, Japan and South Korea. The move highlighted a growing trend towards regional co-operation and especially a rapprochement between ASEAN and China. By contrast, ASEAN leaders threatened to call off a meeting with the EU if the Europeans continued to demand the exclusion from the talks of ASEAN member Myanmar, widely criticised in Europe and the West for its human rights abuses.

ASEAN Foreign Ministers held their 33rd annual meeting in July in Thailand. The chief concrete outcome of the meeting, promoted principally by Thailand's Foreign Minister Surin Pitsuwan, was an agreement to set up a "troika", a team of three Foreign Ministers led by ASEAN's current chairman, as a mechanism to help the organisation deal more effectively with regional crises. However, the stipulation that the troika should adhere to ASEAN's principle of non-interference in the internal affairs of member states severely limited its scope for action. The meeting was followed by the ministerial conclave of the ASEAN Regional Forum (ARF), which included amongst its 23 participants China, the USA and the EU. For the first time North Korea's Foreign Minister Paek Nam Sun attended the ARF, holding unprecedented meetings with his counterparts from South Korea, Japan and the USA.

ASIA-EUROPE MEETING. The third Asia-Europe meeting (ASEM) of President of the European Commission Romano Prodi and heads of government and senior ministers of the 15 EU states and 10 Asian states was held in October in Seoul, the capital of South Korea. The Asian states attending were China, Japan, South Korea, Brunei, Indonesia, Malaysia, the Philippines, Singapore, Thailand and Vietnam. On the opening day of the meeting the leaders adopted the Seoul Declaration for Peace on the Korean Peninsula in support of the process of rapprochement between North and South Korea. It was reported, however, that President Jacques Chirac of France had expressed reservations about the speed with which some EU countries had opened or were proposing to open diplomatic relations with North Korea. Chirac indicated that he preferred to wait until the North granted its citizens human rights and renounced weapons of mass destruction.

The summit endorsed 16 projects to be promoted by the member states, including an annual ASEM roundtable on economic globalisation, the establishment of a Trans-Eurasian information network and co-operation on combating transnational crime. The ASEM closed with the adoption of an Asia-Europe Co-operation Framework (AEFC), a charter for the development of the group. The fourth ASEM was scheduled to be held in 2002 in Copenhagen (Denmark). ASEM was launched by the EU in 1996 as a counter-balance to the influence of the US-led Asia-Pacific Economic Co-operation (APEC) forum.

ASIA-PACIFIC ECONOMIC CO-OPERATION In November heads of government of the 21-member APEC forum held an informal summit meeting in Bandar Seri Begawan, the capital of Brunei. The summit's closing statement called for the start "as soon as possible" in 2001 of a new round of multilateral trade negotiations under the auspices of the World Trade Organisation (WTO). The communiqué also called for the trade talks to have a "balanced and sufficiently broad-based agenda", which was seen by analysts as reflecting a compromise between the more ardent proponents of trade liberalisation, such as the USA, Japan and Australia, and the more cautious attitudes of APEC members such as China and Malaysia.

US President Bill Clinton's national economic adviser Gene Sperling said that the USA hoped to complete a bilateral trade agreement with Singapore by the end of the year, following a groundbreaking agreement concluded in mid-November between New Zealand and Singapore. A number of such regional bilateral accords were in the pipeline, which led some participants at the summit to reflect that the effect of their proliferation might be to weaken rather than strengthen the world trading system.

APEC leaders agreed to invite North Korea to participate in the forum's working committees, an offer which fell short of full membership. New Zealand's Prime Minister Helen Clark announced at the meeting that New Zealand was abolishing tariffs on imports from the 48 least-developed countries (LDC) and urged other APEC leaders to follow this example.

APEC Finance Ministers had met in September in Bandar Seri Begawan. Whilst the ministers presented an overall picture of economic and social recovery from the Asian financial crisis of 1997-98, a group of advisers from private sector financial institutions urged member governments to develop viable bond markets to cushion their economies against future market volatility. The meeting's official agenda of continuing financial, institutional and corporate reform was overshadowed by concern over the region's vulnerability to currently rising oil prices.

SOUTH ASIAN ASSOCIATION FOR REGIONAL CO-OPERATION. The poor state of relations between India and Pakistan (see VIII.2.i.) meant that the 11th summit meeting of the South Asian Association for Regional Co-operation (SAARC), scheduled to be held in late 1999 in Nepal, also failed to take place in 2000. An extraordinary meeting of SAARC senior officials was held in Sri Lanka in mid-November. The meeting, attended by representatives of all member countries, covered a wide range of items on the Association's economic, social, technical and cultural agenda. The 15th anniversary of the signing of the SAARC charter was commemorated at the SAARC secretariat in Nepal in early December.

INDIAN OCEAN RIM ASSOCIATION FOR REGIONAL CO-OPERATION. The council of ministers of the Indian Ocean Rim Association of Regional Co-operation (IORARC) met in Oman in January. At the meeting China, Egypt, Jordan and the UK were accepted as "dialogue partners on trade and investment". Applications for full membership by France and Pakistan were rejected. The conflict between India (a founding member of the IORARC) and Pakistan was said to have "complicated" the latter's application, which was formally rebuffed on the grounds of non-compliance with the organisation's charter on foreign trading links. The French bid for full membership was turned down because it was not an Indian Ocean state. France had claimed membership through its sovereignty over the island of Réunion, to the east of Madagascar.

PACIFIC ISLANDS FORUM. Foreign Ministers of the Pacific Islands Forum (PIF—formerly the South Pacific Forum) held their first meeting under the organisation's new name in August in Samoa. The object of the meeting was to develop a regional strategy for coping with crises such as the recent coups in Fiji and the Solomon Islands (see X.2.ii). PIF trade officials in late August met in Nadi, Fiji, to consider a draft of a Pacific Area Regional Trade Agreement (PARTA).

A second PIF meeting took place in October in Tarawa, Kiribati. The 16-member group departed from its usual practice of avoiding consideration of member countries' internal affairs, welcoming both the Townsville agreement and the commitment by Fiji's interim government "to return the country to constitutional democracy". The Forum also expressed its "deep concern about past and recent violence and loss of life" in West Papua, urging the Indonesian government and secessionist groups "to resolve their differences peacefully through dialogue and consultation".

Forum leaders adopted a statement known as the Biketawa Declaration, which reaffirmed the principle of non-interference in member states' internal affairs but at the same time expressed a commitment to democratic processes and ideals of equality for all citizens. The importance of indigenous rights and cultural values was also emphasised. As a result of the deterioration in the Pacific Islands' security environment, the Forum approved a series of steps to be taken by its Secretary General in the event of any future crises.

Other issues addressed by the Forum included fisheries management, the economic vulnerability of island states, climate change and sea level rise, and shipments of radioactive materials through the region. The need for member states to protect themselves against criminal activities, including drug trafficking and the misuse of banking systems, was also stressed. The economic repercussions of ethnic violence for Fiji and the Solomon Islands was also noted, as instability had proved damaging both for tourism and trade.

PACIFIC COMMUNITY. Lourdes Pangelinan took over as director general of the Pacific Community (formerly, the South Pacific Commission), based in New Caledonia, in January, succeeding Australian Bob Dun. Pangelinan had served as a deputy director general of the Pacific Community for four years, and she was formerly a senior civil servant in Guam.

ASIAN DEVELOPMENT BANK. The Asian Development Bank (ADB) held its annual meeting in May in Chiang Mai, Thailand. South Korea and other Asian borrowers came under some pressure from the USA, the ADB's second largest shareholder, to repay early loans from the ADB and other agencies made during the 1997 Asian financial crisis. On the sidelines of the meeting the 10 ASEAN members together with Japan, China and South Korea agreed in principle to establish a system of currency swaps as a defence against the kind of speculation which had caused the 1997 financial crisis. Although the agreement fell short of Japan's long-standing proposal for an Asian Monetary Fund, analysts regarded it as a significant step in regional economic co-operation, particularly because of China's involvement.

In its 1999 annual report, published in April, the ABD offered to mediate in regional water disputes, citing its successful role in support of water-sharing schemes in the Mekong river delta in south-east Asia and on the Red River (Song Hong) flowing through China and Vietnam. In what the report described as a "major human tragedy", some 830 million people in Asia and the Pacific had no access to safe drinking water and more than 2 billion lacked sanitation. Of the bank's total lending of US$4.98 billion in 1999, some US$1.24 billion had been devoted to water-related projects. It was reported in April that the ADB had signed Poverty Partnership Agreements with Bangladesh and Mongolia, setting targets for the reduction of poverty in both countries.

iv. AMERICAN AND CARIBBEAN ORGANISATIONS

Organisation of American States (OAS)
DATE OF FOUNDATION: 1948   HEADQUARTERS: Washington DC, USA
OBJECTIVES: To facilitate political, economic and other co-operation between member states and to defend their territorial integrity and independence
MEMBERSHIP (END-'00): Antigua & Barbuda, Argentina, Bahamas, Barbados, Belize, Bolivia, Brazil, Canada, Chile, Colombia, Costa Rica, Cuba (currently excluded), Dominica, Dominican Republic, Ecuador, El Salvador, Grenada, Guatemala, Guyana, Haiti, Honduras, Jamaica, Mexico, Nicaragua, Panama, Paraguay, Peru, St Kitts & Nevis, St Lucia, St Vincent & the Grenadines, Suriname, Trinidad & Tobago, United States, Uruguay, Venezuela (*total* 35)
SECRETARY GENERAL: César Gaviria Trujillo (Colombia)

Rio Group
DATE OF FOUNDATION: 1987   HEADQUARTERS: rotating
OBJECTIVES: To provide a regional mechanism for joint political action
MEMBERSHIP (END-'00): Argentina, Bolivia, Brazil, Chile, Colombia, Ecuador, Guatemala, Mexico, Panama, Paraguay, Peru, Trinidad & Tobago, Uruguay, Venezuela (*total* 14)

Southern Common Market (Mercosur)
DATE OF FOUNDATION: 1991   HEADQUARTERS: Montevideo, Uruguay
OBJECTIVES: To build a genuine common market between member states
MEMBERSHIP (END-'00): Argentina, Brazil, Paraguay, Uruguay (*total* 4)
ADMINISTRATIVE SECRETARY: RamonDíaz Pereira (Brazil)

Andean Community of Nations (Ancom/CA)

DATE OF FOUNDATION: 1969 HEADQUARTERS: Lima, Peru
OBJECTIVES: To promote the economic development and integration of member states
MEMBERSHIP (END-'00): Bolivia, Colombia, Ecuador, Venezuela (*total* 4)
SECRETARY GENERAL: SebastianAlegrett (Venezuela)

Latin American Integration Association (ALADI)

DATE OF FOUNDATION: 1980 (as successor to Latin American Free Trade Association founded in 1960)
HEADQUARTERS: Montevideo, Uruguay
OBJECTIVES: To promote Latin American trade and development by economic preference
MEMBERSHIP (END-'00): Argentina, Bolivia, Brazil, Chile, Colombia, Cuba, Ecuador, Mexico, Paraguay, Peru, Uruguay, Venezuela (*total* 12)
SECRETARY GENERAL: Juan Francisco Rojas Penso (Venezuela)

Latin American Economic System (SELA)

DATE OF FOUNDATION: 1975 HEADQUARTERS: Caracas, Venezuela
OBJECTIVES: To accelerate economic and social development in member states
MEMBERSHIP (END-'00): Argentina, Barbados, Bolivia, Brazil, Chile, Colombia, Costa Rica, Cuba, Dominican Republic, Ecuador, El Salvador, Grenada, Guatemala, Guyana, Haiti, Honduras, Jamaica, Mexico, Nicaragua, Panama, Paraguay, Peru, Spain, Suriname, Trinidad & Tobago, Uruguay, Venezuela (*total* 27)
PERMANENT SECRETARY: Carlos Moneta (Argentina)

Caribbean Community and Common Market (Caricom)

DATE OF FOUNDATION: 1973 HEADQUARTERS: Georgetown, Guyana
OBJECTIVES: To facilitate economic, political and other co-operation between member states and to operate certain regional services
MEMBERSHIP (END-'00): Antigua & Barbuda, Bahamas, Barbados, Belize, Dominica, Grenada, Guyana, Haiti, Jamaica, Montserrat, St Kitts & Nevis, St Lucia, St Vincent & the Grenadines, Suriname, Trinidad & Tobago (*total* 15)
SECRETARY GENERAL: Edwin Carrington (Trinidad & Tobago)

Association of Caribbean States (ACS)

DATE OF FOUNDATION: 1994 HEADQUARTERS: Port of Spain, Trinidad
OBJECTIVES: To foster economic, social and political co-operation with a view to building a distinctive bloc of Caribbean littoral states
MEMBERSHIP (END-'00): Caricom members plus Colombia, Costa Rica, Cuba, Dominican Republic, El Salvador, Guatemala, Haiti, Honduras, Mexico, Nicaragua, Venezuela (*total* 25)
SECRETARY GENERAL: Simon Molina Duarte (Venezuela)

Organisation of Eastern Caribbean States (OECS)

DATE OF FOUNDATION: 1981 HEADQUARTERS: Castries, St Lucia
OBJECTIVES: To co-ordinate the external, defence, trade and monetary policies of member states
MEMBERSHIP (END-'00): Antigua & Barbuda, Dominica, Grenada, Montserrat, St Lucia, St Kitts & Nevis, St Vincent & the Grenadines (*total* 7)
DIRECTOR GENERAL: Swinburne Lestrade (Dominica)

THE ORGANISATION OF AMERICAN STATES (OAS) mediated a boundary dispute between Nicaragua and Honduras which had arisen from the ratification by Honduras of a maritime frontier agreement with Colombia which had infringed Nicaraguan claims. Nicaragua claimed that Honduran forces had occupied the Pacific offshore islet of Cayo Sur, to the north of the 15th parallel, which it regarded as the frontier line, on December 30 1999. The islet, however, was to the south of the 17th parallel which Honduras regarded as the boundary. Despite attempts at mediation, which had led on February 7 to an agreement in principle to submit the boundary question to the International Court of Justice (ICJ), Nicaragua subsequently demanded that Honduras evacuate Cayo Sur within 30 days and between February 19 and 25 naval patrols in the Gulf of Fonseca exchanged gunfire on three occasions. Finally on March 7 (pending the decision of the ICJ) both parties signed an accord regulating the conduct of naval patrols in the Caribbean and joint operations in the Gulf of Fonseca, and providing for the withdrawal of all forces in the vicinity of their land border, and the exchange of information on military flights.

The OAS withdrew its observer mission from Haiti on July 7 in protest against alleged ballot-rigging in the first round of elections to Congress and the failure of the government of President René Préval to act on complaints, noting that even on its own figures the official result of the first round of Senate elections was incorrect.

The Peruvian government decided in January to accept the jurisdiction of the Inter-American Court of Human Rights (IACHR) in the case of the retired army officer Gustavo Cesti Hurtado, who had been sentenced to three years' imprisonment after denouncing high-level corruption in the armed forces. Later, at a Meeting of Consultation of Foreign Ministers held in Washington on May 31, the USA failed to gain sufficient votes to condemn the controversial re-election of President Alberto Fujimori under Resolution 1080, which called for a collective response to any interruption of democracy in a member state. The governments of Mexico and Venezuela, which themselves had both faced criticism of their democratic credentials, strongly opposed any action. The matter was remitted to the meeting of the OAS General Assembly at Windsor, Ontario, on June 4-6, when the chief of the OAS observer mission, Eduardo Stein, presented a report which concluded that the whole electoral process had been irregular. Instead of openly questioning Fujimori's victory, the meeting resolved to send a high-level mission to Peru to explore ways in which Peruvian democracy could be strengthened. The mission, led by OAS Secretary General César Gaviria and the Canadian Foreign Minister, Lloyd Axworthy, visited Peru from June 27-30 and presented proposals, but only the US State Department mentioned enforcement and, in the event, Fujimori fell as a result of a domestic crisis. Financial matters remitted to a second plenary session held on October 12 in Washington, DC, included approval of the budget and a resolution on the future financing of the organisation.

On May 18 US President Bill Clinton approved a bill enhancing the Caribbean Basin Initiative (CBI), which had become uncompetitive following the conclusion of the NORTH AMERICAN FREE TRADE AGREEMENT (NAFTA). The bill granted NAFTA parity to products from 24 countries in the region from October 1. On June 29 Mexico signed a free-trade agreement with the so-called Northern Triangle of El Salvador, Guatemala and Honduras. The agreement, which would come into effect on January 1 2001, excluded key export products such as bananas, coffee and sugar.

In mid-March Argentina and Brazil reached agreement on a transitional regime for intra-regional trade in motor vehicles, disputes over which had held up the business of the SOUTHERN COMMON MARKET (Mercosur/Mercosul). They also agreed to shelve long-standing disputes over footwear, pigs, poultry, steel, sugar and textiles. At the 18th presidential summit held in Buenos Aires on June 30, however, Paraguay and Uruguay rejected the agreement, although they joined the others in reaffirming their willingness to enhance integration and improve macroeconomic co-ordination. All members reaffirmed the Ushuaia Protocol of July 1998, affirming their support for democracy, agreed to hold consultations in the event of interruption to democratic government in any member state, and approved the Buenos Aires Charter on Social Commitment. On June 13 Chile, already an associate member, announced that it would apply for full membership of Mercosur in December.

At the 12th annual summit of the ANDEAN COMMUNITY (ANCOM), held in Lima, Peru, on June 9-10, members reaffirmed their determination to create a unified market by 2005, to co-ordinate macroeconomic policy and to start a dialogue with Bolivia and Mercosur. A political declaration reaffirmed their common commitment to democracy and the rule of law and plans to discuss the political aspects of integration, and the development of a social agenda. At a meeting in Buenos Aires on June 30 delegates welcomed Bolivia's offer to host an extraordinary summit later in the year to which Suriname and Guyana would also be invited.

Nineteen states were represented at the 14th summit of the RIO GROUP, which took place on June 15 at Cartagena de Indias, Colombia, to discuss preparations for the UN's Millennium Summit in September. In a new development, a summit of the 12 Presidents of the South American countries to discuss economic integration was held in Brasília on August 31-September 1. Concern that increasing US aid to Colombia would lead to an escalation of the civil war there was strong, and the leaders, whilst supporting the Colombian peace negotiations in their final communiqué, did not express support for the US-backed "Plan Colombia". However, the US plan was conditionally supported by Brazilian President Fernando Henrique Cardoso at the fourth meeting of Defence Ministers of the Americas, held in Manaus, Brazil, on October 17.

The 10th IBERO-AMERICAN SUMMIT took place in Panama City, Panama, on November 18-19. It was attended by the Presidents of all Latin American states except Nicaragua and Peru. The summit unanimously called for the repeal of the Helms-Burton Act, the US legislation which aimed to restrict non-US trade with Cuba. However an acrimonious dispute broke out between Cuba on the one hand and Spain and El Salvador on the other when the Cuban President, Fidel Castro Ruz, refused to endorse a declaration which condemned the activities of the Basque separatist group ETA, on the grounds that it was "selective". In a reversion to pre-1989 practice, the meeting was also asked to call for the re-opening of negotiations between the United Kingdom and Argentina over the future of the Falkland Islands (Islas Malvinas).

Representatives of 28 countries expressed their continuing support for the LATIN AMERICAN ECONOMIC SYSTEM (SELA) at the 26th regular meeting of the Latin American Council in Caracas, Venezuela, on October 18.

At the 11th inter-sessional meeting of the heads of government of the CARIBBEAN COMMUNITY AND COMMON MARKET (CARICOM) held in St Kitts and Nevis on March 13-14, agreement was reached to establish a Caribbean Court of Justice, which in January 2001 would replace the UK Judicial Committee of the UK Privy Council as the final court of appeal for, in the first instance, Guyana, Trinidad & Tobago and Barbados. Specific portfolios were allocated to the heads of government of the member states to provide an institutional structure for a single market and economy. In May a free trade agreement was concluded with the Dominican Republic, following a decision to exclude soft drinks from the list of duty free products and to postpone a decision on some 50 lesser exclusions. The new agreement would extend the sub-regional market covered by the Central American-CARICOM Free Trade Agreement to a total of some 42 million people.

In February the group of AFRICAN, CARIBBEAN AND PACIFIC (ACP) countries declared their full support for Cuba's admission to the trade preferences which they enjoyed with the European Union (EU) under the fifth Lomé Convention due to be signed at the end of May. However the European Commission indicated that Cuba would have to make greater progress on human rights and democratic reform before this would be possible and, after seven EU countries voted on April 18 at the UN Human Right Commission (UNHCR) to condemn Cuba's record, the application was suspended.

XII RELIGION

JUBILEE. Pope John Paul II inaugurated a World Day of Peace on January 1, as "the message of the jubilee, my hope at the beginning of a new millennium". He opened the Holy Door at St Peter's basilica in Rome and gave the blessing Urbi et Orbi—"to the city and for the world"—a ceremony watched on television by 1.6 billion people in over 100 countries. In the UK Catholics from Westminster Cathedral and Methodists from the Central Hall joined in a "Service of Light" in Westminster Abbey attended by Prime Minister Blair and his wife, who went on to a new Millennium Dome at Greenwich. Amongst its exhibits, the Dome contained a Faith Zone, with films and voices from various religions. British diffidence about religion had tended to obscure historical or dogmatic statements in the exhibition, until reminders came from leaders of other religions that the millennium was dated from the approximate time of the birth of Jesus, and was therefore in any case primarily a Christian celebration. At the Dome the Archbishop of Canterbury led prayers, followed by a recitation of the Lord's Prayer and the Beatitudes from the Authorised Version of the Bible by a group of young people. International debt relief for the world's poorest countries was a target for the millennium year and the UK led with the most far-reaching package of relief.

On his 90th trip abroad the Pope visited Egypt in February seeking inter-religious harmony. He embraced the Coptic Orthodox leader, Pope Shenouda III, and the Grand Imam of Al Azhar Mosque and University in Cairo, the senior Muslim authority, and then flew on to St Catherine's monastery on Mount Sinai to view its priceless collection of biblical manuscripts. In March the Pope made a long-planned Jubilee pilgrimage to the Holy Land, spending five nights in Jerusalem and celebrating Mass in Bethlehem and Nazareth. He pleaded for a homeland for Palestinian refugees, visited refugee camps, and demanded "decisive action" from the Israeli government. At Bethlehem he told Palestinians "your torment is before the eyes of the world and it has gone on too long". In December traditional pilgrimages to Bethlehem were severely curtailed because of continuing local violence.

In May the Pope visited Fatima in Portugal where three shepherd children were believed to have seen the Virgin Mary in 1917 (see II.4.iii.). They had claimed a "prophetic vision" of the war of atheism against the Church and a prediction of the shooting of the Pope (see AR 1981, p. 375). Two of these children had died and were beatified by the Pope; the third, Lucia dos Santos, was a nun with whom the pontiff had a private meeting.

In September the Congregation for the Doctrine of the Faith published a document entitled *Dominus Jesus* (the Lord Jesus) which insisted on the uniqueness of Christ and appeared to confine the fullness of the faith to the Roman Catholic Church. Non-Christian religions were said to be "still in search of the absolute truth and still lacking assent to God who reveals himself". Critics of the publication referred to a statement of the Second Vatican Council that "the Catholic Church rejects nothing of what is true and holy in these religions", for they "often reflect a ray of that truth which enlightens everyone". The Pope himself, talking to young Muslims in Casablanca in 1985, had told them that they all believed in the same one God who had revealed himself to Abraham. According to the Congregation, not only other religions but different churches could be deemed inferior, not churches "in the proper sense". In June a note sent to presidents of bishops' conferences warned of problems in the use of the phrase "sister churches". In recent times the phrase "sister churches" had been used by the Orthodox Patriarch of Constantinople when he addressed the Pope in Rome and expressed a desire for inter-communion in "those family ties which ought to exist between local churches, as between sisters". This usage was extended to Anglican and other churches, but theologians insisted that the term "sister churches" did not appear in the Bible and had only become prevalent in contemporary writings on ecumenism. It was ambiguous and needed to be recalled to correct usage.

TURMOIL. In January Lavinia Byrne left the Institute of the Blessed Virgin Mary, after 35 years membership, in protest against the opposition of the Congregation for the Doctrine of the Faith to contraception and female ordination. In 1994 she had published *Woman at the Altar*, in which she stated that women priests were the "logical conclusion" of all recent Catholic theology about women. She was ordered to recant by the Congregation but rejected this as faceless bureaucracy acting "like the Inquisition to silence people". She refused to sign a declaration in support of Pope Paul VI's ban on contraception. After denunciation by the Congregation her book was destroyed in the USA, but was still in print in Britain.

Religious broadcasting in the UK was weakening, according to the Church of England General Synod, which arranged a monitoring unit to check religious programmes. In *Losing Faith in the BBC* Nigel Holmes criticised the lack of funds for religious programmes, with the issue of religion having "no influence over controllers and schedulers". Religion was relegated to unpopular channels and times and pushed into a broadcasting "ghetto", and staff morale was at "rock bottom". Radio fared better than television, but there was a gap between declared support and what actually happened in broadcasting.

The Catholic Church's relationship to the issue of homosexuality came to the fore during the year. A seminary rector, Fr Donald Cozzens of Cleveland, Ohio, examined some of the problems in a slender volume on *The Changing Face of the Priesthood*. He claimed that growing numbers of Roman Catholic priests and bishops were of homosexual inclination and that this distorted the priesthood in general, making it less representative of the Church at large. A US nun, Sr Jeannine Gramick, ministered to homosexuals in the community and with Fr Robert Nugent founded a New Ways Ministry for lesbian and gay Catholics. They were told by the Vatican that their stance on homosexuality was contrary to official teaching and should be dropped, but Sr Gramick refused to be silent, and continued to give talks and help to homosexuals.

Cases of clerical sexual abuse received widespread publicity, those churches which had a celibate priesthood being especially vulnerable. Allegations of child abuse committed by paedophile priests led to the formation of pastoral procedures, but several priests were convicted in secular courts and sent to prison. The new Roman Catholic Archbishop of Westminster, Cormac Murphy-O'Connor was criticised for his handling of the paedophilia of Fr Michael Hill—the Archbishop had revoked Hill's parish licence but had then appointed him chaplain at Gatwick airport where he later abused a child who had learning difficulties. The Archbishop reported to the press the pastoral guidelines that had been agreed, and expressed his sorrow to the victims of abuses.

A survey from the BBC and Nottingham University examined the religious state of the UK. A total of 26 per cent of people questioned believed in a personal God in the year 2000 compared with over 40 per cent in 1968, but less than 8 per cent were convinced atheists. More than half of the respondents believed in life after death, as people did 50 years ago. Belief in a soul was often linked to Indian ideas of reincarnation and less to heaven and hell than previously. Many people were concerned with the meaning and purpose of life, and nearly 40 per cent regarded prayer as the most important spiritual experience. Organised religion weakened, with the biggest decline being in the Church of England, from 55 per cent in 1955 to 25 per cent in 2000. Roman Catholics remained at 9 per cent. Strongly Protestant churches were reduced by about a half, though "House Church" movements had increased. Yet church-going attendance was constant, with 23 per cent attending a service within the past month, and more appearing at baptisms, weddings and funerals.

SCHISM. In January the 6,000-strong Free Church of Scotland, known as the Wee Frees, was split in two, with the smaller body taking the name the Free Church of Scotland Continuing. Division came over the theologian Professor Donald Macleod, after he was cleared of accusations of molesting several women—the sheriff ruling that he was a victim of a conspiracy. Thirty-one ministers, about a fifth of the whole, left the church after being suspended for breaking ecclesiastical law. Legal actions were planned over the ownership of churches, manses and money.

Roman Catholics in Scotland were concerned over teachings on homosexuality. Cardinal Thomas Winning, Archbishop of Glasgow, demanded the retention of Section 28 of a Local Government Act which banned the promotion of homosexuality in Schools. The Cardinal spoke of an "active and militant homosexual lobby" all over Europe and called it a "perversion" but denied an accusation that he had made a comparison with the Nazis. The Moderator of the General Assembly of the Church of Scotland on the other hand condemned repeal of Section 28 as "completely useless", and creating "fear and stigma against people".

In Australia two traditional clerics, Charles Murphy and John Rodgers, were ordained bishops for evangelical parishes in the Episcopal Church of the USA. But their ordination was criticised by the Archbishop of Canterbury, George Carey, as "quite foreign to the Anglican tradition" which required that ministers should be authorised according to the law of the province in which they wished to work-this had not been forthcoming.

In April the Archbishop of Perth, Peter Carnley, was installed as Primate of the Anglican Church of Australia. Well known as a liberal who had ordained the first women priests in Australia in 1992, Carnley spoke after his election on church affairs and state policy, demanding public apologies for the government's past treatment of aboriginals. In view of the presence of other religions he attacked those who were "hell-bent on exclusion and condemnation".

Women priests were at a disadvantage in the Church of England, according to a survey of 1.560 women, many of whom had met with bullying, harassment, rudeness or disrespect. Women married to clergy or with young children found it "almost impossible to fulfil any priestly role." Women priests were likely to be in jobs away from the parishes, but not in the higher ranks of the clergy. They were generally opposed to the use of itinerant or "flying" bishops who ministered to traditionalist parishes (see AR 1993, p. 448).

AFRICAN TRIALS. In March some 1,000 members of a movement for The Restoration of the Ten Commandments of God were found dead in a burned-out church in south-west Uganda. They had given all their possessions to their leaders, in preparation for the end of the world. At first regarded as mass suicide, the slaughter was later discovered to have been organised by a failed politician, who escaped after the bodies were discovered.

In Rwanda bishop Augustin Misago was charged with having arranged the genocide of more than half a million people in 1994 (see VII.1.ii.). The judge at his trial dismissed the charges as contradictory and based on hearsay, and said that the bishop had always acted to save those under his protection. Misago had spent 14 months in prison awaiting trial. He planned to visit Rome to thank Pope John Paul for his support.

In India churches were damaged by bombs in Andhra Pradesh and Goa in June. Hindu right-wing groups were suspected of these actions and of daubing anti-Christian slogans on the walls of churches (see AR 1999, p. 460).

ORTHODOXY. In August the last tsar of Russia, Nicholas II, and other members of his family, all of whom had been executed by the Bolsheviks in 1917, were canonised at a special synod of the Orthodox Church at Christ the Saviour cathedral in Moscow. Another 1,100 Christians who had been persecuted during 70 years of Communist rule were also declared saints, making this the biggest mass canonisation ever held. There were debates over this action, since the Romanovs had not suffered for their faith but for their political office, but there was strong popular support for the canonisation and the royal family were said to have tried to carry out "the commandments of the gospels".

Following the Vatican document *Dominus Jesus*, the Russian Orthodox Church declared itself "the one, holy, catholic and apostolic Church", the keeper of the sacraments throughout the world. Some 50 per cent of the Russian population was claimed to be orthodox, with 13,000 parishes re-established in the last decade, 460 monasteries reopened and 22 new seminaries founded.

In Athens in June thousands of Greek Orthodox faithful demonstrated against the government decision to omit religious affiliation from identity cards. Archbishop Christodoulos, backed by 80 bishops, protested against this state action, which he said would lead to taking the cross off the Greek flag, removing religious teaching from schools, and stripping the Church of its role in safeguarding Hellenism as it had done under 400 years of Ottoman rule.

CONFLICT. In Nigeria eight northern states introduced the Islamic Sharia legal system, prompting opposition from Christian groups which resulted in over a thousand deaths. The Kano state government said that the laws would not apply to the Christian minority, but Christian shops were boarded up and families were sent to the Christian south of the country. Sentences passed by Islamic courts on Muslims included amputation and lashing.

In the Moluccas, in Indonesia, some 2,000 people were said to have been killed in Christian-Muslim clashes. Muslim crowds called for holy war, but Catholics were convinced that the conflict was a struggle for power. More than 1,000 churches were burned down.

In China the government denied the right of the Pope to appoint bishops and cardinals and in January five new Chinese bishops, chosen by the Chinese Patriotic Catholic Association, were ordained in the Cathedral of the Immaculate Conception, Beijing's oldest church. In secret talks with the Chinese government it appeared that the Vatican would recognise the Chinese indigenous church in return for approving its own bishops.

In October Pope John Paul canonised 123 new saints, of whom 87 were native Chinese martyrs and 33 were European missionaries martyred in China. The Chinese government reacted strongly, denouncing the new saints as criminals who had hated China. However, the Vatican claimed that 50 bishops had asked for the canonisations in this jubilee year. Local churches in Japan, South Korea, the Philippines and Vietnam all had their own saints and martyrs, and now the Chinese church, founded much earlier, was catching up.

BOOKS OF THE YEAR. One of the most informed and attractive was *The Image of Christ*, the catalogue of an exhibition, "Seeing Salvation", at the National Gallery in London. *A World History of Christianity*, edited by Adrian Hastings and others, was valuable for chapters on Europe, the Americas, Africa, India, China and Australasia. A one-man production was *Christianity: a global history* by David Chidester of Cape Town. *A History of the Church in Africa* by Bengt Sundkler and Christopher Steed gave special attention to recent centuries. *The Oxford Companion to Christian Thought* was also edited by Adrian Hastings and others. *Catholicism Contending with Moder-*

nity was edited by Darrell Jodoch, and *Catholics in England 1950-2000* by Michael Hornsby-Smith gave modern assessments. Personal views and histories came in *The Journey is my Home* by Lavinia Byrne, *The C of E: the state it's in* by Monica Furlong, and *Journey to Priesthood* by Helen Thorne. *The Battle for God: fundamentalism in Judaism, Christianity and Islam* sketched a common phenomenon. *Ann the Word* by Richard Francis described the Shakers, and *Star in the East: Krishnamurti, the invention of a Messiah* by Roland Verson gave an account of a movement of theosophy. *Righteous Victims* by Benny Morris described the condition of Palestinian refugees, while *Chasing Shadows: memories of a vanished world*, by Hugo and Naomi Gryn, was a memorial to a well-loved rabbi.

XIII THE SCIENCES

1. SCIENTIFIC, MEDICAL AND INDUSTRIAL RESEARCH

SPACE, ASTRONOMY AND PHYSICAL SCIENCES. A major advance was seen in the long-delayed collaborative project to build an International Space Station (ISS), the only remaining active programme involving manned space exploration. After a false start in April when a US National Aeronautics and Space Administration (NASA) space shuttle supply mission was abandoned because of weather conditions, in May the *Atlantis* shuttle was able to carry out repairs on the ISS and prepare it for the successful launch and attachment by remote control in July of the Russian *Zvezda* living-quarters and service module. The late completion of *Zvezda* (see AR 1999, p. 465), caused principally by dwindling Russian government funding, had prompted some US critics to call for the cancellation of the ISS project. US and Russian supply missions from August to October prepared the space station for the launch of the ISS's first long-stay crew aboard a Russian Soyuz spacecraft which docked with the ISS on November 2. The crew, which consisted of an American and two Russians, established what was intended to be a permanent occupation of the ISS. The crew of the shuttle *Endeavour* in December attached 73-metre solar panels to the ISS, making it reportedly the third brightest object in the night sky after the Moon and the star Sirius. Construction of the ISS was scheduled for completion in 2006, at an estimated cost of US$63 billion. Critics of the project claimed that its justification was political (in fostering a collaboration between the USA and Russia), rather than scientific, saying than any experiments carried out on the ISS could have been conducted more cheaply on unmanned orbiting spacecraft.

Progress on the ISS appeared to have been gained partly at the expense of the veteran Russian *Mir* space station, which remained in Russia a potent symbol of national scientific prowess. In January the Russian Space Agency announced that the space station, shut down in 1999, would be saved by finance from a private international consortium, MirCorp, and in April a crew was launched on a 45-day mission to reactivate *Mir* for use as a commercial venture for scientific experiments, film-making and even tourism. However, despite a further supply mission in October, the Russian Space Agency announced in November that private capital had been insufficient to make up a shortfall in funding and that the 14-year-old *Mir* would be ditched in the Pacific Ocean in February 2001. Russian space technology suffered another setback in February when a new reusable launch vehicle, the Fregat, was lost on its return to Earth after an apparently successful test launch. China in October announced that it intended to land a robot on the Moon to explore possible sites for a manned mission, but no launch date was given.

A NASA report released in March concluded that the loss of the *Mars Polar Lander* spacecraft in December 1999 (see AR 1999, p. 466) had probably been caused by the probe's braking rockets cutting out too early in its descent to the planet, with the result that the spacecraft was destroyed by a crash-landing. The report also suggested that a drive to economise on the project had led to inadequate testing of suspect braking components. The US *Mars Global Surveyor* spacecraft, launched in 1996, continued to orbit the red planet and it was announced in June that analysis of photographs taken of the Martian surface showed channel-like features which could have been formed by water seeping from underground reservoirs. Moreover, whilst previous evidence had indicated that the planet had lacked water for about a billion years, these channels appeared to have almost certainly been formed within the last million years. In December NASA released spectacular photographs recently taken by the *Mars Global Surveyor* showing layers of apparent sedimentary rocks which could have formed the beds of deep-water lakes between 4.3 billion and 3.5 billion years ago. They were taken as the strongest evidence yet that the Martian environment could once have sustained life. Damping this optimism was a report by scientists at the California Institute of Technology, published in September in the journal *Nature*, which concluded from an analysis of Martian soil samples taken by NASA's *Viking Lander* probes in 1976 that the presence of highly reactive "superoxides" would have destroyed organic molecules in the soil and made it unlikely that life would ever have developed on the planet.

It was a good year for water in the Solar System. In August NASA announced that measurements taken by its *Galileo* spacecraft had produced overwhelming evidence of an electricity-conducting global salt sea beneath the frozen surface of the Jovian moon Europa. Subsequently *Galileo* made similar observations of Callisto and Ganymede, Jupiter's largest moon. Another unmanned NASA exploration of the Solar System, the Near Earth Asteroid Rendezvous (NEAR—Shoemaker) probe, went into orbit around the asteroid 433 Eros on February 14 (St Valentine's Day). It was planned that the spacecraft would spend a year surveying the asteroid. In May it was reported that NASA's *Stardust* probe, launched in 1999, had detected large, complex, carbon-based molecules in space beyond the orbit of Mars, lending support to the theory that life originated in outer space. A reminder of an earlier era of space exploration came in March with the reception of a weak signal from the veteran probe *Pioneer 10*, which had left the Solar System in 1983 and was currently some 11 billion km from the Sun.

A major achievement in Earth-based astronomy was reported in May. The Boomerang experiment, using instruments on a balloon 40 km above the Antarctic, measured fluctuations of cosmic background radiation dating from a time when the universe was 300,000 years old. The results confirmed the theory that space was "flat" and that its density of matter was insufficient to stop and reverse cosmic expansion. In June NASA brought down the orbiting Compton Gamma Ray Observatory in a controlled descent into the Pacific Ocean after the failure of one of its stabilising gyroscopes. Launched in 1991, the Compton had made the first major study of gamma-ray sources by a space-based observatory.

In physics, scientists at the European Organisation for Nuclear Research (CERN) near Geneva, Switzerland, announced in February that a series of seven experiments colliding lead ions had culminated in the very brief recreation of conditions existing in the first 10 microseconds of the universe. Analysis of the experiments indicated that the collisions had succeeded in dissolving nucleic particles into a new state of matter, a quark-gluon plasma (QGP—or "quagma"), similar to that which existed before the first atoms were formed. Physicists believed that all atomic particles consisted of combinations of quarks bound together by gluons, but the CERN experiments provided the first observational evidence of their existence. Further research into free quarks would be conducted using the more powerful relativistic heavy ion collider (RHIC) at the Brookhaven National Laboratory in the USA, and later on using CERN's new large hadron collider (LHC) due for completion in 2005. CERN's physicists faced a dilemma later in the year when experiments on the laboratory's large electron-positron collider (LEP)—a circular underground particle accelerator 27 km in circumference—showing evidence of the existence of the elusive Higgs boson, postponed the closure of the LEP, due at the end of September. The Higgs boson, dubbed the "holy grail" of physics and first postulated by British physicist Peter Higgs, had never been observed but was crucial to the standard theory of physics in conferring the property of mass. An extension of the experiments failed, however, to confirm the existence of the Higgs and the LEP was finally shut down on November 2, after 11 years of operations, to enable construction of the LHC to begin. This handed the initiative in Higgs boson research over to CERN's US rival, Fermilab's Tevatron accelerator, near Chicago. Fermilab had in July detected the only other previously unobserved member of the 18-strong family of fundamental particles, the tau neutrino.

In industrial research it was predicted that the internal combustion engine, one of the 20th century's dominant technologies, would be replaced by the hydrogen fuel cell, which produced no carbon gases nor any other pollutants. The cell electrochemically combined hydrogen and oxygen to produce electricity, heat and water vapour. Research into fuel cells, which was backed by several major motor manufacturers, was led by the Canadian company Ballard Power Systems. A number of Ballard-powered prototype vehicles already existed, including one currently undergoing trials by DaimlerChrysler. It was expected that mass-production of fuel-cell-powered cars would begin in 2003. In what was hailed as an important advance in the field of so-called artificial life or artificial intelligence it was reported in September in *Nature* that scientists at Brandeis University, Massachusetts, USA, had created a computerised system that autonomously designed simple robots from scratch, evaluated the designs and manufactured the most successful specimens. It was claimed that the system mimicked the processes of evolution.

MEDICAL AND BIOLOGICAL SCIENCES. Genetic and medical research was dominated by the landmark event of the announcement on June 26 of the completion of the mapping of the human genome, the so-called human genetic blueprint. The much-publicised and acrimonious race between the publicly funded international Human Genome Project (HGP) and the US private biotechnology company Celera Genomics was suspended for a joint announcement in Washington DC. The increasingly bitter rivalry centred on allegations that Celera was patenting stretches of raw data, thus restricting access to basic scientific information, whereas the policy of the HGP was to publish its work-in-progress gene sequencing on the internet (see AR 1999, pp. 467-68). US President Bill Clinton and UK Prime Minister Tony Blair had on March 14 issued a joint appeal for scientists everywhere to be given access to the genome data. The dispute was revived in December when Craig Venter, the founder and chief executive of Celera, said that the company's genome results would be available only to researchers who would not put them to commercial use. The announcement in June was widely acclaimed as the "decoding of the book of life", and Mike Dexter, director of the Wellcome Trust, the UK charity that funded a third of the project, favourably compared the significance of the mapping of the genome with that of the invention of the wheel. What was completed at that point, in fact, was a "working draft" of about 90 per cent of the more than 3 billion chemical letters of human genetic material, and the much longer and more expensive project of analysing the data to identify the individual genes and their functions had barely begun. Nevertheless, even the most cautious commentators recognised that deciphering the genome was a major advance that would in time transform scientific understanding of human biology, and consequently of diseases and their treatments.

The journal *Science* in March published the second complete genome of a living creature, the result of collaboration between HGP and Celera scientists. The fruit fly *Drosophila melanogaster* was a far more complex organism than the Nematode worm decoded in 1999. Larger claims were made, however, for the publication in December of the complete genome, decoded by an international group of scientists, of *Arabidopsis thaliana*, the common wild plant thale cress. Because *Arabidopsis* was closely related to all other 300,000 flowering plants, its genome provided an effective map of key genes for the entire plant kingdom. Study of the plant's 25,000 genes was expected to lead to new ways of developing medical drugs and to a new generation of agricultural crops. Some researchers avowed that the completion of the genome of *Arabidopsis* was more important than that of the human genome.

In May scientists in Japan and Germany working on the HGP published the gene sequence of the human chromosome 21, the second chromosome to be sequenced, which was associated with Alzheimer's disease, a neurodegenerative condition. Research published in *Nature* in December showed that an experimental vaccine against Alzheimer's disease developed in Canada and the USA had halted the progress of dementia in genetically modified mice. Researchers in France obtained positive results from transplanting foetal stem cells into the brains of patients suffering from Huntington's chorea, another form of dementia. The potential of embryonic stem cells, the body's so-called "master cells", for regenerating any kind of human tissue and even growing whole organs, remained the focus of intense scientific interest, although the ethical issues surrounding the use of laboratory-produced embryos for medical research remained unresolved. The US government in August introduced guidelines allowing federal funding of research into embryonic stem cells and by the end of the year the UK Parliament passed legislation permitting the cloning of stem cells for research and medical purposes but not for reproduction. There were proponents of alternative sources of stem cells, for example from bone marrow and from post-natal discarded umbilical cords. Although sceptics doubted that these could be as versatile as foetal stem cells, research published in *Science* in December suggested that adult stem cells could be used to treat neurological disorders. Two teams of scientists in the USA had transferred bone marrow stem cells from adult mice to newborn mice or mice that lacked bone marrow, and in each experiment the cells had migrated to the brain and differentiated into working nerve cells.

Advances using genetic technology were made during 2000 to combat two diseases principally affecting tropical regions. Trials started in the Gambia in September on a vaccine developed from the DNA of the malaria parasite by scientists at Oxford University in the UK. In recent years the disease had become increasingly resistant to treatment. In November it was reported in *Nature* that researchers at the US National Institute of Health had successfully vaccinated four monkeys against the Ebola virus, a haemorrhagic fever that first emerged in Africa in 1976 and which was fatal to 90 per cent of its victims. Although patents were awarded in January to the Roslin Institute in Scotland, UK, for the pioneering techniques used in cloning Dolly the sheep in 1997 (see AR 1997, p. 457), the institute announced in August that it was winding down its project to clone pigs for the purpose of producing organs capable of being transplanted into human beings (xenotransplantation). The Roslin Institute insisted that it had made the decision for commercial reasons and that it was not influenced by the widespread fears that animal viruses might be imported into the human organism. Other developments included the successful cloning in January by scientists in Oregon, USA, of a rhesus macaque monkey. This experiment broke new ground by splitting an eight-cell embryo, whereas the Roslin Institute had implanted an adult cell into an egg from which the nucleus had been evacuated. Also in January scientists in Kagoshima, Japan, succeeded in breeding a male calf from a cell from one of six calves which had themselves been cloned in 1999 from cells from the ear of an adult bull. This was the first large mammal to be cloned from a clone, although scientists in the USA had successfully performed the same feat with a mouse.

In palaeontology it was reported in March that a team of scientists from China and the USA had discovered in Shanxi province in southern China fossils of the earliest known ancestor of the higher primates, or anthropoids, a group including monkeys, apes and human beings. The fossils of *Eosimias*, a tiny creature weighing no more than 55g, were about 45 million years old. A jawbone of *Eosimias* had been discovered on the same site in 1995, but analysis of ankle bones found amongst the new fossils showed that it was a transitional species between the arboreal lower primates, such as tarsiers, and anthropoids. The discovery was announced in April of the most complete skull ever found of a more recent human ancestor, a female of the species *Paranthropus robustus*, a hominid of the genus *Australopithecus*. The remains, unearthed in 1994 near Sterkfontein in South Africa, were between 1.5 million and 2 million years old. Palaeontologists discovered in January in Patagonia, in southern Argentina, the remains of a herbivore dinosaur some 50m long, and therefore thought to be the longest dinosaur ever found, outstripping *Argentinosaurus*, also found in Patagonia in 1990. In recent years the Patagonian desert had proved rich in dinosaur finds and in March it was announced that fossils of the largest specimen of a carnivore dinosaur, 13.7m long, had been found there in 1997, compared with the previous biggest predator, the 12.5m *Gigantosaurus*, another Patagonian native found in 1993. Neither of the two new discoveries had been named or classified by the end of the year. It was reported in *Nature* in April that examination of the fossil of a dinosaur *Thescelosaurus*, found in North Dakota, USA, in 1993, showed that its heart had two ventricles, suggesting that, unlike reptiles, dinosaurs might have been warm-blooded. The discovery of what was probably the oldest surviving life form on Earth was published in *Nature* in October. Biologists found, and subsequently revived in a laboratory, a bacterium that had survived some 250 million years frozen in suspended animation in a salt crystal 550 m below ground level in New Mexico, USA.

Archaeologists announced in June the discovery on the bed on the Mediterranean sea off the coast of Alexandria, Egypt, the remarkably well preserved remains of the Pharaonic and Ptolemaic cities of Herakleion, Canopus and Menouthis, dating back as far as 1500 BC. The cities were thought to have been continuously inhabited until around AD 800, when they were probably destroyed by an earthquake. It was reported in October that researchers had found cave paintings in the Lessini hills near Verona, Italy, that had been dated as 35,000 years old, predating what were previously thought to be the oldest surviving human art works, the cave paintings found in the Chauvet cave in southern France in 1999.

NOBEL PRIZES. The award of the 2000 Nobel Prize for Chemistry was shared between Alan Heeger and Alan MacDiarmid of the USA and Hideki Shirakawa of Japan for the discovery of conductive polymers, plastics able to carry an electrical current. The Prize for Medicine was won by the Swede Arvid Carlsson for the discovery of the role of dopamine as a neurotransmitter, by the American Paul Greenguard for the elucidation of how neurotransmitters work and by Eric Kandel in the USA for work on the biology of memory. The Prize for Physics was shared by Jack Kilby in the USA for the invention of the integrated circuit or silicon microchip (in 1958) and by two scientists working independently, Herbert Kroemer in the USA and Zores Alfarov in Russia, for developing semiconductors used in laser-based communications technology.

2. INFORMATION TECHNOLOGY

WHILST the millennium was ushered in to the tune of millions of tonnes of fireworks, those responsible for Information Technology (IT) systems celebrated the new year to the sound of silence. The "millennium bug" (see AR 1999, pp. 472-73), on which billions had been spent raising awareness and testing and modifying computer systems, passed with virtually no impact. The inevitable questions followed as to whether this was due to stalwart preparations or because the significance of the bug and its effects had been exaggerated from the outset. Russia claimed prudence (as well as poverty), after spending only US$100 million yet experiencing no difficulties with the date change, as opposed to the USA which spent US$43 billion.

The remainder of the year was not so quiet as developments in IT (largely those relating to the internet) challenged the status quo on almost every issue they touched. Perceptions of a number of important issues—including intellectual property and copyright, privacy and freedom of information, and financial and business models—were held up for questioning, subjected to modification, or completely swept aside as the internet phenomenon showed no signs of losing momentum.

INTERNET STOCKS. Although internet developments continued at speed, a great bubble of internet hype and hysteria was certainly burst; with the whole drama played out on the stock market. Investors in high-tech companies had a rocky ride, with technology stocks soaring to all time highs early in the year and internet start-ups, yet to produce a penny in profit, continuing to receive valuations higher than established multinationals. Questions began to be raised about the seemingly limitless extent to which these companies appeared able to raise capital (either privately or via the stock market) and then spend it, without any questions of their current or likely future profitability being asked. Those doing the spending claimed that this was an acceptable short-term strategy, akin to "land grabbing" in the virgin territory of the internet, whilst others drew parallels with the hysteria of the tulip markets in the 17th century and forecast a similar correction. The cynics were proved right as technology stocks did indeed take a major plunge in March—with hundreds of billions of US dollars wiped off technology markets in a matter of days and established IT companies like Microsoft and Oracle saw their market value halved.

This was followed later in the year by a series of high profile collapses of internet companies such as Boo.com and Breathe. Boo.com (an internet-based fashion retailer) had floated in 1999, raising UK£115 million, which it proceeded to burn through in only 18 months before collapsing with debts of UK£25 million. Financial services company PricewaterhouseCoopers issued a report in 2000 predicting that the majority of UK internet business would run out of cash within 15 months, with a quarter of them predicted to run out within six months.

Much was made of these violent market movements and yet it remained clear that important and lasting alterations to the global economy had occurred. This "new economy" ushered in by IT companies had already generated what many commentators described as "the single greatest period of wealth creation in the history of mankind", and had left many still racing to understand and take advantage of these new developments.

THIRD GENERATION MOBILE PHONES. Nowhere was the perceived potential value of the new technologies made more clear than during the UK auction of the radio spectrum that would provide the next generation of mobile phone services. Known as third generation (3G) mobiles, these devices would use technologies similar to those used by computers to communicate with one another, thereby allowing for the better transmission of all types of data (rather than just voice); and enabling services such as mobile access to the internet. The treasury anticipated raising around UK£3 billion from the auction, but this turned out to be somewhat wide of the mark, with the total at close of bidding reaching UK£22.5 billion. The incredible prices paid by phone companies, which believed they could not afford to end up without a licence, left concerns as to the long term effects of the auction. Having already paid UK£3-5 billion each for a licence, telephone companies had then to construct the physical network on which 3G mobile phones would operate, before seeing any revenue.

Although the first step towards 3G (dubbed 2.5G) was based on an existing technology called GPRS (General Packet Radio Services) and was relatively simple to make available (the service was already available to business at the time of writing), true 3G performance (essentially defined by higher data transmission rates) would only come in the form of UMTS (Universal Mobile Telephony Services), and this would require substantial investment in new infrastructure to make it possible. Once this was added to the cost of the licence, there were worries that development of the UK 3G industry would be stunted and any eventual 3G services would be expensive. There was thus serious concern that the UK's decision to extract the maximum possible revenue from the sale would have counter-productive long-term effects. Indeed, a number of countries distributed their 3-G licences during 2000, and many, such as Finland and Japan, instead adopted the "beauty contest" approach—where the government awarded licences to applicants based on specified criteria—whilst others chose some form of hybrid process.

REGULATION OF INVESTIGATORY POWERS BILL. Whilst this miscalculation had fortunate consequences (at least in the short term) in the form of a massive windfall for the treasury, the UK government's limited understanding of the nature and significance of the internet had less beneficial consequences when it attempted to pass the Regulation of Investigatory Powers (RIP) bill. The measure granted government and law enforcement agencies extensive powers to monitor and intercept information transmitted over the internet, and was widely criticised for its lack of insight and the inroads which it made into civil liberties. The more contentious points included the intention to place a substantial part of the burden of installing these monitoring systems on the Internet Service Providers (ISPs) which routed internet traffic. Also, the bill allowed the interception of email hosted by ISPs and the ability to demand the keys to encrypted email messages. Failure to hand over encryption keys (passwords) could result in up to two years' imprisonment; and claims of loss or forgetfulness had the burden of proof reversed from the prosecution to the defence.

Although diluted in its passage through the House of Lords, two parts of the bill became law in October (with the third to become law pending a review in 2001). Soon after the RIP bill was approved, Poptel (one of the countries largest ISP's) and Clara.net (the UK's largest independent ISP) announced their intention to move some of their operations abroad in order to satisfy corporate customers who were concerned about the privacy of their information in the light of the new Act. The legislation was also seen as being at odds with Prime Minister Tony Blair's vision of making the UK a centre for e-commerce by 2002, as it left the UK with an intrusive set of laws for the governing of the internet, parallels of which could be found only in Russia, Malaysia and Singapore.

INTERNET CRIME. Reactionary and heavy-handed though the RIP might have been, as with all new technology, new uses were accompanied by new abuses and internet-related crime rocketed in line with the number of people getting connected. Internet crime statistics were still scant, but credit-card company Visa reported that of all the fraud cases it dealt with in 1999, 47 per cent involved the internet. Security fears were rarely out of the headlines as 2000 saw a number of high profile breaches of company networks via the internet. Microsoft reported that a trio operating from the Philippines had gained unauthorised access to Microsoft's internal network and might have stolen pieces of the source code for the Windows operating system and some of Microsoft's other applications. Other notable incidents in the UK involved Barclays bank and the Halifax, which were both forced to suspend their online services when users reported being able access other account holders' details.

NEW DOMAIN NAMES. Yet despite it all, the internet continued its exponential growth, with 10 million people in the UK alone getting on line for the first time during the year. The newly formed international body for managing the internet, the Internet Corporation for Assigned Names and Numbers (ICAAN) eased the congestion of the existing domain names of .com, .org, .net etc. with seven new names: .aero, .biz, .coop, .info, .museum, .name and .pro. It was noted that even these additions would become quickly congested , however, and there was fierce debate as to how these new names would be distributed.

The growing global importance of the internet was demonstrated when the Pacific nation of Tuvalu leased its country-code (its top level domain name), .tv, for a period of 10 years to a Californian company called DotTV, for a 20 per cent stake in the company and the sum of US$50 million—funds which its government promised would be used to bring electricity and medical care to the outlying islands.

THE DIGITAL DIVIDE. Although the number of people accessing the web was rocketing, the distribution of these new users was by no means even, either from a geographic or economic perspective. New users were likely to be wealthy people living in developed countries and concerns were increasing that a "digital divide", was growing between rich and poor nations and people—that is, a gulf between people and communities who could make effective use of Information Technology and those who could not. This was of increasing importance in the modern economy as effective use of IT went hand in hand with economic prosperity.

Although there was unanimity in recognising that a divide did exist, there was little agreement over the extent of the divide and whether it was narrowing or growing. There were good examples of rapid take-up in South America and Asia; China doubled its internet users from 8.9 million to 16.9 million during the year. Africa, however, continued to suffer from many obstacles: a lack of infrastructure and equipment, low awareness levels and poor copyright regulation. The entire African continent had only 2.5 million users as in June 2000, with numbers only expected to rise to 4.4 million by 2003. There was increasing international concern that countries without the infrastructure to support high technology industry would fall into a cycle of decline, being left further and further behind and without the tools and skills to catch up.

NAPSTER. Of those logging on to the internet many were doing more than just browsing the World Wide Web or checking their email, as one of the highest profile internet-related legal battles illustrated. Napster, a business which facilitated the transfer over the internet of music stored on personal computers in a digital format known as MP3, was prosecuted for copyright infringement by the Recording Industry Association of America (RIA). The RIA claimed that Napster, by facilitating the distribution of pieces of music, the copyright for which belong to the RIA; was party to piracy. Despite its winning, on repeated occasions, the right to remain open pending appeal, the future of Napster in its current form looked bleak at the end of the year. It had settled out of court with Bertlesmann (one of the major recording houses that made up the RIA) by filtering from its free service all material copyrighted by Bertlesmann and placing this in another, subscription-based service. However, this still left the other companies represented by the RIA (including Time Warner Inc and Sony Corp) suing for US$300 million in lost sales.

The case was widely seen as highlighting the many questions which were being raised by the easy transfer of data which the internet made both possible and difficult to monitor or regulate. Napster offered an entirely new method for music distribution which bypassed the existing industry channels and the billions of US dollars that these generated for the recording houses. Commentators, industry analysts, even the artists themselves were divided over whether this represented a threat or an opportunity. What was clear was that future attempts at preventing this type of data transfer via legal channels would become increasingly difficult. Napster was a viable target for prosecution because of its obvious physical presence and its sole focus on MP3 transfer. There already existed freely available software which enabled similar data transfer without any kind of central organisation and which could be used for transferring any type of data capable of being digitally stored (including text, pictures, audio and video). This would remove any target for legal action other than the end users themselves, and with Napster alone anticipating 70 million such users by the end of the year, this would make legal action a practical impossibility. These events indicated the radical change which the internet had already begun to demand, forcing entire industries to rethink the way they did business and to leave adaptation, rather than litigation as their only option.

DISTRIBUTED COMPUTING. The Napster phenomenon illustrated how the internet matured in 2000, moving beyond its role as a global library of text and pictures to a truly universal communications network, where its roles were limited only by the imagination of the user. "Betting the company", in its own words, on new ideas such as these, and the software that made them possible, was the world's biggest software company, Microsoft. Forging ahead, despite the ruling of District Court Judge Thomas Penfield Jackson that the company must be split in two (one half responsible for the Windows operating system and the other for applications and the internet), Microsoft released its .Net (dot net) strategy. The strategy was based on the inevitable increases in internet bandwidth and computer processing power which Microsoft believed would combine to place "distributed computing" at the heart of the information age. This new way of networking would move away from the current model of client machines making requests from dedicated servers, to a network of peer machines that acted as both client and server to one another. Napster provided a prime example of this new way of using the internet, with the music being locally stored on users' machines (rather than on central servers), and with the transfer of the music occurring directly between the users (all Napster maintained was the directory of which members had which music files). The future, as far as Microsoft was concerned, lay with this new network topology and the .Net project involved the ambitious task of writing (or rewriting) all of Microsoft's software so that its applications could be run and rented as services over the internet rather than stand-alone applications bought outright.

Microsoft took this vision of software as a web-based service even further in that another major goal of .Net was to make it possible to integrate the services by enabling "rich" communication between them. In other words, information used or produced by a particular web service would be available to any other web service in a format that it could understand. This second goal was more ambitious than the first, and Microsoft was backing new computer languages such as Simple Object Access Protocol (SOAP) and Extensible Mark-up Language (XML) as the universal translators that would enable the sharing of information between disparate software applications.

It seemed likely that the eventual results would change the way people experienced using computing devices, and businesses could already see the huge benefits that this new way of functioning could bring. There was at the time a great deal of information locked away within business systems (for example in accounting and ordering systems) which had to be rewritten or re-keyed in order to communicate it to others. The XML language was already being used to enable information to be taken from one application (such as the accounting application of the buyer), and translated into a form which could be understood and processed by a totally different application (such as the ordering system of the seller). The ability to communicate this information with other business in an automated fashion carried the potential for major cost savings. A business could order from a supplier or sell to a customer without the need for vital information (such as price and delivery date) to be re-keyed repeatedly, thereby reducing administrative overheads, the chances of errors and the time taken for any given transaction to be completed. Although internet firms were certainly no longer the darlings of the investment community, the race to write web-centric software continued at a pace limited only by the number of software engineers that companies could hire.

3. THE ENVIRONMENT

ANY hopes that the first year of the new millennium would be the dawn of a bright, new and greener era were to be dashed; so far as the environment was concerned, 2000 was figuratively and literally a washout.

The previous year, 1999, had left several issues very much in the news and decidedly in the balance. The Kyoto agreement on limiting carbon emissions had signally failed to get beyond the lofty principles and into the realms of practical measures. The year 2000 should have seen significant developments towards a binding and effective treaty. In the event, it saw only conflict and bickering. The earlier year also saw the emergence of genetically modified organisms (GMOs) as a major environmental issue. Monsanto, not the biggest but certainly the most visible—perhaps even the most arrogant—proponent of GM technology ended the century deeply wounded by the anti-GMO campaigners. In 2000 it gave ground, but also took part in a major regrouping which could perhaps signal a determination within the industry to begin a concerted fight back. The other major casualty of 1999 was the World Trade Organisation (WTO), which retreated behind closed doors to lick its wounds following the appalling scenes in Seattle. But far from listening to its critics, there was no evidence in 2000 to suggest the WTO was in any mood to change tack, rather that it would simply attempt to control dissent.

In January research on the humble fruit fly added weight to the UNEP's (United Nations Environment Programme) warning (*Global Environment Report, 2000*) that accidentally introduced alien species presented an increasing and very serious threat to biodiversity. Raymond Huey of the University of Washington published his study on the evolution of the flies in their new habitat following their accidental introduction to the South American west coast some 20 years earlier. Marked changes in their wing spans suggested that introduced species were capable of rapidly adapting to new environments. Not only did this amplify the warnings from the UNEP but it also, according to Huey, suggested that scientists researching the deliberate introduction of control species to combat accidentally introduced pests should consider the alarming possibility that introduced species might evolve in hitherto unexpected directions.

January also saw the beginnings of the worst ever hole in the ozone layer over the north pole. Despite stringent and effective controls on the release of some ozone depleting chemicals, principally CFCs, the severity of the annual depletion was still projected to get worse for decades before it would improve again. However, the significance of the new findings was more alarming. The loss of ozone was being exacerbated by unusually low temperatures in the stratosphere, conditions which accelerated ozone destruction. This, in turn, was being attributed to climate change which, far from warming the air high above the Arctic, was instead leading to the formation of what had become known as the midwinter vortex—a pool of cool air which more closely resembled the ozone-depleting conditions long familiar above the south pole. The clear implication was that projections that the damage caused by CFCs would eventually reverse would be severely compromised by global climate change.

Global warming was confirmed by Harry Pollack of the University of Michigan, who published the results of his studies of over 600 boreholes around the world. He concluded that the planet had warmed by 1 degree centigrade over the past 500 years, but that half of this had occurred during the 20th century.

GMOs were the subject of debate in Montreal in early February where representatives of 130 of the world's governments finally, after five years of argument, agreed a deal to control the trade in genetically modified organisms. Whilst not everyone was happy with the outcome, the Biosafety Protocol did finally legitimise powers which had been demanded by many states but which had been denied to them by WTO free trade rules. Under the new agreement, a government could invoke "the precautionary principle" and refuse to permit the import of certain GMOs should it regard them as an environmental threat: a major concession to green campaigners. However the agreement failed to consider a great many issues: neither the application of the agreement, nor the future regulation of the biotechnology industry were addressed. Nor did it require exporting nations either to segregate GMOs from natural products or to label them clearly: potentially a major cause for disagreement.

It was also seen by some to be a hollow victory for the green movement. Whilst it provided a level of protection against the unknown threat to natural species from GMOs, the focus on GMOs effectively sidelined concerns such as those expressed by UNEP and others that the careless introductions of "alien" species had not only been seen to cause devastating results but were expected to cause even more dramatic problems in the future. As the first result of the Biodiversity Convention which emerged from the Rio Earth Summit in 1992, the protocol's focus on theoretical risks at the expense of very real observable threats could be seen as a major failure.

It was to become clear during the next few months, however, just how much impact the greens had had on the biotechnology industry. Robert Shapiro, Chief Executive of Monsanto and the most visible and reviled proponent of GM technologies, would be removed from the public eye as his post disappeared in the merger between Monsanto and Pharmacia & Upjohn. The move was part of a significant change of direction for the GM industry and, as a gesture of good faith, one of Monsanto's final independent acts was to release its data on the rice genome into the public domain. Whilst this move was welcome, only time would tell if it was part of a genuine shift in policy or a cynical move to divert criticism.

Developments announced in March by the Marsupial Co-operative Research Centre (MCRC) in Sydney, Australia, illustrated the complexity of the debate over GMOs. The MCRC had created a GM carrot specifically targeted at helping the control of possums in New Zealand. Possums were introduced to the islands around 1900, since when they had gone feral and, with no natural controls, had wreaked havoc. Shooting, trapping and the use of poisoned carrots had achieved a measure of success in population control—but had proved far from adequate. The GM carrot was modified to interfere with the possums' reproduction, effectively rendering females sterile. Using a technique despised by green activists to achieve an ecologically sound aim would clearly present a dilemma for the anti-GMO lobby. However, of more immediate concern was that adequate tests should be carried out to ensure that the carrots would only sterilise their intended targets.

The nuclear industry's newsletter *Nuclear Fuel* revealed that India's nuclear tests two years earlier had almost certainly contaminated its neighbour Pakistan. Whilst Pakistan had exploded its own devices at much the same time, analysis of plutonium samples near the Pakistani test site in the Chagai hills suggested that the dust had in fact escaped from India's test range in the Pokran desert. If this was true, then India had violated the 1963 Partial Nuclear Test Ban Treaty, which committed signatories to ensuring that its tests did not contaminate any other country.

The end of March saw the first indications of what was to become the major theme for the year—climate instability and in particular, floods. Rainfall in Mozambique had been filling dams to capacity and levels were such that unless the rains stopped, breaches would be inevitable. The rains continued and the floodwaters could no longer be held back; emergency releases of water from the dams inundated the land with frightening rapidity. Low-lying land in Mozambique flooded and for weeks much of the country was under water, with roads and railways washed away and crops destroyed (see VII.1.iv.). What became one of the year's most memorable images was a photograph of a young woman who had given birth to her child in the boughs of a tree.

Ironically, in the same week experts were meeting in The Hague to discuss water shortages and the problem of assuring supplies in the developing world. Climatologists had long been warning that meteorological instability, including both droughts and storms, would be a feature in a warmer world, but whilst governments did eventually deliver aid to stricken Mozambique, events would prove that they failed, or refused, to accept the underlying message.

Coco, an African elephant, made history in April when it was announced that DNA tests had confirmed suspicions that Africa had not one but two species of elephant. Coco, it appeared, was the last survivor in a European zoo of a distinct species—the African Forest elephant, which was genetically substantially different from its close relatives inhabiting the savannahs. Confirmation would increase the concerns of conservationists as forest-dwelling elephants were rare indeed.

Later that month, at the CITES (Convention on International Trade in Endangered Species) meeting in Nairobi, delegates once again returned to the vexed issue of the trade in ivory. As ever the battle lines were drawn between those who favoured a total ban in order to simplify enforcement and those who favoured limited trade in order to give the animals an intrinsic value and to provide cash for conservation programmes. In the event, the outcome was a temporary truce: neither a permanent ban nor the resumption of regular trade. Whether trade was to be resumed or permanently halted would be decided by two comprehensive studies set up to examine the link between elephant populations and poaching. The aim was to provide hard data for the next scheduled meeting in 2002, at which a more scientifically informed decision could be made.

Scientific certainty, or the lack of it, increasingly affected decisions in the last decade of the 20th century and was having an immense impact on climate negotiations during 2000. Despite the pronouncements of the UN's Intergovernmental Panel on Climate Change (IPCC) that mankind was responsible for global warming, sufficient room for argument remained to provide a refuge for those who either did not agree or found it politic to dissent.

The theoretical foundations underpinning the observations of global warming continued to build an ever more coherent case. How to tackle it was a more difficult problem. Amongst other measures, the Kyoto Protocol called for the reforestation of the planet in order to sequester carbon dioxide in new biomass. However, climate modellers at the Potsdam Institute for Climate Impact Research in Germany released findings which suggested that the reforestation of the Tundra in northern latitudes would have the opposite to desired effect. Whilst extra tree cover would indeed absorb carbon dioxide from the atmosphere, any benefits would be more than outweighed by heat absorption. Bare snow in the winter reflected sunlight back into space, whereas trees were highly effective at absorbing the sun's energy, and hence warming the environment.

Work by the World Commission on Dams, a World Bank-funded study group, suggested in June that hydroelectricity, often hailed as the perfect green power source, might be as damaging to the environment as coal-fired generators. The reason was that organic material either drowned at the time of flooding or, washed into the dams by the feed waters, settled to the bottom and fermented anaerobically, releasing methane—a potent greenhouse gas.

The UK's meteorological office warned in July that transport would be a major victim of climate change. Roads, rivers and rail were all susceptible to disruption caused by climatic extremes such as floods, extremes of temperature, higher winds and increased lightning strikes.

In August the International Institute for Applied Systems Analysis (IIASA) in Austria released a study into the assumptions on which the Kyoto agreement was based. After a study of Russia's forests, the IIASA concluded that any potential gains from increasing forest cover as a way to mitigate carbon release could neither be verified nor policed and any reliance on forestry to achieve overall atmospheric carbon reductions was fundamentally flawed. The conclusion called into question the foundations upon which much of the Kyoto Protocol was based. The argument also defined the opposing factions for the forthcoming discussions to be held at The Hague in November: on the one side were those nations which wished to rely on forestry for carbon sequestering, notably Australia and the USA, and on the other were European countries which wished to see the targets attained through verifiable reductions in actual emissions.

Throughout the second half of 2000, the signs were there that global warming was having an effect. Whilst scientists were careful to avoid any claims of certainty, climate instability was wreaking havoc around the globe. The number of what had become known as EWEs, Extreme Weather Events, was alarming aid and disaster relief agencies.

September saw flooding make 15 million homeless in Bengal, India, and claim over 600 lives in under 10 days. At least 48 people died in Brazil. Mud slides claimed victims in Switzerland and Italy, and hundreds died in China. In Australia the heaviest rains in decades flooded vast areas, and a typhoon in Russia flooded the island of Sakhalin. Over a hundred died in Vietnam, Laos and Cambodia along the banks of the swollen Mekong river, where 4 million were affected by the rising waters. The UK experienced the highest rainfall and the worst flooding for over a century. By contrast, in Kenya, Ethiopia and Afghanistan the worst droughts in decades caused severe famines.

Meanwhile in Europe, where substantial eco taxes had been imposed on petrol and diesel, a measure designed to reduce fuel use, a sudden rise in pump prices triggered widespread protests. Initially popular, the gradual realisation that the severe weather conditions in the region were a probable result of global warming eventually helped to diminish support for the campaign.

The GM debate was revived briefly when it emerged in October that maize contaminated with GM modified crops intended only for animal feed had found its way into the food chain. Of particular concern was that the maize involved had been engineered to produce an insecticide which was known to share the characteristics of recognised allergens and thus might be presumed to have potential health impacts for people. Whilst its manufacturers, Aventis CropScience of America bought back the entire year's crop, the incident raised serious doubts about the feasibility of producing crops solely for animal feed and then attempting to ensure that they never contaminated crops intended for human consumption.

More evidence that a warming climate was affecting the planet was revealed at the International Coral Reef Symposium held in Indonesia. Rich Aronson of the Dauphin Island Sea Lab in the USA had drilled through reefs off the coast of Belize looking for an effect known as bleaching. Bleaching occurs when warmer sea temperatures result in the corals losing the symbiotic algae which give them their colours and which they require to survive. Aronson found that the die-back observed in reefs during the extreme El Nino event of 1997-98 was the first such event for 3,000 years. Scientists at the conference unanimously called for controls on carbon emissions to be agreed immediately.

November saw two further reports which confirmed bleak prospects for the future. In time for the conference on climate change held at The Hague, the Tyndall Centre for Climate Change issued its analysis of the rates at which climate change would affect different regions of the world. Far from being an even temperature rise, some countries, it suggested, would warm by significantly more than others. In particular some of the hottest countries in the world in the arid belt between Saudi Arabia and Kazakhstan would suffer severely with a rise of 5 degrees centigrade over the century. Island states such as New Zealand and the UK would warm the least, by around 3 degrees. However the greatest rises would be in the Arctic, with Canada and Russia seeing a 6 degree rise over 100 years.

From the UN's IPCC came a draft report released early to world leaders to add urgency to the discussions at The Hague. The IPCC had been predicting an eventual sea level rise of no more than three metres over 500 years. According to *New Scientist* magazine, the new report revised this estimate sharply upwards, predicting at least twice as much and suggesting a 13 metre rise as the upper limit. Such a rise predicted devastating consequences for large parts of the world and for vast numbers of people, drowning whole countries and inundating many major cities. A key part of the analysis was the fate of the ice cover, not just of the poles but also of Greenland's ice sheet. Models suggested the sheet would begin melting at an average rise of 2.7 degrees and once started would be impossible to stop. Eventually it would add 7 metres to sea levels. Such rises would, said the report, displace a billion people and eradicate the majority of the world's most productive farmland.

In the face of such dire warnings logic might have predicted that the climate talks at The Hague would recognise the need for progress and that finally a consensus would emerge. In fact the opposite occurred and the talks broke up in disarray with no progress and little chance that the next round would be able to resolve the entrenched views of the opposing factions.

At the core of the disagreement was the issue of carbon sinks—the use of forestry to absorb emissions whilst continuing to allow industry to emit at the same levels. The USA, Australia and a few others were adamant that forestry should be an option. Europe was adamant it should not. In addition, the USA wanted to retain the concept of "carbon trading", the option for rich nations such as the USA to buy the right to emit carbon dioxide from poorer nations. In that way, proponents argued, the USA could pay for the privilege of avoiding imposing controls on its industry whilst helping developing nations to pay for a cleaner development path. However, many others regarded this as the USA, the world's richest and most heavily polluting nation, simply attempting to avoid its responsibilities and to ensure its industrial pre-eminence.

In the face of looming deadlock the UK's Environment Secretary, John Prescott, and US negotiator Frank Loy worked out a last minute compromise, a complex rule book covering how forest sinks and carbon trading could be part of an agreement. The deal was presented to the European delegates, led by the French Environment Minister Dominique Voynet. Voynet, Jurgen Tritten of Germany and Svend Auken of Denmark rejected the deal and the discussions fell apart in a welter of criticism and counter-criticism. Greenpeace was amongst those supporting the EU refusal to sign the deal on the grounds that it was too flawed to be of any value. Other campaigners were less sanguine, observing that any deal would have been better than none.

At the time of the conference Bill Clinton was serving out his last days as President of the USA, but the election for the new President hung in the balance: Clinton's Vice-President Al Gore, an avowed green, had achieved more votes but fewer delegates and the decision remained poised in an unseemly scramble for advantage in Florida (see IV.1). It looked probable that his opponent George W Bush would become President. Even if he did not, an Al Gore presidency would have been compromised by the balance in both the Senate and Congress, but the alternative looked decidedly worse. George W Bush, son of ex-president George Bush—the man who had attempted to scupper the Rio summit with the declaration that its aims would be achieved, as he suggested, "over my dead body"—would clearly be no ally of the greens in any conflict between the environment and industry. The conference at the Hague represented the last chance for the rest of the world to negotiate a deal with the USA before it lurched to the political right for four, possibly eight years. This was surely an opportunity, however imperfect, that should not have been missed. But it was. In the event, George W. Bush was confirmed as the new President of the USA.

XIV THE LAW

1. INTERNATIONAL LAW—EC LAW

i. INTERNATIONAL LAW

THE United Nations Millennium Summit in September included an unprecedented treaty-signing and ratification ceremony; 40 instruments were signed, ratified or acceded to by the leaders of 84 states in an action which significantly advanced the impact of the international rule of law. The largest number of signatures was made to two new protocols to the Convention on the Rights of the Child: one to prevent the use of children in armed conflict and the other to eliminate the sale of children, child prostitution and child pornography.

Amongst other developments in treaty-making, the Cartagena Protocol on Biosafety (the first protocol to the 1992 UN Convention on Biological Diversity) was opened for signature on January 29; this regulated trade in genetically modified products. The UN General Assembly adopted on November 15 a Convention against Transnational Organised Crime to provide a basis for stronger common action against drug trafficking and money laundering and to secure greater ease of extradition, better protection of witnesses and enhanced judicial co-operation. Two protocols supplemented the Convention, one to prevent, suppress and punish trafficking in persons, especially women and children, and the other against the smuggling of migrants by land, sea and air. The Optional Protocol to the UN Convention on the Elimination of All Forms of Discrimination against Women, providing an international remedy for violations of women's rights, came into force on December 22, just over a year after it had been adopted by the UN General Assembly.

The INTERNATIONAL COURT OF JUSTICE continued to be busy, with 24 cases before it. It concluded the hearings in several cases but did not decide on the merits of any case. A new President, Gilbert Guillaume (France), and a new Vice-President, Shi Jiuyong (China), were elected on February 7 to serve for three years; Thomas Buergenthal (USA) was elected to replace Judge Stephen Schwebel. The new President called on the United Nations to provide the Court with the increased resources it required to handle its large case load effectively. He said that it was for states "to decide whether the Court is to die a slow death or whether you will give it the wherewithal to live".

On October 17 the Democratic Republic of Congo (DRC) instituted proceedings against Belgium for violation of its sovereignty and of the diplomatic immunity of the Minister for Foreign Affairs, Yerodia Ndombasi, by the issue of an international arrest warrant for the minister for serious violations of international humanitarian law committed on the territory of the DRC. The DRC also requested provisional measures: because the arrest warrant effectively barred the minister from leaving the state and from carrying out his duties it should be immediately discharged. The dispute concerned the scope of national jurisdiction over crimes against humanity and genocide and the scope of diplomatic immunity. During the case there was a Cabinet reshuffle in the DRC and Ndombasi became Minister of Education. Belgium accordingly argued that the request for provisional measures was without object and should be struck out, but the Court rejected this because the international arrest warrant had not been withdrawn. Nevertheless it refused the request for provisional measures; because Ndombasi was now Minster for Education, less frequent foreign travel was involved and, therefore, it had not been established that irreparable prejudice might be caused in the immediate future nor that the degree of urgency was such that provisional measures were required. However, the Court would ensure that a decision on the DRC's application would be reached with all expedition.

In another case brought by the DRC, the *Case Concerning Armed Activities on the Territory of the Congo*, it was successful in its application for provisional measures. The DRC accused Uganda of acts of armed aggression in flagrant violation of the UN Charter, the OAU Charter and human rights obligations. The DRC asked the Court to indicate that Uganda must order its army to withdraw immediately from Kisanjani and to cease all military activity in the DRC. Uganda argued that its troops had been in the DRC at the request of the government, that they had now withdrawn from Kisanjani and that it was ready to withdraw all troops from the DRC in accordance with the Lusaka Agreement, but that immediate, unilateral withdrawal would contravene that Agreement. The Court found that it had *prima facie* jurisdiction to decide on provisional measures. It was not disputed that Ugandan forces were present on the territory of the DRC, that fighting had taken place between those forces and those of Rwanda, that the fighting had caused a large number of civilian casualties and material damage, that the humanitarian situation remained one of profound concern and that grave and repeated violations of human rights had been committed. Accordingly the Court found that there was a serious risk that the rights at issue in the case might suffer irreparable prejudice and that the situation was urgent. Circumstances required it to indicate provisional measures. However, the measures that it indicated were even-handed and did not impute any responsibility for the breach to Uganda. The Court called on both parties to prevent and refrain from any action which might prejudice the rights of the other party or which might aggravate or extend the dispute.

In the *Case Concerning the Aerial Incident of 10 August 1999,* brought by Pakistan against India for shooting down a Pakistani aircraft, the Court found that it had no jurisdiction. Firstly, Pakistan argued that the Court had jurisdiction under the 1928 General Act. The question of whether this treaty was still in force so as to give jurisdiction to the Court had been raised in earlier cases, but never settled. In this case again the Court did not decide this difficult issue; instead it found that even if India had succeeded to the treaty it had terminated its acceptance at the latest in 1979. Secondly, Pakistan argued that the Court had jurisdiction under India's acceptance of the Court's jurisdiction filed on September 15, 1974. However, India had made a reservation excluding disputes with any state which was, or had been, a member of the Commonwealth. Pakistan argued that this reservation had no legal effect because it was in breach of good faith and in conflict with the principle of sovereign equality; also the reservation was obsolete as it was made at a time when the Commonwealth was a close-knit family. The Court firmly rejected these radical arguments. It followed its earlier case-law to interpret the reservation in a natural and reasonable way, having due regard to the intention of the state concerned. Whilst the historical reason for the Commonwealth reservation might have changed, such considerations could not prevail over the intention of a state as expressed in the actual text of its declaration. Since Pakistan was a member of the Commonwealth the Court had no jurisdiction.

The INTERNATIONAL CRIMINAL TRIBUNAL FOR THE FORMER YUGOSLAVIA (ICTY) and the TRIBUNAL FOR RWANDA (ICTR) were given increased resources by the UN Security Council to enable them to expedite the conclusion of their work. Additionally, the number of judges on the Appeals Chamber common to the two international tribunals was to be enlarged by the election of two additional judges to the Rwanda Tribunal. The Security Council also decided to establish a pool of 27 *ad litem* judges to be appointed to specific trials as and when needed. The ICTY reported that it was still encountering difficulties in securing custody of those accused who remained at large. However, the change of government in Croatia and the overthrow of President Slobodan Milosevic in Yugoslavia (see III.2.vi.) improved the prospects for co-operation with the tribunal.

The Appeals Chamber made final decisions in the cases of *Tadic, Aleksovski* and *Furundzija*. In the first it reduced the sentence to a maximum of 20 years because of the relatively low position of Tadic within the Bosnian Serb hierarchy; in the second it accepted the appeal of the prosecutor that the conflict was international rather than purely internal and increased the sentence of the Bosnian Croat prison commander for war crimes to seven years; in the *Furundzija* case the Appeals Chamber affirmed the conviction for war crimes and upheld the original sentence of 10 years. The Trial Chamber imposed its heaviest sentence to date in the *Blaskic* case. The Bosnian Croat commander was found guilty of individual and superior responsibility for crimes against humanity, grave breaches of the Geneva Conventions and war crimes for the killing, wounding and rape of Bosnian Muslims in the Lasva Valley in April 1993. The Tribunal ruled that Blaskic had been implementing policies formulated at the highest levels of the Croatian government. The conflict was international because of the direct involvement of the Croat army in Bosnia and also Croat overall control of Bosnian Croat forces. Blaskic was sentenced to 45 years' imprisonment. In *Kupreskic and others* the Trial Chamber found five Bosnian Croat soldiers guilty for their part in the massacre of over 100 Bosnian Muslims and the destruction of their houses in central Bosnia in April 1993. In response to complaints made since mid-1999, the Court Prosecutor, Carla del Ponte, reported on the NATO 1999 air campaign against the Federal Republic of Yugoslavia and decided not to open a criminal investigation. Although some mistakes had been made by NATO, she was satisfied that there was no deliberate targeting of civilians or unlawful military targets.

The ICTR reported that its performance had improved and its work had accelerated. Several ground-breaking decisions were made. It reached the final stage in *Serushago* when the appeal was dismissed by the Appeals Chamber and the sentence of 15 years for genocide and crimes against humanity was confirmed. The Appeals Chamber also upheld the genocide conviction and sentence of life imprisonment of former Prime Minister *Jean Kambanda*, the first head of government to be convicted for the crime. *Georges Ruggiu*, a Belgian journalist who had worked at the state-owned radio station that incited people to kill Tutsis, pleaded guilty to incitement to commit genocide and crimes against humanity and was sentenced to 12 years' imprisonment. *Alfred Musema*, director of a tea factory, was the first non-military and non-government official to be sentenced. He was given life imprisonment for individual and superior responsibility for genocide and crimes against humanity for his part in transporting armed attackers, including employees of the factory, to western Rwanda to take part in massacres and for his personal part in the killing and rapes.

The EUROPEAN COURT OF HUMAN RIGHTS in the second year of its existence as a permanent court was faced with an ever increasing case load. The vast majority of cases concerned the right to a fair trial under Article 6 of the European Convention on Human Rights. Delays in criminal and civil cases led to a mass of cases, especially against Italy and France. Many cases were brought against Turkey for violations of the right to life, the prohibition on torture, and freedom of speech with regard to its treatment of the Kurds. Denmark brought a case against Turkey for interrogation techniques involving torture and ill-treatment in police custody, the first case to be brought by one state against another on behalf of a national. It resulted in a friendly settlement whereby Turkey made an *ex gratia* payment, issued a declaration regretting the occurrence of "occasional and individual cases of torture and ill-treatment", and accepted a far-reaching regime designed to end inappropriate police interrogation techniques. The claim of the Kurdish leader, Abdullah Öcalan, who had been sentenced to death in Turkey in June 1999 (see AR 1999, p. 108), was declared admissible; the Court then relinquished jurisdiction to the Grand Chamber of 17 judges, the body responsible for hearing the most sensitive and controversial cases.

The INTERNATIONAL TRIBUNAL FOR THE LAW OF THE SEA gave judgment in two cases arising from the seizure by France of vessels fishing for Patagonian toothfish in its exclusive economic zone in the Southern and Antarctic Territories. The *Camouco* and *Monte Confurco* cases arose out of applications by Panama and the Seychelles respectively for the prompt release of their vessels which had been arrested by French frigates for illegal fishing. The Tribunal rejected the French argument that a state could, by failing to act promptly, lose its rights under article 292 of the United Nations Convention on the Law of the Sea to request prompt release; it also held that the remedy under article 292 was not limited by the requirement that local remedies be exhausted. It was for the Tribunal to determine the reasonableness of the bond which the detaining state could set as security. Following its previous judgment in the *M/V Saiga* case, the Tribunal elaborated on the factors relevant in an assessment of the reasonableness of the bond: these included the gravity of the alleged offences, the penalties under the law of the detaining state, the value of the detained vessel and of the cargo seized. In both cases the Tribunal concluded that the bond imposed by France was not reasonable and determined a lesser amount.

The *Southern Bluefin Tuna* case, which had begun before the International Tribunal for the Law of the Sea in 1999, continued before a five-member arbitration tribunal established to hear the claims of Australia and New Zealand against Japan. This was the first arbitral tribunal to be constituted under the dispute settlement provisions of the UN Convention of the Law of the Sea. The parties disagreed as to whether the stock of southern bluefin tuna had begun to recover after severe overfishing; Japan sought an increase in the allowable catch and initiated a unilateral fishing programme. This complex case turned on the interpretation of two inter-related treaties, the 1982 UN Convention on the Law of the Sea (which came into force for the three parties to the case in 1996) and the 1993 Convention for the Conservation of Southern Bluefin Tuna. The Tribunal found that the dispute arose under both Conventions. However, the 1993 Convention effectively excluded unilateral reference to compulsory arbitration and the UN Convention fell significantly short of establishing a truly comprehensive regime of compulsory jurisdiction. Therefore, the arbitral tribunal found that it lacked jurisdiction to entertain the merits of the dispute and revoked the order of provisional measures.

ii. EUROPEAN COMMUNITY LAW

THE European Council at Nice in December was important not so much for what it decided but for what it started and for the initiatives which it trailed behind it. The change in tempo and in depth of reform of the European Union (EU), which had been visible the previous year, gained in strength by, and alongside, the Intergovernmental Conference (IGC) that ran throughout the year 2000. Thus, by the end of the year it was clear that a fundamental and permanent change had taken place in EU mentalities: it was extending its grasp beyond merely commercial law to embrace the other, deeper, legal sectors which formed the hard core of a legal system; it was replacing the internal market by the concept of the citizen as its main driving force; and it was visualising an increasingly complex and sophisticated judicial structure. More surprising, and significant, was the willingness of the member states to follow this path.

The Treaty of Nice was not signed at the December summit meeting. Merely its contents were agreed, because the political changes (qualified majority voting and weighting of votes in the Council, size of the Commission after enlargement), which were its raison d'etre, had not been adequately prepared and required long and fraught meetings of the heads of government themselves to reach agreement. The two matters (major, albeit marginal to the IGC) which were adopted at Nice without any disagreement, had both been extremely well and efficiently prepared. One related to the Court of Justice (of which more below). The other, the Charter of Fundamental Rights of the European Union, had been drafted in an original manner, using a large and widely representative drafting committee which had been open, via its website, to massive input of opinion from the citizenry at large. Its text was finalised in September, and thereafter remained unchanged. The only disagreement was as to its status. (For full text of Charter see XVII.1.)

Opposition to the desire of most member states to incorporate the Charter in the EC Treaty, and to its having legal force derived from its treaty status, resulted in it being adopted not by the member states but by the EU's political institutions (the Commission, Council and Parliament) in the form of a declaration. Consequently it would not be binding on the member states nor, probably, on the institutions, but would instead constitute a statement of intent and a useful gathering together of the various rights both within the European Convention on Human Rights and scattered in EU treaties and elsewhere. Apart from the status of the document itself, the legal nature of the individual rights was disputable, given that many of them were not absolute but were subject to "Community law and national laws and practices". The Charter itself was addressed to the institutions and bodies of the Union, in spite of the inclusion of clauses prohibiting practices such as capital punishment, slavery, and torture (taken from the European Convention), which were only appropriate to a state. The member states were, however, included "when they are implementing Union law". Even were it part of the EC Treaty the legal effect of the Charter would be subject to numerous and serious questions.

Whilst the IGC was concerned with specific aspects of the EU structure in relation to the future enlargement, underlying it was a deeper interest in more fundamental change. The member states gave expression to that interest by a declaration in the Treaty of Nice providing for a new IGC in 2004 to consider in effect the drafting of a federal-style constitution. This had already been started during 2000 in a general manner by a Commission paper in February on "Shaping the New Europe" and another in April on reforming the Commission. More substantial, indeed vital to the whole enterprise, was consideration of a treaty redraft, to simplify all three EU treaties (Euratom, EC and EU - the ECSC would have expired in 2002 on completion of its 50-year life) and merge them into a single, clearer document, possibly by splitting the result into a "constitution" and a "policy" document, only the former having true treaty status. The hard work on this project was completed during 2000 by the European University Institute at Florence, which at the request of the Commission produced two reports on a "Basic Treaty of the EU" and on reforming the treaties' amendment procedures. The issue was then taken up by the European Parliament in a report on the constitutionalisation of the treaties in October and by the Commission in a communication to the IGC in July.

Parallel to these constitutional developments, the Court of Justice had been urging the member states to take seriously the long-standing problems of the judicial branch of EU governance, resulting from an ever-increasing workload (which would become even heavier upon further enlargement), which was leading to unacceptable delays in delivering judgments. Supported by the Commission and by thoughtful and thorough reports produced the previous year, the Court succeeded in getting its reform proposals onto the IGC agenda and, to a large extent, accepted into the Treaty of Nice. The most far-reaching change was the power to create "judicial panels" to hear specified classes of case such as staff disputes or intellectual property cases. When this power was exercised, the judicial panels would in effect form a first tier of Community courts. Above them would be the Court of First Instance (CFI) which, in spite of strong proposals for change, would keep that name. The CFI was given a strengthened status by the transfer of its main attributes into the EC Treaty (previously in a Council decision) and, in a separate action outside the IGC, was given approval by Coreper for an additional six judges. The division of jurisdiction between the CFI and the European Court of Justice (ECJ) was made more supple, with the CFI having in principle all direct actions, even involving member states or EU institutions, except for Commission "prosecutions" of member states under Article 226.

The purpose of these changes was to free the ECJ from part of its burden and enable it to fulfil the role of ensuring uniform application of Community law. Consequently it retained in principle the giving of preliminary rulings to national courts; although even there the possibility was now provided for the CFI to take on some of them in certain special cases. One further revolutionary change was introduced by allowing jurisdiction to be conferred on the ECJ to try cases between private parties—normal private litigation—in cases involving Community intellectual property law. This was a glance forward to the time when a Community patent law might be enacted (disputes under Community trade mark law were currently heard by special panels at the Community trade mark office in Alicante). ECJ procedure was lightened slightly by giving the Court power to dispense with an Advocate General where appropriate in certain cases, thus saving one stage in the process. The fear that after EU enlargement the Court would become too large (one judge per member state) to maintain a single identity and would split into permanent sub-courts of a more manageable size, was allayed by borrowing from the European Court of Human Rights the concept of a Grand Chamber. Quite apart from the IGC, the two Courts revised their rules of procedure to remove some long-standing irrelevancies and to bring the rules into the electronic age by allowing documents to be lodged by fax. The Courts also introduced a simplified procedure, an accelerated procedure, an expedited procedure and other changes.

Against this background, the ordinary legal work of the EU continued, much of it also being innovative. Thus the new Title IV of the EC Treaty, aiming to create an area of freedom, security and justice in the EU, added by the Treaty of Amsterdam, began to produce texts not only in the field of immigration and asylum but also that of judicial co-operation and civil and criminal law. The most dramatic example was the adoption of a new regulation on jurisdiction and enforcement of foreign judgments in December. This repeated mostly word-for-word the existing Convention on the same subject, with some slight amendments, but moved its text from member state control as a treaty subject to national ratification and placed it under Commission, Council and European Parliament control. The special Scoreboard to review progress on this legislative area, introduced by the Commission in March, was up-dated in November with 34 pages of tabulated legislation being prepared, progressing or being adopted. These covered criminal law and procedure and civil law and procedure, as well as aliens and refugees and collaboration between justice professionals (courts, prosecutors, and police).

The ECJ caused a stir in October when it annulled Directive 98/43 (which prohibited tobacco advertising) on the grounds that it was not necessary to promote the internal market and that its real basis was public health (for which the EC had no legislative power). It had never before annulled a directive on such grounds.

2. LAW IN THE UNITED KINGDOM

THE Human Rights Act 1998 came into force in October, incorporating the European Convention on Human Rights into domestic law. It immediately led to litigation. The Court of Appeal held that the Act required that limitations be imposed on the imposition of automatic life sentences required by the Crime (Sentences) Act 1997;[1] that the denial of a fair trial would almost inevitably result in a conviction being regarded as unsafe,[2] but that the English mode of conduct of proceedings relating to contempts in the face of the court did not infringe the requirements of a fair trial;[3] and that the withdrawal of medical treatment was not to be regarded in itself as a breach of human rights.[4] Press freedom was enhanced when the House of Lords held that a press conference constituted a public meeting, with the result that newspaper reporting of it was covered by the statutory defence of qualified privilege;[5] and individuals' rights against the government were improved by the enactment of the Freedom of Information Act. The Armed Forces Discipline Act made further provision to bring military law and practice in line with the human rights requirements; and the Regulation of Investigatory Powers Act updated the law relating to the governmental monitoring and interception of communications, imposing for the first time a comprehensive regulatory structure. The relationship between English and European law was explored by the House of Lords, and it was held that it would be wrong for English law to take a different stance from other EU member states towards the granting of interim relief when an application was made to enjoin the government from implementing a directive.[6]

The Representation of the People Act amended the law relating to voting in parliamentary and local elections; further changes relating to local government were made by the Local Government Act; and political processes at a national level were regulated by the Political Parties, Elections and Referendums Act, which provided amongst other things for the appointment of an Electoral Commission to oversee the operation of the legislation. The Royal Commission on the House of

Lords chaired by Lord Wakeham recommended sweeping reforms, proposing the creation of a second chamber of appointed working peers.[7]

New structures for the provision of public services were contained in the Postal Services Act, the Utilities Act, the Transport Act and the Police (Northern Ireland) Act. A modern framework for sixth-form and further education was introduced by the Learning and Skills Act.

The courts continued to be active in overseeing how public bodies exercised their powers. The House of Lords held that, in determining where a child with special educational needs should be educated, a Local Education Authority was entitled to take into account the efficient use of its own resources in order to override the preference of the child's parents;[8] but that a local authority could be liable to such pupils for failures of care on the part of council employees.[9] The Ministry of Defence was held to have acted properly in refusing to give compensation to a British soldier injured in the course of military duties on behalf of the United Nations.[10] Further definition was given to the law relating to political refugees: a person seeking asylum was held to satisfy the requirement of a "well-founded fear of persecution" if a state failed to provide adequate protection against persecution by non-state agents.[11]

Two statutes significantly affected the law relating to children. The Care Standards Act created a new regulatory body to oversee children's care homes and similar institutions. The Child Support, Pensions and Social Security Act introduced substantial reforms to the system of child support, as well as creating a completely new system of state pensions in place of the old earnings related pensions scheme and making a host of amendments to the provision of social security benefits. In the courts the House of Lords held that a care order might be made on the grounds that a child was suffering serious harm notwithstanding that it could not be identified who was responsible for the harm,[12] and the High Court ruled that a woman who had been given care and control of a child could lawfully refuse her consent to blood samples being taken from the child with a view to determining the identity of the father.[13]

Employment law was left relatively free from changes. The House of Lords held that the requirement that a person should have been employed for two years before being entitled to bring a claim for unfair dismissal, introduced in 1985[14], was lawful, even though it was shown that fewer women than men were able to satisfy the requirement. A minority of the House thought that the disparity was not significant enough to ground a claim based on indirect sexual discrimination, the majority holding that it was discriminatory but that the discrimination was justifiable.[15] The Court of Appeal held that pupil barristers were not "workers" and were hence excluded from the national minimum wage legislation.[16]

Wholesale reorganisation of the legal regulation of the financial services industry was brought about by the Financial Services and Markets Act, replacing the previous regulatory bodies by a single Financial Services Authority. In the wake of fears about the potential personal liability of members of partnerships, the Limited Liability Partnerships Act created a framework within which the benefits of limited liability could be extended beyond incorporated companies. Amendments to the law relating to trustees and bankruptcy were contained in the Trustee Act and the Insolvency Act. In three far-reaching cases the House of Lords gave consideration to the nature of contractual remedies. It was held that where the normal contractual remedies of compensatory damages, specific performance and injunction were inadequate to compensate a claimant, it might be open to a court to require the defendant to disgorge any profits which had been made as a result of the breach.[17]. A restrictive approach was taken to the circumstances in which contractual damages could be recovered in respect of a third party's losses[18] and an insurance company was required to fulfil its obligations to holders of its policies, despite the enormous costs involved.[19] The House of Lords settled long-standing difficulties in the law relating to the tracing of misappropriated assets into their proceeds,[20] and the Court of Appeal reiterated that whilst liability for knowing assistance in breach of trust depended on the defendant's dishonesty, there was no such requirement where an action was brought against a person who had received property in breach of trust.[21]

Problems stemming from the mortgaging of matrimonial homes continued to arise. The Court of Appeal stressed that, until the House of Lords resolved otherwise, a court should only set aside a bank's charge over a matrimonial home on the grounds of a husband's presumed undue influence over his wife if it was proved that she had suffered some "manifest disadvantage"; but a legal executive's certificate that the wife had received independent legal advice was sufficient to rebut the presumption.[22] The High Court decided that the doctrine of undue influence extended to any situation involving the abuse of a position of trust.[23] The House of Lords took a pragmatic approach in holding that a transfer of a joint tenant's share in land could not have different effects depending on whether it was achieved by release or assignment.[24]

In the latest of the series of cases in the House of Lords relating to psychiatric injury, it was held that parents could sue a public authority who had placed a known child-abuser for fostering by them.[25] Subsequently the Court of Appeal held that a person negligently inflicting injuries on himself was not responsible for psychiatric injury suffered by another person witnessing the event,[26] and that the restrictive rules relating to the compensability of psychiatric injury did not apply in suits for breach of contract.[27] The Court of Appeal gave guidance as to the relationship between issues of causation and quantification of loss in the tort of negligence,[28] and introduced higher awards of damages for negligently caused pain and suffering and other forms of non-pecuniary loss.[29] The recoverability of interest on damages for personal injury was considered by the House of Lords, and difficulties in the interpretation of the Social Security (Recovery of Benefits) Act 1997 were resolved by taking an approach allowing for the most straightforward application of the statutory regime.[30] In an important case on the tortious liability of the emergency services, the Court of Appeal held that the Ambulance Service fell under a duty of care to provide an ambulance within a reasonable time of being called;[31] and the Ministry of Defence was held to owe a duty of care to prevent a drunken soldier injuring himself.[32] The House of Lords departed from its own previous decisions in laying down that an advocate was not immune from liability in negligence at the suit of a client whom he had represented in civil proceedings;[33] and held that a local authority was liable to children who were injured after it had failed to remove an abandoned boat from its land,[34] though not where it had installed lockable windows which had prevented the escape of a tenant's children when fire broke out.[35]

Important definition was given to the law of non-negligent torts. In litigation arising out of the failure of the Bank of Credit and Commerce International the House of Lords sharpened the tort of misfeasance in public office;[36] in other cases the Court of Appeal refused to allow the award of exemplary damages in the tort[37] and held that policemen were not immune from suit by former defendants in criminal proceedings.[38] The House of Lords held that the tort of malicious prosecution could not be extended to situations not involving the institution of legal proceedings.[39] The tort of false imprisonment was held to be a tort of strict liability, and so lay against a prison governor who failed to release a prisoner at the due time notwithstanding that he was acting in accordance with the law as it was then thought to stand.[40] The defence of contributory negligence was held not to apply to the tort of deceit.[41]

Wholesale reforms in the law relating to the prevention of terrorism were contained in the Terrorism Act. In the teeth of opposition from the House of Lords, the Sexual Offences (Amendment) Act reduced the age of consent for homosexual acts and introduced a new offence where a person in a position of trust engaged in sexual activity with a person below the age of 18. The Home Office issued a voluminous consultation paper as a prelude to sweeping reforms in the law relating to sexual offences.[42] The House of Lords reversed an earlier decision of the Queen's Bench Divisional Court, holding that a person could not be convicted of inciting a minor to commit an act of gross indecency with him if he honestly albeit unreasonably believed that she was above the relevant age of consent;[43] but in a subsequent decision the Court of Appeal stressed that it was not necessary for the prosecution to offer positive proof that the defendant did not in fact believe that the victim was over the relevant age.[44] After several years of uncertainty in the law, the House of Lords resolved that the scope of the defence of provocation to a charge of murder was a matter for the jury and that it was wrong for the trial judge to lay down hard and fast rules about its availability, thereby allowing its use by those suffering from diminished mental capacity;[45] and their lordships upheld the decision of the Court of Appeal that the word "appropriation" in the Theft Act 1968 should be given a broad meaning in order to ensure that dishonest people should not escape criminal liability.[46] The Court of Appeal refused to depart from the orthodox view that a corporation could not be liable for manslaughter in the absence of evidence of the guilt of a human being capable of being identified with the corporation;[47] and a centuries-old anomaly in the criminal law was removed when the Court of Appeal held that a battery might be inflicted indirectly.[48]

The law relating to criminal sentencing was consolidated in the Powers of Criminal Courts (Sentencing) Act. The decision of the Home Secretary that a person imprisoned for life should never be released from prison was held to have been lawful.[49] The House of Lords held that time spent on remand in non-secure accommodation should not be treated as time spent in custody which fell to be deducted automatically from a subsequent prison sentence;[50] and the Court of Appeal held that brief periods of remand necessary for the orderly conduct of a trial were similarly not deductible.[51] The Court of Appeal held that it was appropriate to add an additional two years to a sentence for violent assault if the assault was racially motivated.[52]

The House of Lords clarified the law relating to the procedure to be followed after the defendant to a criminal charge had been found unfit to plead;[53] and a strict view was taken of the obligation to hold an identification parade when a suspected person disputed an eyewitness's identification.[54]

It was held that improperly intercepted telephone communications could not be adduced in evidence,[55] but that this restriction did not apply to communications intercepted abroad.[56] Evidence obtained by entrapment was not automatically to be excluded,[57] nor evidence obtained from a DNA sample that had been unlawfully retained.[58]

The House of Lords explained the rare circumstances in which it was appropriate for the court to disregard express statutory words in order to give effect to presumed parliamentary intention.[59] In the face of serious concerns over its increasing workload and the attendant delays on the administration of justice, the House of Lords declined to hear an appeal from the refusal of the Court of Appeal to grant permission to appeal from the order of a single judge, emphasising the need for it to concentrate on cases involving points of major public importance,[60] and in a case involving breach of copyright reiterated that appellate courts should be very slow to interfere with findings of fact made by the trial judge.[61] The Court of Appeal laid down guidelines for the making of vexatious litigant orders.[62]

In a number of cases the work of the courts excited enormous public interest and concern. In an action raising fundamental issues of morality, the Court of Appeal held that it was lawful for doctors to operate to separate conjoined twins, even though the result of the operation would inevitably be that the weaker twin would die,[63] and the operation was subsequently carried out.[64] A Manchester doctor, Harold Frederick Shipman, regarded as Britain's worst serial killer, was convicted of the murder of 15 elderly patients.[65] The historian David Irving lost a libel action against Penguin Books after he had been accused of being a "Hitler partisan" and denying the existence of the Nazi holocaust.[66] A Norfolk farmer, Tony Martin, who killed a burglar who had broken into his home, was sentenced to life imprisonment for murder;[67] though another farmer who shot a poacher was held not to be guilty of unlawful wounding.[68] In the light of medical reports that he was not fit to stand trial, the Home Secretary refused to extradite the Chilean former dictator Gen. (retd) Augusto Pinochet Ugarte to Spain;[69] but, despite having given undertakings of confidentiality, he was required to disclose the contents of medical reports.[70]

1. *R v. Offen, The Times*, November 10.
2. *R v. Togher, The Times*, November 21.
3. *R v. MacLeod, The Times*, December 20.
4. *NHS Trust A v. M, The Times*, November 29 (Family Division).
5. *Turkington v. Times Newspapers Ltd., The Times*, November 3.
6. *R v. Secretary of State for Health, ex parte Imperial Tobacco Ltd., The Times*, December 20.
7. *The Times*, January 21.
8. *B v. Harrow London Borough Council* [2000] 1 WLR 223.
9. *Phelps v. Hillingdon London Borough Council* [2000] 3 WLR 776 (House of Lords).
10. *R v. Ministry of Defence, ex parte Walker* [2000] 1 WLR 806.

11. *Horvath* v. *Secretary of State for the Home Department* [2000] 3 WLR 379 (House of Lords).
12. *Lancashire County Council* v. *B (a Child)* [2000] 2 AC 147.
13. *The Times*, January 27.
14. *Unfair Dismissal (Variation of Qualifying Period) Order* (SI 1985 No 1782).
15. *R* v. *Secretary of State for Employment, ex parte Seymour-Smith (no 2)* [2000] 1 WLR 435.
16. *Edmonds* v. *Lawson* [2000] QB 501.
17. *Attorney-General* v. *Blake* [2000] 3 WLR 625.
18. *McAlpine (Alfred) Construction Ltd.* v. *Panatown Ltd.* [2000] 3 WLR 946.
19. *Equitable Life Assurance Society* v. *Hyman* [2000] 2 WLR 798.
20. *Foskett* v. *McKeown* [2000] 2 WLR 1299.
21. *Houghton* v. *Fayers* [2000] 1 BCLC 511; *Bank of Credit and Commerce International (Overseas) Ltd.* v. *Akindele* [2000] 3 WLR 1423.
22. *Barclays Bank Plc* v. *Coleman* [2000] 3 WLR 405.
23. *Naidoo* v. *Naidu*, *The Times*, November 1.
24. *Burton* v. *Camden London Borough Council* [2000] 2 AC 399.
25. *W* v. *Essex County Council* [2000] 2 WLR 601.
26. *Greatorex* v. *Greatorex* [2000] 1 WLR 1970.
27. *Gogay* v. *Hertfordshire County Council*, *The Times*, October 3.
28. *Holtby* v. *Brigham and Cowan (Hull) Ltd.* [2000] 3 All ER 421.
29. *Heil* v. *Rankin* [2000] 2 WLR 1173.
30. *Wisely* v. *John Fulton (Plumbers) Ltd.* [2000] 1 WLR 820.
31. *Kent* v. *Griffiths* [2000] 2 WLR 1158.
32. *Jebson* v. *Ministry of Defence* [2000] 1 WLR 2055.
33. *Arthur J.S. Hall & Co (a Firm)* v. *Simons (a Firm)* [2000] 3 WLR 543.
34. *Jolley* v. *Sutton London Borough Council* [2000] 1 WLR 1082.
35. *Adams* v. *Rhymney Valley District Council*, *The Times*, August 11.
36. *Three Rivers District Council* v. *Governor and Company of the Bank of England (No 3)* [2000] 2 WLR 15.
37. *Kuddus* v. *Chief Constable of Leicestershire*, *The Times*, March 16.
38. *Docker* v. *Chief Constable of West Midlands Police*, *The Times*, August 1.
39. *Gregory* v. *Portsmouth City Council* [2000] 1 AC 499.
40. *R* v. *Governor of Brockhill Prison, ex parte Evans (No 2)* [2000] 3 WLR 843 (House of Lords).
41. *Standard Chartered Bank* v. *Pakistan National Shipping Corporation (No 4)* [2000] 3 WLR 1692.
42. *The Times*, July 27.
43. *B (a Minor)* v. *Director of Public Prosecutions* [2000] 2 AC 428.
44. *R* v. *K*, The Times, November 7.
45. *R* v. *Smith* [2000] 3 WLR 654.
46. *R* v. *Hinks* [2000] 3 WLR 1590.
47. *Attorney-General's Reference (No 2 of 1999)* [2000] QB 796.
48. *Haystead* v. *Chief Constable of Derbyshire* [2000] 3 All ER 890.
49. *R* v. *Secretary of State for the Home Department, ex parte Hindley* [2000] 2 WLR 730 (House of Lords).
50. *R* v. *Secretary of State for the Home Department, ex parte A* [2000] 2 AC 276.
51. *Burgess* v. *Secretary of State for the Home Department*, *The Times*, November 14.
52. *R* v. *Saunders* [2000] 1 Cr App Rep 458.
53. *R* v. *Antoine* [2000] 2 WLR 703.
54. *R* v. *Forbes*, *The Times*, December 19.
55. *Morgans* v. *Director of Public Prosecutions* [2000] 2 WLR 386.
56. *R* v. *P*, *The Times*, December 19.
57. *R* v. *Shannon*, *The Times*, October 11 (Court of Appeal).
58. *R* v. *B*, *The Times*, December 15.
59. *Inco Europe Ltd.* v. *First Choice Distribution (a Firm)* [2000] 1 WLR 586.
60. *R* v. *Secretary of State for Trade and Industry, ex parte Eastaway* [2000] 1 WLR 2222.
61. *Designers Guild Ltd.* v. *Russell Williams (Textiles) Ltd.* [2000] 1 WLR 2416.
62. *Attorney-General* v. *Barker*, *The Times*, March 7.
63. *In re A (Minors) (Conjoined twins: Medical treatment)*, *The Times*, October 10.
64. *The Times*, November 8.
65. *The Times*, February 1.
66. *The Times*, April 12.
67. *The Times*, April 20 .
68. *The Times*, June 9.
69. *The Times*, March 3.
70. *The Times*, February 16.

3. LAW IN THE USA

SUPREME Court decisions in 2000 concerning the respective powers of the state and federal governments continued the trend towards limiting the federal government's powers and expanding the states' freedom from federal interference, with one notable exception. In *US* v. *Morrison* the Court held invalid the federal Violence Against Women Act of 1994—which permitted female victims of sex crimes to sue, under federal law and in a federal court, their male attackers—because Congress did not have the power under either the Commerce Clause of the US Constitution—under which Congress could enact laws to regulate interstate commerce—since gender-motivated crimes were not considered economic activity, or the Equal Protection Clause of the Fourteenth Amendment—under which Congress could enact laws to protect citizens from discrimination—since such crimes were considered to be acts of private individuals, not states.

In *Kimel* v. *Florida Board of Regents* the Court held that an employee of a state agency, in this case Florida State University, could not sue that agency under the Age Discrimination in Employment Act of 1967, because states had a sovereign immunity from claims arising out of federal laws enacted under the Commerce Clause. The Court also ruled that Congress could not override that immunity by using its power to enforce equal protection rights under the Fourteenth Amendment because the Equal Protection Clause did not forbid discrimination on the basis of age. The exception was *Bush* v. *Gore*, an unprecedented action by the Republican candidate for the presidency (George W. Bush) to stop the counting, ordered by the Florida Supreme Court under Florida law, of ballots not previously counted in three Florida counties in the 2000 presidential election, because those ballots had not been properly punched (see IV.1; and XVII.2). The Court concluded that the different standards that might be applied in those three counties would deny equal protection to voters. The equality that trumped the state's right to determine its own election procedures was neither racial nor gender, but the equality of voters in different counties of Florida.

A federal district court concluded in *United States* v. *Microsoft Corporation* that Microsoft had violated the 1890 federal Sherman Antitrust Act by acquiring and abusing its monopoly as a supplier of software, and ordered that the company be split into three companies. Because of Microsoft's size and importance to the economy, the decision was considered as significant as the decisions in the landmark Standard Oil and American Telephone and Telegraph cases in 1910 and 1982, respectively. Microsoft appealed against the decision, but the Court of Appeals decision was not expected in 2001.

The litigation against tobacco companies continued to set unprecedented damage awards. In the first class action against the tobacco companies by a plaintiff representing 500,000 cigarette smokers, a jury in a Florida court awarded US$12.7 million in compensatory damages and US$144.8 billion in punitive damages, which was the largest award in US history. The tobacco companies appealed against the awards. A New York court ruled in another class action by smokers that they could not sue as a class. The Illinois Supreme Court in *Jones* v. *Chicago HMO Ltd. of Illinois* held that a health maintenance organisation (HMO) could be liable for the tort of institutional negligence because it had a duty to be reasonably careful in its decisions about the care that its members should receive. The Supreme Court, however, in *Pegram* v. *Herdrich*, was considered to have insulated HMOs from mass tort claims (for institutional negligence) arising from cost-conscious decisions about the care which their members received. The Court held that if patients could sue and win damages by merely showing that such decisions were motivated by profit, then the for-profit HMOs would be eliminated.

The Court's decisions on the divisive social issues of abortion and the separation of church and state reflected the philosophical differences amongst the justices as well as the country. In *Stenberg* v. *Carhart,* the Court held invalid a Nebraska law that prohibited midterm abortion procedures, as violating a woman's constitutional right to an abortion. The decision of the five justices, with four dissenting justices, was the first significant decision of the Court on the question since 1992 and the first such decision, since 1986, to hold that state laws which restricted abortion procedures unduly burdened a woman's right to choose. In *Santa Fe Independent School District* v. *Doe* the Court found that Texas had violated the Establishment Clause of the First Amendment when it permitted students at a school in Santa Fe, Texas, to vote on whether to have prayers at football games and other school events. The Court also ruled that a Louisiana school could not, when teaching the scientific version of evolution, require that teachers tell their students that such teaching was not intended to dissuade them from the biblical version of creation. In *Mitchell* v. *Helms*, however, the Court concluded that federal funds provided for education could be used to buy computers and other equipment supplied to both state and religious schools. One justice gave as her reason for permitting such use of funds that the equipment was not used for religious instruction.

The federal courts continued to prescribe minimum standards of police conduct in their enforcement of the law. Contrary to the expectations of some observers, who had hoped that the conservative court would overturn the famous 1966 decision in *Miranda* v. *Arizona*, which held that a police officer must warn a suspect before the admissions of the suspect could be used as evidence against him, the Court in *Dickerson* v. *US* ruled that the Miranda warnings had become too established in US culture to be set aside. The Court also ruled in *Bond* v. *US* that a federal agent could not, whilst checking the immigration status of passengers on a bus at a border checkpoint, squeeze bags in the overhead bin for drugs. The Court also held that the police could not, acting on information—such as that a black youth in a plaid shirt at a specific bus stop was carrying a revolver—from an anonymous source, stop and search a suspect fitting that description. The Court said that information concerning its reliability was lacking.

XV THE ARTS

1. OPERA—MUSIC—BALLET & DANCE—THEATRE—
CINEMA—TELEVISION & RADIO

i. OPERA

The Royal Opera's year began well. An elegant staging of Rossini's *Otello*, imported from Pesaro, was highly enjoyable, with Bruce Ford bringing a fine, ringing tone to the title-role, especially in his duet with the charismatic Rodrigo of Juan Diego Florez—a veritable battle of the high Cs. Mariella Devia's Desdemona was magnificent, her singing exciting and her acting expressive. Gianluigi Gelmetti conducted helpfully, and the Royal Opera's chorus and orchestra were on top form. Richard Strauss's ever-popular *Der Rosenkavalier* returned in a revival of John Schlesinger's 16-year-old staging, with Renée Fleming and Susan Graham close to ideal as the Marschallin and Octavian, Christine Schäfer an engaging Sophie, and Franz Hawlata a youngish, amiable Baron Ochs.

Another outstanding revival was Graham Vick's refreshingly direct, unfussy and respectful staging of Wagner's *Die Meistersinger von Nürnberg* with John Tomlinson's lovable Hans Sachs and Thomas Allen's hilarious Beckmesser. Bernard Haitink, always at his best in Wagner, conducted with warmth and convincing tempi. In the summer, St. Petersburg's Kirov Opera came to the Royal Opera House with several lavishly staged Russian operas. The Royal Opera returned in the autumn with a revival of the popular Franco Zeffirelli production of *Tosca*, interest centering on Roberto Alagna who made a handsome Cavaradossi, compensating in vocal volume for what his timbre lacked in sweetness. However, he behaved like a typical Puccini tenor, prolonging his sustained top notes, and the musicianly conductor Carlo Rizzi had his work cut out following him.

On the first night of a new production of *Tristan und Isolde*, no-one was surprised when the director-designer, Herbert Wernicke, was roundly booed at his curtain-call, for he had staged Wagner's masterpiece in meaninglessly abstract decor, with the two lovers kept on opposite sides of the stage and allowed no contact with each other throughout the entire work. Gabrielle Schnaut's singing as Isolde was erratic, and Jon Frederic West shouted his way through Tristan's music.

The Royal Opera's year ended more happily with a glorious production by Moshe Leiser and Patrice Caurier of Rossini's *Cenerentola*, sung by a magnificent cast headed by Sonia Ganassi and Juan Diego Florez. On the day after its first performance in mid-December, the Royal Opera's Executive Director Michael Kaiser, who had announced his resignation at the beginning of the season, flew back to his native USA.

English National Opera provided London with a new opera, *Silver Tassie* by Mark-Anthony Turnage, its libretto based on the play by Sean O'Casey. For some years, most new operas produced by this company had been turgid disappointments, so it was a huge pleasure to welcome one which was gripping, tuneful, and beautifully orchestrated. And if Turnage's score revealed something of the influence of Benjamin Britten, that was surely no bad thing. In the leading role of the young football hero who leaves Dublin to fight in World War I and returns home confined to a wheelchair, Gerald Finley gave an exemplary performance. The rest of a large cast was fine, and the orchestra played superbly for Paul Daniel.

Verdi's *Ernani* profited from Mike Ashman's staging which was refreshingly gimmick-free, and faithful to the spirit of the work. Later in the year however, the company offered in its autumn season of Italian operas what most of the critics agreed were some of the silliest productions they had ever experienced. Keith Warner's confused and confusing staging of Puccini's *Manon Lescaut* did no favours for an uneven work that needs help if it is not to seem rambling. Rossini's *The Turk in Italy*, directed by David Fielding, was turned into something entirely different and absolutely dreadful, with the action taking place on the set of a Fellini-type movie, and the dialogue delivered in groan-inducing rhymes attributed to Kit Hesketh-Harvey.

David Pountney's production of Verdi's early masterpiece, *Nabucco*, was one of those updated affairs that try to look sensitive by making references, however inappropriate, to the Holocaust. The captive Jews toiling by the banks of the Euphrates in Biblical times were dressed as concentration-camp inmates, whilst across the front of the stage was a line-up of shoes and boots whose owners had presumably already disappeared into the gas-chambers. The orchestra, also dressed as prisoners, occupied the stage, with the conductor wandering about and getting in the way of what little action was possible in the constricted space allowed to the singers.

Even more offensive was a staging of Verdi's *Requiem* with the chorus acting like maniacs, cowering, throwing their chairs around, and indulging in even sillier antics. At one point, they parted to reveal a completely naked woman who looked more than eight months pregnant. All of the operas in this autumn season were staged in variations on a semi-permanent set by Stefano Lazarides with scaffolding that extended into the auditorium.

Glyndebourne, renowned for its Mozart, offered highly disappointing stagings of this year's three Mozart operas. The summer season began with Graham Vick's production of *Le Nozze di Figaro*, which was a disaster. The rot set in early with pointless visual distractions during the overture, and the entire work was played in a minimalist set by Richard Hudson which might just have proved acceptable as a modern hairdressing salon, but which made the action almost impossible to follow. Hudson's costumes could not make up their mind which period they were in, offering 18th-century frock coats worn with 20th-century trainers. Musically, things were somewhat better, though the conductor, Sir Andrew Davis, allowed the singers to observe or ignore appogiaturas at will.

A revival of Graham Vick's senseless production of *Così fan tutte* looked no better than when it was first staged in 1998. Set in a bare rehearsal room, it was made tolerable only by the performances of a superb cast and conductor. But the worst of all by far was Vick's *Don Giovanni*, his final production before leaving Glyndebourne forever. It was ugly to look at, reaching its depths in the final supper scene in which Giovanni dragged the entrails from a dead horse and consumed them greedily. If, as more than one critic surmised, Vick's intention was to make a final insulting gesture to Glyndebourne's well-heeled audience, then his *Don Giovanni* was a success.

ii. MUSIC

WESTERN classical music in the 20th century, particularly since 1950, presented a confused, many-sided picture. On the one hand, greatly improved standards of performance, and technical advances in recording and broadcasting, led to the wider acceptance of excellence. On the other, the separation and proliferation of different strands and trends of music, many of them irreconcilable with each other, led to the fragmentation of the culture. The listener had thrust at him a huge array of musical performances of every sort and style, live and recorded, to meet every taste and no taste. If he was to comprehend the new developments, and differentiate between them, he needed a broadening also of his artistic understanding, a fresh awareness of new aesthetic standards.

Classical culture became divided. As each new strand of it broke away, and struck out with a fresh identity, it either flourished, as in the case of jazz, or faded away, as in the case of Viennese serialism. Many other less distinctive strands proved to be shorter lived. They all contributed to a greater or lesser extent to make the 20th century a period of transition. Moreover, as the musical language itself, hitherto unified by the common usage of the diatonic scale, became splintered into a thousand fragments, so the listener came to perceive the lack of a commonly accepted standard for aesthetic judgement. In the course of the 20th century the main divisions in the musical culture, each exerting its own influence, became clear: classics—pop; concert music—folk music; contemporary music—early music; jazz—rock; electronic music—live music; serialism—tonality; unified language—plurality of style; populist—elitist.

By the close of the 20th century two broad tendencies appeared: a general reaction against modernism, and a general questioning of the nature of music. In 2000 the established repertoire of the classical and romantic periods continued, as before, to make up the greater part of concert performances. As for anniversaries, the greatest attention focused on the 250th anniversary of the death of Bach, with performances worldwide too numerous to specify. What musicians in the year 2000 had to add to what was already known and generally accepted about Bach were, firstly, even further refinements in the style of performance, particularly with the use of "period" instruments, and, secondly, a certain aesthetic questioning, very much in accordance with the prevalent mood, about the "meaning" of Bach's instrumental, absolute music. A particularly colourful contribution to the year consisted of a tour of European churches by the conductor John Eliot Gardiner and his Monteverdi choir and orchestra, in the course of which all Bach's cantatas were performed as they were originally intended to be performed, as part of the liturgy.

A hardly less wide-ranging anniversary, the hundredth of his birth and the fiftieth of his death, brought Kurt Weill's more controversial, less universal music to general public attention. There were numerous performances worldwide, and major festivals in Dessau (his birthplace), Berlin, London and New York. More or less all of the 20 or so stage works were produced, whilst new books and recordings, films and seminars, again following the general mood of the year, challenged and questioned the existing aesthetic assessment of Weill's music.

New music in 2000 for the most part reacted against modernism. The greatest activity seemed to lie with opera, with many premieres worldwide: *Bernarda Albas Haus* by the German Aribert Reimann in Munich; *King Lear* by the Finnish Aulis Sallinen in Helsinki; *L'amour de loin* by the Japanese Kaija Saariaho in Salzburg; *Ion* by the Indian Param Vir in Aldeburgh and London; and *The Handmaid's Tale* by the Danish Paul Ruders in Copenhagen. The one explicitly avantgarde work of the year was Harrison Birtwistle's *The Last Supper* in Berlin. Its style was one of tonal and structural anarchy, in line with his earlier works (see AR 1998, p.512); its creative volition that of ugliness and brutality. This was in marked contrast to the other chief British operatic premiere of the year, Mark Anthony Turnage's anti-war opera *The Silver Tassie* at the London Coliseum—itself in marked contrast to Turnage's earlier work, *Greek*.

For the record world, as far as the commercial aspect of classical music was concerned, 2000 was a leaner year than usual, with the announcement in April that BMG Classics was to be wound down. This demise of one of the last flagships in an ever-decreasing fleet, was proof yet again that the commercialism of pop music held sway over the recording industry. Whilst classical music, in the case of BMG, accounted for just 4 per cent of annual turnover, one single appearance on stage by "the queen of pop, Madonna", at Brixton in November, relayed and hyped on the internet, provided sales, and "hits" during the 30 minute Webcast, of UK£30 million. Faced with such overwhelming commercial logic, what need was there for other considerations of the music, such as artistic judgement?

If for pop music the spread of computer technology vastly increased profits, for the classical musician it affected both the technique of composition and the quality of sound itself. But the speed of technical change had outstripped the listener's capacity to make corresponding artistic judgements. By the century's end most teaching institutions in the UK had installed electronic music studios, as a necessary teaching resource; yet not one of the 74 universities and colleges which offered a degree course in music included music aesthetics as an academic discipline.

Informed opinion on the many trends of music in 2000 was reflected to some extent by the books of the year. These were not only more numerous than usual in previous years, but they also continued with the recent change of emphasis in attitudes to music. Of the 21 books listed below, out of the many that were published, 10 were studies of individual composers, many being biographies in depth, such as the second volume of David Cairn's monumental work on Berlioz (see AR 1999, p. 506); and 11 were attempts to enquire more deeply into the aesthetics of music.

Many writers attempted to give a summary view of the 20th century. Daniel Chua's *Absolute Music*, a study in musical basics by an articulate anti-modernist, was addressed to all would-be philosophers and analysts of music. A fresh view was taken by the Australian composer Andrew Ford, whose *Illegal Harmonies* was written with all the refreshing clarity of someone viewing the European scene, of which he was not a part, from the outside. He described the national origins of the Australian musical tradition, of which he was very much a part, from the inside, thus adding greatly, and at first hand, to the powerful impact of the book.

An academic writer who also attempted to give a broad account of the 20th century was Arnold Whittall. He had been an ardent, almost dogmatic proponent of serialism since the 1970s, with his *Music since the First World War*. When, however, the claims which he made there proved not to have occurred, and his theories were overtaken by events in the 1990s, he retreated further from considering matters relating to the practical performance of music, into a world of purely speculative theory, with *Musical composition in the twentieth century*. Theory always follows practice, and this sort of writing had been least successful in the 1950s, when the spread of avant-garde experimentalism was at its strongest, and writers in certain magazines—*Perspectives* in the USA, *Die Reihe* in Germany—presented theories of matching complexity, in a language of aesthetic mumbo jumbo. New, esoteric musical techniques, it seemed, needed new words, equally obscure, to describe them.

An echo of this trend occurred in the course of a review of Howard Pollock's *Aaron Copland*, when an English academic, Robin Holloway, described Copland's *Piano Variations* in these nostalgic terms: "The notes make a pool of pitch-resources, a highly characterised clench of harmony fused into itself or separated out into intervals forming a repertoire of shapes, a sonorous image-cluster with the material and its total potential locked into a nugget of heavy-density plutonium." Who would have thought it? Leonard Bernstein had a much more telling, first hand description of that particular piece: "I could be relied on to empty my room within three minutes by sitting down at the piano and starting it."

That musical aesthetics are anything but vague, or unintelligible, or otherworldly, was demonstrated by Mark Steyn, in the quote of the year from his book about the Broadway musical. The language of sensationalism exactly captured the essence of the USA's chief cultural institution, and the Jewish hegemony over it: "There are Bernsteins and Blitzsteins / And flop Steins and hit Steins / And Hammersteins with Mama Steins and Pops; / There are Feinsteins and Fiersteins / And Bornsteins and mere Steins / And Jule Styne is tops".

BOOKS OF THE YEAR. *Settling the Score: a journey through the music of the twentieth century*, ed. Michael Oliver; *Musical composition in the twentieth century*, by Arnold Whittall; *Saint-Saens: a critical biography*, by Stephen Studd; *Illegal Harmonies: music in the twentieth century*, by Andrew Ford; *Webern and transformation of nature*, by Julian Johnson; *Four American minimalists: La Monte Young,Terry Riley, Steve Reich, Philip Glass*, by

Keith Potter; *Schubert Studies*, ed. Brian Newbould; *The life of Schubert*, by Christopher Gibbs; *Harrison Birtwistle : Man, Mind, Music*, by Jonathan Cross; *The music of Harrison Birtwistle*, by Robert Adlington;*Berlioz: vol.2 Servitude and greatness*, by David Cairns; *In quest of spirit; music and inspiration*, by Jonathan Harvey; *The music of silence*, by John Tavener, ed. Brian Keeble; *Janacek studies*, ed. Paul Wingfield; *The essential Bach Choir*, by Andrew Parrott; *Bach's works for solo violin: style, structure, performance*, by Joel Lester; *The social and religious designs of J.S.Bach's Brandenburg Concertos*, by Michael Marissen; *Absolute music and the construction of meaning*, by Daniel Chua; *Aaron Copland: the life and work of an uncommon man*, by Howard Pollock; *Broadway babies say goodnight : musicals then and now*, by Mark Steyn.

iii. BALLET & DANCE

2000 was an interesting although not innovative year for dance. The performances that generated most excitement revisited works from the past rather than revealed new choreography. Nevertheless, a number of new dancers attracted attention and some whose dancing careers seemed over (notably Frederic Franklin as Madge in *La Sylphide* in New York, and Christopher Bruce in his own *Moonshine* and Kevin Richmond as Scrooge in Christopher Hampson's *A Christmas Carol*, both in London) returned to the stage with considerable authority.

Problems arose when past treasures were given new settings that distorted their appearance, but during the year there were opportunities to re-evaluate major works by August Bournonville, Marius Petipa and Frederick Ashton and review ballets created originally for the Ballets Russes. London saw the reconstruction of *Jeux* as well as more familiar productions. *Les Biches*, *L'Après-midi d'un faune* and *The Firebird* by the Royal Ballet and the Kirov had all received better performances in past revivals. However, when, to honour the Queen Mother's one hundredth birthday, Valery Gergiev flew in to conduct *Schéhérazade*, he drew such drama from the score that the Kirov's dancers were galvanised to give mesmerising performances.

The Kirov's production of George Balanchine's full-evening *Jewels* ("Emeralds" to music by Fauré, "Rubies" to Stravinsky, and "Diamonds" to Tchaikovsky) was the surprise hit of the year. This also entered the repertory of the Paris Opéra although the first performances were cancelled by a theatre strike. The New York City Ballet participated in the Edinburgh Festival. The company and in particular the dancers, Kyra Nichols, Maria Kowrowski, Peter Boal, Albert Evans and Damien Wotzel were admired, but they brought none of their recent "Diamond Project" creations with them. In New York, City Ballet linked up with Dance Theatre of Harlem to "salute" their younger sibling, giving performances of Balanchine's *Agon* and *Slaughter on Tenth Avenue* with casts drawn from both companies, as well as *Tributary*, jointly created by Harlem's Robert Garland and NYCB's Robert La Fosse. Balanchine's choreography was also celebrated in a two-week programme in September in Washington, danced by the Bolshoi and Joffrey Ballets, Suzanne Farrell's dancers, and companies from Miami, Pennsylvania and San Francisco. Between them they danced 14 different ballets emphasising the universal appeal of the choreographer's work.

More exclusive were the works by August Bournonville, some of which were danced in a mini-Bournonville Festival by the Royal Danish Ballet in January. The centrepiece was a new *Kermesse in Bruges* staged by Dina Bjørn. This extended production seemed misguided, especially by those who loved the former Hans Brenna production, particularly as the score, revised and modernised by Kim Helweg, lost part of its charm. It contained some excellent performances, notably by Thomas Lund as the hero, Carelis, but the new cast was unable to erase the memory of great character performances by earlier casts. It was marvellous to see again *A Folk Tale*, another ballet of considerable charm not in the international repertoire. The hero of the festival was Johan Kobborg, guesting with his former company from London's Royal Ballet, who danced James in *La Sylphide* and Gennaro in *Napoli*.

Kobborg was one of the dancers of the year, in Ashton's ballets too. The detail and precision learnt in his Danish training was an asset that enhanced the clarity of Ashton's choreography. He was a joy to watch in *Ondine*, *Les Rendezvous* and *Symphonic Variations*. Very different, but equally inspiring in his virtuosity and emotional power, was Nicolas Le Riche. In Paris, as the suicide in *Le Jeune homme et la mort*, he was riveting in his turmoil and vertiginous leaps. In London, a few days later, he breathed life into the romantic hero of *La Dame aux camelias*. Ashton's *Marguerite and Armand*, performed for the first time by anyone but its creators, Margot Fonteyn and Rudolf Nureyev, was now rethought by Sylvie Guillem and Le Riche and revealed as a powerful fresh ballet. Performances without Le Riche lacked the required intensity. Similarly Guillem's Caroline, in Antony Tudor's *Lilac Garden*, would have benefited from a more emotionally involved Lover than Jonathan Cope, although he made an able partner and brought drama to his performances of *Manon* with her.

The most important Ashton revival was *Dante Sonata* (unseen since 1950), his reaction to conditions in 1939, which was the centrepiece of two Ashton programmes toured by Birmingham Royal Ballet. With Sophie Fedorovitch's brilliant designs faithfully reconstructed it was strikingly modern, influenced by symphonic ballets and expressionist works and it remained powerful and moving with the Children of Light symbolically struggling against the Children of Darkness. Unfortunately the Royal Ballet's *Les Rendezvous*, which paid homage to Dame Alicia Markova in her ninetieth year, was garishly redesigned. The men were given boaters and blazers with candy cane stripes and the women frocks covered in polka dots and hats of plastic coils. A new colourful semi-circular set negated the architecture of the choreography. Fortunately other productions by the two Royal Ballets were more faithful. Bruce Samson, who retired from dancing in July, was missed in the November performances of *Symphonic Variations* but the trio of women; Alina Cojocaru, Tamara Rojo and Sarah Wildor were excellent. The nineteen-year-old Romanian, Cojocaru, was catapulted to stardom in Fonteyn's role and later proved a sympathetic Clara in Peter Wright's *Nutcracker*. His enchanting 1984 production, with its clearly presented narrative and respect for its heritage, which Wright revised over many seasons, became the definitive production of this ballet.

Rojo made a terrific impact with the Royal Ballet, which she joined in July, particularly in *Swan Lake* where she enchanted as the betrayed Odette, and seduced Siegfied with a stunning array of triple fouettes. Dramatically and technically this was a performance to treasure and gave the company the world-class ballerina it required (Guillem was officially a Guest). Also memorable was Lloyd Riggins in Hamburg Ballet's Paris performances of *Illusions Lake Swan Lake*, which imaginatively linked Tchaikovsky's ballet with the biography of Prince Ludovic of Bavaria. American Ballet Theatre (ABT) and English National Ballet created respectable *Swan Lakes* both adding prologues showing Princess Odette's transformation by Rothbart. Kevin McKenzie's ABT production made Rothbart a central dancing role (strongly danced by Marcelo Gomes) with him seducing all princesses who vied for Siegfried's hand in Act III. Derek Deane's clear, conservative production which drew on 1960s stagings was more satisfactory overall. Last minute injuries and cast changes necessitated that Brazilian dancer Fernanda Olivera, who had just joined English National Ballet's corps de ballet, made her company debut as Odette at the production's first performance (the dual role being divided between two young dancers).

Deane's choice of *The Sleeping Beauty* for arena performance was misguided (this ballet belonged on a proscenium arch stage) and his production tasteless. The revival of New York City Ballet's zippy, video-age *Beauty*, in May, was justified by Jennifer Ringer's performances as stylish, innocent Aurora, but all productions of Petipa's masterpiece were overshadowed by the Kirov's reconstruction, as far as was feasible, of the 1890 production. In this London audiences were privileged to see Zhanna Ayupova and Altynai Asylmuratova amongst the ballerinas who interpreted the youthful heroine.

On the modern dance front Matthew Bourne adapted Merimée's story to 1940s mid-West America as *Car Man*. This entertaining and raucous "auto-erotic thriller" was rich in movie references and benefited from using adaptations of Bizet's score by Terry Davies and Rodion Schhedrin. Siohban Davies created *Oil and Water* in which the elements deliberately failed to mix. Use of video projections and a travelator were distracting but the stunning dancers were strong enough to engage the audience's attention. Creations by the choreographer/dancers Akram Khan (equally at home in Western modern and Kathak dance) and Wayne McGreggor (who in 2000 worked with classically trained ballet dancers) suggested other truly creative artists were at work. Lloyd Newson's *Can We Afford This?*, commissioned for DV8 by the Sydney 2000 Olympic Arts Festival, was provocative in its juxtaposition of ideas yet rich in humanity and humour and remarkable for the variety of its 17 performers. The death of Jeremy James at the age of 38 curtailed the career of one of Britain's most original choreographic talents.

Rambert Dance Company invited Mats Ek to mount *She was Black* which proved the hit of that company's programme and was welcomed as the first of Ek's dances to enter the British repertory. Its disadvantage was that Ek's work needed a vast stage on which to be performed so could not be seen at all of the venues to which the company toured. Nevertheless the opening of the Lowry at

Salford (to which the Paris Opera brought its luxurious *La Bayadère* in May) added another excellent facility for large-scale dance productions. The companies of Paul Taylor and Merce Cunningham were acclaimed on visits to London. Cunningham programmed his *Biped*—with computer images joining live dancers on stage—with two much older productions, *Summerspace* and *Rainforest*. It should be recorded that Martha Graham's company ceased to exist, largely because of legal wrangles over the copyright of her dances.

iv. THEATRE

IN the UK the year 2000 brought some poor musicals, a scattering of good new plays, and the sight of two famous blondes briefly naked in *The Graduate*. In New York, where the mixture was otherwise much the same, it was a group of middle-aged male strippers who appeared naked, in *The Full Monty*. Both shows became smash hits. Both were based on successful films.

Shakespeare continued to be the staple product of English theatre. Into this crowded marketplace Michael Boyd's production of *Romeo and Juliet* at Stratford for the Royal Shakespeare Company (RSC) injected one idea fresh to the over-familiar play. He kept the dead characters on stage, as ghosts, gazing down from a rampart at those still temporarily alive, even interacting with them. The principal actors were unremarkable but the steadily increasing troop of spectres gave the production a seldom experienced sense of tragic necessity.

The RSC's major enterprise in this Millennium Year was the launch of an ambitious season of the eight Histories from *Richard II* to *Richard III* under the title "This England". The directors of this project chose different styles of production. In the opening play, with Samuel West as a quiet, ironic, poignant Richard, Steven Pimlott's choice was a Brechtian method where actors often directly addressed the audience. John of Gaunt's famous speech, from which the phrase "This England" comes, set the despairing tone, bitterly spoken by Alfred Burke (from a wheelchair). The two parts of *Henry IV* followed (director: Michael Attenborough), where David Troughton's guilt-wracked king battled for his son against a Falstaff subtly played by a watchfully jovial Desmond Barrit. William Houston, too controlled as Prince Hal, became a charismatic hero in the title role of *Henry V*, although the direction here (by Edward Hall) suffered from foolish modern clutter, such as lager-drinking soldiers chanting football songs. The three parts of *Henry VI* are Shakespeare's earliest work; the poetry is scarce but the sense of catastrophe can be overwhelming as the warring Planatagenets rip the country apart. The horror was superbly brought out in Michael Boyd's production—best seen as an all-day marathon—with David Oyelowo as a fine and gentle king. (He was the first black actor to play an English king at Stratford.) Aidan McArdle's malevolently smiling Crookback was to be the lead in *Richard III* when the cycle was completed in 2001.

At the Royal National Theatre (RNT) the quality ranged between the sensationally good (revivals of Arthur Miller's *All My Sons*, Michael Frayn's wonderful theatre farce *Noises Off*) and the disastrous. The directors of two productions (another *Romeo and Juliet* and *Peer Gynt*) withdrew before the first previews and Trevor Nunn, the RNT's artistic director, took over the final rehearsals. An award-winning performance by Simon Russell Beale, one of the country's finest actors, empowered an otherwise ordinary *Hamlet*, directed by John Caird on a stage puzzlingly stacked with luggage. *Remembrance of Things Past*, an adaptation by Di Trevis of the screenplay which Harold Pinter distilled from Marcel Proust's vast novel, was only partially successful (and how could it have been otherwise?). A felt sense of time passing did not develop but the pains of insane jealousy came strongly across. Pain of a different nature was vividly revealed in the best new play staged at the RNT since Frayn's *Copenhagen* three years earlier. Joe Penhall's award-winning *Blue/Orange*, set in a psychiatric hospital, presented the contest between two doctors over whether a young Ugandan patient was well enough to be released back into the community. Set on a boxing-ring stage in the well of the Cottesloe, the arguments explored rival psychiatric theories, lurking racism and the sorry state of the nation's hospital system. The writing was astute, unsettling and extraordinarily funny, and Roger Michell's direction drew fine playing from Bill Nighy and Andrew Lincoln as the embattled doctors, and from Chiwetel Ejiofor an outstanding performance as the patient who could see though the tactics of the bullying medics yet was pitifully dependent upon them.

Three other Shakespeare productions proved well worth seeing: Michael Grandage's fast-moving *As You Like It* (Crucible Theatre, Sheffield), graced by Victoria Hamilton's Rosalind, a performance of exquisite vivacity, charm and honesty; in the Open Air Theatre, Regent's Park, a merry *Much Ado About Nothing* updated to the close of World War Two (director, Rachel Kavanaugh); and at Shakespeare's Globe on Bankside, the replica Elizabethan theatre that had proved such a popular success, the rarely performed *Two Noble Kinsman*, part-authored by John Fletcher, strongly directed by Tim Carroll with Will Keen and Jasper Britton as an endearing pair of heroic chumps. The same company dug up Richard Brome's *The Antipodes*, unperformed since 1642, which not only proved a delightful comedy about a pretended trip to the other side of the world but in its play within a play offered rare insights into backstage posturing in 17th century theatres.

Taken as a whole, the year's productions offered the public more revivals than new plays. Some offered the chance to see plays famous in their time but now virtually forgotten, such as James Barrie's *Dear Brutus* (Nottingham Playhouse), with its sentimentally tragic theme of lives unlived, or Jean-Paul Sartre's *Les Mains Sales*, retitled *The Novice* (Almeida), exploring the ethics of political assassination, with a commanding performance by an avuncular Kenneth Cranham as the man to be killed. Tennessee Williams's *Orpheus Descending* was vividly and steamily revived by Nicholas Hytner at the Almeida, with Helen Mirren an outstanding Lady, trapped in the xenophobic Deep South; and his *Baby Doll* proved so successful at Birmingham Rep that it transferred to London for a healthy run at the RNT. Lucy Bailey spliced together the original play and its screen version, and cunningly retained the Peeping Tom impression of the 1956 movie by opening with a black curtain across the stage in which a peephole gradually opened to reveal the blonde nymphet curled up in her kiddie-cot sucking her thumb. Bailey brought a saving humour to her production, so that the steamily sexual encounter between Baby (Charlotte Emmerson) and the muscular stud (Jonathan Cake), a seduction but also a courtship, never declined into the solemn or the absurd, and was the more erotic because of it.

An astonishing feature of the London season was the procession of Hollywood movie stars and blonde celebrities who took to the boards. Jessica Lange was magnificent as the morphine-addicted mother in Eugene O'Neill's *Long Day's Journey Into Night* (Lyric, directed by Robin Phillips), and Macaulay Culkin gave a most accomplished and touching performance in Richard Nelson's *Madame Melville* (Vaudeville) as the emotionally needy 15-year-old studying at the American School in 1960s Paris, where he has a relationship with a ravishing teacher twice his age (Irène Jacob). In outline the story sounds like the familiar rite-of-passage play but the depth and resonance of Nelson's writing, and the subtlety of the playing created an event of profound beauty. Nelson, an American who had lived in the UK for many years, writing plays for the RSC about Americans abroad or Englishmen in the USA, achieved with *Madame Melville* a long-deserved commercial hit.

Daryl Hannah, with no stage experience, appeared in a frail stage version of George Axelrod's *The Seven Year Itch* (Queen's), directed by the similarly inexperienced movie director Michael Radford. Neither this nor Ferenc Molnar's *The Guardsman* (Albery), starring Greta Scacchi, lasted long, unlike Terry Johnson's adaptation of *The Graduate* (Gielgud), an unimaginative piece of work apart from the decision to allow the actress playing Mrs Robinson to appear naked—for about 20 seconds in a dim light. News of this brought mobs of male theatregoers to the box office and the production became a smash, first with Kathleen Turner letting fall the fluffy white towel and then the model Jerry Hall.

Belfast-based writers contributed strong work. Marie Jones's excellent *Stones in his Pockets* successfully made the journey from the Fringe (Tricycle) to a pocket-sized West End theatre (New Ambassadors) and finally to the much larger Duke of York's. The awesomely versatile actors Conleth Hill and Sean Campion played all of the roles in this tragi-comic account of the disruptions caused when an American film company descends on a remote Irish village. Gary Mitchell's *The Force of Change* (Royal Court) was a nail-biting drama about corrupt practises within the Royal Ulster Constabulary, whilst at the other extreme Joanna Laurens re-created a lost play by Sophocles, *The Three Birds* (Gate), using a complex language of punning verse and nursery talk, Joycean in its range and beautifully combining the classic and the contemporary. Hauntingly directed by Rebecca Gatward on a shallow amphitheatre inserted into the Gate's small space, the play won an award for its author, who was still a student at Belfast's Queen's University.

Belfast was the setting for the most satisfying Andrew Lloyd Webber musical for some years, *The Beautiful Game* (Cambridge, lyrics by Ben Elton). This harsh story of a group of football-playing youngsters growing up in a city traumatised by sectarian violence was largely free of the sentimentality that too often marred Lloyd Webber's work, and his use of Irish folk music was effective. The satiric wit of *The Witches of Eastwick* (Drury Lane) came as welcome relief after the banal lyrics of so many other musicals. *Napoleon* (Shaftesbury) revealed that the Battle of Waterloo was lost because the Emperor was distracted by the ghost of Josephine; songwriter Charles Aznavour's first musical *Lautrec* (also Shaftesbury) proved bland and unexciting, and *Notre Dame de Paris* (Dominion) musically inert. *La Cava* (Victoria Palace) at least had the advantage of an uncommon setting—8th century Visigothic Spain—and a sensational final battle scene. True lovers of musical had to rely on work from times gone by: Jude Kelly's production, based on the MGM movie, of *Singin' in the Rain* (Leeds, then RNT); and *Pal Joey* (Chichester) and *Guys and Dolls* (Sheffield), both directed by Loveday Ingram with zestful choreography by Craig Revel Horwood.

In New York the musical *Jane Eyre* (Walter Kerr), created by John Caird and Paul Gordon, was rated a dismal affair, despite a praised performance by Maria Schaffel as Charlotte Brontë's heroine. *Seussical* (Richard Rodgers), Frank Galati's imaginative musical staging of the popular Dr Seuss rhyme-books (music: Stephen Flaherty, lyrics: Lynn Ahrens) enjoyed a cult success, although it was not about to become another *Cats*. A revival of Meredith Willson's *The Music Man* (Neil Simon) created an enormous success for Scott Bierko, giving a punchy, knowing performance as the fast-talking travelling salesman, and for Rebecca Luker, rapturous as the spinster librarian who longs for him. But the season's runaway hit proved to be a stage version of *The Full Monty* (Eugene O'Neill), adapted from the British movie by Terrence McNally, in a setting altered from Sheffield to Buffalo, with music and lyrics by David Yazbek. The story of six unhandsome, unyouthful, unemployed mill workers who decide to bare all was developed with zest and charm.

Neil Simon's latest play (his 41st) *The Dinner Party* (Music Box), set in a Paris restaurant, proved a disappointment. Arthur Miller's *The Ride Down Mount Morgan* (Ambassador) was also a flawed work but the presence of Patrick Stewart in the lead proved popular. Similarly *The Unexpected Man* (Promenade) by Yasmina Reza, author of *Art*, and a slow-burning, subtle work, was sustained by the fame of its two players, Eileen Atkins and Alan Bates.

Copenhagen opened at the Royale and repeated the success that it had found in London, where it continued to run after three years. Again directed by Michael Blakemore, and with Philip Bosco, Blair Brown and Michael Cumpsty as its cast, Michael Frayn's absorbing account of the calamitous 1941 visit by Werner Heisenberg to his fellow nuclear physicist Niels Bohr in Nazi-occupied Denmark showed how readily audiences appreciate work that on the face of it might seem forbiddingly learned provided that its treatment was passionate, thrilling and powerfully theatrical.

In another British three-hander, Harold Pinter's *Betrayal* (AA/Symons), superbly directed by David Leveaux, Juliette Binoche's ably nuanced performance showed her as fully the equal of her more stage-experienced partners, Liev Schreiber and John Slattery.

Gore Vidal's The Best Man (Virginia) was a shrewd choice for revival in a presidential election year—with the author's name now treated as part of the play's title. Originally produced in 1960, and following the manoeuvres to choose a candidate and outwit rivals, Vidal's play revealed his shrewd understanding of political behaviour. Spalding Gray, best known as a monologist, played an erudite Harvard candidate pitted against a ruthless opponent (Chris Noth), both angling for the endorsement of Charles Durning's rascally ex-President.

Another revival, this time from 1985, was Jane Wagner's zippy one-woman show *The Search for Intelligent Life in the Universe* (Booth) which brought back its original award-winning star, Lily Tomlin, as energetic as ever, to delight audiences with this richly comic portrait of the 1970s. In David Auburn's interesting *Proof* (Walter Kerr) Mary-Louise Parker played a daughter in conflict with her mathematician father over the relative importance of scientific proof and instinctive feeling; and Charles Busch's *The Tale of the Allergist's Wife* (Ethel Barrymore) brought an irresistibly comic performance from Linda Lavin.

Amongst the Off-Broadway successes came the New York premiere of August Wilson's first play *Jitney* (Second Stage), a moving account, set in 1977, of the lives of a group of unlicensed cab drivers in Pittsburgh.

A unique theatrical event occurred in Denver, Colorado, where *Tantalus*, a 10-hour modern Greek epic, received its world premiere in October. Written by the RSC's director John Barton over a period of 15 years, to give familiar and less familiar myths a stark contemporary relevance, its director Peter Hall despaired of finding a venue after plans to stage it in London or in Greece fell through. Donald Seawell, founder of the Denver Centre for the Performing Arts, made the resources of his company available, and as a result this monumental and absorbing show avoided becoming one of theatre's sad might-have-beens. Plans to bring it to England were under way.

Back in London *Les Miserables* completed its 15th year, *The Phantom of the Opera* and *Starlight Express* their 16th years, and *Cats* its 19th year. Agatha Christie's *The Mousetrap*, which opened in 1952, celebrated its 20,000th performance.

v. CINEMA

A look at the nominations for the 2001 Oscar awards would not persuade many that Hollywood had had a Millennium year to remember. But if real quality seemed to be at a premium for the most successful film industry in the world, one might think that at least it made a lot of money for itself. In fact, most of the major companies found themselves in financial trouble, largely because the expense of making and distributing the product was becoming more and more prohibitive. Currently, a Hollywood film equipped with a star cast and expansive locations cost US$50-80 million to make. An even bigger amount had to go towards worldwide publicity, prints and exhibition fees. Therefore, at its lowest, such a film needed to make well over US$120 million at the box office to succeed financially, and only a handful of films could gather such largesse. Admittedly, of the Oscar nominations for Best Film, four out of the five contenders had managed to do so. But, as a general rule, only one in 10 major productions went into profit, and with an actors' strike looming, Hollywood felt distinctly uneasy with itself.

Because of this, fewer and fewer risks were being taken. Films were being made to please as many people as possible as easily as possible, with the proviso that the core audience was under 25 years of age and, if a film failed to attract this audience, then it had a minimal chance of success. British director Ridley Scott's *Gladiator*, a spectacular, old-style epic about the gladiators of the Roman Empire certainly succeeded, as did Steven Soderbergh's *Erin Brockovich*, which gave superstar Julia Roberts the best role of her career to date as a working class single mother who decides to get up and fight for her rights. Soderbergh, in fact, had an amazing year considering the way that his career had fluctuated—mostly downwards—since winning worldwide plaudits, including the Cannes Palme D'Or, with *Sex Lies and Videotape*. *Traffic*, his next film after *Erin Brockovich*, won golden opinions, if less box office success, as a three-story exposition of the drug culture in America. He was now one of the few directors working with Hollywood money who could do exactly what he wanted.

Two other film-makers had a year to remember. Ang Lee, the Taiwanese director now making his films for Hollywood, went home to the Far East to make *Crouching Tiger, Hidden Dragon*, a martial arts film, in Mandarin and sporting a Hong Kong cast, which surprised everybody, including its director, by proving the crossover hit of the year. Whether this was because so many of its audiences had never seen a classy kung fu film before, or because Hollywood gave it the kind of hype generally reserved for more orthodox fare, was a moot point. The second film-maker was Scott, who in addition to seeing Russell Crowe's *Gladiator* conquer the world, also made *Hannibal*, the sequel to *The Silence of the Lambs*, in which Anthony Hopkins reprised his role as Hannibal Lecter, the murderous cannibal. That film too had huge success commercially, despite gaining far less critical approbation.

If Hollywood had a year that was only patchily successful, the rest of the world could hardly be said to have taken up the slack. There were great hopes for Lars von Trier's European musical *Dancer In The Dark*, which won both the Cannes Festival and the European Film award. But it eventually transpired that this story of a young single mother unjustly accused of murder and eventually hanged—which also won Bjork, the Icelandic pop star, Best Actress prizes first at Cannes and then at the European Film awards—divided the critics to such an extent that, even in its home territory of Scandinavia, the film did not do the expected business. It was so mauled in the UK that its distributors offered audiences the inducement that they would refund their money if they did not like the film. Not many took up the offer, or saw the film. The Scandinavian cinema, however, did better than most European countries outside its own shores, with Liv Ullman's excellent *Faithless*, written by Ingmar Bergman, leading the way. This intimate story of a marriage breakdown because of an illicit affair contained one of the most impressive performances of the year from Lena Endre, a prominent Swedish stage actress, as the erring wife. Sweden also produced Roy Andersson's *Songs From The Second Floor*, a highly original surrealist story of economic collapse and human suffering in the new Millennium.

However, it was left to the UK to produce any commercial successes from Europe, and three films did make their mark in an otherwise disappointing British year which saw one new film after another fail badly at the domestic box-office, which remained dominated by Hollywood products. The most triumphant of the three was undoubtedly *Billy Elliot*, the first feature of stage director Stephen Daldry, about the young son of a miner who trains to become a ballet dancer during the miners' strike of the early 1980s. Jamie Bell, the teenage star of the film, won many nominations for his acting and dancing, and became the youngest performer ever to win the Best Actor award at the British Academy of Film and Television. The film proved a big attraction everywhere, as did the animated feature *Chicken Run*, made by Peter Lord and Nick Park of the highly successful Aardman Company—but with US money and Mel Gibson voicing the leading part. The third success was Guy Ritchie's *Snatch*, a gangster movie with Brad Pitt in the cast, which was undoubtedly helped on its way by the highly publicised marriage of the director to Madonna.

Another three British films of considerable quality which had a harder time finding commercial success were Terence Davies' stylish *The House of Mirth*, his first period film, adapted by Davies for the screen from the novel by Edith Wharton and starring Gillian Anderson, the American star of television's popular *X-Files*; Pawel Pawlikowski's *The Last Resort*, about an immigrant with her child cruelly holed up in a Kent detention centre; and Nicola Bruce's imaginative first feature *I Could Read The Sky*, about the life and times of a working class man who moves from the West Coast of Ireland to London. Palikowski's film won him the Michael Powell award at Edinburgh for the best British film of the year.

France was still the European country which staved off the Hollywood invasion best, even without many hit films. There US films claimed just over 60 per cent of the box office, compared with over 90 per cent in much of the rest of Europe . Two of the best French films were veteran Agnes Varda's superb documentary *The Gleaners and I*, about the scavengers of Paris, and Philippe Cantet's *Human Resources*, which had a young business executive trained in Paris arriving at the provincial factory where his father worked and finding that modernisation has its human cost.

Elsewhere in Europe there was little to note, and Russia, once the home of outstanding cinema, seemed only able to produce a plethora of gangster movies, many of which were said to have been financed by the Mafia. However, Alexander Sokurov, thought by many to be the true successor to the great Tarkovsky, pursued his lonely way with *Moloch*, a stunningly atmospheric portrait of the relationship between Hitler and Eva Braun, and announced that his next film was to be about Lenin's last years.

There was better news from both Iran and the Far East. At Cannes, Iran, South Korea, Taiwan and Japan had films presented that became prize-winners. One of them, the Taiwanese *Li Li (A One and a Two)*, a superbly fashioned family portrait, won the Best Director award for Edward Yang and later beat the hot favourite, *Crouching Tiger, Hidden Dragon*, in the New York critics contest for the best foreign film of the year. It was less of a surprise that Iran did well, since the film-makers of that country, led by Abbas Kiarostami, considered one of the best directors in the world, had won more film festival awards than most others in recent years. Their success continued when Jafar Panahi's *The Circle*, a brave depiction of the treatment of women in Iran, won both the Golden Lion and the International Critics' Prize at the Venice Festival. India had no such luck, though Bollywood, the Hindi version of Hollywood based in Bombay, not only continued to shoot many of its musical sequences outside India but succeeded in breaking into the multiplex circuits in the UK, Canada and the USA for the first time. Latin American film making showed some signs of revival, after many years of financial impoverishment and audience neglect, and at least one film, the Mexican *Love's A Bitch*—three stories about life in Mexico City by newcomer Alejandro Gonzalez Inarrito—won international praise.

In all, it was not a bad year of cinema, since audiences continued to grow around the world. The warning note was that Hollywood productions dominated almost everywhere, making many national cinemas fight for their right to exist at all outside the film festival circuit. Not all the flowers in the garden were allowed to grow. But there were fortunately still a few film-makers who managed to buck the trend towards a cinematic version of MacDonald's culture.

Amongst those who died during the year were stars Alec Guinness, Walter Matthau, Douglas Fairbanks Jr, Hedy Lamarr, Jason Robards, Loretta Young, Claire Trevor, George Montgomery, Vittorio Gassman and Richard Farnsworth; and directors Roger Vadim, Claude Sautet and Claude Autant-Lara from France, Bernhard Wicki from Germany, Bernard Vorhaus from the UK, Lionel Rogosin from the USA and Wojciech Has from Poland. (For obituaries of Fairbanks, Guinness, Lamarr, Matthau and Robards, see XVIII).

vi. TELEVISION AND RADIO

THERE is no doubt at all that the UK television phenomenon of the year was *Big Brother*, the controversial Channel 4 series that was condemned by some as exploitative but which captivated audiences and generated massive newspaper coverage. It seemed to epitomise a new genre in popular television around the world, in which the contestants exposed themselves to new levels of intrusion, humiliation and rejection in new forms of "reality television". In *Big Brother*, a programme originally created by the Dutch company Endemol, the contestants were isolated for weeks in a specially created house in which virtually all of their intimate moments were captured on camera. In the biggest ever collaboration between a mainstream television programme and the internet the inhabitants could also be seen online 24-hours a day. The inhabitants nominated candidates for expulsion and the viewers were able to make the final choice by a telephone vote on who should go, and who would, thereby, lose the chance of winning a large prize. The Independent Television Commission (ITC) found that despite the controversy there had been no serious complaints about the programme and none at all from the participants. At its peak Channel 4 got a 6.8 million audience for *Big Brother* and during the weeks that the programme was on air Channel 4's share of viewing swelled to 11.6 per cent compared with 10.7 per cent in the same period in 1999. During the year ITV extended the reality TV approach with a national search, sometimes involving brusque rejection, for members of a new pop group and commissioned a UK version of the massively successful US programme *Survivor*, a series to be filmed in Borneo where the castaways would vote for those least useful to the enterprise.

The BBC joined the rush to harder-nosed television with its answer to ITV's *Who Wants To Be A Millionaire*—Anne Robinson's *The Weakest Link*. The formidable Robinson coined a new catch phrase by curtly telling unsuccessful players in the quiz—"You are the weakest link. Goodbye."

One of the most praised dramas of the year was the Channel 4 adaptation of Dava Sobel's *Longitude*, a programme designed to mark the start of the millennium. The documentary that won most awards was the Panorama programme *Who Bombed Omagh?*, which also attracted controversy by naming those members of the Real IRA it believed had been involved in the bombing of the Northern Ireland market town in 1998 (see AR 1998, p. 49).

Internationally two huge media mergers dominated the media climate. By far the biggest (and the largest merger to date) was the coming together of America Online (AOL) internet group, and Time Warner in a US$350 billion deal. The other, in June, brought together Vivendi, owners of the French pay television company Canal Plus, and Seagram, the Canadian owners of Universal, a Hollywood studio, in a combined deal worth US$100 billion. The AOL-Time Warner deal, announced in January, was given regulatory clearance in December. It was remarkable because it was the most dramatic example of a leader of the new internet economy taking over such an established media name whose businesses ranged from the Warner Brothers film studio to CNN, the 24-hour news service and *Time* magazine. Both sides persevered with the merger even though by the end of the year the dot com bubble had burst and values had dropped dramatically. In a powerful example of the benefits of the merger, AOL Time Warner claimed 1 million new subscriptions for *Time* magazine as a result of promotion online to AOL subscribers. Regulators also gave permission for the creation of Vivendi Universal, although Vivendi was required to sell its 22 per cent stake in BSkyB, the UK satellite television operator, as a condition of acceptance. In the UK there was a smaller version of the union of a content company with a cable network group when Flextech, which ran cable and satellite channels, took over Telewest, the UK's second largest cable group in a multi-billion deal.

At the BBC Greg Dyke succeeded Lord Birt as director general and was soon being credited with improving morale at the corporation. Under the slogan "One BBC", Dyke introduced a much flatter management structure and made some progress towards a pledge to cut the bureaucracy of the BBC and move more money into programme-making. He was helped enormously by the government, which rejected the idea of a digital licence fee and instead decided to increase the existing licence fee by one-and-a-half percentage points a year above retail prices until 2006—the year the corporation's Royal Charter ran out. The effect of the licence fee increase and cuts in costs was forecast to mean more than UK£400 million for programmes in 2001. The government made it clear that in return it would be taking a closer interest in the overall public purpose of the BBC, particularly the introduction of new services. At the year's end the government had still to rule on BBC plans to re-launch its digital channels, BBC Choice and BBC Knowledge, as BBC 3 and BBC 4 and introduce two services for children of different ages during the day—a proposal that was controversial with owners of commercial children's channels. The plan envisaged that BBC 3 would be largely for young adults and that BBC 4 would be "unashamedly intellectual", the television equivalent of Radio 4.

Dyke did, however, suffer one conspicuous defeat—over football rights. The director general, a keen football fan, had made it a priority to retain the rights to highlights of the Premier League in order to protect one of the BBC's flagship sports programmes, *Match of the Day*. He was heavily outbid by ITV, however, and the latter was due to take over the rights in August 2001 for three years. The BBC did win the rights to the FA Cup and home internationals in a joint deal with satellite broadcaster BSkyB, which retained its rights to live Premiership games in a UK£1.1 billion deal.

One of the BBC's most controversial decisions, and one that angered the government, was the opportunist move of the *Nine O'Clock News* to 10pm to take advantage of the fact that the ITV news was on its way back to 10pm after moving to 11pm in 1999. The ITC had insisted that ITV move back its news because audiences for the 11pm news and associated regional programming had declined. The ITV companies won the right to have the ITC's decision reviewed by the High Court, but a compromise was reached before the case was heard under which ITV would now play the news at 10pm on at least three nights each week and there would be flexibility on a fourth if there were a major sporting event or drama. In return the ITV companies would get two minutes and 30 seconds of extra advertising a night.

Two weeks after the compromise Greg Dyke struck by announcing that after 30 years the *Nine O'Clock News* would move to 10pm on October 16. Dyke and BBC chairman Sir Christopher Bland said that the news would get a larger audience at 10pm than at 9pm in a highly competitive, multi-channel world. Culture, Media and Sports Secretary Chris Smith, however, insisted that the issue should be reviewed by the BBC governors in six months if the change led to lower audiences. "It is obviously a changing moment for the BBC but the management unanimously believes it is the right decision and the governors believe unanimously it is the right decision," Dyke said. Thus, for the first time there was the prospect of the two main news bulletins going head-to-head on at least three nights a week. Critics argued that such a move would lead to a reduction in the opportunity to see mainstream news bulletins throughout the evening.

There was further controversy when the BBC director general also decided to move the current affairs programme *Panorama* from its traditional Monday slot to 10.15pm on Sunday evenings. By some this was seen as a sidelining of current affairs and a sign that Dyke was fighting too enthusiastically for ratings. Ironically the last *Panorama* programme to be broadcast on a Monday evening was *Who Bombed Omagh?*

ITV fought back in the ratings in the autumn, after an alarming dip in audiences during the summer, partly the result of the growing strength of digital television. By concentrating on creating more "event television"—for example by running *Who Wants To Be A Millionaire* at the same time every night—ITV fought its way back to a 38 per cent share of viewing in evening peak time.

The consolidation of ITV continued, but not in the way that had been expected. In July Stephen Byers, the Trade and Industry Secretary, effectively blocked the merger of Granada, chaired by Gerry Robinson, and United News and Media, run by the Labour Peer Lord Hollick. Byers ruled that the proposed merged company could not own Meridian, United's lucrative south of England franchise—a decision that effectively killed the deal. Hollick sold United's ITV interests to Granada for UK£1.75 billion and Granada sold on HTV, the commercial television franchise for Wales and the West, to Carlton in order to stay within current ownership rules. As a result ITV became totally dominated by Granada and Carlton and both companies expressed the hope that before long the ITV network, which a decade earlier had been made up of 15 separate regional companies, could be owned by a single company.

The possibility came a step closer when in December the government published its long-awaited White Paper, *A New Future for Communications*. The aim, the government said, was " to make the UK home to the most dynamic and competitive communications and media market in the world." ITV rules that prevented one company owning both London franchises would be revoked, as would the system that prevented any company owning more than 15 per cent of the total audience. Any further mergers in ITV would, however, still be subject to competition law. As ITV continued to control some 60 per cent of total television advertising in the UK the Competition Commission appeared likely to block the creation of a single TV company for some time on grounds of market dominance.

The proposed legislation also envisaged a new three-tier structure designed to protect high quality programming. The basic tier would apply to all broadcasters and the other would impose further obligations on public service broadcasters. The new system would be monitored by a newly created Office of Communications which would bring together five regulatory bodies, including the ITC and the Radiocommunications Agency, the body responsible for the allocation of the radio spectrum.

The White Paper disappointed broadcasters because it postponed one of the most important issues—future ownership rules, particularly for radio. The only consolation was a government commitment to review the system. The largest commercial radio station, Capital, was able to expand within the rules by acquiring Border Television, which had extensive radio interests, for UK£151 million.

The plan was to keep the three Century radio stations and sell the television franchise on to Granada for UK£50.5 million to help fund the deal. In another example of a crossover between television and radio, Scottish Media Group, the main TV company in Scotland which also owned Virgin Radio, took a large minority stake in Scottish Radio Holdings. Scottish Media clearly planned to expand in radio if the ownership rules changed.

One of commercial radio's most flamboyant characters, Kelvin MacKenzie, former editor of *The Sun*, successfully floated The Wireless Group. MacKenzie also turned the company's main asset, the national commercial speech station Talk UK, into an all sport station, Talk Sport. MacKenzie and GWR, owners of Classic FM, were enthusiastic supporters of digital radio, although the number of digital receivers was still low. Despite the growing number of commercial stations the BBC held on to just over 50 per cent of total radio listening and had its own ambitious plans for new digital radio services.

During the year digital multi-channel continued its advance with Telewest and NTL, the largest cable group, installing digital in more than 800,000 homes. Ondigital, the digital terrestrial service, just managed to reach its end of 2000 target of 1 million subscribers. Satellite broadcaster BSkyB reached 5 million homes by satellite by the end of 2000, more than 4.5 million of them digital.

However, in a world of 200-channel digital television there was still evidence of both tradition and loyalty. Nowhere was this better illustrated than in the BBC's preparations to celebrate the 50th anniversary of *The Archers*, its long-running radio soap-opera, in February 2001.

2. VISUAL ARTS—ARCHITECTURE

i. VISUAL ARTS

THERE were some major losses to world heritage during the year. About one-third of the Roman legionary city of Zeugma, in southeast Turkey, was flooded by the waters of the Euphrates as part of a dam project. In response to the defection of the Kamaka Lama, the Chinese government returned to its policy of destroying the outward manifestations of Tibetan culture and expelled Tibet Heritage, an international non-governmental organisation which had been restoring the historic centre of Lhasa. In Afghanistan, the prolonged drought encouraged further looting of archaeological sites, the antiquities surfacing mostly in the Peshawar market. An international inspection of the Buddhist site of Tepe Sardar, near Ghazni, reported that many statues had been smashed, but could not find out whether this had happened before or after the take-over by the Talibaan, who viewed such works as "infidel".

On the credit side, there was the discovery in a church in Bassano di Sutri, north of Rome, of a life-size sculpture by Michelangelo, the first version of the Risen Christ that he had carved for Santa Maria sopra Minerva, but abandoned because it had a grey vein running through the face. A baroque sculptor finished the work, but up to chest level it was created by the master himself.

The delayed aftermath of World War II looting and confiscation continued to weigh on museums and the art trade, with a handful of works of art returned to the heirs of the original Jewish owners, amongst which a large triptych by Leopold von Kalkreuth, shown in the Royal Academy's "1900: Art at the Crossroads" exhibition and lent by the Bayerisches Nationalmuseum. An international conference on the issue took place in Vilnius, at which representatives of 37 countries declared, amongst other things, that all governments should "undertake every reasonable effort to achieve the restitution of cultural assets looted during the Holocaust". The UK Minister for the Arts, Alan Howarth told the newly created Spoliation Advisory Panel that he recommended legislation to allow national museums to dispose of any items in their collections wrongfully taken during the period 1933-45.

The Millennium Dome, the government-backed, Lottery funded (UK£538 million) exhibition that was supposed to entertain and enlighten 12 million people, closed at the end of the year having attracted only 6.5 million visitors. The failure was attributed variously to its absence of true purpose and the banal nature of its "info-tainment". Other Lottery funded projects were more successful, notably, Tate Modern. This adaptation of an Art Deco power station on the Thames, to house international art from 1900 to the present day, performed the feat of making art hip, with pop stars present at the opening, huge international publicity and a million visitors in just its first month. Other Lottery projects in London included extensions to the National Portrait Gallery, the Wallace Collection and Dulwich Picture Gallery. The British Museum Reading Room reopened in December, its courtyard revealed for the first time in 150 years and covered by a vast geodesic glass ceiling designed by Norman Foster.

The globalisation of museums continued, with a branch of the Hermitage Museum opening in Somerset House (this, with the Gilbert Collection of goldsmiths' work also inaugurated in 2000, was being restored and turned into a stylish centre for the arts). The Guggenheim Museum in New York also announced a collaboration with the Hermitage, in St Petersburg, and, more surprisingly, in Las Vegas, where it entered a partnership with a hotel/casino complex that had built reproductions of many of the most famous landmarks in Venice, complete with gondolas, and which also owned a group of Impressionist paintings.

For the first time in six years, there was no Impressionism show amongst the 10 most attended exhibitions in the world. Instead, these were: "El Greco", in the Athens National Gallery (an average of 6,483 visitors per day); Islamic art, Hermitage (5,876); icons from Mt Sinai, Hermitage (5,495); images of the face of Christ and their theological meaning, National Gallery, London (5,002); "Picasso's world of children", National Museum of Western Art, Tokyo, (4,290); "Dutch art: Rembrandt and Vermeer", National Museum of Western Art, Tokyo (3,892); women artists of the Soviet Avant-Garde, Guggenheim, Bilbao (3,879); "The Glory of the Golden Age", Rijksmuseum, Amsterdam (3,808); Van Gogh portraits, Museum of Fine Arts, Boston (3,762); ditto , Detroit Institute of Arts (3,706).

The huge attendance in Athens for El Greco could be attributed to nationalist feeling, just as the Mt Sinai exhibition in St Petersburg attracted large numbers of Orthodox and nationalist Russians. The greatest surprise, in secular, youth-obsessed Britain, was the success of the face of Christ exhibition, which had failed to find any commercial backer and happened solely because the gallery director, Neil MacGregor, felt that the religious significance of the millennium had been ignored amongst all of the official jollifications.

In Rome, it was not the millennium, but the Catholic Jubilee that was being celebrated. The Italian government joined with the Vatican and the Church at large to prepare for this religious festival and voted to allocate US$1.76 million for the sprucing up of Rome and its surroundings. Churches, monasteries, historic secular buildings, museums and some of the infrastructure were restored and improved, a lasting benefit of a year that was a great success. Nero's Domus Aurea was now open for the first time in decades and so was the whole Capitol complex and the vast white marble monument to Victor Emmanuel—to give just three examples of what Rome now had to offer. Twenty-four million pilgrims and tourists came to Rome and the gloom-mongers who said that the city's services would collapse under the strain were confounded.

But if the Italian government showed enlightened and nimble thinking where the Jubilee was concerned, it failed yet again to decide on what should be done to protect Venice from flooding. On November 6 the city suffered the third-worst flood since 1900, 144cm above mean sea level and 93 per cent of its area under water. In 1998 a report commissioned from international experts by the Italian Cabinet concluded that mobile barriers at the entrances to the lagoon were the only sure protection for the city, but the decision to build them, opposed by the Green party, was repeatedly delayed. Yet another deadline, December 31, set by Prime Minister Giuliano Amato himself, passed without any progress.

In the art market, the two biggest auction houses, Sotheby's and Christie's became involved in law suits in the USA. At the beginning of the year, in exchange for conditional immunity from prosecution, the latter presented evidence to the federal Department of Justice that there had been collusion over the rate of buyers' commission. This infringed the US Sherman Act against price-fixing. Sotheby's and its Chief Executive officer, Diana Brooks, were charged with criminal conspiracy, and a separate, class action suit was brought by aggrieved clients in the civil courts against both auction houses. In September, the two auction houses agreed to pay the plaintiffs US$512 million (UK£350 million). The next month, Brooks pleaded guilty to the price-fixing charge, thereby facing a maximum of three years in prison, a personal fine of US$350,000 and US$10 million for Sotheby's. Sentencing was postponed to 2001.

Sotheby's position in the market was further weakened by the failure of its web auctions to generate the expected income. Sothebys.com and the related sothebys.amazon.com reported a loss of US$28.1 million for the first six months of the year, only a quarter of the items offered on the web selling, and most at prices below US$5,000.

A widespread belief at the beginning of the year that the web would rationalise and open up the art market in general was dashed by the end. By September, 41 art selling internet companies had closed down, and 30 had been disposed of in "firesales", according to Webmerger.com, the internet mergers and acquisitions watchdog. No art sites turned a profit.

Meanwhile, the real life art market boomed as huge gains on the stock exchange were put into art. Top auction price of the year was US$55 million for a Blue Period Picasso, "Woman with folded arms". Unlike the boom of the 80s, however, only top quality items did well, with those which were second-rate often being left unsold. The contemporary art sector did especially well, with prices at auction often outstripping those in the galleries. As the fashion for sleek modern interiors took over, for the first time prices for Art Deco rivalled or exceeded those for French 18th-century furniture, the traditional rich man's taste.

Deaths in the British art world included: the artist Patrick Heron (aged 79); the collector, Sir Brinsley Ford (93); Sir Robert Sainsbury, collector and benefactor (93); Professor Francis Haskell, art historian (72); and Sir Steven Runciman, Byzantinist (97). Internationally, deaths included: the US Pop art sculptor, George Segal (75); the German-American photographer Horst P. Horst (93); Leo Castelli, the Italo-American dealer for many major US artists of the 1950s and 1960s (including Jasper Johns, Rauschenberg and Frank Stella); the Austrian architect and painter, Friedensreich Hundertwasser (71); the French painter, Bernard Buffet (71), and the American, Charles Schulz (71), creator of the "Peanuts" comic strip. (For obituaries of Runciman, Sainsbury and Schultz, see XVIII).

ii. ARCHITECTURE

As was to be expected, the architecture associated with the Millennium year took on more than usual significance, although not always for the right reasons. The most spectacular new structure in London also turned out to be an embarrassing failure. The Millennium bridge, linking the new Tate Modern on the south bank of the Thames to St Paul's Cathedral, had to be closed almost as soon as it opened, because of swaying which resulted in feelings of panic amongst those using it. The bridge was designed by Britain's most famous architect, Lord (Norman) Foster, with the engineering firm Ove Arup & Partners. The engineers received most of the blame, and it was not entirely clear at the end of the year how the problems would be resolved. The bridge was expected to reopen in the autumn of 2002.

However, the Tate Modern itself was opened to triumphant acclaim. The redundant 1940s power station was transformed by the Swiss practice Herzog & de Meuron into the home for the Tate's collection of 20th Century art. It was an instant hit with the public, its popularity helped by a forward-thinking free admission policy. The success of this project, with a clear programme laid down by its director, Sir Nicholas Serota, was in marked contrast to the dubious fortunes of the Millennium Dome in Greenwich. The Dome opened as the new Millennium began, with a disastrous party, with shambolic scenes as people waited for hours to board special trains taking them to the venue. The opening set the tone for decidedly sniffy comments about the contents of the Dome, although there was general praise for the design of the venue itself, by Richard Rogers Partnership. Expected visitor numbers did not materialise, and throughout the year there was speculation as to what would happen to the project when the year ended. Nothing emerged with certainty.

Problems of a different sort affected another major venue, the British Museum, during the year. Lord Foster's refurbishment and upgrade of the Great Court and the Round Reading Room within it would have been greeted with universal acclaim but for one not so small detail: the replacement Portland stone portico at the southern end of the space. When it was too late to do very much about it (other than start again at vast expense), it was realised that the stone which had been used was in fact a French limestone, geologically related, but certainly different in colour to the Portland stone which had been specified. The mistake was embarrassing, but in the end the general support for the project overcame suggestions that the portico be ripped down and replaced.

The final embarrassment for Lord Foster concerned his ambitious proposals for the replacement Wembley Stadium. The Culture, Media and Sports Secretary, Chris Smith, initially welcomed the proposals, but after lobbying by the athletics community, declared that the stadium was inadequate and ordered a redesign. This ill-advised action immediately threw doubt on the viability of the project, which struggled on until the end of the year without certainty as to its future. Smith ordered the creation of a new athletics stadium on the edge of London, at a venue with no public transport links.

Lord Foster had one triumph, however. His City of London headquarters design for the insurance company, Swiss Re, received all of its planning approvals after a long battle with some conservationists. The torpedo form of the building led to its nickname of the 'erotic gherkin'. It was certain, on completion, to be one of the capital's iconic buildings. Lord Foster was also successful in winning the competition for a major redesign of the Elephant and Castle area, with a team of other architects including the Malaysian Ken Yeang. Work started on Foster & Partners' designs for the Greater London Authority headquarters near Tower Bridge, whilst outside London, the practice completed a huge greenhouse in Wales.

Apart from the Tate Modern, the other great architectural attraction to open in London during the Millennium year was the "London Eye", a giant wheel designed by Marks Barfield, which proved both a popular and a commercial success, unsupported by National Lottery funding. On an even bigger scale, designs were produced by the Italian architect Renzo Piano for the tallest building in London, at 1,000ft. The mixed-use structure, planned for a site above London Bridge Station, was going through its early planning stages as the year ended.

Another international architect, the Californian-Canadian Frank Gehry, won the RIBA Royal Gold medal for Architecture, whilst the Dutch architect and master-planner, Rem Koolhaas, won the Pritzker Prize. A new library in Peckham, south London, won the Stirling Prize for its architect, Will Alsop, to much acclaim, although there was strong support for a new art gallery in Walsall, designed by the young practice Caruso St John, also short-listed. Alsop went on to win a major arts centre project in Toronto. In the British Construction Industry Awards, the building of the year was a new campus at Nottingham University, designed by Sir Michael Hopkins & Partners, with heavy competition from a new arts centre in Armargh, Northern Ireland, designed by the young architect Glen Howells. Two major buildings by Michael Wilford & partners were completed and opened to general congratulation: the Lowry Centre in Salford, Manchester, and the new British Embassy in Berlin. Amazingly the practice then had to close down because of a shortage of work.

Standards of public architecture in Britain needed to improve to match the ambitions of our forbears, said the Prime Minister, Tony Blair, during the year. He launched a document, Better Public Buildings, in the autumn, the nearest thing that the UK had had to a national architecture policy. It was drafted by the government's Commission for Architecture and the Built Environment, which lobbied successfully for a Cabinet office committee to be created, comprising ministers responsible for architecture and design within spending departments. On the broader urban front, the government published a White Paper responding to the report prepared by Lord (Richard) Rogers on the regeneration of Britain's towns and cities. Rogers also took up an appointment as architectural and urban advisor to the new mayor of London, Ken Livingstone.

In Cardiff, the Richard Rogers Partnership designs for a new Welsh assembly building attracted fresh criticism over rising costs, and the project began to look doubtful. In Edinburgh, the cost of the parliament building designed by the Spanish architect Enric Miralles (who died unexpectedly) increased greatly, provoking general criticism which ignored the client's continual changes to the brief.

Other major figures who died during the year included Sir Leslie Martin, a key figure in the creation of the Royal Festival Hall; John Hejduk, the US architect/artist and teacher; Christian Norberg-Schultz, theorist and historian; landscape architect Derek Lovejoy; and the Italian architect, theorist and polemicist, Bruno Zevi.

3. LITERATURE

THE centenary of Oscar Wilde's death fell on November 30 2000 and was a time for stock-taking about the literary century that had succeeded him. There was now no more iconic figure in the cultural landscape than the playwright and wit, though at the time of his demise in a Paris hotel he was a social pariah. Wilde's particular brand of humanity, combined with iconoclasm and style, appeared much more in tune with the 21st century than had been the case in his own age. To mark the centenary his grandson, Merlin Holland, produced the first edition of Wilde's *Complete Letters*.

The celebration of Wilde was only one of many ways in which the birth of a new century was acknowledged by the literary world. It seemed that all over the planet millennial festivities at the commencement of the year were accompanied by the publication of national histories recounting the last one hundred or one thousand years. In Britain the most successful of these was Simon Schama's *A History of Britain*, mainly because it was based on a television series. A related genre of books appeared which explored national identities, including Susan Sontag's *In America*, Bill Bryson's *Down Under* (a look at Australia in its own centenary year) and Yasmin Alibhai-Brown's *Who Do We Think We Are? Imagining the New Britain* (with its controversial image on the cover of a black Queen Elizabeth II). Two books which explored early inter-connections of Europe and America made a particular mark: Caryl Phillips's *The Atlantic Sound*, which linked up points of embarkation, transit and disembarkation in the slave trade, and Giles Morton's *Big Chief Elizabeth: How England's Adventurers Gambled and Won the New World*.

Some writers seemed to reach back into pre-history and to points of origin, an approach best summed up by Alasdair Gray's *The Book of Prefaces*. This original compilation of scene-setting pieces, all of which had once been yoked to a longer work of quality, took on a credible independent life when brought together in a new cross-referencing way. Gray's exquisitely designed book—physically as well as linguistically—paid quiet tribute to centuries of print design and book production, as well as to generations of fine writers. It was an appropriate contribution to a year that saw many polls name Johan von Gutenberg, creator of the printing press, the "Man of the Millennium". Blake Morrison's novel *The Justification of Johan Gutenberg* was a boldly fictionalised rendering of the life of this most practical and visionary of inventors.

Gutenberg had released medieval Europe from dependency on scribes and illuminators. The next comparable revolution was electronic communication, and the year 2000 saw the first foray into online publishing by a prominent writer. Hitherto, publication on the internet had been handicapped by the lack of quality control and the reluctance of a major author to use it for the launch of a new work. Stephen King, if not regarded as an artist of the novel, undoubtedly had one of the largest commercial followings in the world. His decision to publish a novella entitled *Riding the Bullet* online resulted in 400,000 orders in the first 24 hours of internet access. However, King withdrew the project before its completion, for reasons which were never made wholly clear but which seemed to put a hold on any further web development of this nature involving globally marketable authors.

The launch of an online edition of the *Oxford English Dictionary* fared better. Apart from being a remarkable technical achievement, it inspired much discussion about whether English had become a world-dominating language which might one day destroy all other languages. As if to counter such aggrandisement, it emerged that 60 per cent of the global use of the internet was conducted in languages other than English. Indeed, after years in which it had been felt that minority languages were doomed to early extinction, the internet—previously regarded as one reason for this—began to emerge as an unexpected provider of sustenance to them.

With their level of sales, certain authors seemed unstoppable. Chief amongst them was the writer for children, J. K. Rowling, who let it be known that she had chosen to be known by her initials so as not to alienate young male readers, who might have been put off her if they had realised that she was a woman. (A market survey amongst Western readers indicated that women were more flexible in their choice of reading and that men were often guided by the cover of a book, rejecting titles with the word "love" in them or designs which used the colour pink.) *Harry Potter and the Goblet of Fire* was by far the longest of Rowling's four Potter novels. It was published in circumstances of great secrecy, and queues formed at shops where it was due to be sold at midnight on publication day. The BBC devoted the whole of Boxing Day to broadcasting the Rowling *oeuvre*, and the author herself visited Toronto to give a live reading from her work before an audience of 35,000 people, the largest authorial appearance ever recorded. Doubts were expressed about Rowling's durability, but no other writer in the year enjoyed her celebrity or financial rewards. Jeffrey Archer had for many years been synonymous with best-selling success, but, even with impressive sales of 188,000 paperbacks, he fell a long way behind Rowling's achievement. There was a certain amount of glee in the tone of those reviewing his play *The Accused*, in which Archer appeared in person on the London stage, because it was manifestly a flop from the moment it opened.

Celebrity authors continued to make fortunes from their writing. Tom Clancy was thought to have set a world record with an advance before publication of approximately US$90 million. Jamie Oliver, a young British chef of no discernible literary skills, found himself selling well over 1 million hardback copies of *Return of the Naked Chef*, a sequel to an earlier success. Catherine Cookson, though now dead, remained the most widely read novelist in Britain, whilst "airport literature"—voluminous fictions about sex and shopping—flooded the bookshops of the world, threatening the sustainability of indigenous publishing and local creativity.

In an attempt to counter this, at least in one part of the world, a major new literary prize was launched, named to commemorate Michael Caine, a businessman who had propelled the Booker Prize for Fiction and the Russian Booker Prize to success. It sought to recognise the best African short story of the year. Though Western publishers were eligible to enter, the award was conceived partly as a way of encouraging indigenous African publishers, short fiction being chosen as the category because it often appeared in out-of-the-way journals or from obscure sources. The first winner was Leila Aboulela, a young part-Egyptian, part-Ethiopian writer, for her story "The Museum".

Fortunately 2000 was a year notable for the burgeoning of new talent. Zadie Smith made the greatest impact with her novel *White Teeth*. Praised as an acute dissection of modern multiculturalism, it might well come to be seen as the best novel of modern times to capture the spirit of London. In a year when Salman Rushdie announced his intention of living more in New York than London, it helped to restore London's literary sense of itself when Smith made such a mark with a book redolent with London vitality. Overlooked by comparison, but related in theme, was a collection of essays by Asian, Caribbean and African writers who had settled in Britain: *Voices of the Crossing*, edited by Ferdinand Dennis and Naseem Khan.

Although she won the Booker Prize for it, to the general delight of many who felt she should have won this award on earlier occasions, Margaret Atwood was considered by many to be writing below par in *The Blind Assassin*. Amongst established writers of fiction Saul Bellow, Anita Desai, Jean Echenoz, Kazuo Ishiguro, Michael Ondaatje, William Trevor and John Updike all produced original work which took them in new directions, but it was Martin Amis in his autobiographical memoir *Experience* who most caught the public and critical eye. A young Indian writer of short stories, Jhumpa Lahiri, won the Pulitzer Prize for fiction, with an internationally admired collection, *Interpreter of Maladies*.

In the world of poetry—despite the publication of a report in Britain which suggested, on suspect evidence, that sales were even poorer than had been thought—a number of well-established poets confirmed their standing, amongst them the Nobel Prize winners Wislawa Szymborska and Derek Walcott. Another Nobel laureate, Seamus Heaney, gathered more awards for his translation of *Beowulf*. Michael Donaghy was the fastest rising younger talent.

In 1999 there were 110,155 titles published in the UK, and an approximately similar number in the USA, with a population four times as large. Of these, 5,209 of the British titles were fiction, 3,886 were computing books, 9,099 were children's books (the largest category), 11 were on zoology (the smallest category), and 1,968 were works in translation. These figures for the last year of the 20th century were not available until deep into the first year of the 21st, but they told a revealing story. With under 2 per cent of all new books originating in other languages (a similar figure existed in US publishing), parochialism seemed to rule. In no other major publishing countries were the translation figures as low as they were in the two major Anglophone outlets. The award of the Nobel Prize for Literature to a Chinese writer (albeit one living in Paris and clearly at odds with his government) was a significant breakthrough for a modern literature which remained rarely translated. The chosen laureate was Gao Xingjian, author of a large-scale novel, *Soul Mountain,* as well as plays such as *The Other Shore* which had been rendered into English, though never staged outside China.

A number of legendary writers died in the course of the year. The Antipodes lost three of their great poets: A. D. Hope, whose poem *Australia* had found its way into countless anthologies; his fellow Australian, Judith Wright; and Lauris Edmond from New Zealand. The national poet of Israel, Yehuda Amichai, died, as did two influential French novelists, José Cabanis and Roger Peyrefitte. Amongst British writers the death of Malcolm Bradbury was considered especially sad, as he had been so ardent a campaigner for creative writing and had just produced *To the Hermitage*, which many thought his best novel. Penelope Fitzgerald and Anthony Powell, who also died, were amongst the best of post-war novelists. R. S. Thomas, a fiery mixture of Welsh national sentiments, radicalism and Christian ministry, was eulogised as Wales's greatest writer of modern times. Barbara Cartland earned no plaudits for the quality of her work, but she was astonishingly successful internationally and at the time of her death held the strange record for having written the largest number of published books—well over 600. Two highly literate actors, John Gielgud and Alec Guinness, died, leaving behind in both cases some witty and well judged memoirs. (For obituaries of Amichai, Bradbury, Cartland, Fitzgerald, Gielgud, Guinness, Powell and Thomas, see XVIII).

Amongst the leading titles published in 2000 were the following:

FICTION. Diran Adebayo, *My Once Upon a Time* (Abacus); Stephen Amidon, *The New City* (Doubleday); Robert Antoni, *My Grandmother's Erotic Folktales* (Faber); Michael Arditti, *Easter* (Arcadia); Kate Atkinson, *Emotionally Weird* (Doubleday); Margaret Atwood, *The Blind Assassin* (Bloomsbury); J G Ballard, *Super-Cannes* (Flamingo); John Banville, *Eclipse* (Picador); Julian Barnes, *Love, Etc.* (Cape); Saul Bellow, *Ravelstein* (Viking); Neil Bissoondath, *The Worlds Within Her* (Heinemann); Malcom Bradbury, *To the Hermitage* (Picador); A S Byatt, *The Biographer's Tale* (Chatto & Windus); Raymond Carver, *Call If You Need Me* (Harvill); Amit Chaudhuri, *A New World* (Picador); Jason Cowley, *Unknown Pleasures* (Faber); Anita Desai, *Diamond Dust and Other Stories* (Chatto); E L Doctorow, *City of God* (Little, Brown); Helen Dunmore, *Ice Cream* (Viking); Jean Echenoz (trans. by Guid Waldman), *I'm Off* (Harvill); Anne Enright, *What Are You Like?* (Cape); Penelope Fitzgerald, *The Means of Escape* (Flamingo); Namita Gokhale, *The Book of Shadows* (Little, Brown); Juan Goytisolo (trans. Peter Bush), *The Garden of Secrets* (Serpent's Tail); Linda Grant, *When I Lived in Modern Times* (Granta); Rodney Hall, *The Island in the Mind* (Granta); Abdullah Hussain, *Emigré Journeys* (Serpent's Tail); Rachel Ingalls, *Days Like Today* (Faber); Moses Isegawa, *Abyssinian Chronicles* (Picador); Kazuo Ishiguro, *When We Were Orphans* (Faber); Gayl Jones, *The Healing* (Serpent's Tail); Ismail Kadare (trans. by Derek Coltman), *The General of the Dead Army* (Harvill); H R F Keating, *Breaking and Entering* (Macmillan); Matthew Kneale, *English Passengers* (Hamish Hamilton); Jhumpa Lahiri, *Interpreter of Maladies* (Flamingo); John Lanchester, *Mr Phillips* (Faber); Luc Lang (trans. Rory Mulholland), *Strange Ways* (Phoenix House); Doris Lessing, *Ben, In the World* (Cape); Toby Litt, *Corpsing* (Hamish Hamilton); Alistair Macleod, *No Great Mischief* (Cape); David Mamet, *Wilson, A Consideration of the Sources* (Faber); Armistead Maupin, *The Night Listener* (Bantam); Simon Mawer, *The Gospel of Judas* (Little, Brown); Patrick McGrath, *Martha Peake* (Viking); Pankaj Mishra, *The Romantics* (Picador); Blake Morrison, *The Justification of Johan Gutenberg* (Chatto & Windus); Jeff Noon, *Needle in the Groove* (Anchor); Lawrence Norfolk, *In the Shape of a Boar* (Weidenfeld); Michael Ondaatje, *Anil's Ghost* (Bloomsbury); Mike Phillips, *A Shadow of Myself* (HarperCollins); Michele Roberts, *The Looking Glass* (Little, Brown); Philip Roth, *The Human Stain* (Cape); J K Rowling, *Harry Potter and the Goblet of Fire* (Bloomsbury); Will Self, *How the Dead Live* (Bloomsbury); Carol Shields, *Dressing Up for the Carnival* (Fourth Estate); Helen Simpson, *Hey Yeah Right Get A Life* (Cape); Gillian Slovo, *Red Dust* (Virago); Zadie Smith, *White Teeth* (Hamish Hamilton); Susan Sontag, *In America* (Cape); Muriel Spark, *Aiding and Abetting* (Viking); Peter Stamm (trans. Hofmann, Michael), *Agnes* (Bloomsbury); Adam Thorpe, *Shifts* (Cape); William Trevor, *The Hill Bachelors* (Viking); Joanna Trollope, *Marrying the Mistress* (Bloomsbury); John Updike, *Gertrude and Claudius* (Hamish Hamilton); David Foster Wallace, *Brief Interviews with Hideous Men* (Abacus); Jill Paton Walsh, *A Desert in Bohemia* (Doubleday); Edmund White, *The Married Man* (Chatto & Windus); Jeanette Winterson, *The PowerBook* (Cape).

POETRY. John Agard, *Weblines* (Bloodaxe); Patience Agbabi, *Transformatrix* (Payback); Sujata Bhatt, *Augatora* (Carcanet); Jean "Binta" Breeze, *The Arrival of Brighteye* (Bloodaxe); John Burnside, *The Asylum Dance* (Cape); Anne Carson, *Men in the Off Hours* (Cape); Ciaran Carson, *The Twelfth of Never* (Picador); Robert Crawford and Mick Imlah (eds.), *The New Penguin Book of Scottish Verse* (Allen Lane); Michael Donaghy, *Conjure* (Picador); Nick Drake, *The Man in a White Suit* (Bloodaxe); Douglas Dunn, *The Donkey's Ears* (Faber); U A Fanthorpe, *Consequences* (Peterloo); Thom Gunn, *Boss Cupid* (Faber); Michael Hofmann, *Approximately Nowhere* (Faber); Kathleen Jamie, *Jizzen* (Picador); Alan Jenkins, *The Drift* (Chatto & Windus); Derek Mahon, *Selected Poems* (Penguin); Glyn Maxwell, *The Boys at Twilight* (Bloodaxe); Les Murray, *Conscious and Verbal* (Carcanet); Sharon Olds, *Blood, Tin, Straw* (Cape); Tom Paulin, *The Wind Dog* (Faber); Carole Satyamurti, *Love and Variations* (Bloodaxe); Wislawa Szymborska, *Poems: New and Collected 1957-1997* (Faber); Derek Walcott, *Tiepolo's Hound* (Faber); Michelene Wandor, *Gardens of Eden Revisited* (Five Leaves).

AUTOBIOGRAPHY AND BIOGRAPHY. Said K. Aburish, *Saddam Hussain: the politics of revenge* (Bloomsbury); Martin Amis, *Experience* (Cape); Juliet Barker, *Wordsworth: A Life* (Viking); Kate Buford, *Burt Lancaster:An*

American Life (Aurum); John Campbell, *Margaret Thatcher, Volume 1: The Grocer's Daughter* (Cape); Ferdinand Dennis and Naseem Khan (eds.), *Voices of the Crossing:The impact of Britain on writers from Asia, the Caribbean and Africa* (Serpent's Tail); John Drummond, *Tainted By Experience* (Faber); Danny Fields, *Linda McCarney* (Little, Brown); Christopher Frayling, *Sergio Leone: Something to Do with Death* (Faber); Paul Gilroy, *Between Camps* (Allen Lane); Claire Harman, *Fanny Burney: a biography* (HarperCollins); Michael Heseltine, *Life in the Jungle: My Autobiography* (Hodder & Stoughton); Roland Hill, *Lord Acton* (Yale); Merlin Holland and Rupert Hart-Davis (eds.), *The Complete Letters of Oscar Wilde* (Fourth Estate); Richard Holmes, *Sidetracks: Explorations of a Romantic Biographer* (HarperCollins); Karen V Kukil, *The Journals of Sylvia Plath* (Faber); Gavin Lambert, *Mainly About Lindsay Anderson* (Faber); Zachary Leader (ed.), *The Letters of Kingsley Amis* (HarperCollins); F P Lock, *Edmund Burke. Vol. 1: 1730-84* (O.U.P.); Alexis Lykiard, *Jean Rhys Revisited* (Stride); Marion Meade, *The Unruly Life of Woody Allen* (Weidenfeld); Simon Sebag Montefiore, *Prince of Princes: the Life of Potemkin* (Weidenfeld); Caroline Moorehead, *Iris Origo: Marchesa Val d'Orcia* (John Murray); Andrew Motion, *Wainwright the Poisoner* (Faber); Douglas Murray, *Bosie: a Biography of Lord Alfred Douglas* (Hodder); Graham Robb, *Rimbaud* (Picador); Alan Ross, *Reflections on Blue Water* (Harvill); Lorna Sage, *Bad Blood: A Memoir* (Fourth Estate); Robert Service, *Lenin: a Biography* (Macmillan); Robert Skidelsky, *John Maynard Keynes: Fighting for Britain 1937-46* (Macmillan); Charles Spencer, *The Spencer Family* (Viking); David Starkey, *Elizabeth* (Chatto); Anthony Summers, *Nixon* (Gollancz); Jeremy Treglown, *Romancing: the Life and Work of Henry Green* (Faber); Roland Vernon, *Star in the East: Krishnamurti—The Invention of a Messiah* (Constable).

OTHER. Yasmin Alibhai-Brown, *Who Do We Think We Are? Imagining the New Britain* (Allen Lane); Michael Burleigh, *The Third Reich: a New History* (Macmillan); Bill Bryson, *Down Under* (Doubleday); Alain De Botton, *The Consolations of Philosophy* (Hamish Hamilton); Umberto Eco, (translated by Alastair McEwen), *Kant and the Platypus: Essays on Language and Cognition* (Secker & Warburg); Alasdair Gray, *The Book of Prefaces* (Bloomsbury); A L Kennedy, *On Bullfighting* (Yellow Jersey); Frank Kermode, *Shakespeare's Language* (Allen Lane); Andrew Marr, *The Day Britain Died* (Profile); Arthur Miller, *The Crucible in History* (Methuen); Giles Milton, *Big Chief Elizabeth: How England's Adventurers Gambled and Won the New World* (Hodder & Stoughton); Tom Nairn, *After Britain: New Labour and the Return of Scotland* (Granta); Ruth Padel, *I'm a Man— Sex, Gods and Rock'N'Roll* (Faber); Caryl Phillips, *The Atlantic Sound* (Faber); Liz Picard, *Dr. Johnson's London* (Weidenfeld & Nicolson); Andrew Rawnsley, *Servants of the People* (Hamish Hamilton); Yasmina Reza (trans. Carol Cosman), *Hammerklavier* (Faber); Simon Schama, *A History of Britain* (BBC); William Shawcross, *Deliver Us from Evil* (Bloomsbury); Retha M Warnicke, *The Marrying of Anne of Cleves: Royal Protocol in Tudor England* (Cambridge University Press).

XVI SPORT

OLYMPIC GAMES. After the scandal surrounding the vote to stage the 2002 Winter Games in Salt Lake City and a less-than-perfect Summer Games in Atlanta in 1996, the Olympic movement needed Sydney 2000 to be a success. It was rewarded with arguably the best Olympic Games in modern history.

Whilst there were many memorable performances by individuals, the biggest stars were undoubtedly Sydney itself and the host country. No nation in the world was as fanatical about sport and Australians responded to the Games with unrestrained enthusiasm. Crowds were huge, even for events not usually regarded as good spectator sports. The excellence of the facilities won widespread praise, the organisation was silky smooth and even the weather was rarely less than perfect, apart from a chilly evening or two.

Athletics provided many of the most memorable contests, with Australia's greatest moment undoubtedly being Cathy Freeman's triumph in the 400 metres. Freeman went into the Games as the country's greatest sporting icon and defied the overwhelming pressure of expectation to win her gold medal. The sight of Freeman sitting on the track, overcome by the enormity of her achievement, was one of many lasting images of the Games.

It says much for the brilliance of Marion Jones that some observers considered that the 24-year-old US athlete left Sydney without fulfilling her potential. Having gone into the Games hoping to win an unprecedented five gold medals, Jones ended up with "only" three. The 100 metres and 200 metres were won with style and her impressive third leg in the 4 x 400 metres relay helped the US team to take gold. However, Jones was given too much to do on the final leg of the 4 x 100 metres relay, whilst in the long jump Heike Drechsler's outstanding technique gave the German gold.

Many of the men's athletics events were dominated by established champions. Michael Johnson crowned his final Games with victory in the 400 metres and the 4 x 400 metres relay, Haile Gebrselassie retained the 10,000 metres title by winning a thrilling race against Paul Tergat and Jan Zelezny won his third successive javelin gold, relegating Britain's Steve Backley to silver. Maurice Greene lived up to expectations by winning the men's blue riband event, the 100 metres, but the hot favourite for the 1500 metres, Hicham El Guerrouj, was outsprinted by Noah Ngeny.

Britain's Jonathan Edwards made up for his disappointment in Atlanta by winning the triple jump. Denise Lewis was Britain's other gold medal winner in athletics, defying injury to win an intense battle for the heptathlon gold. Remarkably, the UK won another nine gold medals to record the country's best performance at an Olympics for 80 years. The success was hailed by everyone as a triumph for the funding provided by the National Lottery. The funding programme had enabled scores of British competitors across a wide range of disciplines to concentrate full-time on their sport and the reward was there for all to see.

From the first weekend, when Jason Queally won gold on the cycling track, British successes followed with stunning regularity. Yachting was Britain's most successful sport, with Ben Ainslie, Iain Percy and Shirley Robertson all winning gold. Audley Harrison (boxing), Stephanie Cook (modern pentathlon) and Richard Faulds (shooting) also won gold, but the greatest excitement for the British camp came at Penrith Lakes in the rowing competition. Steve Redgrave went to Sydney hoping to become the first man ever to win gold medals at five successive Games. Alongside Matthew Pinsent (who was going for his own third gold), James Cracknell and Tim Foster, Redgrave rarely looked in danger and the British crew dominated their final from start to finish. The coxless four's achievement also provided the perfect inspiration for Britain's men's rowing eight, who won a thrilling final just 24 hours later. It came as no surprise when Redgrave—who at last announced his retirement—mopped up the British sportsman of the year award and was given a knighthood.

Whilst there were some individual disappointments, there was no doubt that Britain's greatest collective under-achievers were the swimmers, who left Sydney without a medal. Britain was completely outclassed in a stunning swimming competition, which saw several memorable clashes between the hosts and the US team. Ian Thorpe—"Thorpedo"—delighted home supporters by living up to his youthful promise with two gold medals, although he was denied a third in the 200 metres by the Dutchman Pieter van den Hoogenband, who also won the 100 metres.

The USA finished on top of the medals table, whilst China ran Russia close for second place and Australia was finished fourth. Almost the only cloud on the Sydney horizon was sport's greatest perennial problem, the abuse of drugs. The highest profile case featured an athlete who was not even competing at Sydney. C J Hunter, Marion Jones's husband, was revealed during the Games to have tested positive for nandrolone, a banned steroid. The women's world hammer champion, Mihaela Melinte, failed a similar test and was informed of the result just as she was about to take part in the qualifying competition. There were positive tests in a number of other sports, particularly weightlifting, showing that the battle against drugs needed to be fought with as much vigour as ever.

Sydney also hosted the Paralympics and any thoughts that they would be an anti-climax following the Olympics were quickly dispelled. The Australian public turned out in huge numbers as the event confirmed its place on the world sporting stage. Britain once again performed with distinction, finishing second behind Australia in the medals table and bringing home 41 golds. Lottery funding was again cited as a key factor.

ASSOCIATION FOOTBALL. If France sprang a surprise by beating Brazil in the 1998 World Cup final (see AR 1998, pp. 548-49), there were few eyebrows raised when the same team triumphed two years later at the European Championship, hosted jointly by the Netherlands and Belgium. Although the French very nearly lost to Italy in the final, there could be little argument that Roger Lemerre's team deserved its success. Remarkably, France's only major weakness in 1998 had been in attack, but in the 2000 tournament the team boasted four young world-class strikers in Thierry Henry, Nicolas Anelka, David Trezeguet and Sylvain Wiltord.

The Italians had stunned one of the co-hosts, knocking out the Netherlands in a penalty shoot-out in the semi-finals. In the Rotterdam final Italy took the lead through Marco Delvecchio's 56th minute goal and held on until four minutes into injury time, when Trezeguet flicked a through ball on to his fellow substitute, Wiltord, who calmly scored. It was a shattering moment for the Italians and in extra time France took control. The third French substitute, Robert Pires, set up the stunning "golden goal" winner, a glorious volley by Trezeguet.

England were the only team from the UK to qualify for Euro 2000. Despite a rare 1-0 win over Germany, Kevin Keegan's team went out after losing both of their other group games to Portugal and Romania, having taken the lead in both matches. With English hooligans again bringing disgrace to the country, it was a sad way for team captain Alan Shearer to end his international career.

Many coaches, including Italy's Dino Zoff and Holland's Frank Rijkaard, chose the end of Euro 2000 as an appropriate moment to resign. Noticeably not amongst them was Keegan. Three months later, however, he quit within minutes of losing to Germany in a World Cup qualifier, the last match ever to be staged at the old Wembley stadium. Howard Wilkinson, the Football Association's technical director, took temporary charge, but a draw in Helsinki against Finland four days later did little to enhance England's prospects. The Swede Sven Goran Eriksson was appointed as Keegan's successor, thereby becoming the first overseas coach ever to take charge of the English national team.

After the initial skirmishes in the 2002 World Cup qualifiers, the Republic of Ireland and Scotland were the best placed UK teams, both unbeaten after three games. Wales and Northern Ireland appeared refreshed by the appointment of Mark Hughes and Sammy McIlroy, respectively, as coaches, but qualification for 2002 remained a tall order.

At club level, it was undoubtedly the year of the Spanish, who provided three of the four European Champions League (the successor of the European Cup) semi-finalists in Real Madrid, Valencia and Barcelona. In the Paris final Real's experience proved crucial as they beat Valencia 3-0. Manchester United, the 1999 champions, had gone out to Real in the quarter-finals. Chelsea had a good Champions' League campaign, failing to reach the quarter-finals only when they lost their last group game at home to Lazio. English clubs also did well in the opening exchanges of the 2000-01 Champions' League, with Manchester United, Leeds and Arsenal all qualifying for the second phase. Glasgow Rangers, however, failed to progress.

In the Uefa Cup final in Copenhagen, Arsenal lost a penalty shoot-out to Galatasary. In the semi-finals the Turkish team had beaten a young and stylish Leeds United whose attacking football in both the domestic and European campaigns had won them many admirers. However, the tie with Galatasary will be remembered more for the killing of two Leeds supporters—both of whom were stabbed to death by Turkish fans in Istanbul the day before the first leg—and for the restrained and dignified way in which the Leeds United chairman, Peter Ridsdale and the team's young manager, David O'Leary, dealt with the tragedy.

In January Manchester United had joined seven other teams in the inaugural Fifa World Club Championship in Brazil. However, from the moment David Beckham was sent off in the first game things did not go well for United, who failed even to reach the third place play-off. Corinthians won an all-Brazilian final against Vasco de Gama.

In order to compete in Brazil, United had to withdraw—because of fixture congestion—from the FA Cup, which they did with the FA's approval. This attracted much criticism, particularly as it seemed that the FA was too keen to please Fifa, the world governing body, in a year when it was campaigning heavily for England to stage the 2006 World Cup. As it turned out, the FA's lavish campaign failed, with Germany controversially winning the 2006 vote. Germany's biggest rivals proved to be South Africa, which was angered to learn that it had lost the prize because one delegate, Charles Dempsey, had abstained rather than follow his mandate to vote for South Africa, saying that he had been put under huge pressure.

Elsewhere in the world Cameroon, which won the Olympic title, confirmed its continental supremacy by beating Nigeria on penalties in the African Nations' Cup, whilst Boca Juniors upheld Argentinian pride by beating Brazil's Palmeiras in the final of the Libertadores Cup.

In England there was no stopping Manchester United. Sir Alex Ferguson's team won their sixth Premiership title in eight seasons, finishing 18 points clear of second-placed Arsenal, while Liverpool's poor run-in enabled Leeds to claim the third Champions' League slot. Liverpool qualified for a Uefa Cup place alongside Chelsea and Leicester, the FA Cup and Worthington Cup winners respectively.

Rangers continued to dominate in Scotland, with Dick Advocaat guiding the Ibrox club to their 49th league title. Nothing symbolised Celtic's problems more than their Scottish Cup defeat to the little Inverness team Caledonian Thistle. Although Celtic won the CIS (League) Cup, their poor league form inevitably meant that Kenny Dalglish's return would end in tears. Having taken over team affairs following the disastrous reign of his appointee, John Barnes, Dalglish was unable to halt the slide. However, the appointment of Martin O'Neill as Dalglish's successor brought promise of a change in fortunes, underlined by Celtic's inspired start to the 2000-01 League campaign.

Whilst the Premiership big guns continued to spend heavily in the transfer market—Rio Ferdinand's UK£18 million move from West Ham to Leeds breaking the record for a deal between two English clubs—Real Madrid splashed out UK£37 million on Luis Figo from Barcelona. With the European Commission threatening to outlaw transfer fees altogether, it could be a world record that will never be broken.

BOXING. Whilst controversial headlines continued to follow Mike Tyson around the world—after one fight in Glasgow he said he wanted to eat Lennox Lewis's children—there was no doubting who was the planet's greatest heavyweight boxer. Lewis ended the year as he had begun it, as world heavyweight champion. New Zealand's David Tua was expected by some to mount a strong challenge to the Briton in Las Vegas, but he proved no match for Lewis.

Britain's other big draw, Naseem Hamed, remained WBO featherweight champion, but nearly lost his title to Augie Sanchez, an unheralded boxer from Las Vegas, in a thrilling fight in Connecticut. Hamed, bleeding from the nose and mouth and having survived a second-round knockdown, counter attacked and knocked Sanchez out with a devastating four-punch salvo in the fourth round.

CRICKET. In cricket the year 2000 will be remembered above all for the match-fixing scandal which blew the game apart. There had been rumours for several years, but nobody was prepared for the revelations which followed the confessions of the South African captain, Hansie Cronje.

The affair began with charges levelled at Cronje by Indian police that he had colluded with a bookmaker. At a hearing in Cape Town, Cronje admitted to taking substantial sums of money from a bookmaker for pitch information and match forecasts. He also confessed to offering bribes to two members of his team, Herschelle Gibbs and Henry Williams, to play badly in a one-day international against India. Both players were banned until the end of the year after admitting that they had agreed to the proposal, although both failed to see the task through and were not paid. Cronje was banned for life.

Salim Malik and Mohammad Azharuddin, former captains of Pakistan and India respectively, were amongst other players banned for life by their cricket boards as the scandal spread. India's highest police authority, the Central Bureau of Investigation, published a report into match-fixing which implicated a number of players around the world, and the year ended with the International Cricket Council investigating the claims through its new anti-corruption unit, headed by Paul Condon, the former commissioner of the Metropolitan Police in London.

On the pitch Australia confirmed their status as the world's best team—winning all eight of their Test matches and completing a world record of 12 consecutive Test victories by beating the West Indies—whilst England continued their resurgence under Nasser Hussain and Duncan Fletcher, captain and coach respectively.

The year began with England losing a Test series 2-1 away to South Africa. English joy at winning the final Test at Centurion—a remarkable match which saw both sides forfeit an innings for the first time in Test history—was tempered later in the year when, during the match-fixing investigation, doubts were raised over Cronje's motives in setting England such a generous target. South Africa then staged a triangular one-day series with England and Zimbabwe, the hosts beating England in the final. England went on to win a one-day series in Zimbabwe 3-0.

England welcomed Zimbabwe as their first visitors of the summer and won a two-match Test series and a three-sided one-day contest which also featured the

West Indies. However, this paled into insignificance alongside England's first Test series victory for 31 years over the West Indies. Darren Gough, with 25 wickets, and Michael Atherton, with 311 runs, were England's leading performers, but the keys were the teamwork of England and the brittle batting of the once-mighty West Indies. Courtney Walsh's achievement in becoming the highest wicket taker in Test history, when he passed Kapil Dev's total of 434, was scant consolation for the West Indies' poor year.

More improbably, England went on to win a series in Pakistan for the first time in 38 years. Neither side looked capable of breaking the stalemate until the final day of the final Test in Karachi, where Pakistan had never been beaten. Graham Thorpe hit the winning runs in near darkness in a thrilling finish.

Elsewhere in the world New Zealand had double reason to celebrate, their men winning the ICC Trophy tournament in Kenya and their women lifting the World Cup in Australia in December.

Surrey confirmed their domestic domination of English first-class cricket by retaining the county championship, whilst there was no doubting Gloucestershire's continued one-day supremacy as they won the NatWest Trophy, Benson and Hedges Cup and the Norwich Union National Cricket League.

GOLF. Rarely can a man have so dominated one sport as Tiger Woods did in 2000. At 24 Woods became the youngest player to win three of the year's four majors and only the fifth in history to win all four majors in his career. The great Ben Hogan was the only other player to have won three majors in the same calendar year. Woods won nine times on the US Tour, put together the best run on the Tour for 52 years with six wins in succession and amassed more than US$10 million in prize money.

The American's only major disappointment came at Augusta, where he finished fifth as Vijay Singh took his first Masters title. In the next two majors Woods was unstoppable. His winning margin of 15 strokes in the US Open at Pebble Beach was a record for any major, whilst in 72 holes at St Andrews he did not find a single bunker en route to an eight-stroke victory in the British Open. At the US PGA at Valhalla, however, Woods met stern opposition from Bob May, a journeyman American professional, who took him to a play-off. It was appropriate that Woods's wonder year coincided with farewell appearances by the legendary Jack Nicklaus at the US and British Opens.

In Europe, Colin Montgomerie's long reign at the top of the Order of Merit was finally ended by Lee Westwood, who denied Darren Clarke by finishing second on a thrilling last day of the season at the World Championship tournament at Valderrama.

The highlight of the women's season was Europe's victory over the USA at Loch Lomond, although the event was soured after the Americans forced Annika Sorenstam to replay a shot because she had played out of turn.

MOTOR SPORT. Ferrari's mammoth investment in the talent of Michael Schumacher finally paid off in 2000 as the Italian team celebrated its first Formula

One world drivers' title for 21 years. Schumacher equalled the record of nine victories in a season as he held off the challenge of McLaren's Mikka Hakkinen, the 1999 champion.

Schumacher made a flying start, only to be pegged back by the Finn's summer resurgence. However, the mechanical problems which Hakkinen suffered at the start and end of the year proved costly as Schumacher secured the title in the penultimate race in Japan.

Rubens Barrichello and David Coulthard were the season's only other winners. It was a remarkable year for Coulthard, who escaped with three cracked ribs after a plane crash that killed the two pilots. Coulthard also won the British Grand Prix at Silverstone, but the event will be remembered most of all for the appalling weather. With car parks closed and spectators forced to trudge through fields of mud, the decision to move the race from its traditional July date to April was widely criticised.

Marcus Gronholm won the world rally championship for Peugeot, although Britain's Richard Burns had the consolation of victory in his home event. On two wheels, Kenny Roberts Jr won the 500cc world title, while the USA's Colin Edwards won the world superbikes championship as injury forced the retirement of Britain's 1999 champion, Carl Fogarty.

RUGBY. It was fitting that a world record crowd of 110,000 flocked to Sydney's Olympic Stadium in July to watch a game that was regarded by many as the greatest in the history of rugby union. New Zealand beat Australia 39-35, thanks largely to three tries in an extraordinary opening five minutes. Australia were level at 24-24 by half-time and when Jeremy Paul put the home side into a 35-34 lead in the 73rd minute it seemed that their revival might be complete. However, Jonah Lomu replied with the 10th try of the match to secure the All Blacks' victory.

Whilst Australia went on to take the Tri-Nations title thanks to a 24-23 win over New Zealand in the return match in Wellington, there were signs of a possible change in the world order in the autumn. England confirmed their growing stature with a pulsating 22-19 victory over the Wallabies at Twickenham, their first triumph over the Australians for five years, whilst France and New Zealand drew a mini-series 1-1. England also beat South Africa again, adding success at Twickenham to their summer triumph at Bloemfontein.

European rugby union welcomed a newcomer to its most famous competition as Italy joined what now became the Six Nations' Championship. The Italians made a fine start, beating Scotland in Rome, although they were unable to maintain that form. England took the title, although a surprising defeat against Scotland at Murrayfield on the final weekend denied them the grand slam.

On the club front, Northampton were beaten by Wasps in the Tetley's Bitter Cup final but were crowned kings of Europe after beating Munster, whilst Leicester retained their domestic league title. Cardiff won the Welsh/Scottish League and Llanelli underlined their ability as cup specialists by beating Swansea in the Welsh Cup final.

The Rugby League World Cup came to the northern hemisphere, but the policy of playing many of the matches outside the game's heartlands did not generally pay off. Attendances were poor and were not helped by the fact that Australia were so much better than everyone else. They were given their toughest test in the semi-finals by Wales, who led 20-8 at one stage but eventually lost 46-22. New Zealand were no match for Australia in the final.

At club level, Wigan finished top of the Super League table to pip second-placed St Helens, who earned revenge by beating Wigan 29-16 in the Grand Final at Old Trafford in front of a record 58,182 crowd. Bradford Bulls beat Leeds 24-18 in the Challenge Cup final at Murrayfield, where the ground staff performed miracles to stage the match after severe flooding.

TENNIS. In June Pete Sampras reinforced his claim to be the greatest tennis player ever when he broke Roy Emerson's record of 12 Grand Slams by winning Wimbledon for the seventh time in eight years. Sampras began the year by losing a five-set thriller in the semi-finals of the Australian Open to Andre Agassi, who went on to win the tournament to claim his third victory in his last four Grand Slam tournaments. Agassi's hopes of successfully defending his French Open title ended, however, with an early defeat to Karol Kucera as Gustavo Kuerten reclaimed the title he had won in 1997.

After his victory at Wimbledon, where he beat Pat Rafter in the final, Sampras was favourite to claim a fifth US Open title. He duly reached the final, but was beaten in straight sets by a wonderful demonstration of skill and power from Russia's Marat Safin. Sampras was still in pole position to end the season as world No 1, but that accolade went to Kuerten thanks to the Brazilian's victory over Agassi in the ATP Masters Cup final in Lisbon. Spain won the Davis Cup for the first time, beating Australia in the final in Barcelona, whilst Yevgeny Kafelnikov claimed Russia's first Olympic tennis gold medal.

Although Martina Hingis finished the year as world number one, women's tennis was dominated by 20-year-old Venus Williams, who beat Lindsay Davenport in the finals at both Wimbledon, which was her first Grand Slam title, and at the US Open, where she inherited the crown from her sister Serena Williams. The sisters won the women's doubles at Wimbledon and the Olympics, where Venus also won gold in the singles. The two other Grand Slam singles titles went to Davenport in Melbourne and Mary Pierce in Paris.

Britain's hopes of success lay, as in previous years, with Tim Henman and Greg Rusedski. Henman won an indoor event in Vienna, ending a run of seven successive final defeats, but failed to make significant progress in the Grand Slam tournaments, whilst Rusedski's year was ruined by injury.

THE TURF A memorable year for Flat racing produced several great horses whose feats will linger long in the memory. It says everything about the year's standards that Sinndar became the first horse to win the Derby, Irish Derby and Prix de l'Arc de Triomphe in the same campaign but was not generally regarded as the horse of the year. That accolade went to Giant's Causeway, who showed remarkable consistency through a tough year. Never out of the first two in 10 starts, the Irish horse rounded off an exceptional year with second place in the Breeders' Cup Classic; Kalanisi upheld European honour at Churchill Downs by winning the Breeder's Cup Turf.

Dubai Millennium won the Dubai World Cup and was hailed by Shaikh Mohammed bin Rashid al-Maktoum as "my best ever horse" after winning the Prince of Wales's Stakes at Royal Ascot. King's Best won the 2,000 Guineas for Sir Michael Stoute, Lahan the 1,000 Guineas for John Gosden, Love Divine the Oaks for Henry Cecil and Millenary the St Leger for John Dunlop.

Frankie Dettori and Ray Cochrane narrowly escaped death after their light aircraft crashed at Newmarket, killing the pilot. Dettori, typically, won with his first ride back later in the summer, but Cochrane's injuries eventually ended his career. In the USA Laffit Pincay became the first jockey in the world to ride 9,000 winners.

Martin Pipe continued to dominate in National Hunt racing and in February saddled his 2,989th winner, a record in British racing. Istabraq was the star of Cheltenham, winning his third successive Champion Hurdle, while Noel Chance trained the Gold Cup winner for the second time in three years, Looks Like Trouble taking the prize this time. An Irish father and son combination won the Grand National for the second year in succession, Ted Walsh and his son Ruby Walsh securing victory for Papillon 12 months after Tommy Carberry and Paul Carberry had performed the feat with Bobbyjo.

OTHER SPORTS. In yachting, Team New Zealand, the defending champions, won the America's Cup, skipper Russell Coutts comfortably holding off the Italians of Prada Challenge, whilst another champion, Lance Armstrong, fought off a rejuvenated Marco Pantani to win cycling's biggest prize, the Tour de France. However, drugs scandals continued to dog cycling. At a sensational court hearing in Lille, Richard Virenque, France's most celebrated rider of recent times, confessed to drug-taking as the systematic use of drugs in the sport was laid bare.

Mark Williams won the Embassy World Snooker Championship for the first time, beating his fellow Welshman Matthew Steven in the final, whilst in equestrianism Mary King won the Badminton three-day event for the second time in her career.

In baseball the New York Yankees won their third consecutive World Series, beating their locals rivals the Mets in the first "Subway Series" for 44 years. The St Louis Rams won the Super Bowl, beating the Tennessee Titans 23-16 to record their first victory in the event. The LA Lakers beat the Indiana Pacers to win the National Basketball Association crown, whilst Shaquille O'Neal fell just one vote short of becoming the first unanimous Most Valuable Player in NBA history. The New Jersey Devils won ice hockey's Stanley Cup, beating the 1999 winners, the Dallas Stars, in the final.

XVII DOCUMENTS AND REFERENCE

1. CHARTER OF FUNDAMENTAL RIGHTS OF THE EUROPEAN UNION

Published below is the official text of the Charter of Fundamental Rights which was signed at the Inter-Governmental Conference in Nice on December 7, 2000.

PREAMBLE

The peoples of Europe, in creating an ever closer union among them, are resolved to share a peaceful future based on common values.

Conscious of its spiritual and moral heritage, the Union is founded on the indivisible, universal values of human dignity, freedom, equality and solidarity; it is based on the principles of democracy and the rule of law. It places the individual at the heart of its activities, by establishing the citizenship of the Union and by creating an area of freedom, security and justice.

The Union contributes to the preservation and to the development of these common values while respecting the diversity of the cultures and traditions of the peoples of Europe as well as the national identities of the Member States and the organisation of their public authorities at national, regional and local levels; it seeks to promote balanced and sustainable development and ensures free movement of persons, goods, services and capital, and the freedom of establishment.

To this end, it is necessary to strengthen the protection of fundamental rights in the light of changes in society, social progress and scientific and technological developments by making those rights more visible in a Charter.

This Charter reaffirms, with due regard for the powers and tasks of the Community and the Union and the principle of subsidiarity, the rights as they result, in particular, from the constitutional traditions and international obligations common to the Member States, the Treaty on European Union, the Community Treaties, the European Convention for the Protection of Human Rights and Fundamental Freedoms, the Social Charters adopted by the Community and by the Council of Europe and the case-law of the Court of Justice of the European Communities and of the European Court of Human Rights.

Enjoyment of these rights entails responsibilities and duties with regard to other persons, to the human community and to future generations.

The Union therefore recognises the rights, freedoms and principles set out hereafter.

CHAPTER I
DIGNITY

Article 1
Human dignity

Human dignity is inviolable. It must be respected and protected.

Article 2
Right to life

1. Everyone has the right to life.
2. No one shall be condemned to the death penalty, or executed.

Article 3
Right to the integrity of the person

1. Everyone has the right to respect for his or her physical and mental integrity.
2. In the fields of medicine and biology, the following must be respected in particular:
   —the free and informed consent of the person concerned, according to the procedures laid down by law,
   —the prohibition of eugenic practices, in particular those aiming at the selection of persons,
   —the prohibition on making the human body and its parts as such a source of financial gain,
   —the prohibition of the reproductive cloning of human beings.

Article 4
Prohibition of torture and inhuman or degrading treatment or punishment

No one shall be subjected to torture or to inhuman or degrading treatment or punishment.

Article 5
Prohibition of slavery and forced labour

1. No one shall be held in slavery or servitude.
2. No one shall be required to perform forced or compulsory labour.
3. Trafficking in human beings is prohibited.

CHAPTER II
FREEDOMS

Article 6
Right to liberty and security

Everyone has the right to liberty and security of person.

Article 7
Respect for private and family life

Everyone has the right to respect for his or her private and family life, home and communications.

Article 8
Protection of personal data

1. Everyone has the right to the protection of personal data concerning him or her.
2. Such data must be processed fairly for specified purposes and on the basis of the consent of the person concerned or some other legitimate basis laid down by law. Everyone has the right of access to data which has been collected concerning him or her, and the right to have it rectified.
3. Compliance with these rules shall be subject to control by an independent authority.

Article 9
Right to marry and right to found a family

The right to marry and the right to found a family shall be guaranteed in accordance with the national laws governing the exercise of these rights.

Article 10
Freedom of thought, conscience and religion

1. Everyone has the right to freedom of thought, conscience and religion. This right includes freedom to change religion or belief and freedom, either alone or in community with others and in public or in private, to manifest religion or belief, in worship, teaching, practice and observance.

2. The right to conscientious objection is recognised, in accordance with the national laws governing the exercise of this right.

Article 11
Freedom of expression and information

1. Everyone has the right to freedom of expression. This right shall include freedom to hold opinions and to receive and impart information and ideas without interference by public authority and regardless of frontiers.
2. The freedom and pluralism of the media shall be respected.

Article 12
Freedom of assembly and of association

1. Everyone has the right to freedom of peaceful assembly and to freedom of association at all levels, in particular in political, trade union and civic matters, which implies the right of everyone to form and to join trade unions for the protection of his or her interests.
2. Political parties at Union level contribute to expressing the political will of the citizens of the Union.

Article 13
Freedom of the arts and sciences

The arts and scientific research shall be free of constraint. Academic freedom shall be respected.

Article 14
Right to education

1. Everyone has the right to education and to have access to vocational and continuing training.
2. This right includes the possibility to receive free compulsory education.
3. The freedom to found educational establishments with due respect for democratic principles and the right of parents to ensure the education and teaching of their children in conformity with their religious, philosophical and pedagogical convictions shall be respected, in accordance with the national laws governing the exercise of such freedom and right.

Article 15
Freedom to choose an occupation and right to engage in work

1. Everyone has the right to engage in work and to pursue a freely chosen or accepted occupation.
2. Every citizen of the Union has the freedom to seek employment, to work, to exercise the right of establishment and to provide services in any Member State.
3. Nationals of third countries who are authorised to work in the territories of the Member States are entitled to working conditions equivalent to those of citizens of the Union.

Article 16
Freedom to conduct a business

The freedom to conduct a business in accordance with Community law and national laws and practices is recognised.

Article 17
Right to property

1. Everyone has the right to own, use, dispose of and bequeath his or her lawfully acquired possessions. No one may be deprived of his or her possessions, except in the public interest and in the cases and under the conditions provided for by law, subject to fair compensation being paid in good time for their loss. The use of property may be regulated by law in so far as is necessary for the general interest.
2. Intellectual property shall be protected.

Article 18
Right to asylum

The right to asylum shall be guaranteed with due respect for the rules of the Geneva Convention of 28 July 1951 and the Protocol of 31 January 1967 relating to the status of refugees and in accordance with the Treaty establishing the European Community.

Article 19
Protection in the event of removal, expulsion or extradition

1. Collective expulsions are prohibited.
2. No one may be removed, expelled or extradited to a State where there is a serious risk that he or she would be subjected to the death penalty, torture or other inhuman or degrading treatment or punishment.

CHAPTER III
EQUALITY

Article 20
Equality before the law

Everyone is equal before the law.

Article 21
Non-discrimination

1. Any discrimination based on any ground such as sex, race, colour, ethnic or social origin, genetic features, language, religion or belief, political or any other opinion, membership of a national minority, property, birth, disability, age or sexual orientation shall be prohibited.
2. Within the scope of application of the Treaty establishing the European Community and of the Treaty on European Union, and without prejudice to the special provisions of those Treaties, any discrimination on grounds of nationality shall be prohibited.

Article 22
Cultural, religious and linguistic diversity

The Union shall respect cultural, religious and linguistic diversity.

Article 23
Equality between men and women

Equality between men and women must be ensured in all areas, including employment, work and pay. The principle of equality shall not prevent the maintenance or adoption of measures providing for specific advantages in favour of the under-represented sex.

Article 24
The rights of the child

1. Children shall have the right to such protection and care as is necessary for their well-being. They may express their views freely. Such views shall be taken into consideration on matters which concern them in accordance with their age and maturity.
2. In all actions relating to children, whether taken by public authorities or private institutions, the child's best interests must be a primary consideration.
3. Every child shall have the right to maintain on a regular basis a personal relationship and direct contact with both his or her parents, unless that is contrary to his or her interests.

Article 25
The rights of the elderly

The Union recognises and respects the rights of the elderly to lead a life of dignity and independence and to participate in social and cultural life.

Article 26
Integration of persons with disabilities

The Union recognises and respects the right of persons with disabilities to benefit from measures designed to ensure their independence, social and occupational integration and participation in the life of the community.

CHAPTER IV
SOLIDARITY

Article 27
Workers' right to information and consultation within the undertaking

Workers or their representatives must, at the appropriate levels, be guaranteed information and consultation in good time in the cases and under the conditions provided for by Community law and national laws and practices.

Article 28
Right of collective bargaining and action

Workers and employers, or their respective organisations, have, in accordance with Community law and national laws and practices, the right to negotiate and conclude collective agreements at the appropriate levels and, in cases of conflicts of interest, to take collective action to defend their interests, including strike action.

Article 29
Right of access to placement services

Everyone has the right of access to a free placement service.

Article 30
Protection in the event of unjustified dismissal

Every worker has the right to protection against unjustified dismissal, in accordance with Community law and national laws and practices.

Article 31
Fair and just working conditions

1. Every worker has the right to working conditions which respect his or her health, safety and dignity.
2. Every worker has the right to limitation of maximum working hours, to daily and weekly rest periods and to an annual period of paid leave.

Article 32
Prohibition of child labour and protection of young people at work

The employment of children is prohibited. The minimum age of admission to employment may not be lower than the minimum school-leaving age, without prejudice to such rules as may be more favourable to young people and except for limited derogations.

Young people admitted to work must have working conditions appropriate to their age and be protected against economic exploitation and any work likely to harm their safety, health or physical, mental, moral or social development or to interfere with their education.

Article 33
Family and professional life

1 The family shall enjoy legal, economic and social protection.
2. To reconcile family and professional life, everyone shall have the right to protection from dismissal for a reason connected with maternity and the right to paid maternity leave and to parental leave following the birth or adoption of a child.

Article 34
Social security and social assistance

1. The Union recognises and respects the entitlement to social security benefits and social services providing protection in cases such as maternity, illness, industrial accidents, dependency or old age, and in the case of loss of employment, in accordance with the rules laid down by Community law and national laws and practices.
2. Everyone residing and moving legally within the European Union is entitled to social security benefits and social advantages in accordance with Community law and national laws and practices.
3. In order to combat social exclusion and poverty, the Union recognises and respects the right to social and housing assistance so as to ensure a decent existence for all those who lack sufficient resources, in accordance with the rules laid down by Community law and national laws and practices.

Article 35
Health care

Everyone has the right of access to preventive health care and the right to benefit from medical treatment under the conditions established by national laws and practices. A high level of human health protection shall be ensured in the definition and implementation of all Union policies and activities.

Article 36
Access to services of general economic interest

The Union recognises and respects access to services of general economic interest as provided for in national laws and practices, in accordance with the Treaty establishing the European Community, in order to promote the social and territorial cohesion of the Union.

Article 37
Environmental protection

A high level of environmental protection and the improvement of the quality of the environment must be integrated into the policies of the Union and ensured in accordance with the principle of sustainable development.

Article 38
Consumer protection

Union policies shall ensure a high level of consumer protection.

CHAPTER V
CITIZENS' RIGHTS

Article 39
Right to vote and to stand as a candidate at elections to the European Parliament

1. Every citizen of the Union has the right to vote and to stand as a candidate at elections to the European Parliament in the Member State in which he or she resides, under the same conditions as nationals of that State.
2. Members of the European Parliament shall be elected by direct universal suffrage in a free and secret ballot.

Article 40
Right to vote and to stand as a candidate at municipal elections

Every citizen of the Union has the right to vote and to stand as a candidate at municipal elections in the Member State in which he or she resides under the same conditions as nationals of that State.

Article 41
Right to good administration

1. Every person has the right to have his or her affairs handled impartially, fairly and within a reasonable time by the institutions and bodies of the Union.
2. This right includes:
   —the right of every person to be heard, before any individual measure which would affect him or her adversely is taken;
   —the right of every person to have access to his or her file, while respecting the legitimate interests of confidentiality and of professional and business secrecy;
   —the obligation of the administration to give reasons for its decisions.
3. Every person has the right to have the Community make good any damage caused by its institutions or by its servants in the performance of their duties, in accordance with the general principles common to the laws of the Member States.
4. Every person may write to the institutions of the Union in one of the languages of the Treaties and must have an answer in the same language.

Article 42
Right of access to documents

Any citizen of the Union, and any natural or legal person residing or having its registered office in a Member State, has a right of access to European Parliament, Council and Commission documents.

Article 43
Ombudsman

Any citizen of the Union and any natural or legal person residing or having its registered office in a Member State has the right to refer to the Ombudsman of the Union cases of maladministration in the activities of the Community institutions or bodies, with the exception of the Court of Justice and the Court of First Instance acting in their judicial role.

Article 44
Right to petition

Any citizen of the Union and any natural or legal person residing or having its registered office in a Member State has the right to petition the European Parliament.

Article 45
Freedom of movement and of residence

1. Every citizen of the Union has the right to move and reside freely within the territory of the Member States.
2. Freedom of movement and residence may be granted, in accordance with the Treaty establishing the European Community, to nationals of third countries legally resident in the territory of a Member State.

Article 46
Diplomatic and consular protection

Every citizen of the Union shall, in the territory of a third country in which the Member State of which he or she is a national is not represented, be entitled to protection by the diplomatic or consular authorities of any Member State, on the same conditions as the nationals of that Member State.

CHAPTER VI
JUSTICE

Article 47
Right to an effective remedy and to a fair trial

Everyone whose rights and freedoms guaranteed by the law of the Union are violated has the right to an effective remedy before a tribunal in compliance with the conditions laid down in this Article. Everyone is entitled to a fair and public hearing within a reasonable time by an independent and impartial tribunal previously established by law. Everyone shall have the possibility of being advised, defended and represented.
Legal aid shall be made available to those who lack sufficient resources in so far as such aid is necessary to ensure effective access to justice.

Article 48
Presumption of innocence and right of defence

1. Everyone who has been charged shall be presumed innocent until proved guilty according to law.
2. Respect for the rights of the defence of anyone who has been charged shall be guaranteed.

Article 49
Principles of legality and proportionality of criminal offences and penalties

1. No one shall be held guilty of any criminal offence on account of any act or omission which did not constitute a criminal offence under national law or international law at the time when it was committed. Nor shall a heavier penalty be imposed than that which was applicable at the time the criminal offence was committed. If, subsequent to the commission of a criminal offence, the law provides for a lighter penalty, that penalty shall be applicable.
2. This Article shall not prejudice the trial and punishment of any person for any act or omission which, at the time when it was committed, was criminal according to the general principles recognised by the community of nations.
3. The severity of penalties must not be disproportionate to the criminal offence.

Article 50
Right not to be tried or punished twice in criminal proceedings
for the same criminal offence

No one shall be liable to be tried or punished again in criminal proceedings for an offence for which he or she has already been finally acquitted or convicted within the Union in accordance with the law.

CHAPTER VII
GENERAL PROVISIONS

Article 51
Scope

1. The provisions of this Charter are addressed to the institutions and bodies of the Union with due regard for the principle of subsidiarity and to the Member States only when they are implementing Union law. They shall therefore respect the rights, observe the principles and promote the application thereof in accordance with their respective powers.
2. This Charter does not establish any new power or task for the Community or the Union, or modify powers and tasks defined by the Treaties.

Article 52
Scope of guaranteed rights

1. Any limitation on the exercise of the rights and freedoms recognised by this Charter must be provided for by law and respect the essence of those rights and freedoms. Subject to the principle of proportionality, limitations may be made only if they are necessary and genuinely meet objectives of general interest recognised by the Union or the need to protect the rights and freedoms of others.
2. Rights recognised by this Charter which are based on the Community Treaties or the Treaty on European Union shall be exercised under the conditions and within the limits defined by those Treaties.
3. In so far as this Charter contains rights which correspond to rights guaranteed by the Convention for the Protection of Human Rights and Fundamental Freedoms, the meaning and scope of those rights shall be the same as those laid down by the said Convention. This provision shall not prevent Union law providing more extensive protection.

Article 53
Level of protection

Nothing in this Charter shall be interpreted as restricting or adversely affecting human rights and fundamental freedoms as recognised, in their respective fields of application, by Union law and international law and by international agreements to which the Union, the Community or all the Member States are party, including the European Convention for the Protection of Human Rights and Fundamental Freedoms, and by the Member States' constitutions.

Article 54
Prohibition of abuse of rights

Nothing in this Charter shall be interpreted as implying any right to engage in any activity or to perform any act aimed at the destruction of any of the rights and freedoms recognised in this Charter or at their limitation to a greater extent than is provided for herein.

Source: *Official Journal of the European Communities.*

2. US PRESIDENTIAL ELECTION: SUPREME COURT RULING

Published below are extracts from the December 12, 2000, Supreme Court ruling on the disputed Florida recount which effectively decided the outcome of the US presidential election between George W. Bush and Albert Gore.

GEORGE W. BUSH, et al., PETITIONERS v. ALBERT GORE, Jr., et al.
ON WRIT OF CERTIORARI TO THE FLORIDA SUPREME COURT

The petition presents the following questions: whether the Florida Supreme Court established new standards for resolving Presidential election contests, thereby violating Art.II, 1, ii of the United States Constitution and. . . whether the use of standardless manual recounts violates the Equal Protection and Due Process Clauses. With respect to the equal protection question, we find a violation of the Equal Protection Clause.

II

A

The closeness of this election, and the multitude of legal challenges which have followed in its wake, have brought into sharp focus a common, if heretofore unnoticed, phenomenon. Nationwide statistics reveal that an estimated 2% of ballots cast do not register a vote for President for whatever reason, including deliberately choosing no candidate at all or some voter error, such as voting for two candidates or insufficiently marking a ballot. . . In certifying election results, the votes eligible for inclusion in the certification are the votes meeting the properly established legal requirements.

This case has shown that punch card balloting machines can produce an unfortunate number of ballots which are not punched in a clean, complete way by the voter. After the current counting, it is likely legislative bodies nationwide will examine ways to improve the mechanisms and machinery for voting.

B

The individual citizen has no federal constitutional right to vote for electors for the President of the United States unless and until the state legislature chooses a statewide election as the means to implement its power to appoint members of the Electoral College. U.S. Const., Art. II, 1. . . . History has now favored the voter, and in each of the several States the citizens themselves vote for Presidential electors. When the state legislature vests the right to vote for President in its people, the right to vote as the legislature has prescribed is fundamental; and one source of its fundamental nature lies in the equal weight accorded to each vote and the equal dignity owed to each voter. The State, of course, after granting the franchise in the special context of Article II, can take back the power to appoint electors. . .

The right to vote is protected in more than the initial allocation of the franchise. Equal protection applies as well to the manner of its exercise. Having once granted the right to vote on equal terms, the State may not, by later arbitrary and disparate treatment, value one person's vote over that of another. . . It must be remembered that "the right of suffrage can be denied by a debasement or dilution of the weight of a citizen's vote just as effectively as by wholly prohibiting the free exercise of the franchise.

There is no difference between the two sides of the present controversy on these basic propositions. Respondents say that the very purpose of vindicating the right to vote justifies the recount procedures now at issue. The question before us, however, is whether the recount procedures the

Florida Supreme Court has adopted are consistent with its obligation to avoid arbitrary and disparate treatment of the members of its electorate.

Much of the controversy seems to revolve around ballot cards designed to be perforated by a stylus but which, either through error or deliberate omission, have not been perforated with sufficient precision for a machine to count them. In some cases a piece of the card-a chad-is hanging, say by two corners. In other cases there is no separation at all, just an indentation.

The Florida Supreme Court has ordered that the intent of the voter be discerned from such ballots. For purposes of resolving the equal protection challenge, it is not necessary to decide whether the Florida Supreme Court had the authority under the legislative scheme for resolving election disputes to define what a legal vote is and to mandate a manual recount implementing that definition. The recount mechanisms implemented in response to the decisions of the Florida Supreme Court do not satisfy the minimum requirement for non-arbitrary treatment of voters necessary to secure the fundamental right. Florida's basic command for the count of legally cast votes is to consider the "intent of the voter." . . . This is unobjectionable as an abstract proposition and a starting principle. The problem inheres in the absence of specific standards to ensure its equal application. The formulation of uniform rules to determine intent based on these recurring circumstances is practicable and, we conclude, necessary.

The law does not refrain from searching for the intent of the actor in a multitude of circumstances; and in some cases the general command to ascertain intent is not susceptible to much further refinement. In this instance, however, the question is not whether to believe a witness but how to interpret the marks or holes or scratches on an inanimate object, a piece of cardboard or paper which, it is said, might not have registered as a vote during the machine count. The factfinder confronts a thing, not a person. The search for intent can be confined by specific rules designed to ensure uniform treatment.

The want of those rules here has led to unequal evaluation of ballots in various respects. . . . The State Supreme Court ratified this uneven treatment. . . . The press of time does not diminish the constitutional concern. A desire for speed is not a general excuse for ignoring equal protection guarantees.

In addition to these difficulties the actual process by which the votes were to be counted under the Florida Supreme Court's decision raises further concerns. That order did not specify who would recount the ballots. The county canvassing boards were forced to pull together ad hoc teams comprised of judges from various Circuits who had no previous training in handling and interpreting ballots. Furthermore, while others were permitted to observe, they were prohibited from objecting during the recount.

The recount process, in its features here described, is inconsistent with the minimum procedures necessary to protect the fundamental right of each voter in the special instance of a statewide recount under the authority of a single state judicial officer. . .

When a court orders a statewide remedy, there must be at least some assurance that the rudimentary requirements of equal treatment and fundamental fairness are satisfied.

Upon due consideration of the difficulties identified to this point, it is obvious that the recount cannot be conducted in compliance with the requirements of equal protection and due process without substantial additional work. It would require not only the adoption (after opportunity for argument) of adequate statewide standards for determining what is a legal vote, and practicable procedures to implement them, but also orderly judicial review of any disputed matters that might arise. In addition, the Secretary of State has advised that the recount of only a portion of the ballots requires that the vote tabulation equipment be used to screen out undervotes, a function for which the machines were not designed. . .

Because it is evident that any recount seeking to meet the December 12 date will be unconstitutional for the reasons we have discussed, we reverse the judgment of the Supreme Court of Florida ordering a recount to proceed.

Seven Justices of the Court agree that there are constitutional problems with the recount ordered by the Florida Supreme Court that demand a remedy. . . The only disagreement is as to the remedy. . .

None are more conscious of the vital limits on judicial authority than are the members of this Court, and none stand more in admiration of the Constitution's design to leave the selection of the President to the people, through their legislatures, and to the political sphere. When contending parties invoke the process of the courts, however, it becomes our unsought responsibility to resolve the federal and constitutional issues the judicial system has been forced to confront.

The judgment of the Supreme Court of Florida is reversed, and the case is remanded for further proceedings not inconsistent with this opinion.

Chief Justice Rehnquist, with whom Justice Scalia and Justice Thomas join, concurring.

. . . Florida statutory law cannot reasonably be thought to *require* the counting of improperly marked ballots. Each Florida precinct before election day provides instructions on how properly to cast a vote, each polling place on election day contains a working model of the voting machine it uses, and each voting booth contains a sample ballot. In precincts using punch-card ballots, voters are instructed to punch out the ballot cleanly:

AFTER VOTING, CHECK YOUR BALLOT CARD TO BE SURE YOUR VOTING SELECTIONS ARE CLEARLY AND CLEANLY PUNCHED AND THERE ARE NO CHIPS LEFT HANGING ON THE BACK OF THE CARD.

. . . No reasonable person would call it "an error in the vote tabulation, or a "rejection of legal votes," when electronic or electromechanical equipment performs precisely in the manner designed, and fails to count those ballots that are not marked in the manner that these voting instructions explicitly and prominently specify.

. . . No one claims there was any fraud in the election. The Supreme Court of Florida ordered this additional recount under the provision of the election code giving the circuit judge the authority to provide relief that is "appropriate under such circumstances."

Surely when the Florida Legislature empowered the courts of the State to grant "appropriate" relief, it must have meant relief that would have become final by the cut-off date. . . In light of the inevitable legal challenges and ensuing appeals to the Supreme Court of Florida and petitions for certiorari to this Court, the entire recounting process could not possibly be completed by that date.

Given all these factors the remedy prescribed by the Supreme Court of Florida cannot be deemed an "appropriate" one as of December 8. It significantly departed from the statutory framework in place on November 7, and authorized open-ended further proceedings which could not be completed by December 12, thereby preventing a final determination by that date.

Justice Stevens, with whom Justice Ginsburg and Justice Breyer join, dissenting.

The Constitution assigns to the States the primary responsibility for determining the manner of selecting the Presidential electors. . . When questions arise about the meaning of state laws, including election laws, it is our settled practice to accept the opinions of the highest courts of the States as providing the final answers. On rare occasions, however, either federal statutes or the Federal Constitution may require federal judicial intervention in state elections. This is not such an occasion.

. . . we have never before called into question the substantive standard by which a State determines that a vote has been legally cast. . . As the majority explicitly holds, once a state legislature determines to select electors through a popular vote, the right to have one's vote counted is of constitutional stature. As the majority further acknowledges, Florida law holds that all ballots that reveal the intent of the voter constitute valid votes. Recognizing these principles, the majority nonetheless orders the termination of the contest proceeding before all such votes have been tabulated. Under their own reasoning, the appropriate course of action would be to remand to allow more specific procedures for implementing the legislature's uniform general standard to be established.

In the interest of finality, however, the majority effectively orders the disenfranchisement of an unknown number of voters whose ballots reveal their intent-and are therefore legal votes under state law-but were for some reason rejected by ballot-counting machines...

What must underlie petitioners' entire federal assault on the Florida election procedures is an unstated lack of confidence in the impartiality and capacity of the state judges who would make the critical decisions if the vote count were to proceed. Otherwise, their position is wholly without merit. The endorsement of that position by the majority of this Court can only lend credence to the most cynical appraisal of the work of judges throughout the land. It is confidence in the men and women who administer the judicial system that is the true backbone of the rule of law. Time will one day heal the wound to that confidence that will be inflicted by today's decision. One thing, however, is certain. Although we may never know with complete certainty the identity of the winner of this year's Presidential election, the identity of the loser is perfectly clear. It is the Nation's confidence in the judge as an impartial guardian of the rule of law.

I respectfully dissent.

Justice Souter, with whom Justice Breyer joins and with whom Justice Stevens and Justice Ginsburg partially join, dissenting.

The Court should not have reviewed either *Bush* v. *Palm Beach County Canvassing Bd.,* or this case, and should not have stopped Florida's attempt to recount all undervote ballots . . If this Court had allowed the State to follow the course indicated by the opinions of its own Supreme Court, it is entirely possible that there would ultimately have been no issue requiring our review, and political tension could have worked itself out in the Congress . . .

1. The statute does not define a "legal vote," the rejection of which may affect the election. The State Supreme Court was therefore required to define it, and in doing that the court looked to another election statute dealing with damaged or defective ballots, which contains a provision that no vote shall be disregarded "if there is a clear indication of the intent of the voter as determined by a canvassing board." The court read that objective of looking to the voter's intent as indicating that the legislature probably meant "legal vote" to mean a vote recorded on a ballot indicating what the voter intended.

2. The Florida court next interpreted "rejection" to determine what act in the counting process may be attacked in a contest. Again, the statute does not define the term. The court majority read the word to mean simply a failure to count. . . A different reading, of course, is possible. The majority might have concluded that "rejection" should refer to machine malfunction, or that a ballot should not be treated as "reject[ed]" in the absence of wrongdoing by election officials, lest contests be so easy to claim that every election will end up in one.

3. The same is true about the court majority's understanding of the phrase "votes sufficient to change or place in doubt" the result of the election in Florida. The court held that if the uncounted ballots were so numerous that it was reasonably possible that they contained enough "legal" votes to swing the election, this contest would be authorized by the statute.

In sum, the interpretations by the Florida court raise no substantial question under Article II. . . In deciding what to do about this, we should take account of the fact that electoral votes are due to be cast in six days. I would therefore remand the case to the courts of Florida with instructions to establish uniform standards for evaluating the several types of ballots that have prompted differing treatments, to be applied within and among counties when passing on such identical ballots in any further recounting (or successive recounting) that the courts might order.

Unlike the majority, I see no warrant for this Court to assume that Florida could not possibly comply with this requirement before the date set for the meeting of electors, December 18. . . .no showing has been made of legal overvotes uncounted, and counsel for Gore made an uncontradicted representation to the Court that the statewide total of undervotes is about 60,000. To recount these manually would be a tall order, but before this Court stayed the effort to do that the courts of Florida were ready to do their best to get that job done. There is no justification for denying the State the opportunity to try to count all disputed ballots now.

I respectfully dissent.

Justice Breyer, with whom Justice Stevens, Justice Ginsburg and Justice Souter partially join, dissenting.

The Court was wrong to take this case. It was wrong to grant a stay. It should now vacate that stay and permit the Florida Supreme Court to decide whether the recount should resume.

The political implications of this case for the country are momentous. But the federal legal questions presented, with one exception, are insubstantial. . . .there is no justification for the majority's remedy, which is simply to reverse the lower court and halt the recount entirely. An appropriate remedy would be, instead, to remand this case with instructions that, even at this late date, would permit the Florida Supreme Court to require recounting *all* undercounted votes in Florida, including those from Broward, Volusia, Palm Beach, and Miami-Dade Counties, whether or not previously recounted prior to the end of the protest period, and to do so in accordance with a single-uniform substandard.

The majority justifies stopping the recount entirely on the ground that there is no more time. In particular, the majority relies on the lack of time for the Secretary to review and approve equipment needed to separate undervotes. But the majority reaches this conclusion in the absence of *any* record evidence that the recount could not have been completed in the time allowed by the Florida Supreme Court. . .

By halting the manual recount, and thus ensuring that the uncounted legal votes will not be counted under any standard, this Court crafts a remedy out of proportion to the asserted harm. And that remedy harms the very fairness interests the Court is attempting to protect. The manual recount would itself redress a problem of unequal treatment of ballots. As Justice Stevens points out, the ballots of voters in counties that use punch-card systems are more likely to be disqualified than those in counties using optical-scanning systems. Thus, in a system that allows counties to use different types of voting systems, voters already arrive at the polls with an unequal chance that their votes will be counted. I do not see how the fact that this results from counties' selection of different voting machines rather than a court order makes the outcome any more fair. Nor do I understand why the Florida Supreme Court's recount order, which helps to redress this inequity, must be entirely prohibited based on a deficiency that could easily be remedied.

Despite the reminder that this case involves "an election for the President of the United States," no preeminent legal concern, or practical concern related to legal questions, required this Court to hear this case, let alone to issue a stay that stopped Florida's recount process in its tracks. . . Neither side claims electoral fraud, dishonesty, or the like. And the more fundamental equal protection claim might have been left to the state court to resolve if and when it was discovered to have mattered. It could still be resolved through a remand conditioned upon issuance of a uniform standard; it does not require reversing the Florida Supreme Court.

Of course, the selection of the President is of fundamental national importance. But that importance is political, not legal. And this Court should resist the temptation unnecessarily to resolve tangential legal disputes, where doing so threatens to determine the outcome of the election.

The Constitution and federal statutes themselves make clear that restraint is appropriate. They set forth a road map of how to resolve disputes about electors, even after an election as close as this one. That road map foresees resolution of electoral disputes by *state* courts. . . . the Twelfth Amendment commits to Congress the authority and responsibility to count electoral votes. A federal statute, the Electoral Count Act, enacted after the close 1876 Hayes-Tilden Presidential election, specifies that, after States have tried to resolve disputes (through "judicial" or other means), Congress is the body primarily authorized to resolve remaining disputes. The legislative history of the Act makes clear its intent to commit the power to resolve such disputes to Congress, rather than the courts . . . However awkward or difficult it may be for Congress to resolve difficult electoral disputes, Congress, being a political body, expresses the people's will far more accurately than does an unelected Court. And the people's will is what elections are about.

. . . I think it not only legally wrong, but also most unfortunate, for the Court simply to have terminated the Florida recount. . . .above all, in this highly politicized matter, the appearance of a split decision runs the risk of undermining the public's confidence in the Court itself. That confidence is a public treasure. It has been built slowly over many years, some of which were marked by a Civil War and the tragedy of segregation. It is a vitally necessary ingredient of any successful effort to protect basic liberty and, indeed, the rule of law itself. . . .we . . .risk a self-inflicted wound - a wound that may harm not just the Court, but the Nation.

I fear that in order to bring this agonizingly long election process to a definitive conclusion, we have not adequately attended to that necessary "check upon our own exercise of power," "our own sense of self-restraint.". . . Justice Brandeis once said of the Court, "The most important thing we do is not doing." . . .What it does today, the Court should have left undone. I would repair the damage done as best we now can, by permitting the Florida recount to continue under uniform standards.

I respectfully dissent.

Justice Ginsburg, with whom Justice Stevens joins, and with whom Justice Souter and Justice Breyer partially join, dissenting.

The Chief Justice acknowledges that provisions of Florida's Election Code "may well admit of more than one interpretation." But instead of respecting the state high court's province to say what the State's Election Code means, The Chief Justice maintains that Florida's Supreme Court has veered so far from the ordinary practice of judicial review that what it did cannot properly be called judging. My colleagues have offered a reasonable construction of Florida's law. . . I might join The Chief Justice were it my commission to interpret Florida law. But disagreement with the Florida court's interpretation of its own State's law does not warrant the conclusion that the justices of that court have legislated. There is no cause here to believe that the members of Florida's high court have done less than "their mortal best to discharge their oath of office,". . . and no cause to upset their reasoned interpretation of Florida law.

. . . As Justice Breyer convincingly explains, this case involves nothing close to the kind of recalcitrance by a state high court that warrants extraordinary action by this Court. The Florida Supreme Court concluded that counting every legal vote was the overriding concern of the Florida Legislature when it enacted the State's Election Code. The court surely should not be bracketed with state high courts of the Jim Crow South. . .

The extraordinary setting of this case has obscured the ordinary principle that dictates its proper resolution: Federal courts defer to state high courts' interpretations of their state's own law. This principle reflects the core of federalism, on which all agree. . . .The Chief Justice's solicitude for the Florida Legislature comes at the expense of the more fundamental solicitude we owe to the legislature's sovereign.

I agree with Justice Stevens that petitioners have not presented a substantial equal protection claim. Ideally, perfection would be the appropriate standard for judging the recount. But we live in an imperfect world, one in which thousands of votes have not been counted. I cannot agree that the recount adopted by the Florida court, flawed as it may be, would yield a result any less fair or precise than the certification that preceded that recount.

. . . But no one has doubted the good faith and diligence with which Florida election officials, attorneys for all sides of this controversy, and the courts of law have performed their duties. Notably, the Florida Supreme Court has produced two substantial opinions within 29 hours of oral argument. In sum, the Court's conclusion that a constitutionally adequate recount is impractical is a prophecy the Court's own judgment will not allow to be tested. Such an untested prophecy should not decide the Presidency of the United States.

I dissent.

3. UNITED KINGDOM LABOUR GOVERNMENT

(as at December 31 2000)

Members of the Cabinet

Prime Minister, First Lord of the Treasury and Minister for the Civil Service	Rt. Hon. Tony Blair, MP
Deputy Prime Minister and Secretary of State for the Environment, Transport and the Regions	Rt. Hon. John Prescott, MP
Lord Chancellor	Rt. Hon. The Lord Irvine of Lairg
Chancellor of the Exchequer	Rt. Hon. Gordon Brown, MP
Secretary of State for the Home Department	Rt. Hon. Jack Straw, MP
Secretary of State for Foreign and Commonwealth Affairs	Rt. Hon. Robin Cook, MP
Secretary of State for Trade and Industry	Rt. Hon. Stephen Byers, MP
President of the Council and Leader of the House of Commons	Rt. Hon. Margaret Beckett, MP
Lord Privy Seal, Leader of the House of Lords and Minister for Women	Rt. Hon. Baroness Jay of Paddington
Secretary of State for Education and Employment	Rt. Hon. David Blunkett, MP
Secretary of State for Social Security	Rt. Hon. Alistair Darling, MP
Secretary of State for Health	Rt. Hon. Alan Milburn, MP
Secretary of State for Defence	Rt. Hon. Geoff Hoon, MP
Secretary of State for Northern Ireland	Rt. Hon. Peter Mandelson, MP
Secretary of State for Scotland	Rt. Hon. John Reid, MP
Secretary of State for Wales	Rt. Hon. Paul Murphy, MP
Secretary of State for Culture, Media and Sport	Rt. Hon. Chris Smith, MP
Chief Secretary to the Treasury	Rt. Hon. Andrew Smith, MP
Minister of Agriculture, Fisheries and Food	Rt. Hon. Nick Brown, MP
Chancellor of the Duchy of Lancaster and Minister for the Cabinet	Rt. Hon. Marjorie (Mo) Mowlam, MP
Secretary of State for International Development	Rt. Hon. Clare Short, MP
Chief Whip	Rt. Hon. Ann Taylor, MP

Other Senior Ministers

Minister of State for Transport and Regions	Lord MacDonald of Tradeston
Financial Secretary to the Treasury	Stephen Timms, MP
Economic Secretary to the Treasury	Melanie Johnson, MP
Paymaster General	Dawn Primarolo, MP
Minister of State for the Environment	Michael Meacher, MP
Minister of State for Local Government and the Regions	Hilary Armstrong, MP
Minister of State for Housing, Planning and Construction	Nick Raynsford, MP
Minister of State for Foreign and Commonwealth Affairs	Peter Hain, MP
Minister of State for Foreign and Commonwealth Affairs	John Battle, MP
Minister of State for Foreign and Commonwealth Affairs	Keith Vaz, MP
Minister of State for Home Affairs	Paul Boateng, MP
Minister of State for Home Affairs	Charles Clarke, MP
Minister of State for Home Affairs	Barbara Roche, MP
Minister of State for Education and Employment	Tessa Jowell, MP
Minister of State for Education and Employment	Estelle Morris, MP
Minister of State for Education and Employment	Baroness Blackstone, MP
Minister of State for Energy and Competitiveness in Europe	Helen Liddell, MP
Minister of State for Trade	Richard Craborn, MP
Minister of State for Small Businesses and E-Commerce	Patricia Hewitt, MP

Minister of State for Agriculture, Fisheries and Food	Joyce Quin, MP
Minister of State for Agriculture, Fisheries and Food	Baroness Hayman
Minister of State for Defence Procurement	Baroness Symons of Vernham Dean
Minister of State for the Armed Forces	John Spellar, MP
Minister of State for Health	John Denham, MP
Minister of State for Health	John Hutton, MP
Minister of State for Social Security	Jeff Rooker, MP
Minister of State for Scotland	Brian Wilson, MP
Minister of State for Northern Ireland	Adam Ingram, MP
Minister of State in the Cabinet Office	Lord Falconer of Thoroton
Minister of State in the Cabinet Office	Ian McCartney, MP

Law Officers

Attorney General	Lord Williams of Mostyn
Solicitor General	Ross Cranston, MP

4. UNITED STATES DEMOCRATIC ADMINISTRATION

(as at 31 December 2000)

Members of the Cabinet

President	Bill Clinton
Vice President	Al Gore
Secretary of State	Madeleine K. Albright
Secretary of the Treasury	Lawrence Summers
Secretary of Defence	William S. Cohen
Secretary of the Interior	Bruce Babbitt
Secretary of Agriculture	Dan Glickman
Secretary of Commerce	(vacant)
Secretary of Housing and Development	Andrew M. Cuomo
Secretary of Transportation	Rodney E. Slater
Secretary of Health and Human Services	Donna E. Shalala
Attorney General	Janet Reno
Secretary of Labour	Alexis M. Herman
Secretary of Energy	Bill Richardson
Secretary of Education	Richard W. Riley
Secretary of Veterans' Affairs	Togo D. West

Other Leading Executive Branch Officials

White House Chief of Staff	John Podesta
Director of Office of Management & Budget	Jacob J. Lew
Chairman of Council of Economic Advisers	Martin N. Bailey
National Security Adviser	Samuel D. Berger
Head of Environmental Protection Agency	Carol Browner
Director of Central Intelligence Agency	George Tenet
Representative for Trade Negotiations	Charlene Barshefsky
Ambassador to United Nations	Richard C. Holbrooke
Director of National Economic Council	Gene Sperling
Director of Small Business Administration	Aida Alvarez

5. INTERNATIONAL COMPARISONS: POPULATION, GDP AND GROWTH

The following table gives population, gross domestic product (GDP) and growth data for the main member states of the Organization for Economic Co-operation and Development plus selected other countries. (Source: World Bank, Washington)

	Population 1999mn	Avg. annual % growth 1990-99	GDP ($000mn) 1998	GDP ($000mn) 1999	GDP growth % 1999	Avg. annual % growth 1990-99
Algeria	30.5	2.2	49.6	47.0	-5.2	1.6
Argentina	36.6	1.3	344.4	281.9	-18.1	4.9
Australia	19.0	1.2	364.2	389.7	7.0	3.8
Austria	8.1	0.5	212.1	208.9	-1.5	2.0
Bangladesh	127.7	1.6	42.8	45.8	7.0	4.8
Belgium	10.2	0.3	247.1	245.7	-0.6	1.7
Brazil	168.1	1.4	778.3	760.3	-2.3	2.9
Canada	30.6	1.1	598.9	612.0	2.2	2.3
Chile	15.0	1.5	78.0	71.1	-8.8	7.2
China	1,249.7	1.1	960.9	991.2	3.2	10.7
Colombia	41.5	1.9	91.1	88.6	-2.7	3.3
Denmark	5.3	0.4	174.3	174.4	0.1	2.8
Egypt	62.4	1.9	78.1	92.4	18.3	4.4
Finland	5.2	0.4	125.7	126.1	0.3	2.5
France	59.1	0.5	1,432.9	1,410.3	-1.6	1.7
Germany	82.0	0.4	2,142.0	2,081.2	-2.8	1.5*
Greece	10.5	0.4	120.3	123.9	3.0	1.9
Hungary	10.1	-0.3	47.8	48.4	1.3	1.0
India	997.5	1.8	383.4	459.8	19.9	6.1
Indonesia	207.0	1.7	96.3	141.0	46.4	4.7
Irish Republic	3.7	0.7	80.9	84.9	4.9	7.9
Israel	6.1	3.0	100.0	99.1	-0.9	5.1
Italy	57.6	0.2	1,171.0	1,150.0	-1.8	1.2
Japan	126.6	0.3	3,783.1	4,395.1	16.2	1.4
Kenya	30.0	2.7	11.1	10.6	-4.5	2.2
South Korea	46.8	1.0	297.9	406.9	36.6	5.7
Malaysia	22.7	2.5	71.3	74.6	4.6	6.3
Mexico	97.4	1.8	393.2	475.0	20.8	2.7
Netherlands	15.8	0.6	382.5	384.8	0.6	2.7
New Zealand	3.8	1.2	54.1	53.6	-0.9	2.9
Nigeria	123.9	2.8	41.4	43.3	4.6	2.4
Norway	4.5	0.5	145.9	145.4	-0.3	3.7
Pakistan	134.8	2.5	63.9	59.9	-6.3	4.0
Philippines	76.8	2.3	65.1	75.4	15.8	3.2
Poland	38.7	0.2	148.9	154.1	3.5	4.7
Portugal	10.0	0.1	106.7	107.7	0.9	2.5
Russia	146.5	-0.1	276.6	375.3	35.7	-6.1
Singapore	3.2	1.9	85.4	84.9	-0.6	8.0
South Africa	42.1	2.0	116.7	131.1	12.3	1.9
Spain	39.4	0.2	551.9	562.2	1.9	2.2
Sweden	8.9	0.4	225.0	226.4	0.6	1.5
Switzerland	7.1	0.7	264.4	260.3	-1.6	0.5
Thailand	61.7	1.2	111.3	123.9	11.3	4.7
Turkey	64.4	1.5	198.8	188.4	-5.2	4.1
United Kingdom	59.1	0.3	1,357.4	1,373.6	1.2	2.2
USA	272.9	1.0	8,210.6	8,708.9	6.1	3.4
Venezuela	23.7	2.2	105.8	103.9	-1.8	1.7

*Estimated

XVIII OBITUARY

Adamson, Sir Campbell (b. 1922), Director-General of the Confederation of British Industry during the turbulent years of industrial relations in the 1970s. Born in Perth and educated at Rugby and Corpus Christi College, Cambridge, Adamson worked with steelmakers in South Wales for more than 20 years. He was seconded to the Department of Economic Affairs in 1967 for a two-year stint, after which he was invited to take charge of the CBI. He was instantly involved in the industrial problems of strikes and the three-day week, constantly being seen on television and having his comments reported in the press. These included some remarks—which he had not expected to be picked up—made at a debate held two days before the 1974 general election, when he appeared to criticise the Industrial Relations Act, a key part of Prime Minister Edward Heath's economic policy. Adamson, accused of contributing to the Conservative Party's narrow defeat, offered his resignation, which was refused, but it was some time before he was able to regain his members' confidence. After his retirement from the CBI in 1976, when he was knighted, he took on a number of directorships and, in 1978, became chairman of Abbey National. During his time there he masterminded the building society's transition into a bank, setting a trend followed by other mutual societies. He retired in 1991. Died August 21

al-Assad, Hafez (b. 1930), President of Syria, was a ruthless ruler of his country whose influence extended throughout the Middle East and beyond, first by linking his country with the Soviet Union and later by adopting policies that seemed to point towards the prospect of peace with Israel. Born to the small minority Alawite sect, Assad made an early career for himself in the armed forces, training in the Soviet Union and Egypt, and rising by 1965 to command the Syrian Air Force. In the following year he became Defence Minister in General Salah Jadid's government, and in 1970, at the age of 40, seized power when Syrian tanks, sent into Jordan to support a Palestinian uprising, were forced out (Assad having withheld the air force from the operation). Once in power Assad maintained his control in Syria by the harshest of methods. In foreign affairs one of his first acts was to join with Egypt to launch the Yom Kippur War of 1973, when Israel was taken by surprise, but the terms of disengagement, and the subsequent efforts of the Egyptian President to make peace, led to the collapse of relations between Egypt and Syria. Assad became preoccupied with Lebanon when civil war broke out there, and in 1976 sent in Syrian troops to maintain some sort of order by helping first one side and then the other with as much force as was necessary. But, as Israel became more involved in Lebanon, Assad and his radical Palestinian allies adopted more direct methods against both Israel and the Western powers. In 1986 Syrian intelligence agents in London were involved in a plot to blow up an El Al airliner, an incident that prompted Britain to break off diplomatic relations. International pressure on Syria grew following the collapse of the Soviet Union, a change that Assad recognised when he agreed to send a token force to join the operation to expel Iraqi troops from Kuwait. The resumption of peace negotiations with Israel and the withdrawal of Israel from southern Lebanon shortly before his death also added to Assad's reputation as a peacemaker in the Middle East. Died June 10

Albert, Carl (b. 1908), Speaker of the US House of Representatives 1971-76 who, because of his office, twice found himself standing in as Vice President. The first occasion was in 1973 when Spiro Agnew had to resign after being found guilty of tax evasion and there was a gap before Gerald Ford was sworn in as his successor. The second was when Richard Nixon resigned the presidency in the following year and there was another pause before Nelson Rockefeller was confirmed as Ford's Vice President. The prospect of Albert being only a heartbeat away from the presidency caused concern to many Americans, for although he was well liked he was not generally regarded as having the necessary strength to run the country. Born in Oklahoma, Albert read law at the University of Oklahoma and, as a Rhodes scholar, at Oxford. He practised law in Oklahoma in the 1930s, but after serving in the army during the war took up politics, being elected to Congress in 1947. He was appointed assistant Democratic leader in 1955, becoming Majority Leader when Sam Rayburn died in 1961 and succeeding John McCormack as Speaker in 1971. In the office he tended to exert his influence behind the scenes. He retired from Congress in 1975. Died February 4

Amichai, Yehuda (b. 1924), Israeli poet who chronicled the hopes and fears of his adopted country. Born Yehuda Pfeuffer in Wurzburg, Germany, he fled with his family at the age of 11 to Palestine, settling in Jerusalem. During the war he joined the British Army's Jewish brigade and later enrolled in the Palmach, the Zionist force, fighting in the War of Independence in 1948 and again in the battles of 1956 and 1973. After the 1948 war he studied Hebrew literature before teaching in secondary schools, in the university and at a number of overseas colleges and institutions. All the while he was writing and publishing poetry as well as writing plays, novels, short stories and children's books. He wrote 13 books of poetry in Hebrew, much of his work being translated into some 30 languages and most of it preoccupied with the strain of living in a land where "last things are expected". He saw himself as one of a generation of new Jews who invented the nation but had doubts about what had subsequently been done in its name. He was awarded the Israel prize for literature in 1982, given an honorary degree at Oxford University and nominated for the Nobel prize. Died September 22

Annan, Lord (Noel), OBE (b. 1916), influential academic, university administrator, author, committee man and pillar of the post-war British Establishment. Educated at Stowe and King's College, Cambridge, Annan served in the military intelligence division of the Army during the war before returning to King's as a Fellow and university lecturer in politics. His first book, *Leslie Stephen: his thought and character in relation to his time*, published in 1951, won the James Tait Black Memorial Prize. At the age of 39 he was elected Provost of King's, and henceforth his life became more administrative. At King's and at the university, and gradually in the wider academic world, he took the lead in working for reforms in education, serving on (and usually chairing) committees on, amongst other topics, university structure, the relationship between university and college teaching, the teaching of Russian in schools, and on the setting up of new universities. He was also a Fellow of Eton, a Governor of Stowe and of Queen Mary College, London, a Trustee of the British Museum, of Churchill College, Cambridge, and of the National Gallery. In 1965 he was created a Life Peer, and in the following year was elected Provost of University College, London. In 1970 he was appointed by Harold Wilson to chair a committee on the future of broadcasting. In 1978 he became the University of London's first Vice-Chancellor, but it was not until he retired in 1981 that he was able to resume writing books. These included *Our Age: Portrait of a Generation*, published in 1990, a hard-hitting account of how many of his generation had failed to fulfil their liberal ideals and ambitions. Died February 21

Bandaranaike, Sirimavo (b. 1914), was three times Prime Minister of Sri Lanka (or Ceylon as it was known until 1972), having become the world's first woman head of government in 1960. Born at Ratnapura, Sirimavo Ratwatte was educated at a Roman Catholic convent, although she remained a Buddhist all her life. As a young woman she was more concerned with social work than politics, even after her marriage to Solomon Bandaranaike in 1940, when he was deeply embroiled in the political activity culminating in Ceylon's independence from Britain in 1948. She remained in the background even after he became Prime Minister eight years later, only involving herself in politics when he was assassinated in 1959. She became president of her husband's Sri Lanka Freedom Party in 1960, and in the general election in July that year led the party to victory. As Prime Minister she followed many of her husband's radical policies, nationalising denominational schools and undertaking to establish the country as a republic and to make Sinhalese its official language in place of English—a promise that angered the minority Tamil population. She was defeated in the 1965 election but returned to power in 1970. An attempt to overthrow her by force was rigorously put down, and Bandaranaike proceeded to create a new republican constitution, with a nominated President replacing the Queen as Head of State, and to change the island's name from Ceylon to Sri Lanka. She also took the opportunity to extend her term of office by two years, finally paying the price in 1977 when her party was defeated and she was found guilty of having abused power whilst in office. She was deprived of all civil rights for six years. Her daughter Chandrika took over the leadership of the SLFP in 1993, and, when elected President in the following year, appointed her mother Prime Minister, which had become a largely ceremonial post. Sirimano Bandaranaike gave up office for the last time in August 2000. Died October 10

Bourguiba, Habib Ben Ali (b. 1903), President of Tunisia for 30 years, led his country to independence in 1956. Born in Monastir, he studied at Sadiqi College in Tunisia, then went to Paris to study law, returning to his own country to take up politics as a nationalist. He first joined the Destour party but later broke away to form a party of his own, the Neo-Destour, and campaigned for full independence from France. He attracted a considerable following but upset the French authorities, who banned the party and imprisoned its leader. On his release in 1936 Bourguiba resumed his campaigning and was again arrested and sent to prison in Marseilles. He was released by the Germans in 1942 and returned to Tunisia. He travelled widely after the war to draw international attention to his campaign for independence, but was again imprisoned after organising an appeal to the United Nations, until in 1955 the French government decided to grant internal autonomy for Tunisia. Bourguiba returned to Tunis as Prime Minister and was elected President when the monarchy was abolished in 1957. He was quick to restore relations with the French government, but found it more difficult to get along with other Arab countries following his early insistence that recognition of Israel was an essential step towards the restoration of occupied Arab territory. At home Bourguiba established a prosperous secular state, relaxing many of the restrictions common to other Arab countries, but he brooked no serious opposition. His Prime Minister in 1986, Mohammed Mzali, was dismissed shortly after being confirmed by the party as Bourguiba's successor-designate. By now Bourguiba was plainly losing his faculties and in 1987, when he determined to arrange the mass execution of Islamic militants, he was deposed on the grounds of senility. For the remainder of his life he lived quietly in his palace at Carthage. Died April 6

Bradbury, Professor Sir Malcolm, CBE (b. 1932), English novelist and critic who contrived successfully to stimulate creativity in others by setting up a writing course at the University of East Anglia. Born in Sheffield, he was educated at West Bridgford Grammar School in Nottingham and at University College, Leicester, then at Queen Mary's College, London, at Indiana University and at Manchester University, where he gained a doctorate in American studies in 1963. He lectured in English Language and Literature at Birmingham University from 1961 to 1963 before moving to the University of East Anglia in Norwich, where he taught English and American studies. The Creative Writing Course was established there in 1970 with the novelist Angus Wilson. Both men had experienced writing courses in America and hoped that something similar might help British writers. It was not an instant success but its only pupil in the first year, Ian McEwan, quickly made his mark, and others who followed in the next decade included Rose Tremain and Kazuo Ishiguro. When Ishiguro won the Booker prize the course became very popular, but as Bradbury pointed out to those who saw it as a fast track to success, of the 200 writers he taught only 60 were published. Bradbury's teaching, broadcasting, scriptwriting and other activities inevitably impinged on his own output as a novelist. His first, *Eating People is Wrong*, was published in 1959 and his second, *Stepping Westward*, in 1965. Both were satires on the academic world, as was his third and most popular, *The History Man*, which recounted the adventures of Howard Kirk, a radical lecturer of the 1960s. Although *Rates of Exchange*, published in 1983, was short-listed for the Booker, and was followed by *Cuts: a very short novel* (1987) and *Dr Criminale* (1992), by common consent *The History Man* was his finest work. Bradbury was appointed CBE in 1991 and knighted in 2000. Died September 7

Budge, Don (b. 1915), American tennis player who became the first to achieve the grand slam of four world titles in the same year when, in 1938, he won the Australian, French, Wimbledon and US championships. Born in Oakland, California, the son of a Glasgow Rangers footballer who emigrated from Wick, in northern Scotland, Budge first showed his potential by winning the California boys' championship in 1930 and, four years later, by taking Fred Perry to five sets in the Pacific Coast championship. In 1935 he met Perry again, losing to him in the Wimbledon semi-finals and in the final of the US Open. When Perry turned professional Budge took over his amateur crown, winning 14 tournaments in a row including the 1937 Wimbledon title, in which he beat the German Gottfried von Cramm in straight sets. He met von Cramm again a few days later, also at Wimbledon, in a Davis Cup match which was tied at 2-2. He later recalled that as the two players were due to go on court von Cramm was called to the telephone to speak to Hitler. He heard von Cramm say "Ja, mein Fuhrer" before coming on court to play every point as if his life depended on it. Von Cramm won the first two sets and saved five match points in the fifth before Budge finally beat him 8-6. In 1938, when Budge won the grand slam, he went through Wimbledon without losing a set, also winning the doubles with his friend Gene Mako and the mixed doubles with Alice Marble. After his success in 1938 he turned professional and had the satisfaction of beating Perry. During service with the US Army in the World War II he injured his right shoulder, which effectively brought his tennis career to a close. Died January 26

Cartland, Dame Barbara (b. 1901), English romantic novelist who wrote more than 700 books during a career that lasted from her early twenties until shortly before she died at the age of 98. Born in Birmingham and educated at Worcester High School, Malvern and at a finishing school called Netley Abbey, to a family that was neither wealthy nor aristocratic, Barbara was nonetheless able to enjoy the London season, "coming out" and becoming fascinated by London society. She began writing gossip paragraphs and articles for the *Daily Express* and in doing so attracted the attention of its proprietor, Lord Beaverbrook, who introduced her to many politicians and other leading figures of the day as well as teaching her to write in the paper's staccato style, which she later adapted for her novels. The first of these, *Jigsaw*, was published in 1923, but it was some time before she settled on the formula which enabled her to produce up to 20 novels a year, usually historical romances with a Cinderella theme, all with a strong love interest and all ending happily. In addition to her fecund literary output Cartland had energy left for other activities, many of them on behalf of charities. She also ran a farm, was a county councillor in Hertfordshire, a popular lecturer, and spent much time in developing and projecting a unique personality and appearance, which was dominated by marshmallow pink. Died May 21

Chaban-Delmas, Jacques (b. 1905), reforming Prime Minister of France, three times President of the National Assembly, mayor of Bordeaux for nearly 50 years, and a wartime hero of the Resistance. He was also a keen sportsman, winning a number of tennis tournaments and playing rugby for his country in 1945. Born in Paris as Jacques Delmas (the name Chaban was used in the Resistance and adopted after the war) and educated mainly at the Lycee Lakanal, he started work as a journalist until he was called up in 1938. He joined the Resistance when the Germans entered Paris, and was brought into de Gaulle's provisional government in 1943. He played an active role in ensuring that the Allied troops reached Paris before the Communists could take control, meeting de Gaulle for the first time when he joined the Free French leader on his triumphant walk down the Champs Elysees in 1944. He went to Bordeaux where he was elected a deputy in 1946 and mayor in 1947, a post he held until his retirement in 1997. During the Fourth Republic he became Minister of Public Works under Pierre Mendez-France, but aroused some distrust in de Gaulle by standing for, and winning, the presidency of the National Assembly in 1949 against de Gaulle's own choice. He was left in that post, and given no ministerial experience, when de Gaulle was back in power between 1958 and 1969, but was appointed Prime Minister by President Georges Pompidou in 1969. It was a popular appointment and Chaban-Delmas responded by quickly introducing his plans for a reforming administration to create what he called a generous free society and less centralised bureaucracy, but met with resistance from the conservative majority. When it was revealed in 1972 that he had not paid any tax for four years (quite legally, as it turned out) he was quickly pushed into resigning. In 1974, following the death of Pompidou, he declared his candidacy for the presidency but was decisively beaten in the first round by Valery Giscard d'Estaing. Although he became president of the National Assembly for two more periods, from 1978-81 and 1986-88, he devoted most of his political activity to Bordeaux and no longer seemed a national leader in waiting. Died November 10

Coggan, The Right Rev Lord (Donald), PC (b. 1909), Archbishop of Canterbury and Primate of All England from 1974 to 1980, committed himself to Church unity and was disappointed that he was not able to achieve more. An Evangelical, he was a good communicator, much in demand as a preacher and author, and was chairman of the committee responsible for the translation of the New English Bible and the Revised English Bible. Coggan was born in London and educated at Merchant Taylor's School and St John's College, Cambridge. His first job was as assistant lecturer in Semitic Languages and Literature at Manchester University, where he worked for three years before becoming ordained, when he was appointed curate at St Mary's, Islington. In 1937 he moved to Canada as Professor of New Testament and Dean of Residence at Wycliffe College, Toronto, where he developed his skills as a speaker, writer and broadcaster. He returned to England in 1944 as Principal of the London College of Divinity, then housed in temporary accommodation but which he re-established in Northwood as one of the country's leading theological colleges. In 1956 he was appointed Bishop of Bradford, a post he took up with great energy, visiting parishes, organising the building of new churches, diocesan offices and a retreat centre, while at the same time chairing the newly-formed Liturgical Commission and touring the world as vice-president of the United Bible Societies. In 1963, when Michael Ramsey became Archbishop of Canterbury, Coggan was appointed to succeed him as Archbishop of York, a post which he tackled with equal energy and enthusiasm, supervising a well-run diocese and launching many new initiatives including the "Call to the North" campaign, but also taking on many overseas commitments which tended to lessen his impact at home. When he succeeded to

Canterbury, on Ramsey's retirement in 1974, it was known that he would have little more than five years before retirement, and he modestly described himself as a caretaker in the post. But he lost no time in making his presence felt, speaking out on moral issues and issuing a "Call to the Nation" and a nationwide initiative in Evangelism. The campaign failed to have the impact intended, partly because it was launched without much consultation within the Church, although it did inspire many letters from people who were concerned about the future and nostalgic for old values. Although the Archbishop was recognised and widely respected for his own spiritual values, he was also criticised for naivety in public affairs. On a visit to Rome he suggested, without prior warning to the Vatican, that immediate intercommunion should be established between Anglicans and Roman Catholics, and he was frustrated by his failure to achieve unity between the Church of England and the Methodists, again perhaps because the ground had not been sufficiently prepared. After his retirement Coggan became chairman of the executive of the Council of Christians and Jews. Died May 17

Comfort, Dr Alex (b. 1920), poet, novelist, biochemist, and anarchist, but best known for one book, *The Joy of Sex*, which he wrote with his wife in two weeks, and which sold more than 12 million copies in many languages. Born in London and educated at Highgate School and Trinity College, Cambridge, he trained in medicine at the London Hospital, having published a book of poetry at the age of 17. During the war, when he was a conscientious objector, he continued to write poetry, some of it critical of the war effort and the patriotism that sustained it, as well as a few not very successful novels. He continued with medical and scientific research, becoming after the war honorary research associate in the department of zoology at University College, London, and director of the Medical Research Council's Group on Ageing, producing a book, *The Biology of Senescence*, which became a textbook on the subject. He also taught psychology at the London Hospital. In the 1960s he joined the anti-nuclear Committee and was sentenced to one month in prison. His interest in sex was often revealed in his poetry, but he also wrote some early books on the subject, including *Barbarism and Sexual Freedom* (1948), *Sexual Behaviour in Society* (1950), *Sex and Society* (1963) and *The Anxiety Makers* (1967), which took a critical view of the medical profession for creating anxiety about bodily functions. His life was transformed when *The Joy of Sex* was published in 1973. Sub-titled A Gourmet Guide, the book was intended, Comfort said, to show that sex could be fun, and it became a standard work in what was then being described as the permissive society. It was followed by *More Joy of Sex* (1974), *The New Joy of Sex* (1991) and *A Gourmet Guide to Lovemaking* (1994), the later books including cautionary words about the dangers of promiscuous sex. In 1974 Comfort became a lecturer at the Department of Psychiatry in Stanford University, California, and from 1980 a professor at the Neuropsychiatric Institute at the University of California. He suffered a stroke in 1990, and retired to a nursing home in London. Died March 26

Cowdrey, Lord (Colin), CBE (b. 1932), cricketer who captained England and his county, Kent, played in 114 Test matches for England, and scored 7,624 runs including 22 centuries. After his retirement he became an administrator and was created a life peer for services to the game. Born in Bangalore, he was given the initials MCC by his father in the hope that he would become a cricketer, an ambition that was soon fulfilled. Educated at Tonbridge (where he was in the first team for five years) and at Brasenose, Oxford, where he captained the university team in 1954 and was chosen to tour for the England team against Australia. In the third Test, at Melbourne, Cowdrey, then 22, scored 102 after England had been reduced to 41 for 4 by the fast bowling of Ray Lindwall and Keith Miller (Len Hutton, Bill Edrich, Peter May and Denis Compton all being back in the pavilion). From then on Cowdrey was a regular member of the England team for more than a decade, taking part in a memorable record stand of 411 with May in 1957 against the West Indies and scoring runs in an elegant if sometimes introspective way wherever he went. Although he captained Kent for a match at the age of 20, and was the county's regular captain from 1957 to 1971, he was only an occasional captain of the England team, initially standing in for May in 1961, when he led England to victory against South Africa, but losing out to Ted Dexter when May retired in 1962. He led England again in 1967 in the tour against the West Indies (winning the series), against Australia in the following year (when England failed to regain the Ashes), and against Pakistan that winter (when the tour was abandoned after riots disrupted the first three Tests). In 1969 Cowdrey was injured and he did not captain England again. By the time of his retirement in 1975 he had scored 42,719 first-class runs, including 107 centuries, at an average of 42, had taken 65 wickets and 638 catches (120 of them for England). After working for some years for Barclays Bank he devoted himself to reorganising, strengthening and acting as a mediator for the International Cricket Council, work for which he was knighted in 1992. Died December 4

Craxi, Bettino (b. 1934), Italy's first Socialist, and longest-serving, Prime Minister, but whose political career ended in a maze of corruption. Born in Milan he first studied law but soon abandoned that to pursue a career in politics. He joined the Socialist Youth Movement and in 1968 entered Parliament as one of the delegates for Milan. After the 1976 election, in which the Socialists did badly, he took over as general secretary of the party and began to distance it from the Communists, abandoning earlier policies of nationalisation and replacing its symbol of hammer and sickle with a red carnation. After the 1979 election, in which the Socialists won less than 10 per cent of the vote, Craxi was asked to form a government but failed to assemble a workable coalition. He was able to play a key role in toppling successive administrations, finally withdrawing support for the coalition led by Amintore Fanfani in 1983. In the subsequent election the Socialists won only 11 per cent of the vote, but Craxi this time was able to form a coalition with the Christian Democrats, Social Democrats and others, and was so successful in maintaining it that he stayed in power for nearly four years, winning a second term at the election of 1985. His coalition fell apart in 1986, when the Christian Democrats pulled out, but they agreed to continue their support after Craxi promised to hand over to them in the following year, which he did. During his term of office Italy enjoyed unusual political stability and a period of fast economic growth, but it was later revealed that much of this prosperity was based on systematic bribery in which Craxi himself was deeply involved. He resigned the party leadership in 1993. In the following year he fled to Tunisia and was sentenced in his absence to imprisonment on charges of illegal party financing and for bribery and corruption in the construction of the Milan Metro. He continued to protest his innocence, and to hope that he might return to Italy, until his death. Died January 19

Day, Sir Robin (b. 1923), television journalist who developed a style of polite but firmly persistent questioning that permanently changed the pattern of political interviewing. He also became better known, and more of a personality, than most of those he interrogated. Educated first at Bembridge School on the Isle of Wight, he then served with the Royal Artillery towards the end of the war before going on to St Edmund Hall, Oxford, where he read law. He was President of the Oxford Union in 1950, and was called to the Bar by the Middle Temple. He did not enjoy the law and left for the USA, where he took a job with the British Information Service in Washington. When he returned to the UK a year later he had a temporary job with the BBC before answering an advertisement for a newscaster on the newly-formed Independent Television News. He made a success of it, reporting as well as delivering the news and conducting studio and outside interviews, flying to Cairo in 1957, soon after Suez crisis, to interview Colonel Nasser. In the 1959 general election Day stood as Liberal candidate, but was defeated and did not make any further attempt to enter Parliament. He then joined the BBC current affairs department, working for Panorama and taking over as anchorman after the death of Richard Dimbleby. He left the programme in 1972, and although he continued to do political interviews, and was always brought into election programmes, he had no regular outlet until he took over as presenter of the Radio 4 World at One and chairman of the BBC television Question Time programme, where he remained for 10 years. During this time he also sought to move into other areas of responsibility, first as director-general of the IBA and then as director-general of the BBC, but failed to land either post. He turned to writing his memoirs. *Day by Day* was published in 1975 and *Grand Inquisitor* in 1989. He also campaigned for the televising of Parliamentary proceedings. He was knighted in 1981. Died August 6

Deutsch, Andre, CBE (b. 1917), publisher who turned down George Orwell's *Animal Farm* but went on to create his own firm with a distinguished list of authors. Born in Hungary, Deutsch came to the UK in 1939, aged 21, and worked first as a bird-scarer and then in a London hotel until Hungary entered the war in 1941, when he was interned on the Isle of Man. Whilst there he was given an introduction to the publishers Nicolson & Watson, where he subsequently learnt his trade, supplementing his income by writing reviews for *Tribune*, where Orwell worked as literary editor. Orwell at that time could not find a publisher for *Animal Farm*, and when Nicolson & Watson also turned it down (against Deutsch's advice) suggested that Deutsch set up his own company to publish it. Deutsch felt he could not take such a risk, but determined to become his own master as soon as he could. In 1945 he set up on his own, taking the name of Allan Wingate and launching the firm with *Operation Cicero* and then finding Norman Mailer's *The Naked and the Dead*, which many publishers had turned down because of its strong language. Deutsch went on to add other American novelists to his list, including Philip Roth and John Updike, but after five years he left to start up again under his own name. Amongst authors added to the list were Laurie Lee, Roy Fuller, Mordecai Richler and George Mikes, the latter being a fellow Hungarian whose *How to be an Alien* became one of the firm's best sellers. As the publishing world changed, with an increase of mergers and takeovers, Deutsch strived to retain his independence, but in 1984 sold a 50 per cent share to Tom Rosenthal, who later exercised an option to buy the rest of the shares. Deutsch left in 1991, becoming chairman of Aurum Press where he remained for the rest of his life. He was created CBE in 1989. Died April 11

Dewar, Donald, PC (b. 1937), Labour politician who steered the Scottish devolution Bill through Parliament at Westminster and became First Minister of the Scottish Executive when a new Scottish Parliament began its life in 1999. Born in Glasgow, Dewar was educated at Glasgow Academy and Glasgow University, where he associated with a group of students who had already determined on political careers. He fought Aberdeen South as a Labour candidate in 1962 and won the seat in 1966, becoming Parliamentary Private Secretary to Anthony Crosland a year after entering the House of Commons. When the Scottish Nationalist Party won the Hamilton by-election in 1967 Dewar worked with John Smith and a number of other Labour Party Scottish MPs on alternative ideas to total independence for Scotland, finally taking up the idea of devolution. Dewar lost his seat in 1970 and three years later also lost his wife, who left him to marry Derry Irvine, who became Lord Chancellor in the Labour Government of 1997. It was a bad time for Dewar, who never remarried and took to an austere and rather lonely life as a partner in a firm of solicitors until returning to politics in 1978, when he won the Glasgow Garscadden seat. In 1983 he was appointed Shadow Scottish Secretary and won a seat in the Shadow Cabinet in the following year. He was appointed Shadow spokesman on Social Security and then Chief Whip, a job which he performed with conspicuous success. After the Labour victory in 1997 he was appointed to the Scottish Office and put in charge of the Scottish referendum campaign. He produced his White Paper within three months and in September of that year won a referendum mandate for a Scottish Parliament with an electoral system based on proportional representation. The result of the first election was to establish an uneasy coalition of Labour and Liberal Democrats which Dewar had some difficulty in controlling, although his sudden death, following a brain haemorrhage, revealed that there was no obvious candidate to succeed him. Died October 11

Dury, Ian (b. 1942), musician, songwriter, and actor, whose unique individual style blended together elements of rock, punk, and music hall. Born in Upminster, east of London, Dury was disabled by polio at the age of seven, and remained partially paralysed throughout his life. Having studied at the Royal College of Art, he taught art until the age of 28 when he began his musical career by playing in pubs and clubs around London. He first emerged during the pub rock era of the early 1970s, with "Kilburn & the High Roads", but it was not until 1977 that he attracted a wider following with "Ian Dury & the Blockheads". In the following year he recorded the album *New Boots And Panties*, which was critically acclaimed for its musical style and irreverently humorous lyrics, and which became a classic of the new wave era. As his popularity waned in the 1980s, Dury increasingly pursued an acting career, and appeared in a number of films and television programmes. In 1998 he became a goodwill ambassador for UNICEF, and worked hard to publicise a polio immunisation programme in Sri Lanka. In the same year he announced that he had developed cancer of the colon in 1995 and that it had spread to his liver and become inoperable. Despite his terminal illness he reunited the Blockheads, and in late 1990s the band toured in support of *Mr. Love Pants*, its first album in almost two decades. He continued to perform until only weeks before his death, and also continued to support a number of children's charities. Speaking frankly about his illness in the last year of his life he said "I don't spend a lot of time shaking my fist at the moon. It doesn't make you feel any better". Died March 27.

Elchibey, Abulfaz (b. 1938), first democratically elected President of Azerbaijan who was forced to give up after a year in office, having failed to defeat Armenian forces in the continuing conflict over Nagorno-Karabakh. Born in Nakhichevan when it was an Autonomous Soviet Socialist Republic, Elchibey was educated at the Azerbaijan State University in Baku, becoming a lecturer at the university from 1969 to 1974. He was arrested by the KGB in 1975 and imprisoned for two years for anti-Soviet activity. On his release he worked as a researcher at the Institute of Manuscripts of the Azerbaijan Academy of Sciences, publishing a number of books on oriental history and philosophy, but continued with his political activities, becoming chairman of the Popular Front of Azerbaijan, which he had helped to found, in 1989. The party was involved in the uprising against Soviet rule which was brutally suppressed in 1990, when the authority of the Communist Party, led by Ayaz Mutalibov, was restored. Once the Soviet Union had collapsed, Mutalibov's authority also waned, and although he became Azerbaijan's first President in 1991 he was deposed in the following year. Elchibey was then elected President, winning nearly 70 per cent of the popular vote. He at once set about launching a new national currency, closing the Russian military bases and establishing closer relations with Turkey. But he failed to resolve the conflict with Armenia and after a series of military defeats was driven from office when disaffected army troops marched on Baku. Elchibey fled to Turkey, and although he remained chairman of the Popular Front and returned to Baku in 1997, he did not recover political power. Died August 22

Fairbanks Jr, Douglas, KBE, DSC (b. 1909), American actor and businessman, who combined these aspects of his career with a busy social life that straddled the Atlantic. Born in New York in 1909, the son of the film star noted for his swashbuckling roles, Fairbanks Junior at first seemed destined to follow a similar career, starring in such films as *Dawn Patrol*, *The Prisoner of Zenda* and *Gunga Din* opposite some of the biggest names in Hollywood, one of whom, Joan Crawford, he had married at the age of 19 (although the marriage lasted only four years). He also acted on the stage, his first appearance being in *Young Woodley* in Los

Angeles in 1929. In England in the 1930s he acted in a number of plays with Gertrude Lawrence, with whom he had an affair. After another romantic involvement, this time with Marlene Dietrich, Fairbanks married Mary Lee in 1939. During the World War II he served in the US Navy, for part of the time commanding a British flotilla of landing craft during a commando operation, and was awarded decorations by many countries, including the UK, France, Greece and the USA. He was also appointed an honorary KBE for his contribution to Anglo-American relations. After the war he concentrated more on his business interests, some of them attached to the theatre and films but others more diverse, such as the making of ballpoint pens. In 1950 he moved to London, where he led a highly social life, although for tax reasons he spent only a limited amount of time in the UK. He was named during the Profumo case, and was also popularly believed to have been the "headless man" receiving fellatio in the sexually explicit photograph featured in the Duchess of Argyll's divorce case in the 1960s. He played in *My Fair Lady* on Broadway in 1968 and in *The Pleasure of his Company* in both New York and London in 1974. He was a governor of the Royal Shakespeare Company and of a boys' club in south London, and published two books of memoirs. After his second wife's death he married Vera Shelton. Died May 7

Fitzgerald, Penelope (b. 1916), English novelist who won the Booker Prize in 1979 and was short-listed on three other occasions, although she did not publish her first novel until she was 60. She was the daughter of "Evoe" Knox, Editor of *Punch*, and was educated at Wycombe Abbey and Somerville College, Oxford. When war broke out in 1939 she worked for a time at the Ministry of Food before joining the BBC as a programme assistant. She met Desmond Fitzgerald, then a soldier, during the war, and they were married in 1942. Together after the war they edited a literary journal, *World Review*, but it did not long survive and the couple moved to Southwold, in Suffolk, where Penelope ran a bookshop. Returning to London they settled in a houseboat on Chelsea Reach and Penelope taught at the Italia Conti School. She began to write in the 1970s, publishing her first book, a life of Edward Burne-Jones, in 1975, and her second, an account of the life of her father's family, *The Knox Brothers*, in 1977. In the same year she published her first novel, *The Golden Child*, a murder mystery set in a museum and written to amuse her ill husband. Her second, *The Bookshop* (1978) was drawn from her experiences in Southwold, and the third, *Offshore* (1979), the Booker prizewinner, was about a family living in a leaky houseboat on the Thames, similar to that which the Fitzgerald family had occupied for a time. She continued to draw on her own experiences for her next two novels: at the BBC in *Human Voices* (1980) and at the Italia Conti for *At Freddie's* (1982), but thereafter chose themes less connected with her own past. These included *Innocence* (1986), *The Beginning of Spring* (1988), a story about an English expatriate living in Moscow in 1917 which many believe to have been her best book, *The Gate of Angels* (1990) and her last novel, *The Blue Flower* (1995). All were short, sparingly and tenderly written books sharpened with wit and erudition. She won the Heywood Hill Prize for a lifetime's achievement in books in 1996 and became the first non-American to win the US National Book Critics' Circle fiction award in 1998. Died April 28

Gielgud, Sir John, OM, CH (born 1904), English actor who was one of the dominant performers and outstanding directors of his time, excelling in the classical roles such as Hamlet, for which his mellifluous voice and fastidious technique were uniquely qualified. Always recognisably himself, he was able to transcend the character he was playing by suggesting inner qualities relevant to all human feelings, not tearing a passion to tatters so much as showing how heart and mind respond. The son of a stockbroker and of Kate Terry Lewis, niece of Ellen Terry, Gielgud was educated at Hillside preparatory school, where he soon showed his talent in performing Humpty Dumpty, Shylock and Mark Antony, and at Westminster, where he made his decision to become an actor and went on to study the art at Lady Benson's dramatic school and at the Royal Academy of Dramatic Art. He made his professional debut at the Old Vic as the English herald in *Henry V*, and in 1924 joined the Oxford Playhouse, playing many classical roles. He returned to the Old Vic in 1929 where he played his first Hamlet and gave a notable performance as Richard II. He played Richard again, in Gordon Daviot's *Richard of Bordeaux*, in 1932, and it was this performance which established his early reputation, and enabled him to develop seasons in the West End which included a five-month run of *Hamlet* (subsequently transferring to New York) and a production of *Romeo and Juliet* in which Peggy Ashcroft played Juliet whilst Gielgud and Laurence Olivier alternated as Romeo and Mercutio. In 1939 he starred with Edith Evans in a memorable production of *The Importance of Being Earnest*, and in 1944-45 organised a season of plays at the Haymarket, including *Hamlet*. After the war Gielgud directed and played in Christopher Fry's *The Lady's Not For Burning*, but he did not quickly respond to the new drama that was emerging at the Royal Court, and his private life ran into trouble when in 1953 he was fined UK£10 in a magistrates' court for "importuning male persons". But theatre audiences proved tolerant and continued to welcome him on stage. His breakthrough into modern theatre, and one which won him new audiences, was Alan Bennett's play *40 Years On*, which was followed by plays by David Storey, Peter Shaffer and Harold Pinter. He did not totally abandon the classics, although his Macbeth and Othello proved less effective than his other classical roles. His Prospero in the Peter Brook production of *The Tempest* was universally praised, and he played the role again for Peter Hall in 1974 and in Peter Greenwood's film version, *Prospero's Books*, in 1991. During his life Gielgud played in many films, most of them in the later years of his life, although he gave memorable performances in Alfred Hitchcock's early film of *The Secret Agent* and as Disraeli in *The Prime Minister* in 1940. He was nominated for an Oscar for his performance in *Becket*, won an Oscar as best supporting actor for his role in *Arthur*, and will be remembered for memorable cameos as Lord Raglan in *The Charge of the Light Brigade*, as Sir Francis Hinsley in *The Loved One*, and as Count Berchtold in *Oh! What a Lovely War*. He was knighted in 1953, appointed CH in 1977 and OM in 1996. In 1994 the Globe Theatre in Shaftesbury Avenue was renamed the Gielgud Theatre in his honour. Died May 21

Giovanna, Queen of the Bulgarians (b. 1907), wife of King Boris III who died in suspicious circumstances after falling ill during a visit to Hitler in 1943. Born Giovanna Elisabetta Antonia Romana Maria, Princess of Italy, the third daughter of King Victor Emmanuel, she married King Boris in the Basilica of St Francis at Assisi in 1930. When war broke out the King tried to preserve Bulgaria's neutrality, but in 1941 was persuaded to join the three-power pact between Germany, Italy and Japan, allowing German troops into his country. Both king and queen were shocked by the Nazis' treatment of the Jews, and helped many to escape the concentration camps, a stance which displeased Hitler who was already angry with the King for not declaring war on the Soviet Union. During a visit to Hitler in 1943 King Boris fell ill in circumstances which led many to believe that he had been poisoned, and he died soon after returning to Sofia. The Queen was not told of his condition until shortly before his death, much to her distress. When Bulgaria was invaded by Soviet forces the Regent, Boris's younger brother Prince Kyril, was tried by a People's Court and shot, and Bulgaria became a republic. Queen Giovanna went into exile with her son, King Simeon, settling eventually in Spain. More recently Giovanna moved to Portugal, where she lived quietly near her brother, the exiled King Umberto II of Italy, although she made one visit to Bulgaria after the collapse of communism to visit the grave in which her husband's heart had been buried. Died February 26

Guinness, Sir Alec, CH, CBE (b. 1914), English actor who was a master of disguise with an ability so to immerse himself into character that his own personality seemed to disappear. He was equally at home on stage, in film and television, achieving memorable successes in all three. An illegitimate child who never knew his father and was badly treated by his mother, he attended a number of schools as well as the Fay Compton School of Dramatic Art, but first found employment in an advertising agency. He wrote to John Gielgud, who cast him as Osric and the Third Player in *Hamlet*, and he had a season with the Old Vic in 1936-37. Enlisting in the Royal Navy during the war, he was commissioned after two years and given command of a landing craft in the Mediterranean, although released for a short time to play on Broadway in *Flare Path*. After demobilisation he was cast as Herbert Pocket in David Lean's film of *Great Expectations* and as Fagin in *Oliver Twist*, and was then given memorable roles in the same director's later films, *The Bridge on the River Kwai*, *Lawrence of Arabia*, *Dr Zhivago* and *A Passage to India*. He also starred in some of the Ealing comedies, notably in *Kind Hearts and Coronets*, in which he played eight members, male and female, of the d'Ascoyne family. Films kept him off the stage for much of his time, though he played the Fool to Laurence Olivier's King Lear in the West End and Hamlet in a not very successful production which he co-directed with Frank Hauser. In the late 1970s and early 1980s he played George Smiley in the television productions of John le Carre's *Tinker, Tailor, Soldier, Spy* and *Smiley's People*, and achieved a new popular following in the film *Star Wars* and its sequels. His last stage appearance was in *A Walk in the Woods*, a play concentrating on the problems of arms control. In 1985 he published a volume of memoirs, *Blessings in Disguise*, with a second volume, in 1996, appropriately entitled *My Name Escapes Me*. Guinness was knighted in 1959, appointed CBE in 1955 and CH in 1994. Died August 5

Harsanyi, Professor John (b. 1920), Hungarian-born economist, philosopher and sociologist who shared the Nobel Prize for Economics in 1994 for his work on game theory. Educated at the Lutheran Gymnasium in Budapest, he went on to study pharmacy. During the war he was rounded up by the Nazis and destined for a concentration camp in Austria, but escaped just as the train was leaving Budapest station. After the war he returned to Budapest to read philosophy, sociology and psychology, but was forced to leave the university, after taking his degree and joining the sociology faculty, because of his anti-Communist views. He escaped from Hungary to Australia, where he took a degree in economics at Sydney University. In 1956 he went to Stanford University in California on a Rockefeller Fellowship, studying statistics, eventually becoming professor of economics at Wayne State University in Detroit and, in 1964, professor at the business school in Berkeley, California. His interest in the game theory, first developed to apply lessons drawn from games such as chess and poker to complex economic and social issues, was prompted by a series of papers by John F Nash Jr analysing how game strategies might be applied to competition between companies. Harsanyi developed the philosophical implications of the game theory, subsequently used to analyse questions of international relations and military strategy. In 1988 Harsanyia co-authored a book on the subject, *A General Theory of Equilibrium Selection in Games*, and six years later shared the Nobel prize with his two co-authors, Nash and Reinhard Selten. Died August 9

Ingrid, Queen of Denmark (b. 1910), was widow of King Frederik IX, great-grand-daughter of Queen Victoria, daughter of the Crown Prince who became King Gustaf VI Adolf of Sweden, and mother of the Queen of Denmark and of Queen Anne-Marie of the Hellenes. Born Princess Ingrid Victoria Sofia Louise Margaret of Sweden to parents who had been married in Windsor Castle in 1905, Princess Ingrid was educated in Sweden but spent much time in England, often staying with her grandfather, the Duke of Connaught. In the early 1930s her name was mentioned as a possible bride for the Prince of Wales, but in 1935 she married Crown Prince Frederik and they set up home in the Amalienborg Palace in Copenhagen, where they remained throughout the war when their country was occupied by the Germans, becoming King and Queen in 1947, when Frederik's father died. They were a popular couple, frequently going to the theatre and restaurants together. Queen Ingrid enjoyed art exhibitions, bookshops and auctions and would happily wait in queues when out shopping. She also enjoyed travelling and was a frequent visitor to the UK, representing her king at the coronation of George VI and attending the weddings of Queen Elizabeth II in 1947 and Princess Margaret in 1960. When King Frederik died in 1972 their daughter Margrethe succeeded to the throne, and towards the end of her life Queen Ingrid, now the Queen Mother, said that her daughter had lived up to all their expectations. Queen Ingrid continued to live in Fredensborg Castle and to take part in public life. Died November 7

Kirchschlager, Rudolf (b. 1905), President of Austria 1974-86. Born in Obermuhl in the province of Upper Austria, Kirchschlager began to study law but when he refused to join the Nazi party in 1938 his education was interrupted and he had to take a number of jobs until joining the army in 1939, finally completing his legal education when he was wounded. After the war he was appointed a district attorney and later a judge, joining the foreign service in 1954 as a legal adviser, assisting in the drafting of the constitutional law on his country's neutrality. He was a member of the Austrian delegation to the UN from 1956-65 and led the Austrian delegation to the law of the sea conference in Geneva in 1960. In 1967 he was appointed Austrian Ambassador to Czechoslovakia, witnessing the suppression of the Prague Spring by Soviet tanks in 1968 and leaving his embassy open to anyone trying to escape the Red Army. In 1970 Kirchschlager was appointed Minister of Foreign Affairs and in 1974 was elected President and re-elected for a second term in 1980, receiving 80 per cent of the vote. A quiet man, he presided over his country's affairs without flamboyance or controversy, an experience his countrymen clearly appreciated. Died March 30

Kitchener, "Lord" (Aldwyn Roberts) (b. 1922), Trinidadian calypso singer and composer whose songs reflected and influenced the development of the island's music for many years. During the 1950s, whilst living in the UK, he also described in song the experiences of West Indian immigrants to the country. After first following his father's trade as a blacksmith he tried his hand at calypso singing and, adopting the name of Lord Kitchener, began to make an impact, four of his songs featuring prominently in the 1946 carnival. In the following year he joined a cargo of immigrants on board the *Empire Windrush* bound for Tilbury from Jamaica. The ship's arrival was widely reported and filmed, with Lord Kitchener prominent as he sang *London is the Place for Me*. His later compositions in London included *The Underground Train*, *Nora* and *Ah, Bernice!* When Trinidad became independent, Kitchener returned to his native land, and his road march for the 1963 carnival, *The Road to Walk on Carnival Day*, won him the title Road March King, granted annually to the composer of the song most performed during the carnival. Kitchener won the title a further nine times. He composed many calypsos specifically for pan orchestras, including *The Beat of the Steel Band*, *Sweet Pan* and *The Bees' Melody*. His portrait appeared on a postage stamp, and a statute was erected to him in Port of Spain. Died February 11

Kung, Cardinal Ignatius (b. 1901), Bishop of Shanghai who spent many years in Chinese prisons for refusing to endorse an official Catholic Church established by the Communists and was made a cardinal without public declaration by Pope John Paul II in 1979. Educated privately and at St Ignatius High School in Shanghai, Kung was ordained as a Catholic priest in 1930, teaching in diocesan schools until he was appointed Bishop of Shanghai and apostolic administrator of Soochow and Nanking in 1950, shortly after Mao Zedong's Communists came to power. The Communist government tried to circumvent religious influence by establishing government-sanctioned churches. Bishop Kung resisted this, calling upon the country's three million Catholics to uphold their faith and organising religious activities in defiance of the authorities. He was arrested in 1955 and sentenced to life imprisonment when he refused allegiance to what was called the patriotic church. He was finally released in 1987 following a visit to China by Cardinal Sin of the Philippines, which provided Kung's first contact with the outside world for more than 30 years. Although surrounded by Chinese officials and kept from speaking directly to the visiting Cardinal,

Kung managed to convey that he had not renounced his faith or the Church, and Cardinal Sin carried this message back to Rome and the Catholic world. After his release Kung was given permission to travel to the USA for medical treatment, settling with a nephew in Stamford, Connecticut. His appointment as Cardinal was publicly announced in 1991, when he was able to visit the Vatican to receive his red biretta from the Pope. Died in exile March 12

Lamarr, Hedy (b. 1914), Hollywood film star best remembered for her role in the 1949 film *Samson and Delilah*. Born in Vienna, her real name was Hedwig Eva Maria Keisler. She was well educated, learning several languages and travelling widely with her parents before going to a finishing school in Switzerland. Blessed with remarkable good looks, she decided to become an actress and joined the Max Reinhardt acting school, after which she made a number of films and appeared in some plays, including the first Austrian production of *Private Lives*. In 1933 she caused a sensation by appearing naked in the film *Ecstasy*, which was banned in a number of countries. In 1937 she was signed up by Louis B Mayer, who gave her the name of Lamarr. Her first Hollywood film was *Casbah*, with Charles Boyer. Although this was popular her subsequent films, even with stars such as Robert Taylor, Clark Gable and James Stewart, were not, and although she set up her own (unsuccessful) production company her career was in serious decline until she was cast as Delilah by Cecil B De Mille. The film was a box office triumph but, sadly for Lamarr, one that she was unable to repeat. Her subsequent films were flops and she eventually retired to New York, where she took up painting. Lamarr was married six times, each union ending in divorce. Died January 19

Lamb, Sir Larry (b. 1929) newspaper editor who transformed *The Sun* into Britain's best-selling daily newspaper but subsequently found it difficult to maintain its impetus. Born in the village of Fitzwilliam in Yorkshire, Lamb first worked at Brighouse Town Hall, where he became branch secretary of his union and edited its magazine. From there he was offered a job on the *Brighouse Echo* and transferred to a number of other papers, joining the *Daily Mirror* in 1958, where he worked for 10 years before becoming northern editor of the *Daily Mail*, based in Manchester. Whilst there he attracted the notice of Rupert Murdoch, who had just bought the ailing *Sun* from the International Publishing Corporation, owners of the *Daily Mirror*, and was looking for an editor who could turn it into a successful paper based on the old Mirror formula but with a more modern, simple and racy style and a regular diet of television, sport and sex. It was Lamb who introduced the daily bare-breasted "Page Three Girl" and gave the paper a sense of fun and some strong political views which, although initially pro-Labour, swung across the political spectrum until, after the strikes of 1979, the paper delivered a message to Labour supporters: "Vote Tory this time: it's the only way to stop the rot". Lamb's formula successfully carried *The Sun* well ahead of the *Mirror*'s circulation, but when the *Daily Star* was launched to try to capture some of the same market *The Sun*'s circulation began to fall and Lamb was quickly replaced, working for a time with other Murdoch publications before taking over the editorship of the *Daily Express* in 1983. He left after three years, having failed to halt its circulation slide, and set up his own media consultancy company. Died May 19

Lindsay, John (b. 1921), mayor of New York 1965-73 who had hopes of becoming a presidential candidate, but never made it to an election campaign. Born in New York and educated at St Paul's School, Concord, New Hampshire, and at Yale. Graduating in law, he was admitted to the New York Bar in 1949, joining the New York law firm of Webster & Sheffield and becoming a partner in 1953. He was elected to Congress in 1957 as a Republican for New York's 17th congressional district. He made his name there as a spokesman for the rights of the individual, but found his political ambitions blocked by the fact that Republicans already held the state governorship and one of the two posts in the Senate, the second being taken by Robert Kennedy in 1964. Mayor of New York seemed the only way forward, and in 1965 Lindsay left Congress to campaign for that post, which he won. In office he made a popular mark by frequent public appearances and by such courageous gestures as riding a bicycle in Central Park, but the city's finances were running out of control and he had to campaign for large tax increases. His popularity among Republicans in New York began to be eroded by the rising tax bill, problems with municipal workers and a teachers' strike during which the National Guard had to be called in. He was re-elected mayor in 1969 but in 1971 left the Republican Party and became a Democrat, announcing that he would not stand for a further term as mayor. Instead he campaigned for the Democratic presidential nomination, but lost some of the early primaries to Senator George McGovern and withdrew. His final political throw was for a Democratic Senate seat in 1980, but again he was defeated in the primary. He went back to the law, worked for a time as a television commentator and published a number of books based on his experiences, together with one novel. Died December 19

Matthau, Walter, (b. 1920), American comic actor who worked for many years on stage and in films before firmly establishing his reputation with a series of irascible and lugubrious characters, notably in *The Odd Couple*, which he played both on Broadway and in the later screen version. Born in New York City, as Walter Matuschanskayasky, he took a number of odd jobs after leaving school before enlisting in the Army Air Force in 1942. After the war he trained as an actor in New York then joined a summer stock company and played small parts on Broadway. He made his first film in 1955 and began also to appear in television dramas. But there were few sizeable parts, and he began to fear that he was destined only for supporting roles. This changed in 1965, when he was cast as Oscar Madison in Neil Simon's play *The Odd Couple*, a comedy about two divorced men trying rather unsuccessfully to live together, one a slobbish sports journalist and the other a fastidious house-proud photographer. Matthau won a Tony award for his performance, and in the following year won an Oscar as best supporting actor in the Billy Wilder film *The Fortune Cookie*, in which he appeared with Jack Lemmon, establishing a partnership which was to feature in several more films, including the film version of *The Odd Couple*, a remake of *The Front Page*, *Buddy Buddy* and *Grumpy Old Men*. Matthau continued to make films at the rate of about one a year, not all of them very memorable, and made a rare return to the stage in 1974 to play Captain Boyle in a production of *Juno and the Paycock*. Died July 1

Matthews, Sir Stanley, CBE (b. 1915), English footballer known as the "wizard of dribble" for his skill at evading opponents as he took the ball down the right wing, presenting it almost to the feet of a succession of defenders before setting off in another direction at a speed that left them floundering. He always tried to avoid physical contact, refusing to play what he called the rough stuff. In a playing career of 33 years, including more than 700 league games and 84 for England, he was never booked. Born in Hanley, Staffordshire, Matthews joined Stoke City football club after leaving school. Having signed on as a professional on his 17th birthday he played his first league match for the club a few weeks later. When he was transferred to Blackpool, for a fee of UK£11,500, in 1947 he won the Footballer of the Year Award in the following year and played in two unsuccessful finals with his new club at Wembley before winning the cup in 1953 in a match which became known as the Matthews final. Blackpool were losing 3-1 to Bolton with only 20 minutes to go when Matthews suddenly took command, sealing victory with a cross that led to a goal in the last minute. His games for England included the memorable match against Germany in 1938, watched in silence by many of the Nazi hierarchy as Matthews scored one of England's goals in a 6-3 victory, and another, 10 years later, when England beat Italy 4-0 in Turin. Matthews returned to Stoke City in 1961, helping its promotion from the second division to the first. He played his last game in 1965 when he was 50. In his retirement he managed Port Vale football club for a short time, and then coached in many parts of the world. He was appointed CBE in 1957 and knighted in 1965, the first footballer to receive that honour. Died February 23

Miller, Merton (b. 1923), American economist who was awarded the Nobel Prize in 1990 for his work on the theory of corporate finance. Born in Boston and educated at Harvard, where he studied economics, Miller worked for three years in the US Treasury and Federal Reserve Board and taught for a year at the London School of Economics before moving to the Carnegie Institute of Technology and finally to the Graduate School of Business in Chicago. During this period he developed, with fellow economist Franco Modigliani, what was called the M&M Theorem, stating that a company's mixture of debt and equity had no effect on its total value, because the more debt taken on the more its shares would be discounted to allow for the increased risk. Managers, Miller argued, should concentrate on maximising earnings, bearing in mind that what counted was what was done with the money, not where it came from, and that no matter how a company was divided up its total value would remain the same. The award of the Nobel Prize recognised his influence on the theory and teaching of corporate finance. Later in his career he worked on the economics of securities and derivatives, arguing that, as instruments of risk control, derivatives made markets safer rather than more dangerous. He set out his views in a book, published in 1997, *Merton Miller on Derivatives*. Died June 3

Mladenov, Petur (b. 1936), Bulgarian Head of State and General Secretary of the country's Communist Party Central Committee for less than a year in 1989-90, but played a significant part in resolving the position of the country's Turks and in restructuring Bulgarian politics. Born in the village of Toshevtsi, he was educated at the Suvorov Military School in Sofia, at the University of Sofia and at the Moscow State Institute of International Relations. He progressed through various local institutions and committees of the Communist Party until, in 1971, he was appointed Minister for Foreign Affairs, a post he held for the next 18 years. In 1984 he was faced with the consequences of the decision by the then Head of State, Todor Zhivkov, forcibly to assimilate the country's one million ethnic Turks, a policy which was widely condemned internationally and which brought the Bulgarian Turks to the verge of rebellion. Mladenov played a leading role in ousting Zhivkov, with the support of the army, in 1989, and was immediately appointed General Secretary of the party and Head of State. He revoked Zhivkov's anti-Turkish policies and survived the subsequent outcry from party hardliners, moving on to restructure the party, in preparation for elections, by abolishing the Central Committee and Politburo, replacing them with a new Supreme Council. He relinquished the party leadership and resigned as Head of State a few months later following charges of interference in the 1990 elections. He had undergone a heart bypass operation a few years earlier, which it was believed played some part in his decision to retire. Died May 31

O'Brian, Patrick, CBE (b. Patrick Russ 1914), English author whose series of 20 seafaring novels set in the Napoleonic Wars eventually captured a wide following, although the first books did not sell well. O'Brian was secretive about his private life and origins, encouraging the long-accepted view that he was born and brought up in Ireland. In fact he was born in Buckinghamshire, the eighth of nine children of a venerealogist whose father had emigrated from Germany in the 1860s.

He began writing early, his first book being published when he was 15 and his second when he was 19. Both were fantasies featuring animals, and both were published under his real surname of Russ. He married in 1936 but separated after a few years, marrying again in 1943 when he was working for the Political Intelligence Department. After the war the couple settled in France, where he wrote his first novel under his new name. The first of his prodigious series about Captain Jack Aubrey, RN, and his friend, the physician and secret agent Stephen Maturin, *Captain and Commander*, was published in 1969 and the last, *Blue at the Mizzen*, was published in 1999. Their strength, and popularity following their sudden rediscovery in the 1990s, lay partly in the intriguing relationship between the two men, one a bluff, simple English sailor and the other a moody half-Irish half-Catalan medical man with a fund of knowledge and mysterious connections, and partly in the accuracy of O'Brian's portraits, not just of the ships and sailing techniques of the day but of the many other subjects that featured in the series. In addition to his novels O'Brian wrote two biographies, one on Picasso in 1976 and the other on Sir Joseph Banks in 1987. He was awarded the Heywood Hill Prize for a lifetime's contribution to literature in 1995 and appointed CBE in the same year. Died January 2

Obuchi, Keizo (b. 1937), became Prime Minister of Japan in 1998, when his country was in deep recession. Given little chance of overcoming Japan's economic problems he nonetheless succeeded in launching an effective short-term recovery programme. Born in the mountainous area of Honshu, Obuchi was educated at Waseda University in Tokyo and first elected to the House of Representatives in 1963 at the age of 26. Seven years later he was given his first office, as Parliamentary Vice-Minister for Posts and Telecommunications, then moved to Construction and subsequently became Director-General and Minister of State. He was not a charismatic politician, as he was the first to admit, but he helped Noburu Takeshita take control of the Liberal Democratic Party and, when Takeshita became Prime Minister in 1987, was appointed Chief Cabinet Secretary. In 1997 he was appointed Foreign Minister in Ryutyro Hashimoto's administration, and when Hashimoto resigned in the following year Obuchi's strong position in the LDP virtually assured him the succession as Prime Minister. Once in office he introduced a massive programme of public spending, personal and corporation tax cuts and legislation to permit the use of public funds to recapitalise the banks, helping them to get rid of bad loans. These and other measures provided the immediate stimulus the economy required, but Obuchi's health did not allow him to stay in power long enough to preside over its complete recovery. He suffered a stroke in April and lapsed into a coma from which he never recovered. Died May 14

O'Connor, Cardinal John (b. 1920), Archbishop of New York, a forceful defender of traditional Catholic teaching, particularly on sexual ethics and on abortion, who in consequence often found himself at odds with many of the inhabitants of a city renowned for its tolerance on such matters. Born in Philadelphia, O'Connor studied for the priesthood there and was ordained in 1945. He was assigned to a Catholic high school until 1952, when he became a chaplain with the US Navy and Marine Corps during the Korean War. He remained with the Navy until 1979, retiring with the rank of rear admiral. Consecrated Bishop by Pope John Paul II in that year he became auxiliary in charge of military chaplains to Cardinal Cooke in New York. In 1983 O'Connor was appointed Bishop of Scranton, Pennsylvania, but within less than a year was promoted to Archbishop of New York, becoming a cardinal in 1985. His hard work, compassion and loving care for the community made him a popular man in spite of the many brushes he had with those angered by his outspokenness. He was opposed to abortion, declaring that Catholics who were in favour should be excommunicated, and to New York's gay rights Bill, suggesting that homosexual men dying of Aids should be refused the last rites until they had repented of their "sin". As he frequently used the pulpit in St Patrick's Cathedral to make such pronouncements, his church was sometimes the scene of angry protests, as when in 1989 militant gay and women's rights activists chained themselves to pews and disrupted Mass. But where his orthodoxy on moral issues roused some criticism it also won him many admirers, as did his positive campaigning on social matters, such as his support for abolishing the death penalty and his opposition to proposed cuts in welfare benefits. His offer to retire in 1995, when he reached the normal age of 75, was refused. Died May 3

Oppenheimer, Harry (b. 1908), South African gold and diamonds magnate who was chairman of the Anglo-American Corporation and of De Beers Consolidated Mines for more than 25 years. Born in the mining town of Kimberley, Oppenheimer was educated in England at Charterhouse and Christ Church, Oxford, joining the diamond business as soon as he graduated and working under his father, Sir Ernest Oppenheimer, who had founded Anglo-American in 1917. During the Second World War Harry served with the South African Armoured Car Regiment in North Africa, and on his return after the war was persuaded to take up politics. He became MP for Kimberley in 1948 as a member of the United Party, effectively becoming the leader of that wing of the party, which wanted to give representation to Africans and other non-whites in government. He resigned his seat in 1957, when he took control of Anglo-American and De Beers following the death of his father, though remaining a member of the United Party until it became more conservative on racial affairs, when Oppenheimer played an influential role in founding the Progressive Party, which later became the Progressive Federal Party. As chairman of Anglo-American Oppenheimer concentrated on earning profits, but in so doing developed it in many directions other than just gold and diamonds. He bought the Rand Daily Mail and interests in many other South African companies, stating that in earning profits on all these enterprises he wanted to do so in a way that made "a real and permanent contribution to the well-being of the people and to the development of South Africa". He sponsored many welfare projects, including the Oppenheimer College in Lusaka and schools in Swaziland and Lesotho. He retired from Anglo-American in 1982, having hugely increased its turnover and profitability and made himself one of the richest men in the world, but stayed on for two more years at De Beers to help it through a period of slump in the diamond market. Died August 19

Pflimlin, Pierre (b. 1907), French politician who became his country's Prime Minister for 15 days at the time of the Algerian War in 1958. Born in Rombaix in the north of France (his parents were from Alsace) he was educated at the Lycee de Mulhouse, at the Institut Catholique de Paris and at Strasbourg University, where he read law. He joined the French Army when war broke out in 1939, was captured by the Germans in 1940 and spent the rest of the war with the Resistance in the Alps, being awarded the Croix de guerre. When the war was over he took up politics and was elected a Deputy for Bas-Rhin as a member of the Mouvement Republicain Populaire. He was given his first Cabinet post in 1946, as Under-Secretary for the National Economy, and continued to serve in the Cabinets of many administrations until, on May 14 1958, he was elected Prime Minister. Pflimlin was determined to maintain Algeria as a constituent part of France, but within 10 days of his taking office the revolt had spread to Corsica and was threatening to engulf France itself. It was becoming apparent that only General de Gaulle could save the situation. Pflimlin accepted the inevitable and resigned on May 31, de Gaulle taking over as President of the Fifth Republic. Pflimlin remained in the Cabinet for four years, but differences over the nature of Europe—he described himself as a fanatic for European unity—persuaded him to resign. He remained mayor of Strasbourg and became a Member of the European Parliament, becoming its President from 1984 to 1987. Died June 27

Pham Van Dong, (b. 1906), Prime Minister of the Democratic Republic of Vietnam (formerly North Vietnam and the Socialist Republic of Vietnam), working first under President Ho Chi Minh and then under Le Duan. Born in the central province of Quang Ngai and educated at the Lycee Quoc-Hoc in Hue and at Hanoi University, where he took part in student protests against the French colonial administration, Dong became a member of Ho Chi Minh's revolutionary youth association before going to China, where he learnt more techniques of revolutionary activity. On his return to Vietnam he was arrested and sentenced to 10 years in prison, but was released after six years under a political amnesty. In 1940 Dong joined Ho Chi Minh in China and became a founder member of the Vietminh. At the end of the war in the Far East he was appointed Minister of Finance in the provisional government set up by the Vietminh in Hanoi. After the French were defeated at Diem Bien Phu in 1954 Dong headed the Vietminh delegation at the Geneva conference which divided the country into the Communist North and the anti-Communist South. In 1955 he became Prime Minister and the North's chief spokesman during the long battle with the South and with the USA. He was never seen as a potential leader of the country's Communist party, even after the death of Ho Chi Minh, but he wielded much influence behind the scenes. Once the war was over he concentrated on the economic problems facing the united country, gradually handing over to younger people until finally retiring in 1986. Died April 29

Pindling, Sir Lynden, PC KCMG (b. 1930), first Prime Minister of the Bahamas who led his country to independence from Britain in 1973. The islands were for many years politically dominated by white businessmen and politicians who formed an oligarchy, known as the Bay Street Boys, to control the House of Assembly. Pindling was not one of these. Born in a poor black area of Nassau, he was educated at a local secondary school before travelling to England to read law at London University. In 1953 he returned to Nassau where he joined the new Progressive Liberal Party, winning a seat in the House of Assembly in 1956 and subsequently becoming the party's leader. In the elections of 1967 both the PLP and the United Bahamanian Party, which had been formed by the Bay Street Boys, won 18 seats, but two independent members joined with Pindling and he became Premier. Introducing a number of reforms in housing and employment, Pindling also declared his intention of making the Bahamas independent, a policy which received some support from the UK. In 1972 he called an election on the issue, which he won, and in the following year the Bahamas became a fully sovereign state, with Pindling as Prime Minister. Reports of narcotic smuggling and money laundering in the islands began to circulate, and it was alleged that Pinding had become involved. A royal commission found no evidence of his direct involvement, but it was noted that he had accepted large sums in gifts and loans. He won the 1987 election, his fifth victory in succession, but lost five years later and did not return to office. He resigned from the House of Assembly in 1997, admitting that he was "less than perfect". He was appointed to the Privy Council in 1973 and KCMG in 1983. Died August 26

Plowden, Lady (b. Bridget Richmond 1910), chairman of the Central Advisory Council for Education 1963-66 and chairman of the Independent Broadcasting Authority 1975-80. Her report on primary education in England and Wales, published in 1967, had an immediate political response and confirmed the importance of primary education, although some of its longer-term effects came in for considerable criticism. Daughter of an Admiral who became Master of Downing College, Cambridge, she was educated at St Alfred's School, Hampstead and at Downe House in Berkshire, marrying, in 1933, Edwin (later Baron) Plowden. Apart from bringing up her family her main early preoccupations were with charities, but in 1963 she was appointed chairman of the Central Advisory Council for Education and almost immediately began work on what was to become known, when it was published four years later, as the Plowden Report, officially entitled *Children and their Primary Schools*. The report transformed attitudes towards primary and nursery education and prompted substantial additional government funding for primary schools, but as the standard in many schools continued to decline the report was criticised for some of its assumptions, which seemed to undermine traditional and more disciplined teaching methods. After the report's publication, Plowden's abilities were much in demand in other areas of public life. She became a governor and vice-chairman of the BBC in 1970, and five years later was appointed chairman of the IBA. Here her independence of mind on occasion led her into controversy, not least with Mary Whitehouse, who was angered by Plowden's defence of the use of a four-letter word in a play by Dennis Potter. Plowden was also a member of the National Theatre Board, President of Relate (formerly the National Marriage Guidance Council), President of the Pre-School Playgroups Association, Chairman of the Mary Feilding Guild and Chairman of the Committee for Education of Romany and Other Travellers. She received honorary degrees from several universities and was appointed DBE in 1972. Died September 29

Powell, Anthony, CH, CBE (b. 1905), English novelist whose sequence of 12 novels *A Dance to the Music of Time* provided a vivid and witty panorama of a part of English life which Powell knew well. Born in London, Powell was educated at Eton and Balliol College, Oxford, where he read history. On coming down he joined the publishing house of Duckworth, where he also began to write. His first novel, *Afternoon Men*, which described the life of a group of bachelors in London, was published in 1931. Four more novels followed during the 1930s, when Powell also worked for a time as a scriptwriter, both in London and for a short unsuccessful period in Hollywood. When war broke out he served with The Welch Regiment before moving to the Intelligence Corps, where he became a liaison officer attached to the War Office. His wartime experiences subsequently provided him with the inspiration for three of the Dance novels, although his first published book after the war was not a novel but a study of John Aubrey. He worked for five years on the staff of the *Times Literary Supplement*, then joined *Punch*, before, in 1957, becoming a regular reviewer for *The Daily Telegraph*, contributing every fortnight for more than 30 years. The first of the Dance novels, *A Question of Upbringing*, appeared in 1951, and others followed at fairly regular intervals until the last, *Hearing Secret Harmonies*, was published in 1975. The fourth in the sequence, *At Lady Molly's*, won the James Tait Black Memorial prize in 1957 and the eleventh, *Temporary*

Kings, the W. H. Smith Prize in 1974. He wrote two more novels after the Dance sequence came to an end, together with four volumes of memoirs and three volumes of Journals, which he wrote after he and his wife (he married Lady Violet Pakenham in 1934) had moved from London to Somerset. Powell was appointed CBE in 1956 and CH in 1988. Died March 28

Robards, Jason (b. 1922), American actor renowned for his stage performances and for his film work. Born in Chicago, the son of an actor, Robards was educated in California at the Hollywood High School, but he did not follow in his father's footsteps (initially as Jason Robards Jr) until after the war, during which he served with the US Navy. He fought in the Pacific, taking part in more than a dozen engagements and was awarded the Navy Cross. In 1946 he studied at the American Academy of Dramatic Art in New York but did not begin to make a mark as an actor until he was cast as Hickey in a stage revival of *The Iceman Cometh* in 1956. Later in the same year he played in the first Broadway production of *A Long Day's Journey into Night*, for which he won the New York Drama Critics' Award for his performance as Jamie Tyrone Jr. He won two more Drama Critic's Awards and a Tony for his stage work in the 1960s, when he was also beginning to establish a reputation in films. One of his first roles was in the film version of *A Long Day's Journey into Night*, with Ralph Richardson and Katharine Hepburn. In 1976 he played Ben Bradlee, the editor of the *Washington Post* during its investigations into the Watergate affair, in *All the President's Men*, for which he won an Oscar as best supporting actor. He won another Oscar in the following year for his performance as Dashiell Hammett in *Julia*, and was nominated for a third in 1980 for the film *Melvin and Howard*, in which he played Howard Hughes. Robards married four times, his third wife being the actress Lauren Bacall, whom he met after the death of her previous husband, Humphrey Bogart. The marriage was dissolved in 1969. Died December 26

Runcie, the Right Rev Lord (Robert), MC, PC (b.1921), Archbishop of Canterbury during the difficult decade of the 1980s, when the Church of England was seriously divided and relations with the State were far from comfortable. The fact that he held things together with some success reflected his personal integrity, intelligence, likeability and pragmatism, but the burden of the office weighed heavily on him and he was relieved to give it up. Born in Liverpool, the son of a Scottish engineer, Runcie was educated at the Merchant Taylors' School, Crosby, and at Brasenose College, Oxford, though his time there was interrupted by war service. Commissioned in the Scots Guards, he served with a tank battalion which landed in France in 1944, and was awarded the Military Cross after rescuing one of his men from a burning tank and leading an attack on a German gun emplacement. Returning to Oxford he took a First in Greats before moving to Westcott House, Cambridge to study theology. Having taken Holy Orders he became a curate at All Saints, Gosforth, before returning to Westcott House as chaplain and, within a year, Vice-Principal. In 1956 he was appointed Fellow and Dean of Trinity Hall, Cambridge, and in 1960 became Principal of Cuddesdon Theological College and Vicar of the parish of Cuddesdon. In 1970 he was appointed Bishop of St Albans. Whilst there he proved a popular preacher and an excellent communicator and administrator, setting up a ministerial training scheme for both priests and laity, one which was widely adopted elsewhere. He also took on other responsibilities, including the Anglican chairmanship of the Anglican-Orthodox Joint Doctrinal Commission and the chairmanship of the BBC and IBA Central Religious Advisory Committee. Whilst at Bristol he turned down an invitation to the Archbishopric of York when Donald Coggan moved to Canterbury, and in 1980 he hesitated for some weeks before finally accepting the appointment of Archbishop of Canterbury when Coggan retired. His term as Archbishop of Canterbury undoubtedly provided some personal disappointments. He worked enthusiastically for communion with Rome, and in 1982 welcomed the Pope to Canterbury, but his hopes foundered when the Vatican made clear that the doctrines of Rome would have to prevail, and that the growing Anglican enthusiasm for the ordination of women (not at that time shared by Runcie) was unacceptable. Runcie's diplomatic skills prevented the issue from disrupting the Lambeth Conference of 1988, but did not erase it from the Church's subsequent agenda, and it was one of the factors that contributed to one of the most painful incidents of his office, the publication of a highly critical preface in the 1987 edition of *Crockford's Clerical Directory*. Although praising Runcie's intelligence, personal warmth and his ability to listen, the article went on to doubt whether he knew what he was doing and had any clear basis for his policies. The preface was anonymous, but it was soon discovered that it had been written by one of Runcie's trusted friends and helpers, Canon Gareth Bennett, who later committed suicide. Some of the criticism stuck, but it ignored the fact that Runcie had to preside over a deeply divided Church, and one which was seen by many supporters of Margaret Thatcher's Conservative government as critical of its policies. When he retired in 1991 Runcie was created a life peer and might have hoped for a quieter time, but he was back in the headlines in 1996 when an official biography was published. Runcie had given its author, Humphrey Carpenter, a series of interviews in which he spoke frankly and at times indiscreetly, assuming they would be for background information. He was distressed to find that he was quoted verbatim on such delicate subjects as the breakdown of the royal marriage and his discussions with the Prince and Princess of Wales at the time. After reading a proof of the book, Runcie wrote in a note to the author that he hoped to die before the book was published. Died July 11

Runciman, Sir Steven, CH, FBA (b. 1903), English historian whose three-volume history of the Crusades became a standard work, although it took a revisionist view of the subject, suggesting that the crusaders were only the last wave of barbarian invaders who destroyed the Roman and Byzantine Empires. Born in Northumberland, he was educated privately by a governess who taught him French, Latin, Greek and Russian before he went on to Eton and Trinity College, Cambridge, where he became a Fellow and university lecturer, publishing a number of books, including *Byzantine Civilization* in 1933. During the Second World War he became press attaché to the British legation in Sofia, and later in Cairo, before becoming professor of Byzantine history and art at the University of Istanbul. From 1945 for two years he was head of the British Council in Athens before devoting himself to the writing of books. His *History of the Crusades* appeared in 1951, 1952 and 1954 and was hailed as a model of narrative history, telling the story of the crusades not just from the Western viewpoint but as it was seen by Islam and Constantinople. Other books followed, notably *The Fall of Constantinople* (1965) and *Byzantine Style and Civilisation* (1975). He travelled constantly and lectured in many countries with a wit and lightness of touch that made him friends wherever he went. He was elected a Fellow of the British Academy in 1957, was knighted in 1958 and appointed a Companion of Honour in 1984. Died November 2

Ryder of Warsaw, Lady, CMG, OBE (b. Sue Ryder 1923), was founder of the international charity which bears her name and which established some 80 homes in Britain and Europe, supported by 500 charity shops. Ryder was born in Leeds and educated at Benenden School in Kent. Aged 16 when war broke out, she immediately joined the First Aid Nursing Yeomanry but was soon transferred to the Special Operations Executive, working for the Polish section for which she would drive agents to airfields at the start of their missions in occupied Europe. After the war she worked with relief units in France and Germany, concentrating on the plight of former prisoners of war, particularly Poles, who had been in German prisons and camps, eventually founding a home for them in Celle. It attracted many volunteers to help in its construction and was so successful that Ryder decided to expand the project. On her return to England in 1953 she set up the Sue Ryder Foundation, buying her mother's house in Cavendish, Suffolk, as its headquarters and first Sue Ryder Home, to house disabled people and others who might otherwise have had to be kept in hospital. More Sue Ryder homes followed, in Germany, Poland, Yugoslavia and Greece as well as in the UK. In 1959 Ryder married the former bomber pilot Group Captain Leonard Cheshire VC, who had set up his own charity, the Cheshire Homes for the Disabled. The two foundations remained separate, except for a joint centre in India, but Ryder and Cheshire worked closely together in promoting their respective charities. Ryder's particular concern and affection for Poland was reflected in her decision to adopt the title of Baroness Ryder of Warsaw when she was made a life peer in 1979, after which she became a regular contributor to debates in the House of Lords as well as continuing to travel many thousands of miles each year to visit her homes. Her later years were troubled by ill-health and a dispute with other trustees of the Foundation. She retired in 1998 and set up a new organisation, the Bouverie Foundation, for charity work. Died November 2

Sainsbury, Sir Robert (b. 1906), former chairman of the British grocery chain and patron of the arts whose generosity led to the establishment of the Sainsbury Centre for the Visual Arts in Norwich. Grandson of the founder of the company and second son of John Benjamin Sainsbury, Robert was educated at Haileybury and Pembroke College, Cambridge, training as an accountant before joining the family business in 1930. He served as company secretary and became a member of the board in 1934. Four years later, he and his brother Alan became joint general managers after their father suffered a heart attack. Robert Sainsbury became chairman of the company in 1967 but handed over to his nephew two years later, when he retired as honorary joint president. Throughout his life Sainsbury was a keen and discriminating collector of art, and in 1973 he and his wife Lisa were able to give some 400 works, including paintings by Picasso, Degas, Francis Bacon and Modigliani and sculptures by Moore and Giacometti, to the University of East Anglia as the basis of what became the Sainsbury Centre, housed in a building designed by Norman Foster for which the Sainsburys also paid. Sainsbury was chairman of the trustees of the Tate Gallery, a member of the management committee of the Courtauld Institute and a member of the Art Panel of the Arts Council. He was knighted for services to the arts in 1967. Died April 2

Salam, Saeb (b. 1905), Lebanese politician who was Prime Minister of his country five times during a career that lasted nearly 50 years. Born in Beirut, Salam was educated at the American University there. He represented the city in the Chamber of Deputies from 1943 until 1992, becoming Prime Minister for the first time in 1952. After the Suez crisis, when he strongly supported Nasser and came into conflict with the pro-Western President Camille Chamoun, he relinquished the office in favour of Abdullah Yafi but remained in the government as Minister of State. The conflict that then split the country on sectarian lines was brought to an end by the landing of the US Marines in 1958, when Chamoun resigned and a neutral government was formed. Salam became Prime Minister again in 1960, forming a new administration in the following year and restructuring it yet again later that year, until he was succeeded by Rashid Karami. In 1970 Salam became Prime Minister for the last time, combining the post with that of Minister of the Interior. He resigned three years later when the President refused to dismiss the Army Commander whom Salam blamed for failing to stop the Israeli commando raid on Lebanon in 1973. During the civil war Salam worked for reconciliation between Muslims and Christians, but subsequently upset the Syrian government by supporting a peace accord with Israel. He retired to Switzerland, where he lived for many years before returning to Lebanon in 1994. Died January 20

Schulz, Charles (b. 1922), American cartoonist who created the *Peanuts* cartoon strip which ran every day for nearly 50 years and became the most widely read and syndicated cartoon in the world, appearing in more than 2,500 papers in 75 countries. Born in St Paul, Minnesota, Schulz was educated at St Paul High School before enrolling in a correspondence art course in which he failed to shine. During the war he served with the US Army in France and Germany, becoming staff sergeant in charge of a machine-gun squad. His first newspaper strip appeared after the war in the *Minneapolis Star*, and in 1948 he began creating some of the Peanut characters which were accepted for publication in the *St Paul Pioneer Press* newspaper under the title *L'il Folk*. In 1950 they began to be syndicated as a strip cartoon, re-titled *Peanuts*, with a gradual development of characters centred upon Charlie Brown, a born loser at everything, constantly put down by Lucy (who offered advice at 5 cents a time), his dog Snoopy, often portrayed lying on top of his kennel dreaming of his exploits as a First World War flying ace, and others such as Schroeder, the young pianist playing Beethoven on a miniature grand piano with no black notes, and Linus, the thumb-sucking philosophical, comfort-blanket-carrying brother of Lucy. *Peanuts*, although essentially American, quickly spread across the world, its characters being adopted for many books, animated films, calendars, and even borrowed for the command and lunar modules on a space mission. They also brought Schulz great wealth and many awards, but he continued to draw the cartoons on a daily basis until, in December 1999, he announced that he was retiring, having completed enough cartoons to run until, as it turned out, the day after his death. Died February 12

Sladkevicius, Cardinal Vincentas (b. 1920), was Archbishop of Kaunas in Lithuania 1989-96, having spent many years under house arrest for his resistance to communist rule. Born in Kaisiadorys he was ordained as a Catholic priest in 1944, when Lithuania was occupied by the Germans. After the Soviet occupation the Church was subjected to a purge which involved the arrest of many Roman Catholics, including priests and bishops, some being deported to Siberia. Sladkevicius was sent to a remote village where he spent the next 25 years, forbidden to carry out any pastoral duties. He continued to campaign for greater freedom for his country, and was finally allowed to return to Kaisiadorys in 1982, when the Pope appointed him apostolic administrator to the diocese. As perestroika began to spread throughout the Soviet Union Sladkevicius was permitted to travel to Rome where, in 1988, he was created a cardinal. When he became Archbishop of Kaunas in 1989 he declared that Lithuania wanted to separate from the Soviet Union, and for a time it appeared that Soviet troops were preparing another crackdown. However the promise of a visit by Pope John Paul II persuaded the Soviet leaders to withdraw their troops one month before the visit took place, in 1993, much to the satisfaction of Sladkevicius and the Catholic community. Died May 28

Sobchak, Anatoli (b. 1937), mayor of Leningrad who presided over the reversion of its name to St Petersburg and played a significant part in the reforms of the Gorbachev era before being charged with corruption and leaving the country. Sobchak was born in Leningrad but lived his early life in the town of Chita, in Siberia, before returning to Leningrad to study law at the university. After obtaining his degree he practised in the Stavropol region, where Mikhail Gorbachev was head of the Communist Party organisation, then returned to Leningrad university to teach, becoming the university's first professor of economic law in 1983. A keen supporter of Gorbachev's reforms, he joined the Communist Party and in 1989 was elected to the Congress of People's Deputies, where he made his reputation with a series of outspoken attacks on the old guard. He became mayor of Leningrad in 1990, winning the vote to change its name in the following year. Later in 1991, when Gorbachev was arrested, Sobchak brought the people of St Petersburg onto the streets to defend the city council and persuaded the military chiefs to halt the tanks which, on orders from Moscow, were heading for the city centre. At that time he was seen as a likely successor to Gorbachev, but his popularity waned under the impact of the city's food shortages, rising crime and collapsing infrastructure. He lost the mayoral elections of 1996 and was charged with a series of corrupt property deals. In the following year he left for

Paris but returned to Russia two years later to campaign on behalf of his former student and assistant, Vladimir Putin. Died February 20

Takeshita, Noboru (b. 1924), Prime Minister of Japan for 18 months before being forced from office after admitting that he had accepted financial gifts and other inducements from a property company. Born in Shimane and educated at Waseda University, Takeshita volunteered as a kamikaze pilot during the last year of the war. Returning to Shimana in 1947 he taught English for a short time before taking up politics, being elected to the prefecture in 1951 and to the House of Representatives in 1958. He was appointed Deputy Cabinet Secretary in 1964, Chief Cabinet Secretary in 1971, Minister of Construction in 1976 and Minister of Finance in 1979. His chief patron during this period had been Kakuei Tanaka, but when Tanaka suffered a stroke Takeshita created his own power base within the Liberal Democratic Party (LDP), becoming its secretary-general in 1986 and president in the following year. From there it was an easy jump to take over as Prime Minister from Yasuhiro Nakasone in 1987. In his quiet enigmatic way Takeshita maintained his predecessor's attempts to raise Japan's profile in international affairs and took an undoubted risk at home by introducing tax reforms, including the imposition of a consumption tax, which inevitably proved unpopular. More damaging to Takeshita was the fact that, even as the tax measures were being introduced, it became known that he was involved in the scandal of the Recruit property company, which had been handing out money, shares and other favours to influential people. Takeshita resigned in 1989 but continued to dominate the LDP until formally announcing his retirement shortly before his death. Died June 19

Thomas, R S (b. Ronald Stuart, 1913), Welsh poet and priest who wrote in English but conveyed in his austere verse the essence of Wales and, in particular, the life of the northern hill farmers. Born in Cardiff, Thomas was brought up in Anglesey and educated at the County School in Holyhead and University College, Bangor. He read theology at St Michael's College, Llandaff, and was ordained in 1936. He became curate at Chirk for four years, where he began to learn Welsh, before moving to Manafon as rector, and it was here that he first began to experience and enjoy the remoteness of rural life. His first volume of poems, *The Stones of the Field*, was published in 1946 and introduced Iago Prycherch as the prototype stolid Welsh hill farmer whose primitive way of life shocked but deeply impressed the poet, who said he could smell evil as soon as he got off the train in any city. Other volumes of poetry followed as Thomas moved to Eglwysfach, north of Aberystwyth, where he remained as vicar until 1967, and then to Aberdaron, on the Leyn peninsula, the poems attracting attention because their severity of tone and moral content was so different from the popular English poets of the day. In his later poems Thomas moved away from the Welsh rural hills to a more intense search for God and a cry of despair for mankind. His final living was at Bwlch-y-Rhiw, also on the Leyn peninsula, where he was rector until his retirement in 1978. He then moved to Llanfairynghornwy, in Anglesey, where he lived quietly with his second wife, writing in prose and in Welsh. He was nominated for the Nobel Prize for literature in 1994. Died September 25

Trudeau, Pierre, CH, PC (b. 1919) Prime Minister of Canada 1968-79 and 1980-84, establishing a new Canadian constitution, striving to unite the country with a unique identity and setting a relaxed a style of government that was enthusiastically welcomed by his countrymen. Born in Montreal, Trudeau was educated at the Jesuit College of Jean-de-Brebeuf and at Montreal University before going on to Harvard, to the Ecole des Sciences Politiques in Paris and to the London School of Economics. On his return to Canada he joined the Privy Council Office in Ottawa for two years before beginning to take an interest in politics, actively promoting federalism against the movement for Quebec independence. He joined the Liberal Party and won a Montreal seat in the parliamentary election of 1965. He became Parliamentary Secretary to the Prime Minister, Lester Pearson, in 1966 and Minister of Justice and Attorney-General in 1967. When the government was defeated in a budget debate Trudeau succeeded Pearson as party leader and won the general election that followed. As Prime Minister he brought a new excitement to Canadian politics, partly because of his personal charisma but also because of his legislative programme. The Official Languages Act of 1969 enshrined French and English as the official languages of Canada, and although this caused some aggravation it eventually helped to promote the unity that the country was lacking. Overseas Trudeau aroused considerable disquiet, particularly in the US, by establishing diplomatic relations with China. The "patriation" of the Canadian Constitution from the UK, which Trudeau eventually achieved in 1982, may have helped to establish Canada as an independent nation, and he was delighted when the Queen went to Ottawa to sign the new Canada Act, but opinion was already beginning to turn against him. There were problems with some of the new constitutional arrangements he had made, his energy policies were bitterly opposed in the western provinces, the latest budget had upset the business community, and his popular marriage to Margaret Sinclair, who was 30 years younger than he, was breaking up. In 1984 he resigned, returning to legal practice in Montreal and in 1993 publishing his memoirs. He was appointed a Companion of Honour in 1984 and a Companion of the Order of Canada in 1985. Died September 28

Zatopec, Emil (b. 1922), Czech athlete who broke 18 world records in long-distance races. Born in Koprivnice, Zatopec was brought up in Zlin, where he started work in a shoe factory. During the German occupation in 1940 he took part in a sponsored 1,500 metre race, for which he had not prepared, coming second in a field of 100. He was then given coaching and two years later came fifth in the national championship 1,500 metres. Wanting to run longer distances he decided to coach himself in fairly unorthodox fashion, training in heavy boots so that his feet felt lighter in races and developing the technique of running sprints of 400 metres interspersed with slower jogs to build up stamina. He used these tactics to good effect in the 1948 London Olympics, when he beat the Finnish world record holder in the 10,000 by nearly a lap and broke the world record by 11.8 seconds. At Helsinki four years later he won three gold medals in a week, beating his own world record in the 10,000 metres by 42 seconds and going on to win the 5,000 metres four days later and then the marathon, which he had never run before but in which he broke the world record by six seconds. He retired in 1956 after coming sixth in the Melbourne Olympics. He then worked as a coach in the Czech Army, but ran into trouble during the Prague Spring reforms of Alexander Dubcek, whose manifesto he had signed. He was present, and recognised, when the Soviet tanks entered Wenceslas Square. He was dismissed from the army, deprived of his membership of the Communist Party and spent the next 20 years in virtual exile working for a geological team in a remote part of the country. He finally returned to Prague in 1990, when his army rank was restored. Died November 22

XIX CHRONICLE OF PRINCIPAL EVENTS IN 2000

JANUARY

3 **Niger:** Hama Amadou was appointed as Prime Minister.
   Tonga: Prince Ulukalala Lavaka Ata replaced veteran Baron Vaea as Prime Minister.
4 **Côte d'Ivoire:** Gen. Robert Guëi, who had led a military coup in December 1999, announced a transitional government with himself as President, to prepare the country for a general election in October.
   Venezuela: the bicameral National Congress was officially dissolved in order to be replaced by an elected unicameral National Assembly, as mandated by the new constitution.
   Croatia: legislative elections were won by the opposition.
   Middle East: Israeli and Palestinian negotiators ended months of deadlock by agreeing to implement a transfer of West Bank land to Palestinian control under the terms of the September 1999 Sharm el-Sheikh agreement.
6 **Tibet:** the 17th Karmapa Lama, the third most holy figure in the religious community, arrived in Dharamsala, India, having fled from Chinese-ruled Tibet.
9 **Uzbekistan:** President Islam Karimov was re-elected for a further five-year term.
10 **Marshall Islands:** Kessai Note was elected President.
14 **Guatemala:** Alfonso Portillo, of the Guatemalan Republican Front, was sworn in as President following his election in December 1999.
15 **Yugoslavia:** Zeljko Raznatovic, the notorious Serbian ultra-nationalist warlord and war crimes suspect better known as Arkan, was gunned down and killed in Belgrade.
16 **Guinea-Bissau:** Kumba Yalla of the Social Renewal Party (PRS) won a presidential run-off election.
   Chile: Ricardo Lagos Escobar, of the ruling centre-left Concertación alliance, defeated Joaquín Lavín Infante of the right-wing Alliance for Chile in the presidential election. Lagos was sworn in on March 11, thereby becoming Chile's first socialist President since Salvador Allende Gossens was overthrown in a military coup in 1973.
17 **Indonesia:** three days of rioting began in Lombok as the sectarian conflict in the Moluccas spread to other islands.
18 **Pakistan:** the trial began of former Prime Minister Nawaz Sharif on charges relating to the alleged hijacking in October 1999 of a plane carrying Gen. Pervaiz Musharraf.
   Burundi: Nelson Mandela, the former South African President, was appointed by the UN Security Council as a facilitator in peace negotiations between the Tutsi-dominated government and Hutu rebels.
   Germany: former Chancellor Helmut Kohl resigned the honorary chairmanship of the Christian Democratic Union (CDU), resisting pleas to reveal the sources of illegal political donations which he had failed to declare whilst in office.
19 **Italy:** Former Prime Minister Bettino Craxi died in self-imposed exile in Tunisia.
20 **Greece:** Georgios Papandreou began the first official visit by a Greek Foreign Minister to Turkey since 1962.
21 **Ecuador:** President Jamil Mahuad Witt was ousted in a bloodless coup.
   Spain: the Basque separatist group ETA killed an army officer in a car bomb attack. It was ETA's first killing in 19 months and the first since it had officially lifted its ceasefire on December 3, 1999.
24 **Sudan:** President Omar Hassan Ahmed al-Bashir appointed a new Cabinet.
   Thailand: Burmese Karen rebels seized a hospital in Thailand to publicise their cause; Thai troops later recaptured the building, killing 10 rebels.

25 **Iran:** Gholamhossain Karbaschi, the former mayor of Tehran—convicted on charges of embezzlement and mismanagement of public funds in July 1998—was pardoned by supreme leader Ayatollah Ali Khamenei.
27 **Comoros:** in a referendum on the island of Anjouan, over 94 per cent of voters rejected rejoining the Comoros federation.
31 **Environment:** the Biosafety Protocol to the UN Convention on Biological Diversity, to regulate the trade in genetically modified (GM) crops, was signed by more than 150 countries.
   Dominica: legislative elections were won by the opposition.

FEBRUARY

1 **UK:** Conservative Party leader William Hague announced a surprise reshuffle of the shadow Cabinet, featuring the appointment of former Defence Secretary Michael Portillo as shadow Chancellor of the Exchequer.
3 **Dominica:** Roosevelt "Rosie" Douglas was sworn in as the new Prime Minister.
4 **Southern Africa:** torrential rains caused severe floods; these were exacerbated from February 21 by two cyclones in Mozambique, South Africa, Zimbabwe, Botswana and Madagascar. At least 650 people were killed and hundreds of thousands left homeless.
5 **USA:** Hillary Clinton officially declared her candidacy for a US Senate seat, thereby becoming the first First Lady ever to run for political office in the USA.
   Austria: President Thomas Klestil reluctantly approved the inclusion of Jörg Haider's far-right Freedom Party (FPÖ) in a new coalition government, against a backdrop of internal and international condemnation.
6 **Finland:** Tarja Halonen, of the Finnish Social Democratic Party (SSDP), was elected as the country's first female President.
   Russia: Grozny, the ruined capital of the separatist republic of Chechnya, fell to Russian forces.
   Afghanistan: a domestic airliner carrying 187 people was hijacked and, eventually, landed in the UK on February 7 amidst considerable confusion over the motives of the hijackers.
7 **Djibouti:** the government signed a peace agreement to end seven years of sporadic guerrilla warfare.
   Yugoslavia: Defence Minister Pavle Bulatovic was gunned down in a Belgrade restaurant.
   Croatia: Stipe Mesic, of the Croatian People's Party (HNS), won the second round of presidential elections.
8 **Turkey:** the presidential council of the Kurdistan Workers' Party (PKK) formally announced that it would back its leader Abdullah Öcalan's calls for peace and would abandon the armed struggle in favour of a political approach.
11 **UK:** the government suspended the Northern Ireland Assembly and executive and reinstated direct rule, following the failure of the weapons decommissioning process.
   Zimbabwe: 55 per cent of voters in a referendum rejected a new constitution giving President Robert Mugabe sweeping new powers.
13 **Iraq:** Hans von Sponeck resigned as the Baghdad-based co-ordinator of the UN's "oil-for-food" programme after voicing criticism of the inadequacies of the UN humanitarian programme in Iraq. The following day, Jutta Burghardt also resigned her post as chief of the UN World Food Programme in Iraq.
14 **Indonesia:** former Defence Minister and former commander-in-chief of armed forces Gen. Wiranto was suspended from the Cabinet by President Abdurrahman Wahid.
15 **Central African Republic:** UN peacekeepers withdrew after the expiry of their mandate.
   EU: membership negotiations with all remaining associate members—Bulgaria, Latvia, Lithuania, Malta, Romania and Slovakia—were formally opened.

UK: Rhodri Morgan was confirmed as First Secretary of the minority Labour administration of Wales, following the resignation of Alun Michael.
17 **Belarus:** President Alyaksandr Lukashenka dismissed Prime Minister Syargey Ling; he was replaced by Uladzimir Yarmoshyn.
18 **Iran:** reformist candidates, associated to varying degrees with President Seyyed Mohammad Khatami, secured two-thirds of the seats in legislative elections.
21 **Nigeria:** three days of sectarian violence between Christians and Muslims in northern state of Kaduna—in which up to 400 people were killed—began after calls for introduction of Islamic sharia law.
23 **Eritrea:** there was a renewal of heavy fighting in the border dispute with Ethiopia.
28 **Rwanda:** the Prime Minister resigned.

MARCH

1 **Uruguay:** Jorge Batlle Ibáñez, of the centrist Colorado Party (PC), was sworn in as President following his victory in elections held in October and November 1999.
Libya: Mubarak Abdullah al-Shamikh was appointed as the new Secretary of a renovated General People's Committee.
2 **Chile:** former dictator Gen. (retd) Augusto Pinochet Ugarte returned from the UK after Home Secretary Jack Straw announced his decision to drop extradition proceedings against him on the grounds of poor health.
3 **Anguilla:** the opposition achieved a narrow win in a general election.
Bosnia: the International Criminal Tribunal for the Former Yugoslavia (based in The Hague) sentenced former Bosnian Croat commander Gen. Tihomir Blaskic to 45 years in prison, the longest sentence thus far handed down by the tribunal.
USA: District Judge Thomas Penfield Jackson ruled against the software manufacturer Microsoft in an anti-trust action against the company.
4 **Thailand:** the first-ever election to the 200-seat Senate was held; after an investigation of malpractice, the election commission ordered re-run contests in 78 seats.
5 **Brunei:** Sultan Hassanal Bolkiah sued his younger brother Prince Jefri Bolkiah for misusing US$15 billion in state funds during Jefri's tenure as head of the Brunei Investment Agency (BIA); the case was settled out of court in May.
6 **Pakistan:** former Prime Minister Sharif was convicted of hijacking and terrorism and was sentenced to life imprisonment.
St Kitts and Nevis: Prime Minister Denzil Douglas's social democratic St Kitts-Nevis Labour Party (SKLP) retained power in a general election.
10 **Norway:** the opposition Labour Party formed a new government under Jens Stoltenberg, who became Norway's youngest Prime Minister, after the defeat of the centrist coalition in a no-confidence vote.
Turkey: former Prime Minister Necmettin Erbakan was sentenced to one year's imprisonment for making an inflammatory speech.
11 **Ukraine:** 82 men died in an explosion at the Barakova coal mine in the Donbass.
12 **El Salvador:** in legislative elections, former left-wing guerrillas of the opposition Farabundo Martí National Liberation Front (FMLN) took more seats than the ruling Nationalist Republican Alliance (ARENA), in the party's biggest success since demobilising in 1992.
Spain: the ruling Popular Party (PP) of Prime Minister José María Aznar won an overall majority in a general election.
13 **Syria:** Mohammed Mustafa Mero was appointed as the new Prime Minister. His predecessor, Mahmoud Zubi, who was accused of corruption, committed suicide on May 21.

Vietnam: William Cohen became the first US Defence Secretary to visit the country since the end of the Vietnam War in 1975.

UN: a report criticised seven African countries, together with Belgium and Bulgaria, for violating sanctions on the sale of diamonds illegally mined by the Angolan rebel group UNITA.

16 **Nepal:** Prime Minister Krishna Prasad Bhattarai, facing a rebellion within his own Nepal Congress Party (NPC), resigned and was succeeded by his veteran party rival, Girija Prasad Koirala.

Japan: former Labour Minister Toshio Yamaguchi was sentenced to four years' imprisonment for arranging illegal loans.

17 **Uganda:** about 500 members of a Christian religious cult were killed in a church fire deliberately started by leaders of the cult; by the end of the month the death toll from this and other massacres at cult sites had reached 924.

18 **Taiwan:** Chen Shui-bian, leader of the pro-independence Democratic Progressive Party (DPP), was elected President, the first holder of the post not to be a member of the ruling Kuomintang (KMT) party.

19 **Senegal:** opposition candidate Abdoulayé Wade won the second round of presidential elections, the first President since independence in 1960 not to be a member of the ruling Socialist Party (PS).

20 **Middle East: Pope John Paul II** began a historic tour of Jordan, Israel and Palestine.

21 **UK:** in the budget the Chancellor of the Exchequer announced a substantial increase in public spending, to be concentrated on the National Health Service and education.

23 **EU:** a two-day summit opened in Lisbon. EU leaders agreed on an ambitious 10-year programme on employment and competitiveness; a Mexico-EU free trade agreement was signed.

24 **IMF:** Horst Köhler, the president of the European Bank of Reconstruction and Development, was appointed as the IMF's new managing director.

25 **Rwanda:** President Pasteur Bizimungu, a Hutu, resigned because of increasing tension with the largely Tutsi National Transitional Assembly.

26 **Russia:** acting President Vladimir Putin won the presidential election with over 50 per cent of the vote.

27 **Iraq:** legislative elections were held.

29 **OPEC:** ministers decided at the end of a two-day meeting in Vienna to raise production quotas by a total of 1.7 million barrels a day (b/d) in an attempt to bring down oil prices.

APRIL

1 **Japan:** Prime Minister Keizo Obuchi suffered a severe stoke and fell into a coma, resulting in his replacement by Yoshiro Mori; Obuchi died on May 14.

Senegal: Moustapha Niasse was appointed as Prime Minister.

3 **Bosnia:** Momcilo Krajisnik, a former Serb member of the Bosnian collective presidency, was arrested and flown to the Hague to stand trial for war crimes.

Azerbaijan: the former Defence Minister of the breakaway republic of Nagorno-Karabakh, Samvel Babayan, was charged with an assassination attempt against President Arkady Gukasyan in March.

6 **Zimbabwe:** the Land Acquisition Act was passed by parliament, enabling the government to take over white-owned farms without compensation and to redistribute them to blacks.

8 **Democratic Republic of Congo:** a new ceasefire agreement was agreed in the civil war, with provision for the deployment of UN peacekeepers and the withdrawal of all foreign combatants after three months.

9 **Peru:** a highly charged first-round presidential election was held. In simultaneous legislative elections President Alberto Keinya Fujimori's Peru 2000 alliance lost its absolute majority.

XIX CHRONICLE OF PRINCIPAL EVENTS IN 2000   563

- **Greece:** the ruling Panhellenic Socialist Movement (Pasok), led by Prime Minister Kostas Simitis, narrowly won a third-successive term in office at a general election.
- **Georgia:** Eduard Shevardnadze was overwhelmingly re-elected as President.
10 **Germany:** Angela Merkel was elected as the first female chairman of the Christian Democratic Union (CDU) following the resignation in February of Wolfgang Schäuble.
11 **UK:** historian David Irving lost a libel action which he had begun in January against a US writer who had described him as a "Holocaust denier".
12 **Latvia:** Prime Minister Andris Skele resigned after the collapse of his three-party coalition; Andris Berzins was nominated as his replacement.
13 **South Korea:** the ruling Millennium Democratic Party (MDP—renamed in January) failed to win an outright majority in legislative elections.
14 **Disarmament:** the Russian Duma ratified the 1993 START II nuclear disarmament treaty and, on April 21, the CTBT treaty. Exploratory talks with the USA on START III began on April 17.
  Samoa: two former ministers were convicted of conspiracy to murder the assassinated minister Luagalau Levaula Kamu, who was shot dead in July 1999; death sentences against the two were subsequently commuted to life imprisonment.
15 **Turkish Republic of Northern Cyprus:** Rauf Denktash won a fourth five-year term as President of the self-proclaimed republic.
16 **Ukraine:** the results of a referendum showed overwhelming popular support for President Leonid Kuchma's bid to reduce the powers of the unicameral legislature.
17 **Italy:** Prime Minister Massimo d'Alema resigned after a heavy defeat in regional elections. Giuliano Amato was sworn in as the new Prime Minister on 26 April.
  Rwanda: Paul Kagame, formerly Vice President, was elected as the first Tutsi President since independence in 1961.
20 **Nauru:** Bernard Dowiyogo was elected as President for the sixth time, following legislative elections on April 8.
22 **Sri Lanka:** the army suffered its heaviest defeat of the 17-year civil war as the Liberation Tigers of Tamil Eelam (LTTE) captured the strategic Elephant Pass military base in a major assault on the Jaffna peninsula.
  USA: armed agents of the US Immigration and Naturalisation Service (INS) seized Elián González, the six-year-old Cuban boy at the centre of a custody dispute, from the home of relations in Miami (Florida) and reunited him with his father in Cuba.
23 **Philippines:** a hostage crisis began after 21 people, including 10 foreign tourists, were kidnapped from a resort in Malaysia by Abu Sayyaf, an Islamic separatist group, and held on the island of Jolo in the Philippines' Sulu province.
24 **Taiwan:** the National Assembly voted to transfer most of its powers to the Legislative Yuan.
25 **India:** the government pledged major intervention to relieve the drought-stricken north-west states of Rajasthan and Gujarat.

MAY

1 **Sierra Leone:** the July 1999 peace agreement broke down as rebel troops attacked UN peacekeepers. With the rebels threatening to move on Freetown, the UK dispatched 700 paratroopers to secure the international airport and stabilise the situation.
  Taiwan: President Chen announced a broad-based new Cabinet, including 13 ministers from the former ruling Kuomintang (KMT).
  Georgia: the government of Vazha Lortkipanizde resigned following presidential elections in April. A new government, headed by Gia Arsenishvili, was later appointed.

2 **Armenia:** President Robert Kocharian dismissed Prime Minister Aram Sarkisian. On May 20 a new Cabinet, headed by Andranik Markarian, was appointed.
3 **Sri Lanka:** as heavy fighting continued on the Jaffna peninsula, President Chandrika Kumaratunga put the country on a war footing.
  Libya: the trial of two Libyans charged with the bombing of Pan Am flight 103 on 21 December 1988, over Lockerbie (Scotland), which had resulted in the death of 270 people, opened in the Netherlands.
4 **UK:** independent left-wing MP Ken Livingstone, who had been expelled from the Labour Party in April, became London's first directly-elected mayor.
  Congo: former Prime Minister Bernard Kolelas was found guilty and sentenced to death in absentia for a range of crimes alleged to have been committed during the 1997 civil war.
5 **Turkey:** Ahmet Necdet Sezer was elected as President.
7 **Russia:** Vladimir Putin was sworn in as President; a new Cabinet, headed by Mikhail Kasyanov, was appointed on May 22.
12 **Pakistan:** the Supreme Court endorsed the legitimacy of the 1999 military coup.
13 **Zimbabwe:** the date of the general election, postponed from April, was announced as June 24-25; by the end of the month 26 opposition supporters had been killed in political violence which had begun in March.
  Netherlands: an explosion at a fireworks depot in the city of Enschede killed at least 15 people and injured some 560 others.
16 **Dominican Republic:** Hipólito Mejía, the candidate of the centre-left Dominican Revolutionary Party (PRD), emerged as the victor in presidential elections.
  Morocco: Abdelsalam Yassine, the leader of the banned pro-Islamist group Adl Wal Ihsan, was released from house arrest.
18 **Paraguay:** the armed forces quashed an attempt to overthrow the government of President Luis González Macchi by supporters of Gen. (retd) Lino César Oviedo Silva.
19 **Fiji:** an armed coup championing "indigenous Fijians", led by failed businessmen George Speight, ousted the multi-ethnic government led by Prime Minister Mahendra Chaudhry. There followed a stand-off between Speight, who held Chaudhry and 30 others as hostages, and the armed forces.
  South Korea: Prime Minister Park Tae Joon resigned following a court ruling on tax evasion; he was replaced on May 22 by Lee Han Dong.
  USA: Rudolph Giuliani, the mayor of New York city, withdrew from the Senate contest against Hillary Clinton because of illness.
23 **Chile:** the Santiago Court of Appeals stripped Gen. (retd) Augusto Pinochet Ugarte of immunity from prosecution, permitting him to be tried in the multitude of human rights cases brought against him. The ruling was upheld by the Supreme Court on August 3.
24 **Lebanon:** Israel's occupation of southern Lebanon ended when the last of its troops departed from its self-declared "security zone", some six weeks ahead of schedule.
25 **Surinam:** former President Ronald Venetiaan's opposition four-party coalition, the New Front for Democracy (NF), won the legislative elections.
28 **Peru:** in the second round of presidential elections, incumbent Alberto Keinya Fujimori won a controversial third consecutive term of office.
29 **Indonesia:** former President Suharto was placed under house arrest to aid corruption investigations.
  UK: power was once again devolved from the UK to the Northern Ireland Assembly, thereby ending the 108 days of direct rule.
31 **Ethiopia:** the government claimed complete victory in its war against Eritrea, having launched massive attacks throughout the month and forced Eritrean units to retreat on all fronts.

JUNE

4 **Disarmament:** US President Clinton and Russia's President Vladimir Putin signed an arms control agreement during a three-day summit in Moscow; Putin reiterated Russian opposition to the proposed US National Missile Defence (NMD) system.

5 **Solomon Islands:** an armed coup mounted by ethnic Malaitan militia forced the resignation of Prime Minister Bartholomew Ulufa'alu; Manasseh Sogavare was elected as the new Prime Minister by parliament on June 30.

6 **Hungary:** Ferenc Madl was elected as President, replacing Arpad Goncz.
   Bosnia: Spasoje Tusevljak was elected as chairman of the all-Bosnian Council of Ministers.
   Poland: the coalition agreement between the Solidarity Electoral Alliance (AWS) and its junior partner, the Freedom Union (UW), collapsed when the UW withdrew its ministers from the Cabinet of Prime Minister Jerzy Buzek.

7 **Slovenia:** a new Cabinet, headed by Andrej Bajuk, was sworn in.

8 **Greece:** UK defence attaché Brig. Stephen Saunders was killed by left-wing "November 17" guerrillas.
   Russia: President Vladimir Putin imposed "temporary" direct presidential rule on Chechnya.

10 **Syria:** President Hafez al-Assad died of a heart attack.

11 **Paraguay:** Gen. (retd) Lino César Oviedo was arrested in southern Brazil at the request of the Paraguayan authorities who then filed extradition proceedings against him.

12 **Yemen:** a "final and permanent" border agreement was signed with Saudi Arabia, ending over 65 years of territorial dispute.

13 **Italy:** Mehmet Ali Agca, the Turkish gunman who attempted to assassinate Pope John Paul II in 1981, was pardoned.
   North-South Korea: Kim Jong Il and Kim Dae Jung began an unprecedented three-day summit in Pyongyang, promising future economic and social co-operation and the pursuit of an eventual peaceful reunification of the two countries.

14 **Ethiopia:** the ruling party was victorious in legislative elections.

18 **Eritrea:** a peace agreement was signed with Ethiopia, in Algiers, accepting UN supervision and an international mission to resolve border disputes.
   UK: the bodies of 58 Chinese illegal immigrants were found in a Dutch-registered container lorry at the Channel port of Dover (UK).
   Jordan: King Abdullah dismissed Abdul-Raouf Rawabdeh as Prime Minister and appointed in his place Ali Abu al-Rageb. A new Cabinet was appointed on 19 June.

19 **EU:** a two-day summit opened in Santa Maria da Feira (Portugal): EU leaders agreed to establish a common EU system to combat cross-border tax evasion; Greece formally won acceptance as the 12th member of EMU.

20 **Bangladesh:** opposition parties ended an 11-month boycott of the legislature.

21 **OPEC:** ministers in Geneva announced a further 3 per cent overall increase in production after earlier increases had failed to bring about a sustained drop in oil prices.

25 **Zimbabwe:** at a general election, the ruling ZANU-PF party was seriously challenged for the first time by the opposition MDC; there was a record voter turnout despite widespread intimidation by government supporters.
   Japan: despite losing its parliamentary majority in the general election, the Liberal Democratic Party (LDP) remained the largest single party and, with the support of its coalition partners, formed a new government on July 4.

26 **Science:** the publicly-funded international Human Genome Project and a US private company, Celera Genomics, jointly announced the completion of a working draft of the human genetic blueprint.
   Indonesia: President Wahid declared a state of civil emergency in the Molucca islands to curb Christian-Muslim conflict.

Northern Ireland: independent inspectors, nominated by the IRA to monitor its hidden arsenals, announced that they were satisfied that the arms were "safely and adequately stored".

29 **Germany:** former Chancellor Helmut Kohl testified before a special Bundestag committee set up to investigate alleged secret donations to the CDU.

Uganda: 90 per cent of voters in a referendum backed a continuation of country's no party "Movement" system; however, the turnout was less than 50 per cent and opponents claimed that the poll had been boycotted by voters.

Indonesia: at least 480 people, many of them refugees from fighting in the Moluccas, died when an overloaded ferry sank in rough seas.

30 **UK:** David Copeland was sentenced to life imprisonment for three nail-bombings in London in April 1999 which had targeted ethnic minorities and homosexuals, and which had killed three people.

JULY

1 **Democratic Republic of Congo:** President Laurent Kabila inaugurated an unelected transitional legislature and constituent assembly.

Denmark: the Oresund road and rail link with Sweden was inaugurated.

2 **Mongolia:** the formerly communist Mongolian People's Revolutionary Party was swept back into power at a general election. A new Cabinet, led by Nambaryn Enhbayar, was approved on Aug 9.

Mexico: after 71 years of uninterrupted rule, the Institutional Revolutionary Party (PRI) lost power in presidential elections.

Russia: over two days, militants in Chechnya carried out five co-ordinated suicide bombings against Russian targets, killing at least 42 Russian troops.

4 **Chad:** a peace agreement was formalised between the government and the rebel group, Armed Resistance Against Anti-Democratic Forces.

5 **Ukraine:** at a two-day conference in Berlin, representatives of 37 states pledged an additional US$320 million towards the cost of reinforcing the concrete shell around the exploded reactor at the Chernobyl nuclear power plant.

9 **Philippines:** after a prolonged battle, in which reportedly 300 rebels and 200 government troops were killed, the army captured the headquarters of the Moro Islamic Liberation Front (MILF) on the island of Mindanao.

WHO: the 13th international AIDS conference opened in South Africa.

Israel: the coalition government of Prime Minister Ehud Barak collapsed when six ministers resigned and withdrew the support of the ultra-orthodox Shas, the right-wing Yisrael Ba'aliya party and the National Religious party.

Haiti: the second round of legislative and local elections was boycotted by the Organisation of American States (OAS) and almost all opposition parties, in protest at alleged vote-rigging in the first round.

10 **Solomon Islands:** a new government was established despite continued ethnic conflict.

Philippines: at least 202 people died when a giant rubbish dump, weakened by typhoon rains, collapsed in a suburb of Manila.

Israel: President Ezer Weizmann resigned over corruption allegations. On 31 July Moshe Katzav, a member of the opposition Likud party, was elected as his replacement.

Syria: in a referendum in which he was the only candidate, Bashar al-Assad was endorsed as President.

11 **Nigeria:** about 250 people were killed by an explosion whilst collecting petrol from a damaged pipeline in Delta state; some 100 people were killed on July 16 in a similar incident at another pipeline.

Middle East: an eight-day Israeli-Palestinian summit meeting began in the USA between US President Bill Clinton, Israeli Prime Minister Ehud Barak and Palestinian President Yassir Arafat.

12 **East Timor:** UN administrators and Timorese representatives formed a government to operate until elections were held in 2001.

Space: after a two-year delay Russia launched the *Zvezda* service module for the International Space Station (ISS); the module docked automatically on July 26.

13 **Colombia:** the US House of Representatives approved a US$1.3 billion aid package; President Clinton supported the package by visiting the country on Aug 30.

Fiji: the Great Council of Chiefs appointed Ratu Josefa Iloilo as the new President after coup leader George Speight released former Prime Minister Chaudhry and the remaining hostages. Iloilo on July 28 swore in new Prime Minister Laisenia Qarase and an all-Melanesian Cabinet. Speight and 16 supporters were charged with treason on August 11.

Vietnam: a bilateral trade agreement was signed with the USA.

14 **Germany:** the Bundesrat approved a landmark tax reform package.

17 **China:** Russia's President Putin began three-day visit; he and President Jiang Zemin issued a joint condemnation of the US NMD system.

Germany: after negotiations begun October 1998, a DM10 billion fund was established to compensate surviving slave and forced labourers under Nazi rule during World War II.

18 **Community of Portuguese-Speaking Countries:** the third summit ended in Maputo, Mozambique.

20 **Macedonia:** a new, reduced, Cabinet was sworn in.

France: Prime Minister Lionel Jospin unveiled a plan granting Corsica limited autonomy.

Zimbabwe: at the opening of parliament, President Mugabe announced an acceleration in the redistribution of land from white farmers to landless blacks.

Kazakhstan: the constitutional court endorsed legislation passed in June granting President Nursultan Nazarbayev lifelong powers beyond his term of office.

21 **G-7/G-8:** a summit opened in Okinawa, Japan, with discussions centring upon Third World development and debt relief.

22 **Pakistan:** former Prime Minister Sharif was convicted of corruption and sentenced to 14 years' imprisonment and banned from office for 21 years.

23 **EU:** a trade agreement was signed with the 77 ACP states in Cotonou, Benin (Cotonou Agreement) which replaced the earlier series of Lomé conventions.

24 **Côte d'Ivoire:** nearly 87 per cent of voters in a referendum endorsed the new constitution which was intended to return the country to civilian rule.

Burma: the military junta allowed 600,000 students to resume their education at colleges which had been closed since 1996.

25 **France:** Concorde's unsurpassed 31-year safety record was shattered as the supersonic airliner crashed outside Paris, killing 113 people.

27 **Northern Ireland:** the final batch of prisoners scheduled for early release under the terms of the 1998 Good Friday Agreement were freed.

28 **Russia:** 21 "oligarchs" (powerful businessmen) met President Putin to resolve the growing tension between the state and the owners of privatised state assets.

30 **Venezuela:** President Hugo Chávez Frías was returned to power at a presidential election held under a new constitution.

AUGUST

1 **Zimbabwe:** President Mugabe extended the list of white-owned farms for compulsory redistribution.

3 **USA:** the Republican National Convention ended with the nomination of George W. Bush as the party's presidential candidate.

7 **Indonesia:** President Abdurrahman Wahid apologised to a session of People's Consultative Assembly for the failings of the first nine months of his presidency. He later agreed to delegate day-to-day tasks of government to Vice President Megawati Sukarnoputri.
8 **Malaysia:** former Prime Minister Anwar Ibrahim was convicted of sodomy and sentenced to nine years' imprisonment. Anwar was already serving a six-year term for his 1999 conviction on corruption charges.
9 **Guatemala:** President Alfonso Portillo admitted the state's responsibility for civil war atrocities.
10 **Sri Lanka:** Sirimavo Bandaranaike, 84, resigned from her third term as Prime Minister, citing ill health, and was replaced by Ratnasiri Wickremanayake.
11 **India:** flooding in north-eastern states, caused by exceptionally heavy monsoon rains, claimed over 300 lives and left 4.5 million homeless.
12 **Russia:** the *Kursk*, one of the navy's most sophisticated nuclear-powered submarines, sank in the Barents Sea after two explosions, killing all of its 118-strong crew.
13 **Somalia:** delegates at a peace conference in Djibouti inaugurated an interim National Assembly of Somalia, the country's first legislature since 1991, which on August 25 elected a new President of Somalia, Abdiqasim Salad Hasan.
14 **Pakistan:** Chief Executive Gen. Pervaiz Musharraf announced district elections from December 2000 to August 2001 as the first phase of a return to democracy.
15 **North-South Korea:** the first family reunions since 1985 took place over four days, with 100 people each from North and South flying to meet relatives in the other country's capital.
16 **Dominican Republic:** newly elected President Hipólito Mejía swore in a new Cabinet.
   Philippines: over three days, the Islamic separatist rebel group Abu Sayyaf released four hostages, kidnapped at Malaysian resort in April. On August 27, after ransoms paid by Libya, six more hostages were freed.
17 **Switzerland:** the country's banks approved a final US$1.3 billion settlement to compensate Holocaust survivors and victims' relatives for assets deposited by Jews and held by the banks since World War II.
   USA: the Democratic National Convention ended with the nomination of Vice President Al Gore as the Democratic presidential candidate.
20 **Kyrgyzstan:** Central Asian leaders issued a declaration of co-operation against terrorism after fighting earlier in month against Islamic insurgents in Kyrgyzstan and Uzbekistan.
22 **Panama:** a new Cabinet was sworn in.
   Azerbaijan: Abulfaz Elchibey, the chairman of the Azerbaijan Popular Front and the country's first democratically elected President, died.
23 **Bahrain:** a Gulf Air Airbus travelling from Cairo to Bahrain crashed near its destination, killing all 143 passengers and crew.
25 **Middle East:** a summit meeting in the USA between Israeli Prime Minister Ehud Barak and Palestinian President Yassir Arafat collapsed without agreement.
26 **Algeria:** a new Cabinet, headed by Ali Benflis, was sworn in.
28 **Lebanon:** the first round of legislative elections took place.
   Burundi: President Pierre Buyoya and 13 political parties signed a peace agreement aimed at ending the seven-year civil war between Burundi's ruling ethnic Tutsi minority and Hutu majority.
   Togo: the government of Prime Minister Eugene Koffi Adoboli resigned after an overwhelming vote of no-confidence in the National Assembly.
   Croatia: a key war crimes witness, Milan Levar, was killed in an explosion outside his house.

SEPTEMBER

1 **USA:** President Bill Clinton formally deferred a decision on the deployment of the National Missile Defence (NMD) system until his successor took office in January 2001.

2 **Burma:** the military junta forced opposition leader Aung San Suu Kyi to return home after a nine-day stand-off with police who were preventing her from travelling by road out of Rangoon, the capital. Her attempt on September 21 to leave Rangoon by train was also thwarted.

3 **Lebanon:** the second round of legislative elections saw defeat for Prime Minister Selim al-Hoss. Former Prime Minister Rafik al-Hariri (1992-98) emerged with most support.

Germany: the Christian Democratic Union premier of Hesse, Roland Koch, was accused of accepting illegal donations to the party and implicated in embezzling party funds.

Vatican: Pope Pius IX was beatified despite allegations that he had been anti-semitic.

5 **Afghanistan:** Talibaan forces launched an assault which captured the strategically important town of Taloqan from the United Islamic Front for Salvation of Afghanistan (led by former Defence Minister Ahmed Shah Masud).

6 **UN:** delegations, including nearly 150 heads of state and government, attended a three-day Millennium Summit at the UN headquarters in New York. UN Secretary-General Kofi Annan called the summit to debate the reform of the UN and its role in the 21st century.

Surinam: President Ronald Venetiaan, who was appointed in August, announced a new Cabinet.

7 **UK:** road hauliers and farmers blockaded the main UK oil refineries in protest against high fuel prices, bringing the country almost to a halt within days by cutting off supplies to consumers. Protesters began to lift blockades on September 14 but threatened renewed action if government did not reduce fuel taxes within 60 days. In the face of similar protests during September French and German governments introduced packages of concessions.

8 **Comoros:** the OAU rejected the August 26 Fomboni declaration by the military government of the Comoros federation and secessionist leaders of the island of Anjouan agreeing on a new decentralised state.

Ecuador: the US dollar was formally adopted as the currency of the country, replacing the sucre.

9 **Sierra Leone:** British troops stormed a militia base in a successful rescue of British hostages who had been held since August. Some 25 militia fighters and one British soldier were killed in the action.

10 **Hong Kong:** elections to the Legislative Council saw a low turn-out of voters and an increase in support for the leading pro-China party.

Palestine: the Palestinian Legislative Council agreed to delay indefinitely the unilateral declaration of Palestinian statehood planned for September 13.

11 **Mauritius:** the ruling coalition government led by Prime Minister Navin Ramgoolam suffered a crushing defeat in general elections to the National Assembly. A new government led by Sir Aneerood Jugnauth (Prime Minister 1982-95) was sworn in on September 17.

Guinea: opposition leader Alpha Condé and 47 supporters were sentenced to prison terms for sedition and other offences.

12 **Austria:** EU sanctions, imposed in February because of the entry of the right-wing Freedom Party into the government, were formally lifted.

14 **Nigeria:** the northern Borno state adopted the Islamic legal code (sharia), the eighth Nigerian state to do so.

Colombia: President Andrés Pastrana issued emergency decrees to increase the effectiveness of the armed forces, authorising an increase in manpower from 10,000 to 52,000 by the end of 2001.

Bangladesh: a study by the WHO found that the exposure of up to two-thirds of the population of Bangladesh to arsenic-contaminated water was "the largest mass-poisoning of a population in history".

15 **France:** police arrested Ignacio Gracia Arregui, widely believed to be the leader of ETA, Spain's Basque separatist group, one of 37 suspected ETA members arrested in a crackdown in Spain and France.
   Olympic Games: the 27th Olympiad opened in Sydney, New South Wales, Australia. By the time the games closed on October 1 they were regarded as amongst the most successful ever held.
16 **Peru:** President Alberto Keinya Fujimori unexpectedly announced that he would step down early to call an election in which he would not be a candidate.
   Philippines: the government launched a military offensive against Islamic separatists holding hostages on the south-western Jolo island. Two hostages escaped, but by end of month rebels still held 16 captives.
19 **USA:** US Senate voted overwhelmingly in favour of a landmark bill granting permanent normal trade relations with China, thereby endorsing an agreement which had been negotiated in November 1999.
20 **USA:** Robert Kay, independent counsel in the long-running Whitewater affair, announced that there was insufficient evidence to prove that President Bill Clinton or his wife Hillary Clinton had committed any criminal acts in regard to allegedly improper loans or land deals.
21 **Japan:** at an extraordinary session of the Diet the government unveiled an economic stimulus package.
22 **EU:** G-7 central banks and the European Central Bank intervened in foreign exchange markets to support the ailing euro, which had lost around 27 per cent of its value against the US dollar since its launch in January 1999.
   Moldova: the legislature approved a constitutional change which provided for the election of a president by parliamentary rather than popular vote.
24 **Yugoslavia:** despite allegations of vote-rigging and intimidation by supporters of Slobodan Milosevic, the incumbent federation President, Vojislav Kostunica, his challenger, was widely regarded as having won the first round of the presidential elections outright with over 50 per cent of the vote.
26 **Prague:** the IMF and World Bank began their annual meetings, amidst disruption by some 12,000 radical demonstrators against global capitalism and third-world debt. At least 160 people were injured in clashes between police and hard-core anarchists.
27 **Canada:** Pierre Trudeau, the charismatic Liberal Prime Minister of 1968-79 and 1980-84, died aged 80.
   Greece: the ferry *Express Samina* hit rocks off the Aegean island of Paros, sinking with the loss of 79 lives.
28 **Jerusalem:** serious rioting broke out amongst Palestinians following an illegal visit by Israeli nationalist hardliner Ariel Sharon to the sacred site of Haram-al-Sharif or the Temple Mount. By the end of the month at least four Palestinians had been killed and around 200 wounded by Israeli security forces.
   Denmark: in a referendum on the European single currency, 53.1 per cent voted to reject the adoption of the euro compared with 46.9 per cent in favour.
   Indonesia: the trial of former President Suharto on corruption charges, which had begun on Aug 31, collapsed when an independent panel of doctors reported that he was physically and mentally unfit to stand trial.
30 **India:** renewed exceptional monsoon flooding since September 18 resulted in a death toll of 758 in the north-eastern state of West Bengal and made 15 million homeless. In neighbouring Bangladesh at least 250 people died.

OCTOBER

1 **Dominica:** Prime Minister Roosevelt "Rosie" Douglas died of a heart attack, aged 58.
3 **Taiwan:** Premier Tang Fei's resignation preceded a government announcement on October 27 cancelling the country's fourth nuclear power plant, which provoked a political crisis.
  Somalia: Ali Khalif Galayr was appointed Prime Minister; appointments to Galayr's interim Cabinet were completed by October 20.
6 **Yugoslavia:** amidst massive popular protests, President Slobodan Milosevic was forced to surrender power and recognise Vojislav Kostunica as winner of September presidential election. Kostunica was inaugurated as President on October 7.
  Argentina: a crisis in the governing alliance was precipitated by the resignation of Vice-President Carlos "Chacho" Alvarez, protesting against President Fernando de la Rúa's failure to dismiss two officials implicated in a recent bribery scandal.
7 **Luxembourg:** Grand Duke Jean, sovereign since 1964, abdicated in favour of his eldest son Crown Prince Henri.
8 **Poland:** President Aleksander Kwasniewski was re-elected with nearly 54 per cent of vote, defeating 11 other candidates, including former President Lech Walesa who received barely 1 per cent of the vote.
9 **Cape Verde:** António Gualberto do Rosario was nominated as Prime Minister following the resignation of Carlos Veiga in August.
  Czech Republic: the controversial Telemin nuclear power plant began operations despite a blockade of the nearby border with Austria by thousands of Austrian protesters who claimed that the plant was unsafe.
10 **Sri Lanka:** in legislative elections President Chandrika Kumaratunga's People's Alliance (PA) won the largest number of seats in Parliament and formed a coalition government on October 19.
  NATO: At a meeting of NATO defence ministers, US Defence Secretary William Cohen endorsed the EU objective of establishing a military rapid reaction force.
  Eurasia: the Presidents of Russia, Belarus, Kazakhstan, Kyrgyzstan and Tajikistan signed a treaty in Kazakhstan establishing a Eurasian Economic Community.
11 **UK:** First Minister of Scotland and former Secretary of State for Scotland Donald Dewar died of a brain haemorrhage; Henry McLeish was elected First Minister by the Scottish Parliament on October 26.
12 **India:** former Prime Minister P.V. Narasimha Rao was sentenced to three years' imprisonment on corruption charges relating to the bribery of MPs in 1993.
  Nigeria: up to 100 people were killed in Lagos, the commercial capital, during ethnic violence.
  Yemen: 17 US sailors were killed and 37 wounded in a suicide bomb attack on the destroyer *USS Cole* in Aden harbour.
13 **Nobel Peace Prize:** in South Korea, celebrations greeted the award in Oslo, Norway, of the Nobel Peace Prize to President Kim Dae Jung.
14 **Saudi Arabia:** a Saudi airliner carrying 85 passengers and 17 crew was hijacked en route from Jeddah to London. The aircraft eventually landed at Baghdad, Iraq, where the two hijackers, Saudi dissidents, surrendered to Iraqi authorities and the hostages were swiftly released.
15 **Solomon Islands:** a peace deal was signed in Townsville, Australia, between two Solomon Islands ethnic militias, to end the conflict which had led to an armed coup in June.
16 **Middle East:** in Egypt, a two-day summit hosted by Egypt's President Hosni Mubarak began at Sharm-el-Shaikh, attended by Israel's Prime Minister Ehud Barak, Palestinian President Yassir Arafat and US President Bill Clinton. The summit concluded with a fragile agreement to end the violence between Israeli troops and Palestinians which since late September had claimed the lives of at least 144 people, mostly Palestinians.

Italy: the government declared a state of emergency in the north-western regions of Valle d'Aosta, Piedmont and Liguria, where 31 people died in the country's worst floods since 1994.

17 **UK:** a rail crash near Hatfield, Hertfordshire, in which 4 people were killed, led to emergency track repairs throughout the country, causing massive disruption of the privatised railway system.

18 **Egypt:** in the first of three rounds of elections for the People's Assembly the ruling National Democratic Party (NDP) won 118 of 150 seats contested.

20 **ASEM:** in Seoul, South Korea, the third Asia-Europe Meeting (ASEM) began, attended by the heads of government of 10 Asian states, the 15 member states of the EU and the President of the European Commission.

Burma: British human rights activist James Mawdsley was released following international pressure, having served 415 days of a 17-year prison sentence imposed for distributing pro-democracy leaflets.

21 **Colombia:** it was reported that at least 54 soldiers and police and an unknown number of left-wing FARC guerrillas had been killed in an army offensive in the north-western Antioquia state, regarded as the most serious fighting for a decade.

23 **North Korea:** US Secretary of State Madeleine Albright began a three-day visit, the most senior US official to visit the country.

East Timor: the UN appointed a 36-member transitional legislature: the East Timor National Council (ETNC).

Lebanon: Prime Minister designate Rafiq al-Hariri appointed a new Cabinet.

24 **Côte d'Ivoire:** President Gen. Robert Guëi declared himself the winner of the presidential election held on October 22 and widely regarded as flawed. After international pressure, popular protests, and fighting between army factions, Guëi fled the country on October 26 and Laurent Gbagbo, believed by many to be the real electoral winner, was inaugurated as President.

26 **UK:** the report of the official inquiry set up in 1997 into the history of bovine spongiform encephalopathy (BSE) was published.

Zimbabwe: the opposition Movement for Democratic Change (MDC) began impeachment proceedings against President Robert Mugabe for unconstitutional rule.

Lithuania: the legislature confirmed Rolandas Paksas as the new Prime Minister, representing the New Policy Bloc electoral alliance, after legislative elections on October 8.

27 **Nepal:** the government began its first direct talks with Maoist rebels, seeking to end an insurgency which had cost 1,450 lives.

St Vincent and the Grenadines: Arnhim Eustace became Prime Minister, replacing long-serving Prime Minister Sir James Mitchell who had agreed to step down in September.

29 **Tanzania:** the outcome of the general election was uncertain after 16 results in Zanzibar were nullified because of alleged electoral malpractice. The election campaign had been characterised by violence and claims by both government and opposition of vote-rigging.

Kyrgyzstan: President Askar Akayev was re-elected with over 74 per cent of the vote amidst reports of widespread electoral malpractice and fraud.

30 **Spain:** three people were killed and more than 60 injured by a bomb in Madrid, the worst attack in the capital by the Basque separatist group ETA since 1995.

31 **UK:** the government pledged to invest in flood defences after the worst floods since 1947 in England and Wales, in which 6 people died. Exceptional weather conditions were widely attributed to global warming.

NOVEMBER

2 **Space:** the first long-stay crew boarded the International Space Station (ISS), currently under construction in orbit and due for completion in 2006.

3 **UK:** the Ilois, or Chagos islanders, won in the UK High Court the right to return to their homes in the British Indian Ocean Territory, whence they had been evicted in the late 1960s when the UK government leased the main island, Diego Garcia, to the USA as a military base.
4 **Yugoslavia:** a new transitional government was sworn in.
5 **Ethiopia:** the remains of Emperor Haile Selassie were reburied at Trinity Cathedral, Addis Ababa, 25 years after his death.
7 **USA:** the presidential election between Vice President Al Gore (Democrat), who won a narrow majority of the popular vote, and George W. Bush remained unresolved by the end of the month because of a disputed result in the crucial state of Florida.
   Burkina Faso: a new Prime Minister, Paramanga Ernest Yoli, was appointed.
8 **Middle East:** President Bill Clinton named an international committee to assess the causes of the continuing wave of violence between Israel and the Palestinians.
9 **Croatia:** the legislature passed constitutional amendments to enhance its own power at the expense of that of the president.
   Lithuania: the legislature approved the programme of the new government, formed following the October legislative elections.
10 **Zimbabwe:** the Supreme Court ruled the government's programme of compulsory seizure of white-owned farms illegal.
11 **Austria:** 155 people died in a fire in the tunnel of a funicular railway above the resort of Kaprun; it was the country's worst peace-time disaster.
   Sierra Leone: a ceasefire was signed by the government and the rebel Revolutionary United Front (RUF).
   Bosnia-Hercegovina: elections were held for the presidencies and legislatures of the Muslim-Croat Federation and Republika Srpska and for the all-Bosnia legislature.
12 **Swaziland:** a two-day general strike began in support of demands for democratic reforms.
13 **France:** Prime Minister Lionel Jospin announced emergency measures to quell public alarm over a rising incidence amongst cattle of bovine spongiform encephalopathy (BSE), linked to the human variant Creutzfeldt-Jakob disease (vCJD).
14 **Egypt:** elections were completed to the 444-seat legislature, with some gains for opposition parties.
15 **Slovenia:** a new coalition government was formed following October's general election.
16 **Vietnam:** US President Bill Clinton began a three-day state visit, the first by a US President to the unified country since the end of the Vietnam War in 1975.
   UN: the International Labour Organisation took the unprecedented step of voting to urge member states to apply economic sanctions to Burma because of its use of forced labour.
20 **EU:** in Brussels, foreign and defence ministers of member states agreed to form a military Rapid Reaction Force.
21 **Mozambique:** 80 prisoners, mostly supporters of the opposition Renamo, died in an overcrowded cell. Nearly 40 people had died in demonstrations by Renamo earlier in the month against the allegedly rigged elections of December 1999.
22 **Mexico:** President-elect Vicente Fox Quesada announced a first batch of Cabinet appointments; the new government was completed by November 27.
   El Salvador: the government formally adopted the US dollar as its currency.
23 **Greece:** former King Constantine won a ruling in the European Court of Human Rights that the Greek government had illegally confiscated royal family properties.
25 **UN:** in the Hague, the Netherlands, the UN Conference on World Climate Change (begun on November 13) failed to reach an agreement on ways of achieving the targets on reducing emissions of greenhouse gases set at Kyoto, Japan, in 1990.
27 **Canada:** the Liberal government under Prime Minister Jean Chrétien was re-elected with an increased majority.

Uganda: An outbreak of the highly contagious and incurable Ebola fever spread from the north to the south-west of the country; by the end of the month 149 people had died.

28 **India:** government troops began a unilateral ceasefire in their conflict with Kashmiri separatists for the duration of the Muslim holy month of Ramadan.

Netherlands: the legislature passed a bill to legalise euthanasia.

Iraq: a Royal Maroc airliner was one of a number of flights during the month to breach the UN ban on commercial air traffic to the country.

30 **UK:** the end of the 1999-2000 parliamentary session saw 10 bills obtain royal assent, including controversial legislation on transport and a lowering of the age of sexual consent for homosexuals.

DECEMBER

5 **Japan:** Prime Minister Yoshiro Mori began implementing structural government reforms with a major Cabinet reshuffle.

Taiwan: President Chen Shui-bian announced the start in 2001 of three "mini-links"—direct travel, trade and communications—between the Taiwanese islands of Kinmen and Matsu and mainland China.

6 **Guinea:** hundreds of civilian refugees from Liberia and Sierra Leone were reportedly massacred by armed groups in the south-east of the country.

Democratic Republic of Congo: government and rebel groups signed an agreement to pull back troops from front-line positions. Fighting, however, continued.

7 **Philippines:** the impeachment trial of President Joseph Estrada, on charges of corruption and violating the constitution, began in the Senate (the upper house of the bicameral legislature).

EU: a five-day summit began in Nice, France. Heads of EU governments agreed on the reform of EU institutions in preparation for an enlargement of the Union.

9 **Israel:** Prime Minister Ehud Barak announced his resignation, calling for a special election of a new Prime Minister on February 6, 2001.

10 **Pakistan:** former Prime Minister Nawaz Sharif was unexpectedly pardoned, released from prison, and flown into exile.

Côte d'Ivoire: the Ivorian Popular Front (FPI), the party of President Laurent Gbagbo, won the largest number of seats but no overall majority in controversial legislative elections from which opposition leader Alasanne Ouattara was excluded.

Romania: the run-off of the November presidential election was won by former communist and former President Ion Iliescu, defeating the ultra nationalist Corneliu Vadim Tudor of the Greater Romania Party (RM). The leading party in the November 26 legislative elections, Iliescu's Social Democracy Party of Romania (SDPR), formed a government under Prime Minister Adrian Nastase on December 28.

11 **Trinidad and Tobago:** Prime Minister Basdeo Panday secured a second term as his United National Congress (UNC) won a majority in legislative elections.

East Timor: UN prosecutors issued the first indictments for crimes against humanity committed in the aftermath of the 1999 independence referendum.

12 **Eritrea:** President Isayas Afewerki of Eritrea and Prime Minister Meles Zenawi of Ethiopia signed a comprehensive peace agreement to bring to a formal end the 19-month border war.

13 **USA:** Vice President Al Gore conceded the November presidential election to Republican George W. Bush after a Supreme Court ruling prevented further recounts in the disputed state of Florida.

Sudan: in presidential and legislative elections held until December 23, President Omar Hassan Ahmad al-Bashir was re-elected with 86.5 per cent of the vote and the ruling National Congress won 355 of 360 seats in the legislature.

14 **France:** President Jacques Chirac denied on television that, whilst mayor of Paris (1977-95), he had been involved in the political corruption scandal currently unfolding, in which several politicians had already been named.

Iran: the popular reformist Minister of Culture and Islamic Guidance Seyyed Ataollah Mohajerani, a close ally of President Seyyed Mohammed Khatami, finally resigned after many months of pressure from conservative hard-liners.

15 **Ukraine:** the last working reactor at the Chernobyl power station, site of the world's worst nuclear accident in 1986, was formally closed.

19 **UN:** the Security Council adopted Resolution 1333, imposing limited sanctions against Afghanistan if the country did not hand over Islamic militant and alleged terrorist Osama bin Laden within 30 days.

Papua New Guinea: Prime Minister Sir Mekere Morauta completed a major Cabinet reshuffle, begun in November after a parliamentary revolt.

Turkey: at least 32 people died in assaults by troops on prisons to break the hunger strikes of political prisoners who were objecting to impending transfers to a new type of prison.

20 **Sri Lanka:** the separatist Liberation Tigers of Tamil Eelam (LTTE) declared a unilateral month-long ceasefire in the civil war.

Denmark: Prime Minister Poul Nyrup Rasmussen announced a major Cabinet reshuffle.

Moldova: the failure of Parlamentul (the legislature) to hold the fourth round of the inconclusive presidential election led to the announcement by incumbent President Petru Lucinschi of its dissolution in January 2001 and a general election in February.

23 **Yugoslavia:** the Democratic Opposition of Serbia (DOS) 18-party alliance, led by President Vojislav Kostunica, won 176 out of 250 seats in the Serbian legislature.

25 **China:** 309 people died in a fire in a department store complex in Luoyang, Henan province

28 **Ghana:** John Kufuor, of the opposition New Patriotic Party (NPP), was elected President in the second round of voting, ending 19 years of rule by President Jerry Rawlings. In legislative elections on December 7 the NPP had won the largest number of seats but had failed to achieve an overall majority.

31 **Russia:** a new national anthem was broadcast, using the tune of the old Soviet anthem, abolished in 1993, but with new lyrics. Legislation had been approved on December 26 adopting the tsarist flag and emblems as national symbols.

USA: President Bill Clinton met the deadline for signing the UN treaty to establish a permanent International Criminal Court (ICC) for trying war crimes.

INDEX

Page references in bold indicate location of main coverage.

Abacha, Sani, 63, 80
Abbott, Anthony John, 189
Abderemane, Lt. Col. Said Abeid, 315
Abdul Aziz Shah, Salahuddin, Sultan of Selangor, 320
Abdulkarim al-Iryani, 213
Abdullah Ahmad Badawi, 320, 321
Abdullah bin Faisal bin Turki, Prince, 212
Abdullah ibn Abdul Aziz, Crown Prince of Saudi Arabia, 210, 211, 213
Abdullah II, King of Jordan, 36, 202, 203, 565
Abgeyome, Messan Kodjo, 253
Aboulela, Leila, 496
Abreu, Antonio, 88
Abubakar, Gen. Abdusalam, 388
Aburish, Said K., 498
Adair, Johnny, 43
Adamkus, Valdas, 102, 105
Adamson, Sir Campbell, 527
Adamsons, Janis, 103
Adebayo, Diran, 498
Adhikari, Bharat Mohan, 307
Adlington, Robert, 475
Adoboli, Eugene Koffi, 568
Advocaat, Dick, 503
Afari-Gyan, Kwadwo, 240
Afewerki, Isayas, 222, 231, 233, 574
Afghanistan, 214, 288, **289-91**, 295-7, 299, 304, 354, 373, 393, 452, 489
Agard, John, 498
Agassi, Andre, 507
Agbabi, Patience, 498
Agca, Mehmet Ali, 565
Agnew, Spiro, 528
Aguirre Martínez, Juan Estaban, 170
Ahern, Bertie, 64, 65
Ahmed, Shahabuddin, 305
Aho, Esko, 72
Ahrens, Lynn, 481
Ahtisaari, Martti, 42, 45, 72, 74
AIDS/HIV, 2, 3, 13, 233, 235, 276, 281, 284, 285, 366, 371, 372, 376, 385, 420, 547
Ainslie, Ben, 501
Ajodhia, Jules, 190, 191
Akayev, Askar, 292, 293, 297, 572
Akihito, Emperor Tsugu no Miya, 341
Akilov, Akil, 292
Akinci, Mustafa, 95

Alagna, Roberto, 470
Albania, **117-8**, 128, 405, 408
Albert, Carl, 528
Albert II, King of Belgium, 60
Albright, Madeleine K., 156, 167, 184, 335, 348, 525, 572
Alegrett, Sebastia, 427
Aleksovski, 457
Alemán, Arnoldo Lacayo, 178, 179, 180
Alexis, Jacques Édouard, 176, 177
Alfonso, Col. (retd) Luis Dávila, 174
Algeria, 225, **226-7**, 229, 230, 231, 419, 420
Ali Abu al-Rageb, 202, 203
Alibhai-Brown, Yasmin, 495, 499
Aliev, Heidar, 137
Aliyev, Geidar, 136
Allègre, Claude, 53
Allen, George, 147
Allen, Thomas, 470
Allende Gossens, Salvador, 165, 559
Almunia, Joaquín, 82
Alsop, Will, 494
Alvarado, José Antonio, 179
Alvares, Elcio, 164
Alvarez, Aida, 525
Alvarez, Carlos "Chacho", 162, 571
Alvarez Bogaert, Fernando, 176
Alvear, María Soledad, 165
Amadi, Ahmed, 313
Amadou, Hama, 248, 559
Amamou, Mohammed, 415
Amaral, Ferreira do, 88
Amarjargal, Rinchinnyamyn, 349
Amato, Giuliano, 56, 57, 58, 491, 563
American Samoa, 364
Amichai, Yehuda, 497, 528
Amidon, Stephen, 498
Amis, Martin, 497, 499
Amnesty International, 34, 167, 189, 225, 226, 262, 417
Amour, Salmin, 237
Amr Musa, 200
Andean Community of Nations, **427**, **429**
Anderson, Gillian, 484
Anderson, John, 355
Anderson, Noel Lynch, 184
Andersson, Roy, 484
Anderton, Jim, 359

Andorra, 79, 80
Andrianarivo, Tantely, 315
Anelka, Nicolas, 502
Angelopoulou-Daskalaki, Gianna, 91
Angola, 34, 54, 61, 160, 252, 253, 259, **268-9**, 274, 275, 278, 373, 419-21
Anguilla, 189
Anguita, Julio, 84
Annan, Kofi, 93, 194, 207, 229, 240, 291, 329, 366, 373, 569
Annan, Lord (Noel), 528
Anne-Marie, Queen of the Hellenes, 541
Anthony, Kenny D., 187, 188
Antigua and Barbuda, 187, 389
Antoni, Robert, 498
Antrobus, Charles James, 187
Anwar Ibrahim, 320, 321, 322, 568
Anyaoku, Chief Emeka, 388, 391
ANZUS Pact, 377
Aoki, Mikio, 342
Aoun, Michel, 207
Aptidon, Hassan Gouled, 233
Aquino, Corazon, 327
Arab League, 209, 213, 224, 234, **415-6**
Arab Maghreb Union (AMU), 415
Arafat, Yassir, 5, 156, 195, 196, 197, 198, 199, 202, 213, 567, 568, 571
Aragona, Giancarlo, 406
Arantes Nájera, Fr Mario, 178
Araque, Alí Rodríguez, 383, 387
Arcaya, Ignacio, 174
Archer, Jeffrey, 496
Architecture, 92-4
Arctic Council, 410-1
Arditti, Michael, 498
Arévalo Lacs, Col Eduardo, 178
Argaña, Félix, 171
Argaña Ferrero, Luis María, 171
Argaña, Nelson, 171
Argentina, 13, **161-2**, 170, 369, 429, 442
Arguedas Mendieta, Antonio, 163
Argyll, Duchess of, 538
Arias Cárdenas, Lt.Col. (retd) Francisco, 174
Arias Sánchez, Oscar, 180
Aristide, Jean-Bertrand, 176, 177
Arkan, 124, 559
Armand, Ducertain, 177
Armenia, 136, 405, 408, 414
Armstrong, Hilary, 524
Armstrong, Lance, 508
Aronson, Rich, 452
Arsenishvili, Gia, 137, 563
Art, see Visual Arts
Arthur, Owen, 184, 389
Aruba, 191

Arzilli, Giuseppe, 79
Ásgrímsson, Halldór, 69
Ashcroft, John, 150
Ashcroft, Michael, 19
Ashcroft, Peggy, 539
Ashman, Mike, 471
Ashraff, Mohammed, 311
Ashton, Frederick, 475
Asia-Pacific Economic Co-operation, (APEC), 132, **422**, **424**
Assad, Bashar al-, 204, 205, 566
Assad, Hafez al-, 156, 193, 204-5, 527, 565
Assen, Ronald, 191
Association of Caribbean States (ACS), 427
Association of South East Asian Nations (ASEAN), 330, 322, 345, 376, 395, **422-3**
Assoumani, Col. Azili, 313, 314
Astiz, Capt (retd) Alfredo Ignacio, 161
Asylmuratova, Altynai, 477
Atherton, Michael, 505
Atkins, Eileen, 481
Atkinson, Kate, 498
Atopare, Sir Sailas, 356
Attenborough, Michael, 478
Atwood, Margaret, 497, 498
Aubry, Martine, 55
Auburn, David, 482
Augustin Misago, 434
Auken, Svend, 453
Aukoso, Toi, 365
Aung San Suu Kyi, Daw, 317, 569
Australia, 318, **352-5**, 358, 363, 377, 424, 434, 452, 453, 459, 474, 500, 501, 504
Austria, 73-6, 107, 402, 541
Autant-Lara, Claude, 485
Axelrod, George, 480
Axworthy, Lloyd, 160, 428
Ayupova, Zhanna, 477
Azam, Golam, 305
Azerbaijan, 136, 137, 288, 405, 408, 414, 537
Azhar, Maulana Masood, 299
Azharuddin, Mohammad, 504
Aziz Hasan, Prince Hasan, 201
Azizah Wan Ismail, Wan, 321
Aznar López, José María, 81, 82, 83, 227, 229, 289, 561
Aznavour, Charles, 481

Ba Thin, 318
Baasan, Dorligjavyn, 349
Babayan, Samvel, 562
Babbitt, Bruce, 525
Bacall, Lauren, 551
Backley, Steve, 500

Badgie, Ousman, 245
Bagabandi, Natsagiyn, 349, 350
Bahamas, The, **189**, 549
Bahçeli, Devlet, 96
Bahrain, **216-20**
Bailey, Lucy, 479
Bailey, Martin N., 525
Baird, Edison, 189
Bajuk, Andrej, 565
Baker, James, 230
Balaguer, Joaquín Ricardo, 176
Balanchine, George, 475
Balcerowicz, Leszek, 99
Ballard, J G, 498
Ballet/Dance, **475-8**
Baltic Council, **410**, **411**
Banda, Hastings Kamuzu, 271
Bandaranaike, Solomon, 529
Bandaranaike, Sirimavo, 311, 529, 568
Bangladesh, 155, **305-6**, 426
Bani, John, 361
Banks, Victor, 189
Banstola, Chakra Prasad, 307
Banville, John, 498
Bánzer Suárez, Hugo, 163
Barahona, Col. José Isaías, 179
Barak, Ehud, 5, 6, 156, 193, 195, 196, 197, 199, 204, 206, 566, 567, 568, 571, 574
Barbados, **184-5**, 430
Barcikowski, Wladyslaw, 100
Barka, Ben, 54
Barker, Juliet, 499
Barnes, John, 503
Barnes, Julian, 498
Barre, Siad, 234
Barrett, Richard, 22
Barrichello, Rubens, 506
Barrie, James, 479
Barrientes, Gen. (retd) Byron, 179
Barrit, Desmond, 478
Barrow, Omar, 245
Barry, Ebrahima, 245
Barschel, Uwe, 48
Barshefsky, Charlene, 525
Barton, John, 482
Bashir, Omar Hassan Ahmed al-, 220, 221, 222, 223, 559, 574
Bassolino, Antonio, 57
Basta, Jaroslav, 106
Bates, Alan, 481
Batlle Ibáñez, Jorge, 173, 561
Battle, John, 524
Bauc, Jaroslaw, 99
Baumhammers, Richard, 152
Bayaganakandi, Col Epitace, 262

Beale, Simon Russell, 479
Beatrix, Queen of the Netherlands, 61
Beaverbrook, Lord, 531
Beckett, Margaret, 524
Beckham, David, 503
Bédié, Konan, 251
Belarus, **133-4**, 295, 297, 405
Belaúnde, Fernando Terry, 172
Belgium, **60-1**, 398, 455, 501
Belize, **185**, 389
Belkadem, Abdelaziz, 227
Bell, Jamie, 484
Bellow, Saul, 497, 498
Bemba, Jean-Pierre, 260
Ben Ali, Gen. Zine el-Abidine, 224, 225
Ben Brik, Taoufiq, 225
Benbitour, Ahmed, 227
Benflis, Ali, 226, 227, 568
Benin, **248**, **253**, 420
Bennett, Alan, 539
Bennett, Canon Gareth, 552
Bérenger, Paul, 312
Berger, Samuel D., 525
Bergman, Ingmar, 483
Berisha, Sali, 117
Berlusconi, Silvio, 57, 58, 59
Berri, Nabih, 207
Berzins, Andris, 102, 103, 563
Bhatt, Sujata, 498
Bhattarai, Krishna Prasad, 562
Bhumibol Adulydadej (Rama IX), 319
Bhutan, 307, **308-9**
Bhutto, Benazir, 303
Bierko, Scott, 481
Bill Richardson, 525
Binoche, Juliette, 481
Bird, Lester, 186, 187, 389
Birendra Bir Bikram Shar Deva, King of Nepal, 306
Birkavs, Valdis, 103
Birt, Lord, 486
Birtwistle, Harrison, 473
Bishop, Maurice, 185
Bisky, Lothar, 50
Bissoondath, Neil, 498
Biya, Paul, 254, 391
Bizimungu, Pasteur, 262, 562
Bjork, 483
Bjørn, Dina, 476
Black Sea Economic Co-operation Organisation (BSECO), **412**, **414**
Blackstone, Baroness, 524
Blair, Tony, 16, 17, 18, 21, 25, 27, 33, 34, 35, 37, 39, 41, 42, 45, 65, 66, 379, 381, 431, 440, 445, 494, 524

Blakemore, Michael, 481
Bland, Sir Christopher, 487
Blaskic, Gen. Tihomir, 457, 561
Blix, Hans, 72, 373
Blom-Cooper, Sir Louis, 188
Blunkett, David, 524
Bo Mya, 318
Bo Yibo, 334
Boal, Peter, 475
Boateng, Paul, 524
Bodström, Thomas, 71
Bogart, Humphrey, 551
Böhmdorfer, Dieter, 74, 75
Bohr, Niels, 481
Bolaños, Enrique, 180
Bolivia, **163**, 429
Bolkiah, Prince Jefri, 322, 561
Bolkiah, Sultan Hassanal, 322, 561
Bollini, Marino, 79
Boloña, Carlos Bohr, 172
Bondevik, Kjell Magne, 69
Bongo, Omar, 254, 256, 257
Bonilla Reyes, Col. Marco Antonio, 179
Bono, José Martínez, 83
Boothroyd, Betty, 17
Borg, Joe, 89
Boris III, King of Bulgaria, 539
Borrie, Mick, 355
Bosco, Philip, 481
Bosnia & Hercegovina, **119-20**, 121, 124, 378, 405, 407, 457
Bossano, Joe, 85
Bossi, Umberto, 59
Botswana, 260, **274-6**
Bourguiba, Habib Ben Ali, 224, 529
Bourne, Matthew, 477
Bourne, Robert, 19
Bournonville, August, 475
Bouteflika, Abdelaziz, 226, 227, 229, 394, 419
Bouterse, Desiré "Desi", 191
Boutros-Ghali, Boutros, 390, 391
Boyd, Michael, 478
Boyer, Charles, 543
Bozhkov, Aleksandar, 115
Bradbury, Malcolm, 497, 498, 530
Bradlee, Ben, 551
Bradley, Bill, 139, 140, 141
Braghis, Dumitru, 133, 135
Brandt, David, 189
Brazauskas, Algirdas, 104
Brazil, 12, 14, 163, **164-5**, 170, 369, 392, 429, 452, 501, 503
Breeze, Jean "Binta", 498
Brenna, Hans, 476

Breyer, Stephen, 147
Brezina, Karel, 106
Britain, see UK
British Indian Ocean Territory (BIOT), 36, 312
British Virgin Islands, **189**, **190**
Brito, Jorge, 169
Britton, Jasper, 479
Brome, Richard, 479
Brontë, Charlotte, 481
Brook, Peter, 539
Brooks, Diana, 491
Brown, Blair, 481
Brown, Gordon, 18, 24, 27, 33, 39, 43, 524
Brown, Nick, 524
Browner, Carol, 525
Browning, Angela, 18
Bruce, Christopher, 475
Bruce, Nicola, 484
Brunei, **322**, 423
Brunner, Christiane, 77
Bryson, Bill, 495, 499
BSE (bovine spongiform encephalopathy), 1, 2, 30, 55, 60, 84, 562, 563
Buchanan, Pat, 140, 142, 145, 150
Budge, Don, 530
Budisa, Drazen, 121
Buergenthal, Thomas, 455
Buffet, Bernard, 492
Buford, Kate, 499
Bugar, Bela, 108
Bühlmann, Cécile, 77
Bujak, Andrej, 124
Bulatovic, Pavle, 125, 560
Bulgaria, 61, **114-6**, 118, 232, 268, 373, 402, 405, 540, 545
Bundum, Vishnu, 312
Burghardt, Jutta, 560
Burke, Alfred, 478
Burkina Faso, **247**, **252**, 373
Burleigh, Michael, 499
Burma, see Myanmar
Burns, Richard, 506
Burnside, John, 498
Burundi, 260, **261-2**
Busch, Charles, 482
Busek, Erhard, 76
Bush, George, 141, 454
Bush, George W., 3, 9, 138, 139, 140, 141, 143, 144, 145, 147, 154, 340, 454, 468, 567, 573, 574
Bush, Peter, 498
Bussi, Gen. (retd) Antonio Domingo, 161
Butler, Richard, 209
Buyoya, Pierre, 261, 262, 568

Buzek, Jerzy, 99, 413, 565
Byatt, A S, 498
Byers, Stephen, 488, 524
Byrne, Lavinia, 432

Cabanis, José, 497
Cacciari, Massimo, 57
Caine, Michael, 496
Caird, John, 479, 481
Cairns, Andrew, 43
Cairns, David, 475
Cake, Jonathan, 480
Caldas Pereira, Eduardo Jorge, 165
Calderón, Sila María, 191, 192
Calles, Plutarco Elías, 181
Cambodia, 329, 452
Camdessus, Michel, 383, 384
Camelia-Römer, Susanne, 191
Cameroon, 254, 255, **256**, 390, 503
Campbell, Gregory, 43
Campbell, John, 499
Campion, Sean, 480
Canada, 157-60, 222, 440, 453, 557, 9, 187
Canavan, Dennis, 18, 38
Cantet, Philippe, 484
Cantwell, Maria, 147
Cape Verde, 263, 264-5, 421
Carberry, Paul, 508
Carberry, Tommy, 508
Cárdenas Solórzano, Cuauhtémoc, 181
Cardoso, Carlos, 267
Cardoso, Fernando Henrique, 164, 429
Carey, George, 434
Caribbean Community and Common Market (CARICOM), 188, **427, 430**
Carl XVI Gustav, King of Sweden, 68, 71
Carlisle, Sir James B., 186
Carlsson, Arvid, 442
Carnahan, Mel, 147
Carnell, Kate, 354
Carnley, Peter, 355, 434
Carpenter, Humphrey, 552
Carper, Tom, 147
Carrillo Olea, Jorge, 181
Carrington, Edwin, 427
Carrión, Gen. Javier, 179
Carroll, Tim, 479
Carson, Anne, 498
Carson, Ciaran, 498
Cartland, Dame Barbara, 498, 531
Cartwright, Dame Silvia, 357, 358
Caruana, Peter, 84
Carver, Raymond, 498
Case, Steve, 154
Casey, Gavin, 32

Castañeda, Jorge, 181
Castelli, Leo, 492
Castle, Barbara, 18
Castro Ruz, Fidel, 175, 429
Cato, Nancy, 355
Caurier, Patrice, 470
Cavallo, Domingo, 162
Cayman Islands, 189, 190
Cecil, Henry, 508
Cem, Ismail, 92
Central African Republic, 254, 257, 260, 371
Central European Free Trade Association (CEFTA), 412, 413
Central European Initiative (CEI), 412, 414
Chaban-Delmas, Jacques, 531
Chaib, Taoufiq, 225
Chakuamba, Gwanda, 271
Chamoun, Camille, 554
Chan, Anson, 337
Chance, Noel, 508
Chang Chun-hsiung, 338, 339
Charles, Pierre, 186, 187
Chaudhry, Mahendra, 361, 362, 388, 564, 567
Chaudhuri, Amit, 498
Chávez Frías, Hugo, 173, 174, 176, 183, 387, 567
Chechelashvili, Valer, 412
Chen Shui-bian, 331, 334, 338, 339, 340, 562, 563, 574
Cheney, Dick, 141, 143, 144, 146
Cheng Kejie, 332
Cheshire, Leonard, 553
Chevènement, Jean-Paul, 54, 55
Chhokar, Surjit Singh, 38
Chi Haotian, 336
Chiepe, Gaositwe , 389
Chile, 36, 61, 162
Chile, 429
Chiluba, 270
Chiluba, Frederick, 269
Chilumpha, Cassim, 270
China, People's Republic of, 4, 11, 14, 36, 63, 156, 198, 232, 288, 296, 301, 304, 328, **331-6**, 338, 344, 367, 377, 386, 404, 423, 424, 426, 435, 437, 441, 446, 452, 501, 542
Chinamasa, Patrick, 272
Chirac, Jacques, 52, 53, 54, 56, 79, 253, 379, 380, 397, 398, 402, 423, 575
Chissano, Joachim Alberto, 265, 266, 267, 392
Chiuz, Elizabeth Sierra, 179
Cho Myong Nok, 348
Cho Seong Tae, 346

Chrétien, Jean, 9, 157, 573
Christie, Agatha, 482
Christodoulakis, Nikos, 91
Christodoulos, Archbishop, 92, 435
Christopher, J. Alvin, 190
Chronicle of 2000, 549-65
Chua, Daniel, 474, 475
Chuan Leekpai, 319, 394
Chung Mong Hun, 347
Chung Mong Koo, 347
Chung Yu Jung, 346
Chygir, Mikhas, 133
Ciampi, Carlo Azeglio, 56, 57
Cinema, 482-5
Cisar, Jaromir, 106
Clancy, Tom, 496
Clark, General, 118
Clark, Helen, 357, 358, 359, 424
Clark, Joe, 158
Clarke, Charles, 524
Clarke, Darren, 505
Clarke, Geoff, 353
Clarkson, Adrienne, 157
Clement, Wolfgang, 49
Clerides, Glafkos, 93, 94
Clinton, Bill, 3, 14, 46, 65, 66, 97, 98, 138, 142, 144, 151, 154, 155, 156, 167, 192, 193, 194, 195, 199, 200, 205, 213, 227, 243, 261, 300, 303, 304, 328, 340, 347, 348, 365, 381, 387, 424, 428, 440, 454, 525, 565, 567, 569, 570, 571, 573
Clinton, Hillary Rodham, 140, 143, 147, 151, 560, 570
Coard, Phyllis, 185
Cobos, Fausto, 169
Cochrane, Ray, 508
Coggan, Donald, 532, 552
Cohen, William, 213, 328, 335, 377, 381, 400, 525, 562, 571
Cojocaru, Alina, 476
Colombia, 155, **167-8**, 367, 429
Colombo, Christian, 162
Coltman, Derek, 498
Colvin, Michael, 17
Comfort, Dr Alex, 533
Common Market for Eastern and Sothern Africa (COMESA), 418, 421
Commonwealth, The, 256, 277, 364, **388-90**, 390, 457
Community of Portuguese-Speaking Countries (CPLP), 86, **390**, **391-2**
Comoros, 313, **314-5**
Compaoré, Blaise, 247, 252, 268
Compton, Denis, 534
Condé, Alpha, 250, 569

Condon, Paul, 504
Condor, Sam, 188
Cong Fukui, 332
Conger, Darva, 139
Congo, Democratic Republic of, (DRC), 160, 238, 256, **259-60**, 261, 262, 263, 269, 273, 368, 419, 420, 421, 455, 456
Congo, Republic of, 256, **257**
Connaught, Duke of, 541
Connor, Joseph E., 368, 369
Constantine, ex-King of Greece, 93, 573
Constantinescu, Emil, 112
Conté, Lansana, 247, 250
Contreras, Gen. (retd) Manuel, 166
Cook, Robin, 34, 37, 272, 524
Cook, Stephanie, 501
Cooke, Cardinal, 547
Cooke, Sir Howard, 182
Cookson, Catherine, 496
Cope, Jonathan, 476
Copeland, David, 566
Corbett, Gerald, 28
Corzine, Jon, 147
Cosgrove, Maj.-Gen. Peter, 353
Cosman, Carol, 499
Costa Rica, 178, 180
Costa, Seixas da, 86
Côte d'Ivoire, 247, 248, 249, 250, **251-2**, 421
Coulibaly, Abdoulaye, 251
Coulthard, David, 506
Council of Europe, 404-6, 407
Council of the Baltic Sea States, (CBSS), 410, 411
Courtney, Annie, 44
Coutts, Russell, 508
Cowan, Brian, 66
Cowdrey, Lord (Colin), 533
Cowley, Jason, 498
Cox, Winston, 390
Cozzens, Fr Donald, 432
Craborn, Richard, 524
Cracknell, James, 501
Cramm, Gottfried von, 531
Cranham, Kenneth, 479
Cranston, Ross, 525
Crawford, Joan, 537
Crawford, Robert, 498
Craxi, Bettino, 57, 534, 559
Creel, Santiago, 181
Croatia, 11, 120, **121-2**, 123, 124, 405, 407, 409, 457
Cronje, Hansie, 504
Crosland, Anthony, 536
Cross, Jonathan, 475
Crowe, Russell, 483

Crvenkovski, Branko, 122
Cuadra, Gen. Joaquín, 179
Cuba, 132, 152, 156, **175-6**, 429, 430
Cubas, Raúl Grau, 170
Culkin, Macaulay, 480
Cumming, Peter, 85
Cumpsty, Michael, 481
Cunningham, Merce, 478
Cuomo, Andrew M., 525
Cyprus, **93-5**, 393, 402, 97
Czech Republic, 76, **105-7**, 109, 111, 402, 413

D'Alema, Massimo, 56, 57, 563
D'Antoni, Sergio, 59
da Costa, Guilherme Pósser, 265
da Costa, Manuel Pinto, 265
Daer, Rodolfo, 161
Dalai Lama, 346
Daldry, Stephen, 484
Dalglish, Kenny, 503
Dalli, John, 90
Dalziel, Lianne, 358
Danforth, John, 153
Daniel, Paul, 471
Danzig, Richard, 192
Darboe, Oussainou, 245
Darling, Alistair, 524
Davenport, Lindsay, 507
David, Ibolya, 110
Davies, Siohban, 477
Davies, Terence, 484
Davies, Terry, 477
Daviot, Gordon, 539
Davis, Sir Andrew, 471
Day, Sir Robin, 535
Day, Stockwell, 157
De Botton, Alain, 499
de Brun, Bairbre, 45
de Carvalho, Louis Pereira, 248
de Chastelain, General, 41, 42, 45
de Gaulle, General, 548, 532
de la Calle Lombana, Humberto, 168
de la Rúa Bruno, Fernando, 161, 571
de la Rúa, Jorge, 162
de Marco, Guido, 89
De Mille, Cecil B, 543
de Soto, Alvaro, 93, 317
Deane, Derek, 477
Deane, Sir William, 352
Déby, Col. Idriss, 254, 255, 256
Deerpalsingh, Kishore, 312
del Ponte, Carla, 121, 457
del Turco, Ottaviano, 57
Delmas, Jacques, 531

Delvecchio, Marco, 502
Demirel, Süleyman, 96
Dempsey, Charles, 503
Deng Xiaoping, 333, 334, 335
Denham, John, 525
Denktash, Rauf, 93, 94, 95, 563
Denmark, 9, **67-8**, 398, 401, 458, 541
Dennis, Ferdinand, 497, 499
Desai, Anita, 497, 498
Dettori, Frankie, 508
Deutsch, Andre, 535
Dev, Kapil, 505
Devia, Mariella, 470
Dewar, Donald, 17, 36, 37, 536, 571
Dewinter, Filip, 60
Dexter, Mike, 440
Dexter, Ted, 534
Dhlakama, Afonso, 267
di Tella, Guido, 162
Diallo, Amadou, 151
Diarra, Souleymane, 251
Dias, José Carlos, 164
Díaz Pereira, Ramo, 426
Didiza, Thoko, 284
Diego, Garcia, 36
Dieng, Ousmane Tanor, 249
Dietrich, Marlene, 538
Dimbleby, Richard, 535
Ding Guangen, 331
Dini, Ahmed, 234
Diodato, Marino, 163
Diouf, Abdou, 248, 249
Djibouti, **231**, 233, **234**
Djukanovic, Milo, 124, 128
Dlamini, Sibusiso Barnabas, 274, 280
do Rosário, Antonio Gualberto, 263, 264
Dobson, Frank, 17
Doctorow, E L, 498
Dodds, Nigel, 43
Dodik, Milorad, 119
Doherty, Pat, 45
Dologuélé, Anicet Georges, 254
Domingos, Raul, 267
Dominica, **186**, **187**
Dominican Republic, **176**, 177, 395, 430
Dominique, Jean Léopold, 177
Donaghy, Michael, 497, 498
Donaldson, Jeffrey, 45
Dorligjav, Dambyn, 350
dos Santos, José Eduardo, 268, 269
dos Santos, Lucia, 431
Douglas, Denzil, 186, 187, 561
Douglas, Michael, 41
Douglas, Roosevelt "Rosie", 187, 560, 571
Dowiyogo, Bernard, 360, 563

INDEX 583

Doyle, Noreen, 409
Drake, Nick, 498
Draskovic, Vuk, 125, 126
Drechsler, Heike, 500
Drnovsek, Janez, 123, 124
Drummond, John, 499
Dubai, 209, 215
Dubcek, Alexander, 558
Dugan, Angel Serafin Seriche, 255
Dumas, Edgardo Rodríguez, 179
Dumas, Roland, 53
Dun, Bob, 425
Dunlop, John, 508
Dunmore, Helen, 498
Dunn, Douglas, 498
Durie, David, 84, 85
Durkan, Mark, 44
Durning, Charles, 482
Dury, Ian, 536
Dyke, Greg, 486, 487, 488
Dyson, Ruth, 357
Dzaiddin Abdullah, Mohamed, 320
Dzhabrailov, Umar, 129
Dzurinda, Mikulas, 107, 108

East African Commission (EAC), 235, **419, 421**
East Timor, 12, **325**, 352, 358, 363, 368, 377, 392
Eberle, Roland, 77
Ecevit, Bülent, 96
Echenoz, Jean, 497, 498
Eco, Umberto, 499
Economic Community of Central African States (CEEAC), **418, 421**
Economic Community of West African States (ECOWAS), 243, 250, 253, **418, 421**
Ecuador, 162, **169-70**
Edde, Raymond, 208
Edham, Bicakcic, 119
Edmond, Lauris, 497
Edrich, Bill, 534
Edwards, Colin, 506
Edwards, Jonathan, 500
Egypt, 194, 199, **200-1**, 202, 204, 206, 219, 221, 224, 368, 395, 416, 419, 424, 431, 442
Eichel, Hans, 50
Eiríksson, Leifur, 68
Ejiofor, Chiwetel, 479
Ek, Mats, 477
Ekeus, Rolf, 373
El Guerrouj, Hicham, 500
El Salvador, **177, 179**, 428, 429
El-Avia Ould Mohammed Khouna, Cheikh, 247

Elchibey, Abulfaz, 537, 568
Elias, Dame Sian, 359
Eliot Gardiner, John, 472
Elizabeth II, Queen, 16, 36, 37, 39, 41, 84, 157, 182, 184, 185, 186, 187, 352, 353, 356, 357, 361, 495, 541
Elklit, Jorg, 277
Elton, Ben, 480
Eman, Jan Hendrick (Henny), 191
Emerson, Roy, 507
Emmerson, Charlotte, 480
Endre, Lena, 483
Enebish, Lhamsürengiyn, 350
Enhbayar, Nambaryn, 349, 350, 566
Enright, Anne, 498
Ensign, John, 147
Environment, 28-30, 69, 76, 86, 100, 105, 107, 134, 365, 410-11, 425, **448-54**
Equitorial Guinea, **255, 257-8**
Erbakan, Necmettin, 561
Erdenebat, Badarchiyn, 349
Ergolu, Dervis, 95
Eriksson, Sven Goran, 502
Eritrea, 221, 222, 227, **231**, **233**, 371, 372, 393, 419
Ershad, Hossain Mohammad, 305
Escobar, Ivan, 180
Eshkevan, Hassan Yussefi, 287
Estonia, **102-3**, 402
Estrada, Joseph Ejercito, 12, 73, 326, 574
Estrada Cagijal, Sergio, 181
Ethiopia, 222, 227, **231-3**, 371, 372, 393, 419, 452
Eurasian Economic Union, 132
European Bank for Reconstruction and Development (EBRD), 11, 110, **409-10**
European Central Bank, 64
European Court of Human Rights (ECHR), 111, **458**
European Free Trade Association (EFTA), 69, **412-3**
European Investment Bank, 65
European Union (EU), 4, 9, 14, 35, 51, 63, 66, 68, 69, 71, 73, 77, 89, 95, 96, 99, 103, 105, 107, 109, 111, 114, 118, 123, 124, 126, 128, 132, 167, 224, 225, 229, 246, 253, 288, 301, 304, 330, 336, 378, **396-404**, 405, 412, 413, 416, 420, 423, 430
Eustace, Arnhim, 187, 188, 572
Evans, Albert, 475
Evans, Edith, 539
Evgenii, Primakov, 129
Eyadéma, Gnassingbé, 248, 252, 253, 268, 419
Eyzaguirre, Nicolás, 165
Faamuli, Rosalia Tisa, 364

Fabius, Laurent, 53, 55, 401
Faget, Mariano, 175
Fahd ibn Abdul Aziz, King of Saudi Arabia, 210, 211
Fairbanks Jr, Douglas, 485, 537
Falcam, Leo, 360
Falconer of Thoroton, Lord, 21, 525
Falwell, Jerry, 140
Fanego, Julio César, 171
Fanfani, Amintore, 534
Fanthorpe, U A, 498
Farid, Hatim Muhsin bin, 214
Farnsworth, Richard, 485
Farrell, Suzanne, 475
Faruq, King of Egypt, 201
Faulds, Richard, 501
Fedorovitch, Sophie, 476
Fenech, Edward Adami, 89, 90
Ferdinand, Rio, 503
Ferenc, Jozsef Nagy, 110
Ferguson, Sir Alex, 503
Fermín, Claudio, 174
Fernández, Gen. Manuel, 173
Fernández Estigarribia, José Félix, 170
Fernández Reyna, Leonel, 176
Ferrero-Waldner, Benita, 76, 118, 407, 408
Fhimah, Lamen Khalifa, 224
Fielding, David, 471
Fields, Danny, 499
Figo, Luis, 503
Fiji Islands, 352, 358, **360**, **361-2**, 377, 388, 425
Finland, 72-3
Finley, Gerald, 471
Fischer, Joschka, 50, 301, 399
Fischer, Stanley, 384
Fischer, Tim, 355
Fischler, Frans, 403
Fiser, Bohumil, 106
Fitzgerald, Desmond, 538
Fitzgerald, Penelope, 497, 498, 538
Fivaz, George, 280
Flaherty, Stephen, 481
Flamarique, Alberto, 162
Fleming, Osbourne, 188, 189
Fleming, Renée, 470
Fletcher, Duncan, 504
Fletcher, John, 479
Flores Facussé, Carlos Roberto, 178
Flores Pérez, Francisco, 177
Florez, Juan Diego, 470
Fogarty, Carl, 506
Fonseca, Gautama, 179
Fontaine, Nicole, 403
Forbes, Steve, 139

Ford, Andrew, 474
Ford, Bruce, 470
Ford, Gerald, 528
Ford, Sir Brinsley, 492
Forné, Marc Molné, 79
Forrestier, Gen. (retd) Carlos, 166
Forsythe, Clifford, 44
Fortún, Guillermo, 163
Foster, Lord (Norman), 492, 493, 554
Foster, Tim, 501
Fox Quesada, Vicente, 13, 181, 573
France, 9, 10, 35, 36, **52-6**, 60, 82, 111, 197, 225, 227, 229, 230, 253, 301, 379, 380, 397, 398, 400, 409, 423, 425, 440, 458, 484, 501, 531, 548
Franco, Itamar, 164
Franco, Julio César, 171
Francophone Community, see International Organisation of Francophonie
Frank, Charles, 409
Franklin, Frederic, 475
Frayling, Christopher, 499
Frayn, Michael, 478, 481
Frederik IX, King of Denmark, 541
Freeman, Cathy, 500
Frei Rúiz-Tagle, Eduardo, 166
Fretes, Daniel Ventre, 170
Frick, Mario, 79
Frievalds, Laila, 71
Frlec, Boris, 123
Fry, Christopher, 539
Fuhrer, Rita, 77
Fujimori, Alberto Keinya, 171, 172, 428, 562, 564, 570
Fuller, Roy, 536
Furundzija, 457

Gable, Clark, 543
Gabon, **254**, **256**, 257, 268, 373
Galati, Frank, 481
Galayr, Ali Khalif, 571
Gama, Jaime, 392
Gambia, The, **245**, 249, 389, 421, 441
Ganassi, Sonia, 470
Gandhi, Indira, 300
Gandhi, Sonia, 300
Gangar, Finbar K., 184
Ganic, Ejup, 119
Ganji, Akbar, 287
Gao Changli, 332
Gao Xingjian, 497
Garang, Col John, 221
Garland, Robert, 475
Garzón, Baltasar, 161
Gassman, Vittorio, 485

Gatward, Rebecca, 480
Gautam, Bamdef, 307
Gaviria Trujillo, César, 426, 428
Gayoom, Maumoon Abdul, 313, 315
Gbagbo, Laurent, 247, 251, 252, 572, 574
Gebrselassie, Haile, 500
Gehry, Frank, 493
Geingob, Hage, 274
Gelmetti, Gianluigi, 470
Genjac, Halid, 119
Genscher, Han-Dietrich, 408
George VI, King, 541
George, Ambrose, 187
Georgia, **136-7**, 405
Georgievski, Ljubco, 122
Gerardi Conadera, Bishop Juan José, 178
Gerbeau, Pierre-Yves, 22
Gerbovits, Jeno, 110
Geremek, Bronislaw, 100
Gergiev, Valery, 475
Gerhardt, Wolfgang, 50
German, Mike, 40
Germany, 9, 10, 35, **47-52**, 397, 398, 399, 409, 440
Geymonat, Gen. Juan, 173
Ghana, **239-40**, 421
Ghannouchi, Mohammed, 224
Giannitsis, Anastasios, 91
Gibbs, Christopher, 475
Gibbs, Herschelle, 504
Gibson, Chris, 44
Gibson, Mel, 484
Gidada, Negaso, 231
Gidley, Sandra, 17
Gielgud, John, 498, 539-40
Gil, Francisco, 181
Gilds, Siegfried, 191
Gilroy, Paul, 499
Ginsberg, Ruth Bader, 147
Giovanna, Queen of the Bulgarians, 539
Giscard d'Estaing, Valery, 54-5, 532
Giuliani, Rudolph, 140, 151, 564
Gjellerup, Pia, 68
Glassel, Richard, 152
Glickman, Dan, 525
Godal, Bjørn Tore, 69
Goddard, Philip, 185
Goh Chok Tong, 322
Gokhale, Namita, 498
Goma, Louis-Sylvain, 418
Gomes, Marcelo, 477
Gómez, Camilo, 167
Gonchigdorj, Radnaasümbereliyn, 350
Göncz, Árpád, 109, 565
Gongadze, Heorhiy, 135

Gonzales, Alberto, 150
Gonzalez Inarrito, Alejandro, 485
González Macchi, Luis, 170, 564
González, Antonio Erman, 162
González, Elian, 141, 152, 175, 563
González, Juan Miguel, 152, 175
Gorbachev, Mikhail, 555
Gordon, Ken, 184
Gordon, Paul, 481
Gore, Al, 8, 138, 139, 140, 141, 143, 145, 147, 150, 154, 454, 525, 568, 573, 574
Gorton, Slade, 147
Gosden, John, 508
Gough, Darren, 505
Gourad Hamadou, Barkat, 231
Goytisolo, Juan, 498
Gracia Arregui, Ignacio, 82, 570
Graham, Martha, 478
Graham, Susan, 470
Gramick, Sr Jeannine, 432
Grandage, Michael, 479
Grant, Linda, 498
Grasser, Karl-Heinz, 75
Gray, Alasdair, 495, 499
Gray, Spalding, 482
Greece, 9, **90-3**, 97, 118, 123, 398, 402
Greene, Maurice, 500
Greenguard, Paul, 442
Greenspan, Alan, 8, 154
Greenwood, Peter, 539
Gregori, José, 164
Grenada, **185**
Grímsson, Ólafur Ragnar, 68
Gronholm, Marcus, 506
Gronkiewicz-Waltz, Hanna, 409
Gross, Stanislav, 106
Group of 77 (G-77), **393**, **394-5**
Grulich, Vaclav, 106
Guadalcanal, 363
Gualberto do Rosario, António, 571
Guam, 364
Guatemala, **178-9**, 185, 389, 428
Gueï, Gen. Robert, 251-2, 419, 559, 572
Guellah, Ismail Omar, 231, 234
Guevara de la Serna, Maj. Ernesto "Che", 163
Guigou, Elisabeth, 53, 55
Guillaume, Gilbert, 455
Guillem, Sylvie, 476
Guinea, 240, **247**, **250-1**, 421
Guinea-Bissau, 249, **263-4**
Guinness, Alec, 485, 498, 540
Gukasyan, Arkady, 562
Gulf Co-operation Council, 212, 214, 218, 219, **415-7**
Gündalay, Lamjavyn, 349

Gunn, Thom, 498
Güsenbauer, Alfred, 74
Gusinsky, Vladimir, 131, 132
Gusmao, José Xanana, 392
Gustaf VI Adolf, King of Sweden, 541
Guterres, António, 86-7, 402
Gutierrez, Carl, 364
Gutiérrez, Lucio, 169
Guyana, **183**, 184, 389, 430
Guzmán, Jorge Ortega, 169
Guzmán, Juan Tapia, 166
Gwyther, Christine, 40
Gyngell, Bruce, 355
Gypsies, see Roma
Gysi, Gregor, 50

Haakon, Crown Prince of Norway, 70
Hague, William, 16, 18-20, 25, 560
Haider, Jörg, 59, 73-6, 80, 402, 407, 560
Haile Selassie, Emperor, 573
Hain, Peter, 272, 524
Haiti, **176-7**
Haitink, Bernard, 470
Hajjaran, Saeed, 287
Hakkinen, Mikka, 506
Hall, Edward, 478
Hall, Jerry, 480
Hall, Peter, 482, 539
Hall, Rodney, 498
Halonen, Tarja, 72, 366, 560
Hama, Amadou, 253
Hamad bin Isa al-Khalifa, Sheikh, 216
Hamad bin Khalifa al-Thani, Sheikh, 215, 219
Hamad, Seif Shariff, 236
Hamed, Naseem, 504
Hamilton, Victoria, 479
Hamlyn, Paul, 19
Hammett, Dashiell, 551
Hampson, Christopher, 475
Hannah, Daryl, 480
Hannah, Timothy, 422
Hans Adam II, Prince of Liechtenstein, 79
Hanson, Pauline, 355
Harald V, King of Norway, 69
Hare, Nick, 390
Hariri, 207
Hariri, Rafiq al-, 206, 207, 569, 572
Harman, Claire, 499
Harris, Katherine, 146
Harris, Rene, 364
Harris, Robert, 189
Harrison, Audley, 501
Harsanyi, Professor John, 540
Hart-Davis, Rupert, 499
Hartling, Poul, 68

Harvey, Jonathan, 475
Has, Wojciech, 485
Hasan, Abdiqasim Salad, 231, 233-4, 568
Hasan, Nacem ul, 422
Hasani, Xhavit, 122
Hashimoto, Ryutaro, 343, 547
Hasina Wajed, Sheikh, 305
Haskell, Francis, 492
Hassan II, King of Morocco, 229
Haughey, Charles, 65
Hauser, Frank, 540
Havel, Václav, 76, 105, 106
Hawala, Maj. Gen. Solomon, 279
Hawlata, Franz, 470
Hayman, Baroness, 525
Heaney, Seamus, 497
Heath, Edward, 19, 527
Heathcoat-Amory, David, 18
Heckman, James, 15
Heeger, Alan, 442
Heisenberg, Werner, 481
Hejduk, John, 494
Helveg, Niels Petersen, 68
Helweg, Kim, 476
Henderson, Peter, 219
Henman, Tim, 507
Henri, Crown Prince of Luxembourg, 63, 571
Henri, Grand Duke of Luxembourg, 63
Henry, Thierry, 502
Hepburn, Katharine, 551
Herak, Ivan, 121
Herman, Alexis M., 525
Heron, Patrick, 492
Herrera, René, 180
Heseltine, Michael, 499
Hesketh-Harvey, Kit, 471
Hewitt, Patricia, 524
Higgs, Peter, 439
Hildebrandt, Martha, 172
Hildenberg, Humphrey, 191
Hill, Conleth, 480
Hill, Fr Michael, 433
Hill, Roland, 499
Hill, Ronald, 46
Hinds, Sam, 183
Hingis, Martina, 507
Hirohito, Emperor of Japan, 344
Hitchcock, Alfred, 539
Hitler, Adolf, 531, 539
Hjelm-Wallén, Lena, 71
Ho Chi Minh, 549
Hodac, Jiri, 107
Hofmann, Michael, 498
Hogan, Ben, 505
Höhn, Bärbel, 50

561, 575
Kiarostami, Abbas, 485
Kiep, Walther Leisler, 47
Kilby, Jack, 442
Kiley, Robert, 28
Kim Dae Jung, 345, 346, 347, 348, 565, 571
Kim Il Chol, 346
Kim Il Sung, 348
Kim Jong Il, 345, 346, 347, 348, 565
Kim Jong Pil, 345
Kim Yong Nam, 348
Kim Young Sam, 346
King, Mary, 508
King, Stephen, 495
Kirchschläger, Rudolf, 76, 541
Kitchener, "Lord" (Aldwyn Roberts), 542
Klestil, Thomas, 73, 76, 403, 560
Klima, Viktor, 74
Kneale, Matthew, 498
Knox, "Evoe", 538
Kobborg, Johan, 476
Koch, Roland, 47, 569
Koch, Ursula, 77
Koch-Weser, Caio, 383
Kocharian, Robert, 136, 564
Kodjo, Messan Agbeyome, 248
Koffigoh, Joseph Kokou, 253
Kohl, Helmut, 47, 53, 384, 559, 566
Köhler, Horst, 383, 409, 562
Koirala, Girija Prasad, 306-7, 562
Koirala, Sushil, 307
Kok, Willem, 61
Kolélas, Bernard, 257, 564
Komorowski, Bronislaw, 100
Konaré, Alpha Oumar, 247, 250, 391
Kononov, Vasili, 104
Kontorosky, Ramón, 179
Koolhaas, Rem, 494
Koolman, Olindo, 191
Korea, Democratic People's Republic of (North Korea), 7, 12, 132, **347-9**, 423-4
Korea, Republic of (South Korea), 11, 12, 342, **345-7**, 423, 425, 435, 484
Korta, José María, 82
Korthals, Benk, 62
Kosovo, 122, 368
Kostov, Ivan, 114-5
Kostroman, Ignac, 121
Kostunica, Vojislav, 6, 33, 123, 124, 125, 126, 128, 403, 405, 570, 571, 575
Kouchner, Bernard, 127
Kouyaté, Lamine, 418
Kovac, Roman, 108
Kowrowski, Maria, 475
Kposowa, Col Jonathan, 245

Kraft, Vahur, 102
Krajisnik, Momcilo, 120, 562
Kramer, Susan, 17
Kroemer, Herbert, 442
Krzaklewski, Marian, 99, 101
Kucan, Milan, 123
Kucera, Karol, 507
Kuchma, Leonid, 133-5, 563
Kuerten, Gustavo, 507
Kufuor, John, 239-40, 575
Kuhnl, Karel, 106
Kukil, Karen V, 499
Kumar Nepal, Madhav, 307
Kumaratunga, Chandrika, 309-10, 564, 571
Kung, Cardinal Ignatius, 542
Kupreskic, 457
Kurdistan, 208
Kutle, Miroslav, 121
Kuwait, 210, 211, 213, **215-20**, 393, 417
Kwasniewski, Aleksander, 99, 571
Kyrgyzstan, 292-7
Kyril, Prince, 540

La Fosse, Robert, 475
Laar, Mart, 102
Labastida, Francisco Ochoa, 181
Lachnit, Petr, 106
Laden, Osama bin, 214, 220, 291, 297, 373, 575
Lagos Escobar, Ricardo, 165, 166, 559
Lahiri, Jhumpa, 497, 498
Lahoud, Émile, 206
Lallah, Rajsmooer, 317
Lam, Willy Wo Lap, 337
Lamarr, Hedy, 485, 543
Lamb, Sir Larry, 543
Lambert, Gavin, 499
Lamont, Norman, 27
Lanchester, John, 498
Landívar, Jorge, 163
Lang, Jack, 53
Lang, Luc, 498
Langa, Pius N., 388
Lange, Jessica, 480
Laos, 330, 452
Lapli, Sir John Ini, 361
Laraki, Azeddine, 395
Latin American Economic System (SELA), 427, 430
Latin American Integration Association (ALADI), 427
Latvia, 103-4, 402, 405
Laurens, Joanna, 480
Lavín Infante, Joaquín, 165, 559
Lavin, Linda, 482

Law, International, 455-9, European
  Community, 459-62, UK, 462-7, USA,
  467-9
Lawrence, Gertrude, 538
Lawrence, Neville, 25
Lawrence, Stephen, 24, 25
Layne, Tamrat, 233
Lazarides, Stefano, 471
Lazio, Rick, 140, 143, 147
le Carre, John, 540
Le Duan, 549
Le Kha Phieu, Lt Gen., 328
Le Riche, Nicolas, 476
Leader, Zachary, 499
Leakey, Richard, 235
Lebanon, 193, 194, 204, 205, **206-8**, 372,
  415, 416, 554
Lebranchu, Marylise, 55
Leclercq, Patrick, 79
Lee Han Dong, 345, 564
Lee Hoi Chang, 345
Lee Kuan Yew, 322
Lee Teng-hui, 338, 339
Lee, Ang, 483
Lee, Laurie, 536
Lee, Martin, 338
Lee, Mary, 538
Lee, Wen Ho, 153
Leiser, Moshe, 470
Lemerre, Roger, 502
Lemierre, Jean, 409
Lemmon, Jack, 544
Leon, Ramon, 277
Leon, Tony, 282
Lepper, Andrzej, 100
Lesotho, **276-8**
Lessing, Doris, 498
Lester, Joel, 475
Lestrade, Swinburne, 427
Letelier, Orlando, 166
Letsie III, King, 274
Letwin, Oliver, 18
Leuenberger, Moritz, 77
Levar, Milan, 121, 568
Leveaux, David, 481
Levens, Marie, 191
Levi, Noel, 422
Levy, David, 196
Lew, Jacob J., 525
Lewinsky, Monica, 151
Lewis, Denise, 500
Lewis, Lennox, 504
Li Ka-shing, 337
Li Lanqing, 331, 393
Li Peng, 331

Li Riuhuan, 331
Liberia, 240, **246**, 250, 252, 421
Libya, 38, 116, 221, **223-4**, 225, 232, 255,
  256, 326, 419
Liddell, Helen, 524
Lieberman, Joseph, 142, 144
Liechtenstein, **80**
Lien Chan, 334, 338, 339
Ligetvari, Ferenc, 109
Lincoln, Andrew, 479
Lindh, Anna, 72
Lindsay, John, 544
Lindwall, Ray, 534
Ling, Syargey, 561
Lipponen, Paavo, 72
Lissouba, Pascal, 257
Literature, **494-9**
Lithuania, **104-5**, 402, 555
Litt, Toby, 498
Livingstone, Ken, 17, 28, 494, 564
Llamazares, Gaspar, 84
Lloyd Webber, Andrew, 480
Lluch, Ernest, 82
Lock, F P, 499
Lomu, Jonah, 506
Lone, Abdul Ghani, 304
López de Lacalle, José Luis, 82
López, Margarita, 178
Lord, Peter, 484
Lortkipanidze, Vazha, 137, 563
Louima, Abner, 151
Louisy, Perlette, 186
Lovejoy, Derek, 494
Loy, Frank, 453
Lu Hsiu-lien, 334, 340
Lu Ruihua, 336
Lu, Annette, 334, 340
Luagalau Levaula Kamu, 365
Lubbers, Ruud, 367
Lucas García, Fernando Romeo, 178
Luce, Sir Richard, 85
Lucinschi, Petru, 133, 135, 575
Lukashenka, Alyaksandr, 133, 134, 561
Luker, Rebecca, 481
Lukman, Rilwanu, 387
Lumumba, Patrice, 61
Lund, Thomas, 476
Luo Gan, 331
Lusophone Community, see Community of
  Portuguese-Speaking Countries (CPLP)
Luxembourg, **63**
Luyt, Louis, 282
Luzhkov, Yuri, 129
Lykiard, Alexis, 499
Lykketoft, Mogens, 68

Ma Xiangdong, 332
Macapagal-Arroyo, Gloria, 327
MacDiarmid, Alan, 442
MacDonald of Tradeston, Lord, 26, 524
Macedonia, 116, 118, **122-3**, 124, 405, 408
MacGregor, Neil, 491
Machar, Riak, 222
Machel, Gracia, 390
MacKenzie, Kelvin, 489
Macleod, Alistair, 498
Macleod, Professor Donald, 433
Madi, Ahamadi "Bolero", 315
Madl, Ferenc, 109, 565
Madonna, 484
Magela Quintão, Geraldo, 164
Mahathir Mohamad, 320, 321, 322
Mahdi, 221
Mahon, Derek, 498
Mahuad Witt, Jamil, 169, 559
Mailer, Norman, 536
Major, John, 20, 25
Mako, Gene, 531
Makoni, Simba, 273
Maktoum bin Rashid al-Maktoum, Sheikh, 215, 508
Malawi, 266, **270-1**, 275
Malaysia, **320-1**, 322, 326, 352, 396, 423, 424, 445
Maldives, **315**
Mali, **250**
Malietoa Tanumafili II, Susuga, 361
Malik, Salim, 504
Mallon, Seamus, 45
Malta, **89-90**, 402
Mamet, David, 498
Mandela, Nelson, 261, 273, 355, 390, 559
Mandelson, Peter, 41, 43, 44, 524
Mané, Gen. Ansumane, 249, 264
Manley, John, 160
Manning, Preston, 157
Mao Zedong, 334, 542
Maples, John, 18
Mara, Ratu Sir Kamisese, 362
Maraj, Ralph, 184
Marble, Alice, 531
Marenco, José, 180
Margaret, Princess, 541
Margrethe II, Queen of Denmark, 67, 68, 541
Marisson, Michael, 475
Markarian, Andranik, 136, 564
Markezinis, Spyros, 93
Markova, Dame Alicia, 476
Márquez, Ricardo, 172
Marr, Andrew, 499
Marshall Islands, **364**

Martí, Bishop Joan Alanis, 79
Martin, Atherton, 187
Martin, Michael, 19, 45
Martin, Paul, 160
Martin, Sir Leslie, 494
Martin, Tony, 466
Martínez, Néstor Humberto, 168
Martínez, Rubén Berríos, 192
Marzouki, Moncef, 225
Mascarenhas Monteiro, Antonio, 263
Masefield, Thorold, 188, 190
Masire, Ketumile, 260, 275
Massow, Ivan, 18
Massu, Jacques, 54
Masud, Ahmed Shah, 289, 290, 569
Matthau, Walter, 485, 544
Matthei, General Fernando, 166
Matthews, Sir Stanley, 545
Maude, Francis, 18
Maupin, Armistead, 498
Mauritania, **249-50**
Mauritius, 275, **311-2**, 367
Mawdsley, James, 317, 572
Mawer, Simon, 498
Maxwell, Glyn, 498
May, Bob, 505
May, Peter, 534
Mayer, Louis B, 543
Mayor Oreja, Jaime,, 82
Maza Castellanos, Manuel, 178
Mazuka, Bernard, 261
Mbeki, Thabo, 14, 273, 282, 283, 284, 389, 393, 394
McAleese, Mary, 64
McArdle, Aidan, 478
McCain, John, 139, 140
McCartney, Ian, 525
McClure, Patrick, 352
McCollum, Bill, 147
McCormack, John, 528
McCrea, Rev. William, 44
McDermott, Michael, 153
McEwan, Ian, 530
McEwen, Alastair, 499
McFadden, Daniel, 15
McGovern, George, 544
McGrath, Patrick, 498
McGreggor, Wayne, 477
McGuinness, Martin, 45
McIlroy, Sammy, 502
McKenzie, Kevin, 477
McKinnon, Don, 388, 389
McLean Abaroa, Ronald, 163
McLeish, Henry, 37, 38, 571
McNally, Terrence, 481

McVeigh, Timothy, 154
Meacher, Michael, 524
Meade, Marion, 499
Meciar, Vladimir, 108
Medina, Danilo, 176
Megawati Sukarnoputri, 324, 568
Meguid, Ismat Abdel, 415, 416
Meidani, Rexhep, 117, 118
Mejía Domínguez, Hipólito, 176, 564, 568
Melancias, Antonio, 88
Melchett, Lord, 30
Melinte, Mihaela, 501
Mendez-France, Pierre, 532
Mendoza, Gen. Carlos, 169
Menem, Carlos Saúl, 161
Meri, Lennart, 102
Merkel, Angela, 48, 563
Mero, Mohammed Mustafa, 204, 561, 205
Méry, Jean-Claude, 54
Merz, Friedrich, 51
Mesic, Stipe, 121, 122, 560
Messervy-Whiting, Graham, 35
Meta, Ilir, 117, 118
Mexico, 13, 14, 82, **181-2**, 412, 428
Michael, Alun, 39, 40, 561
Michel, James, 313
Michell, Roger, 479
Micronesia, Federated States of, 364
Migas, Jozef, 108
Mihailov, Mihail, 115
Mihailova, Nadezhda, 114
Mikes, George, 536
Mikhail, Kasyanov, 130
Milburn, Alan, 524
Miller, Arthur, 478, 481, 499
Miller, Keith, 534
Miller, Merton, 545
Mills, Donald, 390
Mills, John Atta, 240
Milo, Paskal, 118
Milosevic, Slobodan, 6, 11, 33, 118, 124, 125, 126, 127, 403, 408, 409, 457, 570, 571
Milton, Giles, 499
Milutinovic, Milan, 124
Miquilena, Luís, 174
Miralles, Enric, 38, 494
Mirren, Helen, 479
Misago, Augustine, 262
Mishra, Pankaj, 498
Mitchell, Dame Roma, 355
Mitchell, Gary, 480
Mitchell, George, 195
Mitchell, Keith, 185
Mitchell, Sir James, 188, 572
Mitee, Ledum, 242

Mitterrand, François, 47, 53
Mitterrand, Jean-Christophe, 53
Miyazawa, Kiichi, 343
Mkapa, Benjamin, 236, 237
Mladenov, Petur, 545
Mladic, Gen., Ratko, 120
Moco, Marcelino, 391
Mocumbi, Pascoal, 265
Modigliani, Franco, 545
Moeller, Heinz, 169
Mogae, Festus, 274, 275, 276
Mohajerani, Seyyed Ataollah, 288, 575
Mohammed VI, King of Morocco, 228, 229
Moi, Daniel arap, 234
Mois, Juri, 102
Mokhehle, Ntsu, 277
Moldova, 135
Molina Duarte, Simon, 427
Möllemann, Jürgen, 50
Molnar, Ferenc, 480
Monaco, 80, 405
Moncada, Oscar, 180
Moncayo Gallegos, Gen. (retd) Francisco, 169
Moneta, Carlos, 427
Mongolia, 70, **349-51**, 409, 426
Montefiore, Simon Sebag, 499
Montenegro, 118, 122, 124
Montesinos, Vladimiro, 172, 173
Montgomerie, Colin, 505
Montgomery, George, 485
Montserrat, 190
Moore, Mike, 383
Moore, Sir Lee, 188
Moorehead, Caroline, 499
Morauta, Mekere, 356, 357
Morauta, Sir Mekere, 356, 575
Morgan, Rhodri, 39, 40, 561
Mori, Yoshiro, 301, 340, 341, 342, 343, 365, 562, 574
Morocco, 197, 199, 225, 227, **228-9**, 230
Morris, Bill, 23
Morris, Estelle, 524
Morrison, Blake, 495, 498
Morrow, Maurice, 43
Morton, Giles, 495
Moscoso de Gruber, Mireya Elisa, 178, 180
Mosisili, Bethuel Pakalitha, 274
Motion, Andrew, 499
Mowlam, Marjorie (Mo), 524
Moyano, Hugo, 161
Mozambique, **265-7**, 275, 391, 450
Mpinganjira, Brown, 270
Mswati III, King of Swaziland, 274, 280, 281
Mubarak Abdullah al-Shamikh, 223
Mubarak, Hosni, 200, 204, 206, 571

Mugabe, Robert, 2, 34, 271, 272, 273, 284, 388, 421, 560, 567, 572
Muhammad Taib, 320
Muhyiddin Yassin, 320
Mulholland, Rory, 498
Mulroney, Brian, 158
Muluzi, Bakili, 266, 270
Muñoz Ledo, Porfirio, 181
Muraliyev, Amangeldy, 292
Murdoch, Rupert, 543
Murphy, Charles, 434
Murphy, Paul, 524
Murphy-O'Connor, Cormac, 433
Murray, Douglas, 499
Murray, Les, 498
Musa, Said, 185
Musema, Alfred, 458
Museveni, Yoweri, 222, 237
Musharraf, Gen. Pervaiz, 298, 301, 302, 303, 306, 388, 559, 568
Music, 472-5
Musonge, Peter Mafany, 254
Mutalibov, Ayaz, 537
Mwencha, Erastus, 418
Mwila, Ben, 270
Myanmar (Burma), 317-8, 319, 330, 423
Mzali, Mohammed, 530

N'Guessan, Affi, 247
N'Tchama, Caetano, 263, 264
Nader, Ralph, 140, 141, 145
Nagako, Empress, 344
Nagamootoo, Moses, 183
Nahmad, Michael, 176
Naidu, Chandrababu, 302
Naif, Prince, 211
Nairn, Tom, 499
Najib Razak, 320
Nakasone, Yasuhiro, 556
Namibia, 259, **278**, 419, 421
Narantsatsralt, Janlavyn, 349
Narayanan, Kocheril Raman, 298, 300
Nash Jr, John F, 541
Nasser, Colonel, 535
Nastase, Adrian, 111, 113, 574
Nathan, Judith, 140
Nathan, S.R., 322
NATO, 35, 103, 105, 127, **377-8**, 399, 400, 413, 457
Nauru, 364
Navarro, Leopoldo, 180
Nawaz, Kulsoom, 303
Nazarbayev, Nursultan, 292, 293, 295, 296, 297, 567
Ndombasi, Yerodia, 455

Nelson, Bill, 147
Nelson, Richard, 480
Nemeth, Miklos, 409
Nepal, 299, **306**, 309
Netanyahu, Binyamin, 196
Netherlands, 60, **61-2**, 398, 501
Netherlands Antilles, 191
New Zealand, 352, 354, **357-9**, 363, 377, 424, 453, 459, 505
Newbould, Brian, 475
Newman, John, 355
Newson, Lloyd, 477
Ngeny, Noah, 500
Nguesso, Denis Sassou, 257
Nguyen Tan Dung, 328
Niasse, Moustapha, 246, 248, 249, 562
Nicaragua, 179-80, 427
Nicholas II, Tsar of Russia, 434
Nichols, Kyra, 475
Nicklaus, Jack, 505
Nigeria, 63, 155, **241-3**, 265, 419, 420, 421, 435
Nighy, Bill, 479
Nixon, Richard, 528
Niyazov, Gen. Saparmurad, 292, 293, 409
Nkhoma, Francis, 270
Nkomo, John, 272
Noboa Bejarano, Gustavo, 169
Non-Aligned Movement (NAM), 393-4
Noon, Jeff, 498
Norberg-Schultz, Christian, 494
Nordic Council, 410-1
Norfolk, Lawrence, 498
Norman, Archie, 18
Norris, Steve, 16, 17
North American Free Trade Agreement (NAFTA), 13, 413, 428
North Atlantic Treaty Organisation, see NATO
Northern Ireland, 41-6
Northern Marianas, 364
Norton, Gale, 150
Norway, 69-70, 367, 400
Note, Kessai, 360, 364, 559
Noth, Chris, 482
Nsibambi, Apolo, 237
Ntoutoume-Emane, Jean-François, 254
Nugent, Fr Robert, 432
Nujoma, Sam, 274, 279, 366
Nunn, Trevor, 479
Nyachae, Simon, 235
Nyboe, Bodil Andersen, 67
Nyerere, Julius, 261

O'Brian, Patrick, 546
O'Casey, Sean, 470

O'Connor, Cardinal John, 547
O'Connor, Joseph, 44
O'Connor, Sandra Day, 146
O'Donoghue, John, 65
O'Leary, David, 503
O'Neal, Ralph, 189, 190
O'Neal, Shaquille, 508
O'Neill, Eugene, 480
O'Neill, Martin, 503
Obasanjo, Olusegun, 155, 241, 242, 243, 393, 394
Obiang Nguema Mbasogo, Brig.-Gen. Teodoro, 255
Obituaries, 527-58
Obuchi, Keizo, 341, 342, 546, 562
Öcalan, Abdullah, 96, 97, 458, 560
Ocampos Alfaro, Rear Adml. José, 171
Ochirbat, Punsalmaagiyn, 350
Oddson, Davíd, 68
Odinga, Raila, 235
Ogata, Sadako, 367
Ogi, Adolf, 77
Okemo, Chris, 235
Olanta, Lt Col. Humala, 172
Oldfield, David, 355
Olds, Sharon, 498
Olechowski, Andrzej, 101
Oli, K.P, 307
Oliphant, Sir Mark, 355
Oliver, Jamie, 496
Oliver, Michael, 474
Olivera, Fernanda, 477
Olivier, Laurence, 539, 540
Olszewski, Jan, 101
Olympic, Games, 91
Ölziybaatar, Dembereliyn, 349
Oman, 220
Omar Hasan Ahmed al-Bashir, 220
Omar, Mola Mohammed, 289
Ondaatje, Christopher, 19
Ondaatje, Michael, 497, 498
Opera, 470-2
Operti, Didier, 173
Oppenheimer, Harry, 547
Oppenheimer, Sir Ernest, 548
Orban, Viktor, 109, 111, 413
Orellana, Gabriel, 178, 185
Organisation for Economic Co-operation and Development (OECD), 80, 190, **386-7**, 389
Organisation for Security and Cooperation in Europe (OSCE), 293, 405, **406-8**
Organisation of African Unity (OAU), 253, 277, 314, **419-20**
Organisation of American States (OAS), **427-8**
Organisation of Eastern Caribbean States (OECS), **427**
Organisation of the Islamic Conference (OIC), 219, 290, **395-6**
Organisation of the Petroleum Exporting Countries (OPEC), 210, 217, 289, **387**
Orwell, George, 535
Ota, Fusae, 341
Otayza, Eliecer, 174
Ouattara, Alassane, 251, 252, 419, 574
Ouedraogo, Kadre Desiré, 247
Ould Daddah, Ahmed, 249
Ould Daddah, Mokhtar, 250
Overviews of the Year, 1-15
Oviedo Silva, Gen. (retd) Lino César, 170, 564, 565
Oviedo, Francisco, 171
Oyelowo, David, 478
Oyuun, Sanjaasürengiyn, 349
Ozeyranli, Brig. Gen. Ali Nihat, 95

Pacific Community, 425
Pacific Islands Forum, 425
Padel, Ruth, 499
Paek Nam Sun, 348, 423
Page, Jennie, 22
Paige, Rod, 150
Paisley, Rev. Ian, 43
Pakenham, Lady Violet, 551
Pakistan, 155, 291, 296, 298, 299, 300, 301, **302-5**, 306, 388, 424, 425, 450, 456, 504
Paksas, Rolandas, 102, 105, 572
Palau, 360, 363
Palenfo, Lassana, 251
Palestine, 197-200
Palestinians, 194, 195, 202, 213, 223, 226, 229, 367, 395, 431
Pamfilova, Ella, 129
Panahi, Jafar, 485
Panama, 172, 176, **178, 180**, 458
Panday, Basdeo, 183, 574
Pangalos, Theodoros, 91
Pangelinan, Lourdes, 422, 425
Paniagua, Valentín, 171, 172
Pantani, Marco, 508
Papadopoulos, Colonel Georgios, 93
Papandreou, Georgios, 92, 118, 559
Papoutsis, Christos, 93
Papua New Guinea, 352, **356-7**, 389
Paraguay, 170-1, 429
Park Tae Joon, 345, 564
Park, Nick, 484
Parker, Mary-Louise, 482
Parrott, Andrew, 475

Parsons, Eileen, 190
Pascal, Lloyd, 187
Pastrana Arango, Andrés, 167, 168, 569
Patassé, Ange-Félix, 254, 257
Patiashvili, Dzhumber, 137
Patten, Chris, 66, 87
Patterson, Percival, J, 182
Paul VI, Pope, 432
Paul, Jeremy, 506
Paulauskas, Arturas, 105
Paulin, Tom, 498
Pawlikowski, Pawel, 484
Payne, George, 184
Pearson, Lester, 557
Peltram, Antonin, 106
Peñate Polanco, Eduardo, 179
Penhall, Joe, 479
Penov, Risto, 122
Pepo, Pal, 109
Percy, Iain, 501
Pereira, Dulce, 390, 391, 392
Pereira, Garcia, 88
Peres, Shimon, 196
Pérez de Cuéllar, Javier, 173
Perkins, Charles, 355
Perosevic, Bosko, 125
Perovic, Zika, 125
Perry, Fred, 531
Persson, Göran, 71
Peru, 171-3, 428
Pesquera, Carlos, 192
Peterle, Lojze, 124
Petipa, Marius, 475
Petritsch, Wolfgang, 120
Peyrefitte, Roger, 497
Pflimlin, Pierre, 548
Pham Van Dong, 548
Phan Van Kai, 328
Philip, Prince, 36
Philippines, 12, 73, 224, 321, **326-7**, 423, 435, 445
Phillips, Caryl, 495, 499
Phillips, Mike, 498
Phillips, Robin, 480
Piano, Renzo, 493
Picard, Liz, 499
Pierantozzi, Sandra, 364
Pierce, Mary, 507
Pilipovic-Chaffey, Dragica, 409
Pimentel Siles, Manuel, 84
Pimlott, Steven, 478
Pincay, Laffit, 508
Pindling, Sir Lynden, 186, 549
Pinochet Ugarte, Gen. (retd) Augusto, 36, 61, 165, 466, 561, 564

Pinsent, Matthew, 501
Pinter, Harold, 479, 481, 539
Pinto Rubianes, Pedro, 169
Pipe, Martin, 508
Piqué i Camps, Josep,, 83
Pires, Robert, 502
Pithart, Petr, 106
Pitt, Brad, 484
Pius IX, Pope, 569
Plowden, Edwin (later Baron), 550
Plowden, Lady, 549
Podberezkin, Alexei, 129
Podesta, John, 525
Pohamba, Hifikepunye, 278
Poland, 99-101, 109, 111, 398, 402, 413
Pollack, Harry, 449
Pollock, Howard, 474, 475
Pomárico, Armando, 168
Pompidou, Georges, 532
Ponnambalam, Kumar, 311
Porta, Giovanni, 117
Portero, Luis, 82
Portillo, Alfonso, 177, 178, 559, 568
Portillo, Michael, 18, 560
Portugal, 86-9, 392, 397, 431
Pósser da Costa, Guilherme, 263
Potter, Dennis, 550
Potter, Keith, 475
Pountney, David, 471
Powell, Anthony, 497, 550
Powell, Colin, 142, 150
Prabhakaran, Velupillai, 309, 310
Pradhan, Sahana, 307
Prasad, Jitendra, 300
Prats, Gen. Carlos, 166
Prescott, John, 26, 28, 37, 453, 524
Préval, René, 177, 428
Primarolo, Dawn, 524
Prodi, Romano, 121, 224, 396, 397, 403, 423
Proust, Marcel, 479
Puapua, Tomasi, 361
Puerto Rico, 191-2
Putin, Vladimir, 3, 10, 128, 129, 130, 131, 134, 155, 288, 295, 300, 336, 342, 343, 348, 350, 386, 556, 562, 564, 565, 567

Qaboos bin Said, Sheikh, 215
Qarase, Laisenia, 360, 362, 388, 567
Qatar, 199, **215-6**, 395
Queally, Jason, 501
Querol, José, Francisco, 82
Quevedo, Hugo, 170
Quin, Joyce, 525

Rabbani, Burhanuddin, 291, 297

Rabbani, Mohammed, 289
Racan, Ivica, 121
Radebe, Jeff, 286
Radford, Michael, 480
Radhakishun, Pratanpnarain, 191
Radisic, Zivko, 119
Rafsanjani, Ali Akbar Hashemi, 61, 287
Rafter, Pat, 507
Rageb, Ali Abu al, 565
Raguz, Martin, 119
Rainha, José Júnior, 164
Rainier III, Prince of Monaco, 79, 80
Rajoy Brey, Mariano, 83
Rakhmanov, Imamoli, 292, 293
Ramadan, Taher Yasin, 202
Ramaphosa, Cyril, 42, 45
Rambally, Melissa, 188
Ramdial, Ganace, 183
Ramgoolam, Navin, 311, 312, 569
Ramírez Ocampo, Augusto, 168
Ramírez Acuña, Francisco, 181
Ramos, Fidel, 326
Ramos Allup, Henry, 174
Ramsamy, Pakereesamy (Prega), 418
Ramsey, Michael, 532
Randerson, Jenny, 40
Rania, Queen of Jordan, 36
Rankalawan, Waved, 314
Rao, P.V. Narasimha, 300, 571
Rasizade, Artur, 136
Rasmussen, Poul Nyrup, 67, 401, 575
Rato Figaredo, Rodrigo y, 83
Ratsiraka, Didier, 315
Rau, Johannes, 47, 49
Rawabdeh, Abdul-Raouf, 202, 203, 565
Rawlings, Jerry John, 239, 240, 575
Rawnsley, Andrew, 499
Raxnjatovic, Zeljko, 124
Ray, Robert, 151
Rayburn, Sam, 528
Raynsford, Nick, 524
Razali Ismail, 317
Reagan, Ronald, 3
Redgrave, Steve, 501
Redwood, John, 18
Rehnquist, William, 146
Reid, John, 524
Reimann, Aribert, 473
Reinhardus, Barbara, 277
Religion, 431-6
Remengesau, Tommy, 360, 363
René, France-Albert, 313
Reno, Janet, 141, 152, 175, 525
Repse, Einars, 104
Rettig, Raúl, 167

Reyes Villa, Manfred, 163
Reynders, Didier, 401
Reza, Yasmina, 481, 499
Rice, Condoleezza, 150
Rice, Susan, 222
Richardson, Ralph, 551
Richler, Mordecai, 536
Richmond, Kevin, 475
Ridsdale, Peter, 503
Riess-Passer, Susanne, 74
Rifa'at al-Assad, 205
Riggins, Lloyd, 477
Rijkaard, Frank, 502
Riley, Jonathan, 34
Riley, Richard W., 525
Ringer, Jennifer, 477
Ringholm, Bosse, 71
Rio Group, 426
Ríos Montt, Gen. (retd) José Efraín, 178, 179
Ritchie, Guy, 484
Rizzi, Carlo, 470
Robards, Jason, 485, 551
Robb, Chuck, 147
Robb, Graham, 499
Roberts Jr, Kenny, 506
Roberts, Julia, 483
Roberts, Michele, 498
Robertson, Georg, 377, 382, 400
Robertson, Pat, 140
Robertson, Shirley, 501
Robinson, Anne, 486
Robinson, Arthur N.R., 183, 184
Robinson, Gerry, 488
Robinson, Mary, 416
Robinson, Peter, 43
Roche, Barbara, 524
Rockefeller, Nelson, 528
Rockwell, Rick, 139
Rodgers, John, 434
Rodríguez Echeverría, Miguel Angel, 178, 180
Rodriguez Zapetero, José Luis, 83
Rogers, Lord (Richard), 494
Rogosin, Lionel, 485
Rojas Penso, Juan Francisco, 427
Rojas, Luis Alberto, 171
Rojo, Tamara, 476
Roma, 108, 111, 116
Roman, Petre, 413
Romania, 110, **111-4**, 116, 402, 414
Romero Hicks, Juan Carlos, 181
Ronan, John, 22
Rooker, Jeff, 525
Rosas, Fernando, 88
Rosenthal, Tom, 536

Rosham, Hrithik, 307
Ross, Alan, 499
Rosselló González, Pedro Juan, 192
Rossier, William, 412, 413
Roth, Philip, 498, 536
Roth, William, 147
Rowland, Kayla, 152
Rowling, J. K., 496, 498
Rúa, Fernando de la, 13
Ruddock, Philip, 354
Ruders, Paul, 473
Ruggiu, Georges, 262, 458
Rühe, Volker, 48
Rúiz, Bishop Samuel, 182
Ruiz, Col. César Augusto, 178
Runcie, the Right Rev Lord (Robert), 551
Runciman, Sir Steven, 492, 552
Rupel, Dimitrij, 123
Rusedski, Greg, 507
Rushdie, Salman, 496
Russia, 3, 10, 11, 36, 70, 104, 111, 115, **128-32**, 133, 155 ,198, 209, 224, 232, 268, 288, 290, 295, 296, 297, 300, 328, 342, 350, 351, 404, 408, 434, 437, 442, 445, 452, 453, 484, 501, 556
Rutelli, Francesco, 59
Rwanda, 238, 259, 260, **261**, **262-3**, 268, 434, 456
Rwigyema, Pierre-Celestin, 262
Ryan, George, 150
Ryder of Warsaw, Lady, 553

Sa'aduddin Ibrahim, 200
Saad al-Abdullah al-Salim al-Sabah, Crown Prince Sheikh, 215
Saariaho, Kaija, 473
Saddam Hussein, 36, 200, 208
Safin, Marat, 507
Sagat, Tibor, 108
Sage, Lorna, 499
Sainsbury, John Benjamin, 553
Sainsbury, Lord, 19
Sainsbury, Sir Robert, 492, 553
St Kitts & Nevis, 186-8
St Lucia, 186-8
St Vincent & the Grenadines 187-8
Salad Hasan, Abdiqasim, 231
Salam, Saeb, 208, 554
Salas Guevara, Federico, 172
Saleh, Field Marshall Ali Abdullah, 213
Saleh, Jaime M., 191
Salim al-Hoss, 206, 207
Salim, Salim Ahmed, 418, 420
Salinas de Gortari, Carlos, 181
Sallinen, Aulis, 473

Salmond, Alex, 38
Salvatierra, Gen. Manuel, 180
Sam Rangsi, 329
Samak Sundaravej, 319
Samoa, 361, 365
Sampaio, Jorge, 86, 88
Sampras, Pete, 507
Samson, Bruce, 476
Samuels, Dover, 357
San Marino, 79, 80-1
Sanan Kajomprasart, Maj.-Gen., 319
Sanchez, Augie, 504
Sandoval, Gen Telmo, 169
Sanguinetti, Julio María, 173
Sanha, Malam Bacai, 264
Sanha, Mohammed Lamine, 264
Sankoh, Foday, 34, 244, 245, 246
Sant, Alfred, 90
Santiago Díaz, Gen. Julio César, 182
Santibañes, Fernando de, 162
Santos Castillo, Francisco, 167
Santos, Jacinto, 264
Santos Calderón, Juan Manuel, 168
São Tomé & Príncipe, 263, 265
Sarid, Yossi, 196
Sarkisian, Aram, 136, 564
Sarovic, Mirko, 119
Sartre, Jean-Paul, 479
Saryusz, 101
Saryusz-Wolski, Jacek, 101
Sassou-Nguesso, Denis, 254
Satyamurti, Carole, 498
Saudi Arabia, 209, **210-3**, 213, 217, 219, 290, 303, 417, 453
Saunders, Brig. Stephen, 91, 565
Sautet, Claude, 485
Sautter, Christian, 53
Savage, Francis, J., 189
Savimbi, Jonas, 253, 269, 393, 419
Savisaar, Edgar, 102
Savostyanov, Evgenii, 129
Sayyid Muhammed Othman al-Mirghani, 221
Sayyid Sadiq al-Mahdi, 221
Scacchi, Greta, 480
Scalia, Antonin, 146
Schäfer, Christine, 470
Schaffel, Maria, 481
Schama, Simon, 495, 499
Schäuble, Wolfgang, 47, 563
Schhedrin, Rodion, 477
Schjott-Pedersen, Karl-Eirik, 70
Schlesinger, John, 470
Schleuber, Heinz, 49
Schling, Jaroslav, 106
Schlüssel, Wolfgang, 73

Schmid, Samuel, 77
Schnaut, Gabrielle, 470
Schreiber, Liev, 481
Schröder, Gerhard, 47, 48, 50, 383
Schulz, Charles, 492, 554
Schumacher, Michael, 505, 506
Schüssel, Wolfgang, 73, 74, 402, 406, 408
Schuster, Rudolf, 107, 108
Schuwirth, Rainer, 35
Schwarz, Charles, 151
Schwebel, Stephen, 455
Schwimmer, Walter, 404
Scientific, Medical & Industrial Research, 437-42
Scotland, 37-9
Scott, Ridley, 483
Seawell, Donald, 482
Sebarenzi, Kabuye, 262
Sebastian, Sir Cuthbert, 186
Seck, Idrissa, 249
Segal, George, 492
Selassie, Haile, 233
Self, Will, 498
Selten, Reinhard, 541
Senegal, 246, 248-9, 264
Seremane, Joe, 282
Sergeyev, Igor, 288
Serota, Sir Nicholas, 492
Serushago, 458
Service, Robert, 499
Seselj, Vojislav, 125, 126
Sessay, Issay, 244
Sestanovich, Stephen, 296
Severino, Rodolfo C., 422
Seychelles, 313-4, 421, 458
Sezer, Ahmet Necdet, 96, 97, 564
Sfinias, Pantelis, 92
Shaffer, Peter, 539
Shaheen, Jeanne, 150
Shalala, Donna E., 525
Shamikh, Mubarak Abdullah al, 561
Shapiro, Robert, 449
Shara', Faruq al, 156, 193, 204
Sharif, Nawaz, 303, 304, 559, 561, 567, 574
Sharon, Ariel, 193, 195, 196, 198, 199, 200, 395, 570
Shaw, Vernon, 186, 187
Shawcross, William, 499
Shearer, Alan, 502
Shearing, Clifford, 45
Shelton, Vera, 538
Shenouda III, Pope, 431
Sheridan, Tommy, 39
Shevardnadze, Eduard, 136, 137, 563
Shi Jiuyong, 455

Shields, Carol, 498
Shipley, Jenny, 359
Shipman, Harold Frederick, 466
Shirakawa, Hideki, 442
Short, Clare, 524
Sidibe, Mande, 247
Sidimé, Lamine, 247, 250
Sierra Leone, 33, 34, 35, 155, 160, 240, **243-5**, 246, 250, 252, 368, 372, 373, 389, 393, 421
Sihanouk, King Norodom, 329
Simeon, King, 540
Simeonov, Teodosii, 116
Simitis, Kostas, 90, 563
Simmonds, Kennedy, 188
Simon, Neil, 481, 544
Simonis, Heide, 48
Simpson, Helen, 498
Simpson, Portia Miller, 182
Sin, Cardinal, 327, 542
Sinclair, Margaret, 557
Singapore, 12, **322-3**, 352, 358, 359, 367, 423, 424, 445
Singh, Gurbux, 25
Singh, Vijay, 505
Singson, Luis, 327
Sinha, Yashwant, 301
Sisavath Keobounphanh, Gen., 330
Skele, Andris, 103, 563
Skidelsky, Robert, 499
Skuratov, Yuri, 129
Sladkevicius, Cardinal Vincentas, 555
Slater, Rodney E., 525
Slattery, John, 481
Slovakia, 107-9, 111, 268, 402, 413
Slovenia, 122, **123-4**, 123, 402
Slovo, Gillian, 498
Smith, Andrew, 524
Smith, Chris, 20, 487, 493, 524
Smith, Jennifer, 188, 189
Smith, John, 536
Smith, Peter John, 189
Smith, Zadie, 496, 498
Smyth, Rev. Martin, 42, 45
Sobchak, Anatoli, 130, 555
Sobel, Dava, 486
Sodano, Cardinal Angelo, 79
Soderbergh, Steven, 483
Sogavare, Manasseh, 361, 363, 565
Soglo, Nicéphore, 253
Sokurov, Alexander, 484
Solana, Javier, 397, 403
Solheim, Eric, 309
Solomon Islands, 352, 358, **361**, **363**, 377, 388, 425

Solórzano, Carlos, 169
Somalia, 231, **233-4**, 419
Somare, 356
Somare, Sir Michael, 356
Sontag, Susan, 495, 498
Soong Chu-yu, 338
Soong, James, 338, 339
Sope, Barak, 361
Sorenstam, Annika, 505
Soros, George, 14
Souter, David, 147
South Africa, 14, 266, 273, 275, 278, **282-6**, 419, 420, 442, 504
South Asian Association for Regional Cooperation (SAARC), 301, 306, **422**, **424**
Southern African Development Community (SADC), 259, 266, 274, 276, **418**, **420-1**
Southern Common Market (Mercosur), **426**, **429**
Space, **437-8**
Spain, 36, **81-4**, 85, 229, 397, 398, 429
Spark, Muriel, 498
Specter, Arlen, 141
Speight, George, 362, 388, 564, 567
Spellar, John, 525
Spencer, Charles, 499
Sperling, Gene, 424, 525
Spidla, Vladimir, 106
Sport, **500-8**
Sri Lanka, 70, 301, **309-11**, 389, 529
Ssendaula, Gerald, 238
Stambolic, Ivan, 125
Stamm, Peter, 498
Stanislav, Govorukhin, 129
Stank, Jozef, 108
Starkey, David, 499
Stathopoulos, Michalis, 91
Stein, Eduardo, 428
Stephanopoulos, Kostas, 90
Steven, Matthew, 508
Stevens, David, 272
Stevens, John, 147
Stewart, James, 543
Stewart, Patrick, 481
Steyn, Mark, 474, 475
Stirling, Guillermo, 173
Stoiber, Edmund, 48
Stoltenberg, Jens, 69, 561
Storey, David, 539
Stoute, Sir Michael, 508
Stoyanov, Petar, 114, 118
Strauss-Khan, Dominique, 53, 54
Straw, Jack, 23, 24, 27, 36, 166, 524, 561
Studd, Stephen, 474
Sturluson, Snorri, 68

Sudan, 219, **220-2**, 233, 238, 367, 395
Sudarsono, Juwono, 324
Suharto, 323, 324, 325, 564, 570
Sultan, Prince, 211, 213
Sultonov, Otir, 292
Sumaye, Frederick, 236
Summers, Anthony, 499
Summers, Lawrence, 525
Sunia, Tauese, 364
Suprowicz, Krzyztof, 214
Surin Pitsuwan, 423
Surinam, 183, **190**
Sveinsson, Atli Heimir, 68
Svilanovic, Goran, 408
Swaziland, **274**, **280-1**
Sweden, 9, 68, 401
Swinney, John, 38
Switzerland, **77-8**, 412, 438, 452
Sword, Greg, 354
Symons of Vernham Dean, Baroness, 525
Syria, 156, 193, 194, 197, **204-6**, 209, 416, 527
Szymborska, Wislawa, 497, 498

Tadic, 457
Taiwan, 11, 331, 334, **338-40**, 367, 484
Tajikistan, 288, 290, **292**, **293-4**, 371
Takeshita, Noboru, 344, 547, 556
Tambalaw, Gen., 318
Tan, Tony, 323
Tanaka, Kakuei, 556
Tandja, Oumarou, 253
Tang Fei, Gen., 339, 340, 571
Tang Jiaxuan, 301
Tanja, Mamadou, 248
Tanzania, 214, 235, **236-7**, 238, 261, 275, 421
Tarar, Mohammed Rafiq, 302
Tarasyuk, Borys, 134
Taufa'ahua Tupou IV, King, 361
Tavener, John, 475
Taya, Col Moaouia Ould Sidi Mohammed, 247
Taylor, Ann, 524
Taylor, Charles, 246, 251, 252
Taylor, Damilola, 24
Taylor, Derek H., 189
Taylor, Paul, 478
Taylor, Robert, 543
Television & Radio, **485-9**
Tembo, John, 271
Tenet, George, 525
Tergat, Paul, 500
Terragno, Rodolfo, 162
Terry, Ellen, 539

Thailand, 318, **319-20**, 330, 423
Thaksin Shinawatra, 319
Than Shwe, Gen., 317
Thani, Sheikh Hamad Bin Khalifa al, 396
Thatcher, Margaret, 552
Theatre, **478-82**
Thomas, Clarence, 146
Thomas, R. S., 497, 556
Thompson, Tommy, 150
Thorpe, Adam, 498
Thorpe, Graham, 505
Thorpe, Ian, 501
Tiberi, Jean, 54
Tibet, **336**, 489
Timms, Stephen, 524
Tito, Teburoro, 360
Titov, Konstantin, 129
Todd, Christine Whitman, 150
Togo, **248**, **252-3**, 268, 373, 419
Togoïmi, Youssouf, 255
Tokayev, Kasymzhomart, 292
Toledo, Alejandro, 171
Tolentino Dipp, Hugo, 176
Tomlin, Lily, 482
Tomlinson, John, 470
Tonga, **361**, **364**
Tonkin, David, 355
Torgyan, Jozsef, 110
Tosovsky, Josef, 106
Trajkovski, Boris, 122
Tran Duc Luong, 328
Treglown, Jeremy, 499
Tremain, Rose, 530
Trevis, Di, 479
Trevor, Claire, 485
Trevor, William, 497, 498
Trezeguet, David, 502
Trimble, David, 41, 42, 44, 45, 66
Trinidad & Tobago, 183-4, 389, 430, 542
Tripp, Linda, 151
Tritten, Jurgen, 453
Trollope, Joanna, 498
Troughton, David, 478
Trovoada, Miguel, 263, 265
Trudeau, Pierre, 159, 557, 570
Truett, Thomas, 139
Tsvangirai, Morgan, 272, 273
Tua, David, 504
Tudela, Francisco, 172
Tudjman, Franjo, 121
Tudjman, Nevenka, 121
Tudor, Antony, 476
Tudor, Corneliu Vadim, 112, 574
Tuila'epa Sa'ilele Malielegaoi, 361
Tuilimu, Lagitupa, 364

Tuleev, Aman, 129
Tuma, Zdenek, 106
Tung Chee-hwa, 337
Tunisia, **224-6**, 529
Turbay, Diego, 168
Turabi, Hasan al, 193, 204-5, 220
Turkey, 72, 92, **96-8**, 219, 289, 395, 400, 414, 458, 489
Turkish Republic of Northern Cyprus (TRNC), **93-5**, 97
Turkmenistan, 291, **292**, 295-7, 409
Turks & Caicos Islands, **189**, **190**
Turnage, Mark Anthony, 470, 473
Turnbull, Charles, 192
Turner, Kathleen, 480
Turner, Ted, 154, 370
Turnquest, Sir Orville, 186
Tusevljak, Spasoje, 565
Tuvalu, **361**, **364**, 367, 390
Tyson, Mike, 504

Ubayd, Atif Mohammed al, 200
Uganda, 222, 235, **237-9**, 259, 260, 434, 456
Ukraine, 114, **133**, **134-5**, 268, 297, 404, 405
Ulakalala Lavaka Ata, 361
Ullman, Liv, 483
Ulufa'alu, Bartholomew, 363, 388, 565
Ulukalala Lavaka Ata, Prince, 364, 559
Umberto II, King of Italy, 540
United Arab Emirates, **215-6**, 416, 417
United Kingdom (UK), 9, 10, **16-46**, 61, 69, 85, 91, 155, 165, 175, 208, 211, 223, 244, 246, 272, 290, 304, 312, 349, 353, 359, 379, 380, 397, 399, 401, 424, 429, 432, 433, 440, 441, 444, 445, 453, 473, 484, 500
United Nations (UN), 65, 68, 70, 72, 116, 122, 127, 137, 160, 175, 176, 194, 206, 207, 208, 209, 222, 226, 227, 229, 231, 234, 240, 243, 257, 259, 262, 268, 273, 276, 277, 284, 288, 291, 293, 296, 305, 308, 311, 315, 317, 325, 329, 354, 364, **366-75**, 393, 396, 406, 416, 417, 455
United States of America (USA), 3, 8, 9, 10, 11, 12, 13, 14, 35, 36, 60, **138-56**, 167, 175, 177, 179, 180, 187, 194, 197, 198, 200, 202, 204, 205, 208, 213, 214, 219, 222, 223, 229, 230, 231, 243, 280, 281, 286, 288, 291, 296, 300, 310, 312, 328, 331, 335, 340, 342, 347, 348, 358, 364, 365, 366, 368, 369, 370, 377, 379, 383, 399, 423, 424, 426, 432, 437, 438, 439, 440, 441, 442, 452, 453, 454, 501
Updike, John, 497, 498, 536
Urdaneta Hernández, Lt. Col. (retd) Jesús, 174

Uruguay, 429
Uskokovic, Zoran, 125
Uteem, Cassam, 311, 312
Uzbekistan, 290, **292**, **293-4**

Vadim, Roger, 485
Vaea, Baron, 559
Vaillant, Daniel, 55
Vajpayee, Atal Bihari, 12, 298, 299, 300, 301
Valdés, Juan Gabriel, 166
Valdez Bautista, Maj. Gen. José Elías, 176
van den Hoogenband, Pieter, 501
van Schalkwyk, Marthinus, 282
Vanuatu, **361**, **354**
Varda, Agnes, 484
Varga, Mihaly, 109
Vargas, Antonio, 169
Vatican, **97**, **80**, 182, 197
Vaz, Helder, 264
Vaz, Keith, 524
Vedrine, Hubert, 301
Veiga, Carlos, 264, 571
Velioglu, Hüseyi, 97
Veltroni, Walter, 58, 59
Vendrell, Fancesc, 291
Venetiaan, Ronald, 190, 191, 564, 569
Venezuela, 168, **173-4**, 176, 183, 389
Venizelos, Evangelos, 91
Venter, Craig, 440
Ventsel, Vello, 102
Ventura, Jesse, 140
Vera, Raúl, 182
Verheugen, Gunther, 89
Verhofstadt, Guy, 60
Vernon, Roland, 499
Vick, Graham, 470, 471
Victor Emmanuel, King of Italy, 540
Vieira, Sisa, 392
Vietnam, 155, **328-9**, 423, 426, 435, 452, 548
Vike-Freiberga, Vaira, 102, 103, 104
Villanueva Ruesta, Gen, José, 172
Vir, Param, 473
Virenque, Richard, 508
Visco, Vincenzo, 57
Visual Arts, **489-92**
Vitale, Eletise, 365
Vitale, Leafa, 365
Vollebæk, Knud, 70
von Gutenberg, Johan, 495
von Sponeck, Hans, 372, 560
von Trier, Lars, 483
Vorhaus, Bernard, 485
Voynet, Dominique, 37, 453

Wade, Abdoulayé, 246, 248, 249, 264, 562

Wagner, Jane, 482
Wahid, Abdurrahman, 323, 324, 325, 363, 560, 565, 568
Wakeham, Lord, 463
Walcott, Derek, 497, 498
Waldman, Guid, 498
Wales, **39-41**
Wales, Charles Prince of, 541
Walesa, Lech, 7, 100, 571
Walker, Edward, 213
Wallace, David Foster, 498
Wallace, Jim, 37
Walsh, Courtney, 505
Walsh, Jill Paton, 498
Walsh, Ruby, 508
Walsh, Ted, 508
Wan Li, 334
Wan Yongxiang, 348
Wandor, Michelene, 498
Wang Enmao, 334
Wang Fengchiao, 337
Wang Hanbin, 334
Wang Zaixi, Maj.-Gen., 335
Wangchuk, Dragon King Jigme Singye of Bhutan, 308
Ware, John, 44
Warner, Keith, 471
Warnicke, Retha M, 499
Wasacz, Emil, 99
Wei Jianxing, 331
Weill, Kurt, 473
Weizmann, Ezer, 196, 566
Wen Jiabao, 331
Wernicke, Herbert, 470
West, Jon Frederic, 470
West, Samuel, 478
West, Togo D., 525
West Papua, **363**
Western Sahara, 227, 228, **229-30**
Westwood, Lee, 505
Weyrauch, Horst, 47
White, Edmund, 498
Whitehouse, Mary, 550
Whiteread, Rachel, 75
Whittall, Arnold, 474
Wicki, Bernhard, 485
Wickremanayake, Ratnasiri, 309, 568
Wickremasinghe, Ranil, 310
Wigley, Dafydd, 40
Wijdenbosch, Jules, 190
Wilde, Oscar, 494
Wilder, Billy, 544
Wildor, Sarah, 476
Wilkinson, Howard, 502
Willey, Kathleen, 151

Williams of Mostyn, Lord, 525
Williams, Brynle, 41
Williams, Henry, 504
Williams, Mark, 508
Williams, Serena, 507
Williams, Sir Daniel, 185
Williams, Tennessee, 479
Williams, Venus, 507
Willson, Meredith, 481
Wilson, Angus, 530
Wilson, August, 482
Wilson, Brian, 525
Wilson, Harold, 529
Wiltord, Sylvain, 502
Wingfield, Paul, 475
Winning, Cardinal Thomas, 433
Winsor, Tom, 28
Winterson, Jeanette, 498
Wiranto, Gen., 324, 560
Wise, Audrey, 17
Wolfensohn, James, 385, 389
Woods, Dr Michael, 45
Woods, Tiger, 505
World Bank, 13, 14, 114, 185, 232, 237, 255, 256, 265, 269, 316, **385**, 389, 451
World Trade Organisation (WTO), 11, 14, 63, 185, 211, 217, 284, 331, 336, **385-6**, 391, 394, 404, 424, 448
Wotzel, Damien, 475
Wright, Judith, 355, 497
Wright, Peter, 476

Xiong Guangkai, Lt-Gen., 334

Yabeh, Gen. Yacin, 234
Yadav, Laloo Prasad, 299
Yafi, Abdullah, 554
Yalla, Kumba, 263, 264, 559
Yamada, Isamu, 341
Yamaguchi, Toshio, 562
Yamassoum, Nagoum, 254
Yang Baibing, 334
Yang, Edward, 485
Yarmoshyn, Uladzimir, 133, 134, 561
Yassine, Abdelsalam, 228, 564
Yavlinsky, Grigorii, 129, 130
Yawdserk, Col, 318
Yazbek, David, 481
Yeang, Ken, 493
Yeltsin, Boris, 128, 129, 350
Yemen, 212, **213-5**, 291
Yoli, Paramanga Ernest, 573
Yohei, Kono, 336
Yona, Daniel, 237
Young, Loretta, 485
Young, Sir, Colville, 185
Youssoufi, Abderrahmane, 228, 229
Yturralde, Luis, 170
Yugoslavia, Federal Republic of, 6, 11, 33, 110, 114, 118, 120, 123, **124-8**, 367, 377, 405, 408, 409, 413, 414, 457
Yushchenko, Victor, 133, 134

Zambia, 260, 266, **269-70**, 275
Zambrano, Timoteo, 174
Zanzibar, **236-7**, 389
Zatopec, Emil, 557
Zawahiri, Ayman al-, 291
Zayad bin Sultan al-Nahayyan, Sheikh, 215
Zedillo Ponce de Leon, Ernesto, 181
Zeffirelli, Franco, 470
Zelezny, Jan, 500
Zeman, Milos, 105, 106
Zenawi, Meles, 231, 233, 574
Zeng Qinghong, 331, 334, 335
Zevi, Bruno, 494
Zhang Erchen, 332
Zhang Wannian, 331, 334
Zhang Zuoji, 332
Zhirinovsky, Vladimir, 129
Zhivkov, Todor, 546
Zhu Rongji, 63, 331, 333, 336, 344, 346
Zia, Begum Khalela, 305
Zimbabwe, 2, 34, 259, 260, 269, **271-3**, 274, 275, 278, 284, 285, 504
Zizic, Zoran, 124
Zlenko, Anatolii, 134
Zoff, Dino, 502
Zongo, Norbert, 252
Zorig, Sanjaasürengiyn, 349
Zu'bi, Mahmud, 205, 561
Zyuganov, Gennadii, 129

REF D 2.A7 2000